1973
YEAR BOOK

COVERING THE YEAR 1972

MARON L. WAXMAN, M.A.   Executive Editor

GEOFFREY M. HORN, M.A.   Managing Editor

LOUIS SHORES, Ph.D.   Senior Library Adviser

ROBERT H. BLACKBURN, M.S., B.L.S.   Consultant for Canada

SIR FRANK FRANCIS, K.C.B., M.A., D.LITT., F.S.A.   Consultant for Great Britain

CROWELL-COLLIER   EDUCATIONAL   CORPORATION

1973 YEAR BOOK

Jean Paradise, Group Editorial Director
Zelda Haber, Art Director

YEAR BOOK EDITORIAL STAFF

Bernard Johnston

Teddy Slater

Nancy L. Freireich
Pauline Piekarz

Felice Bergen
Susan K. Bloom
David O. Currier
Bob Famighetti
Charlotte R. Gross
Fredric M. Kaplan
William A. McGeveran, Jr.
Peter K. Reinhart
Susan Reisler
David K. Thompson
William Kyer West
Abby Rae Zukerman

EDITORIAL ASSISTANT

Bonnie Lee Miner

ART AND PRODUCTION STAFF

Gerald Vogt, Production Coordinator
Trudy Veit, Associate Art Director

Anne Sabin, Art Editor
Lee Davidson, Designer
Joan Gunderson, Designer
Elizabeth Bird, Picture Editor
Diane Glick, Picture Editor
Jane Latta, Picture Editor
Margaret McRae, Picture Editor
Anne Dobrow, Production Assistant
Richard Luna, Production Assistant

PROOFREADING STAFF

Duncan Brown
Douglas Green
Dianna Gruene
Terry Levi
Robert Solomon
Norma Jean Traylor

CONTENTS

Election '72

On Election Day 1972, Richard Nixon won "four more years" by one of the greatest landslides in American history. But the dimensions of that triumph, predicted by pollsters almost exactly, was one of the least surprising events of this election year—a year in which George McGovern became the Democratic candidate five months after Edmund Muskie supposedly had the nomination sewed up and in which Thomas Eagleton became the first vice-presidential candidate in history to resign from the ticket.

In this special supplement of the *Year Book,* Robert Sherrill, noted author and political analyst, will discuss the philosophy of Richard Nixon and some of the personal experiences which helped form that philosophy, will review the primaries and national conventions, and will describe the fall campaign. Additional articles will focus on the other participants in the national race and analyze congressional and state government contests.

BOB FAMIGHETTI, EDITOR, SPECIAL SUPPLEMENT
LEE DAVIDSON, DESIGNER, SPECIAL SUPPLEMENT

Richard Nixon

Robert Sherrill

Aside from whatever other lessons are to be learned from it, the career of Richard M. Nixon at least proves that the most adept politicians are sometimes made, not born. Moreover, as he has made crystal clear, they are sometimes self-made. He got to the White House and stayed there because by brilliant self-analysis (chiefly, perhaps, his awareness that "I'm an introvert in an extrovert profession") he has learned to compensate.

Although he is not an innovative political campaigner, he made up for that by watching and listening to skilled tacticians, by learning from his own mistakes—and by never forgetting a political lesson. Unable to win mass popularity, he settled for general nonantagonism and respect. Lacking both the instincts and the coloration of a born politician, Nixon learned how to substitute laborious homework for the one and impeccable restraint for the other. Although most successful political careers have been built around the three characteristics popularly considered to be basic to electoral

1959
One of the high points of Nixon's vice-presidency was his famous "kitchen debate" with Nikita Khrushchev.

1950
His investigation of Alger Hiss' alleged connection with Communist spies helped launch Nixon's national political career.

politics—charisma, gregariousness, and ideology—Nixon has managed equally well with his own unique combination of doggedness, isolation, and a sometimes ruthless pragmatism.

It is obviously not the worst political formula. In his virgin fling at electoral politics, at age 33, he unseated a five-term congressman. Then with only four years in the House to recommend him to the voters, Nixon stepped up to the U.S. Senate in 1950. And with only two years of Senate service to impress the GOP kingmakers, he was put on the national ticket with Dwight D. Eisenhower in 1952. Nixon has called his political life "a series of ups and downs," but it has been mostly ups. Only twice in a quarter century have the voters denied him the office he sought, and on one of those occasions he was turned away by less than 1 percent of the vote.

Accident, not a deep inner compulsion, brought Nixon into politics. "Even in college," he has said, "political battles as such never appealed to me, but I always seemed to get dragged into them to run for some office or another." He was so indifferent to politics that he did not register to vote until he was 25. When he was sought out in 1946 by Whittier, Calif., businessmen who needed a candidate to run against Democratic congressman Jerry Voorhis, Nixon was, of course, asked whether he was a Republican. "I guess so," he replied. "I voted for Dewey in 1944."

Up to then he had thought of politics only in the abstract. If he had had any flashes of political passion in his early life, they had probably come in response to the tirades of his father, Frank, who seems, from biographical evidence, to have been suspicious of most men of power and especially of those who were lawyers as well as politicians. Of

Robert Sherrill is Washington, D.C., editor for The Nation *and author of a number of books, most recently* Why They Call It Politics.

1972
On the night of his greatest political triumph, a buoyant Nixon is warmly congratulated by his wife, Pat.

1962
After losing the California governor's race, Nixon faced newsmen for what he predicted would be his last press conference.

all the family, Richard Nixon said later, it was his father, drifting into and out of a dozen jobs and succeeding at none, who "loved the excitement and battles of political life" by proxy. From his father, Nixon inherited a competitive spirit and also a temper. But in most other respects—including his looks, as photographs show—Nixon took after the Milhous side of the family. From his mother, Hannah, who held the family and the family grocery store together, he learned to control his temper, hide his feelings, and be patient. "She bottled things up," he says, "with wonderful self-control."

Unlike President Lyndon B. Johnson, who made frequent references to the hard times of his boyhood, Nixon seldom mentions his much more impoverished upbringing. To pay for one son's care in a tuberculosis sanatorium (this brother and another died while Nixon was still in his teens), Mrs. Nixon joined the staff as a kitchen helper and scrubwoman, living away from home for two years. One of Nixon's rare references to such episodes came in 1972 in a speech urging that people on welfare be required to work if possible. Scrubbing floors and carrying bedpans are not nice duties, he said, "but my mother did that kind of work."

Both at Whittier College and at Duke University, where he took a law degree, Nixon's outstanding record was produced, he says, "not because I was smarter but because I worked longer and harder than some of my more gifted colleagues." At Duke, where he haunted the library, he won the nickname "Iron Butt." Nixon has never lost the taste for work. "I have seen those who have nothing to do—I could be one of them if I wanted—the people just lying around at Palm Beach," he told author Garry Wills. "Nothing could be more pitiful."

THE NEXT FOUR YEARS

In an interview on November 5 that was published two days after the election, President Nixon discussed with Garnett D. Horner of the Washington *Star-News* what he looked forward to in his second term. Excerpts from the interview follow:

"We are going to move on SALT II [the second round of the strategic arms limitation talks]. We, of course, will be moving on the European security conference and . . . mutual balanced force reduction. . . . The Middle East will have a very high priority. . . . I am going to look at the Latin American policy and African policy to see how our programs can be improved in those areas."

"This country has enough on its plate in the way of new spending programs, social programs, throwing dollars at problems. What we need is, basically, reform of existing institutions and not the destruction of our tried values in this country. Consequently, the next administration will be one of reform, not just adding more dollars."

"The people are going to have to carry their share of the load. The average American is like the child in the family. You give him some responsibility, and he is going to amount to something. . . . Pamper him and cater to him too much, you are going to make him soft, spoiled, and eventually a very weak individual."

From 1937 to 1946, Nixon's career was caught in the bog of depression and war. He married Pat Ryan, a high school teacher of stenography, in 1940. Shortly after the Japanese attack on Pearl Harbor he joined the Office of Price Administration in Washington but stayed just long enough to develop a deep distaste for the bureaucracy, and in August 1942 he enlisted in the navy as a lieutenant junior grade, sidestepping his mother's Quaker-pacifist unhappiness at the act. As a supply officer, Nixon won ribbons for service in the South Pacific and reputedly won much more than a reputation as a poker player.

A mediocre law practice was all that he could see in his postwar future until the Whittier businessmen proposed that he run against Representative Voorhis. Nixon promised to wage "an aggressive campaign on a platform of practical liberalism"—a promise that was laid aside when his campaign veered into what seemed to be the more effective line of attacking Voorhis as being among those "who front for un-American elements, wittingly or otherwise." Actually Voorhis was a very standard kind of New Deal liberal who had even offered legislation in 1940 requiring Communists to register. Nixon's tough campaign marked him as a politician to watch in southern California. Two years later his exposure of Alger Hiss, a former State Department official, as a probable Communist and perjurer marked Nixon as a man who could perform adroitly, if not comfortably, on the national stage as well.

In 1950, with his work on the House Un-American Activities Committee gaining him headlines, he won a seat in the U.S. Senate by again exploiting the public's growing concern with "the Communist menace." His opponent was Representative Helen Gahagan Douglas, who, though a staunch supporter of heavy defense expenditures and a backer of Harry Truman over Henry Wallace, somehow came out of the campaign thoroughly smeared as "The Pink Lady."

Nixon was not a forceful vice-president. Eisenhower's great popularity overwhelmed him, and Eisenhower himself seemed willing to delegate few responsibilities to his much younger subordinate. Only when he was out of the country did Nixon get a chance to swing for himself, as when he survived sometimes violent crowds during a tour through South America and when, on a visit to Moscow, he engaged Soviet premier Nikita Khrushchev in the celebrated "kitchen debate."

Although John F. Kennedy's electoral victory over Nixon in 1960 was comfortably top-heavy, 303 electoral votes to 219, actually a shift of about 4,000 votes in Illinois and a shift of about 9,000 votes in other key states would have made Nixon president that year. Many believe that Nixon lost because he consented to a series of debates with Kennedy and then lost the debates in the public's eye—not on substantive grounds but because Kennedy was better looking and had a better makeup man. The experience left Nixon contemptuous of "powder-puff politics." But it also left him convinced of the necessity of proper staging. And, as he showed in 1972, he also had learned that for the incumbent to give exposure to the challenger by engaging in debates is too generous.

Nixon's defeat in the California governor's race in 1962 was judged by most observers to have been politically fatal, a judgment accurately summarized by *Time*: "Barring a political miracle, his political career [has] ended. . . ." Nothing would have pleased Pat Nixon more; in fact, she attempted to obtain from her husband a written promise that he would never again become an active candidate.

Pundits and his wife notwithstanding, Nixon climbed out of his political grave in 1964. By actively supporting and campaigning for Barry Goldwater while other major Republican presidential contenders remained in seclusion lest they be identified too closely with a losing cause, Nixon picked up so many political IOU's from party regulars that his

nomination in 1968 was cinched. This time the hairbreadth was on his side; he defeated Hubert H. Humphrey by less than one percentage point.

No incoming president in recent times had been faced with the obstacle that confronted Nixon: a Congress controlled by the other party. This would have been a greater frustration, of course, if Nixon had been eager to pass domestic legislation. He was not. Although Congress rejected two of his Supreme Court nominees, he did finally succeed in "changing the direction" of the Court by appointing four "strict constructionists." Nixon acted most dramatically in his first term where he could do so independently of Congress, as in removing virtually all GI's from Vietnam while expanding the bombing attacks.

Having inherited rampant inflation from the Johnson administration, Nixon was more interested in holding down government spending than in creating new social welfare programs or expanding old ones; he vetoed a number of health, education, and public works appropriations bills. Even so, his first administration ran up a projected deficit of close to $100 billion.

During his 1968 campaign he told author Theodore H. White, "I've always thought this country could run itself domestically without a president; all you need is a competent cabinet to run the country at home. You need a president for foreign policy; no secretary of state is really important; the president makes foreign policy."

Once in office he veered from that stated position by relegating his cabinet to third-rung importance, far below his close advisers within the White House, but he did indeed demonstrate that he looked upon foreign policy as "his" alone. Nixon's favorite modern president is Woodrow Wilson. "Wilson had the greatest vision of America's world role," he once said, adding with emphasis, "But he wasn't practical enough." Nixon set out to show that this was not his defect. Nixon the cold warrior, Nixon the unbending enemy of Communism, Nixon a hero to the right wing, now became Nixon the international pragmatist. For months before his election he had been subtly indicating, as in an October 1967 issue of *Foreign Affairs,* that he thought the time had come for the United States to change its relationship with Mainland China. In a number of speeches in 1968 —"it is time to open an era of negotiation rather than confrontation"—he had dropped rather obvious hints to both China and the Soviet Union that his position was changing, and out of these hints developed the negotiations that ultimately took Nixon to Peking and Moscow, exchanging toasts with one hand and signing trade and disarmament pacts with the other.

Although some of his policies changed when he became president, his style did not. He remained a loner. He bypassed his defense secretary to order troops into Cambodia. Not until the housing secretary read it in the newspaper did he know that Nixon was going to cut his budget for the Model Cities program.

John Kennedy read the major daily newspapers closely and often called reporters to praise or condemn their stories. Lyndon Johnson also gorged on the printed press and liked to keep three television sets tuned constantly to the major networks. Like Kennedy, Johnson tried to manipulate the press by personal flattery and threats. Nixon gets his news reports in digest form from his staff. He rarely deals with an individual reporter, rarely grants interviews. Close associates say that he was permanently burned by the press in 1952 when it revealed that he had taken a "political expense" slush fund, some $18,000, from a group of wealthy California backers; afraid that this disclosure might knock him out as Eisenhower's running mate, Nixon went on television to defend the fund and to arouse public sympathy by talking about his wife's "respectable Republican cloth coat" and about his dog, Checkers. The speech worked, but Nixon felt it was a demeaning experience, and he never forgave

the press. Despite this animosity, however, he has been as skillful as any president at using the press through the timing of White House announcements and events.

Cutting himself off from the kind of publicity that surrounded the White House careers of Kennedy and Johnson, Nixon avoids the risks of public blunders, but he also loses the chance of letting the public identify with him. He apparently is reconciled to that loss. When Dan Rather of CBS asked him why many people thought he "failed to inspire confidence and faith and lacked personal warmth and compassion," Nixon responded in a way that may give at least a glimpse into the loneliness of the long-distance political runner: he equated those characteristics that Rather had mentioned with trivial political fluff and denigrated them. "My strong point," he replied, "is not rhetoric; it isn't showmanship; it isn't big promises—those things that create the glamour and excitement that people call charisma and warmth."

Live and let live is not a moral code that appeals to Nixon; when the Commission on Obscenity and Pornography suggested that laws on the sale of "sexual materials" to consenting adults be relaxed, he went beyond simple disagreement to call the commission's report "morally bankrupt." Anticipating the National Commission on Marijuana and Drug Abuse's recommendation that criminal penalties for the private use of marijuana be removed, Nixon announced ahead of time that he would reject such a finding. In these debatable moral and aesthetic areas he feels he also speaks for the typical American: "What the new majority wants for America and what I want for this nation are basically the same."

The 1972 vote indicated he may be right. To Nixon it was more than reelection. He dotes on firsts. He was the first president to travel to Peking; the first to travel to Moscow; the first to talk to a man in space; the first to win all but one state's electoral votes. And, with the completion of his second term, he will have served 16 years as vice-president and president, the first time any American has served so long at such an exalted plane: an ironic finale for the man who in 1962, at the darkest hour of his career, bitterly informed newsmen, "You won't have Richard Nixon to kick around anymore."

George McGovern

When all the votes were counted, George McGovern had suffered one of the worst defeats in U.S. electoral history. The bearer of that dubious distinction, exhausted by 22 months of relentless campaigning, flew off for a Virgin Islands vacation—and to meditate on it all. Not until a week later did McGovern feel up to calling in reporters to discuss the reasons for his overwhelming rejection by the electorate. Ranking high on his list were the shooting of Alabama governor George Wallace, the Eagleton affair, and the defection of labor.

The media offered other reasons for the resounding defeat of "the prairie populist": the reputation he acquired for holding "radical" views on a number of controversial subjects, his unsuccessful attempts to explain his positions to rank-and-file Democrats, and his subsequent credibility gap. Furthermore, McGovern's most important campaign issue—ending the war in Vietnam—did not really "catch fire" with the electorate, who saw the continuation of Republican foreign policy as promoting world peace, especially after presidential adviser Henry Kissinger's announcement, one week before the election, that peace in Southeast Asia was at hand.

George Stanley McGovern was born July 19, 1922, in Avon, S.D., the eldest son of a Methodist minister. Raised in Mitchell, S.D., McGovern absorbed rural values and the tough ethical teachings of his father. He attended Dakota Wesleyan University and did not have his first real taste of life beyond the prairie until he went to serve as a bomber pilot in World War II. A decorated veteran of 35 missions over Europe, McGovern emerged from the war so agonized over the daily killings and the death of his friends that he enrolled from 1946 to 1947 as a Methodist divinity student and evolved the essential social philosophy, which he termed the applied idealism of Christianity, that would mark his political career. At that time he was already married to Eleanor Stegeberg, whom he had courted as a student at Dakota Wesleyan and wed while in army flight training school in October 1943.

Although he enjoyed giving sermons as a student minister, McGovern soon found clerical life too limiting and transferred to Northwestern University, where he studied from 1947 to 1951, earning an M.A. and a Ph.D. in American history (his dissertation was a sympathetic account of a Colorado miners' revolt in 1913–1914). At Northwestern he became attracted to politics and the liberal internationalism of Henry A. Wallace, although he grew disenchanted with Wallace's Progressive Party followers in 1948. After six years as a political science professor at Dakota Wesleyan, McGovern became a full-time Democratic Party organizer in his home state. This was 1953—a time when South Dakota was overwhelmingly Republican.

But a state Democratic organization developed under McGovern's dedicated direction, enabling him to run successfully for Congress in 1956 and 1958. As a representative he helped pass a food-stamp law and two measures to expand the school milk program. He lost a U.S. Senate bid in 1960 but was appointed by President John F. Kennedy, whom he supported, to head the Food for Peace program.

He finally reached the Senate in 1962 (winning by 504 votes), and once there he became one of the first to question American policy in Vietnam. His first criticism was made in the Senate on September 24, 1963, when he termed U.S. involvement in Vietnam "a moral debacle and a political defeat." He voted for the Tonkin Gulf resolution in 1964, but on the very next day he expressed reservations on the floor of the Senate. He continued to criticize the war, increasing his opposition after visiting Vietnam in 1965.

He was reelected in 1968 and became known nationally when, on the day before the U.S. and South Vietnamese invasion of Cambodia in 1970, he joined with Senator Mark O. Hatfield (R, Ore.) to sponsor an amendment to cut off funds for the Vietnam war by the end of 1971. The measure was defeated in the Senate by a vote of 55–39. The next year, the two senators reintroduced their measure, in several versions, but were again unable to secure passage. McGovern was also active on a number of other highly publicized

issues: he opposed the antiballistic missile system, advocated reduction of U.S. troops in Europe, and criticized the size of the defense budget.

McGovern's first fling at the presidential nomination came in 1968. After Senator Robert F. Kennedy was assassinated, McGovern declared himself a candidate just 16 days before the Chicago convention and managed to capture only 146½ votes. After his reelection to the Senate, he spearheaded reform of the Democratic Party nominating process, which opened the door to greater rank-and-file participation and helped make his 1972 nomination possible. More than a product of reform, however, his candidacy was a tribute to his foresight, his endurance, and his midwestern brand of toughness. A relative unknown when he declared himself in January 1971, well before his opponents, McGovern was still the underdog in the race until late in the hard-fought primary ordeal.

After his defeat in November, McGovern promised to continue pressing for an end to the war. He was not, he maintained, crushed by Nixon's impressive victory and was still confident that his beliefs would be vindicated. In an interview after the election he mused, "I held views that the country was not ready to accept right now. I'm convinced that they'll come to those views very quickly."

Spiro Agnew—Sargent Shriver

In just a decade, Spiro T. Agnew has risen from the obscurity of a seat on the Baltimore County zoning commission to the prominence of a second term as vice-president of the United States. But although his name has indeed become a household word, his real identity remains obscured by the many roles he has played. In the 1970 congressional campaign, he was assigned the low road—excoriating the radicals, the young, and the press with invectives too harsh for a president to utter. But then, in 1972, he charted a new course. Although still sharp-tongued, he was, on the whole, more moderate, diplomatic, and conciliatory—a posture clearly more befitting a possible 1976 presidential candidate.

In fact, Agnew's career reveals a man who has changed direction before and who has often landed in the right place at the right time. Agnew switched his party affiliation from Democrat to Republican, his image as governor of Maryland from liberal reformer to law-and-order conservative, and his political allegiance from Nelson Rockefeller to Richard Nixon.

Agnew was born in Baltimore County on November 9, 1918, to Margaret and Theodore Agnew (his father, a Greek immigrant, changed his name from Anagnostopoulos after arriving in the United States). His father was a successful restaurateur in Baltimore, but the depression brought economic hardship, and Agnew has often recalled standing with his father selling vegetables in those difficult times.

After graduating from public high school in 1937, Agnew attended Johns Hopkins University, where he studied chemistry for three years. Because of trouble with the curriculum, he transferred to the law school at the University of Baltimore, attending classes at night and working during the day as a clerk at the Maryland Casualty Company. There he met Elinor Isabel Judefind, whom he married in May 1942. After serving with the 10th Armored Division during World War II, Agnew returned to his law studies, earning his L.L.B. in 1947.

Agnew came to admire one of the senior partners in the law firm he joined and, as a result, changed his registration from Democratic to Republican. He soon gave up the practice of law and took a $100-a-week job as a personnel director for a supermarket chain in Baltimore. But after serving a year in the army again during the Korean war, he returned to law, established a practice that flourished, and settled down in Towson, a well-to-do Baltimore suburb. In 1957, Agnew was appointed to Baltimore County's zoning board of appeals, the first step in his rise to national prominence. He quickly became the board's chairman, only to be ousted in a coup by local Democrats in 1961. Having gained attention as a result of this furor, Agnew successfully ran for county executive—a position tantamount to suburban mayor—the next year. Four years later he became the fifth Republican governor of Maryland.

In the gubernatorial campaign, Agnew ran against segregationist George Mahoney, an adversary of open housing. With liberal and black Democrats flocking to his support, Agnew won handily. In his first year in office, the new governor proceeded to push through the state legislature most of his campaign promises: tax reform, a budget increasing aid to antipoverty programs and local governments, a sweeping open housing law, a repeal of the statute banning racial intermarriage, a liberalized abortion law, and the country's toughest water pollution act.

But in his second year in the statehouse, Agnew bewildered his liberal supporters with what seemed to be a political turnabout. He cut the state budget, with the deepest slashes in the areas of health and welfare; praised the Supreme Court's decision allowing police to stop and frisk suspicious persons; and attacked the Poor People's Campaign, as well as President Lyndon Johnson for permitting "the so-called poor people—with Cadillacs" to encamp in Washington, D.C. In April 1968, when rioting broke out in black neighborhoods in Baltimore after the assassination of Martin Luther King, Jr., Agnew summoned moderate Negro leaders for a dressing down for their failure to speak out against militant blacks.

Four months later, on August 7, Agnew placed Nixon's name in nomination at the Republican National Convention in Miami Beach. The next day Nixon chose him as his running mate.

Agnew's 1968 campaign was marked by denunciations of what he termed a "permissive climate and the misguided compassion of public opinion." Permissiveness, the vice-presidential candidate contended, was bred by a lack of respect for law and order. Under the Nixon administration,

he vowed, "no individual is going to decide for himself which laws to break and which to obey."

In the 1972 campaign, Agnew continued to extol the president and to expound his belief in hard work, discipline, morality, and patriotism. When heckled, he minced no words: in Idaho he took out a whistle and blew it, startling the protesters and the audience; and in San Diego he called on demonstrators to wear "brown shirts" and "swastika armbands," "the same way your spiritual ancestors did in Germany in the 1930's."

But there was another side to Agnew in the 1972 campaign. As he himself announced, there was a new, more conciliatory Agnew. The man who wore the mantle of Republican power and respectability showed renewed friendliness toward the press—joshing with journalists and even playing the piano for them. Confident of victory, he had also become more relaxed about the campaign's demands. In short, he was a man who may, four years from now, have the press wondering—much as they wondered about the "new Nixon" in 1968—whether there really is a "new Agnew."

By the time R. Sargent Shriver was tapped as George McGovern's second running mate, it was common knowledge that a long list of prominent Democrats already had turned the job down. Senator Edward Kennedy pleaded personal reasons, and Senator Hubert Humphrey couldn't bear another jog down the same old garden path. Senator Abraham A. Ribicoff of Connecticut, Governor Reubin Askew of Florida, and Senator Edmund Muskie of Maine also refused.

Thus, R. Sargent Shriver, the optimistic, ebullient Kennedy brother-in-law, had one thing going for him: he wanted to run. "I'm not embarrassed at all to be George McGovern's seventh choice for vice-president," Shriver told the Democratic National Committee members when they placed him on the ticket in August. "We Democrats may be short of money, but we're not short of talent. Think of the comparison, and then you can pity poor Mr. Nixon. His first and only choice was Spiro Agnew."

With that roundhouse, Shriver was off and running in an exuberant campaign. He chartered a jet, named it *The Fighting Lucky Seven* (for the seven members of his family, including five children from seven to 18 years old), and began an exhausting schedule of barnstorming appearances. Shriver concentrated on the woes of the blue-collar workingman, blaming the Nixon administration for ignoring labor and hobnobbing with big business. He also made appeals for McGovern in the big-city ghettos and barrios.

Shriver's eagerness to run was similar to the attitude of McGovern's first candidate for the vice-presidency, Thomas Eagleton. But the Missouri senator lasted only 2½ weeks, after which the furor over his history of treatment for emotional problems led McGovern to decide he needed a less controversial candidate.

Although he had never held elective office, Sarge Shriver was a familiar face

to Americans. As the first head of the Peace Corps, he made a success of a new venture that skeptical Washingtonians had regarded as an almost certain fiasco. With his energy and salesmanship, Shriver traveled around the world and did a one-man selling and lobbying job that helped make the Peace Corps famous.

Under President Lyndon B. Johnson, Shriver, as head of the Office of Economic Opportunity, was a leading general in the War on Poverty. In March 1968, Johnson appointed him ambassador to France, a post he held until 1970. Shriver in Paris was as exuberant and outgoing as Shriver in Washington, but his disregard for protocol and for the cautious traditions of diplomacy made him less popular with French officials than with the crowds whose hands he shook like a campaigner.

Shriver might be called a natural campaigner. In John Kennedy's 1960 race, he was an effective contact man with minority groups. In 1970 he campaigned for Democratic candidates throughout the nation to build up his standing in the Democratic Party.

Finally, in 1972, after years in the shadow of his brothers-in-law, he got the chance to campaign in his own right. According to many reports, when Shriver stayed at his diplomatic post in Paris in 1968 instead of joining Robert Kennedy's presidential campaign, he antagonized the powerful Kennedy clan, who then squelched his ambitions to run for the U.S. Senate from New York and later for governor of Maryland.

Shriver has said, "No family could have been better to me in every possible way." He has also said, "I don't feel my name is Kennedy. My name is Shriver. I don't have to do things in a certain way because the Kennedys do."

Robert Sargent Shriver, Jr., has every reason to be proud of his own heritage. He was born November 9, 1915, to a rich, socially prominent Maryland family that traces its ancestors back to colonial times. Shriver's banker father lost a fortune in the 1929 crash, but Sarge still attended the exclusive Canturbury School, a Catholic boarding school in Connecticut, and then went on to graduate *cum laude* from Yale.

After graduating from Yale Law School, Shriver joined the Navy and fought in both the Atlantic and Pacific theaters during World War II, attaining the rank of lieutenant commander. After the war he worked briefly for *Newsweek* magazine in New York and soon met Eunice Kennedy at a cocktail party. In 1953 they were married.

It was family patriarch Joseph P. Kennedy who first spotted Shriver's potential as a hard-nosed businessman and, in 1946, gave him a job helping to manage the huge family-owned Merchandise Mart in Chicago.

Shriver first came before the public eye in Chicago by serving as director, chairman, or fund-raiser for numerous civic organizations. He also spent five years as president of the Chicago board of education.

Despite the Democratic ticket's overwhelming defeat in November 1972, Shriver's vice-presidential candidacy may have only whetted his appetite for public office. As his wife observed, "He's awfully able, and his whole life has been public service."

NANCY GAY FABER

Primaries and Conventions

Robert Sherrill

ILLUSTRATIONS BY JOHN HUEHNERGARTH

From the beginning it was clear that the 1972 primaries would be neither orderly nor predictable. Not since 1916 had so many states set up presidential primaries (22, plus the District of Columbia; a 50 percent increase over 1968). And not in modern times were so many politicians lined up for the preliminary race to the White House.

The Republicans had three candidates, but together they added up to only a minor intrafamily fuss. Neither Representative Paul McCloskey of California nor Representative John Ashbrook of Ohio considered himself a real challenge to Richard M. Nixon's renomination. They were asking voters to use the primary ballot simply as a way of scolding the president for various actions he had taken (McCloskey being concerned with the continuation of the Vietnam war, Ashbrook with deficit spending and with Nixon's overtures to Mainland China and the Soviet Union).

For the Democrats—who had at least four major candidates and twice as many boisterous minor candidates—the primaries were a serious battle to decide not only their presidential nominee but also the future character of their party, and like all serious battles this one was marked by confusion and noise and the waste of money and good men.

In the public's eye, the field of major Democratic candidates was evenly divided between liberals, moderates, and moderate-conservatives. But in fact their political records showed that on some issues the moderate-conservatives were more liberal than the liberals. As if that sort of thing were not enough to ensure confusion, the issues debated by the

candidates were so emotionally scalding (school busing) or of such marginal importance (penalties for marijuana use) that the New York *Times* quite justifiably scorned the early primaries as being less trustworthy for predicting the future than were the pigeon entrails used by Roman soothsayers. Not until the nineteenth primary, California's (held on June 6), did the significant domestic issues confronting the nation —such matters as welfare reform, tax reform, and defense expenditures—begin to get the attention they deserved, and by that time there were only two real candidates left to debate them: Senators Hubert H. Humphrey of Minnesota and George McGovern of South Dakota.

Democratic Dropouts

By June, Senator Edmund S. Muskie of Maine, the early "sure thing" favorite, was gone. Governor George C. Wallace, the maverick Alabama Democrat who had dazzled the country with six primary victories, had been paralyzed by an assassin's bullet and was out of the running. So was the defense industry's champion, Senator Henry M. Jackson of Washington. Gone, too, were New York City's Mayor John V. Lindsay, who had futilely hoped that the Democrats would reward him for switching parties, and Los Angeles' Mayor Sam Yorty and his campaign vehicle, the "Yortymobile." Senator Vance Hartke of Indiana had disappeared unnoticed somewhere back down the campaign trail, and former senator Eugene J. McCarthy, hero of the antiwar

movement in 1968, was a dropout shortly before the California balloting. Still hanging on were Representatives Shirley Chisholm of New York and Wilbur Mills of Arkansas.

They were a colorful lot, no matter what their individual staying power, but the truly historic drama of the primaries of 1972 was wrapped around two men and two fortunes: the strange decline of Edmund Muskie, favored by the Democratic establishment, by most union leaders, and by most big-city Democratic bosses, and the unexpected rise of George McGovern, backed by his coalition of suburban liberals, Kennedy-McCarthy organizational remnants, students, feminists, and black and Latino activists.

Until the primaries really got under way, Muskie had been virtually conceded the Democratic nomination. The polls said he was the heavy favorite. Most major newspapers said he had the nomination wrapped up. The list of politicians who endorsed his candidacy read like a who's who of the Democratic hierarchy. But even before the first primary vote —New Hampshire's—was taken, things began to fall apart for him. If his problems can be traced back to one episode— symbolically, if not in fact—it would be to the snowy morning of February 26, when the Maine Democrat stood on a flatbed truck in front of the offices of the Manchester *Union Leader* and, with what appeared to be tears in his eyes, denounced the newspaper's publisher, William Loeb, as a "gutless coward." Loeb had printed slighting remarks about Muskie's wife and also had published a letter (later sus-

pected as a forgery) accusing Muskie of insulting Americans of French-Canadian descent, New Hampshire's largest ethnic minority. Muskie's advisers felt he could not let the attack go unanswered, but the emotionalism of Muskie's speech stunned his supporters and apparently offended many undecided voters, in other primary states as well as in New Hampshire.

Such self-control lapses aside, one of Muskie's most ferocious opponents from the outset was the one that always plagues the front-runner: his percentage. To win was not enough; he had to win big, or he would lose in public esteem—a phenomenon which Muskie called "the phantom candidate, a figment of the press' imagination."

In mid-January the Boston *Globe* poll showed him with 65 percent of the potential vote in New Hampshire; in early March the *Globe* found Muskie's support down to 49 percent, and less than a week before the election it was down to 42 percent. At that point the headlined question was whether he would win a simple majority. And once that question had been firmly planted in the public's mind, it was impossible for Muskie to emerge as the victor simply by leading the pack. He had to take 50 percent plus.

He won 46.4 percent. McGovern took 37.1 percent. But McGovern's showing (and his claim of "moral victory") got most of the favorable publicity.

From that disappointment Muskie moved to the Florida campaign, which exemplified another of his problems as a

11

presidential candidate—a lackluster campaign style. Hoping to imitate Harry Truman's successful whistle-stop tour of 1948, Muskie used a six-car train from Jacksonville to Miami, but the crowds along the way were thin and Muskie's speeches—far from Truman's "give 'em hell" vintage—struck no sparks. Aiming at a moderate, centrist image, Muskie was succeeding only in appearing indecisive and overly cautious.

The Florida race also pointed up the dangers of the Muskie campaign's decision to contest every primary. What was Muskie doing in Florida anyway? With George Wallace on the ballot in a southern state, the primary was hardly a

WHO "WON" THE PRIMARIES?

According to Democratic National Committee figures, George McGovern was the choice of only about one-quarter of the people who cast ballots in the 23 Democratic primaries. And the candidate who got the highest cumulative vote total was not McGovern but Hubert Humphrey. The total vote in the 23 primaries was distributed as follows:

Hubert Humphrey	4,299,886	(26%)
George McGovern	4,264,358	(26%)
George Wallace	3,648,232	(22%)
Edmund Muskie	1,840,217	(11%)
Others	2,229,810	(15%)
Total vote	16,282,503	

test of a candidate's national strength. Wallace had been predicting that "the people are fixin' to assert themselves," and for his benefit they certainly did. Wallace's 42 percent of the vote more than equaled the combined total of the next three candidates: Humphrey, 18 percent; Jackson, 13 percent; and finally Muskie, 9 percent.

Wallace swept all but one congressional district, losing only the 11th District to Humphrey, who campaigned hard for its heavy Jewish vote, promising everything from strong support for Israel to kosher food in the National School Lunch Program. Thus, in Florida, Muskie also discovered the old campaign rule that when there are several candidates running with essentially the same philosophy, the underdogs pitch their appeals to particular ethnic and special-interest groups and leave the strongest candidate with a slender middle base. After Humphrey carved off the blacks, the Jews, and the elderly and Jackson carved off the defense and aerospace workers, very little was left for Muskie.

Because Florida made Muskie appear to be far less than the supercandidate he was previously touted, his financial support immediately began to dry up and his position became more precarious. Then Illinois gave him a new chance. He won 63 percent of the presidential preference vote—nothing but a popularity contest—against Eugene McCarthy's 37 percent; more important, in separate balloting, Muskie won 59 convention delegates against McGovern's 13.

His spirits and prospects revived by these victories, Muskie seemed ready to gamble everything on Wisconsin, and for good reason: with its balanced urban-rural mixture and its progressive attitudes, Wisconsin seemed more typical of the nation than Florida and better able to give a sharp test of a candidate's popularity. Into Wisconsin, Muskie sent almost his entire national political staff on a blitz campaign, juiced with a campaign fund of nearly $500,000. But neither money nor staff expertise could stir the electorate; the action was around McGovern and Humphrey. And the more this became apparent to Muskie, the more desperately he increased his own efforts—and as a result, the more noticeable was his ultimate failure.

Muskie had to finish high to maintain his credibility. Instead he finished fourth, with only 10 percent of the vote, behind McGovern's 30 percent, Wallace's 22 percent, and Humphrey's 21 percent.

Now the seesaw began its swing in earnest: Muskie went down, and in his place McGovern came up, as the 15-month nationwide effort to recruit campaign workers, canvass voters, and register potential McGovern voters began to pay off. Wisconsin, in which McGovern considered a primary victory essential to his candidacy, epitomized that effort. For example, in Madison, the state capital and the home of the University of Wisconsin, McGovern volunteers had, through a registration drive, boosted the number of eligible voters by an amazing 60 percent; they set up a convoy of shuttle buses to carry the newly enfranchised student voters to the polls; between January and March, McGovern's young volunteers visited virtually every home in the city with a personal sales pitch or a campaign leaflet.

In retrospect it is clear that Wisconsin was a watershed after which Muskie was doomed, Humphrey was slated to fill the centrist vacuum Muskie vacated, and McGovern's fortunes would soar. But at the moment this was not clear, and Democratic Party chairman Lawrence F. O'Brien was saying that he had never before in his political life witnessed so much confusion.

Tragic End for the Wallace Campaign

But things were about to clear up, partly by a new trend, partly by tragedy. On May 15, Arthur Herman Bremer, the smiling, 21-year-old busboy and janitor from Milwaukee, Wis., reached through a crowd surrounding the candidate in a Laurel, Md., shopping center and shot Governor Wallace in the chest and stomach with a .38 caliber pistol. Paralyzed from the waist down, Wallace was out of the race, even though, on the next day, May 16, he won the Maryland and Michigan primaries. But even if Wallace had not been removed from the campaign by a pistol, his efforts would have fallen off sharply after May 16 because he had run out of major target states. Somehow he and his advisers had incredibly underrated his chances, and as a result he had failed, for example, to enter the California and Ohio primaries. Worse than that, he had failed to set up the necessary delegate machinery in the states where he did run, thus canceling out his own strength. Placing second in Wisconsin, Wallace nevertheless got not a single delegate, although Humphrey, who placed third, got 13. In Pennsylvania, his most unfortunate oversight, Wallace finished second but won only two delegates, although McGovern, who finished third, got 37 and Muskie, who finished fourth, got 29. The reason: Wallace had failed to file delegate slates or had filed grotesquely incomplete ones.

Meanwhile, Muskie had been finished off as a candidate by two sledgehammer blows in Pennsylvania and Massachusetts. What Wisconsin was to McGovern, Pennsylvania was to Humphrey. Before the vote, he called Pennsylvania "my Waterloo." If he failed here, he said, he was done for. Muskie, misled by promises of strong organizational support from Governor Milton J. Shapp, ran behind Humphrey in both the presidential preference balloting and the delegate competition. (Pennsylvania was the first contested primary election Humphrey had ever won in three campaigns for the Democratic presidential nomination.)

On the same day, in Massachusetts, McGovern was winning a clear majority (52 percent) in a 12-name primary and taking all 102 delegates, which pushed him into the lead with a total of 234½ delegates. Muskie was now a bad second with 128½.

On April 27, two days after the Pennsylvania and Massachusetts setbacks, Muskie told his staff that he was through and that they should feel free to transfer their loyalties to other candidates. In effect, Muskie's withdrawal made it a

race between McGovern and Humphrey, and California was clearly the showdown between them, with Humphrey representing "the regulars"—the residue of the labor-liberal Democratic Party leadership that traced its heritage back to Franklin Roosevelt's New Deal—and McGovern representing the insurgents—the followers of the "new politics."

Since Pennsylvania, Humphrey had won in Indiana and Ohio; since Massachusetts, McGovern had won in Nebraska, Rhode Island, and Oregon. To walk away with California's 271 delegates in the nation's only winner-take-all primary Humphrey and McGovern knew they had to win as many popular votes as in all the previous 18 primaries combined. McGovern's advantage in California, one that any politician could understand, was twofold: more volunteer workers (about 25,000 at peak) and more money.

Five days before the primary, the respected California Poll, sponsored by 17 newspapers and broadcasting stations in the state, reported McGovern leading Humphrey by 20 percentage points (46 to 26). The outcome was as predicted but much closer, as Humphrey came on strong near the end of the campaign, charging that McGovern's proposed defense-spending cuts would leave the nation vulnerable to attack and that his proposed welfare reforms would increase taxes on the middle class in order to pay others not to work. The final vote was 47.2 percent for McGovern to 41.7 percent for Humphrey.

On the same day as the California balloting, McGovern also won primaries in New Jersey, New Mexico, and South Dakota, and two weeks later he won 251 of a possible 278 delegates in the last of 1972's primaries, New York's.

The big news in the preconvention season came from the 22 states that held primaries, and indeed they rated the attention they got because from them came two-thirds of the Miami Beach convention delegates. Nevertheless, it was in the largely unpublicized nonprimary states—where the delegate fight was hammered out in local party caucuses and state party conventions, not at the voting booth—that McGovern cinched his nomination, winning 364 of a possible 1,009 delegates, compared with fewer than 100 delegates for either of his closest rivals, Humphrey and Muskie.

If McGovern had not had his overwhelming success in the caucus states, his rivals might have held him short of victory on the first ballot in Miami Beach, which in turn would have given them time and space to regroup with sufficient strength to prevent his taking the nomination at all. So it is understandable that the anti-McGovern forces looked back at the outcome in the nonprimary states with special unhappiness. Some accused McGovern of having operated by stealth; some accused him of having helped rig the new rules under which the caucuses were required to operate.

Actually, the party's old-line regulars defeated themselves by presuming that their customary power levers would remain available to them and that the national party's reform commission—which McGovern headed until January 1971 and which wrote the new rules that governed delegate selection in 1972—need not be taken seriously. For example, I. W. Abel, president of the steelworkers' union and a Humphrey supporter, was a member of the 26-man commission,

but he did not attend a single meeting. Thus, the regulars did not fully realize that, although previously entire state delegations could be handpicked by the governor or a few state party bosses, the new rules had thrown open the delegate-selection process.

Commitment and Organization

McGovern's crucial twofold advantage was in being intimately familiar with the new delegate-selection procedure and in exploiting it long before any other candidate got wise to what he was up to. As early as the fall of 1970, McGovern's forces were quietly moving in to fill the power vacuum from the precinct level up, with the ultimate objective of packing the caucuses. Even when, as late as February 1972, the polls showed McGovern getting only 5 or 6 percent of Democratic support, his strategists were reasonably content because the entire caucus operation was conducted on the theory that no more than 5 or 6 percent of the voters showed up for caucuses. If McGovern could be sure that they were his 5 or 6 percent, he would win delegates.

McGovern's strength throughout the preconvention season was in what he called the "commitment" of his small band of believers. They always turned out, whether to canvass primary voters or to attend the caucuses in the nonprimary states. The philosophy behind McGovern's grass roots victory was perhaps best summed up by Gene Pokorny, 25, McGovern's Midwest regional coordinator and the man most responsible for success in Wisconsin. "Organization," Pokorny explained to a reporter, "is a very simple thing. All politics is in names. Get their names and telephone numbers and put them on three-by-five cards. The guts of politics is three-by-five cards." Muskie and Humphrey had the big endorsements, but McGovern had the little cards.

After the bruising primary battles and with the nomination seemingly sewed up by McGovern, the Democrats went to

REPUBLICAN

CONVENTION

Credentials Committee, temporarily controlled by anti-McGovern members, upheld the challenge and ruled that 151 of California's delegates should be given to the other primary candidates.

Denouncing the ruling as "an incredible, cynical, rotten political steal," McGovern threatened to bolt the party if the ruling denied him the nomination. Then the McGovern forces regained control of the Credentials Committee and, in retaliation, unseated Mayor Daley and 58 other Illinois delegates as violators of the party's reform guidelines. Both disputes were in and out of court but were still unresolved on the Monday the convention opened—the day on which all the Credentials Committee decisions would be approved or rejected on the convention floor.

Just how perilous was McGovern's position before the floor vote on the California challenge? Not very. A Washington *Post* vote survey—as accurate as any in that highly fluid period—showed that the convention votes (not counting the 151 disputed California delegates) were scattered this way: McGovern, 1,386.8; Humphrey, 558.2; Wallace, 402; Muskie, 275.5; Jackson, 54.75; Chisholm, 40.69; Mills, 33.5; Terry Sanford (former governor of North Carolina), 33; Yorty, 4; McCarthy, 4; Senator Edward M. Kennedy(Mass.), 2; Lindsay, 2; uncommitted, 219.6.

their national convention in Miami Beach hoping to show that, despite the fratricidal feuding, the party was basically unified. The Republicans showed up in Miami Beach six weeks later hoping to convey the idea that although they were militantly unified behind Richard Nixon, the party still smiled upon diversity. Both failed.

Just how far the Democrats fell short of unity can be measured by the facts that the name of the immediate past Democratic president was not mentioned in any important speech during the four-day convention, that the major defeated candidates of the 1972 primary campaign were shunned by the convention managers, and that the most important big-city political boss in the Democratic pantheon, Mayor Richard Daley of Chicago, was voted off the convention floor.

But the severest blow to the prospects for a unity convention was the attempt by some of the "regulars" to take away 151 of McGovern's 271 California delegates. Less than a week after the June 6 primary, four of the losing candidates filed a formal complaint with the Democratic Party's Credentials Committee regarding California's winner-take-all provision, which gave the candidate with a plurality of the popular vote all 271 delegate votes at the convention. The complainants charged that this provision "totally disenfranchised" the 53 percent of California's Democratic voters who cast their ballots for other candidates.

On June 29, just as McGovern thought he was within a dozen votes of the 1,509 needed to cinch the nomination, the

From those statistics it was apparent that the aggressive coalition which newsmen had nicknamed ABM (anybody but McGovern) really had nobody of any impressive strength to turn to. The psychology of the convention was running heavily against them. And to their dismay, the convention chairman, Lawrence O'Brien (who many regulars had assumed was on their side) issued a ruling increasing McGovern's chances of success. O'Brien held that the California credentials challenge should be decided by a majority of the delegates eligible to vote (all the delegates minus the 151 challenged delegates) rather than by a majority of the full convention. Thus, to overturn the California challenge, McGovern needed to get only 1,433 floor votes instead of 1,509.

With that ruling McGovern was clearly in a winning position, his bandwagon started rolling, and the vote on the California question—which went his way by a very comfortable margin of 1,618 to 1,238—was only a formality.

With his 151 California votes back, McGovern easily won a first-ballot nomination on Wednesday, July 12, getting 1,728 votes before the switching started.

The California victory was so decisive that thereafter, as one McGovern aide later boasted, "We had absolute control

of the convention floor. We played it like a violin." One of the losers described it differently: "It's the same stacked deck we've had for a hundred years. It's just a new set of dealers." Indeed, so tightly did McGovern's top hands control all the face cards that they felt no danger from dissent (George Wallace, just out of the hospital, came to criticize the platform and was received politely) and could allow delegates the luxury of talking on at great length. The second session of the convention lasted from about 7:30 P.M. Tuesday until 6:21 A.M. Wednesday—the longest session in political convention history. Aside from conveying the impression of democracy, the dragging out of debate past prime time had the added advantage of keeping potentially embarrassing topics off the air until an hour when most of the television audience was asleep. A freedom-of-choice abortion plank was killed at 4:45 A.M., and a gay liberation plank was voted down as the sun came up.

Despite the open discussion of issues, the platform that emerged was in all essential parts the one that McGovern's advisers had handed the convention at the outset. Contrary to the expectations of many anti-McGovernites, it was not a radical platform. It did not, for example, mention the $32 billion reduction in the defense budget which McGovern, in many campaign speeches, had promised to make; the welfare plank did not promise a $6,500 guaranteed annual income, despite heavy pressure on McGovern from the National Welfare Rights Organization to endorse such a proposal. It was a rather standard liberal Democratic platform with the usual attention to labor and the minorities.

And despite the almost endless nominations for the vice presidency—the only reflection of the delegates' irritation at being taken for granted by McGovern—he also got the running mate he and his advisers had decided on in private: Senator Thomas F. Eagleton of Missouri. Once again the choice was anything but radical. Eagleton was the standard ticket balancer: McGovern is Protestant; Eagleton, Catholic. McGovern has a rural–small-town background; Eagleton, an urban background. McGovern has close ties to the farm bloc; Eagleton, close ties to labor.

The most noticeable traces of the highly publicized "new politics" were not in what was done but by whom it was done. Compared to the 1968 convention, there were eight times more delegates under the age of 30, three times more women, and three times more blacks. Eighty percent of the delegates had never attended a national political convention before. Less well represented than in 1968 were the party regulars. For example, only 60 of the 310 Democratic members of Congress were delegates in 1972.

Republican Coronation

At the Republican convention six weeks later, there was little to disturb the euphoric atmosphere. The only cloud of any size had already appeared briefly on the horizon in the spring, when the Republican National Committee voted against holding the convention in San Diego, Calif., after allegations that the International Telephone and Telegraph Corporation's offer to help finance a San Diego convention was linked to favorable settlements in several antitrust suits against ITT.

Those ugly rumors of conflict of interest and payoff, however, were well past by the time the Republicans came together in Miami Beach on August 21, and if one could only overlook those rowdy yippies and zippies parading through the streets, then the atmosphere would have to be judged as politically perfect as any partisan could wish. Everything was sewed up, and the Republicans had come together, as much of the press put it, not for a nomination but for a coronation.

Ridiculing the seemingly careless way the Democrats allowed their convention program to sprawl past prime television time, the Republican managers maintained a crisp, no-nonsense timetable. There were no surprises and few ad libs. Even invocation and benediction prayers had to be submitted to party officials for clearance two weeks before the convention opened. To ensure a well-disciplined cheering section, 3,000 Young Republicans were organized in squads. Dissent of any significance was virtually nonexistent. Representative Paul McCloskey was refused permission to arrange a 25-minute antiwar speech. Only two amendments were permitted to be offered to the platform (one against deficit spending and one advocating more help for Indians), and only the latter was permitted to pass. The outcome of all issues was so predetermined that the convention chairman, Representative Gerald Ford (Mich.), was given written instructions on when and how to announce the outcome of a procedural vote—before the vote was taken.

A group of 11 reform-minded Republican congressmen attempted to modify party rules in such a way as to give greater representation at the 1976 convention to the more populous states. But delegates from the South and West joined to destroy this—the only significant proposal for change made at the convention—by a 2–1 vote, thus leaving control of the party solidly in the hands of conservatives.

Open Convention?

And yet speaker after speaker emphasized that this, too, was an open convention. They did not mean open in the same way that the Democratic convention had been open—to a sometimes conflicting scramble of interests. The 2,700 Republican delegates and alternates were basically a white (96 percent), Protestant (75 percent), not too young (92 percent over 30), conservative "family" who had come together for some talks and entertainment by Pat Boone and John Wayne and did not have any intention of spoiling the occasion with open disputes. The references to openness simply meant that the Republicans were opening their arms to disgruntled Democrats. In his acceptance speech President Nixon, lamenting the fate of the Democrats whose party had been taken over by allegedly radical McGovernites, told the cheering delegates: "To those millions who have been driven out of their home in the Democratic Party, I say, 'Come home—not to another party but to the great principles we Americans believe in together.' "

If McGovern's course was "socialism," "radicalism," and "convulsive left-wing extremism"—as Nixon and several keynote speakers tried to label it—the president and the Republicans could hope to establish what Nixon called "our new majority." The party platform, written under the close supervision of the White House, for the first time in a generation gave no support to the concept of the open shop (in which workers are not required to join the plant's union)—an obvious concession to George Meany, president of the AFL-CIO, and to other big-labor officials who were enraged by McGovern's nomination. The platform also implicitly approved deficit spending. That change represented quite a swing to the left for the Republicans, and it was clear that such adjustments of traditional policy were aimed at a hybrid majority that, it was hoped, would last beyond 1972.

If it seemed that the entire political spectrum was embraced by the two major parties, this was not quite true. On the left, the People's Party, meeting in St. Louis, Mo., in late July, nominated Dr. Benjamin Spock as its presidential candidate. The American Party, meeting in Louisville, Ky., in early August, at first tried to interest George Wallace in a splinter-party candidacy. When Wallace insisted he was unable to make the race, they picked lame-duck Representative John G. Schmitz (R, Calif.) as their presidential nominee. Some of Congressman Schmitz's supporters brought back the bumper stickers he had used in his first congressional campaign: "When you're out of Schmitz, you're out of gear." Like a lot of other things coming out of 1972's conventions, it had a familiar ring.

Campaign

Robert Sherrill

If a retroactive slogan is permitted for a campaign, " 'Tom Who?' destroyed George in '72" might be the most accurate one to describe what happened to the Democratic candidate. Perhaps President Richard M. Nixon would have won by a landslide under any circumstances; but the man who made Senator George McGovern's defeat inevitable from the beginning was not Nixon but rather McGovern's first running mate, Senator Thomas Eagleton, 42, handsome, brilliant, witty—and disastrously secretive.

Coming out of the Democratic convention the McGovern

forces were euphoric. All their strategy was clicking. Of course, there had been defections among the Democratic regulars, but the factious Democratic Party had traditionally had a way of patching up its quarrels before Election Day. Moreover, the fresh wind stirred by the McGovern primary campaign was still blowing. Recent polls taken in three key states—Illinois, Texas, and California—showed McGovern running neck-and-neck with Nixon, although, to be sure, nationally the Democratic candidate was still far down in the percentages.

Most importantly, no longer would McGovern have to shoulder the burden alone. Eagleton was a fine speaker. His wry self-denigration—"I accepted before George could change his mind"—put him in especially good rapport, it seemed, with the 18-to-21-year-old voters, that powerful new age bloc that McGovern hoped to sweep. Eagleton was also on friendly terms with big labor—the type of liaison that McGovern sorely needed. (Among other things, a vote that McGovern had cast in the Senate against the union shop made him less than the ideal candidate from labor's point of view—even though McGovern later said that he had come to view that vote as wrong.)

Eagleton's record matched his bright looks and bright rhetoric: *cum laude* at Amherst College, again *cum laude* at Harvard Law School, circuit attorney at 27, attorney general of Missouri at 31, lieutenant governor of Missouri at 35, U.S. senator at 39. He never ran for reelection to anything; every four years he staked out a higher office, went after it, and always won, sometimes by bucking tradition; he was (according to local historians) the first Roman Catholic to win a statewide office in Missouri in the twentieth century.

Admittedly, there had been rumors of a drinking problem in Eagleton's background, but alcohol is not exactly an unknown quantity in most politicians' lives, and besides, a cursory check indicated the rumors to be false. Everyone knew Eagleton was a nervous sort. He smoked two packs of cigarettes a day and sweated at the slightest provocation—"Eagleton sweats on Christmas Eve," he would say, mocking himself. But smoke and sweat hardly added up to a reasonable doubt.

If McGovern had been a Lyndon B. Johnson, gnawed by the suspicions that lay heavier than smoke in the back rooms of politics, he might not have been so cavalier about it all. Before Johnson picked Senator Hubert H. Humphrey as his running mate in 1964, he asked a mutual friend, Washington attorney James Rowe, to subject Humphrey to two hours of brutally intimate grilling—an experience which reportedly left Humphrey quivering with anger and embarrassment but which at least set Johnson's mind at rest.

McGovern, less a politician and more a gentleman than Johnson, was willing to settle for hardly any investigation at all before picking up his Doral Hotel telephone at 3:45 P.M. on July 13, offering the job to Eagleton, chatting with him for about 45 seconds, and then turning him over to his aide Frank Mankiewicz, who asked the crucial question: "Are there any skeletons in your closet?" Eagleton said no.

Skeletons in the Closet?

In December 1960, Eagleton had checked into a Missouri hospital for psychiatric care, including shock treatments; his office told newsmen at the time that he was suffering from a virus. In December 1964, he went off to the Mayo Clinic at Rochester, Minn., for more psychiatric care; his office told newsmen that he had gone in for "some tests." In September 1966, his office issued a press release saying he had been admitted to Johns Hopkins University Hospital in Baltimore for treatment of a "gastric disturbance"; this was what Eagleton later called "a little diversionary" falsehood—actually he had returned to the Mayo Clinic for more shock treatment.

On the flight down to Miami Beach for the Democratic convention, Eagleton discussed with his wife what he should say about his hospital record if he was offered the vice-presidential spot; they decided to keep quiet. But he knew it was risky. He said later, "It always goes through your mind, 'When will I be asked? When will somebody know?'" If Eagleton did not consider his mental history a skeleton, he considered it at least a shroud hanging in the closet.

Not until July 25, 12 days after he accepted, did Eagleton sit down with McGovern and explain in detail his pre-

vious health problems, and he did so then only because he had heard that several members of the press corps—alerted by anonymous phone calls—were closing in on the truth. Oddly, McGovern was not particularly worried by what Eagleton told him. He thought a candid public acknowledgment would take care of the matter nicely.

But as it turned out, Eagleton's first official press conference of the 1972 campaign, in which he told nearly all, was the beginning of the end for McGovern. It launched an unprecedented storm of public controversy, some centering on Eagleton's lack of candor, some on McGovern's lack of caution in picking a running mate, and all touching on the question of whether the United States could afford to have a vice-president about whom there was the slightest doubt as to his mental stability.

Eagleton Backed "1,000 Percent"

At the time of the disclosure, McGovern had vowed that he was "1,000 percent for Tom Eagleton"—a percentage that would come to haunt him in the weeks ahead. But as the storm grew stronger McGovern began to tack a different course. Soon he was hinting that he wanted Eagleton to voluntarily leave the ticket. As his hints grew broader, however, Eagleton's stubbornness increased. A week after his first press conference, he announced his "firm, irrevocable intent" to continue his candidacy. But on the same day that Eagleton, appearing on CBS' *Face the Nation*, reaffirmed his intention to stay in the race, Jean Westwood, Democratic national chairwoman, appeared on NBC's *Meet the Press* and urged the senator to do "the noble thing" and withdraw.

It was plain that McGovern would have to pry Eagleton's hands loose from the mast and throw him overboard if he expected to get rid of him. On July 31, McGovern took Eagleton aside for a couple of hours; then they came out and faced the television lights together—Eagleton pale and perspiring, McGovern unruffled and tan—and agreed to go their separate ways. Eagleton, who had the distinction of being the first vice-presidential candidate to step down after accepting nomination, went gracefully, with the kind of flippancy that the public had learned to expect from him. "I started in anonymity," he said, "and I leave with notoriety. I'm no longer Tom Who. People know my name." (A week after the election, however, Eagleton, showing a little more bitterness than flippancy, told reporters, "Toward the end of the campaign there were members of the McGovern staff who were looking for a convenient scapegoat for what appeared to be the inevitable result. And I believe I became the target of that scapegoatism.")

McGovern, even in August, saw no grounds for flippancy. Eighteen days had elapsed since the Democratic National Convention. All the buoyancy and all the momentum were gone. In the public's eye, McGovern's image had changed. His turnabout on Eagleton was unsettling. The polls, ironically, showed massive sympathy for Eagleton rather than for the politician he had misled. A major loss from the McGovern arsenal was the ability to attack Vice-President Spiro Agnew with the aggressiveness that the Democrats had been planning; the less said now about the vice-presidency, the better.

Shriver: At Least the Seventh Choice

McGovern's embarrassment over the Eagleton affair was immediately followed by the humiliation of being turned down by at least six politicians—Hubert H. Humphrey and Edmund Muskie at the head of the list—to whom he offered the second spot on the ticket; more than six may have been approached out of the press' earshot before R. Sargent Shriver—a former director of the Peace Corps and the Office of Economic Opportunity, a former ambassador to France, and a Kennedy family in-law—agreed to become the vice-

Women: A Political Force

In 1972 women became a major force in national politics, as many feminists came to believe that fair political representation of women is fundamental to their hopes for equal employment, equal rights under the law, and opportunity for individual fulfillment.

The effects of the women's movement on politics could be seen in several ways this year. As early as February, Richard Nixon was receiving staff memos on how not to sound condescending to women audiences, and Edmund Muskie, then the front-runner for the Democratic nomination, was publicizing the fact that his staff included the first women ever to handle the preparations (or advance work) for a major candidate's personal appearances. In July women constituted 40 percent of the delegates to the Democratic National Convention—up from 13 percent in 1968. And 30 percent of the delegates to the 1972 Republican National Convention were women—compared with 17 percent in 1968. The National Women's Political Caucus (organized in 1971 by women activists), through its offshoot Women's Education for Delegate Selection, worked in every state to encourage and prepare women to run for convention delegate positions. When state parties failed to take what the NWPC considered effective action to include women delegates, the caucus helped mount challenges to the states' convention delegations.

For the first time in history, both the Democratic and the Republican party platforms included comprehensive women's planks. Top priority was given in both planks to ratification by the states of the Equal Rights Amendment, which had received final congressional approval by the Senate on March 22. Both planks also called for the appointment of women to positions at the highest levels of the federal government, for the elimination of economic discrimination against women, and for the provision of child-care facilities for families at all economic levels.

However, the conventions also produced some disappointments for women activists. Neither party platform contained any reference to elimination of government intervention in the reproductive lives of American citizens. Such a plank would have been, among other things, a statement in favor of a woman's right to an abortion. At the Democratic convention the following minority report on reproductive freedom was brought to the convention floor for a vote on whether it should be included in the party platform: "In matters relating to human reproduction, each person's right to privacy, freedom of choice, and individual conscience should be fully respected, consistent with relevant Supreme Court decisions." This minority report was defeated by a vote of 1,569.80 to 1,103.37 in a session that lasted until after 6:00 A.M. on July 12.

Senator George McGovern, who was to become the Democratic nominee on the evening of July 12, had stated during the primaries that he considered abortion a matter for state regulation on which he would not take a personal stand. (President Nixon had, during the spring, expressed strong opposition to liberalized abortion laws.) At the Democratic convention, McGovern's aides released many of the delegates pledged to his support, allowing them to vote according to their consciences on the abortion plank. But these aides reportedly made sure that the plank would be defeated because they believed it would be detrimental to McGovern's campaign for the presidency. Shirley MacLaine, the actress, who was a delegate and a McGovern worker at the convention, was criticized by some women activists for not supporting a strong abortion plank.

Another defeat for women activists occurred on July 10, at the Democratic convention's first session. McGovern had helped write the party reform rules which increased the number of women at the convention. However, when an attempt was made on July 10 to seat nine additional women on the South Carolina delegation, McGovern aides ordered some McGovern delegates to vote against the measure. Its defeat by a wide margin avoided a floor fight on a procedural question that could have affected the important California-challenge vote, which McGovern later won to pick up 151 more delegates favorable to his nomination.

The Democratic National Convention was nevertheless important for women for at least two reasons: a black woman, Representative Shirley Chisholm (D, N.Y.), attracted national attention as a presidential contender, and a woman, Texas state legislator Frances "Sissy" Farenthold, got the second-highest number of votes for the vice-presidential nomination.

In neither party were women significantly represented at the highest decision-making levels in the fall presidential campaign. But Rita Hauser, cochairperson of President Nixon's reelection committee, and Anne Armstrong, cochairperson of the Republican National Committee (a position subsidiary to Robert Dole's chairmanship), did have high-level policy positions in the Nixon campaign, and women were in charge of the campaigns in some states. In the Democratic Party, women were in charge of the issues staffs in the McGovern and Shriver campaign; there was a national committee, headed by well-known feminists like Representative Bella Abzug, Sissy Farenthold, and Gloria Steinem, to ensure that women's issues would be addressed in the campaign; and there were advance women and women coordinators in many of the states.

Major battles have yet to be fought if women are to gain full equality in national politics. But they showed strength in 1972, and the activists who started the women's movement had attracted enough followers to make a noticeable impact on both the Democratic and the Republican parties. — BRENDA FEIGEN FASTEAU

A CONTROVERSIAL ROLE in the effort to nominate George McGovern was played by Shirley MacLaine at the Democratic convention, where 40 percent of the delegates were women.
WALLY MCNAMEE/ NEWSWEEK

presidential candidate. By now it was clear that, barring a major scandal in the Nixon administration, the McGovern campaign could not be viewed as a serious challenge.

As it turned out, however, not even a combination of major scandals and potential scandals could dislodge Nixon from his lead. The so-called Watergate affair, which began in June with the arrest of five men on charges of burglarizing and bugging the Democratic National Committee headquarters (located in the Watergate apartment and commercial complex in Washington, D.C.), kept expanding. Largely as a result of the aggressive reporting of the Washington *Post*, aided by a veritable deluge of leaks from within the Justice Department and the FBI, a startling number of big-name Republicans were tied, some by fact and some by innuendo, to political espionage. A security officer for the Committee for the Re-Election of the President and two former White House consultants were indicted for direct participation in the Watergate break-in; the *Post* claimed to have documented proof that the president's personal attorney, his appointments secretary, and several of his closest advisers either had unexplained connections with some of the accused political espionage agents or had supervised a $300,000 to $700,000 fund from which the espionage acts were allegedly subsidized. Among those named by the *Post* were H. R. Haldeman, Nixon's White House chief of staff, and former attorney general John N. Mitchell. Republican officials acknowledged the existence of a special fund but claimed the money was used for preliminary planning for the campaign. In general, the Republicans claimed that the *Post* charges were based on "hearsay."

But the Watergate espionage became almost of secondary importance when the *Post* reported uncovering evidence that a corps of 50 or so political saboteurs had deliberately set out during the primaries to commit such acts as would leave the Democratic Party in disarray and shattered by feuding. The main target of the saboteurs, allegedly led by Dwight Chapin, the president's appointments secretary, was said to be Senator Muskie, then the front-runner. Their most devastating act of sabotage—if the *Post* allegations are correct—was fabricating the "Canuck letter" that was printed in the Manchester, N.H., *Union Leader*. The letter alleged that Muskie had insulted Americans of French-Canadian descent, and its publication during the New Hampshire primary is generally viewed as the start of Muskie's decline as a candidate. The Washington *Post* charged that Ken W. Clawson, a former *Post* reporter and now a White House assistant director of communications, had admitted fabricating the letter and signing it with a fictitious name. Clawson later denied having made the admission. Evidence was also uncovered showing that some of Muskie's campaign-schedule snafus had not been accidental, as previously assumed, but had been deliberately achieved by pro-Nixon operatives working within the Muskie camp.

The Soviet Wheat Deal

The completion of a multimillion-dollar wheat trade deal with the Soviet Union during the presidential campaign seemed destined at first to be a plus for the Nixon side; but then it, too, deteriorated under a barrage of charges that Secretary of Agriculture Earl Butz had helped grain corporations get inside information which enabled them to reap excessive profits, at the expense of wheat farmers and the taxpayer, from the grain sale. One of the companies that benefited was Continental Grain Company; shortly before the sale was publicly announced, Clarence D. Palmby quit his post as assistant secretary of agriculture and became vice-president of Continental.

Then there were the allegations that some contributions to the Nixon campaign were linked to special favors for the donors. Exemplifying that kind of charge was Ralph Nader's suit against the Agriculture Department for raising the wholesale price of milk allegedly in response to campaign contributions of more than $300,000 from milk producers' cooperatives.

Despite these and similar events which surfaced during the campaign and which McGovern interpreted as showing "a deeper and more widespread corruption than at any time in our history," the electorate failed to get very excited. A Louis Harris poll released in mid-October indicated that 62 percent of the voters shrugged off the Watergate affair as "mostly politics" and that voters, by a margin of 50 percent to 25 percent, refused to believe that "White House aides ordered the bugging." As for the wheat deal, that apparently was too complicated for most voters to understand.

Why the Voter Apathy?

Perhaps one reason the electorate did not respond to the Watergate scandal was that although a number of his most important aides were mentioned, President Nixon himself refused to be drawn into a discussion of, much less a quarrel over, either that affair or any of the other questionable activities of the season. He remained aloof and "presidential."

Perhaps another reason was that McGovern had succeeded in opening up his own credibility gap and was not in a very good position to convince voters that he would be

WHAT WENT WRONG?

Five days after the election, George McGovern was interviewed by reporters for the New York *Times* and the Baltimore *Sun*. In the excerpts reprinted below, Senator McGovern analyzes his defeat and discusses his plans for the future:

"As I look back on the campaign, we made mistakes. The other side made deliberate deceptions. There's a vast difference, which I think the public did not comprehend. . . . [T]he president really didn't campaign, he just sort of ignored the campaign. . . . And I was resentful of it."

"I think that the first mistake was making my acceptance speech at 2:30 in the morning. . . . I think that I should have gone to Larry O'Brien and refused to speak any time other than prime time. . . . The second thing I should have said is, 'I'm not going to pick the vice-president today; we'll do that tomorrow.' That would have given us another day."

"[I]t may be that it was over when Wallace decided not to run as an independent candidate and also did not throw his support to me. I couldn't make the kind of compromises on issues that would have won the Wallace support."

"I want to continue to speak on national and international issues. I want to exert my leadership there, from the Senate floor. And . . . I want very much to remain as a senator from South Dakota."

more honest than Nixon. McGovern was the one, after all, who had backed Eagleton 1,000 percent. He was also the one who had proposed giving every person a guaranteed annual income of $1,000—until Humphrey's attacks on the plan in the California primary made it a political liability and the initial estimates of the plan's cost turned out to be much too low, and McGovern retracted the idea.

Some political observers, including McGovern aide Frank Mankiewicz, thought that Humphrey's primary campaigns against McGovern were as important as the whole Eagleton affair in causing McGovern's eventual demise. It was

Humphrey who first claimed that McGovern would make the United States a second-rate power (McGovern denied that his pruning of the defense budget would do that). It was also Humphrey who first implied that McGovern's positions on abortion, marijuana, and amnesty were too far to the left (McGovern said he did not favor legalizing pot, would leave the abortion issue to state legislatures, and would be doing no more than Abraham Lincoln had done if he declared an amnesty at the end of a war). The Republicans needed only to pick up on these already well played themes, and they did. A Nixon television commer-

Who Pays the Bills?

In 1968 candidate Richard M. Nixon spent $12 million on television and radio advertising (twice as much as Hubert H. Humphrey). In 1970, Richard Ottinger's mother gave him $2.7 million to help him run for the U.S. Senate.

If those actions had occurred after April 7, 1972, they would have been illegal under the Federal Election Campaign Act, a potentially significant piece of new legislation intended, first, to inform voters

percent) could be used for television and radio. An important omission from the definition of communications media is direct-mail appeals, and many candidates spent unprecedented amounts of money this fall to send "personalized" computer-printed letters to millions of voters.

Another major provision of the new act requires, in essence, that candidates for president, U.S. senator, and U.S. representative and their campaign committees

well as general elections. Primary campaigns—in which $45 million was spent by presidential aspirants alone in 1968—were not covered under the Corrupt Practices Act, which the new law replaces.

Even before the new law went into effect on April 7, Republican compliance with the spirit of its full disclosure provisions was a campaign issue, as Democrats charged that the Republicans' $10 million fund-raising drive in February and March was intended to evade the public identification of large contributors that would have been required after April 7. Finally, one week before the election, in response to a suit by the citizens' lobby group Common Cause, the Nixon campaign committees released a partial list of pre-April 7 contributors. The list included W. Clement Stone, who gave $1 million.

The reports released after April 7 in compliance with the new law showed that only about 1 or 2 percent of American voters contributed to the presidential campaigns, despite the fact that this year, for the first time, political contributions of up to $100 by a married couple and up to $50 by an individual were tax deductible. The reports also revealed that, in general, a relatively small number of large contributions were essential to both major candidates and that these contributions came from traditional sources—wealthy individuals and corporate and labor union "citizenship" committees.

About three out of every five Nixon contributors gave more than $100. About five out of six contributors to McGovern, who made extensive direct-mail appeals for small donations, gave less than $100. However, McGovern never reached his goal of a "Million-Member Club" (1 million donors of $25 each), and during August, when the Eagleton controversy put McGovern's popularity at its nadir, and then again in October, his campaign was saved from insolvency by some six-figure loans and gifts from a few millionaires.

The campaign reports also showed that in the period from April 7 to October 26 (the date of the last required report before Election Day) Nixon outspent McGovern $36 million to $25 million (some of McGovern's total was for the primaries). Total spending in the general election campaign has been estimated at $27 million for McGovern and $45 million for Nixon.

BOB FAMIGHETTI

Spending by Major Parties in Presidential Elections[1]

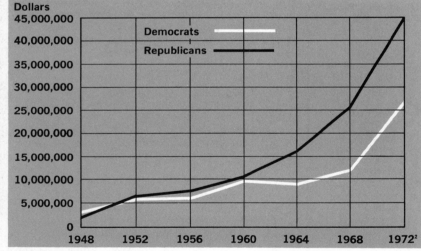

Dollars

Democrats
Republicans

[1]Does not include primaries. [2]Estimated. Source: Citizens' Research Foundation

about where federal candidates' campaign funds come from and go to and, second, to prevent a candidate from winning office solely because he has an unlimited family fortune at his disposal or can afford a "media blitz" right before the election.

A major provision of the new law limits spending by federal candidates for campaigning through communications media, defined in the act as television, radio, newspapers, magazines, billboards and other paid advertising space, and telephone solicitations made by paid staff. Each presidential candidate's media spending ceiling in 1972 was $14.25 million, of which not more than $8.55 million (60

make public the total amounts of money received and spent to seek public office, itemizing each receipt and expenditure of more than $100 (for example, identifying each contributor by name, address, and business affiliation and specifying the amount given).

A third provision limits a federal candidate's use of his own or his family's money to win election. In a race for president, the limit is $50,000; for a Senate seat, $35,000; and for a House seat, $25,000 (all three figures to increase as the consumer price index rises).

All of the provisions of the Federal Election Campaign Act apply to primary as

Loss of a Labor Stronghold

If George McGovern was to win the presidency in 1972, he had to carry the urban-industrial states east of the Mississippi, like Ohio, Pennsylvania—and Michigan, which had voted for every Democratic presidential candidate since 1960, twice rejecting Richard Nixon. Yet on Election Day 1972, Nixon won Michigan by almost half a million votes. An analysis of how McGovern lost a state generally regarded as a Democratic stronghold may be revealing about the weaknesses of his campaign nationwide.

First, it must be noted that Democratic strongholds are not as strong as they used to be. In recent years there has been a marked rise in ticket-splitting in many states. In Michigan, this ticket-splitting has helped elect a Republican governor and give Republicans one of the two U.S. Senate seats and 12 of the 19 U.S. House seats.

Democratic campaigns in Michigan are traditionally directed at the working class —trade unionists in particular—and those of liberal persuasion. But this year, because of the furor in Michigan over court-ordered school busing to assist racial integration, liberalism had become fairly unpopular among working-class groups. During campaign appearances, McGovern's position was that busing was a matter to be left to the courts, a view which was somewhat at odds with his prior statements and which failed to please voters.

Responsibility for the McGovern campaign in Michigan was split between the in-state organization, which was hurriedly constructed after the national convention and actively embraced few regular Democrats; the McGovern national headquarters in Washington, D.C., which bore most planning responsibility; and a regional campaign center in Cleveland, which furnished advance personnel. (It is the advance man or woman who makes sure that a candidate will be met at the airport by the press, local party leaders, and a car and makes sure that a band and a crowd will be at all campaign stops.)

McGovern's Michigan campaign organizers were confronted with an awesome task. Many state Democratic leaders had earlier supported the nomination of Senator Hubert H. Humphrey (Minn.), and at the grass-roots level a schism over the earlier candidacy of Alabama governor George C. Wallace deprived the party of many precinct-level workers. (In the Michigan primary on May 16, Wallace secured 51 percent of the vote, McGovern 27 percent.) Some usually reliable Democratic stalwarts, such as Wayne County AFL-CIO leader Tom Turner, also questioned the abilities of the many young and untried McGovern campaign workers.

McGovern's appearances and statements were orchestrated, in effect, to follow a rigid format allowing little spontaneity. The candidate often appeared in rather formal settings before known supporters, such as labor leaders and party loyalists. A departure—not a particularly fruitful one—from that format brought McGovern before the Detroit Economic Club on October 18. The audience of businessmen was not very receptive to McGovern's views that President Nixon's wage-price controls and the level of unemployment then prevailing in the United States were unbearable.

McGovern met several rather enthusiastic crowds during his Michigan appearances, but even this was sometimes a mixed blessing. Although they were not instructed to turn out a crowd for the candidate's visit, with Senator Edward M. Kennedy of Massachusetts, to a suburban shopping mall in Troy, McGovern workers dutifully advised the news media and sought coverage. At this point in the campaign, media exposure, as such, was being replaced by efforts at greater voter contact. The event backfired, for discussion with voters proved impossible as a crowd of several thousand pursued McGovern and Kennedy through constricted shopping aisles, trampling merchandise. The senators had to be extricated, leaving behind Michigan's Democratic Senate candidate, Frank J. Kelley, who was lost and ignored in the crush.

Most of McGovern's Michigan trips were, in fact, aimed largely at gaining media exposure, in newspapers and on the airwaves. Accordingly, the McGovern schedule was built around quick visits to as many cities as possible during a given day. But the frequency of travel necessarily limited McGovern's stay in any one spot and virtually precluded amplification of remarks on a given subject. Prepared press releases and lengthy position papers were thrust into the hands of local newsmen seeking fuller answers to controversial state issues such as abortion, school busing, or amnesty. Organizationally, the campaign appeared to be a model of efficiency and adherence to a timetable; substantively, it left much to be desired.

This appeared to be the case after his Troy appearance, when McGovern on national television criticized President Nixon for missing opportunities to end the war in Vietnam. However, the next day the nation listened intently to presidential adviser Henry Kissinger discuss a tentative peace agreement with the North Vietnamese. Although his advisers insisted McGovern was aware of the peace deliberations, the candidate was unavailable for several hours and left Detroit for his next stop without making a comprehensive response to the situation.

And in the end, for all of McGovern's hectic and coordinated campaign activity in Michigan, it was not enough to make a difference.

ALLEN PHILLIPS

McGOVERN IN MICHIGAN. During his ill-fated campaign for the presidency, Senator George McGovern courted retired members of the United Automobile Workers of America.
WIDE WORLD

Do Polls Make a Difference?

President Richard M. Nixon's 61 percent to 38 percent victory over George McGovern (1 percent went to other candidates) salvaged what had until then been a poor year for the pollsters. The two best-known pollsters, George Gallup and Louis Harris, reported percentage margins of 62 to 38 and 61 to 39, respectively, in their final surveys. Daniel Yankelovich, whose polls of the 16 largest states appeared in both the New York *Times* and *Time* magazine, did just about as well. During the Democratic primaries, which were harder to call because of low voter interest, lack of party rivalry, and unpredictable turnout, the polls had been consistently wrong.

Although most people's skepticism about the accuracy of polls was erased by the fact that polls called the outcome of the presidential election on the nose, some critics believe that the crucial problem is not statistical accuracy but, rather, the way polls can affect the political process. In September pollsters and their critics debated this issue during congressional hearings on Michigan Democratic representative Lucien Nedzi's proposed "truth-in-polling" act.

The pollsters are always quick to deny that polls can create the so-called bandwagon effect, influencing people to vote for a candidate because he looks like a sure winner. Gallup, who has been polling since the early 1930's, has stated that the influence of poll results on people "is so negligible that it is impossible to measure." Most of his colleagues agree, but at the Nedzi hearings Yankelovich stated that although polls alone may not change many people's minds, they do have a certain influence. In 1972 many lifelong Democrats could not accept McGovern but at the same time regarded voting for Nixon as an act of heresy. Yankelovich suggested that when such Democrats saw polls reporting Nixon's massive appeal, they may well have been reassured that "it's not so terrible to switch party allegiance." However, even though most pollsters refute the bandwagon charge, they do concede that polls may influence some people to vote for the underdog.

Polls can also influence indirectly the conduct and character of a campaign. For example, the polls' prediction from the outset of a Nixon sweep may have been a major cause of the low turnout in 1972. Thirteen million more people were registered in 1972 than in 1968 (largely because the voting age was reduced to 18), but the increase in the number who actually voted was only 3 million; only about 55 percent of those eligible voted, the lowest turnout since 1948. Apathy certainly was another factor in the small vote. One Yankelovich poll showed that

when people were asked, "Forgetting politics, whom do you find more attractive as a personality—Nixon, McGovern, or neither?" 32 percent said, "neither." Many people ultimately voted for "neither" by staying home, putting a symbolic plague on both political houses. In 1968, millions were similarly dismayed at the prospect of choosing among Nixon, Humphrey, and Wallace, but when the final polls called the election a toss-up, most people felt compelled to vote for whomever they regarded as the least of three evils. Because the polls in 1972 seemed to be saying that the election

was over before it had begun, many people felt that they could afford to sit it out.

Polls also influence campaign fund raising. Even the pollsters agree that a candidate who is far behind finds it almost impossible to raise contributions for what seems to be a lost cause. Without money it is equally difficult to close the gap. In 1972 finances may have been relatively less important; the Democrats certainly could have used more money, but McGovern was able to subsist, at least, through an effective grass-roots appeal. He was hurt more by the effect the polls had on the Democratic organization. Local candidates who ordinarily would have rushed to grab the presidential nominee's coattails treated McGovern as if he were the skipper of a sinking ship. He was locked out of many traditional Democratic clubhouses, and even where he was let in, he received only a luke-

warm response. The split within the party was described in ideological terms, but if the polls had put McGovern within striking distance, most Democratic leaders would have fallen into line, no matter what they thought of his politics. In a way, his problem was circular: he could not get help from his party—money, canvassers, wholehearted endorsements—without good polls, but he could not improve his standing in the polls without just that kind of help.

The polls may also have corrupted the quality of the campaign in another, more subtle way. More newspapers and magazines published polls as headline news than ever before. As McGovern's running mate, Sargent Shriver, often complained, "Somebody said, 'These are the times that try men's souls,' but instead of issues everybody discusses polls."

GALLUP'S RECORD OVER THE YEARS

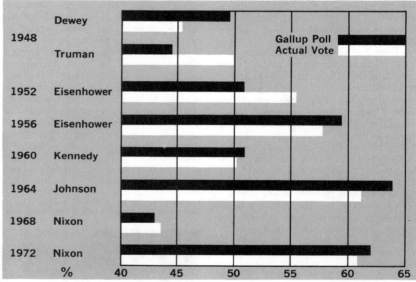

Source: The Gallup Organization

The difficulty in measuring the precise influence of polls in a particular election does not mean that the influence does not exist or is negligible. In any one year the bandwagon effect, the underdog phenomenon, and the other types of influences may cancel one another out. But in 1972 they seem to have combined in such a way as to hurt McGovern more than Nixon. No one has suggested that the polls cost McGovern the election, but they probably made even harder what would have been an extremely difficult task in any case. The pollsters may come to view their accomplishment in calling the election so closely as a mixed blessing. On the one hand, it seems to prove their claim that polling is now a sophisticated science, but on the other, it raises the disturbing possibility that instead of the polls matching the outcome of the election, it may have been the other way around.   MICHAEL WHEELER

cial showed a hand sweeping U.S. planes and warships off the screen and claimed that was what McGovern would do. And Senate Minority Leader Hugh Scott (R, Pa.) called McGovern the "triple A" candidate—for amnesty, abortion, and acid. By Election Day many voters seemed unsure of exactly what McGovern stood for but firmly convinced that, whatever his positions were, they were too radical.

More money for television exposure would undoubtedly have helped McGovern, but he could hardly claim extreme poverty, having an estimated budget twice the size of Humphrey's in 1968. And money alone could not have overcome Nixon's brilliant exploitation of the incumbency. McGovern may not have been the Democratic Party's strongest candidate, but any Democrat would have come up against the fact that, when running for the presidency, nothing beats starting out as president. Only two presidents in the twentieth century tried and failed to win reelection (William Howard Taft in a three-way race in 1912 and Herbert Hoover in 1932); before Nixon, an incumbent president had successfully tried for reelection eight times since 1900.

This year, McGovern kept promising that if he were elected, he would end U.S. involvement in the Vietnam war within 90 days after his inauguration and that he would send Shriver to Hanoi to speed arrangements for the return of U.S. prisoners and an accounting of the missing in action. But these promises for the future hardly equaled in headline value Nixon's sending Henry Kissinger off to Paris for crucial peace talks or Kissinger's announcing, one week before the election, that one more session in Paris would bring about the signing of a truce. It was a hard act for McGovern to follow. And at a more mundane level, McGovern's tour through the flood-wracked areas of Pennsylvania with promises of help if he were elected could hardly equal the immediacy of Nixon's swooping in on his helicopter with a $4 million check to help fix up Wilkes-Barre and a promise of immediate delivery of enough hot dogs for a community picnic.

Nixon's Noncampaign

In the first six weeks of the campaign, while McGovern zealously stumped his way back and forth across the continent, Nixon spent only five days on the campaign trail, but that was a frantic outburst of campaigning compared to what he was going to do during the next month. Not since Franklin D. Roosevelt's reelection campaign—or noncampaign—of 1944 had a presidential candidate spent less time on the road.

When the president did appear in public, so tightly were the appearances orchestrated that many of his crowds consisted totally of persons—very often schoolchildren—screened and bused in for the occasion; the general public was often excluded. The press fared little better. Such television coverage as occurred at Nixon political fund-raising dinners was usually handled by the president's own television crew, which then released to the networks those portions of the film that pleased the president. Newspaper reporters were put in separate rooms to watch on closed-circuit television.

While Nixon stayed above the battle, more than three dozen surrogate "presidents" were on the road. They did not miss a trick. Secretary of Transportation John Volpe went home to Massachusetts bearing the good word and $38.2 million in federal grants. Housing Secretary George Romney, addressing fellow Mormons in Salt Lake City, got out of housing and into foreign affairs to denounce McGovern as "a dangerous isolationist." Agriculture Secretary Butz passed out bumper stickers that warned, "Farmers: Re-elect the President or Lose Your Butz." Defense Secretary Melvin Laird was among several of the surrogates who occasionally came close to labeling as treasonous McGovern's proposal to cut arms spending by $30 billion.

How could McGovern answer them all? More to the point, as he saw it, why should he be expected to? "Nixon's my opponent," he said, scolding the press for giving the surrogates so much space. "I'm not running against Earl Butz or Spiro Agnew." Meanwhile, Nixon, in ten radio talks and a couple of television appearances, did not even mention McGovern's name.

Although McGovern paid a conciliatory call on former president Johnson at his Texas ranch in late August and received his blessing in return (it was the first time the two men had spoken to each other since 1967) and although McGovern got help from some important fellow Democrats—most notably Senator Edward Kennedy (Mass.), who many assumed was putting out I.O.U.'s for 1976—most Democratic politicians acted as though McGovern were a dangerous man to be identified with. Only a dozen U.S. senators and about 20 House members actively campaigned for him.

Democrats for Nixon

On the other hand, many of the old bulls of the Democratic Party were publicly behind Nixon. John Connally, a former Democratic governor of Texas as well as a former treasury secretary in Nixon's cabinet, headed up a campaign organization called Democrats for Nixon. The president's embrace of the Democratic defectors angered some in his own party. For example, Republicans who had been trying for years to build a permanent machine in the South were nonplussed to see such administration spokesmen as Attorney General Richard Kleindienst go into Mississippi, shun the Republican senatorial candidate, and publicly announce that if he were a Mississippian he would vote for Democratic senator James O. Eastland. By cultivating the Democratic switch votes Nixon was cutting off his own coattails, and on Election Day the GOP lost two seats in the Senate, lost one governorship, and won an unimpressive total of 13 seats in the House, with most of this gain creditable to reapportionment.

McGovern kept drawing his hope from the fact that gaps had been closed in previous elections, most recently and most notably by Harry Truman in 1948. But actually 1948 and 1972 were not comparable, for in Truman's victory year more than 21 percent of the American people were earning less than $3,000 a year (in terms of 1971 dollars), and in 1972 only 8.3 percent were under the $3,000 figure. Populism in 1972 clearly had a reduced audience, although McGovern played it relentlessly. One of his favorite pitches to blue-collar audiences was, "A businessman can deduct the price of his $20 martini lunch, and you help pay for it, but a working man can't even deduct the price of his bologna sandwich."

Minority Favoritism?

McGovern promised to close tax "loopholes" totaling $22 billion, but such promises aimed at undoing supposed corporate favoritism probably struck a less responsive chord among most white Americans than did President Nixon's implied promise to undo supposed minority favoritism. In ceremonies at the base of the Statue of Liberty in late September, Nixon indicated his coolness to broader welfare programs by saying that most immigrants to the United States "believed in hard work. They didn't come here for a handout." Elsewhere, in tones and words reminiscent of Alabama governor George Wallace, Nixon spoke indignantly of workingmen's children being bused around "as pawns in the hands of social planners in Washington."

More than the defeat of one man and his platform, McGovern's inability to carry more than Massachusetts and the District of Columbia for a total of 17 electoral votes was generally viewed as the dissolution—whether temporary

or final remains to be seen—of the old New Deal coalition of blue-collar workers, organized labor, Spanish-speaking Americans, Catholics, Jews, and blacks. A CBS survey of 17,000 voters leaving the polls in 143 precincts across the United States showed that only Jewish, Spanish-speaking, and black voters remained loyal to the Democratic standard —although even these groups gave McGovern a smaller percentage of their votes than they had given Humphrey in 1968. The CBS survey, considered by some the best vote profile conducted in 1972, also showed that Nixon won 75 percent of the Wallace vote in the South and 60 percent of the Wallace vote nationwide. Nixon won the Catholic vote and the blue-collar vote and came within two percentage points of getting a majority of the votes of people in households having at least one labor-union member. Nixon's heaviest percentages came from rural, small-town, and upper-income suburban voters; from Protestants; and from retired people and persons 60 years old or older. The core of the "new majority" was, as predicted, composed of the un-young, the un-black, and the un-poor.

Never in recent times has a presidential election been shaped so thoroughly by the voters' negative reactions. Every poll showed that Nixon was elected, to a large extent, as the lesser of two evils; or, as the choice was expressed by ABC commentator Harry Reasoner, voters decided "whether they were more depressed by Nixon than scared by McGovern." In a nationwide survey taken shortly before the election, the Washington *Post* found that nearly half of those interviewed rated Nixon as only an "average"

president; only 36 percent thought conditions in the United States were better in 1972 than they were at the time Nixon took office. But his opponent was held in such low esteem that Nixon carried almost 61 percent of the popular vote, one of the highest percentages in history. Perhaps a more significant measure of the public's mind could be seen in the fact that only 55 percent of the voting-age population went to the polls, the lowest turnout since 1948.

The Other Candidates

If they did not like either Nixon or McGovern, the voters could have, of course, gone the third-party route. Very few did. Representative John Schmitz, the candidate of the American Party (under whose banner Wallace won more than 13 percent of the vote in 1968), spent an estimated $1 million to $1.5 million and received under 1.4 percent of the vote, appealing to people who liked the imagination of such proposals as solving the heroin problem in the United States by defoliating the poppy fields of China. Schmitz' ideological opposite was Dr. Benjamin Spock, the former baby doctor and long-time antiwar activist, whose People's Party spent $20,000 and won 0.09 percent of the vote. There were at least nine minor candidates. What they signified in the year 1972 is hard to say, unless it was the eternal optimism which underpins American politics and which was best captured in Dr. Spock's postelection self-congratulatory appraisal: "Well, after all, I won only two fewer states than McGovern."

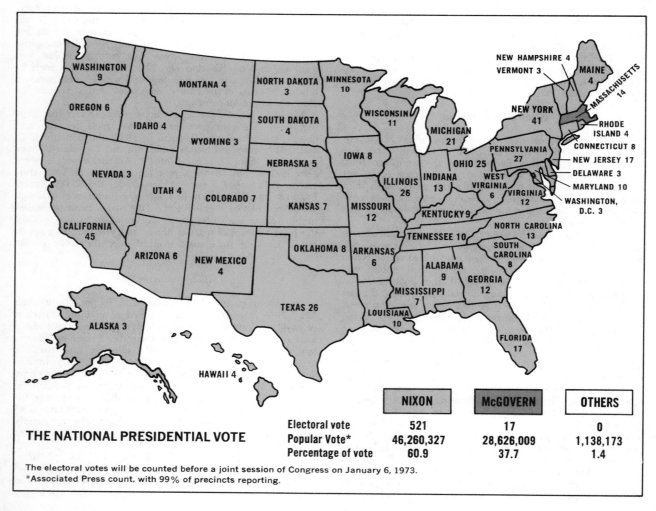

THE NATIONAL PRESIDENTIAL VOTE

	NIXON	McGOVERN	OTHERS
Electoral vote	521	17	0
Popular Vote*	46,260,327	28,626,009	1,138,173
Percentage of vote	60.9	37.7	1.4

The electoral votes will be counted before a joint session of Congress on January 6, 1973.
*Associated Press count, with 99% of precincts reporting.

Anatomy of a Landslide

The overwhelming victory of Richard Nixon over George McGovern indicated to most observers that the Democratic Party's traditional coalition was in danger of breaking up. During the depression of the 1930's, a patchwork of blue-collar workers, blacks, Jews, intellectuals, and southern whites combined their voting strength under the leadership of Franklin D. Roosevelt to create a majority that went on to elect a Democratic president in seven of the nine elections from 1932 through 1964. And in 1968, Hubert H. Humphrey came close to winning by appealing to the same constituencies.

In 1972, however, large holes developed in the Democratic fabric, while nearly all Republican voters remained loyal to their candidate. According to a survey conducted by George Fine Research, Inc., for CBS News, about 36 percent of all Democrats voted for Nixon. They considered McGovern too far to the left—not tough enough with the Communists, too lenient toward abortion and marijuana, and too eager to spend public money—and they had doubts about his ability to make decisions, especially after his handling of the Eagleton affair. Since the majority of registered voters are Democrats, it was this massive defection that buried Senator McGovern under a Nixon landslide—61 percent to 38 percent in the popular vote.

One of the most important sources of Democratic strength has been blue-collar workers, but in 1972, President Nixon captured slightly more than half of their votes. Union families gave a slight edge to McGovern (50 to 48 percent). The Democratic candidate had failed to gain the support of the national AFL-CIO and its president, George Meany, and only two state AFL-CIO organizations (Colorado and Florida) endorsed McGovern.

When the vote was analyzed according to ethnic groups, it appeared that Nixon had made his greatest gains among those referred to as the "ethnics"—Irish-, Italian-, and Polish-Americans, for instance. According to *Newsweek*, 57 percent of the Italian vote went for Nixon, up from 34 percent in 1968, and an Irish election district in Queens, New York City, that had gone 83 percent for Humphrey in 1968 gave only 32 percent of its votes to McGovern. According to the CBS survey, about 53 percent of the nation's Catholics chose Nixon, compared to 33 percent in 1968.

The South, once solidly Democratic, was solidly Republican in this year's presidential contest, giving 72 percent of its votes to Nixon. The South's swing away from the Democrats seemed more permanent than that of other voting blocs who apparently did not trust Senator McGovern or his ideas but have not consistently repudiated the Democratic Party. Barry Goldwater in 1964 and both Nixon and George Wallace in 1968 showed strength in southern states.

Nixon carried not only the South but every other region of the country as well. Even the liberal Northeast gave 59 percent of its votes to the Republican ticket. McGovern's only electoral votes came from antiwar Massachusetts (14) and the predominantly black District of Columbia (3). Cities with populations of more than 500,000 went to McGovern, but smaller cities and towns were Nixon's.

Other sources of great Republican strength were rural and small-town voters, upper-income suburbanites, Protestants, and retired people, all of whom gave about two-thirds of their votes to Nixon. According to *Newsweek* figures, Nixon won 65 percent of the votes of middle-income Americans, who constitute more than half of the electorate. He also captured three-quarters of the upper-income votes but only 38 percent of the low-income total.

Black and Jewish voters remained primarily Democratic, but the percentage of their votes going to the Republicans rose significantly—from 18 percent in 1968 to 37 percent this year among Jews and from 5 to 11 percent among blacks, according to *Newsweek*. McGovern's sponsorship of the quota system used in choosing delegates for the Democratic convention hurt his standing among Jews, who on the average are better educated and hold better-paying jobs than the total population.

Even young voters casting their first presidential ballots (those 18 to 24 years of age), whom McGovern had counted on as his source of greatest strength, gave the Democratic candidate only a little more than half of their votes. The voting

UPI

FIRST-TIME VOTERS get ready to cast their ballots in Berkeley, Calif. Because less than one-half of the potential new voters turned out, they exerted less influence than was expected.

turnout in this group was also far lower than the Democrats had hoped; only about 12 million of the 25.7 million potential new voters actually registered and went to the polls.

The turnout among older voters was higher, but the total number of people voting was still relatively small. Only about 55 percent of the more than 138 million citizens of voting age actually cast their ballots, possibly because neither candidate generated much public enthusiasm.

However, except for the black, Jewish, and Spanish-speaking minorities, the unemployed, and the students, nearly every classification of voter gave a majority to Nixon. For the most part, these results were thought to be a repudiation of Senator McGovern's views and actions, not a permanent rejection of the Democrats, but the Republican Party has gained ground and may seriously challenge the majority coalition of Democrats in future elections. As McGovern admitted, "The president may have been right. He may have had his thumb closer to the public pulse than I did."

PETER K. REINHART

The New Congress

William Robbins

One of the strangest U.S. national elections returned Democrats this year to solid control of Congress while a Republican president swept 49 states by a near-record margin.

It was only the second election in history in which a president winning with more than 58 percent of the votes cast—Richard M. Nixon's total this year was nearly 61 percent—failed to pull a majority of his party's candidates with him and gain control of Congress. The other election was Dwight D. Eisenhower's in 1956.

Instead of winning control, as Republican leaders had hoped, they lost two Senate seats, giving the Democrats a 56–43 edge, with one independent. In the House of Representatives, although the Republicans picked up 13 seats, the Democrats easily retained their majority. The lineup in the new House will be 242 Democrats, 192 Republicans, and one independent expected to vote with the Democrats. The previous figures were 255 Democrats, 177 Republicans, and one vacancy in a seat formerly held by a Democrat.

Other crosscurrents in the voting (aside from the diverging presidential and congressional results) will long puzzle commentators and historians. For although voters rejected in large numbers the left-liberal candidacy of Nixon's opponent, Senator George S. McGovern of South Dakota, they elected many people to Congress who espoused the same views as McGovern had; although the electorate appeared to be reacting in part against the youthful and unconventional presidential campaigners surrounding McGovern, they chose many young candidates over older ones for Congress, including the youngest senator ever to be elected; and although the vote appeared to endorse the Nixon policies on the war in Vietnam, the voters returned to office the antiwar-liberal-moderate Senate majority that had fought those policies at every turn.

Thus, on the morning of November 8, political experts looking at the results that had poured in the night before could say with confidence only the seemingly obvious—that President Nixon had "very short coattails." Despite a resounding personal victory, he had been able to give little help to others running on the Republican ticket.

But even that generality was suspect, questioned by some in words like those of an anonymous Democratic campaigner: "If we were able to do this well with George McGovern as our candidate for president, think how well we could have done if nobody had headed our ticket."

Unquestionably, there were races across the country in which the presidential tide helped sweep uncertain candidates into office. Also unquestionably, Democrats would have seen less erosion of their power in the once-solid South—Republicans gained two Senate and seven House seats in the region—had not a candidate like McGovern, whom many southerners regarded as dangerously liberal, headed their ticket and had not Richard Nixon, in office as in the campaign, recognized long-smoldering southern resentments. But the Republicans had already been making gains in the South, as they vied with Dixie Democrats in the vigor of their support for the traditional southern positions on race-related issues such as school busing.

What chiefly clouded the question of the power of the presidential candidates to influence congressional results was the tactics used by both sides in the campaign. President Nixon ran an exceedingly personal race, attempting in only rare instances to give more than *pro forma* support to his party's candidates for Congress. On the other hand, many Democrats seeking congressional seats pointedly avoided identification with McGovern.

The effects of such tactics were mixed, and it was unclear how much Nixon could have helped if he had made an earnest effort to elect his party's candidates or, on the other hand, to what extent a McGovern label might have hurt the opposition. In one of the few states where the president lent active support, in Delaware, the two-term Republican senator, J. Caleb Boggs, lost to a political newcomer; meanwhile, Andrew Young, a black running in a predominantly white Georgia district, proudly carried the banner of McGovern to victory over a Nixon-supported white Republican.

What was given increased clarity in the congressional election was the great advantage of incumbency. Despite a number of upsets, the vast majority of candidates with the benefit of long exposure to their constituents by virtue of their offices and their free-mail privileges were able to win reelection. In state after state, entire congressional delegations came through unscathed. In California, for example, all the incumbents who had survived primary battles were returned to office, including Representative Paul N. (Pete) McCloskey, the Republican who had fought the president in the primaries.

Yet there were also instances where too many years of incumbency became a disadvantage and where voters appeared to feel that advancing age had withered the effectiveness of current officeholders. Age apparently was a factor in Boggs' loss in Delaware as well as in other upsets in Maine and Colorado. Voters' fears that the candidate was too old may also have hurt 72-year-old Wayne Morse's bid to become once again a U.S. senator from Oregon. Morse, unseated in 1968, this year tried—and failed—to unseat Republican incumbent Mark O. Hatfield.

The election was studded with surprises, the biggest of which, perhaps, was the victory of Young, a youthful black fighter for civil rights and a long-time aide to the late Martin Luther King. Young won in an Atlanta district that is 62 percent white, but Atlanta is a surprising city, considered by some to be symbolic of the "new South," and the electorate reacted favorably to Young's campaign style. From dawn till dark the candidate walked the streets, always holding out his hand and asking for votes. He was also aided by a campaign organization composed largely of young white college graduates who knew their city well.

But the Senate races brought more surprises than did those for the House, in part because the prestige of office makes senators more widely known. One unexpected outcome was the election in Delaware of Joseph R. Biden, Jr., who did not turn 30 years old (the minimum age for a senator) until 13 days after the election. Biden, the youngest senator ever to take office, was a little-known New Castle County councilman when he began his campaign against Boggs, an accomplished vote-getter who had not been defeated in 26 years in politics and whom President Nixon persuaded, at the age of 63, to seek a third term. But Biden canvassed the state from border to coast, aided by an army of 2,000 volunteers and a young campaign organization of family and friends. As late as August he still trailed Boggs in the popular polls, 19 percent to 47 percent, but by Election Day, hammering on issues such as a quick end to the Vietnam war, conservation legislation to save the wetlands, a more equitable tax system, morality in government, and consumer protection, the young senatorial candidate had pulled ahead.

Equally surprising to most election watchers was the upset in Maine of the Senate's only woman member, Republican Margaret Chase Smith, long affectionately known in her state as "our Margaret." But it had been too long, apparently, for many Maine voters. Smith, 74, campaigned sparingly, while her Democratic opponent, Representative William D. Hathaway, 48, stumped every city and town in the state, starting a year before the election, subtly suggesting the advantages of comparative youth over age.

Startling also was the election in Colorado of Floyd K. Haskell, a Democrat, over Gordon L. Allott, a three-term senator who headed the Republican Policy Committee. Haskell, a former state representative, had switched from the Republican Party because of his opposition to the Vietnam war. He campaigned on the war issue, while Allott urged support for the president. The irony was that, although the president carried the state with 63 percent of the vote, his chief supporter there lost. But what apparently turned the tide was Haskell's use of television to

exploit the fact that, although voters were familiar with the Allott name, even after he had served three terms in the Senate they appeared to know little about him. Haskell's chief device was a half-hour film showing his own background, disparaging Allott remarks on the 18-year-old vote and medicare, and publicizing Allott's low rating by ecology groups.

In another upset of major proportions, Iowa's two-term Republican senator, Jack Miller, was defeated by Richard Clark, a former university professor who had been administrative assistant to Representative John Culver. So certain had Miller's reelection seemed that Culver himself had declined to enter the race. When Clark did, he ran—or walked —with vigor, making a much-publicized hike across the state to dramatize his candidacy and his charges against Miller of absenteeism from Senate duties. Miller was also hurt by allegations that he had attempted to legislate tax favors for investors at the behest of a Washington lobbyist.

Another upset that breasted the Nixon tide was the election in Kentucky of Democrat Walter "Dee" Huddleston over former Republican governor Louie B. Nunn for the Senate seat vacated by John Sherman Cooper, also a Republican. Huddleston criticized Nunn for increasing the state sales tax while he was governor and gained strength by supporting a successful drive to repeal the tax on food. On the day that repeal went into affect, Huddleston advertised his role in the drive by promoting a statewide D-Day ("D" for "Dee" and "deductions") celebration.

In North Carolina, Representative Nick Galifianakis had upset Senator B. Everett Jordan in the Democratic primary and had been expected to hold the state safe for his party in the general election. But in one of the few instances when riding the Nixon coattails was effective, Galifianakis was defeated by Jesse A. Helms, a conservative radio commentator. Meanwhile, in Virginia, Senator William B. Spong, Jr., a Democrat, was overwhelmed by the heavily financed campaign of Representative William Lloyd Scott.

Several other senators who had been thought to be in trouble survived. They included Republicans Robert P. Griffin of Michigan, Hatfield of Oregon, and John Tower of Texas and Democrats Claiborne Pell of Rhode Island, Lee Metcalf of Montana, and Thomas J. McIntyre of New Hampshire.

The Senate also kept its only black member, Edward W. Brooke, a Republican who successfully breasted a reverse Democratic tide in Massachusetts, the only state carried by McGovern. And Senators Walter F. Mondale of Minnesota, a Democrat, and Charles Percy of Illinois, a Republican, strengthened their prospects for consideration in future presidential races by winning reelection with wide margins.

| BIDEN | DOMENICI | HATHAWAY | HELMS |

HOLTZMAN

HUDDLESTON

A. YOUNG

Overall, it was being said that the voting had changed little in either house of Congress, but that generalization also was subject to question. In the House, the old seniority system suffered further erosion as younger people came in to take the place of senior representatives. Six Democratic committee chairmen will not return to the House, two who retired and four elderly and powerful men who were defeated at the polls in primary elections.

The primary defeat of Representative John L. McMillan of South Carolina removed the entrenched chairman of the House District of Columbia Committee and one of the most ardent opponents of home rule for Washington, D.C. However, McMillan's conqueror, 36-year-old state representative John W. Jenrette, Jr., was destined not to enjoy the fruits of his victory. He was defeated in the general election by Edward L. Young, a Republican. Also in the primaries, Wayne N. Aspinall of Colorado, 76-year-old chairman of the House Interior and Insular Affairs Committee and a chief target of environmentalists, was defeated by a younger man, 38-year-old Alan Merson. But like Jenrette, Merson was to go down to defeat in the general election at the hands of a Republican, James P. Johnson.

Also defeated in primaries were Emanuel Celler of New York, 84-year-old chairman of the House Judiciary Committee, and George Miller of California, chairman of the House Science and Astronautics Committee. Retiring voluntarily were William Colmer, 82, of Mississippi, chairman of the House Rules Committee, and Edward Garmatz, 69, of Maryland, chairman of the Merchant Marine and Fisheries Committee. Colmer's administrative assistant, 31-year-old Trent Lott, switched to the Republican Party to run successfully for the House seat vacated by his Democratic boss. Another Republican, Marjorie Holt, won the formerly Democratic seat vacated by the Garmatz retirement.

The four defeated committee chairmen were among 14 incumbents who lost in primary elections, generally to younger opponents. The two other chairmen who retired voluntarily were among 30 House members who decided not to seek reelection.

In the general election, the most powerful incumbent representative to go down to defeat was 51-year-old William R. Anderson of Tennessee, whose status stemmed from his seat on the important House Rules Committee, which controls the flow of legislation to the House floor. One overall effect of the House elections was the moving of younger representatives to higher positions on the committee seniority lists.

And among other changes, the elections gave the Republicans a slightly larger representation from the South, including Louisiana's first Republican representative since

Reconstruction. He was David C. Treen, a 44-year-old lawyer, who defeated J. Louis Watkins, a Democrat, despite support for Watkins from retiring representative Patrick T. Caffery. In neighboring Mississippi, Republicans gained two seats, electing Thad Cochran, a lawyer, as well as Trent Lott, Colmer's successor. This is the first time Mississippi has had two Republicans in the House since Reconstruction.

The new lineup in the House will also include 14 women—one more than before the election. Five women are newly elected, including Elizabeth Holtzman, who coasted to victory in November after waging an aggressive primary campaign to defeat Celler. Three women representatives retired and one, Louise Day Hicks, the outspoken Boston opponent of school busing, was defeated. At the same time, the Congressional Black Caucus was strengthened by the election to the House of three new blacks, Young and two of the newly elected women, Yvonne Braithwaite Burke of California and Barbara Jordan of Houston, both Democrats.

In the Senate, the youth movement was as pronounced as it was in the House, with the 13 newly elected senators averaging about 22 years younger than the people they replaced. The new members, ranging in age from Biden's 30 to 57 for Virginia's Scott, have an average age of just under 45 years; those they succeed averaged 67.

Among the most striking age differences were those of J. Bennett Johnston, 40, Democrat of Louisiana, elected to succeed Senator Allen J. Ellender, 82, who died last July, and Sam Nunn, 34, Democrat of Georgia, elected to follow the late Richard B. Russell, 73. There were six new senators besides Johnston in their 40's, all but one of them replacing former senators in their 70's: Pete V. Domenici, Republican of New Mexico, 40, succeeding the retired Clinton P. Anderson, 77, a Democrat; James Abourezk, Democrat of South Dakota, 41, replacing the retired Karl E. Mundt, 72, a Republican; Clark, 43, the Iowan who defeated Miller, 56; Huddleston, 46, succeeding Cooper, 71; James A. McClure, 47, who succeeded his fellow Idaho Republican, Len B. Jordan, 73; and Hathaway, 48, who defeated Margaret Chase Smith, 74.

In turnabouts, overall the Democrats captured six Republican seats, and the Republicans took four seats that had been held by Democrats. As in the House, the younger men taking office generally tend to be less conservative than the people they replace.

But in neither house could the ideological shift be considered substantial. Thus, although the new Senate may offer slightly more resistance to the policies and appointments of the reelected president, the 93rd Congress may well be little different from the 92nd.

THE SENATE: NINETY-THIRD CONGRESS, FIRST SESSION[1]
Spiro T. Agnew, president

State	Senator	Began office	Term expires	State	Senator	Began office	Term expires
ALABAMA	John Sparkman, D	1946	1979	MONTANA	Mike Mansfield, D	1953	1977
	James Allen, D	1969	1975		Lee Metcalf, D	1961	1979
ALASKA	Ted Stevens, R	1968	1979	NEBRASKA	Roman Hruska, R	1954	1977
	Mike Gravel, D	1969	1975		Carl Curtis, R	1955	1979
ARIZONA	Paul Fannin, R	1965	1977	NEVADA	Alan Bible, D	1954	1975
	Barry Goldwater, R[2]	1969	1975		Howard Cannon, D	1959	1977
ARKANSAS	John McClellan, D	1943	1979	NEW HAMPSHIRE	Norris Cotton, R	1954	1975
	J. W. Fulbright, D	1945	1975		Thomas McIntyre, D	1962	1979
CALIFORNIA	Alan Cranston, D	1969	1975	NEW JERSEY	Clifford Case, R	1955	1979
	John Tunney, D	1971	1977		Harrison Williams, Jr., D	1959	1977
COLORADO	Floyd K. Haskell, D	1973	1979	NEW MEXICO	Pete Domenici, R	1973	1979
	Peter Dominick, R	1963	1975		Joseph Montoya, D	1964	1977
CONNECTICUT	Abraham Ribicoff, D	1963	1975	NEW YORK	Jacob Javits, R	1957	1975
	Lowell Weicker, Jr., R	1971	1977		James Buckley, Cons.-R	1971	1977
DELAWARE	Joseph Biden, Jr., D	1973	1979	NORTH CAROLINA	Sam Ervin, Jr., D	1954	1975
	William Roth, Jr., R	1971	1977		Jesse Helms, R	1973	1979
FLORIDA	Edward Gurney, R	1969	1975	NORTH DAKOTA	Milton Young, R	1945	1975
	Lawton Chiles, D	1971	1977		Quentin Burdick, D	1960	1977
GEORGIA	Sam Nunn, D	1973	1979	OHIO	William Saxbe, R	1969	1975
	Herman Talmadge, D	1957	1975		Robert Taft, Jr., R	1971	1977
HAWAII	Hiram Fong, R	1959	1977	OKLAHOMA	Dewey Bartlett, R	1973	1979
	Daniel Inouye, D	1963	1975		Henry Bellmon, R	1969	1975
IDAHO	Frank Church, D	1957	1975	OREGON	Mark Hatfield, R	1967	1979
	James McClure, R	1973	1979		Robert Packwood, R	1969	1975
ILLINOIS	Charles Percy, R	1967	1979	PENNSYLVANIA	Hugh Scott, R	1959	1977
	Adlai Stevenson III, D	1971	1977		Richard Schweiker, R	1969	1975
INDIANA	Vance Hartke, D	1959	1977	RHODE ISLAND	John Pastore, D	1950	1977
	Birch Bayh, D	1963	1975		Claiborne Pell, D	1961	1979
IOWA	Richard Clark, D	1973	1979	SOUTH CAROLINA	Strom Thurmond, R[5]	1956	1979
	Harold Hughes, D	1969	1975		Ernest Hollings, D	1966	1975
KANSAS	James Pearson, R	1962	1979	SOUTH DAKOTA	James Abourezk, D	1973	1979
	Robert Dole, R	1969	1975		George McGovern, D	1963	1975
KENTUCKY	Walter Huddleston, D	1973	1979	TENNESSEE	Howard Baker, Jr., R	1967	1979
	Marlow Cook, R	1968	1975		William Brock III, R	1971	1977
LOUISIANA	J. B. Johnston, D	1973	1979	TEXAS	John Tower, R	1961	1979
	Russell Long, D	1948	1975		Lloyd Bentsen, Jr., D	1971	1977
MAINE	William Hathaway, D	1973	1979	UTAH	Wallace Bennett, R	1951	1975
	Edmund Muskie, D	1959	1977		Frank Moss, D	1959	1977
MARYLAND	Charles Mathias, Jr., R	1969	1975	VERMONT	George Aiken, R	1941	1975
	J. Glenn Beall, Jr., R	1971	1977		Robert T. Stafford, R[6]	1971	1977
MASSACHUSETTS	Edward Kennedy, D	1962	1977	VIRGINIA	Harry Byrd, Jr., ind.	1965	1977
	Edward Brooke, R	1967	1979		William Scott, R	1973	1979
MICHIGAN	Philip Hart, D	1959	1977	WASHINGTON	Warren Magnuson, D	1944	1975
	Robert Griffin, R	1966	1979		Henry Jackson, D	1953	1977
MINNESOTA	Walter Mondale, D	1964	1979	WEST VIRGINIA	Jennings Randolph, D	1958	1979
	Hubert Humphrey, D[3]	1971	1977		Robert Byrd, D	1959	1977
MISSISSIPPI	James Eastland, D[4]	1943	1979	WISCONSIN	William Proxmire, D	1957	1977
	John Stennis, D	1947	1977		Gaylord Nelson, D	1963	1975
MISSOURI	Stuart Symington, D	1953	1977	WYOMING	Gale McGee, D	1959	1977
	Thomas Eagleton, D	1968	1975		Clifford Hansen, R	1967	1979

[1] As of Jan. 3, 1973. [2] Also served in the Senate from Jan. 3, 1953, to Jan. 3, 1965. [3] Also served in the Senate from Dec. 1948 to Jan. 1965. [4] Also served in the Senate from June 30, 1941, to Sept. 28, 1941. [5] Also served in the Senate from Dec. 24, 1954, to Apr. 4, 1956. [6] Appointed to fill vacancy caused by death of Winston Prouty, R, Sept. 10, 1971; elected Jan. 1972 to serve remainder of Prouty's term.

State	D*	Name
ALA.	1.	Jack Edwards, R
	2.	William Dickinson, R
	3.	Bill Nichols, D
	4.	Tom Bevill, D
	5.	Robert Jones, D
	6.	John Buchanan, R
	7.	Walter Flowers, D
ALAS.		(at large)
		Nick Begich, D2
ARIZ.	1.	John Rhodes, R
	2.	Morris Udall, D
	3.	Sam Steiger, R
	4.	J. B. Conlan, R
ARK.	1.	Bill Alexander, D
	2.	Wilbur Mills, D
	3.	John Paul Hammerschmidt, R
	4.	Ray Thornton, D
CALIF.	1.	Don Clausen, R
	2.	Harold Johnson, D
	3.	John Moss, D
	4.	Robert Leggett, D
	5.	Phillip Burton, D
	6.	William Mailliard, R
	7.	Ronald Dellums, D
	8.	F. H. Stark, D
	9.	Don Edwards, D
	10.	Charles Gubser, R
	11.	Leo Ryan, D
	12.	Burt Talcott, R
	13.	Charles Teague, R
	14.	Jerome Waldie, D
	15.	John McFall, D
	16.	B. F. Sisk, D
	17.	Paul N. McCloskey, Jr., R
	18.	Robert Mathias, R
	19.	Chet Holifield, D
	20.	C. J. Moorhead, R
	21.	Augustus Hawkins, D
	22.	James Corman, D
	23.	Del Clawson, R
	24.	John Rousselot, R
	25.	Charles Wiggins, R
	26.	Thomas Rees, D
	27.	Barry Goldwater, Jr., R
	28.	Alphonzo Bell, R
	29.	George Danielson, D
	30.	Edward Roybal, D
	31.	Charles Wilson, D
	32.	Craig Hosmer, R
	33.	Jerry Pettis, R
	34.	Richard Hanna, D
	35.	G. M. Anderson, D
	36.	W. M. Ketchum, R
	37.	Yvonne B. Burke, D
	38.	G. E. Brown, Jr., D
	39.	A. J. Hinshaw, R
	40.	Bob Wilson, R
	41.	Lionel Van Deerlin, D
	42.	C. W. Burgener, R
	43.	Victor Veysey, R
COLO.	1.	Patricia Schroeder, D
	2.	Donald Brotzman, R
	3.	Frank Evans, D
	4.	James P. Johnson, R
	5.	W. L. Armstrong, R
CONN.	1.	William Cotter, D
	2.	Robert Steele, R
	3.	Robert Giaimo, D
	4.	Stewart McKinney, R
	5.	Ronald A. Sarasin, R
	6.	Ella Grasso, D
DEL.		(at large)
		Pierre duPont, R
FLA.	1.	Robert Sikes, D
	2.	Don Fuqua, D
	3.	Charles Bennett, D

State	D*	Name
FLA.—cont.		
	4.	Bill Chappell, Jr., D
	5.	Bill Gunter, D
	6.	C. W. Young, R
	7.	Sam Gibbons, D
	8.	James Haley, D
	9.	Louis Frey, Jr., R
	10.	L. A. Bafalis, R
	11.	Paul Rogers, D
	12.	J. Herbert Burke, R
	13.	William Lehman, D
	14.	Claude Pepper, D
	15.	Dante Fascell, D
GA.	1.	Bo Ginn, D
	2.	Dawson Mathis, D
	3.	Jack Brinkley, D
	4.	Benjamin Blackburn, R
	5.	Andrew Young, D
	6.	John Flynt, Jr., D
	7.	John Davis, D
	8.	W. S. Stuckey, Jr., D
	9.	Phil Landrum, D
	10.	Robert Stephens, Jr., D
HAW.	1.	Spark Matsunaga, D
	2.	Patsy Mink, D
IDA.	1.	S. D. Symms, R
	2.	Orval Hansen, R
ILL.	1.	Ralph Metcalfe, D
	2.	Morgan Murphy, D
	3.	R. P. Hanrahan, R
	4.	Edward Derwinski, R
	5.	John Kluczynski, D
	6.	Harold Collier, R
	7.	George Collins, D
	8.	Dan Rostenkowski, D
	9.	Sidney Yates, D
	10.	S. H. Young, R
	11.	Frank Annunzio, D
	12.	Philip Crane, R
	13.	Robert McClory, R
	14.	John Erlenborn, R
	15.	Leslie Arends, R
	16.	John Anderson, R
	17.	G. M. O'Brien, R
	18.	Robert Michel, R
	19.	Tom Railsback, R
	20.	Paul Findley, R
	21.	E. R. Madigan, R
	22.	George Shipley, D
	23.	Melvin Price, D
	24.	Kenneth Gray, D
IND.	1.	Ray Madden, D
	2.	Earl Landgrebe, R
	3.	John Brademas, D
	4.	J. Edward Roush, D
	5.	Elwood Hillis, R
	6.	William Bray, R
	7.	John Myers, R
	8.	Roger Zion, R
	9.	Lee Hamilton, D
	10.	David Dennis, R
	11.	W. H. Hudnut III, R
IOWA	1.	E. Mezvinsky, D
	2.	John Culver, D
	3.	H. R. Gross, R
	4.	Neal Smith, D
	5.	William Scherle, R
	6.	Wiley Mayne, R
KANS.	1.	Keith Sebelius, R
	2.	William Roy, D
	3.	Larry Winn, Jr., R
	4.	Garner Shriver, R
	5.	Joe Skubitz, R
KY.	1.	Frank Stubblefield, D
	2.	William Natcher, D
	3.	Romano Mazzoli, D

State	D*	Name
KY.—cont.		
	4.	M. G. Snyder, R
	5.	Tim Carter, R
	6.	J. B. Breckinridge, D
	7.	Carl Perkins, D
LA.	1.	F. Edward Hébert, D
	2.	Hale Boggs, D2
	3.	David C. Treen, R
	4.	Joe Waggonner, Jr., D
	5.	Otto Passman, D
	6.	John Rarick, D
	7.	John B. Breaux, D
	8.	Gillis W. Long, D
ME.	1.	Peter Kyros, D
	2.	W. S. Cohen, R
MD.	1.	William Mills, R
	2.	Clarence Long, D
	3.	Paul Sarbanes, D
	4.	M. S. Holt, R
	5.	Lawrence Hogan, R
	6.	Goodloe Byron, D
	7.	Parren Mitchell, D
	8.	Gilbert Gude, R
MASS.	1.	Silvio Conte, R
	2.	Edward Boland, D
	3.	Harold Donohue, D
	4.	Robert Drinan, D
	5.	Paul W. Cronin, R
	6.	Michael Harrington, D
	7.	Torbert Macdonald, D
	8.	Thomas O'Neill, Jr., D
	9.	J. J. Moakley, ind.
	10.	Margaret Heckler, R
	11.	James Burke, D
	12.	Gerry E. Studds, D
MICH.	1.	John Conyers, Jr., D
	2.	Marvin Esch, R
	3.	Gary Brown, R
	4.	Edward Hutchinson, R
	5.	Gerald Ford, R
	6.	Charles Chamberlain, R
	7.	Donald Riegle, Jr., R
	8.	James Harvey, R
	9.	Guy Vander Jagt, R
	10.	Elford Cederberg, R
	11.	Philip Ruppe, R
	12.	James O'Hara, D
	13.	Charles Diggs, Jr., D
	14.	Lucien Nedzi, D
	15.	William Ford, D
	16.	John Dingell, D
	17.	Martha Griffiths, D
	18.	R. J. Huber, R
	19.	William Broomfield, R
MINN.	1.	Albert Quie, R
	2.	Ancher Nelsen, R
	3.	Bill Frenzel, R
	4.	Joseph Karth, D
	5.	Donald Fraser, D
	6.	John Zwach, R
	7.	Bob Bergland, D
	8.	John Blatnik, D
MISS.	1.	Jamie Whitten, D
	2.	D. R. Bowen, D
	3.	G. V. Montgomery, D
	4.	Thad Cochran, R
	5.	Trent Lott, R
MO.	1.	William Clay, D
	2.	James Symington, D
	3.	Leonor Sullivan, D
	4.	William Randall, D
	5.	Richard Bolling, D
	6.	Jerry Litton, D
	7.	Gene Taylor, R
	8.	Richard Ichord, D
	9.	William Hungate, D
	10.	Bill Burlison, D

State	D*	Name	State	D*	Name	State	D*	Name
MONT.	1.	Richard Shoup, R	N. DAK.		(at large)	TENN.-cont.		
	2.	John Melcher, D			Mark Andrews, R		4.	Joe Evins, D
NEBR.	1.	Charles Thone, R	OHIO	1.	William Keating, R		5.	Richard Fulton, D
	2.	John McCollister, R		2.	Donald Clancy, R		6.	R. L. Beard, R
	3.	Dave Martin, R		3.	Charles Whalen, Jr., R		7.	Ed Jones, D
NEV.		(at large)		4.	Tennyson Guyer, R		8.	Dan Kuykendall, R
		David Towell, R		5.	Delbert Latta, R	TEXAS	1.	Wright Patman, D
N. H.	1.	Louis Wyman, R		6.	William Harsha, R		2.	Charles Wilson, D
	2.	James Cleveland, R		7.	Clarence Brown, R		3.	James Collins, R
N. J.	1.	John Hunt, R		8.	W. E. Powell, R		4.	Ray Roberts, D
	2.	Charles Sandman, Jr., R		9.	Thomas Ashley, D		5.	Alan Steelman, R
	3.	James Howard, D		10.	Clarence Miller, R		6.	Olin Teague, D
	4.	Frank Thompson, Jr., D		11.	J. William Stanton, R		7.	Bill Archer, R
	5.	Peter Frelinghuysen, R		12.	Samuel Devine, R		8.	Bob Eckhardt, D
	6.	Edwin Forsythe, R		13.	Charles Mosher, R		9.	Jack Brooks, D
	7.	William Widnall, R		14.	John Seiberling, D		10.	J. J. Pickle, D
	8.	Robert Roe, D		15.	Chalmers Wylie, R		11.	W. R. Poage, D
	9.	Henry Helstoski, D		16.	R. S. Regula, R		12.	Jim Wright, D
	10.	Peter Rodino, Jr., D		17.	John Ashbrook, R		13.	Robert Price, R
	11.	Joseph Minish, D		18.	Wayne Hays, D		14.	John Young, D
	12.	M. J. Rinaldo, R		19.	Charles Carney, D		15.	Eligio de la Garza, D
	13.	J. J. Maraziti, R		20.	James Stanton, D		16.	Richard White, D
	14.	Dominick Daniels, D		21.	Louis Stokes, D		17.	Omar Burleson. D
	15.	Edward Patten, D		22.	Charles Vanik, D		18.	B. C. Jordan, D
N. MEX.	1.	Manuel Lujan, Jr., R		23.	William Minshall, R		19.	George Mahon, D
	2.	Harold Runnels, D	OKLA.	1.	James R. Jones, D		20.	Henry Gonzalez, D
N. Y.	1.	Otis Pike, D		2.	C. R. McSpadden, D		21.	O. C. Fisher, D
	2.	James Grover, Jr., R		3.	Carl Albert, D		22.	Bob Casey, D
	3.	A. D. Roncallo, R		4.	Tom Steed, D		23.	Abraham Kazen, Jr., D
	4.	Norman Lent, R		5.	John Jarman, D		24.	Dale Milford, D
	5.	John Wydler, R		6.	John Happy Camp, R	UTAH	1.	Gunn McKay, D
	6.	Lester Wolff, D	OREG.	1.	Wendell Wyatt, R		2.	Wayne Owens, D
	7.	Joseph Addabbo, D		2.	Al Ullman, D	VT.		(at large)
	8.	Benjamin Rosenthal, D		3.	Edith Green, D			R. W. Mallary, R
	9.	James Delaney, D		4.	John Dellenback, R	VA.	1.	Thomas Downing, D
	10.	Mario Biaggi, D	PA.	1.	William Barrett, D		2.	G. William Whitehurst, R
	11.	Frank Brasco, D		2.	Robert Nix, D		3.	David Satterfield III, D
	12.	Shirley Chisholm, D		3.	W. J. Green, D		4.	R. W. Daniel, Jr., R
	13.	Bertram Podell, D		4.	Joshua Eilberg, D		5.	W. C. Daniel, D
	14.	John Rooney, D		5.	John Ware, R		6.	M. C. Butler, R
	15.	Hugh Carey, D		6.	Gus Yatron, D		7.	J. Kenneth Robinson, R
	16.	Elizabeth Holtzman, D		7.	Lawrence Williams, R		8.	S. E. Parris, R
	17.	John Murphy, D		8.	Edward Biester, Jr., R		9.	William Wampler, R
	18.	Edward Koch, D		9.	E. G. Shuster, R		10.	Joel Broyhill, R
	19.	Charles Rangel, D		10.	Joseph McDade, R	WASH.	1.	Joel Pritchard, R
	20.	Bella Abzug, D		11.	Daniel Flood, D		2.	Lloyd Meeds, D
	21.	Herman Badillo, D		12.	J. P. Saylor, R		3.	Julia Butler Hansen, D
	22.	Jonathan Bingham, D		13.	Lawrence Coughlin, R		4.	Mike McCormack, D
	23.	Peter Peyser, R		14.	William Moorhead, D		5.	Thomas Foley, D
	24.	Ogden Reid, D		15.	Fred Rooney, D		6.	Floyd Hicks, D
	25.	Hamilton Fish, Jr., R		16.	Edwin Eshleman, R		7.	Brock Adams, D
	26.	B. A. Gilman, R		17.	Herman Schneebeli, R	W. VA.	1.	Robert Mollohan, D
	27.	H. W. Robison, R		18.	H. John Heinz III, R		2.	Harley Staggers, D
	28.	Samuel Stratton, D		19.	George Goodling, R		3.	John Slack, D
	29.	Carleton King, R		20.	Joseph Gaydos, D		4.	Ken Hechler, D
	30.	Robert McEwen, R		21.	John Dent, D	WIS.	1.	Les Aspin, D
	31.	D. J. Mitchell, R		22.	T. E. Morgan, D		2.	Robert Kastenmeier, D
	32.	James Hanley, D		23.	Albert Johnson, R		3.	Vernon Thomson, R
	33.	W. F. Walsh, R		24.	Joseph Vigorito, D		4.	Clement Zablocki, D
	34.	Frank Horton, R		25.	Frank Clark, D		5.	Henry Reuss, D
	35.	Barber Conable, Jr., R	R. I.	1.	Fernand St. Germain, D		6.	William Steiger, R
	36.	Henry Smith III, R		2.	Robert Tiernan, D		7.	David Obey, D
	37.	Thaddeus Dulski, D	S. C.	1.	Mendel Davis, D		8.	H. V. Froehlich, R
	38.	Jack Kemp, R		2.	Floyd Spence, R		9.	Glenn Davis, R
	39.	James Hastings, R		3.	William Jennings Bryan Dorn, D	WYO.		(at large)
N. C.	1.	Walter Jones, D		4.	James Mann, D			Teno Roncalio, D
	2.	L. H. Fountain, D		5.	Tom Gettys, D	WASH., D.C.		(delegate)
	3.	David Henderson, D		6.	E. L. Young, R			Walter Fauntroy, D
	4.	Ike F. Andrews, D	S. DAK.	1.	Frank Denholm, D	P. R.		(resident commissioner)
	5.	Wilmer Mizell, R		2.	James Abdnor, R			Jorge Córdova, D
	6.	Richardson Preyer, D	TENN.	1.	James Quillen, R			
	7.	C. G. Rose III, D		2.	John Duncan, R			
	8.	Earl Ruth, R		3.	LaMar Baker, R			
	9.	J. G. Martin, R						
	10.	James Broyhill, R						
	11.	Roy Taylor, D						

* D stands for Congressional District. [1] As of Nov. 27, 1972. [2] Missing in Alaskan airplane crash at time of election.

State Roundup

The following roundup presents state-by-state results of races for both national and state offices. At the end of each article is a list of the winners in that state. Popular vote totals are unofficial, and some state legislative figures are not final. An asterisk (*) next to a victor's name indicates that he or she is the incumbent.

ALABAMA. Seventy-two percent of the Alabama electorate voted for President Nixon in the presidential election. Most of those who had voted for Governor George Wallace in 1968 strongly supported Nixon.

All incumbent congressmen, both Democrat and Republican, were returned to office, and Senator John J. Sparkman defeated Republican candidate Winton "Red" Blount by almost a 2–1 margin, despite the generous aid given the Blount campaign by Republican Party leaders.

In exercising local option concerning the right to sell liquor, 11 Alabama counties all voted dry in the election, the largest number of counties to vote on the wet-dry issue at the same time since Alabama abandoned prohibition in 1937. Two proposed amendments to the Alabama constitution—to require the legislature to meet every year—were defeated.

Presidential vote: Nixon (R), 728,701; Mc-Govern (D), 219,108.
Senator: John J. Sparkman* (D).
House: 4 D, 3 R.

HENRY SEYMOUR MARKS

★ ★ ★

ALASKA. President Nixon carried Alaska in the 1972 election by a more substantial margin than in 1968. Alaskans also returned Republican Ted Stevens to the U.S. Senate with a spectacular 77 percent plurality; his opponent was Gene Guess, speaker of the state house of representatives. In an uncertain, tragedy-struck race for the U.S. House, voters decisively

approved the candidacy of the Democratic incumbent, Nick Begich, over Republican state senator Don Young, although Begich had disappeared on October 16 while on a campaign flight between Anchorage and Juneau.

A proposal to hold a new constitutional convention was overwhelmingly rejected by the voters. In legislative races the Republicans did quite well.

Presidential vote: Nixon (R), 41,809; Mc-Govern (D), 24,362.
Senator: Ted Stevens* (R).
House: 1 D.
State legislature: senate, 11 R, 9 D; house, 21 D, 19 R.

STANTON H. PATTY

★ ★ ★

ARIZONA. As President Richard M. Nixon won an easy victory in Arizona, state senator John B. Conlan, son of a former major league baseball umpire, slugged his way to victory in the new 4th Congressional District, adding one more GOP seat to Arizona's congressional delegation. Conlan's Democratic opponent was state legislator Jack A. Brown, a fellow graduate of Harvard Law School.

Incumbents were returned to office in each of the other three congressional districts: Republican Sam Steiger defeated Ted Wyckoff, a professor at Northern Arizona University; Democrat Morris K. Udall outpolled Gene Savoie, a dentist from Tucson; and Republican John J. Rhodes narrowly defeated Gerald A. Pollock, a lawyer and teacher. Pollock, who had

waged a low-key campaign, surprised pundits with his strong showing; he came within 21,000 votes of defeating Rhodes, who has been in the House of Representatives since 1953.

On the state level, the GOP picked up four seats in the house of representatives to acquire a 16-seat margin over the Democrats. The party alignment in the senate remained the same, with the Republicans leading 18–12. In major judicial races, Fred C. Struckmeyer, Jr., Lorna E. Lockwood, and William A. Holohan won reelection to the state supreme court.

Presidential vote: Nixon (R), 381,532; Mc-Govern (D), 188,892.
House: 3 R, 1 D.
State legislature: Senate, 18 R, 12 D; house, 38 R, 22 D.

CLYDE ANDREW MURRAY

★ ★ ★

ARKANSAS. President Richard M. Nixon became the first Republican presidential candidate to carry Arkansas since Ulysses S. Grant swept most of the South in 1872. But the Republican Party, attempting a comeback in the state after disastrous losses in 1970, was almost annihilated.

Republicans fielded candidates against Governor Dale Bumpers, Senator John McClellan, and three Democratic state officials and launched a campaign aimed at making major inroads in the state legislature. But the results were bleak for the GOP. Bumpers, with almost no campaigning, won 76 percent of the vote to trounce former state welfare commis-

sioner Lee E. Blaylock. McClellan, after a close primary contest in which he defeated Representative David H. Pryor, easily went on to turn away Republican challenger Wayne H. Babbitt. Representative John Paul Hammerschmidt (R) was reelected easily, and the GOP managed to hold onto one seat in the state senate and one in the state house of representatives.

In spite of a strong effort by the state Democratic organization and unprecedented attention from the Democratic national ticket, President Nixon won 70 percent of the popular vote.

Presidential vote: Nixon (R), 427,014; McGovern (D), 190,598.
Senator: John L. McClellan* (D).
House: 3 D, 1 R.
State government: Gov., Dale L. Bumpers* (D); lt. gov., Bob Riley* (D); secy. of state, Kelly Bryant* (D); atty. gen., Jim Guy Tucker (D); aud., Jimmie "Red" Jones* (D); treas., Nancy J. Hall* (D). Legislature: senate, 34 D, 1 R; house, 99 37 R, 28 D.
ERNEST C. DUMAS

★ ★ ★

CALIFORNIA. California's coveted 45 electoral votes went to President Nixon, who carried all but 7 of the state's 58 counties and won 55 percent of the popular vote on Election Day. Senator George McGovern, who had campaigned heavily in the state, garnered 42 percent of the vote, and American Party candidate John Schmitz received some 230,000 votes.

As a result of the 1970 census, five seats were added to California's U.S. House delegation. Democrats retained a majority in the new delegation, capturing 23 of the 43 seats. All 35 incumbents seeking reelection were returned to office by their constituents. Among the newly elected members was Yvonne Braithwaite Burke (D), who had cochaired the Democratic National Convention and who will now become the first black congresswoman from the West.

The contest for control of the state legislature resulted in a mixed verdict. Democrats increased their margin in the assembly to 51–29, wresting 8 seats from the GOP. However, the Republicans gained a 19–19 standoff in the state senate, with two vacancies left to be filled by special elections.

The California ballot included 22 constitutional amendments and initiative proposals. Fifteen won popular approval, including a controversial antibusing initiative, a measure establishing a temporary zoning commission to control development within 1,000 yards of the Pacific coast, and an amendment restoring the death penalty for specific crimes. Voters defeated proposals to restrict the unionization of farm workers, strengthen obscenity control, and place a ceiling on property taxes. Californians also voted, by a 2 to 1 margin, against abolishing penalties for the personal use of marijuana.

Presidential vote: Nixon (R), 4,544,134; McGovern (D), 3,431,824.
House: 23 D, 20 R.
State legislature: Senate, 19 D, 19 R, 2 vacancies; assembly, 51 D, 29 R.
GEORGE S. BLAIR

★ ★ ★

COLORADO. One of the biggest surprises of the 1972 elections was the defeat of Colorado's senior U.S. senator, Gordon L. Allott, one of the highest ranking Republicans in Congress. He lost to Floyd K. Haskell, 56, a Littleton, Colo., attorney. Allott, 65, completing 18 years in the Senate, fell 7,221 votes short of his Democratic opponent, whose campaign emphasized environmental needs.

President Richard M. Nixon posted a wide victory margin in the state, getting 591,352 votes to 328,221 for Senator George McGovern.

Colorado, because of its rapid population growth, was allocated a fifth U.S. congressional seat, which was filled by Republican state senator William L. Armstrong, who defeated former U.S. representative Byron Johnson, a Democrat.

Winners of the remaining seats included two veteran incumbents, both completing five terms: Representative Frank Evans, a Democrat, and Republican representative Don Brotzman. Newcomers to Congress were Republican James Johnson, a Fort Collins lawyer, and Democrat Patricia Schroeder, a Denver attorney who ousted one-term Republican congressman Mike McKevitt.

Numerous initiated laws and amendments were voted on. By far the most controversial were measures denying public funds for Colorado's host role in the 1976 Winter Olympic Games. The measures passed easily, forcing the cancellation of plans to have the winter games in Colorado.

Most of the amendments failed, including one on no-fault automobile in-

"ENTERTAINMENT FOR ADULTS" in San Francisco's North Bay area. Although Californians voted down busing and pot, they rejected a proposal to tighten the reins on pornography.
WIDE WORLD

surance and two others seeking to limit use of the property tax. A "sunshine amendment," requiring lawmakers and other state officials to disclose their personal financial interests, was approved.

Presidential vote: Nixon (R), 591,352; McGovern (D), 328,221.
Senator: Floyd K. Haskell (D).
House: 3 R, 2 D.
State legislature: Senate, 22 R, 13 D; house, 37 R, 28 D.   LEE OLSON

★ ★ ★

CONNECTICUT. After complicated legal maneuvering, the supreme court of Connecticut upheld a lower court order calling for general assembly elections according to a Republican-inspired reapportionment plan. In the wake of the Nixon landslide and the redistricting, the Republicans captured both houses of the legislature for the first time since 1956, winning a 23–13 edge in the senate and a majority of 93–58 in the house of representatives. The reapportionment plan was expected to face a federal court challenge.

George McGovern, Sargent Shriver, Edward Kennedy, and Hubert Humphrey stumped energetically in Connecticut—but to little effect, as Nixon won by a plurality of more than 250,000 votes. The new Connecticut delegation in the U.S. House was split three each—a Republican gain of one seat.

Presidential vote: Nixon (R), 810,763; McGovern (D), 555,498.
House: 3 R, 3 D.
State legislature: Senate, 23 R, 13 D; house, 93 R, 58 D.   ALBERT E. VAN DUSEN

★ ★ ★

DELAWARE. One of the nation's most dramatic political upsets occurred in Delaware, where ticket-splitting voters elected the country's youngest U.S. senator and favored two Republicans and two Democrats in the contests for the four highest statewide offices.

The new Democratic senator, Joseph R. Biden, Jr., only 29 years old on Election Day, edged the two-term Republican incumbent J. Caleb Boggs by about 3,000 votes. On November 20, Biden turned 30, the minimum constitutional age to assume a senatorship. Another Republican incumbent, Governor Russell W. Peterson, was also narrowly rejected by the voters in favor of conservative Democrat Sherman W. Tribbitt, a former lieutenant governor.

U.S. representative Pierre S. duPont IV, a Republican, retained his seat in the House by the biggest margin in Delaware political history (about 58,000 votes), defeating the Democratic contender, Mayor Norma Handloff of Newark.

Delaware voters also gave a one-sided victory to President Nixon, who received 60 percent of the vote.

Republican lieutenant governor Eugene Bookhammer of Lewes was reelected, and the Republicans were left in control of both houses of the newly reapportioned general assembly, but with only a one-vote margin in each.

Presidential vote: Nixon (R), 140,357; McGovern (D), 92,283.

GARY SETTLE/NEW YORK TIMES

THE SKI JUMP near Steamboat Springs, Colo. Voters turned a cold shoulder to a $5 million bond issue that would have enabled Colorado to play host to the 1976 Winter Olympics.

Senator: Joseph R. Biden, Jr. (D).
House: 1 R.
State government: Gov., Sherman W. Tribbitt (D); lt. gov., Eugene Bookhammer* (R). Legislature: senate, 11 R, 10 D; house, 21 R, 20 D.   CY LIBERMAN

★ ★ ★

FLORIDA. A record number of candidates —1,000—contested for state and local offices in the 1972 primaries and general election in Florida, with some small but significant Republican gains in the historically Democratic state. In the U.S. House of Representatives the new lineup is 11 Democrats and four Republicans in contrast to nine Democrats and three Republicans in the 92nd Congress.

Only one statewide office was at stake— a seat on the public service commission.

It was won by Paula Hawkins, cochairman of the Nixon campaign in Florida.

Elected to the new state senate were 14 Republicans and one independent; 43 Republicans, a record number, were elected to the house. In a referendum, Floridians voted overwhelmingly to issue $240 million in bonds to buy environmentally endangered private lands and to create additional state parks. Also approved was a constitutional amendment realigning revenue sources in order to build more schools without new taxes.

Presidential vote: Nixon (R), 1,857,759; McGovern (D), 718,117.
House: 11 D, 4 R.
State legislature: senate, 25 D, 14 R, 1 ind.; house, 77 D, 43 R.   DON SHOEMAKER

★ ★ ★

*indicates incumbent

GEORGIA. Sweeping the state by the largest margin given any presidential candidate since Franklin D. Roosevelt in 1944, Richard M. Nixon was only the second Republican to win Georgia's 12 electoral votes—Barry Goldwater was the first.

However, despite Nixon's overwhelming personal victory, Georgians refused to go along with most of the state-level Republican office-seekers for whom Nixon, Spiro Agnew, and many other GOP stalwarts had fought so diligently, especially Fletcher Thompson, Rodney Cook, and Ronnie Thompson.

Fletcher Thompson lost the U.S. Senate race to Democratic state representative Sam Nunn. Georgia's Republicans must now wait until Herman Talmadge is up for reelection to the Senate in 1974 before they can again try to elect a Republican senator.

Republican Rodney Cook lost the race for the 5th Congressional District seat to Atlanta civil-rights mediator Andrew Young, who is the first black person elected to Congress from Georgia in more than a century. Young emphasized that he will represent a district in which whites constitute 62 percent of the population. Conservative Macon mayor Ronnie Thompson was defeated by 8th District Democratic incumbent William S. Stuckey. Fourth District representative Ben Blackburn is the lone Republican among nine Democrats on Georgia's delegation to the U.S. House of Representatives. With two exceptions—newcomers Young and Bo Ginn, who was unopposed—all incumbent representatives were returned to Congress.

Presidential vote: Nixon (R), 881,490; McGovern (D), 289,529.
Senator: Sam Nunn (D).
House: 9 D, 1 R.
State legislature: Senate, 48 D, 8 R; house, 152 D, 28 R.   JAMES I. ST. JOHN

★   ★   ★

HAWAII. President Nixon became the first Republican ever to carry Hawaii, receiving 62.4 percent of the vote.

In the Honolulu mayoral election, incumbent Frank F. Fasi squeaked through by a 3.5 percent margin to defeat his GOP challenger, D. G. Anderson. Other Democratic incumbents, Spark M. Matsunaga (Honolulu) and Patsy T. Mink (Rural Oahu–Neighbor Islands), were returned to the U.S. House, despite surprisingly strong showings by the two Republican opponents.

On the state level seven new faces were elected to the house, and the Democrats picked up one more seat to better their 2–1 margin. The major upsets on Oahu were won by three Democrats—Steve Cobb, Anson Chong, and Jann Yuen.

Presidential vote: Nixon (R), 167,563; McGovern (D), 100,652.
House: 2 D.
State legislature: Senate, 17 D, 8 R; house, 35 D, 16 R.   PATRICIA L. DOWIE

★   ★   ★

IDAHO. During the campaign in Idaho little excitement was generated by the candidacy of George McGovern. Rather, Democrats avoided presidential politics and campaigned to build Democratic strength in state and U.S. congressional offices. But Republicans won all national elections and consolidated their control of the state legislature.

President Nixon won with 64 percent of the vote, carrying every county, including normally Democratic strongholds. In the House races a political unknown, Republican Steven D. Symms, defeated Edward V. Williams handily in the 1st Congressional District, and in the 2nd Congressional District Republican incumbent Orval Hansen overwhelmed Willis Ludlow with 69 percent of the vote. Also, conservative Republican congressman James A. McClure won over political newcomer William E. Davis in the Senate race.

In the state legislature Republicans increased their three-seat senate majority to 23–12 and their 12-seat margin in the house to 51–19. The voters approved four of nine initiatives, which would limit the executive branch to 20 agencies, require the identification of nonvoting corporate stock prior to sale, allow approval of sewer and water revenue bonds by a simple majority, and replace a constitutional provision limiting the years of compulsory education to three with a requirement of schooling from age six to 18.

Presidential vote: Nixon (R), 186,432; McGovern (D), 80,558.
Senator: James A. McClure (R).
House: 2 R.
State legislature: Senate, 23 R, 12 D; house, 51 R, 19 D.
SIEGFRIED B. ROLLAND

★   ★   ★

ILLINOIS. Democrat Daniel Walker confounded the political experts as he was elected governor of Illinois. U.S. senator Charles Percy and state attorney general William Scott, both Republicans, rolled to easy reelection victories. In the presidential race, Richard Nixon won Illinois' 26 electoral votes.

Walker launched his bid for the Democratic nomination for governor nearly two years before the election, and in the March primary he defeated the popular lieutenant governor Paul Simon, nominated for governor by the state's regular Democratic organization, headed by Chicago mayor Richard Daley. Republican governor Richard Ogilvie had sought reelection, but the coattails of President Nixon and Senator Percy were not enough to overcome Ogilvie's unpopularity among voters.

Controversial Cook County state's attorney Edward V. Hanrahan, who had been indicted in late 1971 by a special grand jury on charges stemming from a police raid in which two Black Panther leaders were killed in Chicago in December 1969, was acquitted a few days before the November election. However, the crossover of normally Democratic black voters to Hanrahan's Republican opponent Bernard Carey gave Carey a narrow win in the election. This was considered a sharp setback for the Daley organization, which had backed Hanrahan after the primary.

Republicans won narrow control of both houses of the Illinois legislature and picked up two seats in the U.S. House of Representatives.

Presidential vote: Nixon (R), 2,747,687; McGovern (D), 1,863,526.
Senator: Charles Percy* (R).
House: 14 R, 10 D.
State government: Gov., Daniel Walker (D); lt. gov., Neil Hartigan (D); atty. gen., William Scott* (R); secy. of state, Michael Howlett (D); comp., George Lindberg (R). Legislature: senate, 30 R, 29 D; house, 90 R, 87 D.
EDWARD H. ARMSTRONG

★   ★   ★

INDIANA. Indiana Republicans, behind President Nixon's victory margin of more than 600,000 votes on November 7, elected a governor and increased their advantage in the state's general assembly and U.S. congressional delegation.

Republican Otis Bowen, a physician and four-time speaker of the Indiana house, was elected governor with 57 percent of the vote, over Democrat Matthew Welsh, a former Indiana governor (1961–1965). Republican state senator Robert Orr was elected lieutenant governor. Under a constitutional amendment approved November 7, Bowen will be the first governor eligible to serve two consecutive four-year terms.

Republicans already controlled the general assembly, but the November 7 vote gave them a 29–21 margin in the state senate and a 73–27 advantage in the state house of representatives.

The Republicans stretched their U.S. House of Representatives margin from 6–5 to 7–4, as William Hudnut, an Indianapolis minister, defeated incumbent Democrat Andrew Jacobs, Jr. All other incumbent congressmen won: Republicans Earl Landgrebe, Elwood Hillis, William Bray, David Dennis, John Myers, and Roger Zion and Democrats Ray J. Madden, J. Edward Roush, Lee Hamilton, and John Brademas.

Presidential vote: Nixon (R), 1,397,744; McGovern (D), 703,098.
House: 7 R, 4 D.
State government: Gov., Otis Bowen (R); lt. gov., Robert Orr (R); atty. gen., Theodore Sendak* (R); supt. of pub. instr., Harold Negley (R). General assembly: senate, 29 R, 21 D; house, 73 R, 27 D.
C. W. VERTREES

★   ★   ★

IOWA. Although President Richard M. Nixon swept Iowa with 57 percent of the popular vote, Democrats achieved a major upset when Richard Clark, a little-known former history professor, beat two-term Republican senator Jack Miller. Clark conducted a tightly organized campaign and dramatized his candidacy by walking 1,300 miles through the state preaching tax reform. He became only the ninth Democrat ever elected to the U.S. Senate from Iowa.

Democrats were also successful in three U.S. House races, gaining an equality with the GOP in Iowa's congressional delegation.

Governor Robert D. Ray, reelected to a third two-year term, led the GOP state ticket to victory. Republicans retained control of all state administrative posts and maintained a majority in both houses of the state legislature. However, Democrats registered impressive gains in both houses, picking up a total of 16 seats.

Voters approved an amendment removing the state's constitutional ban on lotteries and bingo. They also approved amendments increasing the terms for state officers from two to four years and granting the Iowa supreme court the power to remove a lower court judge from office for cause.

Presidential vote: Nixon (R), 703,933; Mc-Govern (D), 493,310.
Senator: Richard Clark (D).
House: 3 D, 3 R.
State government: Gov., Robert D. Ray* (R); lt. gov., Arthur Neu (R); secy. of state, Melvin D. Synhorst* (R); aud., Lloyd R. Smith* (R); treas., Maurice E. Baringer* (R); atty. gen., Richard C. Turner* (R); secy. of agr., Robert H. Lounsberry (R). Legislature: senate, 28 R, 22 D; house, 56 R, 44 D.
LAURENCE M. PAUL

★ ★ ★

KANSAS. Voters in the Republican stronghold of Kansas were in a ticket-splitting mood. They gave President Nixon 605,632 votes, 68 percent of the total cast, but turned down the GOP gubernatorial candidate, Morris Kay, in his effort to unseat three-term governor Robert B. Docking. Running on his record and on a firm stand against tax increases, Docking rolled up the largest margin of votes he ever received, 558,788 out of 891,145, or 63 percent of the total.

Incumbent senator James B. Pearson seems to have benefited less from presidential coattails than from the unpopularity of his opponent, Dr. Arch Tetzlaff, an anesthesiologist who once served in the German Luftwaffe. Pearson won 600,-544 votes, or 72 percent, to his opponent's 195,065 votes.

The state's congressional delegation remained unchanged; William Roy, the lone Democrat, retained his seat along with the four Republicans, defeating Charles D. McAtee with a healthy 61 percent of the vote.

Attorney General Vern Miller was re-elected; aside from the governor, he remained the only Democrat to hold elective office in the state administration. State senator Dave Owens was elected lieutenant governor, and Tom R. Van Sickle, another GOP state senator, became treasurer, succeeding Walter Peery, whom he had defeated in the primary. However, the Republicans lost five seats in the state senate and five in the state house of representatives.

Presidential vote: Nixon (R), 605,632; Mc-Govern (D), 265,158.
Senator: James B. Pearson* (R).
House: 4 R, 1 D.
State government: Gov., Robert B. Docking* (D); lt. gov., Dave Owens (R); atty. gen., Vern Miller* (D); secy. of state, Elwill M. Shanahan* (R); aud., Clay E. Hedrick* (R); treas., Tom R. Van Sickle (R). Legislature: senate, 27 R, 13 D; house, 79 R, 46 D.
JOSEPH W. SNELL

★ ★ ★

KENTUCKY. Ticket-splitting Kentuckians gave Richard Nixon a record-setting margin in the presidential election but also elected a Democrat to the U.S. Senate for the first time in 18 years and kept the 5–2 Democratic edge in the U.S. House of Representatives.

Democratic governor Wendell Ford fought bitterly against the presidential nomination of George McGovern and never offered any active support. Nixon carried every congressional district in the state.

The retirement of U.S. senator John Sherman Cooper left his seat up for grabs. Victory went to state senator Walter "Dee" Huddleston, whose opponent was former governor Louie B. Nunn, a Republican. The sales tax was apparently the main issue with voters. While Nunn was governor, the state sales tax was increased from 3 percent to 5 percent. Democrats claimed credit for the October repeal of the 5 percent food tax.

Former state attorney general John Breckinridge, a Democrat from Lexington, became the only new member of Kentucky's delegation to the U.S. House of Representatives after a very close race. Democrats returning to Congress are Romano L. Mazzoli, Carl D. Perkins, Frank A. Stubblefield, and William H. Natcher. Republicans returning to the house are Gene Snyder and Tim Lee Carter.

Presidential vote: Nixon (R), 671,198; Mc-Govern (D), 369,051.
Senator: Walter "Dee" Huddleston (D).
House: 5 D, 2 R.
CHARLES WALDEN

★ ★ ★

LOUISIANA. After edging out state senator J. Bennett Johnston in the Democratic primary runoff, former congressman Edwin W. Edwards went on to defeat Republican attorney David C. Treen in the February 1 general election and became Louisiana's first Catholic governor in 80 years.

In the November election, President Richard M. Nixon easily won Louisiana's ten electoral votes, capturing 66 percent of the popular vote. State senator Johnston, disappointed in his gubernatorial bid, won the United States Senate seat held by Elaine Edwards (the governor's wife), who was appointed after Senator Allen J. Ellender died in July. Johnston easily defeated Republican Benjamin Toledano and former governor John J. McKeithen, who ran as an independent.

In the contest to represent Louisiana's 3rd Congressional District, Treen, who had already made a strong showing in February's gubernatorial contest, defeated Democrat J. Louis Thompson to become the first Republican in the twentieth century to represent Louisiana in Congress. Representative Hale Boggs, who disappeared in an airplane crash on October 16 while campaigning for fellow Democrats in Alaska, was nevertheless reelected.

Presidential vote: Nixon (R), 701,455; Mc-Govern (D), 314,309.
Senator: J. Bennett Johnston (D).
House: 7 D, 1 R.
State government: Gov., Edwin W. Edwards (D); lt. gov., James H. Fitzmorris (D); secy. of state, Wade O. Martin, Jr.* (D); atty. gen., William J. Guste (D); treas., Mary Evelyn Parker* (D); cont., Roy R. Theriot* (D). Legislature: senate, 39 D, 0 R; house, 101 D, 4 R.
JOE GRAY TAYLOR

★ ★ ★

MAINE. Losers rather than winners stole the political headlines in Maine. Both were U.S. senators, Democrat Edmund S. Muskie, whose bid for the presidential nomination fell apart, and Republican Margaret Chase Smith, whose bid for a fifth term failed despite a 3–2 Nixon win in Maine.

Mrs. Smith, the only woman in the Senate, was upset by Democratic congressman William D. Hathaway partially because of her age, 74. Other factors, in Hathaway's view, were a favorable report on him in Ralph Nader's congressional study and the elimination of simple straight-ticket voting (for example, pressing one lever or marking one X in favor of a whole party slate)—a GOP-backed ballot reform aimed originally at reducing the effect of a Muskie candidacy.

With Muskie and Hathaway, Maine will have two Democratic senators for the first time in the state's 152-year history.

Congressman Peter N. Kyros, a Democrat, won a fourth term. William S. Cohen, 32, won the 1st Congressional District seat vacated by Hathaway and replaced Mrs. Smith as Maine's only Republican in Congress.

Presidential vote: Nixon (R), 256,458; Mc-Govern (D), 160,584.
Senator: William D. Hathaway (D).
House: 1 D, 1 R.
State legislature: Senate, 23 R, 10 D; house, 79 R, 72 D.
JOHN K. MURPHY

★ ★ ★

MARYLAND. President Richard Nixon won Maryland's ten electoral votes, with more than 60 percent of the popular vote. However, Maryland Democrats in Congress held onto their seats. The GOP gained one reapportioned congressional district in which no incumbent ran.

A referendum giving state aid to parochial school children was defeated in a close contest. Another referendum for a state lottery carried overwhelmingly. Some observers viewed both votes as an indication of citizen preoccupation with heavy taxes.

On the eve of the May 16 Maryland presidential primary, George C. Wallace was shot and seriously wounded while campaigning in a suburban Laurel shopping center. Wallace won the primary with 39 percent of the vote.

Although Governor Marvin Mandel endorsed George McGovern's candidacy, several of the governor's most important supporters became Democrats for Nixon.

Presidential vote: Nixon (R), 797,295; Mc-Govern (D), 486,570.
House: 4 D, 4 R.
JEROME KELLY

★ ★ ★

MASSACHUSETTS. With 55 percent of the voters choosing Senator George McGovern over President Richard M. Nixon, Massachusetts became the only state whose electoral votes went to the senator from South Dakota. Many factors were cited for this outcome. For one thing, Massachusetts is the home state of Senator Edward M. Kennedy, a likely Democratic presidential candidate in 1976. Furthermore, this was the first presidential election for some

*indicates incumbent

330,000 voters aged 18–21, many of them college students. Also, there has been long-standing opposition in the state to the Vietnam war; the Massachusetts legislature once sought to prevent the state's youth from being drafted.

The Democratic sweep exempted U.S. senator Edward W. Brooke, a liberal Republican and the only black in the Senate. Retiring Republican congressman Hastings Keith was replaced by antiwar Democrat Gerry Studds, and conservative Democrat Louise Day Hicks was beaten by moderate independent John Joseph Moakley.

Republican forces in the state legislature won only 52 of 240 seats in the house and seven of 40 in the senate. In the 5th Congressional District, Democrat John Kerry, who gained national attention in 1970 when he spoke before a congressional committee on behalf of Vietnam Veterans Against the War, and independent Roger P. Durkin were defeated by Republican Paul W. Cronin.

Voters rejected a constitutional amendment allowing the legislature to replace the state's flat-rate income tax with one similar to the federal graduated-rate tax. They approved an amendment requiring judges to retire at the age of 70.

Presidential vote: McGovern (D), 1,323,843; Nixon (R), 1,104,310.
Senator: Edward W. Brooke* (R).
House: 8 D, 3 R, 1 I.
State legislature: Senate, 33 D, 7 R (Republicans may lose one seat as result of recount); house, 186 D, 52 R, 2 ind.

MICHAEL KENNEY

★ ★ ★

MICHIGAN. President Richard M. Nixon carried Michigan by nearly a half-million votes. Republican senator Robert P. Griffin was reelected to a second term as he defeated Democrat Frank J. Kelley, the popular state attorney general, in a close race. The state congressional delegation of 12 Republicans and 7 Democrats remained unchanged. GOP incumbents Jack H. McDonald and William S. Broomfield faced each other in the Republican primary in the redrawn 19th District; Broomfield won.

Seats on the Michigan supreme court were won by Mary Coleman, the first woman to seek this office, who was supported by the Republicans, and Charles L. Levin, who, although nominally a Democrat, took the unusual step of creating an independent party. The Democrats continued to control the Michigan house.

Of the five statewide ballot proposals, only the one to institute daylight saving time in Michigan passed. Proposals to liberalize abortion laws, use an income tax rather than a property tax to finance public education, graduate the state income tax, and allow a bonus for Vietnam servicemen were defeated.

Michigan politics, especially the senatorial race, was dominated by the issue of court-ordered busing of schoolchildren in the Detroit area. Most candidates assumed an antibusing stance. Busing was also a deciding factor in the May 16 presidential primary, the first such primary in more than 40 years, as George Wallace received 51 percent of the vote.

Presidential vote: Nixon (R), 1,961,721; McGovern (D), 1,459,435.

UPI

THE MARCHING MOTHERS of Michigan helped make busing a big issue; the incumbent Republican senator and his defeated challenger strove to outdo each other in opposing it.

Senator: Robert P. Griffin* (R).
House: 12 R, 7 D.
State legislature: House, 60 D, 50 R. (Senate, 19 D, 19 R; no election for the senate this year.)

ALLEN PHILLIPS

★ ★ ★

MINNESOTA. The 1972 general election in Minnesota came up roses for the Democratic Farmer–Labor Party (DFL). Incumbent U.S. senator Walter F. Mondale coasted to victory over Philip Hansen, and for the first time the DFL won control of both state legislative houses. Although Senator George McGovern lost Minnesota, he got 46 percent of the vote, one of his best performances, partially because of Senator Hubert H. Humphrey's help.

In a television interview over CBS on election night, Senator Humphrey said that he saw Senator Mondale as a likely presidential candidate in 1976 and that he would work toward that end.

At the legislative level Minnesotans elected a total of six women (up from one) and the state's first black senator and representative in this century. Three college students, one only 20 years old, who ran as DFL candidates also won. Hubert H. Humphrey III, the senator's son, was victorious in a state senate race in a Minneapolis suburb. The DFL saw these victories as an opportunity to repeal the law against party designation in the state legislature.

Presidential vote: Nixon (R), 897,569; McGovern (D), 802,346.
Senator: Walter F. Mondale* (D).
House: 4 D, 4 R.
State legislature (officially nonpartisan): senate, 36 liberals, 31 conservatives; house, 77 liberals, 57 conservatives.

AUSTIN C. WEHRWEIN

★ ★ ★

MISSISSIPPI. For the second time since Reconstruction a Republican presidential nominee swept Mississippi (Barry Goldwater, in 1964, was the first). President Richard M. Nixon took 79 percent of the vote and drew two GOP congressmen into office on his coattails: Trent Lott, former aide to retiring Democratic representative William Colmer, and Thad Cochran, a Jackson attorney. The third Republican candidate for the house, however, lost to Democrat David Bowen of Cleveland. With three of the five congressmen retiring—Colmer, Tom Abernathy, and Charles Griffin—it was the largest turnover of the state's congressmen in recent history. Democratic incumbents Jamie Whitten and G. V. Montgomery returned unopposed by Republicans.

Attention was focused on the race for the seat of U.S. senator James Eastland (D). He became president pro tem of the Senate during the year and, as chairman of the Judiciary Committee, had given Nixon powerful support on his Supreme Court

nominations. With a 58 percent majority, Eastland defeated Republican Gilbert Carmichael, who was all but ignored by national Republican leaders. Observers speculated that Carmichael had been encouraged to seek the Republican nomination to keep it from going by default to black activist James Meredith, whose candidacy as a Republican caught state GOP leaders by surprise.

Presidential vote: Nixon (R), 498,680; McGovern (D), 125,756.
Senator: James O. Eastland* (D).
House: 3 D, 2 R.
                                    W. David Brown

★ ★ ★

MISSOURI. The home state of Senator Thomas Eagleton turned down the McGovern-Shriver ticket by a margin of about 450,000 votes and elected a Republican governor for the first time in 28 years. All in all, the election tended to confirm the pessimism of the state Democratic Party, which had been weakened and divided even before Eagleton's ouster from the national ticket.

State auditor Christopher S. "Kit" Bond defeated Democratic candidate Edward L. Dowd to become at 33 the youngest governor in the nation. Bond ran behind the national ticket, winning by about 190,000 votes, but another young Republican, Attorney General John C. Danforth, was reelected by a margin almost equal to Nixon's. A third Republican, state representative William C. Phelps, won a narrow victory to become lieutenant governor.

Democrats were nevertheless successful in winning two other statewide offices; and, in spite of GOP gains in the state senate and house, the party retained control of the legislature. As predicted, Democrats also retained their 9–1 majority in the Missouri congressional delegation. Among the incumbent Democrats returned to Congress were William L. Clay, a leader in the Black Caucus; Leonor K. Sullivan, a longtime consumer advocate; and James W. Symington, son of Missouri's senior senator.

Presidential vote: Nixon (R), 1,132,111; McGovern (D), 682,030.
House: 9 D, 1 R.
State government: Gov., Christopher S. Bond (R); lt. gov., William C. Phelps (R); atty. gen., John C. Danforth* (R); secy. of state, James C. Kirkpatrick* (D); treas., James Spainhower (D). Legislature: senate, 21 D, 13 R; house, 97 D, 66 R.
                            Sally Bixby Defty

★ ★ ★

MONTANA. Encouraged by faith in presidential coattails and by the retirement of one-term governor Forrest H. Anderson (D), the Republicans launched a spirited drive to put Sheridan County rancher Ed Smith into the governor's mansion and regain an office they had held for 16 years prior to 1968. However, although President Nixon carried Montana by more than 60,000 votes, Lieutenant Governor Thomas L. Judge (D) was the victor in the gubernatorial race, winning by a margin of about 26,000 votes.

Democrats also retained control of the new state senate, reduced to 50 seats by reapportionment; and they won a majority in the new state house of representatives, also reduced by reapportionment. Two Republicans and two Democrats won election to lesser state offices, not counting the Republican state auditor, who ran unopposed.

The congressional delegation remained unchanged. Incumbent Democratic senator Lee Metcalf fought off a challenge from Republican Henry S. Hibbard and won by a narrow margin of 12,000 votes. Former congressman Arnold Olsen (D) was unable to unseat his Republican opponent, Representative Richard Shoup, and incumbent John Melcher (D) easily defeated his opponent by almost 80,000 votes.

Presidential vote: Nixon (R), 182,754; McGovern (D), 118,420.
Senator: Lee Metcalf* (D).
House: 1 R, 1 D.
State government: Gov., Thomas L. Judge (D); lt. gov., Bill Christiansen (D); secy. of state, Frank Murray* (D); aud., E. V. "Sonny" Omholt* (R); treas., Hollis G. Connors (R); atty. gen., Robert Woodahl* (R). Legislature: senate, 27 D, 23 R; house, 54 D, 45 R, 1 undecided.
                            Ellen Torgrimson

★ ★ ★

NEBRASKA. Political attention in Nebraska centered on the senatorial race. Three-term incumbent Carl T. Curtis (R), who had expected an easy victory, lagged behind Democrat Terry Carpenter until well toward the end of the vote count. In the end, Curtis won 53 percent of the popular vote, running well behind the na-

PEDAL PUSHERS cross Manhattan's 42nd Street on the last leg of a 526-mile "bike hike" publicizing New York's $1.15 billion environmental bond issue. Voters passed the measure, which will aid construction of sewage-treatment facilities and other public works.

tional ticket's 71 percent. A last-minute television blitz by Carpenter was given credit for the near upset.

Nebraska's three incumbent representatives—Republicans Charles Thone, John McCollister, and Dave Martin—all won handily.

Sixteen state constitutional amendments were on the ballot. Twelve of them, mostly of a housekeeping nature, passed. One of the four that failed would have let state senators set their own salaries.

The youth movement scored in one legislative race. Steve Fowler, University of Nebraska student-body president in 1971, defeated state senator William F. Swanson, who had been a prime prospect for speaker of the 1973 legislature.

Juvenile court judge Seward Hart of Omaha was removed from office by the voters after drawing opposition from the local bar association and some social agencies. He was the seventh judge in the country to be voted out under the Missouri Plan, in which voters mark their ballots yes or no on the question of retention. Governor James J. Exon will appoint a replacement.

Presidential vote: Nixon (R), 384,571; McGovern (D), 162,598.
Senator: Carl T. Curtis* (R).
House: 3 R.

GABE C. PARKS

★ ★ ★

NEVADA. Nevada gave President Richard M. Nixon an almost 2–1 majority over George McGovern. Voters elected a political newcomer, Republican David M. Towell, to Nevada's one seat in the U.S. House of Representatives. Towell defeated Democrat James Bilbray, Jr., a Las Vegas attorney, who had defeated a seemingly unbeatable ten-term incumbent, Walter S. Baring, in the Democratic primary. In the general election, Baring endorsed Nixon and Towell.

The Democrats increased their majority in the state senate and won control of the state assembly.

Nevada voters decidedly rejected an important constitutional amendment to reform the state's courts. The amendment had taken ten years to prepare.

Presidential vote: Nixon (R), 115,119; McGovern (D), 65,564.
House: 1 R.
State legislature: Senate, 14 D, 6 R; assembly, 25 D, 15 R.

DON LYNCH

★ ★ ★

NEW HAMPSHIRE. In the race for the governorship, Republican Meldrim Thomson, Jr., beat out Democrat Roger J. Crowley and independent Malcolm McLane. Thomson received 133,702 votes, Crowley 127,107, and McLane 62,375. Thomson, who beat incumbent governor Walter R. Peterson in the Republican primary after Peterson backed unsuccessful attempts to legislate a state income tax, also ran the fall campaign on an antitax platform.

In the presidential election, New Hampshire gave President Richard M. Nixon 213,724 votes, 64 percent of the vote, compared with 116,435 for Democrat George S. McGovern. Voter turnout was a record 345,013, about 76 percent of those registered.

*indicates incumbent

In the U.S. senate race, ten-year-veteran Senator Thomas J. McIntyre (D) bucked the Republican landslide and defeated former governor Wesley Powell, 184,495 to 139,852. The two U.S. House incumbents, both Republicans, were reelected.

Voters split on the two referendum questions. A proposed constitutional amendment to permit annual legislative sessions narrowly failed to get the needed two-thirds majority. A simple majority was needed to decide the question of calling a state constitutional convention; this measure was approved.

Presidential vote: Nixon (R), 213,724; McGovern (D), 116,435.
Senator: Thomas J. McIntyre* (D).
House: 2 R.
State government: Gov., Meldrim Thomson, Jr. (R). Legislature: senate, 14 R, 10 D; house, 266 R, 134 D.

ROGER TALBOT

★ ★ ★

NEW JERSEY. A dull election campaign in New Jersey was followed by an election that produced no surprising results and was most significant for projecting three Democratic congressmen as possible candidates for governor in 1973. Representatives Henry Helstoski, James J. Howard, and Robert A. Roe all won reelection over their Republican opponents by impressive margins, despite President Nixon's landslide victory in the state.

Even though the reapportionment of the state's congressional districts had produced substantial changes in some districts, the Democrats won an 8–7 majority in the state delegation to the House of Representatives. The Democrat who was the biggest winner was Peter W. Rodino, Jr., a 12-term veteran of the House whose revised 10th Congressional District has a substantial black population and includes Newark. Rodino easily survived a black challenge in the primary and won reelection over Republican Kenneth Miller by more than a 4–1 margin.

Republican senator Clifford P. Case was returned to a fourth term with more than a 700,000-vote margin over Democrat Paul J. Krebs, a former congressman.

The voters rejected a $650 million bond issue for mass transit and highway improvements. Opponents of the measure claimed that it would have provided too much money for highways and not enough for mass transit.

Presidential vote: Nixon (R), 1,788,938; McGovern (D), 1,059,012.
Senator: Clifford P. Case* (R).
House: 8 D, 7 R.

THOMAS J. HOOPER

★ ★ ★

NEW MEXICO. A court ruling eliminating candidate filing fees resulted in a rush of 38 candidates for U.S. Senate and House seats, which included the seat of retiring veteran U.S. senator Clinton P. Anderson, a Democrat, and the House seats of Republican Manuel Lujan, Jr., and Democrat Harold Runnels.

New Mexico, an inherently conservative state, has voted with the winning presidential candidate since its statehood in 1912, and this year the Nixon-Agnew ticket swept all but two of 32 counties to win the biggest vote margin ever re-

corded in the state—which has a heavily Democratic voter registration. Nixon piled up 233,036 votes to McGovern's 138,756.

The new U.S. senator, Pete V. Domenici, who is the first Republican elected to the Senate from New Mexico in 38 years, won an easy victory—by about 29,000 votes—over wealthy Hobbs banker Jack Daniels. Representative Lujan easily won a third term in Congress by about 19,000 votes over his young liberal opponent, Eugene Gallegos. Representative Runnels drubbed his Republican opponent, Ed Presson, in the southern district by nearly 50,000 votes.

In spite of the GOP landslide, the Democrats gained a few seats in the state legislature. However, the election put the Republicans in a position of ascendancy.

Presidential vote: Nixon (R), 233,036; McGovern (D), 138,756.
Senator: Pete V. Domenici (R).
House: 1 D, 1 R.
State legislature: Senate, 27 D, 14 R; house, 47 D, 21 R.

RALPH LOONEY

★ ★ ★

NEW YORK. For only the third time since 1928 the traditionally Democratic state of New York voted for a Republican presidential candidate, giving Richard M. Nixon a margin of more than 1 million votes over his Democratic opponent, Senator George McGovern. Even in the Democratic bastion of New York City, McGovern barely won a plurality, getting 1,341,164 votes to Nixon's 1,259,244. This small edge was easily obliterated by lopsided Nixon majorities in the suburbs and upstate. The president fell just short of the late president Dwight D. Eisenhower's victory in the state (61 percent) in 1956.

Nixon made major inroads in Roman Catholic and Jewish neighborhoods that normally vote Democratic. However, Nixon's coattails proved almost nonexistent as extensive ticket-splitting gave Democrats numerous victories. Westchester County congressman Ogden R. Reid, who switched from the Republican to the Democratic Party during the year, was reelected. Democrats Otis G. Pike of Suffolk County and Lester L. Wolff of Queens and Nassau won reelection to the U.S. House of Representatives, although their districts went heavily for Nixon.

Representative Bella Abzug, whose district had been eliminated by reapportionment, won reelection in a new district on the west side of Manhattan. Abzug had lost the June primary to Representative William F. Ryan, who later died of cancer. Ryan's widow, Priscilla, sought to retain his seat for herself but lost after a bitter, angry campaign.

Both houses of the state legislature increased their Republican majorities slightly as a result of reapportionment. State voters approved a $1.15 billion bond issue to finance antipollution facilities and a constitutional amendment that would make minor changes in the terms of district attorneys. However, two other amendments—one creating a new judicial district on Long Island and the other altering the procedures for amending the state constitution—failed.

Presidential vote: Nixon (R), 4,247,487; McGovern (D), 2,878,513.

39

House: 22 D, 17 R.
State legislature: Senate, 37 R, 23 D; assembly, 83 R, 67 D.   DAVID K. SHIPLER

★ ★ ★

NORTH CAROLINA. President Nixon's coattails helped bring into office North Carolina's first Republican governor and U.S. senator since the turn of the century. George McGovern managed to get only 29 percent of the vote as Nixon carried the state by a huge margin of more than 600,000 votes. James E. Holshouser, Jr., a moderate Republican, and Jesse Helms, a broadcasting executive of extremely conservative views, apparently received decisive help from a final preelection visit to the state by President Nixon.

Helms, running unexpectedly strong in the urban and western parts of the state, defeated a moderate Democrat, U.S. representative Nick Galifianakis, for U.S. senator by more than 120,000 votes. (Galifianakis had defeated incumbent senator B. Everett Jordan in a runoff primary election in May.) Holshouser beat state senator Hargrove "Skipper" Bowles by 40,000 votes.

The makeup of the state's House delegation remained seven Democrats and four Republicans. In state government Democrats were reelected to all seats on the council of state and gained 20 seats in the general assembly. In a referendum, voters authorized the state to acquire land to be preserved in its natural state and also gave themselves a legal right to ecological protection.

Presidential vote: Nixon (R), 1,051,707; McGovern (D), 437,311.
Senator: Jesse Helms (R).
House: 7 D, 4 R.
State government: Gov., James E. Holshouser, Jr. (R). Council of state: lt. gov., James B. Hunt (D); atty. gen., Robert Morgan* (D); secy. of state, Thad Eure* (D); comm. of ins., John Ingram* (D); treas., Edwin M. Gill* (D); labor comm., Billy Creel* (D); supt. of pub. instr., Craig Phillips* (D); aud., Henry L. Bridges (D). General assembly: senate, 35 D, 15 R; house, 85 D, 35 R.   GREG DAVID

★ ★ ★

NORTH DAKOTA. The Democratic Party retained its 12-year hold on the governor's office in North Dakota, a heavily Republican state, as Representative Arthur A. Link narrowly defeated his GOP opponent, Lieutenant Governor Richard F. Larsen. Both candidates had been easy victors in their party primaries. Retiring governor William L. Guy sought no elective office in 1972.

In the presidential election Richard M. Nixon carried the state by nearly 74,000 votes, winning 63 percent of the popular vote. Republican congressman Mark Andrews was an even bigger winner; he outpolled Democratic state chairman Richard Ista by nearly 123,000 votes to gain the single U.S. House of Representatives seat which was allocated to North Dakota after reapportionment.

Besides retaining the governorship, Democrats gained the posts of lieutenant governor and treasurer. The GOP held on to the other major state offices and enlarged its already substantial majorities in both houses of the state legislature.

The ballot also contained a proposal to legalize abortions performed during the first 21 weeks of pregnancy; voters turned it down by a resounding 3–1 margin.

Presidential vote: Nixon (R), 174,109; McGovern, 100,384.
House: 1 R.
State government: Gov., Arthur A. Link (D); lt. gov., Wayne Sanstead (D); secy. of state, Ben Meier* (R); aud., Robert P. Peterson (R); treas., Walter Christensen (D); atty. gen., Allen I. Olson (R). Legislature: senate, 41 R, 9 D, 1 vacancy; house, 77 R, 25 D.   JACK HAGERTY

★ ★ ★

OHIO. President Nixon won 61 percent of the popular vote in Ohio, carrying all but two of the state's 88 counties. The GOP also maintained its 16–7 edge in Ohio's congressional delegation, but Democrats sidestepped the presidential landslide at the state level to grab control of the house for the first time since 1960 and shave the Republican margin in the senate to a perilous 17–16.

Many of the Republicans who lost their seats in the state legislature had advocated repeal of the state income tax, enacted in late 1971 with the support of Governor John J. Gilligan (D). A repeal proposal appeared on the ballot but proved to be extremely unpopular, gaining only 30 percent of the vote.

The state's first presidential preference primary, held May 2, ran into horrendous voting and counting delays; Senator Hubert H. Humphrey was finally determined to have won by a hair, with Senator George McGovern a close second.

Presidential vote: Nixon (R), 2,359,520; McGovern (D), 1,523,716.
House: 16 R, 7 D.
State legislature: Senate, 17 R, 16 D; house, 58 D, 41 R.   LEE LEONARD

★ ★ ★

OKLAHOMA. In the November general election, U.S. representative Ed Edmondson (D) lost his bid for the Senate seat vacated by Senator Fred Harris (D); the winner was former Republican governor Dewey F. Bartlett. James Jones, a former aide to President Lyndon Johnson, picked up a congressional seat for the Democrats when he defeated his Republican opponent, longtime Tulsa mayor J. M. Hewgley. The result of the election was to give the Republicans two U.S. senators and one representative, with the Democrats holding five House seats.

In the presidential election, Richard Nixon beat George McGovern by an overwhelming landslide vote of more than 75 percent. The espousal of conservative ideology was the key to victory for all candidates for federal and state office, regardless of party affiliation.

Efforts to legalize liquor-by-the-drink through an initiative petition went down to defeat. The same petition provided for franchising by liquor companies and for freedom to advertise. The last two items, together with fear of increased prices on bottled liquor, secured success for the opposition forces.

Presidential vote: Nixon (R), 759,025; McGovern (D), 247,147.

Senator: Dewey F. Bartlett (R).
House: 5 D, 1 R.
State legislature: Senate, 38 D, 10 R; house, 75 D, 26 R.   WALTER F. SCHEFFER

★ ★ ★

OREGON. President Richard M. Nixon won Oregon's six electoral votes with a majority of 53 percent. In the U.S. Senate race, Republican incumbent Mark O. Hatfield defeated former U.S. senator Wayne Morse. Morse's age (he is 72) worked against his comeback bid. All four of the incumbent U.S. representatives were reelected.

Of the three state offices that were filled, the closest contest was the race for state treasurer, with Democrat James A. Redden defeating Craig Berkman. Control of the 1973 state legislature was won by the Democrats, who gained a clear majority in both houses.

The most controversial of the nine state ballot measures was an Oregon farm bureau plan to eliminate property taxes as the major support for the public schools. More than 60 percent of the voters opposed the measure. Proponents sought to have the incoming legislature enact a new way to finance the schools; opponents were fearful because no alternative source of revenue had been indicated. Voters also emphatically turned down a measure to reword the constitutional provision regarding religion that had been expected to provide financial aid to parochial schools.

Presidential vote: Nixon (R), 483,229; McGovern (D), 390,867.
Senator: Mark O. Hatfield* (R).
House: 2 D, 2 R.
State government: Secy. of state, Clay Myers* (R); treas., James A. Redden (D); atty. gen., Lee Johnson* (R). Legislature: senate, 18 D, 12 R; house, 33 D, 27 R.   CLARICE KRIEG

★ ★ ★

PENNSYLVANIA. Although the Democrats were in control of both Philadelphia and Pittsburgh, as well as the state government, Richard M. Nixon had no trouble whipping George McGovern for Pennsylvania's 27 electoral votes. Nixon won all of the state's 67 counties except Philadelphia. Thirteen Democrats and 12 Republicans were elected to the U.S. House of Representatives.

In state contests, Auditor General Robert P. Casey and Treasurer Grace M. Sloan, both Democrats, won reelection. In the legislature the GOP captured the majority of house seats, ending four years of Democratic rule. In the senate, the Democrats got 13 of the 25 seats that were up for grabs to maintain their 26–24 margin over the Republicans. Voters overwhelmingly approved the state's first emergency amendment authorizing tax rebates and other direct aid to flood victims. And voters in a number of municipalities voted to start studying ways of taking control of their home areas away from the state legislature.

Presidential vote: Nixon (R), 2,703,975; McGovern (D), 1,788,034.
House: 13 D, 12 R.
State government: Auditor gen., Robert P.

*indicates incumbent

Casey* (D); treas., Grace M. Sloan* (D). Legislature: senate, 26 D, 24 R; house, 103 R, 97 D, 3 undecided.

RALPH C. BREM

* * *

PUERTO RICO. The Popular Democratic Party (PDP) won a surprising and overwhelming election victory in Puerto Rico. PDP gubernatorial candidate Rafael Hernández Colón unseated Governor Luis A. Ferré of the New Progressive Party (NPP) by about 100,000 votes. Hernández Colón, who at 36 will be the youngest governor in Puerto Rican history, campaigned on a platform of reform and continuation of the commonwealth association with the United States. The PDP also won control of both houses of the legislature and 72 of 78 municipalities. The election was viewed as an indication that Puerto Rico wants to remain a self-governing commonwealth rather than become the 51st state as proposed by the NPP or become independent as advocated by the Puerto Rican Independence Party, which received less than 4 percent of the vote and did not elect any members to the legislature.

Gubernatorial vote: Rafael Hernández Colón (PDP), 660,006; Luis Ferré (NPP), 560,966.
Commonwealth legislature: PDP won control of the senate and house of representatives, with the exact number of seats for each party not yet determined.

JAMES NELSON GOODSELL

* * *

RHODE ISLAND. Senator Claiborne Pell (D) won reelection to a third term in the U.S. Senate, easily defeating his Republican challenger, John H. Chafee, former governor and secretary of the navy. More than $1 million was spent on the hotly contested campaign.

Philip W. Noel, mayor of Warwick, the state's second largest city, retained the governorship for the Democrats by defeating Herbert F. DeSimone, former state attorney general. Governor Frank R. Licht did not seek reelection.

Democrats retained all other state seats, with the exception of the attorney general's post, to which Richard J. Israel (R) was reelected.

Normally Democratic Rhode Island gave President Richard M. Nixon an edge over Senator George McGovern, 208,899 votes to 185,158 votes. However, the two incumbent Democratic congressmen, Robert O. Tiernan and Fernand J. St. Germain, easily retained their seats.

The campaigns for senator and governor were particularly hard fought. President Nixon made a last-minute appeal on behalf of Chafee and DeSimone.

Presidential vote: Nixon (R), 208,899; McGovern (D), 185,158.
Senator: Claiborne Pell* (D).
House: 2 D.
State government: Gov., Philip W. Noel (D); lt. gov., J. Joseph Garrahy* (D); secy. of state, Robert F. Burns (D); atty. gen., Richard J. Israel* (R); general treas., Raymond H. Hawksley* (D). General assembly: senate, 37 D, 13 R; house, 73 D, 27 R.

DAVID F. DONNELLY, JR.

* * *

UPI

PICKING UP THE PIECES as floodwaters receded in Pottstown, Pa., last June. Pennsylvania voters later helped to ease the strain by approving an emergency measure for flood relief.

SOUTH CAROLINA. For the third time in a row South Carolina's electoral votes went to the Republican candidate, but this time President Richard M. Nixon's slice of the popular vote was an impressive 71 percent. Republican senator J. Strom Thurmond was also reelected, defeating Democratic state senator Eugene N. Zeigler by about 175,000 votes.

The Republicans also picked up another seat in the U.S. House of Representatives, giving them two out of six. Democratic congressman John L. McMillan, a house member since 1939 and longtime chairman of the District of Columbia Committee, was upset in a runoff primary by state representative John W. Jenrette, Jr., who lost the general election to Edward L. Young, a Republican.

Although Democrats retained overwhelming control of the state legislature, the GOP managed to pick up ten more seats in the house of representatives and one more in the senate. Two counties elected blacks to the state legislature for the first time in their history; the new assembly will contain five women and four blacks. Republicans scored a number of victories in local elections.

Most of the constitutional amendments on the ballot were approved, and voters passed a proposition permitting the sale of whiskey-by-the-drink in minibottles.

Presidential vote: Nixon (R), 477,044; McGovern (D), 186,824.
Senator: J. Strom Thurmond* (R).
House: 2 R, 4 D.
State legislature: Senate, 43 D, 3 R; house, 103 D, 21 R.

R. H. STOUDEMIRE

* * *

SOUTH DAKOTA. South Dakotans cast their votes for President Richard M. Nixon by a substantial margin over the Democratic nominee, George McGovern, their own U.S. senator. Yet they awarded most major offices to Democratic candidates: James Abourezk won the U.S. Senate

seat vacated by Republican Karl Mundt, Richard S. Kneip was reelected as governor, and Frank Denholm was reelected to the U.S. House of Representatives. In addition, South Dakotans gave Democrats control—by one vote—in the state senate and half the seats in the state house of representatives.

The Republicans, still suffering from defeat in 1970, had no incumbents and few attractive candidates to run. Their only major victory came in the 2nd Congressional District, where former lieutenant governor James Abdnor defeated McGovern's former aide Pat McKeever in the contest for the House seat vacated by Senator-elect Abourezk.

Presidential vote: Nixon (R), 161,029; McGovern (D), 139,277.
Senator: James Abourezk (D).
House: 1 D, 1 R.
State government: Gov., Richard S. Kneip* (D); lt. gov., William Dougherty* (D); secy. of state, Lorna Herseth (D); atty. gen., Kermit Sande (D). Legislature: senate, 18 D, 17 R; house, 35 D, 35 R.

HERBERT T. HOOVER

* * *

TENNESSEE. Richard M. Nixon easily won Tennessee's ten electoral votes, outpolling George McGovern by more than a 2–1 margin in the popular vote. Senator Howard H. Baker, Jr. (R), was reelected by an overwhelming majority, defeating Representative Ray Blanton (D).

Reapportionment reduced the number of U.S. congressional districts from nine to eight (Blanton was the officeholder left without a district). Seven incumbents won reelection, but four-term Democratic representative William R. Anderson lost his 6th District seat to Republican Robin L. Beard.

The state legislature will continue to be controlled by the Democrats, although by slightly smaller margins than before the election.

Presidential vote: Nixon (R), 812,484; McGovern (D), 355,817.
Senator: Howard H. Baker, Jr.* (R).
House: 5 R, 3 D.
State legislature: Senate, 19 D, 13 R, 1 A; house, 51 D, 48 R.

STANLEY J. FOLMSBEE

★ ★ ★

TEXAS. President Nixon swept Texas, with 2,170,200 votes to Senator George McGovern's 1,091,808, according to unofficial returns. Nixon did not carry the state in 1968; thus, former governor John Connally's Democrats for Nixon effort was considered a major factor in the president's win in Texas.

The presidential coattails helped pull incumbent senator John G. Tower to victory over Democratic challenger Barefoot Sanders (who had defeated former senator Ralph Yarborough in the June primary) and almost put hard-campaigning State Senator Henry C. Grover in the statehouse. He was just edged out by Dolph Briscoe, who defeated State Representative Frances "Sissy" Farenthold in the Democratic primary but campaigned little in the general election. Grover's total caused speculation that Texas was on the brink of a two-party system. The primary brought defeat for several well-known politicians, including Ralph Yarborough in the Senate race and incumbent governor Preston Smith. Smith was hurt by his connection with a stock-fraud scandal involving a number of prominent Texas Democrats.

The GOP also gained one more seat in the state senate, for a total of three; in the house they raised their total to 17 members in the 150-seat body.

Texas' U.S. congressional delegation grew from 23 to 24, the added seat taken by a Republican; the makeup is now 20 Democrats and four Republicans. Elected to the House of Representatives from Houston's 18th District was Democrat Barbara Jordan—the first black since Reconstruction to be elected to a House seat from Texas.

Presidential vote: Nixon (R), 2,170,200; McGovern (D), 1,091,808.
Senator: John G. Tower* (R).
House: 20 D, 4 R.
State government: Gov., Dolph Briscoe (D); lt. gov., William Hobby (D); atty. gen., John Hill (D); treas., Jesse James* (D); cont., Robert Calvert* (D). Legislature: senate, 28 D, 3 R; house, 133 D, 17 R.

LESLIE H. BENNETT

★ ★ ★

UTAH. The voters of Utah split their ticket during the 1972 elections, giving President Richard M. Nixon a comfortable margin and Democratic incumbent governor Calvin L. Rampton almost 70 percent of the vote, enabling him to defeat his Republican opponent, Nicholas L. Strike. Governor Rampton is the first Utah chief executive to be reelected to a third term.

The president's coattails were neither strong nor lengthy enough to help Republicans running in Utah's congressional races. Four-term veteran U.S. representative Sherman P. Lloyd, a Republican, lost to Democrat Wayne Owens. Owens, a first-time candidate, won much support from young voters and from ecologists. In the 1st Congressional District, incum-

bent Democrat Gunn McKay handily defeated the GOP contender, Robert Wolthuis.

The American Party succeeded in taking 6 percent of the presidential vote (for John G. Schmitz) and 1.5–2 percent in the congressional races.

Republicans captured control of both houses of the state legislature. Utah passed four amendments to the state constitution, streamlining the legislature, restricting bail in some cases, and authorizing consolidated urban school districts and alternate forms of county government.

Presidential vote: Nixon (R), 323,643; McGovern (D), 126,284.
House: 2 D.
State government: Gov., Calvin L. Rampton* (D); secy. of state, Clyde L. Miller* (D); atty. gen., Vernon B. Romney* (R); treas., David L. Duncan (D); aud., David S. Monson (R). Legislature: senate, 16 R, 13 D; house, 44 R, 31 D.

HARRY E. FULLER, JR.

★ ★ ★

VERMONT. The elections had a bitter aftertaste for Vermont's governor, Deane Chandler Davis (R). His handpicked successor, Luther F. Hackett, the 39-year-old former house majority leader and former chairman of the state welfare board, lost to Democratic challenger Thomas Paul Salmon while every other Republican state office-seeker won handsomely. Salmon's election victory (104,533 to 82,491) made him the second Democrat in Vermont history to win a statewide election.

In the presidential race, President Richard M. Nixon won an easy victory over Senator George McGovern, 117,149 to 68,174. The People's Party candidate, Dr. Benjamin Spock, received 1,010 votes.

U.S. representative Richard W. Mallary (R), who won a special election in January for the vacant House seat of Senator Robert T. Stafford, won election to a full term over former Democratic representative William H. Meyer, 120,924 to 65,062. There was no senatorial election in November; former representative Stafford, appointed in September 1971 to succeed the late senator Winston L. Prouty, won election in January to fill the unexpired portion of Prouty's term.

In state legislative elections the Democrats gained eight seats in the house and held steady in the senate.

Presidential vote: Nixon (R), 117,149; McGovern (D), 68,174.
House: 1 R.
State government: Gov., Thomas P. Salmon (D); lt. gov., John S. Burgess* (R); secy. of state, Richard C. Thomas* (R); aud. of accts., Alexander V. Acebo* (R); treas., Frank H. Davis* (R); atty. gen., Kimberley Cheney (R). Legislature: senate, 22 R, 8 D; house, 91 R, 59 D.

ROBERT W. SMITH

★ ★ ★

VIRGINIA. Republicans scored impressive victories in the general election, adding a seventh House of Representatives seat to the six they held already and sending a U.S. senator to Washington for the first time in this century.

Senator William B. Spong, Jr., who ran for reelection with no opposition from fellow Democrats, was beaten by former

representative William L. Scott (R). Spong was partly the victim of a landslide for President Richard M. Nixon, who defeated Senator George McGovern in Virginia by almost 550,000 votes.

Three incumbent Democrats and four incumbent Republicans were returned to the House of Representatives. The GOP also picked up the seat held by veteran congressman Watkin M. Abbitt (D), who decided not to run for a 12th term. Representative Robert W. Daniel, Jr., won Abbitt's seat, defeating Democrat Robert E. Gibson and two independents. Stanford E. Parris (R) and M. Caldwell Butler (R) were elected to seats previously held by Republicans.

Voters approved a state constitutional amendment lowering the minimum state voting age to 18 in conformity with federal standards.

Presidential vote: Nixon (R), 988,493; McGovern (D), 438,887.
Senator: William L. Scott (R).
House: 7 R, 3 D.

WILLIAM R. SAUDER

★ ★ ★

WASHINGTON. As the only mainland state west of the Rockies to fall to the Democrats in 1968, Washington became a prime target for both the Democratic and Republican presidential candidates. When the votes were in, President Richard M. Nixon had carried the state by a 57 percent majority. Incumbent Republican governor Daniel J. Evans also won reelection, to a third consecutive term.

Governor Evans ran against former two-term governor Albert D. Rosellini, who had lost his own bid for a third term when he was defeated by Evans in 1964. In this year's campaign the old issues of a consecutive third term, taxation, and spending were revived, with Evans again taking the more liberal stand.

In other races, it was a good year for Democrats. Washington's U.S. House of Representatives delegation will have six Democrats and only one Republican.

Washington's veteran Republican congressman—Thomas M. Pelly—did not run again. All incumbents won reelection to major state administrative posts, and the Democrats regained control of the state house of representatives, while retaining control of the senate.

The voters supported Governor Evans by approving five of his six "Washington Future" bond issues. A proposal authorizing establishment of a state lottery also won passage. A constitutional amendment to provide sex equality under the law passed by a narrow margin.

Presidential vote: Nixon (R), 721,404; McGovern (D), 504,926.
House: 6 D, 1 R.
State government: Gov., Daniel J. Evans* (R); lt. gov., John A. Cherberg* (D); secy. of state, A. Ludlow Kramer* (R); aud., R.

*indicates incumbent

V. Graham* (D); treas., Robert S. O'Brien* (D); atty. gen., Slade Gorton* (R). Legislature: senate, 30 D, 19 R; house, 57 D, 41 R.

HAZEL EMERY MILLS

★ ★ ★

WASHINGTON, D.C. The District of Columbia joined Massachusetts as the only areas in the country to give their electoral votes to Senator George McGovern. In the only other race, the Reverend Walter E. Fauntroy (D) easily won a second term—his first full term—as the nonvoting delegate from Washington, D.C., in the House of Representatives.

Presidential vote: McGovern (D), 118,993; Nixon (R), 31,987.
Delegate in the House of Representatives: Reverend Walter E. Fauntroy* (D).

JACK E. EISEN

★ ★ ★

WEST VIRGINIA. Arch A. Moore, Jr., a Republican, became the first West Virginia governor in a century to succeed himself. Moore was the first governor to run under a constitutional amendment which permits two consecutive four-year terms. In the process he dealt a heavy blow to the flowering political career of his opponent, Democratic secretary of state John D. Rockefeller IV, who campaigned as a foe of strip mining, an important but subdued issue in the contest.

The poor showing of Senator George McGovern in West Virginia may have affected the gubernatorial results. President Nixon swept all but one of the 55 counties, winning by a 190,000-vote margin.

Veteran U.S. senator Jennings Randolph (D) rolled to an easy 2–1 victory over the only woman member in the state senate, Louise Leonard. Four incumbent members of the U.S. House, all Democrats, were returned to Congress. The House delegation was reduced from five to four seats, forcing a primary race between two Democratic incumbents for one seat. Representative Ken Hechler won, defeating Representative James Kee.

Four constitutional amendments were approved. They authorized the issuance of $200 million in bonds for constructing and equipping public school buildings, removed household goods and personal effects from taxation, permitted state grants to counties and municipalities, and empowered the legislature to call special elections on constitutional amendments.

Presidential vote: Nixon (R), 452,107; McGovern (D), 261,859.
Senator: Jennings Randolph* (D).
House: 4 D.
State government: Gov., Arch A. Moore, Jr.* (R); secy. of state, Edgar Heiskell III (R); treas., John H. Kelly* (D); aud., John M. Gates (R); atty. gen., Chauncey Browning* (D); agr. comm., Gus R. Douglass* (D). Legislature: senate, 24 D, 10 R; house, 57 D, 43 R.

JOHN G. MORGAN

★ ★ ★

WISCONSIN. Wisconsin, one of the states George McGovern counted on winning in the presidential election, followed the landslide to Richard M. Nixon. Wisconsin was the first state in which McGovern won a presidential primary.

Wisconsin reelected five incumbent Democrats to the U.S. House of Representatives—Les Aspin, Robert W. Kastenmeier, Clement J. Zablocki, Henry S. Reuss, and David R. Obey. Obey beat 15-term incumbent Republican Alvin E. O'Konski. (The state lost one of its ten congressional districts as a result of reapportionment.) Four Republicans—incumbents Vernon W. Thomson, William A. Steiger, and Glenn R. Davis, and newcomer Harold V. Froehlich, who replaced the retiring John W. Byrnes—were also elected to the House of Representatives.

The Republicans retained control of the state senate with 18 seats, but the Democrats increased their strength by two, with 15 seats. The Democrats lost four seats in the state assembly but retained control.

Mayor Henry W. Maier was easily reelected to his fourth term as chief executive of Milwaukee.

Presidential vote: Nixon (R), 989,430; McGovern (D), 810,174.
House: 5 D, 4 R.
State legislature: Senate, 18 R, 15 D; assembly, 62 D, 37 R.

HYMAN CHESTER

★ ★ ★

WYOMING. Both President Nixon and incumbent Republican senator Clifford P. Hansen broke the 100,000-vote mark in Wyoming—the first time any candidate has done so in the state's 82-year history. Although both had been expected to win in the state, no one had foreseen the scope of their victories. The president received an unofficial 100,630 votes to 44,348 for Senator George McGovern, while Hansen got 101,034 votes to 40,756 for his Democratic opponent, Mike Vinich.

The Democrats managed to retain the state's one U.S. House seat. Incumbent Democratic congressman Teno Roncalio won reelection over a 28-year-old Casper stockbroker, Bill Kidd, despite preelection predictions to the contrary.

Voters also approved three of six proposed constitutional amendments, two of which extended home rule to cities and towns and lengthened legislative sessions from a total of 40 to 60 days and permitted the legislature to meet annually instead of once every two years. The third, the so-called Missouri Plan, radically altered the method of selecting judges and the system of judicial tenure.

Presidential vote: Nixon (R), 100,630; McGovern (D), 44,348.
Senator: Clifford P. Hansen* (R).
House: 1 D.
State legislature: Senate, 17 R, 14 D; house, 44 R, 18 D.

JAMES M. FLINCHUM

★ ★ ★

STRIP MINING in West Virginia has made its mark on the landscape and has also left an impression in state political contests, such as this year's race for the governorship.

ARTHUR TRESS

יְרוּשָׁלַיִם

Jerusalem

اورشليم القدس

Abba Eban

The city of Jerusalem has religious significance for Jews, Muslims, and Christians. The Jewish people have held it in reverence since Solomon built the great Temple of Jerusalem, almost 1,000 years before the birth of Christ. In the following pages Abba Eban, Israeli minister of foreign affairs, offers his personal reflections on the meaning of Jerusalem, past and present. A recognized scholar of Middle Eastern culture, Eban worked for the establishment of a Jewish state in Palestine, and since the founding of Israel in 1948, he has served as its representative to the United Nations and as ambassador to the United States.

HERITAGE OF PRAYER. The golden Dome of the Rock, built by Muslims on the site of Solomon's Temple, towers above the Wailing Wall, a remnant of the Temple court and a Jewish place of prayer.

It was midmorning on Wednesday, June 7, 1967, when a brigade commander in the Israeli Defense Forces sent a signal back to his headquarters: "The Temple Mount is ours. Repeat: the Temple Mount is ours." Soon the paratroops were moving through the twisting, narrow alleys of the Old City. They walked cautiously, for the sinister whine of a sniper's bullet could be heard at intervals, sometimes too close for comfort. There was still to be some death and havoc before peace set-tled on the silent streets; but the final issue had been sealed and settled. Soon a young soldier, steel helmet askew, looked through an opening in the cobbled alley. First he seemed petrified by an emotion too strong to bear; and then, on recovering his speech, he seemed to tear the very heavens apart with an exultant shout: "The Western Wall! I see the wall!" In a moment he was clutching the wall itself, his body riveted to the stones as if he wished to be glued to them forever.

The Pearly Gates

St. John the Evangelist chose the city of Jerusalem to symbolize the imagined beauty and splendor of the city of heaven. An illumination from a thirteenth-century Anglo-Norman manuscript depicts the "New Jerusalem" of the Apocalypse: "And the twelve gates were twelve pearls ... and the street of the city was pure gold, transparent as glass."

As the news of Jerusalem's unification spread across the world, it evoked a special kind of awe. There were many diverse sentiments about Israel; no modern nation had stirred such contrary passions of devotion and hostility. Indifference was about the only reaction which Israel had not provoked anywhere. But friends and foes alike, so long as they were open to any gleam of memory, could not fail to grasp that the people which had first built Jerusalem had now been reunited with the cradle of its birth. A great wheel of history had come full circle.

There seemed to be no particular reason why there should ever have been a city there, still less a city in which momentous things for the history of mankind would be enacted. There were no rivers or highways or harbors as in other capitals. None of the caravan routes of the ancient East passed through it. It did not even have a sure water supply. Yet it was here in the year 1000 B.C. that King David, whose first capital had been in Hebron, established himself on this Jebusite hill, which straddled the border between the northern and southern Israelite tribes and thus seemed a good vantage point from which to control and mitigate their rivalries. It was here that his son, King Solomon, enriched by foreign trade and taxation from tributary chiefs, built his kingly palace and, above all, the great Temple which made Jerusalem the wonder of all who went up to it in pilgrimage. Excavations now afoot reveal that there is no exaggeration in the biblical story that glitters with lavish descriptions of the Temple's opulence. It is now established that what has been known as the Western Wall is but a small segment of a vaster structure extending many meters on either side and, more surprisingly, reaching down to 14 more layers of carved granite than now appear above the stony surface.

Solomon came as near as anyone in Israel's history to temporal power. Israel was something to be reckoned with in the strategy of the region. But the spacious era was short-lived; on Solomon's death the kingdom was divided into two, and Jerusalem was henceforth the capital only of the smaller realm, Judea. Yet it was already surrounded by a religious aura which overshadowed the northern Israelite capital at Shechem. In the swift and bewildering succession of Judean kings there are five—Uzziah, Jotham, Ahaz, Hezekiah, and Josiah—who kept Jerusalem's fame in constant expansion. Yet in the end Jerusalem would owe its immortality not to the royal masters who held it as their seat of power, but to such citizens as Isaiah the son of Amotz, who made it the arena of prophecy. For it was in this place, inspired perhaps by the scarlet and purple majesty of its sunlight and the swiftly changing colors that spread across its hills, that the prophets gave out their splendid vision of a universe governed by order, righteousness, and grace. It was here that the prophetic thinkers cut through the melancholy and chaos of Middle Eastern idolatries to proclaim the Jewish conviction

about the forward direction of history and the perfectibility of mankind. They rejected the pagan philosophies according to which man's fate is tied to a wheel that revolves eternally in space and time only to come back to its starting point in darkness and chaos. In their revolutionary view, man is not the mere creature of history but a sentient being endowed with a capacity for moral choice. He is thus liberated from the cyclical rhythm of nature to which all the rest of creation is subject. He is not destined merely to be born, to live, and to die in an unceasing and senseless reiteration. He alone of all creatures can inherit, preserve, and bequeath experience and thus keep human life moving upward toward unattainable but inspiring goals. By these ideas, ancient Israel gave man the mastery of his own history; and since, as is the nature of great ideas, these were eternal, something of their eternity rubbed off on the place in which they had been revealed and expressed.

Jerusalem would always have a high spiritual lineage but would seldom possess much physical strength. The Judean kingdom lived a harassed, precarious life in the shadow of the great empires that succeeded each other to the north and south around the opulent waters of the Nile and the Euphrates. Babylon, Egypt, Persia, Byzantium, Greece, and Rome were all endowed at their zenith with a physical might and artistic refinement far beyond the reach of the struggling pastoral kingdom in the Judean hills. The Judean monarchs could maintain some sort of independence only by acrobatic flexibility in playing off one powerful neighbor against the others. Sometimes it was even necessary to yield and to accept foreign hegemony. Even so, Judea was too unstable to endure; and in a dark moment of history in 587 B.C., Nebuchadnezzar, king of Babylon, beleaguered Jerusalem, brought it to submission, and sent its inhabitants into exile. Then, in a savage burst of religious and national envy, the Babylonians laid the Temple waste.

Jerusalem henceforward was not a center of national power; but it became and remained the focus of a deep and endless nostalgia. One of its citizens, the prophet Jeremiah, sang its agony with painful tenderness:

How doth the city sit solitary that was full of people. How like a widow has she become. She that was great amongst nations, princess amongst provinces, how is she now become tributary! . . .

Judea is gone into captivity because of affliction; because of servitude she dwelleth amongst the nations; she findeth no rest.

The ways of Zion mourn because none come to the solemn feasts. Her gates are desolate, her priests sigh, her virgins are afflicted, and she is in bitterness. . . .

Jerusalem remembers in the days of her affliction and of her misery all her pleasant things that she had in the days of old. When her people fell into the hand of the

Where Pilgrims
Cross Paths

In front of the Wailing Wall, a remnant of the court of Solomon's Temple, Hasidic Jews dressed in traditional garb (left) chant prayers in celebration of Simchas Torah, the completion and renewal of the annual cycle of readings from Hebrew law. On the right, throngs of Christian pilgrims relive Good Friday by retracing Christ's steps to Golgotha along the Via Dolorosa. Below, Muslims sit at prayer in the interior of el-Aksa Mosque, a shrine of Islam since the seventh century. It is located near the site where the prophet Muhammad was supposedly transported to heaven after he died.

LOUIS GOLDMAN/RAPHO GUILLUMETTE (LEFT AND RIGHT)
TED SPIEGEL/RAPHO GUILLUMETTE (LOWER LEFT)

enemy and none did help her, adversaries saw her and mocked at her destruction.

(Lamentations 1:1, 3, 4, and 7)

There is a terrible sense of termination in the prophet's lament; Jerusalem's fate was to become a devastated relic in one of the more remote provinces under Babylonian rule. But now there began a drama of resilience in which Jerusalem seemed constantly faced with oblivion beyond recall, only to be called back into the central currents of history by the people that refused to forget its first and only home. The Jewish people was gripped by a conviction that its own persistence and identity were bound up with the place of its original birth. And, indeed, 50 years after the destruction of the Temple, Cyrus, king of Persia, then the head of the greatest empire that mankind had ever known, made a declaration authorizing any Jew in the Persian Empire who wished to go up to Jerusalem and rebuild the House of the Lord to do so with his benediction (Ezra 1).

The biblical narrative tells us that the glory of the Second Temple was no less than that of the original; but this seems to be a sentimental rather than an accurate verdict. The new settlers were assailed by every kind of hardship and obstacle, and they had none of King Solomon's resources. What they built must have been improvised and incomplete. After all, the whole of Jerusalem, not only the Temple Mount, "sat solitary," and the construction went on in an environment of desolation and chaos. But precisely because of these hardships, it must have been a moment of special emotion when the returning Jews were able to celebrate their festival services and to consecrate their sanctuary to the Providence which seemed to have deserted their exiled forebears two generations before. The zest of creation and sanctity was sharpened by the physical danger:

They that builded the wall and they that bore burdens laded themselves, each of them with one of his hands did the work and with the other held his weapon.

(Nehemiah 4:17)

The Jews of the Second Commonwealth (538 B.C.– A.D. 70) were seldom molested in their faith. Alexander the Great overthrew the Persian Empire and became the suzerain of Jerusalem; and in 320 B.C. his viceroy, Ptolemy I Soter, seized the city and expelled part of the Jewish population. But the Ptolemies were succeeded by the Seleucids in 198 B.C.; and 31 years later (167 B.C.) King Antiochius IV Epiphanes polluted the Second Temple and sought to extinguish the independent spiritual existence of the Jews. Against this repression Judah Maccabee and his brothers led a fierce revolt, drove out the oppressor, and consecrated the Temple on a date to be revered ever after as the festival of Chanukah. There now came an astonishing century of Judean freedom under the Hasmonean dynasty—a bright flash of peace and dignity in the long night of disaster. It was at the end of this period that Herod the Great

(reigned 37–4 B.C.) gave Jerusalem a splendor reminiscent of Solomon's glory. The city walls were elevated and reinforced, and, in Herod's crowning achievement, the Second Temple was rebuilt. Josephus is rhapsodic in his description of Herod's accomplishment: "He made a mountain of shining gold and lustrous white marble, beckoning the pilgrim from afar." The population rose to a quarter of a million, and an equal number thronged to the city in pilgrimage three times a year.

There seemed to be no end to the seesaw fluctuation. On Herod's death Roman government became more direct and tyrannical, yet Jerusalem flourished until the outbreak of the Jewish War against the Romans in A.D. 66. In this momentous interlude there took place the birth, ministry, and death of Jesus. A new religion with potent capacity for diffusion had sprung from Jewish loins.

The Romans had not expected Judea to put up such vigorous resistance to their superior force. But the realities of power could not for long be gainsaid. Jerusalem was besieged and overcome by Titus Vespasian (A.D. 70). The Second Temple was burned down, leaving the outer wall of the Temple Court as the only relic of its glory. This became known as the Western or Wailing Wall.

But even this was an episode, not a conclusion. For three years (132–135) Jerusalem was controlled by Simon Bar Kochba. His heroic and poignant revolt against the Romans lives on unfading in Jewish memory; but it so enraged the Romans that they ravaged Jerusalem more violently than it had ever been ravaged before. Its very name was expunged—it became Aelia Capitolina, a grotesque concentration of pagan temples, baths, theaters, and statues glorifying Roman emperors to the point of idolatry.

For nearly 18 centuries there would always be a Jewish foothold in Jerusalem, but never a sense of freedom, still less of power. Constantine the Great (reigned 306–337), who adopted Christianity as the creed of the Byzantine Empire, restored Jerusalem's name and built the Church of the Holy Sepulcher around the Stations of the Cross. The Roman idols were replaced by a group of churches. It was thus that the Persians found the city when they overthrew Byzantium in 614. Eight years later a Christian counterattack took Jerusalem again; but it was a brief respite. A third dimension was to be added to the Jewish and Christian layers in the city's history. The Muslim Arabs, sweeping out of their desert peninsula, took Jerusalem in 638. Islam was to be the controlling power for three and a half centuries. Jerusalem was never the holiest city in Islam, but after Mecca and Medina, the centers of pilgrimage, it was held in special veneration. In honor of the Caliph Omar, whose troops had taken the city 53 years before, his successor Abdul Malik, fifth caliph of the Umayyad dynasty, built the great Mosque of Omar in 691. The site was the Holy of Holies in Solomon's Temple. To this day, it shines forth as the

greatest work of architectural perfection in Jerusalem's ancient history and modern landscape.

Then came the crusading century in 1099–1198. Remnants of the castles still stand in Acre and elsewhere. It was one of the least creditable and effective chapters of Christian history, for the massacre wrought upon Jews and Muslims was hideous, and when the tide rolled back, Islam was still in possession. From 1250, Jerusalem was ruled by the Mamelukes and from 1517, for four whole centuries, by the Ottoman Turks.

All this time there were really two Jerusalems. The actual city had little comfort or splendor, and its aspect must have come as a shock to pilgrims from the flourishing towns of Christian Europe. Yet no matter how great the squalor in the city's narrow streets or the poverty that marked nearly all its communities, Jerusalem could not be deprived of the special legacy that it had won from nature and history. Nature had given it its mountain setting, its sweeping view to the volcanic Dead Sea and the hills of Moab, its distant but lucid glimpse

of the coastal plain. It always seemed to be looking down on the human spectacle from above. Then there is the special quality of its light, sharpening the edges of mountains against the sky, giving an ever-changing design to folds and hollows and illuminating streets and buildings with dramatic shifts of color as the sun ascends and falls. Beyond these possessions, Jerusalem had the pride of history which made men look at it with eyes different from those of flesh and blood. There was quite plainly a tendency to idealize it beyond reality. The rabbis of the Talmud period had boldly stated: "Ten portions of beauty were given to the whole world—and nine of them were taken by Jerusalem." Muslims also looked at Jerusalem with the desire to find its better side. Thus, the Arab geographer al-Mukaddasi wrote in the tenth century: "When it comes to discernment and modesty, the people of Jerusalem are unsurpassed. Unfairness and injustice are unknown to them. Their manners are refined. You will not see one of them drinking wine in public. There are no drunk-

FEAST FOR THE EYES. Picturesque markets brighten the streets of the Old City between the Damascus Gate and the Mosque of Omar.

ards in Jerusalem, nor are there houses of ill repute—for the people of Jerusalem have kept faith with the Lord."

Few Jerusalemites today would give their city such a total certificate of perfection, although it is undoubtedly a better and a cleaner place than Mukaddasi could possibly have visited. The city's remarkable history had taken powerful hold of the world's imagination. It would always be as the prophet had described it: "The perfection of beauty, the joy of the entire earth" (Lamentations 2:15). Men could always feel the breath of years upon it, touched to this day by the vitality of an uninterrupted life.

In particular, any movement to improve or develop the country as a whole placed a special accent on Jerusalem. Between 1855 and 1860, some decades before the rise of the Zionist movement, there was a sudden burst of Jewish piety and benefaction. Sir Moses Montefiore, a London Jew, set up the first durable residential quarter, Yemin Moshe, outside the Old City walls. The Jewish population rose from 300 in 1668 to 5,400 in 1841 and to 10,600 in 1873—exceeding that of the Christian and Muslim communities. There has been a Jewish majority for 100 years. By 1905 the Jews made up two-thirds of the population.

It was thus that the British forces encountered Jerusalem when they expelled the Turks in 1917. General E. H. H. Allenby was accustomed to enter conquered cities on horseback. But there was something about Jerusalem's name and atmosphere that gave him pause. He dismounted and walked through the sacred streets on foot, more humble than dominant. There are cities more ancient than Jerusalem, but they are in ruins. Nineveh is dead, dead also is Babylon, palms grow above desolate Memphis. But Jerusalem goes on. . . .

The proclamation of Israel's independence on May 14, 1948, was made in Tel Aviv, but it was Jerusalem that was named the capital. Soon the United Nations' promise to give Jerusalem an international protection was revealed as frivolous. The UN raised no finger when the Bedouin troops of the Transjordan Arab Legion crossed the river, besieged the Jewish population, and established their guns in the Old City. It refused to nominate its administrators when the Arabs seemed likely to capture the city. Its representative, Count Folke Bernadotte, proposed that the whole city, two-thirds Jewish, come under Arab rule. The formula of internationalization lost all credibility, if only because the United Nations promised to take all and to give nothing. It claimed a title while offering neither protection nor welfare nor service. The city's whole population and the governments in each part, Israel and Jordan, rejected this pretension. Israel alone offered an international control of the holy places. Bread and water had been running low when Israeli forces burst through the ravine at Bab el-Wad and brought relief supplies to the besieged and half-starving city. On the first trucks of the convoy were inscribed the words: "If I forget thee, O Jerusalem, may my right hand forget its cunning" (Psalms 137:5). The people of Jerusalem

Unearthing Jerusalem's Past

Since the 1967 war, archaeologists have uncovered the homes and streets of the ancient city, besieged and almost totally razed by the Roman Army after the Jewish rebellion of 70 A.D. Pictured here is an excavation site at the Western Wall of the Temple Mount, where objects dating back to the seventh century B.C. have been found, including the remnants of a Jewish cemetery alluded to in the biblical books of Jeremiah and Ezekiel.

were not forgotten or alone, though they were still divided.

At this point, and for 19 years until 1967, Jerusalem's story branches out in two directions. The western part was the capital of Israel, seat of the presidents, of the Knesset, and of government departments, center of learning and worship. The Hebrew University, banished from Mount Scopus, built its campus on Givat Ram at a speed that Ezra and Nehemiah would have envied. The speed of growth was steady but decently restrained. Jerusalemites like to feel that they do things slowly but more solidly than their restless brethren on the Mediterranean coast. But the period 1948–1967 is decisive in the formation of Jerusalem's character. Its Jewish population in the west grew from 100,000 to

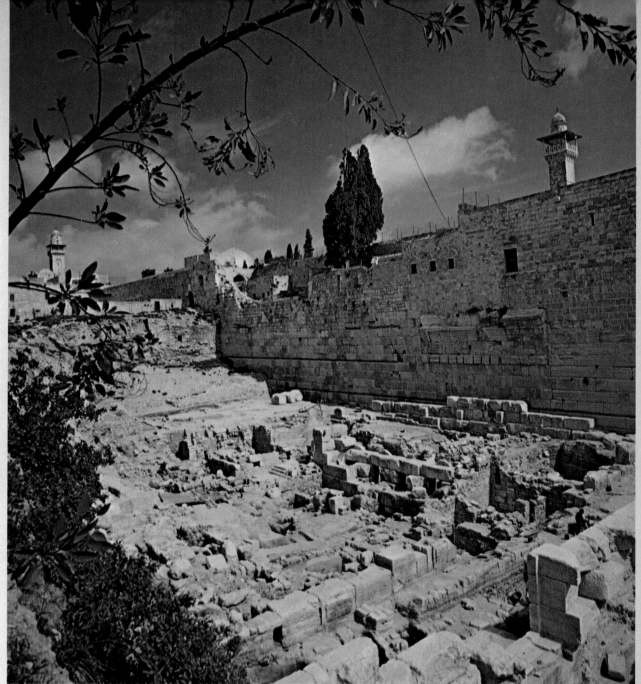

195,000, its highways expanded, and new landmarks—such as the Holocaust Memorial (Yad Va-Shem), the National Museum, and the Shrine of the Book—went up on the appropriate hills. Jerusalem's architects are always standing on tiptoe trying to look over the heads and shoulders of imaginary rivals who would like to deprive them of a view. Meanwhile, in the eastern area under Jordan's rule, tourism and pilgrimage to the holy places gave an impetus to development and to the creation of new wealth. There was, however, little public building, as King Hussein kept his capital in Amman, beyond the river, and brought no organs of government to East Jerusalem where, as a small boy, he had seen his grandfather Abdullah assassinated by Arab extremists in el-Aksa Mosque in 1951.

Jerusalem could not be unaware of the fact that it was tragically divided. There was often sniping across the barbed-wire frontiers. Israeli and Jordanian soldiers looked at each other vigilantly through binoculars and telescopes from positions 100 yards apart. When there was tension in the area, Jerusalemites in the west were careful about how they walked near the armistice line. There was a strange structure called the Mandelbaum Gate at the point of entry and exit between the two sectors. Simcha Mandelbaum was doubtless a worthy man, but the situation of his house at the confluence of the two nations hardly justified his "immortality." The symbolism is that whatever divided Jerusalem in those days seemed worthy of record and notice.

The divided city occasionally gave an outward im-

pression of normality, but there was always a sense of volcanic dissatisfaction in the air. A traveler or pilgrim who wished to go from Israeli Jerusalem to the holy places a few hundred yards away had to travel a few hundred miles to Cyprus and set out from there for Jordan with a different passport, innocent of any visa which might indicate the existence of the State of Israel. None of the 223,000 Muslims in Israel were allowed to cross the line in order to pray at the Mosque of Omar or at el-Aksa Mosque. None of Israel's 58,800 Christians could worship at the Holy Sepulcher. The most they could do was to make a special crossing to the Old City and Bethlehem twice a year, at Christmas and Easter. Time and time again, a murderous burst of fire would come across from the Jordanian troops in East Jerusalem to mow down scholars visiting an archaeological exhibition or civilians in a street near the frontier. Worst of all, Israelis were ominously aware that all the synagogues and cemeteries which they venerated in the city within the walls were being destroyed and polluted in a terrible burst of vandalism. Only in 1967 were they to discover that the gravestones from the Jewish cemetery on the Mount of Olives had been uprooted to pave public latrines.

Yet none of this would have brought Jerusalem into the war had King Hussein heeded a message from Israeli Prime Minister Levi Eshkol on June 5, 1967. Fighting had broken out with Egypt as a result of President Gamal Abdel Nasser's blockade of the Straits of Tiran on May 22 and his intimidatory troop concentrations accompanied by threats to destroy Israel. Eshkol's message, conveyed through the United Nations chief of staff, General Odd Bull, said plainly that if Jordan kept out of the war, Israel would leave everything as it was. The reply was an all-out Jordanian assault on western Jerusalem. Indeed, the fighting in Jerusalem was the fiercest of that in any sector—and it took a heavy toll of Israeli lives. On June 5, Israel hastily improvised troop convoys for the Jerusalem front. By June 7 the laconic message of the brigade commander ("The Temple Mount is ours") conveyed the momentous news that Jerusalem was united. It had known many masters. Now, after 19 centuries, its original builders were back again. Soon the barriers were down—the barbed-wire fences, the tank traps, the Mandelbaum Gate, all the symptoms of ghetto-like separation—and Jews, Muslims, and Christians, with multitudes of pilgrims from all over the world, swarmed together, mingling, jostling, sometimes colliding, but always together in a single human destiny. Requests from United Nations organs that they get themselves divided again—back to their respective cages and compartments—evoked their good-humored derision.

What awaits the city in its new era of reunion? The events of the past five years give some augury of the future. The greatest certainty is that it will remain united. Cities are divided by wars, never by peace. The idea of restoring the barbed wire, the minefields, and the barriers in order to reestablish a Jordanian sovereignty created by the war of 1948 and never recognized by international law has little appeal or prospect. On the other hand, Israel has stated that it does not wish to exercise unilateral control or exclusive jurisdiction in the holy places of Christendom and Islam and would seek agreements with the interests traditionally concerned in order to give expression to that principle. This opens an interesting possibility of reconciling secular democracy with due recognition of the pluralism and universality of Jerusalem's spiritual life. We have seen how at every stage of its history since the Jewish exile began, with the exception of 1948–1967, Jerusalem has been under the political control of a single sovereign. All of these—Babylonia, Persia, Rome, Byzantium, the Arab caliphates, Turkey, and Britain—had their origin and the main center of their devotion somewhere else. None of them could say or, to do them credit, ever said: "Jerusalem made us. It was our only cradle, and it is the single, exclusive focus of our veneration."

If, as is certain, a city has to be under the governance of a state, it makes some historic and theological sense for it to be under the sovereignty of the only state which can make that affirmation. But for Israel the pride is accompanied by a serious challenge. Temporal power in Jerusalem is now in harmony with its spiritual origins. Nevertheless, the idea of Jewish control of Jerusalem has always been conceived with reluctance in the Christian and the Muslim worlds. There is a chance to prove this reluctance to be completely unjustified. There is a chance of making Jerusalem a case history of communal and civic cooperation. There is a chance of ensuring an enterprise of development on behalf of all the city's inhabitants. There is the task, already well begun, of ensuring freedom of worship and pilgrimage for all who "set Jerusalem above [their] chiefest joy" (Psalms 137:6). There is the social predicament, too; for no city in the world strives for its own coherence amidst such a variety of classes, cultures, or conditions. There is the aesthetic challenge, too. It is natural that an offense to a historic landscape or a disruption of its physical perspectives should evoke a healthy roar of protest amongst Jerusalemites themselves. On the other hand, there is no virtue in an excessive conservatism that considers stagnation to be a condition of sanctity. This applies to the archaeological domain as well. It would be a passive form of vandalism to abstain from exposing the full glory of the Temple Wall. But there is every reason for applying safeguards that would prevent the effacement of the Mameluke heritage.

Jerusalem's population distribution (218,300 Jews, 62,300 Muslims, and 11,100 Christians) cannot fail to be determinant in its political status. But on a deeper and higher level of history, Jerusalem represents the confluence of many streams of memory and culture. Its sun has risen and set on a multitude of human longings, passions, agonies, and hopes. It is the capital of one nation and yet also the touchstone of the entire human condition.

> Perhaps more than any other city, Jerusalem has bequeathed a rich historic and spiritual heritage, a living legacy that the encyclopedia article describing the city vividly conveys. For details about its many rulers and their reigns, see such entries as NEBUCHADNEZZAR and BABYLONIA; CYRUS THE GREAT and PERSIA; and PALESTINE. Descriptions of the peoples and religions that have influenced the history of Jerusalem can be found under CHRISTIANITY, JUDAISM, and ISLAM.

Suggestions for Further Reading

AVI-YONAH, MICHAEL, ed. *Jerusalem.* New York, Orion Press, 1960.

COLLINS, LARRY, and DOMINIQUE LAPIERRE. *O Jerusalem!* New York, Simon and Schuster, 1972.

EBAN, ABBA. *My People: The Story of the Jews.* New York, Random House, 1968.

FOX, SARAH K. *Footloose in Jerusalem.* The Center for Jewish Education in the Diaspora of the Hebrew University of Jerusalem, 1971.

KOLLEK, TEDDY, and MOSHE PEARLMAN. *Jerusalem: A History of Forty Centuries.* New York, Random House, 1968.

TUCHMAN, BARBARA W. *Bible and Sword.* New York, Minerva, 1968.

SOCIAL

INSECTS

Peggy Pickering Larson
and Mervin W. Larson

Social insects have long intrigued man, who has gathered their honey, suffered their stings, eaten their bodies, and observed with fascination their intricate societal organization, subtle caste discrimination, and elaborate communication techniques. For centuries man has pondered what organizes these ruthlessly efficient societies of insects, but only very recently has he even begun to unravel the strands of which these societies are woven. The emerging picture is not that of insects directed by love, duty, honor, or selflessness, but rather of insects evolving the most sophisticated social arrangements largely by tastes and smells.

In fact, only four types of insects have reached a truly social level—some wasps, some bees, all ants, and all termites. Their "social" way of life consists of a common pattern: a single egg-laying female whose young are cared for by her daughters, usually sterile, who remain in the nest; a division of labor, oftentimes including specialization even beyond the reproductive duties; and development of varying body forms, known

INSTINCT, not any moral or communal sense, makes social insects act for their common good. When a queen bee (center right) lays eggs, she is surrounded by a court of workers attracted by her secretions. In army ants (above), instinct is literally blind—these sightless creatures will march in an endless circle around a dish, following each other's trails only by smell and touch.

Mervin W. Larson, director of the Arizona-Sonora Desert Museum, and his wife, Peggy Pickering Larson, are the coauthors of All About Ants *and* Lives of Social Insects. *In addition, Mrs. Larson has written* Deserts of America.

as castes, each with its job or jobs. Many variations upon this central theme, however, can be found among the four types of insects.

Only a small portion of the wasps are social. Most of the social wasp species are tropical, although certain species can live in temperate climates. It is about these that the most information is available.

Some of the most familiar wasps in temperate zones belong to the genus *Polistes*. The fertilized queen, produced by a colony the previous summer and fecundated by a male at that time, emerges after having hibernated through the winter to construct her nest in a protected location. The nest, hung from a single pedicel, usually consists of a comb made up of several cells that open downward. Both the comb and the pedicel are composed of a paper the wasp manufactures by chewing bits of plant fibers mixed with saliva.

The female lays an egg in each cell of the comb. The larvae that emerge from the eggs are grublike creatures radically different in form from the adult insect. The adult female cares for these young, feeding them macerated insect prey, although her own diet consists of such liquids as nectar, honeydew (anal secretions of aphids), and insect juices. Eventually, each larva spins a thin silken cap over its cell and enters the pupal stage, a quiescent period during which it assumes its adult form before emerging from the cell. These first individuals, all females, fill the role of workers, foraging for insect prey, wood pulp, and nectar and carrying out all nest duties except for egg laying, which is the prerogative of the queen. In late summer males and queens—that is, larger females capable of overwintering—are produced rather than worker brood. Before winter arrives, the fertile forms leave the nest and mate. Those individuals remaining in the nest and the males eventually die, with only the queen, hibernating singly, living through the winter.

As with the wasps, only a small portion of the many described species of bees are considered social. A vital difference between the bees and wasps is that pollen and honey are used as the basic foodstuffs for the bee larvae and adults, while meat is used for the wasp larvae. To make this pattern of life possible, the basic bee body has unwasplike modifications, which include a long tonguelike structure, the proboscis, for obtaining nectar deep within flowers; numerous body hairs for catching pollen from the flowers; and special body areas for carrying pollen. In addition, the more advanced bees are able to secrete wax, which they use as a building material, rather than producing the manufactured paper of the social wasps.

Although bees, ants, and wasps are justly famous for

HUNTERS, RANCHERS, AND FARMERS

Insects often seem startlingly human in their food-gathering behavior. Below, like a hunter dragging a carcass, a wasp carries a caterpillar home to feed its offspring. At right, ants "milk" aphids for honeydew while protecting the "herd" against predators. The honeybee (extreme right), an efficient farmer, simultaneously gathers food and pollinates flowers to ensure a constant supply.

FROM LEFT, PETER SLATER/PHOTO RESEARCHERS; J. A. L. COOKE; TREAT DAVIDSON/NATIONAL AUDUBON SOCIETY

stings they inflict, there is an important group of social bees, known as stingless bees, which has only a vestigial sting. Nonetheless, these bees have an effective defense. When a colony is disturbed, they rush out in great numbers and swarm over the intruder, biting sharply and repeatedly and smearing a sticky or sometimes caustic solution. Natives of the tropics, the stingless bees have perennial colonies, with populations as great as 80,000. Their queens have become specialized, for they cannot secrete wax, they have no pollen baskets for transport of this vital foodstuff, and their heads and eyes are smaller than those of the workers; hence, new nests must be established by swarming, which in this case is carried out by a young queen with a group of workers. Nests are built in the open, in holes in the ground, and in a variety of crevices. There the workers construct wax cells, the openings directed upward, and eventually add one comb atop another, separating them with wax pillars. Using a mixture of wax and extraneous material, these bees construct oval pots for nectar and pollen storage.

In contrast, workers of the "domesticated" honeybee (*Apis mellifera*) produce numerous vertically hanging combs of double-faced sheets of hexagonal cells, with the cells positioned horizontally, opening to the sides. Cells are used for brood rearing and for storing pollen and honey. In a wild state the honeybees nest in tree hollows or similar crevices, but man-made hives serve captive colonies.

The colonies of *A. mellifera*, which may reach populations of 70,000, have made a major adaptation to the environment, for although their members are cold-blooded, they are able to survive the winter in temperate climates as colonies rather than as single hibernating queens. This survival is due to the presence of sufficient stored food supplies (as much as 100 pounds of honey per colony may be stored in a single season) and to the clustering of the bees as a group on the comb. The metabolism of the food stores they use up can raise the temperature at the center of the cluster as much as 100°F above that of the air outside the hive, so that a life-sustaining temperature may be maintained. This provides tremendous advantages to the colony—the queen is constantly cared for, she need not found colonies unaided, she is allowed to live several years, and a worker force is always present and need not be initiated each spring at brood-rearing time.

As a consequence, it has been possible for the queen's form to become specialized for reproduction. She cannot secrete wax or forage for food, has no pollen baskets, and has reduced senses of sight, touch, and smell compared with the drones and workers. As an egg

ARMY ANTS often perform acrobatics in the line of duty. Here they interlock legs during bivouac to form a living curtain around the queen and brood. Ants at the top support the weight of the entire linked colony.

producer, however, she is phenomenal, producing perhaps a half million eggs in her lifetime of four or five years. When female reproductives are being reared, the old queen and a group of workers leave the hive to establish a new colony before the first virgin queen emerges from her cell. Usually this individual or workers destroy the few other virgin queens as they emerge. The remaining queen leaves the hive for a mating flight, after which she returns to serve as the queen of her home colony, until she later joins the colony-founding swarm as the older queen.

Ants, all of which belong to the family Formicidae, are the most numerous of all social insects in terms of individuals, and the number of living ant species—now 7,600—is greater than that of all other species of social

haviorally evolved to take advantage of a tremendous variety of land habitats and food sources.

Ants can nest all the way from 18 feet within the earth to the tops of trees; they excavate their own galleries or use ready-formed cavities, or they can move into crevices in man's structures. Some build mounds of earth through which they excavate their chambers; others construct carton nests hung high in trees.

Many ants are hunters using prey as food. Among them are not only the most primitive types, with small colonies not highly socially evolved, but also the army ants, which are extremely organized, efficient predators leading nomadic lives in the tropics. One species of army ants has the largest of all ant colonies—up to 20 million individuals! Some of the predatory ants have

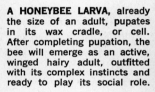

A HONEYBEE LARVA, already the size of an adult, pupates in its wax cradle, or cell. After completing pupation, the bee will emerge as an active, winged hairy adult, outfitted with its complex instincts and ready to play its social role.

LEFT, RUDOLF FREUND/PHOTO RESEARCHERS; ABOVE, TREAT DAVIDSON/NATIONAL AUDUBON SOCIETY

insects combined. An ant colony is normally founded by a single queen who has recently emerged from her home nest, mated during a wedding flight, and lost her wings. Sealing herself in the soil or other location, she lays eggs, which she tends without leaving the nest, and feeds the developing larvae with oral secretions of her body, derived largely from her degenerating wing muscles. Once the first young—workers—are produced, they assume all duties except the reproductive ones.

Ant colonies are perennial and may attain gigantic populations. Three ant castes are produced in most colonies—queens, males, and workers (workers are absent in some parasitic species). Normally, both queens and males are winged, although in some species only one sex may be. Workers are never winged. Within a colony there may be subcastes of workers with differing body forms for specific functions—for example, soldiers may have enlarged mandibles, or jaws.

In adaptation to their environment the ants rank supreme, the group as a whole having physically and be-

become specialized to the point of preying on a single type of organism; for instance, one subfamily preys only on other ants. The harvester ants specialize in collecting, storing, and eating seeds; other types concentrate on collecting sweet juices obtained as honeydew or as plant juices. Some species raise their own food, a fungus, which is grown in underground galleries on a base of plant material, the latter being collected, macerated, and tended by the workers. Other species depend upon "slaves" to garner food for the colony and to tend the brood; they obtain these slaves as larvae and pupae in raids on other species. There are even species that have evolved a completely parasitic way of life—a queen usurps the colony of another species and in some cases then produces only fertile forms of her own species and no workers.

The social organization of termites is built upon an evolutionary base far less advanced than that of the wasps, bees, and ants. There are two basic differences between the termites, whose more than 2,200 described

TERMITES: THE MASTER BUILDERS

Termites are among the foremost insect architects, sparing no effort to construct magnificent palaces for their queens. Certain species create elaborate nests of earth and vegetation mixed with saliva and excreta, like the tube nest (below) and the Kenyan "skyscraper" shown at right. At left, an African queen, her abdomen swollen with eggs, completely dwarfs a king.

living species are all social, and the other three types of social insects. Both male and female termites are present at all times in the castes represented in the colony—usually reproductive, worker, and soldier. Termites undergo incomplete metamorphosis: the young, known as nymphs, which have the same basic body form as the adults, grow by periodically shedding their exoskeleton. In contrast, wasps, bees, and ants undergo complete metamorphosis—larva to pupa to adult.

Termites are usually soft-bodied and vulnerable, and thin-skinned and subject to desiccation; most of the workers, soldiers, and nymphs are blind. They live within soil, wood, or constructions of their own making. The more primitive live directly in galleries in wood which they excavate, the wood serving as their food source. Living within their hindguts are symbiotic protozoa which digest the cellulose in the wood, making its nutrients available to the termite hosts. Some more advanced termite species nest in the soil and do not have the protozoa; these species feed on plant products with lesser quantities of indigestible cellulose, such as grass, decayed wood, dry manure, humus, and lichens.

Some of the African fungus-growing species of termites produce the most outstanding nests, spectacular mounds built over the initial underground nest, some as much as 90 feet wide. The mounds are interspersed with numerous chambers and spaces for air movement that provide air exchange within the nest. As many as 2 million inhabitants may live in such a nest. Earthen nest-building material consists of such mixtures as sand grains cemented with clay and saliva; termite excreta; and combinations of earth, saliva, and fluid fecal matter. Most dry to cement-like hardness. Some tropical termites construct carton nests, the paper-like substance manufactured from fecal materials

H. VON MEISS TEUFFEN/PHOTO RESEARCHERS

containing undigested bits of wood, combined at times with more wood, earth, and saliva. These nests may be several feet in diameter, are composed of innumerable small passages, and may be underground or in trees.

Termite colonies are normally founded by a winged male and female who have emerged from their home nests to participate in a flight. Having encountered one another, they lose their wings; then they prepare a gallery in wood or soil, depending upon their species, and conceal themselves within it. Once they are established, mating and egg laying take place, and the king and queen care for the emerging young until they are able to feed themselves. In some species these primary reproductives live for many years. The queen *Macrotermes natalensis,* for example, has a life expectancy of ten years, during which she produces 100 million eggs.

The nymphs, both male and female, are members of the work force in the lower termites which have no separate worker caste; the higher termites, however, do have a separate worker caste. As the nymphs move through successive molts, various features develop, such as wings on sexual forms. However, for varying lengths of time these nymphs remain plastic, and their development can be changed and directed toward the immediate caste needs of the colony. Some may remain static at a nonterminal stage and are "false workers." The soldier caste is thought to have evolutionarily preceded the worker caste. Some soldiers have enlarged, pigmented, heavily chitinized heads with specialized mandibles used for defense. Others may have a projection on the front of the head through which a chemical is dropped or rubbed on an adversary.

Such highly specialized societies require an efficient system of communication. Basic to insect communication are the pheromones, chemical substances given off by one insect and transferred to another. When pheromones are received as an odor or taste by a member of the same species, they relay a chemical message to the receiver that causes a specific response. Some pheromones are transferred by taste through a process of trophallaxis, the exchange—either mouth to mouth or anus to mouth—of alimentary liquid among the members of an insect colony. Especially in the more highly evolved societies, food and pheromones are passed quickly throughout the colony via this method.

Many of the immature forms of social insects produce body exudates or oral secretions that are eagerly solicited by the adults and that provide motivation for adults to care for the young. The amount of these chemicals present in the colony's mutually transferred food supply keeps the adult members chemically informed of the presence and state of the brood.

In many species pheromones produced by the queen (and in termites, also by the king) are of vital importance in ordering colony affairs. The queen is constantly attended by a retinue of workers who mouth her, obtaining exudates, and also feed and protect her. The secretions produced by the queen frequently prevent or limit the development of additional queens;

herein lies one of the secrets of the success of the queen-dominated, worker-powered insect societies. For example, a queen honeybee produces a combination of pheromones known collectively as queen substance. When these pheromones, present in the food shared in the colony, are in sufficient quantity, the workers are inhibited from building the special cells in which queens are reared. When not enough of these pheromones are present—because of the death or failing of the queen, or because of enlarged colony size—workers build queen cells in which the queen lays eggs or into which workers transfer recently laid eggs, and so begin the production of new queens. The queens develop as a result of a special diet of bee milk, a glandular secretion produced in the workers' pharyngeal glands and fed by the workers to the queen throughout her larval development and adult life.

Similarly, pheromones are considered the primary factor in organizing the caste systems of the termites. The presence in a colony of a king and queen ordinarily prevents the development of secondary reproductives. If a queen is restrained, her head in one group of termites and her abdomen in another, the production of secondary reproductives is inhibited only in the group possessing her abdomen. The reproductive-inhibiting pheromones evidently are obtained by the group members by means of food received from the anus of the queen and passed among the group members through trophallaxis. In a like manner, the production of soldiers in some termite species is inhibited or regulated in proportion to colony size by the presence of other soldiers in the colony.

A highly complicated affair, caste within the social insects is determined by pheromones, among other factors. In the social species of ants, bees, and wasps a fertilized egg produces a female; in almost all cases an unfertilized egg produces a male. Caste within the female group is environmentally rather than genetically determined. Determining factors may be numerous and include pheromones, temperature, and qualitative factors in feeding of the larvae. In a recent study of one ant genus, at least six factors were found to influence caste determination. One major exception to environmental caste determination is that of stingless bees of the genus *Melipona*, which display genetic control of female castes. With termites, both males and females are developed from fertilized eggs. Caste determination appears to be a result of environmental factors, such as nutrition and pheromones, the latter predominating.

In some social insects pheromones received as odors serve as alarm substances, alerting colony members when there is a threat. Pheromones may also be used in trail-laying. Certain ant species lay recruitment trails. In returning to her nest, a worker who has found a good food source marks her trail with glandular secretions from her abdomen. If other workers, following this trail, become excited over the food source, they too will mark the trail. Good sources thus become increasingly well advertised.

Many factors in addition to pheromones contribute to colony organization. The use of an insect's senses, instincts, and, to some extent, the ability to learn (for example, by trial and error) and to retain the memory of a foraging area contribute to organization on the colony level.

The natural odor of a particular social insect species —combined with odors within the nest, the odors of the food being consumed, and the types and quantities of pheromones present in the colony—gives each social insect colony a specific odor. This colony-distinctive odor is used by many social insects to recognize and accept colony members and to identify and deter non-members from entering the colony.

Individual differences exist among the members of a single colony. Some ants appear to be more intelligent and more excitable than their nest mates; they are often the colony members who detect a job to be done, start doing it, and in this way excite other ants to participate. Some honeybees, also, often show more individual initiative than their hive mates and provide impetus within the colony.

Body size or physiological state of the individual insect may also determine its role. Honeybees display temporal division of the work according to their physiology based on age. Early in her adult life the worker remains in the hive; as a young bee her pharyngeal glands develop. She feeds bee milk produced by these glands to the youngest larvae and to queen larvae, thus serving as a nurse bee for approximately a week. After that time these glands begin to shrink; now her wax glands have begun to secrete wax, however, and her duties include secreting and building with wax. After one to two weeks of fulfilling these duties, the worker begins venturing out of the hive and learning the territory, eventually foraging outside the hive.

It is in the honeybees that the most highly evolved communication system contributing to colony organization has developed. A honeybee worker, having located a good source of food, returns to the hive and announces her find by dancing on the comb. If the source is within a certain distance of the hive, she will do an excited "round" dance, turning in circles, clockwise then counterclockwise, forming a figure eight with the two loops of the eight overlapping. The dance serves to excite nest mates, its form tells them generally the distance to food, and the nectar regurgitated to them by the forager advises them of the type of food.

When the food source is located at a greater distance, the forager does a waggle dance, consisting of a true figure eight with the two loops of the figure separated by a straight line. During the straight portion of her run the honeybee wags her abdomen rapidly from side to side. In this dance she relays much more information than in the round dance, specifically the distance to the food source from the hive and the direction in which it lies. Distance evidently is relayed by the duration of waggling in each run, or the number of movements, or the length of time it takes the dancer to

A HORNETS' NEST is a comfortable spot, at least for offspring, which adults care for in the three earliest stages of life: eggs, visible as the white dots in the cells at top right; larvae, which fill the adjacent cells; and pupae, contained in the closed units.

complete a full figure eight. Direction is indicated during the straight run in the figure; the honeybee dances in darkness on the vertical comb, communicating the angle between the position of the sun and the feeding area by making the same angle in her straight run. For example, if the source is directly toward the sun, the straight tail-wagging portion of the dance is made vertically upward on the comb; if the source is 30° to the right of the sun, the straight run points 30° to the right of the vertical on the comb. Experiments have shown that honeybees are not born with the knowledge of the sun's path but must learn it.

Bees need not even see the sun when out foraging to know where it is, for they can detect polarized light. If any portion of blue sky is visible, the pattern of polarized light advises the honeybees of the sun's location. In addition, bees have a sense that enables them to perceive the passage of time. Having found a favorable spot for a group about to swarm, a scout may advertise it within the hive by a waggle dance. She may dance for as long as several hours without leaving the hive, yet she will gradually change the direction of her straight run in keeping with the sun's movement.

This remarkable ability to interact in a wide variety of relationships with other individuals—shown not only by the honeybees but also by the other social insects—is what continues to fascinate man. Indeed, man is only beginning to understand the social insects; they provide a fertile field for creative exploration by layman and scientist alike.

Suggestions for Further Reading

LARSON, PEGGY PICKERING, and MERVIN W. LARSON. *All About Ants.* Cleveland, World Publishing Company, 1965.

LARSON, PEGGY PICKERING, and MERVIN W. LARSON. *Lives of Social Insects.* Cleveland, World Publishing Company, 1968.

MICHENER, CHARLES, and MARY H. MICHENER. *American Social Insects.* New York, D. Van Nostrand Company, 1951.

WILSON, EDWARD O. *The Insect Societies.* Cambridge, Mass., Belknap Press of Harvard University Press, 1971.

The colonies of ants, wasps, termites, and bees seem to rival human societies in their division of labor and their complex communication systems and caste structures. For a different perspective on their intriguing societies, see the encyclopedia article SOCIAL INSECTS. The general characteristics of insects and a classification of various insect orders are offered in INSECTS. For more specific information on the four types of social insects, see the articles ANT, TERMITE, WASP, and BEE.

Nutrition

Charles Glen King

ILLUSTRATIONS BY TOM FUNK

The comfortable feeling after eating an attractive meal has a long and valuable background in human experience. The flavor of fresh food, for example, gave primitive man a valuable guide against eating spoiled meat and many other products that posed a danger of food poisoning. Long before man knew what a vitamin was, this pleasure principle encouraged eating foods that still retained their content of vitamin C, which is normally lost from most foods during drying or storage and is essential for preventing scurvy. Even the appetite mechanism was a good guide for energy needs when nearly everyone was accustomed to hard physical work.

But prosperity has turned this aspect of foods into a major health hazard. About one-half of the world's population is living in technologically advanced countries where food is abundant, marketing is sophisticated, economic resources are large, and population growth is under control. In these countries the most health-damaging form of malnutrition is an excess store of body fat—the result of a persistent intake of excess calories. Nutritional deficiencies in

GLOSSARY

Additive: any substance not naturally found in a food item which is added to improve taste or appearance, increase nutritional value, or retard spoilage.

Calorie: unit of heat; as defined by nutritionists, the amount of heat needed to raise the temperature of one kilogram of water from 15°C to 16°C. The number of calories in a food item represents the amount of energy into which that food can be converted in the body. Excess calories not converted into energy are chiefly stored in the body as fat.

Carbohydrates: nutrients (either starches or sugars) which usually constitute the body's primary source of energy, supplying about 50 percent of caloric needs.

Enriched: fortified with additional nutrients during processing; milk is commonly fortified with vitamin D, white flour with B vitamins and iron.

Fats: ether-soluble nutrients primarily useful as an energy source. Fats provide more than twice as many calories per gram as *carbohydrates*.

Health food: vague term sometimes used synonymously with *organic food* but which may also include foods containing chemical additives or grown with the aid of synthetic fertilizers.

Mineral: as used by nutritionists, one of the approximately 15 mineral elements essential to health, both as materials for body tissue (e.g., calcium in bone tissue) and as regulators of body functions.

Nutrient: a substance that is necessary for the normal functioning of the body or for life itself. There are five classes of nutrients: *carbohydrates*, *fats*, *minerals*, *proteins*, and *vitamins*.

Organic food: food which is produced without the aid of synthetic fertilizers or chemical pesticides and which receives no *additives* before being sold to the consumer; sometimes used misleadingly to refer to food items which do not fit the above definition.

Preservative: any substance added to food during processing to retard spoilage. One of the most common is sodium propionate, a federally approved fungicide which delays the formation of mold on bread.

Proteins: nutrients whose primary purpose is to provide materials—amino acids—for the growth and replacement of body tissue.

Refined: processed, as in grain and sugar, often at the cost of decreased nutritional value. For example, when white flour is refined from wheat, the vitamin-rich germ cell and bran are discarded, leaving the starchy endosperm to be ground up; this product has a longer shelf life than whole wheat flour but, even when enriched, has distinctly less nutritional value.

Trace element: a *mineral* required by the body in minuscule quantities, but essential nevertheless (e.g., fluorides).

Vitamins: chemical compounds, almost always produced in plants, which help regulate bodily functions. Vitamins tend to break down at high temperatures, such as during cooking, and particularly when exposed to air.

such areas are generally marginal and could be almost wholly corrected by good management and reasonable self-discipline. The cliché is valid: our food resources are wasted and waisted.

We must recognize that the rapid trend of our culture is to do less and less physical work and that requirements for specific nutrients do not necessarily decrease as the need for calories decreases. An adult man working in an office and expending only 2,500 calories a day needs food with a proportionately higher nutrient content than does a man expending and consuming 4,500 calories a day as a farmer or ditch digger. The same principle applies among women and children who are not engaged in vigorous exercise or strenuous work; they too need a greater supply of protein, vitamins, and minerals for every 1,000 calories of food they consume.

The tragedy is that while one-half of the world is endangering its health with excessive and nonnutritious calories, the other half of the world lives in countries less advanced technologically, where the basic caloric intake is grossly deficient for a large fraction of the populace, the population growth is unmanageable, and nutrient deficiencies (especially in good quality protein) exact a heavy medical, social, and economic toll. Although the "green revolution"—the production of high-yield grain crops through programs sponsored by the Rockefeller and Ford foundations—has made marvelous headway against starvation in the developing countries, there is still an enormous shortage of proteins, minerals, and vitamins in the diet of the underdeveloped world. There is an acute need for a program to increase the yield and quality of legumes (a family of plants, including peas and beans, that is an efficient protein source) as the "green revolution" has already done with cereals. The shortages that continue to plague the underdeveloped world make our own overconsumption of calories seem all the more wasteful.

The crucial issue in the "overdeveloped" world is not how to produce more food but how to make better

use of the food resources we already have. Most of our population is still illiterate in regard to the use of food. In combating this lack of understanding, the most potent weapon is the relatively recent science of nutrition. Detailed knowledge of what is in foods and the relation of food composition to health has been almost entirely a result of research in biochemistry and nutrition since 1900. Experience taught man which foods were enjoyable and which were immediately harmful, but until this century there was very little knowledge of the many thousands of individual chemical ingredients that practically all foods contain or of the effects of these chemicals on the body.

Between 1902 and 1914 a few biochemists in North America, Europe, and Asia published evidence that such foods as milk, citrus fruits, and brown rice contained minute quantities of organic material that was essential to normal growth and health—and even to survival—in experimental animals and in man. As further research revealed a number of organic materials varying in solubility and associated with various deficiency diseases, a different letter came to be used to designate each substance: A, fat soluble and associated with blindness and rickets; B, water soluble and associated with pellagra and beriberi; C, water soluble, very unstable, and associated with scurvy.

Because several concentrated but crude solutions of these organic materials showed reactions characteristic of what chemists called amines, the name "vitamines" (vital amines) was suggested in 1911 for the whole group of substances. When several of the individual pure products were isolated, however, and their exact compositions were established as not being amines (a fact which was not ascertained until 1932 and later), the popular name for the expanding series was changed to "vitamins." Then, as the initial letter was found to represent a mixture of two or more pure products, new letters or subscripts were introduced, such as A_2, B_{12}, D_2, and E. People often ask why there is no B_3, B_4, B_5, B_7, B_9, B_{10}, or B_{11}. The answer is that these designations all proved to be mixtures, so the proposed names were withdrawn.

As nutrition scientists learned to identify the individual pure organic compounds that were essential to health in man and in experimental animals, it became possible to study diets containing less and less mineral matter and thus to identify the kinds and quantities of minerals that are essential to normal health. Again, amazingly similar results were found in studies of different living organisms, both animals and plants. An early breakthrough was the discovery that a deficiency in minute quantities of both copper and cobalt was likely to become evident by a failure in iron metabolism, with a resultant onset of anemia. The family of essential minerals in nutrition then expanded rapidly from the conventional calcium, phosphorus, magnesium, sodium, potassium, chlorine, sulfur, iron, and iodine to also include fluorine, molybdenum, manganese, zinc, cobalt, chromium, selenium, vanadium, and probably tin and silicon.

Much knowledge of nutrition is very recent. Nearly all that we currently know about the chemical nature and specific functions of the 15 or more vitamins was learned after 1930. The requirements for essential amino acids that food proteins must provide were not established until 1942. The unique nutritional role of the one fatty acid (linoleic) that is essential for man was not identified until 1929. Among the many trace elements now known to be essential, two new ones (vanadium and silicon) were added as late as 1971. Several of the elements known to be poisonous in seemingly small quantities have now been found beneficial in much smaller quantities. A good example of this is fluorine, a very poisonous gas which, as a stable salt, is nevertheless found in minute quantities in all bones and in tooth enamel, where, as many studies have shown, it helps prevent decay.

Some of the recent advances in nutrition have outdated much of what passes for common knowledge. For example, it is now known that vitamin D as eaten in foods or formed in the skin by sunlight does not directly cure or prevent rickets, a childhood disease involving faulty bone growth. Instead, biochemists have shown that vitamin D is transferred to the liver and there changed to a new compound that is distributed to the entire body as a hormone that joins with other chemicals (such as the parathyroid hormone) in regulating the interchange of calcium between the bones and the bloodstream.

Likewise, vitamin A has been found to have a much larger role than protection of the eye structures and prevention of "night blindness." It is essential also in the body's construction of new protein. This partially explains why parallel deficiencies of both vitamin A and good quality protein so rapidly undermine a growing child's health and capacity for survival.

Two major advances related to vitamin C have been announced during the last few years. One group of experimenters isolated an entirely new series of derivatives of vitamin C in the tissues and urine of man, guinea pigs, and fish. As found in fruits and vegetables, vitamin C in a neutral or alkaline solution is easily destroyed when exposed to air. But in the body the vitamin combines with sulfuric acid to form a substance that is very stable, even when boiled in an acid or alkaline solution exposed to air. When synthesized in the laboratory and fed to guinea pigs or fish, this sub-

Charles Glen King is a past president of the American Public Health Association and the American Institute of Nutrition. A member of the National Academy of Sciences, he is currently emeritus professor of chemistry and lecturer in nutrition at Columbia University.

stance still retains its capacity to cure scurvy. This may explain why Eskimos do not suffer from scurvy, even though their diet consists of fish and seal meat without any fruit or fresh vegetables. Vitamin C also promotes protein synthesis and often increases the availability of iron.

Recently, extravagant claims have been made for massive doses (as much as 5 to 10 grams) of vitamin C per day as a method of preventing colds. No solid evidence has yet been published to substantiate such claims.

In many ways, the most exciting progress has been in research on the nutrition of mothers, infants, and small children, both in underdeveloped and overdeveloped nations. The evidence is increasingly clear that protein deficiency in gestation and in the first four years of life places irreversible limits on the composition, size, and functional capacity of the brain. Irreversible stunting in body size had long been recognized but not taken very seriously because the adult had an apparently normal capacity for physical work. Furthermore, it appears that the malnutrition of the mother during gestation may involve greater risk for herself as well as her offspring. At the other extreme, the evidence builds up steadily that excessive caloric intake during gestation and especially during infancy and early childhood tends to produce an excess of specialized fat-storing, adipose tissue. The child or adult burdened with an excess of such tissue tends to consume unnecessary calories and store excess body fat. It is well known that obese adults are distinctly more susceptible to diabetes and cardiovascular disease than adults at recommended weight levels.

Despite the very real knowledge we now have of good nutrition, serious health problems persist. Why is this so?

Nearly all food patterns recommended for general guidance are based on at least one or preferably two servings daily of a high quality protein food such as meat, fish, eggs, milk, or cheese; and two or more servings of vegetables, with emphasis on the green or the yellow varieties, and fruits, including citrus fruits or juices or an alternate choice of berries or tomatoes. This basic food pattern dates back to the Ceramic Age, which marked a turning point in human social development. By learning how to store water and dry, store, and sow seeds, Ceramic Age man could trade a nomadic way of life for settled communities based on simple forms of agriculture. Except in subarctic areas the food pattern for all major civilizations came to consist of cereal products, legumes, meat, and a variety of fruits and vegetables in season. In addition to the few major nutrients for which such foods are usually cited, these groups in combination contain sufficient amounts of nearly all the 45 or 50 chemical nutrients that are essential for health.

The problem is that many people pay little attention to the recommended patterns—for example, eating too many grains and too few vegetables. Others skip breakfast or lunch and have snacks of coffee, tea, or soft drinks along with candy and sweet goods that consist chiefly of sugar, refined flour, and shortening, most of which abound in calories and little else. Others consume frequent cocktails or beer with crackers, potato chips, and pretzels; these calorie carriers provide more social entertainment than nutrition. Another poor practice is to eat a normal meal until feeling satisfied and then add a full-sized high-calorie dessert such as chocolate cake or apple pie a la mode. In this surfeit of empty calories, essential nutrients are frequently shunted aside.

Current surveys show a high incidence of mild to moderate anemia among Americans; this is perhaps the most serious clinical deficiency in the United States. Among small children and fertile women, iron deficiency is the major cause of low hemoglobin and low iron content in the blood. This condition can generally be rectified with an increased intake of available iron in pills, capsules, or tonics. Nevertheless, since excessive iron may result in injury to the liver, caution is called for. One possibly safer remedy is to increase the iron content of the current cereal enrichment formula. Most wheat flour and cornmeal now have iron and vitamins B_1, B_2, and niacin added to them, although this enrichment is not required; since 1940 the U.S. government has regulated the amount of each nutrient a miller or food manufacturer must add if the product is to be labeled "enriched." Many nutrition scientists believe that enrichment should be made mandatory for flour and also should be more widely applied to other products.

The body tends to increase its absorption of iron from the food supply when the body storage (for example, in muscles and blood cells) is low. However, the increased efficiency is not always adequate. Normal adults on a mixed diet generally absorb only about 5 to 10 percent of the iron contained in their food, and even iron-deficient adults absorb no more than 10 to 20 percent.

A second common nutritional deficiency is low iodine intake. Tests with a radioactive isotope of iodine have already shown how widespread this deficiency is, even where there is no conspicuous enlargement of the thyroid gland (goiter). It is inexcusable to delay the adoption of a required optimum addition of iodine in stable, standardized form to all table salt on the general food market or used in preparing commercial food products. Individuals who object on authentic religious or medical grounds could be supplied through local drugstores with salt labeled "noniodized."

A third nutrient deficient in the American diet is fluorine, an element essential for normal tooth and bone development. In many large areas of the United States the low fluorine content of native rock and soil

SUPERBURGER 550
BURGER 350
FRENCH FRIES 300
FRIED CHICKEN 300
CHOCOLATE SHAKE 350
LARGE SODA 160
SUPER SUNDAE 400

OUR SPECIALTY PIZZA 1600 Calories

results in a fluorine concentration in water supplies of less than 0.3 part per million. Artificial fluoridation of public water supplies has been demonstrated in the United States and England to be safe and effective in reducing tooth decay by 50 percent or more.

In addition to these specific nutritional deficiencies, the general quality of the American diet has come under attack, not always on sound nutritional grounds. One of the most frequent and wildly exaggerated charges is that American foods lose nearly all nutritive value in processing and are then preserved, flavored, and colored with substances that may be positively harmful. In fact, food processing by packaging and refrigeration or deep freezing need not result in serious lowering of nutritive values, although the loss imposed by canning bland foods, such as meats, must be recognized, because of the heat treatment needed to minimize the risk of food poisoning. The use of government-approved antioxidants in many foods is a safe and very important service to the public. The resulting retardation or prevention of rancidity both conserves the nutritive value of foods and protects their natural flavor and color. The use of synthetic colors, flavors, and conditioners is more widely subject to criticism, but so far as safety is concerned, health is rarely endangered

when additives are limited to materials approved by government agencies. Techniques of testing for potential risks are steadily becoming more sophisticated, in regard to both the length of test periods and the examination of body tissues for evidence of short-term or cumulative injury.

The general public scarcely recognizes the fact that practically all foods, whether from plant or animal sources, contain in their natural states small quantities of acids, minerals, hormones, and colors that would be toxic in larger quantities. For example, benzoic acid, oxalic acid, and salicylic acid are normally present in a great many plant foods that are consumed regularly and without injury. As has been mentioned, most of the mineral elements now recognized as absolutely necessary for health were long regarded as poisonous.

Loss of nutritional value will result from excessive cooking of food at high temperatures, whether in a home, restaurant, or factory. The use of low-extraction flour, polished rice, sugar, and starch; the substitution of refined protein concentrates for meat; the use of single amino acids instead of good quality protein—all these tend to reduce the nutritive value of the calories we ingest. The task of choosing good foods to eat has further been complicated by the fact that the more

VALUE FOR CALORIES:
How common foods compare

	Calories	Protein (Gm.)	Fat (Gm.)	Calcium (Mg.)	Iron (Mg.)	Vitamin A (I.U.)	Thiamine B₁ (Mg.)	Riboflavin B₂ (Mg.)	Niacin (Mg.)	Ascorbic acid (Mg.)
Banana, raw, 1 large, 8" × 1½"	119	1.6	.3	11	.8	570	.06	.06	1.0	13
Beef, sirloin, 3 oz., cooked[1]	257	20.0	19.0	9	2.5	—	.06	.16	4.1	—
Bread, whole wheat, 1 slice ½" thick	55	2.1	.6	22	.5	—	.07	.03	.7	—
Cheese, cottage, from skim milk, 1 cup	215	43.9	1.1	216	.7	50	.04	.69	.2	—
Chicken, raw, 8 oz.[1]	332	44.4	15.8	31	3.3	—	.18	.36	22.4	—
Cola beverage, carbonated, 1 cup	107	—	—		—	—	—	—	—	—
Corn flakes, 1 cup	96	2.0	.1	.3	.3	—	.01	.02	.4	—
Doughnuts, cake type, 1	136	2.1	6.7	23	.2	40	.05	.04	.4	—
Egg, 1 scrambled	106	6.8	7.9	50	1.3	640	.05	.17	Tr.	—
Flounder, 4 oz., raw, edible portion	78	16.9	.6	69	.9	—	.07	.06	1.9	—
Lamb, rib chop, 3 oz., cooked[1]	356	20.0	30.0	9	2.6	—	.12	.22	4.8	—
Liver, beef, 2 oz., cooked	118	13.4	4.4	5	4.4	30,330	.15	2.25	8.4	18
Macaroni and cheese, baked, 1 cup	464	17.8	24.2	420	1.1	990	.07	.35	.9	Tr.
Mayonnaise, 1 tbs.	92	.2	10.1	2	.1	30	Tr.	Tr.	—	—
Milk, cow: fluid, whole, 1 cup	166	8.5	9.5	288	.2	390	.09	.42	.3	3
Peanuts, shelled, roasted, 1 cup	805	38.7	63.6	107	2.7	—	.42	.19	23.3	—
Orange juice, fresh, 1 cup	108	2.0	.5	47	.5	460	.19	.06	.6	122
Pie, apple, 4" sector	331	2.8	12.8	9	.5	220	.04	.02	.3	1
Potato, baked, 1 medium, 2½" dia.	97	2.4	.1	13	.8	20	.11	.05	1.4	17
Spaghetti, cooked, 1 cup	218	7.4	.9	13	.9	—	.03	.02	.7	—
Spinach, cooked, 1 cup	46	5.6	1.1	223	3.6	21,200	.14	.36	1.1	54

[1] Boneless

sophisticated foods become, whether through special processing or the use of artificial flavors and colors, the more difficult it is for the general public to estimate their nutritive value.

Nevertheless, fad diets are not the answer. Single-mindedly substituting fad foods for common, "suspect" ones is more destructive to health and more wasteful to the pocketbook than is generally recognized.

One current myth surrounds brown rice, the main ingredient of the so-called macrobiotic diet. This diet is actually a series of stages in which the dieter progressively eliminates meats, other animal-source foods, and then other types of food, leaving only brown rice in the diet's highest stage. Each successive elimination supposedly promotes the spiritual and physical health of the follower. Well, brown rice is obviously superior to white polished rice in nutrient content, but it is not a perfect food. Anyone restricted to such a diet would become deficient in protein and other essential nutrients; in a few months he would die from scurvy or other complications. Instances of such illness have been observed by Dr. Fredrick S. Stare of Harvard University and by other physicians in the United States and Europe. Widespread stunting in growth from protein and vitamin (especially A and C) deficiencies are widespread in areas where similar, if less extreme, practices are common.

Several recent weight-loss diets have gone to the other extreme from the rice or vegetarian pattern. The Stillman diet and the "drinking man's diet," for example, advocate extremely high consumption of animal protein, high intake of saturated fat, and very low consumption of carbohydrates.

Many current claims relating to so-called organic foods do not bear scrutiny. For example, the charge that inorganic fertilizers are seriously jeopardizing the health value of food supplies in North America, Europe, and other parts of the world is false, as is well known among nutrition and soil scientists. Agricultural experiment stations have conducted extensive studies of "natural" soils and soils treated in different ways with fertilizers. The results showed that, in most in-

stances, with reasonably good yields, nutritive values tended to be those characteristic of each type of crop, regardless of soil. Hence, in practical farming the use of chemical fertilizers to give the best yields does not impose a risk of lowered nutritive quality.

The pesticide and fungicide problem is indeed a serious one. A farm, garden, or orchard may be isolated from major pests for a short time in newly developed areas, but in nearly all established farming sections, the presence of pests makes the use of chemical sprays essential to successful crops. Governmental surveillance against risks is not perfect, but it has been vigorous in protection of public health and, on the whole, remarkably effective. Accusations that the general food supply on American markets poses a practical risk to health because of the use of pesticides are not valid, as shown by the records of analysis and testing in all major markets.

The current push to establish and patronize "health food stores," on the assumption that the general food supply is not safe or capable of sustaining vigorous health, is grossly in error; this has been shown by accurate sampling and analysis of commercially available products for nutrient loss or harmful materials. Not all farms or stores are perfect, but the normal flow of food commodities is under constant surveillance by federal and state employees who are well trained, competent, and honest—much more so, apparently, than the personnel in health food stores. I have visited health food stores throughout the United States and Europe and have never yet found on their shelves a book, pamphlet, or journal that was written by a competent nutritionist or medical scientist. The major faddists, of course, were well represented. Conversations with the sales staff did not reveal any individuals who could answer inquiries reliably, but they talked freely. Representative purchases confirmed the often-reported fact that costs for produce were substantially above those in normal food stores. Such experiences raise a reasonable question: Why do not more general-purpose grocery stores and supermarkets provide relatively inexpensive but accurate educational material or even professional personnel to assist the public in selecting and preparing the kinds of foods that are truly in the consumer's interest?

The importance of informed food selection from the major food groups—high-quality protein foods, cereals, vegetables, and fruits—becomes increasingly clear with every research program. Researchers are now trying to identify nutritional requirements for optimum health at all ages, as well as the upper limits beyond which the intake of certain nutrients is hazardous to health. In 1968, on the basis of the most recent research at that time, the Food and Nutrition Board of the National Academy of Sciences–National Research Council issued a table specifying the optimal intakes (called recommended daily dietary allowances) of ten vitamins and

five minerals for people of both sexes and various ages. In 1972, the Food and Drug Administration adopted these allowances (with slight modifications) for use in regulating the labeling of enriched foods and vitamin capsules; any manufacturer of processed foods or vitamin supplements making health claims for his product as a result of the addition of vitamins and minerals must specify the quantities added and the percentages of the recommended daily allowances (or RDA's) that those quantities represent. The RDA's will replace the familiar minimum daily requirements, established more than 30 years ago as the minimal amounts of some vitamins and minerals needed to prevent deficiency diseases.

Meanwhile, research continues to determine more accurately the optimum range of human intake of vitamins, minerals, and other nutrients. Quantitative feeding tests are generally conducted with laboratory animals, usually albino rats, under carefully controlled conditions; the findings from these tests are then rechecked with another type of laboratory animal before quantitative tests are conducted with human adult volunteers. Additional studies are then made on infants and pregnant women.

Until such detailed information is available, there is a great risk that too much reliance will be placed on adding a few nutrients to each day's supply of total calories. "Refined" foods may be attractive in terms of flavor, appearance, convenience, packaging, and cost—or so, at least, their advertisers claim—but they are no substitute for a sensibly balanced diet.

Further information on the development and achievements of modern nutritional science can be found in the encyclopedia article NUTRITION. Articles indexed under DIETETICS tell how to plan a well-balanced menu; the subject of FOOD is the production, processing, and delivery of goods to our tables. Detailed analyses of the nutrients vital to health can be found under FATS, PROTEINS, STARCH, SUGAR, and VITAMINS. The articles PELLAGRA, RICKETS, and SCURVY show the diseases that can occur when some of these nutrients are lacking.

Suggestions for Further Reading

DEUTSCH, RONALD M. *The Family Guide to Better Food and Better Health.* New York, Creative Home Library, 1971.

LEVERTON, RUTH. *Food Becomes You.* 3rd ed. Ames, Iowa State University Press, 1965.

Prospects of the World Food Supply. Washington, D.C., National Academy of Sciences, 1966.

Strategy for the Conquest of Hunger. New York, The Rockefeller Foundation, 1968.

A Practical Guide to Combating Malnutrition in the Preschool Child. New York, Appleton-Century-Crofts, 1970.

Toxicants Occurring Naturally in Foods. Washington, D.C., National Academy of Sciences, 1966.

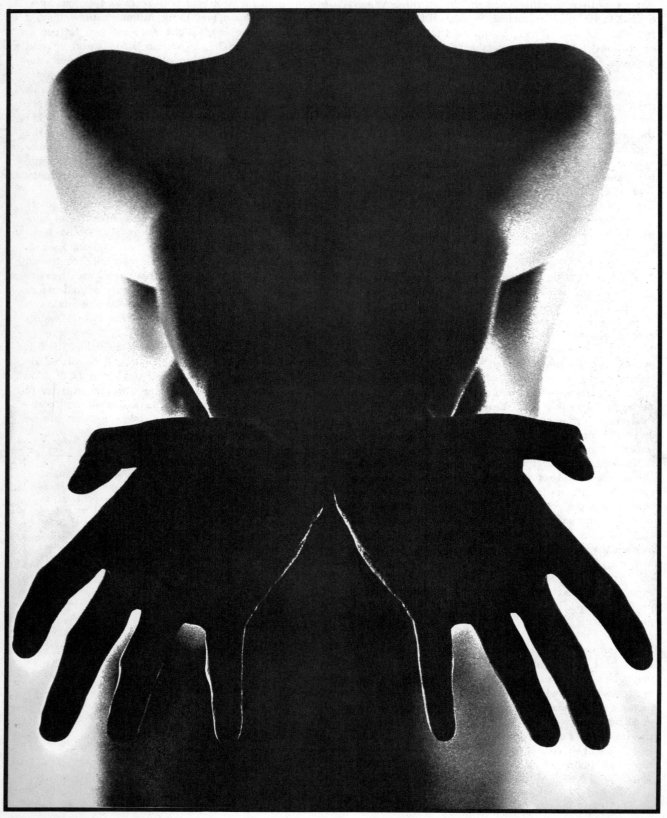

Behavior Control

Geoffrey Horn

Behavior control is the way one person shapes another person's actions. Toilet training, schooling, and advertising are control techniques we have all been exposed to; other techniques can be as brutal as brainwashing or as subtle as seduction. At the deepest level, all these techniques not only shape specific actions but also set general limits on the possibility of human freedom. Taking each instance of controlled behavior as evidence that all behavior can be controlled, psychologists like Harvard's B. F. Skinner project a world in which all our behavior would be shaped by a select few. Utopia or nightmare, that world may be almost upon us. Like Frazier, a character in Skinner's utopian novel *Walden Two,* today's would-be controllers argue that "the science is there for the asking. But its techniques and methods are in the wrong hands—they are used for personal aggrandizement in a competitive world or, in the case of the psychologist and educator, for futilely corrective purposes. My question is, have you the courage to take up and wield the science of behavior for the good of mankind?"

The question Skinner poses is not idle. Over the past 30 years, research scientists—especially José M. R. Delgado of Yale—have presented startling evidence that behavior can be controlled with unprecedented precision. By stimulating animal brains through implanted electrodes, Dr. Delgado and his associates have already made female rhesus monkeys, normally affectionate, completely ignore their young; immobilized a cat lapping milk, with its tongue out; and not only stopped a brave bull in mid-charge but permanently curbed its aggressive instincts. In one experiment on social behavior, an electrode in the brain of a "boss monkey" was connected to a lever within reach of the other monkeys in his cage. One female soon learned that by pressing the lever she could subdue the boss's intimidating behavior. The result was a shift in the balance of power in the colony: whenever the boss made the usual threatening gestures, she could run to the lever and control him instead.

Reversals in human behavior have been just as surprising. Stimulation of a point on the left side of his brain caused an 11-year-old boy to stretch voluptuously, express fondness for his male therapist, and wish to be a girl—an idea which, when presented to him with the current turned off, made the patient anxious and defensive. Another Delgado experiment shows the power of mind control. Under electrical stimulation, one patient began to clench and unclench his right fist without being aware that he was doing so. This behavior was explained to him, and he was then warned of each oncoming stimulus and told to resist it. After many failures he said, "I guess your electricity is stronger than my will."

the soldier "saw" the nonexistent swastika, violently attacked his friend, and had to be forcibly held back.

What these experiments—and all the most controversial behavior control techniques—have in common is the power to change a person's will in ways he is unaware of or unable to resist. The most threatening kinds of control make a sham of voluntary behavior by hiding from the controllee the fact that what he seems to will on his own has already been willed for him by someone else. Indeed, the short-circuiting of awareness—not merely by a hypnotist's trick but by all forms of conditioning—is essential to behaviorist theory as elaborated by Skinner. "It doesn't make any difference to me whether things are conscious or unconscious," he said

MONKEY SEE, MONKEY DON'T

Normally, a monkey reaches out to grab an offered banana. But in experiments conducted by Yale's José Delgado, electrical stimulation of an appetite inhibitory mechanism in the brain compelled this one to spurn food.

BOTH PHOTOS, ERIC SCHAAL/
LIFE © TIME INC.

Behavior control has awesome potential, but there is nothing awesome about the devices used to achieve it. Electrical stimulation is only one technologically sophisticated means to an end. In fact, as Dr. Delgado acknowledges, present electrode implantation techniques control human behavior less effectively than hypnosis, which uses no apparatus at all. Hypnotherapy has enabled overeaters to diet and smokers to quit, but controlled scientific experiments have also confirmed some more sinister uses. A survey of the literature by Paul C. Young of Louisiana State University cited cases in which, under test conditions, army officers were led to "steal" military secrets and test subjects were induced to hurl what they believed to be corrosive acid at innocent victims. In one famous experiment, an American soldier in World War II was told under hypnosis that his best friend was a Nazi spy; the "proof," he was told, was a swastika supposedly engraved on the inside of the friend's cigarette case. By prearrangement with the experimenters, once the soldier was out of the trance his friend came in and offered him a cigarette. The startling result was that

in an interview published in 1968; "the causality in behavior does not depend on awareness." A strict determinist, Skinner denies that we have free will; he claims that explanations based on phrases like "because I wanted to" or "because I chose to" do not explain our behavior at all. Thus, although reason is a useful tool, rational actions no more imply free will than do actions performed through unthinking habit. In either case, according to Skinner, the real cause of our behavior is not mental but environmental.

Conceptually this argument poses many problems, but experimentally it makes good sense. In one of Dr. Delgado's patients, electrical stimulation evoked head turning and "searching" behavior. When asked why he had turned his head, the patient always gave some plausible explanation: "I heard a noise," "I was looking

Geoffrey Horn is senior editor of the Year Book. His research for this article ranged from interviewing B. F. Skinner at Harvard to having electrodes attached to his head in a brain-wave detection experiment.

under the bed," and so forth. Were these accurate descriptions of hallucinations evoked by the stimulus, or were they merely rationalizations invented by the patient so that his apparently unmotivated behavior would not look so foolish? Experimentally there is no certain way to find out. And since from the experimenter's point of view the real cause is always the electrical stimulus, all of the patient's explanations are equally irrelevant. In general, all that matters to the controller is that the controllee behave predictably.

Once we admit that our behavior can be controlled when we don't realize it—and in ways that can horrify us when we do—we must return to the question of values. To what extent and for what purposes should

behavior be scientifically controlled? This question is made doubly difficult by the fact that, in practice, the success of a control program often depends on the prestige of the controller. For example, test subjects who inflict real pain on themselves or simulated pain on others justify their actions by claiming in post-experimental interviews that the experimenter (always wrapped in the white cloak of scientific respectability) would not have asked them to inflict pain without a valid reason. Serious controversies arise when experiments done "in the name of science" run afoul of other social or ethical considerations.

Psychosurgery, the destruction of brain cells in order to modify behavior, is a prime example of such a conflict. Early evidence that different bodily functions were controlled by different parts of the brain came from postmortem examinations of victims of brain disease; it could easily be established that the location of a lesion or tumor was associated with the kinds of disabilities the disease had produced. But the mapping of brain functions took a great leap forward with the use of electrodes on live patients. Electrical stimulation

located the sources, not of general capacities, but of specific physical, emotional, and verbal behavior. It should be remembered that the techniques which neurosurgeons use to determine brain functions themselves constitute behavior control, since it is only by eliciting observable states of behavior in the patient that brain functions can be determined. In this sense, every advance in brain physiology implies an advance in behavior control.

The earliest, best-known, and most discredited version of psychosurgery was the prefrontal lobotomy, a massive surgical incision in the forebrain, usually to suppress violent behavior. The operation made mental patients "manageable," but no one knew quite why. Often, lobotomy worked too well. "The frequent effect . . . was irreversible change in mood, emotion, temperament, and all higher mental functions," observed J. M. C. Holden, physician superintendent of the St. Louis State Hospital Complex. Some patients deteriorated; a few died.

The problem with lobotomies was that they involved massive surgical destruction of a vaguely charted area. Contemporary neurosurgeons argue that the new techniques of psychosurgery avoid unwanted side effects by attacking a highly localized area associated with the patient's specific disability, leaving the rest of his personality intact. A particular advantage of the new stereotactic methods—the destruction of deep brain cells around the tips of implanted electrodes—is that the implants can remain in the brain and be reused if the first dose of electricity has been ineffective; this gradualist approach is supposed to make drastic lobotomy-like effects unlikely.

Using stereotactic methods, Dr. Vernon G. Mark and his psychiatric and neurosurgical associates at the Neuro-Research Foundation in Massachusetts have successfully treated malfunctions of the amygdala, the almond-shaped nucleus that these researchers label the "emotional thermostat" of the brain. Otherwise inexplicable spasms of murderous rage in certain patients have been traced through analysis of deep brain waves to epileptic seizures in the amygdala; electrical stimulation can duplicate such seizures, and stimulation of neighboring areas or stereotactic destruction of portions of the amygdala can control them. Obviously, the ability to turn murderous behavior on and off could be a potent weapon in the hands of an unscrupulous controller. But current psychosurgical techniques remain cumbersome: a single, highly trained, exceptionally skilled neurosurgeon may need months of exploratory measurements to prepare for a single operation that may take a whole day to perform. A malevolent neurosurgeon could become a Dr. Frankenstein, but he could never control enough people to be Big Brother.

Nevertheless, lines of research now advocated by Dr. Mark and Dr. Frank R. Ervin in *Violence and the Brain* raise the specter of 1984 to some libertarians: ". . . we need, but do not yet have, some accurate method of identifying people with deep brain disease, preferably before they commit any violent act, but certainly, at

least, before they commit more than one. . . . Without such a test, we cannot hope to detect, predict, or prevent individual violence related to [deep] brain disease." Since the measurement of deep brain waves is a complex process unsuitable for mass testing, correlations are being sought between deep brain malfunction and more easily applied criteria, such as standard electroencephalograph measurements of surface brain waves. Milder forms of antisocial behavior exhibited by an individual may also be used to diagnose his potential for violence against persons or property; for example, Dr. Mark and Dr. Ervin argue for the diagnostic reliability of a pattern of recurrent traffic violence (at least two accidents involving serious injuries or property damage) on an individual's driving record.

What should happen once the violent or potentially violent have been singled out? In a telephone interview, Dr. Mark indicated that medical and psychiatric treatment should be prescribed in the vast majority of deep brain disease diagnoses. He reserves stereotactic surgery for intractably violent patients with temporal lobe epilepsy, while hoping that future advances in focal chemotherapy of the brain would make destructive brain lesions outmoded.

A very different answer to this question is offered by Dr. Arnold Hutschnecker, formerly President Nixon's internist and currently a psychotherapist in New York. Under his plan, all American children between six and eight years old would be tested for "criminal potential"; those with a high "criminal quotient" would be sent to rehabilitation centers "in a romantic setting out West." The idea was turned down by leading federal officials.

Such proposals leave open the question of who the controllees are likely to be. A psychiatrist bitterly opposed to all forms of psychosurgery, Dr. Peter R. Breggin of the Washington School of Psychiatry, cites evidence to show that psychosurgical patients tend to be old rather than young, female rather than male, black rather than white, and laborers rather than professionals. He concludes that psychosurgical techniques have been used to "blunt those people whom the society found most vulnerable and most easily returnable to relatively nonfunctional or low-level tasks within society." Dr. Breggin's criticisms of psychosurgery could be true of rehabilitation or drug therapy programs if they fell into the wrong hands.

Few people realize that an organized program of behavior control through drug therapy is already under way. Amphetamines and other potent chemicals are currently being administered to about 200,000 American schoolchildren with hyperkinesis, a condition characterized by apparently purposeless muscular activity ranging from inattentiveness and wandering to constant mayhem. Because purposelessness cannot be defined in absolute terms, it is not clear whether hyperkinesis is a medical or a social issue. Proponents of drug therapy see hyperkinesis as a disease impeding normal behavior; critics see the abnormal behavior of many children as a purposeful response to stultifying surroundings. There is no way to resolve the dispute,

but it should be noted that, in the administration of drug therapy, social aims often take precedence over sound medical practice. Dr. Gerald Solomons, director of the University of Iowa's Child Development Clinic, found that many children under drug therapy had not seen a doctor for years and that doctors had often delegated to a child's parents all responsibility for altering the frequency or dosage. Faced with continued disruptive behavior, school personnel had sometimes, without consulting a doctor, asked parents to increase the amount of the drugs their children were receiving.

Programs that single out individuals or groups for special controls may be dangerous to the controllees, but they are at least open to scrutiny by the public at large. This is especially true of aversive controls, the painful or threatening measures that society uses to bring deviants back into line; tyrants can be overthrown because their use of aversive controls makes them obvious, though formidable, targets. In the long run, the less noticeable and more general a control technique, the more successful it is likely to be. The totally controlled society would not require the controller to make a constant show of power. Rather, utopian writers from Plato through Skinner have described environments so controlled that deviant behavior has little chance to develop. What makes a utopia a pleasant place is that no one has to be punished because no one misbehaves. From the standpoint of traditional ethics, of course, a world in which no one has even the urge to misbehave is a world in which no one earns credit for good behavior.

Skinner's utopia, Walden Two, is based on a theory of operant conditioning, a concept which is difficult to express abstractly but which everyone raising a dog or a child practices every day. Skinner developed this concept in the 1930's to fill a serious gap in the learning theory proposed three decades earlier by the Russian physiologist Ivan Pavlov. According to Pavlovian (or classical) theory, learned behavior consists of conditioned reflexes; thus dogs, which salivate instinctively when they smell food, can be taught to salivate at some substitute stimulus (for example, a bell) that has been previously introduced while food was present. But people do not do things just by blind association; they have goals and purposes. Even much animal behavior seems goal oriented, like a mountain lion stalking its prey or a pet dog running in for supper. The challenge was to explain this goal-oriented, or operant, behavior in animals and human beings without making present actions contingent on future goals and without resorting to mental categories like feeling, wanting, and choosing. Skinner's solution was the principle that organisms tend to repeat behavior that is positively reinforced, with positive reinforcement meaning either a sensation of pleasure or the fulfillment of a basic biological need. If a dog hears a bell and comes running, give him food and he'll do it again; comfort a baby after he screams, and he'll be certain to scream for your attention later.

The long-term advantages of positive over aversive

THE CASE OF JULIA:
A STUDY IN SWITCHED-ON VIOLENCE

Between seizures Julia seemed pleasant enough, but suddenly, on at least 12 occasions, she had assaulted other persons without apparent cause. She was referred to Dr. Vernon Mark and his colleagues, who theorized that the trouble lay in epileptic disturbances of her amygdala, the "emotional thermostat of the brain." To prove their hypothesis, the neurosurgeons sought to induce a seizure artificially, using a stimoceiver, a remote-control device for sending and receiving electrical impulses. Before stimulation (left) Julia's face and brain waves both were normal, but shortly after stimulation (below) her expression and brain patterns grew simultaneously contorted. At bottom, jagged waves confirmed that Julia was in mid-seizure.

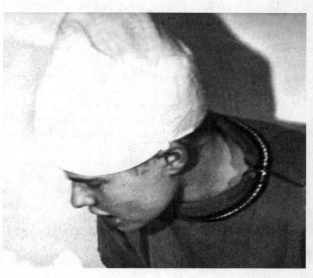

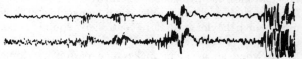

methods are obvious, according to Skinner. Under an aversive system, control over the individual can be increased only through increasingly coercive methods, which magnify suffering and make rebellion more likely. But to intensify control over an organism through positive reinforcement is merely to control more precisely the environmental contingencies under which an organism is positively reinforced. Using a "Skinner box"—a soundproof, airtight enclosure that enables the experimenter to control every environmental stimulus reaching the animal inside it—Skinner has taught pigeons to walk figure eights, make complex color discriminations, play Ping-Pong, and even guide missiles. "In the last 20 years," he remarked in 1968, "pigeons have done things no pigeons had ever done before. It isn't that the pigeons have been improved; the contingencies under which they live have been improved."

In *Science and Human Behavior* (1953), Skinner drew a parallel between operant theory and Darwin's theory of evolution: "Just as genetic characteristics which arise as mutations are selected or discarded by their consequences, so novel forms of behavior are selected or discarded through reinforcement." Substituting systematic controls for the randomness of nature yields the science of cultural design, and according to Skinner, the possibilities for cultural design are as endless as the powers of operant conditioning. Thus, Walden Two is a world in which all environmental contingencies are scientifically controlled in order to secure the greatest degree of personal happiness compatible with survival of the culture. This utopia is said by Skinner to offer "conditions which are described

roughly with such terms as freedom, security, happiness, and knowledge," values reflecting Skinner's own humanism rather closely. He does admit, though, that the same control techniques could produce a society in which all of these humanistic values were suppressed.

How you respond to Skinner's vision of the totally controlled society will likely depend on how seriously you value free choice. Skinner calls behavior control more dangerous than the atom bomb, not so much because a corrupt controller could inflict great pain—weapons for that are already widespread—but because a corrupt controller using positive controls could wipe out the will to resist. But suppose, as Skinner does, that a utopia could be designed in which no controller was corrupt and no controllee exploited: Would such a utopia be worth living in? Believers in freedom have traditionally answered that question by saying that people should not be treated like pigeons, even if they can be; that some free choice is possible; and that we should resist any techniques which foreclose it.

Ultimately, believers in freedom may be comforted by the knowledge that the behaviorist denial of freedom is only an assumption, not a fact. The strongest evidence for free will has always been the subjective experience of making a choice. Sometimes, we know, this experience can be a delusion. But laboratory evidence that human behavior can be controlled does not mean that all behavior is always controlled, any more than amputating one person's legs makes it impossible for everyone else to walk. Skinner maintains that since we are all totally controlled anyway, we might as well be controlled for the good. Those who think free will is more than a myth answer that knowledge of how much our behavior is already controlled requires action to preserve what freedom we have left. Just as it is tragic when an accident makes one person a cripple, so it would be tragic if behavior controllers made moral cripples of us all.

Suggestions for Further Reading

Breggin, Peter R. "The Return of Lobotomy and Psychosurgery." *Congressional Record*, vol. 118, no. 26 (February 24, 1972), pp. E1602–E1612.

Delgado, José M. R. *Physical Control of the Mind: Toward a Psychocivilized Society.* New York, Harper and Row, 1969.

London, Perry. *Behavior Control.* New York, Harper and Row, 1969.

Mark, Vernon G., and Frank R. Ervin. *Violence and the Brain.* New York, Harper and Row, 1970.

Skinner, B. F. *Beyond Freedom and Dignity.* New York, Alfred A. Knopf, 1971.

Skinner, B. F. *Walden Two.* New York, Macmillan, 1948. Paperback edition: Macmillan, 1962.

Ulrich, Roger, Thomas Stachnik, and John Mabry, eds. *Control of Human Behavior.* Glenview, Ill., Scott, Foresman and Company, 1966.

Young, Paul C. "Antisocial Uses of Hypnosis." *Experimental Hypnosis.* Edited by Leslie M. LeCron. New York, Citadel Press, 1965, pp. 376–409.

KEN HEYMAN

HOW DO YOU TRAIN PIGEONS to play Ping-Pong? By operant conditioning—each time a pigeon hits the ball into the opposite trough, food falls into its feedbox. For humans the rewards and behavior are much more complex, but Harvard's B. F. Skinner (above) maintains that such systems of reinforcement underlie all learning by people as well as pigeons.

A VISIT WITH B. F. SKINNER

Born in 1904 and raised in Susquehanna, Pa., Burrhus Frederic Skinner came to psychology after a broad liberal education. His career reflects an astounding variety of interests. He invented the teaching machine, the "Skinner box" for empirical research, and the Air-Crib, a mechanical baby-tender. His publications include technical treatises, popular texts, and a best-selling novel, Walden Two. As a psychologist he is the acknowledged leader of American behaviorism and one of the century's most influential theorists. The following are excerpts from an interview conducted at Harvard University, where he has been Edgar Pierce professor of psychology since 1958.

Q. Do you still favor a utopian approach to social reform?

A. There are two things you can do if you don't like our present way of life (revolution is a third, but after you have revolted you've got to do something). You can either walk away from society and start your own, which is the utopian model, or you can try to improve a way of life as it now exists. I still believe the utopian pattern should be tried, because we could learn a good deal about what people need in order to be happy, and it's hard to find that out with a piecemeal approach in the world at large.

Q. Would this require a rural setting like Walden Two's?

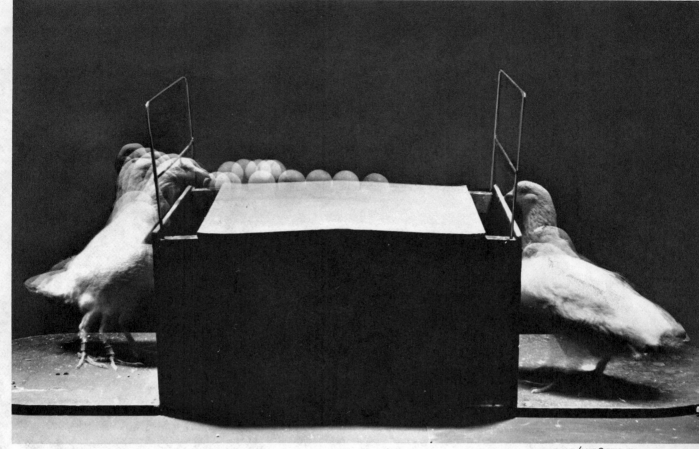

A. Yes, I think that our cities are almost past the point of no return. By making life in smaller communities as interesting as it is in large cities, we could solve all the problems that are now raised by the massive grouping of people in a small space.

Q. Some critics call this a nostalgia for small-town America and for nineteenth-century virtues.

A. It may be. We are all culture-bound. But we must do something about the quality of life. People who don't have to do anything will not, without help, do the kinds of things that develop them as individuals. Drugs, gambling, spectatorship—these may yield a happy life of a sort, but at the end a person won't be any different from when he started. Sex is a special kind of immediate reinforcer because it is concerned with the survival of the species rather than of the individual, and if you can prevent the undesirable consequences, I see nothing against it. But sex also doesn't develop the individual. A person who turns to the arts, crafts, sports, exploration, science, or literature, on the other hand, is constantly changing. He is a different person at the end of his life. But we need a culture to promote these activities. A culture that does so is a strong culture, whereas a culture that allows its people to live a life of pleasant stupefaction is not.

Q. Are you more concerned with the survival of a particular culture—our own—than with the survival of mankind?

A. No. I think in the long run mankind must be the object of cultural design. The major issues have become global, and our decisions must take the future of everyone into account. It's not a question of whether we can still grab more natural resources than anyone else, but whether there will be any resources left.

Q. Survival of the culture, in your terms, seems to require an enormous centralization of power. Couldn't this be called fascist?

A. The culture which makes it impossible for controlling power to be centralized would be a strong culture. What we have to look forward to is not a benevolent dictator but a culture in which no one can become a dictator. That would be a culture that would survive.

Encyclopedia articles indexed under psychiatry explore a wide range of behavior control devices, including drug therapy and psychosurgery. The article on HYPNOTISM describes one of the most potent ways to short-circuit another person's awareness; RHETORIC analyzes how behavior can be controlled through words alone. Essential background information on the discoveries which made contemporary control techniques possible is indexed under brain and psychology. Two founders of modern learning theory are profiled under IVAN PAVLOV and JOHN WATSON; the article LEARNING chronicles the work of their leading disciples and critics. Analyses of the psychological and ethical implications of behavior control can be found in the articles BEHAVIORISM, DETERMINISM, and WILL.

The New Photography

The boundaries of the art of photography have been extended far beyond their original scope. When the camera was a new tool, its accuracy in copying reality helped to drive painters away from representation to ever greater degrees of abstraction—the creation of new realities. Today the art of photography is following a similar path. The camera is becoming not the slave of nature but the photographer's means of personal expression. Because the technical possibilities and the subjects are infinite, each photographer can develop a style as individualistic as a painter's, ranging from almost traditional representations of reality to visions of private hell.

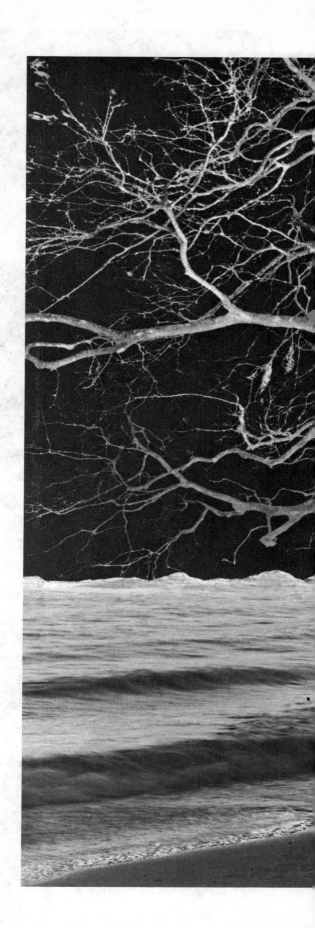

JERRY N. UELSMANN

84

Portrait

At one time the skillful portrait photographer was a careful flatterer whose magic caused warts and blemishes to disappear. The human face, however, can be used in many ways: as a seemingly inanimate object (left), as a study in light and mood (right), or as the center point in a composition (below). The result can express personality and mood as incisively as a painting.

CHARLES GATEWOOD

JACK WELPOTT

Photo Synthesis

Today's photographers no longer feel bound by the two-dimensional flatness of their craft. Instead, a time exposure can free the continuous motion of sports from the constraints of the static news photo or snapshot (above). Or photography and sculpture may be combined in a construction that reveals the inner and outer person (right).

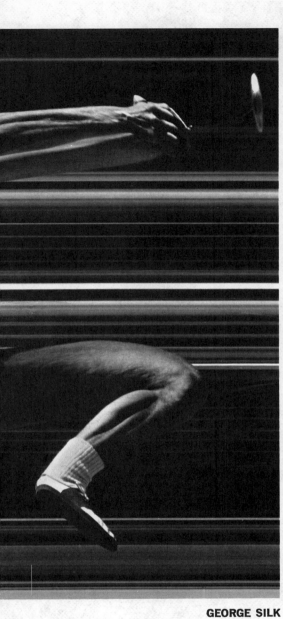

GEORGE SILK

DALE QUARTERMAN

ARTHUR TRESS

Patterns

The creative photographer is always searching for new ways to reshape what is seen by the jaded eye into suggestive arrangements of form and motion. By projecting the acrobatic silhouettes of children at play against the ominous regularity of a playground fence, or the rounded windows of a moving city bus against rigid rows of rectangular office windows, or a free-flowing dance of reflections against a placid watery surface, he abstracts new levels of meaning from everyday experience.

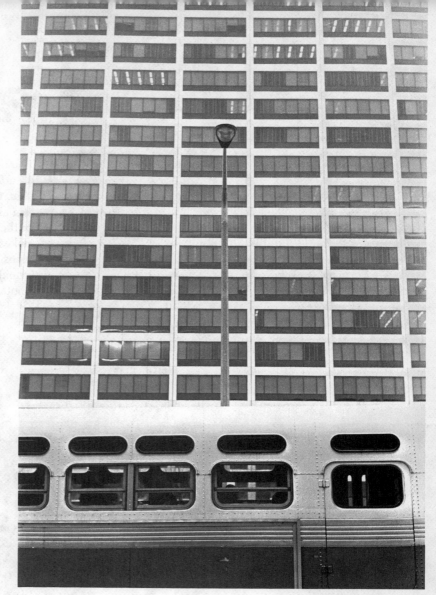

CHARLES HARBUTT

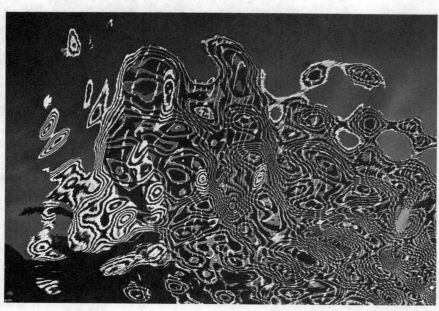

ANTHONY MAINE

89

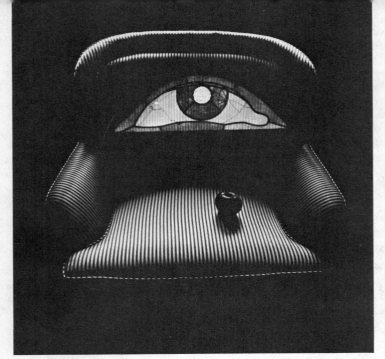

Fantasy

The camera and darkroom can produce dreams, visions, and nightmares—the sense of an object, a place, or a mood captured on film as it was felt by the photographer. In the best of this work, which frequently makes use of double negatives and double exposures, a kind of surrealistic eeriness is achieved that defies analysis and suggests emotions untranslatable into words.

JERRY N. UELSMANN

JON ELLIS STEVENS

PETER ROTH

HOMOSEXUALITY

Arno Karlen

ILLUSTRATIONS BY JACK MARTIN

Less than a century ago, Oscar Wilde shocked a court where he was being tried for homosexuality by defending "the love that dared not speak its name." Even a decade ago, the subject of homosexuality was still nearly taboo. But recently someone quipped that today the love that dared not speak refuses to shut up.

The 1960's brought a wave of sex-revolution rhetoric and a new public frankness. Stage, screen, television, and the press began showing homosexuality in various ways— as a problem, a way of life, or a personal right. Several states have legalized homosexual acts between consenting adults; more will follow. Many newspapers have run neutral or sympathetic articles on militant homosexuals' fights for equal employment and civil rights. In some big-city neighborhoods, it seems that the world's a stage and all the players gay—significantly, that homosexual ingroup word is now known to society at large.

To some this seems a reenactment of the fall of Rome, to others a long-due liberation. Opinion polls suggest that the majority of people are ambivalent; they think homosexuality is a disorder or a mere difference rather than a vice or a crime, yet they want it limited, even penalized. And despite the new air of sexual enlightenment, they have more questions than answers. What causes homosexuality? How common is it in women and men? Is there a homosexual impulse in us all? Do homosexuals seduce the young and favor each other at work? Can and should they be treated?

In fact, many people aren't even sure what homosexuality is. They lump it together with other dysfunctions of sex and gender—hermaphroditism, transsexualism, and transvestism. Hermaphrodites are people whose genes, hormones, or prenatal development gave them some physical traits of each sex. Most hermaphrodites are predomi-

nantly male or female, and heterosexual; many can be treated with surgery or hormones. Transsexuals are physically normal but believe they are victims of a mistake of nature and "really" belong to the other sex. These are the people who seek sex-change surgery. Transvestites get sexual and emotional pleasure from masquerading as the opposite sex. Most are men, and some researchers estimate that about two-thirds are homosexual. Some are heterosexual and married, but many of these are sexually inactive or are potent only if dressed as women.

Far commoner than all of these together are homosexuals—men and women emotionally and sexually drawn to their own sex. Very few are hermaphrodites, transsexuals, or transvestites. Few of the men are effeminate, few of the women mannish. Exhibitionists who act contrary to their sex roles are, of course, the most noticeable homosexuals, but they are a minority of perhaps 10–15 percent. Most homosexuals are secret homosexuals, unremarkably male or female, masculine or feminine. More are men than women in the United States and probably in other societies around the world.

How many homosexuals are there? Alfred Kinsey, in his monumental studies of human sexual behavior, found that 4–6 percent of males in the United States and 2–3 percent of females are mostly or exclusively homosexual during their adult lives. More surprising was the fact that one male in three and one female in eight have at least one homosexual experience. Perhaps most surprising was the discovery that one man in six and half as many women have at least as much homosexual as heterosexual experience for three years or more of their lives.

In some societies a person can perform many homosexual acts without being labeled a homosexual; in certain Marquesan islands, for instance, the majority of men have had homosexual experience. Even in American society, some people wink at sporadic homosexuality, especially among adolescents and among people deprived of heterosexual partners, as in prisons. On the other hand, some people give the label for only one homosexual act or even for not seeming conventionally manly or feminine enough. To the best of our knowledge, the adult who prefers homosexual partners and rejects the roles of spouse and parent is deviant everywhere in the world. Nowhere do parents say, "It's all the same to me whether my child is gay or straight." Homosexuality—adult preferential homosexuality—is apparently a universal deviance (even in ancient Greece, despite myths to the contrary). How societies differ is in what one must do to be labeled homosexual (one sex act or years' worth) and in how they sanction it (from burning at the stake in medieval Europe to relatively mild mockery among the Navaho Indians). American society stands at about the middle of the continuum and is moving toward increased tolerance of most forms of homosexual activity.

Why do some people prefer homosexual relationships? The traditional explanation has been that homosexuals are born different. Some people find the very idea of homosexuality so alien and mystifying that they think only a peculiar, inborn mechanism can explain it. It is their way of saying, "No one like me could feel or act that way." Many homosexuals also have an emotional stake in the view that they are born, not made. If homosexuals are made, perhaps they can be unmade. To some homosexuals that possibility seems an accusation or an emotional threat.

For a century scientists have kept reporting something special discovered in the genes, hormones, brains, or physiques of homosexuals. Not one claim has withstood further tests and criticism. At the turn of this century, some doctors solemnly said most homosexuals are left-handed and whistle poorly. After that fantasy was disproved, others rose and fell in turn. In 1971 researchers reported a hormone imbalance in some homosexuals' urine. Despite some hasty journalism on the subject, the results are still tentative and inconsistent. The researchers themselves warn against calling hormones the cause of homosexuality.

The major drift of recent research has been to stop seeking one or even several direct physical roots of homosexuality. Science now speaks of interplay between constitution and environment. Genes, hormones, and other physical factors may predispose some people to problems in sexual development, with many possible results. Homosexuality, then, arises from family and social forces acting on a more or less vulnerable constitution, and if either factor deserves emphasis, it is probably environment. The idea that homosexuality is an instinctive drive latent within us all stands dis-

credited among all but the most traditional psycho-analysts. Rather, we are all latent heterosexuals.

Our first learning, or mislearning, happens at home. Studies of many homosexuals' families reveal an anti-heterosexual atmosphere. The parents made sex seem dirty, dangerous, or evil—sometimes only tacitly, by shrouding it in silence and anxiety. Some homosexuals, like shrewdly disobedient children, carry out only the letter of the law: "They said never do anything nasty with the opposite sex, but they never mentioned my own!"

Popular lore emphasizes the mother's role in homosexuality. It says the prehomosexual boy is a sissy tied to her apron strings, the prehomosexual girl a tomboy. This is often true, but not all sissies and tomboys become homosexual, and prehomosexual development patterns are more complex. Many homosexuals' mothers are domineering, openly or with a quiet iron hand. They may be harsh or competitive with daughters, who are afraid to bloom sexually. Many are seductive or overintimate with their sons, who remain bound to the mothers by guilt and dependence.

Recent research puts equal emphasis on the father. In most families, each parent compensates for the other's shortcomings. Many homosexuals' fathers abdicated in the face of the mothers' mistakes or were actively destructive—distant, downgrading or even abusive to their sons, scornful or seductive with daughters.

Psychiatrist Irving Bieber, after an exhaustive study of the family backgrounds of male homosexuals, concluded that "a constructive, supportive, warmly related father precludes the possibility of a homosexual son; he acts as a neutralizing protective agent should the mother make seductive or close-binding attempts." In interviewing hundreds of homosexuals, both male and female, of very different backgrounds and lifestyles, I saw Bieber's conclusion illustrated again and again. Talk about parents centered on the mother and left out the father entirely, or the father was described as negative and cold. One male homosexual said, "My father and I haven't spoken since my psychiatrist told him I'm homosexual. The doctor said to him that he was partly responsible, because he didn't play with me when I was a boy, and he was absent from home. Now we can't bear to be in the same room with each other. When we have to be together, we patronize each other." This is actually one of the less virulent descriptions. Some lesbians at first describe their fathers as charming, as great buddies, or even as idols. But as they talk on and details emerge, one often realizes that this is the hungry wishful thinking of a child who magnified every scrap of warmth she saw in a distant parent.

So it takes two parents to teach homosexuality, and even more. A good or poor relationship with a brother or sister, uncle or aunt, or some other relative may help make up for parental deficits or tip the balance toward homosexuality or other psychosexual problems.

Later in childhood, forces outside the family become increasingly important. Many homosexuals were loners in childhood and adolescence; they had few warm, easy relationships, sexual or nonsexual, with other kids. Extensive homosexual experience may have an effect on adult sexuality. So does feeling attractive and successful in life as a teen-ager or as a young husband or wife. Many homosexuals emerge as such early in life, but some do not "come out" until their 20's or even their 30's. The last straw to a vulnerable person may be a shattering love relationship, a bitter divorce, or strong family and career stresses.

Homosexual experience at such times may become a permanent pattern or merely be an interlude in a predominantly heterosexual life. A 35-year-old married woman told me this incident, a not uncommon one: "When I was 18, I fell in love with a guy and gave him my virginity. The next day he deserted me for another girl. I thought I'd die. A lesbian was living in my dormitory, and she seduced me by comforting me and taking charge of my life when I felt so lonely and demoralized. I put up with the sexual part until she began pushing me to reciprocate. Anyway, by then I was starting to feel more confident and go out with boys again. So I broke off with her. That has been my only lesbian experience." For some women, the return to heterosexuality does not happen.

Kinsey showed that our sexuality is also shaped by economic, educational, religious, and ethnic background. For instance, he found homosexuality quite rare among Orthodox Jews and more common in the lower middle class than among the poor or the well-to-do; his work also hints at differences among ethnic subcultures. These and many other such facts are still unexplained and need more research, but they show how many dimly understood social forces add to family influences in shaping sex behavior and attitudes.

Society not only shapes sexual behavior but reacts to it, and the reaction to sexual deviance is now argued about by scientists as never before. The new "sociology of deviance" says that disturbed majorities label people and thus make them a "problem." Only white bigotry, they say, creates of blackness a "Negro problem"; and in the same way, only fearful or angry heterosexuals create a "homosexual problem." Carefully avoiding all judgments of sex behavior, some scientists conclude that if homosexuals are unhappy or emotionally disturbed, it's only because they are labeled and persecuted.

Although some scientists take relativism to extremes in trying to "normalize" homosexuals, they are perform-

Arno Karlen is associate professor of English at Pennsylvania State University. He is the author of Sexuality and Homosexuality: A New View, *the result of five years of study and interviews.*

ing a social and a scientific service—making society realize that it is more accurate and humane to think of homosexuals as people first and as homosexuals second. They balance those scientists who contemptuously write off all homosexuals as "sick" in a tone that implies sin or inferiority.

Advocates of both these polarized views speak loudly through the mass media. The moderate and increasingly common judgment is that homosexuality is neither an illness nor a neutral "alternative behavior," but a dysfunction. The difference in words reflects a difference in viewpoint, and to grasp it one must take a look at recent psychodynamic studies dealing with homosexuality.

At the turn of this century, Freud introduced several revolutionary ideas. He stopped labeling emotions good and evil and began considering them medically. He showed that the magical feelings and irrational thought-processes of childhood survive in our unconscious minds, guiding adult behavior. And he said that behind much nonsexual behavior, sexual motives lie hidden.

Since then, psychiatry has logically extended that last idea: behind much sexual behavior lie nonsexual motives. To some people, sex is more an act of conquest and power than of pleasure or love. Others need affection and security far more than sex; they see sex mostly as a price for being loved and cared for. Such feelings appear in most of us sometimes, but they are exaggerated in many disturbed heterosexuals and in many homosexuals.

For instance, a girl with a cold, puritanical mother may bear through life a terrible thirst for maternal warmth and care. She may become a passive, little-girlish lesbian; a strong, protective woman gives her substitute mother-love as no man can, without rousing old terrors of heterosexual "sin." One lesbian said to me in an interview, "I was married for just a few months in my early 20's and had a child. I leave him with my parents and go out to the gay bars. It's as if I'm the baby. Maybe that's why I can't stand to have my breasts touched in bed—it's like me having to be the mother instead of the baby. Maybe that's why I can't bring myself to break up with a lover, no matter how much we fight or how much she abuses me, even beats me up. I need someone to take care of me." Another young lesbian said bluntly, "I'm looking for a mother, and no matter how perfect my homosexual affairs are, it won't work. You only have one mother. You can't get another one afterward."

Or, for instance, an aggressive male homosexual may equate sex with masculine power; he feels that by "mastering" other men in bed, he exercises the assertive strength that was squelched by his controlling mother, his detached father, his competitive brothers, and his rougher playmates. Psychiatrist Lionel Ovesey, who has done important new work in the emotional dynamics of homosexuality, related to me a good example of the behavior such feelings may lead to. "I had a patient whose behavior was bisexual, a muscle-man who worked out with weights and went out with both men and women. If he made a pass at a girl, and she turned him down, he felt unmanly. So he went to a bar and picked up a male homosexual who would submit to him passively. This made him feel more manly, because he felt he had made a woman out of his partner."

A homosexual who is unable to believe in his ability to subjugate another man may take the passive role and, in an unconscious, irrational way, feel that he has received a sort of transfusion of masculinity. Even the passive role, then, may be a roundabout way of restoring a sense of masculine competence.

Narcissism, or self-love, may be important in homosexuality. Some homosexuals become adoringly protective toward people who remind them of themselves in adolescence, and they lavish on these alter egos the love they craved as youngsters.

Other elements may be involved; studies of animal behavior suggest that misrouted aggression and appeasement are often acted out homosexually, especially where there has been a background of exaggerated power and dependence needs. It is such motives of power and dependence translated into homosexual metaphors ("I was shafted"; "I shafted him") that account for many sporadic homosexual thoughts, dreams, and even acts in people who are predominantly heterosexual.

All this analysis of the motives for homosexuality finally means one thing: to a woman, homosexuality may be the best way she knows to feel lovable and secure; to a male, a roundabout means of salvaging his masculine self-love, of feeling like a man among men. Seen this way, homosexuality ceases to be puzzling or alien. For someone who finds heterosexuality repugnant or fearsome, homosexuality is a way of reaching what we all seek—to be lovable, secure, and strong.

Here lies the conflict in science today. Some say that the things that made a person reject heterosexuality—in many cases exaggerated narcissism, strong power and dependence needs, aggression and passivity problems—are bound to take a toll in friendships, at work, and in the rest of life. They say that homosexuality, like any neurotic, substitutive solution, creates as many problems as it solves, without truly satisfying the needs that created it. The opposing argument is that some people are homosexual because of conditioning or some other nonconflictural process. Or even if the cause was conflict, a homosexual may go on to keep his homosexuality encapsulated in a generally healthy, rewarding life.

Actually, the argument about whether homosexuality is a sickness presents false, oversimplified choices. Homosexuality is not functional biologically or socially, but one dysfunction doesn't make a person sick in even

the simplest physical sense. Is an athlete with astigmatism sick? If physical health is difficult to define, emotional health is doubly so. Let us say that emotional health is a compound of many abilities—to make love; make friends; be joyful, assertive, and creative; live under stress; avoid self-destructive acts; not shrink from life's possibilities. Most of us have some kind and degree of dysfunction yet on balance may be healthy—despite a tendency to overquick temper or depression, despite chronic mild underachievement or strong sense of competitiveness. Why not despite sexual dysfunction?

Whether an individual homosexual is sick can only be measured by how well he copes with life. There are signs, however, of special problems and unhappiness among homosexuals as a group. My own study and interviewing convince me that a small proportion of homosexuals are as flexible, happy, and productive as most of their heterosexual peers; in fact, a very few seem to rank rather high in overall adaptation to life. I am equally convinced that many more homosexuals than heterosexuals fall on the middle-to-low range of the scale and that they would be healthier without their homosexuality. Often it seems entwined with other dysfunctions. For each happy, productive homosexual I have spoken to, I have met many more who suffer deeply, and not just because of social pressures. I find that most homosexuals believe this is true. For every militant homosexual who proclaims that "gay is good," many more mournfully agree with the bitter line in the play *The Boys in the Band*, "Show me a happy homosexual and I'll show you a gay corpse." I have asked many homosexuals whether they would want their children, if they had any, to be homosexual. A very few said "yes." Some said a parent should accept a child no matter what his or her sexual preference; their parents had rejected them. The vast majority said "no" with varying degrees of sadness or dismay at the idea. One young homosexual said grimly that in gay bars he would often have "my two o'clock depression. I see where I am, and I ask, 'What am I doing here?'"

The gay bar is a social club where homosexuals can drop their masks; some are relaxed, even homey. Others, however, are tense sexual marketplaces, "meat racks" that put a terrific premium on youthful good looks. Men over 30 frequently must pay for sex with the male prostitutes who frequent bars, parks,

and cruising grounds. Lesbian bars are far fewer, but no more truly gay; there, as in men's gay bars, one hears many tales of mercurial, brief love affairs, depression, alcoholism, drug abuse, violence, and suicide.

This gay world contains only some homosexuals, and only for a certain period in their lives. After a person comes out, he may plunge energetically into this scene, learning its language, lore, and ideology. He confirms his new homosexual identity by "camping"—commonly called effeminacy, but really a combination of feminine parody and the obverse of stereotyped masculine behavior. The majority of homosexuals are not compelled to camp; they can turn much of it on and off, depending on the social surroundings. Significantly, masculine and feminine sexual patterns are in many ways quite normal despite such displays. Male homosexuals tend to have more sex partners and boast about it; to engage in more one-night stands; to emphasize sex more than love. Most lesbians have fewer partners, fewer brief sex encounters; their love affairs are longer, more domestic; they tend to denigrate promiscuous lesbians and to value love above sex.

Many homosexuals never join the gay world at all. Some live in towns too small (less than about 50,000) to have gay bars. Others are repelled by the predatory "meat rack," its hysterical air and exaggerated role-playing. Many are shy, inhibited; they live in shame and isolation that deepen through their youth and early adulthood. They lie more and more to family, friends, and neighbors; perhaps keep a public front

of "straight" (heterosexual) dates; laugh loudly at jokes that mock them. Their jobs probably demand that they be "closet queens," revealing that they're gay only to trusted gay friends. Gay liberationists find deep satisfaction in "coming out of the closet," abandoning double lives full of fear and paranoia. Many more homosexuals do not.

Some professions have high proportions of homosexuals, but they employ only a small fraction of the gay. Homosexuals live and work in every milieu: they are bartenders, doctors, waiters, policemen, judges, bums, salesmen, and teachers.

Sometimes homosexuals form self-serving professional cliques, but most homosexuals are a secret minority of one at their jobs. They try to keep their sexuality completely hidden from co-workers and bosses. They fear being seen by them in the company of other homosexuals even on evenings or weekends. In gay bars it is a serious breach of etiquette to ask pickups and new acquaintances their last names or where they work; the risk of revelation or blackmail is always there. Many homosexuals have told me something like this: "If I had to choose between hiring someone straight and someone gay, I'd hire the straight. Suppose the gay one camped, tried to make friends with me, got angry at me for some reason? He'd reveal that I'm gay, too."

A small number of homosexuals marry, sustain minimal sex in wedlock, raise children, and have secret gay lives. For more, marriage is a desperate attempt to "straighten out"—usually a brief and dismal one. Married homosexuals should be distinguished from heterosexuals who occasionally perform homosexual acts.

Middle age comes to the straight in their 40's, to the gay a decade earlier. When they no longer can or wish to compete in the gay life, they try harder to achieve long, secure relationships, which many of them consider "marriages." Since only a minority of homosexuals play a supermale or feminine role socially or in bed, homosexual mates aren't often clearly polarized in "husband" and "wife" roles. Lesbian "marriages" are likely to last longer than gay men's, but very many male and female gay mateships eventually dissolve, leaving the ex-partners in lonely middle

age and having to struggle harder for new partners than do comparable heterosexuals. Many young homosexuals are haunted by visions of growing old without lover or family, self-consciously haunting the gay places and getting sex only by paying for it.

Of course most of the gay, like the straight, do survive aging, the end of love, problems, dysfunctions. Although young homosexuals may doubt it, many older homosexuals learn to live somewhat contentedly (or at least resignedly) with the facts of their lives. Still, so many homosexuals of all ages feel outcast, lonely, secretive, and prey to disgrace, arrest, and blackmail that most eventually ponder the question of treatment and change.

Most ponder but reject it. They may think homosexuality is inborn. They may hear friends speak of fruitless or bitter experiences with psychotherapy or of being told to adjust to homosexuality. They do not meet former homosexuals, the small but significant number who have changed.

In the past, psychotherapy helped few homosexuals change. Some very traditional psychoanalysts still consider homosexuality an instinct and deny change is possible; perhaps some don't want to believe other therapists succeed where they fail. But in the past few decades more and more therapists say that among homosexuals who undergo treatment, one in three becomes heterosexual, another moves part way toward heterosexuality, and the third is likely to live more happily while continuing to be homosexual.

High change rates are also reported by some behavior therapists, who "recondition" patients with electric shock, nausea-inducing drugs, and similar methods. Their evidence, though, is incomplete, and volunteers for such strenuous treatment are probably tremendously motivated—the prime precondition for change in any kind of therapy. Interestingly, many psychiatrists and psychologists who report change through psychotherapy do not urge change; they merely help the patient try if he decides he wants to. Many homosexuals enter treatment because of depression, anxiety, troubled love lives, or vocational problems and opt for change after improvement in nonsexual areas.

The strongest opposition to psychiatric treatment and

change comes from gay liberationists, who hold the view that homosexuality should no more be the subject of therapy than heterosexuality. Certainly change should be forced on no one. But many homosexuals, if given a choice, would rather be heterosexual. Change is most likely for those under 35 who have had at least a little history of heterosexual experience or desire and who have not been immersed too long or too deeply in the gay world.

Treatment, whether for change or for a happier homosexual life, is long and expensive. Since therapy, like physical medicine, is as much an art as a science, its success may depend a great deal on each practitioner's personality and skill. In addition, many homosexuals' behavior patterns were set so strongly so early in their lives that change is impossible, given current therapeutic knowledge. Other homosexuals will not seek change for personal reasons; change seems to offer only the threatening loss of their present identities. Since homosexuality will not disappear, gay liberationists properly ask how homosexuals should live in society and how society should live with them.

More and more people consider sexual behavior between consenting adults a matter of private conscience. In a pluralistic society, legislating morality is dangerous, even tyrannical. Since homosexuality is neither contagious nor prevented by law, there seems no reason to make consenting adult homosexual acts illegal. The majority of physicians and lawyers have urged the repeal of antihomosexual laws for years. In the 1960's such laws were repealed in Great Britain and, in the United States, in the state of Illinois. Several other states have recently followed suit, and more will probably do so soon.

The repeals have roused some vague fears of unlocking a dangerous floodgate. Demands to liberalize all sex-control laws—those governing divorce, abortion, and extramarital sex as well as homosexuality—seem to many a threat that mankind is reverting to all fours. But despite all the talk of sexual revolution, recent research reveals only slow evolution. Family and sex-role patterns are changing somewhat, but they are far from revolutionized.

Furthermore, Kinsey's research demonstrated that the proportion of homosexuals in the United States hadn't changed between the 1890's and the 1950's. Recent studies reveal no increase since Kinsey closed his ledgers. Despite a sexual revolution in the 1920's and evolution in the 1960's, despite greater public frankness and changing sex roles, homosexuality has remained limited to about 5 percent of the American population as a way of life and to 10–15 percent as a major life experience. And reliable research suggests that homosexuals are no more likely than heterosexuals to seduce the young.

Homosexuals have always paid a price, great or small, for their proclivity. Today, they are still liable to blackmail, still liable to be sent to jail. And even where they cannot be jailed—in some U.S. states and in those European nations where homosexuality has been legal for more than a century—police still sporadically harass the gay on various pretexts. Most homosexuals still fear exposure before family, friends, employers, and society at large. They are still subject to scorn, prejudice, and ruin.

The Victorians pretended sex didn't exist; our new sexual utopianism pretends sexual limits don't exist. Neither ideal is likely to come true: neither sex nor the need to protect the child-rearing family can be wished away. Our problem is reaching a balance of freedom and restraints that helps society yet demands the smallest human price. During the 1970's, calls for reformed laws and changed attitudes will continue. Some of the loudest voices, for and against, will be those of extremists. Fortunately, research will continue—on the physiology and psychology of sex, on personality development, and on homosexual and heterosexual life-styles. Perhaps by the time society is ready to profoundly consider the question of social controls of sex behavior, it can do so armed with more knowledge and understanding rather than with passion and prejudice.

Suggestions for Further Reading

BEACH, FRANK, ed. *Sex and Behavior.* New York, John Wiley and Sons, 1965. A collection of scientific papers, some quite technical, on the broad, complex problems of sexuality.

CROWLEY, MART. *The Boys in the Band.* New York, Farrar, Straus, and Giroux, 1968. A portrait of the gay world at its worst. Not representative of all homosexual life-styles, but relentlessly accurate about the one it does describe.

HATTERER, LAWRENCE. *Changing Homosexuality in the Male.* New York, McGraw-Hill, 1970. A lengthy work by a psychiatrist, containing interesting tape recordings of the lives and treatment of homosexuals.

KARLEN, ARNO. *Sexuality and Homosexuality: A New View.* New York, W. W. Norton, 1971. A comprehensive volume, providing historical, biological, and social science perspectives and including interviews with homosexuals and researchers.

KINSEY, ALFRED, WARDELL POMEROY, and CLYDE MARTIN. *Sexual Behavior in the Human Male.* Philadelphia, W. B. Saunders, 1948.

KINSEY, ALFRED, et al. *Sexual Behavior in the Human Female.* Philadelphia, W. B. Saunders, 1953. Both volumes by Kinsey and his associates are basic to the scientific study of human sexuality.

RUITENBEEK, HENDRIK, ed. *The Problem of Homosexuality in Modern Society.* New York, E. P. Dutton, 1963. A good sampling of important scientific essays on many aspects of homosexuality.

STORR, ANTHONY. *Sexual Deviation.* Baltimore, Penguin Books, 1964. A good brief explanation from a modern psychiatric viewpoint.

The Open Classroom

Bob Famighetti

A new approach to educating young children is now being tried in hundreds of American classrooms in which the children not only don't have to sit down all day but have no seats; not only don't have to be quiet but are encouraged to talk with each other; not only don't have to pay attention to the teacher's lessons but are given no lessons to pay attention to.

This type of schooling—variously called the open classroom, the free day, open education, or informal education—has been gradually evolving in the British infant schools (for children from five to seven) over the past 40 years. It is now being increasingly advocated by American educators who believe traditional schools fail to impart lasting knowledge and also dis-

Bob Famighetti, a staff editor, is a former elementary school teacher. In preparing this article, he observed open classrooms in schools, both public and private, serving children from all socioeconomic backgrounds.

courage creativity, independent thinking, and self-motivation. And the new approach is being increasingly used. In rural schools in North Dakota, ghetto schools in New York City, and middle-class schools in the suburbs, thousands of children in the early elementary school grades are being educated in open classrooms.

Open education is based on four broad premises about young children and how they learn. These premises are essentially the following: First, learning depends on motivation. What a child wants to learn, he can learn quickly; what he is forced to know, he will not long remember, even if he memorizes it for a test. Second, children are curious about and want to understand the world around them; they come to school with questions which are important to them and which can form the basis for learning. Third, children of primary school age are capable of understanding only those abstract concepts they derive themselves through experience with concrete objects; abstractions

which are told to them will be meaningless. Fourth, different children internalize concepts in different ways and at different speeds.

These four basic premises are a synthesis of the theories of many educators and philosophers, but they probably borrow most heavily from the ideas of the Swiss psychologist Jean Piaget. Piaget has spent more than 30 years studying children's learning processes. He has concluded that the intellectual development of children is a continual process in which the child, who is innately curious, plays an active role by manipulating the objects in his environment and by constantly integrating the information from each new experience with what he already knows.

Piaget has identified four stages of development which he says all children go through in the same order, although not in exactly the same way or at exactly the same age. Extremely young children (about age three or four) tend to have purely mystical or supernatural explanations of events—for example, that wind is caused by God blowing on the world. Slightly older children will generalize from experience as well as resort to supernatural causes, but they can only add experiences together rather than analyze and evaluate them. Thus, a child of five who knows wind occurs outdoors and who feels "wind" when someone claps hands will probably say that hands create wind and also that they somehow call in the wind from outdoors. By the age of about seven (stage three), the child can synthesize experiences to form generalizations, and he will probably be able to conclude, for example, that wind outdoors and the "wind" resulting from clapping hands are both caused by the movement of air. Most children in the early elementary school grades are in this third stage, which Piaget has called the stage of concrete operations. Only at a much later age (about 12 or 13) can a child reason abstractly and reach logical conclusions not based on extensive concrete experience.

Educators who accept Piaget's ideas and the other premises underlying open education see traditional classroom methods as failing because they depend on children putting aside their own questions about the world and trying to learn instead a teacher-determined (and therefore, in the children's view, an arbitrary)

curriculum in an unnatural way—by sitting still and listening to the teacher's verbal abstractions, which the children may not be ready to understand. Thus, Charles Silberman maintained in *Crisis in the Classroom*—a summary of his three-year study of American education, funded by the Carnegie Corporation—that schools were creating their own discipline problems and academic failures by having unrealistic expectations about children's performance and therefore were adversely affecting not only students' eventual employability but their self-esteem and self-confidence as well.

Some critics of traditional American education, including Silberman, argue further that schooling has adverse effects even on those children who apparently succeed in the sense of learning to read and scoring high on standardized tests. They see as a major evil the system of punishments and rewards which exists in most schools. Even if a student has no interest in the subject being taught, he may pay attention and learn (the critics would say memorize) in order to avoid the punishments (whether a verbal reprimand or a note home) and to gain the rewards (whether a gold star, a good report card, or verbal approval from adults). Since the rewards and punishments are based on results, the children acquire a what-is-the-right-answer rather than a why-is-this-so orientation, or as educa-

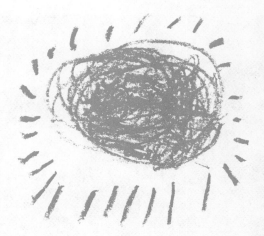

tional reformer John Holt phrased it, they become "producers" rather than "thinkers." In addition, since the rewards flow from mastering what the teacher says is important, the children come to feel that their own questions have no place in school and are somehow less significant.

But if the theory underlying open education is correct, lasting knowledge must spring from the natural curiosity of children. How is this natural curiosity made the basis for academic learning? In other words, how exactly is an open classroom set up, and what exactly do the teacher and the children do? These questions can be answered by some generalizations about open classroom layouts and practices. But the informal approach to education is not a specific formula; its success depends not only on the classroom's physical setting but also on the teacher's ability to be sensitive and responsive to a child and his special needs.

One of the most important duties of the teacher in implementing informal education is to set up an environment which offers the most opportunities for learning—that is, to set up a classroom with a diversity of gadgets and materials for the children to

manipulate. Having done this, the teacher must then give the children freedom to choose their own activities based on their own interests. What this means in practice is that at any given moment during the day there will probably be several children doing something independently, a number working in groups of twos or threes, and a few moving around the room. And there will almost certainly be a lot of noise, which is usually welcomed because the teachers believe children can learn a great deal from talking with each other. This belief has also led many British schools and a growing number of American ones to institute "family grouping," the mixing of children of different ages in the same class, so that the older can help the younger, at the same time reinforcing their own learning by having to express ideas coherently to someone else.

While the children are pursuing their own interests, the teacher is moving from child to child or group to

JONATHAN KING/
EDUCATIONAL FACILITIES LAB

HOW MANY SPOTS DID THAT CARD HAVE?

If you want a child to be able to conceptualize and add numbers, you can teach him to play cards, something he will want to do anyway. A child may quickly learn what "four" is by looking at a four of spades, and he will want to learn to add ten and 11 if he wants to win at blackjack.

group, observing progress, providing individual instruction relevant to a child's activity, asking leading questions, and generally giving the children praise and encouragement for their work. The teacher will seldom try to teach a lesson to the whole class at one time.

Physically, an open classroom looks much different from a traditional one. The walls are covered with the children's original work—drawings, stories, charts. Floor space is not taken up by desks and seats but is instead divided into interest areas. A typical informal classroom might have a library and reading corner; areas for mathematics, art, and science; a playhouse; and a corner containing a cabinet or cubby for each child, so that even though he has no assigned desk, he can feel there is a space all his own for his coat, lunch, books, or toys.

The reading corner will probably have single copies of a number of library books rather than a series of a single reading text. Stories and reports written by the children are included in the library. A piece of rug in front of the bookshelves and a couch or easy chair are often provided, so that the children may read comfortably.

A large number of different materials, many of them common household items or "junk" objects, are usually available in the mathematics area. Bottle caps, nails, and buttons are often used for counting (for example, I saw a first-grade child do a subtraction problem by counting out a number of nails equal to the larger number in the problem, then counting out and taking away the number being subtracted, and then counting out the number of nails left to get the answer). Scales and balance mechanisms are also usually available, and by weighing and comparing the junk objects, the children can come to understand what "heavier" and "lighter" really mean or grasp the concept that weight is not dependent on size. The mathematics area will probably also contain commercially produced materials, such as Cuisenaire rods. (A Cuisenaire set consists of ten wooden rods, each a different color and length. If the smallest rod is considered one unit long, then the others are two to ten units long. Using the rods can help a child develop understanding of the relationships between numbers—for example, by his seeing that a two-rod and a three-rod laid end to end are as long as a five-rod.) Mathematical games are used more frequently in American than in British schools.

Cooking is an activity common to many open classrooms. In preparing a recipe, the children work with fractions and quantity equivalences and also get practice in reading.

The science area of an open classroom might contain such objects as magnets, microscopes, and batteries and wires; in one class I observed, a microscope was used to examine a cockroach killed in the classroom. Most classes also have numerous plants and pet animals which the children must take care of. Ideally this "science" work leads to "math" work, such as graphing changes in a pet's weight or a plant's height.

Many open classroom teachers see science as more than a set of principles or facts. As Professor Lillian Weber of the City College of New York pointed out in *The English Infant School and Informal Education*, British teachers feel science is being learned all day, because the children's process of asking questions and testing hypotheses about objects in their environment is the essence of the scientific method.

Art—original work by the children on topics of their own choosing and in a variety of media—is considered by many open classroom teachers to be a very important activity. Teachers who believe school should be concerned with the development of the whole child, not with the single ability to memorize specific facts, see art as a vehicle through which children can express themselves and be creative. Since the art is the child's own work, teachers often try to integrate other activities or learning with it. A teacher may ask a child just beginning to read what caption he would like to have on the painting or drawing he has just finished. She will then write the caption under the picture for him and ask him to read it and perhaps copy it. Sometimes a group of captioned drawings is made into a book for the child to reread later.

The play area is also an important part of the classroom. It may be just an open space where children play with blocks; it may be a puppet stage; or it may be an elaborate playhouse. The time that groups of children spend in this area is not considered wasted by advocates of open education, since they believe children are capable of learning from everything and everyone in their environment. Thus, building with blocks may help a child develop spatial relationships; playing a role in an improvised puppet show or as a family member in a playhouse may give a child a sense of himself and others as independently motivated human beings, just as role-playing activities do for adults; and fooling around with a replica of a household appliance gives the child who knows how it really works a chance to explain it to one who wants to know.

Many schools gain more space by providing displays or materials and allowing children to work in the corridors, a use of space which also increases contact between children in different classes. Some schools encourage students to visit other classrooms, perhaps to see something other children have made or, as happened in a school I visited, to see a pet guinea pig giving birth. Many British schools encourage the children to work outdoors for a good part of the school day.

A fundamental characteristic of the environment in an informal school is its constant activity. If children acquire lasting knowledge by exploring their own natural interests, then the classroom must give them the opportunity for that exploration and must change as interests change. New books and materials are frequently brought in by students and by teachers, who must be sensitive to the developing interests of children in the class. In one of the classes I observed, several children and a teacher spent a half hour reading riddles

WHO SAYS A SCHOOL BOOK HAS TO BE DULL?

Open classroom teachers believe that a child will learn to read faster if he is interested in the subject matter of the book. There-fore, the class library will usually contain books on a variety of topics, and sometimes even a teacher may be interested in one —something that's not very likely to happen if the only books in the classroom call on the reader to "See Spot run!" While a few children are reading, others, as in the picture at the right, may be writing, drawing, or looking at displays on classroom walls.

from a book one child had brought to school and trying to make up riddles of their own. The book was then added to the class library.

These activities and the materials found in an open classroom point up the fact that basic skills such as reading and mathematics are not ignored in informal schools just because they are not the subjects of distinct, whole-class lessons. Open classroom teachers hope skills are introduced in such a way that the child will view them as tools that can be helpful in pursuing his own interests rather than as ends in themselves with no relevance to his own world. Advocates of open education feel that the traditional 45-minute reading and mathematics periods, which are separated from other activities and in which the teacher determines lesson content, encourage the view that schoolwork is irrelevant and therefore make learning less likely.

Thus, a major function of a teacher in an informal setting is to integrate reading and arithmetic with child-initiated activities. This can be done in a number of ways. In one New York City school I visited, a trip by a combined kindergarten–first-grade class inspired one child to build an elaborate "city" out of blocks.

The teacher then wrote labels on index cards for places in the city—"docks," "Brooklyn Bridge," "World Trade Center," and so forth. The child copied these words, which he could read, onto other index cards and put the cards he had written on his city. Then he decided to string lights along his Brooklyn Bridge, leading to some education in elementary electricity.

In the same class, a play which was going to be presented to another group of children provided the opportunity for a good deal of mathematics and some reading. Two children gained practice in counting and writing by numbering 48 tickets and 48 seats. Other children were in charge of making 48 bags of popcorn. They began by reading the "recipe" (something like "Heat the oil, pop the corn, and put on the salt"). Several times while they were preparing the popcorn, the teacher asked how many bags were already made and how many more were needed for a total of 48. The teacher also wrote out signs for the ticket taker and the popcorn distributor to wear, read the signs to these children, and asked them to copy the signs.

For older children, reading should obviously involve more than single words or phrases. In a third-grade

class I visited, since many of the children were fascinated by their pet turtles, the teacher had added several books about turtles to the class library and had encouraged some children to write their own books describing what they observed about their pets. The child-written books were also put into the class library and, according to the teacher, were widely read.

In the various schools I visited, there were different degrees of encouragement—or pressure—for children to engage in reading or arithmetic activities. Some of the practices seemed to contradict, in part, the theory underlying open education. In a few classes there were reading and mathematics hours, in which the children could still work individually or in small groups but had to do a reading-related or mathematics-related activity. In one class where the children were generally allowed extensive freedom, they were nevertheless required to use a reading text once a week. In another class the children were given great freedom for most of the morning, but at about 11 o'clock the teacher went over to a few of them and in effect told them to do some writing or arithmetic. In still another class, the children were required to write one composition a week.

If incidents or practices such as these are not understood in context, their importance can be exaggerated. Children who have been in traditionally run classes may need a fair amount of teacher direction for a while because they are not used to making decisions about their learning for themselves. Similarly, a teacher who has for years run a traditional classroom may need time to get used to not having to tell the children what to do all the time. Nevertheless, the ambivalence over how directive to be about reading and mathematics does point up a more general problem with open education—the difficulty of the teacher's role. Lillian Weber has defined it as "implementing and opening up a child's purposes," but she added that it also involved "the role of correcting a child's misconceptions, of offering new possibilities, of suggesting new variants for trial, of sharing, as it fits, [the teacher's] own wider experience, of transmitting in this way the culture and the language. Thus, a school called informal ha[s] to have a blend of some direction and a great deal of implementation of a child's purposes."

In other words, the teacher should allow extensive freedom but still control the children's activities to some

extent, and there is no set formula for determining how much freedom to permit or direction to provide. In the classroom, it may be difficult for the teacher to know when to let a child discover something on his own through trial and error and when to make a suggestion or ask a question. It may be difficult for the teacher to keep in mind the level of each child's intellectual development, so that he can ask a question the child can deal with rather than one which is beyond his ability to comprehend. It may also be difficult for the teacher to know how often to suggest that a child read or write about something he is interested in. One principal told me about a child who said he would not answer the teacher's questions any more because he was always asked to write his ideas down.

A private school teacher I spoke with thought that so much training and experience were required to run an open classroom well that the method could never be widely used successfully in the public schools. Nevertheless, a number of school systems are attempting it. The North Dakota education department, for example, is moving toward almost universal use of open education in elementary schools. In conjunction with this effort, the University of North Dakota has established the New School for Behavioral Studies in Education, which provides a master's degree program for prospective teachers consisting of two summers of academic study surrounding a year of practical open classroom experience in an elementary school. When the master's candidates go into a school, they replace experienced teachers, who attend the New School for that year to study open education.

In the New York City public schools, Lillian Weber has been primarily responsible for introducing informal

TRINA LIPTON

The experiences and activities of everyday life form the basis of learning in the open classroom. A child is more likely to learn to write (or so the theory goes) if he wants to write down a recipe for his favorite sandwich and will want to count if he can measure out a fruit cup for everyone.

Solmee and jelly
sandwich

Frst take sum slomee and jelly and Thene take bred and thene miks Them olTo Gether.

Toasted Cheese

you put cheese and bread and cok.

education—very gradually, however, so that the new approach would not threaten or be misunderstood by teachers who had taught in a traditional way for many years, nor be misunderstood by parents concerned with whether their children would really learn if allowed to "play" in school. After Professor Weber had several conferences with teachers, administrators, and members of the community, five classes in a single elementary school (affiliated with the City College student-teaching program) were unstructured for one hour a day, three days a week. As parents and teachers became convinced that learning was going on in the unstructured part of the day, classes became increasingly open. Only after teachers and parents from other schools observed and were favorably impressed by these classes did the use of open education spread, so that by the 1972–1973 school year some classes in well over a dozen New York City elementary schools were being run informally.

Obviously, there are some important questions to be answered about these—and the many other—moves toward open education: Are they successful? What are the children learning? Because open education is a relatively new phenomenon, statistical evidence on its success is scanty. North Dakota has not yet done a statewide evaluation. Its New School, however, has done a study comparing two elementary schools in Fargo, one which began informal education in the fall of 1969 and one which continued the traditional approach. The study concluded that the open classroom students, for the most part, showed greater increases in achievement in language, mathematics, and work-study skills. They also had more positive attitudes toward reading.

At Public School 84 in New York City, one of the first schools at which Lillian Weber helped establish informal classrooms, the average score among second-graders in the open classrooms on the 1970 Metropolitan Achievement Test in reading was 3.35, as opposed to a national norm of 2.7. The open classroom students included 38 black or Puerto Rican children, 17 of whom read on or above grade level; of the 33 black or Puerto Rican second-graders in traditional classes at P.S. 84, four were reading on grade level.

The 1967 Plowden report (formally known as *Children and Their Primary Schools*, the report of the Central Advisory Council for Education of England, headed by Lady Bridget Plowden), a two-volume, comprehensive study, noted that since the end of World War II, the period in which use of informal techniques increased rapidly, reading levels among British students at each grade level increased by about two years; that is, the average 11-year-old in 1967 read as well as the average 13-year-old did in 1947.

On the other hand, a 1963 report on British junior schools (for children from seven to 11) found reading achievement about the same in both formal and informal schools. Similarly, some administrators in American schools told me that reading scores had not changed significantly since their schools began implementing open education.

However, virtually everyone I spoke with about informal education emphasized that the method's success or failure could not be measured solely by scores on standardized tests. They maintained that there were also important intangible benefits—the children are happier and more eager to come to school (many principals have reported declines in both absenteeism and number of discipline problems), they are more self-confident, they are better able to think for themselves and solve problems, and they are more self-motivated, not always needing to be told what to do by an adult.

Open education is not, of course, the instant answer to all the problems of American primary education. It is naive to think that any approach to running schools could be so perfectly conceived or implemented as to turn every child into a genius. Further, as has been noted, the informal approach may be an especially difficult one for teachers to implement, and if it is applied as a success formula (there must be 30 plants, two guinea pigs, one library with two easy chairs, and so on) by people who do not understand the theory, it will certainly not succeed.

Nevertheless, the open classroom approach is being tried by an increasing number of American teachers who are dissatisfied with the traditional approach and are ready to test the hypothesis that children will learn better if given freedom to explore their own interests than if ordered to sit down, shut up, and pay attention to the teacher.

Encyclopedia articles indexed under education and psychology discuss the traditional aims and historical evolution of formal schooling and a variety of theories concerning the intellectual and emotional development of children. Some of the theoretical justification for informal education has been based on the work of JOHANN HEINRICH PESTALOZZI, FRIEDRICH WILHELM AUGUST FROEBEL, MARIA MONTESSORI, and JOHN DEWEY, in addition to Piaget. The informal approach has long been the characteristic method of operating KINDERGARTENS and NURSERY SCHOOLS, both in the United States and Europe.

Suggestions for Further Reading

FEATHERSTONE, JOSEPH. *Schools Where Children Learn.* New York, Liveright, 1971.

HAPGOOD, MARILYN. "The Open Classroom: Protect It From Its Friends." *Saturday Review*, vol. 54 (September 18, 1971), pp. 66–69, 75.

HOLT, JOHN. *How Children Fail.* New York, Pitman Publishing Company, 1964. Paperback edition: Dell, 1965.

Open Door, New York City. New York, Center for Urban Education, 1971.

"Open Education Is Imported From England." *New York University Education Quarterly*, summer 1971, pp. 8–16.

SILBERMAN, CHARLES E. *Crisis in the Classroom.* New York, Random House, 1970. Paperback edition: Vintage, 1971.

WEBER, LILLIAN. *The English Infant School and Informal Education.* Englewood Cliffs, N.J., Prentice-Hall, 1971.

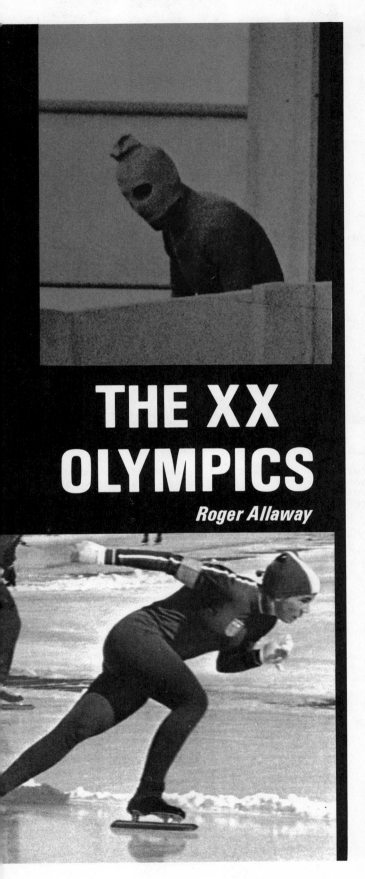

THE XX OLYMPICS

Roger Allaway

They were billed as Olympics of serenity; perhaps in a less turbulent age they could have been. The West German Organizing Committee did its best to ensure that these games would erase the memory of the 1936 Olympics and the show of autocratic strength staged in Berlin by Adolf Hitler. But the Germans may have done their job too well, for in creating the most magnificent sports spectacle ever seen, they made the XX Olympic Games in Munich the focus of world attention and thus, perhaps inevitably, a forum for demonstrating—violently and otherwise—a variety of political and racial conflicts.

A number of incidents shook the Olympic peace, but the one that shattered it, maybe forever, came in the early hours of September 5. Between 4 and 5 A.M. a band of eight terrorists from the Arab extremist group Black September broke into the Olympic Village quarters of the Israeli team, killing two Israelis as they entered and taking nine others hostage. Twenty hours later the reign of terror ended at a military airbase near Munich from which the Arabs had hoped to fly their hostages to Cairo. In a gun battle between German sharpshooters and the terrorists, all nine Israelis, five of the eight terrorists, and one German policeman were killed. The hostages died in the two helicopters in which they had been taken to the airport; all but one succumbed to wounds from an Arab machine gun.

It was not until about 12 hours after the terrorist attack had begun that the day's competition, which had gone on as scheduled throughout the morning and early afternoon, was suspended. By that time, the desperate nature of the situation had been realized, and the attention of the world was centered on Munich more firmly than it could have been for any sports event.

A day later an emotional memorial service was held in the main Olympic Stadium; after much debate as to whether the games should continue, the competition was resumed. Many felt that the games should not have gone on, that to return to athletics in the face of such horror was to dishonor those who had died. Among those holding this position was Willi Daume, president of the West German Organizing Committee and a man who had devoted six years of his life to these now bloodstained games. Others felt that to end the games would be to give the terrorists their victory, to give them the satisfaction of knowing that they had had the power to bring to a halt an imposing, if imperfect, exercise in international relations.

Strong arguments can be made for both points of view, but when the competition did resume, even those who had favored it were somewhat embarrassed. The

SPLENDOR AND TERROR. Far left: Valery Borzov of the Soviet Union sprints to victory in the 100 meters. Center (top to bottom): East Germany's Roland Matthes sets an Olympic backstroke record; a West German youth lights the Olympic torch; and the Soviets sink the controversial layup that beat the U.S. team. Below left: Anne Henning of the United States speed skates against the clock. Like a hooded specter, the Arab guerrilla at upper right peers from the balcony of the Israeli quarters.

BLACK SEPTEMBER AT OLYMPIC VILLAGE

The horror that shattered the Olympic games began shortly before dawn on September 5, when eight Black September terrorists gained entrance to the Israeli quarters, killed two Israelis on the spot, and held nine others hostage during a day of sporadic negotiations. It ended at a nearby airfield, when a blaze of gunfire brought death to all nine Israelis and five of the terrorists as well. Above, a policeman stands guard over the block where the Israelis were being held; at right, a lowered flag commemorates the victims.

International Olympic Committee, in its haste to get back to business as usual, had decreed a day of mourning but had specified that the 24-hour period was to begin at the time of suspension the previous afternoon. Thus, the competition was restarted not even 18 hours after the slayings. Further, many were shocked by IOC president Avery Brundage's speech at the memorial service; it seemed to compare a pre-Olympic boycott threat by several black African nations with the murder of 11 Israelis as equally serious attacks on the games.

The Olympics of serenity were now the Olympics of sorrow, and they moved toward their conclusion in an atmosphere of muted enthusiasm. However, even if the terrorist attack had never occurred, it is unlikely that these Olympics would have been remembered for their peacefulness.

The Olympic year had begun auspiciously enough, with the highly successful winter games at Sapporo, Japan. However, even here, for a week before the opening events, the prospects had been somewhat in

doubt. The big news then was the barring of Austrian skier Karl Schranz from the games on grounds of professionalism. Avery Brundage had originally wanted to bar most of the world's top Alpine skiers, contending that they had flagrantly violated the amateur code of the Olympics by establishing advertising arrangements with ski equipment manufacturers. The Japanese Olympic Organizing Committee, however, protested to Brundage that disqualification would torpedo the games by robbing them of their most glamorous attraction. Brundage eventually relented, although Schranz was chosen as a scapegoat for the transgressions of all. The Austrian was a likely target—his income from skiing has been estimated at $50,000 annually, and he had been openly contemptuous of Brundage's amateur ethic.

Once the games got under way, however, Schranz was quickly forgotten, eclipsed by other heroes and by the general beauty of the show. Sapporo had been something of a surprise when it was selected to host the games; few were familiar with the city on the northernmost island of Japan, which is, in fact, the largest metropolis ever to stage the Winter Olympics. And while the city itself is not particularly beautiful, the sites of the competition were spectacular.

Roger Allaway is a free-lance sports writer whose work has appeared in Sporting Guide *and other publications.*

The most magnificent of the Olympic venues were the men's and women's downhill skiing courses, located on the side of Mount Eniwa, 50 miles from Sapporo. The courses overlooked a giant spring-fed lake, and had the skiers not been so intensely involved in their competitive efforts, they might have been easily distracted by the vista. As it was, the results of the women's competition were rather distracting to the experts. Annemarie Proell of Austria, who had dominated women's Alpine skiing for two years, was upset in the downhill by Marie-Thérèse Nadig of Switzerland, a little-known teen-ager who had never before won a major international race. Miss Nadig went on to continue her mastery over Miss Proell in the giant slalom, winning her second gold medal and emerging as the heroine of the games as well as their biggest surprise.

The Alpine skiers, however, did not provide all the glamour of these Winter Olympics. For even if Brundage had succeeded in barring all the top skiers, the games would still have had speed skater Ard Schenk. It was Schenk—a tall, strikingly handsome Dutchman with a godlike physique—rather than any of the skiers, who was the star of the show. And when the men's speed skating events were completed, he appeared even

more magnificent, with three gold medals to his credit. Schenk skates with a long, powerful stride that isn't quite quick enough for sprinting but which demolished the opposition in the three longer events—the 1,500, 5,000, and 10,000 meters. The only disappointment in Schenk's otherwise perfect performance came when he stumbled and fell at the start of the 500-meter event. But the awkwardness of that display was forgotten at the sight of the Dutchman in the other races, swooping along the ice with awesome grace and strength.

The only other athlete at Sapporo who could possibly rival the preeminence of Schenk was ski jumper Yukio Kasaya of Japan, the darling of the home fans. In recent years the jumping events have been dominated by athletes from Scandinavia and Eastern Europe. But when the 70-meter jumping was completed, Kasaya had led a sweep of medals by the Japanese jumpers, bringing the host nation its first gold ever in the Winter Olympics and setting off a tide of jubilation throughout the Olympic city. A week later the new national hero finished out of the running in the 90-meter jumping, but that couldn't dim the brilliance of his earlier victory.

The Winter Olympics was not totally without controversy, but the problems at Sapporo were relatively minor. The only sport in which any real discontent surfaced was figure skating. As usual in international competitions scored on a subjective basis, many athletes contended that the judges were overrating skaters from their own countries and underrating their rivals. The difficulty was nothing, however, compared with the troubles which developed in subjectively scored events at Munich. With the exception of the Schranz affair, the Winter Olympic Games were as near-idyllic a competition as could have been hoped for. They began in splendor and sunshine, were conducted with a high degree of sportsmanship and a minimum of rancor, and ended in peace and happiness. They may have been the last Olympic gathering ever to enjoy such conditions.

Ironically, until just a few weeks before the summer games, the atmosphere in Munich was relatively free of controversy. The specter of politics first began to haunt the Munich games about ten days before their scheduled opening, when it was reported that several black African nations would stage a boycott if Rhodesian athletes were allowed to compete. A year earlier the sports federations of the African nations had agreed to allow the Rhodesians to participate in the games as long as they played under the British flag, rather than as an independent, white-ruled nation. But in the weeks preceding the opening events, the African governments overruled the sports groups, saying that if the Rhodesians competed, their own athletes would not. Without the Kenyans, Ethiopians, and other Africans, track and field competition—as glamorous to the summer games as Alpine skiing was to the winter—would have been marred. Faced with a similar situation, the International Olympic Committee took a similar way out. The Rhodesians were ousted, thereby sacrificing

Stopped
Before
They
Started

Cannons boomed, trumpets blared, the Olympic flame flared, but for some sad athletes it was all a fizzle before it started. Austrian skier Karl Schranz (upper right, center) had to come in from the cold when he was disqualified from the Winter Olympics on charges of professionalism; the Rhodesians (left) warmed up in Munich only to be barred from play after boycott threats from other African states; and Eddie Hart and Rob Taylor (lower right) were two of three U.S. runners given the wrong starting time by their coach. Only Taylor made it to the heat, with seconds to spare.

UPI

a few athletes in order to keep the rest, and the black Africans called off their boycott.

The attack of the Arab terrorists and the threatened boycott by the Africans, while totally incomparable in human terms, were the major instances of the use of the games as a political forum. However, they were far from being the only cases in which politics mixed with sports.

In one case, two American sprinters who won the gold and silver medals in the 400-meter dash, Vince Matthews and Wayne Collett, were barred from ever again competing in the Olympics. IOC president Brun-

dage took action when he interpreted their behavior during the victory-stand ceremonies as a display of disrespect for the American national anthem. In another, four of a group of seven cyclists from the Irish Republican Army slipped their way into a cycling competition on September 7, allegedly to prove that they were better than the regular Irish entry. One of the IRA riders, however, caused a 15-bike pileup, casting doubt on the contention that they were in the race for purely competitive reasons.

Furthermore, national prejudices were blatantly displayed by judges in subjectively scored sports, such as

AP

AP

and diving arena the judges were playing their nationalistic games with the diving scores, a computerized touch-plate system at the other end determined that swimmer Gunnar Larsson of Sweden had defeated U.S. swimmer Tim McKee in the 400-meter individual medley by the incredibly narrow margin of two-thousandths of a second. And out at the track stadium a prismatic reflector system, used to measure the distances in the weight throws, gave the gold medal in the javelin to Klaus Wolfermann of West Germany over Ianis Lusis of the Soviet Union. The margin of victory—296′ 10″ to 296′ 9½″.

There were other controversies, which, while they may not have been directly affected by politics, involved large elements of national pride. The most notable of these was the dispute over whether the United States or the Soviet Union had actually won the championship final of the basketball tournament. The debate centered on the issue of time—specifically, how much time remained to play when the Russians brought the ball in bounds for the shot that won the game for them, 51–50. Twice they brought the ball in and failed to sink it in the basket before time ran out. Twice the officials ruled that the scoreboard clock had been wrong. Finally, the third time, the Russians scored and had their victory, ending a 63-game winning streak for the United States and American hopes for an eighth consecutive gold medal in basketball. The results did not become official, however, until a 12-hour meeting of the International Basketball Federation finally con-

gymnastics, boxing, and diving. Although scorers from many nations, including the United States, were involved in this practice, the most obvious example came from the East Germans during the finals of the women's springboard diving. The three East German girls finished well out of contention after the scores of all seven judges had been computed, but the one East German judge had rated them first, second, and third.

The scoring of sports like these sharply contrasted with the tremendous array of electronic and mechanical equipment provided by the Germans to call objectively measured events. While at one end of the swimming

RUSH HOUR. Hordes of helmeted riders are off and pedaling. Trying to embarrass the official Irish entry, cyclists from the Irish Republican Army crashed the event and caused a pileup.

firmed the Russian victory. The Americans, feeling that they had been outlegislated rather than outplayed, refused to accept the silver medal.

Another basically nonpolitical but nevertheless rancorous dispute involved drugs; the conflict deprived an American teen-ager, Rick DeMont, of the gold medal he had won in the 400-meter freestyle swimming race. Since the 1960 Olympics the IOC has circulated a list of drugs that are totally banned for use by Olympic athletes; they include ephedrine, a stimulant used in a number of prescription medications. DeMont had been taking Marax, a drug containing ephedrine, for a long-standing asthmatic condition, and had listed the drug on a required medical form before the games. But, apparently, no one on the American team's medical staff bothered to read the form, and DeMont was never informed that the drug was on the banned list. When a trace of ephedrine turned up in the urine test required of all medalists, the youngster was barred from the 1,500-meter final and was later stripped of his 400-meter gold medal. As with most of the Olympic disputes, recriminations flew in all directions, with most of the blame falling on the U.S. team doctors.

And then there was the case of the vaulting poles. A month before the games, the International Amateur Athletic Federation, the ruling body of track and field, decreed that the new-model pole which Bob Seagren of the United States and Kjell Isaksson of Sweden had used to set world records would not be allowed in Olympic competition. The action came after the East Germans contended that their top vaulter, Wolfgang Nordwig, had not had access to the American-made poles. A week before the vaulting events, the IAAF reversed its stand, after learning from the pole manufacturer that an ample supply had been sent to the East Germans months before. But several days later the federation went back to its original position. When Seagren was beaten by Nordwig for the gold medal, he contended that, forced to use the old-style pole, he had lost not on the field but in the committee room.

In the midst of the tragedy, the bickering, and the politics, sports itself was somewhat pushed out of the spotlight. However, there was still plenty of spirited and honest competition going on in Munich during the last week of August and the first week of September.

The dominating star of the games, both summer and winter, was undeniably American swimmer Mark Spitz. At the 1968 Olympics in Mexico City, Spitz had been the 18-year-old wunderkind who predicted that he would win six gold medals but won only two. At Munich, Spitz was no less confident than he had been four years earlier, but he had matured considerably and now channeled all of his energies into swimming rather than boasting. The results were astounding. Spitz swam in four individual events—the 100-meter and 200-meter in both the freestyle and butterfly races—and won all four in world record times. He swam on three relay teams, the 400-meter and 800-meter freestyle relays and the 400-meter medley relay, and again all

three teams won in world record times. Spitz' seven gold medals were the most ever won by an athlete in a single Olympics, surpassing the record of five set in the 1920 games by Italian fencer Nedo Nadi.

The Californian's performance made quite a few waves, and not just in the pool. Some amateur officials, still edgy over the 1968 scandal involving payoffs from track shoe manufacturers to Olympic athletes, chided him for holding up an easily identifiable brand of shoes while acknowledging a round of victory cheers. And one European IOC member suggested, after reports that Spitz might be able to cash in on his fame for as much as $5 million, that in the future swimmers should be limited in the number of events they are allowed to enter. (*See* PEOPLE IN THE NEWS: Mark Spitz.)

Spitz had a very capable, if not quite so spectacular, counterpart in women's swimming. That was Shane Gould of Australia, who as late as August was still the world record holder in all four of the women's freestyle events. She entered five individual races and came away with three gold medals, the 200-meter and 400-meter freestyles and the 200-meter individual medley. The fact that she was beaten by American girls in the 100-meter and 800-meter freestyles (won by Sandra Neilson and Keena Rothhammer, respectively) can be attributed largely to attrition. The Americans specialized in only two or three events and thus did not face such a tiring schedule.

Miss Gould, however, was not the greatest female star of the 1972 Summer Olympics. That honor had to go to 17-year-old Olga Korbut, an 84-pound wisp of a Russian gymnast, who more than any other athlete exemplified the great variety of emotions that are always part of Olympic competition.

On the first night of the gymnastic finals, Olga's emotion was elation, as her stunning performance on the uneven parallel bars (including two maneuvers never before accomplished) helped the Russian girls to the overall team championship. The next night, the overall individual competition championship, was Olga's time for heartbreak. She had just taken the lead in the standings as she moved to the uneven bars, and the crowd of 11,000 was expecting another spectacular performance. But this time the Olympic pressure got to her, and she slipped badly on several moves, losing all chances for any of the medals. The final night, however, saw a return to her earlier form on the bars. However, when the judges gave her a score good enough only for second place, she appeared embarrassed as the crowd, totally sympathetic to her, hooted their decision. And finally, it was joy. In both the balance beam and the floor exercises she was the final competitor and both times needed scores of 9.9 out of 10.0 to win the gold. Both times she succeeded, and she mounted the victory stand ecstatically, probably the most popular winner of the entire competition.

While Miss Korbut's victories may have been the most spectacular for the Russians, they were probably not the most important symbolically. For on their way

to a 99–94 lead over the United States in the final medal totals, the Russians picked up victories in those three most symbolically loaded events—the 100-meter dash, to determine the world's fastest human; the super-heavyweight weight-lifting event, to determine the world's strongest man; and the decathlon, to determine the world's greatest athlete.

UPSET. Alsan Sharmukhamedov of the Soviet Union shoots against Ed Ratleff of the United States in a bitter, chaotic contest that brought official, though disputed, defeat to the Americans for the first time in the history of Olympic basketball.

Valery Borzov gained the first of those three titles, sprinting away from Robert Taylor of the United States to a 1-meter victory in the 100. Some Americans griped that he wouldn't have won if the two Americans who missed their qualifying heats, Eddie Hart and Rey Robinson, had been in the final. But the Russian's performance was impressive, and he solidified his claim on the title with a victory in the 200-meter dash a few days later, the first man in 16 years to score an Olympic sprint double.

The strongman was Vasily Alexeyev, who easily outperformed his weight-lifting competitors, hoisting a record total of 1,410.95 pounds over his head in the three Olympic lifts. But the greatest of the three symbolic winners was Nikolai Avilov, who not only won the decathlon but also set a world mark of 8,454 points, a

particularly difficult feat in Olympic competition, where medals rather than records are the primary goal. Avilov, who had not even been favored to win any medals in the event, destroyed his opposition, setting personal bests in a fantastic eight out of ten decathlon events.

Very nearly matching the greatness of Avilov's feat was the performance of another Russian track star, Ludmila Bragina, who turned the world record for the women's 1,500-meter run into her own private plaything. Usually in Olympic track competition it is wise to hold back as much as possible in the early rounds to save strength for the final. Miss Bragina would have none of this. In her trial heat she went out and broke the world record of 4:06.9 with a 4:06.5 time. The next day, in the semifinals, she lowered that to 4:05.1. And one day later she made her previous efforts look paltry by comparison, as she ran away with the finals in 4:01.4, roughly equal to a 4:21 mile. The accomplishment of lowering the world record three times within a 48-hour span and by a total margin of 5.5 seconds has to be considered one of the greatest in recent track history. The men's record has been reduced only once, by 2.5 seconds, since 1960.

The American track athletes had their stars also, although their medal totals were well below what they had achieved in previous Olympics. The leader was Frank Shorter, who became the first American to win the Olympic marathon since 1908. Shorter, a 24-year-old law student who was born in Munich, easily outdistanced a field that included the three fastest marathon runners of all time. At the finish of the 26-mile race, he was more than two minutes ahead of his nearest pursuer, Karel Lismont of Belgium, clocking a time of 2:12:19.7. His moment of triumph was somewhat marred, however, by an intruder who jumped into the race just outside the stadium and came up the track ahead of him. It was later revealed that the interloper had made the gesture to protest the continuation of the games after the murder of the Israelis.

If the usually dominant American trackmen were surprised at their poor showing, they were not alone, for in track and field these were an Olympics of upsets. Some of the biggest names in the sport found themselves settling for a silver medal, a bronze medal, or no medal at all. Perhaps the biggest surprise of all came in the men's 1,500, where Jim Ryun of the United States and Kipchoge Keino of Kenya were slated to have the ultimate showdown of their great careers. But Ryun was eliminated in the heats when he fell in traffic. That left Keino as the overwhelming favorite, al-

Triumphs for Three Superstars

Olga Korbut, the wispy Russian teen-ager, outclassed tight competition with her enthralling performances on the balance beam (right) and in the floor exercises. Ard Schenk of the Netherlands speed skated for three gold medals to wow spectators at Sapporo. And American Mark Spitz (below) made the biggest splash of all, setting four individual world records and winning seven gold medals, highest ever for one Olympics.

NOT EVERYONE ACCEPTED the suspension of the XX Olympics. But some critics thought the whole future of the games doubtful.

though a few observers thought that Pekka Vasala of Finland, a good runner with a potent finishing kick, might give the Kenyan some trouble. Apparently, Keino did not think so; he played right into the Finn's hands, allowing the early pace to dawdle, thereby turning the race into a last-lap contest. Vasala left little doubt as to who was the speedier, as he roared past Keino in the homestretch, completing the final lap in 53.8 seconds and winning by a solid 5-yard margin.

Vasala's win, on the final day of competition, capped a return by the Finns to their prominent position in distance running, recalling memories of the Flying Finns of the pre–World War II Olympics. Just minutes before Vasala's race, Finland's Lasse Viren won the 5,000-meter run in a record time of 13:26.4, defeating a magnificent field that included eight of the world's ten fastest men in the event. However, Viren's greatest triumph in these games had come earlier, in the 10,000-meter run. Midway through the 25-lap race he lost considerable ground when he fell in a collision with another runner, but he made up the deficit, took over the lead on the final lap, and held off the challenge of Emiel Puttemans of Belgium at the finish to win the race. And his time, despite the fall and a slow pace in the early stages of the race, was 27:38.4, breaking the world record. Paavo Nurmi, the greatest of the Flying Finns, never came within two minutes of that time.

The reemergence of the Finns as the long-distance champions displaced the Africans, who had won every race from 1,500 meters up through the marathon at Mexico City in 1968. In Munich their only gold in the distance events came in the 3,000-meter steeplechase, where Keino, a relative novice at the barrier event, upset a top-notch field in an Olympic record 8:23.6.

The performances of the Munich athletes were generally of an extremely high caliber, but the tragic events off the field nevertheless leave the future of the games in doubt. Many feel that the major problem is one of size—the games have simply grown too large—and point to the $650 million spent by the Germans. They say it would be better to abandon them in favor of separate world championship events in the various sports, which would not attract so much world attention and thus would be less likely vehicles for political expression.

Others say that the real problem is the rampant nationalism exhibited at the games and suggest as remedies the elimination of team sports and victory ceremonies, with their flags and anthems, and possibly even the elimination of national uniforms for the athletes.

Changes are certainly needed if the games are to return to their place as a constructive force in the world, but change will be very difficult to make. Perhaps the Olympics can be saved as a useful meeting ground for the athletes of the world; this is Brundage's last Olympics, and his successor may make some necessary changes. Perhaps they're not worth saving, having failed to adjust to the world as it really exists. But whatever happens, it is certain that despite the athletic feats of young people like Mark Spitz, Ard Schenk, Olga Korbut, and Lasse Viren, the Olympics of 1972 will be remembered for their hours of horror long after the moments of jubilation have been forgotten.

Olympic Medal Winners

EVENT	GOLD	SILVER	BRONZE
SKIING, ALPINE			
MEN'S DOWNHILL	Russi, Switzerland	Collombin, Switzerland	Messner, Austria
WOMEN'S DOWNHILL	Nadig, Switzerland	Proell, Austria	Corrock, U.S.A.
MEN'S SLALOM	Ochoa, Spain	G. Thoeni, Italy	R. Thoeni, Italy
WOMEN'S SLALOM	Cochran, U.S.A.	Debernard, France	Steurer, France
MEN'S GIANT SLALOM	G. Thoeni, Italy	Bruggmann, Switzerland	Mattle, Switzerland
WOMEN'S GIANT SLALOM	Nadig, Switzerland	Proell, Austria	Drexel, Austria
SKIING, NORDIC			
MEN'S 15 KM.	Lundback, Sweden	Simaschov, U.S.S.R.	Formo, Norway
MEN'S 30 KM.	Vedenine, U.S.S.R.	Tyldum, Norway	Harviken, Norway
MEN'S 50 KM.	Tyldum, Norway	Myrmo, Norway	Vedenine, U.S.S.R.
MEN'S 40-KM. RELAY	U.S.S.R.	Norway	Switzerland
WOMEN'S 5 KM.	Kulakova, U.S.S.R.	Kajosmaa, Finland	Sikolova, Czechoslovakia
WOMEN'S 10 KM.	Kulakova, U.S.S.R.	Olunina, U.S.S.R.	Kajosmaa, Finland
WOMEN'S 15-KM. RELAY	U.S.S.R.	Finland	Norway
70-M. JUMP	Kasaya, Japan	Konno, Japan	Aochi, Japan
90-M. JUMP	Fortuna, Poland	Steiner, Switzerland	Schmidt, East Germany
COMBINED	Wehling, East Germany	Miettinen, Finland	Luck, East Germany
SKATING, FIGURE			
MEN'S SINGLES	Nepela, Czechoslovakia	Chetverukhin, U.S.S.R.	Pera, France
WOMEN'S SINGLES	Schuba, Austria	Magnussen, Canada	Lynn, U.S.A.
PAIRS	Rodnina, Ulanov, U.S.S.R.	Smirnova, Suraikin, U.S.S.R.	Gross, Kagelmann, East Germany
SKATING, SPEED			
MEN'S 500 M.	Keller, West Germany	Borjes, Switzerland	Muratov, U.S.S.R.
MEN'S 1,500 M.	Schenk, Netherlands	Gronvold, Norway	Claesson, Sweden
MEN'S 5,000 M.	Schenk, Netherlands	Gronvold, Norway	Stensen, Norway
MEN'S 10,000 M.	Schenk, Netherlands	Verkerk, Netherlands	Stensen, Norway
WOMEN'S 500 M.	Henning, U.S.A.	Krasnova, U.S.S.R.	Titova, U.S.S.R.
WOMEN'S 1,000 M.	Pflug, West Germany	Keulen-Deelstra, Netherlands	Henning, U.S.A.
WOMEN'S 1,500 M.	Holum, U.S.A.	Baas-Kaiser, Netherlands	Keulen-Deelstra, Netherlands
WOMEN'S 1,000 M.	Baas-Kaiser, Netherlands	Holum, U.S.A.	Keulen-Deelstra, Netherlands
ICE HOCKEY	U.S.S.R.	U.S.A.	Czechoslovakia
BIATHLON			
INDIVIDUAL	Solberg, Norway	Knauthe, East Germany	Arwidson, Sweden
RELAY	U.S.S.R.	Finland	East Germany
BOBSLEIGH			
2 MEN	Zimmerer, Utzschneider, West Germany	Floth, Bader, West Germany	Wicki, Hubacher, Switzerland
4 MEN	Switzerland	Italy	West Germany
LUGE			
MEN'S SINGLES	Scheidel, East Germany	Ehrig, East Germany	Fiedler, East Germany
2 MEN	Hildgartner, Plaikner, Italy; Hornlein, Bredow, E. Germany (tie)		Bonsack, Fiedler, East Germany

EVENT	GOLD	SILVER	BRONZE
WOMEN'S SINGLES	Muller, East Germany	Ruhrold, East Germany	Schumann, East Germany
TRACK AND FIELD			
Men			
100 M.	Borzov, U.S.S.R.	Taylor, U.S.A.	Miller, Jamaica
200 M.	Borzov, U.S.S.R.	Black, U.S.A.	Mennea, Italy
400-M. RELAY	U.S.A.	U.S.S.R.	West Germany
400 M.	Matthews, U.S.A.	Collett, U.S.A.	Sang, Kenya
1,600-M. RELAY	Kenya	Great Britain	France
800 M.	Wottle, U.S.A.	Arzhanov, U.S.S.R.	Boit, Kenya
1,500 M.	Vasala, Finland	Keino, Kenya	Dixon, New Zealand
5,000 M.	Viren, Finland	Gammoudi, Tunisia	Stewart, Great Britain
10,000 M.	Viren, Finland	Puttemans, Belgium	Yifter, Ethiopia
MARATHON	Shorter, U.S.A.	Lismont, Belgium	Wolde, Ethiopia
STEEPLECHASE	Keino, Kenya	Jipcho, Kenya	Kantanen, Finland
110-M. HURDLES	Milburn, U.S.A.	Drut, France	Hill, U.S.A.
400-M. HURDLES	Akii-Bua, Uganda	Mann, U.S.A.	Hemery, Great Britain
HIGH JUMP	Tarmak, U.S.S.R.	Junge, East Germany	Stones, U.S.A.
LONG JUMP	Williams, U.S.A.	Baumgartner, West Germany	Robinson, U.S.A.
TRIPLE JUMP	Saneyev, U.S.S.R.	Drehmel, East Germany	Prudencio, Brazil
POLE VAULT	Nordwig, East Germany	Seagren, U.S.A.	Johnson, U.S.A.
SHOTPUT	Komar, Poland	Woods, U.S.A.	Briesenick, East Germany
DISCUS	Danek, Czechoslovakia	Silvester, U.S.A.	Bruch, Sweden
HAMMER	Bondarchuk, U.S.S.R.	Sachse, East Germany	Khmelevsky, U.S.S.R.
JAVELIN	Wolfermann, West Germany	Lusis, U.S.S.R.	Schmidt, U.S.A.
DECATHLON	Avilov, U.S.S.R.	Litvinenko, U.S.S.R.	Katus, Poland
20-KM. WALK	Frenkel, East Germany	Golubnichy, U.S.S.R.	Reimann, East Germany
50-KM. WALK	Kannenberg, West Germany	Soldatenko, U.S.S.R.	Young, U.S.A.
Women			
100 M.	Stecher, East Germany	Boyle, Australia	Chivas, Cuba
200 M.	Stecher, East Germany	Boyle, Australia	Szewinska, Poland
400-M. RELAY	West Germany	East Germany	Cuba
400 M.	Zehrt, East Germany	Wilden, West Germany	Hammond, U.S.A.
1,600-M. RELAY	East Germany	U.S.A.	West Germany
800 M.	Falck, West Germany	Sabaite, U.S.S.R.	Hoffmeister, East Germany
1,500 M.	Bragina, U.S.S.R.	Hoffmeister, East Germany	Cacchi, Italy
100-M. HURDLES	Ehrhardt, East Germany	Bufanu, Romania	Balzer, East Germany
HIGH JUMP	Meyfarth, West Germany	Blagoeva, Bulgaria	Gusenbauer, Austria
LONG JUMP	Rosendahl, West Germany	Yorgova, Bulgaria	Suranova, Czechoslovakia
SHOTPUT	Chizhova, U.S.S.R.	Gummel, East Germany	Christova, Bulgaria
DISCUS	Melnik, U.S.S.R.	Menis, Romania	Stoeva, Bulgaria
JAVELIN	Fuchs, East Germany	Todten, East Germany	Schmidt, U.S.A.
PENTATHLON	Peters, Great Britain	Rosendahl, West Germany	Pollak, East Germany
SWIMMING			
Men			
100-M. FREESTYLE	Spitz, U.S.A.	Heidenreich, U.S.A.	Bure, U.S.S.R.
200-M. FREESTYLE	Spitz, U.S.A.	Genter, U.S.A.	Lampe, West Germany

Olympic

EVENT	GOLD	SILVER	BRONZE
400-M. FREESTYLE	Cooper, Australia[1]	Genter, U.S.A.	McBreen, U.S.A.
1,500-M. FREESTYLE	Burton, U.S.A.	Windeatt, Australia	Northway, U.S.A.
100-M. BREASTSTROKE	Taguchi, Japan	Bruce, U.S.A.	Hencken, U.S.A.
200-M. BREASTSTROKE	Hencken, U.S.A.	Wilkie, Great Britain	Taguchi, Japan
100-M. BUTTERFLY	Spitz, U.S.A.	Robertson, Canada	Heidenreich, U.S.A.
200-M. BUTTERFLY	Spitz, U.S.A.	Hall, U.S.A.	Backhaus, U.S.A.
100-M. BACKSTROKE	Matthes, East Germany	Stamm, U.S.A.	Murphy, U.S.A.
200-M. BACKSTROKE	Matthes, East Germany	Stamm, U.S.A.	Ivey, U.S.A.
200-M. INDIVIDUAL MEDLEY	Larsson, Sweden	McKee, U.S.A.	Furniss, U.S.A.
400-M. INDIVIDUAL MEDLEY	Larsson, Sweden	McKee, U.S.A.	Hargitay, Hungary
400-M. FREESTYLE RELAY	U.S.A.	U.S.S.R.	East Germany
800-M. FREESTYLE RELAY	U.S.A.	West Germany	U.S.S.R.
400-M. MEDLEY RELAY	U.S.A.	East Germany	Canada
SPRINGBOARD DIVE	Vasin, U.S.S.R.	Cagnotto, Italy	Lincoln, U.S.A.
PLATFORM DIVE	Dibiasi, Italy	Rydze, U.S.A.	Cagnotto, Italy

Women

EVENT	GOLD	SILVER	BRONZE
100-M. FREESTYLE	Neilson, U.S.A.	Babashoff, U.S.A.	Gould, Australia
200-M. FREESTYLE	Gould, Australia	Babashoff, U.S.A.	Rothhammer, U.S.A.
400-M. FREESTYLE	Gould, Australia	Calligaris, Italy	Wegner, East Germany
800-M. FREESTYLE	Rothhammer, U.S.A.	Gould, Australia	Calligaris, Italy
100-M. BREASTSTROKE	Carr, U.S.A.	Stepanova, U.S.S.R.	Whitfield, Australia
200-M. BREASTSTROKE	Whitfield, Australia	Schoenfield U.S.A.	Stepanova, U.S.S.R.
100-M. BUTTERFLY	Aoki, Japan	Beier, East Germany	Gyarmati, Hungary
200-M. BUTTERFLY	Moe, U.S.A.	Colella, U.S.A.	Daniel, U.S.A.
100-M. BACKSTROKE	Belote, U.S.A.	Gyarmati, Hungary	Atwood, U.S.A.
200-M BACKSTROKE	Belote, U.S.A.	Atwood, U.S.A.	Gurr, Canada
200-M. INDIVIDUAL MEDLEY	Gould, Australia	Ender, East Germany	Vidali, U.S.A.
400-M. INDIVIDUAL MEDLEY	Neall, Australia	Cliff, Canada	Calligaris, Italy
400-M. FREESTYLE RELAY	U.S.A.	East Germany	West Germany
400-M. MEDLEY RELAY	U.S.A.	East Germany	West Germany
SPRINGBOARD DIVE	King, U.S.A.	Knape, Sweden	Janicke, East Germany
PLATFORM DIVE	Knape, Sweden	Duchkova, Czechoslovakia	Janicke, East Germany

ARCHERY

EVENT	GOLD	SILVER	BRONZE
MEN	Williams, U.S.A.	Jarvil, Sweden	Laasonen, Finland
WOMEN	Wilber, U.S.A.	Szydlowska, Poland	Gaptchenko, U.S.S.R.

BASKETBALL

EVENT	GOLD	SILVER	BRONZE
	U.S.S.R.	U.S.A.[2]	Cuba

BOXING

EVENT	GOLD	SILVER	BRONZE
LIGHT-FLYWEIGHT	Gedo, Hungary	Kim, North Korea	Evans, Great Britain; E. Rodriguez, Spain
FLYWEIGHT	Kostadinov, Bulgaria	Rwarwogo, Uganda	Blazynski, Poland; D. Rodriguez, Cuba
BANTAMWEIGHT	Martinez, Cuba	Zamora, Mexico	Carreras, U.S.A.; Turpin, Great Britain
FEATHERWEIGHT	Kuznetsov, U.S.S.R.	Waruinge, Kenya	Botos, Hungary; Rojas, Colombia
LIGHTWEIGHT	Szczepanski, Poland	Orban, Hungary	Mbugua, Kenya; Perez, Colombia
LIGHT-WELTERWEIGHT	Seales, U.S.A.	Anghelov, Bulgaria	Daborg, Niger; Vujin, Yugoslavia
WELTERWEIGHT	Correa, Cuba	Kajdi, Hungary	Murunga, Kenya; Valdez, U.S.A.

EVENT	GOLD	SILVER	BRONZE
LIGHT-MIDDLEWEIGHT	Kottysch, West Germany	Rudkowski, Poland	Minter, Great Britain; Tiepold, East Germany
MIDDLEWEIGHT	Lemechev, U.S.S.R.	Virtanen, Finland	Amartey, Ghana; Johnson, U.S.A.
LIGHT-HEAVYWEIGHT	Parlov, Yugoslavia	Carrillo, Cuba	Gortat, Poland; Ikhouria, Nigeria
HEAVYWEIGHT	Stevenson, Cuba	Alexe, Romania	Hussing, West Germany; Thomsen, Sweden

CANOEING

Men

EVENT	GOLD	SILVER	BRONZE
KAYAK SINGLES SLALOM	Horn, East Germany	Sattler, Australia	Gimpel, East Germany
CANADIAN SINGLES SLALOM	Eiben, East Germany	Kauder, West Germany	McEwan, U.S.A.
CANADIAN DOUBLES SLALOM	East Germany	West Germany	France
KAYAK SINGLES	Shaparenko, U.S.S.R.	Peterson, Sweden	Czapo, Hungary
KAYAK PAIRS	U.S.S.R.	Hungary	Poland
KAYAK FOURS	U.S.S.R.	Romania	Norway
CANADIAN SINGLES	Patzaichin, Romania	Wichmann, Hungary	Lewe, West Germany
CANADIAN PAIRS	U.S.S.R.	Romania	Bulgaria

Women

EVENT	GOLD	SILVER	BRONZE
KAYAK SINGLES SLALOM	Bahmann, East Germany	Grothaus, West Germany	Wunderlich, West Germany
KAYAK SINGLES	Riabchinskaya, U.S.S.R.	Jaapies, Netherlands	Pfeffer, Hungary
KAYAK PAIRS	U.S.S.R.	East Germany	Romania

CYCLING

EVENT	GOLD	SILVER	BRONZE
1,000-M. TIME TRIAL	Fredborg, Denmark	Clark, Australia	Schuetze, East Germany
SPRINT	Morelon, France	Nicholson, Australia	Phakadze, U.S.S.R.
TANDEM	U.S.S.R.	East Germany	Poland
INDIVIDUAL PURSUIT	Knudsen, Norway	Kurmann, Switzerland	Lutz, West Germany
TEAM PURSUIT	West Germany	East Germany	Great Britain
INDIVIDUAL ROAD RACE	Kuiper, Netherlands	Sefton, Australia	Huelamo, Spain
100-KM. ROAD TEAM TIME TRIAL	U.S.S.R.	Poland	Belgium

EQUESTRIAN

EVENT	GOLD	SILVER	BRONZE
THREE-DAY	Meade, Great Britain	Argenton, Italy	Jonsson, Sweden
THREE-DAY TEAM	Great Britain	U.S.A.	West Germany
DRESSAGE	Linsenhoff, West Germany	Petushkove, U.S.S.R.	Neckermann, West Germany
DRESSAGE TEAM	U.S.S.R.	West Germany	Sweden
JUMPING	Mancinelli, Italy	Moore, Great Britain	Shapiro, U.S.A.
JUMPING TEAM	West Germany	U.S.A.	Italy

FENCING

Men

EVENT	GOLD	SILVER	BRONZE
FOIL	Woyda, Poland	Kamuti, Hungary	Noel, France
FOIL TEAM	Poland	U.S.S.R.	France
SABER	Sidiak, U.S.S.R.	Maroth, Hungary	Nazlymov, U.S.S.R.
SABER TEAM	Italy	U.S.S.R.	Hungary
ÉPÉE	Fenyvesi, Hungary	La Degaillerie, France	Kulcsar, Hungary
ÉPÉE TEAM	Hungary	Switzerland	U.S.S.R.

Women

EVENT	GOLD	SILVER	BRONZE
FOIL	Ragno, Italy	Bobis, Hungary	Gorokhova, U.S.S.R.
FOIL TEAM	U.S.S.R.	Hungary	Romania

FIELD HOCKEY

EVENT	GOLD	SILVER	BRONZE
	West Germany	Pakistan	India

[1] DeMont, U.S.A., won but was disqualified (appealed).
[2] Result appealed by U.S.A., which refused the medal.

Medal Winners

EVENT	GOLD	SILVER	BRONZE
GYMNASTICS			
Men			
TEAM	Japan	U.S.S.R.	East Germany
ALL-AROUND	Kato, Japan	Kenmotsu, Japan	Nakayama, Japan
FLOOR EXERCISES	Andrianov, U.S.S.R.	Nakayama, Japan	Kasamatsu, Japan
SIDE HORSE	Klimenko, U.S.S.R.	Kato, Japan	Kenmotsu, Japan
RINGS	Nakayama, Japan	Voronin, U.S.S.R.	Tsukahara, Japan
LONG HORSE	Koeste, East Germany	Klimenko, U.S.S.R.	Andrianov, U.S.S.R.
PARALLEL BARS	Kato, Japan	Kasamatsu, Japan	Kenmotsu, Japan
HORIZONTAL BAR	Tsukahara, Japan	Kato, Japan	Kasamatsu, Japan
Women			
TEAM	U.S.S.R.	East Germany	Hungary
ALL-AROUND	Turishcheva, U.S.S.R.	Janz, East Germany	Lazakovitch, U.S.S.R.
LONG HORSE VAULT	Janz, East Germany	Zuchold, East Germany	Turishcheva, U.S.S.R.
UNEVEN PARALLEL BARS	Janz, East Germany	Korbut, U.S.S.R.	Zuchold, East Germany
BALANCE BEAM	Korbut, U.S.S.R.	Lazakovitch, U.S.S.R.	Janz, East Germany
FLOOR EXERCISES	Korbut, U.S.S.R.	Turishcheva, U.S.S.R.	Lazakovitch, U.S.S.R.
JUDO			
LIGHTWEIGHT	Kawaguchi, Japan	Buidaa, Mongolia	Kim, North Korea; Mounier, France
WELTERWEIGHT	Nomura, Japan	Zajkowski, Poland	Hoetger, East Germany; Novikov, U.S.S.R.
MIDDLEWEIGHT	Sekine, Japan	Oh, South Korea	Coche, France; Jacks, Great Britain
LIGHT-HEAVYWEIGHT	Chochoshvily, U.S.S.R.	Starbrook, Great Britain	Barth, West Germany; Ishii, Brazil
HEAVYWEIGHT	Ruska, Netherlands	Glahn, West Germany	Nishimura, Japan; Onashvily, U.S.S.R.
OPEN	Ruska, Netherlands	Kuznetsov, U.S.S.R.	Brondani, France; Parisi, Great Britain
MODERN PENTATHLON			
INDIVIDUAL	Balczo, Hungary	Onischenko, U.S.S.R.	Lednev, U.S.S.R.
TEAM	U.S.S.R.	Hungary	Finland
ROWING			
SINGLE SCULLS	Malishev, U.S.S.R.	Demiddi, Argentina	Gueldenpfennig, East Germany
DOUBLE SCULLS	U.S.S.R.	Norway	East Germany
PAIRS	East Germany	Switzerland	Netherlands
COXED PAIRS	East Germany	Czechoslovakia	Romania
FOURS	East Germany	New Zealand	West Germany
COXED FOURS	West Germany	East Germany	Czechoslovakia
EIGHTS	New Zealand	U.S.A.	East Germany
SHOOTING			
FREE RIFLE	Wigger, U.S.A.	Melnik, U.S.S.R.	Pap, Hungary
SMALL BORE THREE-POSITION	Writer, U.S.A.	Bassham, U.S.A.	Lippoldt, East Germany
SMALL BORE PRONE	Li, North Korea	Auer, U.S.A.	Rotaru, Romania
FREE PISTOL	Skanaker, Sweden	Iuga, Romania	Dollinger, Austria
RAPID-FIRE PISTOL	Zapedzki, Poland	Faita, Czechoslovakia	Torshin, U.S.S.R.
MOVING TARGET	Zhelezniak, U.S.S.R.	Bellingrodt, Colombia	Kynoch, Great Britain
TRAP	Scalzone, Italy	Carrega, France	Basagni, Italy
SKEET	Wirnhier, West Germany	Petrov, U.S.S.R.	Buchheim, East Germany

EVENT	GOLD	SILVER	BRONZE
SOCCER	Poland	Hungary	East Germany; U.S.S.R. (tie)
TEAM HANDBALL	Yugoslavia	Czechoslovakia	Romania
VOLLEYBALL			
MEN	Japan	East Germany	U.S.S.R.
WOMEN	U.S.S.R.	Japan	North Korea
WATER POLO	U.S.S.R.	Hungary	U.S.A.
WEIGHT LIFTING			
FLYWEIGHT	Smalcerz, Poland	Szuecs, Hungary	Holczreiter, Hungary
BANTAMWEIGHT	Foeldi, Hungary	Nassiri, Iran	Chetin, U.S.S.R.
FEATHERWEIGHT	Nourikian, Bulgaria	Shanidze, U.S.S.R.	Benedek, Hungary
LIGHTWEIGHT	Kirzhinov, U.S.S.R.	Koutchev, Bulgaria	Kaczmarek, Poland
MIDDLEWEIGHT	Bikov, Bulgaria	Trabulsi, Lebanon	Silvino, Italy
LIGHT-HEAVYWEIGHT	Jenssen, Norway	Ozimek, Poland	Horvath, Hungary
MIDDLE-HEAVYWEIGHT	Nikolov, Bulgaria	Chopov, Bulgaria	Bettembourg, Sweden
HEAVYWEIGHT	Talts, U.S.S.R.	Kraitchev, Bulgaria	Gruetzner, East Germany
SUPER-HEAVYWEIGHT	Alexeyev, U.S.S.R.	Mang, West Germany	Bonk, East Germany
WRESTLING			
Freestyle			
PAPERWEIGHT	Dmitriev, U.S.S.R.	Nikolov, Bulgaria	Javadpour, Iran
FLYWEIGHT	Kato, Japan	Alakhverdiev, U.S.S.R.	Kim-gwong, North Korea
BANTAMWEIGHT	Yanagida, Japan	Sanders, U.S.A.	Klinga, Hungary
FEATHERWEIGHT	Abdulbekov, U.S.S.R.	Akdag, Turkey	Krastev, Bulgaria
LIGHTWEIGHT	Gable, U.S.A.	Wada, Japan	Ashuraliev, U.S.S.R.
WELTERWEIGHT	Wells, U.S.A.	Karlsson, Sweden	Seger, West Germany
MIDDLEWEIGHT	Tediashvily, U.S.S.R.	J. Peterson, U.S.A.	Jorga, Romania
LIGHT-HEAVYWEIGHT	B. Peterson, U.S.A.	Strakhov, U.S.S.R.	Bajko, Hungary
HEAVYWEIGHT	Iarygin, U.S.S.R.	Baianmunkh, Mongolia	Csatari, Hungary
SUPER-HEAVYWEIGHT	Medved, U.S.S.R.	Douraliev, Bulgaria	Taylor, U.S.A.
Greco-Roman			
PAPERWEIGHT	Berceano, Rumania	Aliabadi, Iran	Anghelov, Bulgaria
FLYWEIGHT	Kirov, Bulgaria	Kirayama, Japan	Bognanni, Italy
BANTAMWEIGHT	Kazakov, U.S.S.R.	Veil, West Germany	Bjoerlin, Finland
FEATHERWEIGHT	Markov, Bulgaria	Wehling, West Germany	Lipien, Poland
LIGHTWEIGHT	Khisamutdinov, U.S.S.R.	Apostolov, Bulgaria	Ranzi, Italy
WELTERWEIGHT	Macha, Czechoslovakia	Galaktopoulos, Greece	Karlsson, Sweden
MIDDLEWEIGHT	Hegedus, Hungary	Nazarenko, U.S.S.R.	Nenadic, Yugoslavia
LIGHT-HEAVYWEIGHT	Rezantsev, U.S.S.R.	Corak, Yugoslavia	Kwiecinski, Poland
HEAVYWEIGHT	Martinescu, Romania	Yakovenko, U.S.S.R.	Kiss, Hungary
SUPER-HEAVYWEIGHT	Roshin, U.S.S.R.	Tomoff, Bulgaria	Dolipschi, Romania
YACHTING			
SOLING	U.S.A.	Sweden	Canada
TEMPEST	U.S.S.R.	Great Britain	U.S.A.
DRAGON	Australia	East Germany	U.S.A.
STAR	Australia	Sweden	West Germany
FLYING DUTCHMAN	Great Britain	France	West Germany
FINN	France	Greece	U.S.S.R.

WORLD POWER

Edwin O. Reischauer

DRAWINGS BY GEOFFREY MOSS

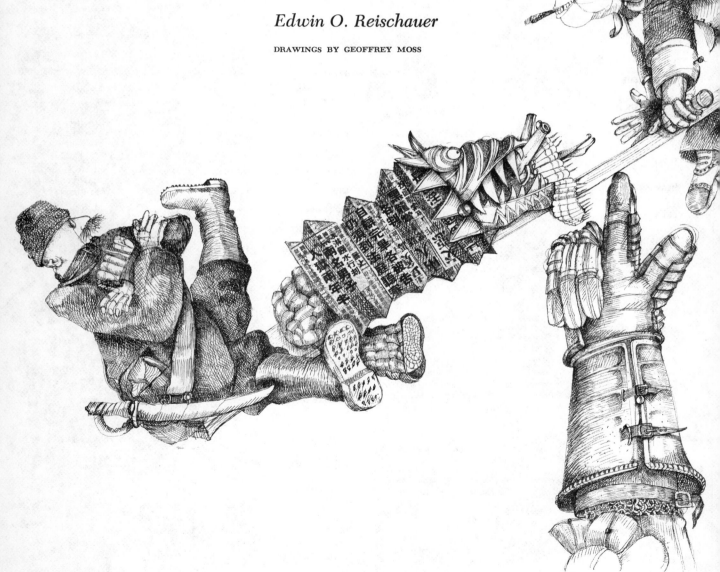

were clearly under strain. The traditional picture of a bipolar world balance of power continued to fade, for it could not explain these moves, and in its place there emerged a picture of a multipolar world balance. President Richard M. Nixon even suggested a specific multipolar model in which there would be a balance among five world powers: the United States, the Soviet Union, Western Europe, China, and Japan.

The concept of the balance of power derives basically from the historical experience of modern Europe, principally in the eighteenth and nineteenth centuries. At that time there existed in Europe a limited number of major states, usually around five or six, of comparable nature and strength. From time to time, these states resorted to warfare to settle clashes of interest and pride when one or another thought it had a military advantage. They also sought to minimize these conflicts by joining together in various combinations to form two groupings of sufficiently equal strength to discourage either side from starting a war.

The lesser European states existed somewhat precariously between these power alliances, finding their security in the stalemate between them or, as happened to Poland, being divided up by them. Because of the supremacy of European military power at the time, this European pattern spread to embrace much of the world. India was part of the booty that went to the British, who played the power game most successfully; Africa, like Poland, was divided up among the contenders; but Siam, as Thailand was called, was preserved as a buffer state between British and French zones in Southeast Asia, much like neutral Belgium in Europe. This was the traditional balance of power, and it is some modern equivalent of this pattern that people have in mind when they speak of the balance of power in the world today.

For a number of years after World War II a simple bipolar balance seemed to be an adequate description of the situation. There were clearly two military giants —the United States and the Soviet Union—roughly in balance; many of the other actual or potential military powers, such as China, Japan, and the nations of Western and Eastern Europe, were closely allied to one of these superpowers, thus creating two great military blocs in uneasy balance with each other. The rest of the nations—sometimes called the Third World—were seen as strung out between the two power blocs, as if all were sitting on the same seesaw. They were considered to be leaning to one side or the other or else maintaining a position of precarious neutrality directly between the two at their point of balance. Any movement in this one-dimensional model could only be away

To nineteenth-century Europe, power was like a seesaw, tilting one way, then the other.

Recent developments have suggested that a major realignment of world power might be under way. Major changes are clearly taking place, if not in world power itself, at least in man's perceptions of it. In 1972 old adversaries, such as the United States and China, sought rapprochement or, as in the case of the United States and the Soviet Union, reached new understandings on arms control. Western Europe further consolidated itself into a major unit. New ties were explored between the Soviet Union and India, the Soviet Union and Japan, and Japan and China, while some old bonds, such as those between the United States and Japan,

Edwin O. Reischauer, a professor at Harvard University, was born in Japan and served as U.S. ambassador there from 1961 to 1966. His works include Japan: The History of a Nation *and* Beyond Vietnam: The United States and Asia.

from one pole and toward the other. Because any shift by any nation was seen as potentially upsetting to the world balance of power, huge military involvements, even in such remote and seemingly unimportant areas as Vietnam, could be justified.

This perception of the world has been shattered in recent years. The split between China and the Soviet Union, which happened more than a decade ago, ruined the basic unilinear model, though Americans continued to cling to it for a long time, as though one end of the seesaw now balanced two boards on the other side. In time it also became obvious that most of the world's population and most national states were not on the see-saw at all. Many had asserted this all along by calling themselves the nonaligned nations. Others, while accepting alignment, clearly added little or no weight to the side to which they belonged but in fact may have been a drain on their patrons. Thus, much of the world was not in any real sense part of the Soviet-American balancing act. Most nations were just going their own way, very little affected by the so-called balance of power in the world.

The Sino-Soviet split gave rise for a while to a triangular model of the balance of power, and China was commonly referred to as the third superpower. But there was never much reality to this picture either. Unlike the historical European model, the units were extremely dissimilar and in any case did not pair up in shifting alliances to maintain the supposed balance. The United States and the Soviet Union were both global military powers still in relative balance with each other. China, which by comparison had a backward and weak economy, was only a regional military power. Its large ground forces made it a formidable opponent in conventional warfare on its own or adjacent territory. But unlike the other two, it had little capacity to project its military power at any great distance. Even its start toward nuclear power was more a matter of future possibilities than present realities. Given the long head start and much greater economic bases of the two superpowers, it seemed unlikely that they would ever slow down enough for China to catch up in nuclear strength. China's limited nuclear forces, more-over, did not give it a capacity for blackmail against its nonnuclear neighbors. Nuclear blackmail to be effective has to be backed up by a credible nuclear threat, which in turn has to be based on a credible capacity to stand up to the great nuclear powers, for they obviously would not stand idly by, permitting nuclear blackmail by China to go unchallenged. The global balance of power thus was not really triangular, nor did the triangular model incorporate the greater part of the world any more successfully than did the bipolar model.

More recently a five-power model has been proposed to explain the rather sudden fluidity in international relations, but it seems no more valid than the triangular model. It, too, leaves much of the world virtually unaffected by the supposed balance between the great powers, and it also suffers from a serious asymmetry between the sizes, natures, and relations of the five so-called world powers. China still remains only a regional military power, and Western Europe and Japan are even less comparable to the United States and the Soviet Union in military terms, the one because it is a conglomeration of states with little unified military purpose, the other because its military power is for the most part only a potentiality not likely to be realized in the foreseeable future because of the Japanese public's strong aversion to war and militarism.

This asymmetry also exists in other fields besides the military, but in different patterns. China, which has a massive population but a largely preindustrial economy, is in no sense an economic power comparable to the other four, which are indeed the four major concentrations of economic strength in the world. In organization and relationships, the United States, Western Europe, and Japan form a closely knit triumvirate of highly prosperous global traders with political institutions based on democracy, economies permitting a relatively high degree of free enterprise, and tremendous and very intimate economic and cultural contacts with one another. The Soviet Union and China, by contrast, are essentially self-contained and isolated societies with minimal contacts with each other or with the other three units of the five-power model. Such characteristics are not just accidental, temporary phenomena but are the natural product of their authoritarian societies and their ideal of a controlled, autarkic economy.

Given these disparities in military power, social and political organization, and economic and cultural relationships, the traditional concept of a balance of power maintained through shifting alliances among a group of basically similar major players is completely illusory. The United States, Western Europe, and Japan have a richness of relationships and a depth of shared interests that are unimaginable between any of them and the Soviet Union or China or between the latter two. For example, trade between the United States and Japan will probably continue to be at least ten times as great as trade between Japan and China and probably 50 or even 100 times larger than trade between the United States and China.

The bipolar, triangular, and five-power balance of power models are all so unsatisfactory that one is forced to wonder if the whole concept of a worldwide balance of power has much validity. There are other flaws in the concept even more serious than the lack of symmetry of the great powers—flaws which probably make it more confusing than helpful in analyzing the present situation in the world.

The historical European balance of power was a very precarious one, not so much because the players might change sides as because war was a readily accepted alternative to peace. A miscalculation that led to defeat rather than victory would of course be painful to a state's pride and might do it some material injury, but the actual damage was far less than that suffered even by the victors in World Wars I and II and incom-

parably less than what would fall on the so-called victor in a nuclear war today. As a consequence, the major powers of that time were ready to go to war for reasons that would now be considered inconsequential or even frivolous and on the basis of only a slight margin of supposed military advantage. In other words, the balance was an extremely delicate one, as easily upset as a finely balanced scale.

This is hardly the situation today between the major military powers. At the present stage of technological advancement, a third world war would all too likely mean the end of higher civilization—conceivably even the end of the human race. War between the two great nuclear nations would amount to a sort of double suicide. War even at the subnuclear level between any actual or potential major military powers would be so devastatingly costly to both contestants and would impose such danger of triggering a nuclear holocaust that all of them would certainly do their best to avoid it. Unlike the European situation in the eighteenth and nineteenth centuries, war between the major military powers can no longer be considered by any of them a really acceptable alternative to peace and could be seriously contemplated only under the most dire or unusual circumstances. Thus, the balance of power between them is very solid, more like a mountain than a

Recent multipolar models

cope with present-day realities

no better than the

discarded seesaw version.

seesaw. It would take some very great shift of forces—like a cataclysmic flood or earthquake—to destabilize the balance and set a great landslide of war in motion.

This is not to say that there is no longer any danger of war between the great powers. There are a number of ways in which one might break out. A serious failure in communication, such as a drastic misunderstanding of what a rival power was doing or intended to do, could trigger a war. "Hot lines" between Washington, D.C., and the Soviet capital have been established in the hope of preventing such mistakes. Or again, a limited confrontation between two or more of the greater powers could, through successive miscalculations of the other side's attitudes and responses, escalate to a general confrontation and eventually to all-out war. It is for this reason that, at least as compared with European states of the eighteenth and nineteenth centuries, the major powers show great restraint in deed, if not in word, in dealing with one another even in relatively minor conflicts of interest or viewpoint.

Another possibility would be that one of the two great nuclear powers established such an overwhelming lead over the other that it became capable of a preemptive first strike which could destroy the capacity of the other to retaliate. This, however, seems very unlikely, and the SALT agreements reached by the United States and the Soviet Union this year, which were designed to limit nuclear defense in particular, appear to be a conscious effort on both sides to prevent such a situation from developing by leaving each side relatively undefended against a nuclear counterattack by the other. One could also imagine war occurring if one of the two great powers went to pieces internally and became incapable of a nuclear response, but again this seems improbable. A more realistic danger might be a great proliferation of nuclear weaponry among a number of nations and the creation of a situation in which a nuclear free-for-all might arise from a nuclear attack of undetermined origin, possibly from some relatively minor power.

These and other possibilities are contingencies that must be guarded against, but they are all extraordinary situations outside the normal meaning of the balance of power. No longer a normal and constantly available alternative to peace between the great powers, war has become only a nightmare possibility that all seek to avoid. Because of the massive ties and closely shared interests between the United States, Japan, and the various countries of Western Europe, war between these warmongers of the recent past is now really unthinkable. War between these three and either the Soviet Union or China may be more conceivable but is nonetheless very unlikely. Only between China and the Soviet Union does war seem a real possibility, and that only because the two, being authoritarian states relatively impervious to the pressures of public opinion, could more easily keep a conflict limited to a tolerable level, as in the small border wars in 1938 and 1939 between the Soviets and a then-authoritarian Japan.

It is the realization of this relative stability of the balance between the great powers, rather than instability or the possible shifting of alliances, that accounts for the present fluidity in big-power relationships. When the bipolar model was accepted as a true picture of power realities, any weakening of alliances or rapprochement of erstwhile enemies was viewed with the greatest alarm. Now all the great powers are a great deal less restrained in their dealings with one another. The Japanese feel less dependence on their defense alliance with the United States and move more freely in developing relations with the Soviet Union and China. The United States views with equanimity the broadening of relationships between Western Europe and the Soviet Union and between Japan and China, while itself seeking closer understandings with the Soviet Union and a rapprochement with China in the hope of increasing American leverage in negotiations with Moscow. Any attempt to interpret these moves in terms of a balance of power is to misunderstand them entirely.

The various balance-of-power models are even more misleading when applied to the areas outside of the five so-called great powers and their close military allies. In the course of the nineteenth century, virtually the whole world became caught up in the European balance of power, but today most nations follow courses influenced only peripherally, if at all, by notions of balance of power between the major nations. The positions of countries such as Austria, Switzerland, Sweden, Finland, and Yugoslavia between the NATO and Soviet defense blocs in Europe do bear some superficial resemblance to the positions of the small countries in the traditional European balance of power, though progressively less so as the possibility of major warfare recedes. The Arab-Israeli conflict may be even closer to the nineteenth-century situation. The two superpowers are involved—the one through old ambitions for power in the Mediterranean area and more recent hopes of influence over the Arab world, the other through emotional and political involvement because of the natural sympathies for Israel on the part of Jews in the United States. But elsewhere in the world, the supposed balance of power between the great powers has little effect upon the other nations, except to give them the hope that they can utilize great power rivalries to extract, for their own purposes, more aid or other concessions from the contestants.

The Korean war two decades ago was seen in purely balance-of-power terms, but the Vietnam war shows the strict limitations of the concept. A balance-of-power viewpoint did account for the original American involvement, but the United States has carefully limited its military efforts in order to avoid a military confrontation with China; and China and the Soviet Union, while bitterly opposed to American actions in Vietnam, have been careful to avoid military involvement themselves. The final outcome is clearly something that will be determined basically by the Vietnamese themselves,

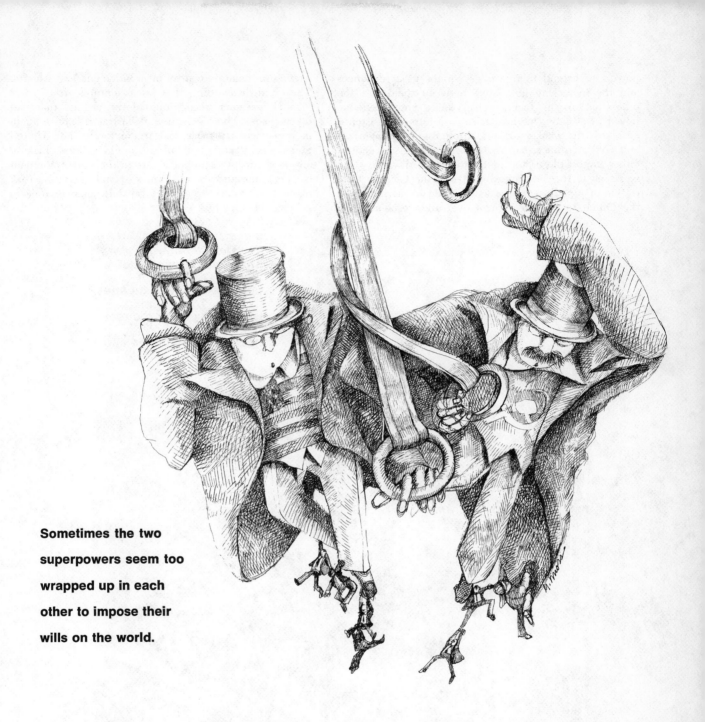

Sometimes the two superpowers seem too wrapped up in each other to impose their wills on the world.

not by a big-power decision on the partition or neutralization of Vietnam, as might have happened in the nineteenth century.

The point is further illustrated by the hands-off policy of the big powers in the wars and general slaughterings of ethnic or political enemies that have gone on in such countries as the Congo (now Zaïre), Indonesia, Nigeria, and more recently Burundi. An even better illustration was the war in December 1971 between India and Pakistan, which resulted in the birth of the nation of Bangladesh—the eighth most populous country in the world. This upheaval in the Indian subcontinent, which involved more than a sixth of the world's population,

did produce sharp reactions by the United States, China, and the Soviet Union, but their threats and alarms amounted to little more than posturings. They had little if any effect on the outcome, which was determined completely by the people on the spot. Clearly, whatever balance of power exists between the great powers affects the rest of the world but slightly.

The rise of nationalism has created another great difference between the present and the nineteenth century, when at relatively little cost the great powers could determine the fate of most of the rest of the world and divide it up between them. Nationalism has more than offset the steadily growing capacity of the great

powers to extend their military might great distances and the increasing imbalance between them and the other nations in technological skills and economic power. Retreating with relative ease into a subsistence economy, the weaker nations, through guerrilla warfare and civil resistance, can make foreign efforts at control either impossible or too costly to be worthwhile. This was seen in the 1930's and 1940's in the Chinese frustration of Japan's war efforts and again in the failure of the Dutch to recover control over Indonesia and the French to maintain control over Indochina and Algeria. The rapid dismantling of overseas empires after World War II was tacit recognition of the change that had taken place. The Vietnam war illustrated it once again in a particularly clear and tragic form. The United States, the strongest of all the world powers, making efforts absurdly disproportionate to the size of Vietnam or the importance of the issues at stake, could wreak havoc throughout the country but has not been able to achieve its objectives.

The worst drawback of balance-of-power theories is that they mask the real need for cooperative efforts.

One by-product of this changed power relationship between the great nations and the less developed countries is a further lessening of the areas and therefore the likelihood of armed conflict between the great powers. In the heyday of the European balance of power, rivalries over trade and political control in other areas were major reasons for wars. The great powers constantly came into conflict over markets for their manufactured goods; sources of raw materials; bases for the further extension of military, economic, and political power; and places where they could fly their flags, largely for the sake of national pride. Most of this conflict is now a thing of the past. Rivalries for markets and raw materials may still exist, but they do not lead to military conflicts, simply because markets and sources of raw materials can no longer be won by war or maintained by colonial control. Open efforts at domination over a less developed country are likely to prove prohibitively costly and end up in the economic expulsion of the great power. Now that the Third World is no longer considered part of a bipolar world balance, it seems improbable that there will be further serious big-power conflicts over these areas or military involvements by any of the great powers on a scale at all comparable to the involvement of the United States in Vietnam.

The stability in the balance between the great powers and their military disengagement from the less developed nations, however, do not mean that the latter too will enjoy stability and peace. They are unstable almost by definition. Their human skills, economies, and social and political institutions are inadequately developed. Many of them are newly created units, sometimes with rather arbitrary boundaries and still unsettled relations with their neighbors. Many no doubt will suffer internal disruptions, and some may be afflicted by wars.

In a sense it is only the less developed countries that can afford war today, because war is much less likely to lead to total destruction for them than for the great industrialized nations. Such local conflicts and disturbances, however, will probably not affect the relationships between the great powers or be much influenced by these relationships. A local balance of power, as between Vietnam, Cambodia, and Thailand or between India, Pakistan, and Bangladesh, may have some meaning for the region affected, but not for a worldwide balance of power.

In the eighteenth and nineteenth centuries the great bulk of international relations had to do with the possibilities and realities of war. Today, at least for the more industrialized nations, warfare has shrunk from the single major concern to a horrible but only peripheral possibility. Other concerns—economic relations, cultural contacts, mutual understanding, and cooperative skills in a very large number of fields—have grown incomparably larger. Under such circumstances, one wonders if an analysis of world power that centers on military strength is any longer valid.

At a time when the horrors of warfare have forced the great powers into a virtual military stalemate, it would seem obvious that economic power is likely to prove a much greater shaper of human destiny than is military might. Will not the capacity for trade, economic investment, and the transfer of technological skills prove more important than nuclear warheads and jet planes as a measure of a country's "power," in the sense of having an impact on the future of mankind? If this is true, then the real superpowers are the United States and its Canadian partner in North America, the grouping of middle-sized and smaller countries in Western Europe, and Japan, the fast-rising superpower of East Asia, while a relatively self-contained Soviet Union and Eastern Europe lag behind, and China is scarcely in the picture at all. Or again, ideologies—that is, the attractiveness of ideas and of patterns of life—may be a more significant measure of world influence today than is military power. Such factors as the affluence, civil liberties, and democratic institutions of North America, Western Europe, and Japan; the cradle-to-grave care in the Soviet Union and the countries of northern Europe; the equalization of distribution and the high sense of morale of the Chinese; or the cultural vigor of a number of nations may be hard to measure in terms of world "power" but may prove much more weighty than warships or tanks.

The traditional balance-of-power approach to international relations actually obscures what are the great problems of the future. Avoiding a great war between the major powers is certainly one of these, but probably not the biggest or most difficult. A more pressing problem is maintaining the community of shared interests and relationships between the United States, Western Europe, and Japan at this time, when the growing solidarity of Europe and the extraordinarily rapid economic growth of Japan are forcing a series of difficult adjustments in their relations with one another. The very misconception that these are three rival players in a balance-of-power game makes these adjustments perhaps all the more difficult.

Another important task for the non-Communist powers is the building of relations and a sense of shared interests with the Soviet Union and China—and, for that matter, with the rest of the world—so that all can cooperate in facing the huge looming problems of the future. I have in mind such problems as the fast-worsening balance between the world's burgeoning population and its limited natural resources, the threat of global pollution and ecological destruction, and the still-growing imbalance between the quarter of the world's population in the industrialized nations, who now have five-sixths of the world's productive capacity, and the remaining three-quarters, who have so little of the world's wealth. These human problems will rise to crisis proportions within the next few decades. None of them has anything to do with the balance of power. In fact, balance-of-power concepts draw our attention away from them and thus make their solution less probable.

Books in Review

The following list is made up of those nonfiction books published in English in late 1971 and 1972 that, in the opinion of the *Year Book* editors, either have broad general appeal or will interest the reader who wants a review of current writings on a given topic. For a broad review of the year's literature—including the most noteworthy poetry and fiction—see AMERICAN LITERATURE, CANADIAN LITERATURE, CHILDREN'S LITERATURE, ENGLISH LITERATURE, and WORLD LITERATURE.

PHILOSOPHY, PSYCHOLOGY, RELIGION

Animals in Art and Thought to the End of the Middle Ages. FRANCIS KLINGENDER; EVELYN ANTAL and JOHN HARTHAN, eds. MIT Press. Monumental analysis, along Freudian lines, of man's often magical relationship to beasts.

The Coming of Age. SIMONE DE BEAUVOIR; PATRICK O'BRIAN, trans. G. P. Putnam's Sons. Engrossing cultural history of aging, whose thesis—that "old age exposes the failure of our entire civilization" and that life itself must be changed before old age can be changed—is supported by findings from history, literature, philosophy, and the social sciences.

Freud and the Americans: The Beginnings of Psychoanalysis in the United States, 1876–1917. NATHAN G. HALE, JR. Oxford University Press. Richly detailed, often brilliant account of the impact of Freudianism on America.

Freud: Living and Dying. MAX SCHUR. International Universities Press. Freud's disciple and personal physician during the decade preceding his painful but dignified death attempts to represent his evolving attitudes toward death and illness.

Mary Barnes: Two Accounts of a Journey Through Madness. MARY BARNES and JOSEPH BERKE. Harcourt Brace Jovanovich. A schizophrenic hits the rock bottom of madness and is helped to achieve rebirth at Kingsley Hall, the therapeutic community founded by R. D. Laing.

Priests in the United States: Reflections on a Survey. ANDREW M. GREELEY. Doubleday. Résumé of the findings of a survey of American priests by the National Opinion Research Center, followed by the author's own reflections and recommendations.

Problems of Knowledge and Freedom: The Russell Lectures. NOAM CHOMSKY. Pantheon Books. Two addresses given at Trinity College, Cambridge, in honor of Bertrand Russell: the first lecture presents modifications of and qualifications to Chomskian linguistics; the second is political, dealing with Vietnam and the American military-industrial complex.

Reinhold Niebuhr: Prophet to Politicians. RONALD H. STONE. Abingdon Press. The intellectual development of Niebuhr and an analysis of his major preoccupations.

The Savage God: A Study of Suicide. A. ALVAREZ. Random House. A meditation on artists' confrontations with self-destruction, creativity's mighty opposite, raising far-reaching questions on the relationship between artists and society.

Science and Philosophy in the Soviet Union. LOREN R. GRAHAM. Alfred A. Knopf. Study of the complex relationship between science and dialectical materialism.

Science and Sentiment in America: Philosophical Thought From Jonathan Edwards to John Dewey. MORTON WHITE. Oxford University Press. Absorbing, coherent treatment of the intricate relationship between the practical and the spiritual in American philosophy.

Souls on Fire: Portraits and Legends of Hasidic Masters. ELIE WIESEL; MARION WIESEL, trans. Random House. A portrayal of the eighteenth-century and nineteenth-century eastern European Jewish mystics, whose resounding call to joy was "a laughter of revolt against a universe where man, whatever he may do, is condemned in advance."

A Theory of Justice. JOHN RAWLS. The Belknap Press of Harvard University Press. A formidable defense of the social contract theory of Rousseau and Kant, formulating principles of justice and negating the claim that systematic political and moral philosophy is extinct.

SOCIAL SCIENCES AND SOCIAL CRITICISM

After the Planners. ROBERT GOODMAN. Simon and Schuster. Advocacy of the "architecture of liberation" in city planning, whereby all people would share society's resources equally.

Children of Crisis. Volume 2: Migrants, Sharecroppers, Mountaineers. Volume 3: The South Goes North. ROBERT COLES. Atlantic–Little, Brown. A psychologist investigates the world of America's rural and urban poor.

Counterrevolution and Revolt. HERBERT MARCUSE. Beacon Press. Superstar of the left calls for revolutionaries to suppress internal ideological differences and build strength in numbers.

Crises of the Republic: Lying in Politics; Civil Disobedience; On Violence; Thoughts on Politics and Revolution. HANNAH ARENDT. Harcourt Brace Jovanovich. Subtle and detailed essays by a political philosopher who sees the "crisis of modern times" as something permanent.

Design for the Real World: Human Ecology and Social Change. VICTOR PAPANEK. Pantheon Books. Consultant to UNESCO and a dean at the California Institute of the Arts, Papanek deplores industrial society's excesses and the role of industrial design as "pimp for big business interests."

Facing Life: Youth and the Family in American History. OSCAR HANDLIN and MARY F. HANDLIN. Little, Brown. General survey culminating in a tirade against radical youth.

Homosexual: Oppression and Liberation. DENNIS ALTMAN. Outerbridge and Dienstfrey. A consideration of two of the "four sexes" and an account of one man's "coming out."

Intimate Behavior. DESMOND MORRIS. Random House. Unintentionally humorous description of human intimacy, featuring these remarkable findings: the human face is the most expressive region of the human body, and an average man spends 2,000 hours of his life shaving. Surprise!

Love and Hate. IRENÄUS EIBL-EIBESFELDT; GEOFFREY STRACHEN, trans. Holt, Rinehart and Winston. Observations on sociability and aggression from the point of view of an old-fashioned new discipline—ethology, the biology of behavior.

Pathways to Madness. JULES HENRY. Random House. The author of *Culture Against Man* documents American family life's complexity; after making extensive visits to five families, he found that survival

often depended upon family members deadening their feelings.

Relations in Public: Microstudies in Public Order. ERVING GOFFMAN. Basic Books. Observations revealing the horror and comedy in our everyday interactions and ritual enactments.

Socialism. MICHAEL HARRINGTON. Saturday Review Press. A fresh interpretation of Marx and the relation between the practical and the visionary, by the chairman of the American Socialist Party.

Where the Wasteland Ends: Politics and Transcendence in Post Industrial Society. THEODORE ROSZAK. Doubleday. The author of *The Making of a Counter Culture* inveighs against science and technocracy.

HISTORY

MODERN HISTORY TO WORLD WAR I

Diderot. ARTHUR M. WILSON. Oxford University Press. Richly detailed account of the life and times of a central figure of the Enlightenment.

The Fatal Friendship: Marie Antoinette, Count Fersen and the Flight to Varennes. STANLEY LOOMIS. Doubleday. Fairly written, carefully researched story of the man who unwittingly contributed to the royal family's downfall.

From Resistance to Revolution: Colonial Radicals and the Development of American Opposition to Britain, 1765–1776. PAULINE MAIER. Alfred A. Knopf. The American Revolution as an ideational affair, depicted from the participants' point of view.

Henry VIII: The Mask of Royalty. LACEY BALDWIN SMITH. Houghton Mifflin. A series of vignettes that contribute to our understanding of a man whose life was a monumental failure.

Napoleon Bonaparte: An Intimate Biography. VINCENT CRONIN. William Morrow. Convincing personal glimpse of the man outside of the social context.

Paris and London in the Eighteenth Century: Studies in Popular Protest. GEORGE RUDÉ. Viking Press. Elegant essays attributing political unrest and mob violence to economic factors.

Samuel de Champlain: Father of New France. SAMUEL ELIOT MORISON. Atlantic–Little, Brown. A sympathetic portrait of a man long neglected by the nation he served, with an appraisal of the French experience in North America during the seventeenth century.

The Sway of the Grand Saloon: A Social History of the North Atlantic. JOHN MALCOLM BRINNIN. Delacorte–Seymour Lawrence. Reminiscences of the great Atlantic ocean liners and of the superrich who traveled on them during a period of artistic and scientific ferment in the nineteenth and early twentieth centuries.

WORLD WAR I AND AFTER

The Double-cross System. J. C. MASTERMAN. Yale University Press. Fascinating account, not originally intended for publication, of the British counterespionage system during World War II.

Eleanor: The Years Alone. JOSEPH P. LASH. W. W. Norton. Moving chronicle of Eleanor Roosevelt's life during the 17 years after FDR's death.

Felled Oaks: Conversation with de Gaulle. ANDRÉ MALRAUX; IRENE CLEPHANE, trans.; revised by LINDA ASHER. Holt, Rinehart and Winston. The mythic figure who embodied the French nation.

Game of the Foxes. LADISLAS FARAGO. David McKay. A diverting, personalized, and uncritical glimpse into the game of espionage during World War II.

In Hiding: The Life of Manuel Cortes. RONALD FRASER. Pantheon Books. Inspiring story of the former mayor of Mijas, Spain, who hid for 30 years to avoid being executed by the Franco regime.

Let History Judge: The Origins and Consequences of Stalinism. ROY A. MEDVEDEV; COLLEEN TAYLOR, trans. Alfred A. Knopf. An insider's meticulous, scholarly analysis of the horrors of the Stalin era.

The Limits of Power: The World and United States Foreign Policy, 1945–1954. JOYCE KOLKO and GABRIEL KOLKO. Harper and Row. Massively researched new interpretations of American policy during the Truman years.

Lloyd George: A Diary by Frances Stevenson. A. J. P. TAYLOR, ed. Harper and Row. The public and private life of "a dynamic force" in British politics, as recorded by the woman who was his confidential secretary for 30 years and then his wife.

Mao's Revolution and the Chinese Political Culture. RICHARD H. SOLOMON. University of California Press. Comprehensive and absorbing depiction of the social and psychological dimensions of governing the old and new China.

Memoirs of Hope: Renewal and Endeavor. CHARLES DE GAULLE. Simon and Schuster. Postwar memoirs by the artist and statesman who considered his mission "to incarnate France."

Nasser. ANTHONY NUTTING. E. P. Dutton. Valuable case history of the Nasser phenomenon.

O Jerusalem! LARRY COLLINS and DOMINIQUE LAPIERRE. Simon and Schuster. Graphic and gripping reconstruction of the 1948 struggle for the Holy City of three religions at the crossroads of three continents; this account helps explain why the outnumbered forces of Israel defeated the Arabs.

A Personal Record: The Labour Government, 1964–1970. HAROLD WILSON. Atlantic–Little, Brown. Image-building by a former prime minister whose "pragmatism" was more rhetorical than real.

Riding the Storm: 1956–1959; Pointing the Way. HAROLD MACMILLAN. Harper and Row. Two volumes of memoirs in which the sun calmly sets on the British Empire.

The Yenan Way in Revolutionary China. MARK SELDEN. Harvard University Press. Scholarly, comprehensive treatment of the legendary Long March and the rise of Communism in China.

AMERICAN HISTORY

American Communism in Crisis, 1943–1957. JOSEPH R. STAROBIN. Harvard University Press. Important personal and political treatment of the American Communist Party's world view in the postwar decade.

The American Heritage History of the American People. BERNARD A. WEISBERGER. A wealth of material to help the reader answer a "specifically unanswerable" question: What is an American?

Benjamin Rush: Revolutionary Gadfly. DAVID FREEMAN HAWKE. Bobbs-Merrill. Skillfully and carefully written biography of the internationally acclaimed American medical scientist who could not rest while there was misery, slavery, or ignorance in the world.

The Children of Pride: A True Story of Georgia and the Civil War. ROBERT MANSON MYERS, ed. Yale University Press. Poignant story of the Old South's destruction, in the form of letters exchanged by members and friends of a Georgia minister's family from 1854 to 1868.

The Discovery of North America. W. P. CUMMING, R. A. SKELTON, and D. B. QUINN. American Heritage Press. A competent narrative about a colorful period of exploration, encyclopedic in scope, with excerpts from original sources.

Half Bitter, Half Sweet: An Excursion Into Italian-American History. ALEXANDER DECONDE. Charles Scribner's Sons. An objective study that may help dispel ignorance and stereotypes about one of America's largest ethnic groups.

Memoirs, 1950–1963. Vol. 2. GEORGE F. KENNAN. Atlantic–Little, Brown. Continued recollections by a distinguished diplomat and historian, treating foreign policy, the cold war, and McCarthyism.

Notable American Women, 1607–1950: A Biographical Dictionary. 3 vols. EDWARD T. JAMES, JANET WILSON JAMES, and PAUL S. BOYER, eds. The Belknap Press of Harvard University Press. Heartening capsule histories of women pushed by adversity to achieve.

Republic or Empire: American Resistance to the Philippine War. DANIEL B. SCHIRMER. Schenkman. A study of anti-imperialism in new leftist terms, taking racism into account.

The Truman Doctrine and the Origins of McCarthyism: Foreign Policy, Domestic Politics, and Internal Security, 1946–1948. RICHARD M. FREELAND. Alfred A. Knopf. The author's thesis is that foreign policy goals in the late 1940's were achieved through the curtailment of domestic civil liberties.

The War for the Union: Vol. 3: The Organized War, 1863–1864. Vol. 4: The Organized War to Victory, 1864–1865. ALLAN NEVINS. Charles Scribner's Sons. Narrative of remarkable scope and character on the American Civil War, published posthumously.

CURRENT EVENTS

The Chilean Revolution: Conversations With Allende. RÉGIS DEBRAY. Pantheon Books. Dialogue with Chile's president, questioning whether socialism can be established without resorting to the use of force.

The Fragile Blossom: Crisis and Change in Japan. ZBIGNIEW BRZEZINSKI. Harper and Row. Intuitive study of the economic and strategic sources of friction with the United States and of political instability in Japan.

The Politics of Heroin in Southeast Asia. ALFRED W. MCCOY et al. Harper and Row. Fascinating, complex, and hotly disputed account of the "international war on the poppy" and the CIA's involvement in it.

Uncensored Russia: Protest and Dissent in the Soviet Union. PETER REDDAWAY, trans. and ed. American Heritage Press. Now organized by subject, these heterodox articles first appeared in the unofficial Moscow journal *A Chronicle of Current Events.*

World Dynamics. JAY W. FORRESTER. Wright-Allen Press. An attempt at predicting the world's future through the use of computer simulation, with the conclusion that growth must end.

U.S. AFFAIRS

The Arnheiter Affair. NEIL SHEEHAN. Random House. Excellent reporting on the almost farcical circumstances surrounding the dismissal of a naval commanding officer in 1966 and its nasty aftermath, revealing some unpleasant details about the American military and its supporters.

Beyond a Reasonable Doubt. SANDOR FRANKEL. Stein and Day. Brilliantly narrated reconstruction of a murder case, both questioning and celebrating the American criminal justice system.

Blood in My Eye. GEORGE L. JACKSON. Random House. Posthumous revolutionary blast of a Soledad Brother.

Citizen Nader. CHARLES MCCARRY. Saturday Review Press. First book-length consideration of the man who could "free others of their indifference."

Cops and Rebels: A Study of Provocation. PAUL CHEVIGNY. Pantheon Books. A New York Civil Liberties Union lawyer examines the extent to which police intelligence work, especially through undercover agents, intrudes on the constitutional rights of ordinary citizens.

A Family Business: Kinship and Social Control in Organized Crime. FRANCIS A. J. IANNI. Basic Books. The revolutionary contention of the author is that Italian-American crime is not rooted in a national crime syndicate called the Mafia but rather is a family business.

Hoax: The Inside Story of the Howard Hughes–Clifford Irving Affair. STEPHEN FAY, LEWIS CHESTER, and MAGNUS LINKLATER. Viking Press. Three British journalists contend that Clifford Irving and Howard Hughes deserve each other.

In Search of Nixon: A Psychohistorical Inquiry. BRUCE MAZLISH. Basic Books. Brief psychological sketch of the president, treating the interplay between the public figure and the private man and finding "an insecurely held self."

In the Name of Profit. ROBERT L. HEILBRONER et al. Doubleday. Assault on the alleged irresponsibility of six corporations, with proposals on how to protect the public interest.

Maximum Security: Letters From California's Prisons. EVE PELL and members of the Prison Law Project, eds. E. P. Dutton. Sickening glimpse of what prison life looks like to the inmates.

A Populist Manifesto: The Making of a New Majority. JACK NEWFIELD and JEFF GREENFIELD. Praeger. Tough-minded program for "a coalition of self-interest between blacks and low- and moderate-income whites" to combat what the authors label the American money and power elite.

Right to Challenge: People and Power in the Steelworkers Union. JOHN HERLING. Harper and Row. A behind-the-scenes view of intrigue and back-stabbing among the union bosses.

Roots of War. RICHARD J. BARNET. Atheneum. This view of foreign policy over the past 30 years condemns America as a threat to world peace.

The Wreck of the Penn Central. JOSEPH R. DAUGHEN and PETER BINZEN. Little, Brown. Cites incompetence, mismanagement, and personal greed as the key elements in the collapse of the nation's largest railroad.

VIETNAM WAR

The Air War in Indochina. RAPHAEL LITTAUER and NORMAN UPHOFF, eds. Beacon Press. A clinical study by the Cornell University Air War Study Group which calls the bombing both tragic and futile.

Cover-up: The Army's Secret Investigation of the Massacre at My Lai 4. SEYMOUR HERSH. Random House. The secret findings of the Peers investigation are made public by a prize-winning reporter.

Fire in the Lake: The Vietnamese and the Americans in Vietnam. FRANCES FITZGERALD. Atlantic–Little, Brown. One of the best books on the subject: all-inclusive, dramatic, and eminently readable.

Papers on the War. DANIEL ELLSBERG. Simon and Schuster. Apologia by the man who released the Pentagon Papers, hoping "that truths that changed me could help Americans free themselves and other victims from our longest war."

War Comes to Long An: Revolutionary Conflict in a Vietnamese Province. JEFFREY RACE. University of California Press. This brilliant study of a strategically located province marks a major breakthrough in understanding the nature of revolution.

YOUTH CULTURE

The Foxfire Book. ELIOT WIGGINTON, ed. Doubleday. Folksy how-to book written by pupils from a school in northern Georgia.

Youth and Dissent. KENNETH KENISTON. Harcourt Brace Jovanovich. A Yale professor of psychology views the youth rebellion as a long-range historical force.

SCIENCE AND MEDICINE

American Medicine and the Public Interest. ROSEMARY STEVENS. Yale University Press. The history and politics of the art and science of healing in the United States.

The Case of the Midwife Toad. ARTHUR KOESTLER. Random House. Defense of the notorious Paul Kammerer, a biologist whose adherence to Lamarck in an age of Darwin led to ostracism and villification by fellow scientists.

The Chinese Art of Healing. STEPHAN PÁLOS; TRANSLAGENCY, LTD., trans. Herder and Herder. Carefully researched account by a Buddhist monk of the revolution in Chinese traditional medicine catalyzed by Mao's mandate that all doctors study acupuncture.

Dr. Kinsey and the Institute for Sex Research. WARDELL POMEROY. Harper and Row. Vivid memoir by a colleague of the man whose scholarly reports on sexual behavior announced the death of Victorian sexual morality.

In Critical Condition: The Crisis in America's Health Care. EDWARD M. KENNEDY. Simon and Schuster. Outrage at a system "that can be so callous to human suffering, so intent on high salaries and profits, and so unconcerned for the needs of our people."

The Insect Societies. EDWARD O. WILSON. The Belknap Press of Harvard University Press. Landmark work, integrating and synthesizing many levels of knowledge about social insects.

The Life of Benjamin Banneker. SILVIO A. BEDINI. Charles Scribner's Sons. The accomplishments of a free-born black tobacco farmer and scientist of the eighteenth century that offered proof to his contemporaries that blacks were not inferior to whites in mental capacity.

THE ARTS

PAINTING AND SCULPTURE

The De-definition of Art. HAROLD ROSENBERG. Horizon Press. Vehement attack on the American avant-garde in art.

Hogarth: His Life, Art and Times. 2 vols. RONALD PAULSON. Yale University Press. A masterful painter, print-maker, and commodity artist of the eighteenth century is considered in the framework of his age.

Terminal Iron Works: The Sculpture of David Smith. ROSALIND E. KRAUSS. MIT Press. Sophisticated yet accessible criticism of the work of one of America's greatest sculptors, defining his modernism and originality.

LITERATURE

Arriving Where We Started. BARBARA PROBST SOLOMON. Harper and Row. Against the backdrops of Washington, New York, Paris, and Madrid, a member of the "un-focused" generation that came of age in the late 1940's and early 1950's unashamedly indulges in self-analysis.

Aspects of Alice: Lewis Carroll's Dreamchild as Seen Through the Critics' Looking Glasses, 1865–1971. ROBERT PHILLIPS, ed. Vanguard Press. Uneven approaches to wonderland.

Camus and Sartre: Crisis and Commitment. GERMAINE BRÉE. Delacorte Press. Two giants are judged, and Camus is declared the better man.

Coleridge, the Damaged Archangel. NORMAN FRUMAN. George Braziller. Passionate indictment of the artist as con man.

The Compact Edition of the Oxford English Dictionary. Oxford University Press. This micrographically reproduced text, reducing the original 13 volumes to two, increases the accessibility of an incomparable reference work which is itself a masterpiece of English prose.

The Diary of Anaïs Nin. Vol. 4: 1944–1947. Harcourt Brace Jovanovich. Beyond gossip or anecdote, this diary records the insights of an extraordinary writer who reveals herself through her relationships with others.

Existential Errands. NORMAN MAILER. Little, Brown. Mailer again speaks out on politics, sports, films, and his favorite topic, himself.

Harlem Renaissance. NATHAN IRVIN HUGGINS. Oxford University Press. Cultural history of a post–World War I literary and artistic flowering among black Americans.

Henry James. Vol. 5: The Master, 1901–1916. LEON EDEL. J. P. Lippincott. Highly illuminating and absorbing conclusion to an opus over 20 years in the making.

Herself: An Autobiographical Work. HORTENSE CALISHER. Arbor House. Meditation on the fiction-writer's craft, defining art as "a statement by an outsider, from within."

Kathleen and Frank. CHRISTOPHER ISHERWOOD. Simon and Schuster. Isherwood's oblique autobiography, based on his mother's letters and diaries and his own memory.

Meyer Weisgal . . . So Far: An Autobiography. Random House. Captivating and provocative tale of the disasters and triumphs of a talented man.

Midnight Oil. V. S. PRITCHETT. Random House. Highly polished, expertly written second volume of memoirs.

No Name in the Street. JAMES BALDWIN. Dial Press. A master of the essay form chronicles and comments on the abortive civil rights movement in America.

People in a Diary: A Memoir. S. N. BEHRMAN. Little, Brown. Delightful anecdotes by a man for whom "comedy is the saving grace which makes life bearable."

Poe Poe Poe Poe Poe Poe Poe. DANIEL HOFFMAN. Doubleday. A scholar and poet gives an exciting account of his involvement, from boyhood on, with the work of an American genius.

The Pound Era. HUGH KENNER. University of California Press. Provocative and demanding study of the controversial poet, by Pound's leading enthusiast.

South to a Very Old Place. ALBERT MURRAY. McGraw-Hill. A black writer's voyage "home" to rediscover the meaning of the history of black America.

Speaking and Language: Defence of Poetry. PAUL GOODMAN. Random House. "How people actually speak" belies other analysts' highfalutin linguistic theories, according to this native skeptic.

FILMS AND THEATER

The Citizen Kane Book: Raising Kane. PAULINE KAEL. Atlantic–Little, Brown. Engrossing study of what the noted film critic calls a "shallow masterpiece," including the original shooting script by Herman J. Mankiewicz and Orson Welles.

Cole. ROBERT KIMBALL, ed. Holt, Rinehart and Winston. Cole Porter, the aristocrat of Tin Pan Alley, is celebrated in this bit of social history through his exuberant lyrics, other writings, and memorabilia.

D. W. Griffith: His Life and Work. ROBERT M. HENDERSON. Oxford University Press. Monumental research on Griffith's life and times that doesn't quite get to the roots of his genius.

George S. Kaufman: An Intimate Portrait. HOWARD TEICHMANN. Atheneum. Original, personal, and adroit examination of an impressive and acerbic master of the American theater.

Run-through: A Memoir. JOHN HOUSEMAN. Simon and Schuster. A substantial account of what it was like to be a producer at a high point in the American theater.

Sean. EILEEN O'CASEY; J. C. TREWIN, ed. Coward, McCann and Geoghegan. Intimate account of the life, career, and 37-year marriage of the Irish playwright.

What Is Cinema? Vol. 2. ANDRÉ BAZIN; HUGH GRAY, trans. and ed. A major contemporary film critic and theorist gives his views on sociology and cinema, Italian neorealism, and cinema eroticism.

MUSIC

American Popular Song: The Great Innovators, 1900–1950. ALEC WILDER; JAMES T. MAHER, ed. Oxford University Press. Attentive examination of hundreds of songs by the greatest craftsmen of popular music: Porter, Gershwin, Berlin, Rogers, and others.

Music and Musical Life in Soviet Russia, 1917–1970. BORIS SCHWARZ. W. W. Norton. How Marxist aesthetics have stifled Soviet composers.

Stravinsky: Chronicle of a Friendship, 1948–1971. ROBERT CRAFT. Alfred A. Knopf. Personal diary by Stravinsky's partner and member of his household, recording the composer's judgments, friendships, travels, and creative activities and treating the themes of old age and death as well as music.

Varèse: A Looking-glass Diary. Vol. 1: 1883–1928. LOUISE VARÈSE. W. W. Norton. Biography of a composer who, rejecting tradition, foresaw the sounds electronic instruments would eventually produce.

JOURNALISM

The Effete Conspiracy and Other Crimes by the Press. BEN H. BAGDIKIAN. Harper and Row. An assistant managing editor and media critic of the Washington *Post* appraises the "community educational institution run for profit," known as the press, and its shortcomings.

Luce and His Empire. W. A. SWANBERG. Charles Scribner's Sons. Massively researched nondefinitive biography of Luce's legendary Life-Time.

The Papers & The Papers. SANFORD J. UNGAR. E. P. Dutton. Important journalism professing to be "An Account of the Legal and Political Battle Over the Pentagon Papers."

Pressures on the Press. HILLIER KRIEGHBAUM. Thomas Y. Crowell. One of the best anatomies of the media, recommending citizen and journalist participation on media review boards to apply moral pressure to media on the local, regional, and (eventually) national levels.

What You Don't Know Can Hurt You. LESTER MARKEL. Public Affairs Press. Improving media will lead to a better informed public and thus to a better country, according to the former editor of the Sunday New York *Times*.

EDUCATION

The English Infant School and Informal Education. LILLIAN WEBER. Prentice-Hall. How an innovative form of state education offers a real possibility for change in our own public schools.

Free Schools. JONATHAN KOZOL. Houghton Mifflin. Manual for setting up a ghetto free school to combat social and political injustice.

Something for Everybody Is Not Enough: An Educator's Search for His Education. WILLIAM M. BIRENBAUM. Random House. Useful book by an administrator who believes schools are for students; a record of his own education and a guide for those who wish to effect change.

Teachers and Power: The Story of the American Federation of Teachers. ROBERT J. BRAUN. Simon and Schuster. A journalist views the teachers union with alarm, outrage, and disappointment.

SPORTS

The Boys of Summer. ROGER KAHN. Harper and Row. Nostalgic account of the achievements of the Brooklyn Dodgers of the 1950's and their later careers.

A Picture History of the Olympics. JAMES COOTE. Macmillan. Competent pictorial account of the Olympic Games.

The Summer Game. ROGER ANGELL. Viking Press. Another summer, another Roger, but this one may be the better book, displaying a "feel" for baseball that few other authors have ever captured.

TRAVEL

Calcutta. GEOFFREY MOORHOUSE. Harcourt Brace Jovanovich. An angry response to British infamy in a disaster area once known as the "second city in the Empire."

800,000,000: The Real China. ROSS TERRILL. Little, Brown. Somewhat skeptical but favorable view by an Australian socialist of the "collective drama of China 'standing up.'"

The New Anatomy of Britain. ANTHONY SAMPSON. Stein and Day. Stylishly journalistic blend of fact, opinion, gossip, and description, attempting to answer the question: Who runs Britain?

HUMOR

Dick Gregory's Political Primer. DICK GREGORY. Harper and Row. How the American government works, from an antiestablishment point of view.

How to Do Things Right: The Revelations of a Fussy Man. L. RUST HILLS. Doubleday. According to the author, this book is "a sequence of apparently complicated solutions to apparently simple problems."

Instant Status, or How to Become a Pillar of the Upper Middle Class. CHARLES MERRILL SMITH. Doubleday. Manual for acquiring "the genteel UMC manners and gracious life style portrayed on television soap operas and cigarette ads."

Poor Russell's Almanac. RUSSELL BAKER. Doubleday. A browser's delight: selections from his New York *Times* columns.

FOOD

The Physiology of Taste, or Meditations on Transcendental Gastronomy. JEAN ANTHELME BRILLAT-SAVARIN; M. F. K. FISHER, trans. Alfred A. Knopf. Philosophical discourses on the pleasures of eating by the eighteenth-century high priest of *la cuisine*.

CHILDREN'S BOOKS

TEEN-AGE

Blow Ye Winds Westerly: The Seaports and Sailing Ships of Old New England. ELIZABETH GEMMING. Thomas Y. Crowell. A look at a vanished era in American history; artfully presented along with contemporary paintings and old maps.

Death Is a Noun: A View of the End of Life. JOHN LANGONE. Little, Brown. Done with candor and common sense, a calm presentation of a subject which often confronts young people at an early age.

Hooray for Peace, Hurrah for War: The United States During World War I. STEVEN JANTZEN. Alfred A. Knopf. Instructive and interesting account drawn from letters, diaries, documents, eyewitness accounts, songs, speeches, and illustrations of the period.

Modern China. ORVILLE SCHELL and JOSEPH ESHERICK. Alfred A. Knopf. From the Opium War to the Communist revolution, an account of how war, famine, and social change affected the Chinese peasant.

More Words of Science. ISAAC ASIMOV. Houghton Mifflin. From ablation to zpg; a sequel to the author's *Words of Science*.

Standing Up for the People: The Life and Work of Estes Kefauver. HARVEY SWADOS. E. P. Dutton. Solidly researched, effectively presented biography of the southern senator.

The Sun Dance People. RICHARD ERDOES. Alfred A. Knopf. Engrossing history of the Plains Indians enhanced by old prints and paintings, with photographs by the author.

Superstition! WILLARD A. HEAPS. Thomas Nelson. Gives a fascinating panoramic view of those old beliefs that modern man still clings to.

The Three Lives of Joseph Conrad. OLIVIA COOLIDGE. Houghton Mifflin. A life of the novelist as a writer, husband, and father

that sorts out the man from the myth, the fact from the fiction.

21 Kinds of American Folk Art and How to Make Each One. JEAN KINNEY and CLE KINNEY. Atheneum. An attractive miscellany of intriguing things to try from America's cultural heritage.

AGES 8 TO 12

The American Heritage School Dictionary. PETER DAVIES, editor-in-chief. American Heritage and Houghton Mifflin. Over 5 million words, aptly defined. A well-produced and valuable reference work for ages up to 15.

The Art of the New American Nation. SHIRLEY GLUBOK. Macmillan. Portraits, public and private buildings, furniture and folk carvings, fine silverware, all presented in a handsome pictorial record of America's first 50 years.

Brave Eagle's Account of the Fetterman Fight, 21 December 1866. PAUL GOBLE and DOROTHY GOBLE. Pantheon Books. Matter-of-factly told in the words of a young Oglala Sioux and magnificently illustrated —a brief account of Chief Red Cloud's six months' war with the U.S. government.

The Cowboy Trade. GLEN ROUNDS. Holiday House. The author's pen-and-ink drawings ramble across the pages of a relaxed but authoritative history of wranglers and wrangling.

The Hodgepodge Book. DUNCAN EMRICH, ed. Four Winds. An almanac of American folklore, brimming with "practical" information, bubbling with wit and humor.

How to Make Whirligigs and Whimmy Diddles and Other American Folkcraft Objects. FLORENCE H. PETTIT. Thomas Y. Crowell. A professional craftsman's detailed instructions for sewing a patchwork quilt, braiding a corn-shuck mat, painting a picture on velvet, and dipping candles.

The Impossible People: A History Natural and Unnatural of Beings Terrible and Wonderful. GEORGESS MCHARGUE. Holt, Rinehart and Winston. A compendium, dazzling in scholarship and delightful in details, about the mythological creatures that may or may not have inhabited the earth.

AGES 7 TO 11

When Clay Sings. BYRD BAYLOR. Charles Scribner's Sons. Prose poem graced by Tom Bahti's primitive-style pictures that explores the archaeology and art of the southwestern American Indians.

Witches, Pumpkins, and Grinning Ghosts: The Story of the Halloween Symbols. EDNA BARTH. Seabury. Back in ancient Celtic times All Hallow's Eve wasn't trick or treat.

PICTURE BOOKS

Behind the Wheel. EDWARD KOREN. Holt, Rinehart and Winston. A dozen double-page spreads show how it looks from the bridge of a tug, the cab of a tractor-trailer, the cockpit of a plane, and so forth.

Count and See. TANA HOBAN. Macmillan. Clear photographs present a numbers game where there are familiar objects to count and dots and numerals to reinforce concepts.

Crash! Bang! Boom! PETER SPIER. Doubleday. A bright, busy catalog of things and the sounds they make.

D'Aulaire's Trolls. INGRI and EDGAR PARIN D'AULAIRE. Doubleday. Bachelors, husbands, wives, and children, hulder maidens, troll hags, trolls with one head, two heads, even 12 heads—a mythological "sociology" of Norway's "creatures of darkness."

Hosie's Alphabet. HOSEA, TOBIAS, and LISA BASKIN, words; LEONARD BASKIN, pictures. Viking Press. A stunning array of animal pictures from armadillo to zebu.

I Saw a Purple Cow and 100 Other Recipes for Learning. ANN COLE et al. Little, Brown. An early learning book for parents and teachers in day-care centers, providing practical and proven activities in recipe form.

Play on Words. ALICE PROVENSEN and MARTIN PROVENSEN. Random House. Engaging verbal and visual gamesmanship for funning and punning with words that make sense and words that make no sense.

Contributors

Adam, Herbert. Professor of political science, Simon Fraser University. SOUTH AFRICA.

Adams, Val. Assistant radio and television editor, New York *News.* TELEVISION AND RADIO BROADCASTING.

Allaway, Roger. Editor, *American Maritime Officer.* Free-lance writer. THE XX OLYMPICS; SPORTS: ICE SKATING; SKIING.

Allen, Philip M. Associate professor, Vermont State colleges. Former African-American Institute director, West Africa. Coauthor, *Traveler's Africa.* GAMBIA; MAURITIUS; SIERRA LEONE.

Anthrop, Donald F. Associate professor of environmental studies, San Jose State College. POWER AND ENERGY SOURCES.

Areskoug, Kaj. Assistant professor of banking, New York University. Free-lance writer. INTERNATIONAL BANKING AND FINANCE.

Armstrong, Edward H. Editor, Illinois *State Register.* ILLINOIS.

Ashbrook, Joseph. Editor, *Sky and Telescope.* ASTRONOMY.

Banki, Judith. Assistant director, interreligious affairs, American Jewish Committee. RELIGION: JEWISH AFFAIRS (coauthor).

Battelle, Kenneth E. President, Kenneth Beauty Salons and Products, Inc. FASHION: HAIR STYLES.

Baxter, R. R. Professor of law, Harvard University. Member, Permanent Court of Arbitration, The Hague. INTERNATIONAL LAW.

Behr, Edward. Paris bureau chief, *Newsweek.* EUROPE.

Bennet-Clark, Henry C. Lecturer, department of zoology, Edinburgh University. BIOLOGY; BOTANY; ZOOLOGY.

Bennett, Leslie H. Associate editor, Houston *Chronicle.* TEXAS.

Bergen, Dan. Associate professor of library science, University of Rhode Island. Contributor, *Library Quarterly.* LIBRARIES.

Blair, George S. Elisabeth Helms Rosecrans professor of social science, Claremont Graduate School, California. Author, *American Legislatures.* CALIFORNIA.

Bloomfield, Irangi C. UNITED NATIONS (coauthor).

Bloomfield, Lincoln P. Professor of political science and director, Arms Control Project, Massachusetts Institute of Technology. Member, Presidential Commission on the UN. UNITED NATIONS (coauthor).

Boughey, Arthur S. Professor of biology, School of Biological Science, University of California (Irvine). Author, *Man and the Environment.* ENVIRONMENT.

Bovey, J. A. Provincial archivist of Manitoba. NORTHWEST TERRITORIES; YUKON TERRITORY.

Bowman, Larry W. Assistant professor of political science, University of Connecticut. Contributor, *Africa Report.* BURUNDI; KENYA; RHODESIA; RWANDA; TANZANIA.

Braynard, Frank O. Director, South Street Seaport Museum, N.Y. Author, *One Square Mile: A Sea Cliff Sketchbook* and eight books on shipping. SHIPS AND SHIPPING.

Brem, Ralph C. Managing editor, Pittsburgh *Press.* PENNSYLVANIA.

Brooks, Allan Yale. Communications consultant. Manager of development, Western Union Corporation. COMPUTERS; ELECTRONICS; METEOROLOGY.

Brown, W. David. Assistant professor of journalism, Morehead State University, Kentucky. MISSISSIPPI.

Bustin, Edouard. Professor of political science, Boston University. Contributor, *An African Dilemma: Refugees South of the Sahara.* GHANA; GUINEA; ZAÏRE.

Butwell, Richard. Chairman, department of political science, State University of New York, Brockport. Author, *Southeast Asia Today & Tomorrow; U Nu of Burma.* BURMA.

Byron, Stuart. Free-lance film critic. Contributor, *Village Voice, Rolling Stone,* New York *Times.* MOTION PICTURES.

Carry, B. Peter. Staff writer, *Sports Illustrated.* SPORTS: BASKETBALL (COLLEGIATE AND PROFESSIONAL); LACROSSE.

Chesher, Richard. Vice-president, Marine Research Foundation. OCEANOGRAPHY.

Chester, Hyman. Special sections editor, Milwaukee *Journal.* WISCONSIN.

Christgau, Robert. Music critic, *Newsday.* MUSIC: POPULAR, JAZZ, AND FOLK.

Cole, Elma Phillipson. Director, Associated Organizations, National Assembly for Social Policy and Development, Inc. SOCIAL SECURITY.

Coleman, A. D. Photographic critic, *Village Voice;* contributor, New York *Times;* instructor, New School for Social Research and Maryland Institute. PHOTOGRAPHY.

Creedman, Theodore S. Former visiting lecturer, University of Costa Rica. Author, *Historical Dictionary of Costa Rica.* COSTA RICA; EL SALVADOR; GUYANA; NICARAGUA; PANAMA AND THE CANAL ZONE.

Curcio, Dominic F. Bureau chief, *Business Week* and McGraw-Hill *World News.* President, International Press Club. SPAIN.

Danforth, Paul M. Author, lecturer, and consultant. TRANSPORTATION.

Danzig, Allison. Former sportswriter, New York *Times.* Author, *History of American Football; The Racquet Game.* SPORTS: FOOTBALL (COLLEGIATE); TENNIS.

Datta-Ray, Sunanda K. Assistant editor, Calcutta and New Delhi *Statesman.* Correspondent, London *Observer,* Canberra *Times,* and *Le monde diplomatique.* BANGLADESH; INDIA; PAKISTAN.

David, Greg. Assistant layout editor, Charlotte *Observer.* NORTH CAROLINA.

Deedy, John. Managing editor, *Commonweal.* Contributor, New York *Times.* RELIGION: ROMAN CATHOLIC CHURCH.

Defty, Sally Bixby. Reporter, St. Louis *Post-Dispatch.* MISSOURI.

Denenberg, Herbert S. Insurance commissioner of Pennsylvania. INSURANCE.

Dommen, Arthur J. Former Saigon bureau chief, Los Angeles *Times* and UPI. Free-lance writer. LAOS.

Donnelly, David F., Jr. Reporter, Providence *Journal-Bulletin.* RHODE ISLAND.

Dow, Richard. Staff officer, Geophysics Research Board and Space Science Board. SPACE EXPLORATION.

Dowie, Patricia L. Owner-manager, Pat Dowie P.R., Promotion, Publicity. HAWAII.

Dowty, Alan. Senior lecturer, department of international relations, Hebrew University of Jerusalem. ISRAEL.

Dudley, Caroline G. Free-lance writer. NOBEL PRIZES.

Dumas, Ernest C. Political reporter, Arkansas *Gazette*. Correspondent, New York Times. ARKANSAS.

DuPre, Flint O. Deputy chief, Air Force Security Review, U.S. Air Force. Author, *USAF Biographical Dictionary; Your Career in Federal Civil Service; So You Want to Be a Professional Officer*. AEROSPACE.

Dutton, John E. Chief librarian, North York Public Library, Ontario. ALBERTA.

Egli, David. Staff writer, *Newsweek*. SWITZERLAND.

Eisen, Jack E. Urban affairs and transportation reporter, Washington *Post*. WASHINGTON, D.C.

Ellsworth, Theodore D. Professor of retail management, New York University Schools of Business. RETAIL BUSINESS.

Elwitt, Sanford H. Associate professor of history, University of Rochester. Contributor, *Science and Society; French Historical Studies*. FRANCE.

Faber, Nancy Gay. Free-lance journalist. Contributor, *Ladies' Home Journal, Time, Life*. PEOPLE IN THE NEWS.

Famighetti, Bob. Staff editor. OPEN CLASSROOM.

Fasteau, Brenda Feigen. Coordinator, ACLU Women's Rights Project. Free-lance writer. ELECTION '72: ROLE OF WOMEN.

Fischler, Stan. Contributor, *Look; Sport; Sports Illustrated*. Author, *Hockey! The Story of the World's Fastest Sport*. SPORTS: ICE HOCKEY.

Fleming, Shirley. Editor, *Musical America*. Contributor, *High Fidelity*. MUSIC: CLASSICAL MUSIC.

Flinchum, James M. Editor, Wyoming *State Tribune*. WYOMING.

Folmsbee, Stanley J. Professor emeritus of history, University of Tennessee. Managing editor of publications, East Tennessee Historical Society. Coauthor, *History of Tennessee*. TENNESSEE.

Foster, James L. Instructor, departments of political science, Massachusetts Institute of Technology and Tufts University. UNITED STATES: NATIONAL DEFENSE.

Franke, Walter H. Professor of labor and industrial relations, University of Illinois at Urbana–Champaign. Author, *Unwanted Workers; The Shortage of Skilled and Technical Workers*. EMPLOYMENT.

French, William. Literary editor, Toronto *Globe and Mail*. CANADIAN LITERATURE.

Frey, Richard L. President, International Bridge Press Association. Associate editor, *Bridge World*. Editor-in-chief, *Official Encyclopedia of Bridge*. Author, *How to Win at Contract Bridge in 10 Easy Lessons*. BRIDGE.

Friis, Erik J. Literary secretary, American-Scandinavian Foundation. Editor, *The American-Scandinavian Review*. Coeditor, *Scandinavian Studies*. ICELAND.

Fuller, Harry E., Jr. Editorial writer, Salt Lake City *Tribune*. UTAH.

Goodman, Donald. Assistant professor of sociology, John Jay College of Criminal Justice (CUNY). CRIME AND CRIME PREVENTION.

Goodsell, James Nelson. Latin America editor, *Christian Science Monitor*. Author, *Quest for Change in Latin America*. DOMINICAN REPUBLIC; HAITI; PUERTO RICO.

Graebner, Norman A. Edward R. Stettinius professor in modern American history, University of Virginia. Author, *Ideas and Diplomacy*. UNITED STATES: FOREIGN RELATIONS.

Greenberg, Milton. Dean of Faculties, Roosevelt University. Coauthor, *The American Political Dictionary*. CIVIL LIBERTIES AND CIVIL RIGHTS.

Greenwood, Gordon. Professor of history, University of Queensland. Member, Australian Commission on Advanced Education. Editor, *Australian Journal of Politics and History*. AUSTRALIA.

Grindrod, Muriel. Assistant editor, *The Annual Register of World Events*. Author, *Rebuilding of Italy; Italy*. ITALY.

Hagerty, Jack. Editor, Grand Forks *Herald*. NORTH DAKOTA.

Hall, Frances L. Director, International Trade Analysis Division, Bureau of International Commerce, U.S. Department of Commerce. INTERNATIONAL TRADE.

Hall, Henry Francis. President, Hall Writing and Research Service, Winnipeg and Calgary. MANITOBA.

Hammond, Allen L. Research news editor, *Science*. PHYSICS.

Hannan, Roger James. Associate editor, *Engineering News-Record*. BUILDING AND CONSTRUCTION INDUSTRIES.

Harrington, Michael. Editor, *Evening Telegram*, St. John's, Newfoundland. NEWFOUNDLAND AND LABRADOR.

Harris, Helen W. Editor, *Home*. Contributing editor, *Town and Country*. INTERIOR DESIGN.

Hartman, Paul T. Associate professor of economics, University of Illinois. Senior fellow, The Brookings Institution. Author, *Collective Bargaining and Productivity*. LABOR UNIONS.

Haverstock, Nathan A. Newspaper columnist on Latin American affairs. Coauthor, *Dateline Latin America*. PARAGUAY; URUGUAY; VENEZUELA.

Hayes, Hal. Sportswriter, Atlanta *Constitution*. SPORTS: GOLF.

Heath, Dwight B. Professor of anthropology, Brown University. Author, *Historical Dictionary of Bolivia; Contemporary Cultures and Societies of Latin America*. BOLIVIA.

Hechinger, Fred M. Member, editorial board and education editor, New York Times. Author, *Pre-school Education Today; The New York Times Guide to New York City Private Schools*. EDUCATION.

Heilbut, Wilfred, D.M.D. Clinic coordinator, Mount Sinai Hospital department of dentistry; associate, department of community medicine, Mount Sinai School of Medicine. DENTISTRY.

Henderson, Harry W. Former writer-economist, Agricultural Service, U.S. Department of Agriculture. Free-lance writer. AGRICULTURE; U.S. PRODUCTION TABLE; WORLD PRODUCTION TABLE.

Hewes, Henry. Drama critic, *Saturday Review*. President, Drama Desk, and president, New York Drama Critics Circle. Editor, *Famous American Plays of the 1940's; The Best Plays of 1963–1964*. THEATER.

Hickey, T. J. O. Member, editorial staff, *The Times* of London. UNITED KINGDOM OF GREAT BRITAIN AND NORTHERN IRELAND; IRELAND.

Hooper, Thomas J. Free-lance writer. NEW JERSEY.

Hoover, Herbert T. Associate professor of history, University of South Dakota. SOUTH DAKOTA.

Jessup, Walter E. Consulting civil engineer. Coauthor, *Law and Specifications for Engineers and Scientists*. CIVIL ENGINEERING.

Joffe, Ellis. Research associate, University of Michigan Center for Chinese Studies. Author, *Party and Army: Professionalism*

and Political Control in the Chinese Officer Corps, 1949–1964. CHINA, PEOPLE'S REPUBLIC OF.

Jones, Bea. Past president, Garden Writers Association of America. Gardening editor, Newsday. Coauthor, Smash the Political Machine. GARDENING.

Keese, Parton. Boating editor, New York Times. SPORTS: POWERBOATING.

Kelley, James R. Assistant professor of history, Georgia State University. MEXICO.

Kelly, Jerome. Editorial writer, Baltimore Sun. MARYLAND.

Kenney, Michael. Massachusetts state house reporter, Boston Globe. MASSACHUSETTS.

Kimbell, Charles L. Physical scientist, U.S. Bureau of Mines. MINERAL AND METAL INDUSTRY.

Krieg, Clarice. Head catalog librarian, University of Oregon. OREGON.

Krooss, Herman E. Professor of economics, New York University. Author, American Economic Development. BANKING AND FINANCE; UNITED STATES: BUDGET.

Lamson, George. Assistant professor of economics, Carleton College, Minnesota. CAMEROON; CHAD; DAHOMEY; LIBERIA; NIGER; TOGO; UPPER VOLTA.

Larkin, Kathy. Fashion editor, New York Daily News. FASHION: WOMEN'S FASHION.

Leifer, Michael. Lecturer in international relations, London School of Economics and Political Science. AFGHANISTAN; KHMER REPUBLIC; NEPAL; THAILAND.

Leonard, Lee. Ohio statehouse correspondent, UPI. OHIO.

Lewis, David L. Professor of business history and director of school relations, Graduate School of Business Administration, University of Michigan. AUTOMOBILE INDUSTRY.

Liberman, Cy. Public affairs editor, News-Journal Papers. Coauthor, The Delaware Citizen. DELAWARE.

Lindgren, Raymond E. Professor of history, California State University, Long Beach. Author, Norway-Sweden. DENMARK; FINLAND; NORWAY; SWEDEN.

Lindo, C. G. Free-lance journalist. BARBADOS; CARIBBEAN COLONIES AND ASSOCIATED AREAS; JAMAICA; TRINIDAD AND TOBAGO.

Lingeman, Richard R. Associate editor, New York Times Sunday Book Review. Author, Drugs From A to Z; Don't You Know There's a War On? AMERICAN LITERATURE; BOOK PUBLISHING.

Litsky, Frank. Assistant sports editor, New York Times. Coauthor, New York Times Official Sports Record Book. Sports editor, The New York Times Encyclopedic Almanac. SPORTS: AUTO RACING; FOOTBALL (PROFESSIONAL); SWIMMING; TRACK AND FIELD; CHAMPIONS IN OTHER SPORTS.

Looney, Ralph. Assistant managing editor, Albuquerque Tribune. Author, Haunted Highways, the Ghost Towns of New Mexico. NEW MEXICO.

Luling, Virginia. Free-lance writer. SOMALIA.

Luter, John. Former coordinator, Advanced International Reporting Program and member of the faculty and administrative staff, Columbia University Graduate School of Journalism. NEWSPAPERS.

Lux, Guillermo. Associate professor of history, New Mexico Highlands University. CUBA; GUATEMALA; HONDURAS.

Lynch, Don. Business editor and political columnist, Nevada State Journal. Journalism instructor, Western Nevada Community College. NEVADA.

MacDougall, Terry Edward. Ph.D. candidate at Yale University. Acting assistant professor, department of government and foreign affairs, University of Virginia. JAPAN.

Magnus, Ralph H. Assistant professor of government, University of Texas (Austin). Former assistant cultural attaché, American Embassy, Kabul, Afghanistan. Author, United States Interests in the Middle East. IRAQ; JORDAN; SAUDI ARABIA; SYRIA; YEMEN.

Marcus, Harold G. Associate professor of history and chairman, Committee on Ethiopian Studies, Michigan State University. ETHIOPIA.

Marcus, Joseph. Billiards, bowling, and soccer editor, New York Post. SPORTS: BOWLING; SOCCER.

Marks, Henry Seymour. Educational consultant and professor of history, Northeast Alabama State Junior College. Author, Who Was Who in Alabama. ALABAMA.

Marsters, Jack. Night city editor, Montreal Gazette. QUEBEC.

Martin, Lee. Editor, Numismatic Literary Guild Newsletter. Director of advertising and columnist, COIN-age magazine. Columnist, Santa Ana Register. COINS AND COIN COLLECTING.

Mathews, Frank P., M.D. Clinical instructor of medicine, University of Washington.

Staff member, Island Hospital, Anacortes, Washington. MEDICINE.

Maynard, Olga. Lecturer, fine arts, University of California (Irvine). Contributing editor, Dance Magazine. Author, Ballet Companion, American Ballet. DANCE.

Mazrui, Ali Al' Amin. Dean, faculty of social sciences, Makerere University, Kampala. Vice-president, International Political Science Association. AFRICA (coauthor).

McGowen, Deane. Sportswriter, New York Times. SPORTS: BOXING; HARNESS RACING; HORSE RACING.

McKay, William A. Special lecturer in history, Scarborough College, University of Toronto. ONTARIO.

Mendy, Justin. Staff editor, L'Afrique nouvelle. Free-lance writer. IVORY COAST; MALI; MAURITANIA; SENEGAL.

Meredith, Laurence. Portugal correspondent, UPI. Free-lance writer. PORTUGAL.

Miller, Lynn H. Associate professor of political science, Temple University, Pennsylvania. INTERNATIONAL REGIONAL ORGANIZATIONS.

Mills, Hazel Emery. Research consultant, Washington-Northwest Room, Washington State Library. WASHINGTON.

Moore, Clement Henry. Associate professor of political science, American University in Cairo. Author, Politics in North Africa. Coeditor, Authoritarian Politics in Modern Society. ALGERIA; LIBYA; MOROCCO; TUNISIA.

Morgan, John G. State editor, Charleston Gazette. Author, West Virginia Governors. WEST VIRGINIA.

Morton, Henry W. Professor of political science, Queens College (CUNY). Coeditor, Soviet Policy Making. Author, Soviet Sport: Mirror of Soviet Society. UNION OF SOVIET SOCIALIST REPUBLICS.

Mudoola, Dan M. Tutorial fellow, department of political science, Makerere University College, Kampala. AFRICA (coauthor).

Mueller, Barbara R. Editor, U.S. Specialist, The Essay-Proof Journal. Author, Postage Stamps and Christianity; United States Postage Stamps. STAMPS AND STAMP COLLECTING.

Murphy, John K. Managing editor, Portland Press Herald, Evening Express, and Maine Sunday Telegram. MAINE.

Murray, Clyde Andrew. Public information director, Maricopa County, Arizona. ARIZONA.

Mytelka, Lynn Krieger. Assistant professor, international affairs, Carleton University. Research associate, Institut de Coopération Internationale de l'Université d'Ottawa. CENTRAL AFRICAN REPUBLIC; CONGO, PEOPLE'S REPUBLIC OF; GABON.

Nahm, Andrew C. Professor of history and director, Center for Korean Studies, Western Michigan University. Author, *Japanese Penetration of Korea, 1876–1910.* Editor, *Studies in the Developmental Aspects of Korea.* KOREA.

Nenneman, Richard. Business and finance editor, *Christian Science Monitor.* WORLD ECONOMIC REVIEW.

Nordstrom, Sherry Chayat. Editor, Marymount College News Office. Free-lance writer. ART.

O'Connell, Margaret F. Assistant children's editor, *New York Times Book Review.* CHILDREN'S LITERATURE; BOOKS OF THE YEAR: CHILDREN'S BOOKS.

Olson, Lee. Editorial writer, Denver *Post.* COLORADO.

Page, Hilary. Ph.D. candidate, Princeton University. Former visiting research fellow, Office of Population Research, Princeton. POPULATION.

Parks, Gabe C. News editor, Omaha *World-Herald.* NEBRASKA.

Patty, Stanton H. Staff reporter, Seattle *Times.* ALASKA.

Paul, Laurence M. Assistant city editor, Des Moines *Register.* IOWA.

Paulsen, Monrad G. John B. Minor professor and dean, University of Virginia. LAW; UNITED STATES: SUPREME COURT.

Peterson, Phyllis J. Former assistant professor of political science, Indiana University. ARGENTINA; BRAZIL; CHILE.

Peterson, Theodore. Dean, College of Communications, University of Illinois. Author, *Magazines in the Twentieth Century.* MAGAZINES.

Petropulos, John Anthony. Associate professor of history, Amherst College. Author, *Politics and Statecraft in the Kingdom of Greece.* GREECE.

Pfaff, Richard H. Professor of political science, University of Colorado. ARABIAN PENINSULA; IRAN; KUWAIT; LEBANON; SOUTHERN YEMEN; SUDAN.

Philips, David M. Boating and yachting writer, Providence *Journal.* SPORTS: ROWING; YACHTING.

Phillips, Allen. Editorial writer, Detroit *News.* MICHIGAN.

Pierce, Gretchen Mary York. Staff reporter, Halifax *Chronicle-Herald* and *Mail-Star.* NOVA SCOTIA.

Pierce, Richard A. Professor of history, Queen's University, Ontario. Author, *Russian Central Asia, 1867–1917: A Study in Colonial Rule.* ALBANIA; BULGARIA; CZECHOSLOVAKIA; HUNGARY; ROMANIA; YUGOSLAVIA.

Potholm, Christian P. Associate professor of political science, Bowdoin College. Author, *Four African Political Systems; Dynamics of Political Development.* AFRICAN DEPENDENT AND ASSOCIATED AREAS; BOTSWANA; LESOTHO; MALAGASY REPUBLIC; SWAZILAND.

Prinz, Martin. Senior research associate, Institute of Meteoritics, University of New Mexico. Coeditor, *Arie Poldervaart—1918–1964.* GEOLOGY.

Pyke, Magnus. Manager, Glenochil Research Station. Author, *Man and Food, Synthetic Food, Technological Eating.* FOOD.

Raskin, Eugene. Architectural critic. Professor of architecture, Columbia University. Author, *Architecturally Speaking; Sequel to Cities.* ARCHITECTURE.

Raymond, John. Regular contributor, Sunday *Times* of London; *The New Statesman; Financial Times.* Author, *The Doge of Dover; Simenon in Court.* Editor, *The Baldwin Age; The Letters of Queen Victoria; The Reminiscences of Captain Gronow.* ENGLISH LITERATURE.

Regan, D. E. Lecturer in public administration, London School of Economics. Contributor, *Public Administration, Public Law, Political Quarterly.* CITIES.

Reinhart, Peter K. Staff editor. SPECIAL REPORT: BANGLADESH: BIRTH OF A NATION.

Reynolds, Christopher B. Lecturer in Sinhalese, University of London. MALDIVES, REPUBLIC OF; SRI LANKA.

Robbins, William. Night news editor, Washington bureau, New York *Times.* UNITED STATES: CONGRESS; ELECTION '72: CONGRESSIONAL ELECTIONS.

Robinson, Kenneth W. Professor of geography, University of Newcastle (Australia). PACIFIC ISLANDS.

Rolland, Siegfried B. Professor of social science and history, University of Idaho. Former president, Pacific Northwest Council on Regional Historical Research in Progress. IDAHO.

Rothman, Theodore, M.D. Clinical professor of psychiatry, University of Southern California. Executive director, Rush Research Foundation. PSYCHIATRY.

St. John, James I. Assistant professor of English, Augusta College. GEORGIA.

Sauder, William R. Special assignment reporter, Richmond *News Leader.* Staff reporter, New York *Times.* VIRGINIA.

Savage, David. Instructor of English, Simon Fraser University, British Columbia. Writer. BRITISH COLUMBIA; CANADA.

Scheffer, Walter F. Professor of political science and director, Graduate Program in Public Administration, University of Oklahoma. OKLAHOMA.

Schmidt, Steffen. Instructor of political science, Iowa State University. COLOMBIA; ECUADOR; PERU.

Schneider, Fred D. Professor of history, Vanderbilt University, Tennessee. NEW ZEALAND.

Schoup, Henri. Free-lance correspondent, *The Guardian* (England); *Elseviers* (Netherlands). Assistant professor of journalism, University of Missouri. BELGIUM; LUXEMBOURG; NETHERLANDS.

Schwarz, Carl Edward. Instructor, Fullerton Community College, California State University. LATIN AMERICA.

Schwarz, Walter. African correspondent, *Guardian.* NIGERIA.

Seymour-Smith, Martin. Visiting professor of English, University of Wisconsin. Author, *Tea With Miss Stockport; Reminiscences of Horma.* WORLD LITERATURE.

Shanor, Donald R. Associate professor and director, international division, Columbia University Graduate School of Journalism. AUSTRIA; POLAND.

Sharkey, John. Assistant foreign editor, Washington *Post.* VIETNAM.

Sherrill, Robert. Washington editor, *The Nation.* Contributor, *New York Times Magazine.* Author, *Why They Call It Politics; The Drugstore Liberal.* ELECTION '72.

Sherwin, James T. Former New York State, intercollegiate, and U.S. speed chess champion and international master. CHESS.

Shipler, David K. Urban affairs reporter, New York *Times.* NEW YORK.

Shoemaker, Don. Editor, Miami *Herald.* Author, *With All Deliberate Speed.* FLORIDA.

Skitol, Robert A. Bureau of Consumer Protection, Federal Trade Commission. CONSUMER AFFAIRS.

Smith, Robert W. Owner-manager, North Country News Service and Vermont Information Agency. VERMONT.

140   CONTRIBUTORS

Smithcors, J. F. Associate editor, American Veterinary Publications, Inc. VETERINARY MEDICINE.

Snell, Joseph W. Assistant state archivist, Kansas State Historical Society. KANSAS.

Snider, Nancy L. Assistant professor of political science, University of Wisconsin (Stevens Point). Contributor, *Asian Survey* and *Christian Science Monitor*. MALAYSIA; SINGAPORE.

Speck, Samuel W., Jr. Associate professor of political science, Muskinghum College. Member, African Advisory Council, U.S. State Department. Member, Ohio house of representatives. MALAWI; UGANDA; ZAMBIA.

Steck, Duncan G. Member, public relations staff, Anna Rosenberg Associates. FASHION: MEN'S FASHION; TEXTILE INDUSTRY.

Stentzel, James H. Communications specialist, United Methodist Board of Missions. Free-lance writer. RELIGION: PROTESTANT AND ORTHODOX CHURCHES.

Stoudemire, Robert H. Associate director, Bureau of Governmental Research, University of South Carolina. SOUTH CAROLINA.

Swenson, Victor R. Associate professor of history, Johnson State College, Vermont. CYPRUS; MALTA; MIDDLE EAST; TURKEY.

Talbot, Roger. Urban affairs reporter, Concord *Monitor*. NEW HAMPSHIRE.

Tanenbaum, Marc. National director, interreligious affairs, American Jewish Committee. RELIGION: JEWISH AFFAIRS (coauthor).

Taylor, Joe Gray. Head, department of history, McNeese State University, Louisiana. Author, *Louisiana*. LOUISIANA.

Tignor, Robert L. Associate professor of history and chairman, African Studies Program, Princeton University. Author, *Modernization and British Colonial Rule in Egypt*. EGYPT, ARAB REPUBLIC OF.

Tobey, Franklin J., Jr. Reports editor, Office of Information Services, U.S. Atomic Energy Commission. NUCLEAR RESEARCH.

Torgrimson, Ellen. Former secretary, Montana Library Commission. MONTANA.

Tsao, Lionel. Associate professor of East Asian studies, Hunter College. ASIA.

Turner, Allan R. Provincial archivist, Saskatchewan Archives Board. Chairman, Historic Sites and Monuments Board of Canada. SASKATCHEWAN.

Van Dusen, Albert E. Professor of history, University of Connecticut. State historian of Connecticut. Author, *Connecticut*. CONNECTICUT.

Vertrees, C. W. Metropolitan editor, Gary *Post-Tribune*. Journalism instructor, Indiana University. INDIANA.

Walden, Charles R. Free-lance writer. KENTUCKY.

Ward, Wallace. Coauthor, *Canada's War at Sea*. PRINCE EDWARD ISLAND.

Watson, Madge C. Statistical clerk, Population Division, U.S. Bureau of the Census. MANUFACTURING TABLE.

Weaver, Edwin S. Professor of chemistry, Mount Holyoke. Coauthor, *Laboratory Introduction to Chemistry*. BIOCHEMISTRY; CHEMISTRY.

Wehrwein, Austin C. Editorial writer, Minneapolis *Star*. Contributor, London *Economist*; *Christian Science Monitor*; Washington *Post*; *Chronicle of Higher Education*. Pulitzer Prize, 1953; American Bar Association Gavel Award, 1969, 1971. MINNESOTA.

Weiskopf, Herman. Writer-reporter, *Sports Illustrated*. Coauthor, *My Life and Baseball; The Gutter and the Ghetto*. PEOPLE IN THE NEWS (SPORTS); SPORTS: INTRODUCTION; BASEBALL; GYMNASTICS; JUDO; WEIGHT LIFTING; WRESTLING.

Wheeler, Michael. Assistant professor of law, New England School of Law. Free-lance writer. ELECTION '72: POLITICAL POLLS.

Whitaker, Donald R. Staff specialist, Fishery Products Research and Inspection Division, National Marine Fisheries Service. Contributor, *Fishing Gazette; Commercial Fisheries Review*. FISHERIES; FISHERIES TABLE.

Wilbur, Richard. Free-lance journalist and historian. Research associate, Sir George Williams University. Author, *The Bennett New Deal: Fraud or Portent; Harry Stevens, The Tory Democrat*. NEW BRUNSWICK.

Willey, Richard J. Associate professor of political science, Vassar College. Author, *Democracy in the West German Trade Unions: A Reappraisal of the "Iron Law."* GERMANY.

Wilson, Dick. Author and journalist. Contributor, *Times* of London, *Spectator*, BBC. Author, *Anatomy of China; Asia Awakes; The Long March*. CHINA, REPUBLIC OF; HONG KONG; INDONESIA; MONGOLIA; PHILIPPINES.

Wood, E. M. Editor and free-lance writer. ANTHROPOLOGY; ARCHAEOLOGY.

Woodcock, John. Cricket correspondent, London *Times*. SPORTS: CRICKET.

Wylie, Charles M., M.D. Professor of public health administration, University of Michigan School of Public Health. Author of papers on public health and medicine. Winner of silver and gold medals, American Heart Association. PUBLIC HEALTH.

Zacher, Robert V. Professor of advertising, Arizona State University. Past president, American Academy of Advertising. Author, *Advertising Techniques and Management*. RETAIL BUSINESS: ADVERTISING.

Zukerman, Abby Rae. Staff editor. DISASTERS; FIJI; OBITUARIES; PRIZES AND AWARDS.

YEAR IN REVIEW
1972

AEROSPACE. Arms limitation. The rush of the United States and the Soviet Union toward their own destruction by the uninterrupted development of deadly nuclear weapons systems was slowed a bit this year by SALT, an acronym for strategic arms limitation talks.

The SALT agreements, or accords, were signed by representatives of both countries in Moscow in May as the highlight of President Richard M. Nixon's visit there. The SALT agreements immediately touched off a round of controversy in the United States, posing the questions of whether they really will slow down the arms race, whether the United States gave away more than it gained, and whether the costly new weapons systems now in development will be funded, as urged by Secretary of Defense Melvin R. Laird simultaneously with Nixon's return from the Soviet Union.

One of the two SALT accords is an executive agreement limiting the number of land-based and sea-launched ballistic missiles to those now operational or under construction. It is called the Interim Agreement on Certain Measures With Respect to the Limitations of Strategic Offensive Arms. The second SALT agreement is called the Treaty on the Limitation of Antiballistic Missile Systems and is a formal treaty limiting deployment of ABM systems by the United States and the Soviet Union. The Senate confirmed this treaty by a vote of 88–2 on August 3 and confirmed the offensive weapons treaty by the same margin on September 14.

The first SALT agreement stops Soviet intercontinental ballistic missile deployment at 1,618 missiles, with a net decrease to 1,408 if the Soviets exercise their option to replace SS-7 and SS-8 ICBM's with submarine-launched ballistic missiles. It also limits the Soviets to 300 of the large SS-9 missiles within the overall 1,618 limit. The agreement limits Soviet SLBM's to 950 modern launchers and 62 modern nuclear-powered submarines. The United States will be limited to the current levels of 1,054 ICBM's and 656 SLBM's but has the option to modernize its 54 Titan launchers or replace them with SLBM's or other ICBM's.

Admiral Thomas H. Moorer, chairman of the Joint Chiefs of Staff, told the House Armed Services Committee that the agreement permits the Soviet Union more strategic offensive launchers than the United States but prevents the Soviets from having the strategically significant lead that had earlier been projected. He said the United States had no program to construct additional strategic launchers in the five-year time frame of the agreement. "We thus reduced the growth of the Soviet lead through negotiations rather than by adding to our force structure," commented the admiral.

The other SALT treaty, affecting antiballistic missiles, limits both sides to a maximum of two sites, with 100 launchers at each site. The Soviet Union currently has a total of 64 launchers deployed around Moscow. The United States has one site under construction at Grand Forks, N.D., which was almost completed by the end of the year. The Soviet Union is allowed one additional site at an ICBM field, and the United States is allowed a 100-launcher site around Washington, D.C. The two countries are just about even in ABM's.

Space shuttle under contract. The space shuttle made significant news during the year in spite of an economy-minded Congress and a public jaded by frequent walks on

JUBILANT EMPLOYEES of North American Rockwell's Space Division throw a champagne party after winning a $2.6 billion NASA contract to build the space shuttle pictured at left; the shuttle will be able to carry up to 65,000 pounds of payload into orbit. The new contract will enable the hiring of about 9,000 new employees.

the moon. In July, the National Aeronautics and Space Administration awarded a $2.6 billion contract to the North American Rockwell Corporation for development of the reusable shuttle craft, which will be about the size of a DC-9 jetliner. Earlier in the year the corporation's Rocketdyne Division received a $450 million contract to develop the shuttle's main engines. The shuttle will be lifted into orbit by its three main engines, supplemented by two powerful solid-fuel boosters; after performing its missions in space the orbiting vehicle will return on wings to earth, flying like an airplane. The first such flight is planned for 1978.

Cape Kennedy in Florida and Vandenberg Air Force Base in California were chosen by NASA as launching sites for the space shuttle program, thus avoiding the extra expense of building new facilities and at the same time putting the military, especially the air force, back in the space business. These sites will provide considerable open space downrange for recovery of the jettisoned boosters, which will be picked up after parachute descent.

The chief purpose of the space shuttle is to reduce drastically the cost of putting men and equipment into orbit and to provide the link between earth and a space station, either in orbit or, in future years, on a distant planet. When fully operational, perhaps by 1980, the space shuttle will deliver both men and supplies to the space station, which will serve as a base for a variety of scientific experiments.

As the only NASA project programmed for the years after 1973, the space shuttle is expected to be the catalyst in revitalizing the aerospace industry.

China. The monthly magazine of the French Air Force, *Air actualités,* reported early in the year that the Chinese Air Force consisted of about 3,600 combat aircraft, including 2,900 fighters, 440 bombers, 300 helicopters, and 400 transports. The fighter category was said to include 100 MIG-15's, 1,700 MIG-17's, 1,000 MIG-19's, and 30–35 MIG-21C's. Among bombers and reconnaissance aircraft, China was estimated to have 100 TU-2's, 300 IL-28's, and approximately 25 TU-16's.

The most recent addition to the arsenal of fighters is known as the F-9. Actually a fighter-bomber, the 10-ton,

twin-jet aircraft is a new design based on the MIG-19, an interceptor. It is thought to have a top speed in the neighborhood of 1,400 miles an hour and a combat radius of 300 to 500 miles. Production may have begun in April 1971 and is now proceeding at a rate of 15 aircraft a month, with 200 already operational. The F-9 is known to be capable of delivering a small nuclear weapon.

In a move thought by observers to herald the appearance of Chinese airliners on European commercial routes, China expanded its civilian air fleet in a series of purchases from foreign manufacturers. The People's Republic has taken delivery of four British-built Trident medium-range passenger planes and has placed orders for six more; the Chinese took delivery of two Ilyushin-62 airliners this year and were reported to have ordered three more. The Soviets consider the four-engine, 186-passenger IL-62 the pride of their air fleet and use it on their Moscow–New York run. On July 24, Chinese and French officials signed a preliminary agreement for the sale of two supersonic Anglo-French Concordes, with delivery expected for late 1976 or early 1977. And on September 10 the Boeing Company announced that an agreement had been signed in Peking for the sale of ten American-made Boeing 707's to the Chinese. The value of this contract, including spare parts, was estimated at $150 million.

China was not in the international market only to buy, however. In April, Tanzania announced that it expected to receive at least 12 Chinese-built MIG's during 1973. Tanzanian pilots and ground crews have been training in China since 1970.

Chinese missile development kept pace with progress in the aircraft field. It was reported that China had started deployment of an intermediate range ballistic missile with a nuclear warhead and an estimated range of 1,500 to 2,500 miles. The propellant system utilizes a storable liquid fuel, which allows the missile to be sited in underground silos. The Chinese had previously deployed around 20 medium-range missiles in the 600–1,000 mile class which, because of their fuel system, had to be launched from the surface. The People's Republic appears to have stopped deploying these earlier model missiles in favor of the new IRBM, of which five to 15 seem to have been deployed.

China also continued development of an intercontinental ballistic missile with a projected range of 3,000 to 6,000 miles, which may be operational in 1974.

Concorde. Princess Margaret, after her ride on the supersonic Anglo-French Concorde, said, "It was a most impressive experience." So was the price, which was estimated to be approaching $60 million for each airliner, including necessary spare parts and auxiliary equipment. Pierre D. Cot, head of government-owned Air France, made it clear that the stiff price tag worried him. "The technical gamble has been won," he said. "The commercial gamble remains to be won."

Nevertheless, in April Britain and France authorized the construction of four more Concordes, in addition to the six already under way, and also decided to order materials for six further production models. In May the Concorde made its first intercontinental flight, from Toulouse, France, to Dakar, Senegal. Averaging 1,140 miles an hour, the airliner covered the 2,800-mile route in two hours and 27 minutes. On a demonstration and sales tour of the Far East in June, the Concorde ran up against stiff protest in Tokyo, where the press and environmental organizations objected strenuously to the smoke from the engines. British Aircraft Corporation and Rolls Royce officials explained that production models of the Concorde are expected to produce little visible smoke and to be no noisier than current subsonic jets.

There are now 11 firm buy orders for the Concorde—five from the British Overseas Airways Corporation, four from Air France, and two from the People's Republic of China.

Lockheed L-1011 Tristar enters service. After receiving a Federal Aviation Administration certificate of airworthiness on April 15, the Lockheed L-1011 Tristar entered commercial service on April 26 with an Eastern Airlines run from Miami to New York by way of Atlanta. At Lockheed's annual meeting in May, Daniel J. Haughton, chairman of the corporation, announced that the company had sold 147 of the wide-body, medium-range airbuses and expected to sell 220 by 1980. He added that the break-even point on the plane was estimated at 255 to 265.

McDonnell Douglas DC-10. The McDonnell Douglas DC-10, a belated competitor with the Boeing 747, is now flying with four U.S. airlines. Commercial service for the huge jet, which can accommodate 250 to 345 passengers depending on the seating configuration, began on August 5, 1971, with American Airlines.

McDonnell Douglas is considering the possibility of producing a twin-engine version of the three-engine jet. With a capacity of 250 passengers, the twin would have a range of 2,200 miles. The range of the current DC-10 models varies from 4,400 to 6,100 miles. An official at McDonnell Douglas pointed out that no decision had been made to produce the craft. "But we have completed our homework, and when the market looks like it's right, we're prepared to move."

F-15 Eagle. The McDonnell Douglas F-15 Eagle rolled out and took its first test flights this summer. The F-15, formerly known as the F-X, is a 20-ton, twin-jet plane able to fly at over twice the speed of sound. It is designed specifically to fight other aircraft rather than attack ground targets, which makes it the air force's first new air-superiority fighter in 24 years, since the F-86 Sabrejet of Korean war vintage.

For short-range fighting, the F-15 is equipped with advanced Sidewinder missiles installed on wing stations; for medium-range engagements, advanced Sparrow missiles are carried on the lower corners of the fuselage. A third weapon system is an internally mounted, rapid-firing M61 20-mm. Gatling gun. A new 25-mm. gun with caseless ammunition is under development for the F-15.

The air force plans to buy 20 test model F-15's and 729 production models at a total cost of $7.8 billion.

A-X developments. The A-X close-support aircraft for the air force was in accelerated development during the year by two contractors, Northrop Corporation and Fairchild Industries, to fill the need for an updated attack plane that can sweep across the battlefield in protection and support of ground forces. When developed, the subsonic A-X will be a simple, rugged, fixed-wing plane capable of short-field takeoff and landing. It will have two engines and a single seat for the pilot. The air force, which wants the plane to have a 250-mile combat radius and a two-hour loiter time over target, expects that it may eventually order as many as 600 production models. It requested $48.1 million for further development of the plane during fiscal 1973.

F-5E sales look good. The Northrop F-5E International fighter rolled out on June 23, ahead of schedule and within cost. An advanced version of an earlier twin-jet plane called the Freedom Fighter, the F-5E is a highly maneuverable supersonic aircraft for air-to-air combat. It is far less costly than most modern jets and easy to maintain.

Saudi Arabia is ordering 30 F-5E's, as is Iran. South Vietnam, Thailand, South Korea, Taiwan, and Jordan are all slated to receive some of the planes. Also interested in the F-5E are Turkey, Greece, Kuwait, Malaysia, Pakistan, and Japan. Northrop officials are confident of at least 650 sales and feel they could sell as many as 1,000 of the aircraft within the next six to seven years.

F-14 difficulties. In January, Grumman told the navy that it was unwilling to accept further orders for the F-14A Tomcat air-superiority fighter unless the 1968 contract was renegotiated. The navy, which wants to buy 313 of the aircraft to replace the F-4 Phantom on carriers, was not impressed. Despite a Grumman threat to close its doors if held to the contract, Admiral Elmo R. Zumwalt, chief of naval operations, told congressional hearings in April, "I believe Grumman will be economically viable for the next year regardless of the losses they expect to take on this contract." E. Clinton Towl, chairman of the board of Grumman, asked if his company would "honor" the contract, replied, "I can't. I don't have the money to do it." The navy sought to exercise its option under the original contract to purchase 48 of the craft during fiscal 1973. Orders placed through fiscal 1972 total 86 aircraft.

During the hearings it came out that Grumman had lowered its bid from $2.9 billion to $2.4 billion in the weeks immediately preceding award of the original contract. Now Grumman wanted to add the $545 million back on. Said Admiral Zumwalt, "I remain convinced that the proper thing to do is stick to the existing contract."

A study by the General Accounting Office said that the F-14 would be inferior in some ways to the modernized F-4, which costs one-fourth as much. It also said that during redesign of the plane in the face of difficulties, 14 of 20 "technical performance" characteristics had been downgraded, while four were improved and two remained the same.

Lockheed C-5A. The Lockheed C-5A Galaxy transport continued to have difficulties with its landing gear, wings, engines, and engine mounts and in its navigational system. The airplane's estimated structural life was 7,000 flying hours instead of the planned 30,000 hours. Secretary of the Air Force Robert C. Seamans, Jr., told Congress that the air force was trying to stretch the aircraft's useful life to 20,000 hours by flying it only two hours a day, without full fuel loads and without practice landings. He mentioned that training flights might be restricted in a further attempt to make the plane last as long as possible.

The air force currently plans to buy a total of 81 of the craft. Of those already received, two have been burned beyond repair in separate fires. A report by the General Accounting Office disclosed that, during a nine-month period in 1971, the average "operational readiness" of one squadron of 12 C-5A planes was 47 percent, instead of the required 75 percent.

Several C-5A production practices also came under fire. The General Accounting Office surveyed Lockheed's 7,000-man assembly line operation for the C-5A, concentrating on the plants at Marietta, Ga., Burbank and Ontario, Calif., and Plainfield, N.J. It determined that "about 8.6 percent of the production assembly employees were idle." In addition, 6.2 percent were absent "and we were unable to determine their whereabouts through discussions with supervisors and co-workers."

B-1 development continues. Although the subject of much controversy because of its expected cost, in the vicinity of $11 billion, the B-1 intercontinental strategic bomber continued to be developed by North American Rockwell as the replacement for the B-52 Stratofortress, which has been repeatedly modified to prolong its active duty life. The B-1 would form the third part of the triad concept of strategic deterrence, the other two consisting of land-based Minuteman ICBM's and sea-launched Poseidon missiles; these three strategic elements would provide the United States with the deterrent force believed necessary against hostile forces in the foreseeable future. The fiscal 1973 budget calls for about $445 million for further development of the B-1.

Designed to fly at over twice the speed of sound, the 200-ton B-1 will carry a crew of four in an airframe with an overall length of 143 feet. The variable-geometry wings will have a span of 137 feet in the forward position and a span of 78 feet fully swept back.

Airborne Warning and Control System. The air force during the year stepped up development of the Airborne

HIJACKING FOR
HIGH STAKES

Hijackers posed a continued threat to the world's airlines. Above, an FBI agent, forced to wear a bathing suit to prove he was unarmed, delivers a record $1 million to three men in a Delta DC-8, which then flew from Miami to Algeria. At right, in Tel Aviv, a wounded woman hijacker is led off a Sabena Boeing 707 which Palestinian guerrillas had held for hours until foiled by the police.

Warning and Control System with competitive flight testing of two different radars produced by Hughes Aircraft and Westinghouse Electric, under supervision of the Boeing Company, the prime contractor. AWACS is designed to assist in the command and control of deployed tactical air forces. Boeing is using a modified 707 aircraft in development, the most notable modification being the addition of a 30-foot-wide mushroom-shaped radome on top of the fuselage. The fiscal 1973 budget calls for $309.9 million for the first three AWACS; a total of 42 are planned to be operational sometime after 1975.

Army cancels Cheyenne helicopter. On August 9 the army announced cancellation of the Lockheed AH-56A Cheyenne helicopter program. The army had hoped the Cheyenne would fill its need for a high-speed, heavily armed antitank helicopter, which still tops its shopping list for new equipment. The program was canceled, six years and approximately $400 million after the award of the first contract, because of rising costs and Lockheed's difficulty in producing a stable rotor system. Lockheed was authorized to continue development of an advanced rigid-rotor control system, utilizing $18 million remaining in the original development contract. The army also asked Congress for $40 million to begin a new advanced attack helicopter program.

The army made its decision shortly after a competitive flyoff evaluation with the Sikorsky S-67 Blackhawk and the Bell 309 King Cobra. "The evaluation board decided none of them was the best," an army official commented. "We're looking now for a brand-new helicopter."

European MRCA fighter. The European multirole combat aircraft, being developed jointly by Great Britain, West Germany, and Italy, is expected to make its maiden flight during 1973. Delivery of production models of the MRCA is planned for 1978. The two-seat airplane will be equipped with variable-geometry wings and will have a gross takeoff weight of 38,000 pounds.

Production work is being split between the three countries. Of the airframe, Britain is responsible for the tail and the front and rear of the fuselage, West Germany the center fuselage section, and Italy the wings. When the program got under way in 1969, it was estimated that 420 of the craft would be required for West Germany, 385 for Britain, and 100 for Italy, but with prices increasing rapidly, total production is expected to run less than 905.

Britain plans to use the MRCA in a deep penetration role. West Germany will use it in a close support role, as a replacement for its fleet of 613 Lockheed F-104G Starfighters.

Britain, West Germany, and Italy are dividing airframe development costs on a 42.5–42.5–15 basis and engine development costs on a 40–40–20 basis. The program has a standard language, English, and a standard currency, the West German mark.

Terrier and Standard missiles. A study by the General Accounting Office called the Terrier and Standard missiles inadequate to their task, which is the defense of the navy's ships from air attack. Prompted by a $1 billion modernization of the fire control systems on 20 missile ships, the report said of the Terrier, "Data on missile firings from frigates modernized to date indicate a high percentage of failures. Most of the identified failures were attributed to the missile itself." The Standard is a replacement for the Terrier that has recently come into service with the fleet. Of it, the report said: "The Standard has experienced a decrease in effectiveness over the last year against aircraft. The rate of successful firings has dropped considerably below that achieved the previous year." Both missiles are products of the General Dynamics Corporation.

Franco-Israeli reimbursement pact. In February, France and Israel reached an agreement whereby France will repay, with interest, the price that the Israelis had paid for 50 Mirage jets which were not delivered because of the outbreak of the Arab-Israeli war in 1967. France will pay the equivalent in francs of $55.1 million to cover the price of the planes and some undelivered spare parts and $17.1 million in francs as interest. The aircraft are being turned over to the French Air Force, which will use them to form a new squadron based in Alsace.   FLINT O. DuPRE

AFGHANISTAN. Politics and government. The government of Prime Minister Abdul Zahir submitted its resignation on September 25, stung by inflation and the economic results of the drought that brought famine to thousands of people over the past winter. The resignation was not accepted, and the government remained in office.

Foreign affairs. Relations between Afghanistan and neighboring Pakistan became strained as the Afghan government once again opened up the issue of Pakhtunistan. Since 1947, Afghanistan has sided with separatist sentiment in the northwest border regions of Pakistan and, at times, pressed for establishment of an independent border state, to be called Pakhtunistan. The issue had shown signs of cooling off, but it was revived in the congratulatory message sent to new Pakistan president Zulfikar Ali Bhutto in December 1971 and in a January speech by Afghan prime minister Abdul Zahir.

Prospects of renewed separatist sentiment in border areas in the North West Frontier Province and Baluchistan prompted Pakistan's president Bhutto to make an unexpected five-hour visit to the Afghan capital of Kabul on January 11. Bhutto, seeking to establish closer ties with Afghan king Muhammad Zahir Shah, indicated a willingness to cooperate in facilitating the flow of trade to and from the landlocked kingdom. But Afghanistan remained unmoved. On May 12, King Zahir Shah received Nawab Akbar Khan Bugti, a prominent Baluchistan leader, for discussions on subjects of "mutual interest." Alarmed by this development, Bhutto sent his wife, along with diplomatic officials, on a two-day goodwill visit to Kabul. But, according to Radio Kabul, the visitors were told that Afghanistan's position on the Pakhtunistan issue remained unchanged. And in June the king welcomed a visit from Khan Abdul Wali Khan, leader of Pakistan's National Awami Party and son of Khan Abdul Ghaffar Khan, a leader in the Pakhtunistan Movement.

The Afghan foreign minister, Muhammad Musa Shafiq, visited Moscow in March, providing an opportunity for Soviet premier Aleksei Kosygin to revive his government's proposal for a system of collective security in Asia. The Soviet government expressed its readiness to provide Afghanistan with economic and technical assistance in executing its five-year development plan beginning this year. However, Premier Kosygin reportedly told the prime minister that his country's revival of advocacy for a Pakhtunistan was inopportune and would only aggravate tension on the Indian subcontinent.

A new agreement was reached between Afghanistan and India, providing increased technical assistance to Afghanistan. Sixty Indian technical experts were to be sent to Kabul, while training would be provided within India for Afghan technicians. Meanwhile, Foreign Minister Musa Shafiq, en route to Peking, met in New Delhi with Prime Minister Indira Gandhi and stressed that his government was reluctant to become involved in any Indo-Pakistani or Sino-Indian disputes.

Relations with China apparently proceeded smoothly. A Chinese trade delegation visited Kabul in April, and a trade agreement was signed. The same month, Musa Shafiq arrived in Peking and, at a banquet held in his honor, heard Chinese foreign minister Chi Peng-fei praise his country for a foreign policy of peace and neutrality. A further indication of cordial Sino-Afghan relations was the signing of a joint civil air transportation agreement in July.

The Afghan government also affirmed close ties with Iraq when that country's foreign minister visited Kabul in July. A common position was expressed on the Palestine question,

and Afghanistan supported Iraq's move in nationalizing the assets of the Western-owned Iraq Petroleum Company.

Economic developments. Afghanistan experienced its worst famine in recent history, pointed up by harrowing reports of sick, starving children, abandoned by their parents, dying by the roadside in provinces in central and northwestern parts of the country. Communications are so backward in Afghanistan that no one knows how many thousands of people starved to death in late 1971 and the early months of this year. But two rainless years, compounded by a severe winter, brought misery to millions of people. Half the livestock had to be slaughtered, including 16 million head of sheep from flocks that provide the staple export commodity.

The situation was aggravated by the fact that the Indo-Pakistani conflict disrupted the flow of food supplies from abroad. Relief from outside was also impaired by washed-out bridges, blocked mountain passages, and a scarcity of trucks. In addition, administrative incompetence and corruption by local officials took their toll.

Area and population. Area, 250,000 sq. mi. Pop. (est. 1971), 17,485,000. Kabul (cap.; 1969), 480,383.
Government. Limited constitutional monarchy. King, Muhammad Zahir Shah; prime min., Abdul Zahir.
Finance. Monetary unit, afghani; official rate, 1 afghani = US$0.0135. Main sources of revenue: land taxation, agriculture, mining royalties, and foreign aid.
Trade. Principal exports: karakul skins, dried and fresh fruit, raw cotton, carpets, and wool. Principal imports: foodstuffs, machinery and equipment, cotton textiles, metals and metal manufactures, fuel products. Major trading partners: Soviet Union, India, United Kingdom, Japan, United States, and Pakistan.
Agriculture. Wheat production reduced considerably by climatic conditions.
Education. Over 90% illiteracy. Secondary schools only in Kabul and provincial capitals. One university in Kabul and a medical school in Jalalabad.
Armed forces. Approximately 83,000 men. 1 armored division. T-34 and T-54 medium tanks. Air force equipped with MIG-21 jet fighters, IL-28 jet bombers, and some helicopters and transports. Gendarmerie strength, 13,000.   MICHAEL LEIFER

AFRICA. Unlike 1971, when black African governments divided over the issue of "dialogue" with South Africa, this year was characterized by an apparent desire, frequently expressed, to develop a common policy toward the white minority regimes of Rhodesia and southern Africa. The pinnacle of unity was reached at a June summit conference in Rabat, which reaffirmed support for black liberation movements. Other signs of unity were the successful staging of an all-African trade fair in Nairobi and increased support for the proposed Pan-African Highway (Mombasa to Lagos), a project which is reportedly under consideration by Japanese developers. But not all was harmonious among African states. Uganda was feuding with Tanzania, with the British, and with the Asian minority within its own borders; the African, Malagasy, and Mauritian Common Organization (OCAMM) was wracked by dissension; and a bloody civil war in Burundi inspired reports of massacres and of refugees fleeing for their lives, with the death toll estimated at 80,000–120,000 by the end of July.

The Rhodesian question and southern Africa. On November 24, 1971, representatives of the British and Rhodesian governments reached a complex compromise formula providing increased political rights for the black majority, eventually leading to majority rule. The British government agreed that if this compromise was found acceptable to the people of Rhodesia as a whole, it would take steps to lift the economic sanctions imposed by the United Nations in 1966, one year after the Rhodesian white minority government had declared independence.

Accordingly, a British commission headed by Lord Pearce set out in January to investigate whether the black population of Rhodesia would accept the compromise. Several African heads of state roundly condemned the establishment of the commission. For example, President Kenneth Kaunda of Zambia called the Anglo-Rhodesian settlement "unrealistic, a negative step, and an exposition of the British government's clear lack of concern for the African population of Zimbabwe [the nationalist name for Rhodesia]." Ugandan

JAMES P. STERBA/NEW YORK TIMES

A STARVING CHILD lies dying on a roadside in the hills of Afghanistan, almost unnoticed by passers-by. No one knows how many men, women, and children starved in the famine brought on by cold and drought and worsened by foul-ups in relief deliveries of much-needed food.

president Idi Amin said the Rhodesian question could only be solved by military means.

African leaders took full advantage of the UN Security Council meeting in Addis Ababa early in the year to conduct a diplomatic campaign against the proposed Anglo-Rhodesian settlement. On January 28 the Organization of African Unity (OAU) called on the Security Council to invalidate the agreement. Mauritanian president Moktar Ould Daddah, then chairman of the OAU, said in a detailed policy statement at the opening meeting of the Security Council that Britain should talk with representatives of the Rhodesian African majority in a neutral place, "away from the oppression prevailing at present in Rhodesia." He called for the immediate withdrawal of the Pearce Commission.

The British permanent representative at the United Nations replied that while Britain subscribed "without reservation on the principle that decolonization should continue," Britain differed over "timing and methods." Britain did not consider that "this is the moment to change course or set ourselves new directions." Thus, on February 4, Britain vetoed a Security Council resolution asking the British government not to implement the Anglo-Rhodesian settlement, Britain's fifth veto on the Rhodesian question. Britain abstained on resolutions calling upon South Africa to relinquish South West Africa (Namibia) and calling for the independence of Portuguese Mozambique, Angola, and Guinea and for the withdrawal of Portuguese government troops. Both resolutions passed.

On February 19 the OAU Ministerial Council, ending a six-day meeting in Addis Ababa, condemned Britain for its persistent use of the veto and called on the Security Council to strengthen and widen the scope of sanctions against Rhodesia. Two days earlier, Emperor Haile Selassie of Ethiopia had criticized the Security Council meeting in Addis Ababa for producing results which were "less than satisfactory." Secretary General Diallo Telli of the OAU told a press conference in March in Kampala that Africans had to accept the fact that the United Nations was dominated by the veto-wielding great powers, three of whom were "colonialist or former colonialist nations."

Despite this opposition, the Pearce Commission went ahead with its mission in Rhodesia, finding strong support for the compromise among whites but overwhelming opposition among blacks. Accordingly, the overall verdict was no. Premier Ian Smith blamed the defeat on the African National Council chaired by Bishop Abel Muzorewa, who had led public demonstrations against the agreement and had traveled to London and New York to arouse international opposition. After the decision, President Hastings Kamuzu Banda of Malawi called on African leaders "not to interfere" on the Rhodesian issue, which he said was Britain's responsibility.

Conditions in other southern African states also excited comment. In a New Year's Day speech at a diplomatic reception, Tanzanian president Julius Nyerere said that a lasting settlement would come in white-ruled southern Africa only when people there have power in their own hands. He pledged Tanzania's continued backing for all those who work to this end and criticized the major Western powers for giving or preparing to give more support to South Africa, Rhodesia, and Portugal.

Organization of African Unity. When the OAU hosted the UN Security Council in Addis Ababa from January 28 to February 4, it was the first time in 20 years that the council had met away from New York. It provided African leaders with a chance to present directly what they consider to be Africa's most burning issues.

This year marked the end of Diallo Telli's second term of office as secretary general of the OAU. In June, at the heads-of-state summit in Rabat, Nzo Ekangaki, President Ahmadou Ahidjo's minister of labor in Cameroon, was elected to the post.

Interstate cooperation. On February 23, President Jomo Kenyatta opened the first All-African Trade Fair at Jamuhuri Park in Nairobi; all African countries were represented except the white-dominated ones of the south.

Economic programs stressed multinational development. Robert Gardiner, executive secretary to the UN Economic Commission for Africa, said this year that the commission had seen the need for heavy industry on the continent and had already set up an electric power plant in West Africa, drawn up plans for multinational iron and other heavy industries, and was in the process of setting up pulp and paper mills in various regions. He was glad to note that the initiative for development had come from African countries themselves. The suggestion made by Malawi's minister of trade and industry that a permanent OAU trade secretariat be set up was received with enthusiasm.

Multinational cooperation through OCAMM was under strain. President Jean Bedel Bokassa of the Central African Republic, who did not attend the OCAMM summit conference in April, denounced the body as a "neocolonialist organization." President François Tombalbaye of Chad, who did attend the conference, complained that decisions were being made behind his back, especially in connection with Air Afrique, OCAMM's airline; in February he had resigned from the chairmanship of the organization. In March, President Mobutu Sese Seko of Zaïre had announced his displeasure with OCAMM, which he linked with the "colonial gravediggers of Africa," and said his country might be leaving OCAMM shortly.

National developments. *Southern Sudan.* The Addis Ababa agreement signed between the southern Sudanese Anyanya guerrillas, led by Major General Joseph Lagu, and the Khartoum government has apparently put an end to the 17-year conflict between the Arab north and the African southern Sudan. The agreement purports to provide for regional autonomy and the eventual integration of the guerrilla forces into the Sudanese regular army. President Amin of Uganda appealed to the southern Sudanese refugees in Uganda to return to the Sudan and urged them to take the Addis Ababa accord seriously.

On his way to Tanzania for a state visit, President Jafaar Muhammad al-Nimery of the Sudan said in July that he thought his country had a constructive role to play as a crucible in which, by the interaction of its different races and cultures, true African unity could be molded.

Tanzania. On April 7 the first vice-president of Tanzania and president of Zanzibar, Sheikh Abeid Karume, was shot dead by an unknown assassin. Tanzania was plunged into a week of mourning. Aboud Jumbe, a graduate of Makerere College in Uganda and a former schoolteacher, was elected by the Zanzibar Revolutionary Council to succeed the assassinated leader.

Ghana. An infantry officer, Lieutenant Colonel Ignatius Kutu Acheampong seized power on January 13 from Prime Minister Kofi Busia, who was in Britain at the time seeking medical treatment. Acheampong announced he had seized power to save Ghana from economic ruin.

Kwame Nkrumah, the first African prime minister in modern times, died in a Romanian sanatorium on April 27; he had been living in exile in Guinea ever since a 1966 coup deposed him. His body was returned to Ghana later in the year, and he was buried at his birthplace, Nkroful.

Uganda. In August, President Amin ordered the expulsion of Asians holding British passports, an approximately 50,000-member minority group which has held disproportionate economic power in the country. The British government made frantic appeals to President Amin to revise the target date, but the general gave every indication that he would abide by his decision, which created the most severe strain on Anglo-Ugandan relations since independence. Asians of Indian, Pakistani, and Bengali nationality were also given notice to leave Uganda.

In September, Ugandan forces beat back an invasion by guerrilla exiles loyal to former president Apollo Milton Obote. The exiles had launched the attack from across the Tanzanian border on September 17; early reports that Tanzanian forces were directly involved were later discounted. Despite mediation efforts, relations between Uganda and Tanzania remained tense throughout the year.

Burundi. Civil war broke out in Burundi after an alleged attempt to overthrow the government of President Michel Micombero. Although authorities in Bujumbura immediately imposed strict censorship, there were widespread reports of massacres against the Hutu majority by their Tutsi rulers. Refugees streamed across the border into Tanzania and Zaïre. On July 10, President Micombero formed a new government, but the fighting continued.

DAN M. MUDOOLA AND ALI AL'AMIN MAZRUI

AFRICAN DEPENDENT AND ASSOCIATED AREAS.
Spanish Sahara. King Hassan II of Morocco once again called on Spain to relinquish its hold on Spanish Sahara, a sparsely populated but potentially rich land of almost 103,000 square miles. Early in the year, the Organization of African Unity asked Spain to implement the various United Nations resolutions calling for a referendum in Spanish Sahara, which is claimed by Mauritania and Algeria as well as by Morocco.

Spain's foreign minister, Gregorio López Bravo, said in May that he favored a referendum in principle but thought the time was not ripe. During a visit to El Aiún, López Bravo declared, "This territory and its riches belong to the Saharans and to nobody else."

The potential richness of Spanish Sahara lies in its extensive deposits of high-grade phosphates. By mid-1972, Spain's state-owned Instituto Nacional de Industria had invested more than $250 million in order to tap those deposits.

French Territory of the Afars and the Issas. There was little political or economic activity during 1972 in the last French-held area in Africa. The ruling Party for Progress and Defense of the Afar and Issa Territory continued to try to cope with an economic slump which has been in effect since the closing of the Suez Canal in 1967.

Portuguese Africa. Responding to increasing demands for greater autonomy on the part of the two African areas, the Portuguese National Assembly enacted legislation in May making Angola and Mozambique states within the unity of the Portuguese nation and providing for greater local involvement in decisions affecting the African areas.

In December 1971 the United States agreed to give Portugal more than $400 million worth of aid in exchange for continued use of an air base on the island of Santa Maria in the Azores.

During 1972, Denmark and Sweden joined the Soviet Union in giving funds to the guerrilla movements in Portuguese Africa.

The rebel group in Portuguese Guinea, the Partido Africano da Independencia da Guiné e Cabo Verde, led by Amilcar Cabral, claimed control over two-thirds of the province. Fighting continued sporadically throughout the year, but no important territory changed hands.

The economic situation in Angola could only be described as booming, and the favorable trade balance of 1971 continued into 1972.

Government forces, numbering some 60,000, managed to keep the guerrilla forces off balance for much of the year.

However, in mid-1972 some hesitant steps toward unity were undertaken by the Governo Revolucionário de Angola no Exilio (GRAE) of Holden Roberto and the Movimento Popular de Libertação de Angola (MPLA) of Agostinho Neto. Meeting in Brazzaville in June, the two leaders, who had been fighting each other for almost a decade, apparently agreed to work for greater cooperation against the Portuguese national government. GRAE was particu-

larly hard pressed by mutinies within its army, and one revolt in March was put down only with the help of troops from the Republic of Zaïre.

In Mozambique the $350 million Cabora Bassa Dam project on the Zambezi River continued on schedule, although attacks continued on the construction crews and garrisons. The forces of the Frente de Libertação de Moçambique launched an offensive in the Tete district.

Heavy air attacks by the Portuguese also led to the shooting down of a Portuguese aircraft by Tanzanian forces in April. The Tanzanian government claimed that the aircraft had been attacking the village of Kitaya when it was hit by antiaircraft fire; the Portuguese government denied that it had violated Tanzanian airspace.

Spanish Sahara. *Area and population.* Area, 102,703 sq. mi. Pop. (est. 1970), 45,000. El Aiún (cap.; est. 1961), 5,500.
Government. Spanish overseas territory. Gov. gen., José María Perez de Lema y Tejero.
Currency. Monetary unit, Spanish overseas peseta; 1 Spanish overseas peseta = US$0.016.
French Territory of the Afars and Issas. *Area and population.* Area, 8,500 sq. mi. Pop. (est. 1967), 125,050. Djibouti (cap.; est. 1969), 61,500.
Government. French overseas territory. High comm., Dominigre Ponchardier.
Currency. Monetary unit, Djibouti franc; 1 Djibouti franc = US$0.0054.
Portuguese Guinea. *Area and population.* Area, 13,944 sq. mi. Pop. (est. 1971), 700,000. Bissau (cap.; est. 1971), 60,000.
Government. Portuguese overseas territory. Gov., Gen. António Sebastião Ribeiro Spinola.
Currency. Monetary unit, Portuguese overseas escudo; 1 Portuguese overseas escudo = US$0.038.
Angola. *Area and population.* Area, 481,350 sq. mi. Pop. (est. 1971), 5,800,000. Luanda (cap.; est. 1960), 224,540.
Government. Portuguese overseas territory. Gov. gen., Lt. Col. Rebocho Vaz.
Currency. Monetary unit, Portuguese overseas escudo; 1 Portuguese overseas escudo = US$0.038.
Mozambique. *Area and population.* Area, 302,329 sq. mi. Pop. (est. 1971), 7,900,000. Lourenço Marques (cap.; est. 1960), 178,565.
Government. Portuguese overseas territory. Gov. gen., Baltazar Rebelo de Sousa.
Currency. Monetary unit, Portuguese overseas escudo; 1 Portuguese overseas escudo = US$0.038.

CHRISTIAN P. POTHOLM

AGRICULTURE.
World agricultural production declined in 1972. Although decreases were reported for a number of commodities, the most significant were in the food crops, notably wheat and rice.

World wheat production was off about 10 percent, despite good crops in Africa and the Middle East. This sharp decline largely reflected weather-shortened crops in the Soviet Union, other Eastern European countries, and Australia. The U.S. wheat harvest was down 6 percent from the 1971 level. The drop in rice output was largely the result of drought in India and Pakistan and floods in the Philippines.

Other food crops also fell off. A decrease in world corn production was paced by an 11 percent decline in the important U.S. crop. Peanut production, hurt by drought in India and West Africa, also was significantly lower. Wool production continued to decline, but cotton production increased about 5 percent.

Although output of some foods increased slightly, demand for them exceeded the supply. For example, sugar output increased about 3 percent, but world demand continued to exceed supply. The results were rising prices and a drawdown on stocks.

Rising meat prices. When President Richard M. Nixon imposed a 90-day wage-price freeze on August 15, 1971, raw agricultural commodities were specifically exempted from his order. A similar exemption from price controls was granted under phase two of Nixon's new economic policy, which took effect in November. The impact of these decisions—coupled with the worldwide inability of beef suppliers to meet increased demand—became one of the hottest domestic issues in the United States in 1972.

Beef was a major component in an overall meat price rise from 118.4 to 127.5 (100 = 1967 prices) on the U.S. consumer price index between August 1971 and June 1972. During the same period, consumer prices for all goods and services increased by only 2.9, with overall food purchases for home consumption even lower. What made the increases all the more startling and painful to the consumer was that meat prices had increased only 1.3 points in the ten months preceding the price freeze. Meanwhile, at the wholesale level, farm commodities were doing much better than average, and livestock prices were soaring to unprecedented levels—from 118.9 to 146.4 between June 1971 and June 1972, a 24 percent increase, with a 3 percent rise between May 15 and June 15.

Federal officials varied in their approaches to the problem. Secretary of Agriculture Earl Butz alternately praised high wholesale prices as the farmers' due and blamed housewives for the "cost of high living." Virginia Knauer, President Nixon's consumer adviser, urged shoppers to purchase meat substitutes until prices leveled off. By June, C. Jackson Grayson, chairman of the Price Commission, was warning that if the president did not impose some kind of controls, the commission would unilaterally freeze meat prices at both wholesale and retail levels. Finally, late in June, President Nixon acted, ending meat import quotas for 1972 and imposing price controls on raw agricultural products as they move from wholesale to retail levels. This effectively clamped down on the middlemen, but farm prices remained free to rise.

Other countries experienced similar meat price increases. On June 5 the European Economic Community suspended import duties on beef and live cattle from nonmember nations to stimulate imports and drive prices down. The tariffs were restored about five weeks later.

U.S.-Soviet grain deal. On July 8, President Nixon announced that the Soviet Union had agreed to purchase at least $750 million in U.S. wheat, corn, and other grains between 1972 and 1975. In fact, by early September Soviet purchases amounted to $1 billion for this year alone. This tremendous sales volume spurred a 25 percent wheat price rise between July and September.

Allegations of impropriety surrounding the deal became fodder for the Democratic presidential campaign. The Consumers Union, the National Farmers Union, and several Democratic congressmen charged that major grain dealers had used inside tips from the Agriculture Department to reap large profits. Specifically, Democrats charged that Clarence D. Palmby was guilty of conflict of interest in resigning as head of the U.S. negotiating team to become vice-president of the Continental Grain Company, a principal exporter. They also complained that dealers had been encouraged by the Agriculture Department on August 24 to register their prior transactions before September 2, when a special 47-cent-per-bushel subsidy would no longer be offered. Registrations during that week amounted to $131.6 million. Agriculture Secretary Earl L. Butz denied that any impropriety was involved in either arrangement.

United States. The index number of U.S. crop production as of August 1972 was 110 percent above the 1967 base year —the second-best crop year of record, but 2 percentage points below the record 1971 level.

Production of corn was forecast at 4.95 billion bushels, 11 percent less than in 1971. Total production of four feed grains (corn, oats, barley, and sorghum grain) also was expected to be down by 11 percent. The wheat harvest, at 1.5 billion bushels, was forecast at 6 percent below the 1971 level. The rice crop, at 85.9 million hundredweight, was predicted to be up slightly. The 1972 soybean crop was expected to be a record high 1.27 billion bushels, 9 percent above the 1971 harvest. Cotton production was forecast at 13.3 million bales, which would be 27 percent above 1971 ginnings. The tobacco crop, at 1.7 billion pounds, was thought to be up 1 percent.

Red meat production in the first six months of the year ran slightly below the 1971 volume. A gain of 2 percent in beef production was more than offset by a decrease of 6 percent in pork output. Production of poultry, probably reflecting a shift in consumer buying from high-priced red

THE BEEF BEEF

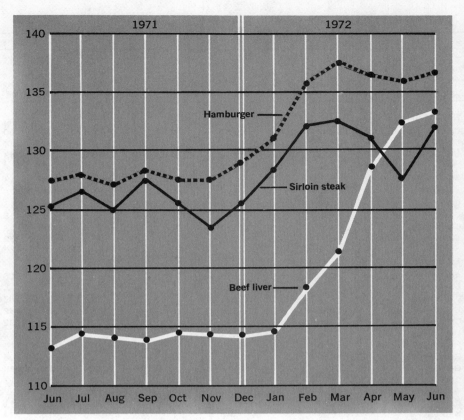

Food shoppers in Keene, N.H. (left), fed up with rising meat prices, staged a one-week boycott at local supermarkets this spring. As the national consumer price index (100 = 1967 levels) confirms, they were not alone in their outrage. Widespread protests forced President Nixon in June to suspend meat import quotas and impose price controls on agricultural products once they leave the farm and are handled before reaching the consumer.

meat, was up 9 percent. Because of the increased supply, poultry prices held steady or suffered slight declines.

Realized net income of U.S. farmers for January–June 1972 was estimated at a record level of $18.4 billion, nearly $3 billion higher than in the same period of 1971.

U.S. agricultural exports in the 12 months ending June 30, 1972, were valued at $8 billion, an all-time high. Leading export commodities were soybeans and soybean products, feed grains, wheat and flour, tobacco, and cotton.

Canada. Canada increased wheat acreage, but crop yields were down somewhat, and final wheat production was expected to approximate the 1971 total of 524 million bushels. Canada's wheat marketing situation was helped greatly by sales to the Soviet Union and China.

The Canadian government in 1971 and early 1972 passed several laws affecting farmers. One set up a nationwide network of marketing agencies; a second established new grade standards for grains in an effort to boost exports; and a third attempted to promote livestock production through incentive payments to farmers who switch from crops and summer fallow to forage crops.

Latin America. Brazil was the brightest spot in Latin American agriculture in 1972, harvesting a record soybean crop of 3.3 million metric tons. Orange production also set a record. Corn and rice harvests were expected to be well maintained. Frost in the states of Paraná and São Paulo in early July damaged coffee trees but had little effect on the 1972 crop, most of which had been harvested.

Argentina's beef slaughter in early 1972 exceeded totals for a comparable period of 1971 by 19 percent, and beef exports rose by 13 percent. But to ensure adequate supplies for export, alternate weekly bans on domestic consumption remained in effect, a measure which provoked dissatisfaction among local consumers. Argentina's wool production was down 8 percent, the lowest level since the 1930's. The corn harvest also declined.

Cuba's sugar production was expected to recover somewhat from the very low output of 3.8 million metric tons in 1971.

A number of Latin American countries are changing their policies toward agriculture. Mexico, for example, is promoting oilseed crops at the expense of feed grains; concomitant policy changes suggest that the country will depend increasingly on wheat imports. In Chile large farm holdings have been passed from private hands to state control. In Peru huge estates are being expropriated for resale to small farmers.

Western Europe. The nations of Western Europe harvested good grain crops in 1972, although weather conditions in July were not too favorable. Sugar output, despite an increase in acreage, was expected to be off because of the low sugar content of the beets. Beef production was about the same as in 1971.

Dairy products, which were in short supply in 1971, were abundant in 1972. Stocks of butter in August totaled 293,-000 metric tons, double the holdings of the previous year. Production was spurred by a boost in the EEC's support price from 80.74 to 88.75 cents a pound. Cheese output also increased.

The EEC approved a modest program of structural reform for agriculture—modest because it provides only $162 million a year, as compared with annual outlays of $1.5 billion projected under the so-called Mansholt Plan. The objectives of restructuring are to guide the process of farm enlargement, facilitate the transfer of young people from farming into other occupations, and ease the hardships of older farmers who cannot be expected to find new work. Several member governments of the EEC already have substantial national restructuring programs under way.

Eastern Europe and the Soviet Union. Extended drought over about half of Eastern Europe's agricultural land in the winter and spring of 1971–1972 damaged the region's winter and spring grain crops. Hungary was the most extensively affected, but Yugoslavia's principal grain area had the driest six-month period in 80 years. Also hard hit were Bulgaria, Romania, and East Germany.

The 1972 grain situation in the Soviet Union has been described as a "disaster." Lack of snow cover, followed by

		Grains[3]				Fibers		Tobacco	Dairy products		Meats		
		Wheat	Corn	Barley	Rice, rough	Cotton[2]	Wool[6]	Tobacco	Butter	Cheese	Beef and veal	Pork	Mutton, lamb, and goat
		th. metric tons	th. metric tons	th. metric tons	th. metric tons	th. bales	million pounds	million pounds	million pounds	million pounds	million pounds	million pounds	million pounds
	NORTH AMERICA												
1	Canada	14,253	2,746	14,257	....	....	4.4	220	290	249	1,929	1,511	19
2	Mexico	1,950	9,000	284	....	1,710	8.6	132	....	....	1,401	617	120
3	United States	44,620	140,728	10,069	3,820	10,473	180.2	1,804	1,143	2,380	22,457	14,772	555
	SOUTH AMERICA												
4	Argentina	5,200	5,800	525	315	475	....	130	76	445	4,537	514	309
5	Brazil	2,000	14,500	....	5,000	3,150	89.3	435	111	279	4,023	1,314	126
6	Chile	1,150	220	100	70	....	55.6	12	13	36	254	141	....
7	Colombia	45	825	110	770	595	....	96	....	....	1,142	165	4
8	Peru	140	625	165	....	420	20.4	12	12	53	180	109	89
	EUROPE												
9	Austria	974	722	1,016	....			1	100	109	351	646	2
10	Belgium and Luxembourg	954	....	636	....		0.6	7	195	100	613	1,032	3
11	Bulgaria	3,053	2,637	1,257	60	70	61.4	....	32	173	....	....	
12	Czechoslovakia	3,978	579	2,724	....			....	192	143	....	....	
13	Denmark	586	....	5,474					272	264	430	1,687	3
14	France	15,100	8,771	8,950	82	....	46.3	97	1,118	1,457	3,556	2,945	291
15	Germany, East	2,050	....	2,000			15.4		500	285			
16	Germany, West	7,142	594	5,774	....		7.9	20	1,039	628	2,998	5,271	
17	Greece	1,933	585	793	78	540	17.4	197	17	304			
18	Hungary	3,850	4,730	782	50		22.0		37	55			
19	Italy	10,070	4,469	367	900	5	28.9	175	121	924	1,823	1,135	25
20	Netherlands	705	....	380	....		3.0		274	679	696	1,659	101
21	Norway	10	....	569					43	120	121	152	34
22	Poland	5,460	....	2,445			18.9	172	282	132			
23	Portugal	835	529	86	190	....	28.4		9	17	220	212	35
24	Romania	5,585	7,762	665	72		63.9		64	156			
25	Soviet Union	79,000	8,100	30,700	1,300	11,100	959.0		2,283	1,027	11,872	7,512	2,250
26	Spain	5,387	2,033	4,611	400	190	65.6	51	15	47			
27	Sweden	964	....	1,964	....				102	137	324	551	8
28	United Kingdom	4,824	....	8,576	....		92.0	....	153	345	2,096	2,286	506
29	Yugoslavia	5,604	7,441	463	35	20	27.1	105	40	....	631	937	....
	ASIA												
30	Burma	....	....	....	8,250	75	....	95	....				
31	China, People's Republic of	23,500	25,340	....	....	6,900	....	....	....	....	....	....	
32	China, Republic of	....	41	....	3,204	....	....						
33	India	23,257	6,500	2,865	66,066	5,600	80.5	771	....	....	....	....	
34	Indonesia	....	2,138	....	17,300			231	....	....	....	....	
35	Israel	190	....	18		170	....	3			42	....	11
36	Japan	440	29	503	13,570	....	....	330	106	....	602	1,658	2
37	Korea, South	322	64	1,857	5,800	21	....	160			106	68	....
38	Pakistan	6,588	711	122	18,994	3,250	44.0	349	....	....	....	....	
39	Philippines	....	2,026	....	5,180	....	....	155	....	....	169	853	12
40	Thailand	....	2,200	....	13,400	75	....	98	....	....	....	....	
41	Turkey	10,500	1,100	4,100	255	2,250	105.8	325	....		397	1	787
	AFRICA												
42	Algeria	....	....	....	....	....		16	....	....	....	....	
43	Egypt	1,724	2,500	....		2,200	....	....	....	....	....	....	
44	Morocco	2,207	395	1,650	3	30	34.2	....	....	....	....	....	
45	South Africa	1,620	10,270	35	....	75	....	76	102	49	1,097	173	476
	OCEANIA												
46	Australia	8,453	281	3,078	281	175	1,933.9	39	432	171	2,309	400	1,819
47	New Zealand	423	143	286	....		727.5	8	473	231	....	....	
	World totals, 1971 final	317,640[1]	291,258[1]	132,595[1]	294,207[1]	56,010[1]	6,068.4[1]	10,015[1]	9,646[7]	12,985[7]	75,291[1]	57,123[1]	10,531[1]
	World totals, 1972 preliminary	286,000	NA	NA	NA	58,818	5,928.7	NA	NA	NA	NA	NA	NA

[1] Includes allowances for any missing data for countries listed and for producing countries not listed. [2] Bales of 480 pounds net. [3] Figures usually related to harvests that ended in 1971 for northern hemisphere countries and early in 1971 for southern hemisphere countries. [4] Southern hemisphere crops harvested from April to June are combined with northern hemisphere crops harvested from September through December. [5] Production in Africa totaled 4,990,000 tons, of which Senegal produced 945,000; Nigeria, 880,000; South Africa, 385,000; and Sudan, 333,000. [6] Greasy basis. [7] Total of countries shown. [8] Production in Sri Lanka (Ceylon) was 214,000 metric tons and total production in Africa was 115,400 tons. [9] Production in Central American and Caribbean countries totaled 12,010,000 bags, including the 3,300,000 bags shown for Mexico. Output

AGRICULTURAL COMMODITIES
thousands)

Lard	Oilseeds			Fruits			Beverages			Sugar,	
	Peanuts	Cottonseed	Soybeans	Apples	Pears	Oranges and tangerines	Coffee	Tea	Cocoa beans	raw value	
million pounds	th. metric tons	th. metric tons	th. metric tons	million 42-pound units	million 45-pound units	th. boxes of 70 pounds each	th. bags	th. metric tons	th. metric tons	th. metric tons	
140	....	....	274	21	2.2	......	....	....	....	149	1
135	70	745	240	9	2.2	35.0	3,300	....	25.0	2,531	2
1,967	1,357	3,974	31,825	152	32.2	247.6	174	....	....	5,546	3
77	388	181	59	23	2.4	31.9	....	24.0	....	991	4
224	900	1,392	2,100	5	......	83.0	23,600	5.0	205.0	5,660	5
21	....	....	....	....	1.0	1.4	7,500	....	....	179	6
25	....	252	120	....	......	......	....	....	18.5	793	7
16	....	178	....	....	......	......	1,030	1.4	1.7	918	8
72	....	....	....	8	2.4	......	....	....	....	295	9
82	....	....	....	15	3.0	......	....	....	....	837	10
......	....	33	....	....	......	......	....	....	....	249	11
......	....	....	....	....	......	......	....	....	....	680	12
93	....	....	....	4	0.4	......	....	....	....	325	13
143	....	....	....	87	25.2	......	....	....	....	3,200	14
......	....	....	....	....	......	......	....	....	....	517	15
754	....	....	....	97	19.3	......	....	....	....	2,354	16
11	12	249	....	12	5.1	11.8	....	....	....	154	17
......	....	....	....	....	......	......	....	....	....	280	18
......	2	3	....	93	86.7	55.6	....	....	....	1,255	19
189	....	....	....	25	4.9	......	....	....	....	827	20
3	....	....	....	3	0.4	......	....	....	....	....	21
......	....	....	....	....	......	......	....	....	....	1,712	22
23	....	....	....	....	......	......	....	....	....	18	23
......	....	....	....	....	......	......	....	....	....	445	24
1,843	....	4,485	....	....	......	......	....	60.0	....	7,877	25
......	6	85	....	30	19.6	68.6	....	....	....	1,048	26
19	....	....	....	2	0.3	......	....	....	....	267	27
28	....	....	....	25	3.4	......	....	....	....	1,148	28
276	....	....	....	17	5.6	......	....	....	....	421	29
......	....	36	....	....	......	......	....	....	....	113	30
......	2,700	2,915	6,700	....	......	......	....	....	....	2,268	31
......	98	....	70	....	......	7.0	....	28.0	....	780	32
......	5,500	2,400	....	....	......	......	1,100	425.0	....	3,817	33
......	475	....	390	....	......	......	2,250	44.0	1.0	680	34
......	21	65	....	....	......	32.6	....	....	....	....	35
207	111	....	122	54	22.5	89.8	....	92.0	....	441	36
......	....	....	246	....	......	......	....	....	....	....	37
......	90	1,436	....	....	......	......	840	20.0	....	707	38
124	19	....	1	....	......	......	....	....	4.0	1,916	39
......	223	36	74	....	......	......	....	....	....	644	40
......	40	785	13	37	6.9	17.4	....	34.0	....	910	41
......	....	....	....	....	......	14.5	....	....	....	....	42
......	....	833	....	....	......	......	....	....	....	454	43
......	....	....	....	....	......	25.7	....	....	....	....	44
28	385	34	3	13	4.6	16.1	....	....	....	1,865	45
......	31	74	12	22	8.1	10.6	....	....	....	2,866	46
......	....	....	....	7	1.0	......	....	....	....	381	47
8,273[1]	17,714[1,4,5]	22,986[1]	43,387[1]	761[7]	259.4[7]	768.7[1]	71,227[1,9]	1,090.1[1,8]	1,593.7[1,10]	70,881[1,11]	
NA	16,895	NA	45,000	NA	NA	NA	72,634	NA	NA	73,000	

in Africa was 19,817,000 bags.   [10] Production in Africa was 1,169,000 metric tons, of which Ghana produced 465,000; Nigeria, 265,000;
Ivory Coast, 225,000; and Cameroon, 120,000.   [11] Centrifugal beet and cane sugar. Cuba's production was 3,800,000 metric tons.

PREPARED BY HARRY W. HENDERSON

State and rank	Value[4] $1,000	Wheat[1] th. bushels	Corn[1] th. bushels	Oats[1] th. bushels	Barley[1] th. bushels	Sorghum grain[1] th. bushels	Soybeans[1] th. bushels	Hay[1] th. tons	Peanuts[1] million pounds	Principal vegetables and melons[6] th. cwt.	Potatoes[1] th. cwt.	Sugarcane and sugar beets[1,3,9] th. tons
1 Alabama (26)	871,256	....	23,520	600	....	1,088	18,408	785	413.7	1,667	2,444	....
2 Alaska (50)	4,601	....	....	....	....	....	....	....	....	....	....	....
3 Arizona (28)	775,486	11,560	420	....	8,175	10,575	....	1,290	....	12,550	2,400	242
4 Arkansas (16)	1,319,897	11,880	1,116	6,298	32	7,500	84,840	1,152	....	864	91	....
5 California (1)	5,037,325	17,339	20,900	4,600	52,000	22,862	....	8,057	....	88,611	NA	8,250
6 Colorado (14)	1,402,142	58,608	32,760	2,000	12,455	10,800	....	3,140	....	3,456	NA	2,414
7 Connecticut (43)	166,129	....	....	....	....	....	....	213	....	750	NA	....
8 Delaware (45)	144,363	975	11,968	84	820	....	4,032	72	....	324	1,360	....
9 Florida (13)	1,436,908	810	16,611	544	....	....	6,264	302	127.2	30,912	4,634	8,568
10 Georgia (15)	1,322,662	3,740	70,500	3,570	525	1,160	16,675	896	1,254.4	3,524	....	....
11 Hawaii (41)	231,091	....	....	....	....	....	....	....	....	225	....	10,788
12 Idaho (29)	755,295	47,712	2,460	3,300	35,828	....	....	3,768	....	1,953	NA	3,168
13 Illinois (4)	2,975,303	52,800	897,250	28,670	714	4,875	247,764	3,210	....	905	320	....
14 Indiana (9)	1,731,702	39,715	453,840	11,800	570	3,250	118,880	2,066	....	2,009	NA	....
15 Iowa (2)	4,228,390	1,480	1,076,350	78,300	225	4,675	202,851	6,846	....	1	624	....
16 Kansas (5)	2,473,648	309,205	110,565	8,580	3,360	200,750	21,390	5,239	....	....	....	578
17 Kentucky (24)	969,821	7,488	81,276	560	3,120	1,160	25,839	3,026	....	73	161	....
18 Louisiana (30)	747,578	960	3,895	1,350	....	1,600	38,341	559	....	734	256	8,750
19 Maine (38)	244,707	....	....	2,100	....	....	....	449	....	....	NA	....
20 Maryland (36)	402,844	4,332	35,100	1,540	3,977	....	6,912	696	....	1,361	245	....
21 Massachusetts (44)	165,216	....	....	....	....	....	....	233	....	1,373	NA	....
22 Michigan (22)	1,023,847	23,400	127,140	18,240	846	....	14,304	3,026	....	6,893	NA	1,479
23 Minnesota (7)	2,395,612	44,465	402,550	135,000	33,970	....	79,775	8,375	....	799	NA	1,456
24 Mississippi (19)	1,140,839	5,640	6,720	1,680	....	1,785	52,095	1,043	10.8	660	180	....
25 Missouri (8)	1,814,533	39,390	205,000	7,700	760	26,000	108,000	5,028	....	1,262	....	....
26 Montana (31)	711,617	93,570	468	9,430	53,380	....	....	3,849	....	....	NA	846
27 Nebraska (6)	2,413,849	94,646	459,000	21,511	1,976	103,700	22,260	6,883	....	....	NA	1,577
28 Nevada (47)	90,031	760	....	180	900	....	....	847	....	....	NA	....
29 New Hampshire (48)	55,779	....	....	....	....	....	....	212	....	98	NA	....
30 New Jersey (39)	242,775	1,433	4,828	336	900	....	1,404	310	....	4,912	2,408	....
31 New Mexico (34)	515,689	4,628	1,054	....	976	20,026	....	1,108	18.4	1,892	600	....
32 New York (20)	1,139,805	5,733	17,340	15,930	440	....	152	5,180	....	10,541	NA	....
33 North Carolina (11)	1,567,478	7,616	103,180	3,995	2,795	4,400	27,375	553	434.2	3,370	1,963	....
34 North Dakota (23)	994,518	206,636	6,480	104,615	104,676	....	2,884	4,269	....	....	NA	925
35 Ohio (12)	1,486,596	45,150	263,755	19,642	864	....	83,897	3,107	....	2,598	NA	817
36 Oklahoma (17)	1,239,554	90,850	5,100	4,995	7,905	25,714	3,400	3,089	209.4	1,000	....	....
37 Oregon (33)	608,546	36,523	803	5,130	12,150	....	....	2,283	....	4,748	NA	506
38 Pennsylvania (21)	1,087,043	9,376	70,455	21,995	7,920	....	1,075	4,099	....	1,616	NA	....
39 Rhode Island (49)	19,989	....	....	....	....	....	....	26	....	....	....	....
40 South Carolina (35)	510,569	3,036	22,940	3,040	792	1,014	24,750	408	32.3	3,260	....	....
41 South Dakota (18)	1,192,264	57,921	120,540	103,390	20,748	11,817	5,145	6,680	....	....	NA	....
42 Tennessee (27)	796,038	9,024	29,160	1,260	1,044	1,325	34,272	1,917	....	426	371	....
43 Texas (3)	3,722,414	44,000	35,000	9,000	1,560	336,000	5,670	3,944	434.7	22,162	3,529	575
44 Utah (40)	233,636	5,833	....	848	6,519	....	....	1,519	....	219	NA	396
45 Vermont (42)	171,156	....	....	240	....	....	....	884	....	....	NA	....
46 Virginia (32)	632,935	7,104	33,880	2,024	4,674	1,092	7,875	1,894	275.4	1,402	4,204	....
47 Washington (25)	903,571	125,455	6,760	2,135	12,320	....	....	2,401	....	2,204	NA	2,279
48 West Virginia (46)	109,346	462	3,540	559	420	....	....	955	....	....	266	....
49 Wisconsin (10)	1,702,242	1,478	182,078	85,492	1,700	....	3,087	10,074	....	2,541	NA	....
50 Wyoming (37)	278,954	8,059	1,694	4,512	7,049	....	....	1,860	....	....	NA	1,140
Totals	56,207,589	1,540,792	4,947,996	736,775	409,085	803,168	1,269,616	127,822	3,210.5	223,895	NA	54,796

[1] August 1972 indications.   [2] July 1972 indications.   [3] Sugarcane in Florida, Hawaii, and Louisiana; sugar beets in other states.   [4] Estimated cash receipts from farm marketings plus government payments received by farmers in 1971.   [5] Units of 42 pounds.   [6] Units of 48 pounds.   [7] 1971 production.   [8] Included in the 7,929,000 units reported for the New England states as a whole.   [9] Total includes undistributed figures.   [10] Total not exact because of rounding.

AGRICULTURAL COMMODITIES—1972
thousands)

Cotton[1,10]	Cottonseed[7]	Tobacco[1]	Citrus fruit[2]	Commercial apples[1,5]	Peaches[1,6]	Milk[7]	Eggs[7]	Cattle and calves[7]	Hogs[7]	Sheep and lambs[7]	Wool[7]	Broilers[7]	Turkeys[7,9]
th. bales	th. tons	th. pounds	th. tons	th. units	th. units	million pounds	millions	th. pounds	th. pounds	th. pounds	th. pounds	th. pounds	th. pounds
675	256	923	....	....	833	827	2,765	599,180	332,327	223	33	1,345,215	368
....	....	....	....	....	....	17	6	1,165	231	....	225	....	....
597	221	....	382.1	....	....	620	195	627,879	29,840	21,446	3,772	....	....
1,600	495	....	....	188	875	708	3,476	602,384	106,587	405	44	1,666,501	155,232
1,460	494	....	2,314.2	10,476	33,542	9,708	8,728	1,972,556	44,710	78,396	11,580	356,932	320,899
....	....	....	....	143	146	905	355	1,743,079	142,479	77,969	12,081	....	57,412
....	....	5,583	....	8	121	659	912	23,680	2,782	259	33	18,610	1,584
....	....	....	....	286	42	133	131	9,188	17,038	101	12	490,749	375
9	......	23,620	8,774.0	....	....	1,785	2,732	469,750	106,780	210	22	174,982	....
400	153	120,599	....	....	3,958	1,202	5,532	562,080	581,272	114	25	1,552,705	40,428
....	....	....	....	....	....	133	211	59,660	13,154	....	....	....	....
....	....	....	....	1,024	42	1,556	186	643,767	51,859	61,831	6,911	....	....
1	......	....	....	2,310	250	2,778	1,878	1,169,919	2,780,889	21,075	2,010	....	13,406
....	....	14,400	....	1,786	4	2,470	3,135	630,629	1,827,421	14,831	1,628	35,531	84,075
....	....	....	....	348	....	4,577	2,861	2,947,236	5,171,195	46,679	5,160	....	130,503
....	....	....	....	214	35	1,717	800	2,811,006	805,040	20,295	2,715	....	5,741
6	......	410,695	....	369	125	2,480	659	906,783	504,003	5,434	518	....	675
850	229	150	....	....	167	1,129	757	545,105	55,936	581	119	199,556	40
....	....	....	....	8	....	632	1,528	30,779	2,931	815	99	309,660	93
....	....	26,000	....	1,429	313	1,564	326	112,624	61,905	1,076	124	705,264	1,180
....	....	1,737	....	8	73	663	513	24,565	20,433	410	53	....	3,840
....	....	....	....	17,143	208	4,755	1,499	491,038	285,414	12,775	1,708	....	22,022
....	....	....	....	619	....	9,618	2,478	1,653,665	1,389,605	33,507	3,468	....	307,614
2,200	663	....	....	....	354	1,021	2,317	773,896	196,802	561	56	892,159	537
491	169	5,520	....	1,429	419	2,999	1,531	1,741,616	1,785,182	13,756	1,820	91,161	170,187
....	....	....	....	....	....	337	257	1,122,595	90,382	53,214	9,016	....	....
....	....	....	....	....	....	1,569	1,050	2,668,870	1,428,192	19,311	2,610	....	17,599
3	......	....	....	....	....	141	3	209,558	2,957	10,390	1,751	....	....
....	....	....	....	8	23	360	312	16,260	3,451	251	33	....	437
....	....	....	....	2,500	521	684	745	38,322	30,201	435	59	....	2,205
158	59	....	....	71	....	312	219	593,479	19,461	24,933	6,858	....	....
....	....	....	....	23,810	375	10,388	2,319	346,275	29,481	4,116	606	....	6,290
125	49	667,975	....	5,952	521	1,535	3,597	259,843	715,057	712	97	1,101,719	183,208
....	....	....	....	....	....	1,012	208	823,598	146,203	22,129	2,873	....	20,400
....	....	20,250	....	3,214	63	4,463	2,263	699,566	895,041	36,663	5,015	....	78,765
254	75	....	....	....	129	1,260	589	1,870,938	188,017	6,710	952	....	34,869
....	....	....	....	2,357	104	1,008	561	563,585	41,681	25,069	4,312	49,400	29,353
....	....	26,400	....	11,071	1,667	7,142	3,626	408,246	180,912	7,423	1,051	240,836	53,172
....	....	....	....	8	8	71	66	2,378	2,668	90	11	....	252
280	110	134,400	....	476	5,417	514	1,341	189,589	207,283	27	8	98,662	52,176
....	....	....	....	....	....	1,493	1,025	1,814,916	798,702	70,529	9,585	....	22,596
600	212	113,630	....	202	169	2,144	1,194	713,233	325,383	1,377	162	177,520	200
3,631	1,050	....	629.0	....	604	3,239	2,607	4,219,109	527,707	175,115	30,397	618,235	173,425
....	....	....	....	119	42	855	267	277,297	17,660	56,670	9,167	....	91,815
....	....	....	....	8	....	2,030	143	68,620	2,170	289	43	....	247
2	......	122,343	....	10,714	458	1,800	1,032	445,770	197,014	11,874	1,023	256,529	91,680
....	....	....	....	35,714	667	2,230	968	435,954	29,497	7,834	1,296	58,231	10,733
....	....	2,560	....	5,476	271	376	316	120,941	26,252	10,568	798	56,592	9,405
....	....	23,485	....	1,619	....	18,879	1,385	1,050,058	722,038	8,577	960	....	64,013
....	....	....	....	....	....	142	40	512,427	11,770	71,628	16,185	....	....
13,343	**4,244**	**1,720,270**	**12,099.3**	**148,988**	**52,546**	**118,640**	**71,644**	**40,624,656**	**22,927,995**	**1,038,683**	**159,084**	**10,496,749**	**2,261,786**

PREPARED BY HARRY W. HENDERSON

CENTRAL PRESS

TOBACCO, Rhodesia's leading export crop, is loaded onto trailers for transportation to drying barns. Hopes that the United Nations might lift its embargo on Rhodesian goods faded after an Anglo-Rhodesian agreement on independence fell through late in May.

drought, brought heavy winterkill of winter wheat. Continued drought affected harvests not only of winter grain but also of spring-planted crops. Hard statistics on output are not available, but the size of Soviet grain purchases by September prove the extent of the damage: from the United States, close to 11 million metric tons of wheat, 2 to 3 million tons of feed grains, and 1 million tons of soybeans; from Canada, 5 million tons of wheat; and from Western Europe, 1 million tons of grains, equally divided between wheat and feed grains. Purchases from the United States alone will almost certainly amount to billions of dollars between 1972 and 1975.

However, the Soviet Union probably would have been a substantial buyer of grain even in the absence of crop problems. All evidence points to a drive by the Soviet Union to upgrade the diets of its people by providing them with more meat and other animal proteins. This drive involves greatly expanded use of grain—much of which must be imported—and stepped-up livestock production.

Africa and the Middle East. North Africa and the Middle East had record wheat crops in 1972. One sign that this was a good year was Syria's sale of 150,000 tons of 1972-crop durum wheat for export, its first substantial wheat export since 1964–1965. Turkey's cotton production was up, and the country harvested an above-average crop of filberts.

Africa's coffee crop was expected to about equal the 1971 production of 19.8 million bags. Earlier hopes for record peanut production in Senegal and Nigeria were dashed by prolonged periods of dry weather during the growing season. South Africa harvested a record crop of corn.

The British government announced in late May that it would continue its embargo on all trade with Rhodesia—a

decision discouraging to Rhodesian tobacco producers. Rhodesia had sold over 200 million pounds of tobacco at the peak of its trade with major markets.

Asia. Food production declined on both a total and a per capita basis in South and East Asia, an area that contains almost 60 percent of the world's people.

India's seasonal rains were light and poorly distributed over two-thirds of the country. Rainfall was especially deficient in June and July, a critical growing period for India's crops. The drought cut grain production some 20 million tons below earlier expectations; rice, corn, and other coarse grains were affected. Peanut production was cut back to an estimated 4 million metric tons from the 5.5 million harvested in 1971. Cotton production was off 15 percent.

The 1972 drought could well threaten India's hoped-for self-sufficiency in food grains. In a politically popular decision shortly after India's victory over Pakistan in December 1971, the Indian government discontinued imports of food grains on concessional terms from the United States. India's confidence in its ability to go it alone had been bolstered by its remarkable success in boosting wheat production with high-yielding Mexican varieties.

In the Philippines, heavy rains in July and early August caused the worst floods ever to hit the islands. Most extensively damaged was the major rice bowl area of central Luzon, with an estimated loss of 300,000 metric tons of rice.

In the People's Republic of China, early harvested crops did well; most notable were rapeseed, barley, winter wheat, beans, and peas. The early rice crop also was good. However, drought in the northern wheat-growing area hurt production, so total grain production probably will not exceed the 1971 harvest. China bought 4.5 million tons of wheat from Canada for delivery by March 1973 and also arranged to buy substantial quantities of U.S. wheat.

The Japanese government continued its program to cut back rice acreage and production. The support price remains high—it was $395 a ton in 1971—and the government has been trying to ease the drain on the treasury. Although increased yields have been offsetting the acreage reductions to some extent, the government has been fairly successful in holding down output.

The new nation of Bangladesh, still suffering from the natural disasters of 1970 and reeling from the bloody civil war through which it gained independence, was forced to seek enormous imports of rice, wheat, vegetable oils, cotton textiles, tallow, and tobacco.

Australia and New Zealand. Drought hit Australia's 1972 wheat crop; production was expected to decline to 6.8 million metric tons, as compared with 8.5 million in 1971. Beef production continued to expand in response to strong export demand. The decline in wool production continued. Prices, which had been very weak in recent years, strengthened sharply; they were up 12 to 15 cents a pound by the middle of 1972.

New Zealand's beef output declined somewhat, but the wool clip was larger.   HARRY W. HENDERSON

ALABAMA. Politics and government. The most significant event in Alabama in 1972 was the assassination attempt upon the life of Governor George C. Wallace while he was campaigning for the Democratic presidential nomination. On May 15, on the eve of the Maryland and Michigan primaries, Wallace was shot by Arthur H. Bremer after speaking at a shopping center in Laurel, Md., a suburb of Washington, D.C. Wallace was taken to Holy Cross Hospital in Silver Spring, Md., where he underwent five hours of surgery. All of the bullets were removed except for the one lodged against his spine, which caused paralysis from the waist down. This last bullet was removed on June 15, but the paralysis continued. Lieutenant Governor Jere Beasley functioned as acting governor until Wallace came back to Alabama, shortly before the Democratic National Conven-

tion. Wallace entered the capital on August 25, his 53rd birthday, but returned to Birmingham on August 27, to the Spain Rehabilitation Center, where he had been undergoing treatment and therapy since July 14. While in the center he was operated on twice to drain abscesses caused by the shooting. He returned to the executive mansion in Montgomery for the first time on August 20, after being released from the center. The mansion had been remodeled to make it easier for the governor to move about in his wheelchair, and physical therapy equipment had been installed for his use. (*See also* CRIME AND CRIME PREVENTION; PEOPLE IN THE NEWS: George Wallace.)

Legislation. In May, voters approved, by a 3–1 margin, a new classification of property taxes called the three-class system. Under this new system, utilities will be appraised at 30 percent of market value; residences, farmlands, and timberlands at 15 percent of market value; and all other property at 25 percent of market value.

Economic developments. In January there was a major oil discovery in Escambia County. Jones Bluff Lock and Dam, just south of Montgomery, was officially opened on April 15, making barge traffic on the Alabama River possible as far north as the capital. In August the Alabama Power Company announced plans to construct a $400 million coal-fired steam-generating plant in Jefferson County. The company also won approval from the Atomic Energy Commission to complete its nuclear power plant near Dothan. Republic Steel's Sayre Coal Mine, located northwest of Birmingham, was closed after 69 years of operation. The creation of the Illinois Central Gulf Railroad from the merger of the Gulf, Mobile, and Ohio with the Illinois Central is expected to expand the economy of Mobile.

Education and culture. A master plan was developed which aimed at concentrating state money and talent in order to avoid overlapping or duplication of academic programs by state-supported institutions of higher learning. As a part of this plan, Alabama's high school vocational departments, trade schools, and junior colleges were placed under a new division of vocational technical and higher education by the state board of education in May. Shake-ups in two of the state-supported universities occurred in 1972. Dr. John E. Deloney, president of Livingston State University, was fired by the trustees of the institution in August, and Robert Guillot, mayor of Vestavia, was appointed president of Florence State University after a controversy developed between Governor Wallace and some members of the institution's board of trustees. The governor appointed two new trustees, and the board voted 6–3 to accept the governor's choice of Guillot as president.

Municipal developments. Republic Steel Corporation announced in March that a $22 million 533-acre residential community will be developed on Birmingham's east side.

Tuskegee Study. In August a nine-member panel was appointed to investigate a U.S. Public Health Service program which allowed more than 430 black males in the state to remain untreated for venereal disease in a study of the long-term effects of syphilis. The 40-year-old Tuskegee Study received national attention for the first time in July, when it was made public through the media. The most controversial aspect of the study was the fact that after the development of antibiotics that could control and cure the disease, the blacks were not treated and none of the patients involved was ever informed that he had syphilis.

Minority employment. As the result of a suit filed by the National Association for the Advancement of Colored People, a federal court ordered the Alabama department of public safety to hire only blacks as state troopers until the ratio of blacks on the force equaled the ratio of blacks in the state. At the time of the instigation of the suit, there were no black troopers on the state force.

Military scandal. Major General Reid Doster resigned his air national guard commission on August 21, after he and three other officers were indicted by a federal grand jury in March for allegedly violating the Hatch Act by pressuring junior officers to make political contributions.

For election results and campaign highlights, see the special supplement ELECTION '72.

Area and population. Area, 51,609 sq. mi. Pop. (1970), 3,444,-165. Principal cities: Montgomery (cap.), 133,386; Birmingham, 300,910; Mobile, 190,026; Huntsville, 137,802.
Government. Gov., George C. Wallace (D); lt. gov., Jere Beasley (D); secy. of state, Mabel Amos (D); treas., Agnes Baggett (D); cont., Roy W. Sanders (D); atty. gen., Bill Baxley (D). Legislature: senate, 35 D; house, 103 D, 2 R, 1 NDPA.
Finance (year ending Sept. 30, 1970). Cash balance, $208,081,-776; gross receipts, $2,014,405,525; gross disbursements, $1,977,-690,948.
Education (1970–1971). Elementary schools, 677; elementary pupils, 454,596; teaching positions, 15,024. Junior high schools, 302; junior high pupils, 223,108; teaching positions, 7,370. Senior high schools, 402; senior high pupils, 172,453; teaching positions, 9,099.

HENRY SEYMOUR MARKS

ALASKA. Oil vs. ecology. Controversy continued over whether a consortium of seven companies should be allowed to build a $5 billion oil pipeline stretching almost 800 miles from the North Slope oil fields at Prudhoe Bay in the Arctic to the ice-free port of Valdez. An environmental-impact report issued March 20 by the U.S. Department of the Interior confirmed fears that the system cannot be guaranteed leak-proof. But the department also cited the economic importance of the pipeline in the development of Alaska's oil.

The issue dominated everything from statewide politics to budgets this year. However, the question is apparently nearing a final decision in the courts. On August 15, U.S. District Court Judge George L. Hart, Jr., in Washington, D.C., lifted his two-year-old injunction against construction of the pipeline. The injunction had been granted in April 1970 to three conservation organizations—the Wilderness Society, Friends of the Earth, and the Environmental Defense Fund. The basis of Judge Hart's new ruling was that publication of the March 20 environmental-impact report fulfilled all legal requirements of the National Environmental Policy Act. The environmentalists are appealing the decision, and the case is expected to be decided by the U.S. Supreme Court. No construction will begin meantime.

Native land claims. Alaska's native peoples—Eskimos, Indians, and Aleuts—moved swiftly to prepare for implementation of an aboriginal land-claims settlement approved by the U.S. Congress in December 1971. That settlement, largest in American history, eventually will award the natives 40 million acres of land and cash compensation of $962.5 million. Enrollment of natives eligible for the benefits must be completed by March 30, 1973. Meanwhile, as required by the settlement act, the natives have organized 12 regional business corporations to administer the settlement proceeds, and each corporation has received $500,000 in advance money from the federal government.

Legislation. The Alaska legislature stayed in session 161 days, a new record. Steered by the policies of Governor William A. Egan (D), the lawmakers passed a number of controversial bills for tight regulation of the oil industry. The industry has indicated it may challenge several of the measures in court. Major bills in the package include a right-of-way leasing bill, a new form of production taxation, and a "local hire" bill aimed at requiring the pipeline company and its contractors to give employment preference to Alaskans. The governor signed a general-fund budget totaling $330.4 million for the 1972–1973 fiscal year, a reduction of $11.3 million from the budget approved by the legislature. The largest cut was $8 million from the University of Alaska's capital-improvements program.

Other news. Eskimos of the oil-rich North Slope voted overwhelmingly in June to incorporate a borough covering some 56.5 million acres. It has been described as the world's largest local government in area.

Confrontations with foreign fishing fleets in the northern Pacific Ocean continue to be a problem for Alaskans. In January authorities seized two Soviet fishing vessels in the Bering Sea for violations of the 12-mile exclusive-fishing zone enforced by the United States. In July four Japanese salmon-fishing boats were detained for operating inside the boundary set by the tripartite fishing treaty of the United States, Canada, and Japan.

For election results and campaign highlights, see the special supplement ELECTION '72.

Area and population. Area, 586,412 sq. mi. Pop. (1970 census), 302,173. Principal cities: Juneau (cap.), 6,050; Anchorage, 48,081; Fairbanks, 14,771; Ketchikan, 6,994.

Government. Gov., William A. Egan (D); lt. gov., H. A. Boucher (D); atty. gen., John E. Havelock (D). Legislature: senate, 10 D, 10 R; house, 31 D, 9 R.

Finance. Cash on hand for state government at close of 1972 fiscal year, including earnings from oil leases, $988,562,947; total revenues available to state in 1972 fiscal year, $401,430,620; total expenditures by state in 1972 fiscal year, $508,479,046.

Education (1972). Elementary schools, 265: enrollment, 60,754; teachers, 2,431. Secondary schools, 60: enrollment, 18,706; teachers, 1,771. Colleges and universities, 3.   STANTON H. PATTY

ALBANIA. Foreign affairs. Continuing to reflect the views of the People's Republic of China, Albanian press and radio muted their attacks on the United States temporarily during President Richard M. Nixon's China visit in February, but in May condemned the president's visit to Moscow as "another stage in the plotting and counterrevolutionary activities of the chieftains of the two 'superpowers' to legalize at a summit meeting their new plots at the expense of

the free peoples." The Soviet-U.S. arms agreement was denounced, and the U.S. and Soviet "zones of influence" were said to be identical in nature. The United States was accused of intimidating national liberation movements around the world, and the Soviet Union was charged with oppressing its own national minorities.

Economic developments. Albania's planners claimed impressive statistical advances for the country's modest economy. The draft plan of industrial development for this year provided for an overall increase in production of 12.5 percent over that planned for 1971. Total agricultural production was to increase by 9.2 percent. The Mao Tse-tung Hydroelectric Power Station at Vau-i-Dejes was to be fully commissioned, and production increased in the Gogova Hydroelectric Power Station, in the machinery plant in Patos, and in Tirana factories for the construction of power lines and for the manufacture of waxed cardboard. The copper enrichment factory in Spac and the cement factory in Fushe-Kruje were to be expanded, and the rate of construction increased in the ferrous metallurgy industry and on the Fierza Hydroelectric Power Station.

Under the fifth five-year plan, electric power generation in 1975 was to be up 100 percent over 1970, chemical production up 124–128 percent, productivity in industry up 26–28 percent, construction and assembly work up 34–36 percent, road transport up 15 percent, and rail transport up 46 percent. In 1975 the production of crude oil is expected to reach 2.7 million tons, compared with the 1.2 million tons planned for 1970 in the fourth five-year plan.

Production of field crops in the 1971–1975 period is to be

NO FISHING. A U.S. Coast Guard icebreaker (below) guards the flagship of a Soviet fleet, caught fishing in rich halibut grounds 10 miles off St. Matthew Island in the Bering Sea. It was intercepted within the 12-mile zone regarded as off-limits for foreign vessels.

UPI

60–65 percent over 1966–1970, with corresponding rises of 38–41 percent for livestock production and 49–53 percent for fruit.

Organization of an advanced type of agricultural cooperative, which began in the lowland areas in 1971, continued. It was anticipated that 50 such cooperatives would be set up this year. These will be large units, with a stronger material and technical base and better financing than those previously organized.

Production of ferronickel ore, which began only after World War II but has become one of Albania's main exports, was said to have increased 4.5 times since 1958. A large metallurgical combine at Elbasan, which is being built with Chinese assistance, will go into operation in 1975, at which time production of ore is expected to reach 650,000 tons, an increase of more than 60 percent over the present output.

Chinese aid is also important in a new coalfield at Valias, in the Tirana District; the field will be Albania's largest.

Area and population. Area, 11,100 sq. mi. Pop. (est. 1970), 2,135,600. Principal cities (1967): Tirana (cap.), 169,000; Durrës, 53,000; Shkodër, 50,000.
Government. Socialist republic. Pres., Haxhi Lleshi; prem., Mehmet Shehu; first secy., Workers' (Communist) Party, Enver Hoxha. Legislature: unicameral People's Assembly with 240 members elected for 4-year terms by all citizens over 18. The assembly elects a Presidium headed by the president and approves appointments of ministers.
Finance. Monetary unit, lek; 1 lek = US$0.20. Budget (1972): revenue, 5.9 billion leks; expenditure, 5.9 billion leks.
Trade (1964). Imports, US$98 million; exports, US$60 million.
Economy. Agricultural production (est. 1969, in thousands of metric tons): corn (maize), 270; wheat, 192. Livestock (est. 1970, in thousands): sheep, 1,610; cattle, 435; pigs, 150; asses, 62; horses, 42. Industry and mining (1970, in thousands of metric tons): crude oil, 1,307; lignite, 592; cement, 220; chrome ore, 194; copper ore, 6; nickel ore, 4. Electric power, 788 million kw.-hr.
Education (1969). Enrollment: primary, 506,683; secondary, 58,900; institutions of higher learning (including the university in Tirana), 16,649.
Armed forces (est. 1969). Army, 30,000; security police, 12,500.

RICHARD A. PIERCE

ALBERTA. Politics and government. The changeover from the 36-year-old Social Credit regime to the Progressive Conservative government of Premier Peter Lougheed was achieved with a minimum of upset. The new leaders were faced with the monumental task of learning how to govern, since no Progressive Conservative members had ever served in the government before. Two major changes were made. First, the department of federal and intergovernmental affairs was established, which reflects the government's concern over relations with the federal authority. Second, recognizing the growing importance of higher education, the government created a department of advanced education, which is independent of the department of education. To acquaint the new government with the needs of the province, legislators formed task forces to study such questions as urban problems, rural life, and censorship.

The new premier established the policy of having the legislative assembly meet twice a year (spring and fall) because he felt that the legislature had developed into a rubber stamp under the old government. A written report of the daily proceedings of the legislature was also introduced. Finally, television coverage of some sessions was authorized.

Legislation. The government introduced 106 bills during the three-month legislative session. Of major importance was the Alberta Bill of Rights and the Individual Rights Protection Act. The Bill of Rights, which establishes basic freedoms, has precedence over all other laws of the province. The Individual Rights Protection Act establishes a human rights commission and reaffirms the rights of the individual against discrimination and oppression. It, too, has precedence over all other laws of the province.

Massive changes in the treatment of mental illness are contained in the Mental Health Act, which provides for mental health care in general hospitals, use of nonmedical personnel in therapy, establishment of regional clinics, and decreased reliance on the services of specialized mental institutions for less serious cases.

The Alberta Opportunity Fund of Can$50 million was established to assist business and secondary industry with loans at low interest. Senior citizens will no longer pay for medicare, and the 30-mill education tax on all property owned by senior citizens was eliminated.

Economic affairs. The increase in the provincial budget is one of the smallest in years. The operating budget is estimated at $1,145,525,000. The major items are education ($254,652,000), advanced education ($143,018,000), and health and social development ($409,778,000). Major sources of income are income taxes ($224,000,000), oil, gas, and mineral revenues ($311,900,000), and the federal government ($228,393,000). The major increases occurred in the health and social development services and in environmental control, areas to which the government has given priority. The province will be required to borrow almost $200 million to cover the deficit.

The province's economy is reflecting a healthy upsurge in activity. Demand for gas and oil is increasing and is being reflected in new refinery construction and in expansion of existing facilities. A $200 million refinery is being constructed, and construction of a second extraction plant at the site of the tar sands has been approved. This plant will produce 125,000 barrels per day and will cost $600 million.

In other areas, coal production, which continues to increase as a result of Japanese orders, reached a total of 9 million tons last year. In addition, increased wheat sales and diversification have stabilized the agricultural scene, as farm income rose in 1971 and was expected to rise again this year.

Education. The change in government brought a review of higher education; one result was deferral of the opening of Athabasca University. A government-initiated study of education recommended major changes in the education system. Proposals by Dr. Walter Worth, who conducted the study, include establishing the Alberta Academy, which would provide higher education through television, radio, and correspondence courses and seminars; establishing a preschool system for five-year-olds and special systems for disadvantaged children three and four years of age; abolishing the colleges and universities commissions, with many of their functions to be taken over by the new department of advanced education; and abolishing permanent teachers' certificates. He also proposed speeding up professional and general education studies.

The committee to inquire into non-Canadian influence in postsecondary education in Alberta published a report containing recommendations to ensure proper Canadian balance in the universities. The committee recommended, among other things, that Western University Press produce the Canadian materials required; that selection processes be improved to ensure that Canadians are given a fair opportunity for university teaching; and that provisions be made to ensure that Canadian viewpoints are presented in appropriate subject fields.

Other issues. Two important events attracted wide attention. The first involved the proposal to hire an American citizen as chief of police in Calgary. The proposal was turned down and resulted in the ruling that chiefs of police must be Canadian citizens. Second, a proposal to establish a year-round recreational complex at Lake Louise was successfully fought by citizens concerned with pollution.

Area and population. Area, 255,285 sq. mi. Pop. (est. 1971), 1,614,000. Principal cities (1969): Edmonton (cap.), 450,000; Calgary, 422,418.
Government. Prem., Peter Lougheed; lt. gov., John MacEwan; prov. treas., Gordon Miniely; atty. gen., Mervin Leitch.
Education. Enrollment: schools, colleges, and universities, 474,700.

JOHN E. DUTTON

ALGERIA. Agrarian reform. President Houari Boumedienne concentrated this year on the extremely complex, politically delicate task of reforming and modernizing Algerian agriculture—an operation promised and postponed almost since independence ten years earlier, first by Ahmed ben Bella, who was Algeria's first president, and then by Boumedienne.

Perhaps it was already too late. Increasingly since 1967, the president's power has rested upon the capable young technocrats who staff Algeria's gigantic state bureaucracy and its growing nationalized industries. Not only were the technocrats a growing privileged class, but many among this educated elite were also related to those 16,500 individuals, 3 percent of all rural freeholders, who owned one-quarter of the nation's land. It was questionable whether the state bureaucracy, called upon to execute agrarian reform, would act against the landowners and thus against the family interests of many of its leading members. A handful of landowners, amid much publicity in late February, donated their land to the state for distribution. But no one really knew which or how much land the rural bourgeoisie possessed, since there had not been any accurate survey, the obvious precondition of any reform, for 20 years. Thus, if the land reform seemed overdue on political or ideological grounds, it also seemed premature on technical grounds.

Meanwhile, the mass media were expected to gain the peasants' confidence, but there were doubts about whether the local authorities would cooperate. The Front of National Liberation, Algeria's official party, remained weak, and the presidents of the communal assemblies, Algeria's only viable local institutions, expressed concern at their annual national conference in late February about the loss of communal lands to the agrarian reform fund. They also questioned whether the "cooperatives" the regime was planning to install in agrarian reform areas would be voluntary, as Boumedienne seemed to promise, or compulsory for reform beneficiaries, as a spokesman for the Ministry of Agriculture had indicated.

In principle, some 300,000 landholdings were subject to the reform. Aside from the "self-managed" farms and cooperatives allocated to veterans of the guerrilla war for independence, only properties of less than 12 unirrigated acres farmed directly by their owners were exempt from reform, and traditional sharecropping practiced by large numbers of small peasants was outlawed. But as of May, not one square inch of private land had been nationalized, although some symbolic donations had begun to be distributed by the government.

Economic affairs. Despite the 1971 decline in Algeria's petroleum production—the cost of nationalizing the French installations that had produced two-thirds of Algeria's total—the ambitious US$6 billion four-year plan (1970–1973) for national investments (mainly in heavy industry) was retained without any fundamental revisions. Because of price increases and the growing Western demand for both crude oil and liquefied gas, Algeria expected revenues of $1 billion in 1972, twice its 1970 earnings. In late 1971 it concluded a 25-year deal with an American company for the sale of up to $260 million annually of petroleum products, and in spring 1972 the U.S. Federal Power Commission finally approved another long-term contract, almost as big, whereby the El Paso Natural Gas Company is to import liquefied Algerian gas. The petroleum earnings were expected considerably to alleviate Algeria's serious balance-of-payments difficulties, caused by capital goods imports for the four-year plan.

However, the highly centralized, state-run economy was experiencing some management difficulties. Even in the state's model oil company giant, Sonatrach, there were indications that too much responsibility was placed in the hands of too few men at the top. The results were avoidable delays in decision-making. At least one factory closed down

in late 1971 because necessary import licenses were not processed in time.

Foreign affairs. Algeria continued to harbor Eldridge Cleaver, who was joined in 1972 by two sets of black skyjackers. The government also retained an interest in Palestinian liberation and in Third World revolution, symbolized by Cuban premier Fidel Castro's visit in May. But Algerian diplomacy was more concerned with its North African neighbors and with the European Common Market. While attending the June summit conference of the Organization of African Unity in Morocco, President Boumedienne ratified with King Hassan II a final settlement of the Moroccan-Algerian border dispute which had precipitated a desert war in 1963. Boumedienne also visited Tunisia for the first time as chief of state in April and then welcomed Tunisian president Habib Bourguiba to Algiers in May, thus consolidating their growing number of bilateral technical and commercial accords.

Of greater potential political import was an accord signed November 1, 1971, with the Common Market which reduced duties on Algerian wine by 40 percent. This augured closer relations in other areas. Algeria also tried to concert its Common Market diplomacy with Morocco and Tunisia; however, any substantial increase in North African economic integration was impossible until their respective economies acquired greater strength in the European and international markets.

Educational affairs. A year after their union was dissolved by the authorities in 1971, university students quietly accepted the "entry of the revolution into the university" in the form of a thorough reorganization which tended to replace the French model with the American model of higher education.

Area and population. Area, 919,595 sq. mi. Pop. (est. 1971), 14,500,000. Principal cities (1966): Algiers (cap.), 943,142; Oran, 328,257; Constantine, 253,649.
Government. Military junta, controlling a one-party, revolutionary government. Pres., Houari Boumedienne; for. min., Abdelaziz Bouteflika.
Finance. Monetary unit, Algerian dinar; DA1 = US$0.2325. Budget (est. 1972): revenue, DA8.7 billion; expenditure, DA15.4 billion. Foreign loans, advances from the treasury, and unbudgeted increases in petroleum revenues are expected to make up the huge deficit.
Trade (1969). Imports, US$1.009 billion; exports, US$934 million. Principal exports: crude petroleum, wine, natural gas, citrus fruits. Principal trading partners (1968): France, West Germany, Great Britain, United States, Italy.
Agriculture and industry. Agricultural production (1968): wheat, 1,534,000 metric tons; wine, 10,000,000 hectoliters. Mining (1969): crude petroleum, 46,000,000 metric tons; iron ore, 2,964,000 metric tons.
CLEMENT HENRY MOORE

AMERICAN LITERATURE. The hoax. If December 7, 1941, was the "day that will live in infamy," December 7, 1971, might be called the day that will live in flimflammery. That was the date that McGraw-Hill proudly announced that the publishing plum of the year, if not the decade, had fallen into its lap—the autobiography of Howard Hughes. Sixty-seven days later, the world's largest publishing company grudgingly admitted that what it had was not a plum but a lemon. It was indeed sour fruit. McGraw-Hill had been roundly hoaxed; Howard Hughes' prickly, garrulous, randy "confessions" had been invented—but not out of whole cloth—by a little-known novelist named Clifford Irving and his sidekick-researcher Richard Suskind.

Hoaxes are not new in the publishing industry, nor is their close relative, plagiarism. But the Irving hoax was a grandiloquent con-job involving hundreds of thousands of dollars and the reputations of a great publishing house and a mass-circulation magazine (Life). And it had all been pulled off by a journeyman writer whose Howard Hughes was his most successful characterization—almost.

The story began on a blustery December day in 1970 on the island of Majorca, off the coast of Spain. Irving, passing

AN UNCOMMON SEAGULL
CLIMBS THE CHARTS

Turning his back on the humdrum, beak-to-mouth existence of his fellow gulls, one Jonathan Livingston Seagull learned to fly higher than they could dream. An odd premise for a best seller, but Richard Bach's childlike fable, at first uncelebrated by bookstores and book reviewers, soared on its own to the top of the best-seller list. By the end of the year, it had gone through 19 printings and sold well over 1 million copies in hard covers.

through on the ferry to his home on the neighboring island of Ibiza, had coffee with his friend Suskind. In the course of their talk he mentioned a *Newsweek* article on the upheavals in the Hughes Las Vegas empire that had caused the old man to flee to the Bahamas. Why not cook up an "autobiography" of Hughes, Irving fantasized; the man never made public appearances and would probably not deny it; even if he did, who would believe him? Perhaps he was even incapacitated, if not dead.

The idea simmered on the back-burner as Irving returned to Ibiza, a sort of lotus-land for the artistic fringe and a stopover on the international hippie underground railroad. Unlike many of Ibiza's permanent residents, Irving did write things—several novels that had sold indifferently and a biography of his friend Elmyr de Hory, an art forger, titled with unintended prescience *Fake!* Irving had a $150,000 four-

book contract with McGraw-Hill and was well into a novel. He loved his fourth wife, Edith, and their two children but compulsively continued a long on-and-off dalliance with the Baroness Nina van Pallandt, a beautiful blonde Danish singer.

But the novel would not come, and the Hughes fantasy in all its gorgeous grandiosity would not down. Irving's mind began, like a self-willing computer, to whir out a plan. He would casually mention to Beverly Loo, an editor at McGraw-Hill, that he had sent Hughes a copy of *Fake!* and that the old curmudgeon had seemed impressed. Perhaps, he would suggest temptingly, the relationship could ripen into a collaboration. If McGraw-Hill bit, well and good; if not, *que será, será*, as they say on Ibiza.

McGraw-Hill bit after Irving showed them two letters in Hughes' own hand—forgeries he had done using a photo-

graph of a Hughes letter that had accompanied the *Newsweek* article. (The forgeries were terrible, Irving later admitted, and he was forced to redo them using a much larger photograph that had appeared in *Life*.) McGraw-Hill was dazzled. No reporter had spoken to Hughes in 15 years; his autobiography would be the Everest of American publishing. His minions had paid off two would-be writers of unauthorized biographies, but three others had been published.

Now the caper was gathering momentum. Irving signed a contract with McGraw-Hill for a $500,000 advance, of which $400,000 was to go to Hughes and $100,000 to his amanuensis. Irving and Suskind fanned out to various libraries digging up every scrap of information about Hughes. A lucky break came when Time-Life, which had bought first serial rights, opened its rich file of raw Hughesiana to Irving, who surreptitiously photographed it. A second break came when Irving met, quite by chance, a Hollywood executive named Stanley Meyer, who had a copy of a manuscript by former Hughes aide Noah Dietrich, done in collaboration with James Phelan, a hard-nosed investigative reporter. The book was unpublishable as is, said Meyer; would Cliff like to look at it with an eye to a rewrite job? Irving's Hughes book was still top secret, of course (McGraw-Hill had christened it Project Octavio), so Cliff merely allowed he'd look at it. He did, xeroxed it, and returned it with thanks, saying he was too busy on another book about famous billionaires.

Using this wealth of material and their own imaginations and even childhood experiences, Irving and Suskind worked through the summer alternating playing the parts of Hughes and Irving and concocting a biography of Hughes in question-and-answer form.

More letters were forged; handwriting experts eventually declared them genuine. Irving even took a lie-detector test that was ruled "inconclusive." A contretemps arose when "Hughes" upped his price to a cool million; McGraw-Hill grudgingly but promptly agreed to a total advance of $750,-000—but not a penny more. Knowing that hanging about Hughes' hotel in the Bahamas might create suspicion, Irving traveled all over the Western hemisphere, ostensibly meeting the eccentric billionaire but actually carrying on his dalliance with Nina; there was also an interlude with a blonde lady skin-diving instructor. The checks that had been paid were made out to "H. R. Hughes," thanks to Irving's shrewd foresight. Employing forged passports made out to "Helga R. Hughes" and the identity card of her ex-husband's second wife, which she had stolen, Edith Irving deposited the checks in Swiss banks, where they lay snugly tucked away, protected by the rigid code of secrecy of the Swiss banking system.

The finished manuscript was pronounced brilliant and saleable by all who read it—a blockbuster. Irving and Suskind had done their work well, probably writing a much more interesting book than the real Howard would have done.

But then the tide in the affairs of Clifford Irving, as it must with all men, began to turn; truth began to bombard him from all sides. The Hughes Tool Company denied the book's authenticity as soon as its publication was announced; insiders, of course, merely nodded knowingly. Swiss authorities learned that "H. R. Hughes" was a woman. As bits of the Hughes biography were leaked to the press, James Phelan began to notice similarities to his own manuscript and, more damaging, anecdotes that only he knew about. The chief counsel of the Hughes Tool Company, Chester Davis, and his detective agency, Intertel, worked overtime to discredit the manuscript. Hughes himself held a bizzare press conference by telephone and denied knowing Irving. Then, in a confrontation at Martin Ackerman's house (a millionaire mainly known as the man who presided over the demise of the *Saturday Evening Post*, he was acting as Irving's attorney), Frank McCulloch of *Time*, a mild skeptic,

showed Irving pictures of men who might be the mysterious "George Gordon Holmes," who had allegedly acted as intermediary between Hughes and Irving and who McCulloch firmly believed was John Meier, a former Hughes employee. But when Irving heard that McCulloch "knew all about" Meier, Irving thought he was referring to Stanley Meyer—which meant he knew about the Dietrich manuscript. After failing to recognize John Meier's picture, Irving broke, partially, and confessed that Edith was Helga R. Hughes.

By that time U.S. postal inspectors were in the act. They tracked down Nina van Pallandt, who agreed to testify that during one of their trysts in Mexico, Irving had not had time for any interviewing as he had claimed. Federal and New York state authorities were also involved, and a grand jury was empaneled. The last bastion—the manuscript—fell when, at a dramatic confrontation in the McGraw-Hill offices, Phelan demonstrated that much of the material closely paralleled his Dietrich book. Stanley Meyer's confession to a grand jury that he had innocently turned over the Dietrich manuscript to Irving completed the demolition job. All that remained was for the Irvings and Suskind to confess and hope for lesser sentences. On June 16, 1972, Clifford Irving was sentenced to 2½ years in federal prison; Edith Irving drew two months and Richard Suskind six months from the state court. After serving her sentence, Edith Irving was extradited voluntarily to Switzerland to face further charges.

Ironically, the year of the hoax brought forth a rash of similar cases. Another McGraw-Hill book, *The Memoirs of Chief Red Fox*, supposedly the reminiscences of a 101-year-old Indian chief, was found to contain plagiarized material.

EDMUND WILSON, considered by some to be America's greatest contemporary social and literary critic, died in June at the age of 77. Since the publication of "Axel's Castle" in 1931, he had been known as an especially erudite and cantankerous man of letters.

JILL KREMENTZ

Bound to Violence, a highly praised novel by Yambo Ouologuem, an African writer, had a scene that echoed one in Graham Greene's *It's a Battlefield* with more than coincidental fidelity. Dan Kurzman, the author of *Genesis 1948,* let slip in a gossip column that sections of *O Jerusalem!,* a current best seller, were remarkably like his own earlier book. And a battle raged among three memoirists of the late Igor Stravinsky as to who was truly the great man's Boswell; the critical verdict was straight out of *Rashomon:* probably all of them.

Fiction. The Irving case aside, however, it was not a particularly strong year for fiction. The year's major literary event was the publication of *August 1914,* Aleksandr I. Solzhenitsyn's profound moral inquiry into the sociomilitary roots of the Russian defeat at Tannenberg in World War I. The first of a projected cycle of novels about prerevolutionary Russia, the book had the critics mentioning Tolstoy in the same breath. Sadly, the translation of *August 1914* was not first-rate—more adaptation than translation. The American publishers, Farrar, Straus and Giroux, were not at fault, however, since the translating was done under the supervision of the British and German publishers under impossible deadline pressures.

There were new novels by John Barth, Philip Roth, and Vladimir Nabokov to cheer and argue about. Barth's *Chimera* was a complex inside-out view of a writer writing, as he retold the myths of Scheherazade, Perseus, and Bellerophon. Roth in *The Breast* employed an extreme symbol of the grotesque, a man who is transformed into a large female breast, in order to affirm the truths embedded in ordinary experience. Nabokov was at his most intellectually playful, brilliantly dancing on the high wire of the English language as he created a funhouse-mirror world of dream and reality in *Transparent Things.* John Updike was represented by a collection of short stories, as were Joyce Carol Oates and Donald Barthelme. Other writers of lesser reputation, such as D. Keith Mano, Larry McMurtry, Frederick Buechner, Thomas Rogers, Harry Crews, John Seelye, and John Gardner, produced interesting fiction. Hortense Calisher played a doubleheader for her readers—a novel, *Standard Dreaming,* and an autobiography, *Herself.* Eudora Welty was masterful in delineating American types in *The Optimist's Daughter.*

Other women writers continued to probe their own condition as women—Rosalyn Drexler, Helen Yglesias, Janet Frame, Anne Richardson Roiphe, and Lois Gould among them. Alix Kates Shulman's *Memoirs of an Ex-Prom Queen* was touted as a *vraiment* woman's liberation novel, but its literary merit was questioned. A small counterrevolution to the women's lib manifestos of past years appeared in the form of Midge Decter's *The New Chastity,* which branded the movement as an escape from freedom.

Nonfiction and poetry. Nonfiction seemed to supply the rent-paying books (in an analysis of books on the best-seller lists in 1971, *Publisher's Weekly* estimated that the nonfiction best sellers sold twice as many copies as the fiction winners). Fads abounded, as usual, and there was a spate of ephemeral books on topical problems. Books on China were in fashion, many of them scholarly studies that did not find a large public. The Bobby Fischer-Boris Spassky world championship chess match inspired a fast turnover in chess books. The David McKay Company, which had 30 chess books in print, sold more of them during the match than it usually sells in a year. Then there were the back-to-the-land, do-it-yourself, handicraft books. Ecology books continued to appear, with Barry Commoner's *The Closing Circle* and David Ehrenfeld's *Conserving Life on Earth* two of the more noteworthy titles. There was an unusually large number of books on the media, stimulated perhaps by Vice-President Spiro Agnew's attacks of the previous year.

The most remarkable *arriviste* on the best-seller lists was a bird named *Jonathan Livingston Seagull,* who occupied the top perch for most of the year. First classified as non-

fiction—it had pictures; perhaps the booksellers thought it was a calendar—it became apparent that this inspirational allegory about a talking seagull who aimed for aerial perfection was pure fantasy.

There always seems to be a do-it-yourself psychoanalysis book on the charts, and this year was no exception. *I'm O.K.—You're O.K.,* which had been around for a couple of years, suddenly took off and led the nonfiction titles.

Three books about or by show-biz celebrities were also popular—*George S. Kaufman, Tracy and Hepburn,* and David Niven's string of anecdotes, *The Moon's a Balloon.* Two baseball books also made the list, belying the sport's replacement by pro football as the national pastime. One, *The Boys of Summer,* by Roger Kahn was heavily nostalgic; the other, *The Summer Game,* featured *New Yorker* editor Roger Angell's perceptive essays on the tactics and grace of the game. Sex was represented (sort of) by *Open Marriage,* which was really not about wife-swapping, and self-improvement by *The Peter Prescription,* Laurence Peter's unfunny successor to his spoof *The Peter Principle.* Joseph Lash's *Eleanor and Franklin* gave way to the same author's sequel, *Eleanor: The Years Alone,* which described the active widowhood of the first lady of the world.

The Vietnam war, once the subject of so many books, faded from a benumbed public's eye. Yet reminders of it would not down. A revised edition of *The Air War in Indochina,* a scholarly analysis of the horrible price this country has been paying for the bombing, financially and morally, was particularly timely as the president substituted B-52's for GI's. Frances FitzGerald, a young reporter who had spent six years in Vietnam, wrote one of the best books yet on the war, on Vietnamese culture, and on the systematic destruction of that culture by the American presence in *A Fire in the Lake.* And Daniel Ellsberg, purveyor of the Pentagon papers, bared his soul in the appropriately impersonal manner of an ex-Rand Corporation systems analyst in *Papers on the War.*

Meanwhile, scholars were probing into the roots of the cold-war thinking that had led us into the quagmire. The "revisionist" school portrayed the United States as the aggressor, driven to organize the world as a fiefdom of capitalism and suppress authentic national liberation movements. This view was best expressed in *The Limits of Power* by Joyce and Gabriel Kolko. A more orthodox approach was that of John Lewis Gaddis in *The United States and the Origins of the Cold War 1941–1947,* which emphasized domestic political pressures as controlling in foreign policy. Other historians attempted to lay the blame for evangelical anti-Communism and McCarthyism on Harry S Truman, while John F. Kennedy's role in passing the torch of this policy along was analyzed critically in two books. The motives of the men responsible for the war in the Kennedy-Johnson administrations were probed by David Halberstam in his ironic *The Best and the Brightest.*

The death of Edmund Wilson left a giant empty place in American letters. His last book, *A Window on Russia,* a collection of studies in Russian literature, and the reissue of his masterpiece *To the Finland Station* coincided with numerous eulogies placing him among the greatest American critics of this century.

If not the greatest, certainly the most controversial American poet of this century, Ezra Pound, died in self-imposed exile on November 1. It may be decades before the remarkable contribution of Pound the poet and critic can be separated from the viciousness of Pound the social thinker and wartime Fascist propagandist.

The death also of John Berryman, by suicide, robbed us of a poet of the first rank. His last collection, *Delusions, Etc.,* which he had edited before his death, was a nervous dialogue with God and a profound evocation of sadness. Two veteran poets were represented by collections: W. H. Auden, whose *Epistle to a Godson* was his first book of

poetry since 1969, and Archibald MacLeish, who at 80 gathered together a collection of past and present poems he wished to be remembered by. Poets such as John Ashberry, Philip Levine, Jon Anderson, Nikki Giovanni, Jay Wright, and Eleanor Ross Taylor had impressive collections published. And Michael Casey, a young Vietnam veteran, wrote some taut, bitter poems about the war, fittingly entitled *Obscenities*.

Leon Edel finished his masterful five-volume biography of Henry James, and it was generally agreed that it was one of the finest literary biographies ever written. There were also noteworthy biographies of Samuel de Champlain by Samuel Eliot Morison, Diderot by Arthur M. Wilson, and Henry Luce by W. A. Swanberg. Other subjects of biography and autobiography included Ralph Nader, Reinhold Niebuhr, John Marquand, S. N. Behrman, James Thurber, Richard M. Nixon, John Foster Dulles, Robert A. Taft, Franklin Roosevelt, Florenz Ziegfeld, Rudolf Bing, Drew Pearson, Marion Davies, Tallulah Bankhead (three!), Mao Tse-tung, Henry Kissinger, and Mary Todd Lincoln.

National Book Awards. The National Book Awards for 1971 proceeded with their usual crisis-ridden deliberations. One judge resigned in the new contemporary affairs category, and the remaining two judges' choice of *The Last Whole Earth Catalog*, a sort of Sears-Roebuck of the counterculture, was not popular. Other winners were arts and letters, *The Classical Style* by Charles Rosen; biography, *Eleanor and Franklin* by Joseph P. Lash; children's books, *The Slightly Irregular Fire Engine, or The Hithering Thithering Djinn* by Donald Barthelme; fiction, *The Complete Stories* by Flannery O'Connor; history, *Ordeal of the Union*, vols. 7–8, by Allan Nevins; philosophy and religion, *Righteous Empire: The Protestant Experience in America* by Martin E. Marty; poetry, *Selected Poems* by Howard Moss and *Collected Poems* by Frank O'Hara; the sciences, *The Blue Whale* by George L. Small; translation, Austryn Wainhouse's translation of *Chance and Necessity* by Jacques Monod.
RICHARD R. LINGEMAN

ANTHROPOLOGY.

Tasadays. The Tasadays, 1971's anthropological sensation, received increased attention this year. The cave-dwelling tribe of the Philippines grew in 1972 from 24 to 27 members and was paid visits by scholars, celebrities (such as Charles Lindbergh), photographers, journalists, and others, although there were happy indications that the flare-up of attention will end shortly and that the gentle people of the Mindanao forests will soon be allowed to return to their former isolation.

On April 6, Philippine president Ferdinand E. Marcos set aside about 50,000 acres in Cotabato Province, 600 miles south of Manila, as a reservation for the Tasadays and one slightly more advanced tribe. Logging and other economic exploitation within the area will not be allowed. Manual Elizalde, Jr., who "discovered" the Tasadays and has been more or less their patron and protector, was named a presidential assistant for cultural minorities. His influence should help to hold down encroachments on the Tasadays' preserve.

The award of the reservation did not occur, however, until after the flood of outsiders had come and gone, leaving, inevitably, an impact on the previously untouched tribal life of the Tasadays. Machetes had come in, along with other small items of modern technology, all of which will have subtle but definite effects on the fabric of Tasaday society. Even more important was the growing awareness by this "lost tribe" that there was an outside world and that one day they may want to see it and perhaps join it.

The Maroons. Attention was called this year to the urgent need for a research program devoted to one of the world's most fascinating ethnic isolates, the Maroons of Jamaica and of Sierra Leone. Although widely known to travel writers, these descendants of the first blacks ever to win and hold freedom in the Americas have not been studied in depth.

The origin of the Maroons is obscure, but apparently their existence as an independent community began in the mid-seventeenth century, just as the British were forcibly taking over Jamaica from the Spanish empire. A number of slaves escaped during the general turmoil, and many took refuge in the ruggedly mountainous interior. The original group may have been Ashanti, but whatever its specific tribal origin, the community even today has a highly African cultural and linguistic complexion.

The Maroons held firmly to their independence, harassing the British settlers and using guerrilla tactics with such skill that finally in 1738 they won a treaty giving them a permanent guarantee of freedom from slavery, full title to their lands, and a high degree of self-government in return for loyalty to the British crown. They also agreed not to harbor escaped slaves.

In general, the Maroons were loyal to their treaty with the British; the one major exception to this compliance produced one of the most interesting population movements of recent times. In 1795 a particular Maroon community rebelled against the British but was quickly defeated because the other communities refused to cooperate. The rebels were captured and deported to Nova Scotia. Abjectly miserable in these cold and unfamiliar surroundings, they refused to work and became a serious social problem. Finally, their repeated petitions for removal met with some success, and in early 1800 the entire community was sent to Sierra Leone.

The Maroons have remained rigidly separate in Africa as well as in the New World, but the inevitable assaults have begun on their independence and distinctiveness, as the societies in which they are embedded undergo rapid modernization. A fascinating cultural mixture, the Maroons provide many excellent opportunities for anthropological research; fortunately, there are indications that the life of these people will be recorded before it is too late.

Voodoo death. An interesting article in the *American Anthropologist* by David Lester discusses voodoo death. It has long been observed that in many societies—especially tribal societies—people can and do die under the influence of voodoo or hex. Many explanations have been offered for this phenomenon, including the possibility that it is strictly physiological (overstimulation of the sympathico-adrenal system).

Lester offers the view that voodoo death must be seen in the perspective of the social context of illness in general. Studies he cites on the onset of illness tend to indicate that a common condition is the experience of helplessness (a failure of belief that the outside world can offer any succor) and hopelessness (a sense of personal and unalterable responsibility for the inability to cope). The "giving up" that accompanies severe disease is akin to the psychological state of a hexed individual. Cultural tradition leads the individual to believe that others can doom him through bad will or through acts of black magic; others around him believe it as well. He will therefore feel either utterly helpless or utterly hopeless in such a situation, depending on whether he tends to externalize or internalize blame. The individual in such a condition has become worthless or damaged and can no longer obtain gratification from his social relationships. To others he is as good as dead, and the moment he accepts that fact he becomes psychologically obliterated. A common response to the hex is to give up all food and water, since nothing can be done anyway. Medical studies show that in this condition the individual is more susceptible to infectious diseases and other pathological conditions.

Lester thinks that this general view is ascertainable in field studies, and he urges those doing field research in areas where voodoo or hex is a cultural pattern to apply these principles to the specific cases that they observe.

Sexist vocabulary. One of the more diverting issues that occupied the attention of social anthropologists during 1972

was the vocabulary of gender. Sensitized by an energetic feminist movement within the field and already attuned to questions of this sort through their concern with kinship and ethnolinguistics, anthropologists took to the issue of discriminatory sexual reference like ducks to water.

The central problem is the third-person pronouns—he, she, him, her, his, hers—which in English indicate gender in a manner that some regard as gratuitous. Various suggestions have been offered to correct the situation. One possibility is a set of asexual forms:

Subjective: *shis* (Who does shis think shis is?)
Objective: *shim* (The idea hit shim like lightning.)
Possessive: *shim(s)* (That is shim book; it is shims.)
Reflexive: *shimself* (Shis hurt shimself.)

Not surprisingly, there were those who felt that adjustment to such a system would be entirely too difficult, and among the alternative approaches was a suggestion that the already available neuter third-person pronoun "it" be employed. However, as anthropologist Paul Kay of the University of California at Berkeley pointed out, this usage would violate an important principle in the English language, which is the discrimination between human and non-human. Besides, Kay added, "sentences such as 'I want no one but it to be the mother of my children' sound odd."

The issue was far from resolved at year's end.

E. M. WOOD

ARABIAN PENINSULA. United Arab Emirates. Twice United Arab Emirates defense forces were required to quell disturbances within the federation. In January they suppressed an abortive coup in Ash Shariqah (Sharja), while in June they restored peace between feuding tribesmen of Ash Shariqah and Al Fujayrah (Fujaira).

In February, Ras al-Khaimah joined the UAE as its seventh member. Now the UAE embraces all the former Trucial sheikhdoms.

Bahrain. In July, Sheikh Isa bin Suleiman al-Khalifa initiated action to bring some democracy to the island sheikhdom. A 44-member constituent council was established, with 12 seats to be held by members of the cabinet, ten appointed by Sheikh Isa, and 22 filled by election.

In January it was announced that Bahrain had agreed to lease part of the former British naval base to the United States as a station for the small American naval contingent assigned to the Persian Gulf.

Qatar. On February 22, Sheikh Khalifa bin Hammad al-Thani deposed his cousin Sheikh Ahmad bin Ali al-Thani in a bloodless coup. The deposed sheikh had spent most of the time abroad and was even away when Qatar was declared independent. Sheikh Khalifa formed a 20-member advisory council on April 23 as the sheikhdom's "first experiment in democracy."

Oman. Sultan Qabus bin Sa'id moved vigorously against rebel forces in Dhofar this year. By May, government troops were gaining hegemony in the province, but several border incidents with Yemen marred these successes. On May 7, Muscat acknowledged that its air force had bombed Yemen, this time in retaliation for alleged attacks on the Omani border post at Habrut.

At the beginning of the year, Sultan Qabus dismissed Prime Minister Tariq bin Tarmain and assumed his duties personally.

United Arab Emirates. *Area and population.* Area, 35,000 sq. mi. Pop. (est. 1969), 185,000.
Government. A federation of seven sheikhdoms. Pres., Sheikh Zayed bin Sultan; pres. of Council of Ministers, Sheikh Maktorim.
Petroleum (1971). Crude oil production: Abu Dhabi, 44.8 million long tons; Dubai, 6.5 million long tons.
Bahrain. *Area and population.* Area, 400 sq. mi. Pop. (1971 census), 216,000.
Government. Independent sheikhdom under the rule of Sheikh Isa bin Suleiman al-Khalifa.
Petroleum (1971). Crude oil production, 3.8 million long tons.

ROBERT AZZ/MAGNUM

SHEIKHS OF ARABY. In December rulers of six former Trucial sheikhdoms joined to form the new United Arab Emirates. But only two months later, Sheikh Khalid bin Muhammad (far left) had dropped out of the picture, murdered in an attempted coup.

Qatar. *Area and population.* Area, 8,500 sq. mi. Pop., 130,000.
Government. Independent sheikhdom under the rule of Sheikh Khalifa bin Hammad al-Thani.
Petroleum (1971). Crude oil production, 20.2 millon long tons.
Oman. *Area and population.* Area, 82,000 sq. mi. Pop. (est. 1971), 750,000.
Government. Independent sultanate under the rule of Sultan Qabus bin Sa'id.
Petroleum (1971). Crude oil production, 14.4 million long tons.

RICHARD H. PFAFF

ARCHAEOLOGY. New Jerusalem finds. With Jerusalem fully in Israeli hands as a result of the six-day war in 1967, a massive program of archaeological excavations has begun, and in this historically richest of cities the first results are already being seen. One important dig is on Mount Zion. Excavating in the courtyard of a medieval Armenian convent atop the mount, a team of archaeologists led by Magen Broshi has been searching for the house of Caiaphas the high priest, where, according to the Gospels, Jesus was taken after he was betrayed in the Garden of Gethsemane. There he was tried before the Jewish elders and kept the night before the Crucifixion. Although Caiaphas' house has not specifically been identified, an entire neighborhood of aristocratic and priestly residences dating from around A.D. 10 to A.D. 70 has been unearthed. The walls of the houses were covered with rich frescoes, the fragments of which are being painstakingly picked up and restored. Although the work has barely begun, there is every indication that this will be a spectacular find. (*See the special article* JERUSALEM.)

Han Dynasty tomb. Late in the summer, the Chinese news agency Hsinhua announced an impressive find at Changsha in south central China. Workmen digging a tunnel sometime earlier in the year had uncovered a remarkable tomb characteristic of the Han Period (206 B.C. to A.D. 220). Leading Chinese archaeologists descended on the site, and the magnitude of the find soon became clear. Behind the

UNDER THE VOLCANO

entrance, sealed with foot-thick layers of charcoal covered by white clay, was the incredibly well-preserved body of a woman of about 50, wrapped in 20 layers of rich silks and surrounded by all of the handsome burial objects characteristic of the period. In addition to six coffins (one covered with a dazzling silk painting), the archaeologists found more than 1,000 accessories, including 120 wooden figurines and a banquet table with the identifiable remains—2,000 years old—of peaches, pears, melons, eggs, pickled vegetables, rice, and rice cakes. Never before had a tomb or a corpse from so early a date been discovered in quite such fine condition. The government paper *Jenmin Jih Pao* hailed the discovery but added that the tomb "bears witness to the extravagance of the feudal ruling class and its ruthless exploitation of the laboring people."

Suits of jade. Earlier in the year, it became known that China had unearthed two magnificent jade burial suits dating from the second century B.C. Each suit, consisting of jacket, trousers, and boots, contains more than 2,000 rectangular pieces of jade fastened together at the corners with gold wire. The suits were used to bury Liu Sheng, king of Chung-shan, and his queen. Liu Sheng died in 113 B.C. after ruling over his kingdom for 41 years.

Exciting statues near Athens. Greek archaeologist Efthymios Mastrokostas, digging 25 miles southwest of Athens, discovered this summer two amazingly well-preserved marble statues, one of a young man (*kouros*) and the other of a young woman (*kore*). The two statues, originally painted and still bearing traces of color, seem to date from approximately 2,500 years ago. Possibly buried (they were found in an orderly state, lying side by side) to protect them from the threatened Persian invasion (which finally occurred in 490 B.C.), the statues are graceful and light in appearance. Both figures have curly hair and faintly smiling expressions. It seems likely that the figures (that of the *kouros* is 6 feet high, that of the *kore* about a foot less) stood over the graves of a brother and sister. Especially exciting is the fact that the female figure fits exactly onto a pedestal inscribed with the words, "Aristion the Párian made me." Aristion, who came from the island of Páros and worked in the middle of the sixth century B.C., had been known previously only by four other pedestals bearing his name; this is the first figure sculpture of his ever found. Now that scholars have an indication of his style, many unascribed museum pieces may be attributed to him.

Aegean art treasures. Work continued throughout the year on a spectacular 3,500-year-old Minoan city—first discovered in 1967—on the Aegean island of Thíra. The island was nearly destroyed by a massive volcanic eruption in 1500 B.C., and the painstaking work of Spyridon Marinatos and his team is only now beginning to recover the glories of the ancient Thíran city of Akrotíri.

Excavators recently found some of the most remarkable frescoes of the entire Mediterranean region. The colors are

In the rubble of the town of Akrotiri, buried 3,500 years ago under the pumice and ash of a massive volcano, archaeologists unearthed fragments of delicate frescoes; pieced together, they showed Bronze Age art at its peak. The "Fresco of the Princes" (left) shows two boys playfully boxing. Workers at right make casts at the Aegean site where a huge three-sided fresco of lilies and birds (partly visible) was discovered almost completely intact.

bright and lively and, for this early period, the compositions imaginative and even daring. One stunning figure is of a woman, her breasts exposed, stooping to pick flowers; another is a fine profile of a teen-aged priestess, her ear and lips painted bright red. The walls of one magnificent room are covered with a wild, undulating, lily-filled landscape.

The city buildings are two and three stories high, with 50-foot street fronts and double doors, and there are indications of balconies. Although no valuables have been found (the inhabitants may have had forewarning of the island's destruction and fled), more than 3,500 ceramic pots have been discovered so far, many exquisitely painted.

Stone Age town. Remains of a 5,000-year-old town of about 20,000 people were discovered 115 miles south of Kiev. Its excavation is expected to shed new light on the Tripolye culture of the prehistoric Ukraine and on the Neolithic "urban revolution."

Isotopes and marble. Harmon and Valerie Craig, of the University of California at San Diego, reported in the journal *Science* a new technique for establishing the provenance of the marble used in ancient buildings and statuary. They collected 170 samples from the old Greek quarries on the islands of Náxos and Páros and at Mounts Pentelikon and Hymettus, both on the mainland near Athens. These four areas were the most popular sources of marble in classical Greece. Samples were tested for their content of the isotopes carbon-13 and oxygen-18. The samples from Páros,

Mount Pentelikon, and Mount Hymettus showed remarkable consistency in their carbon-13 and oxygen-18 contents. The samples from Náxos formed two groups according to the variation in oxygen-18 content. Next, around 20 samples taken from various ancient Greek buildings were studied. Several of the archaeological samples were matched with their quarries; others contained carbon-13 and oxygen-18 in quantities that would indicate they came from none of the quarries studied. Archaeologists would appear to have a powerful new tool which, when fully developed, may be able to establish the origin of the marble used by the ancients in their monuments.

Racing the bulldozers. Efforts continued throughout the year to develop programs around the world that might slow the rampant destruction of archaeological sites before they can be properly studied. The threats have been many—highway construction and large-scale residential and industrial developments; dam construction and watershed projects; strip-mining; deep soil plowing; and massive assaults by amateurs who despoil sites of their artifacts and leave them useless for research. The epidemic of destruction has become worldwide. In Mexico a valuable Indian ruin in Chiapas state will go under water when a new dam is completed in 1973; in Arkansas one-fourth of 1,000 archaeological sites known in 1960 had been lost by 1965; in London the remains of a fifteenth-century fortress are about to be destroyed by construction of a new boys' school.

Systematic salvage programs are still rare, but archaeologists continue to press for educational programs directed at government agencies and the public.

Glass slippers in Cologne. A pair of glass slippers, buried with a woman in the third century A.D., has come to light in Cologne, West Germany. Cologne, which in Roman times was known as Colonia Claudia Ara Agrippinensis, was the glass-making center of the Western Empire during late antiquity. One expert speculated that a glass-blower had made the slippers—which are interesting more as curiosities than for their intrinsic value—to bury with his wife.

The slippers were actually discovered at a building site by a group of amateur archaeologists in September 1971, but public knowledge of the find was delayed because the discoverers failed to report it to the police, as required by law. Under the law, the city claims the right to purchase an archaeological find for preservation in one of its museums; the proceeds go in equal shares to the discoverer and to the owner of the property where the artifact was found.

Viking cathedral to be restored. St. Magnus Cathedral, in Kirkwall, Scotland, has become the object of a restoration campaign to prevent its collapse, which had been predicted to occur within five years if no measures were taken. The cathedral, begun in 1137 under the Viking earl who ruled the area at the time, was finished three centuries later. Considered the most important Viking monument in Britain, the building contains elements in both the Romanesque and Gothic styles. In October it was announced that emergency strengthening of the nave was nearly complete.

E. M. WOOD

ARCHITECTURE. Though not new, one trend in architecture became sufficiently important this year to merit special attention. It might be irreverently referred to as the mystique of contradiction. What is boring is now exciting, and what was thought of as common is now seen to be most unusual. In this approach, of course, architecture has lagged behind the world of art, with its giant soup cans, and the world of literature, with its endless attention to prosaic detail —to say nothing of the world of music, where it is not totally uncommon for audiences to sit raptly listening to significant silences for unendurable periods.

In architecture, the main prophet of the new dullness is Robert Venturi, whose followers are now so numerous and fervent that the whole business takes on a bit of the air of

a religious movement. Venturi and his associates, including his wife, the architect Denise Scott Brown, find that today's leading architects, who fondly imagine themselves to be building structures that are handsome, functional, and expressive, are in fact deluding themselves. American tastes, say the Venturis, stem from a culture dominated by mass-produced plastic objects, foil-wrapped technology, and a computerized mentality which equates originality with error. If anything is "different," something must have gone wrong. Thus, for instance, the new Boston City Hall, which only a year or two ago was being touted as a highly revolutionary example of the latest architectural theory (the new brutalism), is considered by Venturi and his devotees as old hat to the point of sentimentality. True inspiration, they insist, is to be found in the traffic lights and neon signs of Las Vegas.

As illustrations of the architecture Venturi espouses, he presents us with his Guild House—a home for the aged in Philadelphia—and the fire station of Columbus, Ind. If to create architecture that will be warmly overlooked is his aim, Venturi has succeeded beyond his wildest dreams.

AIA awards. Of course Venturi is young; but an even younger architect, Claude Samton, has, with his associates, designed a new YM-YWHA day camp in Mt. Olive, N.J., which stems from an earlier movement, one that might perhaps be thought of as closer to cubism than any other easily named trend. In simplicity of form, in comfortable relationships of elements, Samton displays no effort to alarm, excite, or otherwise titillate his viewers. Yet the whole is so refreshingly right that one is not in the least surprised to learn that the design won a 1972 Honor Award of the American Institute of Architects, at its annual convention held this year in Houston, Texas.

By coincidence, another award winner at the same convention is a building the delegates had no trouble viewing, as it is in Houston itself. It is the Alley Theater, designed by Ulrich Franzen. Here the tradition goes even further back, for the forms, although of massive concrete, nevertheless have a fluidity that is more baroque than modern.

A further contrast is provided by another award winner, the New York State Bar Center in Albany, N.Y., for which James Stewart Polshek served as architect. The need to blend "historic preservation and imaginative design," as the awards committee put it, made severe demands upon the architect's talents, and though the results are not, by their nature, as spectacular as the other winners, the jury is to be commended for having given this work proper recognition.

Bunshaft builds on. Always an innovator, Gordon Bunshaft (designer of Lever House) is exhibiting his daring again—twice again, actually—in New York City by putting up two office buildings, one on 57th Street, the other on 42nd Street, the bottom stories of which taper outward in apparent defiance of the characteristics of frame structure. The silhouettes of these buildings are very striking, to say the least. What will happen when the imitators get busy, as they surely will, is hard to predict. Can originality survive repetition? There's a question that has plagued everyone from Raphael to garment center manufacturers. Incidentally, Bunshaft has been awarded the commission to design the New York City Convention and Exhibition Center.

World's tallest story. The Empire State Building is no longer the tallest skyscraper. Not to be topped, its owners announced in October that they were considering tearing down the top stories and replacing them with a modern 33-story office structure on top of the 80th floor.

Blueprint facade. Originality, it goes without saying, is unpredictable; this is nowhere more evident than in a storefront design created by a group of young architects headed by James Doman. The building, in New York City, is oc-

The New
Blandness

For many young architects the 11th commandment reads, "Thou shalt not startle." Robert Venturi tried to make the Columbus, Ind., fire station (left) almost aggressively dull. Claude Samton, architect of the Mt. Olive, N.J., YM-YWHA camp (right), tried to make it simple but not too simple and wound up with more pleasing results.

cupied by the firm itself. The group feels that its first task is to make itself known to the community—known, that is, not only for what it is but also for what it can do for the neighborhood. The result, credited to project architect Amado M. Ortiz, resembles a blueprint at large scale, reproduced over the facade of the building. Reports are that reactions to this "blueprint storefront" vary from enthusiasm to anger, but that no one, absolutely no one, passes it by without at least stopping to scan it. East 25th Street knows a great deal more about James Doman and Associates than hours of talk would produce.

Olympic site. The site for the tragic XX Olympics in Munich represents one of the most successful designs yet for an Olympic site. The availability of a large open space—a former airfield and dumping area for debris from World War II—within the city limits and only 4 kilometers from downtown Munich allowed almost all facilities to be concentrated in one spot, something that was not possible in Mexico City or in Tokyo.

The architects for the major sports facilities, Behnisch and Partner of Stuttgart, conceived of their task as the creation of an integrated landscape. The essentially flat site was sculpted by earthmovers, creating large earth berms that serve as natural access routes; the changing levels of the berms offer the visitor a continually changing variety of views. The stadium, sports arena, and swimming arena were depressed into the ground and then covered with tent structures that flow into the gently undulating surface of the land. These tent structures, of prestressed cable net construction with transparent acrylic infill, were designed by the engineer Frei Otto and incorporate important advances in design technique.

The Olympic Village, temporary home for 12,500 athletes, is programmed for two permanent uses: The men's village will add 4,800 condominium and rental apartments to Munich's housing stock, and the women's village will house the students of a college of physical education, which itself will be located in the press, radio, and television center.

Aalto's latest. Finlandia Hall in Helsinki, the latest effort of the septuagenarian Alvar Aalto, is a $10 million concert and congress center that houses a 1,750-seat concert/congress hall, a 350-seat hall for chamber music, three 100-seat conference rooms, and 20 smaller rooms that can be used for meetings or as rehearsal rooms for musicians. Built to last, the structure employs Carrara marble and white-painted plaster in combination with native black granite—both polished and unpolished—to produce interesting black-on-white and white-on-white effects.

As happens more often than not these days, there has been an uproar over the quality of the acoustics in the main concert hall. Some of the objectors will undoubtedly be pacified as the room is tuned with the help of sliding hatches hidden in the space above the ceiling grilles. But unlike the standard plush-stuffed nineteenth-century concert hall, it will remain a hall with an extremely dry sound and strong separation between the instruments. Some people like it that way.   EUGENE RASKIN

ARGENTINA. Political turmoil, terrorism, and economic difficulties marked the Argentine scene. President Alejandro A. Lanusse had promised to end direct military rule and hold elections "without proscriptions or exclusions" on March 25, 1973. These scheduled elections stood at the center of political and economic life, but some observers felt that they would never take place.

Politics and government. The dominant figure in Argentine politics did not reside in Buenos Aires but in Madrid. Juan Domingo Perón, exiled since being deposed from the

presidency in 1955 and now 76 years old, still cast his ubiquitous, disruptive shadow over Argentine political life.

Encouraged by an embryonic alliance between the Peronists and part of the middle-class Radical Party, President Lanusse had envisioned a "great national accord," a national coalition supporting him or some other candidate acceptable to both the military and the Peronists. He expected Perón to renounce any personal ambitions because the military had sworn to fight Perón's return to power. Numerous representatives of Lanusse and other party leaders constantly beat a path to Perón's door to effect this national coalition. At Lanusse's request, the courts set aside the last indictments against Perón in April, so that he could return to Argentina without fear of legal action. In June, Lanusse announced that all Argentine citizens could run for the presidency, even those resident abroad, an obvious bow to Perón, whose followers in Argentina formally nominated him for president. Lanusse, while appearing to be trying to placate Perón, apparently believed Perón's attachment to his luxurious lifestyle in Madrid and his fear of assassination would dissuade him from returning to his homeland. However, Perón would not, as Lanusse desired, renounce his presidential candidacy, nor publicly denounce various terrorist acts committed by Peronist extremist groups. Finally, Lanusse lost his patience and challenged Perón directly in July. He declared that neither he nor his colleagues among the joint chiefs of the military would be candidates for the presidency and suggested that Perón return to Argentina immediately and be an open candidate. Then he decreed that those who wished to be candidates had to be residents of Argentina by August 25. He also attacked one of the main centers of Peronist strength by withdrawing legal recognition from the General Confederation of Labor, the nation's largest labor union, and took control of its financial accounts to see that the funds would not be spent in support of any candidate, particularly Perón.

Perón refused to return to Argentina by the deadline, but he still would not renounce his candidacy or appoint a successor to lead his supporters within Argentina. Instead, he tried to promote dissension within the armed forces, hoping to provoke yet another revolt to oust Lanusse.

As the year ended, the political scene remained in turmoil. Five political parties had gained legal registration and could participate in the March elections: the Peronist Justicialist Movement; the Radical Party led by Ricardo Balbín; the Movement for Integration and Development (MID) led by former president Arturo Frondizi; the New Force, a new group led by former finance minister Alvaro Alsogaray; and the smaller Popular Left Front. Four candidates had been announced: Perón, whose candidacy was not legal because he had not returned to Argentina, supported by the Peronists and Frondizi's MID; Balbín and his Radical Party; Alsogaray and his New Force; and Francisco Manrique, a long-time personal friend of Lanusse, who resigned dramatically from his position as secretary of social welfare, suggesting that the administration was involved in some kind of potential plot to stop or manipulate the elections. His candidacy was backed by no existing political group, but some felt that he might become a compromise candidate.

Terrorism and violence. Terrorism and violence continued to be a persistent problem. Six main terrorist organizations, four Peronist and two non-Peronist, carried on an almost continuous series of robberies, kidnappings, and bombings. The two most active organizations were the Montoneros, a nationalist-Catholic-Peronist group, and the People's Revolutionary Army (ERP), composed mainly of Trotskyites. The Montoneros, responsible for the killing of former president Pedro Eugenio Aramburu in 1970, culminated their activities with the assassination in March of Mario Roberto Uzal, a leader of the New Force Party.

The most publicized act, however, was the ERP shooting in April of Italian industrialist Oberdán Sallustro, the direc-

tor of Fiat's Argentine subsidiary, whom the ERP had kidnapped in March, blaming him for the layoff of 400 workers in Fiat factories in Córdoba. The government refused demands of $1 million ransom and the release of 50 political prisoners. (Sallustro was killed as the police attacked the terrorists' hiding place.) On the same day, the ERP and the Revolutionary Armed Forces killed General Juan Carlos Sánchez, who had boasted of his success in ridding the countryside of guerrillas.

Violence of another type erupted in the province of Mendoza in April when workers, striking in protest of an increase in electric power rates, clashed with the police and army. In May, a strike of some 250,000 workers in the province of Tucumán, protesting the death of a worker tortured in jail, also had some violent consequences. Civilian forces feared that if the elections were scuttled through a new military coup, the result would be increased terrorism and perhaps civil war.

Economic developments. President Lanusse's defeat in securing a "great national accord" in the political arena could in part be traced to unrest stemming from the nation's severe economic problems. A high rate of inflation, coupled with a low rate of internal growth in 1971, led the General Confederation of Labor to call a 48-hour general strike from February 29 through March 1. The strike was so successful that President Lanusse ultimately restructured his cabinet and froze prices on milk, bread, butter, and fish.

In 1971 the cost of living went up 40 percent and salaries rose 44.4 percent, while the gross national product rose only 3.8 percent. Private investments grew at a relatively low rate, and there was a pronounced dip in construction. Exports were down 3.6 percent from 1970, while imports were up 12.2 percent, resulting in a commercial trade deficit of $180 million. Only $178.1 million of new capital entered the country, while $374.4 million left.

The nation suffered a continued crisis in its beef industry, which normally supplies one-quarter of the funds needed to finance necessary imports. World beef prices and the demand for beef in 1971 were the highest in some time, but the Argentine beef industry could not keep up with this demand. As a result, internal beef prices went up, contributing to the severe inflation. Beef consumption within Argentina in 1972 went down from a previous average of nearly 200 pounds of meat per person a year to about 100 pounds.

By the end of the first quarter of 1972 there were some encouraging signs. The gross national product increased by 5.5 percent, compared to 1.1 percent in the same period of 1971. Exports were up by 19.7 percent, with imports up only 1.1 percent. The result was a $22 million favorable trade balance compared to a $64.5 million deficit for the same period of 1971. However, Argentina had a 60 percent rate of inflation, the highest in the world. The administration was generally attempting no more than a holding action in the economic field, intending to leave major changes in economic policy to the new regime to be elected in 1973.

Foreign affairs. President Lanusse continued his policy of visiting other South American countries to promote commercial expansion and regional economic integration. He visited Ecuador, Colombia, Venezuela, and Peru. His most difficult trip was to Brazil in March. Argentina showed concern over its growing commercial trade deficit with Brazil and the planned Brazilian projects in the upper portion of the River Plata basin that Argentina foresaw as being detrimental to its downstream interests. There was also a general suspicion of Brazilian commercial and political penetration in Latin America and fear that the United States regarded Brazil as the "key" state in Latin America. After Lanusse and Brazilian president General Emílio Garrastazú Médici met, it was generally felt that there had been little positive response from Brazil.

Another diplomatic defeat occurred in May as the Andean Pact nations refused Argentina's entry into the group on the

grounds that this would be "prejudicial to the objectives of the pact."

Area and population. Area, 1,072,072 sq. mi. Pop. (est. 1971), 24,700,000. Buenos Aires (cap.), 3,160,000.
Government. Nominally a constitutional federal republic, but under military rule since 1966. Pres., General Alejandro A. Lanusse.
Finance. Monetary unit, peso; 1 peso = US$0.104.
Trade (est. 1971). Exports, US$1.71 billion; imports, US$1.90 billion. Principal exports: cereals, meat, hides and wool, oils. Main imports: machinery and electrical equipment, heavy chemicals, iron and steel, fuels.
Agriculture and industry. Agricultural production (1971, in millions of metric tons): corn, 9.8; sorghums, 4.9; wheat, 4.3. Cattle population, 49.6 million; beef production (in millions of metric tons), 2.48. Manufacturing (1970): steel, 1.8 million metric tons.
Education (1968). Enrollment: primary, 3,480,534; secondary, 887,236; higher, 265,313.
Armed forces (1971). Army, 85,000; navy and marines, 35,000; air force, 17,000. PHYLLIS J. PETERSON

ARIZONA. Farm labor. The United Farm Workers union began its 11th year of operation with a vigorous campaign to organize lettuce workers in Arizona and California. Expected resistance from lettuce growers in the two states, coupled with resistance from the Teamsters Union in California, led UFW's Cesar Chavez to call a national lettuce boycott. However, the boycott failed to do the damage that an earlier table-grape boycott had done to large growers in California. Early in the year Chavez, now 45, shifted his center of operation to Arizona to drum up opposition to a farm labor bill being proposed in the state legislature. Passed by the senate and the house, the bill was quickly signed into law by Governor Jack Williams, a Republican, who then became the target of a recall movement promoted by Chavez and the farm workers and fragments of the Democratic Party in Arizona. By September, Chavez supporters claimed to have the 103,000 petition signatures necessary for a recall election but had not filed the petitions. Governor Williams publicly urged his foes to file the petitions so that the election could be held concurrently with the November 7 general election, thereby saving taxpayers the estimated $500,000 it would cost to conduct a separate election. In May, to publicize his opposition to the farm labor bill, Chavez went on a 24-day hunger strike. He also received local support from a number of Arizona clergymen. The Arizona Ecumenical Council sent out a "truth squad" in an attempt to clarify the issues. The report of the truth squad related that a majority of Arizona farm workers interviewed were against the Chavez movement. To the union members, the most objectionable provision of the farm labor bill called for a mandatory court injunction against a strike if the grower could demonstrate that the strike caused irreparable harm to his crop. However, supporters of the bill labeled the piece of legislation a fair one since it guaranteed,, among other things, a supervised secret ballot in union elections.

Chavez' impact on the Arizona labor scene remained uncertain, but his movement in the state apparently did solidify the Mexican-American voting bloc for the first time. This was reflected in the primary election which saw Mexican-American candidates score some upset victories.

Indian developments. It is ironic that a domestic feud should occur between the Navahos and Hopis at a time when Americans are beginning to reexamine their dealings with the Indians with increased concern. Years ago the Navahos started migrating into the outer fringes of the Hopi Reservation. Possession and use of the land have been issues ever since. Although the Navaho and Hopi reservations in northeastern Arizona are vast, overgrazing and underrestoration by the Indians have caused environmentalists to fear that the region is becoming a dust bowl. In 1962 the U.S. Supreme Court directed that the 1.8 million acres in dispute should be used jointly by the two tribes, but the Hopis later complained that they were harassed by the

Navahos on what they consider their own land. U.S. representative Sam Steiger, a Republican, tried unsuccessfully this year to get a bill through Congress that would divide the 1.8 million acres equally between the two tribes. Later in the year a U.S. district court ordered the Navahos to reduce the number of horses, sheep, goats, and cattle—estimated at 50,000—they were grazing on the disputed land.

Legislation. The state legislature passed bills to reduce the powers of the Arizona Corporation Commission to setting and regulating utility rates, to lower the level of alcohol presumed necessary to induce intoxication in motorists, and to pave the way for eventual introduction of a cost-accounting system in public schools.

For election results and campaign highlights, see the special supplement ELECTION '72.

Area and population. Area, 113,909 sq. mi. Pop. (est. 1972), 1,925,000. Principal cities: Phoenix (cap.), 675,000; Tucson, 290,000.
Government. Gov., John R. Williams (R); secy. of state, Wesley Bolin (D); treas., Ernest Garfield (R). Legislature: senate 18 R, 12 D; house, 34 R, 26 D.
Finance (1971–1972). Revenue, $1,421,344,937; expenditure, $1,411,780,760. Cash on hand (June 30), $175,995,408.
Education. Public elementary and secondary schools, 767; enrollment, 510,146; teachers, 20,742. Private and parochial schools, 475; enrollment, 48,952. CLYDE ANDREW MURRAY

ARKANSAS. Government. A state government accustomed to austerity suddenly found at midyear that its treasury was overflowing. The general fund finished fiscal 1972 with a surplus of about $36 million, a sum equaling 12 percent of the total general revenue spent during the year and five times as large as any previous surplus. One reason for the surplus was the fact that Governor Dale L. Bumpers and the legislature had underestimated the productivity of the new 1971 tax program and an unusual rate of economic growth. Also, the first receipts from federal revenue sharing, which had not been anticipated when the legislature appropriated funds in 1971, seemed likely to swell the 1973 surplus to nearly $100 million. Bumpers promised to seek legislative authority to use a large part of the surplus to enlarge the University of Arkansas Medical Center. He also advocated spending part of the money to purchase new parklands and wilderness lands threatened with agricultural or commercial development, to start a free textbook program for high schools and a self-insurance plan for all public schools, to construct a state library and archives building, and to improve state educational and health institutions.

At a special legislative session called by the governor in February, the major legislation was a bill juggling appropriations to allow the state to get matching federal funds for establishing a statewide network of community centers for mentally retarded children and a variety of new social services for the poor.

Educational developments. The busing of students to end segregation increased in the Little Rock schools after the federal courts ordered new steps to end a dual system still existing in the lower five grades. Little public outcry accompanied this move, although enrollment in private schools increased. Most of the public protests were from parents who lived within two miles of their schools and objected to the district's not busing their children.

Campus disturbances and an emotional campaign by supporters of Arkansas Agricultural, Mechanical, and Normal College at Pine Bluff, the only black college supported by the state, failed to persuade the governor and the legislature to postpone a merger with the University of Arkansas. In 1971 the legislature had ordered the merger after administrative problems resulted in large deficits. Blacks charged that the merger was a white takeover. Bills to delay the merger failed at a special legislative session in February, and the change took place on July 1.

Environment. Federal Judge G. Thomas Eisele, who had stopped construction by the U.S. Army Corps of Engineers

of a dam on the Cossatot River in 1971, allowed the work to resume after the corps filed an acceptable environmental impact statement. Environmental groups suffered another setback when Federal Judge J. Smith Henley refused to stop the corps from channeling the lower Cache River in east Arkansas. While opponents appealed the judge's decision, the corps started work. Governor Bumpers demanded that the corps stop until the appeal was settled and until it kept its agreement to furnish 30,000 acres of wooded bottomlands to the state for wildlife management. The corps, backed by the congressman from the district, refused, but bills were introduced in Congress for the purchase.

Economic developments. Some 20,000 new industrial jobs, easily a record for the state, were created by new factory locations or expansions. A big surge of tourism, a good crop year, and vigorous business activity brought the state heightened prosperity.

For election results and campaign highlights, see the special supplement ELECTION '72.

Area and population. Area, 53,104 sq. mi. Pop. (1970), 1,923,-295. Principal cities: Little Rock (cap.), 132,483; Fort Smith, 621,-802; North Little Rock, 60,040; Pine Bluff, 57,389.

Government. Gov., Dale L. Bumpers (D); lt. gov., Bob Riley (D); atty. gen., Ray H. Thornton, Jr. (D); secy. of state, Kelly Bryant (D); treas., Nancy J. Hall (D).

Finance (1972). Revenue, $836,411,138; expenditures, $826,092,-843.

Education (1971–1972). Elementary schools, 675; enrollment, 241,227; teachers, 11,250. Secondary schools, 482; enrollment, 214,-002; teachers, 10,438.   ERNEST C. DUMAS

ART. After several years of seizing upon what was "radically new" and avant-garde in art, the art world seems to be settling in for a period of reflection and evaluation. Many artists and critics are finding new inspiration in old styles. A type of abstract expressionism which took shape last year as "lyric abstraction" has gathered adherents and admirers. Several New York school painters who continued to develop abstract modes during the years of pop, minimal, and conceptual frenzy are now being rediscovered. And the many varieties of figurative painting continue to appear in galleries and museums throughout the United States, only now under the labels "new," "sharp-focus," or "postpop" realism.

Whitney Annual. Among the many figurative and abstract selections at this year's Whitney Annual, few members of the traditional American school were included; even the big names of recent years were scarce. A great number of the artists were under 35, and there were many more women and black artists included than ever before. This year's annual was the 40th and also the last. From now on, the

UPI

Assault on a Masterpiece

The classic repose of Michelange-lo's "Pietà," sculpted in Rome almost five centuries ago, was shattered in May by a hammer-wielding fanatic. He managed to smash the Virgin's nose and left eye, chip part of her veil (left), and break off one arm before being led away.

shows will be biennials and will occupy the entire museum. One of the advantages of this, according to director John I. H. Baur, is that "with a biennial, you only get clobbered every other year." In the past few years the Whitney has been accused of discrimination by women and black artists and of being overly trend-conscious by critics.

Venice Biennale. The 1972 Venice Biennale was more interesting for what it said about the art world than for the art selections themselves. The concept of the biennale has changed from a place for established artists to display their latest pieces to a showcase for new talent, and, in addition, the prize system has been discontinued. As a result, there were few big-time collectors around. The atmosphere was more relaxed, more egalitarian; the format was more diffuse, with exhibits spread out all through the city, in plazas and local museums. The organizers of the biennale, faced with so many radically different styles, used a thematic approach, dividing the work into separate shows: historical-critical, informational, and experimental. The main Italian exhibit was billed as "Work and Behavior" and was characterized as an "open confrontation between those artists who still believe in the work of art as the lasting communication of a 'message' and those who no longer believe in the work of art, and use the most varied forms of 'behavior.'"

The U.S. contingent, chosen by Walter Hopps of the Corcoran Gallery of Art, Washington, D.C., was noteworthy, in Hopps' words, for its "fruitful coexistence of diversity." Some 25 artists were included, among them photographer Diane Arbus, who died last year. Her pictures were judged some of the most dramatic and powerful works in the biennale.

Women. The women's movement in art was more active than ever, organizing exhibitions, forums, conferences, and festivals. At the New York Women's Interart Center, which opened in July 1971, workshops and open shows included some big names like Kate Millett and Yoko Ono. In Los Angeles the Feminist Art Program at the California Institute of the Arts opened a series of "dream-space" environments. During March and April the Women in the Arts

Festival was held at the Finch College Museum of Art in New York, and the Conference of Women in the Visual Arts took place at the Corcoran Gallery. Issues discussed at the conference included discrimination against women's art in museums and galleries, prejudice against women's art by the press and critics, and discrimination with regard to hiring, promotions, salaries, and art school education.

American Indians. The American Indian was well represented in the art world this year. The entire July-August issue of *Art in America* was devoted to articles about Indian artists and the role of the Indian throughout the history of American art and film. At the Brooklyn Museum Community Gallery this summer, the exhibition "Native North American Art" included paintings, wall hangings, and mixed media combining natural and man-made materials.

The first comprehensive show of Navaho blankets opened at the Los Angeles County Museum of Art in June. It included the earliest-known fragments from 1805 and focused on the last half of the nineteenth century. Blankets in those days were worn, not used as rugs, and each seemed to have its own unique spiritual presence. The exhibition traveled from Los Angeles to the Navaho Tribal Museum in Window Rock, Arizona, and then to the Brooklyn Museum in October. From there, the blankets were sent on an extended tour.

Looking backward. Nostalgia for the 1950's manifested itself in a panoramic show of abstract expressionism at Buffalo's Albright-Knox Art Gallery. All of the 56 paintings were drawn from the gallery's own permanent collection. It had acquired 46 of them between 1955 and 1960, at a time when few other museums or galleries were seeking out abstract expressionist works. There were, consequently, many major paintings by such artists as Jackson Pollock, Willem de Kooning, Arshile Gorky, Philip Guston, Hans Hofmann, Clyfford Still, Helen Frankenthaler, Franz Kline, Mark Rothko, and Robert Motherwell.

At the Whitney Museum a free-form abstraction exhibition—conceived, selected, and installed by students in the Whitney Independent Study Program—included some of the most important abstract expressionist works in the

museum's collection. And at the Museum of Modern Art in New York, a small show of seven of de Kooning's new lithographs conveyed the message that the master of abstract expressionism was as robust and inventive as ever.

Major exhibitions. The New York Museum of Modern Art, which has the single greatest public collection of Pablo Picasso's works in the world, ran an exhibition from February through April commemorating the master's 90th birthday (October 25, 1971). Among the 84 paintings and sculptures were many of the most important ones Picasso has ever produced. Twenty-three drawings and a selection of prints rounded out the show, which took up a full quarter of the museum. Also on view was the famous *Guernica,* on loan from the artist since 1939.

Another modern master, Henri Matisse, is known primarily for his paintings that revolutionized the art world with their broad, flat planes of color, their ordered abstract spaces, and their decorative flow of line. Thus, it was both surprising and rewarding to see all 69 of his sculptures at the Museum of Modern Art, on view simultaneously with the Picasso show. Sculpted mainly during periods when his painting was especially involved with flatness, these little bronzes—some only 3 or 4 inches high—were rough, spontaneous, and experimental.

Another unusual show, this time of drawings by a famous sculptor, Auguste Rodin, was on view at the Guggenheim Museum from March to May. Organized by the National Gallery of Art, Washington, D.C., the exhibition, "Rodin Drawings: True and False," included some 150 drawings and prints from public and private collections. The final segment of the show was a group of several unlabeled

authentic and fake Rodins, and the viewer was challenged to identify which was which.

The Metropolitan Museum of Art in New York presented one of its most esoteric but thoroughly successful exhibitions this spring, about Chinese calligraphy. This 3,000-year-old art form, called by the Chinese the highest form of art, was represented by over 115 works dating from 1300 B.C. through the nineteenth century A.D. and included hand scrolls, hanging scrolls, albums, fans, and artifacts. There were many examples of calligraphy by great masters of long ago, including one in running script, written by Wang Hsi-chih, that has been studied for more than 1,000 years.

Two especially impressive shows were mounted in Paris this year. One, "English Romantic Painting: From Gainsborough to the Pre-Raphaelites," which was at the Petit Palais, coincided with the new accord in Anglo-French cultural relations. The show featured some of the finest examples of Romantic painting, from early examples like George Stubbs' *Cheetah With Two Indians* (1764–1765) to Holman Hunt's *Lady of Shalott* (1887). In addition, there were several famous paintings by members of the British school, such as William Blake and John Constable.

At the Louvre the entire Orangerie of the Tuileries was given over to an exhibit of Georges de la Tour. Although la Tour's work was admired in his time by Louis XIII and Louis XIV, it passed into obscurity after the artist's death and was virtually unknown until the early part of this century. Now his paintings rank higher than ever.

The Museum of Modern Art also ran a retrospective of the photographs of Diane Arbus and an exhibition entitled "African Arts and Textiles."

JOHN G. ROSS

SOMETHING OLD, SOMETHING NEW. Atop Florence's Forte di Belvedere, overlooking the tranquil city and its apricot-domed Renaissance cathedral, Henry Moore's 170-ton "Square Form With Cut," part of a spectacular Moore retrospective, radiates a modern glow.

Important retrospectives. An extensive exhibition of the work of Théodore Géricault, the French Romantic painter who was already an international celebrity when he died in 1824 at the age of 33, began at the Los Angeles County Museum, traveled to the Detroit Institute of Art, and made its last stop at the Philadelphia Museum of Art. Géricault is most famous for his *Raft of the Medusa*, an enormous painting that never leaves the Louvre. This retrospective was nevertheless a thorough survey of his development from a student of French Academy formulas to the embodiment of Romantic expression.

At the Metropolitan Museum of Art this summer was a Jacques Lipchitz retrospective. Beginning with his early work 60 years ago, there were some 100 sculptures, including portraits of Gertrude Stein, Jean Cocteau, and Marsden Hartley. Along with the pieces were videotaped excerpts from Lipchitz' autobiography, *My Life in Sculpture*.

Also during the summer, a large group of Wassily Kandinsky's paintings was displayed at the Guggenheim Museum. Inspired by the spiritual teachings of theosophy, Kandinsky was a pioneer of abstract art, using nonobjective imagery to convey a world beyond the experiential one. Concurrently, there were important exhibitions of Kandinsky's work at Beyeler's in Basel and at the Museum of Modern Art in Paris.

James Rosenquist was given a retrospective at the Whitney Museum in the spring. Some 50 works were shown, including sculptural and environmental pieces as well as paintings. Rosenquist, who had a job as a commercial billboard artist in 1959, began painting in a dark and somber abstract expressionist vein during the early 1960's. A synthesis of these two antithetical forms led him to his recent style.

In Florence, at the Forte di Belvedere, Henry Moore was given a large exhibition this summer. Although Moore's sculpture evokes the early civilizations of pre-Columbian America and Africa, he himself attests to a strong bond with Michelangelo, and in much of his work there is a fusion of Western and "primitive" cultures. In addition to this retrospective, a new book of Moore's drawings was published this year by Abrams.

Vandalism and thefts. On May 21, Michelangelo's *Pietà* was severely damaged by a man who jumped over the marble railing in front of the Renaissance masterpiece and attacked it with a 12-pound hammer. Most Italian newspapers criticized the Vatican for not having provided better protection for the famous marble sculpture, citing all the security precautions taken for the transfer of the *Pietà* to the New York World's Fair. Restoration work began promptly.

Art thieves seemed to be everywhere this year. The centerpiece of a rare early collage-painting by Picasso was stolen from Harvard's Fogg Art Museum in Cambridge; and at the Worcester, Mass., Art Gallery, two robbers shot a guard before making off with a Rembrandt, two Gauguins, and a Picasso worth over $1 million in all. Museums across the United States increased their security measures by hiring more guards, charging admission, and installing complex electronic systems. The Italian government, dismayed by the fact that churches were the scene of more than half that country's art thefts during 1972, decreed that burglar alarms be installed in the nation's churches by the end of the year.

New museum. In October the new $6.5 million Kimbell Art Museum opened in Fort Worth, Texas. Designed by Louis I. Kahn of Philadelphia, it stresses the old masters.

Gifts, auctions, and acquisitions. A major work by Francisco Goya y Lucientes was given to the Metropolitan Museum of Art in July. Valued at $2 million, the painting, a full-length portrait of a young boy, is considered one of Goya's masterpieces. It was the gift of Mrs. Umberto de Martini, an American collector living in Paris.

The W. Averell Harriman Foundation presented a multi-million-dollar collection to the National Gallery of Art, Washington, D.C., in memory of Marie N. Harriman. The gift included a well-known Picasso, a famous Gauguin, and five Cézannes.

Seventy-eight miniatures from the great Iranian *Shah-Nameh* (Book of the Kings), painted by the best artists of sixteenth-century Iran, were given by Arthur A. Houghton, Jr., to the Metropolitan Museum of Art.

The Metropolitan Museum of Art touched off a controversy in late September, when it was confirmed that two of its modern masterpieces—Vincent Van Gogh's *The Olive Pickers* and Douanier Rousseau's *Monkeys in the Jungle*—had been sold.

On the auction scene, a major portion of the Cranbrook Academy collection was sold at Parke-Bernet from March through May. Cranbrook, one of the country's leading art schools, sold the works in a fund-raising effort for endowment money. Henry Moore's *Reclining Figure*, said to be the most important sculpture auctioned in many years, was auctioned for a record $260,000. Other important works auctioned off included a Canaletto, a Jan Gossaert, and paintings by Rembrandt, Dürer, Goya, Blake, and Hogarth. Considered by many art specialists as a "unique" work in the career of Thomas Anshutz, *Steelworkers—Noontime* was auctioned for $250,000, a record for an American painting.

The Norton Simon Foundation paid the highest price ever for a still life—$3 million—for a painting by seventeenth-century Spanish painter Zurbarán, the only one signed and dated by him.   SHERRY CHAYAT NORDSTROM

ASIA. The wondrously contagious spirit of détente, sparked by President Richard M. Nixon's epochal journey to China in February, has permeated much of Asia, from the Korean peninsula in the north to the Indian subcontinent in the south. Although this year of busy diplomacy marked but a beginning of normalization of relations and reconciliation of differences, it nevertheless meant a triumph of pragmatism over long-held prejudice.

The People's Republic of China made its debut at the United Nations in November 1971, and its diplomatic posture was further enhanced by the Sino-American rapprochement. Japan, too, moved dramatically onto the world stage as an independent power, willing and prepared to shoulder greater responsibilities commensurate with its national strength. And Peking and Tokyo were moving toward the normalization of relations which was so important to a stable order in Asia. In July came the twin agreements between Asia's most stubborn antagonists for a quarter-century: First, in the aftermath of the December war, India and Pakistan agreed to undertake step-by-step normalization of relations and to renounce the use of force in the settlement of disputes. Second, North and South Korea surprised the world with a joint communiqué, pledging to work toward national reunification by peaceful means.

Meanwhile, the war in Indochina lingered on, as the Paris peace talks and negotiations through other channels remained stalled through August. The United States claimed that Vietnamization was proceeding on schedule, but bombing of the North reached unprecedented levels and the Communists mounted a new offensive. Finally, in September, the pace of secret peace talks quickened, and by the end of October, though the stumbling blocks were many, it seemed that peace might be near.

Sino-American rapprochement. At the invitation of the Chinese government, President Nixon paid an eight-day visit to China, beginning February 21. It was noteworthy that the escalation of U.S. bombing in Indochina had not jeopardized the meticulously planned visit. Understandably, the establishment of full diplomatic relations was impossible until the Taiwan question could be resolved. In the words of the joint communiqué issued at the conclusion of the visit: "The United States acknowledges that all Chinese on either side of the Taiwan Strait maintain there is but one China and that Taiwan is part of China. The United States

Government does not challenge that position. It reaffirms its interest in a peaceful settlement of the Taiwan question by the Chinese themselves." The United States further declared that it would "progressively reduce its forces and military installations on Taiwan as the tension in the area diminishes." Both Washington and Peking agreed that neither "should seek hegemony in the Asia-Pacific region and each is opposed to efforts by any other country or group of countries to establish such hegemony."

New diplomatic initiatives followed in the wake of the president's visit. Within two weeks, agreement was reached for an exchange of ambassadors between Peking and London, which was among the first to recognize the People's Republic of China in 1949 and which now acknowledges Taiwan as a province of China. By August, Premier Kim Jong-pil of South Korea expressed misgivings over the speed with which Japan was proceeding to establish relations with the Chinese, thus "putting small nations of Asia in a difficult position."

Taiwan, of course, viewed the rapidly changing climate with grave concern, despite United States assurance that it remained committed to the 1954 mutual security treaty. The Nationalist government continued to follow a "positive and outgoing" approach to its external relations and indicated an interest in developing trade, economic, and other relations even with Socialist states "if they are not puppets of Communist China."

Japanese diplomatic efforts. On May 15 the Ryukyu Islands (including Okinawa) formally reverted to Japanese sovereignty after 27 years under American administration. Having thus achieved one of his long-sought goals, Premier Eisaku Sato shortly thereafter announced his intention to retire. On July 6 he was succeeded by Kakuei Tanaka.

In his best-selling treatise *A Proposal for Remodeling the Japanese Archipelago,* published in June, the new premier had urged no less than an economic and social revolution in order to cure the many domestic ills born of postwar prosperity. In foreign policy he was known to favor close ties with Washington, improved relations with Moscow, and establishment of diplomatic relations with Peking, even if that meant breaking political ties with Taipei.

Tanaka conferred with President Nixon at the latter's invitation in Hawaii, August 31–September 1. The president clearly acknowledged that Japan was an economic giant whose leadership potential was indispensable to peace in the Pacific. Japan, too, was fully prepared to realize that potential. As a preeminent economic power not only in Asia but throughout the world, Japan had budgeted a total of $2.13 billion for foreign aid during the fiscal year ending March 1973, a one-year increase of 39 percent. At the mid-Pacific meeting the two leaders also exchanged views on trade. Japan agreed to purchase some $1.1 billion in American products as an interim arrangement to ease this year's projected U.S. deficit of $3.8 billion in bilateral trade.

Premier Tanaka also received friendly overtures from China and the Soviet Union. Premier Chou En-lai, who had consistently refused to deal with Sato, wasted no time in inviting Tanaka to Peking. China reportedly would no longer demand that Japan pay war reparations or alter its defense treaty with the United States. It was anticipated that a Japanese-Soviet summit meeting would soon follow Premier Tanaka's Peking visit. While Japanese-Soviet economic relations were developing fast, no formal peace treaty had yet been signed, nor had Japan's claim to four islands seized by the Soviet Union been resolved.

Aftermath of Indian-Pakistani war. The result of the December 1971 war between India and Pakistan was that the Bengali separatists finally won their independence, but at the staggering price of widespread bloodshed and economic hardship. The new government of Bangladesh, led by Sheikh Mujibur Rahman, had a formidable task ahead, probably for some years to come. Pakistan, or what remained

of Pakistan, emerged from the two-week war a humbled and demoralized nation. Zulfikar Ali Bhutto, the new president, found the task of securing his country's spiritual and economic rehabilitation hindered by restive ethnic minorities pressing claims for increased autonomy.

Pragmatic statesmanship by both President Bhutto and Indian premier Indira Gandhi led to their meeting at Simla more than six months after the cessation of hostilities. After five days of intense negotiations, the two leaders agreed on July 3 to resolve their differences by peaceful means, to effect mutual withdrawal of troops from captured territories, and to undertake step-by-step normalization of relations, "so that both countries may henceforth devote their resources and energies to the pressing task of advancing the welfare of their people." The accord left unsettled the festering issue of Kashmir and the repatriation of over 91,000 Pakistani prisoners of war still held by India. The Indian government insisted that Bangladesh, as a cobelligerent, have a voice in the disposition of war prisoners. However, Pakistan was not yet prepared to recognize Bangladesh, the precondition Sheikh Mujib had set for negotiations on the prisoners.

As a permanent member of the UN Security Council, China cast its first veto on August 25 to bar the admission of Bangladesh, contending that Bangladesh stood in violation of two UN resolutions calling for the return of all prisoners of war and for the removal of all foreign troops on Bangladesh soil. Thus, the guns were silenced, but a durable peace on the troubled subcontinent remained to be negotiated. (*See the special report* BANGLADESH: BIRTH OF A NATION.)

Reunification of Korea. For over a quarter century, North and South Korea had confined their dialogue to exchanges of venomous rhetoric. It was known that Red Cross officials of the two Koreas had been meeting regularly at Panmunjom since August 1971, but secret talks between high officials of the two governments were not revealed until this July, when a dramatic joint communiqué called for efforts to achieve national reunification by peaceful means, without external interference and regardless of ideological differences. The same document also called for an end to mutual propaganda vituperations and to military provocations. In addition, the two sides agreed to establish direct telephone communications between Seoul and Pyongyang. Most signs indicated that President Nixon's trip to China had played a catalytic role in bringing about this dramatic change. Premier Kim Il-sung of North Korea hinted to American journalists in June that even prior to the withdrawal of American troops in the South there could be expanded political, economic, and cultural ties between the two Koreas.

After one full year of informal, preliminary discussions, Red Cross officials for each half of the divided nation opened formal talks in Pyongyang on August 30. The delegations were led by Lee Bum-suk of the South and Kim Tae-hui of the North, both veteran diplomats. The first agreement was signed after the first session, pledging that both parties would "make every effort to dissolve the agonies of the families dispersed in the North and the South and thus lay a stepping-stone for unification of the fatherland." It was clear that the scope of exchanges would be gradually expanded to include political issues.

Peace at last? For months there was not the slightest glimmer of peace in Indochina. As the war escalated, peace talks remained deadlocked. The United States, as an ally of South Vietnam, had offered a de-escalation of the fighting, a cease-fire with a deadline for withdrawal of all American forces, and a formula for internationally supervised elections with Communist participation. President Nguyen Van Thieu of the South had even offered to resign one month before the elections. But all these offers had met with continued North Vietnamese insistence on total U.S. withdrawal and abandonment of the Thieu regime. The

North Vietnamese launched an ambitious offensive of conventional warfare on March 30, threatening the tenuous stability of the South. On May 8, President Nixon responded to this threat by ordering the mining of all entrances to North Vietnamese ports and massive retaliation by air and naval strikes against military targets in the North, including rail links with China. Meanwhile, the withdrawal of American ground combat troops was proceeding on schedule. On September 1 troop strength was reduced to 37,700; by December 1 it was to be further reduced to 27,000.

Since there seemed to be no movement at the public sessions in Paris, popular interest shifted to private talks between Henry Kissinger, President Nixon's special assistant for national security affairs, and Le Duc Tho, a member of the North Vietnamese Politburo. By mutual agreement, the substance of these negotiations was not to be revealed. But on October 26, Hanoi insisted that a peace agreement had, in fact, been reached but that the United States was reneging on a promise to sign it by the end of the month—that is, a week before U.S. elections. Claiming that the deadline was all a "misunderstanding," Kissinger publicly announced that peace was "at hand." Even as Hanoi's deadline passed, the Nixon administration remained confident that agreement was near. All sides, it was clear, were willing to accept a cease-fire. But proposals for the political future of South Vietnam were vague enough to arouse President Thieu's worst fears. With both sides trying to gain as much territory as possible before a cease-fire, the "settlement" began to seem like just another tactic in a long, long war.   LIONEL TSAO

ASTRONOMY. Eclipse of the sun. On July 10 a total solar eclipse was visible from North America along a narrow path across Alaska, northwest Canada, Hudson Bay, and Nova Scotia. The maximum duration of totality was 155 seconds. Weather conditions were mostly unfavorable for ground observers, except in the Canadian arctic. Photographs of the corona showed a shape intermediate between the globular form typical at maximum sunspot activity and the long rays typical at minimum sunspot activity. Probably the most important scientific results were those obtained by Canadian researchers, who sent instrumented rockets aloft into the moon's shadow to measure the complex changes occurring in the earth's ionosphere when direct sunlight is briefly blocked off. Four of these Black Brant rockets were launched from East Quoddy, Nova Scotia, and four from near Fort Churchill, Manitoba.

Solar activity. Although the peak of the 11-year sunspot cycle occurred as long ago as late 1968 and the minimum should arrive in 1975, the sun showed major disturbances in August 1972. On August 7 a brilliant flare appeared on the solar disk and lasted for four hours. It was an intense source of X rays, ultraviolet radiations, and radio waves. This flare, the greatest since that of November 12, 1960, was of the rare high-energy type known as white-light flares; fewer than a dozen have ever been photographed.

The flare appeared inside a large sunspot group that had come into view on July 29. Complex magnetic fields with particularly steep magnetic gradients made this region of the sun unusually active. It was also the seat of three major flares on August 2 and another on August 11.

This sequence of solar activity produced widespread terrestrial effects, including brilliant auroras on several nights. On August 7 the excess ultraviolet radiation disturbed the ionosphere, disrupting shortwave radio communications. A moderate geomagnetic storm occurred, and significant increases in the flux of solar cosmic rays and neutrons reaching the earth were monitored. At the height of the flare, solar X rays grew so intense that X-ray detectors carried on the Solrad 9 and 10 artificial satellites became saturated.

Solar neutrino mystery. Astrophysicists are facing a deepening dilemma over neutrinos, uncharged and massless subatomic particles that travel at the speed of light; they are produced in large numbers as by-products of thermonuclear reactions in the extremely hot, dense central core of the sun. Because they interact only weakly with matter, neutrinos escape virtually unhindered through the sun and out into interplanetary space. For the same reason, the detection of solar neutrinos in a terrestrial experiment is exceedingly difficult.

Such detection has been accomplished by the American nuclear physicist Raymond Davis, Jr. His equipment consists primarily of a 100,000-gallon tank of carbon tetrachloride buried 4,850 feet deep in a South Dakota gold mine to shield it from cosmic rays. When a solar neutrino traverses the liquid and collides with a chlorine-37 atom, there is a very small but calculable probability that this atom will be converted into radioactive argon-37, which has a half-life of 35 days. Thus, the neutrino flux can be determined by counting the individual decays of argon-37 nuclei.

Conducted with meticulous precautions, Davis' experiment has been operating for five years with increasing refinements, yet it consistently counts fewer neutrinos than predicted. During this period, the structure of the solar interior has been searchingly studied by theoretical astrophysicists, who have made improved calculations of the expected neutrino flux. But these have tended to widen the gap.

Since the experimental techniques seem impeccable, astrophysicists are faced with an uncomfortable dilemma. Either there has been some important oversight in the currently accepted theories of stellar interiors, or else neutrinos have some unexpected physical properties. Until the solar neutrino problem is solved, present theories of stellar evolution are more or less suspect because they depend in part on an understanding of solar structure.

Jupiter. The passage of Jupiter in front of a bright star is a very rare phenomenon which will not recur until 1996. But on May 13, 1971, Jupiter occulted two stars, Beta Scorpii A (magnitude 2.6) and its neighbor Beta Scorpii C (magnitude 4.9). Moreover, one day later Jupiter's bright inner satellite Io passed in front of the latter star.

Much new information about Jupiter is now available from the observations of these events made in South Africa, India, Java, Australia, and Antarctica, largely through expeditions sent by the University of Texas. The most spectacular phenomenon was the series of bright flashes of Beta Scorpii A as the star gradually faded for several minutes before completely disappearing behind the thick atmosphere of Jupiter. Similar flashes were recorded as the star reappeared and, less conspicuously, at the ingress and egress of the fainter companion star, Beta Scorpii C. The correlated patterns of flashes indicate that Jupiter's atmosphere contains at least four distinct refractive layers, probably permanent and extending nearly or completely around the planet.

Analysis of timings of the stars' disappearances and reappearances as seen from different stations has yielded very accurate dimensions for Jupiter: an equatorial diameter of 44,664 miles and a polar diameter of 41,984 miles, both figures referring to that atmospheric level at which there are 10^{14} molecules per cubic centimeter.

The occultation of Beta Scorpii C by Io was observed in Florida and the Caribbean islands. Photoelectric recordings of the star's light changes show that Io has no appreciable atmosphere and that, if it is spherical, it has a diameter of 2,274 miles, with an uncertainty of ± 3 miles. Thus Io is very slightly larger than our own moon.

On June 7, 1972, Jupiter and its largest satellite, Ganymede, both occulted an eighth-magnitude star. This sequence of events was photographed at the Bosscha Observatory in Indonesia.

Meanwhile, a rich yield of new information about Jupiter can be expected from the Pioneer 10 spacecraft, which was launched March 2 on a mission that should carry it past the planet at a distance of 87,000 miles on December 3, 1973.

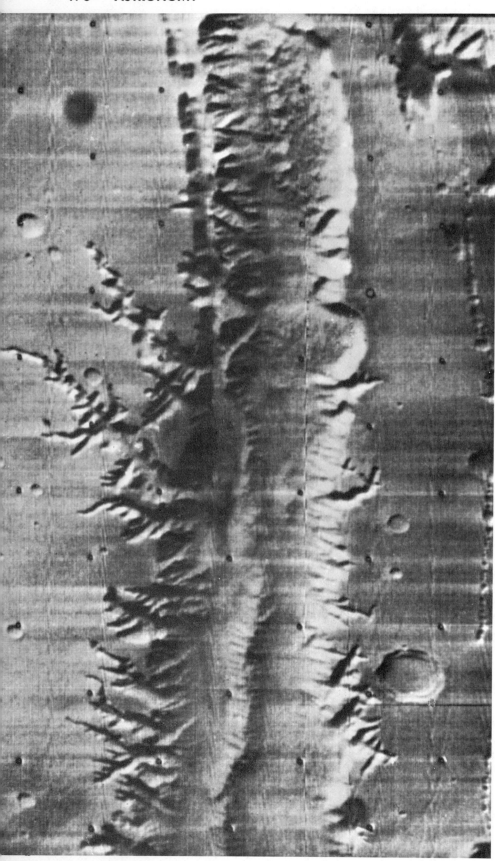

A CLOSER LOOK AT MARS

Early this year the American spacecraft Mariner 9 snapped the most detailed photographs ever published of another planet. Above, Mars as seen by Mariner from 445,000 miles away. At left, from an altitude of 1,225 miles, a 300-mile canyon shows signs of erosion on a planet once thought to be dead. At right, a spectacular 70-mile-wide crater near the Martian equator can be seen.

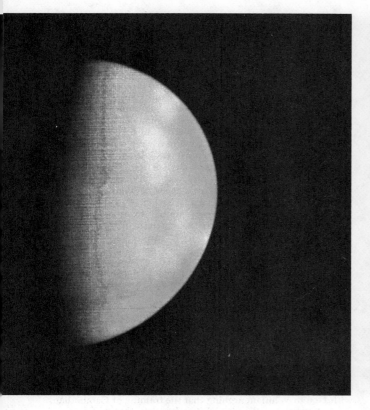

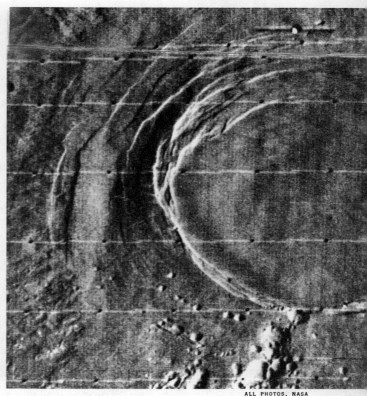

ALL PHOTOS, NASA

Bright supernova. NGC 5253 is a fairly inconspicuous elliptical galaxy a few million light-years from earth in the southern constellation Centaurus. Charles T. Kowal of Hale Observatories in California discovered, on a photograph of the galaxy taken on May 13, a new star of magnitude 8.5 in the southwestern part, at a location where no star as bright as magnitude 16 was present on a photograph made March 12. The new object was considerably brighter than NGC 5253 itself.

Photographs of the spectrum of the supernova were quickly obtained at U.S. observatories in California and Ohio and in Italy and Chile. The character of the bright and dark bands in the spectrum indicated that the great stellar explosion had taken place some days earlier, with maximum light probably around May 4. This finding was confirmed by a later examination of sky patrol photographs taken at a New Zealand observatory and by photographs taken by two California amateur astronomers.

By late summer, the star had faded greatly. It was the second supernova detected in NGC 5253, the first being Z Centauri (magnitude 8) in 1895.

Cygnus X-3. The celestial X-ray source now known as Cygnus X-3 was first detected in October 1966. In June 1972 radio astronomers in Holland and the United States reported that Cygnus X-3 was also a weak radio source at wavelengths of a few centimeters.

On September 2, Canadian scientists using the 150-foot radio telescope at Algonquin Park, Ontario, were startled to find that Cygnus X-3 had greatly increased in radio brightness. This same outburst was also monitored at the National Radio Astronomy Observatory in West Virginia. The West Virginia observations also revealed that the diameter of the strong radio source is less than 0.5 second of arc.

Although slight, irregular variability on a time scale of hours or days is common among celestial radio sources, the giant outburst by Cygnus X-3 is the first known case of its kind. The physical explanation of this distant explosion is not yet known.   JOSEPH ASHBROOK

AUSTRALIA. During 1972 the Australian community lived in an atmosphere of unusual uncertainty. In part, this uncertainty was political: the Liberal–Country Party government, in office since 1949, appeared to be losing the allegiance of the country as national elections drew near. But the changing international situation and the need for Australia to reshape its foreign and defense policies along with it contributed to this unease. In addition, the chaos in the international currency market had serious domestic repercussions; inflation mounted, the wage spiral continued to rise, and unemployment threatened to reach unacceptable levels.

The election campaign. The Liberal–Country Party coalition is suffering from the kind of inertia which often besets a government after a long tenure of power. Its leading figures have departed, and their successors appear to be lesser men. The current prime minister, William McMahon, is a competent professional politician, but he lacks an appealing personality and, even more, a sense of style. By the end of 1971 his popularity was at a low ebb, and Gallup polls revealed that a large majority believed that the Liberals were divided among themselves. By July a poll by the newspaper *Age* assessed the popularity of the prime minister at 16 percent, whereas his Labor opponent, Gough Whitlam, could at least muster 35 percent. Subsequent polls of popular opinion have given little encouragement to the government.

Whitlam himself has adopted a quietly confident pose. Above all, Labor has sought to present a united party front and to prevent the emergence of the deep divisions that have cost the party votes in the past. In this it has met with considerable success, though some divisive issues have emerged. The breach between influential members of the Victorian executive and Gough Whitlam has never been wholly healed. The endorsement of Barry Johnson, a draft resister, by the Victorian branch as a federal candidate for Hotham and the further resolution of the Victorian branch expressing satisfaction at the success of North Vietnamese

forces in their spring 1972 offensive were hardly helpful to Labor solidarity or to its public image. Even more divisive was the question of industrial unrest, which was closely connected with the tactics of the trade unions in promoting one strike after another in essential services. Labor's deputy leader, Lance Barnard, felt it necessary to appeal to the unions not to "rock the boat," but the dynamic leader of the Australian Council of Trades Unions, Bob Hawke, replied that the unions could not guarantee to subordinate the interests of their members to the party's desire to win office. Yet Hawke undoubtedly wishes to see Labor in power, and his more restrained public attitudes in the months before the election were undoubtedly a Labor asset.

For its part, the government also faced some awkward issues. One was the proposed reduction of the voting age to 18, a matter which was thought to hinge upon the interpretation of the word "adult" in the Australian constitution. The High Court's decision that this was not really a constitutional issue but a matter within the legislative control of the Commonwealth Parliament put the onus squarely on the government. Another awkward question was that of the 35-hour workweek, which the government saw as injurious to the economy at the moment. Judging from the polls, the government commanded majority community support for its position. Potentially the most difficult of all was the aboriginal question. Controversy this year centered on two issues: first, the demand by aboriginal leaders that they be given land rights, especially in the Northern Territory and Queensland, and second, the erection of a tent "embassy," staffed by aboriginals and sympathizers, outside Parliament House in Canberra. After much government clumsiness, the tent was removed.

Foreign affairs. The China issue overshadowed all others internationally. Australian policy toward seating the People's Republic of China in the United Nations had been framed in close concert with the United States, Japan, and other Southeast Asian countries. Given the mounting pressure for representation of Peking, there was never any question of opposition by Australia and its partners to UN seating of Peking, but a very strong effort was made by the group to maintain separate representation for Taiwan. These initiatives failed, but realities had to be accepted, and the government detailed its attempts to develop a dialogue with the People's Republic. The subsequent eagerness of the United States and Japan to redefine their China policy made it abundantly plain that Australian policy would have to follow the same path of realignment. Prime Minister McMahon has indicated his desire for a ministerial visit to China. At a lower level, a Chinese table tennis team visited Australia, though the value of this attempt to marry sport and diplomacy was largely nullified by the presence at the same time in Australia of a Taiwanese women's basketball team, a political blunder which should have been avoided. While the government moved cautiously, Gough Whitlam, who in 1971 had led a Labor team to China for informal discussions, argued strongly for immediate recognition of Peking and for the abandonment of diplomatic relations with Taipei. Gallup polls have shown Australian opinion moving steadily toward recognition of Peking. In March 1971 only 39 percent were in favor of recognition, but by April 1972 their number had increased to 53 percent. Interestingly enough, 51 percent also wanted their government to continue to recognize Taiwan. Thus, both the government and public opinion were clinging to an apparently unrealistic policy of attempting to have it both ways.

The momentous changes occurring on the international front spurred Foreign Minister Nigel Bowen to the United Nations and to Tokyo in 1971 and led Prime Minister McMahon to visit Washington and London in October and November 1971 and to tour three Southeast Asian capitals in June 1972. The results of these visits were reflected in the general lines of Australian policy elaborated in the ministerial statement by Nigel Bowen in May 1972. The central points were these. Despite the new orientations discernible in both American and British policy, Australia was determined to preserve major relationships with these two great and powerful Western friends. The United States continued to be of dominant importance. McMahon on his visit to Washington had secured once again a strong public reaffirmation by President Nixon of the continuing significance attached to the ANZUS treaty, the alliance between Australia, New Zealand, and the United States.

Relations with the United Kingdom were also to be preserved and developed. Emphasis was placed on the hope that Britain would exert its influence to ensure that the European Economic Community was "outward looking and international in its approach, that it should be flexible ... to world trade, rather than regionally exclusive in its attitude." The government sees a large potential for trade with the EEC, and this is reflected in the strengthening of missions to the capitals of the community's current and prospective members.

A special relationship was also to be consolidated with Japan, Australia's largest market, on the basis of common interests not only in trade but in policy toward China and the United States. In Southeast Asia the Vietnam war was no longer the crucial issue it once had been, especially since the removal of Australian forces. Nonetheless the government continued to see North Vietnam as the aggressor and supported the intensified bombing of North Vietnam and the mining of Haiphong harbor as appropriate countermeasures to the North Vietnamese offensive. Australia had also agreed to assist in the training of Cambodian troops. Both attitudes were strongly assailed by the Labor Party, with Gough Whitlam arguing that the training of Cambodians carried the same dangers of involvement that had accompanied comparable earlier steps in Vietnam and that President Nixon's action at Haiphong involved the kinds of risks to international peace that had existed at the time of the Cuban missile crisis, when President Kennedy blockaded the island. Elsewhere in Southeast Asia, Australia was primarily concerned with economic and technical development through regional and bilateral cooperation.

In February 1972, President Suharto of Indonesia visited Australia, the first Indonesian head of state to do so. It was agreed that regular meetings should take place between Indonesian and Australian officials from the departments of Foreign Affairs and Trade and Industry. Experts were to meet to delineate seabed and land border boundaries. Australian aid to Indonesia was being steadily stepped up, and efforts were made to encourage Australian businesses to invest in that country. In July, Deputy Prime Minister John Douglas Anthony announced the conclusion of a new trade treaty between the two countries.

Defense policy. A new attempt to redefine Australian defense commitments in light of the changing international situation was spelled out in a government white paper released in late March. Concepts of isolation and "fortress" Australia were rejected, and a three-pronged policy emerged. The basic relationship with the United States was to be sustained and intensified, which meant that the ANZUS treaty and interlocking defense arrangements were central to the Australian position. Combined with this was to be a greater degree of self-reliance, including, if need be, an ability to act alone in certain situations. Self-reliance, the white paper argued, would not only produce greater flexibility but it would also strengthen the impact of Australian foreign policy and increase the likelihood of allied support. Finally, Australia would increase military cooperation with its northern neighbors, as had already been done in the case of Indonesia. The emphasis on self-reliance would not be cheap. It would mean that in the 1970's Australia would be forced to "spend very substantial sums on modern weapons systems and capital installations

and facilities which represent long-term investment in defense capabilities."

This policy required reform in conditions of military service. With conscription still intensely controversial after the Vietnam experience, the government introduced a national service bill which reduced the period of service from two years to 18 months but would still enable the army to sustain a professional force of 40,000.

Attention was also focused on committing ANZUS defense forces to Malaysia and Singapore, strengthening Australia–New Zealand defense cooperation, and maintaining a better balance of forces in the Indian Ocean in view of strong Soviet penetration of the area. Australia welcomed the United States decision for periodical patrols by the Seventh Fleet in the Indian Ocean. The United States for its part undoubtedly welcomed the development of Cockburn Sound as a base for joint use.

The Labor Party's reaction to the white paper was cautious; overall, the white paper and the government statement received a good press.

Population and immigration. Australia's population on March 31, 1972, was estimated at 12,943,000. For the 12 months ending in March the total population increase was estimated at 148,700, with 40,108 from net natural increase and 108,592 from net migration.

The question of maintaining an "attractive" migration program of the magnitude of recent years has come under serious discussion. The Department of Immigration and the Academy of the Social Sciences are making separate studies which may well become the basis for a rethinking of Australian immigration policy. Some advocates of a more restrictive policy believe that the costs are overly high, and with a sluggish economy and mounting unemployment there is less enthusiasm for absorbing the substantial inflow of new migrants.

The program has, in fact, been somewhat scaled down. Net arrivals were a little under 133,000 for 1971–1972, a drop from the previous year's total of slightly more than 170,000. Among assisted settlers the decrease was even more noticeable—82,343 for 1971–1972, compared with 119,847 for 1970–1971.

One striking fact is that some 57.9 percent of the settlers were British nationals, primarily from the United Kingdom. The Yugoslavs have now become the second largest national group, with 10,749 arrivals.

Economics and trade. Currency instability during 1971 and 1972 adversely affected the Australian share market and had repercussions on industry and trade, as the Japanese economy slowed down and the Japanese took a tougher line on contracts with Australian firms, especially over minerals.

A NEW AGE IN NEW GUINEA. A native teacher sent by the Australian government gives a beginning lesson in civics to illiterate tribesmen. In February and March, 2.5 million inhabitants of the trust territory elected a partly autonomous assembly to represent them.

AUSTRALIAN NEWS AND INFORMATION BUREAU

BOTH PHOTOS, ERIC WADSWORTH/AUSTRALIAN INFORMATION SERVICE

Responding to the currency crises of 1971, the government began by restricting foreign exchange dealings, though this was a temporary measure. In December the Australian dollar was linked directly with the United States dollar instead of sterling. But the continuing weakness of the U.S. dollar remained a matter of concern for Australia, since this implied the possibility that Australian currency might become undervalued against other hard currencies, a situation which could lead to further take-overs of Australian firms by foreign investors.

The uncertain economic climate tended to discourage long-term business commitments. Of course, as the *Economic Review* pointed out in May 1972, almost every developed nation had been experiencing "a downturn in economic activity." Australia was no exception, suffering from what has come to be called stagflation. The economy remained sluggish, the rate of growth slow, and consumer demand disappointingly low. The lack of buoyancy was also accompanied by continued inflation, estimated in March 1972 at 9 percent, which was no doubt related to constant trade union pressure for higher wages and from the generous judgments of arbitration bodies. Inflation was also accompanied by a growth in unemployment, which passed the 100,000 mark. This total, lower than in almost any other developed country, was nevertheless intolerably high for the Australian public.

The political consequences were severe. By February the prime minister had been converted from a policy of austerity to one of economic stimulation. At that month's premiers' conference the states fared well from Commonwealth distributions. Such pump-priming methods as the restoration of the investment allowance to the manufacturing industry and a lowering of interest rates were also adopted by the govern-

ment. Treasurer Billy Snedden's minibudget, designed to provide the community with a "psychological boost," followed shortly thereafter.

Even more active measures of stimulation were to come in the budget of August, which was designed to produce strong growth in the economy. Many viewed it cynically as the government's major bid to retain office. Whatever its motivation, it was an intelligently conceived document, offering substantial concessions to individuals and special groups but also sponsoring a number of overdue progressive social and economic developments. The treasurer budgeted for an increased defict of A$630 million and produced concessions costing more than A$565 million in the next year. Its most notable features were a record 10 percent cut in income tax and marked rises in all social services for the aged, including old age benefits, health services, and housing grants; in addition, there were travel subsidies for the unemployed. In the long run, other aspects of the budget may prove to be even more important. The means test on pensions is to be progressively eliminated over three years, and the long demanded inquiry into poverty has begun. Significant advances were made in other necessary areas. Expenditure on aboriginal advancement is to be substantially increased by almost $22 million, to over $53 million. Equally realistic, at a time when foreign aid is being viewed more critically in many countries, is the Australian provision for an increase of some $20 million, to an overall figure of about $220 million. The major recipients are Papua–New Guinea, the Colombo Plan countries, and Indonesia.

In a disappointing year for the domestic economy, trade was a spectacular bright spot, as the figures released by the Commonwealth statistician show. The surplus on the trade account is double that for 1970–1971; exports have

Champagne for "Clutha"

The massive "Clutha Capricorn," biggest ship ever built in Australia, placidly awaits christening (left) in the harbor at Whyalla, South Australia. Mrs. Sonia McMahon (above), wife of the prime minister, whacked the bow of the 83,000-ton ore carrier with a bottle of champagne in traditional ceremonies. Clutha Development Proprietary Ltd. owns the ship.

increased by $4,758 million, and official reserves have risen by $1,443 million. The major trade fact is the startling recovery in many of Australia's primary export industries. The prospects for meat, especially for beef, exports were always good and now look even better. The demand for meat in the American market is steadily increasing, and the Australian position is helped by President Nixon's desire to hold meat prices in check. The meat quota to the United States has been increased by 7.2 percent, and since Australia did not export its full quota in 1970–1971, the new figure allows a potential rise of 13 percent. Changes in Japanese food habits are also likely to be significant in stimulating meat production, and the Soviet Union may also enter the market.

The wheat industry is today in very much better shape than could have been anticipated after the virtual loss of the Chinese market. There have been important purchases by East Germany and by Chile and Peru, as well as sales in the more traditional markets. Wool is showing a heartening recovery, and provided the industry can make the necessary adjustments, there is no reason why wool cannot remain a major export industry.

Domestic politics. Two state elections were held during the year, in Queensland and Tasmania. The Queensland election for an enlarged but single house saw the government returned. The Country Party–Liberal coalition maintained much the same equilibrium, which meant that the junior partner—the Liberal Party—failed in its attempt to become dominant. The results were Country Party, 26 seats; Liberals, 21; Labor, 33; and two independents.

The other major development in Queensland was the decision by the government to make a first-time application to the Commonwealth Grants Commission for special funds

as a claimant state—that is, a state suffering special disabilities because of geographical size, dispersion of population, and the cost of maintaining services to sustain an Australian average. The outcome was an interim grant of $9 million for the financial year.

In Tasmania the relative position of the political parties was reversed. There the Liberal Party was in office, with the support of a Center Party representative. The government suffered from internal divisions and ultimately from the virtual defection of the Center Party member. In combination, this produced an unexpected election and a decisive victory for Labor, 21–14, an unusually decisive result for this state. Tasmania thus became the third state in which Labor holds office; the other two are South Australia and Western Australia.

In Western Australia the Labor grip on power is precarious because the government, which holds only a one-vote majority, is confronted by serious problems. After a period of boom, largely attributable to the mining industries, the state faces the highest unemployment figures in the country at 2.94 percent and is also suffering from a rise in the cost of living.

In New South Wales, Sir Robert Askin made major alterations in his cabinet. The main controversy in the state revolved around conservation, pollution, and measures to prevent a further deterioration in the environment. The government has now adopted the principle that, in the future, major developmental projects will be approved only after studies have been made of their environmental impact, an attitude which puts New South Wales in the forefront on this issue.

In Victoria, Premier Henry Bolte, after a record period of 17 years in office, announced his retirement. He was succeeded by his deputy, Rupert Hamer.

In South Australia, where Don Dunstan is in office as Labor premier, deep divisions have emerged in the opposition party, the Liberal-Country League. Former premier Steele Hall, leader of the party, is a man of stature and integrity, but he was overthrown by a party revolt which led to the election of a new opposition leader, Bruce Eastick.

Federal aid to the states increased this year, largely to stimulate the sluggish domestic economy. At the February premiers' conference the prime minister found another $85 million for the states, and by May a grant of $229 million in new federal money for education had been added. At the June premiers' conference the state premiers made extensive—and largely successful—demands upon the Commonwealth, obtaining an additional $230 million, for a fiscal year total of over $3,188 million acquired from the Commonwealth to carry on state functions. The August budget provided still further assistance for the states, notably for improvements in education and for the reconstruction of primary industries.

Papua–New Guinea. The Australian territory of Papua–New Guinea continued its steady march toward eventual autonomy. In general elections held between February 19 and March 11, a coalition led by the Pangu Pati, the major advocate of self-government, won 60 out of 100 elective seats in the House of Assembly. On April 27, Michael Somare, a schoolteacher who is the leader of the Pangu Pati, became deputy chairman of the administrator's executive council and chief minister of Papua–New Guinea. Somare had indicated one week earlier that he expected the territory to gain self-government within four years. Sir Paul Hasluck, the federally appointed governor general, indicated the Australian government's willingness to confer with the newly elected leaders on preparations for autonomous rule and praised the new House of Assembly as the most representative in the territory's history. Not only had the number of elective seats been expanded and appointive seats diminished, but also the voting age had been lowered

184 AUSTRIA

from 21 to 18 and an extensive effort had been made to enroll and instruct new voters. The territory will become self-governing December 1973.

Education. The Commonwealth is playing an ever more active role in education, primarily through finance and planning. The reports for the triennium 1973–1975 by the Australian Universities Commission and the Australian Commission on Advanced Education indicate that federal and state governments will spend a record $1,467 million on higher education, with the universities receiving $1,017 million and the colleges of advanced education $450 million. Two new universities will be established—Griffith in Brisbane and Murdoch in Perth—and the university college at Wollongong will be upgraded to become an autonomous university. Additional colleges of advanced education are being established in Adelaide, in the Northern Rivers district of New South Wales, and in the western suburbs of Sydney.

There have been significant developments in other areas, again sponsored by Commonwealth initiative. The highly important decision has been taken to provide Commonwealth financial support for teachers' colleges. In most cases, these will become colleges of advanced education, which will add another 38 institutions to the 49 which already come under the aegis of the Commission on Advanced Education.

Cultural developments. In music the federal government, through the Commonwealth Assistance to Composers Fund and in association with the Australian Broadcasting Commission, is producing a wide range of recordings covering some 24 Australian composers and some 32 works. The series, titled "Australian Festival of Music," will feature symphony orchestras from Sydney, Melbourne, Adelaide, and Perth and will include the work of such composers as Peter Sculthorpe, Richard Meale, Barry Conyngham, and the late Alfred Hill.

The extent of government assistance can be seen in the federal grants announced in the budget. Assistance to the performing arts increased by $1.5 million, to reach $5.7 million. Some 71 organizations will benefit from the grants, the major beneficiaries being the opera, the ballet, the Elizabethan Trust orchestras, and the Elizabethan Theater Trust. In addition, the treasurer announced that works of art, regardless of origin or nationality, would be exempt from sales tax.

Other notable developments have been federal government approval for construction of a national gallery in Canberra, with James Mollison as director, and the announcement by Sydney University that a $5 million arts center, including an art gallery and a 780-seat theatre, would be financed by the Seymour and Power bequests.

The books produced late in 1971 and 1972 were impressive in their diversity and quality. Among the most important titles were Bernard Smith, *Australian Painting 1788–1970;* T. B. Millar, editing *Australian Foreign Minister: The Diaries of R. G. Casey 1951–1960;* J. A. A. Stockwin, editing *Japan and Australia in the 70's;* W. K. Hancock, *Discovering Monaro: A Study of Man's Impact on His Environment;* T. Keneally, *The Chant of Jimmie Blacksmith;* A. D. Hope, *Collected Poems 1930–1970;* Robin Boyd, *The Great, Great Australian Dream;* Morris West, *The Summer of the Red Wolf;* David Ireland, *The Flesheaters;* Dennis Altman, *Homosexual: Oppression and Liberation;* Kath Walker, *Stradbroke Dreamtime;* and Hal Porter, *The Right Thing.*

The winners of major art awards were Archibald Prize, Clifton Pugh, for *Sir John McEwen* (portraiture); Wynne Prize, Margaret Woodward, *Karri Country* (landscape); Sulman Prize, James Meldrum, *Pyramid Shelf* (genre painting).

Death of a statesman. This year many mourned the death of a very distinguished Australian, Sir Owen Dixon, who was widely regarded as one of the most eminent lawyers and judges of the English-speaking world. Sir Owen Dixon served during World War II as Australian minister to Washington and was subsequently a United Nations mediator in the Kashmir dispute. He was on the High Court bench for 35 years, and for 12 of these years he served as chief justice.

Area and population. Area, 2,967,909 sq. mi. Pop. (est. March 1972), 12,943,000. Principal cities (est. June 1971): Canberra (cap.), 158,594; Sydney, 2,799,634; Melbourne, 2,497,993.
Government. Gov. gen., Sir Paul Hasluck; prime min., William McMahon; deputy prime min. and min. for trade and ind., John Douglas Anthony; treas., Billy Snedden; min. for foreign affairs, Nigel Bowen; def. min., David Fairbairn; min. for labor and nat. service, Phillip Lynch.
Finance. Monetary unit, Australian dollar: A$1 = US$1.194. Budget (est. 1972–1973): receipts, A$9,447,465,000; expenditure, A$10,077,606,000.
Trade (1971–1972). Total imports, A$4,007 million; total exports, A$4,902 million.
Production (1970–1971). Gross national product, A$33,087 million (at market price).
Education. Primary and secondary schools (1971), 9,588; enrollment (Aug. 1971), 1,452,838; full-time teachers (Aug. 1971), 118,030. University enrollment (Apr. 1972), 128,642; full-time teaching staff (Apr. 1972), 8,216. Colleges of advanced education: enrollment (1971), 44,468.
Armed forces. Expenditure (est. 1972–1973), A$1,323 million. Strength (June 1972): army, 41,290; air force, 22,720; navy, 17,134.

GORDON GREENWOOD

AUSTRIA. Austria made important progress in 1972 in improving relations with neighboring Italy after a generation of postwar conflict and in moving toward agreement with the expanding European Economic Community (EEC, or Common Market). Chancellor Bruno Kreisky, in his third year as head of a Socialist government, took charge of both foreign policy initiatives and a domestic struggle against inflation.

Foreign political and economic relations. Chancellor Kreisky, touring the capitals of the Common Market nations, attended a series of conferences concerning Austria's wish for a special arrangement with the European Economic Community when it expands its membership to 10 nations next year. The three new Common Market members—Britain, Ireland, and Denmark—are all partners with Austria in the European Free Trade Area Association; when they leave EFTA, Austria must seek other economic ties. However, the Soviet Union has insisted that, according to the state treaty of 1955 which provided for permanent neutrality, the Austrians must not even enter into an association with the EEC. Their objection is that as the market moved toward political union, neutral Austria would become a part of the Western system. Kreisky's task has been to work out an arrangement providing for ties close enough to satisfy the integration-minded EEC members and at the same time loose enough to satisfy the Soviet Union.

Chancellor Kreisky in April and President Franz Jonas in November 1971 made official visits to Italy—the first since the end of World War II. Austrian officials believed this signified the end of the long conflict over the South Tirol, or Alto Adige, the former Austrian territory that became part of Italy after World War I. The visits were made possible by the ratification of a compromise agreement in July 1971 which provided for a greater measure of home rule and educational and cultural improvements for the area's German-speaking citizens.

A third and unexpected foreign political event was the two-day stopover of President Richard Nixon in Salzburg on his way to the Moscow summit conference. The president used his stay in Klessheim castle to prepare for his meeting with Soviet leaders but took time out to dine with Chancellor Kreisky. Nixon's arrival was greeted on May 20 by over 1,500 demonstrators protesting the United States' mining of Haiphong harbor. Among the demonstrators was Kreisky's son Peter. The visit was concluded without serious incident.

Domestic economic scene. Chancellor Kreisky's year was as busy on the domestic scene as on the international front. Because of wise budgetary moves Austria's growth in gross national product, at 6 percent, was well above the European average in 1971 and was expected to surpass this figure in 1972. Furthermore, the government pledged to maintain last year's full employment, even if it meant higher prices. Indeed, charges for gasoline, electricity, and transportation rose at the beginning of the year. Unfortunately, the 4.7 percent increase in the price index in 1971 was expected to reoccur this year; the government continued to consider this its main economic problem.

Other development. Two former Nazi SS officers, Walter Dejaco, 63, and Fritz Karl Ertl, 64, were acquitted on March 10 of murder charges arising from their roles in designing and constructing the gas chambers at the Auschwitz death camp. The court found a "remote responsibility" for the murders on Ertl's part but concluded he was forced to act under orders.

On March 1, Austrian Airlines, with Scandinavian Airways, became one of the first non–Western-allied companies to be permitted to fly into West Berlin. Both airlines had already concluded agreements with East German authorities for use of the city's other airport.

In late January, Karl Schranz, Austria's world champion downhill skier, was barred from the Winter Olympics in Sapporo, Japan, on the grounds that his job as a ski company executive conflicted with his amateur status. The Austrian team, which first threatened to leave the games but was persuaded by Schranz to remain, finished ninth with five medals, including a bronze in Schranz's specialty. The Austrian government created its own medal for Schranz.

Area and population. Area, 32,374 sq. mi. Pop. (1971), 7,443,809. Principal cities (1971): Vienna (cap.), 1,603,408; Graz, 249,211; Linz, 204,627; Salzburg, 127,455; Innsbruck, 115,293.
Government. Federal republic with bicameral parliament. Pres., Franz Jonas; chancellor, Bruno Kreisky; for. min., Rudolf Kirchschlaeger.
Finance. Monetary unit, schilling; 1 schilling = US$0.0435. Budget (1972 est., in U.S. dollars): expenditure, 4.96 billion; revenue, 4.57 million. Deficit, 392 million.
Trade (1971, in billions of schillings). Exports, 79; imports, 104.5. Main exports: machinery, motor vehicles, textiles, iron and steel, timber. Main imports: machinery and transportation equipment, foodstuffs, coal. Main trading partners: West Germany, Switzerland, Italy, Britain; 55.9% of imports and 38.7% of exports with the EEC; 19.1% of imports and 26.7% of exports with EFTA.
Agriculture and industry. Most important agricultural product, timber and timber by-products. Industrial production (1970, in millions of tons): steel, 4.1; iron ore, 4.0; brown coal, 3.7; oil, 2.8.
Education (1970–1971). Elementary and special schools, 5,778; enrollment, 963,579; teachers, 44,512. Polytechnic schools, 113; enrollment, 30,896. Secondary schools (1969), 476; enrollment, 186,643. Higher education (1970), 11 universities and colleges, 5 art schools ranking as universities; enrollment, 51,431; faculty, 6,811.
Armed forces. Total strength, 55,000. Compulsory service of six months for all men 18 to 50.
DONALD R. SHANOR

AUTOMOBILE INDUSTRY. Sales and prices. The industry sold a record 12,794,000 vehicles during the 1972 model year, topping the old high of 11,608,014 set in 1969. Of the total, 10,735,000 were passenger cars and 2,059,000 were trucks, including pickups, the industry's newest sales darling. Sales of all cars were spurred by the 1971 repeal of excise taxes on new cars and light trucks. The 1971 realignment of monetary exchange rates, which raised prices on imported cars between 10 and 14 percent, also helped American auto-makers to reverse a ten-year trend and increase their share of the U.S. market from 84 percent in 1971 to 86 percent in 1972. General Motors paced domestic producers, capturing 49 percent of the passenger-car market. Ford had 30 percent of sales, Chrysler 18 percent, the American Motors Company 3 percent.

Manufacturers sought to raise their prices from 2.2 to 5 percent to cover extra costs of installing federally mandated safety and pollution-control equipment, of offering as standard equipment certain items previously offered as options, and in the instance of Chrysler and AMC, of meeting increased labor and material expenses. None of the requests included provision for profit-making on safety and emissions equipment. The Price Commission, pointing to record sales and profits in 1972, asked the companies to withdraw their requests for price hikes. In response, GM and Ford substantially reduced the amounts sought, and Chrysler and AMC also scaled down their demands. Price increases were denied for new-model introduction time in September, but Chrysler and American Motors won increases in mid-October. Ford and General Motors immediately announced somewhat smaller price hikes.

Engines. Interest in the rotary engine—popularly known as the Wankel, after its German inventor—soared in 1972. Spurred by competitive and governmental pressures to develop suitable alternatives to the conventional piston engine, 20 companies—among them General Motors, Ford, Volkswagen, Rolls-Royce, Alfa Romeo, Toyota, and Datsun—have spent tens of millions of dollars to acquire licenses from Audi-NSU Auto Union AG, Wankel G.m.b.H., and the Curtiss-Wright Corporation to develop, manufacture, and market their own versions of the rotary engine. The rotary concept dates to the 1920's, when engineers first foresaw the advantages of replacing the up and down motion of regular piston engines with the smooth, circular motion of rotary power. But Felix Wankel's first prototype was not completed until 1957, and the engines were not available to the motoring public until the mid-1960's, when Japan's Toyo Kogyo Company, Ltd., installed some in its Mazda models. Mazda introduced its Wankel engine in the United States in 1970. Light, compact, simple, and powerful, the Wankel permits greater flexibility in styling and may result in fewer service repairs. But it gobbles gasoline at a rate 20 percent higher than piston engines of equal power and does not yet meet down-the-road emissions requirements. General Motors announced that it may introduce the Wankel engine on its 1975 Chevrolet Vega. Toyota and Datsun are also planning to offer the Wankel as optional equipment.

Ford signed an agreement for a license and development program for Stirling engines with N. V. Philips, a company based in the Netherlands. The Stirling engine, invented more than 150 years ago by a Scottish clergyman, Robert Stirling, operates by external continuous combustion, burns almost any fuel, and has clean-burning characteristics. Philips has been working on the engine since 1938. Not all auto-makers share Ford's enthusiasm for the Stirling engine, since it is said to have poor acceleration.

Meanwhile, developmental work continues on gas turbine and diesel engines as well as piston motors, as the auto industry seeks ways to meet pollution-control requirements. In June auto-makers went to court in an effort to reverse an Environmental Protection Agency decision to deny their request for a one-year extension of 1975 standards calling for a 90 percent reduction in pollutants from 1970 levels. The industry continued to maintain that it does not have the know-how to meet the 1975 standards. Starting with 1973 models, auto-makers are warranting emission-control equipment for five years or 50,000 miles. Ford had to retest engines extensively for its 1973 models to win Environmental Protection Agency certification, after the company itself revealed that illegal adjustments had invalidated the first round of tests.

Safety. Bumpers, air bags, and seat belt/shoulder harness reminder systems were in the forefront of safety design developments. To meet federal standards that require cars to successfully withstand a 5-mile-per-hour crash from the front and a 2½-mph impact from the rear, Ford, Chrysler, and AMC improved the mountings and reinforced the metal on conventional bumpers. But GM came up with two new designs; some of its Chevrolet and Cadillac models have a bumper-grille assembly that absorbs shock by swinging back

MAZDA

THE WANKEL ROTARY ENGINE, now used in the Japanese-made Mazda (right), is lightweight and efficient. A three-sided rotor sweeps clockwise inside a pinched-oval combustion chamber (above), performing the same four functions as a piston in a reciprocating engine. As one rotor tip passes the intake port (upper left), the fuel-air mixture enters; as the rotor turns, the mixture is trapped and compressed until the rotor side is next to the spark plugs, which ignite the mixture. Gases are then expelled from the engine through an exhaust port.

into the engine compartment on a hinge; two Pontiac models have no visible bumpers, just front ends made of urethane, which deforms on impact and returns to its original shape. Most of the new bumpers protrude 3 to 4 inches and weigh 40 to 100 pounds more than their immediate predecessors. Federal standards for 1974 models will require bumpers to be of uniform height and to withstand a rear impact of 5 mph.

Anticipating a government requirement that 1976 models be equipped with a passive-restraint system, auto-makers have installed air bags on a few thousand current models for fleet use. Activated by release of a cap on a container of gas kept under pressure, the bags open in a twinkling of an eye when a car crashes at 15 mph or more. Manufacturers say they cannot guarantee the reliability of the bags, and many motorists share their apprehension.

Auto-makers also are installing safety interlock systems on a limited number of models in advance of a government edict that all 1974 models be equipped either with a passive-restraint system (air bags) or devices which prevent cars from being started until front seat belts and shoulder harnesses are fastened.

1973 models. With most auto-makers having substituted a six-year styling cycle for their traditional three-year "planned obsolescence" cycle, fewer cars boast major styling changes. But all of GM's intermediate-size autos and Ford's

standard-size cars and pickups were new this year. A total of 301 models are on sale, as compared to 297 last year and a record 375 in 1970. Only nine convertibles are available, down from 17 in 1972 and a record 57 in 1966.

Recalls. Since passage of the National Traffic and Motor Vehicle Safety Act of 1966, more than 31 million vehicles—almost half of the number sold during the past half-dozen years—have been recalled for inspection and, in most instances, repairs. Surprisingly, the number of recalls has been increasing rather than decreasing. A total of 11,710,000 vehicles were called back in 1971, and more cars and trucks were recalled than were built during the first nine months of 1972. However, the majority of recent recalls have been for defects newly discovered in vehicles produced from three to ten years ago.

Worldwide developments. Chrysler announced plans to produce in plants around the globe by 1975 a highly standardized "world car." Chrysler and Japan's Mitsubishi Motors, 35 percent owned by Chrysler, have divided many markets, Chrysler taking charge of exports to Latin America, the Middle East, and Africa while permitting the Japanese firm to manage all new Chrysler-Mitsubishi dealerships in Southeast Asia. Chrysler has offered to buy the 3.3 percent interest it does not already own in Société Chrysler-France.

General Motors and Japan's Isuzu Motors, 34.2 percent owned by GM, are developing a small car which Isuzu will

start building in 1974. GM is marketing in America a small pickup truck manufactured by Isuzu, and Ford sells a similar vehicle made by Japan's Toyo Kogyo. Ford and Toyo Kogyo terminated negotiations for a capital tie-up, leaving Ford as the only member of America's Big Three without a capital investment in a Japanese auto company. The two firms failed to agree on the extent of Ford's participation in Toyo Kogyo's management.

DAVID L. LEWIS

BANGLADESH. Few countries can have suffered such protracted and agonizing birth pangs as those endured by the infant republic of Bangladesh in 1971. But the country not only has survived but has also restored parliamentary democracy after 13 years of repressive military rule as part of Pakistan.

In February the United Nations secretary general, Kurt Waldheim, issued an appeal for $565 million in contributions from the international community by the end of 1972. With 5 million houses razed to the ground, Bangladesh has a homeless population of 30 million, including almost 10 million refugees who trekked back from India but are now accommodated in suppurating shantytowns. The Pakistanis also destroyed hundreds of bridges, schools, and colleges. No jute or paddy crops were planted, and farmers had to eat their seed grain.

Government. Sheikh Mujibur Rahman's Awami League, which won a landslide victory in 1970, is probably heading for a split. The league's amorphous ideological character has always encouraged divisive tendencies, but they have been held in check in the past by the fervent nationalism that converted the 1970 general elections into a referendum on autonomy as well as by Rahman's charismatic personality. Both forces appear to have lost some of their compelling power, and a polarization between right and left is evident.

The breach became open on the eve of May 20 student elections at Dacca University, when the leaders of the student Chhatra League split into two groups, one dedicated to socialism through parliamentary democracy ("Mujibism") and the other demanding Marxist economics and a "revolutionary" government. Two months later, the rival factions called separate conferences on the same day in Dacca. Rahman inaugurated the meeting favoring parliamentary government. He was flanked on the ceremonial dais by the leader of the pro-Moscow National Awami Party (NAP) and by several dignitaries of the Bangladesh Communist Party, which is also aligned with the Soviet Union.

Rahman's plea for socialism, secularism, nationalism, and democracy was received with thunderous applause, the massive gathering roaring "Mujibism! Mujibism!" each time he stood up to speak. The breach became final and Mujibism was approved as the country's guiding philosophy.

Marxist revolutionaries are being expelled from unions and are being weeded out of the Awami League's ranks, but the radicals are believed to be waiting only for an opportune moment to announce the formation of a new party. When that happens, many prominent Awami Leaguers are expected to defect. Up to now, opposition groups seem to have made little headway. A "hunger march" staged by the pro-Peking United Front in September fizzled out, and even the well-organized NAP has only one representative in the Constituent Assembly.

See also PEOPLE IN THE NEWS: Mujibur Rahman.

Constitution. A meeting of more than 400 National Assembly and provincial assembly members, together forming the Constituent Assembly, took place on April 10. A provisional government, with Sheikh Mujibur Rahman as president, had been formed in April 1971. But with Rahman in a West Pakistani jail and the secessionist leaders exiled in India, the government did not really start operating until the cabinet-in-exile returned to Dacca on December 22, six days after the Pakistani surrender. On January 10, Rahman returned by way of London and New Delhi, having been released by Pakistani president Zulfikar Ali Bhutto, and a provisional constitution order was promulgated the very next day. Rahman became prime minister on January 12 with the intention of working toward a parliamentary government on the British model. The transition to legislative government appears to have been remarkably orderly after the upheavals of last year, and on October 12 a draft constitution with a strong socialist bias was announced. This document, providing for a unicameral legislature, a responsible cabinet and prime minister, a president as head of state, and universal franchise at the age of 18, was approved by the assembly November 4, to become effective December 16, the first anniversary of Bengali liberation. Until the new constitution was approved, the assembly had no legislative powers; all laws had been promulgated by presidential ordinances. General elections for the new legislature have been scheduled for March 7, 1973.

Economic planning. The United Nations launched a $100 million crash program in April when the director of the UN relief operation, Toni Hagan, predicted that Bangladesh was "heading for disaster." The feared food riots did not materialize, but the price of rice (the staple diet) and all other essential commodities rose sharply under the pressure of hoarding and black market sales.

WITH MALICE TOWARD NONE. In a ceremony at Dacca, Bengali leader Sheikh Mujibur Rahman received arms from the Mukti Bahini guerrillas and urged them not to retaliate against the Bihari minority which had supported Pakistan in the civil war.

MUKTI BAHINI guerrillas patrol their territory during the Pakistani civil war.

SPECIAL REPORT : BANGLADESH

BIRTH OF A NATION

"Joi Bangla" ("Victory to Bengal") was the cry that celebrated the birth of the new nation of Bangladesh in late 1971. Independent nationhood was a long time coming for this fertile corner of the Indian subcontinent. Before 1947, Bangladesh, formerly known as East Bengal, was part of British India; then it became East Pakistan, separated from West Pakistan by almost a thousand miles of Indian territory and by fundamental differences in race, language, and culture. The martial peoples of West Pakistan, an arid land of deserts and hills, thoroughly dominated the more populous eastern region; jute and tea exports from East Pakistan earned revenues that were largely diverted to economic development in the distant western region.

The Bengali independence movement flourished in the rubble left by perhaps the worst natural disaster in human history—the cyclone and tidal wave of November 1970, which may have claimed half a million lives. After the floods subsided, there were charges that the national government's relief efforts were far less efficient and enthusiastic than they could have been. It looked to the Bengalis as if the government did not care if they lived or died.

Two months later, after the Awami League—a party that advocated autonomy for East Pakistan in most matters—had won a majority of seats in a national assembly empowered to write a new constitution, the military government of Agha Muhammad Yahya Khan appeared unwilling to abide by the results. When the convening of the national assembly was postponed, the Bengalis held mass demonstrations. In response, Yahya Khan imposed martial law and curfews. Sheikh Mujibur Rahman, leader of the Awami League, then called a general strike, and East Pakistanis continued to run provincial government agencies in defiance of the military.

On March 25, 1971, the situation boiled over into open warfare. Pakistan's army launched attacks in Dacca, and the fighting escalated rapidly. Most of the damage was done by the Pakistani soldiers, with the aid of non-Bengali irregular militiamen called Razakars. The army had the allegiance of most of East Pakistan's Biharis, members of a Muslim minority who migrated from India at the time of partition in 1947. Fighting on the other side were the East Pakistan Rifles (the regular provincial militia) and local police forces. A new guerrilla movement, the Mukti Bahini (Bengali liberation army), soon made the countryside too hot for small groups of Pakistani soldiers. The government troops, for their part, took reprisals against any village thought to be helping or harboring the Mukti Bahini—reprisals that consisted of mass killings, rapes, and destruction.

Typical of the tales of reprisal was the account given to Sydney H. Schanberg of the New York *Times* by refugees from

After India entered the war on the side of Bangladesh independence forces in December 1971, Pakistan's army in the east found itself looking down the gun barrels of numerically superior Indian forces. Here, the business end of an Indian howitzer points toward retreating Pakistani troops.

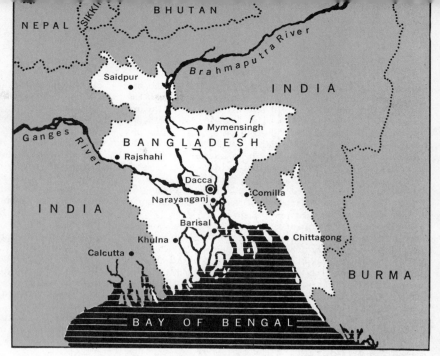

Faridpur District. In mid-September the Pakistani army shelled a village of 5,000 inhabitants and burned the huts. Then, when some of the villagers did not escape soon enough, the soldiers bound their hands and feet and threw them into the flames. In this case as in many others, there was not a hut left standing.

No one can tell how many died in this one-sided civil war. Estimates were as high as 3 million killed by the Pakistani army; certainly the toll was in the hundreds of thousands. Another 10 million easterners fled to India, where they had to live in crowded makeshift camps that soon became sinks of filth and disease. India, normally hard pressed to support its own people, was put under a severe strain to feed the newcomers. Although the Indians sympathized with the victims of Pakistani reprisals, many of them Hindus, the prospect of providing never-ending support for the refugees and guerrillas seemed prohibitively expensive.

The old rivalry between India and Pakistan, which had erupted into war in 1965, made it natural that India would not be disappointed to see Pakistan lose its Bengali "colony." Thus, as the refugees streamed into India during most of 1971, border clashes between Indian and Pakistani troops grew more frequent and more serious, and Indian support for the guerrillas became more open. All-out warfare looked inevitable.

On December 3, 1971, Indian troops pushed into East Pakistan in force. Within four days they had captured two cities. Outnumbering the Pakistani forces by about 200,000 to 80,000 and gaining total air control right from the start, the Indians could not be held back. Of course, India's geographical advantage was a major factor; India's announced strategy was to aim for the complete surrender of Pakistani troops in the east but only to contain attacks from West Pakistan. The strategy was successful. On December 16, Lieutenant General A. A. K. Niazi, Pakistan's eastern commander, surrendered all his forces. The Indian advance had been so rapid that Dacca was surrounded two weeks after India had begun the offensive. By that time, India had recognized the government of Bangladesh, and its independence from Pakistan had become an accomplished fact.

The atrocities committed by the Pakistani army and its collaborators continued for as long as they had the power to commit them. On December 18, 1971, more than 100 Bengalis—physicians, professors, writers, and teachers—were found murdered in a field near Dacca. Since these killings apparently had taken place just before the Pakistani commanders surrendered, they exemplified the seemingly limitless and pointless cruelty of the war.

After the Pakistani army was defeated, it appeared that the Bengalis, especially the armed Mukti Bahini guerrillas, might take massive vengeance on the Razakars and on all non-Bengalis, whether they had cooperated with Pakistan's army or not. The wholesale bloodbath that was feared did not take place, but there were scattered acts of vengeance against collaborators, including the torture and bayoneting of four young Razakars before a crowd of 5,000 in Dacca. Open fighting broke out between Bengalis and Biharis in late January in the Dacca suburbs and mid-March in Khulna. Casualties were estimated to be in the hundreds in both clashes, including Bangladesh security forces and both Bengali and Bihari civilians. Most Biharis have remained isolated in ghettos and refugee camps, afraid to venture out though often short of food and other necessities. Accusations against alleged collaborators, both Biharis and Bengalis, have been common. In early April about 10,000 people were reported to be under arrest and awaiting trial.

The government of Bangladesh has resided almost entirely in the hands of one man, Sheikh Mujibur Rahman. During 1971, Mujib had been captured and tried on 12 charges by the West Pakistanis, but the verdict was never announced. After suffering solitary confinement for nine months, Mujib barely escaped death, according to his own account, when Yahya Khan decided to hang Mujib the same day East Pakistan fell. He was saved by Zulfikar Ali Bhutto, a popular Pakistani leader, who arranged to have him taken from the jail to the house of a police superintendent at 3:00 A.M. Mujib remained in the house for two days, until Pakistani forces had surrendered in the east and Yahya had relinquished his power to Bhutto. Mujib was finally released on January 8, 1972, and returned to his people by way of London.

Mujib, a symbol of salvation to the Bengalis, soon began receiving petitioners from early morning until late at night. He has been called upon to make numerous minor decisions that would normally be handled by subordinates. Unfortunately, Bangladesh suffers a serious lack of experienced leaders because of the many years of Pakistani domination; also, many Bengali civil servants and technicians were either killed by government troops or were caught in West Pakistan when war broke out and have had to remain there.

Bangladesh would have liked to bring these Bengalis back from Pakistan and send the Biharis there in exchange, but such an agreement did not seem likely to be reached soon. India was also involved in the problem because of the thousands of Pakistani army prisoners it still held. The Indian government considered the prisoners to be in the joint custody of Bangladesh, and Bangladesh has insisted that about 1,500 of them be tried as war criminals.

Despite the shortage of experienced leadership and the hatreds left over from the war, Bangladesh has avoided the worst of the horrors that had been predicted. There has been no major postwar bloodbath and no famine. After the cyclone of 1970 and the civil war of 1971, many had expected 1972 to be a year of widespread starvation, but the relief effort, though hampered by distribution problems and even by corruption, was sufficient to prevent mass starvation. This was accomplished despite the fact that nearly all of the 10 million refugees in India had returned to Bangladesh by late March.

Bangladesh has received diplomatic recognition from at least 85 nations and has applied for membership in the United Nations. (The application was vetoed by China.) With a population of about 75 million, it is now the world's eighth-largest nation, and although the most horrible of its trials is over, it still has countless problems to solve. As Sheikh Mujib told a correspondent from *Time* magazine, "I am very happy about the progress my people have made, but every problem is a crisis."

PETER K. REINHART

Though Rahman's threats to shoot down clandestine operators have made little impact, he has gone ahead with the economic promises of his 1970 election campaign. Luxury imports were banned; monthly salaries were frozen at $134; and all locally and Pakistani owned tea estates, banks, insurance companies, and jute, cotton, textile, and sugar mills were nationalized. Workers have been promised a share in the management of 253 nationalized factories.

This year's modest budget shows a slight surplus, while a $668 million development plan for 1972–1973 aims to spend $137 million on the raising of rice. Bangladesh hopes to launch its first five-year plan in 1973.

Law and order. Frequent labor strikes, riots, and murders indicate that only Rahman's personal influence underwrites stability in Bangladesh. The basic problem is the peacetime role of the Mukti Bahini (liberation fighters). All through the turbulence of 1971, 150,000 guerrillas probably had as many as 200,000 unlicensed weapons, some seized from the Pakistani army and others acquired in India. About 30,000 men, organized into the Niyamita (regular) Bahini, fought along with the Indian army; the rest—Gana (people's) Bahini—defended villages on their own. In addition, lone operators ran their private armies, and the political parties had their armed forces. The Awami League's crack Mujib Bahini, believed to have received professional training in India, was estimated to have more than 60,000 men.

Rahman's appeals to such forces to disband and surrender their weapons have not been very effective. Many weapons have been handed over, but at least 20,000 rifles, light machine guns, and mortars are believed to have gone underground. A new private army, called the Lal Bahini (red guards), was formed in April with 110,000 members; there are also at least half a dozen armed Marxist-Leninist groups operating in "liberated zones." About 5,000 Maoist rebels were arrested in July, and Rahman warns that Marxist-Leninists will be shot on sight. But the government's 250,000-man militia has proved itself quite unable to maintain the peace.

Industrial anarchy is, perhaps, even more explosive. Over 100 people were killed in Khulna factory riots in June, and the Narayanganj jute mill (the biggest in Bangladesh) shut down in August after bloody battles between workers.

Foreign policy. Bangladesh was admitted this year to a number of international organizations. Its United Nations application failed only because of China's veto in the Security Council.

GOING HOME. These Bengalis were some of the estimated 10 million refugees who returned to Bangladesh at the end of the conflict.

India. Since independence, India has poured massive funds into the war-torn country. Aid commitments for 1972 and 1973 were $275 million, and India had provided 52 percent of Bangladesh's food by March. Visiting Calcutta in February, Rahman pledged the two countries to eternal friendship; the bond was formalized when a 25-year peace treaty on the Soviet pattern was signed during Mrs. Indira Gandhi's Dacca visit.

The donor-recipient relationship is not without strain, though critics of India are still confined to pro-Peking politicians and fanatical Muslim parties. Anti-Indian slogans have been heard; "Down with Indian expansionism" posters appeared on the walls of Dacca University during the student elections.

Rahman has given warning that India and Pakistan cannot settle the future of Pakistani prisoners of war without Bangladesh. His insistence on putting 1,500 Pakistanis to trial for war crimes—and India's discreet efforts to restrain him—could disrupt a relationship which is still delicately poised. Dacca's decision to set up over 200 border check-posts and impose passport and visa restrictions on Indian visitors suggests a cautious edging away from 1971's rapturous unity.

Soviet Union. It is significant that Rahman's first state visit outside the subcontinent was to Moscow. The Soviet Union, whose ships and minesweepers had earlier cleared the blocked roadsteads to Chittagong and Chalna Anchorage, has, in effect, agreed to underwrite the regeneration of Bangladesh. A grant of nearly $47 million was followed by a trade pact for $431.6 million; the joint communiqué with Soviet prime minister Aleksei N. Kosygin lent indirect support to the Brezhnev doctrine for collective security in Asia.

Pakistan. Relations with the former parent government are understandably bitter because of the events of 1971. Rahman insists on recognition of Bangladesh's independence before he will discuss anything. Pakistani president Bhutto, on the other hand, is under domestic pressure to dissuade Rahman from going ahead with war crimes trials.

The situation is further complicated by minority communities who are virtually imprisoned in each other's countries. Bhutto demands guarantees of safety for the 1.5 million Urdu-speaking Muslims (Biharis) in Bangladesh but will not have them in Pakistan. Rahman says that 400,000 Bengali civilians and 30,000 Bengalis in the Pakistani Army have been jailed in concentration camps. He wants the UN to supervise an exchange of these captive minorities and links the future of Pakistani civilians who surrendered to the joint command in Bangladesh (and are now in India) with the repatriation of his 430,000 Bangladeshis.

The deadlock appears insoluble; Dacca's stand perceptibly hardened after August 10 when, in spite of earlier hints to the contrary, Bhutto told his National Assembly that Bangladesh would not be recognized.

United States. Despite lingering resentment toward American support of Pakistan in 1971, the Bangladesh government has taken a moderate stance with respect to the United States, possibly because of U.S. aid. In the first six months of 1972, the United States contributed $267.5 million of the $800 million received from abroad. But U.S. recognition on April 4, when Bangladesh had already been recognized by 55 countries, was too late to have any dramatic effect on the country's international status.

China. Hopes of an understanding collapsed on August 25 when, even though 84 nations (including four of the five permanent Security Council members) had recognized Dacca, China vetoed Bangladesh's U.N. application. There were widespread protest demonstrations and a day of strikes in Dacca to condemn the Chinese action, but pro-Peking leaders in Bangladesh have maintained a studied silence. Even in the government, many hope that China will soon buy Bangladesh jute and resume the aid projects announced

JEFF LOWENTHAL

MONEY WENT CHEAP at Chicago's United of America Bank, which offered discounts on dollars for its tenth anniversary party.

during the 1971 war. More important, Bangladesh, seeking a new identity, may wish for a counterpoise to its present powerful patrons. But Peking, obsessively suspicious of India, is unable to respond without embarrassing its ally in Islamabad.

Area and population. Area, 55,126 sq. mi. Pop. (est. 1972), 75 million. Dacca (cap.; est. 1969), 829,000.
Government. Republic with unicameral Constituent Assembly and majority party rule. Pres., Abu Syeed Choudhury; prime min., Sheikh Mujibur Rahman.
Finance. Monetary unit, taka; T1 = US$0.1325. Budget (est. 1972–1973): revenue, T2,853.8 million; expenditure, T2,184.3 million; surplus (including capital deficit), T588 million. Development plan (est. 1972–1973): T5,010 million (including T3,750 million foreign aid); agriculture, T1,030 million; education, T437.2 million; defense, T400 million.
Trade (1970, including trade with West Pakistan). Exports, T2,500 million (1973–1974 target, T4,000 million); imports T1,380 million.
SUNANDA K. DATTA-RAY

BANKING AND FINANCE. The year was marked by adjustment to devaluation of the dollar in December 1971 and by a progressive economic recovery beginning late in 1971 and continuing through the first three quarters of 1972.

International monetary troubles. The international monetary crisis, which had been boiling intermittently, was temporarily cooled off in December 1971 by the Smithsonian Agreement, a compromise accepted by the major non-Communist trading nations. The United States agreed to devalue the dollar 8.57 percent, making the price of monetary gold $38 an ounce. Revaluations by other nations brought to 12 percent the total change in the official international value of the dollar. It was also agreed that currency fluctuations would be held to 2.25 percent from par. On April 3 the Smithsonian Agreement received formal approval when President Richard M. Nixon signed a bill authorizing him to devalue the dollar. It was apparent, however, that the agreement had not eliminated international difficulties, for the

MONEY SUPPLY
Monthly averages of daily figures
(seasonally adjusted)

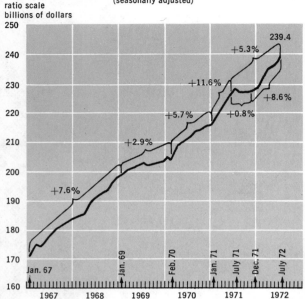

Percentages are annual rates of change for periods indicated
Latest data plotted: July 1972
SOURCE: FEDERAL RESERVE BANK OF ST. LOUIS

YIELDS ON SELECTED SECURITIES,
SEPTEMBER 1971-OCTOBER 1972
(averages of daily rates for week ended Friday)

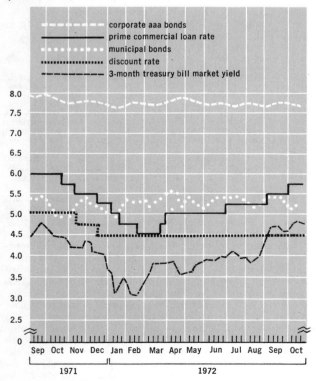

Latest data plotted: week ending October 27
SOURCE: FEDERAL RESERVE BANK OF ST. LOUIS

American balance of payments continued to deteriorate, and the price of gold in the free market continued to soar, passing $70 an ounce on August 1 in London.

Hunt report. Another important development was the publication of the so-called Hunt Commission Report on Financial Structure and Regulation. The report recommended, among other things, the gradual elimination of Regulation Q, which imposed ceilings on interest rates for time deposits; and authorization of savings banks and savings and loan associations to become full-service intermediaries.

The fourth quarter, 1971. *Economic activity.* The economy advanced at an accelerated pace. The real gross national product rose at an annual rate of 6.7 percent, more than double the rate in the third quarter. The rise in industrial production was also encouraging, but unemployment continued to hover around 6 percent, and the cost of living index in December was rising at an annual rate of 4.8 percent.

Money and credit. Money supply expansion slowed down to an annual rate of about 1 percent, bringing the year's increase down to 6 percent. Interest rates fell sharply, as investors took a more sober view of future inflation. The yield on treasury bills dropped to 3.73 percent, compared to 5.45 in late July 1971. The prime rate fell to 5.5 percent in October and to 5 percent in December. The rediscount rate followed, dropping to 4.75 percent in November and 4.5 percent in December.

The stock market. The stock market experienced a new burst of activity. There were 23 days when trading exceeded 15 million shares; two of these, both in December, were over 21 million shares. Yet, despite the activity, the averages did not go anywhere. The Dow-Jones industrial average opened the quarter at 893.98, rose to 901.80, fell to 797.97, and in late November began to climb rapidly, closing the year at 890.20.

First half, 1972. *Economic activity.* The GNP rose 12 percent in the first quarter, but the GNP deflator was also up over 5 percent, so that real growth was 6.5 percent. In the second quarter, real GNP gained at an annual rate of 9.4 percent, the highest since 1965. The GNP deflator advanced relatively slowly; the rise in the cost of living declined steadily during the first half; industrial production did much better than in 1971; productivity showed impressive gains after five years in the doldrums; and unemployment fell to 5.5 percent in June.

Money and credit. In the first quarter, the money supply, following the rise in the monetary base in the last quarter of 1971, resumed the sharp upward advance that had characterized the 1960's. It rose at an annual rate of 9.3 percent, and the more broadly defined money supply (including commercial bank time deposits) rose at a 13 percent annual rate.

Because of the increase in the money supply and dampened inflationary expectations, short-term interest rates fell. A Cincinnati bank lowered its prime rate to 4.25, but most held to 4.75. The yield on bills, just over 3 percent, was the lowest in ten years. New industrials sold at yields between 6.5 and 7 percent.

In the second quarter, the money supply rose at a much slower rate, 5.6 percent. Interest rates reversed their course. Prime rates in most banks rose to 5.25 percent, but in the few banks where it was tied to the commercial paper rate, it advanced to 5.375. Treasury bills, reflecting a general rise in short-term rates, were up to 3.96 percent by June 30, but yields on longer term securities were much as they had been during the first quarter.

The stock market. The stock market was strong from February to the end of May. The Dow-Jones opened the year at 890.20, reached a high of 971.25 on May 26, and then fell off to close the second quarter at 929.03. On May 24, Standard and Poor's 500-stock index reached an all-time high. Activity during the upward swing was brisk. There were 96 days of 15 million shares or more and 22 days of 20 million or more.

Third quarter, 1972. *Economic activity.* The economy continued to improve in the third quarter of 1972. The GNP rose at an annual rate of 8.3 percent, and real GNP growth (after discounting the effects of inflation) was at an annual rate of 5.9 percent.

Money and credit. The money supply increased at an annual rate of about 8.5 percent, a faster pace than monetary authorities desired. The continuous expansion of the economy and the money supply raised fears of renewed inflation. Because of these fears and swelling investment spending, interest rates continued to rise. Treasury bills sold at a 4.75 percent yield; the prime rate in most banks reached 5.75 percent in early October; long-term government bonds paid 5.75 percent; and top corporates yielded 7.25 percent.

The stock market. The stock market was inexplicably lethargic in the third quarter. The Dow-Jones opened July at 928.66, fell to 910.45, rose to 973.51 in August, and then declined to 953.27 at the quarter's end. Once again, the only thing that was able to lift prices out of their doldrums was any rumor of peace in Vietnam.

Volume was also low. On only 21 days were more than 15 million shares traded, and on no day did volume exceed 20 million. HERMAN E. KROOSS

BARBADOS. Religion. The Anglican Church helped to give nationalism a rude jolt when 35-year-old Drexel Gomez of the Bahamas was appointed bishop of Barbados. The Anglican Synod, composed of clergy and laymen, had twice failed to select a Barbadian clergyman as bishop under the rules which demanded a two-thirds vote of both clergy and laity in favor of a candidate. The impasse agitated the whole country, in which religion plays a large part, there being a minister of government in charge of ecclesiastical affairs; furthermore, only in 1969 was the church disestablished. The matter was passed to the Right Reverend Alan Knight, who is both archbishop of the West Indies and bishop of Guyana, and he called a meeting of the Provincial Synod, which then appointed the Reverend Drexel Gomez.

Public and press were incensed, it was suggested that the government refuse to grant the new bishop a work permit, and several clergymen proposed that a government committee be appointed to sound the views of the clergy. There was talk of boycotting the consecration ceremony, but it took place quietly, and the new bishop has become so popular that one newspaper, strongly against him at first, has referred to "an Anglican revival."

Other developments. The largest award for libel ever handed down in a Barbadian court was given against a weekly newspaper, the *Democrat,* which is the organ of the ruling Democratic Labour Party, and against its former editor, who is now speaker of the Barbados House of Assembly. The case arose from an article which appeared in September 1971, just before Prime Minister Errol W. Barrow and his party were returned to power in the general election. The article attacked two lawyers standing for election for the opposition Barbados Labour Party, claiming that they were unfit to hold public office. It received much publicity, as the prime minister distributed copies of the paper by plane at various points on the island. One of the lawyers, who was defeated in a surprise victory by a newcomer to the ruling party, was awarded US$15,000, and the other lawyer was given US$17,500.

Barbadians, often said to be more reserved than the English, broke with tradition in menswear when the prime minister and members of his party appeared at the opening of Parliament not in coat and tie but in "shirtjacs." In January the speaker of the House doffed his usual wig and gown. Since then several firms and organizations have officially instructed their employees that collar and tie are not necessary and they may appear in garb more suited to the tropics.

Area and population. Area, 166 sq. mi. Pop. (est. 1971), 300,000. Bridgetown (cap.), 92,000.

Government. Independent state in the Commonwealth of Nations. Prime min., Errol W. Barrow; gov. gen., Sir Winston Scott.

Finance. Monetary unit, Eastern Caribbean dollar; EC$1 = US$0.50. Revenue (est. 1971–1972), US$50.2 million; expenditure, US$53 million.

Trade (1970–1971). Exports, US$41 million; imports, US$122.3 million.

Education (1970). Enrollment: primary, 42,216; secondary, 16,272; technical, 1,121; university (1971), 550. C. G. LINDO

BELGIUM. Politics and government. In November 1971, Belgian premier Gaston Eyskens called early elections to receive a firm mandate for completing a sweeping program of constitutional reform and applying drastic economic measures, which appeared necessary at that time in view of the international monetary crisis. The election results made it possible for him to continue at the head of a Christian Social–Socialist coalition cabinet, sworn in January 21.

In accordance with the newly reformed constitution, both national communities (Flemish-speaking Flemings and French-speaking Walloons) were represented in the cabinet on a 50–50 basis. Eyskens, a Catholic Fleming, was seconded by a Socialist Walloon, André Cools, as vice-premier; the Economic Affairs Ministry went to the French-speaking

PAUL-HENRI SPAAK, the Belgian statesman who devoted his career to the cause of European unification and cooperation, died in July at the age of 73. A former prime minister and lifelong Socialist, he helped forge the UN charter and the NATO alliance.

UPI

Socialist Henri Simonet, and a Flemish Catholic, Andries Vlerick, became head of the Treasury Department.

As a further expression of Belgium's will to transform itself into a "regionalized" state, two cultural councils were created (one Flemish-speaking, one French-speaking), giving shape to the principle of cultural autonomy for the two national groups. The same principle was applied to the country's economic life.

While these reforms went a long way toward eliminating intercommunity friction in this bicultural state, there was growing awareness, mainly in business circles, that this multiplicity of institutions might endanger the efficient working of the state.

In Parliament, a Socialist member proposed a reform of Belgium's strict abortion law, but it met with strong opposition from the medical profession. The National Medical Council insisted that the law banning abortion except on medical grounds remain unchanged, and Parliament buried the proposal under other business.

The government, conscious of the growing threat to the environment, especially in the industrialized north, proclaimed the principle that in matters of ecological protection "the polluter pays." It announced a five-year plan for protecting surface waters, calling for purifying plants on the Albert Canal, linking Antwerp with Liège, and along the North Sea coast. Experts found that the Scheldt River, originating in France and reaching the sea through the port of Antwerp, had become an "open sewer," but industries in the Antwerp region, anticipating more stringent legislation, moved to build facilities for treating their wastes, and it was confidently predicted that the river would be "alive" again within ten years.

Economic developments. The economy, after a slowdown in the first half of the year, took an upward turn by summer's end. Export orders, vital to a country where about half of the working population produces for the world market, picked up again, and home demand also grew. The government continued its ambitious program of road building and public investments, and private industry was expected to join this trend early in 1973. Inflation, compared with the loss of monetary values in other member states of the European Common Market, remained minimal. Yet, by the end of the year, Belgians had digested a series of drastic price increases, ranging from doubled telephone rates to higher taxes on motor fuel and an increase in university fees.

In September, the state-owned Sabena Airlines decided on drastic cuts in expenditure. Its staff of 10,000 was scheduled to be reduced by 7 percent, and several short-haul services inside Europe were scrapped. Plans for buying a supersonic Concorde aircraft were canceled. These far-reaching economies were made necessary by some ten consecutive years of mounting losses, culminating in an estimated $40 million deficit at the end of the year.

Foreign affairs. Belgium continued its traditional policy of promoting European integration. The country had its share of the worldwide terrorist wave when a Sabena aircraft was hijacked on a run to Tel Aviv on May 8, and an Israeli embassy official was seriously injured by an unknown Arab in a Brussels café on September 17.

Foreign Minister Pierre Harmel engineered an agreement with Iceland securing continued fishing rights for the Belgian fleet within the newly proclaimed 50-mile territorial limit.

At the European Court for Human Rights in Strasbourg, France, however, the Belgian state suffered a defeat when the court accepted a complaint submitted by three vagrants who had been deprived of normal appeal facilities after being interned under the Vagrancy Act. The court established that any Belgian magistrate could order the internment of homeless, unemployed persons who had been found by the police or who had turned to the authorities for help themselves. The three plaintiffs claimed that they had been wrongfully deprived of their liberty and had been barred from appealing to a higher judge. When their claim was allowed, the Belgian government immediately revised the application of the Vagrancy Act.

Death of Spaak. On July 31, Belgium lost its elder statesman, lifelong Socialist Paul-Henri Spaak, who died at the age of 73 in Brussels. Spaak acquired a worldwide reputation as the first president of the United Nations General Assembly (1946), as secretary-general of the North Atlantic Treaty Organization (1957–1961), which he helped create, and as one of the founding fathers of the Common Market.

Area and population. Area, 11,779 sq. mi. Pop., 9.6 million.
Government. Constitutional monarchy with bicameral parliament. Head of state, King Baudouin; prime min., Gaston Eyskens; for. min., Pierre Harmel.
Finance. Monetary unit, Belgian franc; 1 Belgian franc = US$0.0227. Budget (1972): balanced at $8.6 billion. Gross national product: $31.5 billion.
Trade (Belgium-Luxembourg Economic Union, 1971). Exports, $13.4 billion; imports, $13.9 billion. Principal exports: iron and steel, rolling stock, textiles, machinery and industrial equipment, chemicals.
Education (1971). Enrollment: universities, 81,000; secondary and technical schools, 728,000; elementary schools, 1,023,670.
Armed forces. Total strength of army, navy, air force, and state police: 114,275.
                                                    HENRI SCHOUP

BIOCHEMISTRY. Interest in biochemistry during the past year focused on the study of cell membranes; the search for a human cancer virus; a new hormonal system, the prostaglandins; and the concept of chalones.

Membranes. The decade of the 1970's may well bring the same kind of advances in our understanding of membranes as the 1950's brought to protein structure and the 1960's brought to DNA (deoxyribonucleic acid, the basic genetic material). Membranes are the envelopes which surround cells; because a cell gets all its nourishment and reacts with its environment through the membrane, an understanding of exactly how membranes work is basic to the understanding of biochemical processes.

The original model for membrane structure was proposed by James F. Danielli and H. Davson in the 1930's (see drawing). A membrane was assured to be a "lipid bilayer" or "bimolecular leaflet" in which the lipid molecules arranged themselves with their hydrophilic (water-seeking) "heads" on the outside and their hydrophobic (water-excluding) "tails" on the inside of the membrane. Although this model has long been accepted as essentially correct, it has been clear for some time that it was too simple to explain how membranes perform their great variety of known functions.

Cell membranes contain protein molecules in addition to lipid molecules, and biochemists have begun to investigate the role of these protein molecules in the functioning of the cell membrane. The proteins associated with membranes may be divided into two types, according to their distribution within the membrane. S. J. Singer of the University of California, San Diego, has labeled the two types peripheral and integral. The peripheral proteins, although they may perform important membrane functions, are essentially just stuck on the surface of the membrane and can be washed off with a mild buffer solution or chelating agents. More important structurally and functionally are the integral pro-

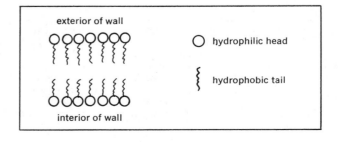

exterior of wall

○ hydrophilic head

{ hydrophobic tail

interior of wall

teins, which are embedded in the lipid bilayer. Experiments with human red blood cells have provided important insights into the actual distribution of these integral proteins.

One technique for isolating integral proteins is "freeze-etching," in which the cells are frozen and then fractured with a microtome knife. Some of the frozen water is then sublimed off, leaving behind an "etched" surface. This surface is shadow-cast with a metal and examined with an electron microscope.

This technique usually splits the membrane along its interior hydrophobic face; the resulting surface consists of a rather smooth background with some distinct particles dispersed at random on the background. Singer and his coworkers have shown that these particles are indeed protein and appear to be randomly spaced throughout the cell membrane.

Further investigation has shown that the protein protrudes all the way through the membrane, so that the hydrophilic portions of a single protein molecule can be found on both the inside and outside surfaces of the membrane, while its hydrophobic portions are found in contact with the hydrophobic parts of the lipid molecules on the inside of the membrane. Singer has also proposed that the protein molecule is not rigidly fixed and has called the model the "fluid mosaic" model of membrane structure.

The usefulness of a scientific model lies in the number of properties it can explain and the number of experiments it suggests for testing predictions based on the model. One such prediction based on the fluid mosaic model may shed some light on the nature of cancerous cells. Normal cells, growing in a culture, stop growing when the surface of the culture is just covered with cells and the cells begin to touch each other—that is, when a cellular monolayer is achieved. This phenomenon is called contact inhibition of cell growth. Cancer cells, however, do not show this contact inhibition; the cells overrun the monolayer and pile up several cells thick, in the uncontrolled growth that is characteristic of cancer cells.

The fluid mosaic model would explain the difference in behavior by saying that normal cells have the sites or molecules responsible for contact inhibition distributed relatively uniformly throughout the membrane, causing the necessary repulsions over the whole surface of the cell. In a malignant cell, however, the molecules which confer the contact inhibition would tend to cluster in small regions, leaving large areas of the cell free to contact other cells and thus allowing the characteristic buildup shown by cancerous cells.

It is clear that membranes are going to continue to be studied intensely in the next few years and that our knowledge of the complexity of membrane function is going to be matched by development of an equally complicated model for the structure of the membrane.

Human cancer virus. The link between cancer and viruses continues to be explored, with the evidence increasingly indicating that at least some kinds of cancer in humans can be caused directly by a virus. In particular, Donald W. Kufe, Rudiger Hehlmann, and Sol Spiegelman of the Institute of Cancer Research, Columbia University, have shown that RNA isolated from certain human breast cancers shows extreme similarity to the RNA (ribonucleic acid) of the virus known to cause leukemias in mice. It is known that in mice the viruses which cause breast tumors work in conjunction with a leukemia-causing virus to produce the breast cancer. The discovery of a similar virus (identified by its similar RNA) in human breast cancer supports the idea of a similar mechanism for the human case. As these workers point out, however, the experiments are not conclusive.

Prostaglandins. The past year saw vastly expanded interest in the subject of prostaglandins. The body produces a great variety of different prostaglandins. The quantities produced are quite small, but nonetheless prostaglandins appear to have a large variety of biological functions. Several important new uses for these materials were uncovered during the past year.

One of the problems associated with using blood platelets for treatment of hemorrhage and in radiation therapy is that platelets from whole blood do not keep very well, and thus fresh donors are needed to provide an adequate supply. However, it was discovered that addition of prostaglandin E_1 to the freshly drawn blood permitted storage of the platelets for several days with only a small loss in effectiveness. There do not appear to be any harmful effects to other blood components from the small amounts of prostaglandin E_1 used.

Another area of research involving prostaglandins is fertility control. It is possible, in laboratory animals, to induce abortions early in pregnancy by injection of the appropriate prostaglandin; the uterus is made to contract and expel the conceptus. The application of this technique to humans on other than an experimental basis is still a long way off, and it will have to wait for the development of prostaglandins that limit the side effects, which have included nausea, vomiting, diarrhea, racing or irregular heartbeat, headache, low blood pressure, and collapse.

Prostaglandins may also have something to do with the long-mysterious action of aspirin in relieving pain. Cells in inflamed areas are known to produce prostaglandins, and it appears that aspirin and similar drugs in the bloodstream effectively inhibit the formation of prostaglandins.

Chalones. A concept with a promising future is the chalone. A chalone is postulated to be an endocrine type of material existing in mature cells for the purpose of inhibiting or regulating further growth or division of the cell. Cancerous cells, which grow and divide without control, are postulated to lack the capability to produce enough chalones to control division. This is an interesting theory, and there is general agreement that there are such substances, but there is as yet no substantive evidence for the existence of chalones. However, the usefulness of the concept and the easy demonstration of "chalone activity" in preparations from whole cells mean that the concept will receive increasing attention in the future.

See also MEDICINE.   EDWIN S. WEAVER

BIOLOGY. Biological clocks. It is of vital importance to many organisms that they should be able to determine the time of day. This need is fulfilled by a "clock" which runs with a fairly precise 24-hour period and which can determine such processes as emergence and diapause—a sort of hibernation—in insects and flowering in plants. Until recently, little has been known of the nature of the clock or of its apparent insensitivity to temperature changes, but work by Arthur Winfree, of the University of Chicago, shows that the clock can be regarded as a 24-hour oscillator.

Winfree used a system that has been examined by Colin Pittendrigh, formerly at Princeton University and now at Stanford University. If pupal fruit flies are kept in the dark they emerge as adults after about 96 hours, but if they are transferred from light to dark, they emerge in groups with a periodicity of 24 hours, which implies that there is some 24-hour clock in control. If the insects are given a single pulse of light at some point after being placed in darkness, the rhythm is shifted, and emergence starts at a different time but with the same 24-hour periodicity. The effect of the light pulse depends both on its duration and on the lapse of time between transfer from light to dark and the stimulus pulse. Light pulses given between 17 and 21 hours after the beginning of darkness shift the rhythm two hours either way, and the pulse duration is not critical; however, at six hours after the onset of darkness, the rhythm can be shifted 12 hours by a ten-second pulse but is unaffected by a 100-second pulse. By a series of experiments of this type, Winfree was able to predict that there should be a critical combination of pulse length and timing that would cause randomization of the insects' clocks and result in a population

IT'S A WISE MOUSE that knows its own mother—at least in Tennessee's Oak Ridge Laboratory, where scientists developed a method for extracting mouse embryos, storing them, and implanting them in surrogates. The method may be applied to livestock.

that emerged at random. Indeed, there was a critical combination, which turned out to be a 50-second pulse given 6.8 hours after the pupal flies were placed in darkness.

If a population that has had its clocks randomized by the critical combination of stimuli is given a second light pulse, emergence takes place with a series of single peaks at 24-hour intervals. If the clocks had not been stopped but had been reset at random, theory predicted that emergence should occur with two daily peaks, so the critical pulse must stop the clock. Winfree's experiments therefore establish that the insects' clocks have the properties of an oscillator and not those of an interval timer, as had been suggested by Anthony Lees, of the Imperial College of Science and Technology, London.

The nature of the clock is not known, but other experiments by Winfree show that the light sensitivity of the clock increases as the pupae age, which suggests that bleaching of some photosensitive pigment may be important. Raising the temperature causes resetting of the clocks but does not upset the 24-hour rhythm, which suggests that biochemical processes are involved.

These oscillator clocks appear also in plants and fungi. J. M. Kinet of the University of Liège has shown that white mustard, which normally flowers in conditions of long days and short nights, can be inhibited by a single exposure to an eight-hour day or by two hours of darkness late in the normal long day. The plants are insensitive to the short day if it occurs out of step with the preceding long days, which demonstrates that there is a 24-hour clock.

Solar navigation by birds. There has been considerable argument about how pigeons find their home roosts. Mechanisms involving the sun's altitude, the sun's change of altitude, Coriolis forces, and terrestrial magnetism have all been proposed to explain this phenomenon. The technique of taking birds away from the roost, releasing them, and estimating their direction of departure is expensive, inaccurate, and inconclusive. A recent technique of operant training used by A. Whiten of the University of Bristol overcomes these problems. The birds were trained to peck keys arranged in a circle around them and were rewarded when they pecked the key that pointed toward home. Therefore, when the birds were taken north, they pecked the south-facing key.

When the birds were taken north—but the apparent altitude of the sun was changed to that of a position south of home by means of a prism—the birds reacted as if they had been taken south. Then, in the laboratory the birds considered home, artificial suns were set up with arcs corresponding to solar arcs visible at positions away from home; the birds reacted as if they had been moved from home to the spots indicated by the artificial suns. In this way, Whiten demonstrated the importance of solar position in the homing behavior of pigeons.

How the pigeons perceive and use this solar information is not clear, but a fairly accurate clock is required. Pigeons can also navigate in overcast conditions, but their performance is seriously affected by altering the magnetic field, as William Keeton of Cornell University has shown. Even in sunny conditions, inexperienced pigeons or pigeons released far from home are upset if magnets are glued to their backs. So it is likely that pigeons use a variety of cues in their homing, with the importance of each depending on the weather conditions.

A contractile rubber in protozoa. The stalks of various ciliated protozoa contain a contractile thread, or spasmoneme, which is used to pull the animal away from danger. This thread is a rubbery rod of protein and shows neither the structure of muscle nor the dependence on adenosine triphosphate or magnesium that is found in other contractile systems.

One species of ciliate, found in colonies of several thousand individuals, is so large that the contractile thread can be extracted and manipulated. Torkel Weis-Fogh and W. B. Amos of the University of Cambridge have used these "giant" threads—they are 1/25 of an inch long and 1/800 of an inch in diameter—to find out how contraction takes place. If the thread is moved from a solution containing no calcium to one with calcium, the thread either contracts or, if it cannot contract, develops tension; at the same time, the molecular structure becomes less highly organized. When the calcium is removed, the rod extends. Weis-Fogh and Amos suggest that without calcium the protein of the thread forms cross-links into the ordered extended state, but when calcium is added the cross-links break and the thread returns to the random contracted state.

Most striking is the speed of contraction. High-speed movies of protozoa show that contraction takes 1/200 of a second and that the thread contracts 50 percent in this time, which gives the protozoa a contraction speed about ten times faster than the contraction speed of muscle. A simple organism does not have to be slow.

Symbiosis: Who benefits? There are many associations between organisms that are not obviously advantageous to either party. Lichens and corals both contain photosynthetic algae, and both live in environments that are well lit but poor in nutrient materials.

When corals are kept in the light in seawater with radioactive carbon sources, the carbon is incorporated into a variety of fatty acids and sugars by the algae and is then released into the surrounding animal cells. Robert K. Trench of the University of California at Los Angeles has estimated that half the algal photosynthetic products are passed to the animal. The algae also produce the amino acid alanine, which subsequently appears in the protein of the animal, so the symbiosis is of real benefit to the animal.

If algae are cultured outside their host coral, they retain organic compounds; but if extracts of host cells are added to the culture, the algae release the compounds within a few hours. The host clearly can exert some control over the alga as a result of the symbiosis, and extracts from corals that do not normally contain algae do not cause release of organic compounds, so there is a close biological association in the system.

Other experiments by D. H. Lewis and D. C. Smith, working at the University of the West Indies Marine Labora-

tory, Jamaica, showed that algae release amino acids if they are provided with a substrate of ammonium chloride. Thus, they may make use of the nitrogenous waste products of the host cells. This finding bears out a suggestion made in the 1930's made by the British marine biologist Maurice Yonge.

Trench, Lewis, and Smith have studied a stranger symbiotic relationship. Various sea slugs feed on marine algae and retain intact chloroplasts from the algal cells. The chloroplasts are kept in branches of the digestive system of the slug, giving it a brilliant green color. When exposed to light, the chloroplasts photosynthesize and release their products to the animal.

Chloroplasts contain their own nucleic acid, and it has been suggested that their presence in plant cells arose as a form of symbiosis. This view is supported by the work of K. L. Giles, formerly of the British Department of Scientific and Industrial Research, and V. Safaris, of Massey University, New Zealand, who isolated marine algal chloroplasts and cultured them in white of egg, where they survived for many days. In the light, the chloroplasts photosynthesized, retained their chlorophyll, synthesized nucleic acids, and, most importantly, divided for the first five days of the experiment. This finding is the first evidence that chloroplasts can survive and grow outside the plant cell. Meanwhile, the sea slug seems well on its way to establishing a suitable environment for chloroplast culture and eventually becoming the first photosynthesizing animal.

HENRY C. BENNET-CLARK

BOLIVIA. Political and economic uncertainties prevailed throughout Bolivia during most of this year. Colonel Hugo Banzer Suárez, the president of a military-dominated coalition, survived repeated threats from both the right and the left. He remains in power, although not securely so, with dissension rife even within the military and his own party, as well as among Castroite guerrillas and a broad spectrum of other groups. On the positive side, economic ties with neighboring countries were strengthened, the activities of the Soviet diplomatic staff were curtailed sharply, and plans for the development and diversification of production were announced.

Internal affairs. Banzer heads an uneasy coalition of former enemies in both the armed forces and the political parties. Although the military brought him to power in a coup last year, they themselves are not united. The most outspoken critic of this relatively depersonalized technocratic administration is Colonel Andres Selich, the former minister of the interior, whom peasants around Cochabamba declared their leader, the successor to the late president René Barrientos Ortuño. As leader of the Rangers, a modern regiment trained in U.S. methods of combatting guerrilla warfare that defeated the guerrilla National Liberation Army (ELN), Selich is a colorful and popular hero resented by his colleagues. Relieved of his position in the Interior Ministry, he was named ambassador to Paraguay. But in May he was dismissed and charged with plotting to oust Banzer and make himself dictator. He is supported by Barrientos' followers in the Bolivian Revolutionary Front, but frequent arrests of leaders have weakened that party. Other top-level army officers, including the commander-in-chief, Colonel Federico Arana Serrudo, were retired abruptly, often without pensions, ostensibly for being "soft on Communism."

The two political parties that are within the ruling coalition, the Nationalist Revolutionary Movement (MNR) and the Bolivian Socialist Falange (FSB), are rent by internal dissension. The founders of the MNR, former presidents Victor Paz Estenssoro and Hernán Siles Zuaso, have been repudiated by younger Bolivians for having been *caudillos* and treating the party as personal fiefs. Their traditional base of popular support among the peasantry has also been eroded. MNR has none of the vitality that characterized its 12-year incumbency after the 1952 revolution. MNR's

traditional opposition, the FSB, is also weakened by factionalism and by a scandal in which one of its high officials stole national funds.

Successive reshufflings of the cabinet reflect Banzer's suspicions of his colleagues. Despite public announcements that detention camps in the Amazon lowlands have been closed, opposition members continue to disappear and hundreds are said to be political prisoners.

The Castroite ELN has variously been reported as having been decimated, posing an imminent threat, and being prepared to shift to urban guerrilla tactics. Many of its members have probably been killed and imprisoned. Relations with the Roman Catholic Church are strained because some churchmen have allegedly aided the ELN. Soldiers have searched convents, sometimes uncovering caches of arms, and several priests and nuns have been arrested.

Strict control of the press has created an atmosphere in which rumors flourish and few have confidence in what they hear. The universities have been closed since Banzer came to power.

Foreign affairs. Mounting anti-Communist sentiment, encouraged by the government, culminated in April in the expulsion of 119 members of the Soviet Embassy. The government claimed that the embassy was financing rebel groups. However, diplomatic relations were maintained, and technical assistance continued.

Relations with Chile have been cool ever since Bolivia lost its coastline in the War of the Pacific at the end of the nineteenth century. Banzer accused Chile of encouraging Bolivian Communists to emigrate there in order to plot his overthrow. Uruguay is also said to be the staging area for another leftist plot against Banzer.

On the other hand, Banzer visited Paraguay, where he and another military man, General Alfredo Stroessner, the president of Paraguay, issued a joint statement condemning the extension of territorial waters as prejudicial to landlocked countries such as their own. Economic ties with neighboring countries, especially with Brazil, were strengthened.

Finally, a naturalized Bolivian, Klaus Altmann, was "exposed" as Klaus Barbie, the notorious wartime head of the Nazi Gestapo in France. Even when he confessed to being Barbie, he still denied wrongdoing, and Bolivia has not acceded to France's request for extradition.

Economic affairs. Bolivia experienced economic difficulties and continued its traditional dependence on foreign aid. Since the expiration of a contract with a U.S. firm, the state mining corporation (COMIBOL) has been having trouble selling its lead, silver, cadmium, and zinc. The Soviet technical assistance mission recommended building a zinc refinery and exploiting nonmetallic minerals such as asbestos, borax, kaolin, mica, and phosphates. The World Bank delayed a loan for the development of the Mutún iron deposits, which are near the Brazilian border and far from transportation, because no foreign investors expressed interest. The government tried with little success to renew confidence in the private sector by such measures as the effective denationalization of the large Matilde tin mine.

The state oil company (YPFB) claimed success in the Soviet-aided exploration for oil on the *altiplano*, but seismic tests and drilling next year will determine whether the strike is significant. Peru offered to buy crude petroleum, which Bolivia has had difficulty in selling since the Bolivian Gulf Oil Company was nationalized in 1969; in June, Brazil started buying 12,000 barrels of oil a day. In April the Santa Cruz–Yacuiba pipeline began carrying natural gas for sale to Argentina. The national development corporation (CBF) announced plans to build a plant for processing vegetable oils in Tarija, and the government expects to improve facilities for generating and transmitting electricity.

The Inter-American Development Bank will help finance a microwave network linking the major cities and an im-

Fake!

From a Mediterranean island to a Pennsylvania prison, the saga of Clifford Irving unreeled before the public with all the intrigue of the latest thriller. At first almost everyone believed Irving's tale that he had met Howard Hughes, wormed a life story out of the billionaire recluse, and, under instructions, opened a Swiss bank account for deposit of the checks written to Hughes by McGraw-Hill, prospective publisher of the "autobiography." But Irving later admitted that the "H. R. Hughes" who opened the account and cashed the checks was his own wife, Edith, and the Irvings pleaded guilty to charges of larceny and conspiracy for their role in the great Hughes hoax.

proved highway connecting La Paz with its airport, El Alto. In April, Brazil's president, Emílio Garrastazú Médici, promised technical and financial aid for such infrastructure development projects as road and railroad construction in the jungle area, low-cost housing, and bridges across some of the rivers that form the frontier between the two nations. Since the middle of 1971, Brazil has extended officially $13.5 million and has also sent military and technical assistance.

Area and population. Area, 424,162 sq. mi. Pop. (est. 1971), 4,931,000. Principal cities (est. 1970): La Paz (de facto cap.), 562,000; Cochabamba, 149,900; Santa Cruz, 124,900; Sucre (legal cap.), 84,900.
Government. Unitary republic. Head of state, Col. Hugo Banzer Suárez; for. min., Mario Gutiérrez Gutiérrez.
Finance. Monetary unit, peso; 1 peso = US$0.085.
Trade (1969). Imports, US$167 million, mainly food staples, motor vehicles, mining equipment, iron and steel products; exports, US$181 million, mainly tin, petroleum, silver, tungsten, antimony, copper. Major trading partners: United States, West Germany, Japan, Andean Common Market.
Education (1970). Enrollment: primary schools, 661,423; secondary schools, 192,435; technical and vocational schools, 11,491.
Armed forces (1969). Army, 17,000; air force, 2,200.

DWIGHT B. HEATH

BOOK PUBLISHING. Economics. For American book publishers this year was one of cautious optimism. The economic recession of 1970, the cutbacks in federal school library funding of the late 1960's, the rising production costs, and the absorption of smaller houses by large conglomerates had all been weathered. Although there were gloomy spots in the picture, this year's slogan could well have been, "Look, we've come through!"

Especially bullish were the paperback publishers, who began throwing their financial muscle around in the marketplace. Avon reported a 12 percent increase in sales in 1971 and continuing progress in 1972; Dell broke all records in 1971; Pocket Books had an increase of 20 percent. Statistics being what they are in the book industry, the full performance of 1972 will not be known until well into 1973. However, a straw in the wind—Bantam Books reported a record net income of $3,108,000 for the first half of 1972, compared to $2,644,000 in the same period in 1971.

A major factor in the increased take was a hike in cover prices. Publishers found they could charge $1.25–$1.65 and up for a paperback and the public would pay. (Between 1967 and 1971 the average price of a paperback book had risen 33⅓ percent.) The only danger signal noticed by some publishers was a somewhat higher rate of returns, which, it was thought, reflected a possible public rebellion against the high prices. Nobody knew for sure; in the meantime, bids for paperback reprint rights to hard-cover best sellers were monotonously in six figures, and sometimes seven—Fawcett paid more than $1 million for the rights to James Michener's novel *The Drifters*. In addition, Avon acquired reprint rights to *I'm O.K.—You're O.K.* for $1 million and rights to *Jonathan Livingston Seagull* for more than $1 million (based on a minimum sale of 3 million copies).

Prestigious authors were quick to jump on the gravy train, threatening the long-standing contractual arrangement whereby the author and his hard-cover publisher split paperback royalties 50–50. Philip Roth parted company with Random House and went to Holt, Rinehart and Winston because he wanted better paperback terms. And that steady best-seller producer Irving Wallace signed a $2.5 million contract for four books with Bantam, under which he will receive full paperback royalties; Bantam, in turn, sold hard-cover rights to Wallace's books to Trident, thus reversing its traditional role as reprinter.

Original publishing was becoming a significant tendency among the paperback houses. Avon, long a pioneer in this area, issued all original titles in a single month in 1972. What this meant for hard-cover publishers was increased competition for hot literary properties. Of course, the higher

advances being paid by the paperback houses still flowed into their treasuries under the traditional 50–50 arrangement, and that could not help but brighten their finances. Still there was much talk of hard-cover–only publishers entering the mass-market paperback fields themselves. As one publisher put it: "If this goes on—and alas it will—I can see a situation three to five years from now when we're all going to be in the paperback business."

Another indirect financial windfall to the traditional houses was the robust prosperity of the book clubs, which were also flinging about large advances. Book-of-the-Month Club's net sales, for example, were $25,642,190 for the six months ended December 31, 1971, compared to $21,039,692 for the same period in 1970. This, too, caused concern, as publishers wondered if the clubs with their cheaper prices were cutting into bookstore sales.

With all the multimedia, big-money wheeling and dealing going on, publishers, who live on subsidiary rights sales, felt a subtle pressure toward the so-called big book and away from literary merit. To the hard-cover publishers this trend meant that the middling author, the first novelist, and the quality work of fiction were becoming increasingly precarious economically. Perhaps the ultimate in big-book psychology was reached with the Howard Hughes "autobiography" (*see* AMERICAN LITERATURE); with subsidiary rights sales to Fawcett, *Life,* and Book-of-the-Month, McGraw-Hill, the would-be publisher, stood to make a tidy profit before the book was out, even with an advance of $750,000 to the putative Mr. Hughes and his imaginative "collaborator," Clifford Irving. That incident seemed to sum up all the best and a good deal more of the worst of the frenetic publishing money game.

Nonetheless, overall book sales (and book prices) continued merrily upward. In 1963 total sales were $1.5 billion; the estimate for 1972 was upward of $3.2 billion, and total number of titles pushed past the 37,000 mark. Even textbook sales showed an increase of 4 percent in 1971, although this figure was nothing to crow about. In academe, however, the situation continued to be depressed, as the university presses slashed staffs and cut back on their lists. As the primary source of serious, noncommercial scholarly works, the university presses were indispensable, and any diminution in their activities would be a severe blow to American intellectual life.

Censorship. While generally counting their profits with satisfaction, publishers were becoming increasingly concerned about governmental censorship. Beacon Press, which published a version of the Pentagon Papers released by Senator Mike Gravel of Alaska, had its financial records examined by the FBI and faced a grand jury investigation that was later dropped, although it could presumably be revived. Such fishing expeditions into the financial waters of the Unitarian Universalist Association, which owns Beacon, posed threats to freedom of religion as well as freedom of the press. In another example of governmental hazing, the Central Intelligence Agency requested a prepublication review of Alfred W. McCoy's *The Politics of Heroin in Southeast Asia,* which was critical of the agency's role in the heroin traffic in that part of the world. Over McCoy's objections, Harper and Row gave in to the request, although no classified information was involved. The principle that a governmental agency shall have the right to preview for "inaccuracies" any book critical of it is dangerously close to prior restraint, and most bookmen agreed that Harper should not have complied. The book was published without changes, the CIA's criticisms of it having been "underwhelming" in the words of one Harper executive.

RICHARD R. LINGEMAN

BOTANY. Recent research in botany has included studies of the mechanisms of disease resistance in plants and of the ways in which hormonal systems control growth and mat-

uration in higher plants. Probably the most interesting developments have been with transport mechanisms; they are still largely unexplained, but the developments of the past year seem likely to lead to a fuller understanding of these essential processes.

Weltwitschia mirabilis: key to phloem transport? It is still not clear how sugars and other substances are transported in plants. A key to this problem comes from study of a very unusual plant found in the Namib Desert of coastal South West Africa. This plant, *Weltwitschia mirabilis,* has both one of the longest life spans and some of the longest leaves in the plant kingdom, and it differs markedly in both anatomy and physiology from other plants that are found in the desert.

The Namib Desert, the home of *Weltwitschia,* is one of the oldest and hottest deserts in the world. Its fauna include a beetle whose long legs keep its body above the scorching sand. The plant *Weltwitschia,* which is a gymnosperm and is related to conifers, lives in small colonies. Two leaves grow continuously throughout the life of the plant from the rim of a stem shaped rather like a turnip. In a 2,000-year-old plant the stem may be 4 feet high and 5 feet across, and the leaves may be 4 feet wide and 20 feet long. The leaves grow from the base at a rate of 3 to 6 inches each year and, at the free ends, are scorched where they touch the desert sand. Christopher Bornman of the University of Natal has been studying the life history and physiology of the plant. He finds that, unlike most plants of the desert, *Weltwitschia* has numerous stomata, or pores, on both sides of its leaves; although these stomata are protected, they are not in deep pockets. The root system is sparse and goes only about 6 feet deep in a plant 4 feet high; the sand is dry and probably does not supply much water —there is virtually no rain in the Namib Desert.

However, between dawn and about 10 A.M. there is often a coastal fog in the Namib, and then the humidity can be high. Over this part of the day, *Weltwitschia* opens its stomata and soaks up the fog. As the fog lifts and the air dries, the plant shuts up for the hot part of the day. It is the only plant that is known to collect water in this way, and if by chance there is less fog than usual, it may die. Most years have 50 to 100 foggy mornings, and the plants can survive under these conditions.

The conduction system differs from that of other plants. In most plants, the phloem cells lose the nucleus and contain a protein slime. In *Weltwitschia,* the phloem retains many features of more conventional cells, including the nucleus, mitochondria, and endoplasmic reticulum. There has been uncertainty about whether the phloem acts as a pipe for transport in plants or whether diffusion is more important. Any cell that contains cytoplasmic structures is most unlikely to act as a pipe, so it appears from Bornman's studies that botanists will have to discard theories of mass-flow phloem transport and look more closely at diffusion inside the cell.

How water moves in tall trees. The pressure produced at the root of a tree is only sufficient to force the sap a few feet into the air, but some plants grow over 300 feet high. The classical theory explaining this phenomenon was proposed in 1895 by Henry H. Dixon and John Joly of Trinity College, Dublin. The Irish researchers suggested that the tensile strength of the water in the xylem was sufficiently high to allow suction at the leaves to pull water up the tree. They supported this theory by measuring the tensile strength of water at many atmospheres. Since then, their theory has been widely accepted, but very little real evidence has appeared in its support, and certain observations are perplexing, including Dixon's own observation that water can move in the xylem down the tree and against the suction gradient.

A new theory proposes that instead of a pressure gradient up the tree there is a chemical energy gradient which allows the water column to be supported at a constant pressure and does not require vast suctions to be exerted. Robert C. Plumb and Wilbur B. Bridgeman of the Worcester Polytechnic Institute have made calculations which show that the hydrostatic pressures in a long vertical water column can be made constant if the chemical energy at the upper end is increased by solutes or active molecules. To work, the solute molecules must not move in the column, and the gradient can thus be maintained if the column is compartmented—as xylem vessels are.

If the active molecules were glucose polymers attached to the inner walls of the vessels, the concentration required would be about 1 percent in a 30-foot-high tree or 10 percent at the top of a 300-foot redwood. Plumb and Bridgeman imagine these filaments as forming a delicate gel-like mat in the xylem vessel which may be easily damaged in the course of conducting water; they point out that old vessels contain a feltlike mat at their upper ends and that most of the transport of water in tall trees follows a path up the outer, newer xylem vessels, which presumably have intact xylem gels.

The theory is attractive because it explains how tall trees can obtain water without active transport in the xylem and without large suction pressures, which would be hard to maintain and which would have to change during the life of the tree as it grew taller. The theory is as yet untested but is unlikely to remain so for long.

HENRY C. BENNET-CLARK

BOTSWANA. Government and politics. The government of Sir Seretse Khama and his ruling Botswana Democratic Party remained in firm control of the country in 1972. The problem of refugees and the danger that Botswana would become an international battleground diminished during the year, and the government concentrated on its many economic problems.

Economic developments. The economy remained highly vulnerable to adverse economic trends in South Africa; the steadily worsening inflation in that country constantly added to the cost of Botswana's development.

Nevertheless, Botswana's economic pace quickened in 1972, as the mining sector began to contribute more and more to the general picture. The Orapa diamond mine was put into production, and work began on the giant copper-nickel project at Selibe-Phikwe. Also of great importance for this generally arid country were the heavy rains early in the year, which made farming and ranching better than usual; near record numbers of cattle were brought to market.

An International Development Association credit of US$2 million and a Swedish government grant of $4 million were awarded Botswana to finance improvement of the road between Gaborone and Lobatse. The improved road will help both livestock and mining operations. Additional surveys indicated Botswana's potential in the area of coal production, with reserves at Morupule estimated at 150 million tons and those at Mnamabula, which are estimated at 408 million tons.

Although most of the people of Botswana are currently involved in subsistence agriculture and are earning less than $100 a year, the economic picture could brighten considerably in the years ahead, as more of the mining projects reach full production.

Area and population. Area, 231,805 sq. mi. Pop. (est. 1970), 648,000, including 4,000 persons of European descent. Principal cities (est. 1969): Gaborone (cap.), 14,000; Serowe, 37,000.
Government. Independent republic within Commonwealth of Nations. Pres., Sir Seretse Khama.
Finance. Monetary unit, South African rand; 1 R = US$1.29. Budget (fiscal year ended March 31, 1970): revenue, R21,404,000; expenditure, R20,394,000.
Trade. Primary exports: cattle products and asbestos.
Armed forces. None.   CHRISTIAN P. POTHOLM

OPENING UP THE JUNGLE. Jeeps carry construction workers along an unpaved portion of the 3,000-mile Trans-Amazon Highway. When completed, the road will open to settlement and exploitation a remote, unexplored jungle area half the size of the United States.

BRAZIL. Economic developments. This year, as Brazil marked its 150th anniversary as an independent nation, economic rather than political developments took center stage.

Late in 1971, President Emílio Garrastazú Médici announced an economic development plan to be implemented during his last three years in office, 1972–1974. The plan was designed to continue the nation's rate of economic growth, double the per-capita income by 1980, and make Brazil a fully developed industrial nation within a generation. Problems to receive special attention were those of illiteracy, backward agriculture, and the uneven distribution of income. Specific provision was made for investments, public and private, of $800 million each year to develop the northeast and the Amazon Basin. Expansion was programmed for the steel, petrochemicals, shipbuilding, highway construction, power, communications, and mining industries. Also, large-scale production of atomic fuels for Brazil's first nuclear power plant was planned.

The first of the president's goals—that of continuing the nation's rate of economic growth—was an ambitious one. In 1971, Brazil's gross national product (GNP) went up 11.3 percent to $40 billion. Although modest by world standards, this represented the largest increase since the nation began keeping statistics in 1947 and included an 11.2 percent increase in manufacturing, 12.8 percent in commerce, and 8.4 percent in transportation and communications. The automotive industry increased production by 24 percent in 1971; by the end of the year Brazil was making more vehicles than all the rest of Latin America, including Argentina and Mexico. In 1971, 516,067 units were produced. The textile industry, after slow growth in 1969 and 1970, also experienced a high growth rate in 1971. Two new petrochemical complexes were opened in São Paulo and Bahia. Agriculture grew 11.4 percent, mainly in the production of coffee, soybeans, cotton, and wheat. The growth rate this year was expected to be slightly lower than in 1971 but still a substantial 9 percent.

The cost of living, which rose 19.5 percent in 1971, was up 5 percent in the first quarter of 1972. It was expected to increase only 15 percent in all of 1972, a rate considered minimal by Brazilians.

In the first half of the year exports were up 33 percent over the same period in 1971 and were expected to reach $3.6 billion by the end of the year. In 1971, $2 billion of new capital entered the country and $1.371 billion left. The government's foreign currency reserves remained adequate.

During the year the government reduced the interest rates banks were permitted to charge, introduced an income tax withholding system, and eliminated taxes on industrial production of many processed foods. A special investment tax credit was introduced through which Brazilians could divert

12 percent of their income tax obligations into mutual funds. One of the results was a 250 percent increase in volume on the São Paulo stock exchange.

In September the first part of the Trans-Amazon Highway opened—750 miles of road (of a total of 3,000 miles) in the state of Pará. While the opening of this road was expected to greatly expand the economic development of the area, technicians were faced with problems in keeping some stretches open to traffic. The route had been selected through use of aerial photographs, but actual construction had brought surprises in the form of swamps and hills and rocky terrain. The cost of construction is already double the original calculation.

Also in September, President Médici presented to Congress a legislative proposal for agrarian reform along the important Rio de Janeiro–São Paulo Highway. This was the first time since the military take-over in 1964 that the administration had dared to bring agrarian reform to the industrial south of Brazil. Under the proposal owners of properties of from 2,470 acres to 12,350 acres would have to sell 20 percent of their lands to their sharecroppers, and owners of over 12,350 acres would have to sell 50 percent of their properties. Although causing a storm in the conservative-controlled Congress, this limited measure was sure of passage, for the Congress still acts on the president's wishes.

Politics and government. The principal hope of the opposition for an easing of the political controls exercised by the military-dominated administration centered in a constitutional provision calling for the direct election of state governors in 1974. In April, President Médici dashed this hope by sending a proposal to Congress asking for a change in the constitution to keep the indirect election of state governors in 1974. He indicated that this would be necessary in order to keep "a climate of tranquillity, confidence, and work indispensable to the consolidation of political and social institutions."

The nation's voters responded with great apathy to the municipal party conventions held throughout the country to select local leaders for the two legal political parties. Subsequent state-level party conventions of the majority party generally ratified slates submitted by the governors, who followed the president's instructions to include a majority of the governor's backers and representatives from the other wings of the party proportionate to their strength. The opposition party did little better, having a contested convention in only one state, São Paulo.

The only arena for direct political participation remained local elections for mayors and councilmen. These were scheduled on a nationwide basis for November. Here divergent wings of the dominant party could present separate slates and battle for power with relative freedom. The opposition party could also participate but was given little chance for widespread success.

Opposition to the regime was not lacking this year, but with the strict controls exercised by the police and military over "subversive" action, the government censorship of the press, and the general public willingness to be for the moment more concerned with economic rather than political activity, it was relatively silent. The battle between the Roman Catholic Church and the administration continued but on a more muted basis than in 1971.

Foreign affairs. Although still a debtor nation on the world scene, Brazil's economic surge recently permitted it to become a creditor nation in Latin America. Brazil gave a total of $70 million in aid to other Latin American countries, including Uruguay, Bolivia, Ecuador, Chile, Guyana, El Salvador, Costa Rica, Nicaragua, and Honduras. The Brazilians were also accused of having a hand in Hugo Banzer Suárez' successful take-over in Bolivia, ousting a relatively leftist military regime and replacing it with one more on the Brazilian model.

In May, Brazil and the United States signed an agreement regarding U.S. shrimp fishing fleet activities in Brazilian waters. Although neither side gave ground on the dispute over the 200-mile territorial limit, it was in fact the first break in the U.S. position on the subject; the agreement did permit regulation by the Brazilians of U.S. shrimp fishermen in an area beyond the U.S.-supported 12-mile limit.

While this agreement did reduce U.S.-Brazilian tensions over a hotly debated subject, it did little to assuage the fears of the Argentines that the United States had selected Brazil to be the key industrial nation of Latin America. In March, President Alejandro A. Lanusse of Argentina came to Brazil for talks with President Médici over two prime Argentine concerns—that nation's trade deficit with Brazil and Brazilian plans for hydroelectric and other projects in the up-river portions of the River Plata basin. The Argentines came away from the talks feeling that they had gained little.

Area and population. Area, 3,286,487 sq. mi. Pop. (1970), 92,-237,570. Brasília (cap.), 544,862; São Paulo, 5,901,533; Rio de Janeiro, 4,296,782; Recife, 1,078,819.
Government. Constitutional republic dominated by the military since 1964. Pres., General Emílio Garrastazú Médici.
Finance. Monetary unit, new cruzeiro; 1 new cruzeiro = US$0.1675.
Trade (1970). Exports, US$2.28 billion; imports, US$2.74 billion. Principal exports: coffee, sugar, cocoa, tobacco, iron ore, processed wood, prepared foods. Main imports: wheat, fuel and lubricants, machinery, chemicals. Principal trading partners: United States, West Germany, Argentina, United Kingdom, France, Italy, the Netherlands.
Education (1971). 53 universities, 13,000 median level schools, 135,000 primary schools. Enrollment (1968): primary, 11,943,506; secondary, 3,205,699; higher, 278,295.
Armed forces. Army, 120,000; navy, 40,600; air force, data not available.
PHYLLIS J. PETERSON

BRITISH COLUMBIA. Government and politics. Premier W. A. C. Bennett's Social Credit government was defeated by the New Democratic Party in the August 30 provincial election. In power for 20 years and nearly 72 years old, Bennett was personally reelected, even though his party lost. David Barrett, a 41-year-old former social worker first elected to the legislature in 1960, led his moderately socialist party through a low-key grass-roots campaign that took 38 seats in the 55-seat legislature, 25 of them from the Social Credits. British Columbia became the third Canadian province in three years to elect a New Democratic Party government. (The others were Manitoba in 1969 and Saskatchewan in 1971.)

The Liberals, who had five seats in the previous legislature, have five in the new one. They have a new leader, David Anderson, a federal Liberal member of Parliament, who became provincial Liberal leader after Dr. Patrick McGeer resigned the post. Anderson, who won a seat in the new legislature, was in the news for his fight in Washington, D.C., to stop the shipment of Alaska oil by tanker down the British Columbia coast because of the danger of oil spillage. The Progressive Conservatives' new leader, Derril Warren, failed to win a seat but planned to seek one in a by-election.

There were two important factors in Barrett's victory, the size of which surprised even his supporters. In many ridings (electoral districts), Progressive Conservative candidates drew votes from Social Credit to the advantage of the New Democratic Party candidates. The leadership of the Social Credit Party became a major issue in the last days of the campaign, when Rehabilitation Minister Phil Gaglardi allegedly stated in a newspaper interview that he was the only real choice as successor to Premier Bennett. Gaglardi, who denied the statement and sought legal action over it, lost the seat he had held since 1952.

Premier Barrett's first words on being elected were a tribute to Bennett "for the service he has given this province." After two decades of Bennett government, it was indeed the end of an era. Premier Barrett faced the task of

carrying out his preelection pledges to establish a guaranteed pension of $200 a month for senior citizens, provide a government-owned auto insurance plan, and reform provincial labor legislation.

Municipal affairs. Fred Quilt, a British Columbia Indian, died two days after he was picked up for drunkenness. Royal Canadian Mounted Police officers were exonerated at the inquest from allegedly beating up Quilt at the time of his arrest. Many Indians protested, and the provincial attorney general, Leslie Peterson, ordered a second inquest. At this inquest, the jury did not attribute blame to anyone and said the injury to Quilt had been applied by an unknown force and an unknown blunt object. Another British Columbia Indian, August Jack of Westholme, the province's oldest man, died at 107. Indians at Cape Mudge, Quadra Island, defeated by four votes a plan to incorporate their lands as Canada's first Indian municipality. Proponents of the scheme planned to try again.

Mayor Tom Campbell of Vancouver flayed opponents of the proposed third crossing of Burrard Inlet between Vancouver and the communities of North and West Vancouver. Alderman Art Phillips announced he would be a mayoralty candidate. Plans were approved to replace Vancouver's old Christ Church Cathedral with a high-rise office and a partially underground church.

A proposed 550-lot subdivision on Gabriola Island in the Strait of Georgia was rejected by the provincial cabinet after lengthy public hearings. At Prince Rupert, a multimillion-dollar fire destroyed a dock, fish cannery, and warehouses, but the National Harbors Board announced a plan to give Prince Rupert improved port facilities.

Economics. The province had labor problems. Prime Minister Pierre Trudeau called the federal Parliament into session to order British Columbia longshoremen to end a strike that halted prairie grain shipments through the province's ports. Woodworkers halted the forest industry until a new contract gave them increased pay. Civic workers of the Lower Mainland municipalities walked out to win increases. Strikes and lockouts crippled the province's construction industry until a provincial cabinet order referred the dispute to the British Columbia Mediation Commission for binding arbitration.

Despite labor difficulties and unemployment, the economic picture was brighter. Census figures showed British Columbia had the highest growth rate of any Canadian province. MacMillan and Bloedel Ltd., Canada's largest forestry company, showed earnings for the first half of 1972 more than double those of the first half of 1971. Other major companies also showed big increases in earnings. Afton Mines Ltd. discovered an ore body 10 miles from Kamloops that showed unusually high grades of copper, and this sparked much interest in the area. A new deep-sea terminal at Squamish heralded its becoming a major shipping center. Chetwynd looked forward to doubling its population after the announcement of a project for mining coal at a site 35 miles south of Chetwynd.

Education and culture. The Victoria city council voted to eliminate all billboards in the next three years. Engineering students at the University of British Columbia designed a car fueled by natural gas, which won the overall award for excellence at the urban vehicle design competition for North American universities at Ann Arbor, Mich. Justice Nathan T. Nemetz was elected chancellor of the University of British Columbia.

Area and population. Area, 366,255 sq. mi. Pop. (1971), 2,184,-621. Principal cities: Victoria (cap.; met. area, est. 1971), 195,800; Vancouver (met. area, est. 1972), 1,082,232.

Government. Lt. gov., John Nicholson; prem. and pres. of executive council, David Barrett; atty. gen., Alex MacDonald. Legislative assembly: New Democratic, 38; Social Credit, 10; Liberals, 5; Progressive Conservatives, 2.

Finance (est. 1972–1973). Revenue, Can$1,453,456,000; expenditures, $1,451,963,421.

Education (1970–1971). Public schools, 1,507; enrollment, 527,-106; teachers, 21,755. College and university enrollment (1971), 36,348. Total expenditure (est. 1972–1973), $448,671,000 (includes colleges and universities).   DAVID SAVAGE

BUILDING AND CONSTRUCTION INDUSTRIES. In perspective, the construction industry will be viewed as passing through a period of critical transition in 1972. It has emerged, owing to a combination of private and government efforts, from several years of rampant inflation into an atmosphere of stabilization that should continue through 1973.

But it was also a year of challenge, in which controversy was stirred by the federal government's new occupational safety and health regulations, a greater use of construction management services by public and private users, and government assaults on designers' professional ethics that prohibit competitive bidding. In other developments, construction users, subcontractors, and open shop contractors made the industry aware of their growing power in the building process.

The cost retreat. Although 1971 was the year the Nixon administration created the Construction Industry Stabilization Committee (CISC) to put a lid on wage inflation, it was not until this year that CISC's impact and that of the administration's later-imposed phase two price controls could accurately be measured. Results were encouraging, with cost inflation slowing considerably on labor, material, and machinery, paving the way for a faster real growth in construction volume in 1973.

After several months of reconciling his authority and practices with those of the new Pay Board, CISC chairman Dr. John Dunlop of Harvard has been successful in bringing increases in new construction wage agreements closer to the Pay Board guideline of 5.5 percent. According to the Labor Department's quarterly survey of union wage rate hikes for seven trades, the average increase for the 12 months ending July 13, 1972, was 6.5 percent, compared to 11.4 percent for the same period one year ago. When fringe benefits are included, the average increase was 7.3 percent, compared to 12.2 percent the year before. In terms of cents per hour, this reflected an average increase of 56.4 cents in wages and fringes, compared with 83.6 cents a year earlier. The sharpest downturn came for the plumbers' union, where the average hourly increase a year ago was $1.24, compared to this year's 54.8 cents. If this trend continues, the average wage increase for the construction trades is expected to be the lowest in about five years.

In addition to this considerable reduction in the size of new wage increases, the CISC's success in cutting back deferred increases in existing long-term contracts should help reduce the size of new settlements negotiated in 1973. Moreover, the CISC has sought to encourage wage agreements that cover broader geographic areas and a greater number of trades, to increase productivity, and to provide for common expiration dates, the absence of which has led to the leapfrog bargaining and whipsaw tactics that have produced numerous and costly strikes.

On the materials side of the cost inflation, phase two price controls were effective in curbing the rate of increase in the prices of such prime construction materials as cement and steel. The lone exception was lumber and plywood products; despite controls that covered virtually all firms in this industry, prices continued to climb, owing primarily to the home-building surge that continued longer into the year than most economists expected. However, an inevitable leveling off in new housing starts should bring prices lower in 1973, accompanied by a possible rollback in prices by lumber firms that find their widening profit margins in violation of Price Commission limitations.

Steel-product producers kept a lid on prices for much of the year, but with wage agreements tied in with cost-of-

A BIG BOOM IN BUILDING

City authorities blew up two 11-story apartment houses this spring as part of a $39 million renovation project designed to make St. Louis' massive Pruitt-Igoe apartment complex livable once again. Hailed as the ultimate in public housing when it was completed in 1954 for $36 million, the project was all but abandoned by 2,800 families unable to put up with poor maintenance, rising crime, and red tape.

living increases and with profit margins narrowing, some firms may have enough evidence by early 1973 to justify higher price quotes than could be approved by the Price Commission.

Another major construction expense, equipment and machinery, also showed signs of stabilized prices. A surge in new orders from manufacturers, and subsequent soaring profits for many equipment firms, should discourage any major price increases and, in fact, could lead to rollbacks by firms that violate profit ceilings. Equipment list prices, according to the Labor Department, increased an average of 3.5 percent in the year ending in July, compared to a 6.1 percent increase in the previous 12-month period.

A boon to profits. The stabilized cost situation has put many contractors back on a sound profit path after several years of shrinking profits and profit margins. This reverses the profit trend of the late 1960's and 1970, when no matter how fast revenues were increased, profits would slide as costs escalated even faster. The particularly dismal showing of many publicly owned contractors in 1970 prompted major organizational changes and tighter cost controls which this year began to bear fruit. Probably the best performance of the year will be shown by the major housing developers, who have benefited from the ready availability of mortgage funds. But just as important is an earnings turnaround for large industrial builders, who, having borne the brunt of a low demand for new facilities during the 1969–1970 recession, are showing signs of pulling out of the profit doldrums. Buoying their prospects is an expected 9.7 percent increase in capital expenditures this year over 1971, compared to an actual gain of 1.9 percent in 1971.

The industry in general should continue to benefit from the significant increase this year in the value of new construction contracts awarded. Supported by a 9 percent in-

crease in the value of residential building contracts, total construction contract value is expected to come close to the $86 billion level, or 8–9 percent higher than in 1971. Non-building contracts, on the strength of an expected upturn in highway-related and sewage and water supply contracts, are also expected to climb considerably from 1971 levels. In nonresidential building, contracts could reach the $28 billion level, sparked by a surge in store and shopping-center construction as a result of the housing boom. And just as important, perhaps the blunting of construction's cost spiral could mean a slight increase in the physical volume of new construction put in place.   ROGER JAMES HANNAN

BULGARIA. Foreign affairs. In May, the Presidium of the Supreme Soviet of the U.S.S.R. awarded the Order of Hero of the Soviet Union posthumously to Bulgarian general Vladimir Zaimov, who in May 1941, when Bulgaria was formally allied with the Axis powers, warned the Soviet Union that it would be attacked by Germany on June 22. Zaimov was later shot by the Germans. On June 1 ceremonies were held throughout Bulgaria honoring the 80th anniversary of Zaimov's birth and the 30th anniversary of his death.

Politics and government. In April, the Central Committee of the Bulgarian Communist Party and the State Council approved a decree providing for the organization of organs of state and people's control. These bodies are to ensure prompt implementation of party directives and of laws and other enactments and will study complaints of the people regarding any of these measures. They can also point out inefficient personnel, deliver reprimands to those at fault, and oblige them to give explanations.

A May decree of the Central Committee of the Bulgarian Communist Party provided for the further development of

technological and scientific creative work by youth, aiming at more active participation of the younger generation in building a socialist society. Young inventors, organized in local clubs for technological and scientific work, have solved a number of problems, saving the country over 170 million leva.

In June an international conference to mark the 90th anniversary of Georgi Dimitrov's birth opened at the National Assembly building in Sofia, attended by 113 Communist Party delegations from various parts of the world. Dimitrov was the pro-Stalin head-of-state who reorganized Bulgaria along Soviet lines in the late 1940's. The Dimitrov Prize was awarded to a number of foreigners "for their active participation in the people's struggle against the old society and for the victory of peace, democracy and social progress."

Economic developments. In April, a Soviet economic delegation arrived in Sofia. An agreement to further Bulgarian-Soviet economic integration was signed at the end of the visit.

Over 13,000 Bulgarian experts were reported working in the Soviet Union, helping to build projects that would be important for the Bulgarian national economy. After completing a long-distance gas pipeline now under construction, Bulgaria will be supplied annually with 13 billion cubic meters of Soviet natural gas. Other Soviet projects on which Bulgarian workers are employed include forestry, mining, and ore-processing operations. In June a Soviet-Bulgarian agreement was signed in Sofia regarding the delivery of equipment for the extension of the Burgas and Pleven oil-processing works. After the extension of the Burgas works an additional six million tons of Soviet oil will be processed annually.

Trade with the Soviet Union will increase by 10 percent in 1972 over 1971 to an amount of over 2.25 billion rubles.

A 38,000-ton collier was scheduled to be launched in 1972, beginning the serial production of this type of vessel. During the current sixth five-year plan (1971–1975) the Bulgarian merchant fleet will be increased by two 100,000-ton, one 70,000-ton, and two 50,000-ton tankers. Over a million tons of shipping vessels are built in Bulgarian yards annually. About 70 percent are exported, mostly to Poland, the Soviet Union, Britain, Norway, Switzerland, India, and some African countries.

One of the biggest projects of the sixth five-year plan is the 628-kilometer U.S.S.R.-Sofia main gas pipeline under construction by Soviet experts. The underground pipeline will begin at the Shebelinka deposit in the Ukraine, will reach the Danube in the Izmail area, and will then cross Romania and Bulgaria to Sofia. It will supply 3 billion cubic meters of natural gas annually to Bulgaria. The equipment was provided by the Soviet Union, Hungary, and Czechoslovakia. An Italian firm is to supply the pipe.

The 600-megawatt Teshel hydroelectric power station, the first of seven on the Vŭcha cascade, will generate 180 million kilowatt-hours a year. Construction continued on the first Bulgarian atomic power station, near Kozloduy. With a capacity of 880 megawatts, it will generate 6 billion kilowatt-hours of electricity a year when it is completed in 1975. A new port has been built on the Danube for the atomic power station. In June the Soviet ship *Tashkent* arrived with the first 200-ton reactor from Izmail.

The Devnya soda ash factory, which is being built with Soviet and Hungarian help, will be based on local raw materials and will have an annual output of 1.2 million tons of soda ash. It will be one of the biggest soda ash plants in Europe.

The Ministry of Forest and Environment Protection and the Ministry of Architecture and Public Works put into

effect special programs for environmental protection. A national program has been elaborated to construct stations for the purification of waste water, and a total of 22 research institutes and laboratories are working on problems connected with the control of noise.

Area and population. Area, 42,823 sq. mi. Pop. (est. 1972), 8,600,000. Principal cities: Sofia (cap.), 885,700; Plovdiv, 252,500; Varna, 230,500.

Government. People's republic. Chmn. of National Assembly, Georgi Traikov; chmn. (pres.) of State Council and first secy. of Communist Party, Todor Zhivkov; chmn. of Council of Ministers (prem.), Stanko Todorov. Unicameral National Assembly is elected every four years. Communist Party membership (1971), 699,476.

Finance. Monetary unit, lev; 1 lev = US$0.95. Budget (1972): revenue, 5.92 billion leva; expenditure, 5.91 billion leva.

Trade (1971). Imports, US$2.10 billion; exports, US$2.19 billion.

Economy (1970). Principal agricultural products: wheat, corn (maize), barley, tobacco, livestock. Principal industrial products: hard coal, lignite, iron ore, pig iron, steel, lead ore, metallurgical coke, crude oil, cement. Electric power, 19.51 billion kw.-hr.

Education (1970). Enrollment: general educational schools, 1,-300,000; polytechnic schools, 290,000; institutions of higher learning, 99,000.

Armed forces. Army, 125,000; security police, 45,000; air force, 20,000; navy, 4,000.

RICHARD A. PIERCE

BURMA. After ten years of ruling Burma as a soldier, General Ne Win resigned his military rank (and doffed his uniform) on April 20, thereby signaling the "civilianization" of Burma's hitherto military-dominated government.

Politics and government. Extensive changes took place in government during the year, as part of Premier Ne Win's avowed plan to make Burma a "socialist democracy." Ne Win announced in March a major overhaul of the administrative structure, including the elimination of the district-level of government and of the once-key office of the district commissioner (a holdover from the British colonial period). The other surviving subnational levels of government—village, township, and division—were henceforth to be administered by security and administrative committees representing the army, police, civil service, government party, and workers' and peasants' councils. Nationally, the once-powerful central Secretariat was abolished in a move to put ministers in more direct contact with their administrative subordinates.

Premier Ne Win's departure from the military in April was accompanied by similar action on the part of 20 of his top aides. The subsequent new "civilian" government included, besides Ne Win, ten other recently resigned officers, three still active-duty military persons, and only two bona fide civilians.

On April 22, Ne Win announced the draft of a new constitution which would provide for the establishment of the Socialist Republic of Burma; a one-chamber, 600-member "elected" People's Congress; and a single political party—the government-sponsored Burma Socialist Program Party. The constitution was scheduled to take effect in 1974.

A "judicial revolution," announced in August, provided for the replacement of professional judges with laymen-run "people's courts." Former judges, however, would act as advisers to the new courts.

Insurgencies. An unidentified aircraft overflying Rangoon in early April dropped safe-conduct passes to territory held in eastern Burma by the National United Liberation Front (a coalition of minority insurgents opposed to the Ne Win regime), revealing the apparent vulnerability of the capital to any kind of air activity. This attention-seeking action was overshadowed, however, by the resignation in the same month of former premier U Nu from the front's leadership. U Nu, who had been ousted by Ne Win in 1962, split with the front's ethnic minority leaders on their demand that Burma's various ethnic minorities have the right of secession from the state.

Central Burma remained largely free of rebel activity, and ethnic minority insurgents made no serious headway against government forces in the eastern part of the country. Strong insurgent activity continued in the north, however, where Communists with Chinese support and ethnic minority rebels frequently clashed with government elements. No more than two-thirds of the national territory was in the government's hands at year's end.

Economy. Implementation began in earnest on the 1971–1975 development plan. But the economy remained stagnant, and there were serious shortages of almost all commodities, including some foodstuffs.

The government continued to severely restrict imports, and this policy, together with the December 1971 devaluation of the national currency, seemed likely to give Burma a small trade surplus by the year's end. Also, the government made an effort to duplicate last year's increase in all major exports.

Internally, the government policy of requiring peasants to market their produce wholly through official channels has apparently eased. A greater governmental tolerance of the "free" (or black) market seemed designed to stimulate incentive for higher output.

State figures released in 1972 indicated an impressive government effort to develop the economy. Direct government investment in the economy doubled between 1962 and 1972, from US$600,000 to US$1,200,000, and government spending on industry advanced from 5 percent to 40 percent of that total during the same period. Allegedly, output similarly increased, but this was not visibly apparent in terms of goods available on the Burmese market.

Foreign policy. On January 13, Burma recognized neighboring Bangladesh, despite continuing Chinese opposition to the new country and its chief sponsors. The Burmese, however, were fully aware of the danger of having a new arena for Sino-Soviet conflict to their immediate west, and the Ne Win government indicated to Peking that it was not aligning itself with the new nation.

Relations with neighboring India remained good, and Burma sought to improve ties with Thailand to the east and Malaysia to the southeast. Malaysian prime minister Tun Abdul Razak visited Rangoon, and after it became apparent that the April leaflet-dropping "air raid" had been launched from an airfield in Thailand, Thai authorities agreed to greater restrictions on Burmese political refugees on their soil.

Burma's relations in general with other countries seemed to improve in 1972, as the Rangoon government appeared to relax its ultraisolationist pose somewhat. Japan, the country's chief source of foreign aid, increased its assistance, and relations generally improved between the two governments. The second-largest donor, West Germany, considerably expanded its aid program during the year. The Burmese also began taking advantage of the resumed Chinese aid program, but it was apparent that there would be far fewer than the 400 Chinese technicians that were residing in the country in 1967, when the Chinese suspended their aid program.

Two American firms were conducting offshore oil exploration on a fee-contract basis for the Burmese government—the first such new U.S. business venture in the country since Ne Win took over in 1962. Burma would own and exploit any oil discovered.

Area and population. Area, 261,790 sq. mi. Pop. (est. 1970), 27.6 million. Rangoon (cap.), 1,758,731.

Government. Civilian rule. Revolutionary Council chmn., Ne Win; army chief of staff, General San Yu; deputy min., Brigadier Tin U. The only official political party is the Burma Socialist Program Party.

Finance. Monetary unit, kyat; 1 kyat = US$0.19.

Trade. Major exports: rice, teak, lead, zinc, raw cotton, rubber.

Agriculture. Key crops: rice, sugarcane, peanuts, beans. Leading forestry products: hardwood, teak.

Armed forces. Army, 145,000; navy, 6,000, including reserves; air force, 6,480.

RICHARD BUTWELL

BURUNDI. Tragic tribal warfare occurred in Burundi this year as the Hutu majority again vainly attempted to end the domination of the ruling Tutsi elite, who control the government, economy, and army. The cost in human life and the intensity of Tutsi reprisals against the entire Hutu educated population have been ferocious, with over 100,000 persons believed killed.

Rebellion. The immediate background to the warfare was the return of the former king, Ntare V, to Burundi at the end of March. Ntare V, previously a supporter of the current president of Burundi, Michel Micombero, had been ousted by Micombero in 1966 and had been in exile in West Germany. In March, Ntare returned to neighboring Uganda, where he received a written guarantee that he would be allowed to return safely to Burundi. Upon his return, however, Ntare was immediately imprisoned.

On April 29, an attempt to free Ntare and a general rebellion against Micombero's government began. The conspirators were some Tutsi royalists from the northern part of Burundi (who desired the return of Ntare V to his throne rather than the continued rule of Micombero, a Tutsi from southern Burundi) as well as the Hutu, who sought an end to Tutsi domination.

During the first days of the rebellion, Ntare was killed, along with perhaps 2,000 Tutsi, largely in southern Burundi and along the shore of Lake Tanganyika. Friends and relatives of President Micombero and many of his senior army officers were among those apparently killed at this early stage.

REFUGEES FROM TERROR, Hutu tribesmen rest up in the countryside of Zaïre. They had fled their homes in neighboring Burundi, where a minimum of 100,000 Hutus have been killed by members of the ruling Tutsi tribe, in reprisal for an attempted coup.

WIDE WORLD

Reprisals and aftermath. The toll taken during the early stages of the rebellion pales when compared with what was to follow. The Burundi Army and all government supporters (that is, the Tutsi minority) quickly turned the curbing of the rebellion into a generalized massacre of the entire Hutu educated population. Nearly every Hutu teacher, government administrator, churchman—indeed almost any Hutu with a secondary school education—was systematically killed. This was particularly true throughout the southern part of the country. At least 100,000 Hutu are believed to have been massacred.

The tragic outcome of the warfare is that all the tensions that led to the killing remain. The Tutsi minority is still in power; Hutu grievances have hardly been eliminated.

In July, President Micombero named a new government, placing in key positions Foreign Minister Simbabanyie and Albin Nyamoya, the new prime minister and executive secretary of the ruling UPRONA Party. Whereas before the troubles five of the ten ministers were Hutu, now only four of 14 are. At least three of the five former Hutu ministers have been killed.

In addition to the killing, there has been widespread destruction throughout much of southern Burundi. The situation in Burundi, already one of the world's poorest countries, is graver than ever. It is estimated that there may be as many as 50,000 Burundian refugees in the neighboring countries of Zaïre, Tanzania, and Rwanda—mainly Hutus fleeing the Tutsi massacres.

In July, perhaps signaling the end of the current troubles, Micombero paid a state visit to Zaïre, where he was welcomed by President Joseph D. Mobutu. During the early stages of the troubles, Zaïre supplied Micombero with paratroopers to defend the airport and palace. Zaïre has thus become Micombero's most important ally.

Area and population. Area, 10,747 sq. mi. Pop. (est. 1970), 3,600,000 (not accounting for civil war deaths). Bujumbura (cap.; est.), 100,000.

Government. Republic. Pres., Michel Micombero.

Finance. Monetary unit, Burundi franc; 1 Burundi franc = US$0.012.

Trade (1970). Exports, US$31.3 million ($21.2 million to USA; $4.5 million to Britain). Imports, US$22.3 million.

LARRY W. BOWMAN

CALIFORNIA. Major tax reform and property tax relief died again this year because of partisan political bickering between Republican governor Ronald Reagan and the Democratic-controlled state legislature. However, Californians did experience income tax withholding for the first time and paid other new taxes as the result of the adoption of a record-high state budget. In other major developments, the California supreme court banned the death penalty; the west coast dock strike, the longest waterfront tie-up in U.S. history, ended after 134 days; and George McGovern defeated Hubert Humphrey and seven other opponents in the winner-take-all Democratic presidential primary.

Legislative session. In January, Governor Reagan presented a record $7.6 billion budget but indicated that his "cut, squeeze, and trim" philosophy of government had not been abandoned, although he added an additional $80 million in a later revision. By mid-June, the legislature passed a compromise $7.96 billion budget that substantially increased state aid to schools and pay raises for state employees and higher education faculties over the governor's requests. Vetoes totaling $257.9 million were exercised by the governor, resulting in a final record-high budget of $7.7 billion. The final budget did contain $190 million more for public school assistance than was granted the previous year.

The legislature failed to accomplish one of its major assignments—an acceptable reapportionment plan. On January 18, the California supreme court ordered that present state senate and assembly legislative districts be used in the 1972 elections and that the realigned congressional districts (Cali-

fornia had gained five new seats), vetoed by the governor, be followed this year.

June primary. Nationwide attention was focused on the Democratic presidential primary of June 6. Senators McGovern and Humphrey both campaigned extensively throughout the state in pursuit of California's 271 convention delegates. The California Poll released a week before the vote showed McGovern with a 20-point margin of victory. George Wallace's name did not appear on the ballot, but spirited efforts for a write-in vote on his behalf enabled him to finish third behind McGovern (45 percent) and Humphrey (40 percent), with Congresswoman Shirley Chisholm winning fourth spot among the nine candidates. President Richard M. Nixon won nearly 90 percent of the Republican primary vote, registering a lopsided victory over Congressman John M. Ashbrook of Ohio after California congressman Paul N. McCloskey, Jr., withdrew.

Two California congressmen—ultraconservative John G. Schmitz, a first-term Republican, and hawkish veteran Democrat George P. Miller, dean of the state's delegation—were defeated in reelection bids. Schmitz was later nominated for president by the American Party, which had supported Wallace in 1968.

Ten ballot propositions were on the June primary ballot. By far the most controversy centered on Proposition 9, a tough, comprehensive pollution-control measure that opponents claimed was extreme, unworkable, and devastating to the California economy; it was defeated by a 2–1 proportion. All nine other proposals were victorious, including measures providing for an open presidential primary, for senatorial confirmation of gubernatorial appointments to the university's board of regents, and for bonds for veterans and schools.

Law and justice. The death penalty was ruled unconstitutional by the California supreme court in a 6–1 decision on February 18. The historic decision held that the penalty violated the state constitutional ban on "cruel or unusual punishments" when judged by contemporary standards. The court found that the death penalty is "unnecessary to any legitimate goals of the state and is incompatible with the dignity of man and the judicial process." The ruling, made in the case of Robert Page Anderson, a convicted murderer, was made applicable to the other 101 men and five women facing execution in San Quentin's gas chamber. Strong opposition to the decision led to the qualification of a constitutional initiative on the November ballot to restore the death penalty by declaring it not to be cruel or unusual—in effect overruling the court decision.

Angela Davis, one-time acting assistant professor of philosophy at UCLA, was found innocent in her trial on charges of murder, kidnapping, and conspiracy in connection with a 1970 shoot-out at the Marin County courthouse. She was also a winner in January when the state court of appeals held that her firing from the university on grounds of admitted membership in the Communist Party was unconstitutional.

Education. The name of the California state colleges officially became the California State University and Colleges in March. Fourteen campuses of the 19-campus system were redesignated as California state universities.

Economy. California continues to be the top agricultural state, producing 25 percent of all the fresh fruit and vegetables sold in the United States. An attempted boycott of lettuce not picked by the United Farm Workers appeared to have little impact on consumption.

The 134-day west coast dock strike, which tied up 24 Pacific coast ports, resulted in losses estimated in the hundreds of millions of dollars. The longest waterfront tie-up in U.S. history ended February 19, when 71 percent of the members of the International Longshoremen's and Warehousemen's Union ratified a new 18-month contract.

A quarantine on poultry and allied products from most of southern California was announced March 13 by the U.S.

UPI

ACQUITTED black activist Angela Davis hugs her mother at the conclusion of her trial in June. She was cleared of kidnap-conspiracy charges in connection with the Marin County courthouse shoot-out in 1970, in which four persons died.

Department of Agriculture in an effort to halt the spread of Newcastle disease. The affected area, one of the top poultry areas, has some 54 million chickens and 3.4 million turkeys.

For election results and campaign highlights, see the special supplement ELECTION '72.

Area and population. Area, 158,693 sq. mi. Pop. (est. 1972), 20,425,000. Principal cities: Sacramento (cap.), 254,413; Los Angeles, 2,816,061; San Francisco, 715,674.
Government. Gov., Ronald Reagan (R); lt. gov., Ed Reinecke (R); secy. of state, Edmund G. Brown, Jr. (D); cont., Houston I. Flournoy (R); treas., Ivy Baker Priest (R); atty. gen., Evelle J. Younger (R); supt. of public instruction (nonpartisan), Wilson Riles. Legislature: senate, 21 D, 19 R; assembly, 43 D, 37 R.
Finance. 1972–1973 budget, $7.7 billion. Principal sources of revenue: sales, personal income, motor fuels, bank, and corporation taxes. Principal items of expenditure: education, tax relief and shared revenues, welfare, transportation.
Education (1970–1971). Elementary schools, 5,519; junior high schools, 445; high schools, 754; junior colleges, 93. Enrollments: kindergarten, 335,975; grades 1–8, 2,832,464; grades 9–12, 1,288,-886; junior college (1970), 393,032; adult education (1970), 686,954.　　　　　　　　　　　　　　　GEORGE S. BLAIR

CAMBODIA. *See* KHMER REPUBLIC.

CAMEROON. Politics and government. In late May a popular referendum approved the end of the federal structure which, since independence, had divided Cameroon into two separate administrative and legislative systems, the French-speaking east and English-speaking west. The official results of the referendum—99.97 percent yes, with only 1.5 percent of the 3 million eligible not voting—were nearly unanimous in favor of a new constitution creating a unitary state, to be known officially as the United Republic of Cameroon. The results were seen by many observers as further evidence of the widespread support and personal power of President Ahmadou Ahidjo. The new constitution establishes a unicameral, 120-member national assembly and formally proclaims Cameroon a bilingual state.

Foreign affairs. For President Ahidjo, late 1971 and 1972 was a period of intense personal diplomacy in the pursuit of African unity. A member of the Organization of African Unity's peace mission to Cairo and Tel Aviv in November 1971, Ahidjo was also part of an OAU mediation commission which successfully brought Senegal and Guinea together in Monrovia in mid-May. In addition, Ahidjo attended the summit conference of the African, Malagasy, and Mauritian Common Organization in mid-April, but it was clear that Cameroon's enthusiasm for OCAMM was cooling.

This multilateral diplomacy was supplemented by a series of bilateral negotiations, including visits to Nigeria in March, Guinea in May, and Senegal in June. Each visit resulted in a joint pledge of economic cooperation and in condemnations of apartheid and the Rhodesian regime. The most important of the meetings, the one with Nigeria, also established a joint commission to work out trade agreements. However, Cameroon-Nigerian relations were marred somewhat by a May announcement that negotiations over a boundary dispute had reached a "temporary impasse."

Economic developments. Economic activity remained brisk. Official estimates placed the annual growth rate in agricultural and industrial production at 16 percent, even though production estimates on the major export crops were marginally down from 1970–1971 record levels. The 1972–1973 budget forecasts reflected the general optimism.

Area and population. Area, 183,569 sq. mi. Pop. (est. 1970), 5.7 million. Principal cities (est. 1971): Yaoundé (cap.), 130,000; Douala, 210,000.
Government. Single-party republic. Pres., Ahmadou Ahidjo.
Finance. Monetary unit, Communauté Financière Africaine franc; 1 CFA franc = US$0.0041. Budget (est. 1972–1973): balanced at 52.7 billion CFA francs.
Trade (1970). Exports, 62.8 billion CFA francs; imports, 67.2 billion CFA francs. Principal exports: cocoa, coffee, aluminum, timber, cotton.　　　　　　　　　　　　　　GEORGE LAMSON

CANADA. On September 1, Liberal prime minister Pierre Elliott Trudeau dissolved Parliament and called a general election for October 30.

The election proved the closest ever in Canadian federal politics. Opposition leader Robert Stanfield's Progressive Conservatives nearly tied the Liberals, who won 109 seats in the 264-seat House of Commons. Few expected this upset after a dull campaign. David Lewis' New Democratic Party took 31 seats, Real Caouette's Social Credit 15, and there were two independents. Minority government in Canada was a certainty, and another election before many months was a strong possibility. With no clear result, Trudeau chose to remain prime minister until Parliament could be convened. All four political leaders gained personal reelection. It was felt that the Liberals lost their big majority because, despite foreign policy successes, they were unable to check high unemployment, hold down the cost of living, and prevent abuses of unemployment insurance payments and welfare grants. (*See* PEOPLE IN THE NEWS: ROBERT STANFIELD and PIERRE ELLIOTT TRUDEAU.)

Before the election was called, Parliament wrangled over unemployment, the economy, relations with the United States, and the actions of various members of Trudeau's cabinet.

The economy. A senate committee, the Science Policy Committee, recommended a new economic policy for Canada. The committee said "drastic revolutions" must occur in Canadian life, with close to $5 billion spent by 1980 on research and development of science and technology. The cost of choosing to remain passive will be much higher, the committee warned, stating such a choice "will almost inevitably lead to the economic dead end that only annexation to the United States could delay." The report urged Canada to become an innovative nation in order to survive.

A more optimistic note was sounded by the 23-member international Organization for Economic Cooperation and Development, which in its midyear economic forecast said that of the seven major industrial states of the world, Canada in the ensuing 12 months would be exceeded in growth rate only by Japan. The report predicted that Canada's high unemployment rate of 6.2 percent of the labor force in mid-1972 should be reduced to 5.5 percent early in 1973. Nonetheless, opposition members hammered at the Trudeau government over the rate of unemployment. In June, the nation had 568,000 unemployed, the highest June unemployment figure ever. Then in July food prices rose to 142.5 percent of 1961 food prices, a rise of 5 percent over the previous month. Louis Rasminsky, governor of the Bank of Canada, said in his annual report that "the pace of cost increases remains high."

Robert L. Stanfield, the Progressive Conservative Party's opposition leader, said "jobs and justice" were his goals. Stanfield criticized increased government expenditures allegedly designed not to create growth but to prevent the governmental system from collapsing. New Democratic Party leader David Lewis added his voice in criticism, saying there were ten or 12 persons out of work for every job available. Lewis also accused the government of patronage, saying Trudeau had "equaled or surpassed every pork-barreling prime minister in the country's history" when it came to providing jobs for party workers. Finance Minister John N. Turner pledged jobs were his top priority and claimed Canada's real growth rate would be "even faster in 1972" than in 1971, when the increase was a record 6 percent.

Turner presented his first budget in May. It offered aid to industry by reducing corporation income tax in 1973 from 49 percent to 40 percent for companies in manufacturing and processing. It also provided for annual adjustment in old-age pensions and for veterans' allowances which will reflect full cost-of-living increases. Turner also introduced a two-year write-off for machinery and equipment acquired for manufacturing and processing in Canada. But he failed

to make general cuts in personal income taxes, explaining he did not want to risk the inflationary pressures that might result. He described the aids to manufacturing as lasting steps toward "a new industrial strategy." The budget also provided a $50 a month income tax exemption for full-time trainees and students taking post–high school training courses for every month of school attendance. In his budget speech, Turner reiterated that jobs remained his first priority.

The discovery of oil in the Canadian arctic showed promise of aiding both jobs and the economy. Panarctic Oils Ltd., a consortium in which the federal government owns a 45 percent interest, took oil from the world's most northerly oil well on Ellesmere Island, in the eastern arctic some 650 miles from the north pole. The company was cautious, however, terming the find significant but not necessarily commercial. Prime Minister Trudeau announced the federal government was starting to build a 750-mile all-weather highway from Fort Simpson in Canada's Northwest Territories to Tuktoyaktuk on the Arctic Ocean as the first stage of a $10 billion oil, gas, and road corridor.

Canada's world trade surplus for the first half of the year was $556 million, down sharply from the surplus of $1.2 billion for the same period the year before. The drop was attributed to the fact that Canada's formerly favorable trade balance with countries other than the United States had turned downward to a deficit. The surplus in trade with the United States recovered in the first half of the year, but Canadians still worried about trade prospects with the Americans. Some Canadians felt that the U.S. Domestic International Sales Corporations (DISC) gave aid to American firms to an extent that could harm Canadian business. Because of the American DISC program, Revenue Minister Herb Gray announced new procedures under which foreign exporters have to declare to Canadian customs whether they receive any corporate tax incentives or benefits in connection with these exports. The procedure will apply to all countries.

Revenue Minister Gray's long-awaited report on foreign investment in Canada reached two main conclusions: that foreign ownership of businesses in Canada will increase and that new government moves can reduce the dangers of such foreign control and increase benefits to Canadians. But the government introduced legislation far milder than anticipated. The government will have power to stop foreign take-over bids that offer no real benefit to Canada and will be able, with jail terms or fines, to punish executives seeking to avoid government take-over legislation. Opposition leader Stanfield called the bill "a weak document," and New Democratic Party leader Lewis labeled it "one big zero." Many businessmen approved, however, and the Canadian Manufacturers' Association called it "a moderate position" which helped lay the groundwork for "a policy of constructive nationalism."

Statistics Canada announced that the Canadian gross national product was $102 billion for the year ending June 30, a record.

Parliament. Paul Hellyer, former Liberal cabinet minister who resigned and formed a new party, Action Canada, switched again and joined the Progressive Conservatives. Douglas Harkness, former Progressive Conservative defense minister, retired after 27 years in Parliament. Long-time Liberal cabinet minister Arthur Laing was made a senator.

Opposition members attacked the government over the release of convicted murderer Yves Geoffroy. Under a life sentence for strangling his wife, Geoffroy was released on a 50-hour leave to marry his mistress. He fled to Spain but after about two months of freedom was brought back to Canada and imprisonment. Solicitor General Jean-Pierre Goyer bore the brunt of the criticisms.

Former Progressive Conservative prime minister John Diefenbaker angrily attacked the government for hiring Pierre Vallières, a former leader of the terrorist Front de Libération du Québec, for a federally financed winter works

job. "This is a shocking situation," Diefenbaker told the House. Opposition leader Stanfield attacked the government many times over unemployment. He also strongly attacked the Canadian Development Corporation, designed to put federal money into Canadian businesses. Stanfield said the venture was confused and ambiguous. Opposition members slammed Information Canada, the government's information service, which spent almost $7 million in its first year.

The LeDain Drug Inquiry Commission reported to the federal government in January. It recommended heroin be made legally available for treating drug addicts in special circumstances and recommended an immediate search for a chemical to block the effects of "speed" drugs. The report was pessimistic about early solutions or permanent cures and laid heavy emphasis on prevention. In addition, it labeled alcoholism as Canada's "most widespread drug-dependence problem."

Provincial affairs. Premier Frank Duff Moores and his Progressive Conservatives triumphed in a Newfoundland provincial election held in March, winning 33 of the 42 seats against nine for the Liberals. The election came about six months after Moores' party had taken 21 seats against 20 for the Liberals, led by former premier Joseph Smallwood, and one for the New Labrador Party. The Liberals had previously won six straight elections, so Moores' twin victories marked a major change in Newfoundland politics.

Quebec had a difficult week in May when the jailing of three union leaders led to widespread walkouts and demonstrations. In Ontario, the Progressive Conservative government presented a provincial budget showing a $597 million deficit and $134 million in new indirect taxes on beer, wine, liquor, tobacco, and gasoline.

Federal-provincial relations. Prime Minister Trudeau called W. A. C. Bennett, then premier of British Columbia,

Canada Roars Back

After being humiliated on Canadian ice by the Soviet all-stars, Team Canada (a collection of NHL greats) vowed to recoup its honor by trouncing the Russians back in Moscow. With only seconds left in the deciding game, Paul Henderson of the Toronto Maple Leafs untied the score with a dramatic goal. An excited teammate waved his arms (below), and Canadian fans, flown in for the historic series by charter plane, gleefully chanted away the few remaining seconds (left.)

LEFT, UPI; BELOW, AP

a "bigot" in an Ottawa speech. Former prime minister Diefenbaker called Trudeau's remark "intellectual arrogance." Bennett said nothing, but Leslie Peterson, then attorney general of British Columbia, replied by attacking the federal government's policy of bilingualism and threatening to go to court to have equalization grants ruled illegal. Peterson said that under the equalization grant system British Columbia, Ontario, and Alberta have contributed $5.5 billion to the other provinces.

Provincial premiers met for their 13th annual provincial premiers' conference. Alberta's Progressive Conservative premier, Peter Lougheed, won support for his strong stand against federal government interference in provincial affairs. The premiers asked Ottawa to make plans for combating winter unemployment.

Foreign affairs. U.S. president Richard M. Nixon began his two-day visit to Ottawa on April 14 with reassurances about Canadian identity, saying, "We respect the separate Canadian identity. We respect the right of the Canadian people to pursue, in their own way, their own destiny." Addressing Parliament, he called for an end to "sentimental rhetoric" in Canada-U.S. relations and said both countries should "recognize that we have very separate identities and that we have significant differences. Nobody's interests are furthered when these realities are obscured." Nixon urged Canada to join the Organization of American States. Trudeau and Nixon signed the Great Lakes cleanup agreement, which provides for construction or upgrading of municipal sewage treatment facilities in all communities bordering on the Great Lakes, such facilities to be completed or near completion by 1975. Cost of the Canadian share of this is estimated at $500 million.

Many Canadians worried over possible pollution of their west coast in the event of spillage from tankers carrying oil from Alaska to the refinery at Cherry Point, Wash. The problem was emphasized when a valve burst at Cherry Point while a tanker was unloading and a small amount of oil escaped to the open sea, some of it appearing at Crescent Beach, British Columbia. Canadians reacted strongly. External Affairs Minister Mitchell Sharp told Parliament the government had asked the United States for "prompt" payment of damages and cleanup costs from the Cherry Point spill. In a tough statement, Sharp declared, "The incident at Cherry Point is a stark reminder of what we have stated on many occasions: that far more serious spills will inevitably take place on other occasions if oil is moved by tanker through the Strait of Juan de Fuca." He said Canada had registered "grave concern about this ominous incident." The Atlantic Richfield Company assured the government it would pay all cleanup costs.

The Cherry Point oil spill occurred during the United Nations environmental conference in Stockholm in June. According to Canada's environment minister, Jack Davis, the news burst on the Stockholm scene "like a bomb." Davis told the conference that pollution laws and standards must be as universal as the laws of nature. "Too often in the past," he said, "the interest of our global community has been sacrificed by the shortsightedness, I might even say the callousness, of the few." Davis urged the nations to adopt the rule, "Thou shalt not pollute the environment of thy neighbor, the ocean, or the atmosphere." Davis gave a 15-point commitment from Canada which included an offer to host the 1977 United Nations environment conference. Despite Davis' efforts and his personal success at Stockholm, the Science Council of Canada warned pollution and environmental problems were appearing faster than they could be solved and called for massive action. "It may be later than we think," the council warned.

Davis released a Canadian government report which predicted a 50 percent chance that a major oil spill involving a supertanker would occur once every 20 years on the route between Alaska and Cherry Point. The report recommended a marine traffic management system be established jointly by Canada and the United States for all major vessels traveling in the Strait of Juan de Fuca, the Strait of Georgia, or Puget Sound. Because of the risk of spillage on the Canadian west coast, many Canadians favor transporting Alaskan oil by a pipeline route through Canada's Mackenzie Valley. The Old Crow Indian band, however, said they would haul the federal government into court if the pipeline is constructed through the northern part of Canada's Yukon Territory before aboriginal land claims are settled with the Old Crow band. The band have lived for centuries on the banks of the Porcupine River, some 80 miles north of the arctic circle.

The parliamentary session passed eight acts concerning national pollution standards, but too hasty enforcement could force many industries, especially pulp mills, to close. Davis said that with the unemployment problem "we will need to go slowly and put jobs ahead of pollution abatement." In Washington, D.C., Davis and Russell Train, chairman of the U.S. Council on Environmental Quality, issued a communiqué stating good progress is being made on developing contingency plans for dealing with oil spills in waters near the Canadian-U.S. boundary. They affirmed the principle that a state is responsible for the damage its pollution causes to another. Davis hailed the U.S. promise to pay all costs of damage to Canada from American pollution as "a big step forward."

The Canadian government backed its Arctic Waters Pollution Prevention Act by setting pollution penalties for land-based industries as well as shipping. These penalties are for the time being a maximum of $14 million but will rise to $30 million and then to $60 million. Canada thus established the principle of "absolute liability" for pollution in disputed waters north of the 60th parallel. The dispute is that Canada has always claimed these are territorial waters, while the United States claims they are international. Ottawa feels that applying Canadian laws in the waters will end the dispute.

External Affairs Minister Sharp visited Peking, conferred with Chinese premier Chou En-lai, and returned with Chou En-lai's pledge that China will continue to consider Canada as a first source of China's wheat imports. Sharp's visit coincided with a visit by 600 Canadians to Peking for a Canadian trade fair.

When Patrick Hillery, external affairs minister of the Irish Republic, asked Canada to try to change British policy in Northern Ireland, Sharp refused, declaring, "We cannot solve other people's problems for them, and we cannot intervene in the internal affairs of either the British or the Irish governments."

Culture. For the first time in its 20-year history, the Stratford Shakespeare Festival in Ontario presented a play by a French-Canadian. The English translation of Roch Carrier's *La Guerre, Yes Sir!* met with favor from the critics. Some critics also praised David Williams' production of *King Lear* and William Hutt's portrayal of the title role. The Shaw Festival's 11th season at Niagara-on-the-Lake, Ontario, opened for the first time with a non-Shavian play, the 1927 George Kaufman and Edna Ferber comedy, *The Royal Family.* Critics praised the performances more than the production. *The Rowdyman,* the first feature film made in

GONE FISSION. Fueling machine operators check instruments in the control room of Canada's first commercial nuclear generating station, which opened in February in Pickering, Ontario. Canada has begun to turn to nuclear power as a source of clean energy.

EDWARD COWAN

Newfoundland, drew plaudits. Gordon Pinsent, a Newfoundlander, wrote the script and played the lead role. The Charlottetown, Prince Edward Island, Festival presented the world premiere of *Ballade*, a musical by Montreal's Arthur Samuels. Roma Hearn was warmly praised as the female lead.

Prime Minister Trudeau named Laurent Picard as new president of the Canadian Broadcasting Corporation. Picard, who had been executive vice-president, succeeded George Davidson, who resigned to become undersecretary general of the United Nations. Hugh Farquhar succeeded Bruce Partridge as president of the University of Victoria. Simon Fraser University acquired one of the continent's largest collections of Eskimo graphics.

Area and population. Area, 3,851,809 sq. mi. Pop. (est. 1972), 21,788,000. Principal cities (met. areas; 1971): Ottawa (cap.), 453,280; Montreal, 2,743,208; Toronto, 2,628,043; Vancouver, 1,-082,352; Winnipeg, 540,262.
Government. Parliamentary government. Gov.-gen., Roland Michener; prime min., Pierre Elliott Trudeau.
Finance. Monetary unit, Canadian dollar; 1 Canadian dollar = US$1.018. Budget (1972–1973; in Can$): revenue, $19,250 million; expenditures, $20,050 million.
Trade (1971, in Can$). Exports, $17,864,924,000; imports, $15,-607,731,000. Principal exports: newsprint, wheat, lumber, minerals. Principal imports: manufactured goods.
Education (est. 1972–1973). Public, federal, and private elementary and secondary schools, 16,397; enrollment, 5,758,520; teachers, 267,701. University and college enrollment, 363,900 in 127 institutions.
Armed forces (1971). Regular forces, 85,000: Royal Canadian Navy, 15,000; Royal Canadian Air Force, 37,000; Canadian Army, 33,000. Reserves, 21,700.   DAVID SAVAGE

CANADIAN LITERATURE. The Canadian federal government, responding to the financial distress of Canadian publishers and a reawakened sense of cultural nationalism, announced measures in February to strengthen the English and French-Canadian publishing industry. The aim is to double the number of Canadian trade (nontext) books produced annually within five years.

In announcing the aid, Secretary of State Gérard Pelletier noted that in 1969, a typical year, books valued at Can$220 million were sold in Canada, but only 5 percent of the books were written, published, and manufactured by Canadians. The largest share, 65 percent, was imported; another 20 percent was published in Canada by foreign-controlled publishers. The remaining 10 percent consisted of foreign books adapted and published in Canada.

Federal aid totaled $1.7 million in 1972, with more assistance promised in subsequent years. It included direct subsidies to Canadian publishers, an expanded budget for the translation of books published in the country's two languages, transfer to private publishers of book projects previously undertaken by the government itself, and a program through which the government will buy sizable quantities of Canadian books for free distribution in foreign countries.

In Ontario, center of English-language publishing in Canada, the provincial government took further steps to strengthen the industry. It acted on several suggestions made by the Royal Commission on Book Publishing, appointed in 1971 after American companies took over two long-established Canadian publishing houses. Low-interest loans totaling $855,000 were made available to four Ontario publishers, and legislation was passed to forestall an American company from gaining a monopoly of paperback and periodical distribution in the province.

Fiction. The younger generation of novelists was prominent this year. Margaret Atwood, who made her reputation as a poet, fulfilled the promise of her first novel in her second, *Surfacing*. Its narrator traveled back to her birthplace in remote Quebec to find her father, but the search was really for herself and her country. In the process, the Canadian experience was beautifully articulated. Two first novels were impressive: Sylvia Fraser's *Pandora*, an evoca-

tion of the early years of school, told from the child's viewpoint; and John Metcalf's *Going Down Slow*, a stinging satire of Canadian high schools. Although Harry Boyle's *The Great Canadian Novel* did not live up to its title, it was an important study of a traditional Canadian problem: the lure of big money in the United States to talented Canadians, this time a Toronto advertising man.

In Quebec fiction, Marie-Claire Blais disappointed her many admirers with her 13th novel, *Le loup*. Her intention was to examine the uses and abuses of love in a homosexual context, but the central character was lifeless. Another prolific author, the irreverent Jacques Ferron, also showed signs of fatigue in *La chaise du Maréchal Ferrant*, a satirical thrust at many of his old establishment targets. More interesting were two novels by immigrants to Quebec—*Le greffon*, by the Spanish-born Jacques Folch-Ribas, and *Une journée un peu chaude*, by a young Belgian, Claude Breuer.

Poetry. Leonard Cohen's *Energy of Slaves*, his first volume since 1968, was notable for its intense and often sensuous lyricism. In *The Armies of the Moon*, Gwendolyn MacEwen used simple language and careful craftsmanship to express her cosmic visions. Elizabeth Brewster's *Sunrise North* was marked by honesty and an absence of pretension. Al Purdy's *Selected Poems*, the best of his considerable output during the past decade, was notable for its revelation of how he uses the familiar Ontario landscape and the familiar stuff of his own life for larger purposes.

Quebec poetry was distinguished by the return of Paul Chamberland with his first work in several years, *Éclats de la pierre noire d'où rejaillit ma vie*, in which he confirmed his reputation as one of Quebec's leading poets. Monique Bosco, who has written distinguished novels, showed that she is almost as adept in poetry with her first collection, *Jericho*. In *Poésie*, Fernand Ouellette revised a number of his older poems and added a section of new ones to make a surprisingly integrated collection.

Nonfiction. Farley Mowat used the controversial shooting of a whale in Newfoundland to write a powerful warning against man's senseless depredations against nature in *A Whale for the Killing*. The ecology theme was continued in *Violated Vision: The Rape of Canada's North*, in which James Woodford warned of the dangers to the arctic ecosystem posed by advancing civilization and oil exploration.

The effect of U.S. ownership of Canadian industry in a typical Ontario community was examined by Robert Perry in *Galt, U.S.A.*, which concluded only that there is a feeling of helplessness about the situation. Nationalist historian Donald Creighton lent historical perspective to the country's present state in his collection of essays *Towards the Discovery of Canada*. He was pessimistic about a Canadian future increasingly dominated by the United States. Critic George Woodcock provided a fascinating tour of his major literary and political interests in *The Rejection of Politics and Other Essays*, in which he warned against the dangers of excessive nationalism. A rare glimpse of Quebec's cultural and political radical movements of the 1960's was provided for English-Canadian readers in *The Shouting Signpainters*, by Malcolm Reid.

In Quebec, Pierre Vallières, notorious author of *White Niggers of America* and one of the founders of the outlawed separatist group Front de Libération du Québec, startled his followers with *L'Urgence de choisir*, in which he renounced the terrorist tactics of the FLQ and announced his decision to join the Parti Québecois, which seeks to achieve independence for Quebec through democratic means. A former senior civil servant in the Quebec government, Claude Morin, discussed Quebec's options in *Le pouvoir québecois . . . en négociation*, then joined the Parti Québecois. One of Quebec's leading women politicians, Thérèse Casgrain, recalled her long career in *Une femme chez les hommes*. Her account of the struggle for civil rights and women's suffrage in Quebec made compelling reading.   WILLIAM FRENCH

CARIBBEAN COLONIES AND ASSOCIATED AREAS. British Honduras.

The century-old dispute between Guatemala and British Honduras (which now likes to call itself Belize) flared again this year, with Guatemala formally accusing Great Britain in the General Assembly of the Organization of American States of keeping troops in British Honduras and planning to attack Guatemala. At the end of 1971, Great Britain had announced that troop maneuvers would take place in British Honduras early in 1972 and that troops would be sent for this purpose and for training. The forewarning was forgotten when the arrival of British troops coincided with Guatemala's dispatch of its own troops to the common frontier with British Honduras, allegedly to combat revolutionary bands operating in the area. Guatemala called on Great Britain to cease its preparations for aggression and asked the OAS for collective sanctions should the alleged threat continue.

At the OAS meeting Senator Dudley Thompson, minister of state for foreign affairs of Jamaica, pointed out that Great Britain had clearly announced that British Honduras could become completely independent whenever it wished, but that the semiautonomous state feared to do so because it believed that as soon as Great Britain withdrew, the country would face invasion from Guatemala.

British Honduras would like Great Britain or the United States to guarantee its independence, but neither seems willing to do so. In its message to the OAS, British Honduras declared that the territorial claim of Guatemala retarded the progress of the people of Belize and perpetuated colonialism in the area. It called on the OAS to take collective measures and sanctions to ensure the right of the people of Belize to independence and to secure an unequivocal declaration by Guatemala that it would not invade Belize. Further, it stated that unless Guatemala made such a declaration, Belize had no alternative but to welcome British forces for defense against possible aggression.

The OAS passed a resolution to send observers to check the number of British troops stationed in British Honduras; Great Britain had said 750, but Guatemala had claimed 1,500. The people of British Honduras expressed resentment at the resolution.

Press freedom. The legislation enacted in Antigua in 1971 requiring newspaper publishers to put up a large surety, pay a stiff license fee, and obtain cabinet approval before publishing, was declared unconstitutional in a court action; two papers that had suspended publication were allowed to resume. The government of Antigua said that it would appeal the decision and if necessary go all the way to the Privy Council of Great Britain. In the meantime, the law and public representations against it attracted the attention of the Inter-American Press Association, which sent a team to investigate the matter and also to visit St. Kitts, where the government had set up a press and publications board which, it was felt, would control the press in that territory. In neither place was the team able to see the premier, although requests for such meetings had been made beforehand. The team gave an adverse report to the IAPA.

In Grenada, also, free comment seemed to be stifled. The government not only acquired a newspaper, refusing to allow a nongovernment group to bid for it, but also took over the Windward Islands Broadcasting Station, which had previously served Dominica, Grenada, St. Lucia, and St. Vincent for 20 years and had built up a reputation for high standards in broadcasting. The station, now fully owned and controlled by the government of Grenada, has been renamed Radio Grenada.

Regional grouping. Ever since the West Indies Federation was dissolved in 1962, there have been moves and proposals for closer unity among the scattered fragments. The Caribbean Free Trade Association, an economic grouping that includes all the countries in the old federation as well as the Bahamas and the mainland territories of Guyana and British Honduras, continues to thrive, but two significant moves this year showed that there are strong feelings in the region for a closer link than that.

Three of the Windward Islands—Grenada, St. Lucia, and St. Vincent—signed a pact providing for complete freedom of movement for inhabitants between the three islands, abolition of passports, and the right to hold land anywhere in the three. Dominica, the fourth island in the old Windward group, was not included in the pact but seems likely to join at a later date. Meanwhile, Montserrat, the smallest of the Leeward Islands, has shown interest in the group, but the government of that island is said to be seeking public comment before making any move.

The other significant move was the publication of a document, prepared by a group of prominent West Indians, that outlines plans for the creation of a federation of eastern Caribbean countries centered around Trinidad and Tobago, with a proposed headquarters on one of the smaller islands. The importance of the signatories, who include Sir Hugh Wooding, chancellor of the University of the West Indies and a former chief justice of Trinidad and Tobago, and Sir Arthur Lewis, president of the Caribbean Development Bank and chancellor of the University of Guyana, suggests that the document cannot be lightly dismissed. It gives as reasons for such a federation the need for national identity, external representation, economic integration, the creation of a federal public service, and the safeguarding of civil liberties.

Politics. An unexpected general election in St. Vincent produced the extraordinary result of a premier without a following of his own. James Mitchell, minister of agriculture and trade in the government of Milton Cato, leader of the St. Vincent Labour Party, resigned because he thought that sufficient attention was not being paid to his constituency, the little offshore islands called the Grenadines. The premier decided to call a general election, but in the election his party secured only six seats, the same number as the rival People's Progressive Party, led by Ebenezer Joshua, who had been defeated by Cato in the previous election. Mitchell won a seat as an independent, completing the total of 13 seats. He refused to serve under Cato, and Joshua produced a masterstroke by saying that his party would serve under Mitchell as premier. This was duly done, and James Mitchell now leads St. Vincent, with Joshua as deputy premier. Mitchell is firmly committed to eastern Caribbean integration and gave evidence of this attitude by signing the freedom of movement pact with Grenada and St. Lucia.

In Grenada, Premier Eric Gairy was returned to power in February, winning 13 of 15 seats; he said that he would seek independence from Great Britain at the earliest possible opportunity.

In Anguilla, which broke away from union with St. Kitts–Nevis in 1967 and reverted to British colonial rule in 1971, constitutional elections were held for the first time since the breakaway. Ronald Webster and his followers won six of the seven elective seats in the new Anguilla council. The seven elective members and not more than six members nominated by the British commissioner form the full council. Webster, who led the breakaway in 1967, was unanimously elected leader and said he would resume negotiations with Great Britain for final separation from St. Kitts–Nevis.

Premier Lynden Pindling of the Bahamas, in a report to Parliament, said he would seek independence from Great Britain after the next general election, which will be held in 1973. The Bahamas will then, he said, seek membership in the United Nations and in the Organization of American States.

Volcanic activity. Soufrière volcano on St. Vincent, long a tourist attraction, showed signs of abnormal activity at the end of 1971, and some 1,100 people living in its vicinity were evacuated on government orders. Seismic research

teams from the University of the West Indies and from the United States had had the volcano under close observation for some time. It last erupted in 1902, with loss of nearly 2,000 lives, in the same month in which Mount Pelée on nearby Martinique blew up and killed 30,000 inhabitants. Soufrière seems to have become dormant once again.

Bahamas. Area, 5,386 sq. mi. Pop. (est. 1971), 190,000.

Bermuda. Area, 21 sq. mi. Pop. (est. 1971), 50,000.

British Honduras. Area, 8,867 sq. mi. Pop. (est. 1971), 120,-000.

British West Indies. *Anguilla.* Area, 35 sq. mi. Pop. (est. 1970), 6,000. *Antigua.* Area, 171 sq. mi. Pop. (est. 1971), 60,000. *British Virgin Islands.* Area, 59 sq. mi. Pop. (1970), 10,840. *Cayman Islands.* Area, 100 sq. mi. Pop. (1970), 10,650. *Dominica.* Area, 290 sq. mi. Pop. (est. 1971), 70,000. *Grenada and the Grenadines.* Area, 133 sq. mi. Pop. (est. 1970), 105,000. *Montserrat.* Area, 38 sq. mi. Pop. (est. 1971), 10,000. *St. Kitts–Nevis.* Area, 118 sq. mi. Pop. (1970), 45,800. *St. Lucia.* Area, 238 sq. mi. Pop. (est. 1971), 100,000. *St. Vincent.* Area, 150 sq. mi. Pop. (est. 1971), 90,000. *Turks and Caicos Islands.* Area, 166 sq. mi. Pop. (est. 1969), 5,500.

French Guiana. Area, 35,135 sq. mi. Pop. (est. 1970), 51,000.

French West Indies. *Guadeloupe.* Area, 687 sq. mi. Pop. (est. 1971), 330,000. *Martinique.* Area, 425 sq. mi. Pop. (est. 1971), 340,000.

Netherlands Antilles (Aruba, Bonaire, Curaçao, part of St. Martin, St. Eustatius, Saba). Area, 371 sq. mi. Pop. (est. 1971), 230,000.

Surinam. Area, 55,144 sq. mi. Pop. (est. 1971), 410,000.

U.S. Virgin Islands. Total area, 133 sq. mi. Pop. (1970 census), 62,468.

C. G. LINDO

CENTRAL AFRICAN REPUBLIC. Government. Early this year a congress of the ruling Movement for Social Evolution of Black Africa (MESAN) named President Jean Bedel Bokassa president for life. President Bokassa soon reshuffled his cabinet, centralizing eight ministerial portfolios in the presidency and retaining personally the Ministry of Defense and Information. Bokassa also tightened up his rein on thieves and petty criminals. Public executions were carried out, and the international press focused on the president's threat to exact biblical retribution for criminal acts.

Foreign affairs. In Libreville, Gabon, President Bokassa and President Albert Bongo of Gabon signed a joint communiqué agreeing to an increase in agricultural trade between the two countries.

Economy. As the internal economic situation continued to deteriorate, President Bokassa requested the Groupement Inter-Professionnel pour l'Étude et le Développement de l'Économie Centrafricaine, an expatriate businessmen's association, to analyze the country's economic difficulties. Its report, criticizing the nation's huge public debt, poor roads and postal services, and inept management of public corporations, created a furor in government circles and among businessmen. In response, Bokassa called in major creditors and paid part of the state's debt to each.

The country's economic situation stood to benefit from plans announced this year for renovation of the Ocean-Congo railroad in the neighboring People's Republic of the Congo. This railroad is the last link in the long river-rail chain that stretches from the landlocked Central African Republic to the sea. But its renovation still would leave the state with no railroads of its own and insufficient access to coastal ports.

In another hopeful development, the Central African and Sudanese governments signed an agreement to study the feasibility of building a railroad line through the rich copper mining area that spans their joint border. Meanwhile, construction began on a 62-mile asphalt road stretching from Mbaiki to the capital city of Bangui. The project was financed by a loan from the United States Agency for International Development.

BEATING IN BANGUI. As 45 convicted thieves cowered in the courtyard of Bangui Prison in the Central African Republic, troops under direct orders from President Jean Bedel Bokassa clubbed them for ten minutes. The bodies of three who died were publicly displayed.

HENRI BUREAU/GAMMA

Area and population. Area, 240,535 sq. mi. Pop. (est. 1972), 1.64 million.

Government. Former French colony, now a single-party republic. Pres., Jean Bedel Bokassa.

Finance. Monetary unit, Communauté Financière Africaine (CFA) franc; 1 CFA franc = US$0.0041. Budget (1972): balanced at US$45,654,300.

Trade (1970). Imports, US$34 million; exports, US$31 million.

LYNN KRIEGER MYTELKA

CEYLON. *See* SRI LANKA.

CHAD. Politics and government. After a brief period of political stability, rebel activity resumed again. It was climaxed in August 1971 by an attempted coup to overthrow President François Tombalbaye. The unsuccessful coup differed significantly from past rebel activity in that it was at least partly of external origin, and much of its aftermath this year involved other countries. The French military in Chad, which had been greatly reduced, had claimed that the country was practically free of rebellion and that the approximately 400 guerrillas left in the Tibesti region were wholly supplied and financed by Libya and other Arab countries. Chad accused Libya of supporting the coup in concert with a foreign imperialist power by providing arms and military training for Frolinat (the rebel National Liberation Front of Chad) and immediately broke off diplomatic relations. Libya, in turn, stated that it only sought Arab unity against Israel and accused Chad of Zionist tendencies. It subsequently recognized Frolinat as the only legitimate government of Chad.

Foreign affairs. With relations with the Arab countries, and particularly Libya, deteriorating to a dangerous level, Chad sought renewed support from France. In February, President Georges Pompidou of France visited Chad, and after finding Libya responsible for Frolinat's activities promised Tombalbaye France's continuing aid. This increase in French military aid was undoubtedly the key to the subsequent improvement in Libyan-Chad relations, but Niger's President Hamani Diori played the active role of international mediator. In April diplomatic relations between Chad and Libya were restored, and a joint statement was issued which condemned apartheid and also called for the return of lands currently held by Israel to the Palestinian people. This was followed in May by a similar improvement in relations with Sudan and the disclosure of Sudanese military action against Frolinat guerrillas using Sudan frontier regions as a staging base.

President Tombalbaye dealt the African, Malagasy, and Mauritian Common Organization (OCAMM) a blow in late February when he resigned as chairman of this French-speaking group of nations comprising most of France's former African colonies and Zaïre. His ostensible reason was dissatisfaction with the management of OCAMM-owned Air Afrique, from which Chad withdrew, although remaining in the parent organization. Tombalbaye's resignation, followed in April by Zaïre's withdrawal, brought into question the viability of OCAMM as anything more than an exclusive club controlled largely by presidents Félix Houphouët-Boigny of Ivory Coast and Léopold-Sédar Senghor of Senegal.

Economic developments. Chad's economy experienced marginal improvement this year. World prices of cotton, its chief export, rose somewhat, and after four years of exceptionally poor weather which had crippled agriculture in all of interior West Africa, output increased by 5 percent. Beef cattle and sheep production, which Chad exports primarily to Zaïre, also increased, and expected revenues from these sources in 1972 were nearly 6 billion CFA francs. Tombalbaye reiterated Chad's policy of de-emphasizing industrialization and concentrating on agricultural development, and this was reflected in the nature of its international development aid. France is currently financing a training program for fishermen on Lake Chad, an extension and

modernization of the slaughterhouse at Foucha, and technical assistance in cotton growing. The International Development Association is providing over $2 million for water wells to increase livestock production, and the European Economic Community's European Development Fund is providing over $11 million to develop cotton for export.

Area and population. Area, 495,800 sq. mi. Pop. (est. 1971), 3.8 million. Fort-Lamy (cap.; est. 1970), 132,500.

Government. Single-party republic. Pres., François Tombalbaye.

Finance. Monetary unit, Communauté Financière Africaine franc; 1 CFA franc = US$0.0041. Budget (est. 1972–1973): revenue, 13.85 billion CFA francs.

Trade (1970). Imports, 17.06 billion CFA francs; exports, 8.21 billion CFA francs. Principal exports: cotton, cattle, tobacco.

GEORGE LAMSON

CHEMISTRY. The environment continued to be a major concern for chemists and chemistry in 1972. The most widely publicized incidents concerned the use of hexachlorophene, an antibacterial agent that appears in over 400 products, from soaps to deodorants. At high concentrations the chemical has been shown to be dangerous (a 3 percent solution used daily for 90 days on monkeys caused some brain damage), and there was ample evidence that some regulation of the material was needed. As a result, the U.S. Food and Drug Administration found it necessary to ban the use of hexachlorophene as an ingredient in cosmetics and to require that antibacterial cleansers have the material present at no greater than a 0.75 percent concentration unless sold by prescription. The hospital routine of washing newborn babies with a solution of the material was also stopped by some hospitals, but the necessity of maintaining a low bacterial level in infant wards required a return to its use, although it is much more strictly controlled than previously.

PCB's. Another class of chlorinated hydrocarbons receiving much attention was the polychlorinated biphenyls. PCB's are formed by chlorinating biphenyl and are used by industry in crude form (a mixture of possible isomers) largely as plasticizers in the plastics industry and as a dielectric fluid or insulator in capacitors and transformers. Such uses are supposed to be permanent. The material is not supposed to find its way into the environment; it is water insoluble and not readily leached out of discarded plastic materials, and capacitors and transformers are sealed. However, PCB's have been detected in rainwater, in human tissue, and in many species of birds and fish. One estimate, in Missouri, found PCB concentration in fish to be 100 times that of DDT. The largest concentrations appear to be along coastlines, in fish and fish-eating birds.

The health hazard of PCB's to humans is considered potential but not immediate; in fact, only in one severe case of PCB poisoning (an industrial accident leading to contaminated food in Japan) are the direct effects of ingesting large quantities of PCB known. There are apparently no effects if PCB in food is below 10 parts per million. It is widely agreed, however, that PCB's, like DDT, can't be good for you. Worry about possible effects of PCB's has led to considerable reduction in the amount of PCB used in any material that might come in contact with food.

Degradable plastics. Der Wienerschnitzel, a chain of fast-food restaurants, has made use of an environmentally degradable plastic lid for its carry-out drinks. One of the problems associated with the use of plastic lids for containers is that the polystyrene or polyethylene plastic cannot be digested by microorganisms and is very stable chemically, which causes the discarded lids to remain intact as litter for long periods of time. Although the exact composition of the degradable plastic is a trade secret, it is basically about 98 percent polystyrene and about 2 percent photosensitizer. The photosensitizer initiates a free-radical reaction in the polystyrene in the presence of ultraviolet light from the sun. Oxygen in the air then continues the breakdown process,

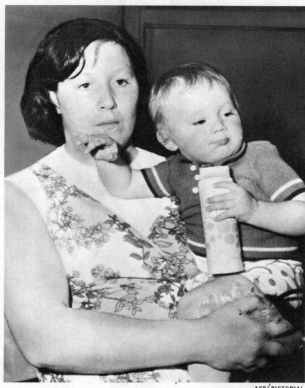

CHEMICAL CULPRIT. A box of talcum powder containing 6 percent hexachlorophene is handed over to authorities after large doses of the germicide allegedly caused the death of 39 French babies. The U.S. Food and Drug Administration limited the nonprescription sale of some 400 products containing the chemical.

AFP/PICTORIAL

which results in disintegration of the caps within about 60 days and complete reduction of the remaining material to water and carbon dioxide within about 120 days.

Rare earth. Control of automobile exhaust emissions requires, among other things, that the level of carbon monoxide in the effluent be kept low. The logical answer to this requirement is a catalytic converter in the exhaust line, to assist in the complete conversion of CO to harmless CO_2 (carbon dioxide). The problem has been that the only long-lasting, effective catalysts have been the commercial platinum-based materials, which, as might be expected, are expensive. Fortunately, it has been found that a mixture of rare earth and cobalt and manganese oxides is competitive with platinum in effectiveness and is less expensive by a wide margin.

This development points up the growing commercial applications of the so-called "rare earths," the elements from lanthanum to lutetium. Up to now there have been only isolated uses of single rare earths, such as europium in color television picture tubes. This is the first commercial opportunity for the group as a whole, which often occurs as a complex mixture in nature.

Mercury and selenium in fish. A study of the amount of mercury in old stuffed fish in museum cases shows that the level of mercury in old fish is about the same as the level in fresh fish caught today. There is also some evidence that selenium, which by itself is toxic, may serve to reduce the toxicity of mercury when both elements are present in fish. Fish such as tuna regularly contain both selenium and mercury.

Resistance of rats to warfarin sodium. Warfarin sodium is an anticoagulant drug often used as rodent poison. It has been particularly useful recently in the control of the vam-

pire bat in South America. Ordinarily, the drug is smeared on the back of a captured bat; the bat is then released and returns to its colony. As the bats preen one another, the drug is licked off, and one treated bat becomes responsible for the death of itself and many others, without endangering other species. There is, however, evidence, both in laboratory rat colonies and in at least one wild population in North Carolina, that a genetic resistance to warfarin sodium is building up. Presumably, this resistance is developing because only resistant rats are surviving to produce offspring.

Outer space. Results of the analysis of many of the lunar samples brought back on the Apollo 15 mission became available this year. The samples brought back by the Apollo missions have been subjected to the most intense analyses of single pieces of rock that have ever been made; the Apollo 15 mission was considered particularly important because of the varied terrain in the Hadley Rille area. A variety of techniques have been used, ranging from simple microscopic observation to gamma ray spectroscopy. The results of these investigations are quite complicated and pose as many questions as they answer. A few general findings, however, appear to be conclusively indicated by the data. First, the moon clearly is not a piece of the earth that fell off some time in the far distant past; this conclusion is almost certain because the ratio of potassium to uranium in moon rocks is quite different from that in earth rocks. Second, there is almost certainly no evidence that there is now or ever has been any life on the moon: There is almost no carbon, the basic atom of living things on earth, and what little there is seems to have come from the sun, carried along in the so-called solar wind, a stream of particles emitted from the sun during solar flares and sunspots. Third, there is evidence that the moon was molten on its surface for about 350 million years and that many of the present surface features have resulted from the fractional crystallization of that primitive surface.

Mariner 9 has provided strong evidence for the existence of both CO_2 and water on Mars, particularly in the area of the southern polar cap. There is also evidence of both hydrogen and oxygen atoms in the atmosphere of the red planet. No form of life has yet been detected, but the conditions of any possible life are now much better understood, so that more discriminating experiments can be devised to look for it. The Viking spacecraft, which is supposed to land on Mars, will explore this question further.

The Venera and Mariner probes of Venus indicate that the upper layers of the Venusian atmosphere are most probably composed of impure hydrochloric acid: that is, water vapor containing about 25 percent hydrogen chloride by weight, plus some impurities. (*See* ASTRONOMY *and* SPACE EXPLORATION.)

New analytical tools. For a number of reasons, but especially for understanding catalysts, the exact nature of surfaces is an important concern. A new technique, electron spectroscopy for chemical analysis, is one method which provides the kind of detailed information about surfaces that is required. In ESCA, the surface is bombarded with X rays of precisely known energies. These X rays cause the surface to emit electrons, the energies of which are determined by the curvature of their courses in a magnetic field. Because the energy of the emitted electron is equal to the difference between the energy of the initial X ray and the binding energy of the electron, the method allows precise determination of the amount of energy holding the electron in place.

Some applications of this technique outside the catalyst industry include study of the formation of silicon dioxide on the surface of the extremely pure silicon used in transistors and study of the nature of the alloy formed when gold is plated on aluminum—a process used to produce high-quality electrical contacts.

When heavy ions instead of X rays are used to knock off the electrons, the technique produces more information,

UPI
POPPERFOTO

Checkmating the Soviet Champ

Intense, temperamental Bobby Fischer, who spent his childhood shattering egos at the Brooklyn Chess Club and used to sleep with a chessboard set up beside his bed, finally realized his life's dream at Reykjavík, Iceland. There he got his chance to meet and beat world chess champion Boris Spassky in a match that lasted 21 grueling games and made chess a household word for the first time in recent U.S. history. The Fischer-Spassky battles were personal as well as tactical. First, Fischer held out for more money, arriving in Iceland a week late (above) only after a British investment banker agreed to augment the purse. Soon after, the Russian grandmaster, already a bit unnerved, walked out in protest over the delay (right). The battle of wits got off to a bad start for Fischer, who blundered in the first game (facing page) and forfeited the second by refusing to play in the presence of cameras. But he went on to win five and draw three of the next eight games, driving Spassky into a corner from which he never escaped, and on September 1 became the first American to win the official world title.

because the heavy ions knock off surface atoms as well as electrons. Thus, deeper and deeper layers of the surface can be exposed, and the analyst can get a layer-by-layer unveiling of the surface characteristics.

Another technique, this one for separation of complicated mixtures, became prominent this year. The technique is liquid chromatography, and although the principles involved have been well known for a long time, there was an explosion of interest this year because of the newly discovered power of the method for separating nucleotides, the sugar-base compounds that are the building blocks of DNA and RNA. A number of commercial instruments for liquid chromatography appeared on the market this year.

Unlike gas chromatography, wherein a mixture is separated by passage as a gas over a solid phase, in liquid chromatography a solution of material is passed through a liquid or solid bed. The method is extremely useful for those compounds that cannot be vaporized without decomposition and for materials with high molecular weight that cannot be gotten into the vapor phase to any extent.

EDWIN S. WEAVER

CHESS. World championship match. Bobby Fischer at age 29 became the 11th world chess champion, the first American to hold that title, by beating Boris Spassky of the Soviet Union, 12½–8½, in a best-of-24-game match.

Fischer qualified to play Spassky by winning the 1970 interzonal tournament at Palma de Mallorca and elimination matches against Mark Taimanov of the Soviet Union and Bent Larsen of Denmark; he then won the semifinal match against Soviet former world champion Tigran Petrosian.

Ten countries put in competitive bids for the championship match, with Belgrade at $152,000 and Reykjavík at

GAME OF THE YEAR

Third match game

Boris Spassky (White)–Bobby Fischer (Black)

White	Black	White	Black
1. P–Q4	N–KB3	22. QR–K1	Q–N3
2. P–QB4	P–K3	23. P–N3	R–K2
3. N–KB3	P–B4	24. Q–Q3	R–N1
4. P–Q5	PxP	25. PxP	PxP
5. PxP	P–Q3	26. P–N4	P–B5
6. N–B3	P–KN3	27. Q–Q2	QR–K1
7. N–Q2	QN–Q2	28. R–K3	P–R4
8. P–K4	B–N2	29. R/3–K2	K–R2
9. B–K2	O–O	30. R–K3	K–N1
10. O–O	R–K1	31. R/3–K2	BxN
11. Q–B2	N–R4!	32. QxB	RxP
12. BxN	PxB	33. RxR	RxR
13. N–B4	N–K4	34. RxR	QxR
14. N–K3	Q–R5!	35. B–R6	Q–N3
15. B–Q2	N–N5	36. B–B1	Q–N8
16. NxN	PxN	37. K–B1	B–B4
17. B–B4	Q–B3	38. K–K2	Q–K5ch
18. P–KN3	B–Q2	39. Q–K3	Q–B7ch
19. P–QR4	P–N3	40. Q–Q2	Q–N6!
20. KR–K1	P–QR3	41. Q–Q4	B–Q6ch!
21. R–K2	P–QN4	Resigns	

(If 42. K–K3, Q–Q8; 43. B–N2 (B–Q2, Q–B6 mate), Q–B6ch; 44. K–Q2, Q–K7ch; 45. K–B3, Q–B7 mate. Or 43. Q–N2, Q–B6ch; 44. K–Q4, Q–K5ch; 45. K–B3, Q–K8ch and 46. Q–K4 mate.)

$125,000 submitting the highest bids. When Spassky and Fischer failed to agree on a site, Dr. Max Euwe of the Netherlands, a former world champion and the president of the International Chess Federation, declared that the match would be split between the two cities. After Fischer demanded more money and the Belgrade organizers demanded a guarantee that Bobby would show up, Belgrade dropped out of the bidding, and the entire match was scheduled for Reykjavík on July 2.

Spassky went to Iceland early, but Fischer, still insisting on more money, didn't show. Finally, Dr. Euwe set a July 4 deadline for his appearance. At the last minute, a British chess enthusiast and investment banker, James Slater, contributed an additional $125,000 to the purse, and Fischer flew to Reykjavík, where the match finally began on July 11.

Completion of the match, however, remained in doubt. Fischer, having blundered and lost a drawn endgame in the first game, demanded that all camera and television equipment be removed from the playing hall. While the dispute continued, he forfeited the second game. He booked passage back to the United States but was eventually persuaded by his advisers—and, reportedly, a call from Henry Kissinger —to play the third game. Spassky agreed to Fischer's demand to play the game in a closed room, and Fischer won in a fine positional struggle. (*See* GAME OF THE YEAR.)

The fourth game, a draw, was played in the regular exhibition hall after the television equipment was removed. Thereafter, the extracurricular part of the match, despite some squabbles over spectator noise and seating and the size of the boards, was not quite as stormy—for Fischer at least. In the next six games Fischer scored 5 points, to establish a 3-point lead. Spassky battled hard thereafter but was unable to narrow the lead.

Fischer's play, though not up to his usual impeccable tactical standards, was steady and confident. He blundered and lost the opening game, played sloppily for a draw in a won position in the seventh, and made another blunder in the 14th, which he drew when Spassky also faltered. Fischer walked into Russian opening analysis in the fourth, 11th, 15th, and 16th games when he played variations for which Spassky was well prepared; but he fought his way to a draw in all of those but the 11th. On the other hand, Fischer's analyses were better than any that the best Soviet players could cook up for him, and he kept Spassky off balance by varying his previously inflexible opening repertoire. Thus, in the third, fifth, sixth, and 13th games, Bobby emerged from prepared openings with a big advantage and won all four.

Perhaps Spassky was disturbed by the circus atmosphere, for he was hardly the detached, flexible, psychological strategist who had previously outperformed all his contemporaries —including Fischer, against whom he had a record of three wins and two draws before the match began. He blundered and lost the fifth game in a bad position, the eighth in an even position, and the 13th; he blundered but drew the 14th and 15th games when both seemed to be sure wins. Late in the match, Spassky's second, Efim Geller, possibly acting on orders from Moscow, charged that Fischer was using electronic and chemical means to affect Spassky's play. The Icelandic organizers examined the lighting and took apart Fischer's and Spassky's chairs, but after finding nothing more sinister than two dead flies in the lighting, they rejected the charges.

Thus, Bobby gained the title to which his fighting play, genius, and complete dedication entitled him. He will defend that title in 1975, but at the moment it seems there is no one really in his class.

Meanwhile, the excitement generated by the extensive media coverage of the match transformed chess from an elitist game to a popular sport in the United States. Channel 13 in New York carried a five-hour daily telephone replay of the games for an estimated 1 million viewers.

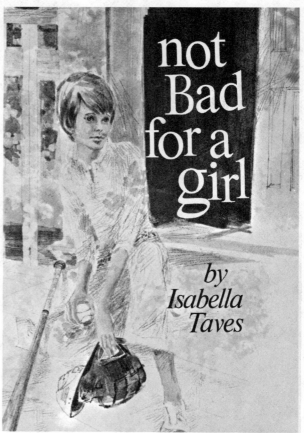

LEFT, M. EVANS; RIGHT, HARPER AND ROW

Children's Lib: New Heroes and Heroines

What makes a boy a boy and a girl a girl? This year children's books have begun to get the message from feminists preaching equality between the sexes. *Not Bad for a Girl* attracted wide attention for its realistic treatment of the travails of 12-year-old Sharon Lee, who slugs it out on the baseball diamond despite torrents of abuse. On the other side of the fence, the hero of *William's Doll* stays home to cuddle his doll, practicing for paternity leave despite his father's efforts to lure him with electric trains.

Television commentator Shelby Lyman became an instant celebrity; chess books and equipment were snapped up by an eager public; and Bobby received a flurry of fabulous commercial offers. Not since Paul Morphy, America's other chess *wunderkind*, was acclaimed the unofficial world champion in the 1850's had chess enjoyed such popularity in the United States.

See also PEOPLE IN THE NEWS: Bobby Fischer.

Other tournaments. Here are the other major winners during the year: U.S. championship: Robert Byrne, Lubomir Kavalek, Samuel Reshevsky (tie). U.S. Open: Walter Browne (Australia). Hastings: Anatoly Karpov, Victor Korchnoi (both U.S.S.R.; tie). Beverwijk: Lajos Portisch (Hungary). World Chess Olympics: U.S.S.R. Alekhine Memorial (Moscow, December 1971): Leonid Stein, Anatoly Karpov (both U.S.S.R.; tie).

JAMES T. SHERWIN

CHILDREN'S LITERATURE. Trends. This year a fourth "r"—relevance—was added to reading, 'riting, and 'rithmetic. The new juvenile titles reflected almost every current adult concern: women's lib, divorce, politics, pollution, the stock market, sex, narcotics, taxes, consumerism, cooking, China. But conspicuously, there *was* a troll or two.

WILLIAM'S DOLL
by CHARLOTTE ZOLOTOW
pictures by WILLIAM PÈNE DU BOIS

HARPER & ROW, PUBLISHERS
New York, Evanston, San Francisco, London

he'll know how to
take care of his baby
and feed him
and love him
and bring him
the things he wants,
like a doll
so that he can
practice being
a father."

Many of last year's economic problems continued to plague publishers. There was continued sluggishness in sales of children's books. Still, some companies reported that their sales picture had brightened and that they had high hopes sales would jump substantially by year's end. However, as one house put it, "We're skating on thin ice. We're not scared exactly, but cautious." New books were selling exceptionally well, but back lists were not because educators, faced with slashed budgets and spiraling administrative costs, were consolidating libraries and classes. Also, the impact of the downturn in the U.S. birthrate in the late sixties was beginning to be felt in lower enrollments in elementary schools. Perhaps reflecting the times, the number of new hard-cover titles brought out was 2,000, about even with last year.

This year paperbacks for children came of age. They seemed to be genuinely accepted by librarians and teachers, who, once forced by necessity to buy paperbacks, have found them just as suitable as hard-cover books for individualized reading programs.

Another word in the news was "reevaluation," and to children's librarians in northern California it meant the re-

reading of ten classics (*The Secret Garden, Mary Poppins, Charlie and the Chocolate Factory, The Story of the Treasure Seekers,* among others) with an eye to withdrawing them from the shelves. It caused a stir in the field, with cries coming from all sides claiming "a violation of the constitutional rights of minors" and "the value of the whole book must be weighed against what is in some cases a very minor racist or sexist incident." A new wrinkle was added to last year's suppression campaign against Maurice Sendak's popular picture book *In the Night Kitchen,* "censorship by mutilation." A number of librarians in Louisiana and Pennsylvania had used white tempera paint to diaper the nakedness of Mickey, the book's hero.

Books for blacks. Black authors talked directly to black children this year, and the message was right now, right on. A delight in being black was the dominant mood of two vibrant picture books: Ernest Gregg's creation story *And the Sun God Said: That's Hip,* with G. Falcon Beazer's glowing illustrations, and Julius Lester's Aesopian retelling of six animal tales from slave days, *The Knee-High Man,* appropriately accompanied by Ralph Pinto's sly and wry pictures. For teen-agers, Julius Lester's *Long Journey Home*

took six footnotes to history and fashioned them into a collection of moving short stories about slaves and ex-slaves. One of the most talented black authors writing today, June Jordan, produced a highly original "hip history," *Dry Victories.* An alive, bitter, cool, controversial, and very subjective book, it compares, in the form of a rap between two teen-agers, the Reconstruction and civil rights eras. An ironic juxtapositioning of photographs and pictures points up the author's anger at the broken promises made to black Americans.

Women's lib. Continuing the close scrutiny given children's books by the Feminist Collective on Children's Media last year, Letty Pogrebin compiled for *Ms.,* the feminist magazine, a basic library for liberated children, complete with books to "boycott (and girlcott)." Stephanie Spinner's fine anthology, *Feminine Plural: Stories by Women About Growing Up,* offered a judicious selection of ten stories by well-known writers but illustrated one problem of creating a consciousness-raising literature: the most feminist story was the least literary; the most literary, the least relevant.

Divorce. With nearly one in three marriages now ending in divorce, it was welcome to find ten authors dramatizing the emotional problems that children encounter when their parents split up. Most therapeutic of the novels was Judy Blume's *It's Not the End of the World,* outlining how a 12-year-old girl adjusts to a pending divorce in her family. Most poignant and psychologically honest was Constance C. Greene's *The Unmaking of Rabbit,* which focuses on the relationship between a boy (unwanted by both his parents) and his grandmother, the only person who loves him.

Teen-age fiction. One critic asserted this year that in literary grace and skill American writers could not compete with the British, stating that the best of the novels for teen-agers were all by British novelists. Most impressive was Jill Paton Walsh's *Goldengrove,* which sensitively sounds the depths of one girl's thoughts and feelings during her last summer of childhood. In *The Summer People,* John Rowe Townsend accomplishes the same kind of evocation of emotions, but from a boy's point of view. Two more British novelists to salute: Mollie Hunter with *A Sound of Chariots* and Catherine Storr with *Thursday.* The Vietnam war finally filtered down into teen-age fiction with Joe W. Haldeman's GI diary *War Year* and Gail Graham's powerful story of an American soldier and four Vietnamese children, *Cross-Fire.* After the outcry last year over the brief homosexual scene in John Donovan's *I'll Get There. It Better Be Worth the Trip,* the silence that greeted Isabelle Holland's *The Man Without a Face* and Lynn Hall's *Sticks and Stones* was deafening. Both books are told with understanding, with the latter book not as much about homosexuality as it is about the power and injustice of gossip.

Nonfiction. Of the many volumes prompted by President Richard M. Nixon's visit to China, Orville Schell's and Joseph Esherick's *Modern China,* for ages 12 and up, was the most readable and balanced of the batch. In *Hooray for Peace, Hurrah for War,* Steven Jantzen presents from an antiwar point of view an excellent picture of the United States during World War I. Last year's torrent of books on ecology still flowed strong and steadily.

Imaginative stories. Most notable among the original stories for children eight and over was Mollie Hunter's *The Haunted Mountain,* a Scottish suspense story of magic and the supernatural, about a farmer who defies the Sidhe (fairy folk) and his son who rescues him. Zilpha Keatley Snyder's *The Witches of Worm* weaves the theme of witchcraft through a thoughtful, gracefully written story of a girl who thinks she's being bewitched by her cat when in reality the demons are her own anger and alienation. In *The House of Wings,* Betsy Byars presents a strong, poignant portrait of a boy's frustration and anger and how his grandfather helps him tame a crane and learn to love. Norma Klein's *Mom, the Wolf Man, and Me,* a very human and honest story of a fatherless girl and her unmarried mother, was considered controversial and relevant.

Picture books. Interestingly, the best picture books for the youngest set dealt not with the real world but the realm of magic, myth, and fairy tales. In *d'Aulaires' Trolls,* Ingri and Edgar Parin d'Aulaire give an authoritative tour of the troll world that existed long ago under Norway's "moss-grown mountains." Randall Jarrell's retelling of the Grimm Brothers' *Snow-White and the Seven Dwarfs* was lovely, especially with Nancy Ekholm Burkert's double-page tableaux, medieval in mood, intensely magical. Blair Lent added luminous cutaway pictures of an underground world populated by wicked *oni* to Arlene Mosel's retelling of an old Japanese folktale, *The Funny Little Woman.* From "A the Armadillo, belted & amazonian" to "Z a ruminating zebu," *Hosie's Alphabet* is a stunning album of animals drawn by Leonard Baskin. A contemporary counterculture family appears in Robert Andrew Parker's soft, tender watercolors for Amy Ehrlich's *Zeek Silver Moon.* For beginning readers there were "short" short-story collections, including two gently wise and witty books written and illustrated by Arnold Lobel: *Mouse Tales* and *Frog and Toad Together.*

Awards. Ursula Nordstrom, publisher of Harper Junior Books, received the Constance Lindsay Skinner Award for her 30 years of distinguished contribution to the world of books and to society. In May, Scott O'Dell became the second American to be given the Hans Christian Andersen Award, the highest international recognition for a children's book author. Donald Barthelme's *The Slightly Irregular Fire Engine, or The Hithering Thithering Djinn* captured the National Book Award. Robert O'Brien's *Mrs. Frisby and the Rats of NIMH* was awarded the Newbery Medal for the most distinguished children's book. The Caldecott Medal honoring the most distinguished picture book of the year was given to Nonny Hogrogian for her *One Fine Day.* Book World's 1972 Spring Book Festival prizes were: picture book, Theodor Storm's *Little John,* retold by Doris Orgel and illustrated by Anita Lobel; 8–12, Charlotte Baker's *Cockleburr Quarters;* and 12–16, Mary Rogers' *Freaky Friday.* The 30th annual Child Study Association Children's Award was given to *John Henry McCoy* by Lillie B. Chaffin. The CSA also presented a special citation to *The Pair of Shoes* by Aline Glasgow.

See also BOOKS IN REVIEW: Children's Books.

MARGARET F. O'CONNELL

CHILE. Growing polarization of forces and increasing confrontation, occasionally violent, beset Chile in 1972. On one side was President Salvador Allende Gossens and his Popular Unity coalition, made up of the Socialist Party, the Communist Party, a portion of the middle-of-the-road Radical Party, and various other leftist groups. The opposition was led by the Christian Democratic Party on the left, the National Party on the right, part of the Radical Party, and other center and rightist groups. In October this polarization led to Allende's worst crisis; in a general strike that lasted over a week, the middle class in effect demonstrated against Allende's efforts to make Chile a socialist country. Truck drivers and owners began the strike, and other workers, small businessmen, and farmers joined them. To restore order, Allende had to declare a state of emergency in 19 of Chile's 25 provinces, call in the armed forces to rule, seize all radio stations for 24 hours, jail many of the striking truck drivers and owners, and threaten to seize the small businesses that had closed down to support the strikers. On October 31, Allende's cabinet resigned at his request, to permit the installation of a new cabinet with heavy military representation. After a government ultimatum, unions ordered all strikers back to work by November 6.

Elections. There was no clear-cut trend from several elections held during the year. The opposition won two congressional seats in a by-election in January. In July a

ALIGNED AGAINST ALLENDE. An estimated 200,000 Chileans held a "march for democracy" in April, demanding that the Marxist regime of President Salvador Allende submit to a plebiscite. The Allende government has been confronting a very severe economic slump.

Communist Party deputy retained his congressional seat as representative of the arid northern province of Coquimbo, but his margin of victory dropped from some 20,000 votes in the 1971 election to 8,000.

In nonlegislative electoral contests in April, the opposition won the rectorship and control of the council of the University of Chile. But in June the Communist Party retained control of the nationwide Central Labor Confederation. The labor elections were the first in which union members participated in the direct selection of their leaders. Some 800,000 workers were eligible to vote. When early returns appeared to favor the Christian Democrats, the Communist leadership announced that, to facilitate greater participation, the polls would be kept open for a few more days. However, the final results, showing the Communists retaining the presidency of the union, were not announced until mid-July.

Both the government coalition and the opposition looked to the nationwide elections scheduled for March 1973 as the first significant test of Allende's popularity.

Mass protests. Both sides used the mass march as a means of demonstrating the scope of their support. In April the opposition staged a peaceful "march for democracy," joined by more than 200,000 people, in the streets of Santiago. On August 21, Chile's 150,000 shopkeepers staged a one-day general strike against government economic policies; the strike led to four days of general protest and to Allende's declaring a state of emergency in Santiago Province.

Allende supporters turned out in September in a highly successful march celebrating the second anniversary of Allende's electoral victory. But violence erupted in the streets in succeeding days, as young members of the conservative Fatherland and Liberty Party clashed with police and with members of the Movement of the Revolutionary Left (MIR).

A few days later, primary and secondary schools were closed for vacation ten days early to stem street violence in Santiago; students had demonstrated almost daily for two weeks to protest Allende's education policies.

Violence also erupted sporadically in the countryside, especially in the fertile south, as squatters, led principally by members of the MIR, took over farmland. In the province of Cautín, dispossessed farmers banded together and began to retake some of their properties. Local police did little to protect or restrict either side, and some observers reported that, in effect, a civil war was being waged.

Congress. The opposition-controlled Congress continued to fight most of Allende's economic program. After Allende announced plans to expropriate an additional 91 major corporations, Congress passed a constitutional amendment, retroactive to October 1971, which required the president to obtain congressional approval before certain kinds of private property could be nationalized. Allende retaliated by vetoing the measure.

The opposition in Congress also impeached and removed from office two ministers of interior. After each congressional action, Allende reappointed the minister to a different cabinet post. On March 9, Congress overrode Allende's veto of a bill that permitted Santiago's university television stations to extend their coverage throughout the country. Previously, there had been one state-owned national television station.

At midyear Allende was faced with a serious split within his own forces. The moderate wing, composed of the Communist Party, the Radicals, and the Social Democrats, counseled that the pace of expropriation and other reforms be slowed in order to consolidate the gains already made. The radical elements, made up of the Socialist Party, the Christian left, and the MIR, advocated more vigorous action, including the dissolution of Congress. Allende appeared to

follow the suggestions of the more moderate wing rather than those of his own Socialist Party. In June he talked with the Christian Democrat leaders in an attempt to moderate that party's absolute opposition to the government, but the Christian Democrats broke off the talks in July.

Economic developments. The Chilean economy continued the growth that had begun in 1971, but the signs of strain were apparent. In the first six months of 1972, the gross national product was up 6 percent; in the same period of the preceding year it had risen 8 percent. Industrial production was up 8–10 percent, as opposed to 12 percent in 1971. Many observers felt that the increases in production would create problems. Although Chilean industry was producing at near capacity and demand was growing, new private investment had almost stopped, and government funds were being used to purchase industries rather than to expand or modernize them. Among the results was an increasing rate of inflation, as the cost of living rose 22 percent in 1971 and 33 percent in the first seven months of 1972.

Serious food shortages developed as agricultural production was disrupted by the agrarian reform program and by the illegal seizures of land. Fowl and eggs were in particularly short supply; meat was rationed and sold only three days a week; milk products were difficult to get; and a black market developed for some foods. It was estimated that Chile imported $300 million to $400 million worth of food products.

Many of Chile's economic difficulties could be traced to the decline of copper prices from 80 cents a pound in 1969 to 50 cents a pound in 1971. Copper sales provide more than 70 percent of the nation's foreign exchange, and a foreign exchange shortage prevented larger food imports. Although large gains in copper production had been hoped for in the industry's first full year of operation after nationalization, by midyear output was only slightly above that of 1971, even though a major new mine was put into production. In May copper miners, demanding higher wages and better working conditions, struck two major mines, Chuquicamata and El Teniente.

Chile succeeded in April in obtaining refinancing by 12 creditor nations of part of Chile's more than $3 billion foreign debt. However, little new private credit was being extended, and Allende accused the United States of withholding credit.

ITT. U.S. newspaper columnist Jack Anderson reported that officials of the International Telephone and Telegraph Corporation (ITT) had expressed fears to the U.S. government that their properties in Chile would be nationalized without compensation if Allende became president in 1970 and had wondered what could be done to prevent Allende's election. Although there was no proof that the U.S. government took any action to influence the Chilean elections, Anderson's allegation was sufficient to loose a storm of protest in Chile against U.S. "imperialism." In April 1972, all ITT properties in Chile—including investments valued at approximately $200 million, shares in the telephone company, a factory making telephone equipment, a telegraph agency, and two hotels—were expropriated.

Area and population. Area, 292,258 sq. mi. Pop. (est. 1972), 10,044,900. Santiago (cap.; 1970), 2,586,212.
Government. Republic with bicameral Congress. Pres., Salvador Allende Gossens.
Finance. Monetary unit, escudo; 1 escudo = US$0.0225.
Agriculture and industry (1971). Steel production, 600,000 metric tons of ingots; copper production, 730,000 tons.

PHYLLIS J. PETERSON

CHINA, PEOPLE'S REPUBLIC OF. Two central events, both sensational in their public manifestations and both momentous in their ramifications, dominated China's external and internal affairs this year. In foreign affairs, China played host to the historic visit in late February of President Richard M. Nixon, a major milestone in the slow but steady rapprochement between the two countries. In its dealings with other countries, China continued to pursue a "diplomatic" rather than a "revolutionary" foreign policy, setting up new contacts and strengthening relations with a wide range of governments. On the internal scene, the key event was the stunning purge of Lin Piao, chief of the armed forces and Mao Tse-tung's heir. It was announced that Lin had been killed in a plane crash in September 1971 while attempting to flee to the Soviet Union. Several top-ranking military leaders were also toppled amid spectacular accusations that they had conspired to assassinate Mao. Whatever the validity of these charges and the details of the infighting, it is clear that during the fall of 1971 the Chinese leadership was rocked by a profound and bitter power struggle, injecting new elements of instability into leadership relations at the highest levels.

The Peking summit. President Nixon's trip to China was a historic watershed in U.S.-China relations. It marked both an end and a beginning: an end to the open hostility that had marked these relations prior to the Nixon administration's shift to a policy of reconciliation; and the beginning of progress toward full normalization of relations between the two countries. Although covert moves aimed at a détente were begun shortly after Nixon assumed office, the president's China trip came as a remarkable climax to these moves, out of all proportion to their modest beginnings. It stamped the détente with the grandeur of a summit meeting and imparted to it a dimension of drama and import that no other single event could have given. While the visit could not dissipate all the suspicions and problems that had accumulated during more than two decades of hostility, it managed, in one bold stroke, to open a new era in relations between the two nations.

The atmosphere surrounding the Peking summit was highly cordial. As expected, the Chinese, led by Premier Chou En-lai, proved to be thoughtful and gracious hosts, and the Americans responded enthusiastically. After a completely correct though somewhat frosty airport reception, the Chinese went out of their way to emphasize their sincerity. A meeting between Chairman Mao and President Nixon a few hours after the president's arrival—much sooner than anyone in the American party had expected—conferred Mao's indispensable blessing on the whole venture.

The visit's public events were dazzling. With the entire world watching their every move, President Nixon and Premier Chou attended a series of banquets, ballet performances, and gymnastic displays. Visits to the Great Wall and to other historic sights rounded out the social schedule. At all these events, Nixon and Chou exchanged friendly toasts and acted more like old friends than leaders of governments that had been bitterly antagonistic for more than 23 years. Behind this curtain of public cordiality, intensive private talks between the two leaders were conducted throughout the week.

The talks were wide-ranging and apparently involved much hard bargaining. The groundwork for the talks had largely been laid by Chou and Henry Kissinger, the president's adviser for national security affairs, at meetings held in China in July and October 1971. But it remained for the president and the premier to refine and ratify whatever arrangements had been made, as well as to announce them to a waiting world. Since both sides had gone this far and since each side, for its own reasons, had a very high stake in reaching at least some kind of agreement, it was clear from the outset that the two leaders would not part without attaining some accord. The content of this accord, however, still had to be hammered out, and here, it appears, the two men hit a serious snag from the start.

The main bone of contention apparently was the nature of the future ties between China and the United States, a question that was inextricably linked with the delicate issue

of Taiwan. The Chinese, it appears, pressed for a rapid move toward formal and full-scale diplomatic relations, a move that would require Washington to sever its ties with and abandon its commitment to the Nationalist government on Taiwan. The Americans, on the other hand, were obviously not prepared to go so far at this juncture, and they apparently argued for less formal ties with Peking, which would enable the United States to maintain its ties with Taiwan.

Although these basic differences remained unresolved, they did not prove fatal. Reflecting accord on some issues and continued disagreement on others, the joint communiqué issued at the close of the talks alternated between statements of agreement and disagreement. Both sides agreed on the basic principles of international conduct. Even as they acknowledged the differences in their social systems, they pledged to abide by the principles of peaceful coexistence and emphasized that international disputes should be settled without threat or use of force. With these principles in mind, the two sides promised to cooperate in four broad areas: They would work toward the normalization of relations. They would try to rescue the world from the danger of international war. Neither side would seek hegemony in Asia or permit any other country to extend its power in the area. And they agreed not to negotiate on behalf of any third party or to assist each other in any operation directed against another nation.

On Indochina and Korea, each side expressed support for its allies. With respect to Japan, the United States underlined its desire for "friendly relations," while China expressed its concern about Japanese "militarism."

Concerning Taiwan, the United States, in a significant shift, stated that it did not challenge the claim of both the Chinese People's Republic and the Nationalist government that "Taiwan is part of China." Underscoring its desire for a peaceful settlement by the Chinese themselves, Washington stated its "ultimate objective of the withdrawal of all United States forces and military installations from Taiwan." In the meantime, but without a specific timetable, the United States pledged to progressively reduce the American forces on Taiwan "as the tension in the area diminishes." The Chinese, for their part, reaffirmed their long-standing position that Taiwan is a province of China and that its "liberation" is consequently "China's internal affair in which no other country has the right to interfere."

In conclusion, the two sides agreed that it would be desirable to "broaden the understanding between the two peoples." To this end, they said they would encourage an exchange of scientists, artists, journalists, and sportsmen. They also agreed to increase bilateral trade. In the absence of diplomatic relations, the two governments decided to remain in contact through various channels in order to exchange views on issues of common interest.

Inevitably, the communiqué raised the question: who won? But viewed from a broad vantage point, the main significance of the summit lay not in specific concessions but in the momentous fact that it started a process of negotiation and paved the way for future cooperation, rather than continued confrontation. As such, the Peking summit constituted a decisive turning point in the relations between the two countries, whatever the scorecard results on specific issues.

As for the specific issues, both sides demonstrated a new realism and flexibility which had been so sorely lacking in U.S.-China relations since the ascension of the Communists. With respect to Taiwan, the most critical and sensitive question in the summit negotiations, both leaders moved away from their previously rigid positions. Since both the Communists and the Nationalists consider Taiwan to be an integral part of China, President Nixon was prepared to concede this point and to view the eventual settlement of the conflict as an internal affair of the Chinese (although for-

gotten here were the native Taiwanese, the vast majority of whom probably want a separate and independent nation). And since there is no real possibility of military action by the People's Republic to take Taiwan, the president could refrain from mentioning the 1954 U.S.-Nationalist mutual defense treaty in the communiqué. The Chinese were no less realistic. Since they are incapable of capturing the island by military force, Premier Chou was prepared to hold out the "prospect" of a peaceful settlement by the Chinese themselves, without American interference.

In the context of global politics, the Peking summit had the effect of ratifying China's new stature as a great world power. A concomitant of this was the final disintegration of the bipolar structure that had characterized the Cold War era. Although this disintegration had begun with the rift in Sino-Soviet relations, it was not until the U.S.-China summit that the shift toward a multipolar world structure may be said to have been consummated. Appropriately, Moscow viewed the Peking summit with considerable suspicion. Indeed, the détente not only freed China and the United States from the straitjacket of mutual hostility but also gave both countries new ground for maneuver vis-à-vis the Soviets.

China's new diplomatic posture. After the Peking summit, China and the United States began to take small and cautious steps designed to develop their new relationship. The American and Chinese ambassadors to Paris soon began a series of contacts intended to establish a permanent channel for discussions. At the same time, limited "people-to-people" contacts, which had begun with the visit to China of the U.S. table tennis team in April 1971, were continued, as a trickle of Americans made their way to the mainland.

Aside from Taiwan, the major immediate stumbling block to the normalization of relations was the Vietnam war. The continuation of the war and the bombing of their ally by the United States placed China in an extremely difficult position. The Chinese are now believed to favor an early end to the war. Abandoning their hard line of several years ago, which exhorted the North Vietnamese to fight to the bitter end, the Chinese now support a negotiated settlement. However, they have reaffirmed their support of North Vietnam as a cardinal political and ideological principle of their foreign policy, and they have continued to assist Hanoi's war effort. The difficulty of the Chinese position was illustrated by the fact that immediately upon Nixon's departure from China, Chou met with North Vietnamese leaders, apparently in Hanoi, to reaffirm China's enduring support.

It was clear, however, that the Chinese would not permit the Vietnam war to jeopardize their emerging relationship with the United States. If any doubts existed on this score, they were dispelled in May, when the Nixon administration, in response to a major North Vietnamese offensive, sharply escalated the war by blockading and mining North Vietnamese harbors and by greatly intensifying the bombing of North Vietnam. Although the Chinese strongly denounced these actions, they avoided any move which might rupture their fragile ties with the United States.

In fact, even as the bombing of North Vietnam was going on, China and the United States continued to solidify their new relationship. In June, Henry Kissinger paid a five-day visit to Peking, where he presumably reassured the Chinese leaders that the American bombing of North Vietnam posed no threat to China's security, a charge which Peking had raised for the first time shortly before Kissinger's visit.

China's lower "revolutionary" profile in foreign policy resulted in an easing of tensions with the Soviet Union, but there was no basic change in their relations, and no progress seems to have been made toward eliminating the border dispute that is the most volatile source of the conflict between them. Although the Soviets, probably suspicious about the U.S.-China détente, seemed to signal a desire for improved relations, the Chinese, perhaps confident in the

American and Chinese Leaders
Find a Breach in the Wall

On February 21 the "Spirit of '76" landed at Peking Airport, and President Nixon disembarked to begin a historic eight-day summit visit with the leaders of the People's Republic of China. Escorted past an honor guard (left) by Premier Chou En-lai, the president almost immediately met with Chairman Mao Tse-tung at the latter's residence (below). The rest of the trip included banquets in the Great Hall of the People, a visit to an anti-imperialist ballet, and a trip to the Great Wall of China. While the president was active in private talks, the first lady practiced her own brand of personal diplomacy in visits to a hotel kitchen, a people's commune, an ancient palace, and the Shanghai Municipal Children's Palace (right).

flexibility which the détente has given them, did not appear to respond. For example, the Soviets tried to convey the impression that the American blockade of North Vietnam had fostered a new collaboration between Moscow and Peking, in the form of joint arrangements for the shipment of Soviet supplies to North Vietnam via China. But the Chinese, while agreeing to increased Soviet rail shipments through China, apparently stopped short of opening their ports to Soviet freighters.

In the meantime, the Soviets reportedly continued their military buildup along the Soviet-Chinese border. In August the Soviets published a hard-hitting attack on the Chinese for making "absurd demands" with respect to the border issue. This suggested that a new deadlock had developed in the Sino-Soviet border talks, under way since the clashes of 1969.

On other diplomatic fronts, the Chinese vigorously emphasized an increased range of contacts. Delegations from Asia, Africa, Latin America, and Western and Eastern Europe traveled to Peking, while Chinese diplomats abroad worked hard at fostering China's image as peacemaker. The increased level of China's foreign activities, which has included the establishment of diplomatic relations with at least 20 countries since 1970, was reflected this year in the appointment by China's Foreign Ministry of seven new deputy and assistant foreign ministers to cope with the new workload. One of the most notable contacts set up in 1972 was with Great Britain, as the two countries agreed to establish full diplomatic relations by raising their representatives in Peking and London to ambassadorial level.

High on the list of Peking's foreign policy priorities was Japan. After Kakuei Tanaka replaced Eisaku Sato as Japanese premier, the Chinese, who had detested Sato, ceased their fulminations about the revival of Japanese "militarism" and expressed a willingness to normalize relations. Both sides began courting each other with public gestures and signals. A major breakthrough came in July, when Chou invited Tanaka to visit Peking in order to discuss the establishment of diplomatic relations. Tanaka accepted the invitation and was scheduled to go to China in late September.

During its first full year of membership in the United Nations, China's delegation left little doubt that its role in the world body would be an active one. In addition to squelching UN membership for Bangladesh, China wielded its Security Council veto in September by joining the Soviet Union in killing a U.S. resolution condemning Arab terrorism against Israel. Earlier, China succeeded in terminating all UN statistical coverage of Taiwan. Besides being represented at the Security Council and General Assembly, China also took up membership in UNESCO and sent representatives to the April meeting of the UN Conference on Trade and Development in Santiago, Chile.

A special focus of China's attention was the Third World, over which Peking is increasingly seeking to assert leadership. China has proclaimed that it will not play superpower politics but will instead encourage nations to remain nonaligned. These protestations of purity came into serious doubt, however, when China, in what was clearly a bigpower play, used its first Security Council veto in August to block the admission of Bangladesh to the United Nations.

In an obvious effort to solidify their political contacts with Third World countries, the Chinese have embarked on a program of trade and economic aid which since 1970 has resulted in the inauguration of aid agreements with Chile, Guyana, and Peru in South America; Equatorial Guinea, Ethiopia, Mauritania, Sierra Leone, Somalia, and the Sudan in Africa; Iraq in the Middle East; and Ceylon in Asia. In addition, the Chinese have resumed aid to such neutral countries as Burma, with which it has had political difficulties in recent years, and have increased aid to such countries as Pakistan, which had already received substantial Chinese aid.

The decline and fall of Lin Piao. In dealing with foreign affairs, China's leaders appeared to be self-assertive, confident, and relaxed. But hidden from both the outside world and from the Chinese people, a major struggle—the roots of which went back to the cultural revolution—was still raging. Only this year did a published account reach the outside world of the internal upheavals that had resulted in the purge of Lin Piao, commander of the armed forces and Mao's designated successor, and several top-ranking military officers.

The bizarre external manifestations of the struggle began to surface in September 1971. They included a mysterious crash the night of September 12–13 of a Chinese plane in Mongolia, presumably en route to the Soviet Union; the almost complete grounding of the Chinese Air Force for several weeks; indications of hasty high-level meetings in mid-September; the abrupt cancellation of the October 1 military parade; the disappearance and "unpersoning" of Lin Piao; the disappearance of several top military leaders; and the fantastic story, soon given out to lower-level officials, that Lin had led a plot to assassinate Mao and that he had been killed in the plane crash.

In subsequent months the press launched a campaign which, though couched in oblique terms, was unmistakably aimed at Lin Piao. Now termed a political swindler and a charlatan, Lin was accused of having "illicit relations with a foreign country" (the Soviet Union), advocating an "ultraleftist" political line, overemphasizing the role of politics in the army, manipulating the cult of Mao for his own benefit, and masterminding intrigues and conspiracies. After several months of secrecy, officials in Peking published a statement abroad naming Lin Piao as the leader of an abortive assassination attempt on Mao.

The fall of Lin Piao was not only stunning in its external manifestations but also highly significant in its internal effects. Purged along with Lin were several of China's top military leaders, including Chief of Staff Huang Yung-sheng, the commander of the air force, the political commissar of the navy, the director of the general logistics department, and at least a few more high-ranking officers on the general staff. This sweeping action constituted the most extensive purge of the army high command since the Chinese Communists came to power. But it clearly went far beyond the bounds of a strictly military matter. Given Lin's party position and national stature and given the political role of the military, it is clear that the shake-up in the army high command cut to the very core of intraleadership politics.

Although the purge has been treated by the Chinese as essentially a "palace affair," its implications are much more far-reaching. First, it has reopened the whole question of succession, setting the stage for a period of uncertainty and perhaps for another violent struggle when Mao dies. Second, it has demonstrated that despite consolidation and stability since the cultural revolution, leadership relations are still extremely unstable. Third, it has forced a reexamination of the political role of the military in the aftermath of the cultural revolution. Finally, it has cast a new and glaring light on internal divisiveness in the army.

But if these ramifications of the Lin Piao affair are clear, the reasons behind it and the circumstances surrounding it are still shrouded in mystery. Despite fragmentary, vague, and contradictory information, it is possible to suggest a plausible hypothesis—the purge of Lin and his allies was not a sudden eruption but the climax of a campaign against ultraleftist leaders that began to take shape in response to Red Guard excesses at the height of the cultural revolution. The most prominent victim of the antiradical drive prior to Lin was Ch'en Po-ta, Mao's close associate for many years and one of the most important figures in the radical wing of the leadership during the cultural revolution. In internal party accounts circulated after Lin's fall, Lin was accused of conspiring with Ch'en against Mao in order to consolidate

the position of the radicals. However, Lin's real links with the radical wing of the leadership are far from clear. Nor is it clear to what extent the policies he espoused, especially concerning the army's political role and the role of politics in the army, were, in fact, ultraleftist. This much, however, is clear: during the turmoil, Lin became increasingly identified with the radical wing of the Maoist leadership. As the chief link between the radicals and the army, Lin infuriated and alienated the powerful regional commanders, as well as the professionally oriented officers and moderate civilian leaders who had been attacked by the radical wing of the Red Guard.

If so, it is conceivable that because of his identification with the ultraleft, Lin had indeed been the ultimate target of the antiradical campaign which was pushed relentlessly by a coalition of moderate military and civilian leaders, presumably led by Chou En-lai. It is possible that, in the atmosphere of intrigue and instability that had apparently enveloped the Chinese ruling group, Lin and his associates were prompted to consider some rather drastic and desperate action.

We do not know the role of Mao in this affair, nor can we be certain about the role of policy issues in the power struggle. Subsequent revelations point to at least three major areas of policy conflict: the détente with the United States and its effect on relations with the Soviet Union; mass-oriented, revolutionary policies versus more orderly and pragmatic methods of development; and the political and professional role of the army. Whatever may have been Lin's stand on these issues, the direction of policy in these areas after Lin's purge is clear enough: the détente with the United States has, of course, continued; the trend away from mass-oriented methods of development has been markedly accelerated; and the army has lowered its profile, though not its impact, on the political scene. His fall gave a new impetus to the policies of moderation and relaxation.

Economy. The importance of material incentives and technical expertise received greater emphasis than at any time since the cultural revolution began. Consumer spending was officially in favor, and the regime made an effort to supply the population with a variety of goods. Official statements advocated a less puritan life-style for the people, cultural activities were noticeably less political, and banned classical works, both Chinese and Western, reappeared in bookstores. Numerous officials and intellectuals who had been attacked or had simply disappeared from public view during the cultural revolution were reinstated. Reflecting the new trend, the official party newspaper this year indulged in what was for China a relatively lighthearted critique of the dull and turgid prose that usually fills Chinese publications.

China's economy continued to grow at what appeared to be a steady and impressive rate. For 1971 the Chinese announced a gain of about 10 percent in the value of industrial and agricultural output. For the first time since 1959 the Chinese released absolute figures, rather than percentage increases, for grain and steel, claiming outputs of 246 million tons and 21 million tons, respectively. For other items only percentage gains were given, but these depicted an economy rapidly moving forward in the industrial sector. Although no absolute figures were as yet announced for 1972, the Chinese reported substantial grain output increases in several key provinces.

The new internationalist spirit in Chinese diplomacy had concrete parallels in China's 1972 foreign trade. By October, China had concluded arrangements for purchasing three British-French Concorde supersonic airliners and ten American Boeing 707's, the latter deal valued at $150 million. Other significant purchases from the United States included a satellite communications station and about 18 million bushels of wheat, the first U.S. grain export to Mainland China in 20 years.

CHINA, REPUBLIC OF (TAIWAN) 229

Area and population. Area, 3,691,500 sq. mi. Pop. (est. 1971), 773 million. Principal cities (est. 1968): Peking (cap.), 7 million; Shanghai, 10.7 million; Tientsin, 4 million.
Government. "People's democratic dictatorship," with rule by the Chinese Communist Party through the government administration. China is without a chief of state. Party Central Committee chmn., Mao Tse-tung; prem., Chou En-lai; for. min. functions directed by Chou En-lai.
Finance. Monetary unit, yuan; 1 yuan = US$0.44. No details regarding the budget have been published for several years.
Trade (1970). Imports, $2 billion; exports, $2.2 billion. Main source for imports, Japan; chief imports, industrial goods. Main market for exports, Hong Kong; chief exports, agricultural produce and light industrial goods.
Education. No figures on enrollment have been made available for several years.
Armed forces. Total strength estimated at 2.7 million, of which 2.3 million make up the ground forces, the remainer the air force and the navy. ELLIS JOFFE

CHINA, REPUBLIC OF (TAIWAN). Generalissimo Chiang Kai-shek had to face the humiliation of President Richard Nixon's hobnobbing with Chiang's archenemy, Mao Tse-tung, in Peking. But his government and party machines were given a good shake-up, and the authorities and people of Taiwan were able to show that the island could survive Peking's entry into—and their own expulsion from—the United Nations.

Politics and government. President Chiang was sworn in for his fifth term of office in May, retaining C. K. Yen as his vice-president. But with Yen laying down his concurrent premiership, interest turned to Chiang Ching-kuo, the new prime minister and the generalissimo's 62-year-old son. After the Legislative Yuan confirmed his appointment, 381–13, President Chiang reaffirmed the traditional avowal to return to the mainland, but on this occasion hinted also at domestic reforms.

His new cabinet showed some significant changes. The Taiwan-born members doubled their number to six, and Henry Kao, the colorful former mayor of Taipei and a leading Taiwanese political figure, was appointed to the key post of minister of communications. Hsu Ching-chung, former minister of the interior, was named vice-premier, and Shen Chang-huan was brought back as foreign minister to succeed S. K. Chow.

Foremost among the sweeping changes at the provincial level was the appointment of Hsieh Tung-min as the first Taiwanese governor of Taiwan Province.

There were similar alterations in the look of the central committee of the Nationalist Party. These changes confirmed the younger Chiang's position in the party and strengthened his control over its apparatus. Finance Minister K. T. Li was replaced as head of the party's financial affairs committee by Yu Kao-hwa, a close associate of the new premier.

Foreign relations. Taiwan's internal changes came in the aftermath of the Nixon visit, which was openly condemned in Taiwan as ill-advised and deeply damaging to Nationalist China. The journey to Taipei immediately thereafter of Assistant Secretary of State Marshall Green helped to allay the Chiangs' worst fears, but could not undo the profound damage to Nationalist morale and to U.S.-Taiwan relations.

A second diplomatic blow was the closure in March of Britain's sole official representation on Taiwan—its consulate at Tamsui, after the British government had acknowledged "the position of the Chinese government that Taiwan is a province of the People's Republic of China" and agreed with Peking to an exchange of ambassadors.

Even worse was the move toward China by Japan, which had been regarded as the most loyal of the great powers after the United States. The Nationalist Party secretary general, Chang Pao-shu, flew to Tokyo in August to seek to dissuade the new Japanese prime minister, Kakuei Tanaka, from seeking a détente with Peking. Although he was unsuccessful, the Taiwanese worked pragmatically to salvage as much as possible of the island's valuable trade with Japan.

Even UN technical aid to Taiwan had to be phased out in deference to Peking's membership.

But there were small compensations. Taiwan's progressive diplomatic isolation tended to move the Nationalists inexorably into the same boat with the Taiwanese independence movement. Nevertheless, action against Taiwan's domestic critics continued, and in May it was announced that eight government opponents had been convicted of sedition. A well-known writer, Lee Ao, and a prominent editor, Hsieh Tsung-ming, were among those imprisoned.

The Nationalists' reaction to their new predicament included new diplomatic and trade initiatives with the Soviet Union and Eastern Europe, and these were warmly reciprocated. Chiang Ching-kuo had, in fact, been educated in the Soviet Union and is married to a Russian, two factors that may be relevant to this trend. A trade ban with Eastern Europe was revoked, and cultural exchanges with the Soviets were under discussion.

Controversy continued over the status of the Tiaoyutai (or Senkaku) Islands, lying between Taiwan and Okinawa. The islands are claimed by Taiwan, China, and Japan. Angry diplomatic notes flowed between Taipei and Tokyo on this question, with offshore oil rights over an adjoining part of the continental shelf as one of the prizes.

The economy stabilizes. Contrary to some expectations, the Taiwan economy did not collapse after the UN and U.S. switch to Peking. There was a drop in Japanese investments and some temporary flight of capital, but Taiwan had too much going for it economically to suffer much or for too long.

Foreign trade rose by 42 percent in the first quarter of 1972, compared with an increase of 30 percent for the full year 1971; this enormous increase reflected a devaluation of the Taiwan dollar. Industrial production was also up by 26

percent in the first quarter of 1972. This followed a growth in gross national product during 1971 of 11.4 percent and the attainment of a per capita income of $329, among the highest in Asia.

The 1972–1973 budget provided for expenditures of NT$16.2 billion, with particular emphasis on the development of the Taichung International Seaport.

Area and population. Area, 13,885 sq. mi. Pop. (est. 1971), 14.35 million. Taipei (cap.; est. 1969), 1,712,108.
Government. Republic, ruled by a single party, the Kuomintang (Nationalist Party). Pres., Chiang Kai-shek; vice-pres., C. K. Yen.
Finance. Monetary unit, New Taiwan dollar; NT$1 = US$0.0255. Budget expenditure (1972–1973), NT$16.2 billion.
Trade (1970). Imports, US$1.5 billion; exports, US$1.4 billion.
Education (1969–1970). Enrollment: primary schools, 2,411,725; secondary schools, 1,024,298; institutions of higher learning (including 9 universities), 184,215.
Armed forces (1970). Army, 400,000; navy, 35,000; marines, 27,000; air force, 85,000.

DICK WILSON

CITIES. "The major problem facing nearly all the great cities in the world is uncontrolled growth. For the most part, efforts to control growth so that it does not exceed the capacity of urban areas to absorb it have failed." This is the conclusion of one of the documents prepared for the United Nations Conference on the Human Environment, held in Stockholm in June.

Between now and the end of the century, world population is expected to double, thus reaching about 7 billion. Although this projection indicates an approaching crisis, the way population is currently distributed means that the crisis is upon us *now*. Mankind is already heavily concentrated in cities, and throughout the world, in both developed and developing countries, men and women are flocking to cities from rural areas in ever-increasing numbers. Roughly one-third of mankind now lives in urban areas; by the year 2000

BOTH PHOTOS, RUSS KENNEDY

Handwriting on the Wall

Crayoned valentines and inked obscenities have yielded to a new "art form," urban scrawl. Spray-painted signatures like those defacing this Philadelphia grade school (left) cost cities millions of dollars a year. But the University of Pennsylvania has a remedy: a "graffiti workshop" (right) for kids caught in the act.

the figure will be about one-half. In the industrialized countries, the proportion of urban population will rise from 65 to 80 percent during the same 30 years. In the less industrialized countries, the rise will be from 25 to 45 percent.

It may appear that this trend is contradicted by the experience of some cities, especially in the United States and Europe, which are growing very slowly or even losing population. This experience is, however, confined to central or inner cities in metropolitan complexes where people are migrating from the centers to the suburbs. The trend is not contradicted in such circumstances but merely reformulated. City boundaries are often constricted and often difficult to expand, and thus suburban migrants technically leave the city. In economic and geographical terms, however, cities and their suburbs are a unity; looked at in this way, suburban migrants are still city dwellers.

Quality of life. Despite every technological advance made by mankind, the quality of life for many city dwellers is poor and sometimes declining. It is not only that many people are unable to satisfy their social aspirations (in education, employment, recreation) but also that many find it difficult to obtain even basic physical necessities in cities (clean air, pure water, adequate housing).

According to the United Nations, in 1972 more than 1 billion people lived in degrading housing conditions. The problem is particularly acute in the metropolitan areas of the Third World. Many famous cities are disfigured by overcrowding, slums, shantytowns, squatter settlements, and filthy conditions.

Calcutta, economic nucleus of eastern India and wealthy center of commerce and industry, is nevertheless known with some justice as the cesspool of Asia. Two-thirds of its 7 million inhabitants live in *kutcha* buildings—insubstantial dwellings made of mud, bamboo, or similar materials.

Thousands of others sleep every night in the streets or the railway stations. Furthermore, over half of Calcutta's multimember families live in no more than one room.

Manila in the Philippines is not in such desperate straits; nevertheless about 20 percent of its households live in ramshackle, makeshift homes (called *barung-barongs*) in slum and squatter areas. In Mexico City the older city is surrounded by hundreds of *colonias proletarias* (proletarian colonies or squatter settlements), in most of which basic facilities are lacking and housing is substandard and overcrowded. The *colonias proletarias* cover one-third of the metropolitan area and house over one-third of the 8 million inhabitants.

In city after city in Africa, Asia, and Latin America the situation is similar, although the extent of the problem varies. In Taipei about 25 percent of the population lives in slums and uncontrolled settlements; in Seoul the proportion is about 30 percent; in Dar es Salaam, 34 percent; Guayaquil, 50 percent; and Ankara, 60 percent.

Water supply and sewerage present a similarly melancholy catalogue. The muddy waters of the Hooghly River, which bisects Calcutta, provide both the main source of drinking water and the principal sewer for the city. The supply of filtered water has not kept pace with the burgeoning population; in consequence the per capita supply has declined, and people are compelled to use unfiltered sources (a major factor in cholera infection). Most areas outside the city center are without underground drainage and have to rely on privies. A few hours of tropical storm are enough to set the streets awash.

Again, example after example of inadequate water supply and sewerage could be cited from the cities of Africa, Asia, and Latin America. In 1972, according to the United Nations, 75 percent of the urban population of the developing

countries was not supplied with water in houses or court-yards. Moreover, the remaining 25 percent was often supplied with unsafe water or an inadequate quantity. Similarly, only 12 percent of urban families in the Third World had sewage facilities at their disposal.

The cities mentioned are not necessarily the worst examples, although it would be hard to find more appalling conditions than those in Calcutta. Moreover, the situation in such cities is not necessarily indicative of a failure of political will, although it sometimes is. The main factor is the simple overwhelming of financial and administrative resources by the sheer size of the problem—excessive growth. Many cities have tried and are trying to attack these problems vigorously, but the massive dimensions of the difficulties have made it impossible to achieve more than a modicum of success.

Indeed, few cities of the developed world, despite their greater resources and administrative experience, can be complacent about the quality of the lives of their citizens. Although their problems may be less extreme, they are often grave enough. Most European, American, and Japanese cities have areas of overcrowding and of obsolescent housing; many have difficulty in meeting water and sewerage demand. If factors like air pollution are considered, to say nothing of social services like education, the task before such cities often seems as intractable as that facing the cities of the Third World.

The Tama River, which supplies 40 percent of Tokyo's drinking water, is too contaminated for fish to survive in it. Purification of its water is ten times as expensive as purification of water from other sources. In the same city, the sewerage system serves less than one-third of the 9 million inhabitants of the special ward area—the central city of the Tokyo metropolis. Between half a million and a million households were domiciled in substandard housing in 1972.

London, despite a massive public housing program since the war, still had about 30,000 substandard dwellings in 1972. Even Stockholm, surely the most favored of cities, had in 1972 several tens of thousands of apartments lacking one or more of toilet facilities, central heating, or bath. Still, a slum to a Swede may well appear a dream home to an Indian.

Nevertheless, in a number of the cities of the developed world—and most have greater problems than Stockholm—there seemed in 1972 some prospect of problems being overcome. Public housing programs, investment in public utilities, and provision for education were often not grossly behind need. There was even an occasional example of improvement in the purity of city air and water.

For the third year running, fish were caught in London's Thames River after a previous half century of poisonous sterility. In the same city, rigorous smoke control measures have effected a constant improvement in the atmosphere. Londoners in 1972 enjoyed cleaner air and more sunshine than they had for many decades previously.

Although the impact of urban growth is often more appalling in developing countries than in developed, the problems are essentially the same for both. Is any solution equally applicable to both? One approach is strict regulation of population movement. In the People's Republic of China, peasants moving to the cities without permission are simply sent back. Such authoritarian controls would be unacceptable in most countries of the non-Communist world. Is there any alternative?

The only one that offers any prospect of success is energetic metropolitan planning. It must be accepted that most cities will continue to grow. Governments and municipal authorities must try to ensure that they grow coherently. Land use must be carefully allocated to avoid environmentally destructive mixed uses (for instance, a combination of heavy industry and housing) and to reserve some areas for amenity and recreation. Road routes and other communica-

tions must be planned with both efficiency and environment in mind. All new air and water pollution must be rigorously checked. Services must be provided where new development is taking place. Above all there must be an adequate supply of low-cost housing.

This is an ideal picture, but many cities are making strenuous efforts along these lines. Paris, in a plan first published in 1965, is guiding its inevitable growth in a linear fashion. The expanded metropolis will form a sort of horizontal Y with its trunk extending west towards Rouen and the arms extending upstream of Paris along the valleys of the rivers Seine and Marne. Recreational land—especially wooded hill country—is being preserved, and the main centers for urbanization are being carefully selected.

In Great Britain, metropolitan planning has a slightly different orientation. There an attempt is made to check the growth of major cities, often by means of an encircling "green belt" of agricultural and recreational land. Population growth, including people displaced from cities by slum clearance, is concentrated in publicly built new towns sited beyond the green belt. Industry and commerce are encouraged to move with the population so that the new towns do not become commuters' dormitories. New towns are also a feature of planning in Poland and the Soviet Union.

Even in London and Paris, metropolitan planning is far from completely successful, and in most of the world's great cities far, far less is possible. There are two massive obstacles. First there is the problem of administrative boundaries. Many of the world's metropolises sprawl across state and local boundaries. Effective planning of the whole is made difficult if not impossible by the need to secure agreement and concerted action among different local or state authorities.

Thus, New York City contains only 2.5 percent of the land area and 42 percent of the population of its metropolitan region. As defined by the Regional Plan Association in 1968, the region consists of 31 counties—five in New York City, nine additional ones in New York State, 14 in New Jersey, and three in Connecticut. Metropolitan planning for New York has been constantly hamstrung by this plethora of authorities.

Some cities have been reorganized administratively in recent years to take account of metropolitan growth. London, Paris, Stockholm, and Toronto all now have upper-tier regional authorities that should facilitate planning. However, inadequate resources, especially finance, present an even greater obstacle to effective metropolitan planning than do administrative boundaries.

Probably not a city in the world is entirely satisfied with its municipal revenues, and many are in dire financial straits. Rome, for instance, is unable to contract any more loans (except those guaranteed by the government) because existing sources of income are already earmarked as security for previous loans. Moreover, a city with an apparently sound financial position often has achieved that position only by severe curtailment of services. Mexico City (the federal district), pursuing conservative fiscal policies, has shown a surplus for every year since 1952 and has entirely retired its funded debt. Yet hundreds of thousands of its citizens still live in primitive conditions in the *colonias proletarias.*

To sum up, all cities are finding it difficult to cope with the problems of growth, and some seem to be losing the battle. The only realistic solution, metropolitan planning, has been hindered in some cases by out-of-date boundaries and in almost all by inadequate finance. In many of the cities of Africa, Asia, and Latin America, even if the population stopped growing this year it would take decades for the backlog of service provision to be made up—in slum clearance, water supply, education, and many other areas. Because growth is continuing and often accelerating, consideration of the future of such cities gives rise to the gloomiest forebodings.

"SCATTER-SITE HOUSING" sounds feasible on paper, but this empty lot in Forest Hills, N.Y., shows what sometimes happens when the concept is applied. New York City's plan to relocate 840 low-income families in three 24-story buildings here bogged down in a mire of opposition from middle-class neighbors.

Transportation. In 1972 few cities seemed to be making much headway in solving their transportation problems. Moreover, these problems were, if anything, more intractable in the cities of the developed world than in those of the developing. The problems fall into two main categories: the adverse impact that transport has on the city environment and the sheer inefficiency of most transportation systems.

Virtually all transport creates some disturbance, but the main villain in cities today is undoubtedly road traffic. The noise, dirt, vibration, air pollution, visual intrusion, and physical danger that result from road traffic threaten to turn parts of our cities into environments as adverse to humans as the Antarctic or the Sahara, and a good deal uglier than either. The casualties from road accidents alone have reached epidemic proportions; indeed, future generations may well look back at the carnage on our roads with the same horror that we view the cholera epidemics of the nineteenth century or the plagues of the fourteenth. Heavy traffic movement sometimes threatens the collapse of older buildings. On September 8, Milan was forced to close to vehicles the square and streets around its cathedral because structural cracks had appeared in the famous Gothic building. There is also concern over noxious emissions, especially lead, from car exhausts. In France, Japan, West Germany, Sweden, and the United States, the lead content of gasoline is now restricted by law, but other potentially dangerous substances are more difficult to cope with. In California, regulations requiring the fitting of devices to limit the emission of hydrocarbons and carbon monoxide from car exhausts increased the discharge of oxides of nitrogen into the atmosphere. This jump in one type of emission produced a new and severe smog crisis in Los Angeles and other southern Californian cities. Accordingly, in September, the California state air resources board made mandatory some new exhaust control equipment designed to reduce the emission of these oxides, even though engineers warned that the equipment might cause overheating in some vehicles.

These drawbacks might possibly be acceptable if, in return, cities enjoyed efficient transportation. Many, especially the larger ones, do not. Citizens find it difficult and often expensive to travel within their city. Traffic congestion may make the use of a private car unsatisfactory; public transport may be inconvenient; cycling unpleasant if not dangerous. Pedestrians may be inadequately provided for (in Tokyo, for instance, only 5 percent of the streets have sidewalks), and in any case some journeys are too lengthy to be walked comfortably.

Such difficulties stem in large part from overreliance upon the private automobile. The strange thing is that highway engineers are still promising eventual success if only more and yet more urban roads are built. The utter futility of such a policy needs to be emphasized. Even given unlimited capital for road investment, even if every citizen had easy access to a car (both unlikely eventualities), it would never be the way to create effective city transportation. The reason is simple but basic. The transport problem in cities is essentially that of terminating journeys. More roads could possibly solve the problem of through traffic, but it is physically impossible to provide in cities for every potential terminating journey to be made by private car.

A growing body of opinion recognizes the absurdity of the highway engineers' approach, although in most countries it is still a minority. Also, opposition to the environmental destruction caused by the motor car is becoming stronger and more articulate.

In London this year, the protagonists of urban motorways staged a noteworthy retreat. The greater London council's plan to build three large concentric rings of motorways in the metropolis—plus radial links—would have cost £2,000 million and destroyed some 20,000 homes. It attracted fierce and well-argued opposition, but for three years the greater London council clung obstinately to the design. In Septem-

ber, however, Richard Brew, chairman of the council's environmental planning committee, announced that sections of two of the proposed ringways would be amalgamated to form one inner ring road; the eventual outcome will be two, not three, concentric rings of motorway. Although this modification is an unsatisfactory compromise, it nevertheless represents a major climb-down by the Conservative-controlled greater London council.

The university city of Oxford, 57 miles west of London, was saved by a change of political control. The ruling Conservative group had backed a £30 million inner-city motorway. In the municipal elections of April, however, Labour captured the city council and promptly threw out the scheme. Instead, private automobile traffic is to be restricted to the city center, and bicycles and buses are encouraged.

In 1972 there were also some interesting developments in public transportation. Rome conducted a ten-day experiment in free public transport. The results were inconclusive; perhaps they might have been more interesting if the experiment had been combined with restrictions on private cars. In Stockholm a new system of fare payment has had a significant impact on the city's public transportation system. Passengers may now purchase a monthly card that allows unlimited travel; so many people are using the cards that delays at bus stops have been cut and the services operate more speedily.

Such developments are interesting and often important. Nevertheless, none of them alone can solve a city's transport problems. No mode of transport should be developed in isolation. The only sensible approach is to regard private vehicles, public transport, bicycles, and pedestrians as forming a system of transport and for a city to plan the system as a whole. Private cars should have a role in the system, though in most cases a restricted and subordinate one.

A few cities are pioneers in this comprehensive approach. San Francisco halted all new expressway construction as early as 1966. Also it has levied a 25 percent tax on city parking spaces to subsidize public transport, increased tolls for commuters on the Golden Gate Bridge, revived ferryboats to carry passengers, and instituted a system of exemption from road tolls for cars carrying three or more passengers. Modern buses running in priority lanes have shown increases of up to 35 percent in passengers. The city is not even afraid to use road congestion to divert people to the increasingly attractive alternative of public transport. Most important, one leg of the Bay Area Rapid Transit system opened on September 11. When finished in 1973, BART will be a fully computerized, 75-mile network of underground and elevated railway, and it should revolutionize transportation throughout the entire San Francisco Bay area. (*See* TRANSPORTATION.)

Pedestrians must also have a place in transportation planning. (It is interesting that few traffic engineers regard pedestrians as "traffic.") In certain parts of cities they must have priority. A number of cities, especially in Europe and North America, have tried pedestrianizing some streets or squares. Not all of these experiments have been successful, and some have been abandoned. There is a danger of overenthusiasm in this field; it is essential that such schemes form part of a comprehensive urban plan. Nevertheless, many pedestrian ways have been successful, and such areas are likely to form a permanent feature of the city scene. One of the most successful is in the cathedral city of Norwich in England. Pedestrianizing of London Street, the narrow, winding, commercial center of the city, has proved an unqualified success. Shopkeepers' trade has improved, and citizens have been enthusiastic. Several West German cities —Kassel, Kiel, and Düsseldorf—have equally successful schemes. Dublin has had favorable response to the pedestrianizing of Grafton and Henry streets.

Thus, in 1972 city transport was generally destructive of the environment and provided inadequately for its citizens.

Too much has been sacrificed on the altar of private traffic flow. There is, however, a growing volume of protest against this state of affairs. And some cities are tentatively feeling their way toward systematic transportation planning, with public transport playing a central role and with due provision made for pedestrians.　　　　D. E. REGAN

CIVIL ENGINEERING. The American Society of Civil Engineers has chosen the California Water Project as the outstanding civil engineering project of 1972. This project began operation on April 14, when the big valves were opened in Castaic Dam, the terminal storage facility of the West Branch of the project, 35 miles north of Los Angeles; at the same time, Feather River water, stored behind Oroville Dam, 70 miles north of Sacramento, began flowing into the distribution system of the Metropolitan Water District of Southern California (MWD).

Scope of the project. The California Water Project is a 685-mile aqueduct system comprising oversized dams, storage and flood-control reservoirs, natural channels, pipelines, tunnels, huge concrete-lined canals, huge pumping plants, and big hydroelectric power stations, all constructed to conserve excess runoff in northern California for domestic, industrial, and agricultural use in the semiarid central and southern parts of the state. Its cost of over $2 billion is being financed primarily from a $1.75 billion issue of general obligation bonds approved by California voters in 1960 and secondarily from other state and federal participation funds.

The project has been characterized as the largest, most complex, and most costly water-moving project in history. Dramatic evidence of its immensity came when U.S. astronauts flying to the moon reported being able to identify only two man-made structures on earth. One was the Great Wall of China; the other was the main aqueduct of the California Water Project surging along the west side of the San Joaquin Valley for 300 miles, from San Francisco Bay

Delta to the A. D. Edmonston Pumping Plant at Tehachapi Mountain.

The original objective of the project was to provide water wholesale by contract to local water districts. The first contract with MWD was executed in 1960 to furnish ultimately 2 million acre-feet a year for distribution to the district's service area. There are 31 such agencies to which the project will deliver ultimately a total of over 4 million acre-feet a year. These agencies will repay every cost related to delivering the water, in addition to paying interest on the bonds and repaying the capital.

More than 450 major construction contracts will be required before the project is complete. At present, over 90 percent of the facilities of the project are in operation. The California department of water resources reported that water deliveries in 1971 totaled 697,000 acre-feet. They are estimated for 1972 to be 1.7 million acre-feet; the maximum annual capacity of water deliveries for the project is 4.2 million acre-feet.

Dams and reservoirs. There are 21 dams and reservoirs. The biggest is Oroville Dam and Lake in Butte County, the primary storage and flood-control facility of the project. This great dam is an earth fill 770 feet high, 6,920 feet long at its crest, and 922 feet above sea level, containing 80.31 million cubic yards of material. It stands 44 feet higher than Hoover Dam on the Colorado River and is the highest dam of any type in the United States. A two-lane highway crosses the crest. In 1965 the threat of a disastrous flood from the Feather River was avoided by storing the floodwater in the reservoir behind the half-finished dam. In July 1970, a year ahead of schedule, Lake Oroville was filled to its 3.538 million acre-foot capacity. The underground six-unit Hyatt Power Plant, cut into the rock of the dam's left abutment, has an operating head of 622 feet and will have an ultimate generating capacity of 678,750 kilowatts (kw.).

THE GREENING OF CALIFORNIA. A stretch of the state's new 685-mile aqueduct system winds through the San Joaquin Valley, irrigating thousands of acres of once-arid land. The system has been called the largest and most costly water-moving project in history.

Immediately downstream from Oroville Dam is a pump-storage facility that retains water released from Lake Oroville for power production as required to meet demand during peak daylight hours. This facility has reversible turbine-pumps that lift the water back to the upper lake during the off-peak night hours.

San Luis Dam in Merced County, a joint-use facility with the U.S. Bureau of Reclamation, is an earth fill 382 feet high and 18,600 feet long at its crest, containing 77.67 million cubic yards of material. San Luis Reservoir has a capacity of 2.11 million acre-feet. Its pump-storage plant has an operating head of 327 feet and a generating capacity of 424,000 kw.

Castaic Dam in Los Angeles County, at the terminus of the West Branch, is another big earth fill. It is 425 feet high and 4,900 feet long at its crest, containing 46 million cubic yards of material. It stores 324,000 acre-feet of water, which is being delivered to MWD. The Los Angeles department of water and power is designing and will construct and operate the power plant at Castaic. When completed in 1978, it will be one of the world's largest pump-storage power projects. Its six 200-megawatt reversible pump-turbines will be capable of producing 1.25 billion kilowatt-hours annually.

Oroville and Castaic power plants together will produce 70 percent of the total capacity of the six project plants. Total storage capacity of the project's 21 reservoirs is 6.8 million acre-feet, of which Oroville and San Luis together account for 5.5 million acre-feet.

Pumping stations. Water released from Oroville Reservoir flows down the natural channel of the Feather and Sacramento rivers, through the delta of the San Joaquin River to the Delta Pumping Plant, which can lift a total of 10,300 cubic feet per second (cfs) 244 feet into the main San Joaquin Aqueduct. For the first 70 miles the canal has the same capacity. The Delta Plant is the first of seven pumping stations to lift water in steps up the broad San Joaquin Valley and over the 2,000-foot Tehachapi Mountain summit. Withdrawals by water agencies along the route reduce the required canal capacity gradually to 4,150 cfs at the A. D. Edmonston Pumping Plant, where 14 four-stage pumps, each driven by an 80,000-horsepower (hp) motor, can lift water 1,926 feet over the Tehachapi summit at a rate of 4,000 cfs. No single lift for such a combination of quantity and head had been built anywhere before.

The first pump began operation at a dedication ceremony on October 7, 1971, attended by 3,000 persons, including Governor Ronald Reagan and William R. Gianelli, director of the state department of water resources, under whose direction the project was designed and constructed. On command from the governor, a 35,000-hp motor started the 80,000-hp main motor, which began turning the 200-ton centrifugal pump. When speed reached 600 revolutions per minute, giant valves were opened. Water began to surge up the mountain and through the 5-mile Carley V. Porter Tunnel on its way to southern California. The price tag on this super-pumping station is $138 million.

Construction of branch aqueducts. In the San Francisco area, two aqueducts take water from Lake Oroville: 26-mile North Bay Aqueduct, with a maximum capacity of 115 cfs, serves agencies in Solano and Napa counties; and 43-mile South Bay Aqueduct, with a maximum capacity of 360 cfs, serves San Mateo and Santa Clara counties. In addition, three branches have been constructed from the main California Aqueduct to serve distant water agencies: the 96-mile Coastal Branch, maximum capacity 450 cfs, in San Luis Obispo County; the 32-mile West Branch, maximum capacity 3,100 cfs, to serve south coastal portions of Ventura, Los Angeles, and Orange counties; and the 138-mile East Branch, maximum capacity 2,000 cfs, to serve the high desert and the future Lake Perris, near Riverside, the terminal storage of the East Branch.

Canal foundations. The nature of the soil along the main aqueduct route through the arid west side of the San Joaquin Valley presented a challenging construction problem. When water saturated the soil, the surface of the soil was reduced up to 10 feet. Before canals were constructed, a series of ponds 200 feet by 500 feet were built on the right-of-way and kept filled with water for six months, while filtration wells were drilled up to 145 feet deep in each pond. This method was effective, but several miles of completed canal near San Luis Reservoir settled as a result of deep subsidence caused by the withdrawal of groundwater close to the construction. This problem was solved by raising the canal lining to provide 8 feet more freeboard (the height above the high-water mark) than in the original construction.

Earthquake-resistant design. Early in the design period, a consulting board of knowledgeable engineers and scientists was retained to develop a program of earthquake engineering. Seismometers were placed at facility sites to telemeter data to a control center in Sacramento, where alarm signals can be activated automatically. Research was conducted to determine responses to be expected in embankments from seismic vibrations and to identify and appraise active faults. In the design, ground acceleration standards, both horizontal and vertical, were adopted to agree with data recorded in the 1966 quake: horizontal, one-half the acceleration of gravity (0.5 g), and vertical, 0.33 g. The terminal reservoirs at Castaic and Perris were designed with capacities adequate to maintain water service for 60 days while upstream damage is being repaired. Check gates, which can be closed quickly by remote control in case of rupture, have been installed at intervals in the aqueduct to isolate the damage, conserve water, and permit rapid repair. Then, remaining parts of the system can be adjusted so that service can continue. In addition, construction near to or crossing active faults is close to ground surface to facilitate repair.

Control of the operation. The project is managed by area control centers (ACC's), located in each of five geographic areas, which monitor and adjust water levels and flow quantities at strategic remote facilities. The control center in Sacramento backs up the five ACC's to maintain surveillance over the project. The local control centers are connected to each other, to Sacramento, and to every remote site by closed-circuit television, a high-speed data transmission system, computers, and teletype.

Improvement of the environment. The California Water Project is the first water project with facilities for recreation and the conservation of fish and wildlife. More than 57,000 acres of water surface at major reservoirs will be available for recreational use. Portions of the right-of-way will be planted to create cover for wildlife. Routes to fishing sites and bicycle paths along the aqueduct are being developed. Project water will eliminate the need to pump too much water from groundwater sources and thereby reduce deep subsidence of land. Furthermore, project water will be used to replenish groundwater basins. A fish hatchery downstream from Oroville Dam provides protection for salmon and steelhead and will be capable of processing 20 million eggs a year.

Celebration in Coalinga. The availability of water from the California Aqueduct has brought joy to the San Joaquin Valley community of Coalinga in Fresno County. In April the residents celebrated the arrival of water from the joint state-federal San Luis Reservoir, which came through Coalinga Canal at Coalinga's new $6.5 million waterworks. The new system includes a filtration plant, pumps, and storage reservoirs and is financed by a local bond issue, state aid, and a federal grant.

This oil-rich and water-poor area had depended for years on water hauled in by wagons, tank trucks, and railroad cars. Groundwater from local wells was too brackish to be

HOW DEMOCRACY WORKS. Eighteen-year-olds in Charlotte, N.C., get their first look at a voting machine and learn how to use it. This year, for the first time, millions of Americans aged 18 to 20 could exercise the right to cast ballots in a presidential election.

BRUCE ROBERTS/RAPHO GUILLUMETTE

potable—2,400 parts per million (ppm) of dissolved salts. In 1959 the community installed one of the first municipal desalinization plants in the nation. Three faucets per house became standard—cold, hot, and drinking. In 1965 a reverse-osmosis desalinization plant was successful in increasing the quantity of the potable supply, but the price was still high. Now Coalinga purchases San Luis Reservoir water—no more than 250 ppm of dissolved solids—at $18.50 per acre-foot.

WALTER E. JESSUP

CIVIL LIBERTIES AND CIVIL RIGHTS. The busing of schoolchildren to achieve racial integration in public schools became a central issue in 1972, an otherwise quiet year in race relations. A substantial amount of civil liberties news was generated by decisions of the U.S. Supreme Court, as the Nixon appointees moved the Court toward a more conservative stance on race relations, criminal rights, and First Amendment freedoms. Women's rights and dissent against the war in Vietnam also continued to command public attention.

Busing. The school bus, long a symbol of community commitment to education, became in 1972 the symbol of a major political and emotional issue: busing for the purpose of racial integration. Seldom mentioned in the heated public debate over busing was the fact that more than two-fifths of all public school students in the United States are bused to school—only 2 or 3 percent of them for desegregation purposes. Also frequently overlooked was the fact that in the past, a good deal of busing was undertaken to preserve separate black and white schools in some states; in Alabama, for example, court-ordered school integration decreased the number of children going to school by bus.

Most busing orders have resulted from federal-court approval of proposed busing plans drawn up by local school boards in an effort to dismantle dual school systems or eliminate segregation resulting from separation of the races in all-white or all-black communities. Still undetermined by the U.S. Supreme Court is whether segregated schools resulting from apparently de facto residential patterns are unconstitutional on the ground that those residential patterns are influenced by government-supported housing programs. A case directly on this issue (and in which a lower federal court in Denver, Colo., ordered implementation of a busing plan to integrate the schools) is to be heard by the Supreme Court in its 1972–1973 term.

Adding to the controversy over busing were decisions in 1972 by federal district courts in Richmond, Va., and Detroit, Mich., ordering massive busing, across school district lines, of both inner-city and suburban students to overcome racial isolation in schools. (In both cities, appeals made it unlikely that busing would be implemented in 1972.) Although the southern states have long been feeling the impact of desegregation decisions and busing orders, the Detroit ruling helped reopen the entire issue as one of national rather than regional concern. Public opinion polls showed a substantial majority of Americans opposed to busing—69 percent according to a poll released by *Newsweek* in early March.

On March 16, in a major address, President Richard M. Nixon criticized busing for integration, claiming that it disrupts communities and imposes hardships on children. The following day Nixon sent a two-part legislative proposal to Congress. The first part would have established a moratorium on new busing orders by federal courts until July 1, 1973, or until Congress enacted substantive legislation on the busing issue, whichever came sooner; the second part of the Nixon proposal (the substantive legislation) would have virtually banned busing as a desegregation tool and prescribed the remedies courts could use (for example, redrawing school attendance zones) to achieve integration.

The Nixon proposals raised some constitutional questions as to whether legislation could limit the courts in their enforcement of individual constitutional rights. Many people in and out of Congress advocated proscribing busing through a constitutional amendment. More than two dozen such amendments were introduced in Congress. Exemplifying

WIDE WORLD

UPI

A WOMAN'S PLACE

Traditional male bastions are falling to determined women. Young Joy Kennedy (below) sold about 12 Chevrolets a month in her first smash year as one of six distaff salespeople for a Coronado, Calif., dealership. For further proof that some old sexual ramparts are crumbling, see Dourniese Hawkins (upper left), who wields a pickax for Con Edison in New York, and Alene B. Duerk (lower left), who this year became the first female admiral in the history of the U.S. Navy.

LESTER SLOAN/NEWSWEEK

them was a proposed amendment sponsored by Representative Norman F. Lent (D, N.Y.) which stated: "No public school student shall, because of his race, creed or color, be assigned to or required to attend a particular school." President Nixon did not oppose the proposal, but he said he preferred legislation to the longer constitutional-amendment route.

Congress had the Nixon recommendations and the constitutional amendment proposals under serious consideration but wound up responding to antibusing pressures by attaching to a higher education bill (which President Nixon reluctantly signed on June 23) a rider which did the following: postponed until all appeals are exhausted or until January 1, 1974, implementation of all federal-district-court busing orders; prohibited federal pressure on local school officials to undertake busing to overcome racial imbalance; limited the use of federal funds to pay for busing to situations in which local officials consented in writing to accept the money for that purpose; and barred busing where it would endanger a

child's health or impair his ability to learn. One difference between the higher education rider and Nixon's moratorium proposal is that the moratorium would have prohibited courts from ordering busing, whereas the rider only delays implementation of any such orders.

In August the House of Representatives passed an antibusing bill which went beyond the Nixon request in that it would permit children to attend the school "closest or next closest" to their homes and would authorize the reopening of all desegregation suits and the modification of desegregation orders in keeping with new restrictions. In the Senate permanent legislation was shelved after a filibuster by Northern liberals.

Progress on school integration. A report issued in January by the Department of Health, Education, and Welfare noted that integration efforts in the South had led, for the first time, to a smaller proportion of black students attending totally segregated schools in the South than in the rest of the United States. A survey revealed that 9.2 percent

of black students in 11 southern states attended all-black schools, compared with 11.2 percent in 32 northern and western states, and 24.2 percent in the border states. In 1968, 68 percent of the South's black students had attended all-black schools.

In June the Supreme Court held 5–4 in *Wright* v. *Council of the City of Emporia* that Emporia, Va., could not remove its schools from the county school system, which had a higher percentage of blacks, to evade integration. The four Nixon appointees dissented. Only once previously since 1954 had the Court issued a nonunanimous decision in a school desegregation case, and the Emporia case seemed to be an important break in the Court's tradition. In a companion case, however, *United States* v. *Scotland Neck City Board of Education*, the Court unanimously rejected a similar action by a North Carolina city. The issue in each case was the degree to which the establishment of separate school districts would have impeded the dismantling of a dual, racially segregated school system.

Equal employment opportunity. On March 8, Congress completed action on a bill providing the Equal Employment Opportunity Commission with enforcement powers. The Civil Rights Act of 1964, which established the EEOC, did not give the agency authority to compel compliance with the law. Since then, civil rights groups had actively worked for legislation vesting the EEOC with the power to issue cease-and-desist orders, a power commonly held by governmental regulatory agencies. However, the Nixon administration proposed instead that EEOC be empowered to take cases to federal court for enforcement through court orders, and it was this approach which was adopted by Congress this year. In addition to the court enforcement authority, the new law extended coverage of the Civil Rights Act of 1964 to business and labor organizations with 15 or more employees or members, to state and local governments, and to educational institutions. Further, the act established an independent general counsel to handle EEOC prosecutions after an investigation and a hearing uncover discrimination.

The White House released a report on February 15 noting that federal civilian minority employment had risen to 19.5 percent by May 1971, including seven black ambassadors and nearly 100 "super grade" jobs, compared with 63 in 1969. Minority business aid rose from $200 million in 1969 to $360 million in 1971. The Labor Department reported on April 22 that a ten-month investigation of its Rural Manpower Service (RMS) had disclosed evidence that the agency had failed to curb discrimination against blacks, chicanos, and women and had not done anything to halt exploitation of migrant workers. The report said that the service's procedures often abetted discrimination. The probe, begun after complaints by numerous civil rights, farm, and labor groups, uncovered patterns of discrimination in jobs, housing, and transportation as well as violations of minimum-wage and child-labor laws. Secretary of Labor James D. Hodgson admitted that past reforms had been ineffective and said that RMS would be consolidated at the local level with the Department of Labor's nonagricultural employment service.

Subsidized housing. New regulations were issued by the Department of Housing and Urban Development on February 7 regarding site selection for subsidized housing. The regulations, designed to promote housing opportunities for low-income families outside segregated central cities, favored the location of new housing in areas with few minority residents or in integrated areas where new projects would not upset the population balance, rather than in center-city urban renewal areas. Exceptions would be made for "overriding housing needs in minority areas not caused by discrimination."

FCC protest. On March 8 the Congressional Black Caucus, composed of 13 black members of the House of Representatives, charged that the Federal Communications Commission was failing to heed the needs of blacks in its licensing of broadcasting stations. The caucus charged that the FCC was insensitive to the needs of black television viewers and to discrimination against blacks in employment by the media. President Nixon, on April 12, appointed Benjamin L. Hooks of Memphis, Tenn., a black lawyer and minister, to a seven-year term on the FCC.

Black politics. About 3,300 delegates and 5,000 observers met in Gary, Ind., March 10–12 for the first National Black Political Convention, cochaired by Imamu Amiri Baraka, formerly known as LeRoi Jones; Richard Hatcher, mayor of Gary; and Representative Charles Diggs, Jr. (D, Mich.). The convention endorsed a proposed political agenda calling for radical social and political reform but refused to support any candidate for the presidency, including Representative Shirley Chisholm (D, N.Y.), the only black woman ever to serve in Congress, who had announced her candidacy on January 25. The delegates also voted to establish a representative body called the National Black Assembly to deal with the white power structure.

The convention originally went on record as opposed to school busing to achieve racial balance, labeling it an insinuation that black children could not learn unless in the same setting as white children. However, when the National Black Political Agenda of the convention was released on May 19, this position was modified to criticism of the Nixon administration for making busing an issue. On May 16 the National Association for the Advancement of Colored People withdrew from the black assembly because of its alleged separatist nature.

Private discrimination. In what was regarded by many observers as a legal setback for racial integration, the Supreme Court held in *Moose Lodge No. 107* v. *Irvis* that a private club could refuse to serve Negro guests and that the state government was not sufficiently implicated in the discriminatory act by granting a liquor license to the club. The Fourteenth Amendment to the U.S. Constitution prohibits only state action depriving citizens of equal rights, not discrimination by private individuals or organizations.

Equal rights for women. On March 22 the Senate approved the Equal Rights Amendment, previously adopted by the House in October 1971, and sent it to the states for ratification within seven years. Its effective date is to be two years after receiving the approval of the required three-fourths of the states. The main clause of the proposed constitutional amendment reads: "Equality of rights under the law shall not be denied or abridged by the United States or by any state on account of sex." Efforts in the Senate to restrict coverage of the amendment, particularly regarding military obligations for women, were defeated.

In March the EEOC issued tighter regulations barring sex discrimination in employment. Among the rules was one that no woman could be denied employment solely because of pregnancy and that the same leave and insurance benefits must apply to pregnancy as to any other temporary disability. Another rule required equal fringe benefits for male and female heads of families. Women were generally very active in pursuing individual and class action suits concerning hiring, pay, promotion, and other aspects of employment, as the concept of job equality for women took strong hold. Several colleges and universities were threatened with suspension of federal funds because of discriminatory hiring practices. L. Patrick Gray III, successor to the late J. Edgar Hoover as director of the Federal Bureau of Investigation, announced on May 11 that, for the first time in its history, the FBI would recruit women as special agents.

In *Reed* v. *Reed* the Supreme Court struck down, as a violation of equal protection of the law, an Idaho statute which provided that males are preferred over females to administer estates.

Antiwar protests. The escalation of U.S. bombing in Vietnam and other parts of Indochina provoked a new wave of

protests across the country in mid-April, particularly on college and university campuses. Violence was reported at Harvard, Boston University, the University of Wisconsin, Stanford, and the University of Oregon from April 15 to April 20. National guardsmen were ordered onto the campus of the University of Maryland on April 20 after two days of clashes between students and state police. Classes were suspended April 21 at Columbia University in New York City after a confrontation on the campus. A national student strike called for by some student leaders failed to materialize, but disruptions continued on scattered campuses during the week of April 21–27. Also during that week, protest marches by more than 30,000 people took place in New York City and San Francisco.

President Nixon's announcement on May 8 that North Vietnamese ports would be mined and that bombing would be intensified caused a resurgence of protest on campuses and in major cities. In Washington, D.C., the Capitol was the scene of almost continuous demonstrations by antiwar groups, joined by many members of Congress. More than 400 protesters were arrested May 21–22 after clashes with Washington, D.C., police. On May 22, 15,000 people attended a peaceful antiwar rally on the Capitol grounds.

A rally calling for victory in Vietnam, led by evangelist Carl McIntire, was held at the Washington Monument on May 20 and attended by about 3,500 people.

Protest groups at the Democratic and Republican national conventions, held at Miami Beach in July and August, respectively, made little impact. On the final night of the Republican Convention, when President Nixon made his acceptance speech, efforts were made by demonstrators to block passage to the convention hall. Police broke up the demonstration through use of tear gas, and before the night ended more than 1,000 arrests were made after random street violence around the city.

On the whole, antiwar protest movements, which have put the constitutional rights of speech, association, and assembly to severe tests, were mild in 1972 compared with former years, and the movement seemed to be losing steam.

Protest trials. There were some developments in trials growing out of past well-known protest activities. The jury deliberating charges brought against the Rev. Philip F. Berrigan and six fellow antiwar activists for conspiracy to kidnap presidential adviser Henry A. Kissinger, blow up heating tunnels in Washington, D.C., and raid draft boards reported itself unable to reach a verdict on the major counts on April 5, after 59 hours of deliberation. However, Berrigan and Sister Elizabeth McAlister were found guilty of smuggling contraband letters into and out of prison. In the course of the trial the prosecution called 64 witnesses and the defense none. On September 5, Berrigan was sentenced to four concurrent two-year prison terms, and Sister Elizabeth received one year in jail and three years' probation. After the sentences had been imposed, the government dropped the other charges.

On March 29, 166 protesters were arrested after surrounding the federal building where the trial was being held in Harrisburg, Pa. On April 1 about 10,000 supporters rallied in that city to protest the trial.

On May 11, a U.S. Court of Appeals ordered retrials on contempt of court charges for the "Chicago seven" defendants; their two lawyers, William Kunstler and Leonard Weinglass; and Bobby Seale, whose case had been separated. The ten persons had been sentenced to prison for two months to four years by Federal District Judge Julius J. Hoffman for disorderly behavior during their celebrated 1969–1970 trial for riot and conspiracy charges arising from the 1968 Democratic Party convention in Chicago. The appeals court noted that under Supreme Court rulings, contempt actions deferred to the end of a trial, as was the case here, had to be left to another judge and that contempt sentences of longer than six months required a jury trial.

The Chicago seven included Abbie Hoffman, Rennie Davis, David Dellinger, Tom Hayden, Jerry Rubin, John Froines, and Lee Weiner.

Angela Davis, an outspoken black militant and Communist who was tried for murder, kidnapping, and criminal conspiracy in San Jose, Calif., was acquitted by an all-white jury on June 4. Many people, including Miss Davis herself, had feared that it would be impossible for her to receive a fair trial because of her revolutionary leanings.

In January the Reverend James E. Groppi, a controversial Catholic priest who had led a protest march into the chambers of the Wisconsin legislature in 1969 and had been cited for contempt by the legislature, was acquitted by the U.S. Supreme Court in *Groppi* v. *Leslie* because he had not been afforded opportunity for notice and hearing prior to the legislature's action.

Freedom of speech, press, and association. The trial of Daniel Ellsberg and Anthony J. Russo, Jr., on charges growing out of the publication of the so-called Pentagon papers was halted by Justice William O. Douglas on July 29 to allow an appeal on an issue of government wiretapping. Although the jury had already been sworn in when the stay was granted, Douglas' action, later upheld by the other justices, could delay the beginning of the actual trial until 1973.

A number of other decisions of the Supreme Court, touching on First Amendment freedoms of speech and association, had a bearing on protest activities. In *Laird* v. *Tatum* the Court held 5–4 that the Army could not be brought to court to defend the mere existence of its surveillance of civilian activities unless "actual or threatened injury" could be shown to have been done to an individual. Another 5–4 decision, *Lloyd Corporation, Ltd.* v. *Tanner*, upheld the right of the private owner of a shopping and residential center to prohibit distribution of handbills. The Court struck down a Georgia law that prohibited use of "opprobrious words or abusive language" in public in *Gooding* v. *Wilson*. It invalidated city ordinances banning picketing within 150 feet of a school in *Police Department of Chicago* v. *Mosley* but upheld a provision in a similar ordinance which prohibited noise on grounds adjacent to a school in *Grayned* v. *City of Rockford (Ill.)*. An attempt by a state college to ban formation of a chapter of Students for a Democratic Society was held invalid in *Healy* v. *James*.

In a major reversal of the Warren Court, the Supreme Court in *Cole* v. *Richardson* upheld a loyalty oath law for the first time in many years. The oath required public employees in Massachusetts to swear opposition to violent overthrow of government. In *Papachristou* v. *City of Jacksonville* the Court struck down a vagrancy ordinance which outlawed "vagabonds," "disorderly loitering," "rogues," "nightwalkers," "habitual loafers," or men who live off the earnings of their wives or children. The Court noted that the Jacksonville, Fla., ordinance, typical of many vagrancy laws, was vague, encouraged arbitrary arrests, and was out of step with contemporary community standards.

In a ruling with possible far-reaching implications, the Court held 5–4 in *Branzburg* v. *Hayes* that journalists have no right to refuse to testify before grand juries with respect to confidential information available to them about crime. In *Rabe* v. *Washington* the Court ruled that the owner of a drive-in movie could not be penalized for showing erotic movies visible to passing motorists and neighborhood children unless the law made clear that a more rigid standard applies to outdoor screens than enclosed theaters.

The House of Representatives on May 30 passed a bill expanding the powers of the Subversive Activities Control Board along the lines of a July 1971 executive order by President Nixon which would save the floundering agency by empowering it to investigate and list subversive groups and persons, a power held by the attorney general. On June 15 the Senate deleted all funds for SACB, but funding was

restored at a lower level in the final appropriation. In addition, the SACB was barred from implementing President Nixon's executive order by the House-Senate compromise.

Eavesdropping. The annual report on electronic eavesdropping issued by the Administrative Office of the United States Courts in June, as required by the Omnibus Crime Control and Safe Streets Act of 1968, showed a continuing and significant increase in use. In 1971, the report indicated, there were 794 court-ordered eavesdrops a 36 percent increase over the 583 ordered in 1970 and a very substantial increase over the 271 taps authorized in 1969 and 147 in 1968. The report did not cover those eavesdrops undertaken without court orders—those against foreign interests and suspected domestic subversives. Most of the eavesdropping was done with telephone wiretaps rather than other bugging devices. Nineteen states now authorize wiretapping, but six of these reported no use. Authorities credited eavesdropping with about 2,800 arrests and more than 300 convictions. Gambling, drugs, and larceny suspects accounted for most of the taps, and the majority took place in private homes and apartments. No applications for warrants were denied by courts.

The Supreme Court, however, continued to take a dim view of too free a use of eavesdropping. It held in *United States* v. *United States District Court* that the Omnibus Crime Control and Safe Streets Act does not authorize the president to use electronic surveillance on domestic radicals without a court warrant, a right claimed and used by the Nixon administration. The Court found such use to be a violation of the Fourth Amendment prohibition against unreasonable searches and seizures and a threat to freedom of speech. In *Gelbard* v. *United States* the Court held that grand jury witnesses could refuse to answer questions arising out of information secured through illegally used listening devices; this case involved persons who refused to testify about the alleged plot to kidnap Henry Kissinger.

Criminal procedure. The Supreme Court issued several important decisions in the area of criminal procedure, many of them showing sharp divisions between the Nixon appointees to the Court and the holdovers from the Warren era. In its most widely noted decision, *Furman* v. *Georgia,* the Court held 5–4 that the imposition of the death penalty constituted cruel and unusual punishment. Each of the nine justices wrote an opinion, thereby leaving the issue somewhat unclear. Those voting for abolition of capital punishment noted that the penalty is imposed in an arbitrary manner, that a disproportionate number of minority and lower-class individuals are sentenced to death, and that the penalty seemed out of keeping with current moral standards. The dissenting justices argued that the matter should be left to the policy-making branches in each of the states. According to the New York *Times* of June 30, the decision saved 600 persons awaiting execution: 329 blacks; 14 Mexicans, Puerto Ricans, or American Indians; and 257 whites.

In another major decision, the Court held 5–4 that in criminal cases states may authorize a less than unanimous jury verdict, without violating the standard of proof beyond a reasonable doubt. The Court upheld a 9–3 vote requirement in *Johnson* v. *Louisiana* and a 10–2 requirement in *Apodaca* v. *Oregon.* In federal trials, however, the Court agreed that the common-law rule of a unanimous verdict by a jury of 12 was intended by the Constitution.

In still another significant decision, *Argersinger* v. *Hamlin,* the Court extended the right to counsel to defendants facing imprisonment for misdemeanors or petty offenses as well as for felonies. This ruling will expand public obligation to provide attorneys for accused persons. In *Kirby* v. *Illinois,* however, the Court narrowed the right to counsel somewhat by restricting a Warren Court ruling regarding the right to counsel at a police lineup by holding, 5–4, that the right applied only after a suspect was indicted or otherwise formally charged and not merely after arrest.

ON TRIAL. Daniel Ellsberg (left) and codefendant Anthony Russo hold a press conference near a Los Angeles courthouse. The two were being tried on charges of stealing and improperly communicating the secret contents of the controversial Pentagon papers.

The Court underscored its insistence that juries be racially neutral, holding in *Peters* v. *Kiff* that the indictment and conviction of a white man for burglary must be overturned because blacks were arbitrarily excluded from the grand jury that indicted him. Similarly, a rape conviction was overturned in *Alexander* v. *Louisiana* because of racial bias in the selection of a grand jury.

Faced with a case calling for some definition of the constitutional requirement for a speedy trial in criminal cases, the Court held in *Barker* v. *Wingo* that this can only be done on an ad hoc basis, depending upon the circumstances of delay and the conduct of the prosecutor and defendant. Four criteria suggested by the Court were the length of delay, the reasons for the delay, whether the delay was prejudicial to the defendant, and whether the defendant demanded a speedy trial. In the case at hand the Court held that a five-year delay in a prosecution for murder did not violate the speedy trial requirement because the delay did not seriously prejudice the defendant and the defendant had not pressed for trial.

In *Kastigar* v. *United States,* the power of prosecutors to compel testimony before grand juries or other investigating panels without granting total immunity from prosecution was broadened. The Court held that in any subsequent action against a witness granted immunity, the prosecution must prove that any evidence used was derived from sources wholly independent of the compelled testimony.

A closely divided Court modified requirements on confessions by holding in *Lego* v. *Twomey* that the prosecution

need only show that the confession was voluntary "by a preponderance of the evidence" rather than voluntary beyond a reasonable doubt. In *United States* v. *Bidwell* the Court upheld a provision of a 1968 federal gun control law that authorized federal agents to inspect a gun dealer's shop without a search warrant during business hours.

In *Morrissey* v. *Brewer,* the Court held that due process requires that persons on parole or probation are entitled, if their freedom is revoked, to a hearing to determine the validity of the reasons for imprisonment.

In *Jackson* v. *Indiana,* the Court decided that a person adjudged to be mentally incompetent to stand trial must be committed to a civil institution within a reasonable time or be released.

Religious and family rights. The right of people of the Amish religious sect to refuse to send their children to school beyond the eighth grade was upheld by the Supreme Court in *Wisconsin* v. *Yoder* as within their rights to the free exercise of religion. It was the first time that a religious group had been exempted from compulsory school attendance laws. The Court was careful to point out that the ruling did not automatically apply to any group but that the history of the Amish sect clearly established that their religious beliefs would be gravely endangered, since secondary schools teach worldly values at odds with Amish ways. In *Stanley* v. *Illinois* the Court held that unwed fathers have the same right as unwed mothers to prove their fitness as parents in disputes over custody of children born out of wedlock. A Massachusetts law permitting married persons to obtain birth control devices but prohibiting their distribution to single persons was struck down as a violation of equal protection of the laws in *Eisenstadt* v. *Baird.*

Voting. In a decision likely to enfranchise millions of additional voters, the Supreme Court held in *Dunn* v. *Blumstein* that state laws establishing lengthy residence requirements for voting are unconstitutional as a violation of equal protection of the laws. The Court struck down a requirement in Tennessee, typical of most state residence requirements, of one year in the state and three months in the county. The Court determined that no vital state interest was served by such laws and that a highly mobile population was unduly penalized. The Court suggested that 30 days was sufficient for a state to take whatever steps were necessary to protect the purity of the ballot. In *Bullock* v. *Carter* the Court struck down a Texas law that required candidates in a primary election to pay excessively high filing fees. Milton Greenberg

COINS AND COIN COLLECTING. Government issues.

The U.S. General Services Administration will sell rare, uncirculated nineteenth-century Carson City silver dollars and anticipates a return of $120 million for the almost 3 million coins to be auctioned. Eisenhower proof silver dollars, originally sold at $10 each, dropped below issue price, as demand fell. However, the uncirculated Eisenhower dollar proved a best buy when its $3 price advanced to $5 on the open market. The U.S. Treasury will include an Eisenhower-clad dollar in 1973 proof sets and increase the price of the sets from $5 to $7. The 1972 proof sets were ordered in record numbers, with a target of 3 million quickly exceeded; orders were halted on March 15.

General activities. Silver coins eliminated from circulation since 1964 received attention, as the price of silver rose from $1.29 an ounce to almost $2 an ounce. Silver plates were very popular. Many collectors purchased commemorative 1-ounce silver bars in various designs and the novel holders specially made for them. The prices of silver dimes, quarters, and late-date halves were generally lower than anticipated. However, an 1894 dime, one of five known, sold for $50,000. The most sensational event in coin collecting was the discovery of some double-die cents among the cents struck by the Philadelphia Mint. Early sales of $50 a coin were bargains; dealers later paid $100.

The activities of several newly formed buying syndicates were reflected by record prices. An 1894-S Barber dime, purchased for $25,000, was reoffered for sale at $75,000. The American Numismatic Association convention in New Orleans was hit with a $60,000 burglary, but the culprit was caught when he tried to resell coins to a dealer.

Gold coins. The pressures of the international market caused the price of $20 common-date gold coins to rise about 50 percent. Many more gold coins were added to the list of those licensed for import. Rare gold issues sold for record prices: an 1824 quarter eagle for $4,600, a 1907 high relief Roman Numeral $20 gold piece for $43,500, and an 1875, 2½-dollar gold piece for $7,000.

Medals. Medal manufacturers sold their releases as a series and received record orders. The United States mints and private mints introduced several new medals. The Letcher Mint produced an issue featuring Paul Revere for the bicentennial of the American Revolution. The Franklin Mint, the largest private mint, continued to expand and was placed on the New York Stock Exchange.

Foreign issues. Nepal sold proof sets at $10 each. Special coins, tokens, and medals commemorated President Richard Nixon's visit to the People's Republic of China. Singapore proofs were overpriced at $25 a set and sold poorly. Canada's coins and sets and the Soviet Union's uncirculated sets at $3.85 each were popular. Many nations issued coins with designs suggested by the UN Food and Agriculture Organization's continuing efforts to fight hunger throughout the world. Lee Martin

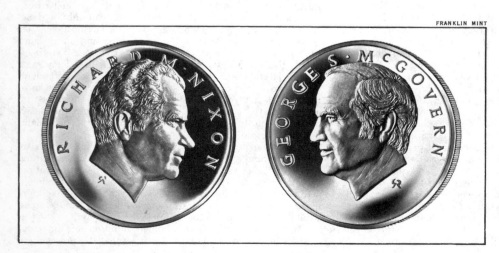

FRANKLIN MINT

CAMPAIGN MINTINGS. Both presidential contenders look the part they want to play, in campaign medals by Gilroy Roberts at the Franklin Mint.

COLOMBIA. Government and politics. In an election eagerly awaited, Colombians went to the polls on April 16 to fill seats in 906 municipal councils and 22 provincial assemblies. While only 2 million of the 8.3 million eligible voters cast their ballots, the results were significant, since they favored the two long-standing political parties, the Liberal and Conservative, and were a blow to the newly formed opposition group, the Popular National Alliance (ANAPO). ANAPO was founded by Gustavo Rojas Pinilla, a retired general of the army and dictator from 1953 to 1957, and his daughter, María Eugenia Rojas de Moreno Díaz. ANAPO had been gaining impressive electoral strength and was widely reputed to have received a majority in the 1970 presidential election, although Misael Pastrana Borrero, of the ruling National Front coalition, won.

The country came under pressure from armed guerrillas of the 250-man National Liberation Army, who periodically staged raids on isolated rural towns. They killed and wounded a few people in each raid, took hostages, released prisoners from jail, robbed banks, set fires, and rounded the townspeople into the central square to lecture them on the need for revolution. In April, seven soldiers and two civilians were killed in an ambush in the state of Antioquia, and in May, two more died in an attack on the town of San Jerónimo. The government revealed that in the first few months of this year, over 20 people were killed by guerrillas and $500,000 in goods and money taken. (In 1971, 74 people were allegedly killed by the guerrillas.)

In a move to ferret out Marxist and other revolutionary groups, security forces arrested over 50 people after a sweep in July. Among those arrested were several people prominent in the theater and television, as well as a number of high government officials, primarily in the National Statistics Service.

Economy. Because of Colombia's dependence on coffee exports, the erratic fluctuation of coffee prices on the world market was of special concern to national planners. However, after low prices in 1971 and gloomy expectations for 1972, coffee prices suddenly rose sharply in June and July, chiefly because of crop failures in Brazil. This "bonanza" was seen as an unexpected windfall for Colombia's programs of economic development and improvement of social services, although President Pastrana warned in July that the excess funds should be "wisely used." This caution reflected a fear that inflation, which reached 18 percent, would accelerate dangerously. Spiraling costs were due chiefly to the unusually severe rainstorms that have lashed the country for almost two years. The Ministry of Agriculture estimated that crop losses from rain and flooding may be as high as 6 percent of the total annual agricultural output, or about US$100 million. Access roads and other parts of the transportation system were also disrupted.

To alleviate economic problems, the government sought to increase steel production and petroleum exploitation. Together with the private sector, it launched an ambitious plan to expand steel production from approximately 300,000 tons to 1 million tons by 1980. This would not only supply the demands of a rapidly expanding internal market but would also provide valuable export opportunities within the Latin American Common Market and more specifically within the Andean Pact. Colombia's steel industry is favorably supplied by the largest coal reserves in Latin America, about 40 million tons. Because of exploration and mining, Colombia will begin to produce the alloy nickel steel on a large scale in approximately three years.

Exploration for new sources of petroleum was encouraged by a new plan under which the state-owned corporation Ecopetrol and foreign companies will undertake joint ventures. Ecopetrol will receive 60 percent of the profits. A strike in the llanos, or plains, in the eastern part of the country by Ecopetrol, Shell, and Continental Petroleum will raise production by more than 50 percent, to over 300,000 barrels of crude petroleum daily. In anticipation of this increase, two new refineries are being built at a cost of some US$130 million, one near Cali, with a capacity of 40,000 barrels daily, and the other on the Pacific coast, near the town of Tumaco, with a capacity of 75,000 barrels daily.

Education. A national teachers' strike became violent in April when students joined to support the teachers. The resulting demonstrations and clashes with police prompted the government to occupy many university campuses; the most violent confrontations took place in Cali. At first, the government refused to negotiate with the teachers, whose demands included higher salaries and accelerated payment of back wages, but the strike was eventually settled.

Area and population. Area (UN est.), 456,535 sq. mi. Pop. (est. 1971), 22,100,000. Principal cities: Bogotá (cap.), 2,512,000; Medellín, 1,089,000; Cali, 917,000.
Government. Constitutional republic with a bicameral legislature. Pres., Misael Pastrana Borrero.
Finance. Monetary unit, peso; exchange rate, 1 peso = US$0.0465. Budget (1970): revenue, US$716.9 million; expenditure, US$788.4 million.
Trade (1969). Imports, US$686 million; exports, US$608 million. Major imports: manufactured consumer goods, heavy machinery, industrial raw materials. Major exports: coffee, petroleum, raw cotton, sugarcane.
Education (1968). School enrollment: primary, 2,733,432; secondary, 577,417; higher, 62,844.
Armed forces. Army, 50,000; navy, 7,200; marines, 800; air force, 6,000.   STEFFEN SCHMIDT

COLORADO. Municipal growth. The year 1972 was dominated by the headlong growth of a strip city along the Front Range of the Rocky Mountains, stretching from Fort Collins and Greeley in the north to Pueblo in the south. Growth in the Denver area was especially heavy.

Denver and four neighboring suburban counties have a total population of 1.3 million, which is more than half the state's population of 2.3 million. To accommodate the new citizens, construction grew rapidly, with the value of building permits for new housing up 41 percent over 1971 and nonbuilding permits up 77.6 percent.

Denver's growth stirred up controversy in a number of ways. Alarmed by the expansion of subdivisions which receive water from the city's municipal system (at higher rates outside the city), residents of Denver voted in July against expansion of their water delivery system. Meanwhile, evironmental and taxpayer opposition continued to build over Denver's role as host city to the 1976 Winter Olympics. Criticism centered on the fear that Olympic events would damage mountain areas, that holding the games would encourage additional real estate activities which were neither conducive to good planning nor consistent with water supplies available, and that the taxpayers would be taxed too heavily in support of the games. A referendum barring further public support for the development of an Olympic site carried in November; almost certainly, the games will now be held elsewhere.

The 1972 session of the general assembly wrestled with the problem and came up with stronger land-use controls. Under legislation passed in April, counties must enact stiff zoning and other land-use regulations or face the prospect of state imposition of such controls. Toward the end of the year, counties were submitting such draft regulations for state approval; the Colorado Land Use Commission said it was pleased with the work being done by the counties.

Transportation. A major transportation development was the "holing through" of the first major bore in the Straight Creek Tunnel, 50 miles west of Denver. With this bore due for surfacing and use in 1973, motorists on Interstate Highway 70 will be spared the necessity of climbing over Loveland Pass, an 11,992-foot-high wintertime hazard. The tunnel will cost more than $50 million.

Economic developments. In the wake of Soviet wheat purchases, which pushed up grain prices, Colorado wheat

growers profited from wheat production which was only fair in some areas but good in others. Although 1972 production—61 million bushels—was not a record, it was far above the average of 40 million for the last ten years. Cattle producers generally had a profitable year, as the national appetite for beef held firm despite complaints of high prices.

The Great Western Sugar Company, the largest sugar beet processor and contractor in the United States, announced that it was seeking to negotiate the sale of the firm to sugar beet farmers. The firm is based in Denver and is part of a conglomerate, Great Western United, which has experienced financial difficulties.

Oil and gas exploration continued to grow, and the Wattenberg Field northeast of Denver—which began yielding gas in 1971—was predicted to have a capacity of 1,000–1,500 wells. Meanwhile, the U.S. Department of the Interior moved a step closer toward possible production of hydrocarbons from oil shale, of which Colorado has vast deposits, by holding hearings to determine the environmental impact of such industrial development.

Retail sales were good, with the metropolitan area of Denver posting increases of nearly 20 percent. New automobiles showed an increase of 20 percent over 1971. Convention visitors and tourists spent more than $600 million in Colorado during the year.

For election results and campaign highlights, see the special supplement ELECTION '72.

Area and population. Area, 104,247 sq. mi. Pop. (est. 1972), 2,363,008. Principal cities: Denver (cap.), 524,458; Colorado Springs, 155,836; Lakewood, 104,482; Pueblo, 102,525.
Government. Gov., John A. Love (R); lt. gov., John D. Vanderhoof (R); atty. gen., Duke W. Dunbar (R); secy. of state, Byron A. Anderson (R); treas., Palmer Burch (R). General assembly: senate, 24 R, 11 D; house, 38 R, 27 D.
Finance (1972–1973). Revenue, $1.287 billion (est.); expenditures, $1.3 billion (appropriated).
Education (est. 1972). Public elementary schools, 850; enrollment, 310,000; teachers, 12,350. Public secondary schools, 350; enrollment, 260,800; teachers, 16,488. Private and parochial elementary and secondary schools, 220; elementary enrollment, 30,000; secondary enrollment, 10,000; teachers, 2,000.   LEE OLSON

COMMON MARKET. *See* INTERNATIONAL TRADE.

COMPUTERS. The computer industry this year enjoyed a modest growth with no startling advances. Gross shipments of United States computer companies were close to $9 billion, up from $7.9 billion in 1971. Some new applications in technology have been helpful, and Soviet markets are beginning to open up, but companies still face the problem of how to stimulate more growth.

The industry. A maturing computer industry appraised itself at a conference of the Institute of Electrical and Electronics Engineers, held March 20–23 in the New York Coliseum. Focusing attention on the practical problems of a still-lingering business slowdown, Robert O. Evans, president of IBM's systems development division in White Plains, N.Y., said the industry must find new applications for computers, develop newer and simpler computer languages, and improve the design of the computer itself.

Kenneth H. Olsen, president of the nation's largest "minicomputer" company, the Digital Equipment Corporation, said he saw the minicomputer industry growing less dramatically than in the past. "The industry's major need is for increased emphasis on quality and systematic engineering in order to keep machines simple and easy to use," Olsen remarked. He noted that small companies often blame their failures on a lack of marketing support or financial resources. "Most of the time," he quipped, "their equipment just didn't work."

Despite a massive corporate commitment over several years, the RCA Corporation elected to drop out of the computer business entirely. Never capturing more than a small percentage of the overall market, RCA had nevertheless been highly regarded for the technical expertise of its equipment. In closing down computer and computer support facilities, RCA wrote off some $250 million in red ink, according to Chairman of the Board Robert W. Sarnoff, Jr. The Sperry Rand Corporation, profiting from the demise of its competition, purchased the bulk of RCA's computer customer base and now, like Honeywell, Inc., has about 10 percent of the market. But IBM remains the giant in the field.

An American exhibit, "Computer '72," opened to enthusiastic crowds of Muscovites. In its current five-year

WIDE WORLD

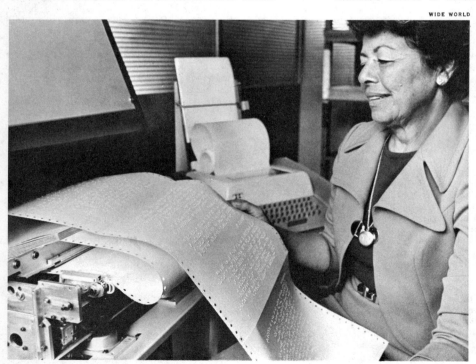

INSTANT BRAILLE. An experimental computer developed at the Massachusetts Institute of Technology converts a full page of typewritten English into Braille characters in only 90 seconds. The same job takes six or seven minutes by hand.

plan the Soviet government calls for 15,000 new computers, which helps explain why some Soviet customers wanted to buy the display computers right off the trade-show floor.

Western computer officials agreed that the Soviet market represents a great potential but noted that the selling costs were extremely high. Computer firms must deal with many levels of officialdom within a given Soviet agency and afterward must convince Elektronorgtekhnika, the central Soviet buying agency for all computers. "An extraordinary amount of red tape is involved in each and every sale," remarked one of the more experienced computer salesmen.

Although the Soviet Union is somewhat behind in the development of very large scale computing machinery, most observers at the show felt the Soviets were well versed in technology and very knowledgeable about their United States counterparts. The Soviet Union is currently developing a Ryat series computer whose capacity is similar to that of the 360/20 and 360/30 series introduced in the 1960's by IBM.

Computer-controlled cash flow. IBM introduced a computer terminal that reads credit cards and directly issues $5, $10, or $20 bills. Operating under the control of a central computer, the "cash issue" terminal permits the holder of a valid credit card to withdraw cash night or day. His bank account number is magnetically encoded on the credit card. After the card is inserted into the "cash issue" terminal, he keys into the computer the amount to be withdrawn and his personal identification number. If the transaction is valid, the cash is dispersed through a tray and the user's bank account is automatically debited by the computer; otherwise, a "check with your bank" light flashes on.

Jury selection. The once-laborious job of jury selection has been transformed into a fast, simple, and foolproof operation by a Univac 9400 computer in Union County, N.J. Once every four months a judge visits the computer installation and tells the Univac processor how many jurors are needed. Within a few moments the computer, choosing at random from a list of eligibles in its memory, prints out the names and addresses of those to be summoned for jury duty. The electronic processor readies jury attendance sheets, prints the summonses to be served by the sheriff's department, and prepares identification tags for each juror. "Before we began using computers, jury selection took a good four to five hours of a judge's time. Now it requires only a few minutes," commented Neil M. Manganella, director of information systems and services for Union County.

ALLAN YALE BROOKS

CONGO, DEMOCRATIC REPUBLIC OF THE. *See* ZAÏRE.

CONGO, PEOPLE'S REPUBLIC OF THE. Government. With President Marien Ngouabi safely off in the coastal city of Pointe Noire, Lieutenant Ange Diawara led an infantry battalion in a take-over of the Congolese radio and television station in the capital, Brazzaville, on February 21. By the time President Ngouabi had returned to the capital, Major Joachim Yhombi-Opango, chief of staff, had brought things back under control. Ngouabi blamed the attempted coup d'état on leftist extremists within the Congolese Workers Party, who were said to oppose Ngouabi's overtures to the West as well as his rapprochement with President Mobutu Sese Seko of Zaïre. A total of 178 alleged participants in the coup, including former prime minister Ambroise Noumazalay and former vice-president Alfred Raoul, were brought to trial before a military court and given long jail sentences. Lieutenant Diawara, who had fled to the south following the abortive coup, was sentenced to death in absentia. However, only two months later, Congolese security forces allegedly clashed with members of a group formed by Diawara, and shots were exchanged.

Foreign affairs. In an apparent effort to soften opposition from leftists, President Ngouabi, speaking at the first con-

ference of the Congolese Workers Party in April, stated that Marxism-Leninism remained the basis of policy in the Congo and that his government had no intention of renewing diplomatic relations with the United States.

On May 5, Abbé Fulbert Youlou, the colorful defrocked priest who had been the first president of the People's Republic of the Congo, died in exile in Madrid. After long discussions within the government, it was agreed that his body could be brought back to the Congo for burial.

Economy. In a Paris meeting with French president Georges Pompidou, President Ngouabi pressed for reorganization of the Central Bank of Equatorial African States and the Cameroon so as to include more Africans in top administrative posts and give individual member countries more latitude in deciding monetary questions. Pompidou promised to consider the matter.

Meanwhile, at home, the Central African Economic and Customs Union, comprising the Congo and three neighboring states, decided to build an oil refinery at Pointe Noire to make use of Congolese oil. Also, it was announced that a massive renovation of the Congo-Ocean railroad would be undertaken with the financial support of the French Fonds d'Aide et de Coopération. The railroad, stretching from Brazzaville, on the Congo River, to the port of Pointe Noire, provides Congolese industry with its main access to the sea.

Area and population. Area, 132,047 sq. mi. Pop. (est. 1972), 979,000.
Government. Former French colony, now single-party Socialist system. Pres., Marien Ngouabi.
Finance. Monetary unit, Communauté Financière Africaine (CFA) franc; 1 CFA franc = US$0.0041. Budget (1972): revenue, US$40.7 million; expenditure, US$46.2 million.
Trade (1970). Imports, US$57 million; exports, US$31 million.
LYNN KRIEGER MYTELKA

CONNECTICUT. Politics. The general assembly session this year proved much more peaceful than the bitter session last year. The Democratic-controlled legislature and Republican governor Thomas J. Meskill agreed on a $1.17 billion budget which involved raising the sales tax from 6.5 to 7 percent.

The legislature lowered the age for full adulthood from 21 to 18 and adopted limited no-fault auto insurance. The lottery began operations in February and after high sales in early weeks produced declining revenues. In the fall, promotional changes, including more weekly prizes, were instituted to increase revenue.

Strong interest in environmental improvement produced one act stating the responsibility of state agencies to determine the environmental impact of their programs and another qualifying thousands of acres of inland wetlands for protection. A large oil spill on Long Island Sound in March caused much damage and aroused widespread concern.

The assembly voted $4.3 million for grants to parents as indirect aid to nonpublic schools. Governor Meskill, however, vetoed a bill to forgive $1 million paid to private schools under a 1969 law declared unconstitutional.

The public reacted unfavorably to a bill raising the pay for legislators from $5,500 to $13,000 for a two-year term. Much criticism also greeted the legislature's enactment of a generous pension system for itself, with ten years' service and age 65 as basic qualifications. Meanwhile, state employees received only a $300 cost-of-living increase after receiving none in 1971.

Again, Governor Meskill vetoed many bills—51 in all—including one providing collective bargaining for state employees. With firm support from Republican legislators, all attempts to override Meskill's vetoes failed.

A federal district court ruled that Connecticut's antiabortion law was unconstitutional, and the U.S. Supreme Court rejected a request for a stay of execution. A special general assembly session on May 23 passed a very tough antiabortion law allowing an abortion only when the life

of an expectant mother is endangered. Then, on September 20, a federal district court again declared Connecticut's antiabortion statute unconstitutional.

The legislature again failed to resolve the problem of reapportionment, and the issue developed into a very complex tangle of legal maneuvering. A federal district court found the 1971 plan drawn by three state judges unconstitutional and ordered Professor Robert H. Bork of Yale to devise a new plan. His purely mathematical plan later was shelved by legal moves. Feeling that an assembly election would be beneficial if held on the regular November date, Republicans pressed for a court-ordered election then. Democrats, hoping for no election or one later, stalled with legal countermoves. Then, on August 23, a federal judge ordered a general assembly election to be held in November under the 1971 plan of apportionment, even though it had been ruled unconstitutional.

Economic developments. Connecticut's economy finally showed marked improvement, although unemployment of 135,400 in June remained only 8 percent below June 1971. The general business index of Connecticut Bank and Trust Company (based on 1957–1959 = 100) reached 278.1 in June—up 11.5 percent in a year. Personal income of $1.4 billion in June reflected an annual gain of 7.5 percent. In 1971, Connecticut again had the highest per capita income figure—$5,032.

Social and civic affairs. Changes in the state welfare system caused much unrest among staff and recipients. After a delay caused by court action, a flat-grant system became effective August 1. A formula based on family size replaced the earlier system based on individual needs. For the second time in three years the U.S. Supreme Court declared unconstitutional Connecticut's one-year residence requirement for welfare.

This was a bad year for state correctional institutions, as serious unrest and disturbances affected several units, especially the maximum security prison at Somers.

For election results and campaign highlights, see the special supplement ELECTION '72.

Area and population. Area, 5,009 sq. mi. Pop. (1970), 3,032,-217. Principal cities: Hartford (cap.), 158,017; Bridgeport, 156,542; New Haven, 137,707; Stamford, 108,798; Waterbury, 108,033.
   Government. Gov., Thomas J. Meskill (R); lt. gov., T. Clark Hull (R); secy. of state, Gloria Schaffer (D); treas., Robert I. Berdon (R); cont., Nathan G. Agostinelli (R); atty. gen., Robert K. Killian (D); Legislature: senate 19 D, 17 R; house of representatives, 99 D, 78 R.
   Finance. (general fund operations, fiscal year ending June 30, 1972). Receipts, $1.03 billion; disbursements, $1 billion.
   Education (1970 to 1971). Elementary (K–8) enrollment, 468,-126; high school (9–12) enrollment, 174,297. Teachers in public schools, 32,346. Vocational-technical schools, 15; full-time enrollment, 8,435; teachers, 584. Private schools, 375; enrollment, 109,353; teachers, 5,579.

ALBERT E. VAN DUSEN

CONSUMER AFFAIRS. Increasing public concern about the safety and quality of basic consumer products, the truthfulness and impact of product advertising, and the imbalance of power and rights as between sellers and buyers in consumer transactions produced extensive and far-reaching regulatory and legislative activity in the name of consumer protection. Although much of this activity was the direct result of organized pressure by consumer organizations and public interest groups, regulatory agencies evinced a new sense of mission and genuine dedication to the cause of consumer protection.

Federal Trade Commission. The most prominent and active consumer protection agency this year was the Federal Trade Commission. This agency mounted a vigorous enforcement program against false and misleading national advertising, proposing a new remedy of "corrective advertising," whereby advertisers found guilty of deceptive advertising would admit to the deception in subsequent advertisements for a period of one year. The objectives of this remedy are to vitiate the effects of deception in past advertising and to restore competitive conditions to the situation existing before the false advertising began.

Many advertisers contend that this remedy is beyond the FTC's statutory authority, and several test cases are presently being litigated. The most important cases now in litigation are a complaint against the Standard Oil Company of California alleging false advertising of the antipollution qualities of F-310 additive in Chevron gasoline; a complaint against ITT Continental Baking alleging false advertising of the nutritional superiority of Wonder Bread; and a complaint against the Coca-Cola Company alleging false advertising of the nutritional value of Hi-C drink.

While these cases and others were being bitterly contested, the FTC obtained three consent orders in which advertisers agreed to engage in corrective advertising. The advertiser of Profile Bread agreed to disclose that, contrary to claims in prior advertising, Profile Bread is not a "diet" bread; the advertiser of Ocean Spray Cranberry Juice Cocktail agreed to disclose that the term food energy, as used in prior advertisements, refers to food calories; and the trade association of the sugar industry agreed to run advertisements refuting the representation in its own prior advertisements that the consumption of sugar before meals will contribute to weight reduction.

In the past the commission has challenged the entire tobacco industry for failing to disclose the health hazards of smoking in cigarette advertising. The challenge ended this year in an industry-wide agreement to include health warnings in all future advertisements.

In the summer of 1971 the commission initiated a bold new approach to advertising regulation in its inauguration of the Advertising Substantiation Program. Under this program, the commission requires all advertisers in selected industries to submit documentation to support factual claims in current advertising. The documentation submitted is placed on the public record for public scrutiny and professional evaluation. Whenever the documentation is found to be inadequate to support the claim being made, the FTC will consider enforcement action against the advertisers involved. This program was implemented vigorously in the past year, with all advertisers in the following product categories ordered to submit advertising substantiation: automobiles, air conditioners, electric shavers, dentifrices, television sets, cough and cold remedies, tires, soaps and detergents, and hearing aids.

The significance of a finding of inadequate substantiation to support a factual claim was highlighted in the commission's final decision in a case challenging Pfizer's advertising of Unburn sunburn lotion. Although the commission dismissed the complaint against Pfizer on the specific facts presented, the commission broke new legal ground in declaring that it is an unfair trade practice, in violation of law, to make a factual claim in product advertising when "no reasonable basis" exists to support the claim. The importance of this ruling is that it is no longer necessary, in the commission's view, for the commission to assume the difficult burden of proving the falsity of an advertiser's claim in order to require the claim to be discontinued; the burden is now upon the advertiser to demonstrate the existence of a "reasonable basis" in support of his claims before such claims may lawfully be disseminated. The exact meaning of the term "reasonable basis" remains to be developed in future cases; and the authority of the commission to establish this policy remains to be tested in appeals to the courts from future commission actions.

In April of this year, the commission began a broad formal challenge to the advertising of analgesics by the Sterling, American Home Products, and Bristol-Myers drug companies, including advertising for Bayer Aspirin, Bufferin, Excedrin, and Anacin. These complaints charged that superiority claims for each of these brands are unfair and decep-

The Whole Truth: The FTC Orders "Corrective Advertising"

Does Profile have fewer calories than other breads? No, Profile has about the same per ounce as other breads.

To be exact Profile has 7 fewer calories per slice.

That's because it's sliced thinner.

But eating Profile will not cause you to lose weight. A reduction of 7 calories is insignificant.

RADIO TV REPORTS, INC.

tive, because of the existence of a "substantial question" as to the validity of each such claim. The proposed relief includes a ban on future claims of therapeutic superiority until such claims are established without question, and an extensive form of corrective advertising. The industry and the commission anticipate a battle that may take several years before the case is over.

The commission has challenged the advertising and marketing practices of the entire breakfast cereal industry, in a multifaceted complaint against Kellogg, General Mills, General Foods, and Quaker Oats. These companies are charged with jointly monopolizing the entire breakfast cereal market by means of such practices as intensive advertising of each brand of cereal, false and misleading advertising of the nutritional value of each brand, brand proliferation, and exclusionary shelf-space programs. The proposed relief includes the creation of new competitors from the sale of existing plants, compulsory licensing of existing brands and trademarks, and various other actions designed to bring about a gradual deconcentration of the cereal industry. The significance of this case is that it may provide a model for similar broad challenges to the advertising and marketing practices of other highly concentrated consumer products industries.

The commission has asserted the authority to attack industry-wide problems or widespread abuses by means of the issuance of "trade regulation rules," considered to be fairer and more efficient than reliance on a case-by-case approach to problems of this nature. Last year the commission issued a rule requiring the posting of octane ratings on all gasoline pumps, as a way of remedying the consumer's current lack of essential comparative information about competing brands of a basic consumer product. The oil industry challenged the commission's legal authority to promulgate the rule, and a federal district court has upheld that challenge. The district court has enjoined the commission's enforcement of that rule pending the commission's appeal of the court's ruling. While that appeal is pending, the commission continues to seek legislation from Congress to clarify its authority to issue trade regulation rules.

One of the commission's most controversial actions this year was its submission to the Federal Communications Commission of a statement in support of "counteradvertising," defined as the right of some access to the broadcast media for the expression of opposing points of view regarding significant public issues expressly or implicitly raised in commercial advertising. Several public interest representatives and groups have urged the Federal Communications Commission to recognize the need for counteradvertising of one type or another to expose the misleading and one-sided nature of commercial advertising. The FTC has lent its support and encouragement to this concept, which it considers to be an appropriate means of supplementing its own efforts to regulate advertising abuses.

Food and Drug Administration. The FTC was not the only federal agency active in consumer protection during the past year. The Food and Drug Administration initiated a number of programs designed to improve the nutritional quality of the food supply and to protect the consuming public from unsafe and ineffective drugs and cosmetics. The most significant action with regard to food was the promulgation of three proposed rules in April: (1) a voluntary nutritional labeling program that would tell consumers at a glance the amount of vitamins, minerals, and proteins in packaged foods; (2) guidelines for "filth tolerance" in foods from unavoidable sources; (3) procedural changes that would allow either the FDA commissioner or any outside person to institute a complete, in-depth reexamination of the safety of a food additive that had previously been declared safe.

On the basis of a report by the National Academy of Sciences–National Research Council that the consumption of large amounts of saccharin by test animals has resulted in the growth of tumors, the FDA removed the widely used artificial sweetener from the list of food additives generally recognized as safe and issued regulations restricting its use while additional safety studies are conducted. On the basis of similar findings regarding the chemical DES (diethylstilbestrol), a stimulant widely used to fatten beef and lamb shortly before preparation for sale, the FDA banned the continued use of this chemical in animal feed.

The most significant action in the drug area was the FDA's announcement, in January of this year, of a massive and unprecedented review of the safety and efficacy of 26 classes of nonprescription drug products, including all antacids, cough and cold remedies, stimulants, laxatives, and analgesics. The agency will establish an expert review panel for each drug category, selected from the membership of the National Academy of Sciences–National Research Council. Utilizing the conclusions of each of these panels, the FDA will consider the need for requiring either changes in the labeling or restrictions on the marketing of drugs which are found to be not as safe or effective as has previously been assumed.

Increasing concern with the safety of cosmetics led the FDA to initiate a program to ensure consumer safety in the use of cosmetics containing antibacterial ingredients. Hexachlorophene was the first and most important such ingredient singled out for action, because it is an active ingredient in about 400 cosmetic, soap, and deodorant products, and there are some indications that it may be toxic when applied or inhaled. The FDA program puts the cosmetics industry on notice that any bacterial agent intended for long-term use must be adequately tested for safety prior to

marketing, bans the continued use of hexachlorophene in all cosmetics, pending further study, and requires a warning label on soaps and deodorants with hexachlorophene.

Industry self-regulation. Government intervention was not the only source of consumer protection news in the past year. Two important developments in industry self-regulation also occurred. First, the advertising industry and the Council of Better Business Bureaus organized the National Advertising Review Board, designed as a form of industry self-policing against false and misleading product advertising. Although it lacks the power to compel advertisers to stop running an advertisement found to be deceptive, the advertising community appears generally inclined to respect and comply with the board's final judgments regarding questioned claims. Consumer groups, however, have begun to doubt NARB's effectiveness and good faith; these groups have been critical of the board's delay in making decisions, the secrecy of its proceedings, and its apparent willingness to approve some advertisements which the Federal Trade Commission would consider deceptive.

The National Business Council for Consumer Affairs, an advisory council of businessmen appointed by President Richard M. Nixon to recommend programs for industry to follow in anticipating and resolving consumer problems, issued its final report this year. The recommendations included unit pricing, open dating, nutritional and ingredient labeling, and care and use directions on package labels. The council strongly urged that labeling for processed foods include serving size, a list of ingredients, nutritional information, and the pull-date (the date at which an article can no longer be sold in its regular shelf space at full price). It also recommended that packaging be designed to protect the quality and form of the product, to protect persons coming in contact with it, and to offer sufficient variety without unnecessarily complicating selection. The Department of Commerce endorsed these suggestions and followed them up by promulgating voluntary guidelines for packaging and labeling of consumer products. The department sent the report to 1,500 of the nation's business and trade association executives urging its adoption.

Legislative activity. Legislative activity during the past year included congressional hearings on five major pieces of consumer legislation. One bill would create a new independent product safety agency, empowered to issue safety standards for all hazardous products and to take swift action against noncomplying products found in the market. The Nixon administration opposed this bill, preferring an alternative bill that would broaden the product safety function of the Food and Drug Administration; nevertheless, President Nixon signed the measure into law. Another bill would create a new, independent consumer protection agency, empowered to intervene in the proceedings of other agencies on behalf of the consumer. This bill passed the House but died in the Senate. A third major bill would expand the powers of the Federal Trade Commission to regulate product warranties, seek injunctions in court against deceptive practices, and issue substantive rules to proscribe or regulate questionable industry practices. The clarification of the FTC's rulemaking power is the most important aspect of this last piece of legislation, in view of the recent court decision rejecting the FTC claim of inherent rulemaking power.

Another major piece of consumer legislation pressed in the past year was the so-called Moss-McGovern Truth-in-Advertising Bill. This bill would give consumers a right to demand and receive substantiating data in support of every advertising claim, and it would make unlawful the dissemination of an advertising claim that lacked adequate substantiation. The Federal Trade Commission has urged that further consideration of this bill be deferred, pending the completion of its evaluation of the impact of its own advertising substantiation program. The FTC, however, has warmly supported another consumer bill that concerns ad-

vertising regulation, the bill to create an institute of advertising, marketing, and society to study all aspects of the relationship between advertising and society.

Legislative activity will continue with regard to all five of these major bills. Other proposals under consideration include the Fair Credit Billing Act, to regulate the billing practices of credit companies and other major creditors, and legislation to create private class-action rights for consumers.

See also RETAIL BUSINESS: Advertising.

ROBERT A. SKITOL

CONTRACT BRIDGE. Return of the Blues. After their two-year retirement from world contract bridge competition, Italy's perennial world champions returned to action with predictable results. The Blue Team consisted of Walter Avarelli, Giorgio Belladonna, Massimo D'Alelio, Pietro Forquet, Benito Garozzo, and Camillo Pabis Ticci—a lineup that included four of the players who began their remarkable winning streak of ten victories in the Bermuda Bowl event in 1957. The Blues added a third successive victory in the quadrennial World Team Olympiad, played in Miami Beach in June. Forthwith, they announced that they would not compete again as a team, though individual members might take part in future world championships.

Events leading up to the Olympiad presaged the Blue Team victory over the world champion Aces of Dallas, who had won the Bermuda Bowl for the United States in 1970 and 1971, while the Blue Team was in retirement. One of

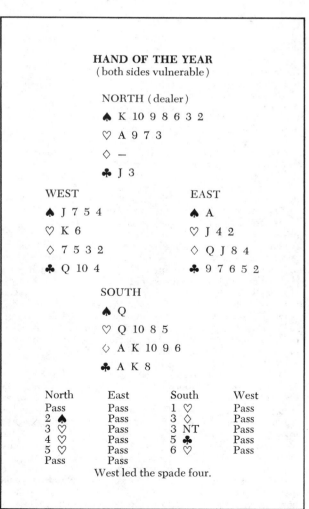

the lures that brought them back into the field was the sponsorship of Chinese-American oil-shipping tycoon C. C. Wei, whose Precision System the Blue Team adopted. Another was the offer of the largest purses in the history of bridge: $15,000 for a head-to-head exhibition match against the Aces (Robert Hamman, Mike Lawrence, Robert Wolff, Bobby 'Goldman, James Jacoby, and Paul Soloway), and another $15,000 to the winner of a knockout team competition, both played in Las Vegas in December 1971. The Italian team won both contests and were heavy favorites to take the 39-nation Olympiad. An Italian team also won the Ladies' World Team Olympiad.

National Championships. The Fall Nationals, the first major event in the 1971–1972 season of the American Contract Bridge League National Championships, were held in Phoenix, Ariz., in November 1971. The Reisinger Board-a-match Teams were won by the team of Lew Mathe and Don Krauss of Los Angeles; George Rapee, William Grieve, and Edgar Kaplan of New York City; and Norman Kay of Philadelphia.

In March of this year, Cincinnati was the site of the Spring Nationals. The Precision Team, twice winners of the Spingold Knockout Teams, scored their first win in the prestigious Vanderbilt Knockout Teams, as Gene Neiger, Peter Weichsel, Alan Sontag, Steve Altman, and Joel Stuart of New York City with Tom Smith of Greenwich, Conn., defeated Jack Blair of Tulsa, Okla.; Fred Hamilton of Berkley, Mich.; Howard Perlman of Bloomfield Hills, Mich.; and Paul Swanson of Morgantown, W.Va., by 23 points, thereby becoming the third team in bridge history to win three out of four consecutive national knockout team events.

The Summer Nationals were held in Denver in July and August. B. Jay Becker, playing on a team which included his son Michael, as well as Jeff Rubens and Andy Bernstein, all of New York City, led the first father-and-son team ever to win the Spingold Knockout Team event, defeating in the finals the team of Curtis Smith of Houston, Texas; Byron Greenberg of Tulsa, Okla.; Pat Brennan of Amarillo, Texas; and Clifford Russell, Albert Weiss, and Edith Kemp of Miami, Fla.

In the final rounds of the competition among the three title winners and the Smith team (who won a playoff against the Blair team in Memphis), B. Jay Becker's team triumphed over the Mathe team to determine the North American team for the 1973 world championship Bermuda Bowl. The Dallas-based Aces will also play in the 1973 World Championship; as defending champions, they are nominally the representatives of the World Bridge Federation in the match.

The most important open pair events of 1971–1972 were the Blue Ribbon title, won by two comparative unknowns, Roger Bates of Tucson, Ariz., and John Grantham of Inglewood, Calif., and the Life Masters Pairs, taken for the second year in a row by Alvin Roth of New York City and Barbara Rappaport of East Orange, N.J., the only pair in history to successfully defend the Von Zedtwitz Gold Cup.

Hand of the year. One deal from the $15,000 challenge match between the Blue Team and the Aces was noteworthy as evidence that even the greatest experts occasionally revoke and that a loophole exists in the present Official Laws of Contract Bridge.

Giorgio Belladonna, West, defending against South's optimistic small slam bid in hearts, opened the seven of spades. East took the ace and returned a club, won by declarer's ace. Recognizing that his only real chance was to find East with the jack of hearts alone, South led the queen of hearts. Belladonna covered with the king and when the jack failed to drop, declarer's hope vanished. He led a low spade from dummy, ruffed with the ten of hearts and led another heart. On this trick, Belladonna revoked, discarding a diamond. The two-trick penalty for this offense would have permitted declarer to make his slam. But South did not know about the revoke, especially when East won the trick with the jack of hearts, East returned another heart, and Belladonna discarded a diamond, revoking a second time.

Had Belladonna discovered his error in time to follow suit on this trick, declarer could have given up a trick to West's spade jack. Then, with a trump left in dummy, spades would have been good for enough tricks to let declarer make his contract with the aid of the two-trick penalty. Instead, he played so as to go down three, and the two-trick penalty still left him down one. The slam was not bid at the other table, so the Aces lost 750 points instead of gaining 780. Since the deal occurred at the halfway point and at a time when the score was close, it may also have cost the Aces $15,000.

Under present laws, a second revoke in the same suit by the same player incurs no additional penalty. Under laws in force prior to 1943, the second revoke would have cost the offender another trick and the slam would have been made. It is entirely possible that when the bridge laws again come up for revision, this deal will be taken into account and the revoke penalty amended.

RICHARD L. FREY

COSTA RICA. Economic problems, highlighted by Costa Rica's virtual withdrawal from the Central American Common Market, dominated the year's events. Costa Rica's balance of trade had worsened over the last two years, and the colón, officially rated at 6.65 to the dollar, was selling at 8.60 under a dual exchange system. Costa Rica's trade deficit with the CACM amounted to a projected $50 million this year, up $25 million from 1971.

In an effort to stem imports and give the government added revenue, new taxes were imposed in February on selected items, mostly luxury goods. However, no new taxes were levied on Central American imports, which continued to come in at an accelerated pace. Instead, Costa Rica announced on August 31 that it would no longer pay for nonessential commodities from CACM at the official rate but would instead apply the 8.60 quotation. This move set off a chain reaction in which trade between Costa Rica and the rest of the common market was virtually suspended.

Government and politics. Throughout the year there were work stoppages by teachers, state-employed doctors and dentists, and railroad workers in the Atlantic Zone. The railroad strike indirectly led to nationalization of the ailing British-owned Northern Railroad.

President José Figueres Ferrer lost a good deal of popularity with the people for some of his actions during the year. In December 1971 right-wing elements marched to protest the opening of a Soviet embassy, which Figueres was determined to open. The next day, when a hijacked Nicaraguan airliner landed in Costa Rica, Figueres used the opportunity to show that he was still the decisive leader of old. He rushed to the airport and, machine gun in hand, led the attack on the airplane in which two of the three hijackers were shot as they tried to surrender. The third hijacker was returned to Nicaragua, a move later condemned by the Costa Rican Supreme Court.

Early in the year, the ultraright Movimiento Costa Rica Libre in league with the Guatemalan Mano Blanco supposedly concocted a plot to assassinate Figueres and other government leaders. The public forces were put on full alert, but nothing happened.

Area and population. Area, 19,575 sq. mi. Pop. (est. 1972), 1,832,081.
Government. Constitutional republic with legislative assembly. Pres., José Figueres Ferrer.
Finance. Monetary unit, colón; 1 colón = US$0.120.
Trade (1971). Exports, $231 million; imports, $350 million. Principal exports: bananas, coffee, beef, sugar.
Education (1971). Enrollment: primary schools, 364,419; secondary schools, 78,171; university, 16,506; normal schools, 2,382.

THEODORE S. CREEDMAN

WALLACE SHOT DOWN

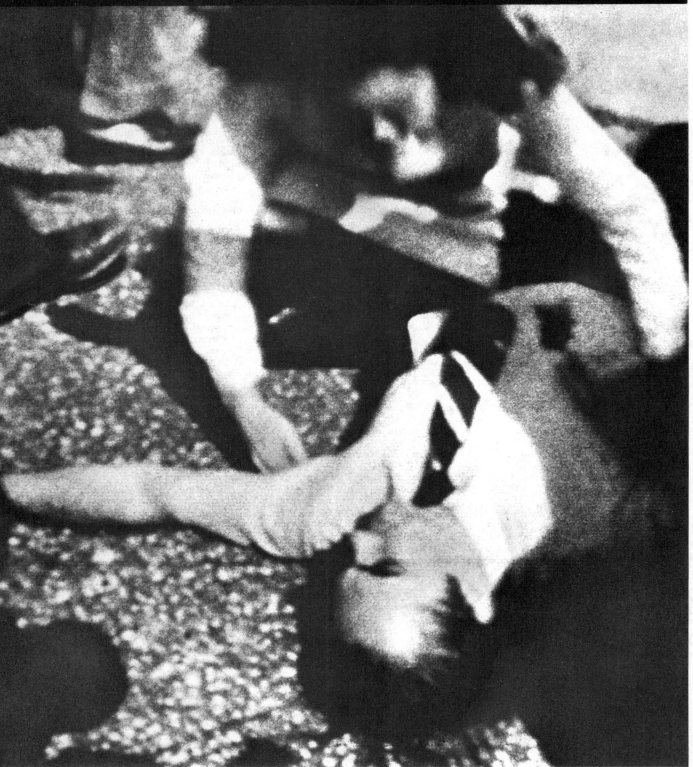

WIDE WORLD

Alabama governor George C. Wallace (far left) lies on the asphalt of a Laurel, Md., shopping center, blood oozing through his shirt. At left, a man in the crowd grabs the arm of Wallace's 21-year-old assailant, Arthur Bremer; below, Bremer is led away. He was later convicted of firing the five shots that paralyzed the governor and cut short Wallace's campaign for the presidency.

UPI

CRIME AND CRIME PREVENTION. In spite of strong measures, the number of hijacked airplanes increased, and the supply of heroin, temporarily diverted, appeared to find new routes to the addict. In certain respects crime in the United States, in keeping with a presidential election year, also took on political overtones. The underworld was busy with its violent feuds, and the United States was again shocked by a political assassination attempt.

Hijackings. On January 29, Garrett Brock Trapnell, a former mental patient, using a gun hidden in a plaster arm cast, took over a Los Angeles–New York TWA jet and demanded a $300,000 ransom. Before the money could be delivered, Trapnell was shot and captured at Kennedy Airport in New York by an FBI agent posing as a crewman. Just two days earlier in Poughkeepsie, N.Y., Heinrich von George was killed by a blast from an FBI shotgun at close range, shortly after receiving the $200,000 he demanded as ransom for the Mohawk airliner he had temporarily commandeered. Early in February the Federal Aviation Administration (FAA) directed domestic scheduled airlines to screen all passengers and baggage to detect potential hijackers. Airline personnel were to check all passengers against a behavior profile, a compiled list of traits common to many past hijackers. The order further directed that each of the nation's 9,000 airline boarding gates be equipped with a magnetometer for the detection of metal objects. Suspicious passengers would be questioned, searched, or even prevented from boarding. According to FAA officials, about 1 percent of all passengers match the profile. For the three-month period April–June, some 349,000 passengers were questioned. Of that number, 1,583 were refused entrance and 514 were arrested. The search for potential hijackers has resulted in arrests for drug possession and a number of other crimes. The right of airline or government officials to search passengers or to deny them boarding rights if they refuse to be searched has so far been upheld in a number of court cases.

Uncertain about the response of travelers to such close scrutiny, some airlines were at first reluctant to implement the program systematically. In March, after one jet was damaged by a bomb while on the ground and explosives were discovered in two others, President Richard M. Nixon ordered the nation's airlines to introduce more stringent security measures. By summer, surveys undertaken by several

WIDE WORLD

airlines indicated that many Americans were avoiding air travel for fear of hijacking, and by August airlines were advertising their newer and stricter security measures, including the inspection of all hand luggage.

The Boeing 727 jetliner, used by many airlines, has an exit door that may be opened while in flight, and inevitably parachutes came to play a role in extortion attempts. On April 7, Richard Floyd McCoy, Jr., a university student majoring in law enforcement, took over a 727 jetliner and directed the plane to fly to San Francisco, where the passengers were set free and a $500,000 ransom was collected. The jet again took off, and McCoy parachuted out near Provo, Utah. He was arrested two days later, and all but $30 of the ransom was recovered in his home. He was later sentenced to 45 years in prison. On the day of McCoy's arrest Stanley H. Speck, a cab driver, took over a 727 in San Diego, demanding $500,000 in ransom as well as parachutes. He was captured when he left the airliner to pick up charts. By midyear most airlines using the 727 announced that the door had been permanently sealed.

In addition to large sums of money, ideological elements also entered the hijacking picture. In July three black men captured a DC-8 jet and, after $1 million in ransom had been paid, ordered the airliner to Algeria. The men com-

KEN REGAN/CAMERA 5

HIS REST DID NOT BRING PEACE. Mourners bury reputed Mafia boss Joey Gallo in a Brooklyn cemetery. The shooting of Gallo in a New York clamhouse, as he celebrated his 43rd birthday with family and friends, started up a new wave of gangland murders.

plained of racial discrimination in the United States; two of them had escaped from prison and were seeking refuge from the police. Eldridge Cleaver, former Black Panther leader now living in Algiers, wrote an open letter to Algerian president Houari Boumedienne asking that the ransom money be kept and used to carry on the Afro-American liberation fight. The million dollars, as well as an earlier ransom of $500,000, was returned to the airline companies. Although Algeria has not granted the hijackers the political asylum they requested, it has not expelled them.

On May 3 four Turks armed with grenades hijacked a Turkish airliner to Bulgaria and threatened to blow up the plane and its passengers unless Turkey freed three condemned guerrillas. The guerrillas had been sentenced to death in October 1971 on terrorism charges which included the kidnapping of four U.S. airmen and the kidnapping and murder of an Israeli consul. After hours of negotiation with representatives of the Turkish embassy in Sofia, the hijackers gave up their demands and freed the passengers and crew.

A political hijacking by Palestinians in late October was more successful. Yielding to hijackers' threats to blow up a Lufthansa Boeing 727 and its 20 civilian passengers, the West German government freed three Arabs held in connection with the shooting of 11 Israeli athletes at the Olympics. The Arabs were turned over to the hijackers at Zagreb, and the plane was then flown to Tripoli, where plane, passengers, and crew were released. The Israeli government denounced Germany's handling of the affair.

Modern piracy took a step backward on May 17, when

Cunard Steam-Ship Company officials received a phone threat that six bombs had been placed on the luxury liner *Queen Elizabeth 2* and would be set off unless a ransom of $350,000 was paid. English bomb-disposal experts were flown to the ship and parachuted into the water. A thorough search of the 13 decks revealed no explosive devices.

Lydda massacre. On May 30, three gunmen, members of a left-wing Japanese group mobilized by the Arab guerrilla movement, attacked a crowd of 250–300 people at Lydda International Airport, outside of Tel Aviv. Armed with automatic rifles and hand grenades, the terrorists killed 25 persons and wounded 77. Among the victims were 15 Puerto Ricans, members of a delegation of pilgrims visiting the Holy Land. One of the attackers committed suicide with a grenade, another was caught by an airport maintenance man, and the third was apparently killed by bullets fired by his companions.

War on drugs. In January, President Nixon established the Drug Abuse Law Enforcement office in the Justice Department and appointed a former commissioner of customs, Myles J. Ambrose, special assistant attorney general to command the 400-agent division. By the end of March, 33 cities had been pinpointed for assistance from teams of federal agents, each headed by a senior Justice Department attorney. By August one team had helped seize approximately $350 million worth of heroin and morphine.

On March 21 the president signed legislation committing $1 billion to a special action office for drug abuse prevention. Headed by Dr. Jerome H. Jaffe, the office will coordinate the antidrug programs spread over 13 different federal agencies. At one time most of the heroin used in the United States originated in the opium poppy fields of Turkey and after processing, most likely in southern France, was smuggled into the United States. At the White House ceremony announcing the new legislation, the president announced that the Turkish government had agreed to completely ban the growing of poppies by the end of 1972. The United States is to provide $35 million in compensation to the growers for loss of income, and U.S. advisers will assist the farmers in developing different crops.

Under some pressure and with American cooperation, French law enforcement agents were able to locate and seize a number of heroin laboratories in France. In January a large secret lab was seized in Marseilles, France. Agents were searching a secluded villa looking for evidence of a fuel-oil smuggling ring when they accidentally uncovered the clandestine laboratory and a large amount of equipment. On March 2 agents captured 935 pounds of pure heroin in the hold of a shrimp boat off the coast of Marseilles. That shipment would have netted $180 million retail and was sufficient to supply every U.S. addict for over three weeks.

With the tightening up of the Turkish-French pipeline, it became apparent that abundant sources in Burma, Thailand, and elsewhere could easily take over the American trade. Nelson Gross, the State Department's senior adviser on narcotics, indicated that the government was aware of the possibilities of Southeast Asian suppliers entering the nation's drug picture and noted that strong efforts would be taken to hinder this. There was evidence that American diplomats were exerting strong pressure on governments in areas where opium is produced. In September, Eugene T. Rossides, assistant treasury secretary, announced that more than $66 million in taxes and tax penalty claims had been charged against suspected drug dealers. He stated that almost $1 million in cash and property had already been collected and that nine persons were convicted on criminal tax charges stemming from drug traffic. Rossides added that 22 persons were under indictment and that prosecution had been recommended in 49 other cases.

Gang war. New York is reputed to have five Mafia families doing business in its busy environs, and for some months that city seemed to be the setting for a bizarre rerun of the best-

selling novel and popular film *The Godfather*. In the early morning of April 7, Joseph Gallo, reputed Mafia boss, was gunned down while celebrating his 43rd birthday with his family and friends in a small New York City restaurant, apparently by associates of the Mafia family of Joseph A. Colombo, Sr. The complex landscape of the underworld was soon further obscured by the clouds of gunsmoke. Over a two-month period the number of riddled bodies found slumped gangland style over the wheels of their cars or lying in the streets rose to more than a dozen, or a total of 25 since the attempted assassination of Joseph Colombo in June 1971. Police initially speculated that a gang war between the Gallo and Colombo factions was responsible for the slayings, although it later appeared that some of the murders were efforts to eliminate individuals cooperating with police investigations into organized crime.

Warfare was not confined to New York nor to Mafia families. On April 3, Tyrone Palmer, identified by police as a millionaire heroin dealer, was among four people killed in an Atlantic City, N.J., nightclub. Eleven other persons were wounded in the gun battle, which officials said had grown out of a gang war for control of the Philadelphia narcotics trade. In September, St. Louis police reported that in the period from June 15 to August 18, 41 persons had been wounded in drug-related disputes.

Angela Davis. The trial of 28-year-old black militant leader Angela Davis began in March after 16 months of pretrial detention. Miss Davis had been charged with supplying the guns and helping plan a Marin County courtroom kidnap attempt in which four people, including the judge, were killed. The prosecution sought to show that Miss Davis and her coconspirators planned to exchange the captured hostages for the release of three additional prisoners. Miss Davis had earlier been dismissed from her teaching position at the University of California because she declared she was a Communist, and she soon became a focal point of radical political causes. Chief prosecutor Albert Harris, Jr., contended that Miss Davis was motivated by a passionate love for George Jackson, one of the prisoners, and would go to any lengths to have him freed. Letters from Miss Davis to Jackson, as well as her diary, were read by the prosecution at the trial. The documents expressed her love for the prisoner and referred to him as her husband. Her active political efforts on his behalf were also described. Witnesses for the prosecution testified that they had seen Miss Davis in the Marin County courthouse only days before the shootout. Defense witnesses disputed that testimony and also stated that the guns used, although registered to Miss Davis, had been taken without her knowledge. On June 4, after 13 hours, the jury voted for acquittal on all charges.

Pentagon papers. Sections of a top-secret study of U.S. involvement in Vietnam had been released to the press in 1971, and on January 4, 1972, Daniel Ellsberg, key figure in the Pentagon papers case, entered a not-guilty plea in a U.S. court in Los Angeles. He and codefendant Anthony J. Russo, Jr., were charged with espionage, conspiracy, and misuse of government property for allegedly leaking large sections of the massive 47-volume secret document, which had been prepared in 1969 under the direction of presidential aide Henry Kissinger. Complex legal maneuvers characterized the proceedings. The trial appeared to be under way in July, with a jury sworn in and lawyers prepared to begin their opening statements, when Supreme Court Justice William O. Douglas ordered a halt so that defense lawyers could appeal to the Supreme Court, then in summer recess, the government's refusal to disclose details of a wiretap. With an anticipated delay of several months, the serious question arose concerning the possibility that the jury could not avoid prejudicial contacts over that period of time. In the meantime the defendants are "in jeopardy," and if the jury is dismissed they may not be tried again unless they waive their Fifth Amendment rights.

Biography hoax. In March, 41-year-old writer Clifford Irving finally admitted that his purported biography of billionaire Howard R. Hughes was a hoax. Irving had earlier claimed that his book was based on extensive personal interviews with Hughes and had signed contracts for publication with the McGraw-Hill Book Company and *Life* magazine. Hughes denied ever having met Irving. The two checks totaling $650,000 and intended for Hughes had been cashed by Irving's wife Edith through a Swiss account she had opened under the name of Helga R. Hughes. The couple, along with research aide Richard Suskind, 46, were indicted in New York in March for attempting to defraud McGraw-Hill of $750,000. All three received prison sentences. After serving two months Mrs. Irving agreed to return to Switzerland to face charges of larceny and forgery. Her husband began serving a 2½-year sentence in August. (*See* PEOPLE IN THE NEWS: Clifford Irving.)

Harrisburg conspiracy. What had promised to be a sensational antiwar conspiracy trial came to an anticlimactic end in April in the courthouse at Harrisburg, Pa. The jury could only agree on one count: that Father Philip F. Berrigan, a 48-year-old Catholic priest, and Sister Elizabeth McAlister, a nun and teacher of art history, had exchanged contraband letters while the priest was imprisoned in Lewisburg Federal Penitentiary. The jury remained deadlocked at 10–2 in rejecting the government's main charges against the seven defendants, mainly priests and nuns and former priests and nuns, of conspiracy to blow up tunnels in Washington, D.C., kidnap presidential adviser Henry Kissinger, and vandalize various draft board records. The allegations first became public knowledge in November 1970, when FBI Director J. Edgar Hoover, testifying before a congressional appropriations committee for additional funds for the bureau, revealed the existence of a dangerous group plotting to disrupt the government. The government's star witness was Boyd F. Douglas, Jr., a Lewisburg prisoner whose criminal record included impersonation of an officer, fraud, and assault with a gun, as well as two escapes from custody. Douglas had had the rare privilege of daytime release for study at nearby Bucknell University. At the trial he testified that after carrying out a letter written by Father Berrigan, he became a paid informer for the FBI. Douglas became active in the antiwar movement and under FBI supervision continued to transport letters to and from the jail. In September, Father Berrigan was sentenced to four concurrent two-year terms and Sister McAlister to a year in prison.

Political bugs. Five men with cameras and electronic surveillance equipment were captured at 2 A.M. on June 17 in the Democratic National Committee headquarters in the Watergate building in Washington, D.C. The five men, apparently caught in the act of bugging the offices and taking photos of documents, all had had connections at one time or another with the Central Intelligence Agency. Then Republican campaign manager John N. Mitchell denied any prior knowledge of the incident and stated that the men apprehended were acting neither on behalf of nor with the consent of the party. In September a federal grand jury indicted seven men on charges of conspiring to break into Democratic headquarters—G. Gordon Liddy, a former Nixon aide and, before his resignation in June, counsel to the finance committee of the Committee for the Re-election of the President; E. Howard Hunt, Jr., a former White House consultant; and the five men caught at Watergate.

Assassination attempt. Since President John F. Kennedy was killed in 1963, assassinations have been an insistent phenomenon on the American scene. In 1965, Malcolm X was gunned down while giving a speech. In 1967, George Lincoln Rockwell was killed. In 1968, Martin Luther King and Robert F. Kennedy were shot. On May 15, 1972, Governor George C. Wallace of Alabama was severely wounded at a political rally in Laurel, Md. The shooting forced the governor out of the campaign for the Democratic

GAMMA

UPI

CASTRO ON TOUR

On an unusual two-month trek through nine countries, Cuban premier Fidel Castro seemed intent on trying everything that came his way. He sampled camel-riding on an Algerian road (above), got into a basketball game in Kraków, Poland (left), and showed his flashy backhand at table tennis in Czechoslovakia (below). But in Moscow, at talks with Party Secretary Leonid Brezhnev and other officials (right), Castro got down to the more serious business, winning acceptance for Cuba as a full member of the Soviet-bloc common market.

WIDE WORLD

nomination for the presidency, in spite of the fact that the next day he swept the Michigan primary and won strongly in Maryland. On May 17 a Senate subcommittee voted to prohibit the general sale of the kind of snub-nosed weapon used in the attempted assassination of Governor Wallace. After several surgical operations, the governor remained confined to a wheelchair. The assailant, Arthur H. Bremer, an odd-job worker from Milwaukee, was seized immediately after firing the five shots which paralyzed the governor and injured three others. He was charged under both state and federal laws. On August 4 he was sentenced by the state of Maryland to 63 years in prison; the federal trial was postponed indefinitely. Films taken at the scene as well as a diary kept by Bremer were important factors in the five-day trial. In the diary Bremer methodically recorded his frustrated attempts to assassinate President Nixon on the latter's April trip to Ottawa and his belated decision to go after Governor Wallace. Jurors later reported that the coherence and calculation exhibited in the document aided them in rejecting the defense plea of insanity. (*See* PEOPLE IN THE NEWS: George Wallace.)   DONALD GOODMAN

CUBA. Politics and government. As premier and first secretary of the Communist Party, Fidel Castro continued to shape Cuba's destiny. The new legal code recognizes only the revolution as power. The courts are under the Council of Ministers and the Communist Party; all judges are Communists, and attorneys are state-appointed. Defense attorneys discreetly limit their cases to pleas for the mercy of the court. Habeas corpus and the right to appeal have been eliminated. At the lowest level are about 2,200 peoples' courts where revolutionary justice is meted out by ordinary citizens. Cubans are tried for listening to U.S. broadcasts or complaining about the revolution.

The creation of the new socialist man remains the primary objective of Cuban education. Children are educated in Communism and atheism at boarding schools and expected to work to bolster the economy. Illiteracy is being eradicated, as prefabricated schools are built all over the country-

TASS FROM SOVFOTO

side. Castro stated that Cuba's goal is 100 new schools a year, with 1,000 by 1980.

These rural schools operate from 6:00 A.M. to 10:00 P.M. and average about 500 students, from 11 to 16 years of age. Individuality is deemphasized, and a communal spirit is stressed. Castro noted, "Now we are substituting the state for papa. Before, the papa paid all of the expenses of the student; now it is the state that pays all expenses."

Economic developments. The Cuban fishing industry has developed from obscurity into one of the largest in Latin America as a result of a $141 million investment in 178 tuna freezers, trawlers, steel-hulled shrimpers, and imported parts to construct more than 700 other boats. In 1971, Cuba exported over $21 million in fish.

Although Cuba is the world's largest sugarcane-producing country and earns 85 percent of its income from sugar exports, sugar for domestic use was rationed. For the first time, Castro did not announce a yearly sugar production goal. It was reported that because of absenteeism, machinery breakdowns, poor transportation, and a decrease in planting, yields were below expectations. Only 138 of the 161 sugar mills in operation in 1961 functioned. Castro said that the 1972 harvest would drop below the 1971 harvest of 5.9 million tons but that there would be uninterrupted growth from 1973 onward. In December 1971, Castro had announced the arrival of 100 cane-cutting machines from Australia, but Cuba needs more than 4,000 to eliminate labor problems in sugar production. One of the largest British banks, the National Westminster, granted Cuba a credit for approximately $7 million to buy equipment and services in Great Britain in 1972–1973.

Foreign affairs. Heavy Cuban economic and military dependence on the Soviet Union continues. The Cuban airline leased Soviet IL-62 aircraft with an option to purchase. Cuban dependence on Soviet aid, which amounts to $750 million a year, increased when Cuba and the Soviet Union signed a new economic pact greatly augmenting Soviet participation in the planning and execution of Cuban development projects.

The maneuvers of Soviet warships, submarines, and other military craft in the Caribbean and Gulf of Mexico and the landing of Soviet long-range naval reconnaissance aircraft in Cuba increased. U.S. Pentagon sources reported that the Soviet Union started sending missile-firing boats to Cuba. Two arrived one month after Cuban gunboat attacks on Panamanian-registered freighters brought U.S. warnings of possible counteraction. U.S. warships in the Caribbean have been ordered by President Richard M. Nixon to prevent, by force if necessary, Cuban vessels from seizing merchant ships of "friendly" nations.

Diplomatic relations were established with Zambia, Somalia, and Peru. The Cuban embassy in Madrid closed, but Spain maintained that ties have not been severed. The primary issues are Cuba's trade debt and compensation to Spain for expropriated Spanish property. Spain also expressed annoyance with Cuban propaganda activities.

Area and population. Area, 44,218 sq. mi. Pop. (1970), 8,553,-395. Havana (cap.; est. 1970), 1,963,000.

Government. Socialist republic. Only active political party is the Communist Party of Cuba (PCC). Pres., Osvaldo Dorticós Torrado; prime min. and first secy. of PCC, Fidel Castro; for. min., Raúl Roa; def. min., Major Raúl Castro.

Finance. Monetary unit, peso; 1 peso = US$1.00.

Trade. Chief exports: sugar, 85%; nickel, 10%; tobacco products, 3%. Imports (est. 1971): $1.4 billion ($840 million from the Soviet Union; $200 million from other Communist countries; and $360 million from non-Communist countries). Major trading partner: Soviet Union (with which over 75 percent of trade is conducted). Estimated debt to the Soviet Union through 1971: $4 billion.

Agriculture and industry. Major crop: sugar. Major industrial products: rum, industrial alcohol, and tobacco products.

Education (1969–1970). Enrollment: primary, 1,560,193; secondary, 160,857; technical, 42,507; higher, 30,708.

Armed forces (1970–1971). Army, 90,000; citizen militia, 200,-000; navy, 6,000; air force, 20,000.   GUILLERMO LUX

CYPRUS. Politics and government. The political and constitutional crisis became increasingly complex during the year, and mounting tensions threatened to destroy the negative stability that has characterized relations between the Greek and Turkish Cypriot communities since the cessation of violence in 1967.

Cypriot president Archbishop Makarios faced three serious challenges to his political leadership during the spring. The first challenge was posed by the threat of a guerrilla coup against his government led by General George Grivas, the 74-year-old hero of the Cypriot war of independence who secretly returned to Cyprus in 1971. General Grivas, a longtime political foe of President Makarios and a strong proponent of *enosis* (political union with Greece) as the basic solution to the Cyprus problem, controlled an underground force of 3,000–4,000 militant followers and appeared to be awaiting an opportune moment to overthrow the Makarios government.

The second challenge to Archbishop Makarios emanated from Athens as a result of deteriorating relations between Cyprus and Greece. The crucial factor in this situation was the secret importation to Cyprus in January of a substantial shipment of armaments from Czechoslovakia. The weapons were ordered by Archbishop Makarios, with the blessing of the Soviet Union, in order to supply a 1,000-man "presidential guard" drawn from loyal elements of the Cypriot National Guard, for the popularity of General Grivas and his program raised doubts about the reliability of regular Cypriot military and police forces. The deal, however, infuriated Athens because it complicated relations with Turkey and seemed to prove the existence of alarming left-wing tendencies in the Makarios government. The Greek government responded sharply by publicly demanding that the Czech arms be handed over to the United Nations peacekeeping force on the island and that the Makarios cabinet be reshuffled to exclude certain left-wing officials.

The third challenge to Archbishop Makarios came from an unexpected quarter. Three bishops of the Holy Synod of the Cypriot Orthodox Church declared on March 2 that it was a violation of orthodox holy canons for a churchman to hold high spiritual and temporal offices simultaneously. They demanded, therefore, that Archbishop Makarios resign from the presidency of Cyprus.

Faced with these difficulties, Archbishop Makarios maneuvered with Byzantine skill to maintain his position. The complaints of the bishops were temporarily submerged in an outpouring of popular support for Makarios, culminating in a demonstration of 150,000 supporters in Nicosia on March 3. At the same time, Makarios made a serious effort to restore good relations with Athens. He agreed in March to the storage of the Czech weapons under a system of double locks controlled separately by Cyprus and the UN force, and in June the Cypriot cabinet was reorganized in line with Greek demands. Meanwhile, Makarios moved to reduce the threat of guerrilla action against his government by entering into secret contacts with General Grivas. The two antagonists apparently met in great secrecy in Nicosia at the end of March to exchange views on the future of Cyprus. Although the talks produced no agreements, observers credited Makarios with a tactical victory in that the initiation of talks made it psychologically more difficult for General Grivas to precipitate an uprising against the government. Makarios' rapprochement with Athens, moreover, coincided with a deterioration in relations between General Grivas and the Greek government; it seemed designed to leave Grivas isolated and without support. Nevertheless, the situation remained highly unstable.

Intercommunal negotiations. The political crises of the spring deepened the hostility and suspicion between the Greek and Turkish Cypriot communities. Intercommunal negotiations, which ended in a stalemate last year, were resumed in July only after the personal intervention of

United Nations secretary general Kurt Waldheim, who visited Nicosia in June. The talks were expanded to include three new parties—the United Nations representative on Cyprus and two expert legal advisers from Turkey and Greece—in addition to Glafcos Clerides, representing the Greek Cypriot government, and Rauf Denktash, representing the Turkish Cypriot community. After a review of accomplishments, during the previous four years of talks, the negotiators turned in August to the difficult issue of local government. The Turkish Cypriot side argued for recognition of the "Turkish Cypriot Administration," which already exercises de facto political control in the 30 Turkish Cypriot enclaves on the island. Although the Greek Cypriot side accepted the principle of Turkish Cypriot autonomy at the village level, it opposed further federalization of the government on grounds that such arrangements would be tantamount to political partition of the island. The two sides remained far from agreement on the local government issue, and few dared hope that the expanded talks would produce much progress toward an overall constitutional settlement of the Cyprus problem.

Foreign affairs. President Makarios continued to pursue a delicately balanced policy of pro-Western nonalignment during the year. Cordial relations with Moscow were encouraged—a cultural exchange agreement was signed in May—as a means of assuring Russian diplomatic support against pressures from Athens and Ankara. At the same time, Cyprus announced the establishment of diplomatic relations with the People's Republic of China and entered a second round of talks with Common Market negotiators to prepare for its ultimate inclusion in the European customs union.

Economic developments. Despite political uncertainties, the economy continued to develop at a brisk pace during the year. The results of the first Cypriot five-year development plan (1967–1971) indicated a growth rate of 8 percent a year. A development budget of C£20 million was planned for 1972, the first year of the second five-year plan. The tourist industry continued to show spectacular gains, with an increase of 34.2 percent over figures for the first half of 1971.

Area and population. Area, 3,572 sq. mi. Pop. (est. 1971), 640,-000, about 77 percent Greek and 18 percent Turkish. Principal cities (est. 1969): Nicosia (cap.), 114,000; Limassol, 51,000; Famagusta, 42,000.

Government. Republic, member of Commonwealth of Nations. Unicameral legislature. Pres., Archbishop Makarios.

Finance. Monetary unit, Cyprus pound; 1 C£ = US$2.55.

Trade (1971). Exports, US$263 million; imports, US$116 million.

Education (1969–1970). Elementary: 553 schools, 2,185 teachers, 70,125 pupils. Secondary: 83 schools (incl. private), 1,781 teachers, 36,269 students. Most higher education is received abroad.

VICTOR R. SWENSON

CZECHOSLOVAKIA. Politics and government. In February, despite assurances by party chief Gustav Husák that "there is and will be no trial and no arrest for political activities in 1968 and 1969," the first mass arrests since the fall of the Dubček regime took place. More than 40 liberal intellectuals and journalists, charged with distributing leaflets denouncing as rigged the National Assembly elections of the previous November, were tried secretly in groups over several months and drew sentences of up to six years. Even Communist newspapers in Western Europe protested the sentences. Husák was believed to have sanctioned the actions in order to fend off demands by two rivals in the Party Politburo, hardliners Vasil Bilák and Alois Indra, that he try such top political leaders as Alexander Dubček, now reported to be in charge of the motor pool for the forest administration in Bratislava.

Police raids and checkups in bars, streets, and even private homes, although intended mainly against the underworld, continued to result in the arrest of many political offenders. A new purge of the union of journalists and mass communications workers led to the expulsion of nearly 40

percent of the membership, bringing the number excluded to 2,000, nearly half of the 1968 membership of 4,600.

Foreign affairs. In May, Austria protested the shooting and abduction of Jaromir Masarik, a Czech émigré, by Czechoslovak border guards when he approached the Czech-Austrian frontier from Austria. Czechoslovakia refused to return the captive, and the country's press condemned the incident as a provocation.

The decision of a U.S. court to leave two children, Vlasta and Bedrich Gabriel, in the hands of relatives of their deceased father in the United States, rather than return them to their mother in Czechoslovakia, was denounced by the Czechoslovak press as "a return to the policies of the Nazis." In April a Slovair plane was hijacked by two men seeking political asylum; they severely wounded the copilot and forced the pilot to land in West Germany. In June another plane was hijacked by seven men and three women and landed near Frankfurt-am-Main. The captain of the plane was shot dead, and the copilot and two passengers were injured. Czechoslovakia demanded the return of the hijackers, but the West German government refused.

Economic developments. The aim of the 1972 economic plan was to stabilize the good results achieved in 1971 and to overcome "negative tendencies." Production in the first quarter was high. Industrial production rose 8.4 percent over production during the same period of 1971. In exchange for high deliveries of oil, pig iron, nonferrous metals, and natural gas, Czechoslovakia was to be supplied with 1 billion kilowatt-hours of electricity from the Soviet Union. The Soviet Union accounted for 33 percent of Czechoslovak trade and remained the nation's biggest trading partner.

A Prague congress on waste disposal in July was attended by 1,000 delegates from 34 countries and 400 delegates from Czechoslovakia. Almost 50 percent of Czechoslovakia's rivers are polluted "to an impermissible degree."

Religion. An antichurch campaign of discrimination, propaganda, and repression attempted to stamp out the religious revival experienced since the fall of the Dubček regime. Attendance at religious classes was held against youths wishing to enter the overcrowded universities. The press frequently attacked religion in general and the Roman Catholic Church in particular. In a series of measures, the Husák government ordered all priests to retire at the age of 60, forced younger priests to move from city to country parishes, and severely restricted attendance at seminaries. Students and teachers in the Bratislava Faculty of Theology went on a hunger strike when 50 out of 80 candidates for admission were rejected on orders from the Ministry of Culture. The refusal of the government to let the Vatican appoint bishops in Czechoslovakia left only one of the country's 12 dioceses in the hands of a Vatican appointee.

Area and population. Area, 49,370 sq. mi. Pop. (est. 1972), 14,442,000. Principal cities (1968): Prague (cap.), 1,031,185; Brno, 337,247; Bratislava (cap. of Slovakia), 285,905; Ostrava, 274,547.

Government. Socialist republic. The highest organ is the bicameral Federal Assembly, elected every six years. Dominant political party is the Communist Party of Czechoslovakia (membership, 1971: 1,200,000). Pres., Ludvík Svoboda; gen. secy., Central Committee of the Communist Party, Gustav Husák; prem., Lubomír Štrougal.

Finance. Monetary unit, koruna (pl., koruny); official rate, 1 koruna = US$0.139 (tourist rate, 1 koruna = US$0.0617). Budget (1971): revenue, 140.1 billion koruny; expenditure, 187.1 billion koruny.

Trade (1970). Imports, US$3.7 billion; exports, US$3.8 billion.

Agriculture and industry (1970). Agricultural production (in thousands of metric tons): potatoes, 4,793; wheat, 3,174; barley, 2,280. Livestock (in thousands): pigs, 5,037; cattle, 4,223; sheep, 977. Industrial production (in thousands of metric tons): lignite, 81,783; hard coal, 28,053; steel, 11,480; metallurgical coke, 8,269. Electric power, 43.16 billion kw.-hr.

Education (1969). Enrollment: primary, 2,002,053; secondary, 390,057; higher, 133,524.

Armed forces (est. 1970–1971). Army, 150,000; air force, 18,-000; security forces and frontier guards, 35,000. About 80,000 Soviet troops occupy western border areas.   RICHARD A. PIERCE

DAHOMEY. Politics and government. Justin Ahomadegbé, whose two-year presidential term began in May, was deposed in late October when an 11-man military junta took over the government; Major Mathieu Kerekou was named president and minister of defense. It was Dahomey's fifth coup in 12 years of independence, and it marked the end of a unique stabilization experiment in which a triad of leaders from different parts of the country were to occupy the presidency in rotating two-year terms. The junta dissolved the ruling Presidential Council and the Consultative Assembly and arrested several civilian leaders.

Ahomadegbé had inherited an explosive situation from his predecessor, Hubert Maga, the first of the triad to take office and, as it turned out, the only one to survive two years. In February a group within the army made an attempt on the life of Colonel Paul-Emile de Souza, army chief of staff. Maga proclaimed a state of alert and urged Dahomeans to disclose any information concerning the whereabouts of the plotters. His successor brought 22 soldiers and one civilian to trial in May; 17 of the soldiers were found guilty and given sentences ranging from death to five years' imprisonment.

Foreign affairs. On June 3, Dahomey, along with all the former French colonies of West Africa except Guinea and Togo, signed a treaty establishing the West African Economic Community. WAEC is, in effect, a formal recognition that the colonial free-trade area of French West Africa and its postindependence successor, the West African Customs Union, had largely disappeared during ten years of unrestrained nationalism. It seeks, however, to reestablish some form of mutual cooperation in the exchange of agricultural goods, industrial location and trade matters and, most important, a preferential tariff regime for industrial goods, which are produced largely in Senegal and Ivory Coast. WAEC will certainly produce conflicts for Dahomey's increasingly close ties with its English-speaking neighbors, particularly Nigeria, which provided a £1 million interest-free loan last year in the name of African unity. Any preferential treatment afforded Ivory Coast manufactures will undoubtedly divert Dahomean purchases of the same products from Nigeria and may also redirect some of Niger's current trade with Nigeria to Dahomey. It is hoped that these conflicts can be mitigated by a broadening of WAEC to include Nigeria, Ghana, Liberia, and Gambia.

Domestic developments. Dahomean economic development, particularly in the disadvantaged north, was given a major boost by the construction of a cotton-textile plant at Parakou. Whereas textiles produced in Dahomey have previously depended on imported raw cotton, the Parakou plant is part of an integrated project that will ultimately provide northern small landholders a profitable new cash crop. To finance the development of cotton production in the north the International Development Association has granted a US$6.1 million loan to the Dahomean National Agricultural Cotton Company.

The long-standing issue of educational reform was raised again in two short-lived student–teacher strikes, one in December 1971 and one in January. Both were provoked by the government's dissolution in late 1971 of the Dahomean Union of Students and Schoolchildren and took place despite a government threat to expel any student who participated.

Area and population. Area, 44,713 sq. mi. Pop. (est. 1971), 2,792,000. Principal cities (est. 1971): Porto-Novo (cap.), 78,000; Cotonou, 111,000.

Government. Republic, now under military rule; Major Mathieu Kerekou heads an 11-man junta.

Finance. Monetary unit, Communauté Financière Africaine franc; 1 CFA franc = US$0.0041. Budget (est. 1972–1973): 11.83 billion CFA francs.

Trade (1971). Imports, 21.20 billion CFA francs; exports, 11.65 billion CFA francs. Principal export: palm oil products.

Education (1965–1966). School enrollment: primary, 130,800; secondary, 11,300.   GEORGE LAMSON

ABOVE, MARTHA SWOPE; RIGHT AND BELOW, NEW YORK CITY BALLET

Homage to Stravinsky

Master choreographer George Balanchine, who had collaborated with the late Igor Stravinsky in a dozen productions, paid homage in June to the memory of the great Russian composer by presenting the New York City Ballet in a week-long festival of 31 compositions, 21 of them brand-new, all set to Stravinsky's music. Above, Edward Villella leaps high in "Pulcinella"; upper right, Kay Mazzo and Peter Martins are caught in the romantic new "Duo Concertant"; and lower right, a scene from "Requiem Canticles," a somber Stravinsky score starkly and solemnly choreographed by Jerome Robbins.

DANCE. Stravinsky Festival. The event of the year in international ballet was the Stravinsky Festival at the New York State Theater, June 18–25, presented by the New York City Ballet. Company directors Lincoln Kirstein and George Balanchine staged the festival to honor the 90th anniversary of the composer's birth, and the week-long presentation drew critics and balletomanes from Europe as well as from all parts of the United States. The participating choreographers were Balanchine, Todd Bolender, John Clifford, Lorca Massine, Richard Tanner, and John Taras. Of Jerome Robbins' works, *Dumbarton Oaks* was the lightest in mood and *Requiem Canticles* the most solemn.

Balanchine was the undisputed genius of the festival, bringing to 28 his portfolio of Stravinsky ballets, of which eight were festival premieres. Featured were *Apollo* (1928), which Balanchine asserts changed his life as a choreographer, and *Agon* (1957), the work that is held to have revolutionized twentieth-century neoclassical dance. *Orpheus* (1948), which earned the Kirstein-Balanchine company, the Ballet Society, its residence and title at the New York City Center Theater 24 years ago, was revived for the festival.

Of the new Stravinsky ballets, Balanchine's *Violin Concerto* was the masterwork, but his *Symphony in Three Movements* ranked high, and he produced a ravishing tour de force to the classical passages of *Baiser de la Fée.* His *Duo Concertant,* a beautiful, long *pas de deux* in which the dancers and the on-stage pianists were integrated, was in a frankly romantic vein. In *Pulcinella,* in collaboration with Robbins, Balanchine produced a ballet in the epic style of *commedia dell' arte;* the work was gross, vulgar, antic, and frantically alive. Sets and costumes were designed by Eugene Berman.

Aside from its own merits, the Stravinsky Festival was instrumental in restoring George Balanchine to the pinnacle of contemporary choreography, where his position had been challenged by several critics in recent years. He had been chastised for the frivolity of *Who Cares?* and the banality of *PAMTGG.* In his 68th year, however, Balanchine proved himself still a master of his craft, and this year his company was invited to present the Stravinsky repertoire in four German opera houses, at the Paris Opéra, and at the Royal Opera House, Covent Garden. In August it performed in Munich and in September made its second visit to the Soviet Union.

American ballet companies. The American Ballet Theater, the official ballet company of the John F. Kennedy Center, presented seasons in Washington, D.C., and New York City and went on a national tour. To its contingent of foreign dancers—the Italian Carla Fracci, the Russian Natalia Makarova, and Michael Denard from the Paris Opéra—it added Paolo Bortoluzzi, formerly of Maurice Béjart's Ballet of the 20th Century. Bortoluzzi was engaged to replace Erik Bruhn, who retired from dancing early in the year. ABT announced the formation of a second company, Ballet Repertory, and the building of a new school in New York City.

The City Center Joffrey Ballet was joined at City Center Theater by the Alvin Ailey Dance Company, and Rebecca Harkness announced the opening of a new theater near Lincoln Center to house the Harkness Ballet and other companies. New York was not the only focus of ballet, although companies outside that metropolis remained convinced that recognition could only be won by a season in Manhattan. Two companies, both drawn from college dance departments, made substantial progress: Ballet West, of the University of Utah in Salt Lake City, and the Pittsburgh Ballet, affiliated with Point Park College. Ballet West, which made a successful European debut in 1971, planned a U.S. tour beginning in the 1972–1973 season and a return to several European cities. The Pittsburgh Ballet, which shares the newly rebuilt Heinz Hall with the Pittsburgh Symphony and Opera, staged a mini-Stravinsky season in the spring, engaged Makarova as guest artist for *Swan Lake,* and sched-

uled regular seasons in Pittsburgh with other internationally known guests. It, too, planned a European tour.

Two other companies, the National Ballet of Washington, D.C., and the Pennsylvania Ballet, presented short seasons at City Center. The National mounted a full-length *Sleeping Beauty* and engaged Dame Margot Fonteyn to make several guest appearances as Aurora. Both companies are recipients of Ford Foundation grants.

Visiting companies. England's Royal Ballet, the company that, along with the Bolshoi Ballet, has exerted the greatest influence on the ballet in America, was presented in a New York season at the Metropolitan Opera House by Sol Hurok. Its ardent New York fans viewed the company with mixed feelings this year. Featuring some of the greatest dancers in contemporary ballet, the company appeared to be suffering from a struggle between the old principles developed by Sir Frederick Ashton, a choreographic genius who is now retired, and the new ones fostered by its current director, Kenneth MacMillan. Current repertoire was not always stimulating, some of the great story ballets were poorly produced, and MacMillan's opus *Anastasia* and a quasi-modern work by Glen Tetley, *Field Figures,* were roundly booed by Met audiences.

The Netherlands Dance Theater presented (at the Brooklyn Academy of Music) Tetley's nude ballet *Mutations,* and Maurice Béjart staged his controversial theater piece, *Nijinsky: Clown of God,* in the Felt Forum at Madison Square Garden.

Modern dance. In theater the barriers continued to shrink between the classical and modern dance modes, largely because each form has long absorbed certain facets of the other. Contemporary ballet dancers can and do make use of modern dance characteristics and are able to extend them through the ballet line and pointes, and modern dance, except for its hardiest eccentrics, has adopted a great many of the ballet's codified movements. Modern dance has been having its greatest influence in England, which had long shunned the form, preferring ballet, whereas in the United States no major dancer of the caliber of the modern dance pioneers has yet emerged in the 1970's. Merce Cunningham, still the radical genius, has been doing his particular thing now for more than 20 years.

Several young modern dancers—James Cunningham, Twyla Tharp, and others—seemed to be making an intense personal search for dance verities in their genre. Among other dancers there was a deliberate attempt to preserve the recent past of modern dance. The Martha Graham studio dancers were resetting some of Graham's works, and other groups—notably that of the Juilliard School of Music's dance department—recreated some of Doris Humphrey's repertoire. Most of the results were of doubtful value, and it has become clear that modern dance has reached another of its crossroads and will have to define future directions in order to retain its validity as a new and constantly evolving form of dance. Audiences still tended to prefer ballet to modern dance performances. However, the most popular of the nonclassical companies, the Alvin Ailey Dance Company, overtly eclectic, indicated a possible trend for the modernists.

Grants. The National Council on the Arts approved continuance of the coordinated residency touring program for dance companies in 1972–1973, and the National Endowment for the Arts again underwrote the program for that period by providing one-third of the fees of dance companies brought into communities. Fifty-one companies were named to the program. The National Endowment also extended from 22 to 27 the number of professional dance companies performing in 36 states for a total of 150 weeks in the fiscal year ended July 1, 1972. Federal funds of $429,197 generated more than $1 million from state and civic sources for the program. In addition, Nancy Hanks, chairman of the National Endowment, announced that the program had been extended to the American Ballet Theater, City Center Joffrey

Ballet, and New York City Ballet. Grants of $822,944 to 15 sponsoring organizations would enable the three major ballet companies to establish resident seasons in 13 cities.

Nonetheless, the dance economy was not appreciably better this year than in years past. Despite popularity with audiences, the companies found it impossible to subsist on box office receipts. Some of them could not even qualify for grants because they could not raise the required matching sum.

Personalities. The retirement of Erik Bruhn, the greatest *danseur noble* of his era, was a shock to the international ballet. Bruhn chose to retire because of persistent illness, which, he said, adversely affected the standards of his performances. He promised to continue working in ballet; he coached the National Ballet of Canada (which has some of his works in repertoire) and accompanied it on its London debut, and he also continued to work with the American Ballet Theater, of which he was the premier for several years. Anthony Dowell (who, with Judith Jamison of the Ailey company, received the *Dance Magazine* Awards of the year) seemed to be Bruhn's heir. Rudolf Nureyev began a long engagement with the National Ballet of Canada, touring Canada and the United States as premier with the company and performing his version of *The Sleeping Beauty.*

Obituaries. Mathilde Kchessinska, *prima ballerina assoluta* of the Russian Imperial Ballet, died in her 99th year in Paris on December 7, 1971. Ted Shawn, revered in his 80th year as the dean of American male dancers, died January 9 at Orlando, Fla. Bronislava Nijinska, choreographer, ballerina, and sister of Nijinsky, died in Los Angeles, February 21.   OLGA MAYNARD

DELAWARE. Constitutional revision. The general assembly gave first passage to a mammoth amendment that would revise the state's 75-year-old constitution. If the next general assembly concurs by giving second passage, the new constitution will be adopted. Ratification by the state's voters is not required.

The 1897 constitution contains about 18,000 words; the new one contains only about 7,000 words. In achieving this reduction, the writers of the streamlined revision dropped many archaic provisions and substituted relatively simple language for the legalese of the old document.

Some of the most basic changes proposed apply to the judiciary system. For example, the supreme court of Delaware, which now has three members, would be expanded to five. Juries would be reduced from 12 members to six, except in capital cases. Jury trials would be abolished in minor civil cases, and the attorney general would be permitted to bypass the grand jury and to proceed by information in criminal cases.

The general assembly's size would fall within a range of 35–45 members for the house of representatives and 15–21 members for the senate. The specific size would be left to the general assembly, which arranges for reapportionment of legislative districts every ten years.

Examples of old provisions that would be left out of the revised constitution are one providing for a three-member state board of agriculture and one providing for a state board of health. The functions of such boards are now carried out by departments of the executive branch of the state government, under the cabinet system. Also omitted from the revision are sections the writers considered adequately covered by law and unnecessary in a constitution. These include sections on gambling, divorce, and liquor.

Politics. Delaware Republicans were seriously split during the summer by a bitter primary election battle between Governor Russell W. Peterson, seeking renomination, and former attorney-general David P. Buckson. In the past such a conflict would have been settled at the party's nominating convention early in the summer, leaving lots of time to heal wounds before election day. However, this year a new

UPI

DENMARK'S KING FREDERIK IX, the rugged sailor, musician, and family man who occupied the Danish throne for 25 years, died in January. At funeral ceremonies his wife, Queen Ingrid (left), beside the new queen, Margrethe II, and Margrethe's husband, Prince Henrik.

PHOTOREPORTERS

election law called for a statewide primary in the event that any contender for nomination at a state political party convention received 35 percent or more of the votes. Buckson received 81 votes—four more than he needed and 37 percent of the total.

Peterson ultimately won the primary by a vote of 24,003 to 19,946. Buckson considered running as the American Party candidate but ultimately rejected that idea and pledged his support to Peterson. However, Buckson did not ask his supporters to follow suit, and the Republican Party appeared weakened by its internal struggles.

For election results and campaign highlights, see the special supplement ELECTION '72.

Area and population. Area, 2,057 sq. mi. Pop. (1970), 548,104. Principal cities: Dover (cap.), 17,488; Wilmington, 80,386; Newark, 20,757.

Government. Gov., Russell W. Peterson (R); lt. gov., Eugene D. Bookhammer (R); secy. of state, Walton H. Simpson (R); atty. gen., W. Laird Stabler, Jr. (R). General assembly: senate, 13 R, 6 D; house, 23 R, 16 D.

Finance (fiscal 1973 projected). Revenue, $298.2 million; expenditures, $297 million. Cash balance expected June 30, 1973, $4.3 million.

Education (1971–1972). Public elementary and middle schools, 154; enrollment, 84,687; teachers, 3,737. Public secondary schools, 51; enrollment, 50,326; teachers, 2,312. Nonpublic schools, 53; enrollment, 18,471; teachers, 909.   CY LIBERMAN

DENMARK. Politics and government. The death of King Frederik IX on January 14 caused sincere sorrow among Danes, but they gave an enthusiastic response to his daughter's succession as Queen Margrethe II. The first queen in modern Danish history chose the motto: "God's help, the peoples' love, Denmark's strength." (Margrethe I, who ruled all the Scandinavian countries, died in 1412.)

The plebiscite on October 2 over membership in the European Economic Community (Common Market) absorbed the country. The cabinet had unanimously voted for membership and confirmed their decision by signing a treaty for entry on January 22 after an overwhelming vote from the Folketing on December 16, 1971. During the spring and summer, however, opponents mounted a campaign against membership that led to conflict in the legislature, the media, and party congresses. Most parties split on the issue, and opposition centered on the costs for Denmark in economic losses and lessening political freedom of action.

Nonetheless, on October 2, 63.5 percent of the Danish voters favored joining the EEC. Only a few hours after the vote—a political victory for Prime Minister Jens Otto Krag's Social Democratic government—the prime minister announced his resignation, for personal rather than political reasons. Krag's successor, designated by the Social Democratic Party, is Anker Jørgensen, prominent in the labor movement. Until the constitutional take-over of the government is accomplished, Foreign Minister Knud Borge Andersen will be interim premier.

Generally the cabinet continued its wobbly course, with the Social Democrats retaining a one-vote majority in the Folketing provided that the Socialist Peoples' Party continues its support as promised. Changes in the defense act made by the legislature were rejected by NATO, which felt that six months' military service was too short a period; thus, new proposals had to be drafted. The Folketing passed legislation increasing pension payments, a stringent law on oil and sewage pollution, a new land act, new regulations governing inheritance and its taxation, and a measure to guard against invasion of privacy through wiretapping, data collection, and photography.

Foreign affairs. The treaty for membership in the Common Market was signed on January 22 in Brussels along with Britain, Ireland, and Norway. Denmark was not affected by the subsequent Norwegian rejection of Common Market membership, and in the October plebiscite Denmark voted to join its population of nearly 5 million in economic union with the 265 million people of the Common Market member nations. Foreign policy debates during the year also included a number of proposals for trade with the People's Republic of China (Commerce Minister Erling Jensen visited Peking) and approval of recognition of the German Democratic Republic (East Germany). To the usual mild condemnation of American policy in Southeast Asia was appended a strong resolution against bombing

North Vietnam. Another controversial item in Danish-American relations was the "salmon war." The United States and Canada requested that Denmark and other countries limit ocean salmon fishing and threatened economic reprisals if catches were not limited. The war ended when the Folketing approved the restrictions. The Portuguese ambassador was withdrawn from Denmark after funds had been approved for freedom groups fighting Portugal's control of its colonies; Denmark responded that provision of such funds conformed to United Nations rules.

Economy. A persistent deficit in its balance of payments and inflation have plagued Denmark for the past three years. A small surplus in the foreign trade balance at the beginning of the year disappeared after a resurgence of Danish consumer spending. The retention of import duties and economic controls enabled the cabinet to halt domestic inflation somewhat. However, a money and credit crisis hit unexpectedly in mid-April, forcing the national bank and other credit institutions into the open market to buy bonds. The cabinet refused to devalue the krone, which remained stable for the remainder of the year. The government started a drastic and emergency reduction of departmental budgets which drew support from all parties except the Socialist Peoples' Party.

Education. The education law was changed to require a total of nine years of school attendance, or until age 17, as well as curricular revisions. The new law brought Denmark into line with other Nordic countries. The state also assumed responsibility for all music conservatories in the same manner as those at Århus and Copenhagen universities.

Area and population. Area: Denmark proper, 16,629 sq. mi.; Greenland, 837,620 sq. mi.; Faeroe Islands, 540 sq. mi. Pop.: Denmark proper (est. 1972), 4,978,106; Greenland (est. 1969), 46,331; Faeroe Islands (est. 1970), 38,681. Principal cities (1972): Copenhagen (cap.), 615,000 (Greater Copenhagen, 1,334,921); Århus, 241,813; Odense, 166,932.

Government. Constitutional monarchy with unicameral legislature (Folketing) of 179 members. Queen, Margrethe II; acting prem., Knud Borge Andersen; fin. min., Henry Grünbaum; def. min., Kjeld Olesen.

Finance. Monetary unit, krone; 1 krone = US$0.14. Budget (1970–1971, in billions of kroner): revenue, 31.7; expenditure, 32.7. Major revenues: income and property taxes, value-added tax, duties and excise tax, auto and gas tax. Major expenditures: social welfare, education, defense, agriculture, investment.

Trade (1971, in billions of kroner). Exports, 26.72; imports, 33.96. Major exports: foodstuffs, machinery, other industrial products. Major imports: machinery and transport, fuels, raw materials. Major trading partners: Sweden, West Germany, United Kingdom.

Agriculture and industry. Leading agricultural products (1971, in metric tons): milk, 4,559,000; pork and meat, 1,129,300; butter, 123,500; cheese, 119,900. Industrial production (1971, in billions of kroner): foodstuffs, 13.8; machinery, 5.2; metals, 4.6; chemicals, 4.06; electrical machinery, 3.17; transport, 3.18; textiles, 2.24.

Education (1970–1971). Enrollment: elementary schools, 591,309; secondary schools, 407,281; folk high schools, 8,356; universities (3), 32,481.

Armed forces. Army, 28,000; home guard, 54,000. Navy, 7,200; home guard, 3,500. Air force, 10,500; home guard, 11,000.

RAYMOND E. LINDGREN

DENTISTRY. The huge rise in the cost of dental services continued to cause problems to a public increasingly aware of the importance of adequate dental care. But the growing use of paraprofessionals and the adoption of group dental practice and group payment plans offered prospects for relieving the situation.

In a continuing trend, hygienists, assistants, and paraprofessionals assumed more of the tasks traditionally performed by dentists. In over twenty states the duties of dental auxiliaries have been expanded to save the dentist's time and energies. Each state has set up legal guidelines limiting what assistants and hygienists would be allowed to do, although many of the state limitations would be unnecessary if adequate professional control could be assured. However, there still exists no national program for the training of auxiliaries and no national system for licensing or accrediting auxiliaries.

Meanwhile, group dentistry kept on growing. Since few dentists can claim to have sufficient versatility to handle all the dental needs of their patients, dentists have turned to group practice so that the various needs of patients can still be met without sacrificing the dentist-patient relationship. This year also saw an increase in the number of "third party" payment plans directed by the patients. The rise of both group dentistry and these payment plans has altered the economic and political structure of dental care.

The new dental consumer groups have begun to seek greater control and review of dental programs affecting members, and government employees, union members, and community organizations are making similar demands. Although changes in dental technology are always important, the introduction of new workers and new organizations of patients will be the most significant feature of the dental care of the 1970's.

Restorative dentistry. New filling materials that chemically bond to tooth structure are on the market. However, not enough is known about their durability or their effects on pulpal tissue. Fluorides have been incorporated in a few types of composite filling material, and the more durable composites have replaced silicates in popularity for anterior restorations. New amalgam alloys are more dimensionally stable, less likely to be dissolved by mouth fluids, and easier to handle as a result of better packaging. Chemicals that remove only decaying tooth structure and do not harm healthy tissue are also being tested.

Periodontics. Several variations in surgical techniques have been developed or improved; however, the dominance of preventive dentistry in periodontal bone surgery has greatly altered the specialty. Many periodontists agree that surgery is rarely indicated for suprabony defects and should only be performed for infrabony pockets after a patient has been carefully counselled in maintenance of his mouth tissue.

Oral surgery and oral medicine. Improvements in orthodontic surgery have facilitated repair of malocclusions that are a result of injury or familial traits. High-frequency oscillations have been used to move teeth for orthodontic or exodontic reasons. The durability of implants is considered questionable, but subperiosteal implants have at least proven more successful than endosteal implants. Meanwhile, more evidence has become available to show the relationship of smoking to oral cancer.

Pain control. The increased use of intravenous sedation in conjunction with local anesthesia has allowed the dentist to perform more procedures on the patient. Already some schools of dentistry are teaching this method of sedation to undergraduate classes.

Prevention. Preventive dentistry has come close to being regarded as a specialty, like endodontics or periodontics. There has been an increased demand for dental health-care programs in schools, to prevent large numbers of children from developing cavities now and periodontal diseases later. The use of tooth sealants, to provide a blanket against tooth decay, has been quite successful in reducing pit and fissure caries.

Since 1947 it has been known that tooth decay is mainly caused by plaque, the formation of a film of food debris that combines with mouth acids to erode teeth. This year, most dentists indicated intentions to launch patients on a full-scale plaque-prevention program. Many patients have been advised to use some type of disclosing solution that makes plaque visible and to use dental floss to remove plaque in places inaccessible to the toothbrush. But some dentists felt that such programs are impractical, since people often do not think they are worth the trouble. Others have warned against overemphasis of plaque control at the expense of other measures considered important: proper diet, not overly sugared and starched, and the use of fluoride to strengthen the resistance of tooth enamel to corroding mouth acids.

WILFRED HEILBUT

Disasters

Some of the major disasters that occurred during late 1971 and 1972 follow.

Aviation

Addis Ababa. Thirty-six people died and 24 were seriously hurt when an East African Airways jet crashed April 18.

Albany, N.Y. A Mohawk Airlines turboprop crashed into a house on March 3, killing 17 people and injuring 36.

Amaseno, Italy. All 18 people aboard an Italian ATI Fokker F-27 were killed when the plane struck a power pylon during a thunderstorm on April 16.

Dhulikhel, Nepal. All 31 people on a Royal Nepalese DC-3 died September 13 when the plane hit a high tension cable and exploded.

East Berlin. In one of the worst disasters in aviation history, on August 14 an East German Interflug charter jet was ripped by a blast shortly after takeoff from Schönefeld Airport; all 156 people on board were killed.

France. An Air Inter plane crashed on a mountaintop near Clermont-Ferrand on October 27, taking 48 lives.

Kalba, United Arab Emirates. Attempting to make a refueling stop, a Danish chartered Super-Caravelle crashed on March 14 in a mountainous region 60 miles east of Dubai, killing 112 persons.

Lobito, Angola. A twin-engined turboprop Angola Airlines plane crashed near Lobito Airport on May 21, killing 20.

Moscow. On October 13, 176 people were killed in the world's worst air disaster when a Soviet Aeroflot Ilyushin-62 jet crashed while attempting to land in the rain at Moscow's international airport.

New Delhi. On June 14 a Japan Air Lines DC-8 crashed while preparing to land at Palam International Airport, taking the lives of 87 of the 89 people on board and killing two persons on the ground.

Orlando, Fla. A flaming B-52 bomber crashed into a residential neighborhood on March 31, killing seven U.S. Air Force crewmen and injuring several civilians.

Sacramento. On September 24 an F-86 Sabrejet had takeoff difficulties at Executive Airport and slammed into a crowded ice cream parlor at the end of the runway, killing 22 people and injuring 26 others.

Sicily. On May 5 an Alitalia DC-8 smashed into a mountainside 6 miles from Palermo and exploded, killing all 115 of its passengers and crew.

Sochi, U.S.S.R. On October 4, over 100 people were killed when a Soviet Ilyushin-18 airliner crashed near Sochi Airport.

Staines, England. All 118 persons aboard a British European Airways jet were killed when it plummeted just after takeoff into a field 4 miles from Heathrow Airport; the June 18 disaster was the worst air crash in British history.

Fires and Explosions

Boston. Nine firemen died on June 17 when the back corner of the century-old Vendome Hotel collapsed after being ravaged by fire for four hours.

Bridgewater, Mass. An explosion in a fireworks factory took the lives of three people and injured 11 others on March 30.

Dallas. On April 5 a series of explosions ripped a chemical plant, killing eight workers.

Montreal. On September 1 a bomb explosion in a nightclub killed about 22 people and injured at least 60 others.

Mufulira, Zambia. Nine freight cars carrying explosives blew up near an explosives factory, claiming the lives of 29 persons on December 14, 1971.

New York City. A fire which swept through a local YMCA killed four persons and injured at least 25 others on March 22.

New York City. Seven people were killed when a steam pipe exploded in an office building on May 3.

Osaka. On May 13 a fire raged through the Sennichi department store building, killing more than 115 persons who were trapped in a top-floor night club and injuring 42 others.

São Paulo. A fire which erupted in a downtown department store and office building claimed the lives of 16 persons and injured more than 400 other people on February 25.

Seoul. A fire which destroyed a 21-story hotel on December 25, 1971, left at least 26 dead and 58 injured among the 203 registered guests.

Valdese, N.C. A May 30 explosion caused by a gas leak killed five of ten children in a backyard bomb shelter.

Marine

Buenos Aires. The *Tien Chee,* a Liberian oil tanker, and the *Royston Grange,* a British cargo ship, collided in the entrance to the River Plata channel on May 11; both ships were destroyed, with 83 persons reported missing.

Kuala Lumpur. On September 13 a ferry capsized in the Krain River, and more than 30 people, mostly schoolchildren, were drowned.

Newport News. Twenty sailors were killed when the cruiser *Newport News* was ripped by explosion off the Vietnam coast on September 29.

Seven Stars. The tanker, drydocked in Hamburg, was ripped by an explosion on March 15, killing four people and seriously injuring two others.

Mine

Kellogg, Idaho. On May 2 a fire broke out about 3,700 feet below the surface of the Sunshine Silver Mine, the country's largest, taking the lives of 91 miners.

REMAINS of a double-decker commuter car, after two trains collided in Chicago this fall.

WIDE WORLD

Salisbury. All 422 Rhodesians working deep within the Wankie Coal Mine were fatally trapped by an underground explosion; four other miners and several surface workers were also killed by the impact of the blast on June 6.

Natural

Eastern United States. On June 23, five states—New York, Pennsylvania, Virginia, Maryland, and Florida—were declared disaster areas after flooding from Hurricane Agnes claimed 134 lives and damaged property worth at least $1.5 billion; the storm, which raged over the east coast for over a week, was termed the worst flood disaster in U.S. history.

Fort Rucker, Ala. Two trailer parks and the army base were struck by a tornado on January 1; four people were killed and at least 50 trailers were totally destroyed.

Hong Kong. A torrential downpour lasting three days caused hundreds of tons of earth and rock to slide down the hills of the crown colony; by June 19 more than 100 people had been killed and thousands more left homeless.

Iran. An earthquake south of Tehran on April 10 leveled some 45 villages and claimed at least 5,000 lives.

Japan. Southwestern Japan was hit by heavy rains which caused flooding and landslides in early July, leaving 105 dead.

Katmandu. An avalanche on the 26,-658-foot Himalayan peak of Manaslu killed 15 members of a South Korean mountaineering expedition on April 10.

Man, W.Va. The known death toll reached 107, with more than 50 people still missing, after the swollen Buffalo Creek smashed a slag dam and flooded the coal-mining valley on February 26.

Philippines. Rising floodwaters in the middle provinces of Luzon Island caused extensive damage, leaving thousands homeless and at least 142 dead in mid-July.

Rapid City, S.D. On June 9 the banks of Rapid Creek overflowed after an exceptionally heavy rainstorm; after two earth dams were wiped out, the resultant flooding claimed at least 226 lives (with over 100 persons missing).

South Korea. On August 19–20 at least 368 persons lost their lives and more than 326,000 were left homeless after floods and landslides caused by a record rainfall of 17.8 inches; property damage was estimated at $17 million.

Texas. At least 11 persons were killed and thousands fled their homes in the central hill country, as the Guadalupe River flooded after heavy rain May 12.

Railroad

Chicago. In the worst U.S. railroad accident since 1958, 44 people were killed and 320 injured when one Illinois Central commuter train was rammed by another.

Congers, N.Y. Five young high school students were killed and 40 more were injured when their school bus was struck by a freight train on March 24; the driver was later charged with failing to stop properly at the crossing.

Potgietersrus, Northern Transvaal. On March 31, 38 people died and at least 174 others were injured when a passenger train was derailed off a bridge 200 miles north of Johannesburg; later investigations showed signs of sabotage.

Saltillo, Mexico. At least 147 deaths and about 700 injuries occurred when a speeding passenger train jumped the track October 5.

Vierzy. At least 63 people died and more than 70 were injured on June 16 when a railway tunnel cave-in derailed one train and caused another to crash into it.

Traffic

Breda the Netherlands. Deaths reached at least 20 and many more people were injured when at least 70 vehicles collided in a thick fog August 25.

Marlow Heights, Md. Five people were killed and 37 were injured on May 4 when their Greyhound commuter bus overturned after swerving to avoid a pickup truck.

Tennessee. A Greyhound bus collided with a tractor-trailer at dawn on May 13; 14 persons were killed.

Thailand. On October 2, 20 fatalities and 21 injuries were caused by the collision of a bus and a truck 85 miles north of Bangkok. ABBY RAE ZUKERMAN

THE WRATH OF AGNES

In a week of wide rampage, Hurricane Agnes raged up Florida's west coast (above left) and finally veered out to sea off Virginia, only to renew its force and capriciously turn inland. Volunteers fled the Susquehanna River (above) when sandbagging could not stem the tide. At right, an old woman dispossessed by floods that struck Elmira, N.Y.

ABOVE LEFT, UPI;
ABOVE AND RIGHT, WIDE WORLD

DOMINICAN REPUBLIC. For the fourth straight year, the Dominican Republic registered substantial economic improvement, but President Joaquín Balaguer's political problems mounted and threatened to erode the island-nation's economic confidence.

Economic developments. Spurred by a sharp rise in world sugar market prices in 1971, the Dominican economy continued to grow substantially during 1972 in exports, new industries, tourism, and mining. The country's gross national product, which grew 12.8 percent in 1971, was expected to increase a similar percent in 1972 and to amount to about US$1.7 billion. Exports jumped an estimated 35 percent to $330 million, with imports leveling off at $360 million. This decline in imports was seen as beneficial because exports are expected to be greater than imports in 1973 for the first time in a decade. The United States remained the Dominican Republic's major trading partner, purchasing 72 percent of its exports as well as supplying more than 50 percent of its imports.

New industries were in part responsible for the improved economic picture. The $200 million Falconbridge nickel mine, which began production in 1971, reached its full $60 million annual output in 1972. A $38 million Shell Oil refinery opened, and a $5 million cardboard mill began operations as the year ended. The dairy and cattle industries also prospered.

Many Dominicans saw tourism as one industry that awaited major development. More than 100,000 tourists visited the island in 1971, spending an estimated $24 million; preliminary figures for 1972 indicated that there had been close to 150,000 tourists who spent more than $40 million. With this in mind, the government announced that it would sell three Santo Domingo hotels to foreign investors in the hope that they would upgrade facilities. The government is also looking for investors to develop tourist areas that were pinpointed in recent World Bank and Inter-American Development Bank studies.

Meanwhile, new studies of mining prospects showed that there are substantial quantities of gold, silver, copper, and zinc in the mountains in the northwest. Several new concessions were granted foreign firms, including one New York company that expects to invest $20 million in 1972 and 1973 in the search for gold and silver.

In contrast to these promising developments, there was a depressingly high unemployment rate, estimated in July at close to one-third of the labor force. Coupled with a cost-of-living increase of 7.9 percent in 1971 and an estimate of a similar rise in 1972, the unemployment picture was a major concern for the Balaguer government. It also provided the president's opposition with a major political issue.

Politics and government. Skirmishing for the 1974 presidential election began as President Balaguer indicated that he might seek a third term. The major opposition force, gathered around former president Juan Bosch's Dominican Revolutionary Party (PRD), sharply attacked Balaguer for setting up what one PRD spokesman termed "a new Trujillo dynasty," an obvious reference to the 31 years in which Dominican strongman Rafael Leonidas Trujillo Molina ruled the island nation as if it were his own political fiefdom. For his part, the self-exiled Bosch continued a series of hard-hitting radio broadcasts attacking prevailing social conditions and "President Balaguer's lack of interest in the common man."

Terrorism, which has long been a major factor in Dominican life, was less evident during the year but flared up on several occasions. One issue of major political comment was the unsolved murder in Europe of two Dominican Communists, Maximiliano Gómez and Miriam Pinedo de Morales. There was widespread speculation that agents of the Dominican secret police were responsible, for the deaths reflected the pattern of murder and intrigue in Dominican politics dating back to the Trujillo years.

Area and population. Area, 18,816 sq. mi. Pop. (est. 1972), 4,750,000. Santo Domingo (cap.), 725,000.
Government. Constitutional republic with bicameral legislature. Pres., Joaquín Balaguer.
Finance. Monetary unit, Dominican gold peso (RD$); RD$1.00 = US$1.00. Budget (fiscal 1971–1972): expenditure, $261 million; revenue (est.), $290 million.
Trade (1971). Imports: $311.1 million; exports, $242.4 million. Principal exports: sugar, cocoa beans, coffee, nickel ore. Principal imports: machinery, iron and steel, food, fuel. Major trading partners: United States, Great Britain, Spain.
Education (1971). Enrollment: primary, 801,000; secondary, 67,100; higher, 9,100. Education budget (1971–1972): $69 million.
JAMES NELSON GOODSELL

ECUADOR. Government and politics. On February 15, the armed forces, led by General Guillermo Rodríguez Lara, removed President José María Velasco Ibarra and sent him into his fourth political exile. The move came after an announcement by Velasco Ibarra that general elections would be held on June 4. Velasco had exercised dictatorial powers since June 22, 1970, and was widely assumed to be ruling for the military rather than in his own right. However, the military feared the elections because it appeared that the populist leader Asaad Bucaram would become president. Leader of the Concentration of Popular Forces Party, Bucaram had made his reputation as mayor of Guayaquil, Ecuador's largest city, and had built up impressive support among Ecuador's masses.

The son of Lebanese immigrants, Bucaram had been declared a citizen of Ecuador in 1960, thus qualifying him for holding political office. When Velasco Ibarra became dictator, he had exiled Bucaram and had not allowed him to return to Ecuador until January. Before Velasco Ibarra's ouster, the military had asked him to deny Bucaram's citizenship and thereby disqualify him from running for the presidency.

The official announcement by the junta was that the president had been "exploiting the people." General Rodriguez announced that the new regime would promote a "nationalist revolution" to eradicate the "anachronistic structures" that kept the country underdeveloped. He revived the radical leftist constitution of 1945 and canceled the June elections. A crisis shook the new regime only four days after it assumed power, when two members of the ruling council, Admiral Reinaldo Vallejo of the navy and General Julio Espinoza of the air force, asked for Rodriguez' resignation, but instead they themselves were forced to resign from the council.

Economic developments. Impressive industrial growth, the start of what promised to be a record year for oil production, and the first serious effort at agricultural development in new areas marked Ecuador's economic picture. According to a report of the UN Economic Commission for Latin America, Ecuador experienced in 1971 a 12 percent growth rate in industry, a 20 percent growth in construction, and a 9.7 percent growth in transportation. These optimistic figures contrasted with a drop in the growth rate from 8.7 percent to 7 percent in the gross national product. This drop was attributable primarily to lower prices on the world market for bananas and coffee, two products on which Ecuador depends very heavily.

The discovery and development of unexpectedly large reserves of petroleum in the northeast may make Ecuador into Latin America's second highest exporter of oil when a pipeline from the Amazon Basin over the Andes Mountains to the Pacific coast is completed this year; Ecuador is expected to become one of the world's leading oil-exporting nations in the near future. The new oil and natural gas production of 83.8 million cubic feet daily represented a saving of nearly US$20 million a year in oil and gas imports. The total investment of the principal firms involved was $330 million. An additional benefit will be the contracting and purchasing of ships to carry 50 percent of the oil to foreign markets.

The regional development of the Guayas River Basin, an area of 13,127 square miles at the confluence of three major river systems—the Daule, Vinces, and Babahoyo—will touch on the economies of nine provinces. The new government made a special point of publicly committing funds from oil for the modernization of rice, citrus, sugarcane, cocoa, banana, coffee, and fibrous crops in this area. This project was planned by a special commission created in 1965 to study the feasibility of major development in the area. The Inter-American Development Bank provided over $1.2 million for the study. The Ministry of Production committed $800,-000 annually for the development of communications, irrigation, electrification, and other infrastructural needs. The plan estimated that 200,000 rural families would be relocated in the newly opened areas. Confident of increased grain production, the government is negotiating for the construction of 14 silos with a capacity of 60,000 tons of grain, to be financed primarily through the sale of coffee and bananas to the countries awarded the contracts. Poland, Yugoslavia, Colombia, Brazil, Sweden, France, and Peru have submitted offers.

International relations. Ecuador's claim of a 200-mile off-shore territorial boundary continued to trigger incidents with U.S. fishing boats. Five vessels were seized in January and February and fined a total of $244,050. The American Tuna Boat Association, whose vessels made up most of the ships seized, decided to defy the U.S. State Department and bought fishing licenses from Ecuador, as Japanese fishermen were doing. The United States has cut off military sales and credit to Ecuador, and the U.S. Congress included in the 1972 foreign aid bill a prohibition of assistance to Ecuador as long as the fishing controversy persists. The United States contends that only a 12-mile limit is sanctioned by international law.

Area and population. Area (UN est.), 104,505 sq. mi. Pop. (est. 1970), 6,028,000. Principal cities: Quito (cap.), 530,000; Guayaquil, 790,000.
Government. Military dictatorship. Chief of state, General Guillermo Rodriguez Lara.
Finance. Monetary unit, sucre; official rate, 1 sucre = US$0.415. Budget (1969), US$244.5 million.
Trade (1970). Imports, US$246.9 million; exports, US$218.2 million.
Education (1968–1969). Primary pupils, 928,687; secondary, 105,362; higher, 22,637.

STEFFEN SCHMIDT

EDUCATION. The fiscal crisis in education was a dominant concern this year of educators at all levels and in both the public and the private sectors. The period of growth and expansion, which had given education planners an optimistic outlook for the past quarter-century, had clearly come to a temporary halt. As the general retrenchment reduced hiring of all personnel, efforts to improve employment opportunities for women and nonwhite minorities in teaching were hampered.

Controversy over school busing once again put the spotlight on the problem of racial integration in the public schools. The question of equal educational opportunity was also raised in the context of school financing, as a number of court actions challenged the constitutionality of huge discrepancies in per-pupil expenditures among local school districts.

Fiscal crisis. As an increasing number of school districts had to struggle to make ends meet—some of them by actually shortening the school year, others by drastically reducing the teaching staff—taxpayers' resistance to higher school taxes stiffened. This resistance was underscored by the fact that a record 53.3 percent of school bond issues were rejected at the polls.

In the United States, 52 percent of all public school funds comes from local property taxes, which have skyrocketed in recent years; 41 percent comes from state governments; and 7 percent comes from the federal government. The Nixon

FERRIS STATE COLLEGE

A NEW ROAD FOR COLLEGES. Vocational students at Michigan's Ferris State College pore over an automobile engine. Colleges have turned increasingly to job-related courses like this one as a means of offsetting declining enrollments and rising deficits.

administration, launching a trial balloon, suggested raising more federal money for education by imposing a national value-added tax, similar in effect to a national sales tax, and then making only those states which reformed their property tax systems eligible for the extra funds. However, a Gallup poll showed that 51 percent of those sampled rejected the value-added tax idea. The same poll showed 56 percent of all adults opposed to any tax increases for education, although 55 percent favored a greater assumption of the school finance burden by the states.

President Richard M. Nixon also promised that he would seek constitutional ways of aiding the Roman Catholic parochial schools, warning that the disappearance of all non-public schools "would saddle the American taxpayer with an additional $3 billion annually in school operating costs, plus as much as $10 billion in new school construction." However, in New York a study by a special state commission concluded that changing parental preferences and a decline in the birthrate among Catholics would reduce the parochial schools' enrollment by as much as 50 percent in the current decade, regardless of their financial situation. The study called for greater stress on the quality of education and administration in a smaller parochial school system.

In higher education the financial crisis also continued. About a dozen colleges, mostly small private institutions, had to close in 1971, and equal numbers were expected to shut down in 1972 and 1973. Nearly two-thirds of the nation's 2,200 colleges and universities, enrolling more than three-fourths of all U.S. students, were considered by the Carnegie

Commission on Higher Education to be in financial trouble or heading for it.

The commission therefore urged U.S. colleges and universities to increase their productivity and trim their budgets. In its study, "More Effective Use of Resources: An Imperative for Higher Education," it estimated that to carry out their responsibilities at a cost that the country and the consumer could afford, colleges and universities must cut about $10 billion by 1980 from their projected annual expenditures. One area in which savings must be made, the report said, is graduate education; it called for a moratorium on virtually all new Ph.D. programs, both to save money and to deal with the growing threat of an oversupply of Ph.D.'s. However, the commission estimated that, even after such reductions, $16 billion in "new" funds would have to be added annually by 1980 to maintain quality in higher education, and it said that most of those new funds would have to come from the federal government.

New York University, a totally private institution located in New York City, emerged this year as the symbol of higher education's financial plight. NYU's budget deficit for 1972–1973 was $14 million, and from fall 1969 through spring 1972 the institution's expenditures exceeded its income by $21 million, seriously depleting cash reserves. A task force appointed by NYU's president, James M. Hester, called for a reduction of the teaching staff by 217 through layoffs and retirement. In addition, each of the university's schools and divisions is being required to pay all of its own expenses and also cover a share of the central university's operating costs.

Campus mood. The turbulence which recently characterized college campuses has given way to peace and, in the view of many observers, to a substantial measure of student apathy, at least about political issues. This change appears to have several causes, including disenchantment with the violent tactics of some radical leaders; increased concern, as jobs became harder to come by, with entering the job market with a good record of academic accomplishment; and reduced feelings of powerlessness and frustration as a result

of the lowering of the voting age and the phasing out of the draft.

There were also indications that some institutions were taking a second look at some of the earlier student demands relating to curriculum requirements and course structure. The University of Chicago attributed its 35 percent increase in applications in part to the fact that its faculty had made a point of maintaining the standards of "basic scholarship." President Kingman Brewster, Jr., of Yale University, in welcoming the new freshmen of the class of 1976, told them: "The demand for relevance, the glorification of the happening, the resort to violence all had one thing in common. They were all shortcuts. They were doomed to frustration and letdown, for there are no shortcuts to understanding, and understanding is essential to true satisfaction and absolutely crucial to real effectiveness."

College admission. For the first time since the arrival on college campuses in the 1960's of the post–World War II baby crop, the pressure for college admission has subsided. Although a few of the most prestigious institutions still had more applicants than places, the 1972–1973 academic year opened with about half a million fewer students than the nation's campuses could accommodate. The reason was not a drop in enrollment but overexpansion by the colleges. The buildings begun during the boom years were still coming off the construction line—faster than they were needed. At the same time, the economic turndown may have slightly reduced the number of students who, under more prosperous circumstances, might have been expected to attend college.

The result was that many colleges were again actively recruiting students. For example, the University of California system, with its high-prestige Berkeley and Los Angeles campuses, announced that it was lowering the requirements for students who wanted to transfer from other universities in their junior year.

Legislation. *Higher education bill.* Congress enacted a landmark higher education measure in 1972—the first law in U.S. history designed to provide general support for colleges

"INTO THE BUS, OFF THE BUS, INTO THE BUS, OFF THE BUS—MAN, WHAT AN EDUCATION!"

and universities, as opposed to funds earmarked for specific purposes (limited in the past largely to building loans and grants, student aid, and research contracts). The new law does, however, attempt to distribute the general aid (up to $1 billion a year was authorized) in such a way as to challenge colleges and universities to provide social service. For every student an institution has in attendance on a federal scholarship, the institution receives a grant which it can use as it wishes. Thus, admitting needy students is doubly rewarded: the college need not provide aid out of its own budget, and it is given additional funds to help close its budget gap. The framers of the legislation also hoped that, by giving needy students a wider choice of where to study, they would be pressuring colleges and universities to improve their offerings in order to remain competitive.

The new bill also authorizes some aid to institutions based on the number of graduate students in attendance, a recognition of the fact that providing graduate education is particularly costly. In addition, an emergency fund at the disposal of the United States commissioner of education will permit the federal government to come to the aid of institutions in immediate danger of insolvency.

Of great long-run significance is a provision in the new law outlining a new concept in student aid. Under this "entitlement grants" provision, every college-aged youth is theoretically eligible for up to $1,400 annually to be applied to the cost of his or her college education. The actual amount payable is reducible in direct relation to the parents' reasonable capacity—as determined by an income formula—to pay for the student's schooling. Thus, the entitlement grant will generally disappear when family income rises above $13,000, except in some hardship cases, such as when a number of children are attending college at the same time. For the moment, the rub of this new aid provision is that it will not become operative until existing federal student aid programs (such as those providing scholarships and work-study grants) and also the entitlement program itself are funded to an extent not likely to be sought by the Nixon administration. Full funding of the entitlement program would involve an appropriation of approximately $900 million annually.

Health, Education, and Welfare appropriation. For the third time in four years, President Nixon vetoed the appropriation bill for the Department of Health, Education, and Welfare. This year Congress had, in a single bill, provided $30.5 billion for HEW and the Department of Labor—$1.8 billion more than the president had requested. A new appropriations package passed by Congress again amounted to $30.5 billion, and again the president vetoed it.

Statistical survey. *Enrollment.* At the beginning of the 1972–1973 academic year, total enrollment in all United States educational institutions, public and private, stood at 60.4 million. Although this figure was larger than 1971–1972 enrollment, the increase was the smallest in 28 consecutive years of growth. High school and college enrollments continued on a moderate growth curve, but for the third consecutive year, elementary schools registered a decrease, reflecting the decline in the birthrate in the early 1960's.

The elementary grades (kindergarten through grade 8) accounted for 35.9 million pupils, about 31.9 million of whom were enrolled in public schools. Of the 4 million attending nonpublic schools, by far the greatest number were in Roman Catholic schools.

In public high schools (grades 9 through 12) enrollment was estimated at 14.1 million. Of the remaining 1.4 million high school students, slightly fewer than 1 million attended Roman Catholic schools.

Fall 1972 enrollment in institutions of higher learning was 9 million; more than two-thirds of the students were attending public institutions. Undergraduates made up 7.9 million of the total.

The high school graduating class of 1973 is expected to exceed 3.1 million, which will make it the largest graduating class in U.S. history. Projected for 1972–1973 are the following statistics on earned college and university degrees conferred: bachelor's and first professional degrees, 958,000 (up 55,000 from 1971–1972); master's degrees, 256,000 (up 18,000); doctorates, 38,000 (up 3,000).

A survey by the United States Office of Education indicated that current school attendance trends make it safe to predict that of students 16 and 17 years of age, more than three-fourths will graduate from high school; 48 percent will enter a college or university; one-fourth will earn a bachelor's degree; 8 percent, a master's degree; and 1.5 percent, a doctorate.

Expenditures. Total expenditures in 1972–1973 for education at all levels, public and private, were estimated at $90.5 billion, compared with $85.1 billion in 1971–1972. About $79.2 billion of the total is expected to be used for operating expenditures, and capital construction will account for $11.3 billion. The nonpublic sector's part of the total expenditure will be $16.6 billion. Of the total 1972–1973 costs, $55.8 billion will go for elementary and secondary education. Federal expenditures for education have risen from $3.4 billion in 1965 to $11.6 billion in 1972, and they are expected to total $12.8 billion for the fiscal year ending June 30, 1973.

The per-pupil expenditure in the public schools in 1971–1972 stood at a national average of $929, compared with $858 the previous year and about $450 a decade ago. However, these figures do not take into account the effects of inflation.

Teachers. The National Center for Educational Statistics estimated that U.S. elementary and secondary schools now employ about 2.3 million teachers, about 2.1 million (20,000 more than last year) in the public schools. College and university faculties are expected to consist of 660,000 people, about 30,000 more than in the fall of 1971. There continues to be a large surplus of teachers in virtually all categories and on all levels.

Uncertain economic conditions and the guidelines of the national Price Commission and Pay Board combined to slow the rate of increase of teachers' salaries. As an indication of the severity of the squeeze, the normally militant teachers union in Detroit, an affiliate of the American Federation of Teachers, agreed to extend the existing contract for one year without a boost in the pay scale. Nationwide, the average teacher salary for 1971–1972 was $9,690, compared with $9,269 the previous year. The lowest average was registered by Mississippi, $6,518; the highest was Alaska's $14,124. The three other states above the $11,000 mark were, in descending order, Michigan, California, and New York. New York City's United Federation of Teachers negotiated a contract which, in its third year, will permit teachers with advanced degrees and seven years of service to get an annual salary of about $20,000.

Union merger. The powerful UFT, the bargaining agent for New York City's 60,000 teachers, merged this year with the New York State Teachers Association to form the United Teachers of New York. The move was viewed as having more than local significance because the federation, an affiliate of the AFL-CIO, had been considered a bitter rival of the association, an affiliate of the National Education Association. In the past the NEA had stressed its role as a professional rather than a labor group. Although there have been a few limited local mergers in the past, many observers believe that the New York agreement, creating a single organization of well over 200,000 teachers, may be an indication of things to come on the national level. The merger has also substantially increased the power of Albert Shanker, the UFT president, thus giving the organized teaching profession a more substantial voice and more significant role in the national labor movement.

JANE LATTA

SCHOOL'S OUT. Amish children play outside a Pennsylvania schoolhouse. This year their parents won a U.S. Supreme Court decision allowing the Amish young to quit school after eighth grade and thus avoid exposure to what the sect considers worldly corruption.

Job outlook. The Bureau of Labor Statistics reported that the market for college graduates seeking jobs will continue to be tight for the rest of the decade. It is estimated that in the course of the 1970's approximately 9.2 million new graduates will enter the job market, competing for an estimated 9.6 million openings. However, an additional 600,000 new job-seekers—"reentrants, delayed entrants, and immigrants"—will be added to the competition. As a result, there will be slightly more than one applicant for each available job.

The report added, however, that the current situation does not reflect any long-term decline in the demand for college graduates; such a decline was seen as unlikely in a "knowledge society." Moreover, the BLS estimated that the average college graduate can expect to earn more than $200,000 more in the course of his life than the average high school graduate. College graduates are forming an increasing part of the U.S. labor force—13.7 percent in 1971, up from 8.1 percent in 1952.

Busing. Federal court-ordered busing intended to desegregate the public schools continued to be highly controversial. President Nixon, who declared he was opposed to busing for integration, called on Congress to enact a moratorium on new busing orders by federal courts. He said that if Congress failed to pass the appropriate legislation, he would favor enactment of a constitutional amendment proscribing busing.

Civil rights spokesmen and other opponents of antibusing legislation accused the president of trying to please segregationists in an election year. They also maintained that the legislation Nixon proposed was unconstitutional.

An antibusing amendment was attached to part of the higher education aid bill. The amendment's major provisions delayed implementation of court-ordered busing (but did not ban new busing orders) and limited the use of federal funds to pay for busing. The wording of the amendment made it appear that it would not permanently stand in the way of busing for purposes of desegregation, provided the goal was not to create a specific "racial balance" in all the schools. In 1971 the U.S. Supreme Court, in upholding an integration and busing order by a lower court in North Carolina, specifically stated that the Constitution does not require such a balance but does require the termination of dual school systems. The court also declared that busing was a legitimate requirement to achieve desegregation, provided the bus ride was not excessively long or detrimental to the children's health.

While the debate continued, there seemed little indication at the start of the 1972–1973 school year that there would be significantly more busing.

It is difficult to obtain definitive statistics on the actual extent of busing for integration purposes. According to government reports, however, it appears that approximately 20 million students are transported to school by bus each day, at an annual public expense of about $1.7 billion. About 97 percent of those students are bused for reasons unrelated to desegregation. (*See* Civil Liberties and Civil Rights *and the special supplement* Election '72.)

School inequality. In March, after two years of study, the President's Commission on School Finance recommended that, in order to eliminate the gap between the amounts spent per child in rich and poor local school districts, the states should take over a major part of the burden of paying for public schools. To induce the states to collect and equitably distribute school taxes, the commission said, the federal government should offer them between $4.6 billion and $7.8 billion in aid over the next five years. The commission was headed by Neil H. McElroy, chairman of the board of the Procter and Gamble Company and a former secretary of defense in the Eisenhower administration.

No action was immediately taken on the McElroy Commission's recommendations, but pressure mounted on the states to wipe out local differences in school financing as a number of court rulings declared widely discrepant per-pupil expenditures unconstitutional. Most of those rulings borrowed heavily from the reasoning used by the California supreme court in its landmark 1971 decision *Serrano* v. *Priest.* That case was brought on behalf of the low-income district of Baldwin Park, which, despite a higher tax rate, could only afford a per-pupil expenditure of $577, while nearby Beverly Hills spent $1,231 per student. The court held that such funding was discriminatory, because it made the quality of a child's education a function of the wealth of his parents and neighbors, and violated the equal protection clause of the Fourteenth Amendment to the U.S. Constitution.

Until the U.S. Supreme Court rules on *Serrano* and the related cases, the advisability of state financing remains a matter for discussion among educators and political leaders. Those who have doubts about a complete take-over by the states of school financing, with equal amounts spent per pupil by all the districts in each state, cite the difficulty of either reducing the expenditures of high-spending localities or finding the funds to bring all districts up to the spending level of the most affluent. In addition, opponents of state financing point to the fact that such a shift of responsibility would still leave considerable per-pupil spending discrepancies in the United States. For example, statewide average expenditures per pupil currently stand at $1,245 in New York and $463 in Alabama. Thus, only a federalization of school financing could equalize per-pupil spending nationwide.

Effect of schooling. Christopher Jencks and his associates at Harvard's Center for Educational Policy Research, in their study "Inequality: A Reassessment of the Effect of Family and Schooling in America," challenged the belief that schooling is a major factor in opening the doors to greater equality of opportunity. According to the study, which was financed by the Carnegie Corporation of New York, the qualities a child brings to school—as a result of heredity, home environment, and other influences—are more important to his cognitive development than anything the school does by way of instruction: "the school budget, its policies, the characteristics of the teacher [are] either secondary or completely irrelevant." The study went on to estimate that, in any case, only a quarter of the variation in adults' incomes is explained by differences in schools, cognitive skills (the ability to manipulate words, numbers, and ideas), genes, home background, and IQ. For the most part, according to Jencks, career success and increased income depend on personality and luck. Moreover, Jencks added, "None of the evidence . . . suggests that school re-

form can be expected to bring about significant social changes outside the schools." Only political reforms, he believes, can do that.

Jencks himself insists that, despite his study's doubts concerning the schools' ability to reform society or improve the individual's economic chances, schools should be adequately financed so that a classroom, not unlike a sound family setting, can offer children pleasant surroundings in which to develop. Inevitably, however, the report's findings—and its statistical approach to the many intangible questions of human success—will be challenged by other authorities and can be expected to be subject to extensive public and professional debate.

Paternity rights. A new contract negotiated for the professional staff of the giant City University of New York is the first such agreement to provide paternity as well as maternity leaves. Under the plan, up to 20 days of paid leave and up to 18 months of unpaid leave would be provided for both men and women. The proposals were developed at the request of the university chancellor's advisory committee on the status of women, which felt that women should have the opportunity to continue working while their husbands stayed home taking care of the children.

Compulsory attendance. On May 15 the U.S. Supreme Court ruled in *Wisconsin* v. *Yoder* that the Amish, who object on religious grounds to schooling above the eighth grade, should be exempt from compulsory attendance laws. The ruling, which did not pass judgment on the legality of compulsory attendance generally (as some educational reformers hoped it would), declared that Wisconsin's interest in having all children in school through grade 10 was outweighed by the Amish's First Amendment right to religious freedom. Fred M. Hechinger

EGYPT. On July 18, 1972, in a dramatic announcement that stunned world leaders and reversed a nearly 20-year trend of increasing military dependence on the Soviet Union, Egypt's president, Anwar Sadat, called for the withdrawal of all Soviet military personnel stationed in Egypt and placed Soviet bases and equipment in Egypt under Egyptian control. Although observers at first were not sure just how many men and how much matériel would be affected, it became increasingly apparent with each passing day that Sadat meant his words to be interpreted strictly. The Soviet Union withdrew nearly all of its estimated 20,000 troops based in Egypt, as well as those fighter and reconnaissance planes flown by Soviet pilots.

Also during 1972, Sadat attempted to consolidate his power by forming a new cabinet, and new economic policies, some of them in sharp contrast to those of Sadat's predecessor, Gamal Abdel Nasser, were initiated.

Soviet-Egyptian relations. Although the announcement of July 18 came as a shock to outsiders, the decision was not made on the spur of the moment but had been coolly and deliberately planned by Sadat. Many Egyptians had grown concerned over Egypt's increasing dependence on the Soviet Union, especially for military supplies. A few weeks before Sadat's proclamation, a small group of former political leaders and associates of the late President Nasser had circulated a letter critical of the Egyptian government for its subservience to the Soviet Union.

The influential editor of the semiofficial Cairo newspaper *al-Ahram*, Muhammad Hasanayn Haykal, had written a series of four editorials designed to show that the military stalemate between Israel and Egypt benefited the United States, Israel, and the Soviet Union, but not Egypt. According to Haykal, Israel, backed by the United States, was able to justify the retention of the Arab territories conquered in the 1967 war on the grounds that Egypt was preparing to renew hostilities. Haykal believed that these tense circumstances forced Egypt to rely on the Soviets for military supplies, but the unwillingness of the Soviet Union to deliver

RUSSIANS GO HOME. In a startling 90-minute speech before the Central Committee of the Arab Socialist Union, Egyptian president Anwar Sadat announced that he was expelling Soviet military personnel and placing Soviet bases in Egypt under Egyptian control.

offensive weapons to the Egyptians meant that Egypt could not alter the balance of power with Israel. The Soviet Union, meanwhile, was using its Egyptian bases for its own purposes, including surveillance of U.S. warships.

An important influence on Sadat's Soviet policy was the Egyptian Army under the leadership of General Muhammad Ahmad Sadek, who later resigned. Egyptian officers resented the loss of military independence to Soviet advisers and high-ranking Soviet officers. It was reported that Egyptian generals had difficulty gaining admittance to several Egyptian bases where Soviet officers were in command. But the unwillingness of the Soviets to supply Egypt with offensive weapons was crucial in causing the alienation of the Egyptian military. Under pressure from the Egyptian government (and from the people themselves) to deal more aggressively with the Israelis, the Egyptian army repeatedly requested from the Soviets long-range bombers and ground-to-ground missiles. When these requests were refused, as they apparently were during at least two major meetings with high-ranking Soviet officials in 1972, the military recommended the cutting of ties with the Soviet Union. Additionally, the Egyptian military leaders felt that the army had become able to handle sophisticated Soviet weaponry without the aid of foreign technicians.

What the Egyptian military could not do without, however, was spare parts for the Soviet equipment, and in October, Premier Aziz Sidki went to Moscow in an effort to get such supplies and to perhaps reduce the level of Soviet-Egyptian hostility. He returned to Cairo with promises that the spare parts shipments would be resumed. Later, the Soviets agreed to restore some SAM-6 missiles that had been removed from Egypt in July.

The reduction, if not the termination, of Egypt's reliance on the Soviet Union for military assistance was all the more shocking because of Egypt's long tradition of dependence on the Soviets. Ever since 1955, when Nasser accepted arms from Czechoslovakia, Egyptian-Soviet military ties had been growing closer, and Egypt's defeat at the hands of the Israelis in 1967 seemed to inextricably link the two countries. The Soviets rearmed Egypt. Soviet ships called at Egyptian naval bases on the Mediterranean. When President Sadat moved into a new house only a short distance away from the Soviet embassy in Cairo, one cynic suggested that a tunnel must exist between the two residences. Yet in a stroke all this was changed.

The Israeli and U.S. governments welcomed the departure from Egypt of the Soviet troops. Within ten days of Sadat's announcement, Israeli prime minister Golda Meir called upon Egypt to sit down and negotiate its differences with Israel. The likelihood of war seemed quite reduced; certainly Egypt was not in a position to challenge the Israelis on the battlefield. The Egyptians no doubt hoped that their expulsion of Soviet troops would lead to important concessions from the Israelis, such as the reopening of the Suez Canal and the return of territory lost in the 1967 war.

Tension with Sudan. In September, Sudan removed most of its troops from the Suez Canal. Relations between Sudan and Egypt became strained after Egypt sided with Libya in a Libyan-Sudanese dispute over aid to Uganda and after Sudan resumed diplomatic relations with the United States. In October, Egypt asked Sudan to remove from the canal area the remainder of its force, which had been sent to Egypt in 1967.

Domestic politics. The expulsion of the Soviets was linked to Sadat's quest to consolidate his power and achieve political stability after the attempted coup d'etat of May 1971. New cabinets were formed in September 1971 and again in January 1972. Yet another round of cabinet changes came in October after General Sadek resigned his posts as vice-premier, war minister, minister of war production, and armed forces commander in chief.

Whereas in 1971 significant challenges to Sadat's power had come from other members of Egypt's political elite, in 1972 the major challenge came from disgruntled students and workers. Both groups were dissatisfied with Sadat's cautious foreign policy, characterized by some as a policy of "no war, no peace" with Israel. They called for a showdown with the Israelis, the reopening of the Suez Canal, and the reacquisition of the land lost in the 1967 war. They also resented the sluggish pace of the Egyptian economy.

After Sadat's formation of the new cabinet in January, Cairo students went on strike, calling for the government to resign and demanding a more energetic foreign policy. An estimated 1,000–1,500 students were arrested. Sadat sought to appease the students by announcing that the Egyptian economy was to be put on a war footing in preparation for an eventual conflict with Israel. Luxury imports were banned, and government expenditures were cut, so that more money could be appropriated for military needs.

New economic policies. While placing the Egyptian economy on a war footing, Sadat also sought to give it new directions. Claiming to be following guidelines for economic change drawn up by Nasser before his death, Sadat promulgated plans to double industrial output in the next ten years, increase agricultural productivity by 50 percent, and attract foreign investment into the country. In each of the three areas, the Egyptian president's proposals represented departures from traditional Egyptian economic practices.

The industrialization program seeks to increase the output of traditionally important industries like steel, cement, oil, fertilizers, and electric power by allowing the managers and boards of directors of industrial firms to make their own decisions and maximize their profits without the close government supervision customary in the past.

Sadat hopes to obtain increased agricultural productivity by bringing new land under cultivation and fostering new agrarian organizations. The government plans to make available 1.5 million acres of new arable land over the next ten years. But in contrast to Nasser's policies, this land will not be turned over outright to small peasant landholders but will be broken up into blocks of at least 50,000 acres and run by independent companies specializing in such export commodities as fruits and nuts; these companies will market their own produce inside and outside the country. Sadat's new policy applies only to new land coming under cultivation, not to land already owned by peasants.

Finally, the government declared "free zones" in industry, agriculture, mining, tourism, and housing. In these areas, foreign investment will be welcomed, and the investors will be tax exempt for five years and be given strong legal guarantees against nationalization and expropriation. The Egyptian government hopes to attract capital from some of the wealthy Arab oil-exporting countries and thus reduce its indebtedness to the Soviet Union, estimated at E£3 billion by mid-1972. In addition, U.S. oil firms are prospecting in Egypt, and a consortium of European investors has signed an agreement to construct an oil pipeline from Suez to Alexandria.

Area and population. Area, 386,661 sq. mi., including territory now occupied by Israel. Pop. (est. mid-1971), 34,900,000. Principal cities (1966): Cairo (cap.), 4,219,853; Alexandria, 1,801,056.
Government. Republic. Pres., Anwar Sadat; prem., Aziz Sidki; war min., Ahmed Ismail.
Finance. Monetary unit, Egyptian pound; E£1 = US$2.32. Budget (est. 1971–1972): balanced at E£2.64 billion.
Trade (1970). Imports, E£342,012,000; exports, E£331,178,-000. Major imports: foodstuffs, manufactured goods. Major exports: cotton, petroleum, certain manufactured goods. Principal trading partners: Soviet Union, Great Britain, France, Japan, India.
Armed forces (1970). Army, 180,000; navy, 14,000; air force, 15,000.   ROBERT L. TIGNOR

SIGN OF THE TIME. Latest in electronic timekeeping, the Longines liquid-crystal display watch flashes the date, hour, minute, and second in milky-white liquid numbers dictated by a minicomputer that receives signals from a regularly vibrating quartz bar.

LONGINES

ELECTRONICS. "Miniaturize" was the byword of the electronics industry this year, primarily in consumer products. As the transistor has supplanted the vacuum tube, so the integrated circuit has replaced the transistor. Now, as a result of technical breakthroughs in manufacturing techniques, large-scale integrated circuitry is replacing the more mundane small-scale integrated circuitry. Thousands of electronic components (transistors and resistors) can be squeezed into an area smaller than a single postage stamp, making possible electronic calculators that fit into a shirt pocket, wristwatches of fantastic accuracy which have no mechanically moving parts, and television sets that are all "solid state" with warranties of a year or more.

Electronic watches. Competition for the $3 billion-a-year world watch market became more frenzied than usual this year, as companies vied for market position with extraordinary engineering innovations. The old standbys tick and tock became things of the past, being replaced by whir, hum, buzz, and, in one instance, by no sound at all. Quartz crystal timing, battery power, and numerical displays on a miniature television screen were novelties for new watch buyers.

The most revolutionary timepiece was introduced by the Longines-Wittnauer Watch Company, Inc. Looking much like the blackboard in a mathematics classroom, the Longines unit displays the time in digital form with numerals for hours, minutes, and seconds and with the day of the month thrown in for good measure. The numerical display, known as liquid crystal digital, uses a liquid which has very peculiar properties. Its molecules normally align themselves in an orderly fashion similar to those in a solid, whence its suggestive name "liquid crystal." When this alignment is upset by an electric field, the liquid crystal loses its waterlike transparency and becomes milky white.

The heart of the quartz watch (from the Bulova Watch Company and the Timex Corporation, as well as Longines) is a single tiny quartz bar that vibrates when charged by electricity from a mercury-oxide battery the size of an aspirin tablet. Quartz has the inherent capability of vibrating at a precise and predictable rate; the rate in each case is determined by the size of the piece of quartz. The reliability of the quartz vibrations has permitted manufacturers to boast of precisions approaching one minute a year

Depending on the brand of watch, the quartz vibrations control several different mechanisms that turn the hour and minute hands. (In Longines' case there are no moving parts but rather a large-scale integrated circuit which links the vibrating quartz to the nonmoving digital display.) Bulova uses the electronic tuning fork developed in its Accutron watch, a battery-powered model that is just a shade less accurate than the quartz model; Timex employs a conventional balance wheel; the Benrus Watch Company and Swiss and Japanese manufacturers use a step-down motor. Linking these mechanisms to the quartz crystal is a small integrated circuit chip.

Despite their accuracy and their unique appeal, there are several drawbacks to the new "space age" wristwatches. They must be returned to the factory to be serviced or repaired, they are not shockproof, and, last but perhaps most important, they are expensive.

Calculators. The great consumer calculator race became increasingly visible this year, as several agile companies leaped to the forefront with electronic machines below the $100 retail price level.

Replacing the larger, noisier, typewriter-sized electromechanical calculators, the new electronic calculators utilize large-scale integrated circuitry to perform their mathematical operations. A variety of digital displays are available—gas discharge tubes, light emitting diodes, and liquid crystals—and it is not yet clear which technology will dominate.

One of the smallest calculators is a British unit claiming a weight of only 2.5 ounces, with measurements of 5.5" by 2.25" by 0.375"—not much larger than a cigarette package.

It became apparent that the smaller, newer firms are finding it easier than the larger, more established business machine companies to adapt to the rapidly changing technologies in the calculator field. The simple $99 calculator appeared to be the divider between the upstart low-overhead technology opportunists and the established firms in the electromechanical business machine market. Some of the latter will participate in the low-price market only with imported machines. Toward the year's end it appeared that close to 1.5 million calculators would be sold.

Healing broken bones. University of Pennsylvania surgeons have reported the first successful case of healing by electricity of an ununited fracture in a human. Further successes could point the way toward the increased use of electrical healing therapy, which would eventually supplant bone grafting in appropriate cases.

Dr. Carl T. Brighton and Dr. Zachary B. Friedenberg began research on the new technique in the early 1960's. At a press conference at the university hospital they described the successful procedure. A small wire cathode was inserted into the fracture under local anesthesia. An aluminum anode was taped to the skin and a cast was applied. The cathode and anode wires were then brought to a small external source of battery power. Ten microamperes (ten one-millionths of an ampere) of current, applied to the ununited fracture for a nine-week period, caused the bone to knit and grow together. Further studies were in progress to determine the optimum amperage and exposed cathode surface area to heal more complicated fractures.

Working under the auspices of the U.S. Navy's Bureau of Medicine and Surgery, the researchers found that the surface of a fractured bone contained a negative charge which was strongest at the fracture site. Further research revealed that the establishment of a current flow produced bone growth at the cathode, or negative pole. Bone growth continued until the current flow exceeded 20 microamperes, at which point there was bone destruction.

The doctors believe that their new electrotherapeutic technique could halve the present five-month to six-month healing time required for a typical leg fracture. Muscle atrophy and stiffness would also be reduced because of the shorter time the bone would need to be immobilized in a cast.

Collision avoidance radar. Once the property of the highway patrolman, radar sets may be installed in future automobiles for the direct protection of the driver. RCA Corporation has demonstrated an experimental radar designed to prevent rear-end collisions by tracking the car ahead and sounding a warning when the separation distance becomes unsafe.

The unit, measuring a very compact 17″ by 8″ by 2½″, transmits a continuous signal which is received by a novel, passive reflector on the rear of the vehicle ahead. The reflector doubles the frequency of the transmitted signal and reflects it back to the unit. The frequency is doubled in order to avoid confusion with the transmitted signals of cars going in the opposite direction.

By measuring the time required for the signal's round trip, the unit calculates the distance to the car in front. A buzzer is sounded when the separation distance decreases below one car length for every 10 miles per hour the car carrying the unit travels.

The developers at RCA feel that their radar could be integrated into a car so that it would automatically release the throttle and apply the brakes in the event of imminent collision. Underscoring the potential significance of the radar is the fact that almost one-fourth of all motor vehicle accidents in the United States are rear-end collisions. National Safety Council figures show that in 1970 there were 3.8 million rear-end collisions.

A key feature of RCA's new device is its rejection of "ground clutter," false targets created by signals bouncing off highway signs, bridges, trees, and other roadside objects. This is achieved by making the radar responsive only to those signals produced by the reflector unit at double the transmitted frequency. Since radar penetrates bad weather and smog, it could play a major role in preventing the multi-car accidents that often occur in heavy fog, rain, or dust storms. The military could use the radar for convoy travel at night without headlights. Each truck in the convoy would be controlled to maintain a preset distance behind the vehicle ahead.

A look into the future. More than 400 electronics industry leaders attended the "Electronics 1985" Conference held in Chicago. United States manufacturers were urged to recognize the growing importance of the international market and to begin developing plans to enter the international marketplace if they had not done so already. The world electronics market in 1985 is expected to be nearly $205 billion, of which the U.S. share will be about $81 billion, almost triple the U.S. market in 1971. Both the United States and Japan are already looking toward Europe as a new and vital marketplace. The Japanese in particular have felt the pinch of the 17 percent upward revaluation of the yen and an erosion of their competitive position in the United States. Preparing for the long term, Japanese manufacturers are setting up sales subsidiaries and preparing to follow European specifications.

Domestically, the color television set will most likely be the predominant consumer electronic product in the home in the 1980's. Attachments to the color television receiver which provide the capability of screening taped material, whether homegrown or rented, will be the consumer's prime demand. These sophisticated television "add-ons," known in the industry as electronic video recording and playback equipment, will probably sell for $400 to $500 and be marketed much as audio components are today. It will be possible to take color tapes of a family picnic and see them on a television receiver the same evening.

Most executives foresaw a demand for large-screen television receivers. Future television display techniques are expected to resemble today's rectangular movie screen rather than the more nearly square television tube. Such applications as televised wide-screen movies or, at the other extreme, flat-screen television receivers in an attaché case were considered definite possibilities.   ALLAN YALE BROOKS

EL SALVADOR. Politics and government. This was a year of intense political ferment, capped by a bitterly contested presidential campaign and a frustrated coup. Presidential elections were held on February 20. Colonel Arturo Armando Molina, the hand-picked choice of outgoing President Fidel Sánchez, emerged as the successful candidate. Molina's major opposition came from a Christian Democrat, José Napoleón Duarte. There were also two candidates from the right, General José Medrano, a hero of the Honduran war, and lawyer Antonio Rodríguez. When the results were announced—amidst cries of fraud from Duarte—no candidate had received a clear majority. Thus, the government-controlled National Assembly, in accordance with constitutional procedures, elected Molina. On March 12, congressional and municipal elections were held in which the ruling National Conciliation party won 206 of the 261 municipal contests and 38 of the 52 seats in the new assembly.

About two weeks later, on March 25, Colonel Benjamín Mejía led an abortive uprising. After the revolt was well under way, Duarte announced his support for the insurgents in a radio address. But most of the armed forces remained loyal to the Sánchez government, and the uprising was quickly subdued. In the course of the fighting, over 100 persons, mostly civilians, were reported killed and at least 200 injured. The leaders fled to various embassies and eventually managed to get out of the country. However, a state of siege continued until Molina's inauguration July 1.

Molina's first problem centered on the national university, which had become a base for antigovernment criticism. Using a disturbance in the medical school as a pretext, Molina rushed a law through Congress reducing university autonomy. Almost immediately, a coordinated military-police force converged on the university and arrested nearly everyone in sight. Most were released, but 15 professors and the university's rector, Dr. Rafael Menjívar, were placed on a military plane and exiled to Nicaragua. This action provoked widespread protests throughout Central America. The institution was closed, and a new law was written giving the government full control over the university's affairs.

During the year, the foreign ministers of El Salvador and Honduras met personally for the first time since the 1969 war between their countries. In September, Costa Rica closed its borders to the free entry of Central American goods. El Salvador retaliated, casting grave doubt on the future of the Central American Common Market.

Economic situation. El Salvador's economic outlook continued to improve in 1972. Exports were up about 12 percent. The overall economic growth rate was about 7 percent, and prices for Salvadoran coffee remained high. Among the important new projects announced were a $40 million dam to produce hydroelectric power on the Lempa River and a new $16 million jetport to be built with Japanese backing. El Salvador was awarded a $90 million loan from the Inter-American Development Bank. President Molina issued a new five-year plan stressing improved housing, medical care, and agricultural assistance.

Area and population. Area, 8,260 sq. mi. Pop. (est. 1972), 3,-500,000. San Salvador (cap.; est. 1967), 281,000.
Government. Constitutional republic. Pres., Colonel Arturo Armando Molina; for. min., Manricio Borgonova.
Finance. Monetary unit, colón; 1 colón = US$0.402. Budget (1969): revenue, 279.2 million colones; expenditure, 255.8 million colones.
Trade (1970). Imports, $214 million; exports, $229 million. Principal imports: wheat, flour, fuel oil, cement, fertilizers, machinery, iron and steel manufactures. Principal exports: coffee, cotton, sugar. Main trading partners: United States, Central American republics, Japan, West Germany. THEODORE S. CREEDMAN

EMPLOYMENT. Improved economic conditions resulted in an impressive increase in employment to a record level in 1972. However, the number of persons in the labor force swelled apace, and no dent was made in the number of unemployed. The situation provided evidence for the presidential nominees of both major parties. The Republicans could boast of their accomplishments in creating an abundance of new jobs, and the Democrats could charge that four years of Nixon administration policies had left millions without jobs.

General economic developments. The Nixon administration's new economic plan for halting inflation, increasing jobs, and stimulating economic growth was initiated on August 15, 1971, with the imposition of a 90-day freeze on wages, prices, and rents. This temporary freeze was followed in November 1971 by implementation of a stabilization program for wages and prices that was operative throughout 1972. The tripartite Pay Board, composed of business, labor, and public members, established a 5.5 percent general standard, with exceptions, as the maximum annual rate of increase for wages. The public-member Price Commission adopted the goal of reducing the level of price increases to an annual average of 2.5 percent by the end of 1972. The theory underlying the stabilization program was that productivity could be expected to increase at the rate of 3 percent a year, and if wages could be held to an average 5.5 percent annual increment, prices could then reasonably be held to a 2.5 percent rate of increase. Within this stabilization framework and with the help of other policies adopted as part of the new economic plan, the administration projected an economic recovery from the 1970–

1971 recession, expansion of employment, and reduced unemployment.

None of these projections was fully realized. The Pay Board found it necessary to approve many negotiated wage increases well in excess of the 5.5 percent standard. Consumer prices increased quite sharply in the months immediately after the 90-day wage-price freeze expired, and organized labor became increasingly disenchanted with a stabilization program that appeared incapable of stopping inflation and which they regarded as unfair to wage earners. In March the AFL-CIO executive board approved the withdrawal of the three AFL-CIO representatives from the Pay Board, concluding that experience with the administration's new economic policy and phase two controls demonstrated that they were "nothing more than a device to make the average worker and consumer both the victim and the goat, while the banks and big business pile up increasing profits. . . . There is no fairness, no equity, no justice in the administration's economic program." Leonard Woodcock, president of the United Automobile Workers, followed AFL-CIO president George Meany, United Steelworkers of America president I. W. Abel, and International Association of Machinists president Floyd Smith off the Pay Board, leaving only International Brotherhood of Teamsters president Frank Fitzsimmons as a representative of organized labor on the board. At that point, President Nixon reconstituted the board, making the membership entirely public.

Some moderation of price increases did occur in 1972. In the eight months prior to the price freeze, prices had increased at an annual rate of 3.8 percent. During the three-month freeze the annual rate of increase was held to 1.9 percent, and in the first eight months of phase two after the freeze the increase was 3.3 percent. Whether the moderation in price increases during the first eight months of phase two was caused by the stabilization program or would also have occurred in the absence of that program was a matter of debate.

That the country was experiencing economic recovery and expansion in 1972, however, was clear. The federal government followed an expansionary monetary and fiscal policy (including a fiscal 1972 budgetary deficit of about $26 billion), and the level of economic activity expanded briskly through the first two quarters of the year. In real terms the U.S. gross national product grew at an annual rate of 6.5 percent in the first quarter of 1972 and 8.9 percent in the second quarter. (See BANKING AND FINANCE and UNITED STATES: Budget.)

Employment and unemployment. The expansion in economic activity resulted in a 1972 increase in civilian employment of about 2.2 million persons, the largest increase in recent years. During the past 25 years the single-year employment increase had previously equaled or exceeded 2 million persons only in 1969 and 1955.

The 2.2 million increment in employment was matched by an equally large increase in the size of the civilian labor force, leaving the number of unemployed unchanged. About 60 percent of the increase in the size of the civilian labor force was attributable to the increase in the size of the population of working age, about 15 percent to a reduction in the size of the armed forces and the transfer of these persons to the civilian labor force, and about 25 percent to the increased rate at which some groups in the population participated in the work force. This third factor added close to 600,000 persons to the labor force, mainly male teen-agers and women of all ages.

As in 1971, unemployment averaged about 5 million persons in 1972. (The comparisons between 1971 and 1972, unless otherwise noted, are based on average monthly figures for the first six months of each year, seasonally adjusted.) The rate of unemployment declined slightly from 6 to 5.8 percent because the 5 million unemployed were part of a larger labor force in 1972, but the duration of unemploy-

BOTH PHOTOS, KEN REGAN/CAMERA 5

Putting Skills to Work

John Mizerny (above) found work on a municipal road repair crew and Felix Garcia landed a job as a housing guard under the first general public employment program in the United States since the New Deal. In its first year the Emergency Employment Act of 1971 provided $1 billion to fund more than 140,000 public service jobs on state and local levels.

TABLE 1. TRENDS IN THE LABOR FORCE[1]
(in thousands)

	1970	1971	1972	Change 1970–71	1971–72
Civilian labor force	82,460	83,620	85,790	+1,160	+2,170
Employment	78,760	78,640	80,830	−120	+2,190
Unemployment	3,700	4,990	4,960	+1,290	−30
15 weeks or more	550	1,120	1,200	+570	+80
27 weeks or more	190	470	610	+280	+140

[1] *All figures are monthly averages for the first six months of each year. Published 1972 figures for the size of labor force, employment, and unemployment are reduced by amounts attributable to the introduction of 1970 census data into the 1972 estimation procedure; these reductions make the 1972 figures comparable to those for earlier years.*

ment for those without jobs increased. Those without work for 15 weeks or more numbered 1.2 million, and the number of those unemployed more than six months reached 610,000, a figure exceeding the 1971 level by nearly 140,000. The average spell of unemployment increased from 11.1 to 12.5 weeks between the two years.

Table 1 summarizes the trends in the labor force for the past two years. Most of the employment growth in 1972 was due to expansion in the service-producing sector, which accounted for 1.4 million of the 1.6 million increase in the number of nonagricultural employees between 1971 and 1972. The largest increase occurred in the wholesale and retail trade segment (474,000), followed by increases of 419,000 in state and local government and 398,000 in the service sector. The service category includes employees in hotels and other lodging places, personal services, medical and other health services, and educational services. The

manufacturing sector, in which employment fell drastically in 1971 (870,000), experienced a modest gain in 1972. Table 2 shows the changes in number of employees on nonagricultural payrolls between the first six months of 1971 and 1972, as well as the June 1972 index, for selected non-agricultural sectors.

TABLE 2. EMPLOYMENT IN SELECTED SECTORS
(in thousands)

Industries	1971	1972	Increase	Index June 1972 (1967=100)
All nonagricultural industries	70,558	72,117	1,559	110.2
Goods producing	22,544	22,670	126	97.8
Manufacturing	18,665	18,806	141	97.2
Service producing	48,014	49,446	1,432	116.9
Wholesale and retail trade	15,094	15,568	474	115.0
Finance, insurance, and real estate	3,770	3,897	127	121.6
Services	11,841	12,239	398	122.4
Government	12,797	13,220	423	116.8
Federal	2,660	2,664	4	96.8
State and local	10,137	10,556	419	123.1

Policy developments. This was more a year of implementation of manpower and employment programs previously adopted than of new policy departures.

Expansion of public service employment under the Emergency Employment Act of 1971 offered an opportunity to experiment with a form of revenue sharing: The federal government allocated about $1 billion in fiscal 1972 alone to units of state and local government to employ some 140,000 unemployed and underemployed workers and to expand essential public services. Preliminary evaluations of the program revealed both strengths and weaknesses. On the positive side, for example, the program was implemented quickly and participants placed in jobs that provided improved wages and fringe benefits. Negatively, training for the participants appeared to be minimal, and the program was not well integrated with other manpower programs and services, perhaps partly because of the swiftness with which the program was made operational. The program will continue into 1973.

Several mayors, in testimony before congressional committees, argued strenuously for substantial expansion of public service employment programs, in large part to provide relief for their hard-pressed budgets. A number of bills were introduced, but congressional action in the manpower and employment field was largely limited to amendment of existing legislation. One amendment to the Equal Employment Opportunity Act granted the Equal Employment Opportunity Commission power to take cases of alleged discrimination into federal courts for resolutions.

WALTER H. FRANKE

ENGLISH LITERATURE. This was a more positive year than last, and one in which almost all branches of literature reflected the country's major preoccupations—Britain's entry into Europe, events in Northern Ireland, and the assorted tensions of society: racialism, overcrowding, pollution, unemployment, the women's liberation movement, and a maximum surrender to the gadarene onrush of materialistic values in this tight island of 55 million people. Some of this (among the popular historians especially) was oddly reflected in the continuing fascination with Britain's vanished empire and its ideals and failures, reassessed in terms of bittersweet nostalgia or acute analysis. (Edward Grierson's *The Imperial Dream* was an excellent example of the latter.) The anguish of public and private conscience was not far to seek; a mood of sharp, bleak irony prevailed, taking many forms, including poetry. In Derek Mahon's *Lives*, for ex-

ample, the poetic image was rusty iron among the hollyhocks—the defunct machinery of a society at odds with itself in terms of aims, values, class, and generation.

Fiction. The clash of values and generations was the theme of C. P. Snow's *The Malcontents*—a novel remarkable in its own right and in the moral problems it raised, faced, and partially answered. The malcontents (they call themselves "the Core") are a group of seven clever, idealistic young people who have discovered something very nasty in the cathedral town they live in. If this wrong is righted, the balloon goes up and a well-deserved national scandal follows. Their motives are impeccable, their means debatable—in fact, illegal. What happens is the exciting narrative peg on which Snow hangs the deeper purposes of his haunting and disturbing novel.

Margaret Drabble's *The Needle's Eye* pleased not just her band of committed admirers but also many of those who have hitherto found themselves allergic to her fiction. This study of a once-rich woman's private conscience explores a heap of issues—exploitation, acquisition, parentage, the social falsities to which we all subscribe—with an unusual depth of mind and feeling. True, the rough, uncertain, would-be sophisticated edges are still there—the lobster thermidor, the Hampstead parties, the theatrical small talk; true, the critic who compared her to George Eliot was well off his compass bearings; but it remained a remarkable book.

For the light fantastic, there was Auberon Waugh's *A Bed of Flowers, or As You Like It*, a blend of fantasy and goodish social satire: only "goodish" because too many targets were the writer's particular and specialized prejudices. A tonic, high-spirited affair, nevertheless—which, considering that Waugh is now the most readable and ferocious reviewer of current fiction, was, for him, just as well.

In *Murgatreud's Empire*, Bamber Gascoigne achieved a similar blending of farce and morality, though here the scene was set among the pygmies of New Guinea and the morality centered around the West's lust for gold. Necessarily, it was a blacker affair altogether. On the Icarus front—the year's consolation prize for aiming higher than most—John Berger's *G* won wide acclaim for its daring attempt to reenact the pre-1914 romantic world of D'Annunzio and the early aviators. G, an Edwardian Casanova turned Don Juan, left the critics agog with the weight of his (and his author's) historical, sexual, artistic, and dialectical assertions. James Hanley, veteran of technique, reastonished his admirers with *Another World*, the hauting study of a group of human beings precariously held together in a set of relationships that collapses into general insanity. Here again near-farce—or black comedy—was a motif throughout.

Partisans of Nicholas Freeling's Maigret-type detective, Van der Valk, cursed his creator for killing off their hero at the climax of *A Long Silence*. Others who have enjoyed the Van der Valk saga but believe Freeling to be one of the most important novelists that the thriller market has produced in the past ten years were left to speculate on his development. Meanwhile, the historical novel produced its usual quota of tushery but little distinction, with the exception of Jill Paton Walsh's *Farewell, Great King* and George Garrett's *Death of the Fox*. The first is a finely sustained self-portrait of the Athenian leader Themistocles. (As the title suggests, the book takes the form of a letter addressed to the king of Persia by the statesman about to die.) The second is an imaginative evocation of the life of Sir Walter Raleigh.

The short story, for so long a relatively underrated form of fiction, took a splendid upward turn in 1972. This may be partly due to the expertise of William Trevor's *The Ballroom of Romance and Other Stories* and partly to William Sanson's brilliantly self-investigatory *The Birth of a Story*, in which he discussed the germ, development, and final manuscript of his famous "No Smoking on the Apron."

Environmental Checklist

AIR POLLUTION ☑ YES ☐ NO ☐ MAYBE

The air over the United States is less polluted than it used to be. The federal Council on Environmental Quality's air quality index, which takes account of three major air pollutants—sulfur dioxide, nitrogen oxides, and particulate matter—showed that in 1970 the air (as measured at 82 sites throughout the United States) was 10 percent cleaner than in 1969, which itself represented a 14 percent improvement over 1968. Only nitrogen oxides increased in quantity between 1969 and 1970.

LEAD PAINT ☑ YES ☐ NO ☐ MAYBE

In an effort to reduce the incidence of lead poisoning, which now afflicts between 50,000 and 100,000 children a year and kills about 200, many of them in ghetto areas, the Food and Drug Administration issued regulations on March 10 limiting the lead content of household paint produced in the United States. Beginning January 1, 1973, such paint may not contain more than 0.5 percent lead, and after December 31, 1973, the figure will be 0.06 percent.

DDT ☐ YES ☐ NO ☑ MAYBE

DDT, hailed as a miracle pesticide in the 1940's, was almost totally banned from domestic use effective December 31, 1972, as evidence mounted of its deadly effects on many species of wildlife and possibly even on man. Nevertheless, U.S. firms will continue to manufacture about 26 million pounds of DDT a year for export, either under the foreign aid program or for the World Health Organization's malaria control efforts. DDT may be used domestically on only 1 percent of all U.S. croplands.

BILLBOARDS ☑ YES ☐ NO ☐ MAYBE

About 35,000 fewer billboards and other commercial roadside signs were obliterating the American landscape in the summer of 1972. The signs were taken down in accordance with the federal Highway Beautification Act, which mandates the removal of all commercial signs within 660 feet of an interstate highway or other primary road, except in industrially or commercially zoned areas. About 800,000 illegal signs were still standing as of June 1, 1972; the target date for removal is 1976.

RECYCLING ☐ YES ☐ NO ☑ MAYBE

Some tentative new solutions to the problem of solid waste disposal appeared during 1972. The Tekology Corporation of Palisades Park, N.J., patented a process for manufacturing strong bricks almost exclusively out of garbage. A Brooklyn firm is using 150 tons of garbage a day as raw material for fertilizer, and the Garrett Research and Development Company of San Diego, Calif., is using 50 tons of solid waste a day to produce fuel oil. About 700 centers were collecting used aluminum cans, which were then recycled by the Reynolds Aluminum Company. One step backward: less paper was recycled in 1971 than in 1960. Contributing to the decline were freight-rate differences making virgin paper more economical than recycled paper.

Elizabeth Taylor's *The Devastating Boys and Other Stories* was the real triumph of this revival, splendiferous in its wit, range of character, and deployment of situation.

Poetry. The appearance of *Scorpion* made a fitting and unforgettable epitaph to the memory of Stevie Smith, who died in 1971. Death confronts the reader in almost all these posthumously published poems—an antithesis to the gay loquacity of the writer's fiction. William Plomer's personal, clubbable *Celebrations* kept the mandarin flag flying; Molly Holden, a permanent invalid whose poems have been described as "tall drinks for grown-ups," revealed her fine sense of nature in *Air and Chill Earth;* Mervyn Peake's *Selected Poems* afforded a powerful sidelight on the world of Gormenghast. Influences abounded: Harold Massingham submerged his originality in the ethos—and prosody—of Anglo-Saxondom (*Frost-Gods*); D. J. Hall (*Journey Into Morning*) was inspired by the wine-dark seas of Homer.

Letters and criticism. Women on women has been a remarkable feature of the year's successes in letters. Most notably, Jane Aiken Hodge's *The Double Life of Jane Austen* broke new ground in what had seemed to be completely developed territory. Marilyn Butler's fine study of *Maria Edgeworth* did break quite new ground—especially in her acute analysis of the Irish novels and of the lessons that Jane Austen and Scott learned from them. (Sir Walter himself towered majestically in W. E. K. Anderson's *The Journal of Sir Walter Scott,* the most distinguished job of editing to be performed in 1972.) The first two volumes of the *Journals and Letters of Fanny Burney,* edited by Joyce Hemlow and Althea Douglas, brought that lively gusher into fresh repute as a social chronicler of her age.

The first volume of Quentin Bell's beautifully skillful and candid biography, *Virginia Woolf,* accompanies Virginia Stephen down to her marriage in 1912—"the wisest decision of her life," as he describes it. Meanwhile, in his study of Aldous Huxley (*Dawn and the Darkest Hour*), George Woodcock contrasted the "intellectual clarity" of Huxley's early novels with Mrs. Woolf's "manifold obscurities." In *A Peep Into the Past,* Rupert Hart-Davis resurrected a sheaf of forgotten sketches and essays to grace Max Beerbohm's hundredth birthday. In *Jean Racine: Dramatist,* Martin Turnell achieved a feat of literary analysis.

History and biography. To take popular history first, the success of the year was undoubtedly Paul Johnson's *The Offshore Islanders,* a brilliant and racy survey of the island story from the Roman occupation to Britain's entry into Europe. Not only popular but also patriotic and spiritedly polemical, the book sets out the historical case for an England free of continental entanglements and international ideologies. Johnson's enthusiasms are for Elizabeth I and Cromwell, his sympathies Pelagian and indigenous, his unsympathetic treatment reserved for renegade Englishmen such as St. Thomas à Becket ("a man of concentrated energy, with second-class brains and no sense of proportion"). His lively layman's erudition left the dons a trifle winded— and for once appreciative. Other popular histories included J. B. Priestley's witty and perceptive survey of the 1850's (*Victoria's Heyday*) and Robert Kee's vivid and exhaustive history of Irish nationalism, *The Green Flag.*

As for the dons, Christopher Hill explored the erratic seventeenth-century sects (the Levelers, Fifth Monarchy Men, Muggletonians, and so on) in *The World Turned Upside Down,* and Richard Cobb continued his learned typology of the tumbril with *Reactions to the French Revolution.* Two great nineteenth-century prime ministers were well served, John Prest's *Lord John Russell* acting as a complement to the concluding volume of Norman Gash's *Sir Robert Peel.* It was a vintage year for biographies of British sovereigns, the most notable being John Brooke's *George III* and Philip Ziegler's *King William IV.* A. J. P. Taylor's vast— and vastly readable—life, *Beaverbrook,* and Christopher Sykes' chivalrous but perceptive study, *Nancy Astor,* helped

to put much near-contemporary history in a new perspective.

Poet laureate. On October 10, Sir John Betjeman was named as the new poet laureate, succeeding Cecil Day Lewis, who died in May. Sir John has achieved great popularity not only for his straightforward verse but also for his many television appearances and his efforts to preserve England from so-called progress. JOHN RAYMOND

ENVIRONMENT. In the United States the Environmental Protection Agency this year reported some heartening news, including prospects of zero pollution by 1985. The National Park Service celebrated Yellowstone's centenary and produced a definitive plan for conservation and recreation over the next 100 years. Also, a controversy erupted among environmentalists over whether population growth or industrial growth is the primary cause of environmental damage. But overshadowing all this was the long-planned United Nations Conference on the Human Environment, held June 5–16, 1972, in Stockholm.

Stockholm conference. The Stockholm conference was attended by some 1,200 representatives from 114 nations. The most conspicuous absentee was the Soviet Union, which objected to the exclusion of East Germany from full participation. However, this circumstance was to some extent offset by a little-heralded treaty of potential significance signed by presidents Richard M. Nixon and Nikolai V. Podgorny in Moscow during their meetings in May. This treaty, which provides for mutual cooperation in the environmental protection field, could serve as a model for further bilateral treaties, supplementing the Stockholm resolutions. Although the ultimate significance of the collective environmental agreements approved in the plenary sessions of the Stockholm conference remains to be seen, the resolutions surely may be considered "the first steps on a new journey for the future of mankind," one speech declared.

At many of the meetings there was obvious disagreement, some of which centered on the insistence of underdeveloped nations that they have a legitimate right to embark upon a path of industrialization unhampered by restrictive antipollution legislation formulated by developed nations. Also, the well-represented Third World countries felt that the developed nations should cease neocolonial resource exploitation and proceed as rapidly as possible to dismantle their war-based technocracies.

The three positive recommendations of the conference were a declaration of broad environmental principles, a plan for environmental management, and a proposal for a global environmental agency. The first, the declaration of general environmental principles, is intended "to inspire and guide the peoples of the world in the preservation and enhancement of the human environment." This statement, which lists in general terms a set of human rights and collective responsibilities for the environment, is essentially the same as the draft prepared some two years ago by an intergovernmental working group. However, some additions to the draft were made at the conference when China and several other nations objected that they had no representatives on the original working committee. In its final adopted version, this document contained four new principles: the conservation of wildlife; the prevention of pollution of the oceans; the stabilization of prices in developing countries; and the right to national self-determination on internal environmental standards. The last of this document's 26 principles, which called for worldwide efforts to attain an early consensus on the abolition of nuclear weapons and other methods of mass destruction, provoked much discussion.

The second proposal, the environmental management project, is an action plan incorporating specific recommendations to deal with pollution and conservation on an international basis. The action plan includes 106 recommendations approved by the conference; these fall into three general areas. The first group is intended to provide a global en-

vironment monitoring service called Earthwatch, which is to "identify and measure environmental problems of international importance and to warn against impending crises." The establishment of a worldwide network of at least 110 atmospheric monitoring stations was suggested. The second group, which deals specifically with environmental management, proposes to "work what is known or learned about the environment, so as to preserve what is desired and to prevent what is feared." The last category of recommendations is aimed at supporting such various ancillary activities as the dissemination of information, environmental education, and the organization and funding of environmental activities.

The third major proposal recommends establishing an environmental coordinating agency, known as the Governing Council for Environmental Programs, to be developed as an agency within the United Nations. As initially constituted, GCEP includes 54 nations. This recommendation was at first opposed from within the UN organization because of possible overlap between this new agency and existing UN agencies, from which the GCEP is to be independent. An environmental fund of some $100 million over a five-year period will be required to support the new agency; contributions totaling nearly two-thirds of this amount have already been promised.

The conference recommended that in 1976 the UN General Assembly review all the organizational machinery set up by the conference. In any case, the General Assembly at its fall meeting must ratify all these recommendations before they can be implemented. No major alterations are expected. There will subsequently, no doubt, be some disappointments. For example, the ten-year moratorium on all whale fishing recommended without dissent by the conference was not upheld by the International Whaling Commission, which met in London shortly afterward. At the insistence of the Soviet Union and Japan, whaling is still to continue but with reduced catch quotas.

Council on Environmental Quality. The third annual report of the President's Council on Environmental Quality, presented this year, reviewed the progress the United States has made in its attempts to control pollution and waste. The report encouragingly states that the United States is "winning the battle against air pollution." Unfortunately, water quality is still getting worse, according to the report, and the cost of the total environmental quality program continues to escalate.

Studies of particulates—carbon monoxide, sulfur dioxide, hydrocarbons, and nitrogen oxides—at 82 sites in the U.S. furnished the statistics for data on air pollution from 1968 to 1970. Emissions of the first two pollutants showed significant declines, whereas those of the second two showed no identifiable change; however, nitrogen oxides increased during this period by 4.5 percent. Fortunately, the Clean Air Act was enacted in 1970 to ensure continued improvements in air quality. Control over nitrogen oxides and hydrocarbons, as well as carbon monoxide, should be further improved with the implementation in 1975–1976 of controls on automotive emissions.

In a survey of major waterways, the council found that in 1970 and 1971 another 5,435 miles of waterways had become polluted, bringing the nation's total close to 80,000 miles. The continuing increase in waters polluted by phosphates and nitrates was attributed to increasing use of chemical fertilizers. Apparently, the extent of water pollution produced by organic wastes has also been underestimated. The Water Pollution Act, passed this year, is intended to permit complete control of water pollution by 1985.

The revised estimate for the cost of total pollution controls during the 1970's is now given as $287 billion—$93 billion for new capital equipment and $194 billion for operating costs. This amount represents 2.2 percent of the projected GNP for the decade, a significant increase over the 1.6 percent originally estimated for total pollution controls for 1970 through 1976. The new figure represents an average annual cost of over $100 per person in the United States.

Items not as yet released from the report of the Council on Environmental Quality include the topics of recycling, land use, and energy. The lack of recommendations on a national energy policy is generally regarded as particularly alarming. General resistance to most proposals for supplementing the number of energy-generating plants was strengthened during the year. Simultaneously, the electric power–producing industry reacted with increased public airing of its opinions on the results of such resistance. The related problem of land use has also become an urgent, highly political issue. Proposals for disposal of some millions of acres of national forest lands are soon to be brought before Congress. This issue cannot be separated from other problems arising from the need for recreational land use.

National Park Service. The National Park Service this year celebrated the founding of the world's first national park at Yellowstone in 1872 and its first 100 years of service to the United States. The Park Service marked this anniversary with a critical self-appraisal of its objectives and achievements, together with an analysis of the needs which it may be expected to fulfill in the future. Conferences at Yosemite and at Yellowstone recommended that while the main function of the National Park Service remains the preservation of wilderness areas and the provision of access to them, a new category of national recreational area is urgently needed to provide more ready access from major urban centers to open space. In the next 100 years the Park Service may have to regulate visitors' use of wilderness areas more closely, while simultaneously developing new and more readily accessible national recreational parks.

Population vs. industrial growth. Environmentalists debated this year over whether population growth or industrial growth was the primary cause of environmental deterioration. Proponents of views originally presented by Paul Ehrlich insisted that the primary action needed to prevent further environmental damage must be immediate reduction of population increase toward the elimination of population growth. Others, including Barry Commoner, maintained that, first of all, uninhibited industrial growth must be controlled. There are indications that these two camps may have reached a rapprochement in the interest of attaining their common objective, the preservation of environmental quality.

Environmental planning. The years 1971 and 1972 may in the future be heralded as the final turning point in the struggle to preserve the American environment and prevent its further deterioration because environmental impact studies became mandatory as essential prerequisites to any federally supported development. This requirement marked the beginning of adequate planning for integrated environmental management in the United States. In some countries—for example, in Great Britain, with its Clean Air Act and its Nature Conservancy Agency—this movement toward environmental conservation began considerably earlier. Although many other countries still are not ready for such concepts, the Stockholm conference may promote more awareness of the universal need for environmental planning.

ARTHUR S. BOUGHEY

EQUATORIAL GUINEA. Politics and foreign affairs. While Equatorial Guinea's ties with the Communist bloc, particularly China, remained close, economic considerations forced the small nation's mercurial president, Francisco Macías Nguema, to seek the cooperation of his African neighbors and to restrain the radical elements which were persistently harassing the few remaining Spanish interests in Equatorial Guinea.

On April 11 it was announced that formal agreement had been reached with Nigeria specifying working conditions and wage rates under which 15,000 recruited Nigerian workers would return to the coffee and cocoa plantations of Equatorial Guinea's island province, Fernando Póo. Since the 1930's the plantations have depended heavily on imported labor, first from Liberia, later, since World War II, from Nigeria. The recruitment system had always been subject to controversy; uneducated and naive immigrants rarely found working conditions consistent with those promised by recruiters. Most recently, the departure of Spanish plantation owners following the country's independence in 1968 led to a marked deterioration in working conditions, and Interior Minister Angel Macia readily admitted that over 20,000 Nigerians had returned home since 1969. Until this year the Nigerian government had been uncooperative in recruitment efforts, making repeated references to "near slavery conditions" in Fernando Póo.

In late 1971, President Macias also sought closer relations with the central African states contiguous to the country's mainland province, Rio Muni. Equatorial Guinea, along with Gabon, was admitted to the seventh East and Central African summit conference, and soon thereafter President Macias signed joint communiqués with the People's Republic of the Congo and Cameroon, pledging economic cooperation.

Economic developments. While labor shortages did not adversely affect cocoa and coffee production in 1970–1971, the 1971–1972 cocoa harvest was expected to drop by as much as 20 percent because beans were simply drying up on the trees. The only encouraging sign was Spain's continued willingness to purchase the entire crop at a figure above world market prices, its only form of foreign aid to the former Spanish colony. At the same time, production of Equatorial Guinea's other major export, timber from Rio Muni, also dropped sharply with the departure of several Spanish timbering companies. To complete this dim economic picture, the country suffered a virtual evaporation of Spanish private capital flows, without sufficient compensation in aid from the Communist bloc that President Macias had assiduously courted for two years.

Area and population. Area, 10,831 sq. mi. (Fernando Póo, 786 sq. mi.; Rio Muni, 10,045 sq. mi.). Pop. (est. 1971), 300,000. Santa Isabel (cap., 1960), 37,237.
Government. Single-party republic. Pres., Francisco Macias Nguema.
Finance. Monetary unit, peseta; 1 peseta = US$0.016.
Trade (est. 1966). Exports, US$26 million; imports, US$18 million. Principal exports: timber, cocoa, coffee.
Education (est. 1966). Elementary, 21,421; primary, 1,565; secondary, 986. GEORGE LAMSON

ETHIOPIA. Foreign relations. For several years the rebels of the Eritrean Liberation Front (ELF) have benefited from the Pan-Islamic position of Sudan and from meddling by Ethiopia in the civil war between northern and southern Sudan; northern authorities supplied the largely Muslim ELF with arms and money in a vain attempt to decrease Ethiopian involvement. After the abortive Communist-led coup against General Jafaar Muhammad al-Nimery's regime in July 1971, it became necessary for Sudan to solve the southern question and to diminish northern revolutionary activity. Nimery's government was receptive when Ethiopia offered to organize a series of meetings between Sudanese government officials and southern revolutionary leaders. After successful preliminary discussions, General Nimery came to Addis Ababa, where he and Emperor Haile Selassie I pledged to restore the status quo ante and to establish a joint frontier commission to investigate any border irregularities that might stem from an inaccurate 1902 demarcation. On January 1 the emperor traveled to Khartoum; he and Nimery signed a frontier protocol and a document that called for the extradition of "criminals," a term always used in Addis Ababa when referring to the ELF. On February 28 in Addis Ababa the Sudanese government negotiated a historic treaty with southern leaders that ended 15 years of bitter internecine strife. For his part in ending the civil war, and also to honor his other efforts at international arbitration and mediation, Haile Selassie became the first head of state to be awarded the United Nations Peace Medal.

Economic developments. Although there was a strengthening of the price of coffee and therefore an improvement in the economy, the government has postponed the completion of the third five-year plan by one year, to 1974. At most, only about 40 percent of the economy can be expressed in money terms, and it seems to be growing at an annual rate of 4–5 percent. Unfortunately, about 87 percent of the population is engaged in subsistence agriculture, the sector which has seen the least development. Manufacturing, which accounts for a small part of the gross national product, is improving at an annual rate of 15 percent and construction at 10 percent. Even so, Ethiopia invariably runs a trade deficit, estimated in 1970 at $44 million, which was covered by short-term capital imports, service charges, and tourism.

There are some economic bright spots: oil prospecting in the Ogaden and off the coast of Eritrea has yielded natural gas, evidence of petroleum reserves; West Germany has loaned Ethiopia $14,573,643 for construction of the first phase of the Dilla-Moyale road, which will open a considerable portion of Sidamo Province to economic exploitation; China stands ready to advance funds for further development of road transportation; a new $1 million steel-rolling mill has opened in Akaki, a few miles south of Addis Ababa; and a Japanese mining concern has discovered large deposits of copper, zinc, and other minerals in a concession area near Asmara.

Student unrest. Ethiopia's activist students, aggrieved by U.S. military and political involvement in their country as well as by parliament's refusal to grant laws regulating tenure and production, have attempted to forge a student-led alliance of peasants, workers, and intellectuals against the coalition of crown, nobility, and landowners. Their failure generally has increased their sense of grievance, and they miss no opportunity to embarrass the government. The February meeting of the Security Council in Addis Ababa proved to be such an occasion. Secondary school students chose that moment to launch protests against poor teaching and dictatorial school administrators. Student leaders at Haile Selassie I University immediately indicated support, and the end result was a general student strike at the university. The government responded with an ultimatum: those not back in classes by February 29 would be expelled. On that date classes were filled, but the next day they were empty again. On March 8 the government expelled all students who had not been in class since March 1; 1,463 students were forced to leave the campus, 48 percent of all full-time students, including 60 percent of the freshmen. Meanwhile, the police broke up a demonstration that had been planned for Africa Hall, where the Security Council was in session, and began arresting student leaders; thereafter, the police rounded up 500 expellees and sent them to detention camps. University faculty members expressed considerable shock at the government's severity, which was capped by the April–May expulsion of four expatriate teachers who were either involved in the student unrest or who had been arrested on drug charges.

There is reason to believe that a large number of expelled students might be readmitted to the university at the beginning of the second semester of this academic year, but there is no indication that student unrest will abate.

Area and population. Area, 471,778 sq. mi. Pop. (est. 1971), 25,600,000. Principal cities (est. 1968): Addis Ababa (cap.), 684,-100; Asmara, 190,500.

Government. Constitutional monarchy, with bicameral legislature (Chamber of Deputies and Senate). Head of state, Emperor Haile Selassie I; crown prince, Asfa-Wossen; prime min., Aklilou Habte-Wold; for. min., Ato Ketema Yifru.

Finance. Monetary unit, Ethiopian dollar; Eth$1 = US$0.40. Budget (est. 1969–1970): revenue, Eth$602 million; expenditures, Eth$631 million.

Trade (1970). Exports, US$122 million; imports, US$172 million. Major export: coffee.

Education (est. 1968–1969). Primary, secondary, and church schools, 2,013; total enrollment, 618,000. Higher education enrollment, 4,000.

Armed forces (est.). Army, 40,000; navy, 1,225; air force, 2,120; police, 32,000.   HAROLD G. MARCUS

EUROPE. There were few dramatic political, social, or economic changes in Western Europe this year, only a confirmation and continuation of trends already discernible in 1971. Stability, however, did not mean an absence of problems. The guerrilla war in Northern Ireland intensified as the Irish Republican Army continued to try to bring about reunification with the rest of Ireland by force; elsewhere in Britain, there were more labor strikes than in 1971, some of them more violent than any since the 1926 general strike. But Britain was not alone in witnessing a drop in prestige caused by internal problems and inflationary cost rises. In France a series of minor scandals weakened the stature of President Georges Pompidou and his Gaullist government, and in the German Federal Republic Chancellor Willy Brandt faced strong opposition throughout the year because of an erosion of his Social Democrat majority and a minor scandal involving two high officials. Finally, in Italy, a protracted presidential election was followed, five months later, by a stormy general election which only resulted in underscoring, once again, the irreconcilable differences between the Italian right and left—without providing any political group with a clear mandate or a ruling majority.

This year also saw the disappearance of several famous, durable personalities: Nubar Gulbenkian, oil millionaire and Riviera socialite of Iranian origin, died in January at 75; King Frederik IX of Denmark, a much loved democratic monarch, died at the age of 72; and the duke of Windsor, 77, died shortly after Queen Elizabeth had called on him while on a state visit to Paris. The whole world also paid tribute to Maurice Chevalier, the French singing star famous for over half a century, who died near Paris at age 83.

Northern Ireland and Great Britain. Headlines continued to focus on Northern Ireland throughout the year, beginning January 30 when a banned march of IRA members and sympathizers was dispersed by heavy fire from British paratroopers, who killed 13 of the demonstrators. The outcry was general and led to an increase in the level of bombings and murders and the increased gunning down by IRA snipers of British troops on patrol in Belfast, Londonderry, and Newry. In Dublin, an angry mob burned down the British embassy, and in protest Irish premier Jack Lynch temporarily withdrew his ambassador from London.

The Conservative government of Edward Heath was determined to try to reduce the grave Irish crisis to manageable proportions before Britain's effective entry into the EEC in 1973, and on March 24 a top-level politician, William Whitelaw, was given the task of restoring law and order in Northern Ireland while meeting the many justified grievances of the Catholic minority there. At the same time that Heath appointed Whitelaw, he dissolved the Ulster provincial government (known as Stormont from the location at Stormont Castle of its parliament and administrative offices), overriding the vocal and violent protests of the Protestant majority in Northern Ireland, which staged massive demonstrations and a two-day general strike. Some coercion was used to compel a minority of nonstriking Protestants to follow the movement, which led to a complete shutdown of factories, shops, and offices. The end of Stormont was deeply resented by the Protestant majority, which rightly saw it as the end of a privileged era and

the beginning of the end of the power wielded by the Orange movement.

Angered by continuing IRA violence, some Catholic housewives began peace demonstrations, but despite the mounting unpopularity of blind IRA acts of violence a short-lived truce was broken on July 9, and on July 31, British troops occupied "no go" fortified enclaves held by the Provisional wing of the IRA in the Londonderry and Belfast Catholic ghettos. This occurred with almost no bloodshed, and the Provisionals went into hiding. The "official" wing of the IRA meanwhile decided to stop all terrorist action, and within the Provisional wing an intense power struggle occurred, leading to the downfall of those Provisional leaders who favored political negotiations with Whitelaw and an end to terrorism. By September the Provisional IRA group seemed shaken and split, but the intransigent Sean MacStiofain was still in command. By the end of 1972, casualties since 1969, both civilian and military, had substantially passed the 600 mark, and the risk of undeclared civil war continued to rise with the growth of the Ulster Defense Association, a paramilitary Protestant extremist body reportedly grouping over 30,000 members with stockpiled small arms.

Apart from the expense of maintaining troops in Ulster and the punishing destruction of facilities, public buildings, and shops, the main reason for Edward Heath's determination to end the conflict was his concern for Britain's image as it was about to enter the EEC. British officials were already being selected and groomed to key jobs in the EEC commission, and a number of senior international civil servants of the original six member nations were prematurely retired to make way for officials from the new member states. But Britain's decision, on June 23, to float the pound in order to put a stop to a speculative run on sterling was severely criticized, especially by the French government, which inferred that Britain, faced with the alternative of obeying EEC rules or protecting its reserves, unhesitatingly chose the latter alternative. Britain's currency and Ulster difficulties were compounded by two lengthy strikes—of coal miners in January and February who turned many parts of the country into a replica of the blacked-out Britain of World War II; and of dockers in August who disrupted trade and were responsible for the temporary closing of pubs in the Shetland Isles.

These adverse conditions notwithstanding and despite continuing unemployment at over the one million mark, one aspect of British business activity proved that despite the slightly weakened pound, the city of London remained powerful as a worldwide and trend-setting banking center, for from early 1972 on, a large number of major British investing institutions began investing heavily in French stocks (both in anticipation of Britain's effective entry into EEC and to take advantage of the largely undervalued French stock market). As a result, some blue-chip French stocks doubled in value, and the average rise on the French stock market was over 30 percent by year's end.

France. The rise in French stock prices, after a ten-year stagnation, was for French industrialists the best news of the year. Otherwise, despite continuing prosperity and less unemployment than either Britain or Italy, the political climate in France was uneasy and almost entirely conditioned by the approaching general elections of 1973.

President Pompidou, who began the year with his prestige intact, inevitably came under fire, and it must be said that some of his detractors used ammunition of Pompidou's own making. Thus, in a press conference on March 16, Pompidou announced that he would hold a referendum in April to ask the French people to ratify by their vote Britain's entry into the Common Market. The referendum project was heavily criticized by opposition parties as a disguised form of personal plebiscite, and despite massive government propaganda on radio and television, the results were disap-

pointing: 39.6 percent of all voters abstained, and of those who voted, 68 percent voted in favor of Britain's entry, with 32 percent against—a poll which weakened, rather than strengthened, Pompidou's domestic status in France and also called into question the validity of France's becoming uncontested leader of the new enlarged European Economic Community.

Despite this disappointing result, Pompidou went ahead with arrangements to hold a summit conference in October with the leaders of the eight other EEC member countries —in the face of considerable reluctance from some of France's partners who would have preferred it to come after the U.S. presidential elections and West German elections. Pompidou's determination to go ahead with a summit conference was in part due to his realization that France was indeed almost alone in seeking a piecemeal approach to European problems and in emphasizing the need for widespread monetary reform, involving a probable further devaluation of the dollar and the pound and the end of the float of sterling. France again was almost alone in wanting to retain the costly European agricultural fund (subsidizing farmers within EEC) on its existing, expensive pattern.

The summit meeting to a certain extent restored Pompidou's image as a leader of the EEC. Although he failed to get a unanimous response to French views, he settled gracefully for a compromise. Hailed as one of the most important meetings since the Versailles Treaty powers met in 1919, the summit conference produced a blueprint for a real "European union" by 1980 but did not define the political scope of such a union. Moreover, several leaders dedicated to European unity felt that by not insisting on a definite date for "international" elections to the European Parliament, the summit had not been sufficiently determined in its bid for political integration.

In other summit developments, a decision was taken to assume a common approach to galloping inflation, the major crisis facing the European Community. Largely at Prime Minister Heath's request, a timetable was adopted for implementing a regional fund that would aid "distressed industrial areas" in EEC countries. The summit also provided for a European monetary fund to cushion, and if possible prevent, the kind of international panic fluctuations in capital which had marked 1971 trading. Regarding gold and dollar devaluation, French views were not adopted, and indeed President Pompidou himself largely skirted these issues in order to preserve the overall harmony.

On domestic issues, France also suffered, like other countries, from a decreasing prestige largely because of the excessive durability of its Gaullist majority. The 1973 elections, observers felt, are almost bound to result in a substantial decrease in the current 287-strong Gaullist majority in Parliament. This became obvious when a series of minor scandals was widely publicized in the French press. The revelation, in a satirical weekly, that Jacques Chaban-Delmas, French premier since 1969, had paid no income tax in 1967 and 1968 and only token sums in 1970 caused a sensation in France and led, on July 5, to his resignation at Pompidou's request. This occurred only partly as a result of the income tax affair, for over the past 18 months there had been a personal falling out between the two men. To replace Chaban-Delmas, Pompidou appointed Pierre Messmer, 56, an "unconditional" Gaullist (and former French Foreign Legion colonel) who, it was assumed, would be more subordinate and receptive to the president's wishes.

The French opposition parties also made considerable political capital out of a real estate scandal in which some members of the Union des Démocrates pour la République (Gaullists) were involved, and in August a police corruption scandal broke in Lyons, involving a ring of senior active and retired police officials allegedly protecting pimps and owners of houses of prostitution. Moreover, one Gaullist

deputy, Edouard Charret was linked to the scandal; he threatened libel suits against his detractors but was nevertheless shown to have had underworld connections. Later, the UDR was brought into further disrepute when Gabriel Aranda, a minor official once on the staff of former public works minister Albin Chalandon, began writing to French weeklies and enclosing photostats of correspondence from deputies and politicians to Chalandon. Each letter writer begged favors for business associates in pending lucrative contracts, and although no contracts were awarded as a result of such pressure, the prestige of the UDR suffered considerably. Aranda, charged with theft, was accused by President Pompidou of being unbalanced. In one field, the French police and customs authorities did produce unprecedentedly satisfactory results: with increased French cooperation with the U.S. Bureau of Narcotics and Dangerous Drugs, a number of clandestine heroin laboratories were raided in the Marseilles area, and several important but middle-level traffickers were arrested, among them Marcel Boucan, aboard his shrimp trawler *Le Caprice des temps,* found to be carrying about 930 pounds of heroin. The pressure put on heroin traffickers and manufacturers was such that, for the first time, U.S. officials in Paris believed that racketeers were contemplating moving their center of operations from Marseilles and seeking alternative routes to the United States by way of West Germany, the Scandinavian countries, and Spain.

West Germany. In the Federal Republic of Germany, Chancellor Willy Brandt's authority was in slight jeopardy after the resignation of his finance minister, Karl Schiller, on policy differences and the resignations of two parliamentary state secretaries found to have links with the popular German illustrated weekly *Quick.* The two men, both Social Democrats, were found to be on the payroll of *Quick* as consultants, and observers linked the leakage of a number of "inside" news items in that paper to their consulting role. The powerful West German business community, understandably wary of Brandt's moderate socialism, was known to be lined up behind the opposition Christian Democrats and Liberals.

All West European countries, whatever their governments, seemed particularly vulnerable throughout the year to inflationary pressures, averaging between 6 percent and 8 percent annually and particularly serious in the Netherlands, West Germany, and France.

West Germany was also the theater of the Olympic games in Munich and of an exceptionally bloody tragedy which overshadowed the athletic competition. On September 5 eight terrorists from Black September, an Arab guerrilla group, raided the Israeli quarters in the Olympic village, killing two team members as they entered and holding nine others hostage in exchange for all Palestinian terrorists then imprisoned in Israel. Although West German authorities reportedly attempted to bargain with the kidnappers, Prime Minister Golda Meir of Israel refused to allow them to save the mens' lives at the cost of releasing Palestinian prisoners. Later that day, all nine hostages, five guerrillas, and one German policeman died in a shootout at a military air base near Munich. Charges and countercharges reverberated. Palestinians blamed the Germans for the deaths; the Germans argued that, with any deals vetoed by Israel, their attempt to stop the kidnapping was the only recourse. In late October, to Israel's fury, the West German government freed three Palestinians arrested in the Munich incident after several Black September guerrillas hijacked a Lufthansa jet and demanded their immediate release.

The Munich tragedy, probably the most memorable single event of 1972, underscored a growing trend of the times— an overall 10 percent increase in crime throughout Western Europe, which, police chiefs claimed, was linked to greater population mobility. EDWARD BEHR

FASHION

comeback
for the
classics

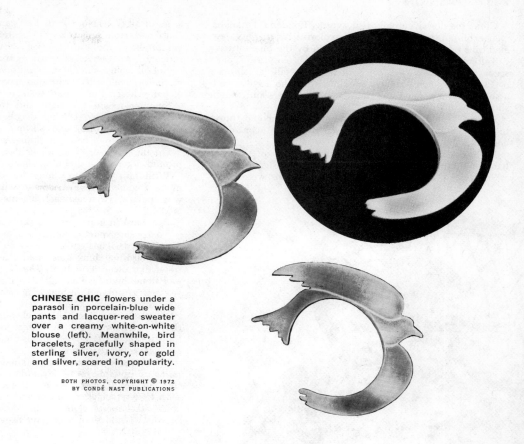

CHINESE CHIC flowers under a parasol in porcelain-blue wide pants and lacquer-red sweater over a creamy white-on-white blouse (left). Meanwhile, bird bracelets, gracefully shaped in sterling silver, ivory, or gold and silver, soared in popularity.

If in the past few years it has seemed to observers that there was a war going on in the fashion world—with designers and consumers as the opposing parties—this year might be viewed as a time of truce. In women's fashion, designers attempted a reconciliation by bringing back the classics, even including an emphasis on dresses and skirts; in men's fashion, there also was a cooling off, with the high-heeled shoe being the wildest innovation.

Women's Fashion

Fashion 1972 was shaped by evolution, not revolution.

It was made as designers wooed back their women, still alienated by the mini-midi aftermath, by an uneasy economy, and the influence of blue-jeaned young who put fashion nowhere compared to basics like ecology and poverty.

But clothes are basic. Clothes as fashion are big business. In New York City alone, the apparel industry houses 9,000 firms; 3,900 employ more than 200 people each.

So fashion designers faced with hesitant customers were bent on reconciliation.

Women everywhere got three fashion gifts. . . .

Variety—because nothing was really out except hot pants, midi hems (a few coats still carried those), and furs from animals on the endangered species list, like the Somali or snow leopard, cheetah, jaguar, tiger, and ocelot.

Newness—because width not length was the measurement of 1972 fashion. Width shaped tent coats, beltless chemise dresses, evening caftans, and batwing dolman sleeves.

Security—because the masquerade was over. Classic, wearable clothes replaced the costume look. And the classics, from twin sweater sets and sweater gowns to coats that wrapped and tied closed, offer an alternative to all that new width.

But costume did not become classic overnight.

President Richard M. Nixon's February trip to Mainland China put designers everywhere on the Orient Express for a brief fling with women in Honan-silk evening pajamas, lotus-patterned gowns, frog closings, mandarin collars, and colors with names like lacquer red.

But kids on both sides of the Atlantic had gotten to China first—with regulation coolie work tunics and trousers. The same group took to American presidential primary scenes in T-shirts marked with slogans from "Vote" to "Archie Bunker in '72." Still others ripped up old clothes and sewed different pieces together, making new jigsaw-patterned clothes that were labeled "recycled fashions." Ecology again.

China yielded eventually to Egypt as London's Tutankhamen exhibit inspired designers to colorful Nile prints, jeweled bibs patterned after the ones worn by the pharaohs.

Taffeta gowns rustled briefly across the early 1972 party scene, inspired by Yves St. Laurent's late fall '71 showing of Proustian gowns, ruffled and bustled. The 1940's made a short revival appearance via broader shoulders and wedgie shoes.

And early in 1972 the kitsch fad—which promoted throw-together clothes in such bad taste they were considered good fun—peaked and died.

Women caught between the ultimate in masquerade and bare closet space made peace with fashion designers.

Scattered throughout spring 1972 collections were proto-types of all the major trends that gained strength as the year continued, from tent coats to sweater looks. Even that fashion prodigal, the little fur jacket, made it back to spring runways. Another classic had returned.

Not all fashions made it. Traditional stocking seams, often in contrast colors like white on navy, legged it up the back of panty hose. But women walked away from the look.

Summer meant the bare and the beautiful. Designers went scissor-happy, cutting décolleté fronts, baring backs, slashing dress sides, and slitting skirts. Most long bare dresses hung by a halter neckline; a few were strapless.

On the cover-up side, an endless parade of long flower-printed organzas and chiffons floated through the nights.

With fall, the short dinner dress and short dinner suit made a comeback. For women who preferred pants, there were palazzo pajamas, each leg measuring 42 inches at the ankle.

Pants lost in importance as skirts and dresses gained.

To be sure, pants remained a major "classic" part of all American designer collections—with many pinstriped, cuffed pants (and matching pinstriped coats) showing a menswear trend that owed its debt to *The Godfather*. But in the Paris and Rome high-fashion collections, pants were in a minority.

Dresses jammed fashion runways, jostling the enduring sportswear separates that stayed in line.

Newest were the beltless chemise (other revivals were the sweater dress and, by year's end, the two-piece dress). Shirtdresses were labeled an all-time popular classic. Jumpers were cut like aprons.

Sportswear continued important—especially when as many parts as possible were layered, one over the other, onto the model. It was like a striptease in reverse. Starting with body stockings, models added sweaters, skirts, jackets, coats; the more clothes, the better. Even short-sleeved dresses were layered over long-sleeved blouses.

STRIKING A CAREFREE NOTE, this bright and breezy shirt-smock, in soft-fluffed wool and mohair, warms the way for a plaid-mad fall. It manages to square in smoothly with this year's soft plaid look.

ESSIE PINSKER ASSOCIATES, INC.

GOSTA PETERSON

MISTY in green and gray wool, this $90 classic, banded in gray and cross-stitched with a touch of red, joins the fall parade of sweaters. Cozy and versatile, packable and sensible, sweaters of every size and shape were big favorites again this year.

The classic suit (matched jacket and skirt with contrasting blouse) made a comeback. It was joined with sporty suits that mixed drawstring cashmere jackets with suede skirts.

Jackets were waist-short or swung like bells to mid-thigh. Long jackets were called toppers and worn most often over pants. Skirts, tied to one side, came pleated or bias-cut.

What was fashion made of?

Everything soft, anything plaid, and, as the year waned, neutral or pale colors.

Fashion fabrics meant warm-weather organza, silk chiffon, linen. Fall and winter produced soft cashmere, fluffy angora, natural alpaca, thick melton, chinchilla, or fleecy wool. Double-faced fabrics that looked reversible but were not joined the fabric list; so did gray flannel, satin, velvet, and winter corduroy.

Long-haired furs like fox, lynx, and raccoon were everywhere. And a little fur trimming proved a big fashion catch.

Designers of regular fabric clothes added fur sleeves, pockets, and bodices. They used fur to collar, cuff, and set foot-deep borders around fashion hems.

By night, the feathers flew as women adopted maribou jackets and trailed ostrich plumes from long gowns.

In patterns, designers were plaid mad—and they swiped tablecloth checks from the kitchen.

Colors eventually calmed down, blending into monochromatic schemes.

The model who once jammed a kaleidoscope of technicolor into one outfit faced fall and winter '72–'73 in one head-to-toe color. She wore neutrals: camel, gray, and white. She wore pastels: ice blue, pale pink. She varied that with all shades of red or a forest green.

And black, once back, stayed throughout the year.

In accessories, small head-hugging knit caps and cloches led the popularity contest, followed by medium or large brimmed felts. Veils, feathers, and jeweled decorations also appeared.

Jewelry ranged through ivory and wood to a revival of pearls. What else would you wear with those sweaters?

Shoes took a woman up in her world, helped by high-stepping platforms. Clogs clumped everywhere. Neat laced boots and saddle shoes (shades of the 1950's) appeared.

One ironic note for 1972: blue jeans swept Europe—and Americans started importing their national uniform from there.

The year also had its collection of promotional ventures and awards.

In Greensboro, N.C., a computer company announced its programmed machine had successfully "designed" fabrics.

BOTH PHOTOS, KEN REGAN/CAMERA 5

HEELS WITH SOUL

While older males settled back to more conservative designs and cuts the under-30 set gave the shoe industry a run for the money by trying on millions of the new multicolored high heels, capable of lifting the hardy soul anywhere from a modest inch or two to a flamboyant 5 inches off the ground.

In New York City, the French set up an apparel office to sell more ready-to-wear in this country. Mayor John V. Lindsay endorsed a new fashion group composed of designers, businessmen, and labor leaders—the Fashion Capital of the World. Its purpose: to promote New York fashions.

Coty fashion awards went to Halston, who did endless sweater fashions, and to John Anthony, who liked the menswear theme. A special award went to Dorothy Weatherford, whose designs are made by Mountain Artisans, a West Virginia group.

Bonnie Cashin was elected to fashion's Hall of Fame. Bonnie, generally credited with originating the layered look, proved designers were practical in 1972. Her innovations included biking fashions and city accessories like the body-pouch bag that fits under coats for foiling pickpockets.

In fashion as elsewhere, life-style was the good word. Never mentioned: the hem, which anchored quietly at the knee.   KATHY LARKIN

Men's Fashion

The only real fashion innovation for men in 1972 was the high-heeled shoe with the bump toe; if there was another, it was the tank shirt, which was simply a sleeveless undershirt that had been tie-dyed.

Otherwise, 1972 was a time of consolidation of trends. For both the wearer and the designer it had become obvious that men's fashion had gone as far as it could in the "peacock revolution" without becoming ludicrous or impractical.

Men's trousers, for instance, while maintaining a hip-hugger waist, were becoming fuller, even taking on the

baggy look of the 1920's, with a return of the cuff to complete the picture. The flared and bell-bottomed looks were still popular, but these were also becoming fuller.

Knits were everywhere, as they had been for some time—in shirts, sweaters, slacks, jackets, and increasingly in men's suits and formal wear. Tailored double knits in blends, all wools, and all polyesters were popular. The great styling possibilities in knits were still being explored, with designers finding knit fabrics more versatile to use than the woven fabrics, particularly for surface textures and colors. Colorful but subdued prints, checks, big herringbones, and other patterns were being used in sweaters, shirts, and jackets.

In jackets the single-breasted made an almost complete comeback. In casual wear the military jacket or the lumberman's jacket was in demand.

The layered look was still popular, with sleeveless sweaters over knit shirts in various color and fabric combinations. Vests made the layered scene, as did turtlenecks.

Topcoats and overcoats were catching the swing to the bigger look with more use of fabric. Coats featured the wide collar, the longer length, and the double breast. Furs and leather appeared as popular trim, with even greater use predicted. Fancy overcoats, in fact, were the symbol of fashion consciousness among the more affluent city dwellers who had to forgo bizarre styles in deference to the demands of the business world.

In shirts the button-down was back, and more white shirts were in evidence Stripings took over most of the patterning in formal shirt wear, with only a scattering of dots and curlicues.

The fashion trend in 1972 was more casual and more informal without extremes; styles were dictated by comfort and not effect. Older men were going in for youthful checks and the more highly styled suit; younger men were trying the high-heeled shoe and the casual knit shirt. Outside of an increasing use of the bare, browned chest and the slim jean, style kept its head all down the line, seeming to reflect the prediction of the Men's Fashion Association of America that there would be a return to elegance in 1973.

DUNCAN G. STECK

Hairstyles

The single most important change in hair for 1972 was the change from an accent on styling to an interest in and demand for scalp and hair treatments to produce healthy hair. As a result, many new "instant" hair-conditioning products were developed. Many hairdressing salons added hair and scalp treatments as a result of the interest shown, particularly by young people, in the organic, or so-called natural, hair care products. In a sense, the beauty business took an ecological direction.

The predominant hairstyle changed only insofar as many shag haircuts were being grown out; the easiest way to do this was to cut off the bottom layers of hair until the top layers caught up and evened out. As a result, the single most evident hairdo looked like the Prince Valiant, the serf, or the Buster Brown, a style that has long bangs and falls fairly evenly around the head but is not longer than the chin.

Hair shapes for other lengths of hair were more graphic. There were styles in all lengths of hair, from the chin to well below the shoulders, but the hair was always cut in a very distinct line—longer in the back and shorter in the front, or vice versa, or an even length all around.

Another interesting development was the return of Egyptian henna—a vegetable coloring agent that is applied to the hair in the form of a mud pack or paste. Henna can produce various shades, generally in the red family, but without peroxide or developers. The shades it produces depend upon the basic color of the hair and how long the henna is left on.

All kinds of hair decorations—barrettes, ribbons, and simple tortoiseshell combs to hold the hair in place or create a line—were in fashion. The demand for acrylic-fiber wigs continued to be great because the fibers have been vastly improved and because the styling has become more sophisticated and up-to-date.

KENNETH E. BATTELLE

FIJI. Domestic affairs. On April 15 and 29, elections were held on the Fiji Islands for the 52-member House of Representatives. The House now consists of 12 Fijians, 12 Indians, and three general members elected on communal rolls, plus ten Fijians, ten Indians, and five general members elected on national rolls.

In early 1973 a royal commission will be appointed to determine the most equitable and appropriate method of election and representation for the islands. The proposal will then be presented to the prime minister and the leader of the opposition for agreement and approval.

South Pacific Festival of Arts. In early May, Fiji hosted the first South Pacific Festival of Arts on Suva. The island swarmed with thousands of dancers, singers, artists, and craftsmen of mixed racial and ethnic backgrounds. More than 100 shows and exhibitions were on view during the two-week festival.

Area and population. Area, 7,055 sq. mi. Pop. (est. 1971), 531,-000.
Government. Appointed gov. gen., Sir Robert Foster; prime min., Ratu Sir K. K. T. Mara.
Finance. Monetary unit, Fijian dollar; 1 F$ = US$1.15.
Trade (1969). Exports, F$43,548,000; imports, F$77,900,000.
Economy. Basic crops: sugar, coconut oil, bananas.
Education (1969). Schools, 686; total enrollment, 231,429.

ABBY RAE ZUKERMAN

FINLAND. Politics and government. The year opened with a caretaker government in power and the holding of elections on January 2–3. The Social Democrats and Christian People's Party gained three seats each, but the political balance remained unchanged. After a month's negotiations a Social Democratic minority cabinet replaced the caretaker government in February, but it resigned on July 19 because it would not take responsibility for the signing of a free-trade agreement with the Common Market or an increase in old age pensions.

The rest of July and August was spent in finding a new cabinet. The first efforts of the Center Party proved fruitless until Kalevi Sorsa, secretary of the Social Democratic Party and foreign minister in the prior cabinet, was given a mandate by President Urho Kekkonen to negotiate for a majority coalition. He succeeded finally on August 29 in obtaining the agreement of the Center Party to increases in the pensions, and on September 4 the new cabinet was presented to President Kekkonen for appointment. Behind the scenes the president challenged tradition by addressing his own party's steering committee to ask them to support a coalition. His intervention helped to some extent in the formation of a ministry of seven Social Democrats, five Centrists, two members of the Swedish People's Party, one Liberal, and one nonpartisan. The new cabinet would have full powers to continue price, rent, wage, and other controls to cope with Finland's serious economic difficulties.

The formation of the prior cabinet by Rafael Paasio, leader of the Social Democrats, forced the selection of a new speaker in February, V. K. Sukselainen. During the spring all parties except the Democratic People's (Communist) agreed that a member of the Center Party should be president; Kekkonen agreed to run for another term in 1974, despite his 72 years and some opposition from members of his own party.

The Democratic People's Party decided to oppose the Social Democrats for their cooperation with bourgeois parties and to increase its fight against the capitalist class. These ideological stands meant the end of cooperation with any other parliamentary group in a coalition government and the exclusion of Communists from the parliamentary system.

The Diet passed laws for control of wiretapping, photography, and other possible invasions of privacy, enacted some changes in communal voting procedures, and abolished the death penalty, unused since 1825.

Foreign affairs. The decision in 1971 to drop negotiations for entry into the Common Market forced the two governments of the first half of the year to negotiate for a trade agreement to replace the European Free Trade Association that would cease when England and Denmark formally enter the European Economic Community. The treaty sought favorable duties on products of forest industries, chemicals, shipbuilding, and, to a lesser extent, the entire metals complex, covering approximately 60 percent of Finnish exports. A caretaker cabinet negotiated a favorable agreement on forest products, pulp, and paper in London on July 20 which allowed favorable prices and quotas on Finnish products and their share in the Common Market.

More than two months of negotiations led to formal recognition of the German Democratic Republic, Finland being the first European state to recognize that country. The government stated that conditions were ripe for such an action in view of the success in negotiations between West Germany and the Soviet Union and the likelihood of a treaty between the two Germanies.

In another move the Finnish government persevered in its attempt to host a European Security Conference in Helsinki during November. Western powers refused to accept the invitation until the Soviet Union made known its plans as to arms agreements and reduction of conventional forces.

Economy. The international recession increased Finnish economic problems. An immense deficit of 1.8 billion

WORLD CATCH OF FISH AND SHELLFISH[1]
(in thousands of metric tons)

	Fresh-water fish	Salmon, trout, etc.	Flounder, halibut, etc.	Cod, hake, haddock, etc.	Redfish, bass, etc.	Herring, sardine, etc.	Tuna, bonito, etc.	Mackerel, billfish, etc.	Crustaceans (shrimp, crab, etc.)	Mollusks, (oyster, clam, etc.)[2]	Other	Total
NORTH AMERICA												
Canada	23	102	172	316	115	473	10	16	19	56	76	1,378
Mexico	7	.....	3	.....	28	35	17	3	60	56	150	353
United States	37	190	86	79	119	967	191	4	310	602	129	2,714
SOUTH AMERICA												
Argentina	5	.....	2	87	33	14	5	10	1	16	42	215
Chile	.....	.....	3	83	8	865	6	12	36	36	115	1,161
Peru	80	.....	1	17	25	12,297	76	9	1	11	96	12,613
EUROPE												
Denmark	3	12	61	549	193	263	.....	27	6	20	95	1,226
France	.....	3	22	322	31	74	50	50	28	94	104	775
Germany, West	15	3	9	269	76	177	.....	2	38	10	17	613
Netherlands	1	3	67	65	3	60	.....	7	10	87	4	301
Norway	3	1,302	20	835	12	365	1	286	10	.....	149	2,980
Portugal	3	.....	1	202	9	66	8	28	1	14	128	457
Spain	9	2	18	554	97	179	69	41	35	238	255	1,497
Sweden	12	1	2	37	3	178	.....	4	3	3	57	294
Soviet Union (Europe and Asia)	410	98	271	2,765	892	1,111	13	326	40	71	1,255	7,252
United Kingdom	1	.....	61	715	17	178	.....	4	17	34	72	1,099
ASIA												
China, Mainland[4]	.....	.....	.....	.....	.....	.....	.....	.....	.....	.....	.....	5,800
China, Nationalist	21	.....	2	.....	98	39	124	44	40	35	210	613
India	670	.....	13	2	238	352	16	173	125	1	156	1,746
Japan	58	162	296	2,506	679	539	609	1,357	146	1,127	1,829	9,308
Korea	3	3	27	16	81	55	95	107	16	148	389	934
Pakistan	222	4	1	.....	68	4	12	14	30	.....	65	420
Philippines	43	.....	4	.....	205	93	23	60	39	.....	523	990
Thailand	107	.....	.....	.....	.....	.....	.....	140	132	266	950	1,595
AFRICA												
South Africa	3	.....	1	78	24	1,311	.....	82	9	2	99	1,606
OTHER COUNTRIES	5,229	217	103	823	592	1,455	355	237	468	376	1,505	11,360
World totals[5]	**6,950**	**2,090**	**1,240**	**10,320**	**3,640**	**21,150**	**1,680**	**3,040**	**1,620**	**3,300**	**8,470**	**69,300**

[1] 1970 data.   [2] Includes weight of shells.   [3] Less than 500 tons.   [4] 1960 data.   [5] Except in "Total" column, figures exclude any possible harvest by Mainland China, which does not report catch by species. Therefore, figures will not add across.

PREPARED BY DONALD R. WHITAKER

markka (approx. US$450 million) in foreign trade, an unwillingness to take strong measures on wage and price controls, and increases in pensions lessened the chances for a successful solution to the dilemma of inflation, lessening exports, and unrestricted consumer purchases. The new cabinet, formed in September, faced serious difficulties in its stated attempt to achieve economic stability and recovery. A wage agreement on March 18 raised hourly payments an average of 7.5 percent and caused dissension in the Diet, widening the gap between the Social Democrats and the Democratic People's Party. When an increase of 7.6 percent in farm prices and adjustments on farm labor wages were made, the Center Party protested and the Democratic People's Party condemned the agreement as class treason. The favorable indexes of the year were a manageable unemployment figure, the possible trade agreement with the Common Market, and an excellent harvest.

Area and population. Area, 130,119 sq. mi. Pop. (est. 1972), 4,638,000. Principal cities (1971): Helsinki (cap.), 523,677; Tampere, 157,697; Turku, 155,069.

Government. Democratic republic with one-house parliament. Pres., Dr. Urho Kekkonen; prime min., Kalevi Sorsa; for. min., Ahti Karjalainen; fin. min., Johannes Virolainen; def. min., Kristian Gestrin.

Finance. Monetary unit, markka; M1 = US$0.245. Budget (1971–1972, in billions of markka): revenue, 12.2; expenditure, 11.9. Gross national product, 42.9.

Agriculture and industry. Leading agricultural products: milk, butter, cheese. Leading industrial products: pulp, paper, metals.

Trade (1971, in billions of markka). Exports, 9.9; imports, 11.7. Leading exports: wood and paper, metals. Leading imports: industrial goods, fuels, raw materials, manufactured goods. Major trading partners: Sweden, West Germany, United Kingdom, Soviet Union.

Education (1970–1971). Enrollment: elementary schools, 474,299; secondary schools, 315,710; folk high schools, 8,098; universities, 57,299.

Armed forces. Army, approx. 31,000; navy, 2,000; air force, approx. 2,000.

RAYMOND E. LINDGREN

FISHERIES. World catch. According to the UN Food and Agriculture Organization, in 1970 the world fish catch rose almost 10 percent, to a new record of 69.3 million metric tons. In 1969 it had dropped to 63.1 million tons, the first decline in almost 25 years. The figures include marine,

freshwater, and diadromous (migratory between freshwater and saltwater) fish and mollusks, crustaceans, and other marine life; they do not include whales and seals.

Peru remained the leading fishing nation in the world, with a catch of 12.6 million tons, up from 9.2 million in 1969. Almost all of Peru's catch was anchoveta, a high-protein fish which is processed into fish meal for export as livestock feed.

Japan had the second largest catch, 9.3 million tons, up from 8.6 million in 1969. The Soviet Union was third with 7.3 million tons (6.5 million in 1969); then Mainland China, 5.8 million tons (estimated, since no official figures are released by the government); Norway, 3 million tons (2.5 million in 1969); and the United States, 2.7 million tons (2.5 million in 1969). Thailand was 8th with 1.6 million tons, and South Africa dropped to 9th with 1.5 million tons.

Catches by continents. All of the continents except Africa caught more fish in 1970 than in 1969. The African catch dropped by 100,000 tons, to 4.2 million tons, mainly because of catch declines in South Africa, the largest African fishing nation.

North American and Central American nations caught 4.8 million tons, compared with 4.5 million in 1969. The United States and Canada accounted for most of the catch. The U.S. catch was its highest since 1964, but still below that of earlier years; in 1956, for example, almost 3 million tons were caught. Cuba, continuing its steady catch rise, harvested 105,800 tons; in 1969 the catch was only 79,700 tons.

South America registered the biggest catch increase of any continent—from 11.3 million tons in 1969 to 14.8 million tons in 1970—largely because of Peru's increased harvest. Chile's catch also rose significantly, from 1.1 million to 1.2 million tons.

Asia's catch, the largest of any continent's, was its highest ever—26.2 million tons, up from 24.7 million tons in 1969. Japan was largely responsible for the increase. Thailand's catch increased significantly, to almost 1.6 million tons, up from 1.3 million tons in 1969.

The catch for Europe (excluding the Soviet Union) was 12 million tons, up from 11.3 million in 1969. Norway, Spain, Denmark, and the United Kingdom each exceeded 1 million tons.

Australia, New Zealand, and the southwestern Pacific islands harvested 190,000 tons, 10,000 tons more than in 1969.

Catches by species and areas. The greatest catch increases during 1970 were in marine fishes—from 48.3 million metric tons in 1969 to 53.5 million tons. Freshwater catches increased slightly—from 6.8 million tons to 7 million tons. There were also small increases in the harvests of crustaceans and mollusks.

Herring sardines, anchovies, and related species constituted almost 40 percent of the marine catch—21.2 million metric tons. The catch of South African pilchards dropped significantly, from 1.4 million tons to 0.7 million. Alaskan pollack, cod, hake, haddock, redfishes, and mackerel were all caught in larger quantities than in 1969.

The Pacific Ocean produced the largest catch—35.3 million tons, compared with 30.1 million in 1969. The Atlantic Ocean yielded 23.6 million tons (up by 1 million), about two-thirds of it caught in the northeast and northwest Atlantic. In the southeast Atlantic, where an international fishery convention is now operative, catches dropped from 3 million tons in 1969 to 2.4 million tons in 1970. The Mediterranean and Black seas, grouped within the Atlantic region, produced 1.1 million tons in 1970.

The Indian Ocean catch was 2.7 million tons, up by about 160,000 tons from 1969.

Disposition of catch. About 37 percent of the combined catch of 151 trading countries in 1970 went into foreign trade in one form or another. This figure was down from 40 percent in 1969 and 44 percent in 1968.

A little less than two-thirds of the world catch went for direct human consumption in the form of fresh, frozen, canned, or cured fish. Of the remainder, 37 percent was used to produce fish meal, and the rest went for miscellaneous purposes. The proportion of the catch used for fish meal was slightly larger in 1970 than in 1969.

DONALD R. WHITAKER

FLORIDA. Politics and government. The state legislature followed up its 1971 "reform" session by enacting a land-use law empowering the cabinet to buy up as much as 500,000 acres of so-called endangered lands. It also strengthened local controls over housing, traffic, and pollution; provided $192 million in a revenue-sharing plan for counties and cities; required Governor Reubin Askew to prepare a 12-year housing program; launched a family-planning service; created a loan fund for college students; and appropriated a record $1.6 million to the general revenue fund and $1.5 million to the trust funds for a total budget approaching $5 billion.

In March in a special referendum the people approved a constitutional amendment creating a two-tier court system with 142 circuit judges and 147 county judges replacing justice of the peace courts, city courts, and all lesser courts. After a California supreme court decision outlawing executions, the governor declared a moratorium on Florida executions. Subsequently, the U.S. Supreme Court declared current capital punishment laws unconstitutional.

Miami Beach was the site of both national conventions. The Democratic convention passed without major incident.

YOUNG AND OLD mingled peaceably in the Flamingo Park greenery as Democrats met in Miami Beach for their 1972 convention.

LAWRENCE FRANK/RAPHO GUILLUMETTE

However, during the GOP convention there were street demonstrations by nondelegates protesting the Vietnam war. Police arrested more than 1,100 (most of whom wished to be arrested) on the final night of the convention. No one was seriously injured.

Florida Power and Light Company got final permission to start up its huge Turkey Point nuclear energy plant. Its operation had been successfully halted for two years by conservationists.

Economy. A new boom developed during the year in Florida. It was so large that a few worried analysts who remembered disastrous 1926 were asking whether the balloon might burst. While expansion was statewide, it was most pronounced in the Orlando area, where Disney World drew over capacity crowds, and in south Florida, where overall business conditions expanded at an annual rate of 20 percent. In populous Dade (Miami) County, where in-migration was running at 48,000 a year, there were 25,983 residential housing starts in the first six months of the year in contrast to 16,431 in the same period last year.

All areas of the state had a banner tourist year, with some 24 million persons visiting Florida. Tourism is believed to yield about 65 percent of the state's income.

In May the unemployment rate fell to a low of 3.8 percent, in contrast to a 5.9 percent national rate. It then rose slightly during the summer.

Florida by law forbids branch banking. A continuing phenomenon this year was the growth in registered bank holding companies. Their number has increased from 17 companies and 175 banks in 1970 to 26 companies and 327 banks in 1972, either subject to Federal Reserve approval or already existing. Four of these companies top the $1 billion mark.

Education. In March the voters overwhelmingly adopted a school busing ban for achievement of integrated schools, despite a vigorous pro-busing campaign in this "straw ballot" election by Governor Askew. The voters also approved overwhelmingly quality education for all children and opposed a return to a segregated school system. In addition, the voters solidly supported allowing prayers in public schools.

Despite the referendum, the state's 1,836 elementary and secondary schools were forced to implement increased court-ordered busing for the purpose of racial balance; the schools opened in September without incident.

Of the $1.6 billion appropriated by the legislature from the General Revenue Fund for the next fiscal year, 65.3 percent—an increase—went to education. The legislature also provided for increased education equalization, raising the required local effort by 1.5 mills to a total of 6 (local financing accounts for 35 percent of all educational spending), and upped the state's per-unit contribution to keep pace with the program.

Florida International University opened its doors in Dade County in September with an enrollment of 6,000 students as the newest unit of the nine-university state system.

The legislature approved $29.4 million in new general fund appropriations for the university system and authorized the issuance of up to $65 million in higher education bonds for university, community college, and vocational-technical construction. At the same time, however, it rejected a comprehensive reorganization of the entire educational structure proposed by Governor Askew and a blue ribbon study commission.

For election results and campaign highlights, see the special supplement ELECTION '72.

Area and population. Area, 58,560 sq. mi. Pop. (1970), 6,671,-162. Principal cities (1970): Tallahassee (cap.), 71,763; Jacksonville, 513,439; Miami, 331,553; Tampa, 274,359.
Government. Gov., Reubin Askew (D); secy. of state, Richard Stone (D); treas., Tom O'Malley (D); cont., Fred O. Dickinson, Jr. (D); atty. gen., Robert Shevin (D); comm. of ag., Doyle E. Conner

FOOD FOR A FRACTION

Instead of idly gnashing teeth over rising costs, 12 Manhattan families formed a food cooperative to shop at the Hunts Point Wholesale Produce Market. Right, a wife takes her turn buying $72 worth of produce, supplying members for two weeks. Far right, food is uncrated and distributed equally.

(D); supt. of pub. inst., Floyd T. Christian (D). Legislature: senate, 33 D, 15 R; house of representatives, 81 D, 38 R.
Finance (fiscal year ending June 30, 1972). Cash on hand, $417,-485,405; total revenue, $5,045,634,221; total expenditure; $4,812,-219,514.
Education (1971–1972). Public elementary schools, 1,435, enrollment, 1,216,490 (grades 1–9). Public secondary schools, 473; enrollment, 327,207 (grades 10–12). Teachers: grades 1–6, 31,159; grades 7–12, 32,162. College enrollment (est. 1970–1971): junior, 147,820; 4-year state, 74,500.   DON SHOEMAKER

FOOD. World food supplies. This year there were signs that the total food supply of the world as a whole was keeping pace with the total population, and the imbalance had become that of a surplus rather than a deficiency. The major exporting countries, including the United States, limited the acreage sown to grain through several plans: the Canadian program called LIFT (lower inventory for tomorrow), which offered farmers $6 an acre not to grow wheat; the European provision for payment to farmers of a "denaturing" premium when their wheat was fed to animals and not to people; and similar arrangements by the Japanese government to restrict the production of rice. The fact that this state of affairs coexisted with recognizable malnutrition, as that resulting from the India-Pakistan war, has historical precedents. Current efforts by technologists to grow yeast and other microorganisms on petroleum hydrocarbons clearly demonstrate the complexity of the factors deciding whether people are well fed or not. Nevertheless, the change from adequacy to surplus in world food supplies must to a significant degree be credited not only to the steady improvement in agricultural techniques but also to extended cultivation of the new high-yielding short-stemmed strains of wheat and rice developed by intense scientific efforts encouraged jointly by the Rockefeller Foundation, the Ford Foundation, and the International Rice Research Institute.

Advances in nutritional science. Knowledge of the chemical composition of foodstuffs advanced significantly during the year. The continual development of increasingly refined methods of analysis has made it possible both to elucidate the molecular structure of the nutrient substances present and to detect the presence of extremely small but harmful concentrations of substances in foods. Some of the most interesting discoveries were related to the trace mineral

BOTH PHOTOS, HELLA HAMID/RAPHO GUILLUMETTE

components of food. For example, minute concentrations of chromium were found to possess nutritional significance. Chromium has been shown to play a part in the way in which glucose is utilized in the body and has been found in a variety of organs and tissues. In certain circumstances, young children appear to have less chromium in their bodies than now seems normal. Whether the metals vanadium, nickel, and zinc have any nutritional significance in human diets is not yet entirely clear; however, selenium has been found necessary. Studies on a variety of animals (with findings that can be assumed to apply to man) have demonstrated that the nutritional significance of traces of dietary selenium is linked with that of vitamin E. In view of the need for an appropriate concentration of selenium as a nutrient in the diet, it is interesting to note that a comparatively small excess is undoubtedly toxic, although an earlier belief that it was carcinogenic is yet unconfirmed.

Research has been done at the University of Wisconsin on 25-hydroxy-cholecalciferol, a substance that appears to be the metabolically effective form of vitamin D–active compounds. The findings culminate nearly 50 years of investigation; in 1924, what Professor Harry Steenbock and his co-workers at the University of Wisconsin first produced synthetically by irradiation as vitamin D, the antirickets vitamin, has subsequently been found to be a group of substances possessing varying antirachitic potency.

Food safety. The hasty banning of cyclamates in the United States in 1969 was followed by similar actions in a number of other countries, despite the fact that cyclamates had been used in substantial amounts for about 20 years without causing any recognizable harm to human beings. Now researchers have been investigating the safety of saccharine, a sugar substitute that has been in use since 1879, as well as other substances long included on the U.S. government's list of ingredients generally recognized as safe (called the GRAS list by food manufacturers). During these studies it has been found that lactose, the sugar naturally occurring in milk, causes untoward symptoms, usually mild and sometimes limited to diarrhea, to a substantial proportion of the adult population in many parts of the world. This condition of lactose intolerance is least common where milk continues to be drunk by

adults from their childhood on. Nevertheless, the widespread incidence of toxic symptoms from a foodstuff such as milk, long esteemed for nutritional value, has drawn attention to the existence of a variety of toxic ingredients in an extensive list of natural foods, ranging from potatoes, containing solanine, and vegetables of the cabbage family (*Brassica*), containing goiter-producing agents, all the way to myristicin in nutmeg. The fact that such admittedly poisonous compounds are consumed in what experience has shown to be wholesome diets is leading to a reassessment of the harm likely to be done by food additives, the toxicity of which can only be shown after their having been administered to experimental animals in concentrations far greater than humans would ever consume.

For all the controversy over the allegedly toxic effects of food additives or of DDT and other contaminants, a far more serious threat to health is evidenced by those persons afflicted by food poisoning as a result of bacterial contamination. They numbered in thousands in every country where medical records are kept. In the United States, a number of cases were reported of canned soup infected with *Clostridium botulinum*, the microorganism which produces a toxin more lethal than any other known compound.

Food technology. Developments continued in so-called fabricated foods, the most notable being texturized vegetable protein (TVP) processed into the form of meat and normally made from soya protein. Production plants were brought into operation for the manufacture of analogues of beef, lamb, pork, bacon, chicken, and much else on a substantial scale. Either a spinning process similar in principle

to that employed in fabricating nylon or one of several extrusion techniques is used. Progress was also made in developing a technique for making meat analogue from the mycelium of a fungus of the genus *Fusarium* grown in a manner similar to that used in making penicillin. These meat analogues found their use largely as ingredients of manufactured meat products in the industrialized countries in which they were produced, just as margarine, developed a century earlier as a butter analogue, is also used as part of the diet of technologically developed countries. The use of fabricated soya protein illustrates the peculiar attractiveness of meat to Western tastes; in the East soya beans are converted domestically by a fermentation process into a kind of cheesecake called *tempeh,* thus contributing equal nutritional value while suiting a different taste.

Another notable development in food manufacture was the continued advance in freezing technology. Liquid nitrogen, of which four parts are present in the liquid air from which it is prepared for every unit weight of oxygen produced, can add a new excellence to food manufacture. Prepared foods, including such items as pizzas, can be taken hot from the cooking and within 90 seconds frozen with flavor intact by liquid nitrogen at a temperature of −198° C.

Community nutrition. Concern over the nutritional adequacy of the food available to communities in different parts of the world has commonly been based on calculations of the nutritional value of the total supplies. Only since significant evidence was presented at the White House Conference on Food, Nutrition, and Health in late 1969 has it become apparent that total food supplies may not give a true picture. Poverty and malnutrition can exist as serious public-health problems even when total food supplies are ample and considerable attention is being given to the manufacture of low-calorie slimming diets. This observation has served in some degree as a turning point in current views on food science. The establishment of standards of composition for

staple foods, including the enrichment of bread with vitamins and iron, the consideration of the protein level of breakfast cereals, and the supplementation with synthetic amino acids of foods used in developing nations can be of nutritional benefit to the communities eating such foods; however, the economic standards of the separate groups of which every community is composed must equally receive the attention of food scientists.

See also the special article NUTRITION.

MAGNUS PYKE

FRANCE. Politics. On July 5, President Georges Pompidou dismissed his prime minister, Jacques Chaban-Delmas, and appointed Pierre Messmer in his place. Several factors led to this change in government leadership. Earlier in the year, Chaban had been embarrassed by the disclosure that he had paid little or no income taxes for the past several years. Although no proof of evasion was forthcoming, Chaban's explanations, made on national television, appeared to be less than convincing. Chaban also had been somewhat of a glamour figure in French politics, enjoyed an independent political base, and thus threatened Pompidou's total control over his government. With general legislative elections scheduled for March 1973, Pompidou wanted to install a man closely identified with the Gaullist political machine. Finally, General Charles de Gaulle had made it a rule (to which Pompidou was the exception) that no prime minister should serve more than 3½ years—that is, one-half the length of time of the president's mandate. Pompidou, in this way, sought to perpetuate some of the Gaullist tradition and underline the difference in status between the chief of state and the administrative head of the government. Messmer, 56 years old, served for many years as defense minister under Michel Debré, Pompidou, and Maurice Couve de Murville, when those men were General de Gaulle's prime ministers. He was minister for overseas and occupied ter-

KEYSTONE

A TAXING SITUATION. Jacques Chaban-Delmas defends his integrity in a television interview after disclosures that he had paid little or no income tax for years. Later, President Georges Pompidou, who had become increasingly disenchanted with Chaban, fired him as premier.

ritories under Chaban-Delmas. Messmer was an old colonial bureaucrat whose overseas administrative service began 30 years ago. He joined the Free French in 1940, went to Indochina in 1945, where he spent some time in a Vietminh prison camp, and held a variety of posts there until 1948. He was thus closely involved with the events that led to the first Indochinese war between the French and the Vietminh under Ho Chi Minh. He left Indochina early enough not to be associated with the French defeat that came in 1954. Messmer, aside from his governmental and administrative posts, has led the national action group of the Gaullist party, Présence-Action du Gaullisme. This has given him direct communication with and control over local party leaders and cadres, placing him in an ideal position to organize the Gaullists for the forthcoming general elections. Unlike Chaban, he does not have an independent political base, relying on his orthodox Gaullism to maintain himself on the right side of Pompidou. His selection as prime minister at this juncture suggests that the right-wing, unimaginative face of Gaullism will be presented to the voters next year. Messmer made few changes in the cabinet. One important addition was Edgar Faure, appointed minister of social affairs, labor, and health. Faure was minister of education briefly after the upheaval of May 1968. At that time he attempted to introduce a series of educational reforms that responded to the criticism of the university system raised by the student revolutionaries. Faure went too far in alienating the established bosses of the Gaullist party and was summarily cashiered. His reappearance will give to the cabinet a modern "progressive" tone that it had lacked. It remains to be seen how Faure will fare in translating this into serious reform, especially since the "tough cop" of 1968 and 1970, Raymond Marcellin, remains entrenched in the Ministry of the Interior.

A further contributing factor to Chaban-Delmas' political execution was the tepid response of the French electorate to a referendum on the enlarged European Economic Community (EEC, or Common Market) April 23. Gaullist political choreography includes at least one referendum every two or three years as a way of sanctifying the regime's claim to be more directly in touch with and responsive to the people. It will be recalled that the late general himself abdicated on the morrow of an unfavorable referendum on a rather trivial issue. This time there was no constitutional issue to be tested; the enlargement of the EEC to include the United Kingdom, Ireland, and the Scandinavian countries needed no legislative or plebiscitary sanction. What Pompidou was doing was testing his own political apparatus to see if it could deliver the votes that would be crucial next March. The apparatus was found wanting. Of those who bothered to vote, 67 percent approved the government's program. But that figure represented only 35 percent of the total electorate, since 46 percent either abstained or handed in blank ballots. Pompidou had launched an extensive propaganda campaign in favor of the referendum and had called for a "massive" yes vote. He cleverly combined an appeal to French nationalism, emphasizing the benefits to accrue to France, with the European's legitimate concern about the massive power of the United States and the Soviet Union, pointing out that only a united Western Europe could match the economic capacity of those superpowers. Most of the opposition, especially the left, campaigned against the referendum. The Communist Party called for a no vote, and its leader, Georges Marchais, claimed full credit for the results. The Socialists supported abstention. They did not oppose the enlargement of the EEC on principle. They did oppose the referendum as a device used by Pompidou to boost his own popularity. On the "radical" (anti-Communist) left, Jean-Jacques Servan-Schreiber supported the referendum as a way of differentiating himself from the rest of the left. But in doing so, he contributed ammunition to the arsenal of those who have never accepted him as a

serious politician representing a distinct political position. Servan-Schreiber is the latest in a long line of contemporary French politicians who hope to stake out a center position between the Gaullists on the right and the Socialist-Communist position on the left, thus aiming to make themselves indispensable. The problem with this tactic recently has been that such men cannot put together a substantial base, and they wind up being used by the Gaullists without achieving any benefit in the shape of a personal political reward. If Frenchmen want to vote anti-Communist, they have no reason to vote for a man like Servan-Schreiber when they can vote for the genuine article, represented by the Gaullist Party.

Shortly before the cabinet change, the leaders of the united Socialist parties and of the Communist Party, François Mitterrand and Georges Marchais, met to confirm the final text of a "united front" political program. For the first time since a similar agreement in 1934 ushered in the short-lived Popular Front, the great majority of the French left rallied behind a common program designed to form the basis of a governing coalition—should the occasion arise. Such efforts had been attempted in the past and invariably foundered on the deep distrust the Communist and the non-Communist left held for each other. It appeared for the moment that Pompidou's conservative economic policies would unite the left in a way that not even de Gaulle could manage. The Popular Front had foundered on the unwillingness of the Communists to take ministerial responsibility in a government that did not provide adequate guarantees for their working-class constituency. This year's united front platform attempts to avoid a repetition of that disaster. Both parties agreed that if in power a serious split develops between them, neither will call for new elections—effectively throwing everything up in the air—and both will try to close the breach. Other items in the program included the nationalization of all financial sectors, the banks and the insurance companies, mines, oil refineries, nuclear plants, chemicals, and pharmaceuticals. It also called for a sharp reduction in the discretionary powers of the president of the republic, a 40-hour week for all wage workers, pensioned retirement at the age of 60, and a minimum wage of 1,000 francs per month (roughly US$200). Servan-Schreiber was invited to join this alliance, but he refused, preferring to take his chances with a centrist "third force" between the Gaullists and the left.

The economy. The economy remains the most important issue in French political life. The regime has prided itself on maintaining ever-increasing reserves of gold and hard currencies. Its gold reserves now exceed those of the United States by almost 50 percent. This monetary strength has been purchased, however, at a high price, namely deflation and a high rate of unemployment. Bowing to pressure from businessmen and faced with a renewed series of strikes by workers in the public sector, the government relaxed its currency and economic controls. It would not have done so had not the signs been exceedingly ominous—for instance, a 39 percent rise in unemployment during 1971. Valéry Giscard d'Estaing, the architect of deflation and tight money, announced a series of measures in the winter and spring designed to reduce the pressure. He realigned currency exchange rates applying to imports and exports to effectively devalue the franc by nearly 3 percent in relation to the currencies of France's major trading partners. In March, he modified a strict system of price controls that had been introduced to hold down inflation. All businesses employing less than 20 workers, which accounts for 97 percent of all French enterprises, were freed from price controls; other enterprises remained limited to price increases of 3 percent a year. Other measures included the large-scale reimbursement of the value-added tax (a form of sales tax) to reduce costs and thereby to increase production and employment and the budgeting of an additional billion francs in loans

DEATH TRAP. A young man is rescued from the wreckage of a six-car train that derailed and was then crashed into by a second train inside a mile-long railroad tunnel near Vierzy. Over 63 persons died in the rail disaster, which was one of the worst in French history.

GAMMA

and subsidies for housing and public works. In a move that appeared to be aimed at increasing French investments abroad, the government relaxed exchange controls and promised more direct support for franc investments in foreign areas. All commercial and business transactions between Frenchmen and foreigners were to be placed under government guarantees rather than allowing the franc to float freely in such instances. In a related move, the French came to terms with the Iraqi government, which had seized a foreign oil-producing consortium, 20 percent of which was French owned. The French agreed to accept the expropriation, in return for which the Iraqi government pledged itself to maintain the regular flow of oil to France. The owners of the other 80 percent were left to make whatever deals they could.

Foreign affairs. President Pompidou met with British prime minister Edward Heath in England in mid-March. They announced a "complete identity" of views on forthcoming European economic and monetary union, galvanized by the entry of the United Kingdom into the Common Market. Three items formed the basis of the agreement: a reduction in the margins of fluctuation among the currencies, Britain's immediate and total participation in the administration of closer economic and monetary union, and joint control of the movement of capital among the EEC nations. Political questions, such as the location of the EEC's permanent secretariat, the staff of the secretariat, its role in the community, and designation of special ministers for European affairs were discussed, but no conclusions were reached. Both men also agreed that the dollar ought to be brought further in line with other currencies and that the gold standard ought to be reinvigorated as a significant element in the international financial system. They also discussed the progress of the Concorde supersonic transport project, which has been running into delays and substantial cost overruns, and the projected under-channel tunnel. Later in the year, the joint French-British channel company received final confirmation of its existence, and the project is expected to get under way shortly. It has

been over a century since the first French under-channel tunnel company was formed.

President Pompidou and West German chancellor Willy Brandt met twice during the year as part of their regular series of semiannual meetings between French and German leaders inaugurated during the de Gaulle regime. In February they concentrated mainly on questions relating to the expansion and solidification of the EEC. They agreed on the need for greater political cooperation among the member nations and on the urgency for moving ahead quickly on economic and monetary union, especially as regards the rate of fluctuation among the various currencies. They also agreed on providing a greater role in monetary controls for the central banks of the member nations as a way of easily coordinating monetary developments. As was the case in the French-British conversations, Pompidou and Brandt agreed on the political secretariat in principle, without spelling out its shape and character. The French also supported West Germany's campaign to sign nonaggression treaties with countries of eastern Europe. The July meeting between Brandt and Pompidou made little progress. German response to French pressure resulted in its fixing tighter exchange controls to prevent speculators from playing on the uncertainties associated with the dollar-gold crisis. Otherwise, the meeting was occupied mostly with a reiteration of positions.

Another important area of foreign affairs involved the development of new markets for France's armaments industry. Israel will be reimbursed, with interest, for the 50 Mirages ordered, paid for, but never delivered. France contracted to sell to Lebanon unspecified "military equipment." In January, Jean de Lipkowski, secretary of state for foreign affairs, visited Greece, the first high-ranking Western European official to do so since the coup of 1967. Lipkowski discussed the possibility of Greek membership in the EEC, dropped hints about selling Mirage fighter-bombers to the Greek Air Force, and expressed great French interest in the financing of public works and industrial projects in Greece. Two bombs exploded near the

French embassy during Lipkowski's sojourn. The Greek government characteristically blamed "terrorists."

"Maoist" militance. Not a year has passed in France since the revolution of 1968 when some small repetition of the violence of protest and related government reaction did not occur. This year was the year of "Maoist" militance. On February 25, René-Pierre Overney, a self-styled Maoist revolutionary, was shot down by guards outside the huge Renault auto plant in suburban Paris. He and his comrades were trying to storm the place and agitate among the workers. These same workers had been among the most militant in 1968 and did not need the agitation of the street revolutionaries. Nevertheless, most of the left denounced the shooting and pointed out that the presence of armed guards at the plant contravened the rules of the state-owned Renault works. On the day of Overney's funeral, a crowd estimated at 100,000 strong followed the cortege. Notably absent from the demonstration was the Communist Party and the Communist Confédération Générale du Travail (General Labor Federation). The Communists denounced both the shooting and the young militants calling them "Maoist provocateurs" exploited by the government in order to oppress honest workers. It does appear that the French left might perform greater services for the French working class by turning out such numbers in the streets for improved conditions and an end to the policy of deliberate high unemployment. On the other hand, the Communists, never noted for their openness to anyone not within the movement, could not be expected to support a confrontation of "Maoists" with the police.

Penal reform. France has shared with other countries the social upheaval inside prison walls resulting from antiquated, if not barbarous, conditions and out-of-date penal philosophies. In December 1971, prisoners in the Toul penetentiary rioted for several days. The following month, an even larger and more destructive prison riot took place at Nancy, where part of the main cell block was burned down. The government commission appointed to investigate the incidents at Toul reported back within the month. It recommended that the entire top echelon of the prison staff, from the warden down, be dismissed and maintained that exces-

sive discipline had been used against the prisoners. The Nancy riot precipitated a general series of reforms, promulgated by the decree of the minister of justice, René Pleven. The reforms provided for the appointment of more highly qualified staff, the improvement of prison inspection boards, improved vocational training within the prisons and higher wages for working prisoners, social security protection for the families of prisoners, and a clearer definition of the rights and status of prisoners to remove them from the discretionary powers of the wardens, some of whom had clearly abused that power. Finally, Pleven fired the warden of the Toul prison and his entire staff.

Reorganization of the ORTF. Since 1968, when the creative and production staff of the ORTF (Office de Radio-diffusion-Télévision Française) joined their fellow workers in the great strike of May, the state-controlled communications complex has staggered from crisis to crisis. The pressure of events in 1968 forced some relaxation of bureaucratic control over the production of programs. Reforms promulgated the following year delivered a certain amount of production control into the hands of the staff—a staff, however, purged of the leaders of the 1968 strike. This year the morale of the ORTF plunged to its nadir. Payola arrived at French television. A series of scandals revealed that announcers and directors had been receiving payoffs under the table in return for pushing products on television and in general promoting clandestine advertising. Several high officials of the ORTF were intimately involved and were forced to resign in May even after the prime minister, Chaban-Delmas, strenuously and unwisely defended their innocence in the Chamber of Deputies. A parliamentary committee convened to probe the scandal ascribed the situation to general inefficiency, top-heavy bureaucracy, ill-defined rules on advertising, and an authoritarian attitude on the part of the ORTF's chief officials. Reorganization of the ORTF later in the year did not go very far in treating the causes of the disease. Some of the symptoms were masked. State control was reaffirmed, and the definition of the public service role of the ORTF carried with it a restricted right to strike on the part of its employees. The director general was given tighter control over the news department and for the first

AT THE GATES. Author Jean-Paul Sartre arrives at a government-owned Renault plant to protest the February 25 killing of a Maoist demonstrator by an armed factory guard. The incident triggered the largest leftist demonstrations in Paris since the violent strikes of May 1968.

time exercised that control directly, without intermediaries. The ORTF's board of directors now is divided equally between representatives of the government, who hold 50 percent of the seats, and representatives of the public, the press, and the ORTF staff, who hold the other 50 percent. This means that in any tight situation the government will maintain control, since it would have to recruit only one extra vote among the public representatives. The redefined news policy, reflecting the reaffirmed state control, if anything will prove to be a regression from the liberalization of 1969. Appointed director general was Arthur Conte, a Gaullist deputy. This appointment was widely criticized as exceedingly inappropriate, since the ORTF will play a major role in the campaigning before the general elections of March 1973. Conte, for his part, pledged himself to absolute impartiality.

Skyscrapers unlimited. Until recently, the height of new buildings constructed in Paris was restricted by law to eight stories in order to preserve the uniform skyline of the city and prevent the blocking of the magnificent vistas for which the city is justly celebrated. These restrictions no longer apply. Since the middle of the 1960's, an orgy of skyscraper building has produced a jagged and, architects and planners say, an aesthetically unpleasant skyline. The building began with the Maine-Montparnasse complex on the left bank. Two massive office buildings and some lesser structures reared up behind the demolished ruins of the old Montparnasse railroad station. The rationale for placing the new buildings at that location was the massive exodus of white-collar workers to the southern suburbs from where, supposedly, they could easily gain access to the new offices by commuter train. Some of this has happened, although the infusion of automobiles by way of the Autoroute du Sud has choked the already impossibly congested streets of southern Paris. Also on the left bank, a series of skyscrapers has risen along the banks of the Seine near the Eiffel Tower, marching downriver from there like so many steel and glass robots. The buildings are neither clustered nor spaced evenly, but simply planted at assorted distances from one another. Finally, due west of the city, at the Place de la Défense, another group of high-rises is being constructed to add to the industrial-commercial complex already implanted in that area. The effect of this building has been to intrude on what is perhaps the most famous urban vista in the world: the sight line from the Place de la Concorde to the Arc de Triomphe along the axis of the Champs-Elysées. While the urban sprawl of Paris has spread to the suburbs, creating a metropolitan area of about 10 million persons, Paris congestion has accelerated unabated. To handle the situation, an east-west express subway is in the process of completion, as well as superhighways along both banks of the Seine. Rather than encourage the reduction of automobile traffic into the city, this latter project and the digging of several underground parking garages in the center of town have delivered Paris totally, and it is feared irrevocably, into the hands of the automobile.

See also INTERIOR DESIGN.

Area and population. Area, 210,039 sq. mi. Pop. (est. 1971), 51.26 million. Principal cities (1968 census): Paris (cap.), 2,590,771 (metropolitan region, 8,196,746); Marseille, 889,029; Lyon, 527,800; Toulouse, 370,796.

Government. Fifth Republic. Pres., Georges Pompidou; prime min., Pierre Messmer; for. min., Maurice Schumann; min. of fin., Valéry Giscard d'Estaing; min. of def., Michel Debré; min. of the int., Raymond Marcellin.

Finance. Monetary unit, franc; 1 franc = US$0.1995 (financial rate). Budget (est. 1972), 190.3 billion francs. Gross national product (1970), 805 billion francs.

Trade (1971). Imports, US$21.006 billion; exports, US$20.327 billion. Major exports: machinery, textiles, automobiles, aircraft, agricultural produce, luxury goods. Major imports: machinery, other capital goods, chemical products, coal, crude oil.

Armed forces. Army, 324,900; navy, 69,300; air force, 104,000.

SANFORD H. ELWITT

GABON. Government. In early February a cabinet reshuffle gave President Albert-Bernard Bongo control over economic decision-making. President Bongo, while remaining minister of defense, information, planning, and national development, assumed the newly created portfolio of territorial organization. The former minister of finance and budget, Augustin Boumah, became minister of state, directly responsible to President Bongo for three economic portfolios. Two former ministers of state, Paul Moukambi and Simon Essimengane, moved out to become, respectively, minister of finance and budget and minister of industry and tourism.

At the opening session of the Gabonese National Assembly on April 18, President Bongo reaffirmed his concern for economic progress and dedicated his government to the principles of directed economic liberalism and national unity.

Foreign affairs. President Bongo announced that on April 28 he had been reconciled with General Yakubu Gowon, Nigerian head of state. Relations between the two countries had been disrupted by the Nigerian civil war, since Gabon had allowed its capital to be used as a staging post for the flying of arms and supplies to Biafran secessionists.

Economy. The Gabonese economy continued to flourish. Production of crude oil reached nearly 6 million tons, with 12 wells producing. The oil refinery at Port-Gentil increased its capacity to over 900,000 tons per year, and officials were studying plans to construct additional refining facilities. Agreement was also nearing on a $250 million project to build the first stage of the trans-Gabon railroad, which will ultimately open up new timber areas and permit the export of iron ore from Mékambo in eastern Gabon. As a result of its mineral and timber wealth, Gabon has the third highest per-capita gross domestic product in Africa.

As elsewhere in Africa, a wave of economic nationalism is beginning to lap the Gabonese shores. In a radio and television address to the nation on June 6, President Bongo urged all foreign firms locating in Gabon to give 10 percent of their stock to the Gabonese government so that the government could represent the Gabonese public and its interests within company councils.

Area and population. Area, 103,347 sq. mi. Pop. (est. 1972), 646,000.

Government. Former French colony, now single-party republic. Pres., Albert-Bernard Bongo.

Finance. Monetary unit, Communauté Financière Africaine (CFA) franc; 1 CFA franc = US$0.0041. Budget (1972): revenues and expenditures balanced at US$125 million.

Trade (1970). Imports, US$80 million; exports, US$121 million.

LYNN KRIEGER MYTELKA

GAMBIA, THE. Politics and government. On March 28–29, in the first elections held under their republican constitution, Gambian voters kept President Dawda Kairaba Jawara's People's Progressive Party in power. The PPP ended up with 28 of 32 seats, the same margin it had held in the previous Parliament, with the opposition United Party retaining three and an independent capturing the remaining seat. In an undramatic campaign, UP and independent candidates attacked government use of administrative facilities for political purposes and urged expansion of educational opportunities, greater attention to young Gambians, and reduction of the country's dependence on foreign businesses and the tourist trade.

Despite such pressures for change, Jawara's new PPP government included only one new face among nine ministers. But the president reassured his opposition that he had no intention of leading the Gambia into a one-party system.

Traditional links with Great Britain, Taiwan, and other Western interests were promptly reaffirmed, and Foreign Minister Andrew Camara pledged to continue his country's cautious pursuit of integration with the Republic of Senegal, which surrounds the Gambia on three sides. In late July the Gambia decided to apply for association with the European Economic Community. EEC association was expected

BEATING THE BLIGHT. The graceful American elm, long a victim of the creeping fungus that blighted this once-shady lane in Waukegan, Ill. (right and below), may again become the nation's most popular shade tree; the Elm Research Institute in Waldwick, N.J., has been developing a promising cure for the deadly Dutch elm disease.

ELM RESEARCH INSTITUTE

to bring increased economic aid from the six current members as well as export benefits for the Gambia's main cash crop when Great Britain, the principal importer of Gambian peanuts, joins the EEC.

Economic developments. Peanut production and exports prospered this year, as did the European tourist trade. These revenues helped offset growing imports, unemployment, and rising prices at home. The current three-year development program stresses agricultural diversification and self-sufficiency; technical assistance from Taiwan and a loan from the World Bank are being used to help curtail increasing rice imports from Burma. The current development plan also calls for the accelerated construction of educational institutions, roadways, and tourist facilities. The port of Bathurst was being improved, and an airport expansion project, assisted by British funds, was soon to begin.

Area and population. Area, 4,361 sq. mi. Pop. (est. 1971), 400,-000. Bathurst (cap.; est. 1971), 40,000.

Government. Presidential republic within the Commonwealth of Nations. Pres., Sir Dawda Kairaba Jawara.

Finance. Monetary unit, dalasi; 1 DS = US$0.5230. Budget (1972–1973): revenue, US$10.3 million; expenditure, US$10.5 million.

Trade (1970–1971). Imports, $22.3 million; exports, $16.1 million. Groundnut sales (1971–1972), 123,769 tons (9% over 1970–1971). Chief items of import (1967–1968): rice, wheat, sugar, beverages. Chief items of export: groundnuts, palm kernels, dried and smoked fish, and groundnut oil.

Education (1970). Enrollment: primary, 16,230; postprimary, 4,012; teacher training, 155; vocational training, 120; students at universities abroad, 99. Schools: primary, 94; postprimary, 28; teacher training, 1.

PHILIP M. ALLEN

GARDENING. Developments in asexual reproduction. Two scientific developments in the asexual reproduction of plants have opened up exciting possibilities for the home gardener. In prospect are the crossbreeding of totally unrelated species to create new hybrids and the propagation of genetically tailored ornamentals, forest trees, and plants that are resistant to both disease and insects.

At Brookhaven National Laboratory in Upton, N.Y., biologists succeeded in growing mature plants by fusing cells of different species in a test tube; previously, plants had to be

hybridized sexually—by transferring pollen from one parent plant to another. (According to Mendel's law, sexually produced hybrids cannot reproduce themselves true to form; to maintain new flower varieties, the seed has to be set each year by hand pollination.) At Brookhaven, the crossbred plants can breed true because they developed from somatic cells, not sex cells, and contain two equal sets of chromosomes.

The other achievement was the first test-tube tree, an aspen now at the U.S. National Arboretum in Washington, D.C. It began with tissue culture in laboratory glassware at the Institute of Paper Chemistry in Appleton, Wis. This process could eliminate decades of inbreeding in pursuit of desirable, genetically mixed strains of trees. It also could be the means of mass-producing trees that do not breed true in nature.

Hope for the American elm. The Elm Research Institute, dedicated to saving the American elm from Dutch elm disease (DED), which has killed tens of thousands of these trees in the United States, has a program expected to protect 95 percent of these trees. It includes a dormant spray of methoxychlor, then a mist spray of methoxychlor combined with the systemic fungicide Benlate, and daily checking during the three crucial months of June, July, and August for signs of wilting. If there is wilting, Benlate is injected into the trunk and the wilted branches are pruned within three days. This institute, in Waldwick, N.J., has been responsible for planting hundreds of thousands of small elms, because it is confident that by the time these young trees reach maturity, DED will be under control.

Other developments. Growth regulators and artificial lighting are being utilized by scientists to speed the growth of many plants. At the University of Minnesota in St. Paul, cyclamen has been raised from seed to flowering size in half the usual time—just nine months—by the use of gibberellic acid. At the U.S. Department of Agriculture's research service in Beltsville, Md., horticulturists used aluminum foil to repel leafhoppers, a minimum of insecticides, and night lighting with floodlamps to grow maples four to six feet tall in three months instead of three years. These and similar results will ultimately reduce the retail cost of ornamental and house plants.

As gardening becomes more popular, the search for biological controls and natural predators of insect pests continues. Because so many pests have been imported, teams from USDA's research service are studying the methods of control of insects and diseases in their native habitats.

BEA JONES

GEOLOGY. The geological sciences continue to make rapid progress in a number of areas in which data are being collected for the first time—and on a grand scale. The Apollo 16 (United States) and Luna 20 (Soviet Union) missions sampled for the first time the moon's highland areas, terrains which make up 70 percent of the lunar surface. The Third Lunar Science Conference was held in January, and much new data and many new hypotheses were presented. The Mariner 9 mission made the most extensive photographic study of the surface of Mars, resulting in several exciting new discoveries.

The moon. The Third Lunar Science Conference was held at the Manned Spacecraft Center in Houston. It lacked some of the excitement of the first conference, which dealt with the initial moon-landing flight, Apollo 11, but scientists showed more confidence in presenting hypotheses.

By far the most important result to come out of the meeting was clear evidence that the moon is layered and contains a crust and mantle. Nafi Toksoz and his co-workers at the Massachusetts Institute of Technology showed that the moon's crust in the Fra Mauro region of Oceanus Procellarum consists of two distinct layers of igneous rocks. The upper layer is basaltic rock and extends to about 25 kilo-

meters (km.). The lower layer, about 40 km. thick, consists of anorthositic or noritic (KREEP) rocks, or both. (The term KREEP was coined to refer to rocks which are richer in potassium, K, rare earth elements, REE, and phosphorus, P, than the moon rocks initially studied.) Beneath the crust is the lunar mantle, which was reported to have an apparent seismic velocity of about 9 kilometers per second (km./sec.), a value much higher than that of the earth's upper mantle. The lunar crust has a seismic velocity of 6.8 km./sec. The 65-km.-thick lunar crust is thicker than the earth's, which is 5 km. for the oceans and an average of about 35 km. for the continents. The lunar crust constitutes 7–10 percent, by volume, of the moon, whereas the terrestrial crust is less than 0.5 percent of the earth's volume.

Verification of the lunar crust's thickness came later in the year, after a meteoroid slammed into the moon on May 13 with an energy equivalent to 2,000 tons of TNT. Geophysicists had been awaiting such an impact so that they could determine the structure of the lunar interior. Study of the event allowed correction of the seismic velocity of the lunar mantle to 8.1 km./sec., which is a figure very similar to that of the earth's upper mantle and implies that the rocks of the lunar mantle are rich in olivine and pyroxene.

Also reported on at the Third Lunar Science Conference were the data gathered by two remote sensing instruments carried on Apollo 15. One was an X-ray spectrometer, which was detecting aluminum/silicon and magnesium/silicon ratios of rocks on the lunar surface. The other was a gamma-ray spectrometer, sensing the natural decay of potassium, uranium, and thorium. The X-ray intensity profile confirmed the widespread occurrence of anorthositic rocks over wide areas of the lunar surface. The gamma-ray profile results were more surprising. Nearly all of the radioactivity was concentrated in one place in Oceanus Procellarum, where it is adjacent to Mare Imbrium, and there was a small concentration on the lunar backside. The radioactive material probably comes from noritic (KREEP) rock. Since that type of rock has been found in widely separated lunar soil and rock samples, scientists were surprised to find that its sources are concentrated in only one or two places on the lunar surface.

Two other important aspects of the lunar interior were reported at the meeting. The heat-flow experiment at Hadley base (Apollo 15 landing site) showed that the moon is giving off more heat than expected, 3.3 ergs/cm.²/sec. This finding has led to the hypothesis that most of the radioactive material has been concentrated near the lunar surface by igneous fractionation, although there has been some speculation that it fell onto the surface in the late stages of accretion. Evidence from lunar electrical conductivity and seismicity indicates that the present-day interior is relatively cool, 800°–1,000°C. The magnetic results indicate that most rocks have definite magnetic remanents. The question of whether the moon had a liquid core and its own magnetic field early in its history remains open. There is also the possibility of shock magnetization caused by impacts, or of an external magnetic field imposed by a nearby planetary body. All of the hypotheses suggested have serious drawbacks, and the origin of the moon's magnetic field remains a puzzle. .

It has now been clearly established that precursors of amino acids were found, in very minor amounts, in Apollo 11, 12, and 14 samples. These compounds are the starting materials for the evolutionary development of life and have recently been found in the Murchison meteorite. Thus, the building blocks of life appear to be present in other parts of our solar system. Evolution on the moon to and beyond amino acids was probably stopped because the water necessary for further changes to life was not present.

The Apollo 16 mission to the Descartes region in the Central Highlands was completed in April 1972. This is the only mission by the United States that is planned for a

terra region, that is, a region believed to be covered by what is left of the outer crust of the moon. The astronauts collected an estimated 212 to 240 pounds of rocks—the biggest haul yet—in what was a highly successful mission, except for the loss of a heat-flow experiment.

The rocks collected by the Apollo 16 astronauts looked like black and white breccias, and some looked like crystalline rocks. However, very few looked like basalt, which is what some lunar geologists were expecting to find. It was not immediately clear whether the rocks represent early lunar crust or later volcanic materials. The Apollo 16 gamma-ray spectrometer revealed that the Fra Mauro region has a high radioactivity level, similar to that discovered by Apollo 15 at Oceanus Procellarum. Another mystery was opened up when a rock which is rusty was found. How the iron could get rusty without the presence of water on the moon presents a puzzle. However, it should be pointed out that earlier missions found highly controversial evidence that small amounts of water may have been present on the moon.

The unmanned Luna 20 mission returned to the Soviet Union in February 1972 with soil and rocks drilled from the Apollonius Mountains, which form an isthmus between Mare Crisium and Mare Fecunditatis. Preliminary results indicate that the rocks are rich anorthositic and KREEP rock materials.

Mars. Mars, the earth's neighbor since the beginnings of the solar system, was photographed in detail for the first time this year by Mariner 9. Photographic coverage of a large portion of the Martian surface was obtained, and the results were spectacular.

Mars, once thought to be moonlike, is actually a geographically complex planet. It has elevation differences of 15 km. and has at least five different geologic areas. Scientists are finding that Mars is differentiated chemically (with evidence of past volcanism), has had extensive tectonic activity, and shows evidence of erosion by wind, water, and thermal effects. Wind patterns are observed to rotate—toward the north at morning, south at noon, northwest at midnight. The ubiquitous channels seem to indicate erosion by water in the past. Surface temperatures range from 81°F in the equatorial zone to −189°F at the poles, but there are temperature differences all over the surface. Strong gravitational anomalies were found which imply that large stresses are at work. Spectacular photographs of canyons with tributary channels caused by water erosion, sand dune fields, volcanic calderas, faults, lava flows, and oval tablelands have caused an upsurge of interest in Martian geology. Scientists are now using Mariner 9 data to select candidate landing sites for two 1976 flights by Viking spacecraft.

MARTIN PRINZ

GEORGIA. Legislation. After a frustratingly factional initial year in office, Governor James E. Carter finally rallied his forces this year and prevailed upon the legislature to approve, in one form or another, his program to streamline state government. In effect, the legislature's action consolidated some 300 boards and agencies into 24 departments. A specific result of reorganization was the creation of a department of administrative services with control over state purchasing, personnel, and transportation.

A record $1.32 billion state budget was approved for fiscal 1973, as was the so-called Sunshine Bill, requiring meetings of government bodies to be open to the public, with certain exceptions. Eighteen-year-olds were given the legal rights of adulthood, including the right to buy liquor, but a bill calling for a liberalized state abortion law was withdrawn by its sponsors when it became clear that election-year opposition to such a measure would prove insurmountable. A positive action was the establishment of the Judicial Qualifications Commission, which will oversee the courts and keep an eye on the conduct of judges.

Economic development. Georgia's burgeoning economy continued to be one of the strongest in the Southeast. Manufacturing output expanded with impressive strength, and the unemployment rate fell somewhat. Banks, enjoying the acquisition of substantial demand deposits and wanting to support expanding consumption, further increased consumer credit.

The state continued as a mecca for tourists, and the tourist industry prospered. Totals for 1971, a record year with total travel spending in Georgia reaching $1.2 billion, were far surpassed this year.

Education. An early childhood development program, the forerunner of a public school kindergarten program, was approved by the general assembly, but in a form considerably reduced from the governor's original request. The $75–100 million program will, at the outset, be planned and implemented by local school boards.

Municipal developments. The 1972 legislature created a new authority to supervise construction of toll roads in the state and also approved a package of bills which could lead to the construction of the $35 million World Congress Center in Atlanta. Financing for the center remained doubtful.

Environment. Strong enforcement powers were given to an environmental division of the state natural resources department. And even though protection legislation for the much-abused Chattahoochee River and a measure for the development of a scenic river system failed, Georgians were not losing their environmental conscience. The "golden isles" region, 525,000 acres of islands, marshlands, and estuaries along the coast, is being earmarked for resorts and public beaches, preserved as national seashores and outdoor museums, restored as historic sites, or reserved for marine science organizations.

For election results and campaign highlights, see the special supplement ELECTION '72.

Area and population. Area, 58,876 sq. mi. Pop. (1970), 4,589,575. Principal cities: Atlanta (cap.), 496,973; Columbus, 154,168; Macon, 122,423; Savannah, 118,349.
Government. Gov., James E. Carter (D); lt. gov., Lester G. Maddox (D); secy. of state, Ben W. Fortson, Jr. (D); treas., William H. Burson (D); comp. gen., John L. Caldwell (D); atty. gen., Arthur K. Bolton (D). General assembly: senate, 49 D, 6 R, 1 ind.; house of representatives, 173 D, 22 R.
Finance (year ending June 30, 1972). Revenue, $1,212,843,449; expenditure, $1,158,220,625. Balance on hand, $90,950,097. Principal sources of revenue: sales tax, income tax, motor fuel tax, and tobacco taxes. Principal items of expenditure: education, highways, and health and welfare.
Education (1970–1971). Public elementary schools, 1,477; enrollment, 628,667; teachers, 29,314. Public secondary schools, 355; enrollment, 333,257; teachers, 15,734. Public institutions of higher education, 16 senior and 12 junior; enrollment (1971–1972), 105,424; faculty, 5,544.

JAMES I. ST. JOHN

GERMANY. In May the West German Bundestag ratified treaties of friendship that the government of Chancellor Willy Brandt had negotiated with the Soviet Union and Poland in 1970. Defections by Socialists and Free Democrats who opposed ratification cost Brandt a working majority in the Bundestag. Thus, a general election was held on November 19, several months before the government had served its full term, the first such occurrence in the history of the federal republic. The Socialists and Free Democrats once again received a majority of the vote between them, indicating the formation of a new coalition government headed by Chancellor Brandt.

The Two Germanys

Berlin accords. The Brandt government in 1970 had set as a condition of treaty ratification a satisfactory settlement of the tensions surrounding Berlin. The four powers governing Berlin—Britain, France, the Soviet Union, and the United States—negotiated a Berlin settlement in August 1971. After difficult negotiations the accords between the Germans were initialed in December. They provided security from harass-

BIRTH OF A BLIMP. The first German-built dirigible since World War II is eased out of its hangar in Mulheim, West Germany. Filled with noninflammable helium, this whale of an airship is specially designed for displaying advertisements and carrying outsize loads.

ment for travelers and goods crossing the German Democratic Republic to and from West Berlin, eliminated a few enclaves on either side of the Berlin border, and allowed West Berliners limited visits to East Berlin and the GDR. In order to shield East Germans from a deluge of affluent West Berliners, automobiles could not be used in most cases and only 30 days of visits could be accumulated each year. The accords represented the first significant political agreement between the two Germanys.

The East German government under Communist Party chief Eric Honecker follows a policy of *Abgrenzung* (fencing off) toward the Federal Republic. But the Soviet Union, in the interest of general détente with the West, apparently pressured Honecker into the Berlin accords as well as into a number of other conciliatory steps taken this year.

Although the Berlin accords would not take effect until West Germany had ratified the friendship treaties, in the spring East Germany allowed West Berliners visiting privileges for two weeks, at Easter and Whitsunday. Restrictions on travel across the GDR were also lifted during those weeks. In May a new traffic treaty was initialed, the first agreement between the two Germanys that held the status of a state-level treaty. It provided for visits by West Germans to the GDR and for very limited visiting privileges for East Germans to the West.

Basic treaty. The outstanding event in relations between the two Germanys this year was the initialing on November 8 of a treaty designed to begin normalizing relations. (Formal signing and ratification would follow the election.) A number of issues were involved in the negotiations.

West Germany considers the two states as one German nation with special relationships—for example, joint athletic and cultural activities. It envisions no exchange of ambassadors, but rather an exchange of representatives of ministerial rank. Also, four-power rights over Germany would remain in force, signifying the existence of a single nation.

East Germany, on the other hand, wants to be recognized as a fully independent nation, with the customary exchange of ambassadors. It also wants to restrict person-to-person contacts. Exposure to the West's higher living standard and freedom of speech and press might produce the same widespread dissatisfaction that led to the emigration of more than one-quarter of the East German population prior to the erection of the Berlin Wall in 1961.

In exchange for a treaty, it was understood that West Germany would drop its policy of requesting friendly states to withhold diplomatic recognition from the GDR. Both the GDR and the Federal Republic would gain admission to the United Nations. The GDR, in addition, would be able to join a number of specialized UN agencies to which the Federal Republic now belongs. In May the World Health Organization rejected the GDR's bid for membership, making the GDR ineligible to attend the UN Conference on the Human Environment in Stockholm.

Actions by several neutral states had shown that a basic treaty would soon be concluded. An agreement on diplomatic recognition of the GDR by Finland was initialed in September; Sweden put out diplomatic feelers on the same subject; and Switzerland and the GDR exchanged trade missions that also carried out some consular functions, such as the granting of visas and the provision of legal assistance.

Optimism about the treaty stemmed chiefly from the East German party communiqué from the Crimean conference of East European Communist Party heads in late July. It spoke of "peaceful coexistence" and "the further development of intergovernmental relations." This indicated continued Soviet pressure on the East Germans to come to terms with the Brandt government.

Federal Republic of Germany (West Germany)

Politics and government. Ratification of treaties with the Soviet Union and Poland negotiated in 1970 was the outstanding political issue in the Federal Republic this year. The treaties committed all parties to a renunciation of force in settling disputes, the recognition of current European borders, including those of the GDR, and cooperation in economic, scientific, and cultural spheres.

The treaties were opposed by the opposition parties in the Bundestag—the Christian Democratic Union (CDU) and its Bavarian affiliate, the Christian Social Union (CSU). The CDU charged that the treaties gave up a great deal in return for few substantive benefits. The Federal Republic had to recognize the existence of a divided Germany, had to renounce its claims to German territories lost to Poland and the Soviet Union at the close of World War II and its claims to be sole representative of Germany in international relations, and had to give up its attempt to keep the GDR isolated.

The coalition government of Chancellor Willy Brandt, head of the Social Democratic Party (SPD), and Foreign Minister Walter Scheel, head of the liberal Free Democratic Party (FDP), answered that the lost eastern territories could not in reality be regained; that the Soviet Union, in renouncing the use of force gave up an alleged right of intervention in Germany under the United Nations charter; that the recognition of existing frontiers and renunciation of force did not preclude the reunification of the two German states by peaceful means, since a supplementary note left open that possibility; and finally, that the treaties did not demand that the Federal Republic extend full diplomatic recognition to the GDR. Most importantly, ratification of the treaties was a condition established by the Soviet Union for the implementation of the four-power Berlin accords of 1971.

The election in Baden-Württemberg scheduled for April was awaited with great interest as a test of voter opinion on the treaties. National political figures of all parties campaigned vigorously there. The CDU gained 53 percent of the vote, in contrast to 44.2 percent in the 1968 state election and 51.7 percent in the 1969 federal election. The CDU benefited from the decision of the right-wing National Democratic Party (NPD) to withdraw from the election and to urge its supporters to vote for the CDU.

Because some 60 percent of the voters favored the treaties in preelection opinion polls, however, the election could not be interpreted as a vote against them. Also, the governing parties registered some gains. The SPD won 37.5 percent of the vote, compared with 29 percent in 1968 and 36.5 percent in 1969. The FDP, with 8.9 percent, did worse than it had in 1968 with 14.4 percent but better than its 1969 percentage of 7.5.

Of greater concern to the government at the time of the state election was the resignation from the FDP of a Bundestag deputy because of opposition to the treaties. Added to a defection by an SPD member earlier in the year, the government was left with 249 votes in the Bundestag, the minimum needed to pass the treaties against the opposition of the Bundesrat, where the CDU had a voting edge of 21–20. One more defection would thus mean defeat for the treaties, and other SPD and FDP deputies were known to be uneasy about ratification.

The CDU in late April submitted a motion of no confidence against the government, the first such motion in the history of the Federal Republic. However, the CDU's motion fell two votes short of the required majority. Voting with the government was at least one Christian Democrat, probably a member of the labor wing of the CDU, which had opposed the submission of the no-confidence vote. Masses of trade unionists had demonstrated vigorously in support of the government throughout the Federal Republic.

Revenge by the CDU came shortly thereafter, when on April 28 the annual budget proposal of the government was defeated in a tie vote. This indicated the lack of a working majority for the government and placed some doubts on the treaty ratification vote, which had been scheduled for May.

At this point, however, negotiations were begun between the government and CDU leaders, eventually leading to ratification of the treaties. In an effort to allay conservative fears, a bipartisan Bundestag resolution interpreting the treaties was drafted. Most importantly, the resolution stated that the treaties did not conflict with West Germany's aim of reunification and did not affect the rights and responsibilities of the four powers. The Soviet ambassador to the Federal Republic indicated his government's willingness to accept the joint resolution, and it was subsequently endorsed by Christian Democrats in the Bundestag. On the ratification vote on May 17, most Christian Democrats abstained, and thus the treaties were approved. An absolute majority was not needed, since the CDU leaders requested that their state governments in the Bundesrat not delay the treaties any longer. On May 19 the treaties were ratified by the Bundesrat.

The surprising acquiescence of the CDU to the treaties after two years of intense opposition was due to several factors. In March, Soviet party chief Leonid Brezhnev had said that treaty ratification would "lead to a qualitatively new and significantly more fruitful stage in the development of Soviet–West German relations in a variety of areas." In the last year the Soviets had permitted 1,200 ethnic Germans living in the Soviet Union to emigrate and had granted an additional 700 exit visas in April. Previously they had refused even to discuss the question. Regarding the CDU's stated intention to renegotiate treaty passages if the party came into power, Brezhnev threatened, "It is not obvious that the opponents of the treaties will have any partner with whom to negotiate."

More important than the Soviet stance was that of the Western allies. Although the United States, Great Britain, and France remained neutral, pressure was brought to bear on the German deputies.

Finally, a number of Christian Democrats led by the nominal CDU leader, Ranier Barzel, took a positive position toward the treaties. A CDU government could not have negotiated more favorable terms. Past opposition had been based more on the desire to unseat the Brandt government, and European détente was much too important for political opportunism. Moreover, according to opinion polls, a majority of the West German electorate favored ratification.

Barzel had been forced by party votes to submit the April motion of no confidence; there was evidence that rivals for leadership of the CDU—Franz Josef Strauss, leader of the CSU, and Helmut Kohl, governor of Rhineland-Palatinate—supported the move, in part to embarrass Barzel when it failed.

Because of the erosion of his Bundestag majority, Brandt had the lower house of Parliament dissolved by asking on September 20 for a confidence vote he intended to lose. The election, slated for November, looked close. A poll during the summer indicated that coalition parties would win 50 percent of the vote, and the CDU opposition 48 percent.

In the campaign the SPD stressed the achievement of the Brandt government in reducing tensions and normalizing relations with the Communist bloc, thus paving the way for general European détente. Domestically, Brandt called for the implementation of democratic socialism oriented toward a humanistic society based on freedom, justice, and community. He promised no political cooperation with Communists in the Federal Republic and embraced the concepts of free enterprise, economic competition, and property. But he also emphasized the importance of the individual in the state, economic system, and society.

The FDP committed itself to a continued coalition with the SPD, after refusing offers of coalition with the Christian Democratic opposition. The party put strongest emphasis on the goal of free competition in the economy and also stressed the very real achievements of its ministers in the Brandt government—Scheel in the Foreign Office, Hans Genscher in Interior, and Josef Ertl in Agriculture. In the 1969 federal election the FDP had come dangerously close to falling short of the 5 percent needed to gain Bundestag representation. Since that election, they had lost representation in three states.

As the opposition, the CDU did not attack the Eastern policies (*Ostpolitik*) of the Brandt government, assuring continuity in this sphere in the eventuality of a Christian Democratic victory. Instead, the CDU emphasized domestic issues, especially the regaining of economic and political stability. Inflation and large currency inflows have plagued the Brandt government for the past two years. Crime and political terrorism have also been important issues. The Christian Democrats also attacked the Socialists as left extremists and hinted at a popular front between Socialists and Communists.

A major campaign problem for Brandt was the resignation in July of his "superminister," Karl Schiller, who held portfolios in both economics and finance. As economics minister Schiller was credited with moving the economy out of the 1966–1967 recession. His popularity then helped the SPD into power in the 1969 election. The ostensible reason for Schiller's resignation was the cabinet's acceptance of restrictions on currency flow. Schiller also had difficulty getting along with other cabinet members and seemed to lack a sense of what was politically feasible. A political sensation was caused when Schiller's resignation letter was published in *Quick*, a popular magazine. Critical of the government for not taking difficult and unpopular but necessary economic and financial decisions, Schiller wrote that he was "not ready to support policy which gives rise to the impression that the government lives according to the motto, 'After us, the deluge.'"

Schiller was replaced by Helmut Schmidt, who had been highly successful as minister for defense. Personable and popular, Schmidt was considered a good politician as well as an effective administrator. Schiller, in the meantime, resigned from all Socialist party offices and eventually from the party itself, allegedly after negotiating with the CDU leader, Barzel, for a cabinet position in a Christian Democratic government. There was no such offer forthcoming, however.

Economy and finance. The overheated economy of the past few years slowed to a more moderate pace in 1972. The index of industrial production in June, for example, was only 0.9 percent higher than the previous year. The slowdown may be attributed to a number of steps taken by the government to reduce inflation, such as the revaluation of the mark. Nevertheless, in July the cost of living was rising at a rate of 5.6 percent—the highest of the postwar period—compared to 5.1 percent for 1971.

A continued shortage of labor helped to feed the inflationary spiral. The unemployment rate in June increased to 0.9 percent from the 0.6 percent of 1971. Yet there were 600,800 unfilled positions for the 190,200 seeking jobs, and the number of workers brought in from foreign countries to take unfilled jobs grew to 2.3 million, an increase of almost 10 percent over 1971. With labor scarce, salaries and wages rose at a rate of 11.9 percent in May, down from the 15 percent of 1971 but still far above the increase in productivity of about 5.9 percent.

A favorable balance of trade also increased the demand, and hence the price, for goods on the West German market. In the first half of 1972 the trade surplus widened to DM8.4 billion from DM6.9 billion in the same period in 1971.

In an attempt to prevent a business slowdown that might result from revaluation and to combat a large inflow of foreign currency, the central bank in February lowered its discount rate to 3 percent, the second lowest level of the postwar period. A number of complementary controls were also placed on currency exchange.

Area and population. Area, 95,932 sq. mi. Pop. (est. 1971), 59,170,000; West Berlin, 2,110,000. Other principal cities: Bonn (cap.), 277,135; Hamburg, 1,788,599; Munich, 1,328,069.
Government. Federal republic with a bicameral legislature. Pres., Gustav Heinemann; chancellor, Willy Brandt; vice-chancellor and for. min., Walter Scheel.

Finance. Monetary unit, deutsche mark (DM); DMI = US$0.31. Budget (1972, proposed): DM109.3 billion. Principal items of expenditure: social security and social services, 29.3%; defense, 23.3%; transportation and communications, 9.1%. Main sources of revenue: income and corporation taxes, 32.3%; value-added tax, 20.9%; gasoline and oil taxes, 12.7%.
Trade (1971, in billions of U.S. dollars). Exports, 39; imports, 34.3. Principal exports: machinery, vehicles, chemicals, electrical products. Principal imports: agricultural goods, textiles and clothing, machinery, petroleum, chemicals, hardware. Major trading partners: France, United States, Netherlands, Italy.
Agriculture and industry. Contribution to GNP (1969): production of goods, 54.8%; trade and transport, 18.2%; services, 14.5%; public sector, 8%; agriculture and forestry, 3.1%; other, 1.4%.
Education (1970). Enrollment: grade school, 6,425,363; nonclassical secondary school, 834,599; classical secondary school, 1,361,426; vocational school, 2,095,333; institutions of higher education, 469,073.
Armed forces (1970). Army, 326,700; air force, 104,100; navy, 36,400.

German Democratic Republic (East Germany)

Politics. One year after replacing Walter Ulbricht as Communist Party chief, Erich Honecker seemed firmly installed at the head of the East German power structure. Although he emphasized collective leadership and appeared as a hard-working, modest "first among equals," a number of changes in party policy indicated either that he was in a position of considerable power or, less likely, lacked opponents.

Honecker's words and actions appeared contradictory in many respects. On the one hand, his domestic and international ideological offensives and activities in line with the policy of *Abgrenzung* from the Federal Republic confirmed the image of Honecker as leader of the hard-line faction in the Politburo. On the other hand, he allowed negotiation of the treaties with the Federal Republic as well as some relaxation in domestic politics. What seemed to be contradictory actions, however, were only an attempt to deal with conflicting situations. Honecker was pressured toward peaceful coexistence with the Federal Republic by the Soviet Union, which desired a European security conference and general détente with the West. But because considerable segments of the East German population did not appear to support the Communist regime and might be liable to influence from the West, relations with the West had to remain minimal. Honecker worked against this threat by continuing his policy of *Abgrenzung* and at the same time attempting to gain support with a number of domestic reforms.

In line with that policy, the United Protestant Church of Germany, the last Protestant denomination to claim organization on an all-German basis, this year divided into independent eastern and western parts. The German Freedom Radio, which had promoted Communist causes in the Federal Republic, ceased broadcasting. The official East German broadcasting organ changed its name from German Broadcasting to Voice of the GDR. And the official newspaper, *Neues Deutschland*, which often devoted at least one-quarter of each issue to events in the Federal Republic, drastically reduced its coverage.

A kind of internal "fencing off" also took place within the GDR. Attempts were made to expunge remnants of the pre-Communist social and economic system. Most of the remaining private enterprises and joint state-private enterprises, accounting for about 13 percent of the national product, were socialized. Ideologists who had adhered to the Ulbricht line of a "Socialist community of mankind" began to emphasize class differences. New benefits—vacation or rest trips, for example—were supposed to accrue to workers, collective farmers, and their representatives rather than to the former privileged of the GDR, such as private employers, tradesmen, scientists, and doctors. A limit of $700 per month was set on salaries in order to lower the income gap between workers and the privileged strata, significantly reducing income for many.

Meanwhile, the churches, claimed by Marx as a mainstay of the bourgeois system, were harassed. Young people active in the church were prevented from entering institutions of higher learning. Prior approval of local authorities was required for all church functions outside of the ordinary service.

Measures to eliminate bourgeois patterns in society were supplemented with domestic reforms. In April a number of changes in social services that are expected to cost more than $2.5 billion through 1975 were announced. Old-age pensions were increased by at least 25 percent. The workweek of mothers with three or more children was reduced from 44 to 40 hours at the same pay, and their annual vacation was increased to a minimum of 21 working days. Child allowances were increased to MDN1,000 for each child. Newly married couples with incomes below MDN1,400 per month could receive loans for housing and furnishings with no interest on the first MDN5,000 in each category. Rents in new apartments were reduced for families earning less than MDN2,000 per month.

For the consumer, prices on quality goods imported from abroad, such as blue jeans and Italian shoes, were drastically reduced to put them within reach of ordinary working people. In the past the markup on such goods was as high as 300 percent. The regime also announced a price freeze on consumer goods through 1975, although prices have been remarkably stable over the past decade.

The status of women was promoted by the Communist regime this year. The government began to actively propagandize the image of emancipated women in such media as the movies. Some 79 percent of women of employable age were working, and the regime was attempting to eliminate the notion that they alone had to be responsible for housework and child care. In March a law was passed permitting abortion on demand during the first 12 weeks of pregnancy, with medical bills and sick leave paid by the state. Birth control pills were also placed on the list of drugs to be dispensed at no charge.

Some relaxation was also noticeable in domestic politics this year. Scientists were invited to be more critical and have more clashes of opinion, although Honecker emphasized the primacy of politics over technical expertise in important decisions. The same applied to art and literature. According to Honecker, there should be "no taboos. This applied to questions of content as well as style," but naturally "with no concessions to conceptions that are foreign to our ideology." In practice, these views resulted in the replacement of conservative officials in the cultural section of the party central committee, the publication of literary works and films that had been forbidden since the crackdown on cultural dissidents in 1965, and a more critical and satirical program for the East Berlin cabaret Die Distel (The Thistle).

Greater freedom to travel abroad was granted with the introduction in January of movement without passport or visa for all citizens between Czechoslovakia, Poland, and the GDR.

Economy. Statistics announced this year for the first year of the 1971 five-year plan indicated good results. Industrial production rose 5.5 percent over 1970. The productivity of industrial labor increased by 4.5 percent, as did overall national income. Net cash income grew by 3.7 percent. Investments were increased overall by 4 percent. Despite a 21 percent increase in capital investment in the power industry, a considerable power supply deficit continued to exist, especially during peak hours; the power target set down in the plan was not reached. About 65,000 dwellings were built, 2,200 of them by private individuals, exceeding the plan's goal. More facilities for children made spaces available this year in child care centers for 28 percent of all infants, in nursery schools for 73 percent of preschoolers, and in after-school centers for 51 percent of those between first and fourth grades.

Area and population. Area, 41,766 sq. mi. Pop. (est. 1971), 17,040,926. Principal cities: East Berlin (cap.), 1,084,866; Leipzig, 583,311; Dresden, 500,051.

Government. People's Republic controlled by the (Communist) Socialist Unity Party (SED). First secy. of the SED, Erich Honecker; prime min., Willi Stoph; chmn. of the state council (chief of state), Walter Ulbricht.

Finance. Monetary unit, East German mark (MDN); official rate, MDN1 = US$0.49; tourist rate, MDN1 = US$0.32. Budget (1969), MDN65 billion.

UPI

LIFTING THE IRON CURTAIN. At Easter, for the first time in six years, West Berliners got passes from the East German regime to visit relatives on the other side of the wall. Later, in May, ratification of friendship treaties permitted future visits.

Trade (1971, in billions of U.S. dollars). Exports, 4.58; imports, 4.96. Principal exports: machinery and manufactured goods, foodstuffs. Principal imports: fuel, metal ores. Major trading partners: Soviet Union, Czechoslovakia, West Germany, Poland.

Agriculture and industry. Contributions to national income (1970): manufacturing, power, and mining, 60.9%; trade and restaurants, 12.6%; agriculture and forestry, 11.7%; construction, 8.2%; transportation and communication, 5.1%; other, 1.5%.

Education. Enrollment (1970): kindergarten, 620,200; primary and secondary school, 2,667,316; vocational school, 430,500; technical school, 163,818; universities and other institutions of higher education (54), 138,541.

Armed forces (1970). Army 92,000; air force, 21,000; navy, 16,000.
RICHARD J. WILLEY

GHANA. Only time will tell whether developments in 1972 signaled the final eclipse of the independence generation and the permanent intrusion of the military in Ghana's political life. Both aspects were very much in evidence in the overthrow by the military of Prime Minister Kofi A. Busia's civilian regime in January and the death in exile three months later of former president Kwame Nkrumah, father of Ghanaian independence.

Political developments. During the last months of 1971, the Busia regime had managed to antagonize almost every segment of the population. Rampant inflation was partly offset by salary raises, but the December 27 decision to devalue the cedi by 44 percent, coupled with the easing of price controls, threatened to send the price of consumer goods skyrocketing and to erode further the average Ghanaian's purchasing power. Possibly anticipating a hostile reaction on the part of organized labor, the government had earlier initiated a bill disbanding the Trade Unions Congress (TUC), Ghana's largest union, in favor of a government-sponsored organization, the Ghana Confederation of Labour. At the same time, the arbitrary dismissal of several hundred civil servants, the high-handed treatment of a number of senior officers, and the elimination of some fringe benefits for both groups had antagonized the bureaucracy and the military.

On January 13, a bloodless military coup led by Colonel Ignatius Kotu Acheampong removed all civilian leaders from office, suspended the 1969 constitution, and set up the National Redemption Council (NRC) of six (later ten) members, none of whom had been members of the military junta set up after President Nkrumah's overthrow in 1966. A desperate attempt by General A. A. Afrifa, leader of the 1966 coup, to foil the military take-over and to bring back Prime Minister Busia, then in London, was easily defeated, and the NRC set about the business of undoing some of Busia's most unpopular measures. The ban against the TUC was rescinded, and the national currency was revalued to regain almost half of the loss it had suffered a few weeks earlier.

Popular reaction to the overthrow of the unpopular Busia regime and to the junta's economic initiatives was predominantly favorable, and a long-lost sense of national pride and purpose appeared to have been regained. Initial speculation that the coup might signal a change of fortune for the disenfranchised followers of Nkrumah was seriously dampened when former TUC leader John Tettegah was arrested upon his return from a six-year exile. As for Nkrumah himself, whatever long-term intentions the junta may have had toward him, he did not live to make a political comeback; on April 27 he died in a hospital in Bucharest, Romania. His body became the focus of a macabre argument between the governments of Ghana and Guinea (where he had sought asylum) over the kind of posthumous recognition that should be awarded to the man who had once been the very symbol of African freedom. The NRC paid a measured tribute to Nkrumah's memory and announced plans to have him buried in Ghanaian soil, but before allowing the body to be flown home, President Sékou Touré of Guinea insisted on a full official rehabilitation for the deposed president and his followers. Colonel Acheampong replied that he would

never disavow the 1966 coup. Touré eventually yielded, and Nkrumah's body was buried in his native village of Nkroful on July 9. Shortly thereafter, following the discovery of an alleged plot by supporters of Busia, the NRC passed a subversion decree specifying the death penalty for a wide range of offenses. Prospects for an early return to civilian rule seemed distinctly unpromising.

Economic developments. Ghana's stagnant economy continued to suffer from the falling world price of cocoa, the country's chief export, and from the growing burden of its huge foreign indebtedness. By the end of 1971 the price of cocoa had sunk to less than half of its 1969 level. Paradoxically, Ghana, a predominantly agricultural country, was increasingly unable to feed itself; in 1970, $186 million had to be spent on imported food and raw materials alone.

Under the Busia regime the country had been falling behind in the repayment of its external debt, which had reached $494 million by 1969. Western creditors had bluntly refused to accept any further rescheduling of Ghana's debts. Perhaps the most spectacular measure taken by the NRC following the January 1972 coup was its announcement that it would reexamine all debts incurred by the Nkrumah regime and repudiate contracts that had been vitiated by fraud or corruption. Debts incurred after 1966 would be accepted, but only on terms comparable with those of the "soft" loans offered by such agencies as the International Development Association. Creditor nations, having previously refused any further repayment facilities to Busia's pro-Western regime, were bound to react unfavorably to such radical, unilateral decisions, and Great Britain, followed by other Western governments, promptly withdrew its credit guarantee on all exports going to Ghana, a measure that quickly resulted in the drying up of the short-term suppliers' credit on which Ghana had been relying heavily since 1970 for the import of consumer goods. This tightening of credit, coupled with the NRC's introduction of a stiff licensing system covering some 350 items, led to a drastic cutback on imports; as a result, Ghana's trade balance from January to April registered an uprecedented surplus of 60 million cedis. At the same time, however, cocoa prices remained depressed and government spending was not substantially reduced, which meant that the country's financial situation continued to be precarious.

Foreign affairs. In the field of foreign relations, the NRC indicated its intention of returning to a position of genuine nonalignment. Unlike its predecessor, the new government declared its unequivocal support for African liberation movements and clearly rejected any thought of a "dialogue" with South Africa. A move to resume relations with China was also announced. To a large extent, of course, the decision to veer away from the Busia regime's marked predilection for the West was conditioned by Ghana's virtual repudiation of a good portion of its external debt. Similarly, pragmatic rather than ideological considerations dictated the dispatching of two Ghanaian delegations to Eastern Europe and to China in search of alternative economic ties.

Area and population. Area, 92,100 sq. mi. Pop. (est. 1971), 8,-860,000. Principal cities (1970): Accra (cap.), 633,900; Kumasi, 343,000; Sekondi-Takoradi, 161,100.

Government. Republic; member of the Commonwealth of Nations. Head of state, Colonel Ignatius Kotu Acheampong, head of National Redemption Council. NRC Commissioners: def., fin., and econ. min., I. K. Acheampong; for. min., Maj. Gen. N. A. Aferi.

Finance. Monetary unit, cedi (formerly known as new cedi); C1 = US$0.80. Expenditure (1972 estimate), C440.5 million; GNP (1970), US$2.32 billion.

Trade (1970). Exports, US$467.4 million; imports, US$422 million. Chief export, cocoa (US$331.5 million). Major trading partners: United Kingdom, United States, Common Market, Japan, Soviet Union, Canada, Yugoslavia.

Education (1969). Enrollment: primary schools, 1,016,457; middle schools, 381,551; secondary schools, 46,512; teachers colleges, 18,728; technical institutes, 4,011; universities, 5,035.

Armed forces. Army, 14,000 men; navy, 9 units; air force, 69 aircraft.
EDOUARD BUSTIN

GREAT BRITAIN. *See* UNITED KINGDOM OF GREAT BRITAIN AND NORTHERN IRELAND.

GREECE. The current regime entered its sixth year of uninterrupted rule in April with all indicators pointing toward its perpetuation under the personal command of Premier George Papadopoulos. On March 21 he replaced General George Zoitakis as regent and prompted speculation that the way was being paved for the abolition of the monarchy and the establishment of a republic under his presidency. His radio speech of April 20, celebrating the fifth anniversary of his 1967 military coup, was notable for the absence of the usual pledges to restore parliamentary democratic rule.

A major government reshuffle at the end of July underscored the military character of his regime. All of the ten new members of the 42-member government were former military men. Seven members of the 18-man cabinet and six of the 25 undersecretaries were members of the military group that planned the 1967 coup. The only organizational changes took place at the beginning of the year, in an attempt to overcome administrative problems that had resulted from the August 1971 merger of several ministries into a single Ministry of National Economy. The authoritarian outlook of the regime persisted, with the continued imprisonment of over 250 persons for political reasons, the introduction of a new loyalty oath for prospective employees of all official and semiofficial bodies (including the priesthood), indirect censorship through government policing of the book trade, and a ban on the right of lawyers to elect the leaders of their corporate associations.

Opposition. The year witnessed the continuation of already established patterns of opposition, such as bomb explosions staged by illegal resistance organizations and public manifestos issued by former political leaders. Claiming responsibility for several bomb incidents, occurring especially in the early part of the year, was a group called AAA, the initials signifying "resistance, liberation, independence." On March 24, 167 former members of Parliament, speaking for the two major pre-1967 political parties (Center Union and National Radical Union), pledged for the first time bipartisan support for any government that would restore democracy to Greece.

New types of opposition included the contemplated addition of kidnapping to the tactics of urban guerrilla groups, the establishment of ostensibly cultural organizations for the public discussion of national issues, and the peaceful pursuit of specific demands by interest groups within the context of the new constitution of 1968. The first of these new moves was revealed by the regime in its announcement on July 15 that eight persons had been arrested in June for alleged conspiracy to kidnap important persons, Greek and non-Greek. Organized intellectual dissent was represented by the Society for the Study of Greek Problems, the Greek-European Youth Movement, and the new monthly *Anti*. The first two organizations were dissolved by an Athens court order toward the end of May, after the first had organized a public debate on human rights. Immediately after this debate, the government banished to remote villages under police surveillance eight intellectuals, among them the celebrated economist John Pesmazoglu, chairman of the Society for the Study of Greek Problems. A raid by tax and security officials forced *Anti* to suspend publication after the appearance of its first issue.

A wave of student strikes and peaceful demonstrations, the first since 1967, took place in Athens and Salonika late in April; 400 physics students and 2,600 engineering students participated. Their major demand was that students elect, rather than have the government appoint, the leaders of their corporate bodies. In response, the government arrested, detained, or in the case of six Cypriots, banished a few students. On May 2 it authorized the police to use firearms at their own discretion in the future. The appointment on

ARRIVING AT ATHENS for a stopoff on his world tour, U.S. secretary of state William P. Rogers met with Premier George Papadopoulos (right) and assured Greek leaders of the close relationship between the two countries in spite of some "differences of view."

July 31 of a former colonel as minister of education was viewed as an indication of stronger government action against future student unrest.

Foreign policy. In the international field, the most important development was the strengthening of ties between the Greek and U.S. governments, marked by the Greek regime's provision of home port facilities for the U.S. Sixth Fleet in the Mediterranean and the virtual abandonment of earlier U.S. pressure for the restoration of parliamentary rule in Greece. The home port agreement, reached early in the year and at the first stage of implementation by July, secured permanent docking facilities for U.S. ships in Piraeus harbor (an estimated six destroyers and one aircraft carrier) and residence facilities in the Athens area for an estimated 6,600 American crewmen and their 3,100 dependents.

On March 29 the Nixon administration announced an agreement to sell Greece 36 F-4 Phantom jets. It was the largest such sale since the Greek regime seized power in 1967.

Indicative of the increasingly warm relations between the Greek and U.S. governments was the inclusion of Greece in the world tour of Secretary of State William P. Rogers, who conferred with Papadopoulos on July 5. Policy toward Greece, long under attack by critics of the Greek regime in Congress, became an issue in the U.S. presidential campaign. Democratic nominee George McGovern announced that, if elected, he would end all aid to the "Greek dictatorship," review the home port agreement, and reduce American military presence in Greece to the "absolute minimum."

In the sphere of regional politics, the major event was a protracted crisis in Greek-Cypriot relations. Behind the crisis lay a deadlock in long-standing talks between representatives of the Greek and Turkish Cypriot communities and a concerted effort of the Greek and Turkish governments to normalize their relations by forcing a settlement of the Cyprus issue. It was sparked, however, by the Cypriot government's importation of a large consignment of Czechoslovak arms in January and by a peremptory note from the

Greek government to Archbishop Makarios, president of Cyprus, on February 11. The note demanded surrender of Czechoslovak arms to the United Nations peacekeeping force, a reshuffle of the Cyprus government, and acknowledgment of a stronger role for Greece in Cypriot affairs. A virtual ultimatum, the note was followed by a demand from the bishops of the Cypriot Orthodox Church that Makarios resign the presidency, generating suspicions that Papadopoulos sought the political downfall of Makarios. The archbishop managed to ride out the storm by fully satisfying the first demand, nominally complying with the second, and minimally acceding to the third by agreeing to resume intercommunal talks with the inclusion of advisers from Greece and Turkey, as well as the UN special representative in Cyprus. The formal resumption of these talks on July 8 did represent a minimal victory for Papadopoulos and his regime.

Greece established diplomatic relations with the People's Republic of China on June 5.

Economic developments. The economy continued to expand in 1972, and per capita income passed the $1,000 mark. With two loans, contracted on the European money market in the spring and totaling $110 million, Greece was able to register an increase in its official reserves. Avions Marcel Dassault and Automation Industries, French and American concerns, were vying for the franchise to establish an aerospace factory. The factory, which is to be sponsored by the government, is estimated to cost approximately $50 million.

The ostensibly bright economic picture was challenged by John Pesmazoglu in a press conference on April 29. According to him, the rate of overall economic growth had declined from 7.65 percent in 1963–1966 to 6.2 percent in 1967–1970, with the average annual rate of increase in agricultural income and in private industrial investment falling by more than 50 percent. The development base created before 1967, rather than the record of the current Greek regime, accounted for the economic gains since then, he added.

In any case, the regime's ability to attract long-term foreign capital investment was less than successful, and the continued freeze on Greek association with the European Economic Community deprived Greece of loans from the European Development Fund and deferred indefinitely the harmonization of Greek agricultural policy with that of Western Europe.

In June it was reported that the government, in an attempt to reverse the low birthrate, planned to provide parents with a monthly bonus of 500 drachmas for each child after the second.

Area and population. Area, 50,944 sq. mi. Pop. (est. mid-1971), 8,960,000. Principal cities: Greater Athens (cap.), 1,853,000; Salonika, 378,000; Patras, 102,000.
Government. Constitutional monarchy now ruled by government edict. Effective power held by military junta. King-in-exile, Constantine II; prem., George Papadopoulos.
Finance. Monetary unit, drachma; DR1 = US$0.0336. Central government revenue (national account basis, est. 1970), $1.6 billion; expenditure, $1.48 billion.
Trade. Principal imports: capital goods, manufactured consumer goods, foodstuffs and live animals, crude petroleum and petroleum products. Principal exports: manufactured goods (iron and steel, aluminum, textiles), foodstuffs, tobacco, raw materials.
Production (est. 1969), $8.41 billion. Percentage of gross domestic product: agriculture (20.3%); industry (28.2%); services (51.5%).
Armed forces (est. 1970). Army, 120,000; navy, 18,000; air force, 23,000.   JOHN ANTHONY PETROPULOS

GUATEMALA. Politics. The state of siege (modified martial law) imposed on the country in November 1970 by President Carlos Arana Osorio to combat acts of violence by both left-wing and right-wing terrorists finally was lifted on November 22, 1971, so that normal political activities could be resumed. Arana's action followed a massive student strike

in October 1971 at the University of San Carlos protesting the violence in the country—almost 1,000 deaths (including 79 policemen), 171 kidnappings, and 174 disappearances in 1971—and demanding an end to the state of siege, during which the government assumed the power to make arrests and search homes without a court order. Journalists, intellectuals, and a group of Protestant clergymen joined the protest. At the time, however, the government maintained that the measures could not be lifted and banned further public demonstrations.

With the state of siege lifted, municipal elections were held in March of this year. The powerful Movimiento de Liberación Nacional gained about 70 percent of the votes. But despite the apparent reduction of tensions, domestic insecurity and occasional violence continued. In June, Olivero Castañeda Paíz, deputy speaker of Congress and an MLN leader, was assassinated; Castañeda was purportedly a leader of La Mano Blanca, a right-wing terrorist organization. During the next month four other MLN leaders were also assassinated.

One proposal to achieve tranquillity sought constitutional reform to establish a one-party state under the MLN. But this was viewed by the opposition as a step toward dictatorship and a poor alternative to civil war. One area that would certainly have been affected had such a state been established was the autonomous university, presently given special protection under the constitution. At midyear, President Arana declared in a radio speech to the nation that parts of the university had become "political parties in disguise."

Foreign affairs. Early in the year, rumors that Guatemalan troops were massing on the Guatemala–British Honduras border led to an announcement by the British that they were sending troops and materiel to the area to conduct maneuvers in the jungle border region. Guatemalan officials maintained that they were pursuing leftist guerrillas and denied any intent to invade.

Economic developments. The government announced in January that the gross national product increased by 5 percent in 1971. Nevertheless, it expected a trade deficit of $50 million. A bilateral trade agreement with Honduras was signed.

Area and population. Area, 42,042 sq. mi. Pop. (1971), 5,350,000. Guatemala City (cap.; UN est. 1970), 730,991.
Government. Constitutional republic with unicameral legislature. Pres., Carlos Arana Osorio.
Finance. Monetary unit, quetzal; 1 quetzal = US$1.00. Budget (1970): revenue, US$165.5 million; expenditure, US$188.9 million.
Trade (1970). Exports, US$298.3 million; imports, US$284 million. Principal exports: coffee, raw cotton, bananas and plantains.
Armed forces (1970). Army, 8,000; national police, 3,000; air force, 1,000.
Education (1969). Literacy rate of persons 10 years of age or older: 38.9 percent. Primary and secondary schools, 5,095; enrollment, 538,094; teachers, 17,599.   GUILLERMO LUX

GUINEA. The scars left by the abortive Portuguese-backed invasion of Guinea in November 1970 were a long time healing, but by spring of 1972 the regime appeared to have surmounted its worst difficulties and perhaps even to have found an unexpected second wind.

Political developments. The year following the attempt against the Guinean regime was in large measure devoted to a protracted purge that reached, in ever-widening circles, deep into the ranks of the political and military elite of the country.

On the anniversary of the invasion, President Ahmed Sékou Touré acknowledged that a startling total of 16 ministers, five ex-ministers, several governors, and a number of high-ranking officers (including the army chief of staff, Major Mara Sékou Khalil) had been arrested or dismissed as a result of alleged implication in the plot. Touré also claimed that "imperialists" had spent more than US$30 million in their vain attempt to subvert his regime. With

the possible exception of dissidents in the Fouta Djallon area, however, the masses apparently remained loyal throughout the crisis, perhaps because of the vigilance of the grassroots cells of the Guinean Democratic Party (PDG), the country's only political party. However, as the devastating effects of the purge depleted the country's political cadres, President Touré was confronted with the threat of being isolated at the top with no heir apparent and no established procedure of political succession. By the end of April, the government underwent its most comprehensive reorganization yet. For the first time since independence, a premier was appointed, in the person of former foreign minister Lansana Beavogui. Even more important, President Touré, while retaining his position as head of state and of party, relinquished a number of key portfolios (army, civil service) into the hands of the new premier, keeping direct control only over matters having to do with ideology—a lifelong concern of his. Economic affairs and finance remained, as they had been for years, under the control of the president's brother, Ismaël Touré, but one of the Guinean leader's oldest associates, El Hadj Saifoulaye Diallo, was for all practical purposes retired from office. The political bureau of the party was also substantially reorganized.

Foreign affairs. While the abortive invasion may have ignited a slow-burning fuse on the domestic scene, it also generated a considerable amount of sympathy for Guinea on the international scene, particularly in Africa. President Touré capitalized on this by renewing some of his traditional attacks against neocolonialist infiltration of the continent—notably through the French-oriented African, Malagasy, and Mauritian Common Organization (OCAMM)—and by calling for the emergence of a counterforce of "revolutionary African states" within the Organization of African Unity (OAU). His appeal, however, met with little visible response. The government of neighboring Senegal showed increasing irritation at Touré's reiterated charges that it had been letting its territory be used as a base for subversive activities against Guinea. The most spectacular result of this hostility between the two neighbors was Guinea's long-anticipated decision to withdraw from the Organization of the Sénégal River States (OERS), which led in turn to that agency's demise and to its tentative reorganization (minus Guinea) as the Organisation pour la Mise en Valeur du Sénégal (OMVS) in March. Guinea's relations with Ghana, which had been seriously strained since the overthrow of Ghana's president Kwame Nkrumah in 1966, showed promising signs of improvement after the military take-over in Accra in January 1972, but the two countries again became embroiled in controversy in May over the issue of the deceased Nkrumah's burial site (see GHANA). Relations with Sierra Leone, on the other hand, have been consistently good since the return to power in that country of Siaka Stevens; the two countries have decided to improve physical communications between them as a matter of "first priority."

In the long run, however, Guinea's mineral resources and strategic potential have always been its most attractive points, and these must have been partly responsible for the unprecedented succession of distinguished visitors who appeared in Conakry during the spring and summer. The series began in March with a state visit by General Yakubu Gowon of Nigeria, followed in May by Cuba's Fidel Castro, Liberia's William Tolbert, and Cameroon's Ahmadou Ahidjo, and in June by presidents Moktar Ould Daddah of Mauritania and Mobutu Sese Seko of Zaire. Their motivations were probably as diverse as the visitors' ideological orientations (the supply of Guinean bauxite for Zaire's planned hydroelectric complex at Inga, for instance, was a central point in the conversations with Mobutu), but no move was greeted with more disbelief than Ivory Coast president Félix Houphouët-Boigny's meeting with Sékou Touré in the small Guinean town of Faranah. The meeting was apparently indecisive, but many observers felt that this move and the

other visits by leaders of French-speaking Africa were related to the gradual erosion of OCAMM and to the decision to set up a separate West African Economic Community. Meanwhile, Sékou Touré's surface reconciliation with President Léopold-Sédar Senghor of Senegal (who was also, incidentally, the new chairman of OCAMM) may have been another episode in this slow-moving diplomatic realignment, but it remains to be seen whether Guinea's desire to emerge from its relative isolation will be stronger than its deep-seated suspicion of any kind of foreign influence.

Area and population. Area, 94,926 sq. mi. Pop. (est. 1971), 4,010,000. Conakry (cap.; 1967), 197,267.
Government. Republic with one-party system. Single party: Parti Démocratique de Guinée. Pres., Ahmed Sékou Touré; prem., Lansana Beavogui; fin. and econ. min., Ismaël Touré.
Finance. Monetary unit: Guinean franc; GF1 = US$0.005. Budget (1970–1971): balanced at US$92.6 million.
Trade (1968–1969). Imports, US$58 million; exports, US$51 million (of which, minerals: US$32.4 million). Major trading partners: Common Market, United States, Norway, Spain, Yugoslavia, Soviet Union.
Education (1968). Primary school enrollment, 167,340; secondary school enrollment, 41,736; technical school enrollment, 5,334; higher education, 942.   EDOUARD BUSTIN

GUYANA. Politics and government. Prime Minister Forbes Burnham struggled to maintain popular support at home, a situation brought on by his economic policies, which have resulted in a severe economic decline. Official figures place unemployment at more than 20 percent. (Sixteen percent is considered average for the Caribbean.)

Because of government banking policies, the nationalizing of the principal Canadian-owned bauxite corporation last year, and other government policies, both domestic and foreign investment are almost nonexistent. The External Trade Bureau, a newly established government agency designed to curtail the power of important East Indian importers, has caused considerable flight of domestic East Indian capital. Nevertheless, Prime Minister Burnham doggedly continued to strive to make the "cooperative" republic, established two years ago, self-sufficient in food, housing, and clothing. To this end he planned to use revenue from increased sugar production—Guyana is the only country in the Caribbean Commonwealth to enjoy such an increase. He also hoped for revenue from newly developed bauxite markets.

Economic developments. Burnham, who has set a rapid national development pace, still relied heavily on United States aid and sugar sales at preferential prices in the protected British market. However, he did not intend to neglect the business potential of the Communist world: Guyana recently established diplomatic relations with the Soviet Union. And in March, the People's Republic of China made an entrée into Guyana, the first Commonwealth Caribbean nation to accept its overtures. A permanent trade mission was established, and an agreement for technical assistance was signed whereby Peking will loan Guyana approximately $26 million, interest free, over the next five years. The loan is repayable in 20 years.

Inherent in Guyana's development program is an element of economic nationalism. One way in which Guyanese are striving to end foreign control of commercial banking is through the new government-supported Guyana National Cooperative Bank, which was founded two years ago. Formerly, the nation's five commercial banks were branches of banks with parent organizations located in the United States, the United Kingdom, Canada, or India; and the Bank of Guyana, which controlled the nation's currency supply, did not loan to individuals—a legacy of colonial rule. Now the Guyana National Cooperative Bank has about 7 percent of the nation's commercial banking business and expects steady increases.

Foreign affairs. Because of litigation with Venezuela over a boundary dispute, Guyana continued to be a "per-

manent observer" at the Organization of American States. In August, Guyana hosted a conference of foreign ministers from nonaligned nations.

Area and population. Area, 83,000 sq. mi. Pop. (est. 1971), 786,000. Georgetown (cap.: est. 1968), 194,473.
Government. "Cooperative" republic. Pres., Raymond Arthur Chung; prime min., Forbes Burnham.
Finance. Monetary unit, Guyana dollar; G$1 = US$0.50.
Trade (1970). Imports, US$134.1 million; exports, US$130.8 million.
Education (1968). Enrollment: primary, 130,836; secondary, 53,078; higher, 816.   GUILLERMO LUX

HAITI. Politics and government. The political apparatus set up by the late dictator François Duvalier before his death in 1971 held together throughout the year. This evidence of Duvalier's continuing influence on the impoverished Caribbean nation was something of a surprise to many observers, given the bitter antagonisms that marked his final years. Luckner Cambronne, the minister of interior and defense, was clearly the power behind Jean-Claude Duvalier, the late dictator's son, who succeeded his father as president for life. The dictator's widow, Simone, also appeared to be exercising increasing power.

Many Haitians and Haitian exiles jockeyed for power and posed frequent threats; the exiles consolidated their newly established organization, La Résistance Haïtienne. However, even an incipient threat from Marie-Denise, the elder sister of the new president, and her husband, Colonel Max Dominique, was cut off before it had an opportunity to make much headway, when Dominique was dismissed as ambassador to France in January. Although Marie-Denise returned briefly to Haiti at midyear, she and her husband spent most of 1972 in France.

In August, at least 20 people, including retired army officers, were arrested in connection with the alleged kidnapping of the young son of Lebert Jean-Pierre, the minister of trade and industry. The incident was cloaked in secrecy,

as are so many events in Haiti, but Cambronne used the kidnapping to charge that it was part of a "vast conspiracy" of "international Communism." François Duvalier had frequently charged Communists with infiltrating the country when he sought to eliminate opponents, and Cambronne's accusation was seen by some observers as a continuation of the old ways.

Jean-Claude, who had acquired the reputation of a playboy before he was named president, notably departed from his father's style. In his last years in office, "Papa Doc" had become something of a recluse in the presidential palace. Jean-Claude, on the other hand, was increasingly seen in public during the year. He and his mother, together with most of the government, made a triumphal 120-mile trip by road to the main southern town of Les Cayes in February, and in April they spent five days in the north, eventually reaching Cap-Haïtien, before returning to Port-au-Prince. The young president was also frequently seen in the capital away from the confines of the palace. Although his bodyguard was massive on all these occasions, his presence among his countrymen helped strengthen the regime.

Foreign affairs. The new government devoted much attention to renewing diplomatic and trade ties with the United States. Cambronne led a top-level delegation to Washington in March in an effort to achieve these aims. Although the United States was wary of becoming too friendly with the new government, it agreed to consider Haiti's request for the resumption of military aid. It also permitted more than $1 million in private arms sales, most of it through a Miami-based firm. In July, a seven-man U.S. military mission made an unpublicized visit to the island nation to weigh the aid request. Haiti also asked France to supply arms aid, and Haiti's minister of information announced, after a visit to Paris in April, that the French government would begin shipping light arms in 1973.

Economic developments. Economists reported that Haiti has nowhere to go but up. In virtually every study of

CHARLES MOORE/BLACK STAR

CHILD'S PLAY. Since the death of Haiti's "Papa Doc," the capital city of Port-au-Prince has been attracting more tourists for fun and games in casinos and palm-dotted pools. Under Jean-Claude ("Bébé Doc") Duvalier, tensions are down and the economy is on the upswing.

economic conditions in the Western Hemisphere, Haiti is at the bottom of the list. But during 1972, there was evidence that the new government was seeking to improve the situation. Cabinet ministers actively sought foreign investment on a variety of trips to the United States and Western Europe. U.S. investment totaled about $50 million at the start of 1972, and estimates toward the end of the year suggested that there had been a $13 million increase. The Overseas Private Investment Corporation, which insures American investors against losses from foreign investments, announced in January that it would again insure new U.S. investors in Haiti. The World Bank and the Inter-American Development Bank announced new loans to Haiti, and the Haitian government applied to these two organizations for additional loans, for a total of $16 million for the year. Much of the loan money will be used to improve agriculture and industry.

The government announced in March that it would welcome tourist investment, and a number of U.S. firms expressed interest. An estimated 95,000 foreign tourists visited the island in 1972, and projections for 1973 called for a 25 percent increase.

Economic conditions improved, as Haiti had a 5.7 percent annual growth rate in 1971 and an estimated 6.1 percent rate in 1972. The government announced in August that, through July, 3,100 new jobs had been created in 1972.

Area and population. Area, 10,714 sq. mi. Pop. (est. 1971), 4.9 million. Principal cities: Port-au-Prince (cap.), 300,000; Cap-Haïtien, 35,000.
Government. Republic with unicameral legislature. Pres., Jean-Claude Duvalier.
Finance. Monetary unit, gourde; 1 gourde = US$0.201. Budget (1971): balanced at US$36.1 million, but figures are reportedly unreliable.
Trade (1971). Exports, US$42 million; imports, US$44.1 million. Principal exports: coffee, sisal, cotton, handicrafts, baseballs. Principal imports: food, machinery, drugs. Principal trading partners: United States, France, Japan.
Education (1966). Enrollment: primary, 283,799; secondary, 24,514; higher, 1,607.
Armed forces. Army, 1,100; air force, 170; coast guard, 290.

JAMES NELSON GOODSELL

HAWAII. Legislation. Among important legislation passed during the regular session of the state legislature was a bill providing comprehensive revision of the state penal code, especially with respect to penalties authorized for severe crimes and rules and procedures for determining penal responsibility. Another measure lowered the age of majority from 20 to 18 and reduced the minimum qualifying age from 20 to 18 in several different categories. Legislators also voted in a landlord-tenant code which lists the basic obligations of both parties and grants the small claims division of the district court exclusive jurisdiction in cases involving disagreements over security deposits. Also, a state commission on the status of women was set up to deal especially with unlawful job practices involving sex discrimination.

But perhaps the most innovative measure of the year was a bill designed to curb air pollution and traffic congestion by setting limits on the number of automobiles and other vehicles to be allowed on each of Hawaii's islands. The bill set up an interdepartmental transportation control commission, consisting of the director of environmental quality control, the director of health, the director of transportation, and the director of planning and economic development, to recommend annually to the legislature the number and size of transportation units to be allowed in operation on or over the ground in each island of the state. It is expected that this bill, the first of its kind in any state, may eventually face court challenges.

Economic developments. Defense, tourism, and sugar and pineapple production, which bring in a total of approximately $1.7 billion annually, continued to be the top sources of statewide revenue. By removing 14,000 acres of sugar-producing lands from production, the state has tightened land-use controls with a view toward diversifying agricultural production. Hawaiian tourism made some recovery after a flat 1971, with a boost from the $179 inclusive group tour fare approved by the Civil Aeronautics Board as standard fare from the west-coast gateways.

After 18 months of negotiations, the longshoremen's union shut down Honolulu's main port in October, seeking to bring four stevedore companies to heel. At issue was an 82-cent-an-hour increase, retroactive to December 1971.

Sports. Jesse Kuhaulua, of Happy Valley, Maui, became the first non-Easterner to win a professional sumo tournament in Japan. The 365-pound Hawaiian wrestler is known professionally as Takamiyama.

Transportation. A $15 million improvement in the Honolulu bus transportation system resulted in 102 new 49-passenger coaches, which brought service to an additional 10,000 persons and opened up the windward, north shore, and Waianae coast areas of Oahu.

In May, the state dedicated a $12 million, three-level airport ticket-lobby extension to accommodate the increasing numbers of 747's serving the islands.

Education. In February, teachers became the first public employees in Hawaii to win collective bargaining rights.

For election results and campaign highlights, see the special supplement ELECTION '72.

Area and population. Area, 6,424 sq. mi. Pop. (1970), 769,913. Principal cities (1970): Honolulu, Oahu (cap.), 324,871; Hilo, Hawaii, 26,353; Kahului, Maui, 8,280; Lihue, Kauai, 3,124.
Government. Gov., John A. Burns (D); lt. gov., George R. Ariyoshi (D); atty. gen., George Pai (D). Legislature: senate, 17 D, 8 R; house, 34 D, 17 R.
Finance (1971). Revenue, $631 million; expenditure, $685 million. Main sources of revenue: federal grants in aid, general excise and use tax. Main expenditures: education, capital improvements, health and welfare.
Education (est. 1970–1971). Primary school enrollment, 154,433; secondary school enrollment, 58,732. Total of 9,646 teachers in all grades.

PATRICIA L. DOWIE

HONDURAS. Politics and government. Late in 1971 ex-president Oswaldo López Arellano—now commander in chief of the armed forces—denied intentions to oust President Ramón Ernesto Cruz through a military coup.

Early this year, President Cruz went on record as being opposed to the establishment of Soviet embassies in Central America. Hondurans, he said, who had returned to Tegucigalpa after periods of study at Patrice Lumumba University in Moscow, were causing problems.

Economic developments. The Honduras National Development Foundation, affiliated with the Pan American Development Foundation (PADF) in Washington, D.C., has launched a self-help cooperative effort program to assist farmers in acquiring housing and land. The program is financed for five years from the PADF's $1.6 million revolving fund.

Foreign affairs. Late in 1971, an agreement between the Honduran government and a consortium of Florida universities, under which United States academics were advising on the reform of secondary education, was canceled at the request of the Honduran government following an extended anti-U.S. campaign by Honduran students and teachers. United States technicians were requested to leave the country.

President Cruz, during a visit to Guatemala, explained that peace with El Salvador was not possible until a general agreement was arrived at to resolve pending problems, some of which date back 110 years. Honduras and El Salvador continued to negotiate to normalize relations interrupted by the "soccer war" of 1969.

In February, at a meeting of Central American foreign ministers in Guatemala City, Honduras, which had withdrawn from the Central American Common Market owing in part to the effects of the war with El Salvador, signed

bilateral trade treaties with Costa Rica, Nicaragua, and Guatemala.

In June, the United States Senate ratified a treaty ceding the Swan Islands, which had been under U.S. sovereignty since 1856, to Honduras.

Mexican president Luis Echeverría Álvarez and President Cruz announced formation of a bilateral agreement to coordinate economic and technical cooperation between Mexico and Honduras.

Area and population. Area, 43,277 sq. mi. Pop. (est. 1970), 2,-583,000. Tegucigalpa (cap.; est. 1970), 232,276.
Government. Constitutional republic with unicameral legislature. Pres., Ramón Ernesto Cruz.
Finance. Monetary unit, lempira; 1 lempira = US$0.501.
Trade (1970). Imports (CIF), US$221 million; exports (FOB), US$171 million. Principal exports: bananas, coffee, lumber, minerals (silver, lead, and zinc), frozen or chilled meat, cotton. Principal trading partners: United States, Central American Common Market countries, West Germany, Japan, United Kingdom.
Education (1970). Literacy rate of persons of 10 years or older: 47.3 percent.
Armed forces. Army and national guard, 2,500; air force, 1,200.

GUILLERMO LUX

HONG KONG. China's entry into the United Nations did not unsettle Hong Kong. The immediate political future of the British colony seemed assured, in spite of economic setbacks from other quarters—from Britain itself, the United States, and Japan.

Politics and government. Soon after China's admission to the United Nations, the Chinese delegation had to take a position on Hong Kong, whose status had been under continual study by the UN Decolonization Committee. China's UN ambassador, Huang Hua, declared in a letter to the committee that while Hong Kong and Macao were "occupied by the British and Portuguese authorities," the fate of the territories was an internal matter of China's and should be left to China to deal with in its own way and in its own time. This reaffirmation of a long-established policy line of the Chinese Communist Party obliged the UN committee to remove Hong Kong from its agenda.

In Hong Kong itself the use of the word "colony" was deleted—apparently at Peking's request—from reentry permits issued to Chinese returning from visits to China. Meanwhile, China continued to derive more than a half of its foreign exchange income from Hong Kong, and the British were given to understand by the leaders in Peking that the status of Hong Kong would not have to change until the expiration of the New Territories lease in 1997.

Governor Crawford Murray Maclehose, who took office in October 1971, pledged to do all in his power to improve the quality of life of Hong Kong's Chinese population, a policy dictated by new internal political forces. This was also a means of deflecting Peking's criticisms of the colonial establishment.

The beginnings of a welfare state were evident in the inauguration of virtually compulsory, free primary education and in plans to extend this legislation to secondary education in the next two years. The government further undertook a public assistance program for aged, handicapped, and sick persons. Both policies marked complete departures from the former laissez-faire policies of the British regime.

Alec Douglas-Home, the British foreign secretary, visited Hong Kong in February to assure the colony of Britain's continuing interest and support. "Hong Kong," he said, "has an almost unique talent for playing a role that offers benefit to all and harms no one." In reality, however, Britain had unequivocally put its own interests before Hong Kong's on two economic issues of overwhelming importance to the colony, and the ties between Hong Kong and London visibly weakened during the year in spite of such ardent assurances.

Economic setbacks and advances. The two sectors threatened by British actions were the textile trade and currency parity. At the end of 1971, Britain decided to with-

draw its promise to Commonwealth producers and established both a quota and a tariff on textile imports from Commonwealth countries. This action weakened Hong Kong's competitive position relative to non-Commonwealth suppliers in the vital British market. In 1973, furthermore, Hong Kong stood to lose its Commonwealth preference status as a result of Britain's entrance into the Common Market.

In June, Britain floated the pound on the open market and Hong Kong responded by cutting itself loose from its sterling link. The Hong Kong dollar was then tied to the U.S. dollar, at the rate of HK$5.65 to US$1.00, thus producing an upward revaluation of 8.6 percent against the U.S. dollar.

As compensation for the loss of Commonwealth tariff preference, Hong Kong had looked forward to profiting from the special preference scheme organized by the United Nations Conference on Trade and Development, which promised tariff advantages in Western markets. But Japan, showing that the United Nations scheme could be readily undermined, won exemption from the scheme's provisions for precisely those articles that were of importance to Hong Kong in the Japanese market, notably textiles.

Meanwhile, Hong Kong suffered from a backlash of America's economic problems. The revaluation of Hong Kong's currency vis-à-vis the U.S. dollar gravely reduced the colony's competitiveness as an export manufacturer, particularly with respect to Taiwan and South Korea. Hong Kong was in turn obliged to sign a five-year agreement limiting its synthetic textile exports to the United States.

In March, Hong Kong's new financial secretary, Philip Haddon-Cave, introduced his first budget, reducing income taxes from 15 percent to 12.5 percent while cutting expenditures to $655 million in 1972–1973. The budget surplus for 1971–1972 was announced at $124 million, with reserves reaching a record $796 million.

Despite threats of further tariff and quota barriers in foreign markets, Hong Kong's trade stood up well, and the economic boom of the late 1960's continued. The colony's fourth stock exchange was opened at the end of 1971.

Area and population. Area, 399 sq. mi. Pop. (1971), 3,950,000.
Government. British crown colony. Gov., Sir Crawford Murray Maclehose.
Finance. Monetary unit, Hong Kong dollar; HK$1 = US$0.179. Budget (est. 1972–1973): HK$3,657 million.
Trade (1970). Imports, US$2,095 million; exports, US$2,514 million.
Education (1970–1971). Enrollment: primary, 765,397; secondary, 279,318; postsecondary technical and special schools, 11,739; universities (1 teaching in English, 1 in Chinese), 4,706.

DICK WILSON

HUNGARY. Economic developments. Nearly 70 percent of Hungarian foreign trade this year was to be carried out with Communist economic bloc countries, with whom agreements were made for an anticipated trade increase of 9–10 percent. The Hungarian National Committee for Technical Development was drafting ten-year and 20-year forecasts on which the long-term economic development plans were based. Hungary was to participate intensively in economic integration schemes in certain areas, including the machine tool industry, where research was to be carried out on the development of numerically controlled metalworking machine tools. In the area of farming, Hungary was to cooperate with other bloc countries in pig breeding and pork production.

Particularly great significance is attached to plans for coordination with the Soviet Union. Difficulties in economic relations arose during the Moscow visit of János Kádár and Hungarian premier Jenő Fock in February and March. Negotiations were to be resumed in November or December. The Soviet Union supplies 80 percent of Hungary's crude oil requirements, its entire demand for iron ore, and much

THE QUEEN IS DEAD. After burning for 24 hours, the "Queen Elizabeth" sank in Hong Kong harbor. Sold after hundreds of Atlantic crossings, the largest luxury liner ever built had been undergoing renovation for use as a floating university. Arson was suspected.

of its pine timber and other vital products. The Soviets are the biggest customers for Hungarian-made laboratory equipment, mechanical engineering products, and vehicles.

The new Friendship II oil pipeline, to link the pipeline at the Soviet-Hungarian frontier with the Danube oil refinery at Szashalombatta, was completed, and the first tons of Soviet oil were to reach the refinery in November. A branch line will carry oil to Leninvaros, where a large petrochemical combine is being set up with Soviet aid.

In May an agreement was signed in Budapest for the first Hungarian-U.S. joint enterprise. To be known as the Euroamerican Technocorporation, registered in Amsterdam and Curaçao, the firm will undertake commercial development of the Hungarian biochemical invention "fibrinbioplast," a tissue substitute which replaces missing tissue and also stimulates regeneration of the body's own tissue.

Because of the slow development of the building materials industry in Hungary, many materials have had to be imported from abroad, particularly from non-Communist countries. This year the Ministry of Building and Urban Development sought to cut the import of building materials from non-Communist countries by 15 percent. This was to be accomplished by construction of new paneling tile plants in the porcelain factories of Budapest and Alföld, increase in the output of ceramic floor coverings in the Budapest building ceramics factory, speeding up of the construction of the Beremend cement works, and bilateral agreements with the Soviet Union and other Communist countries.

The Ozd metalworks was to spend more than 90 million forints on water purification equipment during the fourth five-year plan in order to clean up one of Hungary's most polluted rivers, the Sajo. The works has already paid almost 6 million forints in fines.

Politics and government. The Councils Act was reportedly proving to be a significant step toward decentralization and toward providing more uniform systems of state administration. The placing of towns with county status under the jurisdiction of counties was proving useful, and the formation of county district offices was said to have

taken place smoothly. The sphere of authority of villages was widened. Of particular importance was introduction of the category of the large village. There are at present 276 of these, in which almost 40 percent of the population lives.

Problems concerning youth continued to increase. The number of legally convicted youths rose in Budapest and was ascribed to the numerous broken marriages and increased consumption of alcohol.

Religion. In May, Pope Paul VI received nine Hungarian bishops and 68 priests who led the first pilgrimage of Hungarians to Rome since the end of World War II. The age level of the Hungarian clergy is rapidly rising. In 1969 there were 4,014 practicing Catholic priests in Hungary, of whom 31.3 percent were between 51 and 60 years of age. With only 300 students in six seminaries, it is likely that the number of priests will diminish and the number of vacant posts will increase.

Travel. Travel to the West is increasing greatly. Hungary, the most liberal of Soviet bloc countries in granting permission to visit the West, was to provide a quarter of a million passports for that purpose this year.

Area and population. Area, 35,919 sq. mi. Pop. (est. 1972), 10,374,000. Principal cities (est. 1969): Budapest (cap.), 1,969,000; Miskolc, 175,000.

Government. People's republic. Unicameral National Assembly of 349 deputies represented by 21-member Presidium when not in session. Chmn., presidium, Pál Losonczi; prem., Jenö Fock; first secy., Socialist Workers' (Communist) Party, János Kádár. Party membership (1970), 600,000.

Finance. Monetary unit, forint; 1 forint = US$0.0865; tourist rate, 1 forint = US$0.033. Budget (1972, in billions of forints): revenue, 212.6; expenditure, 215.8.

Trade (1970). Imports, US$2.5 billion; exports, US$2.3 billion.

Agriculture and industry (1970). Agricultural production (in thousands of metric tons): maize, 4,073; wheat, 2,722; potatoes, 1,-813; barley, 553. Livestock (in thousands): pigs, 5,970; sheep, 3,024; cattle, 1,933; horses, 231. Industrial production (in thousands of metric tons): lignite, 23,679; hard coal, 4,151; crude steel, 3,110; cement, 2,771; bauxite, 2,022; crude oil, 1,937; pig iron, 1,835. Electric power, 14.54 billion kw.-hr.

Education (1970). Enrollment: primary, 1,177,887; secondary, 454,552; institutions of higher learning, 53,237.

RICHARD A. PIERCE

ICELAND. Politics and government. The term of Iceland's president, Dr. Kristján Eldjárn, expired at midyear, and elections were set for June 25. The law specifies that presidential candidates must be nominated by at least 1,500 but no more than 3,000 residents of Iceland. By May 20, however, the deadline for nominations, there was only one candidate, the incumbent. Dr. Eldjárn was thus automatically reelected to serve for another four years.

Foreign affairs. On February 15 the Althing (Parliament) voted unanimously to empower the government to extend the fishing limits around Iceland from 12 miles to 50 miles, effective September 1. In accordance with a treaty signed in 1961, negotiations had been going on with both Great Britain and West Germany regarding such an extension, but no agreement had been reached. Great Britain and West Germany thereupon submitted the dispute to the International Court of Justice at The Hague for an advisory opinion. In August the court ruled that Great Britain and West Germany could continue to fish until the next UN Conference on the Law of the Sea, to be held in 1974, when the matter would be settled.

Iceland maintained that the court had no jurisdiction and that the country's vital interests were at stake. On September 1, the Icelandic government proceeded to extend the fishing limits. Iceland was prepared to resume, if necessary, the "cod war" against Great Britain of some years ago. Many foreign vessels continued to fish with impunity within the new limits. Iceland counteracted by having some gunboats and inspection vessels cut the expensive trawler lines of the offending boats.

In early September, Belgium recognized the new limits, and Faeroese vessels were allowed to fish inside the 50-mile zone. At year's end negotiations had been resumed, and the interested nations seemed to have come to terms with the Icelandic action.

The United States and Iceland some time ago agreed to revise the defense agreement and eventually to have all U.S. forces at the Keflavík NATO base withdrawn. The present government has indicated that it will seek the withdrawal of U.S. forces within four years. Further talks were held in the fall. In the meantime the United States began work on the extension of one of the Keflavík runways, at a cost of more than $5 million, leading some Icelanders to suspect that the United States had been permitted to stay longer than four years. The Icelandic government denied that any promise had been made.

Economic affairs. In Iceland all parties agreed that Iceland's best interests would be served by remaining outside the European Economic Community, but there was a strong desire to reach a favorable trade agreement with the enlarged community. Several meetings were held, with no tangible results. One stumbling block in the negotiations was the fact that the EEC objected to the new 50-mile fisheries limit, but Iceland remained adamant and no agreement was immediately forthcoming.

Area and population. Area, 39,800 sq. mi. Pop. (1971), 206,818. Reykjavík (cap.), 82,693.

Government. Republic. Pres., Kristján Eldjárn; prime min., Ólafur Johannesson.

Finance. Monetary unit, króna (pl., krónur); 1 króna = US$0.0117.

Trade (1971). Imports, 13.175 billion krónur; exports, 19.361 billion krónur.

Education. Primary schools, 187; secondary schools, 139; technical and special schools, 107; colleges, 6; universities, 1. Enrollment, 62,500; teachers, 4,466.

Armed forces. None. NATO forces are stationed in Iceland as the Iceland Defense Force. ERIK J. FRIIS

IDAHO. Mine disaster. In one of the worst mining disasters in memory, 91 miners died as fire swept the jewel shaft of the Sunshine Silver Mine in Kellogg on May 2. Flames, smoke, and heat hampered rescue operations, while casualty figures mounted day by day. On May 10 two men who had survived in an air pocket on the lunches of dead comrades were rescued alive; but two days later the last 40 missing men were found dead. After an inconclusive investigation, the mine remained closed.

UPI

BURIED ALIVE FOR A WEEK, Tom Wilkenson is rescued from the Sunshine Silver Mine in Kellogg, Idaho. He and his friend Ron Flory were the only survivors among 93 miners trapped by a flash fire in one of the worst U.S. mining disasters.

Environment. Dedication of the Sawtooth recreation area on September 1 ensured protection to the White Clouds peaks, which had been a center of controversy for the past three years. The measure regulated the use of some 754,000 acres of public and private land. Meanwhile, a moratorium on dam building in the middle Snake River continued to be urged both in and out of government, and pressure mounted to block private development of land adjacent to that stretch of river. Senator Frank Church (D) requested a $4 million appropriation for federal purchase of some 15,000 acres of ranch land for sale in the area.

Fish runs continued to suffer from downriver development on the Snake. Hatchery fish migrating downstream and adult salmon and steelhead trout moving inland were threatened by nitrogen supersaturation at dams from Little Goose to Bonneville. Installation of slotted gates in skeleton generator bays and of flip lips on spillways reduced nitrogen content in the spillage, but the overall effectiveness of these devices remained unproved. Nevertheless, greater optimism about the future of fish runs prevailed this year.

The Dworshak Reservoir on the North Fork branch of the Clearwater River filled throughout the winter. The antagonism of preservationists and sportsmen toward this project was abetted by reports and pictures of deer trapped by broken ice and run down by coyote packs, although the actual extent of the damage to deer and elk herds remained to be determined.

Legislation. The second session of the 41st legislature deliberated for 76 days. Among 416 bills enacted was a bill lowering the age of majority to 18 and making 19 the minimum age for consumption of alcoholic beverages. Another measure brought repeal of the new criminal code. A result of a six-year study financed by the legislature, the new code had gone into effect January 1. It came under attack from law enforcement sources and was repealed outright after unsuccessful attempts to save it by amendment. With no alternative, the old code was reenacted.

From the start of the session, Governor Cecil D. Andrus and the Republican leadership were engaged in a debate on state finances. The Republican-controlled legislature finally appropriated $137.3 million, or $12 million less than the governor had requested and $27 million below major agency requests. For the public schools it provided $47.8 million (up from $44 million) and for higher education $29.5 million (up from $27.7 million).

Nine proposed constitutional amendments, six of which passed this session, were slated to appear on the November ballot. The legislature considered but failed to enact measures providing for a state lottery, legalized abortion, and 100 percent state funding of public schools. It also rejected establishment of a special commission on public school organization, but the issue remained alive.

For election results and campaign highlights, see the special supplement ELECTION '72.

Area and population. Area, 83,557 sq. mi. Pop. (1970), 712,-567. Principal cities (1970): Boise (cap.), 74,990; Pocatello, 40,036; Idaho Falls, 35,776; Lewiston, 26,068.
Government. Gov., Cecil D. Andrus (D); lt. gov., Jack M. Murphy (R); atty. gen., W. Anthony Park (D); secy. of state, Peter T. Cenarrusa (R). Legislature: senate, 19 R, 16 D; house, 41 R, 29 D.
Finance (fiscal 1973). General fund budget, $137 million.
Education. Public schools (est. 1971–1972): elementary enrollment, 93,148; teachers, 3,777; secondary enrollment, 91,966; teachers, 4,232. Nonpublic elementary and secondary school enrollment (est. fall 1971), 7,400. Institutions of higher education (fall 1970): full-time enrollment, 26,890; part-time enrollment, 7,810.

SIEGFRIED B. ROLLAND

ILLINOIS. Legislation. The general assembly devoted the biggest share of its attention to taxes and appropriations during the first of its annual sessions under the new state constitution. The previous constitution had provided for biennial sessions in odd-numbered years.

The tax questions centered on relief for certain groups. Measures approved included a $5,000 personal property tax exemption for both individuals and businesses; special personal property tax relief for farmers, with the state replacing revenues lost to local governments; grants up to $500 authorized as reimbursement for taxes paid by elderly and handicapped persons; and continuation of exemption from personal property tax of one car and one household of furniture per family. The assembly turned down a proposal to freeze real estate taxes for two years, a plan supported by Governor Richard B. Ogilvie and opposed by Chicago mayor Richard J. Daley.

Appropriations were the subject of much debate, but in the end they were approximately the same as recommended by Governor Ogilvie in his record $7.2 billion budget for fiscal 1973.

The general assembly also enacted a new code of corrections for handling convicted felons, restricted billboards along major highways, provided financial aid for mass transportation districts, and created a capital development bond authority, a state agency to replace the quasi-state Illinois Building Authority.

A no-fault insurance plan failed to pass after the courts had voided a previously approved plan. The senate voted to ratify the federal Equal Rights Amendment, but proponents were unable to get enough votes to push the issue through the House.

Economic developments. The Illinois economy rebounded somewhat from the previous year's doldrums but still was not as healthy as in 1969 and 1970. At midyear total nonfarm employment was up from July 1971 but still well below the July 1969 total. The average workweek was 40.4 hours, at an average rate of $4.22 an hour, up 26 cents from the previous year.

The U.S. grain sale to the Soviet Union was a big boost to the Illinois farm economy, as grain prices rose despite a bumper crop of corn and soybeans. Congressman Paul Findley led a trade mission to the Soviet Union in the fall in an effort to increase exports from Illinois, already the top agricultural export state.

Education. State Superintendent of Public Instruction Michael J. Bakalis based the operations of his office on a set of action goals for public education in Illinois in the 1970's which were adopted at a statewide conference of interested citizens. The most ambitious goal, to achieve a 50 percent level of state funding by fiscal 1975, still seemed somewhat remote after the general assembly declined to raise the 1973 figure to 42 percent. Some other goals, such as better financial planning and experiments with 12-month schools, did win approval. Bakalis cited about 20 school districts in the state for failure to desegregate and ordered work on desegregation plans. He and Governor Ogilvie jointly created a task force to seek ways to cut administrative costs in school systems.

Teachers' strikes in the fall of 1972 were fewer than a year earlier, but there was still unrest in the huge Chicago school system, where a strike was avoided only by using bond issue funds to pay teacher salaries.

For election results and campaign highlights, see the special supplement ELECTION '72.

Area and population. Area, 56,400 sq. mi. Pop. (1970), 11,113,-976. Principal cities (1970): Springfield (cap.), 91,753; Chicago, 3,366,957; Rockford, 147,370; Peoria, 126,963.
Government. Gov., Richard B. Ogilvie (R); lt. gov., Paul Simon (D); atty. gen., William Scott (R); secy. of state, John Lewis (R); aud., Michael J. Howlett (D); treas., Alan Dixon (D). Legislature: senate, 29 R, 28 D; house, 89 R, 86 D.
Finance (fiscal 1971). Revenue, $6.28 billion; expenditures, $6.19 billion.
Education (1971–1972). Public schools, 4,545; districts, 1,103; enrollment, 2,379,982; teachers, 108,913. Parochial schools, 1,174; enrollment, 423,124; teachers, 18,505. Public colleges and universities, 47; enrollment, 326,409. Private colleges and universities, 87; enrollment, 132,478.

EDWARD H. ARMSTRONG

MEETING AT SIMLA, Indian prime minister Indira Gandhi and Pakistani president Zulfikar Ali Bhutto agreed to a step-by-step normalization of Indo-Pakistani relations. The July 3 accord ended a rupture dating from December 1971 war.

INDIA. In the aftermath of the 1971 war with Pakistan, India created a friendly and dependent neighbor in Bangladesh, weakened an embittered and intransigent Pakistan, sent home 9.9 million burdensome refugees, and emerged unmistakably as the dominant power in South Asia. Prime Minister Indira Gandhi's stock rose to new heights; Indians were convinced that an era of stability lay round the corner.

But that hope faded as the year wore on and the Indo-Pakistani agreement petered out in objections, hesitations, and legal quibbling. With drought and floods afflicting vast areas, lights were austerely dimmed on August 15 when India celebrated the 25th anniversary of independence from British rule. Even more ominous was the fear of civil war in the northeastern state of Nagaland, where, after a murderous attack August 8 upon the state chief minister, Hokishe Sema, Mrs. Gandhi refused to renew an eight-year-old armistice with secessionists.

The war. Visiting East Pakistani refugee camps in Calcutta, Mrs. Ghandhi was at a government house reception on December 3, 1971, when eight Indian airfields were suddenly strafed by Pakistani bombers. She flew back to New Delhi at once to announce in a dramatic midnight broadcast that "the war in Bangladesh has become a war on India." Indian troops had by then already crossed into East Pakistan at 12 points. Five columns were advancing upon the capital city of Dacca, and Pakistani ports and runways were under aerial and naval attack. Five hours later, Pakistani president Agha Muhammad Yahya Khan broke off diplomatic relations with India for the first time in the strained history of Indo-Pakistani relations.

Events had been moving inexorably to this climax since March 25, 1971, when civil war broke out in East Pakistan. As millions of bruised and battered refugees (90 percent of them Hindus) poured into India with horrendous tales of military brutality, Mrs. Gandhi announced her terms for de-escalating tension: reforms in East Pakistan which would at once stop the exodus, an early return of all refugees, and credible guarantees for their future safety.

The crippling burden of keeping the refugees alive was the official explanation for Mrs. Gandhi's policy of controlled escalation. (India had to carry the major share of the load and spent vast sums from an already overstrained budget to maintain the overcrowded, noisome, and disease-infested camps.) Though she did not admit to aiding East Pakistani liberation fighters until November, war was re-

garded as a certainty in July when the army chief, General S. H. F. J. Manekshaw, drew up his campaign outline; the operational plan was ready at the end of October. Troop movements to a 3,000-mile border in the east and west had been completed by mid-November, and ordnance factories were working overtime. India's success is partly attributed to its capacity to produce its own weapons and airplanes.

Mrs. Gandhi's military strategy reflected her political objectives. In the west, where most of Yahya Khan's 250,000 soldiers were concentrated, the Indian army was content to fight a holding operation. But Lieutenant General Jagjit Singh Aurora, who commanded seven and a half divisions in the east, had explicit orders to obtain the speedy and unconditional surrender of East Pakistan. Having found western leaders unresponsive to her appeals, Mrs. Gandhi decided that in India's long-term interests, as well as for the sake of 75 million East Bengalis, the martial law authority in Dacca would have to be replaced by a representative national regime. Diplomatic recognition of the Bangladesh government-in-exile, followed by the formation of a joint command which brought approximately 150,000 East Bengal liberation fighters (Mukti Bahini) under Aurora's orders, gave the formal finishing touches to this policy.

The battle was for Dacca, and by December 13, Indian forces had the capital city nearly encircled. Forty miles from the capital, the Indian commander broadcast the first of General Manekshaw's three ultimatums. But East Pakistan's martial law administrator, Lieutenant General Amir Abdullah Khan Niazi, announced his determination to fight to the last man.

Others were less courageous. Two days earlier, the government's military adviser, Major General Rao Farman Ali, had proposed a plan of retreat. And within 24 hours of Niazi's announcement, as Indian Gnats (lightweight fighter planes) were pounding Dacca's government house, East Pakistan's civilian governor, Abdul Motaleb Malik, resigned in a letter to President Yahya Khan. The governor and his cabinet took refuge in the Hotel Intercontinental, a neutral zone where 16 senior East Pakistani officials, including the police chief, had already sought asylum. Niazi signed surrender papers on December 16. Mrs. Gandhi promptly announced a unilateral cease-fire in the west, where India had taken a great deal of Pakistani territory and lost very little. It was initially rejected by Yahya Khan, but accepted the next day.

Fruits of victory. Indians expect peace in the subcontinent now that Pakistan has been reduced from one-fifth to one-tenth the size of India and lost 54 percent of its population. Mrs. Gandhi also ensured liberated Bangladesh's goodwill by evacuating Indian troops before March 25, 1972, the first anniversary of the civil war. The rationalization for the conflict was also justified when, following invitations from Bangladesh, the last of the refugees returned on March 25.

But the war has also saddled India with more than 91,000 Pakistani prisoners, whose upkeep costs about $1.3 million a month. Their future, still undecided, could cause friction between India, Pakistan, and Bangladesh. Indian casualties —3,241 killed, 302 missing, 8,561 wounded, and 504 taken prisoner—are not regarded as high, but 73 tanks, 45 aircraft, and a frigate were also lost. Replacement of military hardware has not permitted any reduction in a defense outlay of $1,867 million.

Harvest at the hustings. The Congress Party was in a predictably stronger position to canvass in the fifth general elections, when 193 million people went to the polls in 16 states and two federally administered territories. Mrs. Gandhi also successfully argued that her strong federal government needed regional support to push through a ten-point program of social and economic reform. Promising limitation of private property, free compulsory education, and more jobs, the Congress Party captured 71 percent of state assembly seats in the balloting (March 5–11).

The landslide victory meant, in effect, a return to the pre-1967 single-party system. A discredited Communist Party of India (Marxist), which had dragged its feet over Bangladesh, won only 34 scattered seats. The three major parties to the right of Mrs. Gandhi—the Old Congress, the Jan Sangh, and the Swatantra Party—accounted for no more than 8 percent of the vote. By June the Congress Party controlled, either directly or through alliances, 19 out of 21 state governments. The chief ministers of the two remaining states, Tamil Nadu and Manipur, were accusing it of trying to overthrow their regimes.

Economic and social reform. Heavy imposts seemed inevitable in view of the Congress slogan of *Garibi Hatao* ("Banish Poverty"), as well as war expenditure and aid to Bangladesh. But Finance Minister Yashwantrao Chavan's budget raised an extra $244 million without drastic levies. At the same time, he announced massive expenditures (more than $2 billion) for welfare, agriculture, roads, and power in 1972–1973. But even with a 20 percent rise in exports in the first quarter of 1972, the budget is likely to be in deficit; Chavan kept his options open to impose higher income and wealth taxes. The rich are not yet being soaked, but the government take-over this year of a copper corporation and an iron and steel company dismayed industrialists.

For the first time, India became self-sufficient in food with stocks of 9 million metric tons. A consumer society emerged with the production of bicycles, wristwatches, and sewing machines. Television is being extended beyond New Delhi, and health centers are being set up.

But there are still about 13 million people without jobs, and half the population is unable to spend more than $2.60 a month. Malnutrition remains a major problem, and West Bengal legislators were agitated over 30 alleged starvation deaths. The fourth five-year plan's $2,680 million education budget, spent mainly on colleges, added about 100,000 degree holders to the ranks of the jobless, while only 39 percent of Indian males and 18 percent of females are literate.

West Bengal. There were widespread complaints of rigging when, after five years of chronic instability, the Congress Party swept the polls in March, putting to rout a seven-party Marxist alliance. Former deputy chief minister Jyoti Basu accused Chief Minister Siddhartha Sankar Ray of "gangsterism and manipulation of votes" in 200 out of

280 constituencies; then his 14 legislators (there were 111 in 1971) boycotted the assembly. The decisive rejection of the extreme left was attributed by others to the militancy of the Congress Party's two youth wings. The swing was further consolidated with the capture on July 16 of the Marxist-Leninist (Naxalite) chairman, Charu Mazumdar, after a two-year hunt. A brief recrudescence of Naxalite violence followed the arrest, but the movement was already in disarray because of Peking's ambiguous attitude toward Bangladesh, and it quietly petered out when Mazumdar, a cardiac asthma patient, died 12 days later.

Kashmir. Differences in disputed Jammu and Kashmir appear to be narrowing down to an argument over autonomy within the Indian federation. Formal negotiations were denied by the federal planning minister, Durga Prasad Dhar, a Kashmiri brahmin and architect of the Indo-Soviet treaty of 1971. But Sheikh Muhammad Abdullah, 67-year-old "Lion of Kashmir," met Mrs. Gandhi after a ban was lifted which had kept him out of the state for 17 months. He claimed that the impasse would be resolved if India granted self-government to Kashmir except in the areas of defense, foreign affairs, and communications. Mirza Afzal Beg, chief of the proscribed Plebiscite Front, abandoned his earlier argument that Pakistan is a party to the dispute. Encouraged by a climate of accommodation, Syed Mir Qasim's government, which holds 57 out of 75 seats, released 400 political prisoners and permitted 20 externed leaders to return. But the sheikh refused to accept Qasim's electoral mandate and accused Mrs. Gandhi of double standards over Kashmir and Bangladesh.

Foreign relations. After exhaustive lobbying for world support for its actions in Bangladesh, India is now consolidating its new position on the subcontinent.

Pakistan. Several months of negotiating through the Swiss embassy and a preliminary meeting of Indian and Pakistani officials in the Pakistani hill resort of Murree prepared the ground for Mrs. Gandhi's Simla summit meeting at Simla, beginning June 28. For the first three days, both sides appeared to be reconciled to an innocuous communiqué stressing the need for peace; but late on July 1 the Pakistanis sent a fresh set of proposals to Mrs. Gandhi's headquarters. She had already gone to bed, but the document was studied through the night by her political affairs committee, and further talks were held the next day. It was not until after midnight of July 2–3 that the two leaders ended the suspense and uncertainty.

Although the two countries agreed to a gradual normalization of relations, there was no mention of restoring diplomatic ties, the repatriation of 93,000 Pakistanis still held in India was left to future discussion, and the whole pact was made contingent on prior settlement of the line of control in the disputed state of Kashmir.

The issue of Kashmir was a major stumbling block in later talks. After meeting for five days in late August, officials of the two countries were said to have established general guidelines for setting the line of control, but by the end of the third week in October, Indian and Pakistani military commanders had met eight times without coming to an agreement. Mrs. Gandhi turned down a proposal for a return visit to Pakistan, declined to vacate 5,200 square miles of Pakistani territory, and refused to withdraw troops from a forward position on a 1,400 mile border. Bhutto, for his part, found one reason after another to delay settlement and, at the last minute, laid claim to an additional 2 square miles of territory in Kashmir. On October 22 a terse announcement said that settlement of the difficulties had been postponed, and although Mrs. Gandhi and Bhutto exchanged letters, no date was fixed for another round of talks.

Bangladesh. The 25-year treaty of friendship, cooperation, and peace which Mrs. Gandhi signed with Prime Minister Sheikh Mujibur Rahman in Dacca on March 19 is one of an interlocking series of agreements to promote the

"Brezhnev doctrine" of collective security. India and Bangladesh have also moved toward a customs union and free trade zone with agreements to reduce tariffs, guarantee a trading turnover of $50 million in 1972, and plan jointly for flood control, irrigation, and power. But the economic association is under political attack, and Indian businessmen have been accused of exploiting Bangladesh. Rahman and other leaders have strongly denounced criticism of India. But despite substantial Indian aid (commitments are in excess of $270 million, in addition to food and technical and military assistance), Bangladesh would probably like to write off gratitude for 1971 and start a new relationship on a different basis.

Soviet Union. Agreements on space research and trade have followed the Indo-Soviet treaty of 1971, and Indian foreign trade minister Lalit Narayan Mishra predicted that the Soviet Union would be India's biggest trading partner in 1972–1973. But in spite of Soviet president Nikolai Podgorny's welcome in Calcutta, Mrs. Gandhi has been careful to stress that India remains nonaligned. For instance, she assured Australian television viewers that Soviet warships did not use Indian ports. There is some anxiety because the U.S.-Soviet Statement of Basic Principles is interpreted in India as carving out spheres of influence.

United States. During the December war the U.S. government was highly critical of India's actions, and Indians have resented the U.S. interpretation of events. Hopes of a rapprochement aroused by John B. Connally's arrival to brief Mrs. Gandhi on Nixon's Moscow visit soon fizzled out. The Calcutta *Statesman* called it a "nonmission" which left the impression that the U.S. "tilt" toward Pakistan remained unchanged. It is believed in New Delhi that Ambassador Kenneth B. Keating resigned in July because he saw no hope of improving relations until after the November presidential elections.

Connally's statement that aid was "under review," as well as the Nixon administration's claim that a request to Congress for $90 million for India was only "designed to keep options open," are resented as indicating that India is on probation. Brooding over President Nixon's attitude during the December war, many Indians are convinced that Washington turns a blind eye to U.S. arms routed to Pakistan through Islamic countries and is trying to undermine Indian influence in Bangladesh.

China. Routine diplomatic courtesies were resumed in 1971, but there has been little progress since the war, in which China supported Pakistan. Mrs. Gandhi is ready to raise the level of diplomatic recognition (there are now only chargés d'affaires in New Delhi and Peking) without settling the border dispute and to enter into economic relations, but overtures are persistently ignored. Peking took no notice of an invitation to participate in the Asian trade fair in New Delhi. There is also annoyance at China's veto of Bangladesh's membership in the United Nations.

Area and population. *Federation.* Area, 1,226,480 sq. mi. Pop. (1971 census, final), 547,959,809. Principal cities (met. areas; 1971 census, final): New Delhi (cap.), 4,065,698; Calcutta, 7,031,832; Bombay, 5,970,575; Madras, 3,169,930; Hyderabad, 1,796,339; Ahmedabad, 1,741,522; Bangalore, 1,653,779; Kanpur, 1,275,242; Poona, 1,135,034. *Protectorates.* Bhutan: area, 18,000 sq. mi.; pop. (est. 1971), 1 million. Sikkim: area, 2,745 sq. mi.; pop. (est. 1971), 200,000.

Government. Parliamentary federal republic consisting of 21 states and nine union territories. Pres., V. V. Giri; prime min., Indira Gandhi.

Finance. Monetary unit, rupee; R1 = US$0.129. Budget (est. 1972–1973): total expenditure, Rs68,130 million; overall deficit, Rs2,420 million.

Trade (1969–1970). Exports, Rs14,130 million; imports, Rs15,670 million.

Education (1972). Total enrollment, 90 million, including 1.5 million in colleges. University degree holders, 12 million. Literacy, 29.35%.

SUNANDA K. DATTA-RAY

TUG OF WAR. Grabbing the bottom of a rope barrier from police, New Delhi protesters pull hard to stretch a point about rising prices.

UPI

INDIANA. Education. The continuing and increasing financial crises in public schools moved Indiana closer to a showdown over state and local responsibility for education. The legislature again was unable to enact a tax reform bill or to find new sources of revenue to supplement the old property tax system.

The travail of school corporations throughout the state worsened, with 71 corporations reporting they faced even more serious problems next year. Some units opened their fall terms later than usual to delay the first pay day. Several faced possible strikes, but none had to postpone the opening of the new term.

The legislature passed an emergency bill creating a "distressed school fund" from which qualified schools could draw aid. However, the help available was only minimal. At one point, 14 school corporations were asking for more than $9 million, while the state fund contained only $5 million.

Another emergency bill, setting a precedent in Indiana, gave the giant Gary school system permission to transfer some of its school-building funds to operating expenses in order to obtain a state loan and draw advance money from the state. The new law gave a state control board authority to oversee Gary expenditures.

In Gary a lengthy teachers' strike kept 45,000 students out of school for 22 days in April and May. Governor Edgar D. Whitcomb charged that the teachers' demands forced the school board to contract for money it did not have. The board adopted a 1973 budget totaling $40.6 million, including a $6.6 million deficit.

Government. The legislature, meeting for the first time in an even-numbered year, passed 239 bills out of 794 introduced during the 30-day session. It lowered the legal age of adulthood from 21 to 18 years, with a major exception: citizens under 21 cannot legally buy alcoholic drinks or make sales of liquor, although they can work in package liquor stores. Lowering the legal drinking age was one of six bills vetoed by the governor.

Lake County (Gary, Hammond, and East Chicago) and Allen County (Fort Wayne) were given permission to levy a 3 percent tax on gross incomes of hotels and motels. Lake County was to use the money to create a medical center board, which would plan for a proposed medical school, and Allen County was to finance a convention center board.

Ecology. Northern Indiana Public Service Company was involved in two key projects along the shores of Lake Michigan. It signed an $8.5 million contract with the U.S. Environmental Protection Agency for construction of a sulfur dioxide control system at the utility's generating station east of Gary. Its proposal to build a nuclear plant in nearby Porter County was undergoing hearings conducted by the Atomic Energy Commission.

The legislature created a part-time, 11-member Indiana Environmental Management Board to coordinate antipollution activities of state agencies.

Finance. The state's general fund showed a $39 million surplus at the end of the fiscal year, more than twice the surplus of the previous year. The governor attributed part of the surplus to job freezes and other economic measures.

For election results and campaign highlights, see the special supplement ELECTION '72.

Area and population. Area, 36,291 sq. mi., including 102 sq. mi. of inland water. Pop. (1970), 5,193,669. Principal cities: Indianapolis (cap.), 744,624; Fort Wayne, 177,671; Gary, 175,415; Evansville, 138,764; South Bend, 125,580.
Government. Gov., Edgar D. Whitcomb (R); lt. gov., Richard E. Folz (R); secy. of state, Larry Conrad (D); aud., Mary Aikins (D); treas., Jack New (D); atty. gen., Theodore L. Sendak (R); supt. of pub. instr., John J. Loughlin (D). General assembly: senate, 29 R, 21 D; house of representatives, 53 R, 47 D.
Finance (year ending June 30). Revenue, general fund, $864.2 million; expenditure, $825.2 million. Principal sources of revenue: taxes. Principal items of expenditure: education, highways.
Education. Public schools, 2,198; enrollment, 1,230,853; teachers, 59,435. Parochial and private schools, 440.   C. W. VERTREES

INDONESIA. Since the elections of 1971, President Suharto has had nothing dramatic to offer the Indonesian public, and 1972 brought some rumblings of impatience at the slow pace of both economic progress and sociopolitical reforms.

Politics and government. Strong discontent focused on the Indonesia-in-Miniature project, a $26 million tourist complex partly modeled on Disneyland and supported by Madame Tien Suharto, the president's wife. Although government funds were not involved in the project, it was nevertheless criticized by students, the press, and intellectuals on the ground that it displayed a bad sense of priorities in what remained, basically, a very poor country.

Suharto himself tried to stay aloof from the debate but eventually found himself compelled to move against the demonstrators. Some students were accused of affiliations with the New Left in the United States and elsewhere. Among those arrested were the psychologist Arif Budiman and the journalist H. J. C. Princen, both respected figures who had lent support to the moderate student movement.

General Sumitro, deputy commander of the National Security Council and one of the most powerful military figures after Suharto himself, warned the demonstrators "not to imitate Western youths in this new and dangerous trend of political thinking." Some observers saw the issue as a further instance of rivalry among the president's colleagues in the army hierarchy.

Major General Ali Moertopo, a presidential adviser and organizer of the Sekber Golkar (the political arm of the military group that has ruled the country since the 1971 elections), favored some leeway for intellectuals to express dissent. But the more security-conscious generals, notably General Sumitro and General Maraden Panggabean, the deputy defense minister, pressed for a strong stand against radicalism, whether Marxist or not.

The difference was less a matter of opposing policies than one of emphasis and political tactics among generals who share a strongly anti-Communist platform. Moertopo, however, found himself type-cast as the champion of civilian participation in the government, a movement led by Foreign Minister Adam Malik. The pro-civilian stance was enhanced by the Golkar's nomination of Sultan Hamengku Buwono, a widely respected neutral figure in Indonesian politics, for the key post of minister of economics, finance, and industry.

But civilians (especially journalists) continued to broaden their attacks on the government. They focused in particular on the stranglehold on business exerted jointly by the army and the government—what some commentators called Indonesia's "industrial-military complex." As a result of these criticisms, more generals felt put on the defensive. During 1972, Moertopo lost political ground, to the chagrin of both civil leaders and the Chinese community.

Some consolidations were made in the conduct of national party politics. Only three political groups won the right to field candidates in the 1976 elections. These were the ruling Golkar, the Unity Development (comprising the four established Muslim parties), and the Democratic Development (uniting the Nationalist Party, the Christian parties, and the Proletarian Party). The second of these shotgun alliances looked feasible, but, paradoxically enough, a working coalition of the rival Islamic leaders proved more elusive.

Foreign affairs. President Suharto visited Australia, New Zealand, and the Philippines in February and journeyed to Japan (his third visit in five years) in May. Prime Minister William McMahon of Australia repaid the compliment in June and agreed to give the Indonesians more substantial defense help, notably 16 Sabre jet fighters.

But the dominant international issue centered on the legal status of the Straits of Malacca, the vital commercial waterway lying between Malaysia and Indonesia. Inasmuch as both governments now claim a 12-mile limit for their terri-

torial waters, vast stretches of the straits ostensibly lie within the boundaries of one country or the other.

Indonesia took the lead in asserting, along with Malaysia, the "de-internationalization" of the straits. "We object," said Foreign Minister Malik in March, "to the view that the Malacca Straits is international water. We have nothing against anybody, but we must guard our national safety. We still recognize the right of passage of ships of other nationalities, but we are thinking of coming to some agreement on placing those waters under the joint control of Malaysia, Singapore, and Indonesia."

Proclamations notwithstanding, Indonesia and Malaysia acted to bar ships over 200,000 tons—in effect, all supertankers—from the straits. The Indonesians made it clear that they were upset by the clandestine use of the straits by foreign warships and submarines. Most major maritime nations expressed concern over these developments, but the two that were most directly affected were Japan, 90 percent of whose oil supplies come through the straits, and the Soviet Union. It was the Soviets who made the most open attacks on the new Indonesian policy.

Minor excitement was aroused by border troubles with the Portuguese on Timor, and Malik flew to the island to mollify the situation. A neutral zone installed along the border defused the issue, and Indonesia reaffirmed its policy of nonaggrandizement toward the tiny Portuguese colony.

Economic stagnation—and hope. The growth of the GNP in 1972 was expected to exceed 7 percent, but with an annual population growth of 2.7 percent, the 1972 gain in per capita income (3.5 percent in 1971) was not likely to exceed 4 or 5 percent. With a population enjoying an average income of only $100 a year, the plodding economic growth rate became a matter for grave concern.

The government presented a $1.8 billion budget for 1972–1973, a 28 percent increase over the previous year. Half of the routine expenditure was on civil service salaries, which were to be nearly doubled. The official review of the 1971–1972 performance found cause for optimism, citing the reduction of the annual inflation rate to only 2.5 percent. The review also noted that there was a vastly increased rice harvest of 13 million tons.

Exports in 1972 were expected to rise by 40 percent to over $1.8 billion, but most of this increase was accounted for by petroleum exports, which had doubled during the year to over $1 billion. The production of crude oil passed the million-barrels-per-day mark early in 1972, and the total for the year was expected to reach 400 million barrels. With this year's increases in international oil prices, the Indonesian petroleum industry accounted for an unprecedented 60 percent of the nation's total export revenues and for 40 percent of state income from all sources. New offshore and inland finds were reported by some of the large Indonesian-licensed oil corporations.

The 11 nations and two international banks making up the Inter-Governmental Group on Indonesia pledged $724 million in aid for the year 1972–1973, exceeding Djakarta's initial request by $54 million. Some $118 million was earmarked in the form of food assistance; the United States, Japan, West Germany, and the Netherlands, in decreasing order, were the largest donors. In May, a month after this pledge was announced in Amsterdam, President Suharto went to Tokyo and obtained additional loans for new oil projects totaling $300 million.

Two setbacks to the economy were the stoppage of work on the Asahan hydroelectric project in Sumatra and the decision by the government to force broader ownership patterns in the industrial and commercial sectors—a move clearly directed at breaking the dominance of Indonesian Chinese in the private economy. Completion of the $400 million Asahan scheme, by far Indonesia's most ambitious development project, was placed in jeopardy when the seven U.S. and Japanese firms contracted to build the power station

and an adjacent aluminum plant withdrew from the project. In a controversial economic policy speech in March, President Suharto called for local companies to set aside at least half their shares for indigenous Indonesians. The precise arrangements for such massive transfers of ownership were left unstated, but Suharto left little doubt that the government was fast losing its tolerance for a system by which Indonesian citizens of Chinese origin owned and managed most of the country's wealth, despite whatever benefits in efficiency had accrued.

Area and population. Area, 735,077 sq. mi. Pop. (est. 1971), 124,890,000. Cap., Djakarta (est. 1968), 4.8 million.
Government. Republic. Pres., prime min., and min. of def., General Suharto.
Finance. Monetary unit, rupiah; 1 rupiah = US$0.0025. Budget expenditure (1972–1973), US$1.8 billion.
Trade (1970). Exports, US$1,009,000,000; imports, US$893,-000,000.
Education (est. 1970). Primary and secondary school enrollment, 16,984,594. Higher education enrollment, 604,694.
Armed forces (1971). Army, 275,000; navy, 40,000; air force, 20,000.   DICK WILSON

INSURANCE. No-fault automobile insurance. Pressure for dramatic change in the insurance field continued to mount. The greatest pressure focused on automobile insurance, which represents about $16.5 billion of the over $72.5 billion in premiums paid to insurance companies each year. Supporters of no-fault automobile insurance claim that it is the answer to the automobile insurance miseries of the American public. Under a no-fault law, the victims of automobile injuries are paid promptly for medical expenses, loss of income, and other expenses by their own insurance company without regard to who was at fault or how the accident happened.

Adherents of no-fault maintain that it has been highly successful in the United States whenever and wherever it has been tried. The Commonwealth of Puerto Rico, the first U.S. jurisdiction to enact a no-fault law, found all the no-fault automobile insurance promises were deliverable—lower premiums and prompt, adequate, and equitable benefits to those injured in auto accidents. Enacted in 1968, the Puerto Rican no-fault law became effective on January 1, 1970, and is run by a government corporation. In 1972, the annual premium that each automobile owner paid was cut from $35 to $24. Massachusetts became the first state to enact a no-fault law, which has been in effect since January 1, 1971. There was a 15 percent premium cut when the law went into effect and another 27.6 percent cut in 1972. Later, an additional 27.6 percent cut was granted and upheld by the courts to make up for apparently excessive premiums in 1971. Florida and Illinois both enacted no-fault laws in 1971, but the Illinois law was struck down as unconstitutional in 1972. Although 37 states had no-fault under study, only Connecticut, Michigan, and New Jersey joined the no-fault ranks in 1972.

Other states enacted so-called no-fault laws that were criticized for providing only the first of the two essential ingredients of no-fault laws—compulsory no-fault benefits without regard to fault. However, these laws fail to eliminate the right to sue for "pain and suffering" (the psychic damages resulting from the accident) in the less serious cases. Supporters of no-fault contend that as long as suits for "pain and suffering" are not limited, premiums cannot be reduced, adequate resources are not available for no-fault benefits, too many exaggerated and fraudulent claims may be filed, and excessive and protracted litigation can occur over the value of "pain and suffering." Delaware enacted such a law in 1971 and Maryland in 1972. Even more diluted versions of no-fault, which simply provide no-fault benefits on an optional basis, were passed in Minnesota, Oregon, and South Dakota. Under these laws limited no-fault benefits must be offered to each policyholder or be included in automobile liability insurance if it is purchased.

Because of the apparent inability of most states to enact no-fault laws, the U.S. Congress in 1971 considered a bill cosponsored by Senator Philip Hart (D, Mich.) and Senator Warren G. Magnuson (D, Wash.) which would have required states to enact no-fault laws that met minimum federal standards or be subject to a federal no-fault law. The bill came to a vote in the Senate in August 1972, and by a tally of 49 to 46 it was sent back to the Judiciary Committee for further study, in effect burying the measure.

This defeat returned the battle to the state legislatures. Despite strong if not overwhelming public support, no-fault will continue to face great opposition, mainly from trial lawyers whose over $1.4 billion business of fighting automobile accident cases would be endangered by no-fault.

Flood insurance. Hurricane Agnes, which struck in June, caused such extensive flooding in the eastern United States that it ranks as the worst natural disaster in American history. The brunt of the flood damage was in Pennsylvania, but there was also substantial damage in Florida, Maryland, New York, Virginia, and West Virginia. Estimates of property losses ranged from $1.6 billion to over $3.4 billion, of which only $110 million were insured, less than 5 percent of the total. Flood insurance for homeowners and tenants has generally been unavailable from commercial insurance companies, although larger businesses can sometimes obtain coverage.

Critics alleged that Hurricane Agnes dramatically underlined the failure of the Federal Flood Insurance Program, established by legislation passed on August 1, 1968, to provide protection against flood losses. In Wilkes-Barre, Pa., almost wiped out by the flood, only two residents had flood insurance. The Federal Flood Insurance Program paid for only $108 million of the multibillion dollar flood disaster.

Despite a record $2.1 billion in federal grants for the flood-stricken area, there was a growing demand for a new federal disaster insurance program to pay for such losses on an insurance basis, rather than a relief, grant, and assistance basis. Experience prior to Hurricane Agnes indicated that it was difficult to get property owners to voluntarily buy flood insurance. Therefore, it was proposed that flood coverage be included on a mandatory basis in all property insurance policies. Each policyholder's premium would be surcharged a specified percentage, perhaps 2 or 3 percent, thus generating funds to a public corporation that would pay losses, with supplementary financing to be provided by the federal government.

Shoppers' guides to insurance. Life insurance premiums, unlike automobile and homeowner's premiums, are not subject to rate regulation by state insurance departments. However, the Pennsylvania insurance department pioneered a method of reducing life insurance rates without regulatory authority. This method involved publishing a shopper's guide to life insurance, which showed the highest and lowest cost life insurance companies. The public demand for the guide was overwhelming, because it made clear that life insurance costs for the same coverage varied as much as 170 percent. The determination of the true cost of a life insurance policy requires a calculation taking into account premiums, cash values, and dividends. The guide made this calculation in clear terms that for the first time made the consumer understand that life insurance premiums are not basically the same.

The shopper's guide series began with a shopper's guide to hospitals in the Philadelphia area. Guide's on automobile insurance premiums and surgery have also been published, but the shopper's guide to life insurance clearly had the greatest impact, as life insurance premiums, unlike automobile insurance premiums, are determined on a national basis. Some insurance companies denied the impact of the guide, but critics maintained that their deeds contradicted their claims. Several companies advertised the availability of the guide, one on network television. The guide put high-

cost companies under pressure from policyholders, the public, insurance agents, and security analysts. The Pennsylvania insurance department confidently predicted savings of hundreds of millions of dollars as a result of the guide's pressure on insurance companies to slash premiums. The shopper's guide technique was followed elsewhere; nine other commissioners issued or were expected to issue similar shopper's guides. The Pennsylvania insurance department called on others to put out shopper's guides of their own. For example, it asked the Pennsylvania medical society to put out a series of guides on medical care and ordered one Pennsylvania Blue Cross plan to publish a shopper's guide to hospitals, which it did.

Other developments. The National Commission on State Workmen's Compensation Laws on July 31 concluded that state workmen's compensation laws must provide larger and more liberal benefits to employees injured on the job and use more modern procedures to settle claims. The insurance industry writes over $3.5 billion in workmen's compensation coverage for employers.

The pensions system also came under intensive and continuing attack; it was characterized as a consumer fraud and a "shell game" because of its failure to deliver the benefits promised at the time of retirement. Payments into insured pension plans now exceed $5 billion a year, and proposed reforms before Congress would affect these plans, as well as noninsured plans, which accumulate their assets in trust funds rather than in insurance contracts.

Mail-order health insurance advertising came under heavy attack as being misleading and deceptive. About 20 states issued new regulations or took other special measures to curb abuses.   HERBERT S. DENENBERG

INTERIOR DESIGN. Individualism. Notable trends in decoration have been the pattern-on-pattern idea, the blossoming of crafts and needlework, the expanded interest in plants and indoor gardening, and the interest in art and memorabilia; most of these decorative devices can be interpreted as a pursuit of individuality. Factors that have undoubtedly contributed to this desire for a personal stamp in decoration are the new apartments which are virtually featureless boxes; the remodeled old houses and apartments which may have been warehouses, lofts, foundries, small schoolhouses, or churches; and the second house, which permits great latitude in style. An additional factor is the interior designer himself, who is often given a free hand, with the apparent stipulation that the owner and the designer thoroughly enjoy the project. In the new and unorthodox way of doing interiors, the designers have found an opportunity for genuine creativity, unusual effects, and individual interpretations. No longer are the display rooms in department stores or the other model rooms the only vanguard of startling ideas and offbeat decoration. Private homes are often furnished with little or no trace of the traditional formal design, although there is a great interest in the romantic look with lovely colors and pretty floral prints dominating.

Furnishings. Furniture throughout these interiors has very little resemblance to the commercial furniture made in quantity in the United States (with the exception of the upholstery). Aside from genuine antiques—fine eighteenth-century French, English, and American colonial pieces—furniture is chosen for its quaintness, whimsy, country appeal, and sometimes its general acceptance (for example, such inexpensive items as the wood and canvas director's chair and the Thonet bentwood chair are widely accepted). English regency, provincial French, nineteenth-century American through the cottage styles, and certain Victorian pieces seem to prevail, with a liberal sprinkling of the extremely modern chromed steel and glass and molded plastic pieces. But it is the upholstered pieces that carry the mood of the interiors with large overstuffed or loose-cushioned models covered in fabrics that match or correlate with wall and drap-

From Pompadour To Pompidou

ery treatments. Also, a certain number of wood pieces have frames completely covered in fabric—chairs with totally upholstered legs, Parsons tables, and large "tester" beds with big open rectangular frames. Many times the fabric covering them is vinyl-coated or has a suedelike nap.

Fabrics. Lavish use has been made of fabrics—in fact, the basis of the whole pattern-on-pattern style of decorating has been the use of fabric. Entire walls and ceilings have been draped with fabric gathered on rods around a room. Ceiling fabrics are often gathered into a center rosette, giving a tented look to a room. In the pattern-on-pattern style there is always a play of broken design and color as a background for the full pattern used on sofas, chairs, screens, window shades, and tablecloths. Fabric, as well as wallpaper and other wall coverings, is also hung in flat panels on the walls.

Probably the most exciting fabrics are the florals with their riotous though pretty tones massed all over the surface. Leafy designs are close behind with everything from enormous tropical specimens to delicate vinelike traceries. Geometric designs are also prevalent and are often gigantic. These are used most often in very modern interiors where they complement great architectural expanses of white or colored planes and a very sparse grouping of furnishings.

Pattern and forms. In accordance with the passion for pattern, two fairly neglected areas have sprung up with new excitement—floors and ceilings. Carpeting has long been the bastion of conservatism, with solid-toned broadlooms most popular, along with a few area rugs, including the Scandinavian ryas and the ubiquitous Orientals. However, carpeting has now risen to the occasion, and a great range of designs exists. Where once only hard-surface flooring was looked to for ornamental treatments, now special effects are achieved with carpet. The man-made fibers take color very well, and printed carpeting is the newest phenomenon. Ceilings, also, have come into their own, with the white ceiling not necessarily the rule. Solid colors that complement the wall tones or match them are being used more and more. The high shine of enamel is also used for its greater reflective power. Smaller rooms like baths, dressing rooms, and kitchens have long had ceilings papered, but now wallpaper and wall coverings are often extended to include the ceiling of major rooms. When walls are painted with graphic designs, the design is often carried up and over the ceiling.

Another area that has come increasingly into prominence for its design quality and technical improvement is the field of domestics. The advantages of permanent-press sheets and pillowcases have—with their exciting patterns bearing the names of such well-known designers as Yves St. Laurent, Hanae Mori, Marimekko, and Vera—taken them into the total room scheme for use as draperies and upholstery as well as for bed coverings. Bold colors, lively geometric patterns, flower patterns, and quaint gingham styles have all followed the lead of today's interior design.

The Elysée Palace has long kept up the warmly splendid Louis XV flavor of the salon pictured at left. But this year President and Mme. Georges Pompidou redecorated four rooms of the East Wing in startlingly modern style. The anteroom above features ivory-colored fabric walls and ceilings with abstracts by Delaunay and Kupka. At right, a dining room for semiofficial parties houses two round Plexiglas tables under a pinkish aluminum beehive ceiling.

Currently strong in another direction is the attention to natural forms and materials—an ecological response reflected in the use of various woods, stone, natural fibers, woven objects (everything from baskets and wicker to fabrics), and handcrafted pieces.

Elegance. Elegance appears to be finding its way back into interiors. Heavy upholstery satin in handsome solid colors has appeared at the moderate price level, and the use of leathers of all kinds as well as the many velvets indicate a steady interest in a look of luxury. Another trend—painting walls and ceilings in one tone—might be considered a reaction to pattern-on-pattern. Furnishings are grouped about independently of the wall areas, which are usually not hung with pictures or decorative objects of any kind. Thus, there is a suffusion of tone seeming to recede into infinity—an entirely new treatment that seems to have no real decorating precedent.

HELEN W. HARRIS

INTERNATIONAL BANKING AND FINANCE. The international financial scene was dominated in 1972 by efforts to overcome the monetary crisis that had culminated on August 15, 1971, with the U.S. government's suspension of the convertability of the dollar into gold and imposition of a 10 percent surcharge on imports entering the United States. In an immediate sense, these efforts were quite successful, for they produced a drastic and much-needed realignment of exchange rates. But the underlying weaknesses of the inter-

THAT SINKING FEELING. A Londoner reads up on Britain's latest money crisis. Set afloat on June 23, the pound quickly dropped from its $2.61 high down to the $2.40–$2.50 range, the first major currency to flounder in the wake of the Smithsonian accord.

national payments system remained, and the major industrial trading nations increasingly recognized the need for more fundamental, long-range reforms. It was generally agreed that the evolving new system should permit a high degree of freedom in trade and other international transactions and, at the same time, help minimize the destabilizing effects of international developments on national economies. The international monetary role of the United States also had to be reappraised; considering the long series of U.S. balance-of-payments deficits and the growing reluctance of other countries to accept dollars in settlement of these deficits, it was questionable whether the dollar should continue to serve as the leading official reserve asset. But there was as yet no agreement on how the conflicting financial, economic, and political interests were to be reconciled.

The Smithsonian Agreement. The immediate problem of correcting existing payments imbalances could not await the result of the long-term reform efforts. Pressured by U.S. diplomacy and by the U.S. import surcharge, the ten leading non-Communist industrial countries, meeting in Washington, D.C., agreed on December 18, 1971, to a general realignment of exchange rates and to provisions for increasing the short-run flexibility of these rates. Referred to as the Smithsonian Agreement, this was the most important international monetary accord since the International Monetary Fund (IMF) was established at the end of World War II to provide a reserve of foreign exchange.

As part of the overall agreement, the United States removed the import surcharge and, in a dramatic reversal of policy, conceded to European demands that the dollar be devalued in terms of gold. This was achieved by raising the official monetary gold price from $35 to $38 an ounce—a reduction of the dollar's gold equivalent by more than 8 percent. The new gold price became official on May 8, 1972, after ratification by the U.S. Congress. The dollar devaluation had two important implications. First, it changed the book value of the gold component of each nation's official foreign reserves and created a windfall gain for those countries, such as France, which held most of their international reserves in gold rather than dollars. Second, it destroyed the fiction of an immutable gold-dollar relationship and an undevaluable dollar, thereby aggravating doubts about its usefulness as a reserve asset.

Under the Smithsonian Agreement, most other major currencies retained or increased their gold parities, in either case taking on higher dollar values. The combined effect of the U.S. devaluation and Japanese revaluation brought a total increase in the value of the Japanese yen of nearly 17 percent compared to its position before it was floated in August 1971. The West German mark, floating since May 1971, was similarly upvalued by almost 14 percent, and the Benelux currencies appreciated by slightly smaller amounts. The United Kingdom for the moment decided to leave the pound-gold relation unchanged, the result being an increase in the dollar-pound rate from the old $2.40 to $2.61 —an effective revaluation of 8 percent. The French chose to continue their system, adopted in 1971, of two franc rates, one based on the old gold par and applying to trade in goods and services, the other applying to financial transactions and allowed to find its own value in the international exchange market.

Overall, these complex exchange rate changes meant a reduction in the international value of the U.S. dollar relative to other currencies. If each country's currency is weighted according to the amount of the country's trade with the United States, the overall dollar devaluation can be calculated to about 12 percent—the best available measure of the real shift in the position of the dollar.

Since the major exchange rate shifts of the Smithsonian Agreement were negotiated outside the normally prescribed IMF machinery, the new rates could not legally be designated as "par" values. The term "central rate" was adopted instead, with no indication of any significant practical difference. Of true economic significance, however, was the increase in the permissible deviations of actual spot rates from these official "pegs." Thus, most of the major countries announced that they would permit their exchange rates to deviate by up to 2.25 percent in either direction from the new pegs, as against the former 1 or 0.75 percent. The prices of their currencies are hence allowed to move within a band whose total width is equivalent to 4.5 percent; if they threaten to go outside this band, their central banks are obliged to intervene in the exchange market to prevent this from happening. It was hoped that this modest move toward greater exchange rate flexibility would help prevent large, sudden flows of "hot" short-term capital among the major money markets.

The Smithsonian Agreement appeared to contribute toward maintaining some measure of equilibrium in international payments for the near future. A competitive trade disadvantage had been created for countries with large surpluses, especially Japan and Germany, and a competitive advantage had been created for the major deficit country, the United States. In addition, the volatility of international capital flows had been reduced somewhat. It remained to be seen whether the amounts of currency adjustments would prove sufficient—or whether other adjustments would soon be necessary.

The U.S. payments performance. The currency realignments were officially expected to result in a turnaround in the U.S. balance of payments of between $8 billion and $10 billion a year, but it was recognized that this improvement would take time. In 1972, the U.S. trade balance was

INTERNATIONAL EXCHANGE RATES

COUNTRY	CURRENCY UNIT	DOLLARS PER CURRENCY UNIT[1] Free-market rate New York City October 31, 1972	COUNTRY	CURRENCY UNIT	DOLLARS PER CURRENCY UNIT[1] Free-market rate New York City October 31, 1972
Afghanistan	afghani	.0135	Laos	kip	.0018
Albania	lek	.2025	Lebanon	pound	.3350
Algeria	dinar	.2325	Lesotho	rand	1.29
Argentina	peso	.1040	Liberia	US dollar	1.00
Australia	dollar	1.1940	Libya	dinar	3.11
Austria	schilling	.0435	Luxembourg	franc	.0227
Barbados	dollar	.5000	Malagasy Republic	franc	.0041
Belgium	franc	.0227	Malawi	kwacha	1.19
Bolivia	peso	.0850	Malaysia	dollar	.3625
Botswana	rand	1.29	Maldives[2]	rupee	not traded
Brazil	new cruzeiro	.1675	Mali	franc	.002050
Bulgaria	lev	.95	Malta	pound	2.50
Burma	kyat	.1900	Mauritania	CFA franc[3]	.0041
Burundi	franc	.0120	Mauritius	rupee	.1900
			Mexico	peso	.0801
Cameroon	CFA franc[3]	.0041	Mongolia	tugrik	.2600
Canada	dollar	1.0180	Morocco	dirham	.2225
Central African Rep.	CFA franc[3]	.0041			
Chad	CFA franc[3]	.0041	Nepal	rupee	.1010
Chile	escudo	.0225	Netherlands	guilder	.3100
China, Mainland[2]	yuan	not traded	New Zealand	dollar	1.1970
China, Nationalist	NT dollar	.0255	Nicaragua	córdoba	.1430
Colombia	peso	.0465	Niger	CFA franc[3]	.0041
Congo, Rep. of the	CFA franc[3]	.0041	Nigeria	pound	3.10
Costa Rica	colón	.1200	Norway	krone	.1510
Cuba[2]	peso	not traded			
Cyprus	pound	2.55	Pakistan	rupee	.0925
Czechoslovakia	koruna	.1525	Panama	balboa	1.00
			Paraguay	guaraní	.0080
Dahomey	CFA franc[3]	.0041	Peru	sol	.0232
Denmark	krone	.1450	Philippines	peso	.1500
Dominican Republic	peso	1.00	Poland	zloty	.0475
			Portugal	escudo	.0380
Ecuador	sucre	.0415			
Egypt, Arab Rep. of	pound	2.32	Rhodesia	dollar	1.57
El Salvador	colón	.4020	Romania	leu	.1810
Equatorial Guinea	peseta	.0160	Rwanda	franc	.0112
Ethiopia	dollar	.4400			
			Saudi Arabia	riyal	.2450
Finland	markka	.2450	Senegal	CFA franc[3]	.0041
France	franc	.1990	Sierra Leone	leone	1.25
			Singapore	dollar	.3625
Gabon	CFA franc[3]	.0041	Somalia	somali	.1500
Gambia	dalasi	.5100	South Africa	rand	1.29
Germany, East[2]	ostmark	not traded	Spain	peseta	.0160
Germany, West	deutsche mark	.3125	Sri Lanka	rupee	.1575
Ghana	new cedi	.8000	Sudan	pound	2.94
Greece	drachma	.0336	Swaziland	rand	1.29
Guatemala	quetzal	1.00	Sweden	krona	.2110
Guinea	franc	.0050	Switzerland	franc	.2635
Guyana	dollar	.5000	Syria	pound	.2400
Haiti	gourde	.2010	Tanzania	shilling	.1415
Honduras	lempira	.5010	Thailand	baht	.0483
Hong Kong	dollar	.1790	Togo	CFA franc[3]	.0041
Hungary	forint	.0865	Trinidad and Tobago	dollar	.5200
			Tunisia	dinar	2.12
Iceland	króna	.0117	Turkey	pound	.0725
India	rupee	.1290			
Indonesia	rupiah	.0025	Uganda	shilling	.1415
Iran	rial	.0134	U.S.S.R.	ruble	1.25
Iraq	dinar	3.10	United Kingdom	pound	2.34
Ireland	pound	2.3400	Upper Volta	CFA franc[3]	.0041
Israel	pound	.2400	Uruguay	peso	.00125
Italy	lira	.001720			
Ivory Coast	CFA franc[3]	.0041	Venezuela	bolívar	.2280
			Vietnam, North[2]	dong	not traded
Jamaica	dollar	1.19	Vietnam, South	piaster	.0025
Japan	yen	.003330			
Jordan	dinar	2.85	Yemen	riyal	.2050
			Yugoslavia	dinar	.0625
Kenya	shilling	.1415			
Khmer Republic	riel	.0075	Zaïre, Rep. of		
Korea, North[2]	won	not traded	(Leopoldville)	zaïre	2.05
Korea, South	won	.0026	Zambia	kwacha	1.41
Kuwait	dinar	3.12			

[1] *All information contained in the above list of rates has been obtained from sources believed to be reliable but is tendered without responsibility or guarantee.* [2] *Official rate of exchange set by country in terms of dollars per currency unit was as follows: Mainland China, .45; Cuba, 1.08; East Germany, .3185; North Korea, .9075; Maldives, .2275; North Vietnam, .3175.* [3] *Communauté Financière Africaine.*

adversely influenced by the strong recovery in domestic economic activity, coupled with sluggishness in most of the Western European economies and in the Japanese economy. It was therefore not surprising that the U.S. trade deficit remained uncomfortably high in the first part of the year and that the intended correction became apparent only in the fall and winter. For 1972 the deficit was estimated at about $6 billion, the worst trade result in U.S. history. Income from foreign investment grew further, but the net outflow of long-term private capital remained high, adding to the total deficit.

There was, however, genuine disappointment that the speculative outflow of short-term capital was not reversed immediately after the Smithsonian Agreement. With the slowing of the U.S. rate of inflation, there was downward pressure on short-term interest rates in the United States, reducing incentives for a repatriation of funds invested abroad. Later in the year, the upward drift of U.S. interest rates at last started to pull back most of these funds, to the benefit of the overall U.S. payments position.

In view of the erratic behavior of the short-term capital account in past years, nobody could predict the magnitude of the 1972 payments deficit with any degree of accuracy. As the year drew to a close, it seemed that the figure would not be nearly so bad as the extraordinary $30 billion deficit recorded in 1971 on the "official reserve transactions" basis—that is, when measured by the reduction in official U.S. reserves of gold and foreign currency, changes in the U.S. net position in the IMF, and additions to official short-term foreign dollar holdings. The value of U.S. official reserves

remained at about $13 billion, including $10 billion of newly upvalued gold and $2 billion of special drawing rights (SDR's) in the IMF; the relative stability of these reserves, of course, reflected the refusal by the U.S. government to sell gold to foreign monetary authorities (or, for that matter, to anybody). Instead, the continued deficit was "settled" simply through the grudging acceptance by these authorities of additional dollar balances. As a result, their total dollar holdings soared above the $50 billion mark.

Under the existing payments system, these outstanding dollar balances could be significantly reduced only through a series of substantial U.S. payments surpluses. However, most of the major U.S. trading partners seemed unwilling to permit the deficits in their payments that would have to be the counterpart of such U.S. surpluses. The inherent dilemma could be resolved, if at all, only through an exchange of these accumulated dollars for other reserve assets, preferably with guarantees of value stability and convertibility—one of the major unresolved reform issues.

On its part, the United States took one small but significant step to alleviate the risk of exchange market disturbances and currency crises. In a shift of policy, the Federal Reserve in July started to intervene in the exchange markets to protect the value of the dollar, in this instance by selling large amounts of the speculatively favored West German mark. At the same time, it was announced that the reciprocal borrowing arrangements—the so-called swap lines—with major foreign central banks and the Bank for International Settlements in Basel were reactivated. These swap facilities, which permit the United States to borrow up to

DOLLAR DIPLOMACY. The "Group of Ten" industrial nations met in Washington, D.C., in December 1971. Under the Smithsonian Agreement concluding the international conference, the United States agreed to reduce the dollar's gold equivalent by about 8 percent.

$12 billion on a short-term basis, had been suspended in August 1971. Their reactivation made it possible for the United States to absorb temporarily any excess dollars in the exchange markets—dollars that would otherwise have to be purchased by foreign central banks under their obligation to support the value of the dollar in terms of their own currencies. To many critics of U.S. foreign policy, the move represented an end to the seeming U.S. policy of "benign neglect" toward international monetary problems. In any case, it was a cooperative step that reassured European bankers and governments but that did nothing to solve the longer-term problems of payments adjustment or reserve asset creation.

Eurocurrency markets. The uncertainties regarding the future official status of the dollar did not seem to affect its usefulness and attractiveness to private traders and investors outside the United States as a "vehicle" currency. This was evidenced by the continued growth of the Eurodollar market —the market for dollars placed on deposit in foreign commercial banks or in overseas branches of U.S. banks. In spite of the currency turmoil in the fall and winter of 1971–1972, the market is estimated to have grown to a new record of $50–60 billion in total deposits (excluding redeposits among banks). By comparison, the amount of nondollar Eurocurrencies (mainly Swiss francs and West German marks) similarly deposited outside the countries of issue was still less than $20 billion—an indication of the continued preeminence of the dollar.

Foreign governments, however, took an increasingly critical view of these developments. The ready access to Eurodollar credit makes it difficult for an individual government to control, by conventional monetary policy instruments, the amount of credit-induced spending and activity within the domestic economy; the efficacy of monetary and credit policy is thus impaired. To counter this, several European governments instituted more severe controls on Eurodollar transactions in the form of special reserve requirements applied to dollar deposits and restrictions on corporate activity in the market.

Values of other currencies. There were recurring signs that certain leading currencies might soon be ready for further adjustments. The German mark seemed somewhat undervalued even at its post-Smithsonian rate of 3.22 to the dollar, but the risk of hurting exports and depressing economic activity made a further revaluation an unattractive policy alternative for the German government. The Japanese yen, at its new rate of 308 to the dollar, was in an even stronger position, and the Japanese government took steps to counter tendencies toward continued payments surpluses through a further liberalization of imports and capital inflows.

The first major casualty of the Smithsonian accords was the British pound, which to many observers had seemed overvalued at its new $2.61 rate. Although Britain's trade-and-services account still showed a surplus, the underlying trend pointed to renewed deficits, and a wildcat dock strike in June led to a speculative flight from the pound. European central banks intervened heavily to save it, but the British government on June 23 set it free to float in the exchange markets and tightened controls on capital outflows. The pound swiftly fell to between $2.40 and $2.50—that is, almost to its pre-Smithsonian par. It was generally assumed that the pound would return to a fixed parity in 1973, when Britain enters the European Economic Community.

EEC monetary integration. Members of the European Economic Community continued their efforts toward the creation of a unified EEC currency—one of the final steps in their gradual harmonization of economic policies and their complete economic integration. In April 1972 the community introduced a new currency intervention policy under which the permissible margins of fluctuations in their exchange rates were reduced.

Under the Smithsonian Agreement, the total 4.5 percent band of exchange rate variation against the U.S. dollar had implied a maximum mutual variability of 9 percent between two nondollar currencies; if one currency moved from its lower to its upper limit, and the other conversely moved from its upper to its lower limit, the so-called cross rate between these currencies would actually have shifted by approximately 9 percent—a very considerable margin of gain or loss for short-term speculative international investment. The new community policy meant that the potential swings in intra-Community cross rates were reduced to 4.5 percent. To achieve this, the EEC central banks will have to intervene in the exchange market whenever the value of one of the EEC currencies reaches its new upper or lower limit in terms of any of the other EEC currencies—through sales or purchases, respectively, of the particular currency against other EEC currencies or the dollar.

The main beneficiary of the new policy was the Italian lira. The large support purchases of lira by EEC central banks, however, gave rise to controversy as to how the Bank of Italy should liquidate its resulting lira debts—whether through gold or through dollar payments. At least for the moment, the less-wanted dollars were considered an acceptable form of repayment.

On October 19, EEC member nations agreed to establish a European monetary cooperation fund—a line of credits valued at $1.4 billion for emergency aid to any member state. The fund is to come into existence on April 1, 1973. A timetable for expansion and further development of the fund was also agreed upon. At the same time, the nine members obligated themselves to speak with a single voice in international monetary negotiations.

Longer-run reform prospects. Preliminary discussions of alternative monetary reform proposals were held at the annual IMF meeting in September. At the insistence of the United States, a new negotiating group—referred to as the Committee of 20—had been set up, with national representatives for the major industrial countries and joint representatives for regional groups of smaller industrial and nonindustrial countries. The committee was to work out an acceptable plan for a restructured monetary system and to recommend policy changes in regard to trade and foreign investment. The political reality behind this arrangement was that the United States, in return for stricter payments "discipline" in the future, hoped to gain European concessions in the areas of trade liberalization and commitments to a free flow of private investment capital.

The prevailing view, shared by the United States, was that SDR's would be the most appropriate reserve asset to replace gold and dollars, suggesting a trend toward further demonetization of gold and an internationally managed creation and distribution of reserves. But there was as yet no agreement on what should be done with the large outstanding dollar balances held by foreign central institutions. Since U.S. monetary reserves would not nearly be sufficient to finance their repatriation to the United States, one possibility under increased consideration was for the United States to offer some kind of long-term securities on attractive terms to foreign governments. Barring such funding arrangements, it was proposed that unwanted reserve dollars be deposited with the IMF in return for additional SDR's or in special settlement accounts, thereby providing a guarantee against dollar devaluation and inconvertibility.

Nevertheless, many Europeans continued to advocate a return to a modified gold standard and another, bigger increase in the official gold price, more in line with the $70 price quoted in the private gold market in July and August. The United States conceded that the dollar, at some future date, ought to be made convertible into other reserve assets. This might be accomplished not only through the sale of gold but through the use of U.S. SDR allocations or other IMF facilities.

MARVINE HOWE/NEW YORK TIMES

POINT OF NO RETURN

The notion of increased exchange rate flexibility had gained further acceptance in official circles, and it looked as if the widened bands would be maintained for the near future. This, however, did not solve the question of how more persistent payments imbalances should be corrected—whether through "crawling pegs," temporary floats, or the permanent floating of individual (or blocs of closely inter-linked) currencies. Any of these alternatives might help avoid the disruptive currency crises that in recent years have plagued the international economy.   KAJ ARESKOUG

INTERNATIONAL LAW. Strategic arms limitation agreements. President Richard M. Nixon's nine-day summit meeting in Moscow with Soviet leaders produced a number of agreements, ranging in subject from environmental protection to cooperation in space and including two landmark agreements on arms control. These agreements, negotiated at the strategic arms limitation talks (SALT), which have been going on in Helsinki and Vienna for 2½ years, were a treaty on antiballistic missile (ABM) systems and an interim agreement on limitation of strategic offensive arms. The treaty limits the United States and the Soviet Union to two ABM sites, one for the national capital and one for an intercontinental ballistic missile (ICBM) installation. The number of launchers at each ABM site is not to exceed 100. This agreement will avoid a race to establish ABM systems, which would be staggeringly expensive and have

a destabilizing effect on the strategic balance between the two superpowers.

In essence, the five-year interim agreement on strategic offensive arms freezes the numbers of U.S. and Soviet ICBM's, submarine-launched ballistic missiles, and ballistic missile submarines. There will be no international inspection to check on compliance, but each country pledged "not to interfere with the [other's] national technical means of verification." The Soviet Union has more ICBM's than the United States and also leads in submarine-launched missiles. The United States has more strategic bombers (which are not covered by the interim agreement) and, because many of its ICBM's are equipped with multiple warheads, a two-to-one lead in deliverable nuclear warheads.

A definitive treaty on the limitation of strategic nuclear weapons remains to be concluded. In approving the interim agreement, the U.S. Senate voted, at the initiative of Senator Henry M. Jackson (D, Wash.), to ask the president to seek a treaty which "would not limit the United States to levels of intercontinental strategic forces inferior to the limits provided for the Soviet Union."

The sea. Work on the drafting of new treaties to regulate the uses of the oceans and to regulate exploitation of the resources of the sea, the seabed, and the subsoil proceeded at an agonizingly slow pace during 1972. The UN Committee on the Peaceful Uses of the Seabed and the Ocean Floor Beyond the Limits of National Jurisdiction,

KEYSTONE

Refugees have always existed in a no-man's-land of international law. This year two new groups were forced into limbo: left, two of the 48,000 Iranian nationals deported from Iraq talk things over at a transit camp in the Iranian town of Khosravy, just over the Iran-Iraq boundary; above is a trainload of Asians, some of the 50,000 expelled from Uganda by Major General Idi Amin's edict.

which had been established by the UN General Assembly, was increased to an unwieldy 91 members. The committee met twice during 1972, in New York in March and in Geneva in July and August. Its two visible accomplishments were, first, agreement on an extremely lengthy list of issues to be taken up at the diplomatic conference to be held in 1973 and, second, the drafting of principles (to be incorporated in the ultimate treaty) on the exploitation of the resources of the seabed and subsoil. It was agreed that the diplomatic conference would begin with an organizational session in 1973, but only after two more meetings of the seabed committee. The extra sessions are needed because much preliminary drafting remains to be done.

The United States continued to assert, as a basic element of national policy, that passage through, over, and under straits should be governed by the principle of "free transit," but it declared its willingness to accommodate coastal states' concerns about pollution and safety of navigation in straits.

Moving toward the positions taken by a large number of African and Latin American countries, the United States is willing to accept virtually complete resource management by coastal states in adjacent seabed areas, provided international treaty standards are laid down to prevent interference with other uses of the ocean, to protect the ocean from pollution, to protect existing investment, to provide for a sharing of revenue for international community purposes, and to secure the compulsory settlement of disputes.

Although the measurable achievements of the seabed committee were few, the members were groping their way toward explaining their positions, sounding out the positions of other states, and engaging in a certain amount of bargaining and adjustment. One possible middle path between demands for a narrow territorial sea and the extreme claims to 200 miles of territorial sea made by a few Latin American states was suggested by the Declaration of Santo Domingo, signed by ten Caribbean states on June 9. The declaration incorporated the concept of a "patrimonial sea" of 200 miles within which coastal states could exercise sovereignty over natural resources but would be required to allow full freedom of navigation and overflight.

In an agreement on shrimp fisheries signed by the United States and Brazil in May, the two countries agreed to disagree on the breadth of the territorial sea but made arrangements for U.S. vessels to fish for shrimp in Brazilian waters under certain circumstances, subject to the payment of compensation by the United States to Brazil. Iceland has been less accommodating. It unilaterally established a 50-mile fisheries limit, effective September 1, in the face of strong protests from Great Britain and West Germany that this claim violated agreements with those two countries.

In November representatives of 91 countries agreed on the Convention on the Dumping of Wastes at Sea. When ratified, the treaty will prohibit discharge of poisonous wastes such as crude oil, pesticides, chemical and biological warfare agents, and radioactive waste.

Law of war. The protection of war victims—the wounded and sick, prisoners of war, and civilians in the hands of the enemy—is now regulated by the four Geneva conventions of 1949, to which most of the countries of the world are parties. These agreements were shown to be not fully adequate by events in the Korean war, the continuing conflict between the Arab states and Israel, the war in Vietnam, and other hostilities in the past quarter century. In 1971 and 1972 the International Committee of the Red Cross convened two large meetings of government experts to review the texts of protocols (supplementary treaties) to the Geneva conventions of 1949. On the basis of the advice furnished by experts from approximately 70 countries in May and June of 1972, the International Committee of the Red Cross will draft two protocols, one on international and the other on internal armed conflicts.

American aerial bombardment of North Vietnam and the mining of North Vietnamese harbors aroused a substantial amount of criticism this year. There is no treaty of general application specifically covering aerial bombardment. The Hague regulations of 1907, which have passed into customary international law, contain general prohibitions against the use of weapons calculated to cause "unnecessary suffering" or unnecessary destruction of property and against the bombardment of undefended places. The United States has been accused of bombing North Vietnamese hospitals, schools, and other undefended targets of no apparent military value and of bombing the Red River dikes, whose destruction could result in widespread flooding. The U.S. government has said that any such bombing has been done accidentally or in the course of an attack on a military target but not as a matter of national policy.

The U.S. Department of State has maintained that the legal basis for mining the entrances to North Vietnamese ports is the right of collective self-defense, recognized by Article 51 of the UN Charter—a right exercised in this case by the United States and South Vietnam in the face of a renewed armed attack on South Vietnam from North Vietnam.

Terrorism in the air. Hijackings and other violent incidents involving international aircraft increased this year. Three international conventions deal with jurisdiction over crimes committed on board or against aircraft in the air—but not on the ground. The Tokyo convention of 1963 defines what states have jurisdiction to punish crimes committed

ventions, all of which were concluded under the auspices of the International Civil Aviation Organization, suffer from the fact that the states most likely to be implicated in such seizures or to be places of refuge for hijackers and terrorists are not parties.

To deal with this situation, the United States and Canada jointly submitted to a 17-nation meeting in Washington, D.C., in September a proposal for a new treaty under which the parties would suspend air service to countries refusing to give effect to the Tokyo, Hague, and Montreal conventions. This proposal was rejected by the conference in the face of strong opposition from the Soviet Union, France, and Great Britain, and the conference, after a wider consideration of means of dealing with aircraft hijacking and sabotage, adjourned without taking strong substantive action.

R. R. BAXTER

INTERNATIONAL REGIONAL ORGANIZATIONS. International regional organizations are created through treaty arrangements that commit member states to act together for certain specified goals. At the height of the cold war, a number of such groups came into being as security organizations—that is, organizations whose chief purpose is to encourage joint military planning for common defense. These have declined somewhat in importance in recent years, and those that remain viable are being seen increasingly as the instruments of greater cold war détente. More recently, functional organizations, intended to provide a unified approach to the solution of economic and social problems of a particular region, have grown and, in some cases, flourished. These include loose customs unions, free-trade areas, and common markets. Finally, several multipurpose organizations also exist, combining to some extent the security and functional goals of the first two types of organizations, although usually in somewhat more loosely knit arrangements. Here, emphasis is strongly upon harmonizing political relationships among the members as well as on attempting to provide a common front to the outside world.

Security organizations. *NATO and Warsaw Pact.* Developments this year involving the North Atlantic Treaty Organization and the Warsaw Pact nations gave further evidence of progress—albeit, slow—in the effort to reduce military confrontation in Europe. Much of that confrontation is the legacy of the stalemated effort to achieve a peace settlement, including a solution to the problem of a divided Germany, after World War II. The important moves toward détente that were made this year, therefore, centered, not surprisingly, around German issues.

Not until 1971 did four-power talks on Berlin produce an agreement providing freer access to that divided city and safeguards for the security of the Western sector. The agreement—which is very important in its own right—was the first concrete step toward a more general reduction in the tensions that have long divided Europe. The Soviet Union insisted that the Berlin agreement could not be activated until after ratification by West Germany of the friendship treaties it had negotiated previously with the Soviet Union and Poland. These treaties provided for the acceptance of the Oder-Neisse line as the legitimate border between Poland and East Germany and paved the way for the improvement of relations between the governments of West Germany and Eastern Europe. After a protracted and bitter fight in the West German parliament this spring, the treaties finally were ratified by a narrow margin. Within a matter of weeks, the Berlin accords also were activated.

These developments in turn opened the way for an eventual European conference on security and cooperation—a meeting long urged by the Warsaw Pact countries—and sped preparations for talks between NATO and Warsaw Pact countries on mutual troop reductions in Europe. Just as the Soviet Union had insisted upon Bonn's ratification of the Eastern treaties as a prerequisite to activation of the agree-

HISTORY WAS WRITTEN in Moscow's Great Hall of the Kremlin on May 26, as U.S. president Richard M. Nixon and Soviet Communist Party chairman Leonid I. Brezhnev signed agreements limiting construction of defensive and offensive weapons systems.

aboard aircraft. The Convention for the Suppression of Unlawful Seizure of Aircraft, concluded at The Hague in 1970, deals with hijacking, the seizure of control of an aircraft by force or threat of force. The Convention for the Suppression of Unlawful Acts against the Safety of Civil Aviation, concluded at Montreal in September 1971, was designed as a measure against other terroristic acts, such as violence against a person so as to endanger a plane, the destruction of a plane or navigational facilities, and the placing of a bomb aboard an aircraft. The latter two agreements oblige the parties to make the covered acts crimes, to establish jurisdiction over the offenses, to apprehend suspects, and to either prosecute an alleged offender or extradite him to another state which has jurisdiction to try him. The three con-

ment on Berlin, so the West had regarded the Berlin agreement's implementation as essential before serious discussions could begin regarding mutual troop reductions or the future of European security. Such negotiations would consider reduction of NATO forces between Denmark and the Alps, which now total about 500,000 troops and 1,800 tactical aircraft. Soviet and other Eastern European military strength would be reduced from the present total of approximately 750,000 men and 3,500 tactical aircraft. Should these negotiations succeed in producing positive understandings or agreements, the structure and purposes of both NATO and the Warsaw Pact could be radically transformed.

Meanwhile, however, more immediate problems continued to occupy the attention of the leaders of both alliances during the year. Secretary of State William Rogers of the United States, addressing the NATO council meeting in May, asserted that the Soviet Union bore "a heavy responsibility" for the new North Vietnamese offensive in South Vietnam. Rogers also alleged that any precipitous United States withdrawal from South Vietnam would inevitably lead to questioning of the U.S. commitment to NATO. The fact that the Nixon-Brezhnev summit talks took place despite increased tensions over Vietnam seemed a clear indication of the desire of Soviet leaders to achieve accommodation with the United States.

Early in the year, the NATO governments were faced with a crisis from an unexpected quarter. Ever since Malta achieved its independence from the United Kingdom in 1964, the British have rented naval and air facilities on that strategic Mediterranean island, which is not a NATO member. However, in late 1971 the Maltese prime minister, Dom Mintoff, suddenly demanded a huge increase in the annual rental payment. The government of Prime Minister Edward Heath refused to yield and began withdrawing its 3,500-man force. With that, the United States urged its NATO allies to join in making an increased offer to Malta lest the bases become available for use by the Soviet Union. The Heath government at first objected to this move on the grounds it would undercut the British effort to deal firmly with Malta. By the middle of January, however, Prime Minister Mintoff rescinded the evacuation order, and talks in search of a new base agreement were begun between the British and the Maltese, talks in which the NATO secretary general, Joseph M. A. H. Luns, acted as mediator. Reaching a new agreement proved to be difficult, and it was not until March 26 that Great Britain and Malta signed an agreement providing for the continued use by the British of the Maltese bases. The seven-year agreement grants the government of Malta an annual payment of £9.5 million, nearly three times what it received previously.

Also this year, the defense ministers of ten European NATO countries agreed to intensify their cooperation in research, development, production, and purchase of defense equipment. The move was regarded as indicative of the desire of many European governments to move away from reliance on American research and production in the military field and toward greater independence in the development of weapons, including tanks and antiaircraft missiles.

Central Treaty Organization. The Central Treaty Organization, composed of Turkey, Iran, Pakistan, the United Kingdom, and the United States (in an associate capacity), was originally designed to protect the "northern tier" of the Middle East from Soviet incursions but was never a very important factor in cold war East-West conflicts. This year, however, at CENTO's annual meeting, the United States urged its allies to guard against new Soviet thrusts through the Middle East and southern Asia. In addition, Secretary Rogers reported that the overall quality of the United States naval presence in the Indian Ocean would be improved.

Functional organizations. *Europe.* It was last year that the members of the European Community—composed of the European Economic Community (EEC), or Common Market; the European Coal and Steel Community; and EURATOM—finally agreed to admit four new members. But much of the drama surrounding the community's expansion came this year, when the governments of the proposed new members—Great Britain, Denmark, Norway, and Ireland—sought domestic approval of their decision to join.

On February 17 the British Parliament approved for the second time EEC entry in principle—but by the narrowest of margins, 309–301. The opposition Labour Party maintained its strong stance against EEC membership as parliamentary action to pave the way for entry continued, but by October the government had won final parliamentary approval.

Ireland, Norway, and Denmark all held referenda on joining the EEC. On May 10 the electorate in Ireland approved Common Market entry by a four-to-one margin. However, on September 24–25, in a very close vote, the Norwegian electorate rejected EEC membership, the government's defeat being engineered by a coalition of fishermen (who feared loss of income), conservative nationalists, environmentalists (who opposed Norway's further industrialization), and socialists who favored closer ties with Eastern Europe. Denmark's electorate approved EEC membership in voting held on October 2.

Meanwhile, on April 23 voters in France, one of the original six EEC members (along with Italy, West Germany, Belgium, Luxembourg, and the Netherlands), approved of the community's expansion by a two-to-one margin.

A nine-member European Community would have a total population of about 265 million; the total of its members' gross national products would exceed $630 billion; and the community would account for two-fifths of world trade.

At a summit of the heads of the enlarged community's member nations on October 19–20 in Paris, plans were made to establish a European monetary fund on April 1, 1973. There were also proposals for common social, industrial, governmental, and foreign policies.

As in the past, the question of farm policy divided the EEC members during 1972. Farmers' organizations in the member countries pressed for average increases of 8 percent in cereal prices and 12 percent in the prices of dairy products. After extended discussions, agreement was reached within the community on price increases of only 4 percent for cereals and 8 percent for dairy products. The agreement also included measures designed to modernize agriculture and to encourage farmers to leave the land.

The need to maintain communications among the various economic groupings of the world resulted this year in talks between members of the European Community and a delegation of the Association of Southeast Asian Nations. Members of the latter group are Indonesia, Malaysia, the Philippines, Singapore, and Thailand. The discussions, which took place in Brussels in June, focused on opening new channels of communication and considered the trade consequences of the Common Market's generalized tariff preferences and the impact on the developing countries of EEC enlargement.

Latin America. The success of the European Common Market in producing a highly integrated economy among its members has yet to be duplicated in Latin America. The Latin American Free Trade Association, whose members are Mexico and all the principal states of South America, has been hindered by the divergences in the levels of economic development among the members. In contrast, for a number of years the Central American Common Market (CACM) made considerable progress in stimulating economic growth among its five members, largely through the reduction of internal tariffs. But last year, Honduras withdrew from the market, in part as the result of the drain on its foreign exchange earnings. Intraregional trade patterns were greatly affected as a result. One outcome of the Honduran move was that it encouraged other members to levy duties on "sensitive" products traded within the CACM, thereby vitiating much of the progress previously made toward creation

of a common market. Foreign investment was reduced, and last year market activity fell by about $36 million, to $250 million. During 1972 many of the duties raised the year before were rescinded, although it appeared that the market's full recovery would take some time, if it could be accomplished at all in the continued absence of one of the Central American states.

Africa. With the coming of independence to most of the continent of Africa in the 1960's, a number of associative arrangements have been attempted among various African nations. Last year, tensions arose within one of the associations, the African, Malagasy, and Mauritian Common Organization (OCAMM), the organization of French-speaking African nations. Senegal withdrew, in 1971, from OCAMM's sugar agreement, and Cameroon pulled out of Air Afrique, the regional airline. These problems were further exacerbated early in 1972 when the president of Chad, François Tombalbaye, resigned as president of OCAMM and announced Chad's withdrawal from Air Afrique. The official reason given for the move was the organization's decision to establish the company's headquarters at Libreville, Gabon, rather than at Fort-Lamy, Chad. In April, however, President Tombalbaye met with President Léopold-Sédar Senghor of Senegal and announced, in a public reconciliation between the two leaders, that Chad would remain a member of OCAMM.

This move foreshadowed a promising development two weeks later when ten African heads of state, meeting within the OCAMM framework, agreed to continue planning for the West African Economic Community, which may eventually include English-speaking as well as French-speaking African nations. In addition to the OCAMM members present, Major General Yakubu Gowon of Nigeria took part in the discussions. As the meeting began, there were widespread reports that the planned organization would not survive this initial session, principally because of the growing cleavage in interests and views between OCAMM's Central African and West African members. But by the conclusion of the conference, representatives were convinced that OCAMM had obtained two new missions: to initiate closer economic and cultural contacts with English-speaking countries and to serve as a liaison between the more compact economic groupings to be formed by the West African and, soon, the Central African countries. The West African grouping held its charter meeting on June 1 at Bamako, Mali.

Closely related to these developments was the decision in May between Nigeria and Togo to establish a Nigerian-Togolese economic community as an embryo for a larger West African grouping. It was largely this move, initiated principally by the Nigerian head of state, that suggested that the OCAMM-sponsored West African Economic Community might not long be restricted to French-speaking states.

Multipurpose organizations. *Arab League.* Formed in 1945 in the wake of the British departure from much of the Middle East, the League of Arab States is recognizable as much by its internecine divisions as by its tangible accomplishments. Such was the case this year. In the spring, King Hussein of Jordan launched a diplomatic offensive with his proposal to make Jordan a united Arab kingdom, giving federation status to the West Bank territory of Jordan—now occupied by Israel—in which most of the people are Palestinians. Never a popular figure with more radical Arab leaders, Hussein was immediately criticized in other Arab capitals. Some Arab leaders asserted that the king had made a secret agreement with Israeli leaders, perhaps because his proposal included the suggestion that Israel and Jordan share the administration of Jerusalem as part of a "total and final" peace settlement. Hussein immediately denied the charge and emphasized that his plan was "for the future" and not to be implemented until after a full settlement of the Arab dispute with Israel and recovery of all lands lost in the 1967 war. He insisted that preliminary discussions with Pales-

tinians had brought overwhelming approval of the federation proposal. The Egyptian government soon broke relations with Jordan to voice its disapproval of the plan, and a united Arab position vis-à-vis Israel seemed farther than ever from being realized. Hussein had succeeded, nonetheless, in focusing attention once more upon the Israeli occupation of the West Bank.

New Year's Day saw a somewhat more harmonious manifestation of Arab unity when flags were raised in symbolic creation of the new Federal Arab Republic. The loose federation joins Egypt, Syria, and Libya on the basis of plans announced last year. The new association provides for an eight-member federal cabinet, which is charged with promoting political cooperation among the three member states.

Asian and Pacific Council. This year the Asian and Pacific Council, whose members are the principal non-Communist nations of the Asian Pacific region, modified its anti-Peking posture. At the ASPAC ministerial meeting in Seoul this summer, delegates from Japan, South Korea, Australia, New Zealand, the Philippines, and Malaysia all spoke of the need to improve relations with the People's Republic of China. Only Thailand and South Vietnam insisted upon unequivocal support of the Nationalist Chinese (Taiwan) government.

Organization of African Unity. The Organization of African Unity began the year by sponsoring an all-Africa fair in Nairobi, the first major economic venture initiated by the OAU. The fair was designed to encourage member countries to diversify their economies and to reduce their traditional dependence on trade with their former mother countries.

During the summer, the council of ministers and the heads of state of the OAU met in Rabat, Morocco, where they agreed to strongly worded resolutions criticizing Israel's role in the Middle East conflict and the United States' decision to buy chrome from Rhodesia. (The United Nations has invoked economic sanctions against Rhodesia.) The OAU members also pledged to widen their support of liberation struggles in the remaining colonial and white-ruled African territories. The Algeria-Morocco border dispute of the 1960's was finally laid to rest when the heads of state of those two countries signed documents formally ending the conflict. The agreements also prepared the way for joint mining ventures by the two countries in reserves near the southwestern Algerian frontier. Finally, the heads of state elected Nzo Ekangaki, the minister of labor of Cameroon, to a four-year term as secretary general of the OAU. Ekangaki replaced Diallo Telli of Guinea.

Organization of American States. Although no major crises confronted the Organization of American States this year, ambiguity over U.S. policy toward the other members of the organization was a source of tension. In April, at the second General Assembly of the OAS, held in Washington, D.C., Secretary General Galo Plaza called on the United States for a "concrete definition of the new U.S. policy toward Latin America." He charged that the absence of such a definition had adversely affected international relations in the western hemisphere.

The secretary general's statement reflected the unhappiness of a number of Latin American governments over two recent changes in U.S. policy. First, although Secretary of State Rogers had pledged in 1971 that the Nixon administration would introduce legislation for preferential tariffs for Latin American and other developing nations, this had not been done (largely because of U.S. congressional opposition and economic difficulties within the United States). Second, as the result of a protracted dispute between the United States and Chile over Chile's expropriation of U.S. copper and telecommunications assets, President Richard M. Nixon announced in February a hard-line U.S. policy in such matters. Expropriating countries that did not meet U.S. standards of adequate and effective compensation, he said, could "presume" that Washington would cut off direct aid and use its influence in the World Bank and the Inter-Ameri-

can Development Bank to bar loans. By the time of the 1972 General Assembly meeting, that policy already had succeeded in suspending $30 million in loans to Chile. In his address to the General Assembly, President Nixon seemed to suggest that Latin American criticism would not deflect the United States from its tough position on expropriations of property held by U.S. nationals. "Our basic policy," he said, "is a new, practical acknowledgment that the term Latin America now connotes a plurality of views rather than a uniform voice."

In other action within the OAS this year, the United States fought back a resolution proposed by Peru that would have normalized relations with Cuba, in part by lifting sanctions imposed by the OAS in 1964. At a specially called meeting of the permanent council in June, the United States argued that Cuba was still exporting subversion and should not be permitted to participate in the work of the OAS. A majority of the delegates opposed the Peruvian resolution, and Cuba remains officially under OAS sanctions, although several Latin American governments now maintain normal diplomatic relations with the Castro regime.

LYNN H. MILLER

INTERNATIONAL TRADE. After their 11.5 percent advance in dollar value in 1971, exports in the non-Communist world rose by about 16 percent in the first half of 1972 to an annual rate of around $350 billion. The general upward revaluation of currencies, however, accounted for as much as half of the advance. Thus, it appeared that the growth rate in the worldwide exchange of goods was well below that of the previous year.

Also, a greater rise in prices than in the previous year contributed to the 1972 total, limiting still further the volume increase. The upturn in prices stemmed in large part from a widespread strengthening of agricultural prices, notably those for meat, sugar, jute, sisal, and coffee. By June, prices of agricultural products as a group had risen by 18 percent over 1971 values.

Major developments. An occurrence likely to affect world trade patterns for some years was the realignment of currencies late in 1971. The most widespread since the extensive devaluations of 1949, this realignment was agreed upon at a ministerial meeting of the Group of Ten major nations on December 18, 1971, in Washington, D.C. It has since been referred to as the Smithsonian Agreement.

Although no country was unaffected, the major shifts included the devaluation of the U.S. dollar in terms of gold by 8.57 percent and the upward valuation of the Japanese yen by 16.9 percent and of the West German mark by 13.6 percent in terms of the dollar. Insofar as such currency shifts were carried over into export and import prices as the year progressed, those countries whose products were thereby cheaper vis-à-vis German, Japanese, or any other country's goods stood to expand their sales, while their imports were likely to be inhibited by higher prices. Initially, before market forces worked themselves out, imports would grow in value, and exports would not necessarily expand, because the accomplishment of such extensive adjustments always takes considerable time. Nevertheless, by the second half of 1972, the effects were beginning to be evident in the trade of certain countries.

In Brussels on July 22, representatives of nations belonging to the European Economic Community and the European Free Trade Association signed treaties providing for an industrial free-trade zone that would have encompassed almost all of Western Europe. The new zone, which would have included 300 million Europeans, was prompted by the proposed entrance of three members of the EFTA into the EEC. Ireland (which is not a member of the EFTA), Great Britain, Norway, and Denmark had been slated to join the Common Market on January 1, 1973. Because the Common Market has maintained a tariff barrier separating member

nations from nonmember nations, a trade wall would ordinarily have gone up between Great Britain, Norway, and Denmark and the other members of the EFTA if no special arrangement had been made.

The arrangements called for the existing free trade to continue between the three EFTA nations that were to join the Common Market and the six that were not—Iceland, Sweden, Finland, Austria, Switzerland, and Portugal. Industrial tariff barriers between the rest of the Common Market and the portion of the EFTA that had chosen not to join the Common Market would have been eliminated gradually, with most disappearing by July 1, 1977.

The arrangements were disrupted in September, when the Norwegians voted against joining the EEC in a two-day referendum. In October, however, Denmark voted to join the Common Market by a wide margin.

Great Britain and Ireland remained firm in their commitments to join the Common Market. The trading position of Norway vis-à-vis the Common Market became the subject of negotiations between the countries concerned.

Beginning on April 13, 2,000 representatives from 135 nations met for five weeks in Santiago, Chile, for the third United Nations Conference on Trade and Development. A major theme of the conference was the desire of the developing countries for greater participation in the decision-making process on international economic issues. Agreements reached at this conference, which the developing countries consider their principal forum for a dialogue between the developed nations and themselves, concerned (1) participation in monetary reform discussions, (2) the need for special measures to assist the least developed countries, (3) more favorable allocation of special drawing rights from the International Monetary Fund, and (4) special attention in the 1973 multilateral trade negotiations.

The implementation of the decisions of the Kennedy Round of tariff discussions was completed in January, when the final stage of tariff reductions went into effect. At the March council meeting of the General Agreement on Tariffs and Trade, the major developed nations of the world joined together to initiate "new multilateral and comprehensive negotiations to expand world trade, beginning in 1973."

U.S. deficit deepens. After its first deficit in this century in 1971, U.S. trade worsened in the first half of 1972. Imports advanced to a seasonally adjusted annual rate of $53.7 billion, while exports rose to a $47 billion rate, leaving the rate of deficit at $6.7 billion, compared to a $2 billion total for 1971.

There were several reasons behind this further deterioration. On the one hand, imports were stimulated by a strong advance in U.S. economic activity in the first six months. Further, import prices were 6 percent higher than in the same period of 1971 as the devaluation of the dollar automatically resulted in higher prices for foreign goods. On the other hand, demand for U.S. goods in foreign countries, with the exception of Canada and Japan, was sluggish. Europe in particular was just beginning to recover from a period of lowered production and slower growth. The effects of the U.S. dollar devaluation on exports were not discernible through the first half of the year.

The major part of the $1.3 billion rise in exports in the first six months of the year was due to sales to Canada, which advanced by $850 million, and sales to Japan, up by $200 million. The $4.3 billion import increase, however, was spread throughout the world, although Western Europe, Canada, and Japan—in that order—provided the lion's share.

The growing trade deficits with Canada and Japan, particularly the latter, were of special concern to the United States. Imports from Japan at midyear were nearly double the value of exports. In the spring and summer months, several meetings between officials of the two governments were held to discuss this trade imbalance; at the end of August, President Richard M. Nixon and Premier Kakuei

Tanaka of Japan met for two days in Hawaii. It was announced on September 1 at the conclusion of the mid-Pacific talks that Japan had agreed to augment its short-term purchases of U.S. goods by $1.1 billion. These additional purchases will include enriched uranium, aircraft, and forestry and agricultural products.

Almost half of the 19 percent import rise in the first half of 1972 stemmed from a sharp gain in arrivals of consumer products. A good part of the increase was attributable to the acceleration in personal consumption expenditures on goods, though part came from higher prices. Foreign consumer goods continued to expand their share of the U.S. market, accounting for 6.2 percent of expenditures in the first six months of the year, compared to 5.3 percent in 1971.

Arrivals of automobiles and parts from U.S. subsidiaries in Canada showed further advances. Purchases of foreign consumer electronic products expanded by one-third to nearly $1 billion in the first six months. Tape recorders and players, purchased largely from Japan, posted the biggest advance. Other commodities that exceeded 1971 levels by significant amounts were clothing, footwear, transistor radios, motorcycles, and bicycles.

The rise in imports of industrial supplies, especially strong for petroleum and lumber, was related to the upturn in industrial production. Capital equipment arrivals likewise advanced sharply, exceeding the level of a year earlier by 31 percent. Business machines led the advance; much of the increase came from computer parts shipped by recently opened U.S.-owned facilities in Canada. Food and beverage imports recorded a substantial gain, with fish and meat accounting for the major share.

In contrast to imports, few exports showed large gains in the first half of this year. Shipments of all nonagricultural products, which accounted for over 80 percent of the total, increased by only 5 percent over the first half of 1971. Machinery sales were the biggest gainers.

Sales of transport equipment, which had made a large contribution to export gains in preceding years, were $100 million below those of the first half of 1971. Much of the fall was attributable to a decline in aircraft deliveries. Although they generally posted recoveries from the strike-affected second half of 1971, industrial supplies exports showed little change from the first half of 1971 except for lumber and logs. Exports of those products rose by about $100 million because of greater construction activity and because of demand for hardwood for bowling alleys in Japan.

Deliveries of agricultural products climbed by 9 percent, with grain and tobacco pacing the expansion. Corn deliveries were up sharply as a result of soaring shipments to Western Europe and the Soviet Union. Wheat shipments, however, were lower through June, though new contracts with the Soviet Union, as a result of poor harvests in that country, were expected to boost exports sharply in the second half.

Canadian surplus. As a result of an increasingly favorable balance with the United States, Canadian trade in the first six months of 1972 recorded a surplus of Can$556 million, seasonally adjusted. This value, however, was over Can$300 million below that for the preceding six months and less than half the level for the first six months of 1971.

Canadian exports to the United States, which accounted for 71 percent of the total, were almost $1 billion greater in the first half of 1971, but exports to other regions showed no change on balance. Imports, on the other hand, gained by Can$1,600 million, of which only about Can$900 million was from the United States. Japan, Britain, and the Common Market countries were responsible for most of the remaining expansion.

With the exception of food products, which are of minor importance in total sales to the United States, the largest part of the overall 11 percent advance in commodity exports occurred in products for which demand south of the border was strong or in products that industrial affiliates in Canada were shipping to their parent companies. Among such products were petroleum, lumber, certain nonferrous metals, automotive equipment, newsprint, and computer and aircraft parts.

Despite a high level of unemployment, the Canadian economy moved strongly upward in 1972, stimulating imports of all kinds. Demand was especially high for machinery and consumer goods. Also of major importance was the continued growth of automotive imports, especially of parts shipped from the United States for assembly into new cars and return south under duty-free arrangements in existence since 1965.

The share of imports coming from the United States edged downward to 68 percent, compared to 72 percent three years earlier, as some countries—especially Japan—made new efforts to sell in the Canadian market. Imports from Japan, though small when compared to those from the United States, more than doubled from the first half of 1970. In 1972, Japan became Canada's second major supplier, replacing Great Britain.

Imports from both the Soviet Union and the People's Republic of China, though minuscule in comparison to other countries, continued to grow sharply as those nations tried to market their products to offset the cost of large Canadian grain shipments to them.

Again in 1972, Canada negotiated new contracts with both the Soviet Union and China for further sizable grain sales. The extremely poor Soviet harvest led to contracts with the Canadians for 3.5 million tons of wheat and flour and 200,000 tons of barley for delivery during the 1972–1973 crop year alone.

Pickup in Latin America. After a generally sluggish performance in 1971, a pickup appeared to be under way in Latin American trade in 1972.

Resuming expansionist policies after a period of cutbacks, Mexico was recovering from its 1971 slowdown in economic growth. The stimulation of the economy resulted in a 9 percent rise in imports in the first five months. In the same period exports climbed by 29 percent, with manufactured goods leading the advance. Thus, a sizable cut in the usual deficit appeared in store if these trends continued throughout the year.

The Brazilian economy continued to boom, with an expected growth rate of about 10 percent for the fifth consecutive year. The expansion served to maintain a high level of import demand, following a 30 percent rise in 1971. Exports in contrast did relatively poorly in that year, partly as a result of low prices for coffee, Brazil's chief export. In 1972, prices were considerably higher because the major producing countries held back shipments and also because of a spring frost in Brazil that threatened to reduce sharply the crop in the next season. Thus, in the early months of the year, Brazilian exports were substantially above those for the same period of 1971. It was by no means certain, however, that exports would be high enough to allow the balance of trade, which showed a deficit of $325 million in 1971, to return to its former surplus position when the year's accounts were tallied.

The trade outlook of Argentina, in contrast to that of Mexico and Brazil, was bleak, as the economy stagnated and the balance of payments faced another serious deficit. In an effort to curb the heavy flow of imports following a negative trade balance in 1971, the government made foreign goods more expensive through adjustment of the exchange rate and through imposition of costly mandatory credit terms. But a sharply rising rate of inflation and the possibility of further tightening of controls tended to vitiate efforts to reduce imports. The export forecast for agricultural products in 1972 was even poorer than for the relatively slow year of 1971. Corn yields declined sharply because of dry weather, but beef exports early this year were 13 percent higher

than in the comparable 1971 period. Wool production, however, fell to the lowest level since the 1930's.

The previous rapid disintegration that had characterized the Central American Common Market gave way to a period of consolidation this year, but there were no steps toward further development or toward reincorporation of Honduras into the group. This most promising of Latin American integration groups thus continues to mark time, and the outlook is cloudy. However, the Andean Pact group continued to make some progress toward the eventual establishment of a common market, and trade among the Andean nations gained in 1972.

Currency shifts affect Western Europe. Measured in a common currency such as dollars, Western European exports recorded a 23 percent jump in the first half of 1972 compared to the same period of 1971, while imports advanced by 18 percent. Because of the general upward revaluation of European currencies in December 1971, however, the growth in terms of national currencies was much more modest, perhaps 10–11 percent lower.

The pickup in European economic activity in 1972 after the stagnation of the preceding year was much slower than anticipated, and demand for imported goods was limited. Exports of all countries moved strongly, in part because extra efforts were made to sell abroad because domestic requirements were expanding slowly.

The West German situation was more or less typical and, by the sheer size of its trade, dominated the European scene. Imports grew only marginally in the first half of the year because the slowdown in the economy continued to depress demand. There was little or no growth through June, as industrial investment contracted sharply. Despite higher prices as a result of revaluation, exports were strong, leaving a surplus in the first six months of $2.6 billion.

French export trade benefited from relative improvement in competitiveness because of the various European currency shifts. Sales, both to other members of the EEC and to the rest of the world, moved upward rapidly. Imports, too, speeded up somewhat, particularly because there was an improvement in the investment climate.

After showing a surplus of about £25 million a month in 1971, the British trade balance moved into deficit by about that same amount through the first seven months of 1972. Import values were raised from June 23, when the chancellor of the Exchequer announced that the pound sterling would be allowed to float because of heavy pressure in international markets. The pound declined rapidly to a level near that which had obtained before sterling was revalued relative to the dollar as part of the Smithsonian Agreement. This alteration was reflected in higher sterling values for imports.

Asia continues growth. Japanese exports advanced strongly in the first six months of 1972 in terms of dollars, while imports picked up momentum after their marginal growth in 1971. The Japanese trade surplus thus continued to soar, reaching an annual rate of over $5 billion. Measured in Japanese yen, however, exports showed only a negligible advance over first half 1971 levels and imports actually declined. Thus, the sharp revaluation of the yen at the end of 1971 accounted for the changes relative to the preceding year, rather than any shifts in the actual volume of sales and receipts. With a strong upswing expected in the second half of 1972 in the Japanese economy and with efforts on the part of the government to promote purchases of foreign goods, the large surplus in dollar terms was sure to be reduced.

Incomplete returns for the first part of 1972 for most other Asian countries showed considerable expansion in sales, a much smaller portion of which could be associated with revaluations. Larger quantities of consumer goods and higher prices for jute, tin, and rope fibers caused growing sales by South Korea, Hong Kong, India, Thailand, and Singapore. Malaysia and the Philippines did not share in the expansion.

UPI

YOUNGEST MAYOR in the United States, Jody Smith (left) chats with a constituent in Ayrshire, Iowa. Inaugurated at the age of 19, Smith attends classes at a nearby community college when he is not ministering to the needs of the town's 273 residents.

Slowdown in Africa. With the exception of Libya and Nigeria, where petroleum is the main foreign exchange earner, most developing countries in Africa were not able to expand the value of their sales in 1971 to meet growing needs for imported goods. In 1972, rising prices for petroleum and coffee and stabilization of prices for cocoa and copper—in contrast to previous declines—contributed to an improved outlook.

The Republic of South Africa instituted tight import controls and devalued its currency even more sharply than the U.S. dollar following three years of declining growth in the economy. Despite controls, imports through May, measured in South African rands, were about the same as in the first five months of 1971. Exports, however, jumped by nearly one-third, especially corn, pearls, and precious stones and metals. The trade imbalance was thus lessened considerably.

FRANCES L. HALL

IOWA. Politics and government. Attorney General Richard Turner created a year-long furor when he widened a "gambling" crackdown that he began late in 1971 with a raid on a church picnic in the tiny town of North Buena Vista and the arrest of a parish priest for running a "gambling house." Iowa churches and schools, which for years had raised money with penny pitches, bingo, and dart games, suddenly found themselves in danger of prosecution.

The Iowa State Fair Board and the many county fair associations predicted big revenue losses when Turner also decided that virtually all the traditional midway games were illegal. With fair and midway operators on one side and Turner on the other, a seesaw legal battle was waged throughout a long hot summer, with court injunctions, appeals, and counterappeals reaching all the way to the U.S. Supreme Court, which declined to hear the case.

Turner was upheld by both the state supreme court and federal district court in the definition of "gambling" as it

appears in the Iowa penal code: all games where a consideration is paid in an attempt to win a prize, regardless of whether skill or chance is involved.

Legislation. The 64th general assembly, meeting for the second and final session of its two-year life, passed several important measures. One of the most far-reaching lowered the legal age for various adult activities from 21 to 19. The bill provides, as of July 1, not only for a lower drinking age, but also for a lower age at which one can own property, marry without parental consent, obtain professional licenses, take responsibility for their debts, enter court actions, and obtain permits for dangerous weapons.

Four major governmental reform laws were enacted. The state's justices of the peace, mayors' courts, and municipal courts are to be replaced by July 1, 1973, with a system of magistrates under the control of the 18 district courts. A department of environmental quality was created to consolidate and strengthen the machinery for environmental control. Municipal law was completely recodified to give Iowa's 900-plus cities and towns home rule, allowing them to do anything not specifically prohibited by state law. The office of citizen's aide, or ombudsman, was made formal and will hear complaints against state bureaucracy.

The state election laws were revised, cutting the residency requirement for voting to 30 days and streamlining election administration at the local level. The new residency law was challenged in court, however. The state admitted that, in view of a U.S. Supreme Court decision for another state, the new statute was unenforceable, and a court order wiped out all residency requirements for voting in the state (except the voter registration requirement that applies in metropolitan areas).

The state supreme court, which ruled unconstitutional a reapportionment plan passed by the 1971 session of the legislature, drew up its own redistricting plan providing only one-tenth of a percent deviation between the largest and smallest house and senatorial districts. As a result, more than 40 of the 150 legislators were thrown into combined districts, forcing them to run against fellow incumbents for reelection.

Economic developments. The historic agreement on sales of several types of grain from the United States to the Soviet Union and China promised major boosts for Iowa's agriculturally based economy. Iowa, according to forecasts by the U.S. Department of Agriculture, was once again the nation's leading feed corn state, with a harvest of 1.1 billion bushels predicted (about one-fifth of the national total), and the second largest soybean producer, with an expected harvest of 203 million bushels.

For election results and campaign highlights, see the special supplement ELECTION '72.

Area and population. Area, 56,290 sq. mi. Pop. (1970), 2,825,041. Principal cities: Des Moines (cap.), 200,587; Cedar Rapids, 110,642; Davenport, 98,469; Sioux City, 85,925; Waterloo, 75,533.

Government. Gov., Robert D. Ray (R); lt. gov., Roger W. Jepsen (R); secy. of state, Melvin D. Synhorst (R); treas., Maurice E. Baringer (R); atty. gen., Richard C. Turner (R); aud., Lloyd R. Smith (R); secy. of agr., Lucius B. Liddy (R). Legislature (elected in 1970): senate, 37 R, 13 D; house, 63 R, 37 D.

Finance (state general fund only, year ending July 30, 1972). Revenue, $632,046,234; expenditures, $567,518,613. Major sources of revenue: sales, income, use, and tobacco taxes; federal aid. Major items of expenditure: education, welfare, grants-in-aid to schools and local governments.

Education (1971–1972). Public school enrollment: elementary, 357,711; secondary, 292,092. Private and parochial school enrollment: elementary, 51,998; secondary, 17,939. College and university enrollment: 110,785.   LAURENCE M. PAUL

IRAN. Foreign affairs. Relations with neighboring Iraq continued to deteriorate throughout the year. In January the government of Iran notified the United Nations that Iraq's expulsion since October 1971 of more than 48,000 Iranians had created a "dangerous situation." Iran charged that Iraqi policemen had beaten and tortured some of the refugees before expelling them and that Iraqi spies were attempting to infiltrate by posing as refugees.

The Iraqi-Soviet friendship treaty of April 9, followed by the arrival at the Iraqi port of Basra of a Soviet naval formation on April 11, shifted the dispute to a more serious level. The treaty, which includes a provision for Soviet military aid to Iraq, was perceived in Iran as a possible challenge to Iranian efforts to establish military and political hegemony over the Persian Gulf region. Iran feared that Iraq would now press claims, either directly or in the name of the "Arab nation" (Iran is not an Arab country), to three areas that are now part of Iran: first, the province of Khuzistan, which the Arabs call "Arabistan" and which includes the disputed Shatt al 'Arab River, now shared by Iraq and Iran; second, border territory, particularly in the Khanaqin region; and third, three small Persian Gulf islands (nominally part of the United Arab Emirates, formerly Trucial Oman) that Iran occupied when the British left in late 1971.

On April 11 a border clash occurred between Iraqi and Iranian forces in the Khanaqin region, an action involving both troops and artillery. The following month Iran called up for "fresh training" military reservists in the western provinces (near Iraq), and on July 8 another border clash occurred in Khanaqin. After the Soviet military's expulsion from Egypt in the middle of July, Soviet arms shipments to Iraq increased.

In response to the potential military threat, Iran was especially careful to court the West this year. In March the Iranians were host to West German chancellor Willy Brandt and also received British foreign secretary Alec Douglas-Home, who came to discuss the Persian Gulf situation. On May 30, President Richard M. Nixon stopped over in Tehran on his way home from Moscow and conferred with both the shah and Prime Minister Amir Abbas Hoveida. The visit was interpreted as a symbol of American support for Iranian policy in the Persian Gulf, an interpretation that was affirmed when the United States announced, subsequent to the president's visit, that Washington was prepared to supply Iran with F-14 fighter-bombers and laser-guided bombs. The news came as some surprise inasmuch as production on the F-14 has not even started.

Iran has also sharply increased its military expenditures. Whereas in 1965 Iran spent $250 million for arms, it is estimated that for the fiscal year ending in March 1973 such expenditures will exceed $687 million. In late August, Iran placed a $240 million order for British military equipment.

Internal affairs. On April 10 an earthquake struck southern Iran causing heavy loss of life and extensive property damage. The epicenter of the quake was some 100 miles southeast of Shiraz. More than 45 villages were razed to the ground; about 5,000 people were killed, and an additional 1,300 were seriously wounded. It was the worst earthquake in Iran since 1968.

Iran's economic boom and strengthened military position have generated growing demands within the country that the shah begin to relax his authoritarian rule. In January, Iranian security officials admitted that at least three major rebel networks were operating within the country. These rebel groups are receiving at least tacit support from a number of frustrated middle-class Iranians who aspire to participate in their country's decision-making processes. Although such participation is permitted in the technological sphere, the shah holds the reins of political power tightly in his own hands.

The Iranian government dismisses the rebels either as groups "in conspiracy with Iraq" or as Iranian youths who have been "misguided." On January 1 some 120 rebels were put on trial for being "saboteurs trained in Iraq," and on March 1 six of those convicted were executed. Iran formally filed a complaint before the United Nations in May charging that Iraq was the "main source of support and subsidy for subversive elements in the Middle East."

On August 18, Tehran's police chief, Jaffar Gholi Aadri, announced that 75 percent of Iran's antigovernment guerrillas had been killed or captured. Some observers, however, considered the police chief's statement overly optimistic.

Economic developments. The shah broke the solid front of the Organization of Petroleum Exporting Countries when he announced in June that Iran would not press for 20 percent participation rights in Western oil companies operating in Iran. Instead the Iranian government and the consortium of oil firms entered into a five-year extension of their previous agreement. Under the terms of the new arrangement, Iran may look forward to annual oil revenues in excess of $4 billion.

Area and population. Area, 636,300 sq. mi. Pop. (March 1973 official est.), 30,900,000. Tehran (cap.), 3,229,000.
Government. Constitutional monarchy. Parliament composed of the Senate and the Majlis (National Assembly). Shah, Muhammad Riza Pahlavi; prime min., Amir Abbas Hoveida.
Finance. Monetary unit, rial; R1 = US$0.0134. Budget (1972–1973): balanced at R548.5 billion.
Petroleum. Crude oil production (1971), 226.2 million long tons.
RICHARD H. PFAFF

IRAQ. On April 9, Iraq and the Soviet Union signed a 15-year friendship treaty, and on June 1, Iraq nationalized the Iraq Petroleum Company (IPC), one of the oldest and largest of the foreign-owned oil companies in the Middle East. The immediate effect of both of these important events has been to strengthen the Iraqi government.

Foreign affairs. The treaty between Iraq and the Soviet Union was foreshadowed by the visit of Saddam Hussein Takriti, the vice-chairman of the Revolutionary Command Council (RCC) and secretary of the Ba'ath Party, to Moscow in February. Takriti called for a "solid strategic alliance" with the Soviet Union. A joint communiqué was issued on February 17 which mentioned that the possibility of formalizing mutual relations in a treaty would be given careful study.

In early April Soviet premier Aleksei Kosygin visited Iraq and on April 9 signed the treaty in Baghdad. It denounced all forms of imperialism and colonialism, including "Zionism," and pledged cooperation and consultation in economics, technology, culture, trade, science, and politics. Both countries promised to "continue to develop cooperation in the strengthening of their defense capabilities." Each signatory pledged not to join any pact hostile to the other or to allow its territory to be used for military action hostile to the other.

The Soviet Union had long been ambivalent in its relations with governments of the Ba'ath Party. In both 1963 and 1968 the Iraqi Ba'ath Party had moved ruthlessly against the Iraqi Communist Party. In addition, the Soviet Union wished to maintain good relations with the Kurdish nationalists and with the shah of Iran. Apparently, however, Iraq's great strategic value and the new Soviet policy of seeking formal allies in Asia overcame the obstacles to cooperation.

Many Arab states, including Libya, objected to the treaty because it reminded them of the Baghdad Pact (now CENTO) of 1955. In protest, Libya withdrew its ambassador from Baghdad.

In July the new treaty became even more significant. When Egyptian president Anwar Sadat expelled most of his Soviet military advisers, the possibility was raised that Iraq might become the major base for Soviet influence in the Middle East.

Iraq led the successful opposition to the plan of Jordan's King Hussein for a united Arab kingdom made up of a Jordanian region (the present area of Jordan) and a Palestinian region (the West Bank of the Jordan River and the Gaza Strip, both occupied by Israel since 1967). Takriti went to Egypt and Syria for talks, despite long-standing hostility between the Syrian and Iraqi Ba'ath regimes. Iraqi president Ahmed Hussein al-Bakr called for an immediate union between Iraq, Syria, and Egypt.

Economic affairs. Relations between the IPC, owned jointly by British, U.S., French, and Dutch companies, and Iraq had been strained since 1961 when Iraq had nationalized IPC's unexploited territory. Part of this area was developed by Iraq, with aid from the Soviet Union, as the North Rumaila field. The IPC continued to demand compensation and to take legal action against buyers of North Rumaila oil.

Negotiations between the Iraqi government and the IPC were in progress for months. Iraq demanded equity participation of 20 percent in the IPC. The crucial issue, however, was over oil output. The IPC contended that oil delivered through their pipeline to the Mediterranean ports of Baniyas and Tripoli was more expensive on the world market than Persian Gulf oil shipped by tanker. Thus, it claimed, production decreased because of decreased demand, while production of the Basra Petroleum Company (BPC), which has almost identical ownership but which exports its product by tanker from southern Iraq, increased. Iraq, on the other hand, charged that the IPC was cutting production to put pressure on Iraq during negotiations.

Iraq took immediate steps to lessen the impact of the loss of oil revenues. It obtained the financial backing of the Organization of Arab Petroleum Exporting Companies

FATAL FAULT. A man carries the body of his son, victim of the earthquake that killed about 5,000 persons one April morning in the primitive villages of southern Iran. Continuing seismic activity around the Zagros Mountains means future quakes are likely.

AFP/PICTORIAL

(OAPEC), which it had joined in March, in the form of an interest-free two-year loan of $151 million. The Organization of Petroleum Exporting Companies (OPEC) backed Iraq by refusing to allow oil companies to raise production to offset their Iraqi losses. However, both the IPC and Iraq agreed to the mediation of the secretary general of OPEC, and IPC declared a three-month moratorium on legal action against potential buyers of the nationalized oil.

Iraq also took action to maintain its oil markets in Europe. Italy agreed to increase its purchases. On June 18, France agreed to buy at least 23.75 percent of nationalized production, which is the same percentage as the share of the Compagnie Française des Petroles (CFP) in the IPC. France stated that this was not a settlement for nationalization and that the CFP would remain in the negotiations between the IPC and the Iraqi government. Iraq's success in gaining support from the Soviet Union, from oil-exporting nations, and from other Arab states was beneficial. Libya resumed full diplomatic relations, and Kuwait pledged 25 percent of the OAPEC loan.

At home an austerity program was announced. It called for obligatory "savings bonds" to be deducted from the salaries of all government employees, a drastic reduction in imports, and a readjustment of the five-year plan.

Domestic affairs. The uneasy truce between the government and the Kurds, under the leadership of Mulla Mustafa Barzani, was maintained this year. The Kurds protested when many of the illegal Iranian immigrants expelled by Iraq late last year and early this year turned out also to be Kurds. They were forced to leave the country in retaliation for Iran's occupation of three disputed islands in the Persian Gulf. The government was unhappy when Barzani refused to join the condemnation of Iranian policy.

In May the Soviet Union strengthened the Ba'ath government by arranging for the participation in the cabinet of two Communist Party members. This was the first Communist participation since the fall of Abdul Karim Kassem in 1963. However, a splinter group of the Iraqi Communist Party known as the Central Command organized a coalition of anti-Ba'ath leftists in a "national grouping" and attempted to foment armed uprisings against the Ba'ath regime. Also in May two independent Arab nationalists joined the cabinet.

Miscellaneous. In March hundreds of Iraqis died from mercury poisoning. Farmers and animals had eaten mercury-treated seed grain intended only for planting.

The Christian Syriac-speaking minorities (Assyrians, Chaldeans, and Syrians) were guaranteed special cultural rights on April 22. Their language is to be taught in their community schools and studied at Baghdad University. The information ministry is to produce Syriac materials and a writer's society is to be formed.

Area and population. Area, 167,925 sq. mi. Pop. (est. 1971), 9,750,000. Principal cities (est. 1970): Baghdad (cap.), 1,300,000; Basra, 370,900; Mosul, 293,100.

Government. Nominally a constitutional republic. Power is in the hands of the Revolutionary Command Council of the Ba'ath Party. Pres., Ahmed Hassan al-Bakr.

Finance. Monetary unit, Iraqi dinar; ID1 = US$3.10.

Oil production (1971). 83,772,000 metric tons.

Trade (1971). Imports, US$694,000,000; exports, US$1,538,-000,000.

Armed forces. 92,000, including paramilitary forces.

RALPH H. MAGNUS

IRELAND. Common Market membership. After 11 years of intermittent negotiation by their government, the people of Ireland voted overwhelmingly for membership in the European Economic Community in a referendum on May 10. The governing party, Fianna Fáil, and the principal opposition party, Fine Gael, were united in recommending acceptance to the electorate. Rejection was urged by the Labour Party, trade union organizations, and both factions of Sinn Fein.

The advocates of entry held out the prospect of greater economic prosperity, a change from Ireland's comparative isolation from Europe, and a better chance of bringing the partition of Ireland to an end. The opponents of entry maintained that the economic promises were illusory, that Ireland would lie in an area of peripheral poverty in the enlarged community, that its Gaelic culture would be doomed, and that to vote for Europe was to abandon their fellow Irishmen in the North, who were presumed to be against it.

Seventy percent of the electorate turned out, an unusually high poll for a referendum in Ireland, and of those voting more than four-fifths were in favor. A favorable result had been expected, but the size of the margin surprised everyone. The vote was seen as a personal triumph for Prime Minister Jack Lynch and indirectly as an endorsement of his policy toward the North.

Politics and government. Shortly after the referendum, Prime Minister Lynch had another emphatic success at the polls, this time in a by-election in mid-Cork. Had his party lost the seat (as at first looked very likely) the government's majority in the Dáil, already reduced by defections, would have disappeared altogether; and although Irish governments have been able to carry on in such circumstances, prospective events seemed to require a government more firmly based than that. A general election might have been necessary. Lynch and his senior ministers threw themselves into the campaign, turning a provincial by-election into a national vote of confidence. Again he was richly rewarded by the voters. A breakaway group under the leadership of the former Fianna Fáil minister, Kevin Boland (whose quarrel with his former colleagues is that they do not pursue the goal of Irish unity with sufficient vigor), found only the barest support. Fine Gael and the Labour Party, which had shortly before notified the country that they were prepared to combine in a coalition government as an alternative to Fianna Fáil, remained as far as ever from the seat of power.

The Northern Ireland issue. Prime Minister Lynch's approach to the question of Northern Ireland has been to proceed on the assumption that Irish unity is not to be had and would not be worth having on any basis other than consent; to bring whatever diplomatic pressure he can on the British government on behalf of the Roman Catholic minority in the North with a view to improving their political status and keeping open the route to eventual national unity; and to move against the Irish Republican Army (IRA) within the republic, but in a gingerly fashion so as not to provoke popular disorders or the use of violence. A number of arrests were made of IRA suspects on charges of unlawful possession of arms or membership in an unlawful organization. However, convictions were not easy to secure, partly because some members of juries and local magistrates were succumbing to prejudice or intimidation. Thus, in May the government introduced special criminal courts under emergency powers legislation, in which three judges sit without juries. Thereafter, the conviction rate increased. Nonetheless, there was less legal harassment of IRA leaders, supplies, and sanctuaries within the republic than suited the British authorities or for that matter some domestic critics of the government.

The prime minister's caution was also visible in the matter of constitutional reform. It is now widely acknowledged that if northern Protestant consent to unity is ever to be won, there will have to be major reforms within the republic, especially of those features which make it a confessional state in Protestant eyes, including the special position accorded by the constitution to the Roman Catholic Church.

The Irish government's relations with the British government have varied with the movement of events in Ulster. After "Bloody Sunday" in Londonderry, January 30, when 13 civilians were shot dead by British paratroopers during a

civil rights demonstration, the Irish ambassador in London was recalled; the foreign minister, Patrick Hillery, was sent to the United Nations in New York, where he declared that "If Britain is not visited by sanity, we are dedicated to getting them out"; and Prime Minister Lynch demanded the immediate withdrawal of British troops from sensitive Catholic areas, the end of internment, and a conference to settle the Irish question. A few days later, on a day designated by the government as a day of national mourning, a mob burned down the British embassy in Dublin.

On March 24, when the British government suspended the Northern Ireland parliament and government and assumed direct control of the province, the move was welcomed by Lynch as "a step forward in reaching a lasting solution to the remaining problems of Anglo-Irish relations." The Irish ambassador was restored to London, and the resumed cordiality of relations withstood even the British army's bloodless invasion of the Bogside and the "no-go" areas of Belfast later in the year.

Economy. Although the pace of inflation was unabated and unemployment figures remained high, other economic indicators were encouraging—production, investment, exports, balance of payments—and that in spite of a further falling off in the important sector of tourism, where a hoped-for £125 million of receipts was actually £80 million. Some brake on inflation was imposed by a renewal of the national wages agreement in late summer. This laid down an increase of 9 percent for those earning up to £30 a week, with lower proportionate raises for those earning more. The spring budget introduced by George Colley, the minister for finance, was unusual in that it budgeted for a deficit of £35 million. It increased no taxes, improved social welfare payments, and made larger tax concessions than any previous budget in the history of the state.

Area and population. Area, 27,137 sq. mi. Pop. (1971), 2,971,-000. Principal cities: Dublin (cap.), 566,000; Cork, 128,000.
Government. Republic. Pres., Eamon de Valera; prime min., Jack Lynch; deputy prime min. and min. for health, Erskine H. Childers; min. for external affairs, Patrick J. Hillery; fin. min., George Colley; min. of agriculture, James Gibbons.
Finance. Monetary unit, Irish pound; £1 = US$2.34. Budget (est. 1971–1972): revenue and expenditure, £551 million.
Trade (1971). Imports, £754 million; exports, £537 million.
Armed forces. Total strength, 13,000.   T. J. O. HICKEY

ISRAEL. The year opened under the shadow of Egyptian president Anwar Sadat's unfulfilled pledge to evict Israeli troops from the Sinai Peninsula by the end of 1971. However, as the year progressed and Egypt still did not act, tension moderated and concern shifted to Arab guerrilla activities. Two dramatic guerrilla actions—claiming a total of 31 lives—occurred at Tel Aviv's Lydda Airport in May. Then in September, 11 members of the Israeli Olympic team were killed in Munich, Germany, by Palestinian terrorists who held the Israelis as hostages in an attempt to gain the release of Arab prisoners in Israel.

Diplomatic activity. The Egyptian decision not to seek a "military solution" to the Sinai issue led to renewed interest in diplomatic settlements. On February 2, after the United States had announced its decision to resume sales of Phantom jets to Israel, the Israeli government agreed to renew U.S.-initiated negotiations on opening the Suez Canal. Also in February, UN mediator Gunnar Jarring, who has been seeking an overall settlement, made a series of exploratory visits. However, neither initiative immediately bore fruit, and then, after the deaths of the 11 athletes, Foreign Minister Abba Eban said negotiations could not go forward until "this obstacle [Arab terrorism] is out of the way."

Israel rejected King Hussein of Jordan's March 15 proposal for West Bank (Palestinian) autonomy within Jordan, presumably as part of a peace settlement. (The West Bank of the Jordan River has been occupied by Israel since the 1967 war.) Calling the proposal a step backward, Prime

Minister Golda Meir attacked Hussein for attempting to act unilaterally and for refusing to deal directly with Israel. Israelis also saw Hussein's proposal as primarily aimed at influencing local elections on the West Bank, elections which were held successfully under Israeli auspices on March 28 and May 2.

On other fronts, Israel continued to push for the right of Soviet Jews to immigrate to Israel. From January to August 1972, about 20,000 Jews were allowed to leave the Soviet Union, compared with about 15,000 in all of 1971, and about 2,000 the year before. In mid-August, however, the Soviet government's imposition of stiff new exit fees on educated Jews threatened to reduce the tide of immigrants by up to a third, leading to immediate Israeli protests. In the fall, Soviet immigration policy became less clear. The exit fees were still in effect, but many Jews seeking to leave were exempted from paying them.

Relations with France improved with the conclusion, on February 15, of an agreement returning to Israel the money paid for 50 Mirage jets withheld from delivery since 1967.

A diplomatic setback of serious dimensions occurred in March when several hundred Israeli technicians and advisers—representing the largest aid program to a single country—were summarily expelled from Uganda by President Idi Amin, who accused Israel of subversive activities. The expulsion coincided with improved relations between Uganda and Libya and with plans for Libyan aid to Uganda.

Security issues. The incident at Munich, the site of this year's Olympic Games, began at about 4 A.M. on September 5, when eight Palestinian terrorists broke into the Israeli athletes' quarters in the Olympic Village. Several athletes escaped, two were killed, and nine were taken hostage—to be held, according to one of the Arabs, until about 200 Arab prisoners in Israel were released.

The guerrillas demanded that the West German government provide them with a jet airplane, and after a full day of unsuccessful negotiations between the Palestinians and German officials, the government provided three helicopters to take the Arabs and their hostages to a nearby airport. Shortly after their arrival, at about 10 P.M., police sharpshooters opened fire on the terrorists, but they killed only two of the Arabs. Then, at about midnight, the final exchange occurred. When it was over, all nine Israelis, five of the guerrillas, and one German policeman were dead; the other three Arabs, members of the guerrilla organization Black September, were captured. In late October, however, Palestinian guerrillas hijacked a West German airliner and forced the release of the three terrorists captured in Munich. The Israeli government said that it planned to protest the release. (*See also the special article* THE XX OLYMPICS.)

In the next few days Black September, whose name refers to the September 1970 crackdown on Palestinian guerrillas in Jordan by King Hussein's government, turned to a new tactic—mailing bombs to Israeli diplomats and other officials abroad. Dozens of bombs, each one small enough to fit in a standard letter envelope, were sent to officials throughout Europe and North America, and a counselor with the Israeli embassy in London was killed by a bomb explosion on September 19.

Earlier in the year, Black September claimed responsibility for the hijacking of a Sabena airliner by four Palestinians on May 8. The hijackers ordered the pilot to land at Lydda International Airport and then threatened to blow up plane and passengers unless 317 Arab prisoners in Israel were released. The incident ended the next day when Israeli troops stormed the plane, killing the two male hijackers and capturing the two female hijackers. Five passengers were wounded in the shooting, and one subsequently died.

On the night of May 30, a three-man suicide team, made up of members of a Japanese left-wing revolutionary organization, landed at Lydda and opened fire in the crowded

ABOVE, STARPHOTO; LEFT, RICHARD MELLOUL/GAMMA

TERROR AT LYDDA

Pools of blood and clumps of abandoned luggage grimly testify to the carnage that enveloped the airport at Lydda when three Palestinian-trained Japanese terrorists suddenly opened submachine guns on unsuspecting civilians, killing 25 men, women, and children. The lone surviving assassin was held for trial (left) and sentenced to life in prison.

passenger terminal, killing 25 persons and injuring 77 others; two of the Japanese were also killed. The lone survivor, who claimed the trio was acting on behalf of the Popular Front for the Liberation of Palestine, was 24-year-old Kozo Okamoto, one of the people whose release was demanded by the Arab guerrillas in Munich. By September, Okamoto and the two captured hijackers in the Sabena incident had been sentenced to life imprisonment.

The Munich killings and the subsequent letter-bomb incidents prompted ten days of heavy Israeli air and ground attacks on suspected guerrilla strongholds in Lebanon and Syria—attacks aimed at destroying the guerrillas' capacity to make war against Israel. On September 16, Israeli and

Lebanese troops clashed in southern Lebanon, but the Lebanese army's primary goal in late September was not fighting Israeli forces but rather restraining the guerrillas in order to avoid further raids by Israel. On September 20 the Palestinian guerrillas, under pressure from Lebanese troops, reportedly agreed to limit their border activities.

The Lebanese frontier had been the scene of repeated incursions and bombardment by Arab guerrillas in the first half of the year. This guerrilla activity led to Israeli reprisals in February and June, culminating in the capture of five Syrian army officers on Lebanese territory on June 21 and in a heavy aerial and artillery bombardment of guerrilla strongholds in Lebanon two days later.

Politics and government. Prime Minister Meir's coalition cabinet survived another crisis over religious issues. Meir was forced to invoke coalition discipline against secular parties that sought to introduce civil marriage and against National Religious Party members who wanted to establish as law their definition of conversion to Judaism. An NRP deputy minister who voted against the government on the latter issue was ousted from his post.

Other issues which occupied the country included a four-month-long investigation of mismanagement in the operation of the Sinai oil fields, leading subsequently to an investigation of the investigation and to the resignation of Justice Minister Yaakov Shapiro. The public was also stirred by debate over the appeal of former residents of Berem and Ikrit, two Arab Christian villages on the Lebanese border, to be allowed to return to their former residences. The Arabs had been evicted during the 1948 war and kept out since then so that the villages could not be used by guerrillas infiltrating from Lebanon. Eighteen Israeli Arabs were arrested in August 1972 when they and about 300 other former residents tried to reoccupy Berem and Ikrit.

In October the Israeli government removed Rashad Shawa, the Arab mayor of the town of Gaza, after he refused to provide municipal services (for example, running water) to a nearby refugee camp. The mayor maintained that the existence of the camp as a separate entity dramatized the plight of all Arab refugees. The Palestinian majority in the Gaza Strip still fears that the area will be annexed by Israel, which has already spent $75 million to develop the area.

Maneuvering for the next parliamentary elections, to be held no later than November 1973, continued amid speculation about a successor to Prime Minister Meir, who has announced she will not seek reelection. The appointment to the cabinet in March of former chief of staff Haim Bar-Lev was widely interpreted as an effort by Finance Minister Pinhas Sapir and others to provide a counterweight to Defense Minister Moshe Dayan.

Social issues. Normalization of the country's daily life continued in the second year of cease-fire. An estimated 150,000 Arab tourists visited occupied areas under the summer visit program (up from about 100,000 in 1971). The problem of absorbing the new influx of Soviet Jews was the focus of much attention. Immigration from the United States, which quadrupled in the 1967–1971 period, showed signs of tapering off from the 8,500 peak of 1971.

Economic developments. The economy, functioning at full employment, continued to grow at a 6–7 percent rate, but the combined pressures of defense spending, increased immigration, and a huge trade deficit continued to fuel a rate of inflation called intolerable—12 percent in 1971.

Finance Minister Sapir presented a fiscal 1972 budget which it was hoped would hold price rises in 1972 to the 5–6 percent level. Total outlays were projected at $4.03 billion, up from $3.78 billion in fiscal 1971, but a slight decrease in real terms. More significantly, for the first time in the history of the state there was a projected cut in defense spending—by 11 percent, to $1.2 billion.

By year's end the external debt stood at about $4.2 billion, again giving Israel the highest per capita debt in the world. The growth of exports, which had surged in 1971 under artificial market conditions, slowed down during the year, and the chronic trade deficit (down by $254 million in 1971) widened again. On the positive side, dollar reserves, up by $215 million in 1971 after an earlier crisis, were expected to remain at the new high level.

See also the special article JERUSALEM.

Area and population. Area, 7,993 sq. mi.; occupied Arab territories, 26,500 sq. mi. Pop. (est. Jan. 2, 1971), 2,999,000. Principal cities: Jerusalem (cap.), 283,100; Tel Aviv–Jaffa, 382,900; Haifa, 214,500.

Government. Democratic republic. Power rests with the Knesset, a unicameral parliament. Pres., Zalman Shazar; prime min., Golda Meir.

Finance. Monetary unit, pound; I £ 1 = US$0.24. Budget (fiscal 1972): US$4.03 billion.

Trade (1970). Imports, $1.4 billion; exports, $731 million. Principal exports: polished diamonds, citrus fruits, textiles and clothing, food products, chemicals (potash). Principal imports: crude diamonds, machinery, iron and steel, foodstuffs. Major trading partners: Common Market, United States, United Kingdom.

Education (1970–1971). Primary schools, 1,496; enrollment, 459,-646; teachers, 25,793. Secondary schools, including vocational and technical, 589; enrollment, 140,080; teachers, 13,796. Colleges and universities, 7; enrollment, 49,330; teachers, 6,710.

ALAN DOWTY

ITALY. The center-left coalition which had governed Italy for the past decade broke up in January. After a general election, held on May 7, a new, centrist government was formed in June under the premiership of Christian Democrat Giulio Andreotti. The stagnant Italian economy continued to be a major preoccupation in 1972. Short-term strikes and political clashes between extremists occurred throughout the year, the strikes intensifying with the approach of autumn, when employment contracts in a number of major industries were up for renewal.

Government and politics. The presidential election of December 1971 revealed sharp divisions between the two major partners in the center-left coalition, the Christian Democrats and the Socialists (the other two members were the Social Democrats and the Republicans). The Socialists consistently sided with the Communists against the Christian Democrat candidates—first, Amintore Fanfani and then, when his candidacy failed, Giovanni Leone, who was eventually elected to succeed Giuseppe Saragat as president of the Republic.

A fresh difficulty for the coalition's Christian Democrat premier, Emilio Colombo, arose in January when Ugo La Malfa, leader of the Republicans, announced that his party would join the opposition unless a vigorous program of economic reforms could be produced. The Republicans' withdrawal of support and the continued Christian Democrat–Socialist friction (primarily over whether to consult with the Communist Party) prompted Premier Colombo's resignation on January 15. However, with the agreement of the four coalition parties, he attempted to create a new center-left government, in order to avoid the calling of a general election a year ahead of schedule. Parliament's five-year term was not due to end until mid-1973 and never since the creation of the republic after World War II had Parliament been dissolved early.

On February 1, however, Colombo announced that he had been unable to form a government, and President Leone then called on Giulio Andreotti, chairman of the Christian Democrats in the Chamber of Deputies, to try his hand. Andreotti, 53 years old, started his political career under Alcide de Gasperi's premiership in the late 1940's and had since then been a minister in every government until 1969. However, despite his political experience, Andreotti failed to secure the support of the other center-left parties for a revived coalition and therefore presented a single-party Christian Democrat government. That government gained the support only of the rightist Liberal Party, which had been in opposition for the past 12 years, and it was defeated in the Senate on February 26 by a vote of 158 to 151, thus obviating what would have been a much more decisive adverse vote in the Chamber.

Late that night Andreotti resigned, and President Leone asked him to remain as head of a caretaker government until after the now inevitable national election. On February 28 the president dissolved Parliament and announced that the election would be held on May 7.

As the election campaign got under way, the prospect was for stalemate, for although the center-left coalition pattern of the past decade seemed to be breaking up, it was

difficult to see what could take its place. The former coalition partners made no attempt to present joint lists of candidates or coordinated programs. Indeed, so far had they drifted apart that they often blamed each other for the coalition's shortcomings. The Socialists accused the Christian Democrats of moving rightward and blocking essential reforms; the Christian Democrats, the Social Democrats, and the Republicans vied with each other in attacking the Socialist policy of seeking closer association and consultation with the Communists in the conduct of affairs. At the Communist Party congress, held in Milan in March, the new party secretary, Enrico Berlinguer, declared that the time was ripe for collaboration among the forces of the left, including Catholic workers, to meet a "reactionary attack which threatened democracy."

During the campaign, some violent clashes occurred between extremist groups of the right and left. In Milan in March, two days before the Communist Party congress opened, street battles broke out in which some 80 people were injured, including one policeman. The leftists were demanding the release of Pietro Valpreda, an anarchist charged with bombing a Milan bank in 1969, an incident for which two right-wing extremists were also under detention. Valpreda was subsequently put up as an (unsuccessful) election candidate by the extreme-left group Manifesto.

The results of the general election came near to fulfilling the forecasts of stalemate, for on the whole there was little change in the party positions. The Christian Democrats remained the largest single party, securing 38.8 percent of the total vote for the Chamber (38.1 percent for the Senate) and making a strong comeback after their decline (to 31 percent) in the local elections of June 1971. The Socialists lost one seat in the Chamber, and the Social Democrats maintained their position. The small Republican Party improved its representation in both houses.

The Communists, the second largest party, won 27.2 percent of the total vote and gained a seat in the Chamber, but the party lost seven seats in the Senate, for which it presented joint candidate lists with the extreme-left Proletarian Socialist Unity Party. That party lost all of its 23 seats in the Chamber, and after the election most of its members merged with the Communists. The Manifesto group, which had split from the Communists and entertained high hopes of success, secured only 0.7 percent of the total vote.

The most striking changes of the election came on the right. The attack from that quarter had been seriously feared by the Christian Democrats after the successes of the neo-Fascist Movimento Sociale Italiano (MSI) in the local (mainly southern) elections of 1971. The MSI, under Giorgio Almirante, a former journalist and a government official in the last days of the Fascist regime, mounted a skillful campaign, playing down its neo-Fascist associations and representing itself as a party of law and order. It hoped for spectacular successes, and it did in fact increase its representation from 30 to 56 seats in the Chamber and from 13 to 26 seats in the Senate. It nevertheless still accounted for only some 9 percent of the total vote—a small vote of about 5 percent in the North and a larger following, as much as 14–15 percent, in the South, where some protest votes which had previously gone to the Communists went to the MSI. The MSI also made some inroads on the Liberals, both in the South and in the North. The Liberals' strength dropped from 31 to 21 seats in the Chamber and from 16 to eight seats in the Senate.

Parliament reassembled on May 25 and proceeded to reelect Amintore Fanfani and Sandro Pertini (Socialist Party) as leaders of the Senate and the Chamber, respectively. On June 4, President Leone again called on Giulio Andreotti to form a government—of what kind was not specified. The Social Democrats, now under Saragat's leadership, were anxious to revive the center-left coalition, and the Republicans even suggested an emergency five-party version including the Liberals. But the Socialists flatly refused to enter any coalition of which the Liberals formed a part. In addition, the Socialists' open-minded attitude toward the Communists caused many Christian Democrats to feel that the Socialists had become incompatible as allies and to wish to replace them with the Liberals, whose presence in the government would hearten industrialists and bring back to the center some wavering support that might otherwise have moved to the right. Consequently, on June 14 the Christian Democrat executive authorized Andreotti to form a centrist coalition with the Social Democrats and the Liberals, an authorization which was not wholly supported by the Christian Democrat left wing, led by Foreign Minister Aldo Moro, which still strongly advocated a revival of the center-left. The Republicans, under pressure from Andreotti, eventually agreed to give the proposed centrist coalition their support in Parliament, although they refused to enter the government. The coalition consequently had a majority of 16 in the Chamber and of only three or four in the Senate.

The cabinet which Andreotti presented on June 26 included no left-wing Christian Democrats, since they had refused to take office in a centrist administration. Moro was replaced as foreign minister by another Christian Democrat of long ministerial experience, Giuseppe Medici. Liberal Party leader Giovanni Malagodi replaced Emilio Colombo as treasury minister, a crucial post given the country's precarious economic situation. Colombo had for several years been largely responsible for Italy's economic policies and was regarded as the minister best equipped to deal with European problems.

Left-wing and also moderate opinion was particularly critical of the fact that the ministries of education and justice—both spheres in which reforms were urgently needed—were put in the hands of Christian Democrats of the far right (respectively, Oscar Scalfaro and Guido Gonella).

In presenting his government's program to Parliament on July 4, Andreotti denied that his somewhat conservative coalition with its narrow majority might in moments of difficulty accept some help from the neo-Fascists. He summed up his coalition's aims as reactivating the economy, improving law and order, and bringing Italy in every respect up to the highest European level. He secured a 41-vote majority in the Chamber, thanks partly to some empty seats among the opposition, and in the Senate he won his vote of confidence by only eight votes.

The new centrist government nearly ran into difficulties even before the summer parliamentary recess when it was defeated in the Chamber on a Socialist amendment substantially increasing the planned cost of a measure raising payments to certain categories of pensioners. The government narrowly escaped further defeats over a Senate amendment calling for an even greater increase, which Andreotti said the country could not afford. The bill was finally passed in its original form on August 11. By that time the cabinet had worked intensively to approve 25 bills and revive 103 measures put forward by past administrations but still lacking final parliamentary approval.

Economic affairs. The economic stagnation of the previous two years persisted in 1972, aggravated by the political crises of the year's first half. The annual economic review, appearing at the end of March, showed 1971 as the worst year since the postwar mid-1940's. The gross national product had risen by only 1.3 percent; capital investment had fallen; social investment in much-needed reforms was down by 7.5 percent; productivity had also fallen, but wages and salaries had risen by 13.4 percent. Unemployment was estimated in March 1972 at 613,000, and an additional 312,000 people were underemployed.

The balance of payments for 1971 showed a surplus double that of 1970. The increase resulted, in part, from a

BAD VIBRATIONS. In October workers began repairs on the Colosseum, closed to tourists because of falling rocks. The heavy stresses of modern big-city traffic helped unglue the ancient arena, in addition to unsettling the Roman Forum and shaking up the Palatine Hill.

rise in exports of 6.5 percent in real terms, as manufacturers sold abroad to compensate for weak demand at home.

Forecasts in the autumn suggested that Italy in 1972 would experience an increase in gross national product of between 3 and 3.5 percent and that industrial production would rise by about 4 percent.

Small firms, especially in the textile industry and in industries affected by the recession in building, were particularly hard hit by the economic turndown. One result was the take-over of a number of businesses by foreign companies, primarily firms which had expanded during the "miracle" years but were now finding themselves no longer able to compete. Some industrialists still blamed their plight on the wage increases granted after the "hot autumn" of 1969, but in some, although by no means all, cases the fault lay rather in their own failure to adapt an old family concern to modern conditions.

Regional administrations. The transfer of certain powers from the central government to the regional administrations, agreed to in principle in 1970, came into effect on April 1, almost unnoticed in the midst of the election campaign. This change, however, may eventually have a considerable impact on the economic situation in the individual regions, which are now responsible for the management of their own affairs in such spheres as public health, housing, agriculture, and tourism.

Developing the South. Plans for southern development, carried out for the past 22 years by the Cassa per il Mezzogiorno (Southern Development Fund), were completely reorganized under a law passed in October 1971. The new law, which took into account the need to collaborate with the new regional administrations, authorized the *cassa* to spend almost $12.5 billion over the next five years—more than the total amount previously disbursed—in an all-out effort to reduce the imbalance between North and South. The law also required state-owned corporations to locate 80 percent of their capital investment in the South.

The shortage of jobs in the Mezzogiorno accounted for the continuing high rate of emigration of southern workers to northern Italy or to Germany, and the region's poverty, which many of its people feel the national government in the North has failed to deal with vigorously, was undoubtedly responsible, in part, for the heavy protest vote accorded to the MSI in the May elections.

Common Market relations. Toward the end of June, after the British pound was floated, there was some talk of devaluation of the lira, the weakest of the Common Market currencies. However, Italy was persuaded to remain within the market's system of narrow currency margins. The Common Market agreed, albeit unwillingly, to Italy's request to postpone introduction of a value-added tax from July 1, 1972, to January 1, 1973.

Social issues. One side effect of the spring national election was the postponing of a referendum on Italy's 1970 law permitting divorce in certain circumstances. By the end of 1971, opponents of the controversial law had collected nearly three times the number of signatures (500,000) needed under the constitution to demand a nationwide referendum, and voting had been scheduled for June 11, 1972. However, the constitution also states that a referendum cannot be held until a year after a national election. Most Italian political leaders were pleased to delay any vote on such an emotional and divisive issue as legalized divorce.

Noticeable increases in the general crime rate and in the number of violent incidents precipitated by political extremists concerned the public in 1972. During ceremonies in January marking the beginning of the judicial year, a number of Italy's highest judicial officials devoted their speeches to condemning the increase in crime, especially among juveniles.

On the night of March 15, Giangiacomo Feltrinelli, noted publisher and heir to one of Italy's largest fortunes, was found blown apart near a pylon he was apparently attempting to sabotage with dynamite. Subsequent investigation re-

343

vealed that Feltrinelli was a founder of the Partisan Action Groups, which were planning to disrupt electric-power and transportation systems throughout northern Italy and to kidnap candidates for the May 7 election. Police raids in late March on left-wing and right-wing guerrilla hideouts netted enormous stockpiles of guns, bombs, and explosives.

In May a parliamentary commission report warned against the spread of a better-known type of Italian criminal organization—the Mafia. The Mafia has traditionally been a rather loosely knit association of local criminal groups operating primarily in western Sicily. But recently, according to the report, some of these groups or new ones emulating Mafia tactics have become increasingly active in the Sicilian cities, on the mainland, and in the international drug traffic.

Foreign affairs. President Leone and Premier Andreotti met with French president Georges Pompidou on July 27–28 in Tuscany. The French and Italian leaders discussed Common Market issues and the forthcoming European security conference. At the EEC summit in October, Premier Andreotti stressed regional policies and the European monetary fund. Visiting Moscow at the end of the month, he concluded an agreement for closer economic ties with the Soviets.

Italian diplomats participated in the negotiations over a new lease for British naval and air bases on the island of Malta. These negotiations went on throughout the first quarter of the year after the government of Malta demanded a huge increase in the United Kingdom's annual payment for use of the bases. Because of Malta's proximity to Sicily, Italy's own Mediterranean interests were obviously involved. After an agreement for continued British use of the bases was reached in late March, Italy promised an immediate contribution of more than $6 million in aid to Malta.

Area and population. Area, 116,303 sq. mi. Pop. (Oct. 1971), 54,025,211. Principal cities: Rome (cap.), 2,799,836; Milan, 1,724,723.
Government. Republic with bicameral legislature. Pres., Giovanni Leone; prem., Giulio Andreotti; for. min., Giuseppe Medici.

Finance. Monetary unit, lira (pl., lire); 1 lira = US$0.00172. Budget (est. 1973): revenue, 15,000 billion lire; expenditure, 18,-600 billion lire. Principal sources of revenue: business and turnover taxes, direct taxes, customs duties, consumer and production taxes.
Trade (1971; in million lire). Imports, 9,893,518; exports, 9,358,-735. Principal trading partners: West Germany, France, United States, Benelux, United Kingdom.
Agriculture and industry. Gross value of production (1971, in billion lire at 1963 value): industry (including construction), 16,168; agriculture, 4,581; mining, 289.
Education (1971–1972 figures for enrollment; 1970–1971 figures for teachers). Preschool: enrollment, 1,466,374; teachers, 42,516. Elementary and lower secondary: enrollment, 8,953,080; teachers, 547,703. University: enrollment, 635,776; teachers, 50,394.
Armed forces (est. 1971). Army, 295,000; navy, 45,000; air force, 74,000.

MURIEL GRINDROD

IVORY COAST. Foreign affairs. The Ivory Coast was a leader in moves to foster greater cooperation among the French-speaking nations of West Africa. Especially significant was a dramatic upturn in relations with Senegal, whose president, Léopold-Sédar Senghor, visited the Ivory Coast for nine days in December 1971. On December 16, President Senghor and President Félix Houphouët-Boigny concluded a treaty of friendship and cooperation, agreeing to work for the complete liberation of Africa and to oppose all forms of discrimination in all African states.

With Dahomey, Mali, Mauritania, Niger, and Upper Volta, the two nations also signed an agreement on June 3 to establish the West African Economic Community.

Mrs. Richard M. Nixon toured the Ivory Coast for three days in January on her three-nation West African tour. Arriving in Abidjan on January 7, she was met by a crowd estimated at 75,000. She later conferred with President Houphouët-Boigny.

Economic affairs. The Ivorian economy, West Africa's most prosperous, continued to flourish. Between 1960 and 1970 the economy grew at a rate of 11 percent annually, and present investment programs may sustain or even surpass that record. In this second year of the 1971–1975 five-

PHOTOREPORTERS

MAYHEM IN MILAN. A policeman shields himself from a barrage of rocks hurled by leftist rioters. About 1,000 demonstrators took to the streets with helmets and firebombs, battling police and burning cars, in the March 11 melee. At least 80 participants suffered injuries.

year plan, work continued on the $100 million Bandama River hydroelectric and irrigation project, scheduled for completion in 1973; connecting roads for the new port of San Pedro; and a total of 50 new factories in an industrial development at Vridi. Progress also continued on a plan to make Ivory Coast a major tourist area capable of attracting and accommodating more than 500,000 visitors a year. For this "African Riviera," the Intercontinental Hotel Ivoire, already the largest in Africa, is adding a new 250-room wing and a convention center with space for 2,000 people. New housing, hotels, and a golf course are also planned as tourist attractions.

Education and culture. Started in September 1971, a new educational television network was already reaching almost 26,000 students in 426 classes four months later. Programs will be beamed throughout the country by 1973, and by 1980 it is expected that all schoolchildren at every level will be receiving some televised lessons. The United Nations, the World Bank, and French, Canadian, and American sources have helped fund the project.

Area and population. Area, 124,504 sq. mi. Pop. (est. 1971), 4.42 million. Abidjan (cap.; est. 1968), 380,000.
Government. Single-party republic. Pres., Félix Houphouët-Boigny.
Finance. Monetary unit, Communauté Financière Africaine franc; 1 CFA franc = US$0.0041. Budget (est. 1972), balanced at 68.2 billion CFA francs.
Trade (1971). Exports, 126.6 billion CFA francs; imports, 110.8 billion CFA francs. Principal exports: coffee, timber, cocoa. Principal trading partners: France, EEC, United States.
Education (1971–1972). Primary: students, 516,000; teachers, 8,450. Secondary: students, 75,000; teachers, 1,846. University of Abidjan (1970): students, 3,092; teachers, 189.
Armed forces (est. 1972). Total forces, 4,500.

JAMAICA. Politics and government. On February 29, the opposition People's National Party, which had been out of power for all of Jamaica's ten years as an independent nation, swept to an overwhelming victory in a general election, winning 36 of the 53 seats in the Lower House of Parliament. Michael Manley took over the leadership of this party from his father, Norman Manley, one of Jamaica's national heroes, a year before his father's death in 1970, and was regarded as a left-wing if not doctrinaire socialist until his recent swing to the right. The party campaign promised a government free of the graft and corruption that they charged beset the previous government. Shortly after taking office, the new government carried out an election promise to lower the voting age from 21 to 18.

The new prime minister's immense popularity was dramatically shown on Labor Day, May 23. Manley suggested that the holiday be spent not in celebration but in civic work, such as beautifying slums, clearing and cleaning sidewalks, and planting trees. Tens of thousands of people from all social classes joined in the projects, a most remarkable event in a country whose people are said to be very ready to take a holiday from work at the least opportunity.

Finance. After the international monetary crisis, the government extended its control over foreign currency dealings to include sterling, which had previously been freely exchangeable by Jamaicans. Now all sterling transactions, like transactions in other foreign currency, have to be approved by the Bank of Jamaica. In addition, under threat of prosecution, Jamaicans have to declare all assets held overseas.

Economics. In August, Jamaica learned painfully that no island is a world unto itself. The British dock strike caused a loss of over $1 million, as bananas shipped to Britain in refrigerated ships could not be unloaded at British ports and had to be dumped into the Atlantic Ocean after they rotted. Just two months before, strikes at seven sugar estates had caused a loss estimated at $2 million.

On the bright side, Jamaica may prove to be the source of a new process of profitably exploiting the "red mud" residue left after alumina is made from bauxite, which may bring

millions of dollars in increased earnings and incidentally benefit many other countries. After years of experimentation by two men, Jamaican Robert Lightbourne, who was in the Ministry of Trade and Industry in the previous government, and Barclay Baetz, an American chemist, it appears that an economical process has been found so that iron, titanium, and additional alumina can be obtained from this previously unusable residue. Both Alcoa of the United States and Alcan of Canada have confirmed the feasibility of this chemical process, and a pilot plant is being established to verify its economic feasibility.

Area and population. Area, 4,232 sq. mi. Pop. (est. 1971), 2,000,000. Kingston (cap.; met. area, est. 1970), 506,200.
Government. Independent member of Commonwealth of Nations, with bicameral legislature. Prime min., Michael Manley; gov. gen., Sir Clifford Campbell.
Finance (1971–1972). Monetary unit, Jamaican dollar; J$1.00 = US$1.19. Revenue, US$376 million; expenditure, US$376 million.
Trade (1970). Exports, US$347 million; imports, US$543 million.
Education (1969–1970). Enrollment: primary, 387,924; junior secondary, 33,323; secondary, 22,739; university (1971), 4,564.

C. G. LINDO

JAPAN. Kakuei Tanaka, an unconventional and vigorous conservative politician, succeeded the aging Eisaku Sato as Japan's prime minister in July, after Sato had held the post longer than any other man in Japanese history. Immediately, Tanaka set his government machinery in motion for reestablishing diplomatic relations with China; after only a month in office, he accepted an invitation to visit China in early autumn. Whereas the Sato government had been severely shaken by the 1971 U.S. initiatives toward China, the Tanaka government appeared headed at breakneck speed toward a China policy far outdistancing the limited American objectives. At a meeting with President Nixon in Hawaii in August, the Japanese prime minister reaffirmed the central position of the United States in Japanese foreign relations. Significantly, however, the two leaders agreed to a pursuit of separate China policies, thereby recognizing the beginning of an independent postwar Japanese diplomacy. In September, Japan and China agreed to establish diplomatic relations.

At home, Tanaka set flowing a seemingly unending stream of directives and ideas, including a comprehensive plan to cope with urban congestion, pollution, and high land prices. Tanaka's conservative Liberal Democratic Party (LDP) felt it had to make major breakthroughs in these areas in order to remake its lackluster public image and consolidate its monopoly of national political power, held since its founding in 1955.

Government and politics. Domestic politics in 1972 were dominated by the issues surrounding Prime Minister Sato's resignation and the choice of his successor. In July, after seven years and eight months in office, Sato stepped down. During his leadership, Japan had become the third largest economic power in the world and—in what had become a highly volatile issue for the Japanese—finalized the normalization of relations with South Korea. Sato's final major goal was achieved on May 15, when Okinawa's 27 years of U.S. occupation were terminated and the islands returned to Japanese jurisdiction. Despite these successes, Sato's government had fallen to the lowest level of popular support (21 percent according to an April poll) of any postwar Japanese administration. At age 71, Sato appeared to have neither the flexibility nor the energy to attack Japan's complex domestic, social, and environmental problems or to cope with increased economic strains with the United States and pressures to normalize relations with China.

In the July balloting of Liberal Democratic Diet and prefectural party representatives, the 54-year-old Tanaka defeated Takeo Fukuda to become the majority party's leader and, thus, Japan's youngest postwar premier. Fukuda had long been favored to succeed Sato because of his back-

ing by big business and his close ties to Sato, under whom he served as finance minister and foreign minister. But in the end, Fukuda's association with Sato worked to his disadvantage. Younger LDP Diet members came to feel that Fukuda, at 67, would inherit Sato's low public esteem and thereby hurt their own chances for reelection. In contrast, Tanaka was one of the most popular political personalities in Japan and was the chief architect of the LDP's overwhelming victory in the 1969 Lower House election.

Tanaka's predecessors had come from affluent families, attended prestigious universities, and generally entered politics after serving in the national bureaucracy. Tanaka, however, rose from rural poverty and part-time vocational study to a position of wealth in the construction industry. At age 29 he was elected to the Lower House and has been there ever since. He has served as minister of postal services and telecommunications, minister of finance, and recently minister of international trade and industry as well as secretary general of his party.

Tanaka's administration began at full speed. Besides the frantic pace of his activities in foreign affairs, he intervened to end a marathon seamen's strike and avert another work stoppage by government employees. He met with heads of opposition parties, business and labor leaders, and representatives of housewife and consumer groups to hear their ideas. He laid plans for a rationalization of the government's administrative structure and outlined measures for dispersing major industries from the Pacific coast cities and for facilitating land purchases for use by the national and local governments. Tanaka is, like Sato, a conservative with a strong faith in the free enterprise capitalist system. But unlike his predecessor, he has perceived a need for a stronger government watch over private industry and for potent new initiatives in welfare. The opposition parties and many neutral Japanese remain skeptical about the ability, if not the conviction, of the new prime minister to tackle such problems as pollution, urban congestion, soaring prices, and insufficient urban housing and public facilities—problems which had been allowed to develop to a critical state during Japan's all-out push for rapid economic growth. (See PEOPLE IN THE NEWS: Kakuei Tanaka.)

Japan's four moderate opposition parties have been actively seeking grounds for closer electoral and parliamentary cooperation and even for party union. But they have been bogged down over the issue of including the Communist Party in their alliance, a move favored by the Japan Socialist Party, the largest opposition group, and opposed by the moderate wing of the JSP as well as by conservative factions within the Democratic Socialist and Clean Government (Komeito) parties. A second dilemma for the opposition parties is the fact that increasingly bitter competition among themselves has worked to ensure the continued electoral success of the LDP, despite a steady decline in the latter's share of the popular vote in national elections. The JSP's decision in mid-1972 to switch its major focus from foreign to domestic policy was a long overdue move, inspired by the success of allied independent progressives in mayoral and gubernatorial elections, particularly in urban areas.

Foreign relations. Despite recent readjustments, Japan's foreign policy continues to follow four traditional lines: alliance with the United States; active economic assistance to less developed nations; strong commitment to the United Nations and its councils as vehicles for foreign policy implementation; and renunciation of the development both of nuclear weapons and of a strong offensive military force. However, in October the Japanese cabinet approved a five-year defense plan that calls for a doubling of the military budget. The move was seen as evidence of Japan's increasing vigor and independence in foreign policy.

United States. In January, Prime Minister Sato traveled to San Clemente, Calif., to petition President Nixon for the earliest possible date for the return of Okinawa and to seek reassurance that Japan would be kept on as a key party to U.S. policy decisions in the Far East despite the "Nixon shocks" of 1971. In August, Prime Minister Tanaka and President Nixon met in Hawaii, at the president's request; Nixon wished to learn Japanese intentions vis-à-vis China and Taiwan and to apprise Tanaka of short-term measures by the United States to lower its huge—and politically embarrassing—trade imbalance with Japan.

Since the early 1950's, Japanese foreign policy has been devised to fall within the framework of the Japan–U.S. Mutual Security Treaty as well as within the dictates of America's stance in the cold war. As a result of Japan's newly acquired status as an economic superpower, the relationship has entered a new stage in which "partnership" is being replaced by a more mutual alliance spiced by friendly competition. The Nixon moves of 1971 and the U.S. rapprochement with China galvanized Japan's attention on its relative growth in economic power vis-à-vis the United States and showed clearly how much Japan's pursuit of an independent diplomacy had been hurt by its unqualified allegiance to the United States. The U.S. moves, furthermore, added fuel to a resurgent Japanese nationalism and to a forceful new pan-Asianism. Whereas the aging Sato could not divorce himself from the posture of clientism, the younger Tanaka was quick to recognize and cash in on the imperatives of the changing realities in international affairs and Japanese public opinion.

Sato literally presided over an end of an era when, in May, the United States returned the Ryukyu Islands (Okinawa) to Japanese control. For nearly three decades, Okinawa had symbolized Japan's inferior position: nearly 1 million ethnic Japanese living in Okinawa had to suffer the indignities of a life under alien rule, and the Japanese government had virtually no say in how the U.S. military chose to use a territory that had always been acknowledged as part of Japanese soil. According to the new agreement, American use of bases in Okinawa fall under the same conditions as those in Japan proper—poisonous gas and nuclear weapons are banned, and the Japanese government must be consulted before Japan-based U.S. troops can be deployed to combat areas.

In 1971, Japanese exports to the United States rose by 26 percent to $7.5 billion, while imports from the United States declined to $5 billion. Japanese economic concessions to the United States in 1971 included a substantial 16.9 percent revaluation of the yen, "voluntary" curbs on textiles and other exports to the United States, and speeded-up liberalization of strictures on trade and capital investments. In spite of these gestures, the U.S. trade deficit with Japan in 1972 appeared to be headed for a record $3.9 billion. America's recovery from recession had outpaced that of Japan, resulting in increased U.S. demands for Japanese products. Meanwhile, Japanese requirements for raw materials and machinery—comprising the bulk of Japan's imports from the United States—remained sluggish in the absence of a full business recovery in Japan. The Japanese have combined their currency revaluation with an effort to redirect exports to the consumer markets of Western Europe and Canada. But these measures were not expected to provide the quick results demanded by the timetables of politicians. Thus, Premier Tanaka agreed with President Nixon to authorize a Japanese purchase of $1.1 billion worth of American uranium, agricultural products, and other goods.

China. After China's admission to the United Nations in fall 1971, Prime Minister Sato moved gradually to reopen talks on diplomatic exchanges between the two nations. But Sato was openly snubbed by the Chinese, who were suspicious of both him and his brother, Nobusuke Kishi, a former prime minister who led the LDP's "Taiwan lobby." China hinted it would talk with whoever succeeded Sato and, in fact, bowed graciously to the overtures of Kakuei Tanaka when he became prime minister. The Chinese press

TOASTING A NEW ERA, Japanese prime minister Kakuei Tanaka raises his cup with Chinese premier Chou En-lai at a Peking banquet ending a historic five-day summit meeting between the two Asian leaders.

UPI

began to drop references to Japanese militarism, and Chinese premier Chou En-lai announced support for Japan's claim to a group of islands off Hokkaido that had been seized by the Soviet Union at the end of World War II.

Public opinion in Japan has overwhelmingly backed normalization of relations with China. Campaigns for the recognition of China have involved a formidable coalition of the mass media, local assemblies, opposition parties and labor unions, key business leaders, and an increasingly larger minority of the LDP.

On September 29 in Peking, Tanaka and Chinese premier Chou En-lai signed an agreement to establish diplomatic relations. The joint communiqué ended a period of hostility dating from 1937 and was warmly welcomed in Japan. It was announced that the two countries would open negotiations on a peace-and-friendship treaty and that Japan had broken off diplomatic relations with the Nationalist Chinese.

Taiwan. Japan has over $100 million in open investments and licensing agreements in Taiwan and perhaps even more than that in hidden investments. Japan's trade with Taiwan (1971 exports were valued at $925 million and imports at $284 million) still surpasses its exchange with the Mainland ($578 million in exports and $322 million in imports in 1971). Japan has also signed a peace treaty with Taiwan, officially ending the 1937–1945 war between Japan and China. Nevertheless, Prime Minister Tanaka carried out his intention of proceeding with the recognition of China.

In March the first Chinese trade mission to Japan in six years arrived for a seven-week inspection tour of the synthetic textile industry. The same month the Japanese government repudiated an unofficial promise made in 1964 to Chiang Kai-shek that Japan would not use its export-import bank to finance trade with China. Meanwhile an increasing number of major Japanese banks and corporations have accepted trade conditions laid down by Premier Chou in 1970: no assistance to South Korea or Taiwan or major investments there; no munitions for the United States in Vietnam; and no management affiliation with U.S. companies.

When Japan agreed to recognize Mainland China in September, the accord stated that "Japan fully understands and respects" Peking's position that Taiwan is part of the territory of the People's Republic of China. About a month later, Japanese officials said that they had not actually recognized Peking's claim and that the Taiwan question was still

open. Although Japan broke its diplomatic ties with Taiwan, the countries agreed in November to set up a liaison office for trade and other nondiplomatic relations.

Soviet Union. The new U.S. initiatives toward China, coupled with Japan's growing disillusionment with U.S. foreign policy, helped inspire a new Soviet "smiling diplomacy" toward Japan. The turn in Moscow's attitude was climaxed by a visit to Tokyo in January 1972 by Soviet foreign minister Andrei Gromyko. The two governments thereafter announced the start of negotiations for a Soviet-Japanese peace treaty; agreement to a summit meeting by the leaders of the two nations; the establishment of ministerial consultations on an annual basis; and a joint commitment to tackle questions of economic, cultural, and technological exchanges as well as joint development of resources and bilateral trade. The Japanese were most encouraged with the first indications that the Soviet Union would be willing to discuss the return of the southern Kuril Islands to Japan.

Japan ranks as the Soviet Union's largest non-Communist trading partner. In 1971, Japanese exports to the Soviet Union reached $377 million and imports totaled $496 million. In December of that year an agreement was signed for a $50 million project to explore forest resources in eastern Siberia. At the meeting of the fifth Japan-Soviet Joint Economic Committee in February 1972, it was agreed that Japan would send a survey mission to the Tyumen oil field development project in western Siberia. The Soviets have requested an interbank loan from Japan of $1 billion toward a $2.5 billion Russo-Japanese pipeline that would link that vast Siberian oil field with the Soviet port of Nakhodka over 4,000 miles away on the Japan Sea. If the project were to be carried out, 25 to 40 million tons of oil could be delivered to Japan each year. The Japanese are as yet noncommittal on this proposal, as on a further Soviet request for credit to develop gas and oil resources on the continental shelf of Sakhalin Island.

Economy. Japan's economy in 1971–1972 was characterized by a major recession, a gigantic balance-of-payments surplus, and a huge accumulation of dollar reserves. The country's GNP in 1971–1972 reached $242 billion. The real growth rate of 5.7 percent (nominal rate = 10.5%) was the lowest since the 5.4 percent rate in the 1965 recession.

The government has been forced to adopt an expansionary budget policy and, for the first time, to move to a change in

domestic priorities from productive capacity to social over-head capital, environmental protection, and welfare. The general accounts budget of fiscal 1972 rose by 22 percent to $37.2 billion. Housing allocations increased by 38 percent, education by 37 percent, recreation facilities by 91 percent, airports by 61 percent, and environmental protection by 95 percent.

In 1971–1972, Japan registered a record $8 billion balance-of-payments surplus. The trade surplus was $8.6 billion with exports up 25 percent to $24.8 billion and imports up 5 percent to $16.2 billion. The December 1971 upward revaluation of the yen by 16.88 percent (Y308 = $1) has not yet had any clear impact on trade patterns. By mid-1972 imports of consumer goods and food products had picked up rapidly, although imports tied to the overall level of business activity, such as raw materials, fuel, and capital goods, continued to lag.

In May the government published a seven-point plan to combat the problems of a lingering recession, the balance-of-payments surplus, and the accumulation of dollar reserves. The plan's major features included stepped-up government spending to stimulate the domestic economy; increased imports through enlarged quotas and better distribution of import items; refined methods of export marketing with stiffer government controls; and greater use of foreign exchange reserves in loans for overseas investment, import financing, and export of capital. The administration proposed the use of emergency legislation to implement these measures.

With close to $16 billion in foreign reserves, a Tokyo dollar call market was established in April. This was a step toward making Tokyo an international financial market.

HOME FROM THE WAR. Shoichi Yokoi, a former army sergeant, prays at the family grave on which his own name is also inscribed. He was brought back to Japan from a cave in Guam where he had hidden in shame for 28 years since World War II.

UPI

Environment. A national poll conducted by the prime minister's office in November 1971 found that one out of three Japanese felt themselves to be victims of excessive air, water, or noise pollution. The majority of the remainder feared that they too would soon feel the impact of Japan's environmental destruction, a by-product of the nation's rapid—and virtually uncontrolled—economic growth. Japanese environmentalists were encouraged by recent court decisions against firms responsible for pollution-induced diseases. In July 1972, six large companies were found guilty of causing asthma and other lung irritations through discharges of sulfurous gases. In each case the companies were ordered to pay reparations to the victims. Responding to public pressure, private industry vastly increased its investments in antipollution equipment, spending $1.7 billion in 1971–1972, an increase of 87 percent over the preceding year. All told, environmental protection measures accounted for 10.2 percent of total plant and equipment investment in 1971–1972.

Other events. Thirty-two years after they were first scheduled for Sapporo, the Winter Olympics finally arrived at that northern Japanese city in February 1972. Over 740,000 spectators were on hand to see athletes compete from 35 countries. In addition, as many as 200 million persons were thought to have watched the games on television.

On April 16, Yasunari Kawabata, Japan's first winner of the Nobel Prize for Literature (1968), committed suicide at age 72. His friends speculated that his motives lay either in his declining health or his grief over the 1970 suicide of his gifted protegé, Yukio Mishima. Unlike Mishima, who was a flamboyant political activist, Kawabata was a passive, solitary figure known for his delicate depiction of Japanese values and emotions. He was best known in the West for his novels *Snow Country* and *A Thousand Cranes*.

Members of Japan's extremist United Red Army, which in 1970 had hijacked a plane to North Korea, again rocked the nation with two wanton acts of violence. In February five leaders were captured after a ten-day siege of a mountain hideout. Their arrest was followed by the discovery of 14 bodies of Red Army members who had allegedly been murdered for deviation from the group's revolutionary line. Weakened by hundreds of arrests in the past few years, the Red Army moved to the international front. Acting as agents for the Popular Front for the Liberation of Palestine, three Japanese members of the Red Army killed 25 persons in a brutal massacre of airline passengers at the Lydda Airport near Tel Aviv. The sole survivor, Kozo Okamoto, was sentenced to life imprisonment in an Israeli court. Genuinely shocked and embarrassed, the Japanese government, in a gesture of national repentance and remorse, offered its official condolences and $1.5 million to the families of the victims.

Area and population. Area, 142,727 sq. mi. Pop. (est. 1971), 104,700,000. Principal cities (est. 1971): Tokyo (cap., ward area only), 8,610,000; Osaka, 2,909,000; Yokohama, 2,277,000; Nagoya, 2,035,000; Kyoto, 1,431,000; Kobe, 1,266,000; Kitakyushu, 1,050,000; Sapporo, 1,000,000.

Government. Constitutional monarchy. Symbolic head of state, Emperor Hirohito. Prime min., Kakuei Tanaka; for. min., Masayoshi Ohira; fin. min., Koshiro Ueki.

Finance. Monetary unit, yen; Y1 = US$0.00333. GNP (1971–1972), $242 billion.

Trade (1971–1972). Exports, $24.8 billion; imports, $16.2 billion. Chief exports: steel, automobiles, ships, textiles, radios and televisions. Chief imports: crude oil, foodstuffs, machinery, lumber, iron ore, nonferrous ores, chemical goods. Major trading partners: United States, Australia, Canada, Iran, Federal Republic of Germany, Republic of Korea.

Education (1970). Enrollment: elementary school, 9,493,485; middle school, 4,716,833; high school, 3,859,528; junior college, 263,219; four-year college and university, 1,406,521.

Armed forces (Oct. 1971). Self-defense forces: ground, 155,800 (authorized 179,000); navy, 37,100 (38,323); air force, 41,000 (41,-657).

TERRY EDWARD MACDOUGALL

JEWISH AFFAIRS. *See* RELIGION: JEWISH AFFAIRS.

JORDAN. Having successfully eliminated the Palestinian guerrilla organizations as a political and military force in Jordan in a series of violent clashes during 1970 and 1971, King Hussein faced this year both the unpleasant consequences and the new opportunities created by his victories.

Aftermath of civil war. One effect of the long struggle with the guerrillas was further damage to Jordan's economy, still not recovered from the loss of the West Bank territory to Israel in 1967. Imports rose slightly in 1971, and Jordan's trade deficit exceeded $185 million. Direct economic losses during the civil war were estimated at more than $70 million. Businessmen were understandably reluctant to invest. The gross national product was expected to increase sharply in 1972, but not enough for a full recovery from the 14 percent loss the GNP suffered in 1971.

Economic recovery was hampered by the hostility of other Arab states more sympathetic to the Palestinian guerrillas. The closing of the Syrian and Iraqi borders in mid-1971 seriously affected both Jordan's regional trade and, more significantly, its shipments of phosphates to world markets. Early in 1972, Syria allowed Jordan to resume phosphate shipments. A drastic consequence of Arab hostility was the suspension of the annual subsidies from Kuwait and Libya.

Jordanian initiatives. Moving to stimulate the economy, Jordan devalued the dinar by 8.5 percent in May. In June the Economic Security Committee, headed by Crown Prince Hassan (the king's brother), was formed. It was to study ways to repair the civil war damage and extend loans to businesses. Proposals were also made to encourage foreign investment. Total exemption from all taxes and import duties was to be given for seven years to new companies locating in Amman and for nine years to those locating outside the capital; companies outside of Amman would also be given free land. Under a new three-year development plan, foreign investors were to be guaranteed the freedom to withdraw both profits and capital.

King Hussein acted vigorously to gain foreign support. He visited the United States in March and April, a visit which included a meeting with President Richard M. Nixon and which resulted in a U.S. agreement to sell Jordan 12 to 24 F5 jets over the next two years. In January the United States had contributed $15 million toward Jordan's 1971 budget deficit of $25 million.

The monarch also visited Iran and the sheikhdom Abu Dhabi, and he received a visit from Sultan Qabus bin Sa'id of Oman. The latter visit underscored the new importance of Jordanian military power in the Middle East; hints were dropped that Jordan was giving military aid and advisers to Oman to help the government fight the leftist guerrillas in Dhofar. Saudi Arabia remained one of Jordan's closest allies, continuing its annual subsidy and working to soften the attitudes of hostile Arab governments.

One factor working to restrain hostile Arab governments was the fear that they would drive Jordan into closer relations with Israel. Jordanian-Israeli economic contacts on an unofficial level were increasing during the year.

United Arab kingdom plan. King Hussein's most dramatic diplomatic initiative of 1972 was his plan for a united Arab kingdom. Announced on March 15, the plan called for a dual, or federal, kingdom, consisting of a Jordanian region and a Palestinian region. The Palestinian region would include the West Bank territory and "other Palestinian territories to be liberated"—an obvious reference to the Gaza Strip, which has also been occupied by Israel since 1967 and was under Egyptian administration for almost 20 years before that. Each region would have a governor general, an elected council, and regional ministers. The central executive—controlling foreign relations, defense and security, and development—would be located in Amman, as would the federal supreme court and council of ministers.

Reaction to the plan, which many national leaders considered unrealistic, was primarily hostile. The Palestinian

guerrillas, most Arab governments, and Israel all criticized the proposal. Egypt broke relations with Jordan in protest. The United States was noncommittally silent. Although some U.S. officials reportedly approved of the plan in private, King Hussein failed to obtain any public statement of support during his U.S. visit.

Guerrilla activity. On February 29 the four Palestinian guerrillas accused of assassinating Jordanian premier Wasfi al-Tal were released on bail by an Egyptian court. The assassination occurred in Cairo on November 28, 1971.

On April 1, 1972, the Palestinian guerrilla organization el-Fatah claimed credit for planting a mine which killed four Jordanians. Six days later in Cairo, the Palestinian National Council, composed of various guerrilla organizations, established a special committee for the purpose of planning King Hussein's overthrow.

King's father dies. On July 8 former king Talal ibn-Abullah, the father of King Hussein, died in a Turkish mental hospital. He had reigned for a year in 1951–1952, but when his mental disturbances became too obvious, he was deposed by the Jordanian Parliament. His body was returned to Jordan and buried with full military honors.

Area and population. Area, 37,738 sq. mi. (including 2,165 sq. mi. occupied by Israel since June 1967). Pop. (est. 1972), 2,418,000 (including approximately 700,000 in the occupied territories). Amman (cap.; est. 1971), 450,000.
Government. Constitutional monarchy; effective control of the government is in the hands of King Hussein.
Finance. Monetary unit, Jordanian dinar; JD1 = US$2.85. Budget (1972): balanced at JD124,860,000.
Trade (1971; in thousand dinars). Imports, 76,627; exports, 8,-817.
Education (1968). Government schools, 935; private schools, 156; UNRWA schools, 112. Pupils, 287,396; teachers, 7,923.

RALPH H. MAGNUS

KANSAS. Legislation. The 1972 legislature appropriated $998.5 million to operate the state in fiscal 1973, $84 million more than last year's budget. No new taxes were levied, although corporations can now no longer deduct federal income tax liability from their state taxes.

Despite considerable heated debate, an agricultural employment relations act was passed which provided that agricultural employees shall have the right to form, join, and participate in the activities of employee organizations of their own choosing, to express grievances, and to discuss conditions of employment with their employers. An age-of-majority law reduced from 21 to 18 the legal age of adulthood in Kansas in all things except the purchase and consumption of alcohol. This act includes the right to marry without parental consent, to enter into contracts, to control one's own assets and earnings, to enter into litigation, and to enjoy most other property rights and liabilities.

State employees were given the right of collective bargaining, aid to junior colleges was increased, a tuition grant program for needy youths was funded, and benefits under the state's homestead property tax relief law for citizens over 65 were increased.

On the last day of the session the legislature ratified the amendment to the federal Constitution guaranteeing equal rights to women. Oddly enough, most of the opposition to the amendment was voiced by the women of Kansas, who felt the legislature was rushing into ratification without sufficient study and deliberation.

Economic developments. In 1971 total personal income in Kansas rose 7.4 percent over 1970, much higher than had been predicted and higher than both the national and Plains States growth rates. Per capita income had risen from $3,804 in 1970 to $4,090 in 1971. Farm income showed the greatest growth, with an increase of nearly 24 percent during the same period.

Drastic unemployment in the state's aircraft industry at Wichita eased so that the unemployment rate in the state by mid-1972 was 4.9, as compared to 6.2 a year earlier. In the

Wichita area it had dropped from 11.7 in 1971 to 6.8 in June and to 5.7 in July 1972. Although some smaller manufacturers went out of business because of the implementation of pollution controls and enforcement of the federal safety and health act, increased employment in the meat-packing and mobile home industries more than offset the loss.

Law enforcement. Many Kansans of both political parties have regarded the actions of Vern Miller, the state's first Democratic attorney general in 80 years, as a refreshing change. Miller has conducted a vigorous war against the drug traffic, gambling, illegal sale of alcohol, and crime in general. Gamblers were warned to stay away from the numerous county and regional fairs where they have congregated in past summers. Slot machines were confiscated from institutions where they had enjoyed immunity for years. A law permitting the operation of bingo games by nonprofit organizations was passed when it became clear that the attorney general intended to prosecute gambling at all levels.

Few Kansans argue that Miller has had anything but a good effect on the moral climate of their state, but some regret his penchant for personal involvement in the execution of raids, his apparent assumption of authority over local officials, and his dogged pursuit of lesser lawbreakers.

For election results and campaign highlights, see the special supplement ELECTION '72.

Area and population. Area, 82,264 sq. mi. Pop. (1971), 2,249,-248. Principal cities: Topeka (cap.), 126,364; Wichita, 263,297; Kansas City, 168,957.
Government. Gov., Robert B. Docking (D); lt. gov., Reynolds Shultz (R); atty. gen., Vern Miller (D); secy. of state, Elwill M. Shanahan (R). Legislature: senate, 32 R, 8 D; house, 84 R, 41 D.
Finance (1972). Revenue, $962,659,209.73 (excludes nonoperating revenue); operating expenditures, $928,093,974.05.
Education (1971). Elementary schools, 1,400; enrollment, 281,-515; teachers, 13,391. Junior high schools, 138; enrollment, 105,095; teachers, 3,990. High schools, 421; enrollment, 121,325; teachers, 8,194. Institutions of higher education, 49; enrollment, 101,770.

JOSEPH W. SNELL

KENTUCKY. Legislature. The general assembly had to hold a second special session to redraw house and senate district lines that would meet the federal court's one-man, one-vote requirements. The special session, however, gave legislators an opportunity to vote on the Equal Rights Amendment to the U.S. Constitution, and effective last-minute lobbying by women and civil rights groups resulted in Kentucky's becoming the 17th state to approve it.

During the regular session, the legislature voted to remove the 5 percent sales tax from groceries while leaving it on other retail items, approved the local government option on keeping retail stores open on Sundays, placed a 4 percent severance tax on coal (with a minimum of 30 cents a ton), established an environmental protection department, modernized the state penal code and set an effective date of 1974 after first deleting provisions that would have eased pornography and abortion laws, and authorized a presidential primary beginning in 1976.

Education. Four of the state's largest public school systems were brought to the federal courts during the year on segregation charges made by civil rights organizations. Additional busing of students was ordered for both the Fayette County (Lexington) and Christian County (Hopkinsville) school systems. During preliminary phases of court action in desegregation suits involving Louisville and the Jefferson County school districts, a U.S. district court judge ruled against merger of the two systems as a means of ending segregation. The number of black students in the Louisville system topped 50 percent for the first time, although less than 4 percent of the students in the surrounding county system are black.

The Louisville school system set up an experimental program for creative students. The student body was selected to reflect the racial and economic balance within the system, and open classroom education is provided in grades 1–12.

Parochial schools received some aid when the legislature approved a $10 state income tax credit on tuition. Backers indicated the low figure would permit a constitutional test.

Municipal developments. Urban areas throughout the state began, slowly, to adopt local legislation under limited home-rule provisions approved by the state legislature. If serious conflict develops between urban and county governments, legislators warned that they might withdraw the home-rule authorization at the 1974 session.

Louisville opened the first section of its $1.5 million pedestrian mall in the principal downtown retail section in an effort to bring new economic life to the area.

Several cities faced ecological problems, and Jefferson County established what is reported to be the first ecology court in the nation.

Economic developments. Cattle have replaced tobacco as the principal cash crop for Kentucky farmers. Tobacco dropped from $302,904,000 to $271,234,000, and cattle and calves increased from $258,266,000 to $280,046,000. The cash crop total rose 2 percent to $945,627,000.

The coal industry also continued to adjust, with safety law enforcement and the new severance tax resulting in the closing of some small mines.

For election results and campaign highlights, see the special supplement ELECTION '72.

Area and population. Area, 40,395 sq. mi. Pop. (1970), 3,219,-311. Principal cities: Frankfort (cap.), 21,356; Louisville, 361,472; Lexington, 108,137.
Government. Gov., Wendell H. Ford (D); lt. gov., Julian Carroll (D); secy. of state, Thelma Stovall (D); treas., Drexell Davis (D); aud., Mary Louise Foust (D); atty. gen., Edward W. Hancock (D). Legislature: senate, 27 D, 10 R, 1 vacancy; house, 73 D, 27 R.
Finance. General fund: revenue, $668,732,135; expenditures, $634,983,449. Road fund: resources, $473,644,391; expenses, $437,-952,031.
Education (June 1972). Public schools, 2,748; enrollment, 714,-576; teachers, 28,182. Nonpublic schools, 297; enrollment, 69,911; teachers, 3,270.

CHARLES R. WALDEN

KENYA. Government and politics. Kenya has been governed since independence by the Kenya African National Union (KANU). New KANU elections were to have been held March 1, but on the eve of the elections they were postponed. The official government statement was vague, and it is possible that KANU leaders were uncertain about the results and therefore decided to cancel the elections. Some weeks later, Vice-President Daniel Moi announced that there would be no elections until the majority of Kenyan citizens were officially registered as KANU members. He stated that only 338,000 persons (out of a population of some 11 million) were now so registered and that the party did not want so few people to elect national leaders. This statement, of course, did not confront the issue of why so few were officially enrolled in KANU and the fact that no elections would simply leave the current KANU officeholders in power.

Later in the year trouble broke out at the University of Nairobi, and 56 students were arrested and charged with taking part in a riot. Tensions between the government and university students have grown in recent years, generally over the questions of criticism of the government and the privileges to be occupied by the new educated elite. The government holds that since nearly all students are on government fellowships, their right to protest government actions should be limited to some degree. The students, on the other hand, tend to view themselves as a privileged class —a fact that the government would rather not see flaunted. The students in Nairobi live in quarters far better than the average Kenyan citizen, and that inevitably produces tensions, especially for the government, which both wants and needs more educated manpower but also endeavors to hold the allegiance of the masses.

The issue of Asians flared up with great intensity this year. Asians came to East Africa at the turn of the century

THE PAST RECAPTURED. Angkor Vat, built eight centuries ago by Cambodia's earliest known rulers, was taken by government troops in May but later was rewon by the Communists. Here Cambodian soldiers guard the Bakheng Temple, which was damaged by shelling.

as railway workers for the British colonial government. They stayed on and came to dominate retail trade, textile industries, and import and export firms. About 140,000 of the 309,000 Asians in East Africa live in Kenya.

In August, President Idi Amin of Uganda ordered the expulsion from Uganda of all Asians who were not Ugandan citizens. Kenya immediately stepped up its border guard to ensure that Ugandan Asians did not enter Kenya, and Kenyan Asians in general became increasingly fearful that Amin's actions might in time force President Jomo Kenyatta or his successor to take similar steps against them. Many Kenyan Asians have taken Africans into their businesses as partners, but there is considerable tension between the two communities, largely generated by the superior economic position of Asians despite the fact that the government is African. During the year Kenyatta announced that 300 noncitizen businesses in Nairobi and other main towns would be taken over in the coming year. This step would largely affect Asians.

Economic development. Kenya was the host this year for the first All-African Trade Fair, organized by the Organization for African Unity. The fair, which was designed to promote the growth of intra-African communication and trade, lasted for 12 days and had over 150,000 visitors. Kenya was the logical place to hold this first fair because the East African Community of Kenya-Uganda-Tanzania has so far been the most successful regional organization to promote intra-African trade. Only South African exports to Zambia and Mozambique and Rhodesian exports to Zambia match the volume of intra–East African trade.

The East African Community is not operating without considerable difficulties, however. Uganda and Tanzania have in recent years taken strong steps to limit their imports from Kenya. The advantages that Kenya has long held in development and trade over the other two East African countries is a source of constant tension within the community, and Kenya is reluctant to forgo these advantages.

Kenya's own growth during 1971 was exceptional, up 8.4 percent to an all-time high gross domestic product of K£569 million. At the same time, however, Kenya's trade deficit rose to nearly K£100 million, and therefore tight new import controls were introduced. This was necessitated by the fact that the cost of Kenyan imports was rising faster than the price of Kenyan exports; in fact, the Kenyan coffee crop dropped off nearly 10,000 tons in 1971–1972. Tourism, on the other hand, again rose substantially.

Several new development projects were announced. The Mombasa oil refinery, which presently produces crude oil for Kenya, Uganda, Burundi, Rwanda, and northern Tanzania, is to be expanded substantially in order to keep pace with East Africa's growing petroleum needs. The International Finance Corporation announced that it was about to invest US$3.5 million in new tourist service accommodations, and the International Development Association announced a new US$22 million loan to Kenya for a highway project that would be built with Swedish assistance.

Area and population. Area, 224,960 sq. mi. Pop. (est. 1971), 11,200,000. Nairobi (cap.), 500,000; Mombasa, 250,000.
Government. Independent republic. Pres., Jomo Kenyatta.
Finance. Monetary unit, Kenya pound; 1K£ = US$2.83. Gross domestic product (1971), K£569 million.
Trade (1970). Exports, K£71.6 million; imports, K£142 million. Major trading partners: United Kingdom, United States, West Germany, Japan.   LARRY W. BOWMAN

KHMER REPUBLIC (CAMBODIA). Politics and government. As the military position of the Cambodian government deteriorated in the face of Communist insurgent success, Marshal Lon Nol, despite physical incapacity, consolidated his hold over the political life of the country.

During December 1971 the Cambodian army suffered a crushing defeat when its best-trained units attempted to remove the Communist presence from Highway 6, a key artery that proceeds northward from Phnom Penh, the capital, to the town of Kompong Thom. The government's

columns were decimated by the superior firepower of the intruding North Vietnamese forces and their Cambodian allies. One consequence of this military disaster was a dramatic drop in army morale. At the same time, criticism of Lon Nol—who had initiated and personally run the disastrous operation—became widespread among the political and military elite of the violated country. Although similar criticisms of Lon Nol were voiced by the U.S. embassy in Phnom Penh, it was made known that any coup against him would result in the withdrawal of American aid.

On his return to Cambodia from a vacation in March 1972, Lon Nol acted to disarm his political opponents. His initiatives coincided with the outbreak of antiroyalist student demonstrations directed at the acting prime minister, Sisowath Sirik Matak, a member of the Cambodian royal family. On March 10, Cheng Heng resigned as head of state in favor of Lon Nol, who announced that it was his duty to assume the presidency in order to save the nation. Lon Nol dissolved the Constituent Assembly and nullified its work on the nearly completed republican constitution. On March 12, Lon Nol declared himself president of the Khmer Republic, commander in chief of the armed forces, and president of the Council of Ministers.

Sirik Matak, who had assumed the main burden of administration when Lon Nol suffered a stroke in February 1971, announced his retirement from politics in March 1972. On March 18, the second anniversary of Prince Sihanouk's overthrow, Lon Nol ended the week-long political crisis by naming Son Ngoc Thanh as prime minister. Son had first held the post during the Japanese occupation; a bitterly anti-Sihanouk figure, he had passed many years in exile in South Vietnam. At the end of March, Lon Nol introduced a "presidential constitution" in order to give himself legal basis for ruling. A popular referendum was held one month later to pass judgment on this document, and according to government figures the 1.5 million voters overwhelmingly supported the new constitution.

On June 4, the first presidential election was held under the new constitution. Apart from Lon Nol, the contenders for office were In Tam, who had been president of the National Assembly at the time of the deposition of Prince Sihanouk, and Keo An, dismissed in February by the government from the post of dean of law at the University in Phnom Penh. The election was hampered by Communist attacks near the capital and by the deliberate exclusion from the polling booths of many voters in Phnom Penh. Although his election campaign was well financed and enjoyed the political support—and the votes—of the armed forces, Lon Nol did not poll as well as expected. Out of about 1 million votes cast (roughly half the eligible number of voters), Lon Nol received 54 percent. On July 3, Lon Nol was sworn in as Cambodia's first elected president.

General elections were held on September 3 for the 126 seats in the National Assembly. Three major political parties announced their intention of contesting the elections: the Social Republican Party, led by Colonel Lon Non (Lon Nol's brother); the Republican Party, led by Sirik Matak; and the Democratic Party, led by In Tam. But before polling day, the leaders of the Democratic and Republican parties withdrew from the contest in protest over the electoral law, which, they charged, denied them any chance of winning. As a result, the Social Republican Party, facing opposition in only 17 constituencies, won all of the seats in the assembly. On October 14, Lon Nol designated Hang Thun Hak as the new prime minister, and the cabinet, announced the next day, included Lon Non.

Military deterioration. With the failure of the Highway 6 operation, most Cambodian territory east of the Mekong River was lost almost without a fight. Despite the government's recruitment of an army of about 200,000 men, the military initiative remained fully with the Communist forces, whose ranks had been augmented by indigenous Khmer

Rouge insurgents estimated to number 30,000. The Communists began to chip away at morale in Phnom Penh by assassination attempts against the U.S. ambassador and Prime Minister Son and by periodically launching rockets into the city—on one occasion within yards of Lon Nol's residence. By mid-1972, the insurgents had extended their operations south and northwest of the capital and were able to cut off food and fuel supplies to Phnom Penh. Breakdowns in army discipline were manifested in January with the arrest of an army colonel charged with selling pharmaceuticals to the enemy and, in the same month, with the shooting of civilians by battle-weary troops who claimed to have opened fire on the moon to prevent it from being devoured by a mythical frog. In early September, dire food shortages in Phnom Penh—the result of North Vietnamese interdiction of supply routes—prompted large-scale looting, allegedly led by government soldiers. Lon Nol offered amnesty to the Khmer Rouge in November, but it was not known how many insurgents were accepting the offer and returning to civilian life.

Foreign affairs. United States support remained the key factor in sustaining the Lon Nol government. U.S. economic and military support for 1971 amounted to a record $341 million. In March, U.S. Assistant Secretary of State Marshall Green asserted that the Nixon administration anticipated an ongoing U.S. defense commitment to Cambodia, even after U.S. forces were withdrawn from South Vietnam.

The Cambodian government expressed anxiety over President Nixon's visit to Peking in February and over Nixon's failure to include Cambodia within the terms of his Vietnam peace proposal. These events, together with the desperate military situation, may have prompted Lon Nol to seek, without success, a compromise agreement with the Vietnamese Communists, using the Soviet Union as an intermediary. Lon Nol reportedly offered a de facto partition of the country.

Prince Sihanouk, still in exile in Peking, spent much of the year traveling abroad to win support for his cause. In February, just before President Nixon's arrival, Sihanouk left Peking for a three-week visit to North Vietnam. In April he visited North Korea, and in June he went on an East European and North African tour which included Romania, Yugoslavia, Albania, Algeria, and Mauritania. The Chinese government continued to express strong support for Sihanouk and his government-in-exile. On March 19, Premier Chou En-lai hosted a banquet to mark the second anniversary of Prince Sihanouk's arrival in Peking. The persistence of Sihanouk and his supporters in presenting their case bore diplomatic fruit in August when the Conference of Nonaligned Countries, meeting in Guyana, recognized the Sihanouk delegation as the legitimate representative of Cambodia.

Economic disintegration. The war began to wreak havoc with the economic life of Cambodia. The economy was kept from utter collapse by consumer imports financed through foreign aid and by agricultural products provided by the United States. In January, the government convened an emergency monetary conference made up of nations sympathetic to the Cambodian cause in order to solicit financial assistance in propping up the war-stricken economy and the level of the currency. Contributions totaling $20 million were received from the United States, Japan, Australia, New Zealand, Great Britain, Thailand, and Malaysia.

Area and population. Area, 69,800 sq. mi. Pop. (est. 1972), 7 million. Principal cities: Phnom Penh (cap.), 1 million; Battambang, 50,000; Kompong Cham, 35,000.
Government. Constitutional republic. Pres., Lon Nol; prime min., Hang Thun Hak.
Finance. Monetary unit, riel; 1 riel = US$0.0075. Budget (1972): 24 billion riels.
Trade. Virtually no exports because of the war. Principal imports: petroleum products, vehicles, foodstuffs, and armaments.

Agriculture and industry. Chief products: rice, corn, rubber, pepper, cattle, fish. Insignificant industrial production.

Education (1968). Enrollment: primary, 1,025,000; secondary, 117,000; higher, 10,800; technical, 7,400.

Armed forces. Army (est. 1972), 200,000; air force, 2,400; navy, 1,600.

MICHAEL LEIFER

KOREA. The simultaneous announcement on July 4, 1972, from both Seoul and Pyongyang that South and North Korea had agreed on the goal of national unification marked a historic breakthrough in North-South relations since 1948. The agreement specified that Korean unification would be achieved without external interference and through peaceful means and that the Seoul and Pyongyang regimes would not slander or defame each other or engage in armed provocation, would take positive measures (including establishment of a direct telephone line between the two governments), to prevent inadvertent military incidents which might lead to another war, and would work to foster an atmosphere of mutual trust. The two sides also agreed to cooperate in seeking an early success of the Red Cross talks on reuniting divided families.

After protracted preliminary discussion, the first full-scale Red Cross meetings were held August 30–September 2 in Pyongyang and September 13–15 in Seoul.

South Korea

Government and politics. On December 6, 1971, President Park Chung-hee declared a state of national emergency. Three weeks later the National Assembly, despite vigorous opposition, passed a bill granting Park sweeping emergency powers, enabling him to restrict freedoms of expression, to order the partial or general mobilization of national resources, and to freeze wages, prices, and rents without specific legislative approval.

The subsequent refusal of the ruling Democratic Republican Party, which maintained a slim majority in the National Assembly, to call the body into session caused both press and public to express the fear that parliamentary democracy in South Korea was in danger. Demonstrations by university students against high prices, alleged corruption among high political leaders, and the expansion of compulsory military training programs at colleges were dealt with sternly by government troops. The National Assembly was finally reconvened on July 3, only to be dissolved less than four months later when President Park declared martial law, suspended all political activities, closed all colleges and universities, imposed press censorship, and suspended parts of the constitution. Promising to restore constitutional order by the end of the year, he claimed that the Red Cross talks with the North had made fundamental changes necessary in South Korea's government. The new constitution, announced October 27 and subject to referendum, allows President Park to serve an unlimited number of terms and to appoint one-third of the new National Assembly.

Foreign affairs. President Park instructed chiefs of overseas missions boldly to seek improvements in South Korea's foreign relations and trade and to counter the activities of North Korean agents abroad. On the diplomatic front, Seoul disclosed that it would not sever diplomatic relations with those countries which recognized the government in Pyongyang and that it was prepared to establish diplomatic and commercial relations with Communist countries as long as they held no hostile intentions and carried out no hostile actions against the Republic of Korea.

In response to the U.S.-China détente, South Korea reiterated its "self-reliant" foreign policy; nevertheless, the Seoul government sought stronger ties with the United States, which agreed to help bolster and modernize South Korean defense capabilities. Early in September the South Korean government stated that it had reached a final decision to withdraw all troops from Vietnam by December.

Economic developments. The third economic development plan (1972–1976) was launched this year. Nearly all aspects of the South Korean economy, from food production to job training to public housing, were covered. In conjunction with the plan, the government launched a "new community" movement to promote the spirit of self-reliance and cooperation in rural communities in order to modernize production facilities. The government also sought increased loans and private investments from abroad. For fiscal 1972–1973 U.S. economic aid was reportedly $173 million.

None of these efforts could prevent an economic slowdown this year; mismanagement, a shortage of capital, and U.S. trade restrictions on Korean products were blamed for the slump. In addition, an unusually cool and dry spring, the late arrival of the rainy season, and the heaviest rainfall in 50 years (claiming 550 lives and causing extensive property damage) seriously disrupted the economy.

UPI

A TOAST TO UNITY. South Korea's Kim Yeon-choo and North Korea's Kim Tae-hui celebrate a preliminary agreement on plans for full-scale bilateral negotiations to reunite divided families.

Using the powers granted him the previous December, on August 2 the president froze prices and wages, stopped payment of principal (for five years) and interest (for three years) on private loans by industrial and financial borrowers, and ordered reductions from 19 percent to 15.5 percent on annual interest rates for general loans and from 16.8 percent to 12 percent on one-year time deposits. The government announced that it was prepared to provide loans to private firms in order to encourage economic development.

Area and population. Area, 38,004 sq. mi. Pop. (est. 1972), 34 million. Principal cities: Seoul (cap.), 5.9 million; Pusan, 2.1 million; Taegu, 1.1 million; Inchŏn, 900,000.

Government. Republic with strong executive power. Pres., Park Chung-hee; prem., Kim Chong-pil; for. min., Kim Yong-sik.

Finance. Monetary unit, won; 1 won = US$0.0026. Budget (1972), US$1.7 billion.

Trade (1971). Imports, $2.35 billion; exports, $1.35 billion. Principal imports: capital, iron and steel, raw materials, oil, machinery. Principal exports: plywood, textile and electronics goods, footwear, tobacco.

Education (1971). Elementary schools, 6,856; enrollment, 5,807,448. Middle schools, 1,794; enrollment, 1,529,541. Liberal arts and vocational high schools, 898; enrollment, 647,180. Colleges and universities, 127; enrollment, 244,913.

Armed forces. Army, 600,000; air force, 25,000; navy, 20,000; marine corps, 22,000; home guards, 2 million.

North Korea

Foreign affairs. Kim Il-sung and his younger brother, Kim Yong-ju, director of the Organization and Guidance Department, launched an aggressive campaign to sell his "peaceful plan" for Korean unification both to the South Koreans and to the world. Diplomatic initiatives were undertaken with many countries in Asia, Africa, Latin America, and Southeast Asia. The North Korean regime also invited scholars and journalists from abroad.

As a means to improve its position vis-à-vis China and the Soviet Union, North Korea sent missions to Moscow and Peking. After a Soviet–North Korean agreement on technical and economic development was concluded in December 1971, the Soviet Union made special gestures to North Korea for closer ties and also sent North Korea a new shipment of MIG-21's. Agreements between North Korea and China for military and technical assistance were concluded in September and November 1971, respectively.

North Korea disclosed its interest in gaining a foothold in the UN through its ally, Albania. For the first time, the North Koreans also showed interest in establishing diplomatic, commercial, and cultural relations with the United States.

Economic developments. North Korea divulged no economic statistics but merely stated that the new six-year plan (1971–1976) was progressing satisfactorily. However, available sources indicated that the North had severe shortages of capital, machinery, food, and consumer goods.

North Korea indicated its interest in establishing trade relations with the United States, hoping to export mica, tungsten, coal, and gold in exchange for American machinery for its aluminum and shipbuilding industries. North Korea initiated negotiations with a Japanese automobile manufacturing firm to build a $130 million truck plant with an annual capacity of 10,000 trucks. An agreement signed in January between private Japanese interests and a North Korean trade delegation and the trade protocol signed between North Korea and the Soviet Union in March should increase North Korea's exports substantially in the next five years. The Soviets have also agreed to build 28 new factories in North Korea.

Area and population. Area, 46,540 sq. mi. Pop. (1971), 13.5 million. Pyongyang (cap.), 1.3 million.
Government. Communist republic controlled by Korean Workers' Party. Prem., Kim Il-sung; for. min., Ho Tam.
Finance. Monetary unit, won; 1 won = US$0.0075. GNP (1970): $3.5 billion.
Trade (1970). Exports, $217 million; imports, $371.9 million. Principal imports: machinery, chemicals, raw materials, food. Principal exports: freight cars, farm tools, and iron and steel. Major trading partners: Soviet Union, China, Japan, and East European nations.
Armed forces. Army, 360,000; air force, 33,000; navy, 10,000; home guards, 2 million.   ANDREW C. NAHM

KUWAIT. Foreign affairs.

In view of the power vacuum existing in the Persian Gulf region since Great Britain's withdrawal of its military presence in 1971, Kuwait expressed an interest this year in purchasing arms and military aircraft. Although Kuwait cannot expect to develop any serious military profile, the sheikhdom does hope to sufficiently modernize its armed forces to be able to quell internal disturbances and slow down any sudden attack by Iraq, a potentially hostile neighbor, until outside help could arrive.

United States, British, and French delegations arrived in the sheikhdom early in the year to discuss arms sales. In July, U.S. secretary of state William P. Rogers visited Kuwait and announced that Washington was glad to assist the sheikhdom—"by economic aid and other forms of cooperation"—in preserving peace, security, and stability in the Persian Gulf region.

Kuwait also moved to improve relations with Iraq this year. In April the Kuwaiti National Assembly called for cooperation with Iraq on the use of the Shatt al 'Arab River, and in May, Kuwait joined Iraq in denouncing Iran's occupation of three Persian Gulf islands in late 1971. In addition, Kuwait contributed heavily to a $151 million loan to Iraq from the Organization of Arab Petroleum Exporting Countries. The loan followed Iraq's nationalization on June 1 of the Western-owned Iraq Petroleum Company.

Economic developments. The government expressed some concern this year over the rapid depletion of Kuwait's oil reserves, particularly in light of evidence suggesting that those reserves may be more than two-thirds lower than had been estimated. For this reason Kuwait initiated steps to limit production of oil.

Despite the production cutbacks, Kuwait is expected, for two reasons, to receive higher oil revenues than ever before. First, in accordance with a January 20 agreement with Western oil companies on compensation for devaluation of the U.S. dollar, the posted price of crude oil was boosted by 8.49 percent. Then in October, Kuwait and four other Arab countries reached an agreement with Western oil-producing firms in the Persian Gulf area under which the countries will acquire a 51 percent (that is, a controlling) interest in the oil companies.

Area and population. Area, 6,000 sq. mi. (excluding partitioned zone). Pop. (1972 census), 815,400, of whom 375,000 (46%) are Kuwaitis and 440,400 (54%) are non-Kuwaitis. Kuwait City (cap.), 224,700.
Government. Constitutional sheikhdom. Ruler, Sheikh Sabah as-Salim as Sabah; crown prince and prem., Sheikh Jabir al-Ahmad al-Jabir.
Finance. Monetary unit, Kuwaiti dinar; KD1 = US$3.12. Budget (1972–1973 fiscal year): balanced at KD536,000,000, with 23% of total revenues earmarked for state reserve funds.
Petroleum. Crude oil production (1971), 147,100,000 long tons. Oil revenues (1971–1972 fiscal year), KD332,700,000.
RICHARD H. PFAFF

LABOR UNIONS.

The Pay Board and presidential politics concerned labor unions in 1972. Also during the year, major league baseball players went on strike for the first time.

Politics. One of the year's most surprising developments, and one of the most distressing to many labor union members, was the refusal of George Meany, president of the American Federation of Labor and Congress of Industrial Organizations (AFL-CIO), to endorse a candidate for president of the United States. The presidential campaign was the first since the 1930's in which no major segment of organized labor, acting through a federation, had endorsed the Democratic nominee. Although Leonard Woodcock, president of the United Automobile Workers (UAW), was an early supporter of Senator George McGovern (D, S.D.), many top union officials had backed Senator Hubert H. Humphrey (D, Minn.) in his losing bid for the Democratic nomination. These officials were for the most part not won over by Senator McGovern, who was considered too radical by some labor leaders and who had once voted in the Senate in favor of right-to-work legislation. On the other hand, Meany and many of his supporters had bitterly criticized President Richard M. Nixon's domestic policies, including the wage-price freeze of 1971 and the operations of the Pay Board and the Price Commission in 1971 and 1972. Meeting in late summer, Meany and the executive board of the AFL-CIO decided to endorse neither candidate.

The various national unions belonging to the AFL-CIO were free to support either candidate, but Meany took the position that the state and local federations and councils were bound by the national federation's no-endorsement decision. The Colorado state body openly defied the national leadership by endorsing Senator McGovern, and the state federations in a number of large states, including California, Illinois, and Texas, expressed support for McGovern by "informal" polls and other devices, but most state and local bodies avoided confrontation. The American Federation of State, County, and Municipal Employees and a number of

other unions joined the UAW in supporting Senator McGovern. The International Brotherhood of Teamsters and some other unions, especially in the building trades, endorsed President Nixon. Most national, state, and local groups concentrated their efforts on nonpresidential contests.

Pay Board reorganized. Four of the five labor members of the Pay Board—including George Meany—resigned in March to protest the board's reduction of a wage increase for Pacific coast longshoremen. Only Teamsters president Frank E. Fitzsimmons remained.

The withdrawal of labor support forced the reconstitution of the board, which as originally established by President Nixon consisted of five representatives each of business, labor, and the public. On March 23, Nixon issued an executive order making the Pay Board a seven-member all-public body. Chairman George H. Boldt and the other four original public members continued to serve, as well as Fitzsimmons and Rocco Siciliano, a former business member.

Longshoring settlements. In part by chance, the longshoring branch of the maritime industry, one of the United States' smallest industries, was thrust into prominence out of all proportion to its size during 1972. Labor dissatisfaction with Pay Board decisions peaked with the board's reduction of the negotiated wage and fringe benefit increases in the Pacific coast longshore settlement, affecting about 10,000 longshoremen. The settlement for Atlantic and Gulf coast longshoremen, affecting about 50,000 workers, was the first major agreement reviewed by the newly reconstituted Pay Board in late spring.

The Pacific coast agreement was signed on February 19, 1972, at the end of the nation's longest port strike—134 days. The International Longshoremen's and Warehousemen's Union (ILWU), headed by Harry Bridges, and the Pacific Maritime Association (PMA), an employers' group of 120 member companies, agreed to a basic wage increase of 72 cents an hour, retroactive to December 25, 1971, and another 40 cents an hour, effective July 1, 1972. Pensions were increased from $235 to $500 a month; small improvements in the health and medical programs were made; and a pay guarantee plan was adopted, providing 36 hours of work or straight-time pay a week. The pay guarantee plan was financed by a $1-per-ton royalty on all container tonnage loaded or unloaded by non-ILWU members within a 50-mile radius of each port.

The settlement, submitted to the Pay Board in late February, exceeded the board's guidelines. But both the ILWU and the PMA agreed that above-average wage and fringe benefit increases for longshoremen were appropriate in view of the very large productivity increases in the industry over the life of the preceding five-year agreement, signed in 1966. That agreement provided that the union continue to give up restrictive work rules and other barriers to technological improvements in exchange for a substantial retirement bonus and other benefits for its members. Wage increases were moderate, averaging about 5 percent a year. Sharply increased containerization, continued adjustments to work-rule elimination, and new investment in cargo handling equipment led to productivity increases averaging 15 percent a year, compounded, during the five years of the agreement. The ILWU and the PMA argued that this trend of rising productivity and decreasing costs would continue, making the negotiated settlement noninflationary.

The Pay Board agreed—but only in part. On March 16 the board disapproved the original package negotiated by the parties, which the board's staff calculated to be a 20.6 percent wage and fringe benefit increase in the first year. The board approved instead a reduced settlement of 10 percent in wages and 4.9 percent in fringe benefits, figures still above the board's established guidelines.

The decision almost brought on a nationwide port strike. The International Longshoremen's Association (ILA), headed by Thomas W. Gleason, had gone on strike over

new-contract negotiations on October 1, 1971, closing Atlantic and Gulf coast ports. The strike-ending settlements were substantially above the Pay Board guidelines and were scheduled to be taken up by the board shortly after the ILWU-PMA case. Therefore, the ILA indicated that it would support an ILWU strike against the Pay Board decision and that it would strike to maintain its own settlements. However, the reorganization of the Pay Board delayed the ILA case until May. By that time, an ILWU court challenge of the Pay Board decision had failed. When the reconstituted board finally decided, on May 8, to reduce the ILA wage increases for the North Atlantic, New Orleans, and West Gulf ports from 12.1, 14.5, and 13.8 percent to 9.8, 12, and 11.4 percent, respectively, the ILA leaders grumbled but eventually accepted the decision. The board-approved wage increases for the ILA were about the same as the increase previously approved for the ILWU.

Aerospace. The most important contract negotiations reviewed this year, in terms of number of workers covered, involved the International Association of Machinists (IAM) and the United Automobile Workers on the union side and Boeing, General Dynamics, Ling-Temco-Vought (LTV), Lockheed, McDonnell Douglas, North American Rockwell, and United Aircraft among the employers. All together, some 200,000 aerospace workers were affected by the bargaining. As was true elsewhere, the Pay Board was a tougher obstacle to large wage settlements than the employers.

The IAM and the UAW, working together in accordance with an agreement made early in 1971, sought wage increases of about 10 percent in each year of a three-year contract. Bargaining opened in midsummer 1971, well before the October and November expiration dates of the principal agreements. The talks made little headway during most of the 90-day wage freeze, which ended in mid-November, but in early December the first agreement, between the UAW and North American Rockwell, was signed. The wage terms of the three-year contract provided for an initial hourly increase of 34 cents, retroactive to October 3, plus another 17 cents, effective on December 6. Additional wage increases of 3 percent were to become effective in each of the second and third years of the contract. Negotiations were quickly concluded by similar agreements between the UAW or the IAM and Lockheed, Boeing, LTV, and McDonnell Douglas. The settlement with United Aircraft was slightly smaller.

The first-year increases, about 12 percent, were well above the announced 5.5 percent Pay Board guideline, and representatives of labor and management were invited to Pay Board hearings held in mid-December 1971. The unions asked for an exception to the guidelines on the grounds that the aerospace settlements were closely linked, in a "tandem" relationship, to the automobile industry settlements made before the wage freeze in 1971. On January 5 the board decided that the settlements were not tandem and rejected the two-step first-year increase of 51 cents an hour. On January 13 the board, in its first refusal of a wage agreement, held that the aerospace settlements would be acceptable only if the first-year increase were held to 34 cents an hour, calculated by the board's staff to be about an 8.3 percent wage increase, and if the remaining 17 cents an hour were deferred to the second year of the agreements. Although the two unions filed suit in federal court challenging the legality of the board's action, most of the aerospace agreements had been renegotiated by mid-1972 to incorporate the Pay Board's terms.

Mine workers. On May 1, 1972, U.S. District Court Judge William B. Bryant nullified the 1969 election of W. A. "Tony" Boyle as president of the United Mine Workers. Boyle, the incumbent, defeated Joseph A. Yablonski, who accused Boyle of corruption. Yablonski was murdered three weeks after the election by persons later linked to Silous Huddleston, then president of a Tennessee local of the

UMA, and others. Judge Bryant found that there had been large-scale violations of the union's election laws, including illegal use of the union newspaper and union funds to support Boyle's campaign and denial to opponents of the right to have observers at polling places. On June 16, Bryant ordered a new election to be held in December and specified a detailed set of procedures and reports designed to make the election a fair one. He further authorized the secretary of labor to place representatives in union offices to supervise the union's financial transactions.

On March 31, Boyle had been found guilty on 13 counts of conspiracy and of making illegal political contributions from union funds. Boyle was sentenced on June 27 to two concurrent five-year prison terms and fined $130,000. Judge Charles R. Richey ordered that the fine be paid from Boyle's own funds and that he also pay the union $49,250 as reimbursement for funds illegally contributed to political campaigns (including about $30,000 to the 1968 presidential campaign of Hubert Humphrey). Boyle appealed.

Construction unions. The construction industry was less prominent this year than in the recent past, despite an above-average number of contract negotiations and the continued development of government plans and legal action to attack racial discrimination in the industry. In part the low profile resulted from the delegation by the Pay Board of direct control over wage settlements to the Construction Industry Stabilization Committee, an action which shifted the industry away from the center of attention. (Construction is the only industry with its own separate wage-control apparatus.) More important, there were few significant strikes in the industry, apart from a two-week stoppage by carpenters and cement masons in Chicago in June and July. Finally, the negotiated wage increases in construction have become much smaller; the averages were

about 16 percent in 1970, 11 percent in 1971, but only 5.3 percent in the first quarter of 1972.

Railways. Railroad unions are perennially in the news, and this year was no exception. The railroad signalmen's agreement, signed in November 1971, provided for increases in wages totaling 46 percent over the 42-month period beginning January 1, 1970. The Pay Board ruled on December 9, 1971, that the settlement was closely linked to other rail union agreements concluded earlier and approved the contract. The United Transportation Union's 42-month agreement, containing provisions very similar to the signalmen's contract, was approved by the Pay Board on January 25, 1972. Shopcraft workers, sheet metal workers, and others also settled on the industry pattern.

In July the UTU agreed with representatives of U.S. railroads to eventually eliminate the job of fireman on freight locomotives, apparently ending that dispute.

Baseball strike. One of the year's most interesting developments was the first nationwide strike ever in professional baseball. The players struck for 13 days, beginning April 1, and forced postponement of the start of the 1972 season. The players originally demanded a 17 percent increase in the club owners' contribution to the players' pension fund; the owners originally refused to make any increase; they settled on 8.5 percent.

Hoffa paroled. Former Teamsters president James R. Hoffa was released from federal prison on December 23, 1971, after serving four years, 9½ months of a 13-year sentence for jury-tampering and fraud. President Nixon commuted the sentence to 6½ years, making Hoffa eligible for parole on the basis of the time he had already served. One condition of Hoffa's release was that he not participate in the management of any labor organization until 1980.

PAUL T. HARTMAN

George Meany
Sits This One Out

When the bell sounded for this year's round of electoral politics, both parties wanted AFL-CIO president George Meany in their corner. No fan of President Nixon (left), Meany was expected to side with George McGovern. But as the smoke cleared (right), the national AFL-CIO decided to endorse no candidate for national office.

UPI

LAOS. On June 24, the provisional government of Prince Souvanna Phouma, the veteran neutralist prime minister, observed its tenth anniversary. Unhappily for Laos, the continuation of the Indochina war belied the hopes for peaceful democratic development and national unity expressed by the 1962 Geneva accords, and fighting continued to plague the life of the small kingdom.

Elections to the national assembly were held as scheduled on January 2. Pro-Souvanna Phouma candidates received overwhelming support, but as in previous elections voting took place only in areas controlled by the Royal Laotian forces. The pro-Communist Pathet Lao refused to take part, denouncing the elections as illegal. This year's balloting was conducted under dramatic circumstances, since the North Vietnamese Army had launched its customary dry-season Laos offensive in mid-December, a month earlier than usual, subjecting government positions both in the north and south to heavy enemy pressure.

The fighting. In the north, the North Vietnamese and their Pathet Lao allies rapidly overran the Plain of Jars, which had been captured and held by the government since May 1971. Using long-range Soviet 130-mm. artillery for the first time, the North Vietnamese threatened to drive the government forces from Long Cheng, their principal base in the north. All civilians were evacuated from the area on January 10, but in bitter fighting during the following week, the irregular Meo army of General Vang Pao managed to hold out against the storm. The success was owed in part to the intervention of U.S. aircraft and to the beefing up of Vang Pao's forces by Thai troops. Vang Pao, who has given a good account of himself over the years of fighting against the Vietnamese, once again succeeded in reversing a near-desperate situation, and in early February launched a counteroffensive, advancing as far as the Plain

of Jars in the last few days of that month. In the south, Royalist forces defending the towns of the Mekong Valley were subjected to continuous pressure and were unable to regain their positions on the Bolovens Plateau, lost in 1971.

The main interest of the Vietnamese Communists in Laos since the 1954 partition of Vietnam has been the so-called Ho Chi Minh Trail. This network of mountain trails and roads has enabled North Vietnam to supply the insurgency in South Vietnam across the border of Laos through Khe Sanh, the A Shau Valley, Que Son, Dak To, and other strategic points whose names recall some of the fiercest battles of the war. Each year the trail has been enlarged and improved to keep up with the heavier and more rapid flow of food and equipment required by the war in South Vietnam. On January 19, the U.S. Defense Department reported that reconnaissance photos had revealed the existence of an unprecedented array of armaments along the trail: 130 missile launchers and over 400 antiaircraft guns.

The negotiations. During 1972 the preliminary negotiations begun in 1970 between Prince Souvanna Phouma and Prince Souphanouvong, the leader of the Pathet Lao political faction—the Neo Lao Hak Sat (NLHS)—continued sporadically. Neither the South Vietnamese invasion into southern Laos of 1971 nor the resumption of the American bombing of North Vietnam in the spring of 1972 had put a stop to these contacts. Two of the principal obstacles to more rapid progress had been failure to agree upon a meeting place for a higher-level conference and the fact that the NLHS had refused since 1964 to recognize the competence of the Vientiane government. But on October 14 a delegation headed by General Phoune Sipraseuth, deputy commander in chief of the Lao People's Army, arrived in Vientiane and issued the following statement: "If the Nixon administration is willing to cease its policy of aggression

and intervention in Laos and the Vientiane side regards the national interest as the most important thing, it is certain that the Laos question will be conveniently solved in the forthcoming talks between the two sides."

International relations. Ambivalence continued to mark the stances of the foreign powers involved in Laos. For many years now North Vietnam, while vociferously supporting the aims of the Pathet Lao and acting as a conduit for Soviet and Chinese arms to the Pathet Lao Army, has denied the presence of its own troops in Laos, refusing even to accept repatriation of North Vietnamese soldiers held prisoner by the Royal Lao government (North Vietnamese diplomats in Vientiane have claimed that such prisoners were in fact "soup merchants arrested on the streets of Vientiane"). The day-to-day involvement of the United States in Laos, especially that of U.S. offensive aircraft, was likewise generally conceded to be well over the borderline of what was permissible under the letter of the 1962 Geneva Accords. For its part, the Soviet Union continued to act its role as cochairman of the Geneva Conference. The Soviets maintained an active embassy in Vientiane, while all the time continuing to supply arms to Hanoi which would in turn be used in Laos against Royalist government forces. In addition, following the U.S. mining of North Vietnam's coast in May, the traditional air route from Moscow to Hanoi via Vientiane—flown by civil aircraft immune from U.S. air attack—became the Soviet Union's most rapid and secure link to North Vietnam.

Vientiane remained one of the few capitals in the world to house both North Vietnamese and South Vietnamese embassies. During 1972, Prince Souvanna Phouma maintained his policy of resisting efforts by the Saigon government to involve his armed forces command more deeply in joint planning. The January election victory over rightist candidates of the prime minister's neutralist supporters showed that this policy was fully in accord with popular sentiment. South Vietnam's foreign minister Tran Van Lam visited Vientiane in August, reportedly to reconcile differences between the two governments over proposals made at the Paris conference on Vietnam. Saigon's commitment to President Richard M. Nixon's offer, made on May 8, 1972, of "an internationally supervised ceasefire throughout Indochina" has met some resistance among the Laotians. A decade's experience has taught them the difficulty of enforcing such inspection.

Area and population. Area, 91,428 sq. mi. Pop. (est. 1972), 3.1 million. Principal cities: Vientiane (admin. cap.), 150,000; Luang Prabang (royal cap.), 43,000.

Government. Constitutional monarchy, with bicameral legislature (King's Council and National Assembly). King, Savang Vatthana; prime min., Souvanna Phouma.

Finance. Monetary unit, kip; K1 = US$0.0018 at free-market rate. Budget (1970): revenue, K8.08 billion; expenditure, K18.18 billion.

Trade. Imports (1969), US$46.1 million; recorded exports (1970), US$2.9 million. Major exports: tin ore, coffee, timber, opium. Major trading partner: Thailand.

Armed forces. Royal government forces, 56,800 regulars and 27,000 irregulars. Pathet Lao and dissident neutralist forces, 31,000.

ARTHUR J. DOMMEN

LATIN AMERICA. Conflict in Chile. "Our dilemma is not between democracy and totalitarianism, but between Chilean interests and those of foreign capital, between the authority of the owners or of the workers." Thus did Chile's Marxist president Salvador Allende Gossens keynote the salient political theme in Latin America during 1972—the intensifying conflict between social reform and economic nationalism on the one hand and foreign private investment and concentrated wealth on the other. The trend portended renewed pressures on U.S. private investment in Latin America, which amounts to $14 billion, or 70 percent of U.S. total investment in the developing nations. As head of the ruling Popular Unity coalition of Marxist parties, President Allende tied his difficulties with the Chilean Con-

gress and street demonstrators to interference by foreign corporations, accusing them of conspiring with opposition leaders in the Congress. In March, Allende seized two enterprises in direct defiance of legislation that required congressional approval of such action.

In addition, the Congress impeached Allende's first minister of interior and censured his successor, charging them with carrying out "illegal" expropriations of farms and industries, even though they acted on presidential orders. The opposition overrode Allende's veto of a law granting nationwide broadcasting to university television stations, thus offsetting the government's national television monopoly. The opposition also combined to defeat two of the three government candidates in congressional by-elections in districts where the regime had carried out extensive expropriations of U.S.-owned copper mines and large farming estates. The defeats also reflected dissatisfaction from miners' unions over government attempts to hold down wage increases and prevent a 40–50 percent inflation rate. Strikes in the major cities, motivated by denied pay raises, paralyzed the state-run railroad and private bus lines; in August a state of emergency was declared in Santiago after widespread strikes by retail merchants protesting against continuing food shortages and price controls. The coalition's traditional hold on the University of Chile slipped, as its candidates for the rectorship and council lost. Finally, in October and November, widespread strikes and street violence forced the government to declare a state of emergency in 19 provinces. After the cabinet was reshuffled to permit greater military representation, the strikers returned to work.

On the other hand, the coalition won a key by-election in Coquimbo. In September the six factions of the coalition emerged united from their "national assembly." The elections for a new Chamber of Deputies in March 1973 will provide the first national test of popular support.

Other reform and nationalization efforts. Mexico, Venezuela, Peru, and other Latin American nations made significant efforts to reform or nationalize their economies. In Mexico, the two-year-old administration of Luis Echeverría Álvarez spent more than $100 million during 1971 and 1972 on housing, schools, mobile clinics, roads, and irrigation projects to improve the plight of the 8 million rural poor in the north and central regions. This investment followed national reforms in taxation, banking, industrial decentralization, rural education, modernization of agriculture, expansion of social security, and low-cost housing.

Venezuela sought to unite nine other Latin American countries in the Organization of Oil Exporting Nations to force the United States to grant lower tariffs and import quotas, as well as to mandate a larger share of corporate oil profits for the oil-producing countries of Latin America. Venezuela passed a controversial law in 1971 that called for the reversion of all foreign assets to the state's petroleum corporation when concessions expire in 1983, obliged foreign companies to pay higher taxes when production goes certain percentage points above or below 1970 levels, and increased the government's share of oil profits to more than 80 percent.

The military government of Peru, in power since a 1968 coup, continued to reinforce its nationalist-revolutionary image. It increased worker-peasant control of agricultural production, local government, universities, and commercial enterprises. In May, a new national agrarian confederation and affiliated associations replaced the three major rural agrarian societies traditionally dominated by large landowners. The new confederation will be incorporated into a cabinet-level agency that aims to make the working classes socially conscious through participation in industrial, agricultural, and neighborhood action groups. The regime also took over the foreign-owned telephone company. President Richard M. Nixon's "low profile" policy toward Latin America lessened tensions over the Peruvian expropriation of the International Petroleum Corporation and the 200-mile-limit

controversy. (North American fishermen purchased Ecuadorian and Peruvian licenses rather than risk steep fines and the impounding of their boats.)

Colombia, Bolivia, Ecuador, and Panama registered less spectacular reforms and nationalization. Colombia's agrarian reform law, enacted in January, provided new capital for the farmers' credit bank and enabled depositors to receive savings' interest of up to 8 percent; it also improved rural housing, credit, and free life insurance coverage for small farmers. A special fund will enable a land reform institute to buy up land inefficiently used.

Many observers thought the Ecuadorian military, in staging Latin America's only coup of the year, would follow the Peruvian example of "barracks socialism." After overthrowing the civilian administration of President José María Velasco Ibarra in February, the new regime of General Guillermo Rodríguez Lara promptly annulled all existing oil contracts with Texaco and Gulf, promised the "democratizing" of rural landholdings, cracked down on the press, and advocated a cleanup of the corrupt civilian bureaucracy. However, the regime proved extremely cautious in implementing social reforms.

The coup was due not only to the scandals and ineptitude of the Velasco government but also reflected the confusion and division within the traditional parties as they faced the June presidential elections, which they feared would have resulted in victory for Guayaquil's leftist and immensely popular former mayor, Asaad Bucaram. The military appeared to want to prevent a truly popular revolution in the event the country's economic elite moved against Bucaram after his election.

Panama's military leader, General Omar Torrijos, seemed as determined to make total national sovereignty over the canal the issue of 1972 as he was to assume more dictatorial powers. His government even responded favorably to Cuban offers of cooperation and financial assistance on ending U.S. control of national territories. Negotiations with the United States, now in their eighth year after the bloody rioting in the Canal Zone, were stalemated by frenzied anti-U.S. attacks in the government-controlled press.

Unlike its Peruvian and Panamanian counterparts, Bolivia's new military government exhibited a friendlier attitude toward foreign capital, even while expounding the virtues of national economic controls; it legislated "substantial" but not "exclusive" state control over basic industries and capital investment.

Guerrillas and political crackdowns. Guerrilla violence flared up, with Argentina, which has at least seven extreme leftist groups in the major cities, bearing the brunt of terrorist acts. The Uruguayan government of Juan Maria Bordaberry killed and arrested important members of the ever-active Tupamaros but allowed Congress to end the last curbs on civil liberties decreed by the former embattled president, Jorge Pacheco Areco in 1969. Rebel activity expanded in rural parts of Colombia, spurred in part by state and city elections in April. Quiescent for years, rural guerrilla groups committed scattered acts of violence and kidnappings in Venezuela and southern Mexico. Even Chile's Marxist regime had to take action against illegal rural land seizures by a Castroite guerrilla group once nominally part of the ruling coalition.

There were also widespread official crackdowns on other forms of political dissent. Mexico's increasing sensitivity to criticism was dramatized by the swift arrest, detention, and deportation without explanation of U.S. professor Kenneth Johnson, who had long been critical of the dominant party and had associated openly with opposition political leaders in Mexico. In Peru, the military government ousted Pedro Beltrán as editor of the prestigious paper *La Prensa* in January. The conservative newspaper of Chile, *El Mercurio*, fought the government's systematic efforts to force it into bankruptcy. Political suppressions in El Salvador followed

an unsuccessful coup by leftist army units when the handpicked candidate of President Fidel Sánchez Hernández narrowly won the February election.

Old dictators on the political horizon. Uncertainty continued to cloud the candidacy of 76-year-old ex-president Juan Perón for Argentina's presidential elections in March 1973. The president, General Alejandro A. Lanusse, removed all legal barriers to Perón's eligibility and return from Madrid exile, except one: he had to establish residence in the country by August 25, which he failed to do. His supporters claimed he would return on November 17. In Colombia, the results of April elections for state and municipal offices slowed the momentum of ex-president and dictator Gustavo Rojas Pinilla and his National Popular Alliance for the presidency and control of Congress in 1974, when the 16-year National Front experiment rotating the government between Liberals and Conservatives ends. Former dictator Marcos Pérez Jiménez returned from exile in Madrid, with an eye toward Venezuela's presidential elections in 1973. Democratic forces were alarmed at his candidacy, especially with the refusal of Rómulo Betancourt to run. (Betancourt is the democratic ex-president who had helped lead the coup to oust Pérez in 1958.)

Nixon's "low profile." President Nixon's policy of "realism and restraint" toward Latin America included the refusal to invoke the Hickenlooper Amendment and withhold aid over Chilean expropriations of U.S. copper and oil industries, to confront Ecuador and Peru regarding previous seizures of U.S. fishing boats, and to cut off aid to the Ecuadorian military after its coup. Latin Americans greeted favorably the president's announcement in December 1971 lifting the 10 percent surcharge on imports and promising general trade preferences for Latin American exports, but little action was taken on this pledge in 1972. In keeping with the Rockefeller Commission's recommendations of 1969, the Nixon administration attempted to "multilateralize" nonmilitary aid by asking Congress to quadruple the U.S. contribution to the Inter-American Development Bank, from $262 million in 1972 to $837 million in 1973. At the same time, Nixon submitted the lowest bilateral aid request for Latin America in more than a decade—$224.5 million in economic and development assistance for fiscal 1973—less than 10 percent of the $3.2 billion foreign-aid budget sent to the Congress.

International cooperation. Partially in response to the declining U.S. role in hemispheric affairs, Latin American nations looked more closely to each other, Europe, and Asia on matters of trade and technical development. The chief success story was the dramatic increase in commerce and fiscal cooperation among the five nations of the Andean Group (Colombia, Ecuador, Peru, Bolivia, and Chile). In the three years since the group's founding, trade expanded by $100 million, or 170 percent, a rate ten times the yearly rate of increase of trade among the members of the parent Latin American Free Trade Association during 1961–1969. This achievement, along with the growth rate within the Central American common market, portends increasing Latin American reliance on smaller, regional associations.

Other examples of Latin American cooperation, either in the planning or development stage, were market and refining outlets for Bolivian oil and gas in western Brazil; a highway across the Darien Isthmus by Panama and Colombia, with U.S. financial assistance; agreement among Venezuela, Brazil, and Colombia on linking the Orinoco, Negro, and Amazon rivers; and accords by 15 Caribbean nations for a 200-mile maximum limit on national "patrimonial waters" (sovereign control of subsurface ocean resources). On the diplomatic front, Cuba's wall of isolation, imposed at U.S. urging by the OAS in 1964, cracked even more. Peru became the third Latin American country after Mexico and Chile to establish formal relations with the Castro regime.

CARL EDWARD SCHWARZ

MR. FBI

FEDERAL BUREAU OF INVESTIGATION

J. Edgar Hoover's marathon career in law enforcement began when he joined the Justice Department back in 1917. After serving under Woodrow Wilson and Warren G. Harding, he was given a free hand by Calvin Coolidge to shape and direct an FBI untainted by political influence; only 29 when he took over the post of director (above), he went on to serve under Herbert Hoover and the six presidents seen at right, in a 48-year tenure ending with his death this year at the age of 77.

WITH FRANKLIN D. ROOSEVELT (1933–1945)

BETTMANN ARCHIVE

WITH HARRY S TRUMAN (1945–1953)

WIDE WORLD

LAW. Problems for lawyers. Besides mulling over what former American Bar Association president Charles Rhyne called "a panorama of defects and deficiencies in American justice," delegates to the ABA convention this summer also had two more personal problems to consider.

One was the increasing popularity of no-fault automobile liability insurance. The ABA house of delegates unsurprisingly adopted a resolution opposing any nationwide system of no-fault auto insurance, but it also supported a compromise resolution urging all states to require that drivers carry $2,000 in insurance, covering damages to their own cars regardless of fault. However, under this plan drivers would retain the right to sue.

Another problem was the possibility of severe job shortages for lawyers over the coming ten years. While a heavy stream of law school graduates was expected to swell bar membership at a rate of over 30,000 attorneys a year, the Department of Labor estimated that only 14,000 new law jobs would be available annually. Although it has been suggested that law schools cut back on admissions, an ABA committee took a more sanguine view, arguing that many law students do not pursue law as a career and that the extension of adequate legal services to the lower and middle classes could go far in relieving the pressure generated by heavy law school enrollments. The committee also pointed out that limiting access to professional education for economic reasons has very little precedent in the history of the United States.

Rights of minors. The traditional justification for exercising judicial power over children for "noncriminal behavior" (such as habitual truancy or disobedience to parents) is that children require adult guidance for their proper development. But in the case of *Commonwealth* v. *Brasher,* 270 N.E. 2d 389 (1971), the constitutionality of the Massachusetts "parental command" and truancy statutes was challenged on the grounds that the statutory language was unconstitutionally vague, that a child's freedom (particularly that of a child over 12) ought not to be limited by a universal requirement that parental orders be obeyed, and that since adults are not punished for noncriminal conduct, the equal-protection clause of the Fourteenth Amendment is violated by rules for children that are not equally applicable to adults.

The Brasher case upheld the Massachusetts statute and noted that the duty of parents to "support, provide for, and protect the children they bring forth" is a duty upheld by law, and its breach "a crime against society." The Court of Appeals of New York, in *A* v. *City of New York,* 31 N.Y. 2d 33 (1972), upheld a similar statute permitting the exercise of control over a child who was "disobedient and beyond . . . lawful control" or a "habitual truant." The court said, "The terms . . . as well as the conduct proscribed are easily understood." A court of appeals in the State of Washington agreed in *In re Jackson,* 497 P. 2d 254 (1972), saying, "Children of ordinary understanding know that they must obey their parents . . ."

PHOTO TRENDS, COPYRIGHT © HARRIS & EWING
WITH DWIGHT D. EISENHOWER (1953–1961)

UPI
WITH LYNDON B. JOHNSON (1963–1969)

WITH JOHN F. KENNEDY (1961–1963)

UPI

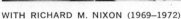
WITH RICHARD M. NIXON (1969–1972)

However, the issue of court power over children for non-criminal conduct was by no means resolved by the year's case law. The question opened up fundamental problems concerning the nature of the family. In a footnote (n. 3) to his dissenting opinion in *Wisconsin* v. *Yoder* (92 S. Ct. 1526), U.S. Supreme Court justice William O. Douglas asserted, "There is substantial agreement among child psychologists and sociologists that the moral and intellectual maturity of the fourteen-year-old approaches that of the adult." If this point is accepted, much legislation concerning the rights of minors must be changed.

Medical decisions and the law. Two recent cases raised perplexing questions about the state's jurisdiction in ordering medical treatment for unwilling individuals.

Kevin Sampson, a 15-year-old, suffered from a massive deformity of the right side of his face and neck, caused by Von Recklinghausen's disease. A New York juvenile-court staff psychiatrist testified that the boy's grotesque appearance inevitably exerted a negative effect upon his personality development. Kevin had also been exempted from school because of his disfigurement; hence, although he had the capacity to be educated to a reasonable level, he remained a virtual illiterate. Doctors said that his facial appearance could be vastly improved by a surgical procedure but that the operation was not necessary to preserve his life, would not cure the disease, and could involve "considerable risks." A juvenile court in New York City faced the question of whether to order young Sampson to undergo the

procedure, in the face of parental urging that surgery be delayed until the boy was old enough to make his own decision. The court ordered the operation to proceed provided that the surgeons would advise that the risk attending the operation was acceptable. The judge grounded his decision on the importance of ensuring some amelioration of the personality difficulties which stemmed from the deformity. His order was upheld by the New York court of appeals (278 N.E. 2d 919) in January.

Generally, the courts do not disregard parental judgment about medical treatments unless intervention is necessary to save the life of a child or the child's condition raises a danger of contagion to others. The approach of the *Sampson* case was much bolder. Surgery of some danger was ordered to attempt the correction of a serious psychological impairment.

In another unusual case of aggressive judicial intervention, *John F. Kennedy Memorial Hospital* v. *Heston*, 279 A. 2d 670 (1971), the New Jersey supreme court approved ordering a life-saving blood transfusion for a young Jenovah's Witness injured in an automobile accident and suffering from a ruptured spleen. A lower court in New Jersey had appointed a guardian who consented to the transfusion; thus, the victim's life had been saved by a means repugnant to her religious beliefs. The state supreme court upheld the decision, asserting that the interest of the state in the preservation of the lives of its citizens justified the interference with religious freedom.

Electronic testimony. When two St. Paul, Minn., policemen were ambushed and shot after responding to a telephone call to assist an expectant mother, the city police department, which routinely tapes all emergency telephone calls, sent a tape of the call to a police laboratory, where an acoustic spectrogram was made. Later, a suspect's phone call was taped, and the laboratory identified the suspect as the person who had made the fateful call.

In *State ex rel. Trimble* v. *Hedman,* 192 N.E. 2d 432 (1971), the Minnesota supreme court decided that spectrograms ought to be admissible at trial to corroborate aural identification. *Trimble* was the first nonmilitary case to approve this addition to the list of technological aids to the police.

The use of any such electronic aid is generally permitted if the relevant scientific community has agreed that the process is reasonably accurate. The Minnesota court was aided in its opinion by some recent research which established that spectrographic identification errors were rare.

Courts and governmental budgets. Courts have frequently added indirectly to the cost of government by stipulating, for example, that hearings be held or counsel be made available. Similarly, if the courts recognize a right to treatment after civil commitment to a mental hospital, the cost of treatment is added to the public budget. More recently, there have been signs that, in some instances, judges are even willing to mandate the direct appropriation of a sum of money. In *Commonwealth ex rel. Carroll* v. *Tate,* 402 U.S. 974 (1971), the Pennsylvania supreme court sustained a lower court order forcing the Philadelphia city council to raise its budget for court operations for the fiscal year 1970–1971. The council had appropriated $2,458,000 less than the lower court thought sufficient to carry out its functions. In its ruling, the Supreme Court cited a state constitutional provision requiring that the judiciary "possess the inherent power to determine and compel payment of those sums of money which are reasonable and necessary to carry out its mandated responsibility and its power and duties to administer justice."

MONRAD G. PAULSEN

LEBANON. The Palestinian guerrillas. Lebanon's most important problems in 1972 stemmed from the presence of 3,000 well-armed Palestinian guerrillas in the southern part of the country, near the Israeli border. Several times during the year, guerrilla raids against Israel or other acts of terrorism by Palestinian organizations led to Israeli incursions into Lebanon for retaliatory attacks. Although the attacks were aimed primarily at guerrilla strongholds, a number of innocent Lebanese villagers were also killed. These events placed Beirut in a dilemma: Suppression of the guerrillas would incur the wrath of leftist and other pro-Palestinian elements within Lebanon, as well as of radical Arab states such as Syria and Iraq. Yet allowing the guerrillas to function freely meant inviting further Israeli incursions into Lebanese territory.

In late February, Israeli military forces crossed the border for four days of raids through southern Lebanon. Attacks were made on several villages claimed to be guerrilla strongholds or sanctuaries and on the Nabatiya refugee camp.

After the Israeli troops withdrew, Lebanon decided to restrain the guerrillas and moved its army into southern Lebanon, provoking sharp reactions from domestic radical parties, who alleged that this action violated the 1969 agreement giving the guerrillas freedom of action in certain parts of Lebanon. The move by the Lebanese Army also prompted Yasir Arafat, leader of the Palestinian guerrilla organization el-Fatah, to meet with President Suleiman Franjieh on February 28. Arafat also met later with Premier Saeb Salam.

The UN Security Council increased the number of its observers in Lebanon from 7 to 21 in April. Nevertheless, guerrilla activity continued along the Lebanese-Israeli border, and on June 21 and then again two days later, Israel launched air and ground attacks against several Lebanese villages, killing some 60–70 Lebanese and Palestinians. This crisis continued to mount until the end of June, when the guerrillas were finally persuaded by the government to withdraw from the areas near the border in order to relieve tension.

JUAN DE ONIS/N.Y. TIMES

DEATH FROM THE SKY. A woman (left) wails for her daughter and grandchildren, reportedly among civilians killed when Israeli bombers hit the Lebanese village of Rafid in a retaliatory raid against guerrillas.

The assassination in Beirut on July 8 of Ghassan Kanafani, a leader of the Popular Front for the Liberation of Palestine, threatened for a time to plunge Lebanon once more into internal upheaval over the guerrilla question. (The guerrillas claimed Israeli agents killed Kanafani.) But by September it seemed that Lebanon had weathered the storm and regained some measure of security along its southern border.

However, after Palestinian guerrillas kidnapped and killed 11 members of the Israeli Olympic team on September 5 and then began mailing bombs to Israeli diplomats throughout the world, Israel retaliated with a series of sharp air and ground attacks on reputed guerrilla positions in Lebanon. On September 16, Israeli troops in Lebanon clashed with units of the Lebanese Army. The Lebanese government reported that its troops suffered 61 casualties.

After Israel's withdrawal, the Lebanese Army again moved in strength into the southern region. Troops reportedly set up roadblocks to prevent guerrillas who had fled north during the Israeli raids from returning to the border area. Palestinian organizations issued new protests, and Premier Salam again met with Yasir Arafat. On September 19, Mahmoud Riad, secretary general of the Arab League, hurriedly flew to Beirut to mediate the talks between the government and the Palestinians, and the next day the guerrillas reportedly agreed, in order to avoid a confrontation with the Lebanese Army, to restrict their activities in Lebanon.

Politics. In April elections were held for seats in Lebanon's unicameral national assembly (Majlis). The elections were staged over three successive Sundays to allow the concentration of security forces in the area where voting was taking place: Beirut, April 16; southern Lebanon, April 23; and Tripoli and northern Lebanon, April 30. Premier Salam was reelected in Beirut, and the speaker of the Majlis, Kamal Assad, was also returned to office.

President Franjieh asked Premier Salam to form a new government, and on June 14 the cabinet received a 77–15 vote of confidence. As is customary, positions in the new cabinet were given out so as to reflect the religious composition of Lebanon's population.

In the spring the Lebanese Communist Party held its third congress in Beirut. Observers from 30 other leftist groups attended the congress, including Ba'athists from Iraq and Syria and representatives from Egypt's Arab Socialist Union, the Kurdish Democratic Party, and the Palestinian resistance movement. The congress was the first to be held openly by any Communist party in the Arab world.

Economic developments. A six-year development plan, covering the period 1972–1977, was launched by Lebanon. The plan calls for total investments of L£7.5 billion (US-$2.38 billion), with the government investing L£1.25 billion, public sector companies and local governments contributing L£490 million, and private investment making up the remainder. The economic targets are a 7 percent growth rate and a shift away from heavy emphasis on the service sector, which currently accounts for some 70 percent of Lebanon's gross national product. Major projects which are planned include land reclamation and construction of irrigation canals, highways, and airports. Expansion of Lebanon's telephone and telegraph facilities is also envisaged. Lebanon may find it difficult to shift away from the service sector at the rate planned. In 1971, Lebanon played host to some 1 million tourists.

Area and population. Area, 4,000 sq. mi. Pop. (est. 1972), 3,-120,000, including 180,000 Palestinian refugees. Principal cities: Beirut (cap.), 720,000; Tripoli, 155,000.
Government. Parliamentary republic. Seats in the 99-member unicameral legislature, as well as positions in the executive branch of government, are apportioned along religious lines. Pres., Suleiman Franjieh; prem., Saeb Salam.
Finance. Monetary unit, Lebanese pound; L£1 = US$0.335. Budget (1972): balanced at L£1,087,948,000. Principal expenditures: defense, L£212,685,000; education, L£171,933,800; public works, L£144,870,000.
RICHARD H. PFAFF

LESOTHO. Politics and government. Continuing a policy of national reconciliation, Prime Minister Leabua Jonathan and the ruling Basutoland National Party sought to integrate their major political opponents into the national life of the country. Jonathan removed all restrictions on Ntsu Mokhehle, leader of the Basutoland Congress Party, and released more than 50 detainees who had been held since the state of emergency was declared in 1970 after the general election. In addition, the government dismissed Lesotho's commissioner of police, Frederick Roach. Roach, who was apparently working too closely with the government of South Africa, had aided Jonathan in his coup d'etat when it became clear that Ntsu Mokhehle and his Congress Party had won the election in 1970.

Prime Minister Jonathan was also outspoken during the year in his opposition to apartheid. Bothered by Lesotho's image as a client state of South Africa, members of the government, as well as leaders of the opposition, urged Jonathan to take a stronger stand against South Africa. It seemed clear that the government was actively seeking to replace South African technical personnel with those from other countries or from the United Nations. Especially interesting was Lesotho's call for black Americans to fill some of the posts.

Economic developments. Whatever the ultimate direction of Lesotho–South African diplomatic and political relations, the economy of Lesotho will continue to be highly dependent upon South Africa. Revenues from the customs union with South Africa, Swaziland, and Botswana remain a critical factor in Lesotho's yearly budget. Receipts from migrant labor in South Africa also continue to be the largest single cash source in the national economy.

Lesotho has budgeted more than US$75 million for development over the next five years. Projects planned by the Lesotho National Development Corporation include diamond mining and the construction of several hotels. Also during 1972, the government announced that it had accepted an offer from a Canadian firm to prospect for oil in the rugged mountains of Lesotho.

Area and population. Area, 11,720 sq. mi. Pop. (est. 1971), 1.1 million, including 2,000 persons of European descent. Maseru (cap.), 14,000.
Government. Constitutional monarchy within the Commonwealth of Nations. King, Motlotlehi Moshoeshoe II; prime min., Chief Leabua Jonathan.
Finance and trade. Monetary unit, South African rand; 1 R = US$1.29. Budget (fiscal year ended March 31, 1971): revenue, R11,704,510; expenditure, R11,041,480.
Trade. Principal exports: wool, mohair, labor to South Africa.
Armed forces. None.
CHRISTIAN P. POTHOLM

LIBERIA. Politics and government. Liberia, on the 150th anniversary of its establishment by freed American slaves, appears to be successfully weathering the succession of the late president William V. S. Tubman by former vice-president William R. Tolbert. Tolbert had been acting president until January, when he was formally acknowledged as president for the remainder of Tubman's term, without popular elections, by a legislative amendment to the constitution. Senator James E. Green of Sino County replaced Tolbert as vice-president in April, after his unanimous nomination by the dominant True Whig Party.

President Tolbert stated that he will follow the lead of his predecessor in both the "open door" approach to foreign investment and the unification policy toward the interior tribes. This was reflected in Tolbert's cabinet appointments. J. Milton Weeks, a sometime critic of foreign investment, was replaced by the president's brother, Stephen Tolbert, in the post of secretary of the treasury, and two men of "purely tribal origin," George Flama Sherman and

James Gbarbea, were appointed secretary of education and minister of lands and mines, respectively.

Foreign affairs. Monrovia was host in May to the nine heads of state, including Tolbert, who constitute the Organization of African Unity's mediation commission. The meeting, whose objective was to achieve a reconciliation between Senegal and Guinea, was concluded successfully on May 31 with the signing of a document outlining the principles to underlie the two countries' "normalized" relations.

Economic developments. The economic recession that began last year with sharp declines in the world prices of Liberia's major exports, iron ore and rubber, continued unabated. By midyear the healthy trade surplus of over US$70 million had become an estimated annual deficit of US$8 million. The economy received a further blow in May when Kawasaki Steel Corporation of Japan gave up its plans to develop a new iron mine in the Wologisi region. As with most recessions in the past, the first group to bear the brunt was the largely foreign-owned import houses. The government warned importers to lower prices and maintain current import volumes or face revocation of their licenses to operate. The seriousness of the situation was underscored by Liberia's negotiation of standby rights with the International Monetary Fund for US$4 million in special drawing rights.

Liberia's current recession brought home even more forcefully that its current development needs lie outside mining and manufacturing, where the potential for further exploitation has been all but exhausted. This was reflected in the international aid obtained for a wide range of agricultural and rural development projects: an International Development Association grant of US$1.2 million for integrated rural development and education projects, a U.S. Export-Import Bank loan of US$3.75 million for the improvement of port facilities at Port Harper, and a World Bank loan of US$1 million to be administered by the Liberian Bank for Industrial Development and Investment to help cover import needs associated with agricultural development projects.

Area and population. Area, 43,000 sq. mi. Pop. (est. 1971), 1,-200,000. Principal city: Monrovia (cap.; est. 1969), 135,000.
Government. Constitutional republic with bicameral legislature. Pres., William R. Tolbert.
Finance. Monetary unit, U.S. dollar. Budget (1971): US$71.6 million.
Trade (1970). Exports, $214 million; imports, $133.5 million. Principal exports: iron ore, rubber. Trading partners: United States, Netherlands, West Germany, Japan.
Education (est. 1969). Enrollment, 147,000.

GEORGE LAMSON

LIBRARIES. United States. It became clear during 1972 that a decade-long halcyon period had ended for the nation's libraries. From New England to the Pacific coast, shortages of funds forced reductions in library services and professional staff. Before the National Endowment for the Humanities offered, in May, a $500,000 matching grant to the privately endowed research libraries of the New York Public Library, both the science and technology division and the collections at the Lincoln Center for the Performing Arts faced cancellation of services. (Earlier in the year the science and technology division had, in fact, suspended service for two weeks because of a lack of operating funds.)

Coinciding with the decline in financial support were some successful efforts to unionize more librarians. The University of Chicago was asked by a group of library staff members to recognize, for the purpose of collective bargaining, a local of the National Council of Distributive Workers of America. On January 1, 1972, the Board of Trustees of the New York Public Library made an agency shop agreement with a local of the American Federation of State, County, and Municipal Employees (AFL-CIO). Under that contract, librarians were required to either join the union or pay an equivalent "contract consideration fee," and staff members who did not

UNBALANCED BOOKS. Forced by rising costs to curtail services, institutions like New York's Public Library pleaded for support.

choose one of the options were subject to dismissal. Some librarians opposed to the agency shop provision contested its validity in a petition to the New York State Public Employment Relations Board. However, a hearing officer for the board ruled that it had no jurisdiction because the library is not a government agency but "a private corporation serving a public purpose with close financial ties to the City of New York."

The National Commission on Libraries and Information Science, meeting February 17–18, 1972, emphasized its concern with libraries as well as with the broader problem of information transmission. Citing court decisions in California and Minnesota which found the local property tax an unacceptable base for public school funding, the commission resolved that if "the current method of funding public schools is changed, library funding must change, too."

The combination of improved photocopying technology and an antiquated copyright law continued to be a problem for U.S. libraries. In 1968, Williams and Wilkins, a Baltimore publisher, filed suit against the National Institutes of Health and the National Library of Medicine for infringement of copyright. The publisher, joined by the Authors League of America and the Association of American Publishers, contended that the two government agencies violated copyright by making available to medical researchers and practitioners photocopies of legally protected works.

Williams and Wilkins initiated its action because library photoduplication was reducing subscriptions to its medical journals. The government, supported by the American Library Association and the Association of Research Libraries, based its defense on the 1935 Gentlemen's Agreement (or "single copy doctrine") between the American Council of Learned Societies and the National Association of Book Publishers which states that a library may make a single

copy of copyrighted material for its scholarly and scientific purposes.

On February 16, 1972, a U.S. court of claims ruled that the publisher is "entitled to recover reasonable and entire compensation for infringement of copyright arising from photocopying." The ruling observed that technological progress had vitiated the Gentlemen's Agreement and that, although the government agencies made only one copy per request, there was no limit on the number of requests for the same article. A final decision in the case awaits the opinion of a U.S. court of appeals and the outcome of any appeal of that ruling to the U.S. Supreme Court. While the Copyright Revision Bill remained stalled in Congress, librarians pondered the implications of the Williams and Wilkins case for the use of photocopies instead of interlibrary loans and for the reduction of in-library materials to microform and their subsequent retrieval as "hard" copy.

Work on the first phase of the James Madison Memorial Building of the Library of Congress was completed in the fall of 1972. The use of compact library shelving in that structure is expected to increase the capacity of its stack areas by about 80 percent over that of the older building.

During 1972 the American Library Association accredited graduate programs of library education in the School of Information and Library Studies of the State University of New York at Buffalo and in the Division of Library Science of Southern Connecticut State College. These actions brought to 57 the number of library schools offering accredited programs.

International developments. By proclamation of the United Nations Educational, Scientific, and Cultural Organization (UNESCO), 1972 was the International Book Year; the theme of the IBY was "Books for All." According to "The Charter of the Book," adopted in connection with the IBY, "Books constitute one of the major defenses of peace because of their enormous influence in creating an intellectual climate of friendship and mutual understanding."

In another development, UNESCO censured the International Federation of Library Associations during 1972 for its failure to take a stand on the discriminatory racial policies practiced in South Africa and several other countries or territories, including Rhodesia and Portuguese Africa. The federation's response to its suspension from "consultative status" by UNESCO was a decision to sever relations with the South African Library Association if that body could not satisfy UNESCO's requirements on race relations. In the late spring of 1972, the South African Library Association withdrew from the federation, making it likely that the federation could satisfy UNESCO's requirements for membership and financial support. DAN BERGEN

LIBYA. Politics and government. Libyan head of state Colonel Muammar al-Qaddafi and Egyptian president Anwar Sadat jointly proclaimed in Benghazi on August 2 that their countries would be merged, subject to a final referendum on September 1, 1973. This latest step toward unity was clearly a personal triumph for Qaddafi, since the Egyptians had intended until the last moment to delay the move. Steps were immediately taken to assure reciprocal work and property rights for citizens of the two countries.

The move came, however, only after apparent dissension within the ruling Libyan military junta. After weeks of press speculation, Libya's premier, Major Abdul Salam Jallud, formed a new 17-man cabinet on July 16. Although Qaddafi nominally retained the presidency of the sovereign Revolutionary Command Council and the ministry of defense, he was not included in the cabinet and had temporarily disappeared from public view—for the second time since September 1971—amid rumors of a military coup. Despite his subsequent reemergence and personal triumph, it was not clear that all the officers, much less the general population, shared his enthusiasm for immediate merger with Egypt.

The regime appeared to be hardening. In November 1971, it sentenced former king Idris to death in absentia. In mid-January all the daily newspapers were suspended for six weeks while 29 journalists were tried for "corrupting public opinion" prior to the revolution of 1969. In April the junta banned all strikes, henceforth considered to be a "crime against the nation impeding its revolutionary march and development." Obligatory labor was also introduced, perhaps as a weapon to be held in reserve against students. Meanwhile, the military regime launched an Arab Socialist Union (ASU) open to all Libyans, "except 200 persons" of the *ancien régime*, according to Qaddafi. Its constituent congress was held at the end of March, and plans were subsequently prepared to merge it with its Egyptian sister organization.

Foreign affairs. Qaddafi told his ASU congress that he felt Libya would play a major role in "unifying the whole Arab nation." Even before his merger plans with Egypt fructified, Qaddafi spent a busy winter visiting Mauritania's Moktar Ould Daddah and Algeria's Houari Boumedienne. Because of Qaddafi's disagreement with Morocco's King Hassan II, Libya was not represented at the summit meeting of the Organization of African Unity held in Rabat in June. Qaddafi managed, however, to pull off a brilliant coup for the Arab cause in Uganda by receiving General Idi Amin and persuading him to oust the Israelis from his country and denounce them as imperialist spies—in return for Libya's diplomatic and financial support of the Ugandan, whom some Africans did not recognize as a legitimate head of state.

Although Jallud signed an agreement with the Soviet Union on March 4 for technical and economic assistance in the petroleum sector, Qaddafi took every public occasion to criticize Communism and Soviet policy on Islamic and Arab nationalist grounds. Apparently on the verge of nationalizing American oil interests in June because of continued U.S. support for Israel, Qaddafi temporarily refrained from doing so.

Economic developments. With billions of dollars of foreign reserves and annual oil revenues in excess of $1.5 billion annually, Libya prepared a $4 billion three-year plan for industrial and agricultural development. The plans were perhaps unrealistic, given the inadequacies of Libyan labor, but the regime was determined to use most of its oil revenues to develop other resources against the day, perhaps in 20 years, when the oil wells run dry. Libya also placed restrictions on current petroleum production.

Area and population. Area, 679,358 sq. mi. Pop. (est. 1971), 1,900,000. Principal cities (cocapitals; est. 1968): Tripoli, 250,000; Benghazi, 150,000.
Government. Libyan Arab Republic. Military regime. Pres. and def. min., Colonel Muammar al-Qaddafi; prem., Abdul Salam Jallud.
Finance. Monetary unit, Libyan dinar; LD1 = US$3.11. Budget (1971–1972): balanced at LD500 million, including LD300 million for development.
Trade (1970). Imports, LD198 million; exports, LD842 million. Principal export: crude petroleum. Major trading partners: West Germany, Italy, United Kingdom, United States.
Education (1969–1970). Enrollment: elementary, 315,106; preparatory, 37,815; secondary, 9,109; teacher training, 3,114; technical, 1,457.
Armed forces (est. 1971). 14,000 men, 4 missile patrol boats, 10 combat aircraft. CLEMENT HENRY MOORE

LOUISIANA. The environment. No major oil spills occurred in the Gulf of Mexico during the first nine months of the year, but lawsuits by environmentalists brought at least a temporary halt to the leasing of offshore tracts. The most publicized environmental issue was an experimental hunting season for alligators, set for September. Alligators, now on the federal list of endangered species, had become rare in Louisiana by the early 1960's. Since that time, however, stringent local protection and federal laws against the interstate transportation of alligator hides have led to a

ALL IN THE FAMILY. Louisiana governor Edwin Edwards hugs his wife, Elaine, after appointing her to fill the unexpired term of the late senator Allen Ellender (D). She promised to resign right after the November elections, giving her successor an edge in seniority.

rapid increase in their numbers. It was estimated that 250,-000 of the reptiles were located in Cameron Parish alone. Under the regulations of the new open season, 4,000 alligators more than 4 feet in length could be killed. The hides could be sold only after inspection and tagging for identification by state authorities.

Government. In an effort to avoid a court-ordered equalization of tax assessments, which vary greatly from parish to parish, the legislature repealed the state property tax. To replace the revenue lost, an increase in the severance tax on natural gas was enacted, despite the obstacle imposed by a constitutional requirement which states that a two-thirds majority is needed in both the senate and house of representatives in order to pass a tax increase.

The most important action of the legislature, however, was the call for a constitutional convention. The present Louisiana constitution is the longest in the United States and the second longest in the world, consisting of some 1,000 pages of text and index. The document contains duplications and contradictions and is so restrictive that it has required from 30 to 50 amendments at every general election. The voters forced the calling of a convention by rejecting almost all amendments offered for approval at the last two general elections.

Race relations. The climate of race relations in Louisiana has definitely improved in recent years. School integration is accepted, albeit grudgingly, and the presence of black people in formerly "white" restaurants, theaters, hotels, etc., is taken for granted. Politicians carefully but definitely seek the black vote.

The improvement in race relations was marred, however, by a confrontation between police and an alleged group of Black Muslims in Baton Rouge, in the course of which a white reporter was beaten into a permanent coma and two blacks and two policemen were killed by gunfire. A number of blacks were charged with murder, but no trials have yet been held.

Education. The election of a new state superintendent of education, Louis J. Michot, was expected to bring significant changes in the administration of public schools in Louisiana. As schools opened in the fall a significant decline was noted in the number of students attending nonpublic schools. Whether this decline was primarily in parochial enrollment, and therefore a reflection of economic factors, or in enrollment at the so-called "segregation academies," which would indicate growing acceptance of public-school integration, could not immediately be determined. Integration continued to advance. Faculties throughout Louisiana were almost wholly integrated. Neighborhood residence patterns preserved some nearly all-white and some all-black schools in the larger cities of the state, however.

Economics. The industrial development of Louisiana has been slowed by the economic recession of the past three years. In the industrial areas of Baton Rouge, New Orleans, and Lake Charles, unemployment was almost twice the national average. Most of the unemployed were young adults with no more than a high school education, including many blacks, but there were substantial numbers of skilled workers who were unemployed or who accepted employment that paid less than they would have earned in their specialty. For the first time in recent history, it was difficult for college graduates with teaching certificates to find positions.

Despite the high rate of unemployment, however, the state was generally prosperous. Cotton, sugar, rice, and soybean prices were high and were expected to remain so through the harvest season. Growers of beef cattle had one of their best years in the past decade. Persons employed in service industries, from television repairmen to doctors of medicine, prospered. The market for houses costing $20,000 and more was excellent, despite high interest rates. Multiple-unit housing with rental value of from $100 to $400 per unit was being built at a rapid pace. In contrast to the previous two years, Louisiana consumers showed little reluctance to go into debt for automobiles and major home appliances.

For election results and campaign highlights, see the special supplement ELECTION '72.

Area and population. Area, 48,523 sq. mi. Pop. (1970), 3,643,-180. Principal cities: Baton Rouge (cap.), 165,963; New Orleans, 593,471; Shreveport, 182,064.
Government. Gov., Edwin W. Edwards; lt. gov., James H. Fitzmorris, Jr.; secy. of state, Wade O. Martin, Jr.; atty. gen., William J. Guste, Jr.; cont., Roy R. Theriot; treas., Mary Evelyn Parker. All are Democrats. Legislature: senate, 39 D; house, 101 D, 4 R.
Finance (fiscal 1971). Revenue, $1,821,171,240; expenditure, $1,821,438,837.
Education (1970–1971). Public elementary schools, 1,191; enrollment, 637,290; teachers, 21,643. Public secondary schools, 520; enrollment, 233,326; teachers, 17,296. Private and parochial schools, 459; enrollment, 165,678; teachers, 7,592. Institutions of higher education (1971–1972), 12; enrollment, 103,479.

JOE GRAY TAYLOR

LUXEMBOURG. Politics and government. The Grand Duchy of Luxembourg passed a year of continued prosperity and political stability. The opposition Socialist Party, being badly split, posed no major threat to the Christian Social-Liberal coalition cabinet of Catholic premier Pierre Werner.

Werner was successful in promoting his master plan for financial and economic union among the member states of the Common Market when, during the international monetary crisis, the six members decided to maintain the narrow fluctuation margins between their national currencies and so act as a bloc toward the rest of the world. This, coupled

with the beginning of a European Reserve Fund, indicated that the plan, despite its sweeping ambition, was on the way to being realized.

Economic developments. Luxembourg shared its Belgian and Dutch partners' preoccupations about rising prices, but inflation was kept well in hand. Since tax receipts exceeded expectations, Werner, doubling as finance minister, was able to introduce a record 1973 budget of 17 billion francs ($340 million) without increasing the overall tax burden. Within the framework of the Benelux excise agreement, taxes on motor fuel, tobacco, and cigarettes were due to be increased on January 1, 1973, but the government was able to announce an end to taxation on radio and television sets in the coming year.

In September, Werner announced the resignation from his cabinet of Mrs. Madeleine Frieden, the minister for public health. Last year, Mrs. Frieden, a ranking member of the Christian Social (Catholic) Party, was reported by a Socialist opposition newspaper to have attended a picnic where at least two men had appeared in the nude. In deeply conservative Luxembourg this caused a nationwide scandal, which prompted the minister to defend herself with a writ for libel. The court case was complicated by the fact that a principal witness, a young man, was convicted in the high court for perjury in another lawsuit. In view of her controversial position, Mrs. Frieden then decided to resign from the government.

Area and population. Area, 998 sq. mi. Pop. (1970), 339,848.
Government. Constitutional monarchy. Unicameral Parliament elected every five years. Head of state, Grand Duke Jean; prime min., Pierre Werner.
Finance. Monetary unit, Luxembourg franc (tied to Belgian franc); LF1 = US$0.02. Budget (proposed for 1973): balanced at US$340 million. Gross national product: US$1.15 billion.
Trade (Belgium-Luxembourg Economic Union, 1971). Exports, US$13.4 billion; imports, US$13.9 billion. Principal export, steel.
Education. Enrollment: elementary schools, 35,000; secondary schools, 19,100.
HENRI SCHOUP

MAGAZINES. One problem continued to overshadow all others for magazine publishers in 1972: the proposed 142 percent increase in postal rates over five years, starting May 1971. Publishers contended that the increase jeopardized the very existence of magazines. The Magazine Publishers Association testified against it and sought legislative support for reductions; some members used editorials and advertisements to take their case to the readers. Andrew Heiskell, chairman of Time Inc., told congressmen that the five-year increase would cost magazines an additional $130 million.

One of the few publishers dissenting over effects of the increase was James Milholland, Jr., chairman of American Business Press, an association of trade and technical publishers. Milholland said he did not believe the increases now scheduled would put magazines out of business. But he did criticize the quality of postal service.

In June the Postal Rate Commission recommended a reduction in the rate increases—from 142 to 127 percent—which would allegedly save publishers more than $21 million.

Some publishers, hoping to bypass the postal service, expanded their experiments with private delivery of copies to subscribers. Tests were under way in Florida, Oklahoma, and Maryland. In Barrington, R.I., publishers of 12 magazines—among them *Time, Life, Sports Illustrated,* and *True*—tested the feasibility of having milkmen deliver copies.

Advertising. As some publishers had predicted, 1972 was a better year for advertising than 1971, when gross advertising revenues of general magazines amounted to $1,251,-388,304 on a page volume of 78,275. A fair estimate was that 1972 revenues would improve by about 5 percent; they were $632,560,157, for the first six months. The largest gains were among magazines appealing to special interests or clearly defined audiences. The Federal Trade Commission reported that magazines were the greatest beneficiaries when

cigarette advertisers were forced out of the broadcast media. Their revenue from cigarette advertising jumped from $38.6 million in 1970 to $98.3 million in 1971.

Trade and technical publishers, whose advertising volume in 1971 had slipped by 2.7 percent to $813.8 million, were also optimistic. Surveyed at midyear by American Business Press, 88 of them predicted a "strong recovery," with jumps of 9.4 percent in net revenues and 4.9 percent in pages. However, the 100 leading technical publications showed a gain of only 3.7 percent in gross advertising revenues in the first half of 1972, according to Bernard Gallagher's industry newsletter.

Old leaders. In February, *Reader's Digest* observed its 50th anniversary with a special issue. DeWitt Wallace and his wife, Lila, started the monthly in a Greenwich Village basement in 1922 on a borrowed $1,300 and $5,000 from subscribers. The magazine's gross annual income from all sources is now more than $300 million, and its paid U.S. circulation exceeds 18 million.

Although *Life* continued to have financial problems, Time Inc. spokesmen denied that the company planned to kill the weekly, and they predicted that *Life* would have its best year since 1968. Time Inc. did decide to decrease *Life's* circulation from 8 million to 5.5 million.

Awards. Winners of the 1972 National Magazine Awards, administered by the Columbia University Graduate School of Journalism, were *Architectural Record,* specialized journalism; *Atlantic,* reportorial excellence; *Esquire,* visual excellence; *Mademoiselle,* fiction; and *Philadelphia,* public service.

New magazines. Norman Cousins, who had headed *Saturday Review* for 31 years, left in late 1971 after policy disagreements with its new owners. A survey convinced

EROS IN CHAINS. Ralph Ginzburg, publisher of the short-lived journal *Eros,* went to prison in February after the U.S. Supreme Court upheld his 1963 conviction for sending obscene matter through the mails. He was out on parole several months later.

WIDE WORLD

him there was a market for a new magazine similar to what *Saturday Review* had been, and in June 1972, joined by several key staff members of *SR*, Cousins launched *World*. The new journal aimed at being "international in scope, concerned with the life of the mind, the principal problems of our time: war and peace, environment, the squandering of human resources." Meanwhile, the new owners of *Saturday Review* converted its supplements into four separate monthly magazines, covering the arts, education, science, and society. Readers could subscribe to the publications separately or as a group.

A number of women active in the feminist movement, including the journalist Gloria Steinem, started *Ms.*, a monthly intended to be both a vehicle for free expression by feminists and a means of communicating with women outside the movement. A 44-page preview appeared as a special feature in *New York* in December 1971. An independent prototype issue came out in January, and the first regularly scheduled issue (dated July) reached the newsstands in early summer.

In October, Time Inc. brought out *Money*, its first new magazine in 18 years. The monthly was intended "to introduce people to better ways of spending their money." Cowles Communications, Inc., which had published *Look*, reentered magazine publishing with *On Arrival*, for airline passengers. *Cosmopolitan* inaugurated a British edition with an initial circulation of 200,000. *Playboy* introduced its first foreign-language edition in Europe. In partnership with a French publisher, Playboy Enterprises, Inc., also brought out *Oui* (written in English) for "the man of the world."

Other new magazines included *Sweet 'n Low* (for weight watchers), *Encore* (for blacks), *PV4* (for pickup, van, and four-wheel-drive enthusiasts), *A.D.* (a joint venture of *Presbyterian Life* and *United Church Herald*), *Doctors' Finances*, *Medical Financial Adviser*, *Epicure*, *Caribbean Sunrise*, *Value Travel*, *Folio*, *Lifestyle*, *Budget Recipes*, *Current Audio*, and *Music Retailer*. Two suspended magazines—*Rod & Custom* and *Pools and Gardens*—were revived.

THEODORE PETERSON

MAINE. Industry and environment. Controversy over industrial development versus conservation continued, with the focus on oil and nuclear power. State residents were jolted when 100,000 gallons of industrial fuel oil spilled into Casco Bay from a gash in a tanker hull, fouling beaches and closing clam flats. A state task force proposed that heavy industry be limited to two coastal areas and that only Portland, already the east coast's second-busiest oil port, be the site of oil refineries. But it said that oil development should be barred until the probe of the Casco Bay oil spill was completed and steps taken to prevent a repetition. The task force also recommended a state coastal industry development corporation to manage the heavy-industry zones. Meanwhile, the state supreme court studied an appeal for the approval of an oil refinery in the mid-coast section, and army engineers continued their study of the Maine coast for deepwater port development.

Conservationists raised a pollution alarm against a plant owned by the Maine Yankee Atomic Power Company. Hearings on environmental dangers continued after the Atomic Energy Commission authorized the plant's operation at three-quarter capacity and the state imposed curbs on the discharge of heated water.

Tourism. The state launched a 15-month study of the multimillion dollar tourist industry to gauge its future and its effects on the state. A controversial survey showed business off for the first time since the summer of 1942, but the state later came up with figures showing a gain of 11 percent despite bad beach weather.

Legislation. A 34-day special session of the legislature was marked by extensive reorganization of state government, meeting most of the governor's proposals to consolidate more than 250 state agencies into 13 departments. Adult rights

were granted to 18-year-olds. Legislators continued to probe the collapse of the embryonic sugar beet industry after appropriating $4 million to help pay off losses.

Marine developments. With unemployment over 8 percent in the state at one point, both of the big shipyards got new work—merchant ships for the private Bath Iron Works and submarines for the Navy's Portsmouth yard in Kittery. The state fisheries research head warned, amid soaring prices, that the lobster industry was periled by overfishing. Toxic "red tide" plankton shut clam flats temporarily.

For election results and campaign highlights, see the special supplement ELECTION '72.

Area and population. Area, 33,215 sq. mi. Pop. (1970), 992,048. Principal cities (1970 census): Augusta (cap.), 21,945; Portland, 65,116; Lewiston, 41,779; Bangor, 33,168.

Government. Governor, Kenneth M. Curtis (D); secy. of state, Joseph T. Edgar (R); atty. gen., James S. Erwin (R). Legislature: senate, 18 R, 12 D; house, 79 R, 71 D.

Finance (year ending June 30, 1972). Revenue, $478,264,702; expenditure, $482,705,878; cash on hand, $17,590,649.

Education (1971–1972). Elementary schools, 779; enrollment, 177,555; teachers, 7,930. Secondary schools, 117; enrollment, 68,854; teachers, 4,472. Private and parochial schools, 96; enrollment, 18,442; teachers, 983.

JOHN K. MURPHY

MALAGASY REPUBLIC. Government and politics. On May 18, after several weeks of disorders and clashes with students and workers, President Philibert Tsiranana dissolved his government, which had led the country since independence in 1960, and relinquished control to General Gabriel Ramanantsoa, the army chief of staff. The 66-year-old Ramanantsoa, a graduate of France's St. Cyr Military Academy, is very popular with the people. Pledging "honesty and austerity," the new leader quickly formed a cabinet that reflected a balance between the Merinas of the inland plateau and the coastal peoples. The key Ministry of the Interior went to his close friend, Lieutenant Colonel Richard Ratsimandrava.

Tsiranana's troubles had been building up for some time, with a great deal of unrest in rural areas. His policies of rapprochement with South Africa and continued economic dependence on France also alienated many of the country's youth. The new government will have to deal with many problems, not the least of which is the assimilation of over 7 million persons representing different languages, cultures, and religions.

Economic development. Most of the island's people are still engaged in subsistence agriculture, especially in rice growing and cattle raising. There is no significant industry, although increased production of coffee, cloves, vanilla, rice, and sugar have helped push Malagasy exports to record levels in recent years. The Tsiranana government had hoped that South African investment would spur the development of a tourist industry, but this seems doubtful. The new government has downgraded Malagasy–South African relations, another serious setback for South Africa's "outward policy." Malagasy's economy should improve when a shipyard and dry dock at Baie de Narinda are completed; an international consortium became interested in establishing a port in Malagasy after the Suez Canal was closed in 1967 and ships were rerouted around Africa.

Area and population. Area, 226,658 sq. mi. Pop. (est. 1971), 7,100,000. Principal cities (est. 1970): Tananarive (cap.), 322,000; Tamatave, 50,500; Majunga, 43,500.

Government. Republic with bicameral legislature, now suspended.

Finance. Monetary unit, Malagasy franc; FMG1 = US$0.0041. Budget (est. 1970): revenue, $152 million; expenditures, $172 million, including $40 million capital expenditure.

Trade (1968). Exports, $114,432,000; imports, $168,096,000. Chief exports: coffee, sugar, sisal, rice, textiles, mineral products. Chief imports: metalware, vehicles, chemicals. Major trading partners: France, United States, Common Market.

Education (1968–1969). Enrollment: primary, 815,307; secondary, 24,672; technical, 59,091; University of Madagascar, 3,500.

Armed forces (1968). Army, 4,000; air force, 400.

CHRISTIAN P. POTHOLM

THINGS WERE LOOKING UP for reform forces in the Malagasy Republic after student rioting induced the unpopular President Tsiranana to relinquish power to General Gabriel Ramanantsoa, here shown waving to cheering crowds in the republic's capital city of Tananarive.

MALAWI. Foreign relations. The journey of South African president J. J. Fouché to the capital of Malawi this year marked a continuing progress in friendly relations between the white-ruled Union of South Africa and its black-governed neighbor to the north. Fouché's week-long visit in March was his first visit to a black African head of state and climaxed a series of diplomatic interchanges between the two countries; Malawi president Hastings Kamuzu Banda had visited South Africa the previous year, and South African prime minister Balthazar Johannes Vorster came to Malawi in 1970. Speaking at a banquet shortly before the end of his visit, Fouché called for all African nations to join together in fighting poverty, ignorance, and disease, which he termed "the real enemies of Africa." The two countries signed an extradition treaty, and arrangements were made for the issuing of passports to allow South Africans to visit Malawi.

Perhaps more significant, South Africa, in December 1971, sold nine armored cars and four planeloads of arms to the Malawi government. Although President Banda was inclined to underplay the matter, his government was clearly nervous about the activities of the Front for the Liberation of Mozambique (Frelimo), which stepped up its attacks within Mozambique, especially in the area of the Cabora Bassa construction site, not far from Malawi's border.

On July 31, President Banda announced that the British government had agreed to grant $2.5 million toward the construction of an army barracks for the Malawi Rifles, which would enable Malawi to carry out plans for doubling the strength of its army.

Meanwhile, Malawi was the only member state to absent itself from the 19th session of the Organization of African Unity Council of Ministers, held June 5–11 in Morocco.

Domestic affairs. The nation's economy appeared to be on the upswing. According to a July estimate, the year's tobacco crop was expected to yield 68 million pounds, up 17 percent from 1971, as trade restrictions against Rhodesia continued to give Malawi an export marketing advantage. The Sugar Corporation of Malawi announced

expansion of its facilities to prepare for sugar exportation to the United States, slated to begin in 1973. Meanwhile, the United Nations International Development Association granted a credit of $6.6 million to support a rural development project, expected to benefit 5,000 farmers in the southwest by improving agricultural production.

Area and population. Area, 45,747 sq. mi. Pop. (est. 1971), 4,600,000. Principal cities (1966): Zomba (cap.), 19,666; Blantyre-Limbe, 109,461; Lilongwe, 19,425.
Government. Republic with unicameral legislature; member of the Commonwealth of Nations. Pres., Hastings Kamuzu Banda.
Finance. Monetary unit, kwacha; 1 kwacha = US$1.19. Budget (est. 1972–1973, in kwachas): revenue, K40.5 million; expenditure, K41.8 million (deficit to be met by British aid).
Trade (1971). Exports, $71 million; imports, $108 million.

WILLIAM A. McGEVERAN, JR.

MALAYSIA. Politics and government. The year was marked by the continued strengthening of the Malay-dominated Alliance Party and its racially based component parties, the Malaysian Chinese Association (MCA) and the Malayan Indian Congress (MIC). This was accompanied by a breakdown in the structure and political power of the various opposition parties. The appointment early this year of Lim Keng Yaik of the MCA as minister with special functions was symptomatic of efforts by the MCA and the United Malays National Organization (UMNO), the third component party of the Alliance, to encourage the younger and more dynamic leaders in the MCA. Lim had gained grassroots support among Malaysian Chinese by promising aid and permanent land titles to the 500,000 mostly Chinese people who had been living in resettlement villages since a state of emergency was declared during the terrorist campaign by Communists in 1948. In June the Alliance announced that Dato S. P. Seenivasagam, leader of the opposition People's Progressive Party, had agreed to assume the Alliance's "Indian seat" in the Perak state cabinet, which had been left vacant when the MIC incumbent was defeated in an election. At the end of the year talks were also being held between the Malay opposition Partai Islam (PI) and UMNO

369

leaders, exploring the possibility of a coalition between the two parties that would bring Kelantan state (controlled by the PI for more than a decade) back into the Alliance fold. Except for the PI, political opposition to the Alliance is now almost nonexistent.

Strong leadership was provided by Alliance prime minister Tun Abdul Razak and his deputy, Tun Ismail, as well as by Tan Sri Ghazali Shafie, minister with special functions and minister of information. Shafie is generally considered the eventual successor to Razak and is currently the moving force behind attempts to assure that the "racial balancing" inherent in the provisions of the government's new economic policy is carried out.

Economic developments. Despite record lows in prices for Malaysia's two major exports, rubber and tin, unemployment declined slightly from 8 percent to 7.8 percent last year, and by the middle of this year industrial employment had increased by almost 100,000 jobs since January. Half of these jobs were new and resulted from government encouragement of foreign investment, particularly in the burgeoning and nonpolluting electronics field.

The new economic policy (NEP), announced in the middle of last year, added a new element to the government's program for economic expansion. As well as providing jobs for the poor of all races, the NEP seeks to ensure that Malays eventually control the management sectors of the economy in proportion to their numbers among the population (about 48 percent). The increase in industrial employment was at the expense of the NEP goal, however, and the growth rate for control by Malays last year fell short by almost 2 percent of the NEP-projected rate of 6 percent. Management and productivity training centers run by the government have found it difficult to attract more than 15 to 20 percent Malays in their classes. Malaysian-owned as well as foreign firms have been unable to find trained Malays to fill the quotas called for in their contractual agreements with the Malaysian government.

Malaysia continued to hold inflation down to a maximum of 1 percent last year, a rare achievement among developing nations. Finance Minister Tun Tan Siew presented the usual balanced budget estimate to Parliament this year, avoiding deficit financing through the imposition of a 5 percent sales tax on all but basic necessities and certain raw materials. Although earnings from the export of timber, rubber, and tin were down last year, palm oil sales increased by 40 percent, and petroleum exports more than doubled. The government moved to establish a national oil corporation, modeled along the lines of Indonesia's Pertamina, to deal with foreign oil companies engaged in exploration and drilling in both East and West Malaysia.

Foreign affairs. Malaysia played a leading role as a member of the Association of Southeast Asian Nations (ASEAN) in attempting to assure the neutralization of Southeast Asia. In this effort government leaders received strong support from Indonesia. Both countries would like to see the disappearance of big-power rivalry in this area of the world.

After some 20 years of sporadic negotiations Malaysia and Indonesia also agreed to standardize spelling and grammar of the Malay and Indonesian languages. The two spoken languages are very similar, but Malay was influenced by English spelling, while Indonesian was influenced by Dutch spelling. Beginning next year all books will be written in the new simplified spelling system. Government agencies and some newspapers in both countries have already made the change.

Indonesia and Malaysia were in basic agreement over the thorny issue of the use of the Straits of Malacca by ever-larger (mainly Japanese and Russian) tankers and other shipping. Late last year the two countries agreed that the straits are not an international waterway. While recognizing the right of "innocent passage" for the approximately 100 vessels using the straits per day, the two countries jointly

claimed the right to close the passageway to any ship posing a threat to their national interests. Reaction from Japan, the Soviet Union, and the United States was basically unfavorable, and once again there was talk of building a pipeline or a canal across the narrow Kra Isthmus in Thailand.

Relations between Malaysia and Singapore were highlighted by the first official visit of Singapore's prime minister, Lee Kuan Yew, to Kuala Lumpur since the expulsion of Singapore from Malaysia in 1965. The two governments could not come to an agreement on Singapore's intention to use the initials MSA (formerly Malaysia-Singapore Airlines) in the name of its airline, even though the joint Malaysian-Singapore company had divided. It seemed that the matter would have to be resolved in the courts, but in July Singapore suddenly announced that it would forgo the publicity advantages of using the old initials and name its national flag carrier Singapore Airlines (SIA). The new Malaysian airline had already been named Malaysian Airlines System (MAS).

Area and population. Area, 128,430 sq. mi. Pop. (1971), 10,-650,000.
Government. Federated constitutional monarchy. Head of state, Sultan Abdul Halim Mu'adzam Shah; prime min., Tun Abdul Razak.
Finance. Monetary unit, Malaysia dollar; M$1 = US$0.3625. Budget (1972): revenue, US$900 million; expenditure, US$860 million.
Trade (1971). Imports, US$1.5 billion; exports, US$1.7 billion. Chief exports: rubber, tin, palm oil, petroleum; chief imports: food, manufactured goods, chemicals, fuels. Main trading partners: Singapore, Japan, Great Britain, United States.
Education (1969). Enrollment: primary, 1,579,812; secondary, 560,654; higher education, 13,412.
Armed forces (1971). Army, 43,000; navy, 3,000; air force, 4,000 men and 30 combat aircraft.   NANCY L. SNIDER

MALDIVES, REPUBLIC OF. Politics and government.
On August 1 the office of prime minister was revived and Ahmad Zaki was named to the post.

Foreign affairs. International fishing agreements were made for the direct sale of fresh fish within the archipelago to the government of Ceylon and to the Marubeni Corporation of Japan. Hitherto fish has always been exported to Ceylon in dried form. Although the government exercises a monopoly over all export trade, permission was also given for private export under license of certain classes of fish.

Queen Elizabeth II paid a state visit to Male in March and also visited the British air-staging post at Gan in Addu Atoll, activities which indicate a lessening of the ill feeling which arose between Great Britain and the Maldives about Gan in the early 1960's.

Diplomatic relations were established with the People's Republic of China.

Area and population. Area, 115 sq. mi. Pop. (1971), 114,469. Male (cap.), 15,129.
Government. Republic. Pres., Ibrahim Nasir; prime min., Ahmad Zaki.
Finance. Monetary unit, Maldivian rupee; 1 rupee = US $0.23.
Trade (1970). Imports, 11.8 million rupees; exports, 22.9 million rupees. Principal exports: dried fish, copra. Principal trading partner: Ceylon.   CHRISTOPHER B. REYNOLDS

MALI, REPUBLIC OF. Foreign affairs.
In April, Colonel Moussa Traoré became the first president of Mali ever to pay a state visit to France. Conferences with French officials centered on economic cooperation. France agreed to help fund Mali's rail transport system and construction of the Selengué Dam on a tributary of the Niger River. On outstanding political issues, Traoré denied that Mali had any intention of joining the African, Malagasy, and Mauritian Common Organization and promised that his government would pursue a policy of "dynamic nonalignment." No decision was made on whether Mali would rejoin the West African Currency Union. Before leaving, Traoré invited French president Georges Pompidou to visit Bamako.

Though remaining aloof from OCAMM, Mali did participate in two moves toward West African unity. On March

11, Mali, Mauritania, and Senegal established the Organization for the Development of the Sénégal River. That same meeting completed arrangements for the dissolution of the Organization of Sénégal River States, which had broken up in November 1971. Not quite three months later, Mali joined Ivory Coast, Dahomey, Mauritania, Niger, Senegal, and Upper Volta in founding the West African Economic Community.

In other diplomatic developments, President Léopold-Sédar Senghor of Senegal visited Mali in December. In a joint communiqué, Senghor and Traoré asserted that bilateral relations between the two countries were and would continue to be excellent.

Internal affairs. Four persons, including former premier Yoro Diakite, were convicted by Mali's State Security Court for their parts in an attempted coup on March 9, 1971. Diakite was sentenced to forced labor for life; penalties for the other three ranged from forced labor for life to five years' imprisonment.

Economy. Despite substantial improvements in agricultural output, Mali remained reliant on foreign aid. Attempts to find gold or oil deposits in the country have so far been unsuccessful.

Area and population. Area, 478,766 sq. mi. Pop. (est. 1971), 5.2 million. Bamako (cap.; est. 1969), 200,000.
Government. Republic, under the Military Committee of National Liberation, headed by Colonel Moussa Traoré.
Finance. Monetary unit, Mali franc; MF1 = US$0.00205. Budget (1971): expenditure, 23.3 billion Mali francs; income, 20.6 billion Mali francs.
Trade (1970). Imports, 19.9 billion Mali francs; exports, 24.9 billion Mali francs. Principal trading partners: France, Soviet Union.

Education (1969–1970). Enrollments: elementary, 210,954; secondary general, 2,923; normal and technical, 2,703.
Armed forces (est. 1972). Army, 3,000.

MALTA. Foreign affairs. A dramatic policy of diplomatic brinkmanship, relentlessly pursued by Labor Party prime minister Dom Mintoff, succeeded in trebling the annual rental payments to be received by Malta for the use of its military base facilities. Shortly after his election last year Prime Minister Mintoff denounced the ten-year treaty of aid and defense that Malta had signed with Great Britain in 1964. Instead of the £5 million paid yearly to Malta under the old treaty, he demanded that Britain pay an annual rental of £18 million (with an immediate down payment of £10 million) or evacuate its forces from the island by the end of March. Tortuous negotiations, which were frequently broken off, followed. Mintoff threatened to pursue a non-aligned foreign policy and to seek alternate sources of aid from Libya and the Soviet Union. Britain refused to offer more in annual rent than the £9.5 million proposed in September 1971 and, in the absence of an agreement, families of British servicemen were evacuated by January 15. As the withdrawal progressed, however, the specter of Soviet ships and planes operating out of Malta increasingly alarmed Britain's NATO allies. Offers of additional funds from the United States, Italy, and NATO raised the Western rental package to a level acceptable to Prime Minister Mintoff, who signed a new, seven-year defense agreement in London on March 26. At the time of the agreement, Britain had removed 50,000 tons of equipment and all but 30 of 3,500 servicemen from Malta.

BEAMING MALTESE PREMIER Dom Mintoff (seated, left) orders a toast after bringing off an agreement to renew Great Britain's lease for base facilities on the island at nearly triple the former annual rent. The agreement climaxed nine months of tortuous bargaining.

Terms of agreement. The new defense agreement provides Malta with an annual rental payment of £14 million from Britain and NATO and a lump sum payment of £2.5 million from Italy, in addition to £7 million in bilateral aid over seven years from other NATO countries and undisclosed amounts of aid from the United States in return for berthing privileges for the U.S. Sixth Fleet. Britain will maintain 3,000 troops on the island and will guarantee employment to a minimum of 3,600 Maltese defense workers. Most important to the NATO allies, Malta will deny the use of its military facilities to Warsaw Pact countries.

Economic developments. The striking success of Mintoff's flamboyant diplomacy helped obscure the real costs of the negotiating period. Unemployment, which stood at 5,000 when Mintoff took office last year, reached 8,000 by September, largely as a result of the rundown of British forces. The anti-British campaign mounted in the spring, coupled with the Labor Party government's termination of special tax advantages to foreign investors and retired Englishmen, contributed to a general economic slump.

Area and population. Area, 122 sq. mi. Pop. (est. 1970), 326,-000. Principal cities: Valletta (cap.), 15,547; Sliema, 21,983.
Government. Self-governing democracy with unicameral parliamentary legislature; member of the Commonwealth of Nations. Prime min., Dom Mintoff.
Finance. Monetary unit, Maltese pound; M£1 = US$2.50.
Education (1970). Elementary schools, 111; enrollment, 44,571. Secondary and vocational schools, 11; enrollment, 9,170. Institutions of higher learning, 2; enrollment, 1,054 regular students. Private schools, 80; enrollment, 17,394. VICTOR R. SWENSON

MANITOBA. Politics and government. Although the general political situation remained relatively calm this year, there were periodic rumblings of disenchantment among rival political parties and among the general public over several major programs and policies sponsored by the New Democratic government. Administrative delays in the servicing of claims under the government's new and compulsory automobile insurance plan caused considerable frustration and heated editorial comment in the media.

The placing in receivership of the large Churchill Forest Industries complex, a multimillion-dollar pulp, paper, and lumber operation financed largely by government funds, led to the appointment of a royal commission to investigate the disposition of capital and operating funds advanced by the government through the Manitoba Development Corporation. Concern over the apparent unsecured advance of almost $100 million of public money was reflected in public outcries and legislative debate.

Citizens and politicians were also embroiled in heated discussion over Manitoba Hydro's decision to erect control structures on Lake Winnipeg as part of the Nelson River power development scheme. Some hydroelectric engineers, water control experts, and ecologists expressed grave doubts as to the economic and ecological validity of the plan.

The prospect that the New Democratic government would introduce legislation seeking public financial support for private schools caused considerable alarm in many quarters, and when Premier Edward Schreyer was reported to have said that he would resign if the measure were not passed, widespread speculation arose as to the future prospects for survival of the New Democratic government. This contentious issue was, however, put to rest, at least for the time being, when a substitute bill asking only for the appointment of a commission to study the subject was defeated in the legislature.

A by-election in the Winnipeg constituency of Wolesley was won by the Liberal Party leader, Izzy Asper, who had not previously held a seat in the legislature. His seat was formerly held by the Conservative Party. There were two defections from the New Democratic cabinet during the year. Joseph Borowski, minister of highways, resigned his cabinet portfolio in protest over his party's liberal stand on legalized abortions and movie censorship. During the 1972 session of the legislature he sat as an independent member. Sidney Green, minister of mines, resources, and environmental management and minister of urban affairs, resigned from the cabinet in March over the issue of government aid to private schools. However, at the invitation of the premier, he later returned to the cabinet, assuming his two former portfolios and retaining his seniority. The premier also retained his office and party leadership despite the defeat of his personally sponsored measure for aid to private schools.

Legislation. The New Democratic Party, with a clear majority over the combined strength of the opposition parties, was able to press forward its social legislation and pass all major measures as introduced in the speech from the throne. The spending estimates for the 1972–1973 fiscal year were passed by the fourth session of the 29th legislature in the total amount of $575.8 million, up $59.2 million over the 1971–1972 estimates. More than two-thirds of the proposed spending, $388.2 million, was earmarked for health, social development, and education. Major increases in expenditure were in the areas of income security, social allowances, child maintenance, and municipal assistance to cover local health and welfare charges. The department of youth and education, with $129.5 million, showed an increase of $13.5 million over the previous year, $11.6 million of which was for increased grants to local school divisions. The increase went to implement the government's decision to underwrite 75 percent of the cost of education, 5 percent more than in the previous year, with corresponding tax savings to property owners.

Economic developments. The government's official assessment of this year's fiscal and economic position was worded as "basically healthy" in the speech from the throne. The gross income of Manitobans in 1971 exceeded $4 billion for the first time, and prospects for 1972 were estimated at 10 percent above this figure. The unemployment rate in the province was considerably below the national level, although it was by no means satisfactory. Public and private capital investments were expected to increase 12 percent, a major stimulus being given by the government's program of borrowing $393.5 million for capital purposes in an expansionary effort aimed at stimulating the economy, a move which would increase the provincial public debt by more than 60 percent.

Area and population. Area, 251,000 sq. mi. Pop. (est. 1972), 993,000. Winnipeg (cap.), 537,000.
Government. Lt. gov., William J. McKeag; prem., Edward R. Schreyer. Legislature; New Democrats, 30; Progressive Conservatives, 20; Liberals, 4; independents, 2; Social Credit, 1.
Finance. Budget (est. 1972–1973): revenue, Can$573 million; expenditure, Can$575.8 million.
Production (est. 1972). Minerals, $250 million; forest products, $30 million; crude oil, $15 million; wild and domestic furs, $6 million; fisheries, $5.5 million; manufacturing (gross value), $1.4 billion.
Agriculture. Farm cash receipts (est. 1972), $360 million; gross farm production, $480 million; number of farms, 37,800.
Education (1972). Elementary school enrollment, 187,460; teachers, 7,341. Secondary school enrollment, 66,780; teachers, 3,801; postsecondary school enrollment (universities and community colleges), 28,765. HENRY FRANCIS HALL

MARYLAND. Legislature. In March, during the legislature's regular 90-day session, Governor Marvin Mandel beat the powerful gun lobby and the even stronger highway lobby to win two highly controversial measures. The first, an emergency bill to control handguns on the street, authorizes policemen to stop and frisk any person suspected of illegally carrying a pistol without a permit. The second bill allows construction of a mass transit subway for metropolitan Baltimore to begin in 1974. For the first time the jealously guarded highway trust fund accumulating from gasoline taxes was freed for transportation needs other than road building. Another innovative and controversial program

was adopted which established a public insurance company to provide coverage for owners of cars who have difficulty gaining liability protection from private carriers.

Economics. All was not success for the administration, however. The governor's attempts to legalize horse betting away from racetracks failed, despite obvious needs for new revenue sources. Since becoming governor in 1969, Mandel has raised state spending from $1.34 billion to the current $2.15 billion. Conversely, he has lifted sales and nuisance taxes only slightly to make up the difference, relying mostly on normal economic growth to produce more revenue. He expects Congress to enact some form of revenue sharing, thus providing heavy doses of federal aid. Meanwhile, some financial and social kinks were beginning to show.

Tropical storm Agnes destroyed many businesses and homes, especially along Maryland's streams and rivers, in mid-June. Property owners without insurance relied on federal emergency aid for recovery. State officials, reacting to appeals to clamp down on "cheaters and abusers," refused cost-of-living increases for welfare recipients. And the state's correctional system, plagued with riots and disruptions in 1971–1972, needs more money to implement reforms.

Education and culture. The complex state formula for funding local public school systems is likely to be challenged in a court suit contending inequitable distribution. A legislative authorization passed in 1971 to grant private school aid was petitioned to referendum on the November ballot. And the local bicentennial commission, responsible for coordinating Maryland's role in the nation's 200th anniversary celebration, was just beginning to function at the end of summer after a poor start.

Municipal developments. Baltimore city's massive redevelopment of its inner harbor continued to move. The latest addition would be a sports palace to accommodate the baseball Orioles and football Colts. This enterprise has the optimistic backing of officials and private business interests.

For election results and campaign highlights, see the special supplement ELECTION '72.

Area and population. Area, 10,577 sq. mi. Pop. (1970), 3,922,399. Principal cities: Annapolis (cap.), 33,000; Baltimore, 905,759.
Government. Gov., Marvin Mandel (D); lt. gov., Blair Lee III (D); atty. gen., Francis B. Burch (D); cont., Louis L. Goldstein (D). Legislature: senate, 33 D, 10 R; house, 120 D, 22 R.
Finance. Budget (appropriated), $2,151,856,239; revenue (est.), $1,794,200,000; federal aid, $357,656,000. Major sources of revenue: graduated income tax and sales tax. Major spending programs: education, health and welfare, transportation.
Education (fall 1970). Public school enrollment: elementary, 522,173; secondary, 391,023. Nonpublic school enrollment: elementary, 96,492; secondary, 31,549.

JEROME KELLY

MASSACHUSETTS. Government.

Pressing economic problems—dramatized by the state's first $2 billion budget—deterred the legislature from enacting many new programs and instead caused it to experiment with an unusual way of budget-cutting. The Democratic-dominated body put 3 percent of the budget in escrow, to be used only in emergencies and then only with legislative approval. The brunt of the cutback fell on the accounts that pay welfare and medical assistance benefits. With welfare accounting for more than 40 percent of the state budget, Governor Francis W. Sargent, a Republican, announced that monthly welfare checks would have to be cut by as much as $12. A month-long campaign by welfare groups forced Sargent to rescind the cuts.

Most of the innovative legislation passed had low price tags. An omnibus prison reform bill, whisked through in the final days of the session, authorizes the creation of a series of community halfway houses and aims to aid rehabilitation by setting up work-release programs and modernizing prison industries to substitute computer and electronic skills for flag-stitching and broom-making. A piece of progressive legislation gave tenants the right to make essential repairs

UPI

PEACE WATCH. While inmates gathered on the balcony of Maryland State Penitentiary and police and firemen waited in the court-yard below, Governor Marvin Mandel convinced rioting inmates inside to release four wounded hostages and return to their cells.

and deduct the cost up to a total of two months' rent; another set a stringent ban on the real estate practice of "blockbusting" in racially changing neighborhoods. Although the legislature balked at lowering the age of majority to 18, it did lower the drinking age to 18. Among the conservation measures was the year's largest capital bond issue: $124 million for Boston's aging Franklin Park Zoo, river and harbor cleanups, sewage treatment plants, and restoration of Fort Independence in Boston Harbor for the 1976 bicentennial.

The new state lottery kicked in with a first-week sale of 4.8 million 50-cent tickets in April, and it was estimated that first-year sales would total $56 million. With 40 percent of the take going to the 351 cities and towns, they were expected to split up some $22 million.

Progress was made toward shuffling and combining some 300 state agencies, boards, and departments under 10 cabinet secretaries newly named by Governor Sargent.

The economy. Continuing high unemployment coupled with a long-term decline in manufacturing jobs provoked fears for the state's economic future. Short-term relief was provided through tax incentives, but at midyear statewide unemployment was 8.4 percent, with 12 percent in the failing textile town of Lowell and 10.9 percent in the stricken fishing port of New Bedford.

The most dramatic business closing was that of the 125-year-old Boston *Herald Traveler* in June. Winner of six Pulitzer prizes and once a strong conservative voice with a

loyal readership in Republican strongholds, the paper was doomed in January when the Federal Communications Commission, in a fight that went to the U.S. Supreme Court, took away its lucrative television franchise, charging that improper influence had been used to obtain the franchise 15 years before.

Culture. William Steinberg stepped down after only three years as musical director of the Boston Symphony Orchestra. He was the last in a long line of European-trained conductors which included Charles Munch and Serge Koussevitzky. He will be succeeded by Seiji Ozawa. Perry Rathbone resigned after 16 years as director of the Boston Museum of Fine Arts. He was credited with virtually creating the museum's strong medieval, renaissance, and baroque collections.

For election results and campaign highlights, see the special supplement ELECTION '72.

Area and population. Area, 8,257 sq. mi. Pop. (1970), 5,689,-170. Principal cities: Boston (cap.), 641,071; Worcester, 176,572; Springfield, 163,905; Cambridge, 100,361; New Bedford, 101,777.
Government. Gov., Francis W. Sargent (R); lt. gov., Donald R. Dwight (R); secy. of state, John F. X. Davoren (D); treas., Robert Q. Crane (D); atty. gen., Robert H. Quinn (D). Legislature: senate, 30 D, 10 R; house, 175 D, 59 R, 6 vac.
Finance (fiscal 1972). Total revenue, $2,122,284,716; total expenditure, $2,094,476,507.
Education (1971–1972). Enrollment: public elementary schools, 861,902; public secondary schools, 365,800; nonpublic elementary schools, 144,806; nonpublic secondary schools, 64,910.

MICHAEL KENNEY

MAURITANIA. Foreign affairs. Led by President Moktar Ould Daddah, Mauritania was part of the general movement among French-speaking West African states toward greater cooperation. On March 11 in Nouakchott, President Daddah, President Léopold-Sédar Senghor of Senegal, and Colonel Moussa Traoré of Mali signed an agreement establishing the Organization for the Development of the Sénégal River (OMVS). Together with Guinea, the three nations had belonged to the Organization of Sénégal River States (OERS), an alliance which fell apart November 1971 when Senegal quarreled with Guinea. The new OMVS is limited to one economic objective, the development of the Sénégal River, and has none of the political implications of its predecessors. The organization will be run by a ministerial council, and the heads of state will meet only when necessary (the OERS had obligatory annual summit meetings).

The new West African Economic Community, established at a June 3 summit meeting in Bamako, has similarly limited objectives. Of the seven founding countries—Dahomey, Ivory Coast, Mali, Mauritania, Niger, Senegal, and Upper Volta—Mauritania is one of the poorest, and it was clearly not in Mauritania's interest to join an integrated customs union that Ivory Coast and Senegal could easily dominate. Agricultural and industrial arrangements among member nations are intended to preserve equality of opportunity for all states. At the close of the summit conference, President Daddah announced that he considered the WAEC as a step toward an expanded West African grouping.

President Daddah's prestige on the continent continued to increase. He was an honored guest at the inauguration of President William Tolbert of Liberia and at the funeral of Kwame Nkrumah in Conakry. In June he stepped down as head of the Organization of African Unity.

Economy. French and Chinese aid contributed considerably to Mauritanian economic development. Mining research, a desalinization program, and road construction in the eastern region were all being financed with French resources, while a long-term loan of $20 million from China was financing construction of a deepwater port at Nouakchott. Meanwhile, the government planned to open training centers to enable Mauritanians to take jobs in French-owned firms. Italian and American firms were engaged in searching for offshore oil.

Area and population. Area, 397,955 sq. mi. Pop. (est. 1971), 1.2 million. Nouakchott (cap.), 20,000.
Government. Single-party republic with unicameral legislature. Pres., Moktar Ould Daddah.
Finance. Monetary unit, Communauté Financière Africaine franc; 1 CFA franc = US$0.0041. Budget (1972): balanced at 10.4 billion CFA francs.
Trade (1970). Imports, 13.1 billion CFA francs; exports, 25.1 billion CFA francs. Principal export: iron ore. Principal imports: agricultural products and manufactured goods.
Education. Primary (1970–1971): enrollment, 31,925; teachers, 1,294. Secondary (1972): enrollment, 3,650.

MAURITIUS. Politics and government. Early in the year Mauritius became the first Commonwealth member to associate with the European Economic Community (EEC) under the terms of the 18-member Treaty of Yaoundé. Since the agreement excludes sugar—95 percent of the island's exports—from duty-free privileges in the EEC countries, Mauritius' main immediate benefit from Common Market association consists of a new $5 million grant aid allowance under the EEC's European Development Fund. Once Mauritius' association is ratified early in 1973, the EEC members will enjoy gradually reduced tariffs for their sales to Mauritius.

A state of emergency, declared in December 1971 after a series of crippling strikes and local election defeats, was extended through 1972. Using special powers obtained from Parliament by a one-vote margin in December, the government jailed 50 members of the radically nationalist Mauritian Militant Movement, including most of its leaders, and banned the party's newspaper and several of its affiliated labor unions as well.

Foreign affairs. In April, Prime Minister Sir Seewoosagur Ramgoolam visited Peking, where he agreed to establish diplomatic relations with China. At the same time, two of his ministers were enjoying the hospitality of the Taiwan regime in Taipei. Foreign Minister Gaëtan Duval had joined the United States as cosponsor of the "two Chinas" resolution in the preceding UN General Assembly. The People's Republic has granted Mauritius a $35 million interest-free loan.

Queen Elizabeth II visited Mauritius for the first time in March, inaugurating the new University of Mauritius and drawing large crowds, despite the ban on assembly under the prevailing state of emergency.

Economic developments. Mauritius' current four-year plan calls for the investment of over $100 million from a combination of sources to create 52,000 new jobs by 1975, open up the islands's scarce remaining arable land, and improve transportation, housing, electrical power installations, and other facilities. In addition to steady British aid and the $5 million pledged by the EEC, France has committed over $5 million toward these goals. Light processing industries are being attracted to the island's new export-processing zone, a free trade area where firms from Hong Kong, France, and South Africa have already begun stocking and processing consumer export articles. The EEC has declined thus far, however, to accord these items duty-free status as "Mauritius exports."

In addition, a dozen new hotels are to be built to house an anticipated rush of tourists.

Area and population. Area, 720 sq. mi. (plus major dependency, Rodriguez Island, 40 sq. mi.). Pop. (est. 1971), 900,000. Port Louis (cap.), 140,000.
Government. Constitutional monarchy within the Commonwealth of Nations; unicameral legislature. Prime min., Sir Seewoosagur Ramgoolam.
Finance. Monetary unit, rupee; R1 = US$0.19. Budget (1969–1970): revenue, $45.1 million; expenditures, $45,024,000.
Trade (1970). Imports, $75.1 million; exports, $67.2 million. Chief products: sugar, molasses, tea. Major trading partners: United Kingdom, Canada, South Africa, United States, Thailand.
Education (1969). Enrollment: primary, 140,853; secondary, 42,444; postsecondary, 550.

PHILIP M. ALLEN

MEDICARE. *See* SOCIAL SECURITY.

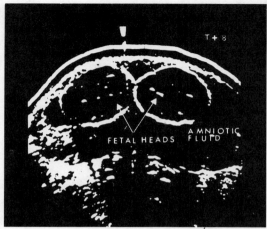

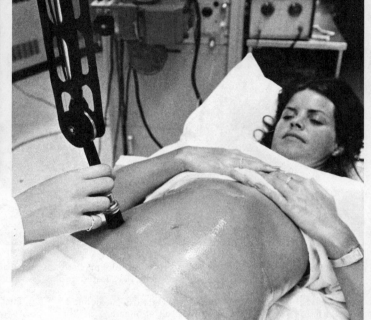

RIGHT, LEONARD KAMSLER/NEW YORK TIMES;
ABOVE, ST. LUKE'S HOSPITAL CENTER

WOMB WITH A VIEW

Physicians have been turning more and more to a new diagnostic tool, the ultrasonic probe, used to scan the uterus as a ship's sonar system scans the bottom of the sea. Sonographic monitoring, unlike the use of X rays, is safe to the fetus; and ultrasonic echoes, translated into TV pictures, can accurately diagnose pregnancy from the fifth week on, identify twins as early as the eighth week (see above), determine the degree of fetal maturity, and detect ovarian tumors or other problems.

MEDICINE. Two impressive biochemical substances will be associated by future medical historians with the year 1972. One is the hormone-like cyclic AMP (cyclic adenosine 3′,5′-monophosphate), for which its discoverer, Dr. Earl Sutherland, Jr., of Vanderbilt University, has received both the Lasker and Nobel prizes. Cyclic AMP turns out to be a missing link in many important biological control mechanisms. An example is the pulse-rate speeding effect of the hormone adrenalin, which actually is mediated by cyclic AMP. The second substance—the existence of which has been postulated but not proved—is a group of hormone-like agents, called chalones; as inhibitors of mitosis, or cell reproduction, they may have important potential in the fields of cancer treatment, skin disease, and immunotherapy. Much of the ground work on chalones has been done by Dr. Edna Laurence of Birkbeck College, London, and Dr. Tapio Rytömaa of Finland's University of Helsinki. (*See* BIOCHEMISTRY.)

Antithetically, medical literature this year was full of references to the ancient Chinese medical practice of acupuncture. Centuries old, this technique involves multiple puncture of certain skin areas of the body with long steel, silver, or gold needles, recently associated with the passing of a current of galvanic electricity through certain of these needles. Claims are made for alleviation by acupuncture of a wide spectrum of human ills, including deafness. Several recent medical observers in the People's Republic of China have reported on major operations performed with no other anesthetic than acupuncture needles. Skeptics (for example, William S. Kroger, M.D., a hypnosis expert) point out that this local anesthesia and other beneficial effects of acupuncture could be the result of a form of hypnosis.

Cardiovascular diseases. Great improvement continues in the salvage of myocardial infarction victims. Attention is now focused on lifesaving measures applicable before the patient can reach a hospital coronary care unit. Dr. Stanley Sarnoff of the National Institutes of Health has developed a "survival kit" to be carried about by coronary-prone individuals. The commonest fatal event early in a coronary attack is ventricular fibrillation (ineffective, chaotic heart rhythm). Since there are two potent antidotes against this killing arhythmia—atropine and lidocaine—Dr. Sarnoff has devised two automatic self-injectors of these drugs, the "Atro-Pen" and the "Lido-Pen." Which to use depends on the preceding pulse rate: for slow hearts, atropine; and for fast hearts, lidocaine. The so-called Cardio Beeper, a portable electronic device, can be used to "pipe" the rate, rhythm, and electrocardiogram of the patient directly by telephone to a physician, perhaps located at a central cardiac care unit. The physician can then tell the patient which drug to inject.

Another common and sinister complication of acute myocardial infarction is cardiogenic shock. It is now increasingly the practice to administer very large doses of the well-known steroid hydrocortisone intravenously, an emergency measure useful in various types of surgical, cardiac, or allergic shock. According to Dr. Richard Lillehei, a thoracic surgeon at the University of Minnesota, steroids increase the effectiveness of other antishock measures.

The drug clofibrate (Atromid-S), which has been used for the last ten years to reduce the blood lipids cholesterol and triglyceride, turns out to provide symptomatic improvement in angina pectoris and to reduce significantly the mortality from myocardial infarction. These findings come from long-term studies carried out in England and Scotland.

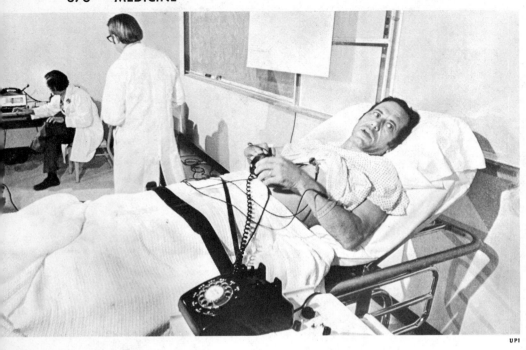

HEART LINE. Testing a new system for cardiac consultation, a patient at Stanford Medical Center phones his EKG on a 51,000-mile round trip out over the Pacific to Manila, then back again via satellite to doctors monitoring the signal.

UPI

In these studies, some 1,700 middle-aged people of both sexes were involved in courses of treatment that lasted for six years.

While visiting the Soviet Union, a Harvard cardiologist, Dr. Bernard Lown, observed a useful application of the well-known anesthetic gas nitrous oxide. Further studied and substantiated by his Boston colleague Dr. Peter Thompson, this gas (a mixture of 35 percent nitrous oxide in oxygen), when inhaled for five minutes, brought much more relief from the pain of coronary insufficiency than did inhalation of pure oxygen. The proportion of nitrous oxide may be increased to 65 percent, if necessary.

Dr. George Burch of Tulane University, long puzzled by the so-called rheumatic damage to heart valves and muscles sometimes found in patients who have never had rheumatic fever, may have incriminated at least one heart-damaging viral culprit. Using the Coxsackie B_4 virus injected into test mice, Dr. Burch produced heart lesions similar to those seen in human rheumatic heart disease. Furthermore, he has isolated B_4 viral antibodies in the blood of several victims of supposed rheumatic heart disease. Dr. Burch has even noted coronary artery-wall lesions produced in B_4 injected mice, and he hypothesizes that viral infections of early life may have something to do with causing the great American disease, coronary atherosclerosis.

Infectious disease and epidemiology. The worst typhoid fever epidemic in years is striking the central Mexican states of Hidalgo, Tlaxcala, México, and Puebla. Apparently caused by a new and virulent strain of typhoid bacillus, this epidemic has struck people who had been vaccinated against previous strains. Ampicillin has proved more effective than chloramphenicol in treating these new cases.

The value of universal vaccination against smallpox in the United States is increasingly being questioned in the light of its potential hazards. Nevertheless, major smallpox epidemics continue to erupt in other parts of the world, such as Yugoslavia, which are supposedly free of the disease. Infecting at least 173 persons and killing at least 34, the Yugoslav outbreak of severe smallpox (*variola major*) was apparently imported from the Middle East by a Yugoslav Muslim pilgrim.

A vaccine against syphilis has been developed by Dr. Mieczyslaw Metzger of the Polish Academy of Sciences.

The treponeme of syphilis is attenuated by washing and storing at 4°C for ten days. Effective in protecting rabbits, the vaccine has not yet been administered to humans.

That gonorrhea may be transmitted nonvenereally has been proved by two Stockholm doctors, Theodore Elmros and Per-Ake Larsson. Viable and transmissible gonococci survived up to 17 hours on dried glass slides and towels.

Infectious mononucleosis is all but proved to be due to the Epstein-Barr virus. Isolating the virus from human cases and injecting it into gibbons, investigators observed serum conversion and tonsilitis six weeks later in three cases, according to Dr. Werner Henle of the University of Pennsylvania. Dr. Georg Springer of Northwestern University has produced a vaccine that induced mononucleosis antibodies in eight out of ten persons so immunized.

A new antiviral antibiotic, adenine arabinoside (ARA-A), related to cystosine arabinoside (ARA-C), has been investigated at the University of Alabama by Dr. Lawrence Ch'ien. Pronounced less toxic to leukocytes than its predecessor, it appears to leave the immune system intact. This drug is effective against herpes zoster and vaccinia.

Chronic disease. Effective nonsurgical treatment is now in view for two major chronic ailments, previously treated almost exclusively by the surgeon.

From the Mayo Clinic comes a report by Dr. Johnson Thistle that gallstones can be dissolved by oral administration of bile acid (cheno-deoxycholic acid) over a period of six to 24 months.

For the estimated 65 percent of American males over 60 who are afflicted with some degree of enlargement of the prostate gland, reports of nonsurgical approach to treatment by Dr. Robert Rangno of McGill University will come as good news. Starting from the known fact that androgens, particularly testosterone and dihydrotestosterone, stimulate enlargement of the prostate, a search was made for an androgen-blocking hormone. Courses lasting 24 weeks of a progestogen named medrogestone produced striking improvement in urinary retention, decrease in gland size, and cellular regression, as observed in serial needle biopsies.

A predisposition to emphysema may turn out to be associated with a hereditary deficiency in the enzyme alpha₁-antitrypsin. In fact, Dr. Jack Lieberman of California's City of Hope Medical Center has evolved a simple serum test for

this AAT deficiency that may eventually prove to be a method for mass screening of emphysema-prone individuals, before irreversible lung damage has taken place.

A program of mass screening for the incurable genetic disease sickle-cell anemia is gathering momentum at Cornell University Medical College. Of primary importance to black people, who are almost exclusively the victims of the disease, this program seeks to discover the sickling trait, rather than the overt disease, by using the reagent Sickledex. Genetic advice is offered to those found positive for the trait, including counseling on the patient's choice of mate and recommendation that afflicted couples raise adopted children rather than have children of their own.

The 1971 storm of controversy over the efficacy of oral hypoglycemic drugs in treating diabetes, which was originally initiated by the University Group Diabetes Program, has temporarily been settled through cautious approval of these drugs by the U.S. Food and Drug Administration. Labeling of all these drugs (Orinase, Tolinase, Dymelor, Diabinese, and DBI) must include a special warning: "To be used in the treatment of adult onset, non-ketotic diabetes mellitus only when the condition cannot be controlled by diet and reduction of excess weight alone."

Malignant disease. Two new early cancer detection techniques are of interest, especially to women.

To spot early cancer of the breast there is now an improvement on the well-known X-ray technique of mammagraphy. Called xero-radiography, this new process embodies some of the principles of a Xerox copying machine. Conventional X-ray exposures are made on a selenium plate sensitized to X rays. When developed electronically, a beautifully accurate rendition of various soft-part structures, including early tumors, is obtained. Credit for the basic research goes to Dr. John Wolfe, of Hutzel Hospital, Detroit.

To extend the "Pap smear" cytological type of screening for early cancer of the female genital tract to include the body as well as the cervix of the uterus, the Upjohn Company has devised and marketed a device called the Gravlee Jet Washer. This mechanism irrigates the interior of the uterus with a weak salt solution, washing out loose endometrial cells. These are collected, stained, and examined for possible cancer by a pathologist.

Two new anticancer drugs sound promising. A nontoxic antimetabolite nucleic acid named Ftorafur by one of its developers, Dr. Salomon Hiller of the Soviet Institute for Organic Synthesis, is claimed to be 50–65 percent effective against breast and intestinal cancers. In metastatic osteogenic sarcoma, Dr. Engracio Cortes of the Roswell Park Memorial Institute in Buffalo reports variable but marked regression in six victims of this tumor when treated with the antibiotic adriamycin, a derivative of the older daunomycin.

Surgery. A new chapter in orthopedic surgery was opened when the FDA approved the medical use of methyl methacrylate, a new cement. This material, reported Harvard surgeon Roderick Turner, has many uses—for example, hip joint replacement. It can also be used to secure solid bone union through bone destroyed by tumor.

To alleviate the pain of active rheumatoid arthritis of finger joints, Dr. Alan Wilde of the Cleveland Clinic has performed an operation called a synovectomy on 39 patients, with partial to complete pain relief in almost all; this operation involves the delicate removal of the inflamed synovial membrane enclosing the diseased joint.

Technical advances are being made in extracting cataracts. Dr. William J. McGannon of Cleveland and Dr. Charles Kelman of New York have developed a small hand-held high frequency vibrator which is applied to the cataractous eyelens through a small puncture in the eye. The vibrator liquefies the lens and then aspirates it. Incision and suturing of the eye are thus avoided.

The present status of transplantation surgery is summarized in the *Medical Letter*. To date, transplantations have been attempted for the liver, heart, lung, and pancreas with some initial success but without long-term survival. The thymus gland and segments of intestine have also been transplanted experimentally. Long-term success in kidney transplantation is attributed to the use of hemodialysis during the postoperative period, as well as customary antirejection measures. Bone marrow transplantation has been accomplished successfully in a small group of children who were deficient in lymphocytes and immuno-globulins. The most successful of these were cases in which the donor was a sibling, with leukocytes immunologically identical to those of the patient.

Obstetrics and gynecology. The technique of obtaining a sample of amniotic fluid during pregnancy by needle puncture (amniocentesis) is becoming increasingly valuable. Amniotic fluid obtained by this method can reveal the sex of the child; furthermore, fetal cells so secured may be cultured, making cytogenetic studies possible. Certain serious genetic disorders may be spotted in the fetus, and the pregnancy may be terminated if the parents so desire. Such anomalies include disorders involving X-chromosomes, such as the Lesch-Nyhan syndrome; various metabolic abnormalities, such as Tay-Sachs disease; and Hurler's syndrome. Down's syndrome, or mongolism, can also be spotted; because the incidence of mongolism varies directly with the age of the mother, amniocentesis is now advised for all pregnant women over 40.

Near term, amniotic fluid may reveal very accurately the maturity of the fetus. This knowledge can be of particular importance in preventing hyalin membrane disease of the newborn. Dr. George Nelson of Augusta, Ga., reports that the concentration of the lipoid lecithin in amniotic fluid bears a direct relationship to the "pulmonary maturity" of the fetus. The use of this test before scheduling the mother for a possible elective Caesarean section or induction of labor thus may help prevent fatal hyalin membrane disease.

To prevent miscarriage because a weak cervix has given way to dilation during midpregnancy (cervical incompetence), the Israeli physician Rudolph Artal and his colleagues in Tel Aviv have devised a strengthening suture around the cervix to be applied in the 12th week of pregnancy, an operation known as cerclage. Fetal salvage rates were markedly improved in these habitual miscarriers. The suture was removed at term to allow the cervix to dilate normally during labor.

Pediatrics. The commonest cause of death in the United States between the ages of one week and seven months is the tragic Sudden Infant Death Syndrome, also known as crib deaths. Abbreviated SIDS, it accounts for some 15,000 infant losses each year. Dr. Bruce Beckwith of the Children's Orthopedic Hospital, Seattle, suspects the cause to be a very acute viral laryngitis which swells the baby's vocal cords so rapidly that crying is impossible and the baby chokes to death. Neither warning technique nor preventive treatment has yet been discovered.

The hyperkinetic child is being recognized as a true behavioral aberration or diagnostic entity. Also called MBD, for "minimal brain dysfunction," this handicap causes children to be extremely overactive, distractible, of short attention span, impulsive, aggressive, and fluctuant in mood. Great trials to their parents and teachers, these children can apparently be calmed down by antidepressive drugs such as imipramine (Tofranil) and methylphenidate (Ritalin). Drug treatment, however, is only a beginning in the management of these problem children. Family therapy, behavior modification, and individual psychotherapy are equally important, according to Dr. Leon Eisenberg, a Boston pediatrician. (*See the special article* BEHAVIOR CONTROL.)

An increase in the incidence of congenital pyloric stenosis in infants born recently in Northern Ireland—coincidently with the rise in the level of conflict in that area—has been noted by Dr. James A. Dodge of Belfast. To account for

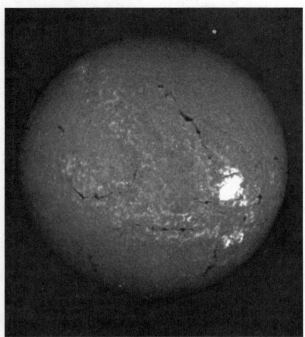

SUN STORM. Giant flares (visible at right) mysteriously exploded on the solar surface this August, jamming radio signals on earth.

this, Dr. Dodge theorizes that an increase of gastrin secretion takes place in the mother because of anxiety; gastrin crosses the placental barrier and hypertrophies the pyloric muscle of the fetus, which leads to obstructive symptoms in the stomach outlet after the child is born.

Dr. J. B. J. McKendry and his staff at the University of Toronto have invented an ingenious technique to prevent bed-wetting—an electrical device in an athletic-type supporter. The first few drops of urine trigger off a buzzer and a slight electric shock, which wake the child. An overall cure rate of 72 percent is claimed for enuretic children by this method.

New drugs and techniques. Analogous to the cardiac pacemaker, a new electrical breathing aid, or respiratory stimulator, may make the iron lung obsolete. Developed by Dr. William Glenn of the Yale University School of Medicine, this device has kept a quadriplegic with respiratory paralysis alive for over a year. The breathing aid rhythmically stimulates both of the patient's phrenic nerves by way of implanted radio receivers hooked up to external antennae, which receive appropriately controlled surges of radio frequency energy.

The administration of oxygen under pressure, with the patient in a pressurized oxygen chamber, is of proven effectiveness in treating decompression sickness, air embolism, and carbon monoxide intoxication. Dr. Jefferson Davis, of the U.S. Air Force, now reports the technique's usefulness in treating gas gangrene, citing 80 case reports. In these cases, oxygen apparently acts as a sort of antibiotic to inhibit growth in the infected tissues of Welsh's bacillus, an obligate anaerobe.

Dr. Harry Arnold, Jr., a Honolulu dermatologist, reports that a quarter teaspoonful of ordinary meat tenderizer, dissolved in one or two teaspoons of water and rubbed into the skin around a fresh insect bite, will dull the pain of the bite, if applied soon enough. The protein-dissolving enzyme papain is apparently the agent which neutralizes the insect venom.

Reported previously as effective abortifacients, the prostaglandins are finding other important medical uses. These substances, which are fatty acids synthesized in the body from linoleic acid, can dilate blood vessels, and some of them can suppress gastric juice secretion. Their eventual practical use in treatment of hypertension and stomach ulcer seems quite likely.

A new inhalant drug, cromolyn sodium, now available for treatment of bronchial asthma, is particularly effective in asthmatic children, reports Dr. Zelda Fox, of McGill University, Montreal.

The drug metronidazole (Flagyl), used for years to treat the gynecological infection trichomoniasis, is now accepted as of value in amoebiasis, especially in amoebic abscess of the liver, reports the Amoebiasis Research Unit of Durban, South Africa.

Flucytosine is a new oral antifungal drug, marketed under the name Ancobon by Hoffmann-La Roche; much less toxic than its predecessor Amphotericin B, it is of particular value against *Candida* and *Cryptococcus* infections.

FRANK P. MATHEWS

METEOROLOGY. Tornado detection. Fifteen sites in ten tornado-prone states were equipped with new portable electronic tornado detectors developed by scientists of the Department of Commerce's National Oceanic and Atmospheric Administration. NOAA scientists, analyzing the data collected by the new instrumentation, will attempt to identify the electromagnetic signals associated with the birth, growth, life, and death of a tornado. Eventually the scientists hope to be able to pinpoint potential trouble spots well before destructive activity begins and to predict the severity and perhaps the direction of the developing tornado.

Meteorological warfare. On July 3, Seymour M. Hersh of the New York *Times* reported that the United States had been secretly using weather-modification techniques in Indochina. Quoting unnamed government sources, the *Times* indicated that cloud seeding had been used in Laos and Vietnam since 1963. The Laos weather program, known as Operation Pop-Eye, was an attempt to "reduce trafficability along infiltration routes." Another aim of the program was to foil North Vietnamese attacks. Also, a method was developed for treating clouds with a chemical that led to highly acidic rainfall that could foul the operation of enemy radar and thus hamper the effectiveness of surface-to-air missiles.

At hearings held by the Senate Foreign Relations Subcommittee on the Ocean and the International Environment, Senator Claiborne Pell (D,R.I.) attempted to investigate the Department of Defense's weather research program, but a DOD spokesman testified that the Indochina program was classified.

Flood control. The National Weather Service announced in May that it had begun operating the first of a new series of automatic flash-flood warning systems. Wheeling, W.Va., was the recipient of the first prototype system, a forerunner of several automatic warning systems to be installed in the United States in places where fast-rising floodwaters from heavy rains are a chronic threat. The new systems connect robot water-level sensors situated upstream with community alarm stations such as police or fire headquarters, which can issue warnings to the public on a 24-hour-a-day basis. It is expected that the new systems will provide valuable minutes' and perhaps hours' notice to streamside residents, allowing them time to seek higher ground.

Solar storms. Puzzled scientists were unable to explain a rash of gigantic solar explosions that took place on the sun's surface this August. The geomagnetic storms jammed radio signals throughout the world and interrupted the flow of electric current in some areas. Covering 2.8 billion square miles of the sun's surface, the energy emitted from the massive solar flare posed no danger to man, since the earth's atmosphere acts as an energy filter. However, scientists feared that the flare could endanger astronauts in space and

warned that space flights or very high altitude experimentation be postponed until the solar activity subsided.

Carbon dioxide and the greenhouse effect. Dr. Lester Machta, head of the U.S. Air Resources Laboratory, predicted that the carbon dioxide content of the earth's atmosphere will increase by 20 percent by the year 2000. Dr. Machta was able to make his forecast by developing a mathematical model of the exchange of carbon dioxide between the atmosphere, the oceans, and plant and animal life coupled with estimates of worldwide consumption of fossil fuels.

Theoretically, an increasing concentration of carbon dioxide should raise the temperature of the lower atmosphere. Carbon dioxide permits solar energy to pass essentially unchanged into the lower atmosphere but traps the earth's radiation outward, creating what is called a greenhouse effect. Contrary to expectations and despite the rising carbon dioxide concentration documented during the past few decades, ground-level air temperatures in the northern hemisphere have cooled since the mid-1940's. "It is apparent," said Dr. Machta, "that carbon dioxide is only one of the factors that determine the temperature of the lower atmosphere."

Neutercanes. A new classification of storms, the neutercane, has been added to the lexicon of meteorological phenomena. The term neutercane is derived from the fact that this type of storm draws equally upon the energy sources of both tropical and frontal storms and thus is, in a sense, neutral between them. Weather satellites have been providing pictures of the progress and development of neutercanes ever since the mid-1960's, but it was not until this May that Dr. Robert Simpson, director of the National Hurricane Center in Miami, officially adopted the term to signify a new type of storm.　　　　ALLAN YALE BROOKS

MEXICO. Politics and internal affairs. President Luis Echeverría Álvarez may well turn out to be the Franklin D. Roosevelt of Mexico. He knows his country is in trouble and he is determined to experiment and reform so that the present system can save itself. He has been under sharp attack from both the right and left, and he is not yet master of his own house. This year, however, he took giant steps to crush his opposition.

His first bold move, in February, was the ousting of the president and secretary-general of the Institutional Revolutionary Party (PRI), the nation's ruling party. The removed president, Manuel Sánchez Vite, and his secretary-general were both regarded as "old guard," and their pressured resignations indicated that Echeverría was moving closer to party acceptance of his reform program. The new president of PRI, Jesús Reyes Heroles, an economist-historian who had been serving as head of PEMEX, the national Mexican petroleum company, is well known for his liberal reformist views. However, the "old guard" is still deeply entrenched, and Echeverría must move cautiously in bringing about necessary changes.

Rightist elements outside of PRI are becoming increasingly active. The year saw the incorporation of the Mexican Democratic Party, a group based on the remains of the neofascist Sinarquista movement, which had its high point during the 1940's. The paramilitary groups called Halcones (Hawks), responsible for the murders of a number of students in 1971, were again present in street riots and demonstrations. They are armed, have radio-equipped cars, and have obviously been well trained. It is strongly suspected that they are backed by rightists from within PRI itself.

On the left, meanwhile, guerrilla activity against the government increased. The death, under rather unclear circumstances, of guerrilla leader Genaro Vásquez Rojas in the southern state of Guerrero was thought to have been a major blow against armed leftist movements. However, Lucio Cabañas, successor to Vásquez and, like him, a former schoolteacher, scored several highly successful ambushes against government troops.

The extreme left wing is rather badly divided. Some concentrate on urban terrorism (bank-robbing, kidnapping, bombing) while others attempt to establish guerrilla *focos* in remote jungle or mountain areas. Despite government claims, and occasional real successes against the terrorists and guerrillas, they remain a constant menace and embarrassment to the Echeverría regime.

The sharp division within the Roman Catholic Church in Mexico showed few signs of healing. The most dramatic incident demonstrative of the rift came at Mexico City's International Airport in midsummer when Cuernavaca's ultra-liberal bishop, Sergio Méndez Acero, was doused with red dye upon his return from a trip to Chile. He had been attending a meeting called Latin American Encounter of Christians for Socialism. The Echeverría reform movement has not gone so far as to embrace the leftist clergy, and after the dye-throwing incident President Reyes of PRI publicly stated that the clergy ought not to engage in politics.

At the same time, the government raised the ire of conservative clergy and laymen alike when it reversed its position on birth control. Echeverría had been known to be against birth control on religious grounds, but apparently the economic realities of Mexico's very high birthrate changed his mind. The government's birth control program is still in the planning stage but is expected to be operational in 1973.

Economic developments. The Mexican economy moved almost briskly forward again after a serious recession in 1971, when the government induced a slowdown in order to curb inflation. The gamble seems to have paid off, for the inflation rate, as measured by the wholesale price index, tumbled from 6 percent to 3.6 percent. Minister of Finance Hugo Margáin has apparently lived up to his reputation as an economic wizard. His problems were complicated by general wage increases for Mexican workers, which in some cases ranged up to 18 percent. An estimated three-quarters of Mexico's population lives near the subsistence level, and the Echeverría reforms aim at raising consumption levels as a means of promoting economic growth and maintaining political peace. The per capita income in Mexico is now thought to be about US$700, but this still reflects the enormous wealth concentrated among a small group of industrialists. In rural areas the figure is only US$200.

The result of the drive against inflation in 1971 was that the increase in gross national product of 3.5 percent scarcely matched the population growth. This year, however, the final figures are expected to reveal a 5.5–6 percent increase. Among areas of notable improvement, agriculture surged forward after a two-year slump as Mexico was spared the hurricanes and severe droughts that have occurred in the past several years. The agricultural problem now centers on finding markets for fresh produce.

Industrial growth was generally sluggish, with increases only in a few specialized areas, such as construction and aluminum. Mining followed the industrial pattern, with the sector generally depressed but with copper and phosphates sharply up because of increased U.S. demand.

The government launched a massive export drive, largely directed away from the United States, seeking new markets in Asia, Europe, and Latin America. Simultaneously, imports were cut back. The result was a 22.2 percent increase in exports for the first half of the year over the same period of last year.

On the home scene, the minister of finance announced an enormous budget increase. For the government to balance its books additional revenue had to be found, and maximum income-tax rates were upped by 10 percent (to 42 percent). But that measure alone will not be enough for a balanced budget. Although the internal debt is not yet a crucial problem, the external debt and the still unequal export-import balance remain as serious matters to be solved.

Meanwhile, the government made two rather startling moves in the economic arena. Echeverría announced in August that several large estates owned by some of Mexico's leading gentry were to be expropriated and distributed among 941 peasant families. The same month, investors and industrialists expressed concern when the government purchased 51 percent of the stock in Teléfonos de Mexico, the largest privately owned corporation in the country. Officials asserted, however, that the telephone company was not being nationalized and that the government intended only to control and not to administer the system.

The political survival of President Echeverría is tied closely in many ways to the economy. He knows this. Consequently, he has been one of the most innovative presidents that Mexico has seen in several decades.

Foreign relations. This year President Echeverría visited the United States, Japan, Chile, Venezuela, Colombia, Costa Rica, Guatemala, Panama, and Honduras. In addition, many key government officials were also globe-trotting. Most of this travel was motivated by the export drive. The Mexican government is even engaged in an in-depth study of Mainland China as a market area. Mexico established diplomatic relations with China in February.

Echeverría managed to seriously annoy the United States twice during the year. First, in April, he visited President Salvador Allende Gossens of Chile and issued a joint statement with the Chilean leader supporting positions somewhat unpopular with the United States government and business community. Declaring their concern with the principle of sovereignty for smaller nations, the two presidents asserted the right of nations to control their own natural resources, endorsed the controversial 200-mile sea boundary, and said that international financing should not be subject to political considerations. Then, in June, Echeverría came to the United States and addressed a joint session of Congress. Ignoring the polite conventionalities typical of such occasions, he attacked the United States, and the superpowers in general, as being insensitive to the needs and aspirations of smaller nations. He called for a more effective program on the part of the United States to control the salt content in the Colorado River water flowing into Mexico. He complained of the increasingly protectionist trade policies of the United States and argued that Latin American nations should be given preferred trade positions. Quite a few congressmen were upset by Echeverría's bluntness, but the Mexican president had little to lose; he could not have expected to gain much from the Nixon administration in an election year.

Mexican relations with the Soviet Union and Cuba remained somewhat cool. The Soviet government has not been forgiven its connivance in the training of Mexican students in urban guerrilla warfare in North Korea last year, and Cuba is suspected of aiding several of the guerrilla groups operating in Mexico. In addition, President Echeverría demonstrated Mexico's traditional diplomatic independence by announcing that his country would never recognize Spain as long as an undemocratic government continued in power.

Area and population. Area, 761,604 sq. mi. Pop. (est. 1971), 50,830,000. Principal cities (1970): Mexico City (cap.), 3,484,000 (met. area, 8,400,000); Guadalajara, 1,352,100; Monterrey, 1,011,900; Ciudad Juárez, 522,000.
Government. Federated republic with bicameral legislature. Pres., Luis Echeverría Álvarez.
Finance. Monetary unit, peso; 1 peso = US$0.0801. Budget (1972): Pl23.4 billion.
Trade (1971). Exports, US$1.44 billion; imports, US$2.41 billion. Principal exports: cotton, sugar, coffee, tomatoes, shrimp, minerals, petroleum. Principal imports: machinery, automobiles, chemicals.
Education (est. 1972). Enrollment: primary, 8,900,000; secondary, 1,100,000; higher, 250,000.
Armed forces. One-year compulsory military training for all males. Regular army, approx. 54,000; navy, 12,000; air force, 6,000.

JAMES R. KELLEY

MICHIGAN. Legislation. The budget adopted by the 76th Michigan legislature in late spring approximated recommendations made by Governor William G. Milliken and totaled $3.5 billion, including both general and restricted fund appropriations. The budget reflected inflationary and built-in costs rather than much new spending. The funding, in part, was established by the legislature, making permanent the temporary changes the year before in state income tax categories. The new rates thus became 3.9 percent on individual income, 7.8 percent on corporations, and 9.7 percent on financial institutions. A balanced budget for fiscal 1972–1973 was achieved by also including as revenue $20 million estimated income from a state lottery not scheduled to begin operation until year's end and a marginal $5 million carry-over surplus.

Public approval for the lottery, a significant departure from Michigan's traditional ban on legalized gambling other than horse racing, was given in a constitutional amendment adopted in the May presidential preference primary election. Legislative approval for the special primary resumed a practice abandoned in 1928.

Major bills passed by the 1972 legislature included state revenue sharing with cities, villages, and townships totaling $237.7 million; enabling acts to extend and clarify the adult rights of newly enfranchised 18-year-olds; and the creation of a state wilderness and natural areas advisory board to recommend properties worthy of preservation by the state.

Education. The Michigan Education Association, a teachers' union, successfully circulated petitions to provide for a statewide constitutional referendum on limiting local property tax millage for school operations. The plan proposed that public school systems be almost fully funded through state aid, instead of being allocated the present 50 percent. Another proposed amendment bases the state's income tax on a graduated rather than a flat rate. Voters will also decide whether to permit legalized abortions through the 20th week of pregnancy by licensed physicians in facilities approved by the state.

Education became enmeshed with racial problems when U.S. District Court Judge Stephen J. Roth ordered massive interdistrict busing of Detroit and suburban students to achieve racial balance and educational equality. His order, stayed on appeal to the federal courts, called for the daily transfer of 150,000 Detroit black schoolchildren with a like number of white suburban pupils. In terms of numbers and school jurisdictions involved, it was the most sweeping school integration case affecting any major northern area.

Economic activity. The Michigan-based automobile industry had a banner year. As the 1972 model run ended in August, domestic car production for the first eight months of the year was just over 6 million units, 10 percent above the comparable 1971 period. However, jobless rates in Michigan and the Detroit area remained above national averages.

For election results and campaign highlights, see the special supplement ELECTION '72.

Area and population. Area, 58,216 sq. mi. Pop. (1970), 8,875,083. Principal cities: Lansing (cap.), 131,546; Detroit, 1,511,482; Grand Rapids, 197,649; Flint, 193,317; Warren, 179,260.
Government. Gov., William G. Milliken (R); lt. gov., James H. Brickley (R); secy. of state, Richard H. Austin (D); atty. gen., Frank J. Kelley (D). Legislature: senate, 19 D, 19 R; house, 57 D, 53 R.
Finance (1972–1973). Revenue and expenditures, $3,466,199,562. Main sources of revenue: state income tax, state sales tax, motor fuel and weight taxes, cigarette tax. Main expenditures: education, health and welfare, highways.
Education (1971–1972). Primary schools (K–6): enrollment, 1,161,284; teachers, 44,122. Secondary schools (7–12): enrollment, 980,477; teachers, 40,280.

ALLEN PHILLIPS

MIDDLE EAST. Cold war rivalries. *Soviets ousted.* The evacuation of Soviet military forces from Egypt was clearly the most surprising and significant development in the Middle East during the year. Egyptian president Anwar

IN LEAGUE. Egyptian president Anwar Sadat and Libyan premier Muammar al-Qaddafi, meeting in Bengasi, agreed to set up a "political leadership" empowered to work out plans for "complete unity" between the two Arab countries.

UPI

Sadat announced unexpectedly on July 18 that he had ordered the immediate withdrawal from Egypt of Soviet military advisers and experts and the restoration of exclusive Egyptian control over all Soviet installations and equipment in the country. The Soviet government reacted to the abrupt Egyptian move with cool restraint. The Soviet news agency, Tass, reported on July 19 that Soviet advisers in Egypt had completed their assignments and on the basis of mutual agreement with the Egyptian government would return home. Airlifts of Soviet personnel began at once, and the exodus grew in magnitude until by October only some 300 Soviet technicians remained out of the 20,000 pilots, advisers, missile experts, and troops who had been stationed in Egypt three months earlier.

Along with departing personnel, the Soviets removed considerable amounts of sophisticated military hardware. Seventy MIG-21 fighter-bombers, six highly advanced MIG-23 interceptors, and the 18 TU-16 reconnaissance bombers which had been used to shadow ships of the U.S. Sixth Fleet, were returned to Soviet bases. Antiaircraft missile complexes were dismantled and sent home along with supporting electronic gear; some were restored later.

Although Soviet naval forces based at Port Said, Alexandria, and Mersa Matruh were also initially withdrawn, by September, Soviet naval activity in Egyptian Mediterranean ports had returned to pre-July levels. The Soviet squadron in the Mediterranean was, in fact, strengthened by the addition of three highly advanced Krivak-class destroyers armed with surface-to-surface missiles.

A tangled combination of factors induced President Sadat to oust the Soviets despite the consequent impairment of Egyptian military efficiency (Egyptian air defenses were reported to be only one-third as effective at the end of September as they had been before July). Faced with student unrest and growing frustration in the officers' corps, President Sadat seemed inclined to explore possibilities of reestablishing ties with the West as a means of achieving some dramatic new turn of policy to improve his government's popular standing. The Soviets, for their part, suffered from increasing hostility in Egypt. Arrogant and exclusive at the personal level, Soviet advisers won their way into few Egyptian hearts. The Soviet Union's firm refusal to provide the long-range offensive weapons sought by President Sadat in three successive trips to Moscow gave

credence to the disillusioned Egyptian belief, expressed editorially in June by Muhammad Heykal in his influential daily, *al-Ahram*, that the Soviet Union gained most from the no war, no peace, stalemate in the Middle East and had no intention of seeing Egypt through to a successful reconquest of the Sinai Peninsula. The extensive use of Soviet radar and reconnaissance facilities to monitor not Israeli, but NATO forces and the pervasive influence of Soviet KGB and GRU intelligence agents on internal affairs further deepened Egyptian hostility toward the Soviet presence.

According to some sources, the clinching factor in convincing President Sadat to send the Soviets home was an ultimatum from Egyptian military leaders. Information indicating that the Soviets disliked the views of Egyptian defense minister General Muhammad Sadek and other governmental officials apparently provoked an army ultimatum that if the Soviets were not removed, the military would overthrow Sadat. Sadek resigned in October, as Soviet-Egyptian relations began to improve.

Western reaction. The unexpected Soviet departure from Egypt was viewed with cautious satisfaction in Western Europe and the United States. After the setback to Soviet interests in the Sudan in 1971, the reduction of Soviet influence in Egypt was seen as a further step in restoring a favorable balance of power in the eastern Mediterranean.

From the Western point of view there were other encouraging developments in the Middle East during the year. The power vacuum in the Persian Gulf, caused by the evacuation of British forces from the area last year, was partially filled by American-Iranian diplomatic and military cooperation. Iran's defense capabilities were strengthened by American pledges to supply the shah's government with an undisclosed number of F-14 and F-15 fighter aircraft armed with laser beam—guided bombs. The United States, meanwhile, quietly established a naval presence at the old British facility on Bahrain. In southern Arabia the government of Yemen reestablished diplomatic ties with the United States in July. A long-standing conflict between Yemen (backed by Britain and the United States) and the Marxist-oriented People's Democratic Republic of Yemen (Southern Yemen) apparently ended in October with an agreement to confederate. Elsewhere, the Western allies could take satisfaction in Britain's improving relations with Algeria and Sudan and could breathe a sigh of relief over

successful NATO negotiations securing exclusive use of Malta's military base facilities for a seven-year period.

Power realities. The Soviet withdrawal from Egypt, however, produced no major alteration of power realities in the Middle East. Egypt remained desperately dependent on the Soviet Union for military equipment, spare parts, and economic aid, and the Soviet Union showed no intention of abandoning its substantial Egyptian investment. Both Cairo and Moscow demonstrated a keen interest in maintaining cordial relations under the new circumstances. Meanwhile, the Soviet Union worked to increase its influence in other areas of the Middle East. On April 9, Iraqi president Ahmed Hassan al-Bakr and Soviet premier Aleksei N. Kosygin signed a 15-year treaty of cooperation and friendship in Baghdad, modeled on the Soviet-Egyptian treaty signed last year. Iraq's strategic geographical location opened the possibility of Soviet penetration in the oil-rich but politically unstable states of the Persian Gulf and exerted additional pressure on NATO and CENTO defensive capabilities in Turkey and Iran. The establishment of a Soviet naval base at Umm Kasr on Iraq's Persian Gulf coast and Iraq's nationalization of the Western-owned Iraq Petroleum Company provided further evidence of Iraq's deepening involvement with the Soviet bloc. The Soviet Union also worked to compensate losses in Egypt by establishing closer ties with Syria.

Arab-Israeli conflict. The departure of Soviet advisers from Egypt temporarily exerted a calming influence on the Arab-Israeli conflict. Egypt clearly abandoned all hope of achieving a military solution to outstanding grievances with Israel, and in September more than 20,000 conscripts who had served in the Egyptian Army since the June 1967 war were discharged from the service. King Hussein of Jordan announced a plan in March designed to establish peace with Israel by creating a united Arab kingdom to be made up of Jordan, the West Bank area, and perhaps the Gaza Strip. Although met by a chorus of Arab denunciations and rejected by Israel, King Hussein's plan represented a negotiating basis for future talks with Israel and indicated Jordan's interest in Gaza as a possible Jordanian outlet to the Mediterranean Sea. Jordan's lifeline to the sea lies across Syria and Lebanon and is currently blocked by a partial Syrian boycott against Jordanian commerce. In February and June, Israel launched extended raids against Palestinian guerrillas based in the foothills of southern Lebanon, but Israel's frontiers were otherwise quiet. Local Arab elections in the West Bank area were held in March and May without incident, and the absence of terrorism in Gaza for most of the year indicated Israel's success in suppressing resistance at least temporarily.

The mood of relative tranquillity and hopes for new diplomatic departures in the Middle East were shattered in September by the attack on Israeli athletes at the Olympic games in Munich carried out by Palestinian terrorists connected with the Black September organization. The death of 11 Israeli competitors in the Munich tragedy catapulted the waning Palestinian resistance movement to renewed prominence and succeeded in inflaming all the old animosities. The slayings drove a wedge of hostility between the Arab states, most of which refused to condemn Black September's activities, and the Western governments, which viewed international terrorism as totally inexcusable. In Israel the events at Munich, the latest of a series of bloody terrorist incidents during the year, hardened the government's determination to crush the Palestinian guerrilla movement and produced retaliatory raids against guerrilla camps in Syria and Lebanon. In the context of renewed Middle Eastern turmoil, the Soviet Union moved to establish closer ties with the Palestinian resistance movement— a policy no doubt prompted by the growth of Chinese influence among radical elements in the area. The Soviets announced in a joint communiqué with Iraq that the Soviet

Union would provide direct material aid as well as moral support to the guerrilla movement.

Political developments. King Hassan II of Morocco narrowly escaped assassination in August when Moroccan fighter planes failed in an attempt to shoot down the Boeing 727 which was flying the king and 100 other passengers back to Morocco from France. The leader of the conspiracy appeared to have been General Muhammad Oufkir, former security chief and trusted associate of the king, who was made defense minister after the unsuccessful military coup in July 1971. In the aftermath of the crisis King Hassan assumed personal command of the armed forces and instituted strict press censorship. It remained uncertain, however, whether severe measures would suffice for long to save the king his throne.

Settlement of the 16-year-old civil conflict in Sudan between government forces and dissident Anyanya rebels in the three southern provinces was announced in March by President Jafaar al-Nimery in Khartoum. Secret negotiations between the two sides in Addis Ababa produced agreement that the southern provinces would be accorded a broad degree of local autonomy within the framework of a federal state.

Libya and Egypt continued to pursue the aims of Arab unity, and in August the two governments formally announced plans to achieve merger by September 1, 1973. The announcement was regarded with considerable skepticism owing to the formidable political, social, and economic obstacles to be overcome before union between the two countries could be realized.

Oil. Soaring world demand for oil placed oil-rich Middle Eastern countries, possessing 70 percent of the world's proved oil reserves, in an unprecedentedly powerful bargaining position relative to the Western oil companies. Representatives of five Persian Gulf oil-producing states and seven major Western oil companies reached agreement in October on a plan allowing producing countries to participate in the ownership of the extracting and refining facilities located on their soil. The plan calls for producing countries to acquire an initial 20 percent interest in the plant and equipment within their borders and to move to a controlling 51 percent ownership of oil facilities by the early 1980's. The oil companies will be compensated for the change in ownership but at a book price value far lower than the value of the oil still underground. Although the October agreement involved only Saudi Arabia, Qatar, Kuwait, Iraq, and Abu Dhabi, the plan seemed likely to be taken up by other oil-producing states in the Middle East.

VICTOR R. SWENSON

MINERAL AND METAL INDUSTRY. The output of the world's mineral industry increased in 1972 in response to the demands of the growing population. Several of the mineral commodity industries that experienced difficulties in 1971 appeared to be having a better year in 1972, although problems of oversupply persisted for some materials. Virtually the entire industry, particularly in the United States but also in other nations with developed economies, was confronted with various problems relating to the environment—problems of controlling plant emissions or of possible dangers from certain uses of products.

World mineral output. The value of total world crude mineral production in recent years has been estimated as follows, in terms of 1968 U.S. dollars: 1968, $88 billion; 1969, $92.8 billion; 1970, $98.3 billion; 1971, $101.7 billion; and 1972, $105.2 billion. These estimates are based primarily on the work of François Callot, the director of the French Bureau de Documentation Minière, and were published in the January 1971 issue of *Annales des Mines.* Data presented therein covering 53 selected mineral commodities were extrapolated from 1968 figures using United Nations indexes of mineral industry production and were extended to

cover a greater variety of crude minerals. It should be stressed, however, that these figures are based on approximations and that the data represent only the value of the crude product, thus excluding the value added through smelting and refining of metals, refining of oil, and similar processing, as well as the value added through transport of the materials to market areas. Thus, the products of the mineral industry when sold to manufacturing firms would be worth several times the crude mineral value.

In world mineral output, fuels are the overwhelming leader. Petroleum heads the list, accounting for almost 36 percent of the 1968 total; coal (including lignite) ranked second and accounted for almost 21 percent in 1968. These two commodities, together with fourth-ranked natural gas, eighth-ranked natural gas liquids, and 20th-ranked uranium, accounted for more than 64 percent of the 1968 total and more than 67 percent of the 1971 total. The broad category of stone, sand, gravel, and common clay was the largest single nonfuel commodity group, ranking third among all commodities and accounting for about one-tenth of the total value of crude mineral output in each year from 1968 to 1971. Copper, iron, and gold ranked highest among the metals (fifth, sixth, and seventh among all commodities, respectively) with copper and iron accounting for somewhat more than 5 percent of the total crude mineral output value each and gold for about 2 percent. Other commodities accounting for between 1 and 0.5 percent each, in order of importance, were: salt, sulfur, zinc, phosphates, nickel, lead, tin, silver, diamonds, potash, and asbestos.

The ranking of various producing nations has not been determined for the years after 1968. In that year the United States accounted for nearly 26 percent of the total, followed by the Soviet Union with about 18 percent; Canada, the People's Republic of China, and Venezuela (4 to 5 percent each); and West Germany, the United Kingdom, Libya,

Saudi Arabia, South Africa, Iran, and Kuwait (2 to 3 percent each). Nine other countries—Poland, France, Iraq, Japan, Australia, Chile, Mexico, Algeria, and East Germany—accounted for between 1 and 2 percent each. In 1968 the first 21 nations produced more than 85 percent of the total value of crude minerals.

Strip mining. Environmentalists have voiced strenuous objections to the practice of strip mining, but the method has become more and more widely used. According to the New York *Times* of September 27, strip mining has passed underground mining as the most common means of mining coal in the United States. Bills were under consideration in committees of both houses of Congress this year to regulate strip mines, but no legislation dealing with the practice passed during the 1972 session.

In the West Virginia primary election on May 9, conservationists won a number of Democratic nominations in a political confrontation with the coal industry. The Democratic candidate for governor, John D. Rockefeller IV, who pledged to abolish strip mining if elected, was defeated by the Republican incumbent in November.

Coal. World coal output continued to advance slowly in 1972, reaching an estimated 3,050 million tons (total anthracite, bituminous, and lignite), despite the widely publicized coal strike in the United Kingdom.

In Rhodesia, the Wankie Coal Mine suffered one of the worst mine disasters in history on June 6, when 426 miners and several surface workers were killed as a result of an explosion and subsequent fire. Much less costly in terms of lives lost was the explosion and fire at the Blacksville No. 1 mine in Blacksville, W.Va. This July 22 disaster claimed nine lives and brought renewed controversy over mine safety.

Crude petroleum. World crude oil output in 1972 topped the recorded 17,638 million barrels of 1971, but the data were not sufficiently complete to establish the 1972 total

A MAKESHIFT MORTUARY was set up near the opening of the mine shaft at the Wankie Coal Mine in western Rhodesia, as hope dimmed for the miners trapped below by fire and explosion. Over 426 men perished in one of this century's worst mining accidents.

UPI

State and 1970 rank by value[1]	Value in 1970[1] $1,000	Coal[2] th.	Coke th.	Natural gas mi. cu. ft.	Natural gas liquids th. 42-gal. bbl.	Petroleum, crude th. 42-gal. bbl.	Copper, mine (recoverable)	Gold troy oz.	Iron ore (usable)[3] th. long tons	Pig iron th.	Steel, raw th.
Alabama (21)	323,245	17,945	.....	355	W	7,832	.....	.....	415	3,945	W
Alaska (20)	338,271	698	.....	121,618	W	79,494	.....	13,012	.....	.....	.....
Arizona (5)	1,166,767	1,146	.....	868	.....	1,236	820,171	94,038	16	.....	W
Arkansas (27)	225,622	276	.....	172,154	1,035	18,263	.....	.....	.....	.....	W
California (3)	1,897,136	W	W	612,629	24,555	358,484	515	2,966	W	W	3,595
Colorado (18)	389,789	5,337	W	108,537	2,582	27,391	3,938	42,031	W	W	W
Connecticut (45)	28,383	.....	.....	.....	.....	.....	.....	.....	.....	.....	W
Delaware (50)	1,615	.....	.....	.....	.....	.....	.....	.....	W	.....	W
Florida (23)	300,042	.....	.....	903	W	5,347	.....	.....	W	.....	W
Georgia (29)	203,225	.....	.....	.....	.....	.....	.....	.....	W	.....	.....
Hawaii (44)	28,965	.....	.....	.....	.....	.....	.....	.....	.....	.....	W
Idaho (32)	119,748	.....	.....	.....	.....	.....	3,776	3,596	W	.....	.....
Illinois (11)	688,697	58,402	2,144	498	W	39,084	.....	.....	.....	6,443	10,897
Indiana (25)	255,786	21,396	7,832	537	.....	6,658	.....	.....	.....	12,696	17,307
Iowa (31)	120,822	989	.....	.....	.....	.....	.....	.....	.....	.....	.....
Kansas (16)	586,161	1,151	.....	885,144	28,602	78,532	.....	.....	.....	.....	.....
Kentucky (9)	847,465	119,389	W	72,723	W	10,692	.....	.....	.....	W	2,291
Louisiana (2)	5,102,321	.....	.....	8,081,907	144,695	935,243	.....	.....	.....	.....	.....
Maine (47)	23,780	.....	.....	.....	.....	.....	2,510	.....	.....	.....	.....
Maryland (37)	88,216	1,644	W	214	.....	.....	.....	.....	.....	W	W
Massachusetts (43)	50,360	.....	.....	.....	.....	.....	.....	.....	.....	.....	.....
Michigan (12)	670,729	.....	3,780	25,662	1,528	11,893	56,005	.....	11,833	} 7,274	6,069
Minnesota (13)	633,006	.....	W	.....	.....	.....	.....	.....	49,054		W
Mississippi (26)	249,973	.....	.....	118,805	W	64,066	.....	.....	.....	.....	W
Missouri (17)	392,996	4,036	W	22	.....	66	8,445	.....	2,727	.....	W
Montana (22)	313,016	7,064	.....	32,720	W	34,599	88,581	15,613	14	.....	.....
Nebraska (39)	72,657	.....	.....	3,496	W	10,062	.....	.....	.....	.....	.....
Nevada (30)	186,349	.....	.....	.....	.....	113	96,928	374,878	W	.....	.....
New Hampshire (48)	8,730	.....	.....	.....	.....	.....	.....	.....	.....	.....	.....
New Jersey (36)	89,281	.....	W	.....	.....	.....	.....	.....	.....	.....	W
New Mexico (8)	1,060,358	8,175	.....	1,167,577	37,034	118,412	157,419	10,681	W	.....	.....
New York (24)	299,564	.....	3,178	2,202	.....	1,126	.....	.....	W	4,195	4,321
North Carolina (33)	98,365	.....	.....	.....	.....	.....	W	W	W	.....	W
North Dakota (34)	96,047	6,075	.....	33,864	W	21,653	.....	.....	.....	.....	.....
Ohio (14)	612,166	51,431	7,575	79,903	.....	8,286	.....	.....	.....	13,695	20,064
Oklahoma (6)	1,137,267	2,234	.....	1,684,260	41,737	213,313	W	.....	.....	.....	W
Oregon (40)	68,101	.....	.....	.....	.....	.....	3	244	.....	.....	W
Pennsylvania (7)	1,095,743	81,562	15,510	76,451	W	3,798	3,349	W	W	18,786	27,655
Rhode Island (49)	4,386	.....	.....	.....	.....	.....	.....	.....	.....	.....	W
South Carolina (42)	56,365	.....	.....	.....	.....	.....	.....	.....	.....	.....	W
South Dakota (41)	61,576	.....	.....	.....	.....	233	.....	513,427	.....	.....	.....
Tennessee (28)	220,465	9,271	W	89	.....	398	13,916	192	W	W	W
Texas (1)	6,402,462	W	W	8,550,705	306,721	1,222,926	.....	.....	W	W	W
Utah (15)	601,997	4,626	W	42,418	W	23,630	263,451	368,996	1,681	W	W
Vermont (46)	27,843	.....	.....	.....	.....	.....	.....	.....	.....	.....	.....
Virginia (19)	374,321	30,628	W	2,619	.....	1	.....	.....	W	.....	W
Washington (35)	90,922	1,134	.....	.....	.....	.....	W	W	.....	.....	W
West Virginia (4)	1,285,364	118,258	W	234,027	W	2,969	.....	.....	.....	W	W
Wisconsin (38)	87,670	.....	W	.....	.....	.....	.....	.....	824	.....	.....
Wyoming (10)	705,533	8,052	.....	380,105	7,988	148,114	.....	.....	1,809	.....	.....
Undistributed	.....	.....	17,417	.....	21,338	.....	3,176	55,434	9,319	14,265	28,244
U.S. totals	29,789,668	560,919	57,436	22,493,012	617,815	3,453,914	1,522,183	1,495,108	77,692	81,299	120,443

Note: W indicates data withheld to avoid disclosing individual company information. [1] Value data are for all crude minerals produced, including a number of items not reported in this table, and excluding some processed commodities listed here (coke, pig iron, raw steel, and ferroalloys). Corresponding 1971 data are not yet available. [2] Includes 8,727,000 tons of Pennsylvania anthracite. [3] Includes 586,000 tons of by-product ore not distributed by state, but included in undistributed. [4] Frasch process sulfur only; excludes elemental sulfur, sulfur content of

MINERAL COMMODITIES, 1971
or mi. indicates thousands or millions)

Ferroalloys	Lead, mine (recoverable)	Molybdenum, mine th. lb.	Silver th. troy oz.	Uranium, mine (recoverable U3O8 content) th. lb.	Zinc, mine (recoverable)	Cement, Portland and masonry th. 376-lb. bbl.	Clays th.	Lime th.	Phosphate rock th.	Potash (K2O equivalent) th.	Salt th.	Sand and gravel th.	Stone th.	Sulfur (elemental)[4] th. long tons
W	.....	.....	.....	.....	.....	14,006	2,915[5]	761	.....	.....	W	6,674	17,773[6]	.....
.....	.....	.....	.....	W	.....	.....	.....	.....	.....	.....	.....	23,617	2,658	.....
.....	859	22,684	6,170	.....	7,761	W	119[5]	296	.....	.....	.....	19,791	2,873	.....
.....	.....	.....	.....	.....	.....	W	936[5]	157	.....	.....	.....	11,630	17,116	.....
.....	2,284	W	444	.....	3,003	48,493	2,822[5]	630	.....	W	1,887	115,468	43,336	.....
.....	25,746	W	3,390	2,536	61,181	W	625	193	.....	.....	W	27,000	3,785	.....
.....	.....	.....	.....	.....	.....	.....	174	W	.....	.....	.....	6,921	7,193	.....
.....	.....	.....	.....	.....	.....	.....	14	.....	.....	.....	.....	2,205	.....	.....
.....	.....	.....	.....	.....	.....	W	993[5]	159	W	.....	.....	23,228	42,816	.....
.....	.....	.....	.....	.....	.....	6,791	5,791[5]	.....	.....	.....	.....	3,697	30,669	.....
.....	.....	.....	.....	.....	.....	2,051	W	8	.....	.....	W	836	6,056[6]	.....
.....	66,610	.....	19,140	.....	45,078	W	W	W	W	.....	.....	11,279	4,149	.....
.....	1,238	.....	W	.....	12,706	7,967	1,788	W	.....	.....	.....	45,364	61,991[6]	.....
.....	.....	.....	.....	.....	.....	W	1,324	W	.....	.....	.....	24,982	26,233	.....
.....	.....	.....	.....	.....	.....	13,078	1,028[5]	W	.....	.....	.....	18,279	25,389[6]	.....
.....	.....	.....	.....	.....	.....	9,473	879	8	.....	.....	1,240[7]	11,862	14,908[6]	.....
.....	.....	.....	.....	.....	5,268	.....	956[5]	W	.....	.....	.....	8,202	32,514[6]	.....
.....	.....	.....	.....	.....	.....	W	1,073	960	.....	.....	13,352	19,228	9,688[6]	3,681
.....	.....	.....	41	.....	5,850	W	42[5]	.....	.....	.....	.....	8,292	1,133	.....
.....	.....	.....	.....	.....	.....	W	1,027[5]	W	.....	.....	.....	12,842	15,912	.....
.....	.....	.....	.....	.....	.....	.....	186	W	.....	.....	.....	17,343	7,816	.....
.....	.....	.....	670	.....	.....	33,759	2,458	1,444	.....	.....	4,458	56,613	40,705	.....
.....	.....	.....	.....	.....	.....	W	223	W	.....	.....	.....	44,916	5,838	.....
.....	.....	.....	.....	.....	.....	W	2,278	W	.....	.....	.....	11,289	848	.....
.....	429,634	.....	1,661	.....	48,215	24,403	2,354[5]	W	.....	.....	.....	10,327	41,099	.....
.....	615	.....	2,748	.....	361	W	264[5]	199	W	.....	.....	15,781	W	.....
.....	.....	.....	.....	.....	.....	W	69	29	.....	.....	.....	13,224	4,175	.....
.....	111	W	601	.....	71	W	W	W	.....	.....	W	9,379	2,531	.....
.....	.....	.....	.....	.....	.....	.....	37	.....	.....	.....	.....	8,404	429	.....
.....	.....	.....	.....	.....	29,977	.....	201	W	.....	.....	.....	18,511	13,469[6]	.....
.....	2,971	W	782	10,567	13,959	W	76[5]	35	.....	2,291	146	8,869	2,913[6]	.....
41	877	.....	18	.....	63,420	W	1,588[5]	W	.....	.....	5,303	23,221	37,778	.....
.....	.....	.....	W	.....	W	W	3,503[5]	.....	W	.....	.....	14,240	30,917	.....
.....	.....	.....	.....	.....	.....	.....	W	W	.....	.....	W	8,196	W	.....
710	.....	.....	.....	.....	.....	16,168	3,973	4,007	.....	.....	5,709	40,797	46,891	.....
.....	.....	.....	W	.....	W	W	845[5]	W	.....	.....	W	5,713	19,449	.....
W	.....	.....	4	.....	.....	W	157	106	.....	.....	.....	20,230	13,794	.....
362	.....	.....	W	.....	27,438	43,982	2,325[5]	1,760	.....	.....	.....	19,668	64,467	.....
.....	.....	.....	.....	.....	.....	.....	.....	.....	.....	.....	.....	2,252	3[6]	.....
W	.....	.....	.....	.....	.....	W	2,049[5]	.....	.....	.....	.....	6,438	11,047	.....
.....	.....	.....	107	W	.....	W	150[5]	W	.....	.....	.....	16,727	2,199	.....
W	.....	.....	131	.....	103,255	9,955	1,537[5]	W	2,571	.....	.....	8,018	32,369	.....
.....	.....	.....	.....	W	.....	39,187	4,615	1,612	.....	.....	9,217	32,788	41,168	3,075
.....	38,270	W	5,294	1,445	25,701	W	198	172	W	W	614	10,505	2,556	.....
.....	.....	.....	.....	.....	.....	.....	.....	.....	.....	.....	.....	3,761	2,498	.....
W	3,386	.....	.....	.....	16,829	W	1,710	759	.....	.....	W	12,796	34,643	.....
.....	5,177	.....	W	W	5,782	W	255[5]	W	.....	.....	.....	22,702	12,436	.....
W	.....	.....	.....	.....	.....	W	232[5]	197	.....	.....	1,174	7,107	9,880	.....
.....	752	.....	.....	.....	10,645	W	4	246	.....	.....	.....	38,561	15,568	.....
.....	.....	.....	.....	6,986	.....	W	1,798	27	W	.....	.....	9,820	2,894	.....
1,056	.....	75,198	363	2,986	6	152,076	1,075	5,872	36,315	297	976	.....	9,144	.....
2,169	578,530	97,882	41,564	24,520	486,506	421,389	56,666	19,637	38,886	2,588	44,076	919,593	875,716	6,756

sulfuric acid, H2S and SO2 recovered from oil and gas operations and from pyrite and nonferrous metal smelting operations. [5] Partial figure; excludes certain varieties of clay; total of such clays included under undistributed. [6] Partial figure; excludes certain varieties of stone; total of such stone included under undistributed. [7] Excludes brine.

PREPARED BY CHARLES L. KIMBELL   SOURCE: U.S. BUREAU OF MINES

WORLD PRODUCTION OF SELECTED
(metric tons unless otherwise indicated; th.

		Alumi-num th.	Bauxite th.	Asbestos th.	Cement th.	Chromite th.	Coal (including lignite) mi.	Copper, mine[1] th.	Copper, smelter th.	Fluor-spar th.	Gold, mine[1] th. troy oz.	Iron ore th.	Steel th.	Lead, mine[1] th.
	NORTH AMERICA													
1	Canada	1,002	.....	1,483	8,649	.....	17.6	648	462	73	2,243	43,976	11,004	387
2	Mexico	40	.....	.....	7,360	.....	3.4	63	59	1,181	151	4,698	3,809	157
3	United States	3,561	2,020	119	72,863	.....	508.9	1,391	1,421	247	1,495	78,943	109,264	525
4	West Indies	.....	14,722	.....	3,039*	NA	.....	13*	.....	.....	3	.....	55*	.....
5	Central America	.....	.....	.....	1,031*	.....	.....	4	.....	.....	129	2	.....	18*
	SOUTH AMERICA													
6	Argentina	.....	.....	p	5,552	.....	.6*	p	.....	30*	NA	240*	1,913	38
7	Bolivia	.....	.....	.....	206	.....	.....	8	.....	.....	22	6	.....	23
8	Brazil	80	500*	20*	9,803	28*	2.5	5	5	35*	157	42,700*	5,997	28
9	Chile	.....	.....	.....	1,369	.....	1.6	708	625	.....	64	11,228	600*	1
10	Colombia	.....	.....	.....	2,943	1	2.7*	.....	.....	.....	189	442	330*	p
11	Ecuador	.....	.....	.....	470*	.....	.....	p	.....	.....	7*	.....	.....	.....
12	Guyana	.....	3,817*	.....	.....	.....	.....	.....	.....	.....	4*	.....	.....	.....
13	Peru	.....	.....	.....	1,150*	.....	.1*	213	167	.....	99	8,830	190*	178
14	Surinam	60	6,261*	.....	.....	.....	.....	.....	.....	.....	1*	.....	.....	.....
15	Venezuela	24	.....	.....	2,700*	.....	p	.....	.....	.....	19	20,500	950*	.....
16	Other	.....	.....	.....	469	.....	.....	.....	.....	.....	2*	3	16*	.....
	EUROPE													
17	Austria	91	.....	.....	5,491	.....	3.8	3	11	.....	.....	4,171	3,960	8
18	Belgium	.....	.....	.....	6,931	.....	11.7	.....	65	.....	.....	93	12,444	.....
19	Bulgaria	.....	.....	3*	3,880	NA	27.0	45	45	NA	.....	3,001	1,948	100*
20	Czechoslovakia	31*	.....	.....	7,274	.....	113.0	4	4	90*	.....	1,608	12,069	18*
21	Denmark	.....	.....	.....	2,733	.....	.1*	.....	.....	.....	.....	30*	471	.....
22	Finland	.....	.....	14*	1,811	112	.....	28	33	.....	17	744	1,025	5
23	France	384	3,115	1*	28,947	.....	35.0	3	7	300*	65*	55,873	22,859	30
24	Germany, East	65*	.....	.....	8,000*	.....	266.1*	2	2	80*	.....	318	5,350	10*
25	Germany, West	428	.....	.....	32,689	.....	215.3	1	205	88	2	6,391	40,314	41
26	Greece	116	3,088	.....	5,546	24	11.0	.....	.....	.....	.....	687	477	10
27	Hungary	67	2,090	.....	2,713	.....	27.4	1	1	.....	.....	.....	3,110	2*
28	Ireland	.....	.....	.....	1,381	.....	.2*	12	.....	.....	.....	.....	90*	46
29	Italy	120	191	119	31,730	.....	1.6	2	.....	291	.....	683	17,452	30
30	Luxembourg	.....	.....	.....	262	.....	.....	.....	.....	.....	.....	4,507	5,241	.....
31	Netherlands	117	.....	.....	4,045	.....	3.8	.....	.....	.....	.....	.....	5,930	.....
32	Norway (including Svalbard)	529	.....	.....	2,722	.....	.8	23	34	.....	.....	3,911	863	3
33	Poland	100	.....	.....	13,082	.....	180.0	89	89	.....	.....	2,078	12,738	65*
34	Portugal	.....	.....	p	2,458	.....	.3	4	4	15*	15	100	410*	1
35	Romania	110*	305*	.....	8,528	.....	21.9	15	15	15*	60*	3,467	6,803	38*
36	Spain	127	2*	.....	16,993	.....	13.6	43	71	400	.....	7,307	7,759	70
37	Sweden	76	.....	.....	3,827	.....	p	28	58	.....	44*	33,338	5,271	78
38	Switzerland	94	.....	.....	5,220	.....	.....	.....	.....	.....	.....	.....	532	.....
39	U.S.S.R.	1,180*	4,500*	1,150*	100,300	1,800	635.0*	990	990	420*	6,700*	203,000	121,000	450*
40	United Kingdom	119	.....	.....	17,896	.....	146.6	.....	.....	245	116	10,229	24,175	4
41	Yugoslavia	47	1,959	15	4,954	34	30.9	107	94	.....	.....	3,724	2,672	125
42	Other	41	.....	.....	460	600*	.7	7	7	.....	.....	567	.....	.....
	ASIA													
43	Burma	.....	.....	.....	176	.....	p	p	.....	p	p	.....	17	10
44	China, People's Republic of	140*	550*	160*	12,000*	.....	410.0*	100	100	250*	50*	55,000*	21,000*	110*
45	China, Republic of	27	.....	2	5,043	.....	4.1	4	4	.....	19	.....	392	.....
46	Cyprus	.....	.....	23	308	41	.....	18	.....	.....	.....	.....	.....	.....
47	India	178	1,437	11	14,894	261	72.8	11	10	3	119	32,288	5,950	2
48	Indonesia	.....	1,238	.....	571	.....	.2	.....	.....	.....	11	.....	.....	p
49	Iran	.....	.....	.....	4,200*	200*	.4	1	1	.....	15	.....	.....	24
50	Iraq	.....	.....	.....	1,400*	.....	.....	.....	.....	.....	.....	.....	.....	.....
51	Israel	.....	.....	.....	1,405	.....	.....	11	.....	.....	.....	.....	120*	.....
52	Japan	893	.....	22*	53,750	32	33.6	120	661	13	255	1,420	88,557	71
53	Korea, South	18	.....	.....	6,872	.....	12.8	2	6	58	29	504	518	17
54	Malaysia	.....	977	.....	1,096	.....	.....	.....	.....	.....	6	.....	70*	.....
55	Pakistan (including Bangladesh)	.....	p	.....	2,652	24	1.3	.....	.....	.....	.....	.....	70*	p
56	Philippines	.....	.....	1*	3,117	432	p	197	.....	.....	637	2,243	86	.....
57	Saudi Arabia	.....	.....	.....	712	.....	.....	.....	.....	.....	.....	.....	.....	.....
58	Sri Lanka (formerly Ceylon)	.....	.....	.....	385	.....	.....	.....	.....	.....	.....	.....	.....	.....
59	Thailand	.....	.....	.....	2,779	.....	.4	.....	.....	427	.....	40	120	2
60	Turkey	.....	127	2*	7,543	603	10.0	30	18	1	.....	2,080	1,122	7
61	Vietnam, South	.....	.....	.....	.280*	.....	.....	.....	.....	.....	.....	.....	.....	.....
62	Other	.....	.....	.....	9,774*	NA	35.7	12*	12*	110*	164*	8,700*	2,542	80
	AFRICA													
63	Algeria	.....	.....	.....	1,000*	.....	p	1	.....	.....	.....	3,050	18*	6
64	Angola	.....	.....	.....	530	.....	.....	2	.....	.....	.....	6,158	.....	.....
65	Cameroon	51	.....	.....	.....	.....	.....	.....	.....	.....	p	.....	.....	.....
66	Egypt, Arab Republic of	.....	.....	p	3,883	.....	.....	.....	.....	.....	.....	510	500*	NA
67	Ethiopia	.....	.....	.....	211	.....	.....	.....	.....	.....	21	.....	.....	.....
68	Gabon	.....	.....	.....	.....	.....	.....	.....	.....	.....	14	.....	.....	.....
69	Ghana	111	329	.....	445*	.....	.....	.....	.....	.....	698	.....	.....	.....
70	Kenya	.....	.....	.....	804	.....	.....	.....	.....	7	.....	.....	.....	.....
71	Liberia	.....	.....	.....	90*	.....	.....	.....	.....	.....	1	23,179	.....	.....
72	Malagasy Republic	.....	.....	.....	77	140*	.....	.....	.....	.....	p	.....	.....	.....
73	Morocco	.....	.....	.....	1,475	.....	.5	4	.....	NA	.....	623	.....	74
74	Mozambique	.....	6*	p	425*	.....	.4*	.....	.....	.....	p	.....	.....	.....
75	Nigeria	.....	.....	.....	664	.....	.2	.....	.....	.....	p	.....	.....	.....
76	Rhodesia (Southern)	.....	.....	80*	500*	360*	3.4*	23	23	p	500*	510*	150*	.....
77	Sierra Leone	.....	590	.....	.....	.....	.....	.....	.....	.....	.....	2,547	.....	.....
78	South Africa, Republic of	.....	.....	319	5,861	1,644	58.7	158	160	239	31,389	10,678	4,956	.....
79	South West Africa	.....	.....	.....	.....	.....	.....	25	29	.....	.....	.....	.....	67
80	Swaziland	.....	.....	35	.....	.....	.1	.....	.....	.....	.....	2,887	.....	.....
81	Tanzania	.....	.....	.....	178	.....	p	.....	.....	.....	p	.....	.....	.....
82	Tunisia	.....	.....	.....	584	.....	.....	.....	.....	33	.....	936	100*	21
83	Uganda	.....	.....	.....	200	.....	.....	16	16	.....	.....	.....	27	NA
84	Zaïre (formerly Congo-Kinshasa)	.....	.....	.....	360*	.....	.1	407	407	.....	179	.....	.....	28
85	Zambia	.....	.....	.....	470*	.....	.8	651	644	.....	10	.....	.....	.....
86	Other	.....	2,640*	.....	1,101	21	.....	4	.....	.....	7*	8,446	.....	.....
	OCEANIA													
87	Australia	223	12,541	1	4,719	.....	72.3	170	151	.....	670	62,100	6,736	399
88	Fiji	.....	.....	.....	77	.....	.....	.....	.....	.....	89	.....	.....	.....
89	New Caledonia	.....	.....	.....	.....	.....	.....	.....	.....	.....	.....	.....	.....	.....
90	New Zealand	.....	.....	.....	823	.....	2.1*	p	.....	.....	9	576	200	1
91	Other	.....	.....	.....	.....	.....	.....	.....	.....	.....	24	.....	.....	.....
	World totals	10,250	63,005	3,580	590,911	6,357	3,003.1	6,427	6.716	4.636	46.505	782,837	582,342	3,408

[1] Metal content of ore.   [2] Withheld to avoid disclosing individual company data.   [3] Includes estimated production of Sinai Peninsula.   * Estimate.   NA Not available.   p Indicates small unknown production or less than one half of indicated unit for column.

MINERAL COMMODITIES, 1971
or mi. indicates thousands or millions)

Lead, smelter (th.)	Manganese ore (th.)	Mercury 76-pound flasks	Nickel, mine[1] (th.)	Petroleum, crude (mi. bbl.)	Phosphate rock (th.)	Pyrite, gross weight (th.)	Salt (th.)	Silver, mine[1] (th. troy oz.)	Sulfur, elemental (th.)	Tin, mine[1] (long tons)	Tin, smelter (long tons)	Titanium, ilmenite and rutile (th.)	Tungsten, mine[1]	Zinc, mine[1] (th.)	Zinc, smelter (th.)	
157	....	18,000*	267	496	....	289	4,839	45,950	4,727	131	....	775	1,379	1,268	372	1
136	267	35,390	p	156	58	....	4,360	36,657	8,772	471	471	....	238	265	78	2
590	p	17,627	14	3,454	35,277	[2]	39,986	41,564	1,178	[2]	[2]	620	3,130	446	695	3
....	....	....	36*	48	110*	....	1,550*	17	21	....	....	....	....	....	....	4
p	....	....	....	....	....	....	114*	4,118	8	....	....	....	....	23	....	5
44	32*	....	....	155	....	....	960*	2,050*	40*	1,000*	....	....	141	40	33	6
p	....	....	....	13	....	....	....	6,800*	20*	27,441	7,116	....	1,837	46	....	7
26	2,602	....	3	64	800*	....	1,477	624	10*	2,560*	2,352	20*	898	13*	11*	8
....	24	310	....	13	13	....	425	5,360	40*	....	....	....	....	2	....	9
....	....	p	p	79	12*	....	638	67	35*	....	....	....	....	p	....	10
....	....	....	....	1	....	....	....	70	....	....	....	....	....	p	....	11
....	....	....	....	....	....	....	....	....	....	....	....	....	....	....	....	12
67	8	1,800*	....	23	22	....	180*	38,398	....	100*	....	....	....	387	57	13
....	....	....	....	....	....	....	....	....	....	....	....	....	....	....	....	14
....	....	....	....	1,295	49	....	260*	....	10*	....	....	....	....	....	....	15
....	....	....	....	....	....	....	....	....	....	....	....	....	....	....	....	16
9	....	....	....	18	....	....	482	225	3*	....	....	....	47	21	16	17
80	....	....	....	....	....	....	....	....	15	....	3,878	....	....	....	207	18
100*	30*	....	....	2	....	150*	135*	....	8*	....	....	....	....	70*	76*	19
18*	....	7,000*	....	1	....	360*	180*	1,100	....	....	....	....	....	12*	....	20
....	....	....	....	....	....	133	....	....	....	....	....	....	....	....	....	21
....	....	135	5	....	....	861	....	623	101	....	....	139	....	51	64	22
108	....	....	....	14	27*	85*	6,546*	2,000*	1,816	317	....	....	300	15	219	23
24	....	....	....	p	....	140*	2,200*	5,000*	115*	1,000*	1,200*	....	....	10*	15*	24
95	....	....	....	54	....	554*	8,413	1,800	205	....	1,151	....	....	131	255	25
12	6	....	11	15	....	214	70*	462	....	....	....	....	....	14	....	26
1*	170*	....	....	....	....	....	....	6*	2*	....	....	....	....	5*	....	27
....	....	2,000*	....	....	....	....	....	2,200*	....	....	....	....	....	88	....	28
48	31	42,671	....	9	....	1,518	4,400*	1,222	82	....	....	....	....	104	139	29
....	....	....	....	....	....	....	....	....	....	....	....	....	....	....	....	30
24	....	....	....	12	....	....	3,167	....	35*	....	824	....	....	....	41	31
....	....	....	p	2	100*	781	....	....	3	....	....	642	....	11	62	32
60	....	....	2*	3	....	200*	2,959	200*	2,778	....	....	....	....	190*	220	33
1	5	....	....	....	....	561	435*	250*	5	515	500*	1	1,338	2	....	34
36*	....	....	....	102	....	840	2,270*	1,000*	....	....	....	....	....	40*	40*	35
72	18	67,528	....	1	....	2,429	2,020*	1,640*	7	170	4,751	24	531	86	89	36
32	....	....	....	....	....	663	....	4,823	6	....	....	....	....	96	....	37
....	....	....	....	....	....	291	....	....	....	....	....	....	....	....	....	38
450*	7,000*	50,000*	120*	2,778	21,650	4,300	13,000*	39,000*	2,180	28,000*	28,000*	NA	6,350	650*	650*	39
39	....	....	....	1	....	....	9,245*	....	43	1,787	22,787	....	....	....	116	40
99	16	15,564	....	22	....	276	209	3,354	....	....	....	....	....	100	53	41
....	....	....	....	9	....	....	3*	....	....	....	....	....	....	....	....	42
10*	....	20,000*	p	7	....	....	186	952	....	680	....	....	181	4	....	43
100*	1,000*	....	....	168*	1,200*	2,000*	15,000*	800*	250*	20,000*	20,000*	....	8,000	100*	100	44
....	....	....	....	1	....	46	669	73	11*	....	....	....	....	....	....	45
....	....	....	....	....	....	781	6	....	....	....	....	....	....	....	....	46
2	1,779	....	....	52	249	....	5,790	124	5	....	....	94	16	8	21	47
....	12	....	27	326	....	18*	285	1*	....	19,411	9,260*	....	....	....	....	48
p	20*	....	....	1,662	....	....	390*	....	495*	....	....	....	....	58*	....	49
....	....	....	....	624	....	....	55*	....	....	....	....	....	....	....	....	50
....	....	....	....	45[3]	765	....	80	....	8*	....	....	....	....	....	....	51
215	285	5,700*	....	6	....	2,363	946	11,540	404	777	1,355	9	706	294	601	52
3	2	....	....	....	....	....	372	1,543	....	5	....	....	1,841	28	9	53
....	....	....	....	25	....	....	644	....	....	74,253	85,719	156	113	....	....	54
....	p	....	....	4	....	....	227	....	....	....	....	....	....	....	....	55
....	5	5,022	....	....	305*	....	227	1,940	5	....	....	....	....	4	....	56
....	....	....	....	1,642	....	....	....	....	....	....	....	....	....	....	....	57
....	14	....	....	p	....	....	86	160	....	....	....	88	....	....	....	58
p	13	9,500*	....	25	....	59	660*	....	25*	....	....	....	2,507	1*	....	59
....	....	....	....	....	....	....	120	....	....	....	....	....	....	25*	....	60
....	....	....	....	....	....	....	....	....	....	....	....	....	....	....	....	61
65	....	....	....	2,029	3,181*	500*	991	700	30*	1,548	....	....	2,100	135*	100*	62
....	....	7,136	....	280	500*	33*	100*	100	....	....	....	....	20	....	....	63
....	23	....	....	41	....	....	91	....	....	....	....	....	....	....	....	64
....	....	....	....	....	....	....	....	....	....	22	....	....	....	....	....	65
....	4*	....	....	107	745*	....	500*	....	1*	....	....	....	....	....	....	66
....	....	....	....	....	....	....	290	....	....	....	....	....	....	....	....	67
....	1,869	....	....	42	....	....	....	....	....	....	....	....	....	....	....	68
....	599	....	....	....	....	....	47	....	....	....	....	....	....	....	....	69
....	....	....	....	....	....	....	44	....	....	....	....	....	....	....	....	70
....	....	....	....	....	....	....	....	....	....	....	....	....	....	....	....	71
....	....	....	....	....	....	....	28	....	....	....	....	....	....	....	....	72
19	101	....	p	p	12,008	441	53	809	....	7	12	....	12	....	....	73
....	....	....	....	....	....	....	29*	....	....	....	....	....	....	....	....	74
....	....	....	....	558	....	....	....	....	....	7,005	7,243	....	93	....	....	75
....	....	....	12*	....	....	....	....	71*	....	600*	600*	....	....	....	....	76
....	....	....	....	....	....	....	....	....	....	....	....	5	....	....	....	77
....	3,237	....	13	....	1,729	750	353	3,378	25	1,997	703	....	141	p	20	78
59	....	....	....	....	....	....	110*	1,426	....	949	....	....	122	44	....	79
....	....	....	....	....	....	....	....	....	....	12	....	....	....	....	....	80
....	....	....	....	....	....	....	35	36	....	53	....	....	....	....	....	81
19	....	340	....	32	3,162	....	351	58*	....	146	....	....	12	....	....	82
....	387	....	....	....	13	....	3	....	....	6,400*	1,330*	....	68	120	64	83
28	....	....	....	....	....	....	....	1,800	....	....	....	....	....	57	57	84
....	52	....	....	....	....	....	....	768	....	1,465*	....	....	172	p	....	85
....	....	....	....	1,008	3,271	....	304*	....	....	....	....	....	....	....	....	86
324	1,076	....	31*	113	15	255	3,080*	21,615	10	9,365	6,233	1,182	1,544	448	259	87
....	8	....	102	....	....	....	....	27*	....	....	....	....	....	....	....	88
....	....	....	....	....	....	....	....	....	....	....	....	....	....	....	....	89
....	....	....	....	1	....	....	44	66	....	....	....	....	2	....	....	90
....	15	....	....	....	2,585*	....	....	18	....	....	....	....	....	....	....	91
3,172	20,710	305,723	643	17,638	87,541	20,754	142,809	294,709	23,535	229,533	226,821	3,755	33,652	5,558	4,739	

with reasonable certainty. In the table of 1971 world production, substantial figures are credited to "Other" under the continental headings of Asia and Africa. In Asia, the 2,029 million barrel "Other" total was distributed as follows (in million barrels): Kuwait, 1,068; former Kuwait–Saudi Arabia Neutral Zone, 199; United Arab Emirates (Abu Dhabi and Dubai), 387; Qatar, 157; Oman, 107; Bahrain, 27; Syria, 36; and Brunei, 48. In Africa, Libya accounted for the overwhelming part of the 1,008-million-barrel total, with 130,000 barrels coming from the People's Republic of the Congo.

Natural gas. World 1972 marketed production was estimated at about 43 trillion cubic feet, about 8 percent above the 1971 level. The United States accounted for about half of the total and the Soviet Union for about one-fifth, with Canada and the Netherlands ranking third and fourth. International marine shipment of liquefied gas continued to receive newspaper attention. There was substantial growth in such shipments, but the total amount of gas so transported was an insignificant part of 1972 world supply. However, marine transport and international pipeline movement of natural gas cannot be regarded lightly. Sizable quantities of natural gas produced in association with oil production are burned at the production site and lost as an energy resource, owing to the lack of markets in many producing areas.

Aluminum. Partial returns for most major non-Communist producers of both bauxite and aluminum were at lower levels than in the same period of 1971, indicating that annual 1972 world totals for both the ore and the metal may have fallen below the record 1971 high. As early as late 1970, some non-Communist world producers reduced output because world aluminum demand was not increasing at the anticipated rate. However, other producers increased activities, and the expected production slump did not materialize in 1971.

The U.S. aluminum price, unchanged since 1970 at 29 cents a pound, registered a decline to 25 cents in early May of 1972 and held that level through the third quarter.

This year Australia replaced Jamaica as the world leader in production of bauxite. Considering development plans and available reserves, it appears likely that Australia will retain first rank for the foreseeable future.

Copper. A buildup of copper stocks and consequent price decline anticipated in 1971 failed to materialize on a worldwide basis, and in the first half of 1972 there was a slight increase in the U.S. copper price. A modest U.S. price decline was recorded in July 1972, but preliminary figures indicated that 1972 world output would reach a new record high.

In Chile, the recently nationalized industry had a disappointing 1971 performance. Chilean output capacity was increased by about 135,000 metric tons in that year; however, output was little changed from the 1970 level, which itself was below the nation's capacity. The Chilean state agency, Codelco, attributed the low production level to such factors as inadequate water supply, unsatisfactory training of employees, and defective equipment, but did not allude to the departure of managerial and supervisory employees or to the annoyance of at least a part of the labor force with government intervention in the mines—two causes postulated by others as contributing significantly to the shortfall.

Gold. Preliminary returns indicated that world gold output in 1972 would exceed the 46.5 million ounce level of 1971 and thus that a new record high would be reached.

Output in South Africa, the world's leading producer, advanced, as some lower grade ores were sent to mills; the marked increase in world gold prices made these ores processable at a profit.

In the United States, the increase in the gold price led to a decision to reopen a Colorado mine closed in 1961 by the squeeze between rising costs and the then-fixed $35 per ounce price. In September, it was announced that produc-

tion by the Cripple Creek Gold Corporation might begin in 2½ years.

Iron and steel. Preliminary returns indicated that world iron ore output topped 800 million metric tons in 1972, with the bulk of the increase attributed to rising production in the Soviet Union, Australia, and the People's Republic of China. While final U.S. production results were not available, preliminary information suggested that it certainly did not reach the record high 1970 level of 88,580,000 metric tons, and may not have topped the 78,943,000-ton 1971 level. The lower level of U.S. output was attributed to a substantial buildup in stocks by both mines and consumers during a period of very low steel production in the last half of 1971.

Preliminary figures indicated growth in world steel output during 1972, with the United States registering a substantial recovery after the sharp decline in 1971; however, output growth elsewhere, particularly in Eastern Europe, apparently was greater, judging from figures for the first half of the year. In 1971, the United States was displaced by the Soviet Union from its position of world leadership in steel output for the first time in the twentieth century.

Lead and zinc. The world's lead and zinc industry in general enjoyed a better year in 1972 than in 1971, and total production of both metals advanced as world demand increased. Industry representatives indicated that they expected demand for both metals to grow substantially during the 1970's, but pointed out that for the industry to meet this demand, higher prices would be essential. During 1971, four major zinc smelters in the United States were closed owing to declining economic returns that resulted from increasing wages, substantial capital improvements for pollution control, and a variety of other factors. This loss in capacity substantially increased U.S. dependence upon foreign sources for zinc.

New facilities with an aggregate capacity of more than 1 million tons of zinc annually (none in the United States) were projected for completion by 1975.

One economic problem which threatens the industry is the market-glut of sulfur that could stem from sulfur recovery efforts required under new antipollution laws. The lead-zinc industry produces considerable sulfur in the form of sulfuric acid as a by-product of metal recovery. Falling prices for this by-product could necessitate price rises for the metals.

Both metals registered price increases on U.S. markets during the first eight months of 1972; lead advanced from 14 cents a pound on January 1 to 15.5 cents in August; zinc increased from 17 cents a pound to 18 cents in the same period.

Mercury. Following the 1970 slump in mercury mine output to a level of less than 285,000 76-pound flasks, production advanced sharply in 1971 to almost 306,000 flasks, chiefly as the result of a 22,000-flask increase in Spain (primarily an increase in production of mercury in ore rather than in smelter recovery).

Incomplete data on 1972 output indicated that the level of production was falling, with Spain's production receding to the 1970 level. The U.S. price for the metal, which averaged $407.77 per flask in 1970 and $292.41 in 1971, fell to $213.24 (monthly average) in January of 1972 and $152.50 in February, and then began moving upward, reaching a level of $261 to $270 per flask in September. The world market for mercury in recent years has been affected quite appreciably by environmental considerations as well as by the commodity's high price during the late 1960's. The influence of environmental problems was dual—not only was mercury use reduced in an effort to moderate pollution, but also secondary recovery efforts were intensified. Thus, total demand was reduced, and a larger share of this reduced demand was met by reclaimed mercury. Furthermore, lower-cost materials are replacing mercury for some uses.

Nickel. Despite an estimated 16 percent decline in non-Communist world nickel demand in 1971, output reached a new record high of 643,000 metric tons in that year. Production cutbacks were initiated at some facilities in late 1971 and continued into 1972. Late in the year, it was not clear whether these reductions would be outweighed by increases resulting from new openings and output increases elsewhere. However, industry representatives maintained expectations of a 7 percent annual growth in demand over the long term, and development of new mines and smelting facilities continued through 1972.

Plans were announced to export $60 million in U.S. goods, mostly mining and petroleum equipment, to the Soviet Union on a barter basis in exchange for unreported quantities of metals, mainly nickel. In contrast, Canadian producers completed negotiations to ship nickel to the People's Republic of China.

Platinum. It appeared that 1972 output would top the 4,076,788 troy ounce production of 1971. Looking hopefully to the future, major producers announced plans for expansion.

Silver. The price of silver rose during the first nine months of the year, and it was expected, on the basis of incomplete returns, that world output would top the nearly 295 million ounce level of 1971.

In the United States, silver output was dealt a crippling blow on May 2 by the Sunshine Silver Mine disaster in the Coeur d'Alene mining district of Idaho. This mine fire claimed 91 lives and resulted in the closure of the mine for the balance of the year. The loss in production was estimated at 5.4 million ounces of silver.

Tin. Available partial data indicate that world output advanced slightly, for both mine and smelter output, over the 1971 levels. The New York market tin price advanced during the early months of 1972, registered an 11 cent decline in May from the April average of $1.82 a pound, and then began rising again through September. Tin price fluctuations were less violent in 1971 and early 1972 than in previous years. These stable market conditions, if they continue at a reasonably high level of early, may provide some stimulus to development of additional reserves. In the past, efforts to increase output had a reasonable chance of being met with plunging prices, making investment in major facilities quite risky.

Bolivia, long a major mine producer, became a significant smelter producer of tin in 1971–1972. Indonesia registered a modest gain in mine output in 1971 and a substantial gain in smelter output, an increase which seemed likely to be maintained in 1972.

Fertilizer materials. Available information again pointed to modest gains in world output of all three major fertilizer materials—nitrogen, phosphate, and potash. However, productive capacity remained in excess of demand and prices seemed destined to remain low, particularly since capacity continued to increase.

Environmental considerations continued as a threat to increased use of phosphates for some applications in the United States, but there were contradictory views on the seriousness of the phosphate pollution problem. Moreover, the hazards of phosphate substitutes were not known.

Sulfur. World sulfur output reached a new high in 1972, more than meeting the rising demand, with the result that stocks continued to increase and the depressed prices of the previous four years continued. However, the decline in the price at least was checked; the U.S. export price remained at $25 to $26 per ton through the first nine months.

Poland has become a major world producer of sulfur, and Iraq was also expected to become a significant producer. A substantial part of Iraq's output was slated for the People's Republic of China.

Industry spokesmen generally expected demand to go on increasing, but environmental control projects aimed at re-covering sulfur from fuels and from smelter stack gases promised to result in a growing potential source of sulfur in addition to mining pyrite and elemental sulfur.

CHARLES L. KIMBELL

MINNESOTA. Government. A power struggle over legislative reapportionment developed early in the year between the Democratic Farmer-Labor governor, Wendell R. Anderson, and the Republican-controlled legislature. The deadlock, whose origins lay in the 1971 legislative session, was broken by a three-judge federal court, which as part of its reapportionment formula cut state senate membership from 67 to 35 and house membership from 135 to 105. This result was welcomed by the governor as an alternative to a special session. However, the U.S. Supreme Court, acting on an appeal brought by the state senate, said the reduction exceeded the doctrine laid down in the previous "one man, one vote" reapportionment cases. Ordered to try again, the lower court produced a "remap" that cut the lower house by only one seat. This was not challenged.

Minnesota became one of the first states to move systematically away from reliance on the local property tax to support public schools, after a federal court ruled in 1971 that such financing discriminated against children in low-wealth school districts. This year, the yield from new taxes was channeled into the school aid formula.

Racial issues. A U.S. district court ordered Minneapolis schools desegregated, in effect embracing a moderate program previously endorsed by the city's school board. Although the plan stressed such devices as school pairing and clustering, it would increase busing. However, busing was not at issue in the case, which was brought by integrationists who felt the school board had not gone far enough. The two antibusing members on the seven-member Minneapolis school board served notice that bitter battles were ahead for control of the board. However, inasmuch as the federal court retained jurisdiction over the integration plan, a general aim of which is to prevent any school from having more than a 43 percent minority enrollment, it could block efforts to dismantle the board's program.

An agreement between the Chippewa Indians on the Leech Lake Reservation and the state gave the Indians the right to charge non-Indian sportsmen hunting and fishing on the reservation a special $1 fee. The agreement implemented a federal court decision restoring the Indians' historic right to hunt and fish without state control on reservation land. Under the agreement the Indians pledged to refrain from commercial fishing and to abide by an Indian-devised fish and game code.

Business and agriculture. A generally healthy economic situation, characterized by rising profits, was marred by a protracted strike begun on June 30 by pilots for Minnesota-based Northwest Airlines.

The agricultural picture was somewhat mixed. Crop prospects were dim in 14 counties that suffered such heavy rains and flooding that they were declared disaster areas. However, in areas unaffected by excessive moisture there were indications of a record corn crop.

The value of the tourist industry was estimated at $950 million in 1972, up 10.4 percent from 1971 but short of the projected $1 billion.

The arts. Ground was broken for a $15.9 million "arts complex" that will enlarge and improve the interconnected Minneapolis Institute of Arts, Children's Theater, and Minneapolis College of Art and Design. The new complex, one result of a $26 million fund-raising drive, is designed to generate more community involvement and financial support. The Tyrone Guthrie Theater, which succeeded in 1971 in reversing a financial and artistic decline, had another successful season.

For election results and campaign highlights, see the special supplement ELECTION '72.

Area and population. Area, 84,068 sq. mi. Pop. (est. 1972), 3,896,000. Principal cities: St. Paul (cap.), 313,206; Minneapolis, 436,425.

Government. Gov., Wendell R. Anderson (DFL); lt. gov., Rudy Perpich (DFL); secy. of state, Arlen Erdahl (R); treas., Val Bjornson (R); atty. gen., Warren Spannaus (DFL). Legislature (officially nonpartisan): senate, 33 conservatives, 33 liberals, 1 independent; house, 70 conservatives, 65 liberals.

Finance (fiscal 1972). Budget: revenue, $3,403,431,426; expenditure, $3,403,720,680.

Education (1971–1972). Public primary schools: enrollment, 502,678; teachers, 23,190. Public secondary schools: enrollment, 444,025; teachers, 26,908. Private and parochial schools: enrollment, 106,392; teachers, 6,442.

AUSTIN C. WEHRWEIN

MISSISSIPPI. Legislation.

The largest public works program in state history, a $600 million highway bill, was passed by the legislature, along with a 1-cent increase in gasoline taxes. A $425 million budget was approved, as were a 5 percent teachers' pay hike; a $25 million park renovation program, to include two new parks and five tourist facilities; a workmen's compensation increase from $40 to $50 a week; a recharting of congressional districts according to the 1970 census; a law allowing branch colleges to confer degrees; a drug law reform reducing marijuana-possession penalties; and a broadened absentee ballot provision for college students and out-of-town workers. Governor William L. Waller, favoring a 12 percent limit for credit card interest, tried to veto an 18 percent maximum, but courts ruled him a day late.

The state prison came under scrutiny after revelations dealing with poor living conditions, an escape attempt, and slayings of two guards. In September, Governor Waller authorized spending $1 million in federal funds to improve facilities. One new policy made the prison the first in the nation to allow conjugal visits to women prisoners from their husbands, a privilege already allowed male prisoners.

Racial issues. Blacks made official gains as Governor Waller fulfilled promises by naming several blacks for the first time to top posts, including membership on boards governing state universities, the state prison, public welfare, educational television, and a new drug enforcement bureau. Three blacks were added for the first time to the 379-man highway patrol.

A longtime fighter against racial injustice, Pulitzer Prize-winning (1946) publisher-writer Hodding Carter, Jr., died of a heart attack at 65 in Greenville. He was lauded by the 1972 state legislature—an earlier session had censured him for his expressions about racial issues.

Education. The flight of whites to private schools to avoid desegregation appeared to have ended. Statistics showed a decline of 5,000 public school students from the 1970–1971 school year to 1971–1972, but officials said that 83 percent of these were black and 3,500 were first graders, reflecting a birthrate decline. Private school enrollment leveled off, despite the highest rate of integration to date. There was rising sentiment to restore compulsory school attendance laws, abandoned after the 1964 school desegregation ruling. The Mississippi Teachers Association reported 28,000 school-age children not in schools.

Economics. New openings this year included a $400 million Mississippi Power and Light Company nuclear generating plant at Port Gibson, to employ 1,500 people, and a $280 million Pennzoil Company synthetic natural gas plant at Pascagoula, to create 300 new jobs. Total industrial investments, for 56 new plants and 59 expansions, totaled over $775 million by the end of July.

In agriculture, the August forecast of 2.2 million bales of cotton was 507,000 bales above the 1971 output; and rice, at 2,321,000 hundredweight, was 51,000 over 1971. But corn, at 6,720,000 bushels, was down 37 percent from 1971; soybeans, at 52,095,000 bushels, were down 4 percent; and hay, at 1,043,000 tons, was down 15 percent.

For election results and campaign highlights, see the special supplement ELECTION '72.

Area and population. Area, 47,716 sq. mi. Pop. (1970), 2,216,-912. Jackson (cap.), 153,968.

Government. Gov., William L. Waller; lt. gov., William Winter; secy. of state, Heber Ladner; atty. gen., A. F. Summer; treas., Brad Dye; aud., W. H. King. All are Democrats. Legislature: senate, 50 D, 2 R; house, 119 D, 2 R, 1 I.

Finance (1971–1972). Revenue, $1,372,525,306.26; expenditure, $1,342,180,747.13; cash on hand July 1, $153,767,073.82.

Education (1971–1972). Public elementary schools, 655; enrollment, 287,354; teachers, 12,824. Public secondary schools, 396; enrollment, 248,512; teachers, 10,005. Private and parochial schools, 305; enrollment, 64,196; teachers, 3,060. Institutions of higher learning, 25 public, 16 private; enrollment, 101,893.

W. DAVID BROWN

MISSOURI.

Many Missourians will remember 1972 as the year they had their first vice-presidential candidate since 1944—at least for 19 days. Harry S Truman, chosen by President Franklin D. Roosevelt, went on to assume the presidency in 1945 after Roosevelt's death. But Senator Thomas F. Eagleton, chosen by the 1972 Democratic nominee, Senator George McGovern of South Dakota, was forced to resign from the ticket after he disclosed that he had, on three occasions, received psychiatric treatment for exhaustion and depression. Feelings ran high in the state over Senator Eagleton's ouster. (*See* PEOPLE IN THE NEWS: Thomas F. Eagleton.)

Legislation. Major legislation passed in 1972 included state constitutional amendments to give tax relief to the elderly and to completely reorganize state government. The legislature created a statewide public defender system and brought Missouri, long called the billboard capital of the United States, into compliance with federal regulations regarding billboards.

Measures defeated by the legislature included ratification of the proposed Equal Rights Amendment to the U.S. Constitution, liberalization of the state abortion and divorce laws, an antibusing state constitutional amendment, a law that would have instituted no-fault automobile insurance, and abolition of capital punishment. In September, however, the Missouri supreme court reduced to life imprisonment the death sentences of eight convicted murderers after the U.S. Supreme Court had declared the death penalty unconstitutional.

A state fire marshal's office was created by the legislature after newspaper investigations showed that a wave of arson-for-insurance had been going on in St. Louis. Unscrupulous speculators were buying buildings at low prices in changing neighborhoods, insuring them for many times their market value, and then having them burned.

Education and culture. This year Missouri's public schools received their largest appropriation ever—$70 million. In addition, a bill was passed that would give aid to needy youths to enable them to attend the college of their choice within the state. That bill is expected to be challenged in court, as is another that would provide funds for textbooks to be used in parochial schools.

The rise in quality of the St. Louis Symphony Orchestra was noted by many critics during the orchestra's 1972 tour. The Missouri state council on the arts received $215,000 from the state this year, with which it sponsored traveling art exhibits, tours by Kansas City's Lyric Opera Company, and performances in schools.

Economic developments. Business and industrial expansion was slower in 1972 than in 1971, largely as a result of higher interest rates and the Nixon administration's economic stabilization programs. Unemployment (still lower than the national average) increased in the industrial sector in the first half of 1972. Agriculture and agriculture-related manufacturing remained the major industry in the state.

Per-capita income in Missouri increased 6.7 percent during 1971, slightly less than the national average over the same 12 months.

For election results and campaign highlights, see the special supplement ELECTION '72.

Area and population. Area, 69,686 sq. mi. Pop. (1970 census), 4,677,399. Principal cities: Jefferson City (cap.), 32,407; St. Louis, 622,236; Kansas City, 507,087; Springfield, 120,096.

Government. Gov., Warren E. Hearnes (D); lt. gov., William S. Morris (D); secy of state, James C. Kirkpatrick (D); treas., William E. Robinson (D); atty. gen., John C. Danforth (R). Legislature: senate, 23 D, 11 R; house, 112 D, 51 R.

Finance (fiscal year ended June 30, 1972). Revenue, $1,573,-973,497.75; expenditure, $1,550,260,782.52. Principal sources of revenue: sales and income taxes. Principal expenditures: health and welfare, highways, education.

Education (1970–1971). Public elementary schools, 1,625; enrollment, 788,469; teachers, 32,941. Public secondary schools, 702; enrollment, 296,364; teachers, 16,878. Private and parochial schools, 586; enrollment, 137,938; teachers, 6,230.

SALLY BIXBY DEFTY

MONGOLIA. Politics and government. President Zhamsarangin Sambu died in May at the age of 77. In the first move of an expected series of top-level realignments, Damdinjavyn Maydar was named to replace Sonomyn Luvsan—a career diplomat—as first deputy chairman of the Council of Ministers.

As the new chief lieutenant of the council's powerful chairman, Premier Yumzhagiyn Tsedenbal, Maydar thus rose to a key role in Mongolian national affairs. A Soviet-educated expert on veterinary services (a critical skill in Mongolia's livestock-centered economy), Maydar had been chairman of the Planning Commission for the past 20 years. In that post he earned a reputation for expertise in industrial matters as well. Soon after his promotion, Maydar flew to Moscow to discuss new prospects for Soviet economic, technical, and scientific assistance.

The central committee of the ruling Workers' Party—the country's sole legal political organization—was enlarged after the 1971 meeting of the 16th party congress. The expansion reflected a growth in party membership, which had reached 58,000.

Foreign relations. Contacts with the outside world by this isolated and landlocked country continued to expand. A Mongolian team attended the Olympics Games in Munich. Diplomacy continued to echo the familiar themes of close dependence on the Soviet Union and unveiled hostility toward China.

Economy. The belated drafting of the 1971–1975 five-year plan was the highlight of the year. It projected an increase in sheep and other livestock to 25 million head, a rise of 11 percent. The plan also envisioned a 50 percent growth in crop production and electrical output, both important indicators of economic development in Mongolia.

An expanding trade volume with Japan was probably responsible for the sole surprise in the plan: the target growth rate for mineral production jumped from an earlier estimate of 80 percent to 150 percent for the five-year period. Japan was expected to buy more fluorspar for its steel mills as well as more Mongolian tungsten.

Area and population. Area, 604,250 sq. mi. Pop. (1971), 1.3 million. Ulan Bator (cap.), 250,000.

Government. People's republic. First deputy chmn. of Presidium (acting chmn.), Sonomyn Luvsan; first secy. of Mongolian People's Revolutionary (Communist) Party and prime min., Yumzhagin Tsedenbal.

Finance. Monetary unit, tugrik; 1 tugrik = US$0.255. Budget (1970): revenue, 1.92 billion tugriks; expenditure, 1.91 billion tugriks.

Trade. Principal exports: cattle, horses, wool, hides, meat, butter. Principal imports: industrial and consumer goods. Chief trading partner: Soviet Union.

DICK WILSON

MONTANA. Legislation. No legislative session was held this year, but the capitol building was taken over by a constitutional convention, delegated to write the first new constitution since Montana achieved statehood in 1889. The new constitution, which voters approved by a narrow margin in a special election in June, is less than half as long as the 1889 document and makes some important changes. It provides for 60-day legislative sessions every year, instead of every two years, and makes the legislature more directly responsive by providing single-member districts. The constitution also permits amendment by the legislature or by the people through the initiative process; removes the 2-mill limit on statewide property taxes; and requires protection of the environment and reclamation of spoiled land.

Economic developments. The U.S.-Soviet agreement to limit nuclear-missile arsenals resulted in abrupt cancellation of the Safeguard antiballistic missile project in north-central Montana. Construction had reached phase two by the end of May, when the order came to stop. Construction workers, many of whom had moved their families to Montana with assurances that the project would last until 1976, lost their jobs, while towns with half-finished or newly expanded schools, sewerage projects, and other facilities had to face sudden declines in population and tax revenue. To help counteract the impact of the ABM shutdown, Montana's congressional delegation summoned federal agencies to the state to discuss financial problems and offer assistance.

The state faced other shutdowns as well. In March the government announced deactivation of the 319th Fighter Interceptor Squadron at Malmstrom Air Force Base in Great Falls. Effective June 30, 600 military personnel were transferred, and some civilian employees were laid off. Also, the Anaconda Company, forced to retrench after nationalization of its holdings in Chile, closed down plant operations in Anaconda, Great Falls, and East Helena.

Surveys of mineral resources have estimated that Montana has more than 4 billion tons of underground coal, most of it readily available by strip mining. Ecologists urged that further development be delayed until more stringent laws could guarantee restoration of land to its original condition, adequate protection of surface and subsurface water, and an equitable method of taxing this nonrenewable resource.

For election results and campaign highlights, see the special supplement ELECTION '72.

Area and population. Area, 147,138 sq. mi. Pop. (1970), 694,-409. Principal cities: Helena (cap.), 22,730; Billings, 61,581; Great Falls, 60,091; Missoula, 29,497; Butte, 23,368.

Government. Gov., Forrest H. Anderson (D); lt. gov., Thomas L. Judge (D); atty. gen., Robert L. Woodahl (R); secy. of state, Frank Murray (D). Legislature: senate, 30 D, 25 R; house, 49 D, 55 R.

Finance (1971–1972). Revenue, $796,494,033; expenditure, $444,732,196.

Education (1970). Elementary schools, 751; enrollment, 107,827; teachers, 5,259. Secondary schools, 201 (including 5 vocational-technical schools); enrollment, 67,037; teachers, 3,143. Private and parochial schools, 62; elementary enrollment, 8,322; teachers, 370; secondary enrollment, 3,570; teachers, 240. Institutions of higher learning, 10; enrollment, 26,662.

ELLEN TORGRIMSON

MOROCCO. Politics and government. On August 16, for the second time in little more than a year, King Hassan II narrowly escaped assassination at the hands of discontented officers. Three Moroccan Air Force F-5 fighters failed at point-blank range to shoot down the king's unarmed Boeing 727 as it approached Rabat from France. The F-5's also strafed the airport, killing eight people and wounding 47, including four ministers awaiting the king's arrival. Hassan's plane, two of its engines on fire, landed on an airstrip outside the main airport. Two hours later dissident air force pilots were shooting rockets and machine guns at his palace in Rabat, but Hassan had already driven to a secret hideout in Meknès. Only part of the air force seems to have been implicated in this year's coup, and it was quickly put down once the king had escaped. In October, 220 air force personnel were put on trial for alleged participation in the attempted coup.

The major casualty of the abortive coup was the defense minister, General Muhammad Oufkir, the man who had foiled last year's plot. Oufkir allegedly committed suicide in the king's palace at Skhirat shortly after the coup failed. Interior Minister Muhammad Benhima subsequently announced that Oufkir had plotted the coup, thus contradict-

ing initial reports that he had committed suicide for failing to prevent such happenings.

Earlier in the year, King Hassan had failed to ally the opposition parties with his regime as a counterweight to the military. Quiet "consultations," really negotiations, went on for four months beginning in late 1971 with the National Bloc, which consists of the Istiqlal Party, the National Union of Popular Forces (UNFP), and the Moroccan Union of Labor. But just when agreement on a new constitution seemed imminent, the king announced his own new constitution on February 17 and scheduled a March referendum.

Taken by surprise but unwilling to burn its bridges with the palace, the National Bloc opted for "nonparticipation in the referendum operation" rather than participation in the small Communist Party's campaign against the constitution. From the bloc's point of view, after all, the new text was a distinct improvement. Although the cabinet continued to be responsible to the king as well as to Parliament, both the prime minister and Parliament gained greater and more precisely defined powers than they enjoyed under previous constitutions. According to official figures, 92.92 percent of the registered voters went to the polls on March 1, and 98.75 percent of them voted in favor of the new text.

Subsequently, however, the king postponed parliamentary elections, and by the end of March negotiations between the palace and the National Bloc on the makeup of a new government broke down. The king then ordered Prime Minister Muhammad Karim Lamrani to form a new government of ministers loyal to the king.

Foreign affairs. Hassan's policy of mending fences with his neighbors paid off handsomely in June when he hosted a summit meeting of the Organization of African Unity. The meeting finalized his settlement with Algerian president Houari Boumedienne of the Moroccan-Algerian border dispute, which had led to war between the two states in 1963. Relations with Mauritania also improved, but relations with Libya's Muammar al-Qaddafi remained strained. Qaddafi had verbally supported the 1971 coup attempt against Hassan.

Hassan also moved to further consolidate his already close relations with France. A new cultural and technical cooperation agreement was signed in Rabat on January 13, guaranteeing continued French financial aid for at least five years. Hassan also received substantial U.S. aid but nevertheless managed to acquire modest Soviet assistance for mining and water control projects.

Economic affairs. Since October 1971, Hassan has been moving actively to stamp out the corruption that pervades all levels of the Moroccan administration. He has also imposed a direct and retroactive personal income tax on the wealthiest members of Morocco's elite. But these measures have had little impact on the economy, which continues to be plagued by private investors' lack of confidence in the government's stability and by numerous strikes in the industrial sector. Minimum wage increases of 12 to 29 percent were not enough to satisfy the workers, but Hassan insisted that any further increases would produce inflation.

Student unrest. University and high school student agitation hit new peaks, even for Morocco, in the winter and spring. The high school students (and many parents) opposed a new baccalaureate examination system, and the university students objected to overcrowded dormitory conditions, to tight scholarship funding, and, in the medical faculty, to the existing internship program. Widespread student strikes in January led to predictably brutal responses by the police. Hundreds of students were beaten or arrested or both, and some professors sympathetic to the students were kidnapped by the police. Agitation and strikes continued through April, and the authorities resorted to drafting some of the more rebellious youths. Finally, a general amnesty was declared, and the students voted to return to their classes.

THE KING WASN'T DEAD

Morocco's King Hassan II, casually embarking from a Paris airport (above) after a few weeks' vacation, had a surprise in store for his homeward flight: three Moroccan Air Force F-5's fired point-blank through his Boeing 727 as it neared Rabat. But the cool-headed king saved his life by rushing to the cockpit to deliver a radio message (right) that tricked rebel pilots into thinking he was dead and allowing his plane to land safely. He escaped unharmed.

Area and population. Area, 172,415 sq. mi. Pop. (est. 1971), 15,359,000. Principal cities (est. 1969): Rabat (cap.), 370,000; Casablanca, 1,120,000; Marrakech, 270,000; Fez, 255,000.

Government. Constitutional monarchy. Head of state, King Hassan II; prime min., Muhammad Karim Lamrani.

Finance. Monetary unit, dirham; DH1 = US$0.2225. Budget (est. 1972): revenue, 5.8 billion dirhams; expenditure, 6.2 billion dirhams.

Trade (1969, in millions of dirhams). Imports, 2,844; exports, 2,455. Principal imports: wheat, sugar, motor vehicles, petroleum. Principal exports: phosphates, citrus fruits, fresh vegetables. Major trading partners: France, West Germany, United Kingdom (for exports).

Agriculture and industry (1969, in thousands of metric tons). Agricultural production: barley, 2,040; wheat, 1,470; citrus fruits, 742; olives, 320. Industrial production: phosphates, 12,294; cement, 1,165; iron, 742.

Education. Enrollment (1969–1970): primary school, 1.14 million; secondary school, 293,193; university, 12,970.

Armed forces. Army, 50,000 men.

CLEMENT HENRY MOORE

MOTION PICTURES. The road to recovery. After three years of agonized reappraisal, during which the American film industry registered losses in the hundreds of millions of dollars, Hollywood began to recover in 1972. Most major companies posted profits for the first time in several years, and there were none of those proxy fights, conglomerate buyouts, and vast overhauls of management personnel which had so disrupted the industry in the recent past. But the turnaround was relative; since most studios had adjusted their asset values to realistic levels, they needed to make fewer films with smaller returns in order to earn profits. Thus, although movie production increased, it by no means

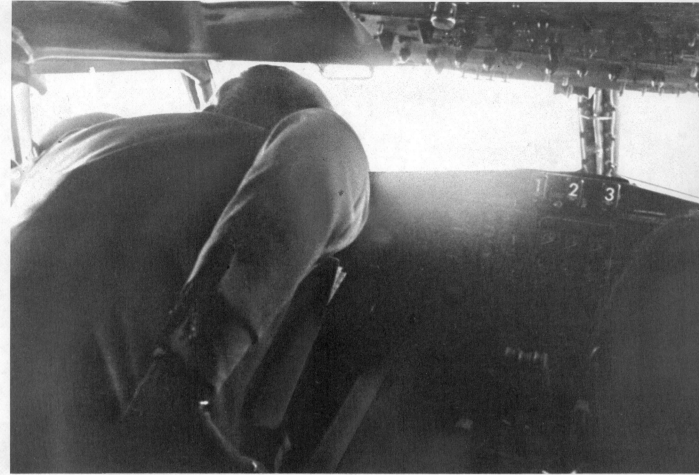

approached the mid-1960's level, and the unemployment situation in Hollywood remained serious.

Nevertheless, business was clearly on the upswing in "absolute dollar" terms, with the Motion Picture Association of America claiming that Americans spent an astounding 20 percent more money to see movies during the first eight months of 1972 than they had during the corresponding period of 1971. There was an ominous fly in this ointment, however, and it was the suggestion that the increase was attributable entirely to the existence of a few big successes, especially Paramount's unprecedented smash, *The Godfather,* which was responsible for about 12 cents out of every dollar spent at movie houses during 1972.

Only two important motion picture companies closed up shop during the year, the feature film division of the ABC and CBS television networks. As if to fill the production vacuum, there was a significant increase in film-making by small companies financed by "angels," that is, banks and industrial concerns. Most of these companies' completed productions were sold to and distributed by the major studios.

A conservative vision. As if to give a political reflection to Hollywood's new fiscal stability, the great majority of the year's major successes displayed a fairly conservative philosophy. The days when films with a socially or culturally liberal or radical point of view could become big hits—*2001: A Space Odyssey, Midnight Cowboy, Blow-up, Easy Rider* —seemed very long ago. The musical *Cabaret,* in which Liza Minnelli, daughter of the late Judy Garland, gave a dynamic performance as Sally, a nightclub entertainer in

pre-Hitler Berlin, dealt openly with sexual libertarianism, striking a note reminiscent of the 1960's. But the film's message was against moral decay and political apathy.

The year's other big musical hit, *Fiddler on the Roof,* was based on Broadway's long-running nostalgic look at a small Jewish town in tsarist Russia. Like the play, the film celebrated some of its characters' reverence of "tradition" (the title of one of the score's most famous songs, sung in the film by Topol, whose performance as Tevye disappointed critics).

Stanley Kubrick's *A Clockwork Orange,* adapted from Anthony Burgess' political science-fiction novel of the same name, contained a savage attack on social control (seen as the logical outcome of ever-bigger government). The film showed how a young hoodlum (Malcolm McDowell), homicidal in his employment of "ultraviolence" (a term that immediately entered the language), was subjected to brainwashing by government scientists—the greater of two evils, the film implied, because it robbed him of his free will.

Peter Bogdanovich, who directed the 1971 success *The Last Picture Show,* came up with a highly successful piece of nostalgia this year, *What's Up, Doc?,* a G-rated imitation of the "screwball" comedies of the 1930's. *What's Up, Doc?,* starring Ryan O'Neal as an absentminded professor and Barbra Streisand as a screwball who pursues him, far outgrossed all other comedies in 1972, including many with overt sexual content. (Two Woody Allen satires, *Play It Again, Sam* and *Everything You Always Wanted to Know About Sex*/*But Were Afraid to Ask,* also did well.) There

THE LITTLE TRAMP COMES BACK

Charlie Chaplin, for three decades one of America's great comic stars, was barred from returning to the United States in the early 1950's because of his political views. But on a triumphal return trip this year, the beloved tramp, now a portly old gentleman, won a tearful welcome in New York and a special Oscar in Hollywood (left). Two unforgettable Chaplin films: "The Great Dictator" (right), a 1940 spoof on Hitler, and "Modern Times" (below), a 1936 tragicomedy of industrialism.

LEFT, J. PLAFFONT/GAMMA

was also an X-rated cartoon, *Fritz the Cat,* with sexual content galore, but it, too, reflected a conservative bias. The compleat put-down of the revolutionary youth culture of the 1960's, the film was disowned by R. Crumb, the creator of the comic book characters on which it was based.

But it was in the year's violent action dramas that the conservative mood received its most popular manifestations. No longer did audiences flock to see romantic celebrations of antiestablishment outlaws like Bonnie and Clyde or Butch Cassidy. The new heroes were policemen whose attitudes toward civil rights were indifferent, intellectuals who learned the necessity of brute force—or, in the case of the year's most popular film, the kingpins of organized crime.

The success of Francis Ford Coppola's *The Godfather* was a phenomenon so singular as to inspire discussion and analysis for years to come. By the end of the year this saga of a New York Mafia "family" was in a class with *Gone With the Wind* and *The Sound of Music* as one of the biggest-grossing films of all time. Employing a good deal of Monday-morning quarterbacking, the industry thought it saw the reasons for this achievement. Mario Puzo's novel was one of those rare "properties," occurring no more than once in a generation, which had everything but forced nothing. It was an action melodrama; it was a family drama; it was a love story; it had a "generation gap" angle. In addition, the novel's lengthy career as a best seller had cleared the way to all markets; *The Godfather* was so familiar to moviegoers that its advertisements featured little more than its title. Needless to say, such a massive success required a final ingredient. The film must be one of overriding excellence—and was loudly proclaimed such by the critics. Most reviewers found that Coppola had made *The Godfather* a superb compendium of everything good about the various genres developed by Hollywood over the years. Its action (featuring everything from restaurant shoot-outs to car explosions) was imaginative; there was a moving relationship established between Marlon Brando's earthy but dignified father and Al Pacino's initially aloof but ultimately loyal and devoted son; and the love scenes were pastoral and poignant. Made up to look way beyond his years, Brando gave what many critics considered his best performance in almost two decades, and Pacino entered the front ranks of young actors.

Yet a question, much debated on the nation's editorial pages, emerged in the wake of the film's unprecedented success. *The Godfather* may be superb entertainment, but what is its moral stance? Does it placidly accept, or even defend, the existence of organized crime? And not only *The Godfather* was at issue. For right behind it in box-office popularity stood several other action-packed dramas which likewise took amoral or at best neutral attitudes toward their violent subjects. Released late in 1971, William Friedkin's *The French Connection* won the Academy Award for the best film of that year as well as several other Oscars, including one for Gene Hackman, who played a New York narcotics policeman not above beating up black junkies in order to extract information. Another coast was heard from with *Dirty Harry,* by the veteran action director Donald Siegel. This film presented Clint Eastwood as a San Francisco detective prevented by recent U.S. Supreme Court decisions from arresting a mad killer.

Then there were the movies which postulated an evil universe kept in order only when the forces of good learn to be as violent as the forces of villainy: Sam Peckinpah's *Straw Dogs,* in which Dustin Hoffman is a mathematics professor who assumes the "territorial imperative" in protecting his home from a gang of marauding villagers, and Mark Rydell's *The Cowboys,* in which John Wayne teaches a group of teen-agers the rudiments of war. And Sean Connery returned to play James Bond in *Diamonds Are Forever,* this time enlisting CIA assistance to once more defend the British Isles from colorful madmen.

The American electoral process was the subject of Michael Ritchie's *The Candidate,* in which a liberal challenger (Robert Redford) sells out his ideals in order to defeat a crusty conservative incumbent and become a U.S. senator from California. *The Candidate* and *Fritz the Cat* were the only movies to score by aiming directly at the "youth market," viewed as an industry panacea only a few years ago. But college students seemed to share the general interest in violent action and showed scant desire to spend money on such subjects as drugs (*Dealing, Cisco Pike*), neurotic love affairs (*Made for Each Other, Minnie and Moskowitz*), antiwar films (*The Trial of the Catonsville Nine*), mistreatment of Indians (*Journey Through Rosebud*), or transvestism (*I Want What I Want*).

As if to prove that the success of *The Godfather* was not entirely preordained, such pictures derived from best sellers as *Portnoy's Complaint, Slaughterhouse-Five,* and *The Other* were disappointments (*Deliverance,* from James Dickey's novel, opened to good business in New York and Los Angeles during the summer but was not seen in the rest of the country until late in the year). Several Broadway-derived comedies also fared poorly.

The industry awaited with curiosity the fates of a number of films released fairly late in the year: *Young Winston, 1776, Man of La Mancha, Travels with My Aunt, The Life and Times of Judge Roy Bean, Savage Messiah, A Separate Peace, Up the Sandbox, Play It as It Lays, The Assassination of Trotsky, Sleuth,* and *The Getaways.*

Among the veteran directors, only Siegel with *Dirty Harry* and Alfred Hitchcock with *Frenzy* struck chords with the

LOVE MAFIA-STYLE. In a scene from Paramount's smash box-office melodrama "The Godfather," aging boss Don Vito Corleone (Marlon Brando) shows his tender side as he counsels his son Michael (Al Pacino), on plans for war with a rival organization.

© 1972 BY PARAMOUNT PICTURES

public. The latter represented Hitchcock's return to his native England, after 20 years, to film a suspenseful story of a man wrongly accused of a series of rape-murders. Other old-timers received critical but not box-office attention: John Huston with *Fat City,* a Gorkyesque tribute to life's failures; Otto Preminger with *Such Good Friends,* the awakening of a young wife to her dying husband's infidelities; Blake Edwards with *The Carey Treatment,* a murder mystery with a medical background; and Budd Boetticher with *Arruza,* a documentary about bullfighting. Elia Kazan's *The Visitors* and Richard Brooks' *Dollars* pleased few.

The reissue of a number of Charlie Chaplin films, unseen since 1952 in most cities, culled much publicity, peaking in April when the 83-year-old comedian-director returned to the United States and received gala tributes in New York and at the Academy Award ceremonies in Los Angeles.

Black cinema. Meanwhile, the newly established "black market" expanded and flourished. Harlem police detectives Godfrey Cambridge and Raymond St. Jacques, introduced two years earlier in *Cotton Comes to Harlem,* enjoyed popularity anew with a sequel, *Come Back, Charleston Blue.* Similarly, private eye Richard Roundtree of 1971's *Shaft* returned with *Shaft's Big Score.* Equaling them in success was Gordon Parks, Jr.'s *Super Fly,* financed by a group of black businessmen, which told the story of a Manhattan cocaine dealer (Ron O'Neal) who gets out of the business by beating the white man at his own game. Most interesting of all, perhaps, was the smash success of *Lady Sings the Blues,* with Diana Ross as Billie Holiday.

But a significant backlash, perhaps inevitable, developed among leaders of organized black groups. They complained that the new films had replaced the "shuffling Negro" of yore with an equally unrealistic "supernigger," that black people were pictured in the films largely as prostitutes and thieves, and that the film industry was not hiring black technical personnel to any degree commensurate with the success of black movies. Most vociferous in opposition was Roy Innis, president of the Congress on Racial Equality, who unleashed a list of seven "demands" on the industry in June, the most controversial of which asked that responsible black leaders be allowed to censor scripts and finished films. In August the Black Artists Alliance was formed in Hollywood to pressure for increased employment of minority group members.

Foreign-language films. "No longer does the elitist end of the American audience look solely to the foreign films as the source of intellectual stimulation in the 'wasteland' of U.S. commercial 'trash,'" observed *Variety* during the year. And indeed, only Vittorio de Sica's *The Garden of the Finzi-Continis,* a romantic tragedy about Jews under Italian Fascism, was an important success among foreign films in 1972. Others, such as Marcel Ophuls' documentary of the Nazi occupation of France, *The Sorrow and the Pity,* and Alain Tanner's Swiss drama *La Salamandre,* achieved critical accolades which did not translate into box-office results. The French director Claude Chabrol came up with a thriller, *Le Boucher,* which many considered his most accomplished work to date, and the Italian film-maker Pier Paolo Pasolini made a raucous interpretation of *The Decameron.* U.S. audiences were also offered *My Uncle Antoine,* a touching French-Canadian story, and the Russian-made *Uncle Vanya,* which many critics considered the best Chekhov adaptation ever filmed. A number of new movies by acknowledged masters opened late in the year, including Eric Rohmer's *Chloe in the Afternoon,* François Truffaut's *Two English Girls* and *Such a Gorgeous Kid Like Me,* Federico Fellini's *Roma,* and Pasolini's *Canterbury Tales.* Bernardo Bertolucci's sexually explicit *Last Tango in Paris,* starring Marlon Brando, and Luis Buñuel's *The Discreet Charm of the Bourgeoisie* received critical acclaim.

Censorship. The rating system inaugurated by the Motion Picture Association of America in 1968 remained in a

state of instability in 1972, the first full year of the system's administration by psychologist Aaron Stern. The rating originally termed M continued to be a source of contention. Once, as a result of exhibitors' complaints that the original letter implied adult content, this unrestricted category had been renamed GP (for general audiences, parental guidance recommended). But then, the opposite opinion came to the fore: GP seemed too close to G for parents' comfort. And so, in February, the category was renamed for the second time, becoming PG, for parental guidance.

An even greater furor occurred this year over the X category. During the rating system's first few years, a score of small newspapers had banned advertisements for and editorial references to X-rated movies, but it was only in 1972 that they were joined by major dailies—namely, the Cleveland *Plain Dealer* and the Detroit *Free Press*. The most important film to suffer from the ban was *A Clockwork Orange*, and in April director Stanley Kubrick wrote a vociferous letter to the two newspapers protesting their action. In May the New York Film Critics urged "drastic revision or abolition" of the rating system in the light of the controversy, but the MPAA replied with the suggestion that the critics direct pressure at the newspapers rather than at the ratings. In August, Kubrick reedited his film for an R rating.

STUART BYRON

MUSIC. The year in classical music was marked by a number of opera "firsts" and marred by the death of the Metropolitan Opera's new general manager, Goeran Gentele. Popular music saw the return of old-time rock and roll and boogie and a black music renaissance. The Newport Jazz Festival was successfully moved to New York City.

Classical Music

The most interesting musical events in the United States centered around opera, with a number of important premieres and U.S. first performances. Overshadowing the fall season of New York's Metropolitan Opera, however, was the tragic death of its new general manager, Goeran Gentele, aged 54, in an automobile accident in Sardinia on July 18. Gentele, formerly director of Stockholm's Royal Opera House, had been scheduled to commence his opening Met season in September with a new production of *Carmen*, directed by himself and conducted by Leonard Bernstein. Because of the very complete stage instructions he had already made out, the opening went on as planned. The thoroughness of his administrative groundwork would be felt long after his death: three full seasons were almost completely mapped out, and his guidelines continued in effect.

Before he died, Gentele had quietly accomplished important tasks at the Met, a company normally plagued by labor problems: he had negotiated contracts with the company's 14 unions, and it was the first time in the Met's history that a contract with the musicians' union had been signed before expiration of the preceding one. Gentele's basic administrative philosophy was one of teamwork, and he had appointed Rafael Kubelik as the first music director the company has ever had. He had also chosen James Levine as principal conductor. The teamwork concept proved effective at his death: his assistant manager, Schuyler Chapin, was immediately appointed acting general manager and was able to take over the reins smoothly. Chapin would hold the post indefinitely.

The spring opera season. Three new productions early in the year rounded out the Met era of general manager Rudolf Bing. In January, Debussy's *Pelléas et Mélisande* caused some critical misgivings because of the extrovert quality of its staging and directions but brought high praise to Thomas Stewart for his Golaud (the first French role he had sung in New York) and to Barry McDaniel for his Pelléas (this was his Met debut). Colin Davis conducted. In February came Donizetti's *La fille du regiment* in a pro-

duction adapted from Covent Garden, starring Joan Sutherland. It was judged by one critic to be "ultimately boring," but Luciano Pavarotti, as Tonio, was complimented for his ease in singing the famous nine high C's of his first-act aria. Richard Bonynge conducted. The final Bing production was Verdi's *Otello* in March, with James McCracken magnificent in the title role and a "splashy and spectacular" staging by Franco Zeffirelli. Karl Böhm's conducting was deemed placid. Sir Rudolf's last appearance in the house was at a gala farewell on April 22, when many of the great stars of his 22-year regime stepped forth in brief performances, serious and otherwise. In September, Bing took up new duties as distinguished visiting professor of music at Brooklyn College and published a book about his years at the Met.

At the New York City Opera the spring season was highlighted by a new production of Donizetti's *Maria Stuarda,* with Beverly Sills brilliant in the title role; the opera was nicely balanced by a revival of Donizetti's opera about Queen Elizabeth, *Roberto Devereux*, also starring Miss Sills. The fall season inaugurated an experiment: *Don Giovanni* was presented in both Italian and English, with some overlapping of casts. The second new production was *The Tales of Hoffmann*, with Sills singing the three heroines and Norman Treigle the villains.

The Juilliard School also contributed to the operatic activity around Lincoln Center. Virgil Thomson's *Lord Byron*, commissioned by the Metropolitan but not produced, was given its premiere on April 20 by the Juilliard American Opera Center. The story, libretto by Jack Larson, opens after Byron's death, as a group of his friends stand in Westminster Abbey pondering the prospect of placing his statue with the immortals there. The main portion of the opera consists of flashbacks touching upon episodes in the hero's not very heroic life. Thomson's music and orchestration are deliberately old-fashioned (a number of old popular tunes are quoted), and so is the inclusion of a long ballet, à la French opera. Some critics were cool, but at least one judged it to be a masterpiece. Thomson had another showing in St. Paul, where the St. Paul Opera Company presented a semiconcert version of *Four Saints in Three Acts*.

Opera outside New York. Operatic news outside New York included the premiere in Seattle of *Black Widow,* by a young New Yorker named Thomas Pasatieri. Joanna Simon sang the principal role of a thwarted and conniving woman who ensnares both her lover and his wife in her destructive web; the libretto, by the composer, is based on a story by Miguel de Unamuno. Pasatieri had an earlier success the same season with a television opera, *The Trial of Mary Lincoln*, commissioned by NET. Elaine Bonazzi was splendidly dramatic in the title role.

A premiere of quite another sort was that of a ragtime opera, *Treemonisha*, by the early twentieth-century black composer Scott Joplin. It was presented in January, to great acclaim, by an all-black cast at the Memorial Arts Center in Atlanta, sponsored by Morehouse College and the Atlanta University Center. A summer production was given by some of the same forces at Wolf Trap Farm Park for the Performing Arts, the one-year-old summer festival site near Washington, D.C.

Another first occurred in Boston, where in February the Opera Company of Boston, under Sarah Caldwell's direction, gave the first complete performance in this country of Berlioz's *The Trojans*. The first portion, dealing with the sacking of Troy, occupied one full evening; the second, concerned with Aeneas' stay at Queen Dido's court in Carthage, followed the next evening; both were given as a double-header the next Sunday. There was nothing but praise for the adventurous undertaking itself, done with limited means in less than ideal surroundings, although some details came in for criticism. The 22-foot-high Trojan horse swamped the scene in which it appeared, and the Cassandra of Maralin

WIDE WORLD

PASSING THE BATON

A new crop of conductors is luring young ears to the sound of symphonic music: Seiji Ozawa (left), who will lead the Boston Symphony in 1973; Zubin Mehta (far right), who jets between the Los Angeles and Israel philharmonics; and Michael Tilson Thomas (right), taking over Leonard Bernstein's podium at the New York Philharmonic's Young People's Concerts this year.

Niska was judged by one critic to have been badly misinterpreted. But the Dido of Régine Crespin was "grandly erotic" though vocally unpredictable, and the Aeneas of Ronald Dowd was impressive.

In San Francisco, Spring Opera Theater had great public success with three works: Rossini's *Barber of Seville,* in a pert production capped by a plea for women's lib (Alan Titus sang the Figaro); Monteverdi's *Orfeo,* judged by one critic to be inept and amateurishly staged; and Kurt Weill's *The Rise and Fall of the City of Mahagonny,* which the same critic deemed a failure. Still, the season was sold out, and additional performances were added.

The San Francisco Opera, celebrating its 50th anniversary, got underway in September with a new *Norma* (with Joan Sutherland), a complete *Ring* cycle (the components of which were not new), and the U.S. premier of Gottfried von Einem's *The Visit.*

In Houston a new Spring Opera venture took place in a large open-air theater in one of the city's parks: 50,000 people turned out to see ten performances of three operas. The most successful was Carlisle Floyd's *Susannah;* Donizetti's *Elixir of Love* and a modern opera, *Postcard From Morocco,* by Dominick Argento, completed the bill.

Another promising summertime event was the return of opera to Central City, Colo., where none had been given the preceding year. Sparkling productions of *The Marriage of Figaro* and Verdi's *Falstaff* seemed to ensure the future success of similar undertakings in the small historic opera house in the Rocky Mountains.

Santa Fe continued its policy of presenting at least one U.S. premiere. This summer's was Aribert Reimann's *Melusine,* which had some masterfully scored moments and some extremely difficult, jaggedly florid vocal writing.

In Cincinnati, the so-called Zoo Opera, which had been held every summer to the accompaniment, musical and otherwise, of the inmates of the city zoo, moved indoors to the century-old refurbished Music Hall, and everybody was pleased with the results, visually and acoustically. The New York City Opera's production of Boito's *Mefistofele,* starring Norman Treigle, was the opener, followed by good productions of *The Marriage of Figaro* and Puccini's *Tosca.*

Orchestras. In the orchestral field, the New York Philharmonic completed its first full season under the direction of Pierre Boulez, who devoted his inaugural year to a survey of works by Alban Berg and Franz Liszt. Critics were pleased with his work and welcomed the fresh approach in programming; more conservative members of the audience were less enthusiastic, but there seemed to be no large-scale exodus or reduction in the number of subscribers. The 1972–1973 season highlights Stravinsky and Haydn.

The Philharmonic made efforts to come to terms with demands of black musicians who had claimed, three years before, that hiring practices discriminated against them. New York City's commission on human rights, after an investigation, found no evidence of discrimination in the hiring of permanent players, but it did criticize the method of hiring substitutes. The orchestra announced plans for concerted efforts to add black players to its substitute lists and made it known that 18 such substitutes had been added in the past two years. It also arranged new methods for letting minority musicians know when permanent posts became available. The Philharmonic will continue to file progress reports with the human rights commission every 90 days through 1973.

Elsewhere, Anshel Brusilow led the Dallas Symphony in its first foreign venture—a six-day tour of Central America. The British conductor Colin Davis arrived in the United States in October to lead his first performances with the Boston Symphony in his new position as principal guest conductor.

The San Francisco Symphony's music director, Seiji Ozawa, created some stir (and a bit of discontent on his

UPI

CONSTANTINE MANOS/MAGNUM

home ground) by announcing that he had accepted Boston's invitation to become music director and would divide his time between Massachusetts and California. His Boston job would begin in the 1973–1974 season. Other appointments included that of conductor Aldo Ceccato to the Detroit Symphony for a two-year term beginning in 1973 and that of Michael Tilson Thomas as Leonard Bernstein's replacement for the New York Philharmonic's Young People's Concerts for the next two years. Thomas, as well as Davis, was named a principal guest conductor of the Boston Symphony.

People and places. Another musician in the news was soprano Maria Callas, who arrived at the Juilliard School in February to give the second segment of the master classes initiated the previous fall. A limited number of visitors were permitted to audit, and they returned time and again to the twice-weekly sessions. All concerned were impressed with Mme. Callas' artistic insight and sympathetic approach.

Two new opera halls opened this year to great acclaim. The Musical Arts Center at Indiana University at Bloomington was judged by one visitor to be one of the half-dozen great opera houses in the world in design, construction, and equipment. It seats 1,460 persons in a wide, shallow pattern that has proved flattering to voices in the smaller German houses. A much more intimate theater is the 400-seat Patricia Corbett Pavilion at the College-Conservatory of Music at the University of Cincinnati, named after its donor. There are only 12 rows of seats in a square concrete hall; the lighting was described as "magically planned" to ensure that the stage, which has no curtain, remains in absolute darkness when the house lights are on. The hall was inaugurated on April 10 with a performance in Raymond Leppard's updated version of *La Calisto,* by the seventeenth-century Venetian Pier Francesco Cavalli. The opera, in which Jupiter is disguised as Diana (for characteristically seductive purposes), proved to be a merry romp.

One particularly ominous event took place on January 26, when bombs exploded in the New York offices of Columbia Artists Management and of impresario Sol Hurok, in protest against the importation of Russian artists. At the Hurok office a young receptionist was killed. Three members of the Jewish Defense League were indicted in June.

The Pulitzer Prize for music this year went to Jacob Druckman, a 44-year-old member of the Juilliard faculty, for his orchestral work *Windows,* premiered by the Chicago Symphony on a program led by guest conductor Bruno Maderna. *Windows* was greeted, along with other works like George Rochberg's Third String Quartet (also a 1972 premiere, in New York), as indicating a return to a more communicative kind of music than has been fashionable in recent years.

Obituaries. In addition to Goeran Gentele, these music figures died during the year: violinist Michael Rabin; pianists Victor Babin, Jean Casadesus, Robert Casadesus, Rudolph Ganz, and Oscar Levant; conductor Vladimir Golschmann; contralto Jean Madeira; soprano Helen Traubel; and composers Ferde Grofé and Stefan Wolpe.

Europe. In Italy the 35th Maggio musicale got underway with a splendid *William Tell* (Rossini) in an uncut version that lasted from 8 P.M. to 2 A.M.; it was beautifully produced, excitingly conducted by Riccardi Muti, and well sung by Norman Mittellmann in the title role. Contemporary opera has always been a feature of the Maggio, and this year's choices were two one-acters of the 1950's (Petrassi's *Morte dell' Aria* and Peragallo's *La gita in campagna*), with the world premiere of a short work by Bruno Bartolozzi, *Tutto cio' che accada ti reguarda* (Everything that happens concerns you). One critic summed it up as "reprehensible sentiments and boring, relentlessly 'advanced' music." The Spoleto Festival, in its 15th year, gave Weill's *Mahagonny* in a rather unsuccessful production; the other major operatic offering was Menotti's *The Consul.*

In England, André Previn made an impressive showing as organizer and chamber music performer of the South Bank Music Festival, and an opera called *Time Off? Not a Ghost of a Chance,* by Elisabeth Lutyens, was described as full of "imaginative intensity." Pierre Boulez, in his first season as successor to Colin Davis as music director of the BBC Symphony, inaugurated three tripartite concerts at Festival Hall, lasting from 7:30 to 10:30 with two brief breaks. Described as virtual cram courses in contemporary music, these sessions were received with considerable enthusiasm. Boulez's other innovation—a series of avant-garde concerts at the converted locomotive shed called the Round-house—was less successful. Covent Garden's premiere of Peter Maxwell Davies' opera *Taverner* was among the season's provocative events; the staging was complex but the music "less brutal" than some critics had anticipated.

Elsewhere, the Israel Philharmonic presented the first Wagner concert ever to be held in Israel. Zubin Mehta conducted the concert in Tel Aviv. In Salzburg, Herbert von Karajan was booed for the first time, at the close of his first *Tristan und Isolde* at the Easter Festival. The problem with this handsomely staged presentation seemed to be that the Isolde of Helga Dernesch was vocally inadequate and the Tristan of Jon Vickers much less impressive than had been hoped. Karajan, confronting these difficulties, let the orchestra play at full volume and completely drowned out his singers—an "orchestral deluge" according to one listener.

SHIRLEY FLEMING

Popular, Jazz, and Folk Music

In popular music, 1972 was a year of escape into the simplistic answers of the past. Such forebodingly complex trends as audience fragmentation and corporate conglomeration were almost forgotten, even by those who had noted them dimly the year before, which did not mean that they lost any of their efficacy. In fact, it was just the opposite. Young people became so skeptical of their own generational cohesiveness (although not of the rectitude of their own particular subgrouping) that the old calls to "get-it-together-people" sounded like pathetic throwbacks when they sounded at all. Industry spokesmen conveniently blamed the slowdown in the rapid audience and market growth of the post-Beatle era on general economic sluggishness, instead of questioning whether the monopolistic tendency of the record business—Warners and Columbia controlled an estimated 50 percent of sales—was at all related to the decline. But on the surface, the music business was cheery. The reason was the return of old-time rock and roll.

Good old rock and roll. There had been talk and random indications of a rock-and-roll revival since the so-called art-rock movement began to show its seams in 1968, but the aptest corroboration didn't appear until October 1972, when Elvis Presley, Chuck Berry, and Rick Nelson reached the top five of the lowly singles chart simultaneously. Presley's "Burning Love" ranked with his early classics for drive and sexuality. As it happened, neither Berry's "My Ding-a-ling," a naughty novelty, nor Nelson's "Garden Party," a plaintive, countryish account of how his long-haired band was booed at a rock-and-roll revival—the first major hit for either in seven or eight years—qualified as a rocker. Nevertheless, the symbolism was real. It was no surprise that Richard Nader's touring revival shows played Las Vegas or that *Grease,* a self-described " '50s rock musical" which began as an off-Broadway longshot, was selling out the Broadhurst Theater on West 44th Street before the year was out.

Among the hip, album-selling bands which accrued fame and fortune on the collegiate circuit, the rock-and-roll revival was summed up in the word "boogie." Originally re-popularized by the Grateful Dead, its basic meaning was "get up and shake it." The Dead, clinging cheerfully to their reputation as the world's most peripatetic rock band, rode the crest of the phenomenon they originated, playing

throughout the year to large audiences in the United States and Europe, where they recorded a three-record live set. It was a rare band that didn't climax a concert by imploring the crowd to rise to its feet and dance. The term itself became such a cliché that veteran boogie-men like Leon Russell were starting to avoid it before the year was out. No matter. The giveaway was always in the encore, which was invariably a 1950's classic, most often by the infinitely imitable Chuck Berry.

A few major bands resisted the rootsy, blues-based music. Jefferson Airplane, with the departure of folk-rock founder Marty Balin, crystallized its rather cerebral sci-fi rock around Paul Kantner and Grace Slick. Ian Anderson's Jethro Tull reached number one with the year's biggest concept album, *Thick as a Brick,* and also scored with a two-record live set that captured the band's somewhat hostile relationship to its adoring audience. Anderson's chief influence, Frank Zappa, reserved some choice putdowns of the good-vibes boogieing idea not only with the Mothers but with the Big Wazoo, an extraordinary 20-piece jazz-rock orchestra which played eight dates in the United States and Europe. Emerson, Lake, and Palmer combined heavy clichés with electronic noodling, and the Moody Blues continued their homage to Mantovani in two tours, two hit albums, and several hit singles.

But in general the boogie predominated. Of the four major male singer-songwriters—James Taylor, Cat Stevens, Neil Young, Elton John—only Young failed to move away from the folky or lush settings of his previous album, and only Young received bad reviews, although his sales were unaffected. Thriving survivors like the Kinks and the Beach Boys, country-rockers like Poco and Commander Cody, and most of the heavy music groups—Led Zeppelin, Humble Pie, the James Gang—geared their stage shows and, to a lesser extent, their records to the new trend. The blues-based Allman Brothers, who rivaled the Dead in both stage and road energy, emerged as America's premier touring band, and the rhythm-and-blues reproductions of Boston's J. Geils Band also gained in popularity. Even Three Dog Night, the most commercial of rock groups, ended every sold-out concert by getting its relatively straight audiences up on the chairs for "Celebrate."

But the most impressive success of good old rock and roll was the Rolling Stones' 1972 tour. Playing 54 concerts in 30 cities for a gross of between $3 million and $4 million, the Stones reached well over half a million fans, a figure they probably could have quadrupled if they had wanted to. Deliberately downplaying the arrogance that culminated in 1969's Altamont disaster, both the Stones and tour manager Peter Rudge went to unprecedented lengths to prevent ticket scalping and to channel the audience's ecstasy non-violently. The Stones' double LP, *Exile on Main Street,* confused critics at first but was frequently acclaimed as the year's best after many listenings.

In any case, the Stones were definitely kings of the music. The other members of the traditional triumvirate—Bob Dylan and the individual Beatles—were virtually silent musically all year. Only John Lennon, who was engaged politically in benefits, a failed agitprop album, and a court fight against his own deportation, was even visible.

Resurgence of soul. Another aspect of the return of rock and roll this year was the renewed vitality of black music. But whereas in white music the trend was basically a downward move, toward the roots, in black music it was a function of upward mobility. Soul LP's sold better than ever, not because the old soul audience was any richer—although it was apparently more willing to buy long-playing records—but because the music itself was more acceptable to middle-class blacks and to whites. Respectability was everywhere. Isaac Hayes won a Grammy and an Oscar for his soundtrack to *Shaft,* and by year's end Curtis Mayfield's *Super Fly* score, a number one album, seemed a good bet to do

the same. Berry Gordy's Motown Records moved from Detroit to Los Angeles, and Gordy was coproducer of *Lady Sings the Blues*, in which Diana Ross made a creditable screen debut as Billie Holiday. B. B. King was an international phenomenon who even sold out in Asia.

The old soul stars were slipping away: Wilson Pickett wasn't selling, there was a final retrospective on the late Otis Redding, and Smokey Robinson retired as a stage performer to devote more time to his duties as Motown vice-president. Not counting the perennial James Brown, only Motown's Temptations and Atlantic's Aretha Franklin, whose *Young, Gifted, and Black* LP was an effective departure in the direction of black pop and who also released a well-accepted double album of live gospel music recorded with the Reverend James Cleveland, held their own. But for the first time in five or six years, two new soul heroes emerged. Significantly, both were decidedly middle-class in image and appeal, and both wrote most of their own material. Bill Withers, whose "Ain't No Sunshine" became an instant standard in 1971, proved himself with an even bigger standard, "Lean on Me," as well as several other top ten hits. Al Green, working from Willie Mitchell's Hi studios in Memphis, turned into a soft-spoken sex symbol, teasing the women in the predominantly black audiences that turned out at showcases like New York's Copacabana into oohing and aahing every time he squealed, moaned, or made a face.

Willie Mitchell was the most promising new black producer of the year. He worked not only with Green but with two talented women singers, Ann Peebles and Denise LaSalle, who is also a composer. Philadelphia's perennial local phenomena, Kenny Gamble and Leon Huff, softened their sound even further, producing a major soft ballad for Harold Melvin and a major soft rocker for the O'Jays and several in-betweens for Joe Simon. Their former associate, Thom Bell, who also formerly worked with the Delfonics, was in the forefront of the boom in falsetto groups with big hits for the Stylistics and the Spinners. And a group called the Chi-Lites, who had been working out of Chicago for over a decade, suddenly came up with two classics in the genre, "Have You Seen Her?" and "Oh Girl," both written by leader Eugene Record.

Jazz. The black music renaissance had a correlative in the major jazz upswing symbolized by the surprise success of George Wein's Newport Jazz Festival. After years of mild mayhem, the staid Rhode Island community barred Wein's festival from its traditional site, and Wein decided to transform it into a month-long series at various locations in New York City. Surprisingly enough, this proved immensely popular. Suddenly, new labels like Cobblestone and Kudu and the revived Prestige were flooding the market with jazz.

For the most part, this represented a trend against the avant garde, also signified by the continued success of white horn bands like Chicago and the black vogue for multipercussion and soul progressions. Roberta Flack had a number one hit, and black composers and groups from War and Osibisa to Donny Hathaway and Curtis Mayfield successfully integrated watered-down jazz techniques into their music.

Even Miles Davis went back to the roots, defying two broken legs to climax his year with a multipercussion show at Harlem's Apollo Theater. But the avant-gardists—from Archie Shepp and Pharoah Sanders to the Art Ensemble of Chicago and the Jazz Composer's Orchestra—also gained in popularity. Ornette Coleman produced a highly acclaimed symphonic work, *Skies of America*. And several very progressive white-dominated jazz-rock groups, notably John

FRENZIED FINALE. Clad in leather jacket and skintight silver jumpsuit, Mick Jagger, lithe lead singer of the Rolling Stones, turns it on for the 20,000 fans who packed New York City's Madison Square Garden for the flashy climax of the group's North American tour.

N.Y. TIMES

ABOVE, BRADFORD FARRAR/WOLF TRAP FARM PARK FOR THE PERFORMING ARTS; INSET, NONESUCH RECORDS

RAG REVIVAL

Ragtime, a new rhythm that swept the United States and Europe early in the century but tarnished in the glitter of the jazz age, has captured a whole new audience. Fittingly, Scott Joplin (inset), the pianist-composer whose "Maple Leaf Rag" (1899) sold over a million copies in sheet music, is at the crest of the revival. Above, a scene from his opera, "Treemonisha," performed this year for the first time since Joplin staged an unsuccessful production in 1915, two years before he died.

McLaughlin's Mahavishnu Orchestra, captured large portions of the electronically sophisticated rock audience in what may prove the year's most important trend.

Freaks and novelties. It was, however, a year of freak events, not trends. It seemed that the realities of radio programming and concert booking were discouraging prolonged work on lengthy product, so that together with a deplorable thinning-out of talent, the single record, the novelty, the comedy album, and the weirdo act were in some sort of ascendancy.

A group of Mormons called the Osmonds sold 11 gold records in a year, more than the Beatles ever had. After Grand Funk Railroad sued him for allegedly skimming off two-thirds of their grosses, producer-promoter Terry Knight announced that the group's hubris resulted from their believing the lies he had told about them. The most promising new male stars—Alice Cooper, who hanged himself on stage, and David Bowie, who predicted the end of the world in five years—both wore dresses and makeup, and the most promising female star, Bette Midler, got her start singing at a gay steam bath. Rod Stewart and Van Morrison and Joni Mitchell and Randy Newman and Paul Simon came up with some startling aesthetic successes. Carole King and Stephen Stills and the Doors made startlingly bland records.

The boogie was more or less a holding action until something new could happen. The question was whether it ever would. Rock and roll had come from nowhere to become the most important artistic expression of the 1960's. It's difficult, and probably impossible, to come from nowhere more than once. ROBERT CHRISTGAU

NEBRASKA. Legislation. The veto of two tax bills by Democratic governor James J. Exon highlighted the 1972 session of the legislature. One veto, against a proposed $125 million increase in state aid to schools, was upheld. The second veto, on a bill cutting personal property taxes, was overriden. Besides exempting some farm equipment and some farm and business inventories from state taxation, this act reduced the property tax 12.5 percent for the first year and provided for an eventual property tax reduction totaling 62.5 percent.

The legislature also lowered to 19 the age for adulthood, bringing with it the right to drink, sign contracts, and assume debts; approved "no-fault divorces," which dissolve marriages without court contest provided both parties agree that their relationship is "irretrievably broken"; abolished justices of the peace, setting up a new county court system throughout the state; and named the cottonwood the official state tree, replacing the American elm.

402

Agriculture. Center-pivot irrigation systems continued to spread throughout the state, like large green polka dots, irrigating nearly half a million acres of corn and pasture. The system, patented by Frank Zybach of Columbus, operates by means of a long water pipe mounted on wheels. The pipe, propelled by water pressure, moves around a pivot, as sprinkler heads disperse water over a circular field.

However, the year was somewhat disappointing to farmers and cattlemen. Nebraska's winter wheat harvest was about 95 million bushels, relatively small and of lower quality than the 1971 yield. Corn production also declined, from nearly 6 million acres in 1971 to 5.1 million acres this year. And, although Omaha retained its position as the biggest livestock market in the nation, the number of head sold slipped from 3.1 million to 3 million.

Industry. The Nebraska Public Power District announced plans to build a $180 million generating plant near Sutherland, a small town on the Platte River, 20 miles west of North Platte. The plant, to be fueled by coal, will produce 600 megawatts of power. Meanwhile, two nuclear energy installations on the Missouri River neared completion, and ground was broken for an $11 million steel mill.

Education and culture. New chancellors for the three University of Nebraska campuses were named. They are James H. Zumberge, the University of Nebraska at Lincoln; Ronald W. Roskens, the University of Nebraska at Omaha; and Robert D. Sparks, the University of Nebraska Medical Center.

In April, the University of Nebraska at Lincoln dedicated a $5.1 million engineering laboratory. The school also issued $12 million in revenue bonds for a new field house, the bonds to be paid off by a cigarette tax. Meanwhile, for the second straight year, the University of Nebraska football team was voted number one by the Associated Press.

Municipal developments. Construction began on a 12-story, $16.3 million city-county building in downtown Omaha. Also, the Omaha Transit Authority, created this year, bought out two privately owned companies and started operating the buses in Omaha and in the neighboring city of Council Bluffs, Iowa.

Area and population. Area, 77,227 sq. mi. Pop. (est. 1971), 1,500,081. Principal cities (est. 1971): Lincoln (cap.), 153,869; Omaha, 357,780; Grand Island, 31,919; Bellevue, 24,548; Hastings, 23,881; Fremont, 23,544.
Government. Gov., James J. Exon (D); lt. gov., Frank Marsh (R); secy. of state, Allen Beermann (R); treas., Wayne R. Swanson (R); aud., Ray A. C. Johnson (R); atty. gen., Clarence A. H. Meyer (R). Unicameral legislature, 49 members elected on nonpartisan ballot; four-year terms, one-half elected every two years.
Finance (fiscal year ending June 30, 1972). Revenue, $1,651,-136,845; expenditure, $1,661,524,088; cash on hand, $72,332,151.
Education. Public enrollment (est. 1971–1972): elementary, 188,500; secondary, 142,500. Nonpublic enrollment (est. fall 1971): elementary, 32,300; secondary, 13,100. Higher education enrollment (fall 1970): full time, 51,994; part time, 14,381.

GABE C. PARKS

NEPAL. Politics and government. On January 31, Nepal's King Mahendra died from a heart attack at the age of 51. Within hours, 26-year-old Crown Prince Birenda Bir Bikram Shah Deva was enthroned as the country's new king.

Against a background of growing political dissent in the Rashtriya Panchayat (National Council), a major cabinet reshuffle took place on April 16. Although eight ministers were dismissed, Prime Minister Kirti Nidhi Bista held firm to his post. Concurrently, the king issued directives to his ministers on the execution of their functions, specifically warning them against the employment of relatives. On June 17, the opening day of the Panchayat's budget session, a motion of no confidence in Prime Minister Bista was offered by two former premiers (K. I. Singh and Surya Bahadur Thapa). The move was interpreted as an indirect attack on the king for sustaining the narrowly based political system inaugurated by his late father. On August 13, four dissident Panchayat members—including Thapa—were arrested

after an unprecedented public meeting at which the prime minister was bitterly assailed for failing to take action on food shortages, rising prices, and unemployment. After the meeting, hundreds of university students clashed with the police while attempting to march through the center of Katmandu shouting their demands for reform. On August 17, in the midst of a riotous session of the Panchayat, several members of the opposition were manhandled by police. Subsequently, 12 assembly members were suspended.

Foreign affairs. Nepal moved early to recognize the independence of Bangladesh, announcing its decision on January 16. In June the new nation's foreign minister, Abdus Samad, visited Katmandu. Agreements were announced on bilateral trade and the sharing of transport facilities. Relations with India were marked by increased cordiality as Prime Minister Bista visited New Delhi in April. The same month, technical plans were completed for a 79-mile canal to irrigate land in India's Bihar Province and Nepal.

In June, Nepal halted parcel post exchanges with the People's Republic of China because of the southerly flow of Tibetan propaganda material to refugees in Nepal. But relations with China were not materially affected, as indicated by China's offer to build a road encircling the Katmandu Valley.

Economic developments. Excessive rainfall in 1971 destroyed much of Nepal's corn and millet crops, producing a food crisis in various parts of the country. In March thousands of people staged a hunger march from the Tibet border to Katmandu.

Area and population. Area, 54,000 sq. mi. Pop. (est. 1967), 10,294,000. Katmandu (cap.), 195,300.
Government. Constitutional monarchy. King, Birenda Bir Bikram Shah Deva; prime minister, Kirti Nidhi Bista.
Finance. Monetary unit, Nepali rupee; NR1 = US$0.101.
Trade. Principal exports: jute, timber. Principal imports: textiles, cigarettes, salt, petroleum, kerosine, sugar, machinery, cement, iron. Major trading partner: India (approx. 90 percent).
Education. Literacy rate, 12 percent. Schools (1969): primary, 6,319; secondary, 741; colleges of higher education, 31; 1 university in Katmandu.
Armed forces. 20,000 regulars, mainly infantry.

MICHAEL LEIFER

NETHERLANDS. Politics and government. Throughout the year the Netherlands presented a picture of great political and social instability. The fragmented state of public opinion had created a precariously balanced government coalition in which no less than five parties were represented under the Protestant prime minister Barend W. Biesheuvel. His cabinet started the year with an attempt to economize on public expenditure and to achieve wage and price restraint, both designed to halt the inflation that was the highest among members of the European Economic Community. But while consumer prices in 1971 had risen by 7.6 percent compared with the previous year, by the end of 1972 an overall price increase of 8 percent was anticipated. And the labor unions could not be persuaded to lessen their wage demands, which in 1971 had resulted in an increase of the national wage bill by 13.5 percent.

On July 20, Premier Biesheuvel's cabinet resigned over a conflict about the $1 billion budget deficit expected in 1973. The five-party coalition government lost its majority in Parliament when two ministers seeking cuts in defense spending and a wage-price freeze were the first to resign. The crisis was resolved in early August when four of the parties agreed to remain as a minority government under Biesheuvel until the late November elections.

Church affairs. Early in the year Dutch Catholics openly attacked Pope Paul VI for appointing a noted conservative as bishop of Roermond, in the southern province of Limburg. When the Holy See announced the appointment of 40-year-old Johannes M. Gijsen on January 22, the cathedral chapter issued a statement revealing that Rome had completely ignored the three names it had proposed for the post.

This unprecedented statement was followed by a communiqué from the diocesan pastoral council that expressed "bewilderment at the way in which Rome has ignored the minutely prepared procedure" of consultations among the local priesthood and lay members of the church. In the same week, 51 Limburg priests signed an appeal urging Gijsen not to accept his appointment. The Dutch episcopate requested the pope to withhold his official investiture and warned that a consecration ceremony in Rome under these circumstances "would split the Dutch Catholic community."

However, Gijsen was consecrated and subsequently deepened the controversy over his allegedly reactionary views by warning Catholic politicians that they could no longer claim to be Catholics if they supported a bill liberalizing abortion which was then before Parliament. Finally, a policy statement insisting on the absolute authority of the pope and the bishops in religious affairs, which Gijsen had drawn up for the benefit of priests and lay members working under him, was rejected by the diocesan pastoral council. By that time Gijsen was completely isolated in his bishopric.

War criminals. The government found itself in deep trouble over a decision to free the last three war criminals being held in a Dutch prison. Excercising his right to shorten or end prison sentences, Justice Minister A. A. M. van Agt planned to release three Germans, aged 62 to 70, who had spent 27 years at Breda maximum security prison. Van Agt told Parliament that their continued imprisonment could no longer be justified as a means of reforming them or of protecting society. When, in view of the exceptional nature of the case (Holland suffered cruelly under the German occupation and lost most of its Jewish community), Van Agt allowed a parliamentary debate on his decision, a wave of emotion swept the country. The parliamentary debate ended in a motion "advising" the government not to free the "three of Breda." Van Agt complied but reserved the right to set them free at a later date after consulting experts who would include former members of the wartime underground movement.

Universities. The universities were in a ferment over new legislation concerning their management. Protest movements culminated in the "occupation" of faculties in Amsterdam. The situation deteriorated further when the government increased college charges from 100 guilders to 1,100 guilders, withdrew fee concessions previously granted to families with several members at a university, and scrapped the no-fee rule for students who had paid a college money for four consecutive years. Student organizations, in some cases supported by professors, unleashed a boycott movement that university administrations found hard to check. A further cause for student unrest was a decision to limit the number of new admissions to certain overcrowded faculties (mainly medicine, veterinary science, and sociology) for a period of two years. The cabinet pushed the measure through Parliament by threatening to resign.

Armed forces. In the armed forces, pressure for "more democracy" and "humanization" prompted a reform of military law. In most cases, fines were substituted for the usual punishment of confinement to barracks. Demotion was abolished, as was the military prison. A right of appeal to the military court was granted against any punishment imposed by a unit commander, and it was established that a refusal to carry out an order would be punishable only if this endangered military or other general interests. Moreover, any enlisted man or officer was permitted to disobey any order which he thought would lead to committing a criminal act, even if a subsequent military tribunal were to rule to the contrary.

Area and population. Area, 15,785 sq. mi. Pop. (est. 1971), 13,100,000.
Government. Constitutional monarchy with bicameral parliament (States General). Head of state, Queen Juliana; prime min., Barend W. Biesheuvel; for. min., Norbert Schmelzer.

Finance. Monetary unit, guilder; 1 guilder = US$0.31. Budget (projected for 1973): expenditure, US$11.61 billion; revenue, US$10.8 billion.
Trade (1971). Exports, US$15 billion; imports, US$15.93 billion. Principal exports: oil products, electrical equipment, machinery, meat and meat products, tissues and yarns.
Education (1971). Enrollment: universities, 80,608; vocational schools, 339,300; secondary schools, 96,854; elementary schools, 1,-540,790.
Armed forces. Total strength: 144,581, including 50,704 professionals.
HENRI SCHOUP

NEVADA. Economic developments. Business and population growth were the most distinctive economic developments in Nevada this year, as they have been for most of the preceding decade. In fact, Nevada has the highest rate of population growth of any state in the United States.

A conservative business activity index prepared by the College of Business Administration of the University of Nevada at Reno showed a 9.2 percent rate of gain in the first five months of 1972. Population growth at least kept pace with the record rate of the 1960's, but no dependable new census figures were available.

Business leaders gave credit for this growth to several influences—the developing popularity of outdoor living, which is easy in Nevada; the state's determination to preserve its unspoiled environment; and an unusual approach to taxes. The state constitution contains a free-port provision that exempts from taxation any merchandise in warehouses awaiting reshipment to other destinations. Futhermore, Nevada has neither personal, corporate income, nor inheritance taxes.

Gambling receipts were up approximately 15 percent over 1971 for the first six months of 1972. Building continued to flourish, with thousands of new dwellings being occupied as soon as they were built.

Environment. The Tahoe Regional Planning Agency began its long-awaited effort to save Lake Tahoe and the Tahoe Basin from environmental destruction. This new interstate agency—the first government unit of its kind in the United States—passed new ordinances affecting land use; shorelines; air, water, soil, and vegetation protection; sewage disposal; population density; and zoning. Within a few months the new agency was besieged by lawsuits claiming $53 million for damages that the new regulations had allegedly done to real estate developers.

In another environmental area, a long-time conflict over the use of water in the Truckee River became more intense. Pyramid Lake, the big desert lake on the Paiute Indian reservation northeast of Reno, has been shrinking ever since the Newlands Irrigation Project began taking water from the river early in this century. A federal-state task force has recommended changes on the irrigation project that would return 95,500 acre feet of water to Pyramid Lake.

In November a district court judge, acting on behalf of the Indians, ordered the secretary of the interior to deliver enough water to Pyramid Lake to maintain present levels or show cause why he could not do so. Farmers and state officials reacted bitterly to the decision, and the manager of the Newlands Project, defying the court order, said the irrigation district would continue to take the same amount of water from the Truckee River.

Education. Early in 1972, Nevada received a windfall that benefited higher education when Congress authorized the federal government to refund 80 percent of the slot machine tax paid on Nevada's 39,000 slot machines. The 1971 refund for a period of less than a year amounted to $8.7 million, $5 million of which went to higher education. The state's new community college division received $3.9 million, which financed construction of its first three buildings—in Elko, Carson City, and North Las Vegas.

The new community college division made rapid growth with an enrollment at the start of its second year (September 1972) of more than 4,200, a figure three times the first year's enrollment.

Municipal affairs. Port-of-entry status was given to both Reno and Las Vegas, with customs offices being established to service international trade. Economic leaders hoped this would stimulate future expansion in air commerce.

For election results and campaign highlights, see the special supplement ELECTION '72.

Area and population. Area, 110,540 sq. mi. Pop. (1970), 488,-738. Principal cities: Carson City (cap.), 15,468; Las Vegas, 125,-787; Reno, 72,863.

Government. Gov., D. N. (Mike) O'Callaghan (D); lt. gov., Harry Reid (D); secy. of state, John Koontz (R); atty. gen., Robert List (R); cont., Wilson McGowan (R); treas., Michael Mirabelli (D). Legislature: senate, 13 D, 7 R; assembly, 21 R, 19 D.

Finance (1971–1972). General fund budget: revenue, $108 million; expenditure (est.),$100 million.

Education (1971). Elementary schools, 170; pupils, 74,394; teachers, 2,760. Secondary schools, 74; pupils, 51,359; teachers, 2,207.

DON LYNCH

NEW BRUNSWICK. Politics and government. The two-year-old administration of Progressive Conservative premier Richard Hatfield seemed to be characterized by a lack of dynamism and direction. During a 15-week legislative session, one of the longest on record, 48 bills were passed, including a Community Planning Act requiring over 50 amendments. Changes were also approved in succession duties, gift, and income tax acts. The Liberal opposition charged that these changes were really tax increases instead of adjustments to meet new federal acts, as the government argued. In addition, the legislature lowered the voting age to 19 and granted women the right to serve on juries. Amendments to the Industrial Relations Act established a projects bargaining authority for the Lorneville area of Saint John, where the provincial and federal governments are trying to establish a multi-industry complex. Finally, members granted themselves substantial salary increases.

Finance Minister Jean-Maurice Simard reported a surplus on ordinary accounts of Can$36.8 million, more than double his prediction, and a $13.1 million increase in the net debt, or half his forecast. He credited an unexpected increase in federal equalization grants for the improvement.

A Progressive Conservative victory in a Kent County by-election ended 59 years of Liberal domination of that Acadian area. In February, Le Parti Acadien announced its formation in Bathurst, in the economically and predominantly French region. Its organizers, mostly at Collège de Bathurst, claimed growing grass-roots support among hard-pressed woodcutters and fishermen. But despite several opportunities, party leaders declined to contest by-elections, deciding instead to wait until after a general convention.

In August, Premier Hatfield fired his colorful minister of tourism, J. C. Van Horne, after the popular figure repeatedly ignored demands to stop overspending.

Economic developments. In January industrialist K. C. Irving, New Brunswick's most influential citizen, left Saint John to reside permanently in the Bahamas, amid speculation that he was escaping new federal succession duties. His empire, valued at more than Can$500 million, includes all five English language newspapers in the province, a pulp mill, an oil refinery and deep-water terminal, several television and radio stations, the only provincial busline, a shipbuilding firm, and dry dock facilities.

Saint John and Moncton in southern New Brunswick continued to outstrip the northern areas in economic activity. The New Brunswick Electric Power Commission began building a Can$184 million generating station at Lorneville and later received permission from the National Energy Board to export two-thirds of the new output to Maine and New England. Lorneville is also the site of a proposed deep-water terminal. But Continental Oil of Houston, Texas, reconsidered its plans to use Lorneville to transship Middle East crude after Ottawa placed a levy of 15 cents a ton on ships transporting oil in Canadian waters—the money to be used for emergency cleanup of oil spills.

In the Bathurst area, 1,500 workers were laid off in January as pulp mills and base metal mines were hit by foreign exchange restrictions and declining overseas markets. In April, 300 salmon fishermen were both shocked and angered when Ottawa, in a conservation move, placed a five-year ban on commercial salmon fishing along the east coast. The ban did not affect sports fishermen, who reported the best catches in years as salmon mysteriously returned to the famed Restigouche and Miramichi rivers.

Biculturalism. Students at L'Université de Moncton continued to pressure local authorities to provide full bilingual services, but Mayor Leonard C. Jones argued that most of Moncton's citizens understood English, despite the fact that 35 percent claimed French as their first language. The controversy spawned several lawsuits and a testing of the provincial Official Languages Act, which gives French equality with English in the provincial civil service. Evidence of an English backlash to this French militancy came with the formation of a rightist English Language Association pledged to keep Canada a unilingual (that is, English) country. Meanwhile, the influential National Acadian Society, centered in Moncton, demanded that the Hatfield government, which has only four French-speaking members out of 33 legislators, revamp the education department to overcome the English domination of the provincial school system.

Area and population. Area, 28,354 sq. mi. Pop. (1971), 634,557. Principal cities (1971): Fredericton (cap.), 24,250; Saint John (incl. metro. area), 105,227; Moncton, 47,781.

Government. Lt. gov., H. J. Robichaud; prem., Richard Hatfield. Unicameral legislature: Progressive Conservatives, 33; Liberals, 25.

Finance. Budget (1972–1973): revenue, Can$545.8 million; expenditure, Can$588.6 million.

Education (1972). Public school enrollment, 175,997; teachers, 7,968. University enrollment (1971), 14,395.

RICHARD WILBUR

NEWFOUNDLAND AND LABRADOR. Politics—the end of an era. This year the era of Premier Joseph Smallwood, who had ruled Newfoundland since its confederation with Canada in 1949 and presided over 23 years of unbroken Liberal Party government, came to an end. The people had to begin an adjustment to the Progressive Conservative (PC) Party and a new style of administration.

THE TASTE OF DEFEAT. Joseph R. Smallwood, premier of Newfoundland for 23 years, was forced to step down in January.

UPI

It began when Smallwood, elected for the sixth successive five-year term in September 1966, called a general election for October 28, 1971. The Liberals tried to play down the longevity of their 71-year-old veteran and his regime, emphasizing his younger colleagues in order to counter the new look and team approach of 38-year-old PC leader Frank Moores.

The election proved a cliffhanger. The PC's got 51.2 percent of the vote and 21 of the 42 legislature seats; the Liberals won 20, with New Labrador Party leader Tom Burgess, a former Liberal, coming out with the crucial remaining seat.

It was a crushing defeat for Smallwood. He lost seven cabinet ministers and was himself barely reelected by a relatively small majority in Placentia East. Even the speaker of the house of assembly was rejected. In addition, Burgess intimated that he would support the PC's, thus giving Moores a bare majority after electing a speaker.

But Smallwood refused to resign until the official count was made, demanding judicial recounts in several districts where margins were close. The recount in St. Barbe South, which the PC's had won by a razor-thin majority, was stopped when it was discovered that a returning officer in one small village had burned the ballots through an error of judgment. Smallwood took the case to the supreme court for a decision, saying he would resign if the Liberals lost the case. The court decided that the PC's had in fact won St. Barbe South, and Smallwood could stall no longer. On January 18 he resigned, and Moores and his cabinet were sworn in as the first Progressive Conservative regime since confederation.

But the machinations continued. A couple of days later, Gus Oldford (L, Fortune Bay) resigned his seat. This seemed to establish a PC majority, though Burgess was now blowing hot and cold. He shocked the public by announcing that he was returning to the Liberal fold, although he lost his bid for the party leadership to Ed Roberts, former health minister and Smallwood protégé. Then Hugh Shea (PC, St. John's South), disgruntled at not being included in the new cabinet, also switched to the Liberals, and, as the 35th general assembly met on March 1, the government found itself in a minority: PC's 20, Liberals 21, and one vacancy. Before the house met, Roberts promised cooperation, but the Liberals made it clear that the government would survive only as long as the Opposition wished. Moores went to Lieutenant Governor E. John A. Harnum and asked for a dissolution on the grounds that William Saunders (L, Bay de Verde) had resigned, creating a 20–20 standoff in the legislature, with two vacancies. The dissolution was granted, and a new election, the second in five months, was held March 25.

Even the PC's were astonished at the extent of their 33–9 victory—reminiscent of the previous Liberal sweeps—in which Shea and Burgess, the two weathervanes who in a way had started it all, both lost. The Smallwood era had ended.

The "liquor lease scandal." One of the government's first moves was to appoint a royal commission, under former lieutenant governor Fabian O'Dea, to inquire into the ownership of certain premises leased to the Newfoundland Liquor Commission. As the Opposition, the PC's had charged that the costs and rents of several buildings were exorbitant and that the deal smacked of corruption. Smallwood had refused to give the names during the sessions of 1970 and 1971.

The O'Dea commission identified the mysterious owners as Smallwood, O. L. Vardy, a longtime civil servant and Smallwood's confidant, and Arthur Lundrigan, a prominent Liberal and Corner Brook businessman whose family firm, Lundrigan's Ltd., had prospered from its government connections. The report said the three held equal shares in a dummy corporation that built and owned a number of liquor stores and rented them to the government at inflated costs. It was also revealed that the trio had borrowed over Can$1.5 million from the Bank of Montreal to buy shares in British Newfoundland Corporation (BRINCO), which was then involved with the Newfoundland government in developing hydroelectric power in Churchill Falls, Labrador, and that the bank subsequently forgave "hundreds of thousands of dollars" of interest on the loan. The bank, it turned out, was simultaneously acting for BRINCO, Lundrigan's Ltd., and the Newfoundland government, and Lundrigan was publicly revealed to be a director of both the bank and the trust company.

The O'Dea report was passed to J. J. Robinette, a leading Toronto lawyer, who advised that both criminal and civil charges could be laid. But the PC cabinet backed away from criminal action, and Moores opined that Smallwood, Vardy, and Lundrigan had already been tried in "the court of public opinion." He said the government was only interested in getting its money back and preferred to settle out of court. However, the government also went to work to prepare comprehensive conflict-of-interest legislation to introduce at the next session of the legislature.

The revelations of the "liquor lease scandal" made headlines all across Canada and badly tarnished the Smallwood image. Smallwood stubbornly denied his connection with the company that had dealt with the Newfoundland Liquor Commission, and the O'Dea report did state that the evidence in his case was "circumstantial."

Economic problems. The new government had to feel its way through a maze of political and financial wheeling and dealing from the Smallwood era. The linerboard mill at Stephenville, a project of expatriate American promoter John C. Doyle, another longtime Smallwood backer and beneficiary, was in difficulties, and its cost had escalated to Can$154 million, twice the original estimate and treble the financial guarantee envisioned by the Smallwood government. The PC's decided to take over the mill and pay Doyle Can$5 million for his equity.

The huge Bowater paper mill at Corner Brook had announced in August 1971 that it would soon close down its largest machine because of market conditions, throwing one-third of the work force out of jobs. In a political grandstand play, Smallwood had threatened nationalization unless the government was given an option to buy the complex, valued at about Can$100 million. He got the option for a Can$200,-000 payment, and the shutdown was postponed to December 31. In January the Moores administration dropped the option and tried unsuccessfully to recover some of the payment. The mill, in the meantime, showed a remarkable recovery, and No. 7 machine was back in production by August.

The Save Our Fisheries Association kept up pressure on Ottawa to take a tougher stand with foreign fishing fleets that have been operating on the continental shelf and in Canadian coastal waters.

Labor. The province was plagued with wildcat strikes against the advice and orders of union leaders. They were partially attributed to the flexing of new-found muscle by a rank and file ignorant of the process of collective bargaining and their responsibilities within a bona fide labor-management contract. The worst strike, involving 1,500 men, occurred in the iron ore region of the Labrador City–Wabush community. One result was the appointment of a royal commission to study the "psychological malaise" affecting Labrador residents and their grievances (real or imagined) vis-à-vis their compatriots in Newfoundland.

Area and population. Area, 156,185 sq. mi. Pop. (1971 census), 522,103. St. John's (cap.), 78,103.

Government. Lt. gov., E. John A. Harnum; prem., Frank D. Moores.

Finance. Budget (est. 1972–1973): gross revenue, Can$401,736,-900; gross expenditure, Can$589,172,700.

Education (1972). Enrollment: public schools, 164,700; university (full-time), 6,954.   MICHAEL HARRINGTON

BITTERNESS ON THE CAMPAIGN TRAIL. Senator Edmund Muskie (D, Me.), in front of the Manchester "Union Leader" office, emotionally denounces publisher William Loeb for printing lies about him and his wife.

WIDE WORLD

NEW HAMPSHIRE. Legislation. The Granite State retained the distinction of being the only state with neither a tax on earned personal income nor a general sales tax, when the legislature voted 217–154 against a 4.5 percent income tax bill supported by Governor Walter R. Peterson (R). The tax would have produced about $150 million annually to relieve cities and towns of the burden of financing local schools. It was the second time an income tax plan sponsored (in spite of a campaign pledge) by Governor Peterson died in the giant 400-member house.

The 15-day special session did approve an $8.4 million supplemental budget, providing a 5.5 percent average pay hike for 7,000 state workers and allocating $700,000 in school building aid, $300,000 in parochial school aid, and $1.3 million for 199 new state positions, half of them in the health and welfare department.

Environment and the economy. A clean river clashed with 275 jobs in Lincoln this spring, and the river won. Closing of the Franconia Manufacturing Company's paper mill, the only factory in the town of 1,300, dramatized the plight of the state's pulpwood industry when faced with pressure for a cleaner environment. The plant's $5 million worth of pollution-abatement equipment proved inadequate, and, faced with state orders to install more expensive equipment, the owners declared bankruptcy.

The environment was also victorious in January when the New England Regional Commission, after an 18-month survey, abandoned further study of construction of an east-west interstate highway to help develop the depressed areas in northern New England. Attention turned to the alternative of improving existing feeder routes.

Meanwhile, the Merrimack River, an open sewer for industrial and domestic waste from the state's rapidly developing south-central region, was scheduled to be clean enough to drink from by 1975. Plans called for 24 more sewage-treatment plants along its banks and four regional water-filtration and water-renovation facilities to clean and reclean the river water for each city's water supply. Also, the

legislature authorized the state water supply and pollution control commission to build and operate a regional pollution-abatement system tying in nine communities in the Winnipesaukee River basin.

Accreditation lost. New Hampshire Hospital in Concord lost its accreditation in August. The Chicago-based Accreditation Council for Psychiatric Facilities refused to certify the 1,800-patient state mental hospital because of insufficient staff. Earlier in the year, the hospital's doctors had petitioned for a $6,000 raise, complaining that low salaries made it impossible to recruit and retain trained staff.

Education. The state's three-year-old dual enrollment program was ruled unconstitutional in September. U.S. District Court Judge Hugh H. Bownes ruled on a case involving the Nashua school district and Holy Infant Jesus School, where the city rented five classrooms and paid teachers to instruct parochial school children in secular subjects. The state considered appealing the decision or trying to change the method of implementation before the ruling would take effect in September 1973.

For election results and campaign highlights, see the special supplement ELECTION '72.

Area and population. Area, 9,304 sq. mi. Pop. (est. 1972), 778,-566. Principal cities: Concord (cap.), 29,670; Manchester, 96,657; Nashua, 60,136.

Government. Gov., Walter R. Peterson (R); secy. of state, Robert L. Stark (R); treas., Robert W. Flanders (R); cont., John T. Flanders (R); atty. gen., Warren B. Rudman (R). Legislature: senate, 12 R, 8 D, 3 R-D, 1 D-R; house, 213 R, 135 D, 39 R-D, 13 D-R.

Finance (fiscal year 1971–1972). Revenue, $350,671,031; expenditure, $313,268,620.

Education (1971–1972). Public elementary schools, 364; enrollment, 95,419; teachers, 4,097. Public secondary schools, 104; enrollment, 70,239; teachers, 3,353. Parochial elementary schools, 52; enrollment, 15,604; teachers, 516. Parochial secondary schools, 9; enrollment, 19,413; teachers, 204.   ROGER TALBOT

NEW JERSEY. Tax reform and taxes. Governor William T. Cahill's sweeping program for fundamental tax reform went down to defeat in the assembly. Acting on the recom-

mendations of a special commission that studied the tax structure of the state, Cahill had proposed a state income tax, revisions in the existing sales tax, a limited statewide property tax, an increase in the corporate income tax, and other taxes on business, banks, and utilities to relieve the burden now carried by property owners through local real estate taxes. Under the proposals, the state would assume all costs of welfare and the court system and the major share of the costs of primary and secondary public school education. Tax reform has become especially important because of a superior court ruling that New Jersey's system of financing public education through property taxes is unconstitutional because it discriminates against school districts with low property taxes.

Both the state AFL-CIO, which was suspicious of the effect of an income tax, and the state chamber of commerce, which feared an adverse impact on business and industry, opposed the reforms. There also appeared to be no support at the grass roots level. However, the mayors of the state's largest cities vowed to keep the movement for tax reform alive. In his efforts to balance New Jersey's $2 billion budget, the governor had more success with the legislature. A corporate tax hike and an excise and sales tax package were enacted, which increased some existing taxes, including 1 cent on gasoline, 50 cents on a gallon of liquor, 30 cents on a gallon of wine, and 5 cents on a pack of cigarettes, and for the first time levied a 5 percent tax on beer.

Other legislation. A no-fault auto insurance law was enacted to go into effect on January 1, 1973. Regarded as one of the best state laws in the country, it guaranteed a 15 percent reduction in the cost of liability insurance and provided generous compensation. The legislature lowered the age of legal majority from 21 to 18, effective January 1, 1973. Cahill's prison reform program advanced when a three-member, full-time parole board was established. A bill was adopted which permits voters in counties to change and thus strengthen their form of government.

Legislative reapportionment. The state supreme court, in a suit that challenged the apportionment of the legislature, broke with tradition and ruled that county boundary lines could be ignored in drawing up new legislative districts to achieve population equality.

Crime and corruption. The most notable public figure to be jailed in the continuing federal and state crackdown on crime and corruption was John V. Kenny, Democratic leader of Hudson County, one of the most powerful political bosses in the nation. As his machine crumbled around him, the ailing, 80-year-old Kenny pleaded guilty to income tax evasion charges and was sent to a federal medical center, where he was found not well enough to serve a prison term. Former Democratic secretary of state Robert Burkhardt was let off lightly by a federal court on his guilty plea to a charge of conspiring to extort $30,000 as a campaign contribution from a contractor; he was fined $5,000.

The press. The state's most influential newspaper, the Newark *News,* ceased publication on August 31. The 88-year-old paper, shut down by a long strike, resumed publication on April 10 but failed to recover its advertising and circulation levels.

For election results and campaign highlights, see the special supplement ELECTION '72.

Area and population. Area, 7,836 sq. mi. Pop. (1970), 7,168,164. Principal cities: Trenton (cap.), 104,638; Newark, 382,417; Jersey City, 260,545; Patterson, 144,824; Elizabeth, 112,654; Camden, 102,551.
Government. Gov., William T. Cahill (R); atty. gen., George F. Kugler, Jr.; treas., Joseph M. McCrane; secy. of state, Paul Sherwin (on leave of absence). All state officers are appointed by the governor. Legislature: senate, 24 R, 16 D; assembly, 39 R, 40 D, 1 I.
Finance (fiscal 1972–1973). Budget, $2 billion.
Education (1971–1972). Elementary school enrollment, 1,003,556; teachers, 44,560. Secondary school enrollment, 516,983; teachers, 30,331; nonpublic school enrollment, 313,300.

THOMAS J. HOOPER

NEW MEXICO. Legislative action. Governor Bruce King learned at age 14 that the best way to break a wild horse was to lead him on a short cinch, mocking his every move. Applying the same methods to later life, the tall, cowboy-booted Democrat piloted his programs through the New Mexico legislature, with the help of comfortable majorities in both senate and house. Typical was the success he enjoyed with his $291 million budget proposal. The powerful Legislative Finance Committee had urged a budget $4.8 million below that figure, but, when the sound and fury of the 30-day session was over, King had won all but $25,000 of the amount he had sought. The governor was similarly successful in the area of education. Starting before the session, King got legislators and educators together and hammered out agreement on an education bill. Without the usual bitter battle, an education bill boosting appropriations by $32.8 million glided through to passage. King also obtained a $1.08 million appropriation for the Department of Development and $100,000 in funds for continuation of a successful program to lure motion-picture production to the state. He also joined in the successful fight led by Representative Eugene Cinelli (D, Albuquerque) to pass a new weight-distance system of truck taxation over opposition from the trucking lobby. Supporters claimed the bill would produce $3 million in new revenues and put truck taxes on an equitable basis for the first time.

In line with Governor King's pledge, no general tax increases were voted by the legislature. Instead, an income tax credit for low-income families was adopted. Meanwhile, bills to tax electricity, place stiff regulations on land subdividers, and adopt a form of "no-fault" automobile insurance fell by the wayside.

Economy. The U.S. government chose a site on the high, flat San Augustin Plains near Magdalena for erection of a $76 million radio-telescope observatory, designed to search out weak radio signals from outer space. U.S. Senator Clinton P. Anderson (D), who announced the selection, said the giant observatory would be 10 to 100 times more powerful than any other radio observatory in the world. The project was expected to contribute significantly to the New Mexico economy.

Sports. It was a good year for New Mexico sports fans, who saw the Albuquerque Dukes win a pennant and three New Mexicans win honors in the 1972 Olympics. The Dukes won the Pacific Coast League (Triple-A) pennant, then came in runner-up in the Triple-A World Series in Hawaii, losing to a team of Venezuelan all-stars. Cathy Carr of Albuquerque captured two gold medals in Olympic swim competition for the women's 200-meter breaststroke and for the 400-meter relay. Frank Shorter, of Ranches of Taos, won a gold medal in the marathon race, and Janet Ely, of Albuquerque, came in fourth in two of the Olympic diving competitions.

Natural disasters. Flash floods created havoc at widely separated points. A cloudburst brought extensive flooding to the historic Black Range country of southern New Mexico, and a wall of water hit the old mining town of Hillsboro, causing heavy damage and killing four persons. Other serious floods occurred in Gallup and Las Cruces.

For election results and campaign highlights, see the special supplement ELECTION '72.

Area and population. Area, 121,666 sq. mi. Pop. (1970), 1,016,000. Principal cities: Santa Fe (cap.), 41,167; Albuquerque, 243,751.
Government. Gov., Bruce King (D); lt. gov., Robert A. Mondragon (D); secy. of state, Betty Fiorina (D); aud., Frank M. Olmstead (D); treas., Jesse D. Kornegay (D); atty. gen., David L. Norvell.
Finance (year ending June 30, 1972). Total expenditure, $670 million; total revenue, $688 million.
Education (1971–1972). Enrollment: public elementary schools, 142,680; public secondary schools, 129,721; private and parochial schools, 9,329; state-supported institutions of higher education, 40,231; private institutions of higher education, 3,580. Teachers: public elementary schools, 6,234; public secondary schools, 5,773; private and parochial schools, 714.

RALPH LOONEY

HEADLINES, WASHINGTON POST; PHOTO, DON CARL STEFFEN/RAPHO-GUILLUMETTE

SUPERSNOOP. Since taking over the ''Washington Merry-Go-Round'' column from the late Drew Pearson in 1969, Jack Anderson has earned a reputation of his own as the nation's top muckraker. Never overcautious, Anderson made headlines this year by leaking secret transcripts of national security meetings on the Indo-Pakistani war and by releasing a memo, purportedly written by ITT lobbyist Dita Beard, linking a corporate contribution to the Republicans with the settlement of an antitrust suit. But Anderson's zeal backfired in the summer, when he had to retract charges that Democratic vice-presidential nominee Thomas Eagleton had a drunken driving record.

NEWSPAPERS. The U.S. Supreme Court, which last year refused to restrain newspapers from publishing the Pentagon papers, this year ruled against the press in a decision that had far-reaching implications. By a 5 to 4 vote, the Court in June held that constitutional guarantees of freedom of speech and press are not abridged when journalists are required to testify before state or federal grand juries.

At issue were three separate cases involving reporters who had been cited for contempt for refusing to testify. The most widely publicized case was that of Earl Caldwell, a west coast correspondent for the New York *Times,* who had reported extensively on the Black Panthers. After Caldwell had been judged guilty of contempt in 1970 for refusing to appear before a federal grand jury investigating the Black Panthers, a U.S. court of appeals vacated the contempt citation, ruling that the government could not require a reporter to give evidence unless a "compelling need" could be shown. The Justice Department then sought a ruling from the nation's highest court, which considered

the Caldwell case along with those of two other journalists: Paul Pappas, a newsman-photographer for a New Bedford, Mass., television station, who also had been called before a grand jury probing the Black Panthers, and Paul M. Branzburg, a Detroit *Free Press* reporter whose eyewitness account of hashish production in Kentucky had aroused the interest of a county grand jury in that state.

The Supreme Court's majority decision, in which President Richard M. Nixon's four appointees to the Court joined with one Kennedy appointee, Byron White, referred only to appearances before grand juries and did not deal with requests for testimony in court cases. But the ruling established a legal precedent in the long-disputed issue between government and the press. The Justice Department has long contended that journalists have the same duty as other citizens to answer questions put by grand juries—and to produce notes and unused portions of news film—unless state law provides otherwise. The press, on the other hand, has traditionally argued that a journalist must have the

409

New Twist for a Crooked Cop

As star witness in the Knapp Commission hearings on police corruption in New York City, Patrolman William Phillips, admitted grafter turned informant, shocked the public (above) with tales of police on the take. But even as the commission readied its recommendations, Phillips was indicted for the murder of a pimp and a prostitute in a Manhattan brothel four years earlier. Phillips claimed he had been framed and appeared confident (left) of the outcome during proceedings that ended in a mistrial on August 9.

right to a confidential relationship with his source, because such a relationship is often necessary to the gathering of significant information. By striking down claims to journalistic privilege under the First Amendment, the Court renewed pressure on Congress to give journalists the right to protect their sources by passing a federal "shield law" comparable to the laws already in force in 19 states.

In October, while committees in both the Senate and the House considered proposed "shield" legislation, Peter J. Bridge, a city hall reporter for the now-defunct Newark *Evening News,* became the first journalist since the Supreme Court decision to go to jail for refusal to testify before a grand jury. Bridge had written about a reported bribe-offer to a member of the Newark Housing Authority but balked at telling the grand jury who had allegedly offered the bribe, on grounds that the information was confidential and had not been included in his printed story. He was jailed for contempt until either he relented or the grand jury's term expired.

Politics and the press. Meanwhile, the continuing tension between the Nixon administration and some sectors of the press was increased by events related to the national election campaign (even though Vice-President Spiro T. Agnew had declared at least a partial truce at a July publishers' convention, calling for discussion in place of harangue and cliché). The Democrats seized on the Nixon administration's troubled relations with the press as an issue in the presidential campaign. The party's platform accused the administration of excessive secrecy and intimidation of the media and promised that the Democrats, if elected, would make more information available to the press and the public.

Another political note was sounded in July when the American Newspaper Guild departed from its traditional neutrality in presidential elections and, by action of its executive board, endorsed the presidential candidacy of Senator George McGovern. Earlier, delegates to the guild's convention in San Juan, P.R., had rejected a move to endorse McGovern for the Democratic nomination, but by a vote of 220 to 114 they had empowered the union's executive board to consider endorsing a candidate following the party conventions. The guild's action was promptly disavowed by some guild locals and by many individual journalists. Through an advertisement in the Washington

Post, nearly 300 Washington-based reporters and editors, mostly guild members, disassociated themselves from the endorsement, declaring that the guild had no business interjecting its members into a partisan political role and that its efforts to do so "demean us as professionals whose hallmark is fairness."

Pulitzer Prizes. The awarding of the year's Pulitzer Prizes was accompanied by another disavowal—this one from the trustees of Columbia University, who cannot initiate Pulitzer awards but have the power to veto the choices made by the 14-member advisory board, composed almost entirely of prominent editors. In announcing the Pulitzers for 1972, the trustees said in a formal statement that a majority among them "had deep reservations about the timeliness and suitability of certain of the journalism awards" and would not have made the same choices if the decision had been theirs alone. Although the trustees named no names, their reservations concerned the Pulitzer for meritorious and distinguished public service, awarded to the New York *Times* for its controversial decision to publish the Pentagon papers, and the national reporting prize, given to columnist Jack Anderson for his disclosure of secret U.S. policy papers on the India-Pakistan conflict. (*See* PEOPLE IN THE NEWS: Jack Anderson.)

U.S. dropouts. The United States also had its troubled newspapers, and three long-established major dailies ceased publication during the year. After losing a lengthy court battle to retain control of a profitable Boston television station, the owners of the Boston *Herald Traveler* in May sold the newspaper, its modern printing plant, and a sales and distribution subsidiary to the Hearst Corporation, publisher of the rival Boston *Record American.* In July, the Washington *Evening Star* bought and absorbed the 50-year-old Washington *Daily News,* the Scripps-Howard chain's flagship in the nation's capital. And at the end of August, the Newark *Evening News,* once New Jersey's largest and most prestigious newspaper, closed permanently, only 21 weeks after it had reopened following a strike-induced shutdown that lasted more than ten months, during which time it had lost many key editorial employees and had sold its printing plant and Sunday edition to the opposition Newark *Star-Ledger.*

The death of the Washington *Daily News,* a tabloid evening paper with a circulation of 207,000, reduced the number of Scripps-Howard papers to 19 and left New York as the only city in the country with more than two publishers of general circulation dailies.

Outlook. On the whole, however, the business outlook for U.S. newspapers was encouraging, and some publishing groups, including Knight Newspapers, Inc., and the Los Angeles–based Times Mirror Company, reported record earnings. Although costs for all papers continued to mount, the pace of inflation slowed, and total linage showed a modest gain. The American Newspaper Publishers Association said that advertising revenues for 1971, aided by a late surge, had risen 9 percent over the previous year, to an all-time high of more than $6 billion. Forecasting continued growth, the ANPA predicted a total advertising income of $10.3 to $12.6 billion by 1980. Another ANPA survey disclosed that only 29 U.S. daily newspapers were currently selling for a nickel, the usual price ten years ago. The largest number of dailies had risen to a dime, almost as many were at 15 cents a copy, and six were even higher.

Employment. The editorial job market remained tight in 1972, but there were more openings than in the previous year, especially for journalists from minority groups. The American Society of Newspaper Editors' Committee on Minority Employment reported that the number of blacks, Mexican-Americans, Puerto Ricans, Indians, Cubans, and Orientals in U.S. news jobs was only about 300, or less than 1 percent of the estimated 40,000 persons employed as reporters, writers, photographers, and editors. But the committee further noted that there was "no pool of adequately qualified minority professionals presently available."

New acquisitions. Showing confidence in the future of the newspaper industry, many major publishing groups shopped for new properties. The Texas-based Harte-Hanks Newspapers, Inc., continued to extend its holdings, buying an assortment of small papers in other states, and the Gannett Company made two more major acquisitions. In January, Gannett bought the 95-year-old Nashville, Tenn., *Banner* for $14 million in cash and notes, and in June, through a stock exchange valued at $26.7 million, the company added the El Paso, Texas, *Times.* The transactions bolstered the Gannett group's position as the largest U.S. newspaper chain in number of papers, giving it a new total of 54.   JOHN LUTER

NEW YORK. Abortion. One of the nation's first states to legalize abortion nearly became the first to repeal the legalization. Under the pressure of determined lobbying by the Roman Catholic Church and citizen "right-to-life" organizations, both houses of the state legislature voted to erase the two-year-old statute permitting abortions up to the 24th week of pregnancy. The legislators rejected a compromise offered by Governor Nelson A. Rockefeller that would have reduced the legal period for abortions to 18 weeks of pregnancy and voted instead to reinstate the original law, which prohibited terminating pregnancy except to save the mother's life. Governor Rockefeller vetoed the change, however, leaving the liberalized abortion law on the books.

The debate over abortion was one of the most emotional ever to occur in the capital. On the floor of the assembly, legislators fighting for repeal of the liberalized law circulated photographs of aborted fetuses to illustrate the contention that abortion was murder. Their opponents passed around wire coat hangers to dramatize what they saw as the alternative for women who wanted abortions but could not get them legally.

Even President Richard M. Nixon stepped into the debate, sending a letter to Terence Cardinal Cooke of the Archdiocese of New York, asserting that he "would personally like to associate myself with convictions you deeply feel and eloquently express" in opposition to legalized abortion.

Since the liberalized law was passed in 1970, more than 350,000 abortions have been performed, according to the state health services administration in May, many of those sought by women from other parts of the country. A long dispute over whether the state's medicaid program for the poor should pay for abortions was resolved by a court decision ordering such payments.

Welfare. As the state's population on welfare reached a high in 1971 of 1.7 million at a record cost of $4.1 billion, the United States Supreme Court struck down a New York law designed to curb welfare spending. The law, enacted in 1971, barred aid to persons who had not lived in the state for at least a year. The law was part of a sweeping package of legislation designed to tighten controls on welfare spending. One feature was a requirement that able-bodied recipients work in government jobs in exchange for their welfare checks, a program that enrolled 130,000 people in New York City, just over 10 percent of the city's welfare rolls. The effort has proved largely symbolic, however, since it has made virtually no impact on the percentage of recipients found to be ineligible and therefore removed from welfare.

Corruption. A lengthy report by the Knapp Commission, which had been appointed by Mayor John V. Lindsay to investigate the problem of police graft in New York City, confirmed that widespread corruption existed among the city's police. The commission, headed by Whitman Knapp, a Wall Street lawyer, urged Governor Rockefeller to name a special deputy attorney general to combat corruption

among policemen, prosecutors, and judges. The suggestion encountered immediate opposition from the city's five district attorneys. However, in September the governor named Maurice H. Nadjari, an experienced city prosecutor, to the post, placing all cases of corruption in the city under his jurisdiction.

The commission's other recommendations included the suggestion that some potential sources of graft be removed by legalizing gambling and withdrawing the police from the enforcement of laws concerning construction, restaurants, and the sale of liquor. It also called for a shift in the strategy of prosecutors so that those who pay bribes, as well as those who take them, could be arrested.

The New York *Times*, which had brought the police corruption problem to light, also turned its attention to graft in the construction industry, where it estimated that $25 million a year was paid in bribes. The published reports prompted a series of arrests and investigations.

The New York *Daily News* ran a series of articles documenting the Lindsay administration's use of provisional jobs and emergency employment funds to make political payoffs to those who had supported Lindsay in his unsuccessful bid for the Democratic presidential nomination.

Attica. Another investigative commission, this headed by Robert B. McKay, dean of the New York University Law School, studied the events at Attica Prison that left 43 persons dead in September 1971 and concluded that the blame fell not only on the rebelling inmates but also on Governor Rockefeller, for failing to go to the prison personally, and on the state police, for using lethal ammunition during the assault to retake the prison.

Organized crime. An underworld war erupted in New York City, beginning with the April slaying of reputed Mafia family head Joseph Gallo in a Little Italy clam house. Two days later, an associate of Joseph Colombo, Sr., who had been shot and incapacitated in June 1971, was murdered outside his south Brooklyn restaurant. In succeeding days, four more bodies were found, and, in the weeks that followed, numerous Mafia men turned up dead, including Thomas Eboli, acting head of the Genovese clan.

Tragically, the gangland killings took some innocent lives. In early August, two businessmen were killed, apparently in error, after they took seats in a bar that had just been vacated by mobsters who were the intended targets. The incident prompted Mayor Lindsay to pledge that gangsters would be "run out of town." It turned out later that one way this was to be accomplished would be for the police to reveal the names of businesses with "known" Mafia links. There were immediate protests by civil liberties advocates.

Low-income housing. New York City's plan to build high-rise public housing in the middle-class neighborhood of Forest Hills, Queens, touched off one of the nation's most acute conflicts over the issue of where the poor are to live. Community groups in Forest Hills, playing on neighborhood residents' fears of an influx of crime and social disorganization, pressured Mayor Lindsay into a compromise that would halve the size of the project. This seemed to do little to ease the residents' fears, however, and the fate of the housing—and of the entire program to open the way for low-income families out of ghetto neighborhoods—remained in doubt.

A similar battle was launched in Westchester County, where the state's powerful Urban Development Corporation announced plans to build low-income housing in several rural towns, even if the towns objected. A flurry of protests and court suits forced a pause in the plans, but the state declared its resolve to go ahead.

Economic developments. Jobs continued to flow from cities to suburbs in New York State. Although factory jobs had been dropping in New York City for some years, 1971 was the first year since 1963 that nonfactory positions also declined. The city lost 36,600 private jobs outside factories

in 1971 and lost 43,000 factory jobs. Government employment rose by 7,600.

For election results and campaign highlights, see the special supplement ELECTION '72.

Area and population. Area, 49,576 sq. mi. Pop. (1970), 18,190,740. Principal cities: Albany (cap.), 114,873; New York, 7,867,760; Buffalo, 462,768; Rochester, 296,233; Yonkers, 204,370; Syracuse, 197,208.

Government. Gov., Nelson A. Rockefeller (R); lt. gov., Malcolm Wilson (R); atty. gen., Louis J. Lefkowitz (R); cont., Arthur Levitt (D). Legislature: senate, 32 R, 25 D; assembly, 79 R, 71 D.

Finance. State budget (April 1, 1972–March 31, 1973): $7,870,000,000. New York City expense budget (July 1, 1972–June 30, 1973): $9,407,000,000. New York City capital budget: $1,840,000,000.

Education (est. 1972). Elementary schools, 2,965; enrollment, 1,922,567; teachers, 88,204. Secondary schools, 1,471; enrollment, 1,832,900; teachers, 97,091. Private and parochial schools, 1,946; enrollment, 753,313; teachers, 35,667.   DAVID K. SHIPLER

NEW ZEALAND. Politics and economics. On February 2, Prime Minister Sir Keith Holyoake announced his resignation from the premiership, an office which he had held for nearly 12 years. A caucus of the ruling National Party chose John Marshall, deputy prime minister, as his successor. Marshall was sworn in on February 7 and announced the membership of his cabinet two days later. Robert Muldoon, finance minister, became deputy prime minister, while Sir Keith retained the portfolio of foreign affairs. In a major reorganization of the government, Marshall appointed five new ministers to replace retiring members of the cabinet and created three new posts, covering environment, fuel and power, and social welfare. The changes were designed to revitalize the party's image in preparation for the general elections in November.

Marshall at once took a series of steps to deal with inflation and unemployment. Immediately on assuming office he announced a price, wage, and salary freeze, to remain in effect until March 31, as part of a comprehensive effort to stabilize the economy.

At the end of March, the new prime minister announced to a nationwide television audience a comprehensive economic stabilization program, including price controls on a wide range of goods and services, restraints on wage increases, and limitations on dividends and interest rates on money borrowed for relending. He also announced several measures to promote growth, including an easing of "hire-purchase" (installment plan) restrictions and a reduction in the Reserve Bank discount rate. Defending these actions, he pointed out that in the past two years prices in New Zealand had risen by 20 percent and wages by 35 percent and that the proposed measures were both corrective and temporary. Strong action was necessary, he declared, to reduce the risk of "rekindling the fires of inflation," but the new regulations would continue only until the economy had been restored to a healthy state. The plan was said to contain the strictest anti-inflationary measures since World War II and provided new enforcement authority which permitted spot checks on accounts. The Federation of Labour, New Zealand's largest trade union, said it would not cooperate in implementing the program.

Foreign and Commonwealth affairs. In January the New Zealand government, along with Australia and the United Kingdom, announced its intention to recognize Bangladesh, whereupon Pakistan withdrew its membership in the Commonwealth of Nations. New Zealand extended formal recognition to Bangladesh on January 31.

In February, the seven nations of the South Pacific Forum, including New Zealand, met in Canberra, Australia, and agreed to create a regional research and advisory body, to be known as the South Pacific Bureau for Economic Cooperation. The forum members also agreed to upgrade telecommunications throughout the region, in particular by a submarine cable system, and to establish a regional disaster

fund for its island members. New Zealand and Australia, in response to a sharp attack on their policy of restricting non-white immigration to skilled persons, agreed to give "sympathetic consideration" to proposals for allowing more people from the Pacific Islands to enter for training in technical skills.

On May 31, New Zealand trade union representatives declared a month-long boycott of services to French vessels and supplies as a protest against an imminent French nuclear test in the South Pacific. The New Zealand government subsequently entered a formal protest to the Geneva Disarmament Conference over the planned tests. The French government in turn denounced the "hypocrisy" of New Zealand for protesting the French tests but not previous U.S., British, and Soviet atomic explosions.

On July 7, U.S. treasury secretary George P. Shultz announced that foreign countries increasing their supplies of meat exported to the United States could expect higher meat quotas in 1973. The announcement was heard with great interest in New Zealand, and a few days later the New Zealand ambassador in Washington welcomed a statement from the State Department that the American meat market was "wide open and we will take all you can send."

On June 20, Prime Minister Marshall stated that Australian and New Zealand defense equipment, armaments, communications, training, and strategic and tactical planning should be coordinated. The prime minister's statement was followed on July 27 by an announcement that the two governments had agreed to set up the joint Consultative Committee on Defense Cooperation, comprising high officials of both countries.

Area and population. Area, 103,736 sq. mi. Pop. (1971), 2,862,-431. Principal cities (est. 1970): Wellington (cap.), 179,300 (excluding Hutt); Auckland, 603,500; Christchurch, 260,200; Hutt, 122,000; Dunedin, 110,100.
Government. Self-governing member of the Commonwealth of Nations. Gov. gen., Sir Arthur Porritt; prime min., John Marshall. Parliament (unicameral): National Party, 44; Labour Party, 40. (Does not incorporate results of November 1972 elections.)
Finance. Monetary unit, New Zealand dollar; NZ$1.00 = US$1.197.
Trade (1971). Imports, US$1,346 million; exports, US$1,364 million. Major exports: butter, cheese, meats, fruit, wool, pulp, and paper. Imports: raw materials and machinery, capital equipment, certain foods, and consumer goods. Chief trading partners: Australia, Great Britain, United States, Japan.
Education (1969). Public primary schools, 2,200; enrollment, 450,850. Registered primary schools, 344; enrollment, 52,407. State secondary schools, 204; district high schools, 66; private secondary schools, 116; total enrollment, 183,783. Universities, 6; enrollment, 31,542. Total public expenditures on education (1969–1970), NZ$209,064,524.
Armed forces (1970). Army, 5,782 all ranks; territorial personnel, 11,169. Royal New Zealand Navy, 2,975 officers and ratings; 2,378 reserve. Royal New Zealand Air Force, 4,475 regular; 1,850 non-regular.
FRED D. SCHNEIDER

NICARAGUA. Politics and government. The year was one of great political activity, but despite many outward changes in the governmental structure, the situation remained the same. General Anastasio Somoza Debayle remained firmly in control.

After a long series of negotiations between President Somoza and Fernando Agüero Rocha, leader of the opposition Conservative Party, a pact was signed in August 1971 in which Somoza would resign from the presidency at the end of April and Nicaragua would then be ruled by a three-man junta and a 100-seat Constituent Assembly until the next general election in 1974. The assembly would be divided 60–40 between the majority and minority parties, with the minority party entitled to name one of the triumvers. In addition, the agreement provided for a new electoral law that is supposed to make free elections possible in the future.

It was a foregone conclusion that Somoza's Liberal Party would win the February 6 elections, and Agüero's acceptance of the pact lost him a great deal of support. When the election results started to come in, Somoza led by better than a 9–1 proportion. At this point Agüero reportedly begged Somoza to do something to help him save face. A lavishly planned public computation of the vote was therefore abruptly halted, and several days later when the results were announced, Agüero was awarded 26 percent of the vote. On the local level the Conservatives did not win one municipal contest, but for the first time in 47 years there actually were municipal elections.

The triumvirate, which took office on May 1, consisted of Agüero and two of Somoza's most trusted friends, retired general Roberto Martínez Lacayo and Alfonso Lobo Cordero. Somoza remained chief of the national guard (Nicaragua's combined military and police force) and assumed a new title, supreme commander of the armed forces, with responsibility only to his Constituent Assembly.

The Constituent Assembly was not expected to make any substantial changes in the present constitution, except to extend the presidential term of office to six years and make it possible for Somoza to succeed himself.

Economic developments. Nicaragua improved its economic position slightly. Exports for the first half of the year were up 23.7 percent, while imports were up only 10 percent. However, severe problems developed in September with Costa Rica's suspension of Central American Common Market concessions. This could affect as much as 25 percent of Nicaragua's exports.

The most important new project announced this year was a $3 million refinery to be built at Punta Mico on the Atlantic coast by Maritimo Mundial, a company chiefly owned by Somoza. Initially it will have a capacity of 250,000 barrels a day but can be expanded to 1 million.

Howard Hughes made two visits to Nicaragua, each of which provoked many rumors. It is certain, however, that Hughes made a deal with Lanica, the Nicaraguan national airline (owned by the Somoza family) to trade 25 percent of Lanica stock for two Convair 880 jets. Supposedly, this is the first step in a merger of Hughes' Air West with Lanica.

Area and population. Area, 50,193 sq. mi. Pop. (gov. est. April 1972), 1,894,690. Principal cities (1967): Managua (cap.), 300,000; Léon, 61,649; Matagalpa, 61,383.
Government. Triumvirate with Constituent Assembly (until general elections of 1974). Triumvers: Gen. Roberto Martínez Lacayo (Liberal), Alfonso Lobo Cordero (Liberal), and Fernando Aguero Rocha (Conservative). Ex-president Anastasio Somoza Debayle, head of the Liberal Party, holds actual power. For. min., Dr. Lorenzo Guerrero.
Finance. Monetary unit, córdoba (C$); C$1 = US$0.143. Budget (est. 1970): balanced at US$98.03 million.
Trade (1970). Imports, US$198,747,507; exports, US$178,623,-292. Principal exports: cotton, coffee, sugar, beef. Principal trading partners: United States, Japan, CACM.
Education (1972). School enrollment: 334,940, or 34.5 percent of persons between age 6 and 29. Illiteracy: 52.5 percent.
Armed forces. National guard, 5,410 (plus 4,000 in reserve); air force, 1,500.
THEODORE S. CREEDMAN

NIGER. Politics and government. Niger's customarily quiet political scene was marred somewhat by an issue that first erupted in 1970 and has festered ever since: educational reform. Most of the nation's secondary schools were closed in early February by a strike of both students and teachers. They remained closed until early March when the government told students to sign unconditional agreements to return to classes or face expulsion. The reopening was accompanied by a National Assembly resolution that supported the government's handling of the affair but characterized the educational system as a "resounding failure" and called for reform.

Foreign affairs. On June 3, Niger joined the other former French colonies of West Africa (except Guinea and Togo) to form the West African Economic Community (WAEC). Creation of the WAEC represented, in effect, formal recognition by the signers that the colonial free trade area of French West Africa and its postindependence derivative,

THOMAS A. JOHNSON/NEW YORK TIMES

CHANGING MONEY. A Nigerian government official gives an illustrated lecture in the Ikeja marketplace to explain the country's new decimal money system, scheduled to go into effect in 1973.

the West African Customs Union (UDEAO) were defunct concepts—buried by ten years of unbridled nationalism. The WAEC was viewed as a means for reestablishing some form of regional cooperation in the selection of industrial sites, in trade matters, and, most important, in forming a preferential tariff regime to promote industrial goods produced largely in the coastal countries of Senegal and Ivory Coast. While the coastal countries will thus stand to gain by a widening of their markets, an interior country such as Niger would end up paying more for manufactured goods, normally bought from cheaper sources in Europe or from its English-speaking neighbors. As in the East African Economic Community, the WAEC treaty foresees the eventual application of the compensation principle, whereby the interior countries—also including Mali, Upper Volta, and Mauritania—would receive payments from a community development fund in proportion to the rise in prices on imported goods they purchased from manufacturers within the community. On his return to Niamey, President Hamani Diori hailed the creation of the new community but emphasized the need for its extension to the English-speaking countries of West Africa. He pointed out that Niger's trade with Nigeria already far exceeded the volume of commerce with Niger's neighbors in the WAEC.

Diori's cultivation of Niger's Arab neighbors to the north last year permitted him to take a role as mediator in the Libya-Chad dispute. Chad had accused Libya of supporting the Chadian guerrillas (Frolinat) in a coup attempt in September 1971. By mid-May, Diori had succeeded in restoring peaceful diplomatic relations between the two African nations.

Economic developments. After suffering more than three years of economic depression, particularly in agriculture, Niger's economy in 1971–1972 experienced a significant turn for the better. Owing to a combination of drought and declining prices, peanut production had dropped by almost 30 percent since the record 1966–67 crop. But in 1971–1972, production began to show an upswing: estimates placed the crop at 140,000 tons, compared to 128,000 tons in the previous crop year. The uranium processing plant at Airlit began production on schedule in mid-1971, and this

new source of income had an immediate impact by producing a 9 percent rise in public revenues for the 1972–1973 fiscal year. In less than 12 months, Niger had become the world's fourth largest producer of uranium.

Area and population. Area, 489,190 sq. mi. Pop. (est. 1970), 4.02 million. Niamey (cap.), 75,000.
Government. Single-party republic. Pres., Hamani Diori.
Finance. Monetary unit, Communauté Financière Africaine franc. 1 CFA franc = US$0.0041. Budget (est. 1972–1973), 11.9 billion CFA francs.
Trade (1970). Imports, 16.2 billion CFA francs; exports, 8.8 billion CFA francs. Principal exports: peanuts, cotton, livestock.
Education (1968). Enrollment: primary, 77,261; secondary, 3,900; technical, 900.   GEORGE LAMSON

NIGERIA. Further progress was made during 1972 in healing the wounds of the civil war of 1967–1970, as the government's policy of nonvindictiveness against former secessionists remained the keynote of efforts toward national reconciliation. Soldiers and civilians from the Ibo areas of East-Central State—formerly Biafra—returned to the mainstream of national life, taking up their old jobs and businesses with surprising ease and speed.

Political developments. The popularity of the military government, led by General Yakubu Gowon, cannot be said to have improved during the year. Corruption appeared to be fully as common as it had been under the civilian regime overthrown in 1966. Official efforts to check corruption were made; a number of soldiers, including officers, were charged, and some executed, for corrupt practices.

A military board of inquiry, established to investigate disruptions in the army, completed its work in December 1971. Sixteen officers were dismissed for their roles in the attempted secession of Biafra. But about half the officers investigated, numbering 65—most of them Ibos—were permitted to return to the army. It was an encouraging sign of the revived sense of national unity that all of them did in fact resume their commissions.

The inordinate size of the army as a result of the civil war has been a serious economic and social burden on the country. From its prewar size of 10,000, the army has swelled to 250,000, costing £8.9 million in pay and £15 million in maintenance each month. Aside from the staggering economic cost this represents, the army has itself posed a threat to law and order. Economic hardship and rising prices combined with the large number of people possessing weapons have produced a postwar crime wave that continued unabated during 1972, despite the government's policy of public execution of convicted armed robbers.

General Gowon was not able to improve on his still-distant date of 1976 as the "target" for return to civilian rule. Committed to the completion of a new constitution before giving up power, the government made little progress in drawing up the document during the year, especially in formulating a distribution of power and revenues between the federal and state governments. The senior civil servants who control the federal government continued to advocate a greater degree of centralism; but efforts to increase the power of the central government raised the possibility of renewed demands for greater regional autonomy, especially on the part of oil-rich River State and cocoa-producing West-Central State.

A crisis related to the problem of constitution-making may arise in November 1973, when a new census is scheduled. The previous census, in 1963, was heavily rigged by tribal politicians and has been challenged ever since. Not until the new census enables the government to prepare new voter lists can a constituent assembly be elected to approve the country's new constitution.

Foreign affairs. Nigeria continued to play a leading role in African affairs, both in the Organization of African Unity (OAU) and in efforts to establish closer economic ties with

its neighbors in West Africa. In December 1971, General Gowon visited Israel and Egypt as part of the OAU's Middle East peace mission. In April 1972 he visited Togo, where a Nigerian-Togolese Economic Community was established as the embryo of a larger West African economic community.

Relations with African countries that had been sympathetic to Biafra during the civil war—Ivory Coast, Tanzania, Gabon, and Zambia—had been reestablished at the diplomatic level by the end of the year. Nigeria also opened its first embassy in the People's Republic of China during 1972; Peking's embassy in Lagos had opened the year before. During the summer General Gowon helped mediate the dispute between Guinea and Ghana over the disposition of the body of Kwame Nkrumah.

Economic developments. Nigeria's economic progress continued to be dominated by the remarkable oil boom the country has enjoyed in recent years. Oil revenues rose from £4.4 million in 1960 to £489 million in 1971, when they accounted for 73 percent of export earnings. Income from oil was expected to contribute £500 million to Nigeria's total estimated federal revenues of £650 million in 1972–1973.

The economy as a whole registered a highly satisfactory growth rate of 9.6 percent during 1971–1972, double the rate projected in the current four-year plan. A growth rate of 12 percent was projected for 1972–1973.

Damage resulting from the civil war was estimated during the year at £300 million. Reconstruction efforts were concentrated in the hardest-hit area, East-Central State, which was still troubled by massive unemployment. The mounting oil revenues enabled the federal government to increase its contribution to the state budget by 40 percent, allowing the state almost to balance its budget for the first time since its creation in 1966.

Satisfactory recovery was also reported in River State, which was also seriously hurt by the civil war. Almost all private businesses were back in operation, and the state government showed a substantial budget surplus.

On the debit side, however, it was clear that the benefits of the oil boom had hardly begun to seep down to the less privileged sectors of the economy. The overall expansion of the economy overshadowed the poor 2 percent growth of the agricultural sector, which accounts for 40 percent of Nigeria's total economic production. Unemployment, always higher than indicated by official figures, rose to record levels, especially in East-Central State. An unprecedented rise in prices also helped generate widespread discontent.

Nigerianization. Perhaps the most prominent feature of the economy in 1972 was the effort to increase the government's share in all phases of the oil industry and to "Nigerianize" the industrial sector in general. A new policy requiring 51 percent participation by the Nigerian Oil Corporation in all new exploration ventures was first implemented in November 1971, when 51 percent of three Japanese offshore oil exploration companies was taken over. In April 1972 the government announced that the oil corporation was also to participate in the production, refining, and marketing of oil and that no additional foreign concessions would be granted.

The Nigerianization of the oil industry brought a new note of pessimism over the future of the country's oil boom. Producers feared that the investments necessary for continued growth would not be forthcoming in the changing political and economic climate. They complained of "overzealous" enforcement of previously established regulations, bureaucratic delays in the granting of permits, and the forced reductions in foreign staff when there was an apparent shortage of Nigerians qualified to replace them.

Nigerianization was not restricted to oil. A decree was issued on March 1 requiring 40 percent Nigerian participation in most industries and the total exclusion of foreigners

from retail trade, certain light industries, and services such as haulage. The decree is to become fully operative by 1974 and to be implemented by a Nigerian Enterprises Promotion Board. In his budget speech in April, General Gowon also announced a government take-over of 40 percent of the equity of all commercial banks.

Other developments. In April, Nigeria eliminated one of the remaining legacies of British rule by changing over from driving on the left to driving on the right. The change was effected smoothly and accompanied by significant road improvements around Lagos.

A good part of the year was spent in preparing the population for the introduction of a new currency in January 1973. The new currency, which replaces the Nigerian pound, is the naira, made up of 100 kobo.

Area and population. Area, 356,669 sq. mi. Pop. (est. 1971), 56,500,000. Principal cities: Lagos (cap.; est. 1970), 875,000; Ibadan, 746,000; Ogbomosho (1963), 319,881; Kano (1963), 295,-432.

Government. Federal military government; member of Commonwealth of Nations. Head of state and of government, General Yakubu Gowon; commissioner for foreign affairs, Okoi Arikpo; commissioner for finance, Alhaji Shehu Shagari.

Finance. Monetary unit: Nigerian pound; £1 = US$3.10. Pound replaced by the naira (= 100 kobo) on Jan. 1, 1973; 1 naira = 0.5 Nigerian pound. Budget (1971–1972): revenue, £462 million; expenditure, £219 million.

Trade (1971). Exports, US$1.8 billion; imports, US$1.5 billion. Principal exports: petroleum, peanuts, cocoa, palm kernels and oil, rubber, raw cotton, cottonseed, tin. Principal imports: manufactured goods, machinery and transport equipment, chemicals. Principal trading partners: United Kingdom and other Commonwealth nations, United States, Japan, Netherlands, West Germany, Italy.

Education (1967, excluding the three eastern states). Primary enrollment, 1,778,976. Secondary enrollment, 142,837. University enrollment: Nigeria Nsukka, 3,482; Ibadan, 2,559; Ahmadu Bello, 1,351; Ife, 1,258; Lagos, 1,436.   WALTER SCHWARZ

NOBEL PRIZES. Out of the 11 Nobel Prizes that were awarded for 1972, nine went to Americans, two to Britons, and one, the prize in literature, to a German for the first time in over four decades. The peace prize was withheld this year for the 19th time since 1901. The awards were given under the terms of the will left by the Swedish scientist and inventor Alfred Nobel.

Chemistry. Three Americans, Christian B. Anfinsen of the National Institutes of Health in Bethesda, Md., and Stanford Moore and William H. Stein, both of Rockefeller University, shared the 1972 Nobel Prize in chemistry for making "fundamental contributions to enzyme chemistry." The Swedish Royal Academy of Sciences explained that "enzymes must in many respects be considered the key substances of life" since they accelerate the chemical reactions in cells that result in growth, motility, and reaction to external stimuli.

Christian Boehmer Anfinsen was born in Monessen, Pa., on March 26, 1916. After graduating from Swarthmore College in 1937, he received his M.S. from the University of Pennsylvania in 1939 and his Ph.D. in biochemistry from Harvard in 1943. Since 1950 he has worked as a biochemist at the National Institutes of Health. He received the Nobel Prize for his investigations of the formation of the enzyme ribonuclease in living cells.

Stanford Moore was born in Chicago on September 4, 1913. He earned his B.A. from Vanderbilt University in 1935 and his Ph.D. in organic chemistry from the University of Wisconsin in 1938. Since 1939 he has been on the staff of Rockefeller University. Together with Stein, Moore received his Nobel prize for pioneering studies that illuminated important principles related to the biological activity of the enzyme ribonuclease.

William Howard Stein, born in New York City on June 25, 1911, was educated at Phillips Exeter Academy and received his B.S. from Harvard in 1933 and his Ph.D. from Columbia University in 1938. A member of the staff at Rockefeller University since 1938, he has been a professor

there since 1952 and also has served as a visiting professor at the University of Chicago and at Harvard and as editor of the *Journal of Biological Chemistry* from 1968 to 1971. He has been investigating the biochemical mysteries of proteins, peptides, and amino acids for over three decades.

Economics. The Nobel Prize in economics for 1972 was conferred on one American, Kenneth J. Arrow of Harvard, and one Briton, Sir John R. Hicks, a retired Oxford fellow and economics professor. The Swedish Royal Academy of Sciences cited Hicks and Arrow for "their pioneering contributions to general economic equilibrium theory and welfare theory." Their contributions have been the basis for most economic theories now applied to investment, foreign trade, and price structure.

Sir John Richard Hicks was born near Stratford, England, on April 8, 1904. He studied mathematics, philosophy, politics, and economics at Oxford University's Balliol College, where he received his bachelor's degree in 1927 and his master's in 1931. His first book, *The Theory of Wages*, published in 1932, was followed by more than a dozen others, including several written with his wife, the economist Lady Ursula Hicks. His most important work, *Value and Capital*, published in 1939, laid the theoretical groundwork for the renewal of the equilibrium theory. Sir John, whose teaching career spans more than 40 years, retired as a professor of political economy at Oxford University in 1965 and as a fellow at Oxford's All Souls College in 1972. He was knighted in 1964.

Kenneth Joseph Arrow was born on August 23, 1921, in New York City, where he attended public schools and received a B.S. from the City College of New York in 1940 and an M.A. from Columbia University in 1941. In 1949 he joined the staff of Stanford University, and in 1968 he moved to Harvard. He received a Ph.D. from Columbia in 1951 with his dissertation *Social Choice and Individual Values*, which established his reputation and developed Hicks' equilibrium theory with new theories on risk and uncertainty in business judgment. In the words of Paul A. Samuelson, a Nobel laureate in economics, Arrow's "two greatest contributions . . . were . . . his revolutionary formulation of welfare economics and his pathbreaking theory of risk."

Literature. A West German writer representing his country's World War II generation won the Nobel Prize for literature in 1972. The laureate, Heinrich Böll, was the first German citizen to receive the literature award since it was given to Thomas Mann in 1929 (although two German-born expatriates have since won the prize—Herman Hesse in 1946 and Nelly Sachs in 1966). Böll, whose works include novels, short stories, and plays, was cited for writing "which through its combination of a broad perspective on his time and a sensitive skill in characterization has contributed to a renewal of German literature."

Heinrich Theodor Böll was born on December 21, 1917, in Cologne, where he still maintains a residence. During World War II he was an infantryman in the Wehrmacht and was captured by the U.S. Army. Soon after his release in 1947, he published his first short story and began to concentrate on writing as a career. His first novel, *Adam, Where Art Thou?*, appeared in West Germany in 1951. In this and subsequent works he has provided a satirical and often bitter view of German society in its wartime defeat and gradual recovery, chronicling its hypocrisy, obtuseness, and despair as well as its moments of hope, decency, and courage. He interprets institutions as mainly inhuman and oppressive and people as largely the instruments of group prejudices. In the United States his best known works are *Billiards at Half Past Nine* and *The Clown*.

Physics. The 1972 Nobel Prize in physics, like the chemistry award, went to three Americans: John Bardeen of the University of Illinois, a Nobel laureate for the second time; Leon N. Cooper of Brown University; and John

Robert Schrieffer of the University of Pennsylvania. The three scientists were honored for their jointly developed theory of superconductivity, an effect characteristic of certain metals which at very low temperatures lose their resistance to the flow of an electric current. Although superconductivity was discovered in 1911, it was not explained until now. According to the Swedish Royal Academy of Sciences, superconductivity "involves a number of possible new ways of defining the units of voltage [and] is important not only for scientific instruments, but also for accelerators and motors." At present, superconducting materials are being used in atom smashers and some large electric motors and may soon also find application in transmission lines.

John Bardeen was born on May 23, 1908, in Madison, Wis. He received his B.S. and M.S. degrees from the University of Wisconsin in 1928 and 1929 and his Ph.D. from Princeton in 1936. While employed at Bell Telephone Laboratories from 1945 to 1951, he was a member of the research team that was awarded the Nobel Prize in physics for 1956.

Leon N. Cooper was born on February 28, 1930, in New York City. He studied at Columbia University, where he received his B.A. in 1951, his M.A. in 1953, and his Ph.D. in 1954. In 1958 he joined the faculty of Brown University and in 1966 became Henry Ledyard Goddard professor of physics there.

John Robert Schrieffer was born in Oak Park, Ill., on May 31, 1931. He received his B.S. degree from the Massachusetts Institute of Technology in 1953 and his M.S. and Ph.D. from the University of Illinois in 1954 and 1957. At the University of Illinois from 1957 to 1959 he collaborated on the superconductivity research. In 1962 he became a member of the faculty of the University of Pennsylvania, where he now is the Mary Amanda Wood professor of physics.

Physiology or medicine. An American molecular biologist, Dr. Gerald M. Edelman, and a British biochemist, Dr. Rodney R. Porter, shared the 1972 Nobel Prize for physiology or medicine in recognition of their separate research on the chemical structure of antibodies, a group of blood proteins that play an important part in the body's defense against infection. Although the two scientists were in frequent contact after their initial meeting in 1957, each worked independently and developed his own methods for deciphering the structure of the antibody. Each broke the antibody molecule into different fragments and ended up with different sets of information, which were put together to form a map of the molecule. In this way the structure of antibodies, which consist of heavy and light chains of amino acids, was determined. According to the Nobel Prize Committee, these discoveries "incited a fervent research activity the whole world over, in all fields of immunologic science, yielding results and practical values for clinical diagnostics and therapy."

Gerald Maurice Edelman was born in New York City on July 1, 1929. He was graduated from Ursinus College in 1950, received his medical degree from the University of Pennsylvania in 1954, and then served a one-year residency at Massachusetts General Hospital. From 1957 to 1960 he was on the medical staff of Rockefeller University, and after receiving his Ph.D. there in 1960 he became a member of the faculty, attaining the rank of full professor in 1966.

Rodney Robert Porter was born in England on October 8, 1917. He attended Liverpool and Cambridge universities and worked at the National Institute for Medical Research from 1949 to 1960. While serving as the Pfizer Professor of Immunology at St. Mary's Hospital Medical School from 1960 to 1967, he conducted research on antibodies, using the protein-splitting enzyme papain. Since 1967 he has served as the Whitley professor of biochemistry at Oxford University.   CAROLINE G. DUDLEY

NORTH CAROLINA. Mental health.

In January the state bureau of investigation delivered an 871-page report on conditions at the Cherry state mental hospital to Governor Robert W. Scott. As the contents of the report leaked out, substantiating charges that patients had been mistreated, mental health became a frequent subject of headlines.

Warrants were issued against 11 staff members at Cherry, and by the end of the year six persons had been convicted with more cases yet to be heard. Continuing investigations of the state's mental hospitals disclosed less than ideal conditions, and in May the chief of the state department and his aides were forced to help the overworked Cherry staff on a regular basis.

Both candidates for governor, Hargrove "Skipper" Bowles and Jim Holshouser, used mental health as a campaign issue. Legislators predicted that mental health would be the number one issue of the biennial session beginning in January.

Trials. North Carolina had three trials this year involving two of the state's leading black militants.

Ben Chavis, a member of the Virginia–North Carolina Commission on racial justice and a minister in the First American Church of the Black Messiah, and James Earl Grant, a field representative of the Southern Conference Education Fund, were charged with helping two men under indictment on federal weapons charges to leave the country. Grant and three others were tried in Charlotte for the burning of a horse stables during the tense summer of 1968 which followed the assassination of Martin Luther King, Jr. In Wilmington, Chavis and ten others were alleged to have fire-bombed a grocery and conspired to attack firemen who arrived to put out the blaze in February 1971.

In the first trial, the state relied on the evidence of Walter Washington and Thomas Hood, the two men Chavis and Grant allegedly helped to leave the country. Both Hood and Washington previously had been convicted of felonies and agreed to testify in return for immunity from prosecution. The jury found Chavis not guilty, but it convicted Grant, who was sentenced to ten years.

In the Charlotte trial, known as the Lazy B case after the stables where several horses died in a fire, the state again based its case on the testimony of Hood and Washington. This time the jury returned guilty verdicts against all the defendants (one had pleaded guilty just before the start of the trial), and the judge, calling the men dangerous, handed out stiff sentences of 25 years to Grant and 20 and ten years to his codefendants. (The man pleading guilty received a suspended sentence.)

In the Wilmington disorders, Chavis was sentenced to 34 years. His followers received 20 to 26 years.

Liquor by the drink. Continuing efforts to allow the sale of hard liquor in bars and restaurants received a severe blow when the state supreme court ruled a local option law unconstitutional. The law, passed by the 1971 legislature and approved in a local referendum, would have allowed the sale of hard liquor in Mecklenburg County (Charlotte).

Education. On July 1 a restructuring of the state's system of higher education went into effect. The plan, a result of a bitter struggle during a special session of the legislature in 1971, places all 16 campuses in the state system under the control of a consolidated university board.

For election results and campaign highlights, see the special supplement ELECTION '72.

Area and population. Area, 52,712 sq. mi. Pop. (1970), 5,082,059. Principal cities (1970): Raleigh (cap.), 121,577; Charlotte, 241,178; Greensboro, 144,076; Winston-Salem, 132,913; Durham, 95,438.

Government. Gov., Robert W. Scott (D); lt. gov., H. Pat Taylor (D); secy. of state, Thad Eure, Jr. (D); atty. gen., Robert Morgan (D). Legislature: house, 96 D, 24 R; senate, 43 D, 7 R.

Finance (1972). Revenue, $1,093,909,181; expenditure, $1,096,-244,272.

Education (1969–1970). Primary schools, 1,801; enrollment, 859,-949; teachers, 35,883. Secondary schools, 620; enrollment, 357,075; teachers, 17,584.

GREG DAVID

NORTH DAKOTA. Constitution.

Voters of North Dakota rejected the first new constitution submitted to them in nearly 85 years in a special election on April 28, after the proposed document had been drawn up by the state's second constitutional convention. The vote was 107,643 to 64,073 against approval.

Among the major factors conceded to have influenced the vote was the opposition of organized labor, which objected to retention of a "right-to-work" provision in the charter. Opposition was also sparked, at least in part, by a proposition submitted separately which would have increased the number of signatures needed to refer or initiate measures for popular vote. Another item submitted separately which contributed to the defeat would have made 18-year-olds adults for all purposes, including the right to drink alcoholic beverages.

Reapportionment. In July three federal judges ordered minor revisions in the legislative districting for the 1973 session and added two senators and four representatives.

The court did not change provisions under which some largely urban districts elect their legislators at-large but indicated it might do so in 1973 if the session that year does not enact a satisfactory reapportionment law.

North Dakota Democrats claim the at-large election in districts including major cities prejudices their chance of equitable representation. They believe that subdivision of such districts would give them a better chance of winning control of the legislature, which has been denied them historically in North Dakota, even when they hold the governorship, as during the past 12 years.

Education. In the September primary election voters ratified the decision of the 1971 legislature to close the Ellendale branch of the University of North Dakota.

Late in 1972, the state board of higher education decided that no future graduate study programs will be approved except at the University of North Dakota at Grand Forks and North Dakota State University at Fargo. It also decided to embark upon a review of present graduate programs at all state institutions of higher learning, in view of stabilizing declining enrollments.

Industry. Major economic activities in North Dakota during the year involved the state's sugar and lignite coal industries. The Red River Valley Sugarbeet Growers Association began negotiations for the purchase of refineries owned by American Crystal Sugar Company. The growers hope that by operating the refining plants themselves, as a cooperative, they will be able to expand production and, eventually, build additional or replacement plants. Other growers or potential growers organized to establish new refineries at Hillsboro and in the Wahpeton, N.D.–Breckenridge, Minn., area.

Further development of the state's lignite resources seemed assured. Only controversy over reclamation of the areas uncovered by strip mining seemed to present any hurdle to the development.

ABM site. Construction is scheduled to be completed in 1973 on the Grand Forks Safeguard antiballistic missile site, one of two permitted the United States under the strategic arms limitation agreement signed by President Richard M. Nixon in Moscow.

With the completion of construction next year, installation of radar and other technical equipment will begin. Army troops to man the ABM complex will move in once installation is completed, in 1974 or 1975. The Grand Forks complex is designed to protect the major U.S. Air Force bases near Grand Forks and Minot, where more nuclear destructive power is located than anywhere else in the Western world. Federal funds are being funneled into the ABM impact area to help cope with the population increase which has resulted from the project.

For election results and campaign highlights, see the special supplement ELECTION '72.

Area and population. Area, 70,665 sq. mi. Pop. (1970), 617,-761. Principal cities: Bismarck (cap.), 34,703; Fargo, 53,365; Grand Forks, 39,008; Minot, 32,290.

Government. Gov., William L. Guy (D); lt. gov., Richard Larsen (R); atty. gen., Helgi Johanneson (R); secy. of state, Ben Meier (R); aud., Curtis Olson (R); treas., Bernice Asbridge (R). Legislature: senate, 35 R, 14 D; house, 58 R, 40 D.

Education (1971). Public elementary schools: enrollment, 100,-527; teachers, 4,807. Public secondary schools: enrollment, 47,605; teachers, 2,926. Private and parochial schools: enrollment, 12,095; teachers, 567. Higher education enrollment: state and public supported, 27,470; private, 1,189.

Finance (year ending June 30, 1972). General fund revenue, $115,278,000; expenditure, $111,612,000.   JACK HAGERTY

NORTHERN IRELAND. *See* UNITED KINGDOM OF GREAT BRITAIN AND NORTHERN IRELAND.

NORTHWEST TERRITORIES. Government. Dissatisfaction with the federal government's ultimate control over territorial affairs dominated the public life of the Northwest Territories this year. In June the council defied Ottawa by creating two committees, one to study the transfer of responsibilities of a provincial level to the territorial government and a second to review the development of northern resources in the Northwest Territories. Local politicians were distressed because, although the territorial government had responsibility for health, education, and social welfare, the federal government retained control of revenue-producing natural resources.

A joint committee of the Canadian legislature stated that the government should foster self-government and eventual provincial status for the Northwest Territories and that the territories should be given representation in the Senate as well as in the House of Commons. However, proposed federal redistribution plans announced in April again earmarked the Northwest Territories for only one House seat.

Arctic corridor. Construction began during the summer on an all-weather highway, to run 1,000 miles from the Arctic Ocean to the Alberta border, where it would link up with a 206-mile stretch already reaching from the Alberta border to Fort Simpson. The road has been planned as part of a proposed oil, gas, and highway corridor which, it was estimated, would cost up to $10 billion to complete. In March, federal minister of energy and resources Donald S. Macdonald stated that Canada favors the construction of an overland pipeline up the Mackenzie Valley which could carry Alaskan oil to the United States. However, the council and the general public continued to voice concern over the possible environmental effect of the corridor.

Resources. Pending the formulation of new regulations, the federal government announced in March an embargo on oil search permits in the Northwest Territories and a temporary prohibition of offshore drilling on the east and west coasts of Canada, as well as in the waters of Hudson Bay. Meanwhile, federal northern development minister Jean Chretien announced on October 10 that Panarctic Oils had found gas on Melville Island, which would bring estimated reserves to 15 trillion cubic feet. It was said that reserves of 25 trillion cubic feet would justify construction of a gas pipeline to eastern Canada.

Area and population. Area, 1,304,903 sq. mi. Pop. (1971 census), 34,807. Yellowknife (cap.), 6,122.

Government. Comm., Stuart M. Hodgson.

Production. Minerals (1971), Can$124,004,060.

Education (1971–1972). Total enrollment, 11,049.

J. A. BOVEY

NORWAY. Politics and government. The plebiscite in which Norwegian voters on September 24–25 turned down Common Market membership climaxed a year of bitter de-

NORWAY SAYS NEI. In a torchlight parade, Oslo residents hoist a banner reading ''Vote no!'' That's just what Norwegians did in a referendum this fall, ending hopes that their country would be among the European nations added to the Common Market in January 1973.

NORSK TELEGRAMBYRA

bate and brought the downfall of Trygve Bratteli's government and its replacement by a minority coalition.

Opponents of entry had steadily gained strength as the vote neared. Even Knut Hoem, fisheries minister in the Labor cabinet, resigned in protest and allied himself with opponents. Most members of the Labor Party in northern Norway had been against membership because of competitive disadvantage to fisheries. Farmers also felt they would be seriously endangered by competition, as did the chemical, shipbuilding, engineering, and metals industries. Other opponents pointed out serious constitutional questions. Opponents in the Storting did not marshal enough strength, however, to defeat the measure approving entry, although they needed only one vote to block it. They argued for a free trade agreement, similar to the one signed by Sweden in July, which would not threaten fisheries, farming, or the social security and health programs. In debate in August, Prime Minister Trygve Bratteli stated that the Labor cabinet would resign if the plebiscite disapproved Norwegian membership.

When the referendum was held in September, nearly 54 percent of the electorate voted against Common Market membership. Norway's rejection of the EEC was seen as both a setback in the effort to build a united Europe and a handicap to Norway's own economic growth. (Present and prospective Common Market members now purchase 65 percent of Norway's exports; however, it is expected that tariffs will restrict these markets.) Prime Minister Bratteli and the Labor cabinet, choosing not to serve in an anti-market government, were replaced (until the 1973 elections) by a minority coalition caretaker government headed by Lars Korvald, chairman of the Christian People's Party, as the new premier. Seven members of the new cabinet are members of the Center Party, five are Liberals, and four are members of the Christian People's Party. The negotiation of a free trade agreement with the Common Market is the first major task of the new government.

Foreign affairs. Foreign policy debates in the Storting in January and June concentrated on the Common Market, but special note was made of West German negotiations to resolve conflicts with the German People's Republic and to extend détente in Europe. Funds were approved for harbor development for Chile and Cuba and for aid programs in several other countries, specifically for refugees and education in Pakistan and Bangladesh. Increases in Soviet military forces in the northern part of the Scandinavian peninsula on the Norwegian border caused concern and encouraged continued Norwegian support of NATO. In July, Norway joined with Britain, Sweden, and Finland in negotiations on pulp, paper, and forest products exports to ease Common Market adjustment problems. One part of the debate in June contained strong opposition to American bombing of North Vietnam.

Economy. The international recession affected Norway less than other European countries, but this year saw a lowered gross national product and a drop in industrial productivity. Wage agreements in June provided for a 5.6 percent increase, which was also reflected in agricultural and fish price adjustments. Unemployment showed a slight increase, but not of alarming proportions. Both fish catches and farm harvests were excellent, with international prices for fish improving and the grain harvest enabling Norway to lessen its import of grains. Control of inflation seemed to require special effort after the various increases, including those in retirement pensions. Despite export gains early in the year, a deficit higher than that of 1971 was expected.

The government organized a state-owned oil directory to manage the oil and gas production of the North Sea field. The directory would work out details of transport of oil and gas from the field to markets. An outlet through England seemed the most feasible and it seemed cheaper to refine oil there. However, some refineries would be built

in Stavanger, which has become a "gold rush" town with all the expansion in facilities.

Educational developments. Two committee reports proposed changes of some consequence. One report recommended alterations in higher education to allow the district colleges to offer courses for university credit, and another commission proposed a broadened entry into the university through examinations, acceptance of work taken at professional schools, and other means. Another proposal recommended the extension of the school requirement to nine years, or age 17, with reforms in instruction and methods.

Area and population. Area, 125,181 sq. mi. Pop. (est. 1971), 3,922,000. Principal cities: Oslo (cap.), 481,548; Trondheim, 127,595; Bergen, 113,351; Stavanger, 81,847.
Government. Hereditary constitutional monarchy with unicameral parliament (Storting). King, Olav V; prime min., Lars Korvald; for. min., Dagfinn Vaarik.
Finance. Monetary unit, krone; 1 krone = US$0.151. Budget (1972–1973, in billions of kroner): revenue, 23.3; expenditure, 22.1. Principal sources of revenue: value-added tax, excise duties, income and property tax. Principal items of expenditure: social welfare, investment, defense. Gross national product, 100.7.
Trade (1971, in billions of kroner). Imports, 28.7; exports, 18. Major imports: transport, 3.45; fuel, 2.16; textiles, 1.58; machinery, 1.44; chemicals, 1.07. Major exports: metals, 4.55; paper and pulp, 2.23; machinery, 1.12. Major trading partners: United Kingdom, Sweden, West Germany.
Agriculture and industry. Agricultural production (1971, in metric tons): milk, 1,704,000; cheese, 34,978; butter, 20,431. Industrial production (1971, in billions of kroner): metals, 8.6; forest products, 6.5; transport, 5.2; machinery, 4.3; chemicals, 2.7; textiles, 1.37.
Education (1969–1970). Enrollment: elementary schools, 517,563; secondary, 83,804; folk high schools, 6,720; universities (3), 27,414.
Armed forces. Army, 21,000; navy, 6,000; air force, 9,000; home guard, approximately 70,000. RAYMOND E. LINDGREN

NOVA SCOTIA. Politics and government. Recent discoveries of gas and oil off the coast of Nova Scotia have provoked vigorous controversy over the issue of whether the federal or provincial government has jurisdiction over the offshore areas. In August, after Prime Minister Pierre Elliott Trudeau met with the premiers of the five eastern provinces, the federal government retreated from its stand that royalties from the offshore finds be divided equally with the federal government, with all ten provinces sharing their half. The meeting resulted in the establishment of a joint federal-provincial fact-finding commission that will report on the costs of developing the offshore industry, as well as concentrate on a formula for revenue sharing rather than decide who has jurisdiction.

The relationship of Nova Scotia to its sister Maritime Provinces is being studied by the Council of Maritime Premiers. Although premiers Gerald A. Regan of Nova Scotia, Alexander B. Campbell of Prince Edward Island, and Richard Hatfield of New Brunswick are exploring ways in which the provinces might benefit each other through mutual cooperation, no moves are being made to unite politically.

Legislation. The Liberal government of Premier Regan put through legislation designed to deal with the disposition of legal rights to oil and gas resources onshore and offshore, a measure for the management of oil as a resource, and a pipeline act to be administered by the oil and gas conservation board.

The provincial legislature passed several other important pieces of legislation, including a trade union act that provides for a single arbitrator when a collective bargaining agreement does not contain provision for final settlement of disputes and a labor standards code that protects the rights of workers. The minimum wage was raised to $1.65 an hour for adults, and a long-standing wage differential based on sex and geographic location was abolished. In September the government enacted an amendment to the Nova Scotia Human Rights Act ending discrimination between male and female workers.

Economic developments. Although unemployment continued at a high rate—7.6 percent of the labor force—the

province's leading industries maintained a high level of production. In 1971 manufacturing was valued at $760 million in total factory shipments. Construction followed with a value of $526 million, agriculture with a value of $62 million, and fishing and mining with a value of $59 million.

Pulp and paper, the leading exports, brought in $73 million, followed closely by $72 million for fish products. Petroleum products showed the highest jump, from $5 million to $27 million between 1970 and 1971, largely due to the new Gulf refinery on the Strait of Canso. This unique port is capable of handling tankers as huge as the 326,000-deadweight-ton *Empress of Japan* and is considered a major terminal for transshipment.

The discovery of oil and gas off the coast of Nova Scotia in the past year has stimulated the economy of the province. Four wells—two on Sable Island, about 180 miles southeast of Halifax, and two others near the island—have produced a positive show. The discoveries were made by Mobil Oil of Canada Ltd. and Shell Oil. Mobil's first discovery, in October 1971, produced 10 million cubic feet of gas per day and started avid speculation on the possibility of a major oil industry in the province.

Not only have the offshore finds precipitated hopes of broadening the economic base of the province but they have also resulted in a spinoff industry, the construction of multi-million-dollar offshore drilling rigs at the shipyards in the port of Halifax, the provincial capital. Over $85 million has been spent or contracted for five rigs. Total spending on offshore exploration and drilling along the east coast is currently estimated at $75 million annually, and between 1972 and 1975 the minimum amount spent on exploration is expected to reach $200 million. Since the early 1960's, 70 oil companies have taken out exploration permits on more than 300 million acres.

Halifax has become a leader in the production of containers, boosting the local economy by about $150 million each year. Cargo passing through its port on the way to markets in the United Kingdom and Northern Europe continued to increase in 1972. A total of 11.2 million tons of cargo moved across its piers in 1971. An autoport with a capacity of 100,000 cars, jointly operated by the province and Canadian National Railways, opened November 1971.

National park. In 1973, Nova Scotia will become the site of Canada's 29th national park. Situated 40 miles east of Halifax, the park will encompass 225 square miles and will feature several aspects of the coastal environment, including a number of offshore islands.

Area and population. Area, 21,425 sq. mi. Pop. (1972), 794,-000. Principal cities: Halifax (cap.), 122,035; Dartmouth, 64,770; Sydney, 33,230.
Government. Lt. gov., Victor deB. Oland; prem., Gerald A. Regan. Legislative assembly: Liberals, 24; Progressive Conservatives, 20; New Democrats, 2.
Finance. Budget (est., fiscal year ending March 31, 1972): revenue, Can$475 million; expenditures, Can$478 million.
Education (1969–1970). School enrollment: elementary, 125,124; junior high, 52,494; senior high, 37,251; higher education, 17,132.

GRETCHEN MARY YORK PIERCE

NUCLEAR RESEARCH. The Los Alamos Meson Physics Facility's accelerator achieved an 800-Mev (million electron volt) beam on June 9, one month ahead of schedule. The new device, capable of producing one of the most intense beams of pi-mesons (pions) ever attained, is the central feature of the $57 million installation. It is being built by the Atomic Energy Commission for basic research in nuclear physics, for radioisotope production, and for practical use in biology and medicine. Experimental facilities surrounding the accelerator are to be completed in 1973.

The highest energies ever achieved by a man-made machine have been reached at the National Accelerator Laboratory. On March 1, the laboratory's particle accelerator reached its original design energy of 200 Gev (billion elec-

tron volts). On July 16, researchers at the laboratory boosted the energy level of the giant 4-mile circular magnet to 300 Gev, or 50 percent above its design level. Robert R. Wilson, director of the National Accelerator Laboratory, and his staff are confident that the accelerator will eventually operate at energies of 400–500 Gev. The higher energies were made possible by improvements in design and advances in technology during construction.

Since the achievement of 200 Gev, ten experiments have been initiated. A group of American and Soviet scientists are jointly studying proton-proton scattering. The team of seven scientists from the Soviet Union is composed entirely of high-energy physicists from the Joint Institute for Nuclear Research; they are visiting this country as part of the reciprocal arrangement for joint Soviet-American projects in high-energy physics research.

Radioactivity in humans decreasing. The level of radioactive cesium contamination in a test group of humans has decreased since 1963, when the limited test ban treaty reduced the number of nuclear explosions occurring in the atmosphere. A study at Brookhaven National Laboratory has measured the level of cesium-137 in ten employees each month for the past 12 years. In addition, 900 other employees were checked occasionally as a backup measure. None of the persons involved in the test "had significant occupational contact with radioactivity." Cesium-137, which has a half-life of 30 years, is a product of nuclear fission and is present in the fallout of atmospheric tests. It enters the body through food and drink and, mimicking potassium, localizes primarily in the large muscles of the body. In 1963, the average cesium-137 levels were 80 picocuries for each gram of body weight. By 1970–1971, these levels had dropped to 18–20 picocuries. The regularly measured employees' levels compared rather closely with those of the 900 who were measured less frequently. Cesium-137 levels in females averaged 20 percent less than those for males.

Stanton H. Cohn, head of the monitoring project, emphasized that "the conclusions are based on a relatively small population and should not be extrapolated to the world population at large." He noted, however, that the findings agreed substantially with the results of similar experiments that have been conducted in Denmark and the Soviet Union.

"Sniffer" detects dirty air. Heavily polluted air can easily be detected—without analytical instrumentation. But how can very small amounts of pollutants be detected? A prototype electronic "sniffer" the size of a hatbox has been built at the Lawrence Livermore Laboratory of the University of California.

If full-scale production of the device proves feasible, the instrument would have widespread application in environmental control and in the confines of a manned space capsule. For both reasons, the Lawrence Livermore Laboratory received $97,000 from the National Aeronautics and Space Administration and the Environmental Protection Agency to perfect the model and explore its potential.

The "sniffer"—a microwave rotational spectrometer—will test air samples for formaldehyde, a by-product of automobile exhaust that contributes to smog. The research team is hoping to produce an instrument that will clearly and quickly identify up to six gases, including oxides of nitrogen, carbon, and sulfur, when they are present in the air in minute quantities.

ICONS program. ICONS (isotopes of carbon, oxygen, nitrogen, and sulfur) are of growing scientific interest. These nonradioactive minor constituents of the environment have great potential as research tools, but until recently they have been rare and, therefore, expensive. The Atomic Energy Commission has supported a program for expanding production of ICONS, and the success of the program has been reflected in a sharp drop in prices. Over the past two years, for instance, the price of carbon-13 has dropped from $3,000 to $30 a gram.

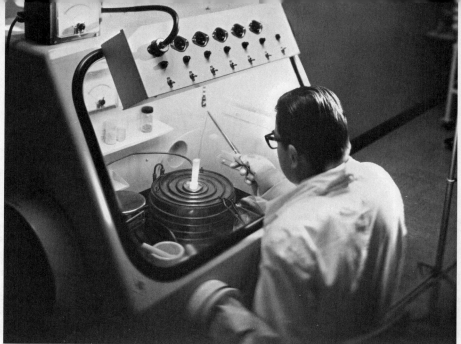

NUCLEAR NURSERY. Crystals containing transuranium isotopes are grown in special furnaces at AEC's Oak Ridge National Laboratory.

U.S. ATOMIC ENERGY COMMISSION

The expansion of carbon-13 production at the Los Alamos Scientific Laboratory has made that installation one of the world's largest producers of this rare isotope. In the production process, carbon-13 is separated from normal carbon-12 (98.9 percent of all earthly carbon) by a cryogenic distillation process using liquid carbon monoxide at −192° C, which in turn is obtained by cooling carbon monoxide with liquid nitrogen. Enrichment to 95 percent carbon-13 has been achieved.

The uses of carbon-13 in research have expanded recently because of the introduction of the nuclear magnetic resonance spectrometer, which permits much more refined analyses of carbon-13 labeled compounds than had been possible previously.

Carbon-13 can be added to organisms: Algae and yeast in which 90 percent of the carbon content was carbon-13 have been grown successfully at Los Alamos. Algae and yeast rich in carbon-13 have been fed to mice in a series of studies to determine whether high levels of carbon-13 have toxic effects on organisms and to demonstrate the usefulness of carbon-13 in basic research.

Large-scale production means that carbon-13 will be available for diagnostic medicine. One possible application would be the use of carbon-13 labeled glucose in diagnosing diabetes. To facilitate the use of such tests in hospitals, a clinical carbon-13 dioxide breath analyzer is being developed at the Argonne National Laboratory.

Preliminary investigations of environmental applications have been under way at Los Alamos to determine how long carbon dioxide composed of carbon-13 and oxygen-18 will persist in normal air. The experiments are designed to determine whether the labeled carbon dioxide will remain detectable long enough for subtle meteorological measurements to be made, and to determine whether it will dissipate quickly enough not to upset the balance between carbon-13 and carbon-12 in localities for long periods. If the labeling technique itself is environmentally acceptable, it may find an application in pinpointing sources of pollution. If it were known that the air in a given locality was being polluted by industrial wastes, the offenders might be singled out by adding carbon-13 to incoming raw materials. Effluent from the operation selected for scrutiny would then also be carbon-13 labeled and would serve to confirm the source.

Natural plutonium believed found. The heaviest isotope ever found in nature, plutonium-244, is believed to have been separated from an ore concentrate. It was discovered by a team from the Los Alamos Scientific Laboratory and the Knolls Atomic Power Laboratory in a rare-earth mineral,

bastnäsite. The barely detectable amount of plutonium-244, about 20 million atoms, was chemically isolated from a concentrate obtained by processing nearly 200 pounds of the ore. A Knolls Laboratory mass spectrometer was used to make positive identification of the isotope. Plutonium-244, the most stable known isotope of plutonium, decays by emitting alpha particles. However, the sample obtained was so small that it would emit only one alpha particle in six years—far too low a count to permit identification by that method.

New isotopes produced. A systematic search for new isotopes has been undertaken at Brookhaven National Laboratory. Proof of the existence or nonexistence of many isotopes that have been predicted theoretically would fill in some of the gaps in our knowledge of the natural relationships of the chemical elements.

The search was launched following the fortuitous discovery of a new isotope of silicon: silicon-33. The objective in the first experiment of the new series was phosphorus-35. Researchers used tandem Van de Graaff accelerators to bombard oxygen-18 with fluorine-19 ions. The fluorine and oxygen nuclei merged to produce an isotope having a total of 37 protons and neutrons; two protons were emitted instantly, leaving the sought-for phosphorus-35 isotope. Phosphorus-35 has a 48-second half-life and decays by emitting beta particles and gamma rays, decaying eventually to sulfur-35. Silicon-33 had been produced in a similar manner as a by-product to another experiment.

Discovery of phosphorus-35 brings to seven the number of radioisotopes of phosphorus with known half-lives. The information bears out theoretical predictions.

Princeton-Penn accelerator closes. After an 18-month struggle for survival, the Princeton-Pennsylvania Accelerator, located on the campus of Princeton University, ceased operation early in the year. The accelerator had originally been designed as a medium-energy proton accelerator (3 Gev) with a particularly high intensity of protons per pulse. In 1970, the Atomic Energy Commission, faced with the choice of cutting budgets for all its laboratories or eliminating one, decided that the Princeton-Penn accelerator was expendable. The accelertor's director, Milton G. White, thought that if the accelerator was no longer needed in particle physics it could be converted to accelerate heavy ions, which are just now coming to be studied intensively and which may have important implications for the study of cancer. Sufficient funds were not forthcoming, however, and the accelerator finally had no alternative but to shut down.

FRANKLIN J. TOBEY, JR.

Obituaries

Alinsky, Saul David, 63, American social reformer and antipoverty organizer whose teaching stressed pragmatism in politics. June 12 in Carmel, Calif.

Athenagoras I, 86, ecumenical patriarch of the Eastern Orthodox Church since 1948; he attempted to heal the 900-year-old schism with the Roman Catholic Church. July 6 in Istanbul.

Austin, Gene, 71, crooner whose versions of "When My Sugar Walks Down the Street" (his own composition) and "My Blue Heaven" were the rage in the 1920's and 1930's. January 24 in Palm Springs, Calif.

Balenciaga, Cristobal, 77, influential Spanish couturier who introduced the chemise, semifitted suit, and pillbox hat to modern fashion. March 24 in Valencia.

Békésy, Georg von, 73, Hungarian-born physicist and Harvard professor who won the 1961 Nobel Prize in medicine and physiology for his research on human hearing. June 13 in Honolulu.

Benson, Sally, 71, author and screenwriter most famous for the "Junior Miss" stories and for *Meet Me in St. Louis,* which Hollywood turned into a musical. July 19 in Woodland Hills, Calif.

Berryman, John, 57, poet and professor who won the 1965 Pulitzer Prize for *77 Dream Songs* and the 1969 National Book Award for *His Toy, His Dream, His Rest.* Drowned January 7 after jumping from a bridge in Minneapolis.

Blocker, Dan, 43, the popular Hoss Cartwright, a gentle giant in the TV series *Bonanza.* May 13 in Inglewood, Calif.

Bonfils, Helen G., 82, chairman of the board of the Denver *Post* and a longtime patron of the theater. June 6 in Denver.

Boyd, Louise Arner, 84, a former debutante who, as an explorer and aviator, became world famous for her arctic exploits. September 14 in San Francisco.

Boyd, William, 77, reformed playboy who became Hopalong Cassidy, the movie and television western star who never kissed a girl and always defended virtue. September 12 in South Laguna Beach, Calif.

Bunche, Ralph Johnson, 67, former UN under secretary general and winner of the 1950 Nobel Peace Prize. A peerless mediator, he arranged the Palestine armistice in 1949 and later supervised UN peacekeeping efforts in Suez, the Congo, and Cyprus. Although not principally identified with the civil rights movement, he was active in the NAACP. December 9, 1971, in New York City.

Bush, Prescott, 77, former Republican senator from Connecticut (1952–1963). October 10 in New York City.

Byrnes, James Francis, 92, influential South Carolina Democrat who, as FDR's director of war mobilization, was popularly labeled "assistant president"; he also served as state governor, U.S. senator, Supreme Court justice, secretary of state, and United Nations delegate. April 9 in Columbia.

Cabot, Bruce (Jacques de Bujac), 67, handsome leading man who rescued Fay Wray from the hairy clutches of King Kong; his film career spanned 40 years. May 3 in Woodland Hills, Calif.

Style and Substance

Four people who died this year put a special style into their lives and work: at right, Yasunari Kawabata, whose melancholy novels of Japanese life won him a Nobel Prize; below, Congressman Adam Clayton Powell, whose life-style and early prominence as a black politician made him both a symbol and a target; left (facing page), Marianne Moore, a prize-winning poet almost as renowned for her devotion to the Dodgers; and Maurice Chevalier (far right), the agelessly ebullient French chanteur, lovable in any language.

Carroll, Leo G., 80, British-born character actor in such Hollywood classics as *Spellbound* and *Rebecca* and in the TV series *Topper* and *The Man from U.N.C.L.E.* October 16 in Hollywood.

Carter, Hodding, Jr., 65, editor and publisher of the Greenville (Miss.) *Delta Democratic-Times* whose editorials supporting racial tolerance won him the 1946 Pulitzer Prize. April 4 in Greenville.

Casadesus, Robert Marcel, 73, French concert pianist. September 19 in Paris.

Ceram, C. W. (Kurt W. Marek), 57, German-born author of *Gods, Graves and Scholars* (1949), a best-selling history of archaeology. April 12 in Hamburg.

BURT GLINN/MAGNUM

UPI

Chapman, John, 71, blunt drama critic of the New York *Daily News.* January 19 in Westport, Conn.

Chevalier, Maurice, 83, French chanteur whose buoyant and elegant manner made him his nation's most popular entertainer for more than 50 years; through films like *The Merry Widow* and *Gigi* he came to symbolize France to the world. January 1 in Paris.

Chichester, Sir Francis, 70, redoubtable British solo adventurer who at 65 circumnavigated the globe in his 53-foot ketch, *Gipsy Moth IV.* August 26 in Plymouth.

Churchill, Peter, 63, British liaison to the French resistance during World War II. May 1 in Cannes.

Clark, Walter Van Tilburg, 62, writer and teacher whose most popular novel was *The Ox-Bow Incident.* November 10, 1971, in Reno.

Colum, Padraic, 90, Irish-born lyric poet, critic, historian, and storyteller; a founder of the world-famous Abbey Theater, this key figure in Ireland's literary renaissance settled in the United States in 1914. January 11 in Enfield, Conn.

Correll, Charles J., 82, radio and television comedian who, in dialect and blackface, played Andy in the popular *Amos 'n' Andy* show. September 26 in Chicago.

Cowan, Jerome, 74, Hollywood character actor whose debonair presence graced such films as *Miracle on 34th Street* and *Mr. Skeffington.* January 24 in Hollywood.

Delderfield, R(onald) F(rederick), 60, prolific British author whose pastoral novels chronicled the English way of life. June 24 in Sidmouth.

De Wilde, Brandon, 30, child star who made a stunning Broadway debut in *Member of the Wedding* and moved millions in the western film classic *Shane.* July 6 in a traffic accident in Lakewood, Colo.

Dixon, Owen, 86, Australian statesman. On the High Court for 35 years and chief justice for 12, he was also minister to Washington and a UN mediator in the Kashmir dispute. July 10 in Melbourne.

Donlevy, Brian, 71, Hollywood character actor who played likable tough guys in such films as *Barbary Coast* and *What Price Glory?* April 5 in Hollywood.

Dreyfuss, Henry, 68, U.S. industrial designer whose talents ranged from the *Twentieth Century Limited* to household appliances and artificial limbs. Committed suicide on October 5 in South Pasadena, Calif.

Edward VIII, duke of Windsor, 77, former king of England who assumed the throne for less than 11 months and abdicated on December 11, 1936, to marry an American divorcee. May 28 in Paris.

Ellender, Allen J., 81, Louisiana Democrat who, during 35 years in the Senate, had become president pro tem and chairman of the powerful Appropriations Committee. July 27 in Bethesda, Md.

Escher, Maurits C., 73, witty Dutch printmaker whose two-dimensional worlds belied three-dimensional reality. March 27 in Hilversum.

Fisher, Geoffrey Francis (Lord Fisher of Lambeth), 85, former archbishop of Canterbury. As Anglican primate from 1945 to 1961, he was an outspoken supporter of conciliation between the Anglican and Roman Catholic churches. September 14 in Sherborne, Dorset.

ERNEST SISTO/NEW YORK TIMES

BETTMANN ARCHIVE

Fleischer, Max, 89, Austrian-born artist whose *Out of the Inkwell* was the first popular animated cartoon series. September 11 in Los Angeles.

Fleischer, Nat(haniel) S., 80, fight writer and historian who founded and edited *Ring* magazine. June 25 in New York City.

Franklin, Sidney, 79, Hollywood film producer and director whose credits include the Oscar-winning *Mrs. Miniver*. May 18 in Santa Monica, Calif.

Frederik IX, king of Denmark, 72, robust monarch whose informality won him his subjects' affection throughout his 25-year reign. January 14 in Copenhagen.

Friml, Charles Rudolf, 92, operetta king who composed *Rose Marie* and *Vagabond King*; his best known songs include "Indian Love Call" and "Donkey Serenade." November 12 in Hollywood.

Gallo, Joseph ("Crazy Joe"), 43, reputed leader of an underworld syndicate in New York City. Assassinated April 7 while celebrating his birthday at a restaurant in Little Italy.

Gentele, Claes-Goeran Herman Arvid, 54, Swedish opera director who had recently replaced Rudolf Bing as general manager of New York's Metropolitan Opera. July 18 in a car crash in Sardinia.

Gilbreth, Lillian Moller, 93, industrial engineer and management consultant memorialized in *Cheaper by the Dozen*. January 2 in Phoenix.

Goodman, Paul, 60, author, social critic, and psychotherapist whose radical humanism made him a campus hero in the 1960's. August 2 in North Stratford, N.H.

Grant, William Thomas, 96, founder of the billion-dollar W. T. Grant department store chain. August 6 in Greenwich, Conn.

Griebling, Otto ("Otto the Clown"), 75, German-born showman who became world famous with the Ringling Brothers Circus. April 19 in New York City.

Grofé, Ferde, 80, American composer of the *Grand Canyon Suite* and other Americana. April 3 in Santa Monica, Calif.

Harlan, John Marshall, 72, leading conservative on the U.S. Supreme Court from 1955 until his retirement in September 1971; he vigorously dissented from many of the Court's most momentous decisions, insisting that it could not be the sole remedy for all social ills. December 29, 1971, in Washington, D.C.

Hayden, Carl Trumbull, 94, quietly influential Arizona Democrat who served 56 years in Congress, a record. January 25 in Mesa.

Heatter, Gabriel, 82, radio commentator whose trademark was his introductory "Ah, there's good news tonight." March 30 in Miami Beach.

Hodges, Gil(bert Ray), 47, star first baseman for the 1950's Dodgers; in 1969 he managed the New York Mets to an amazing world championship. April 2 in West Palm Beach, Fla.

Hoover, J(ohn) Edgar, 77, FBI director since 1924. Celebrated for his gangbusting exploits, he transformed a small, inefficient agency into the computerized headquarters of the nation's war on crime. In later years his personal power and fervent anti-Communism became increasingly controversial. Found dead April 2 in Washington, D.C.

Hopkins, Miriam, 69, tough leading lady in *Becky Sharp* and the first film version of *The Children's Hour*. October 9 in New York City.

Ireland, Charles T., Jr., 51, corporate lawyer and financial expert who was named president of the Columbia Broadcasting System in 1971. June 7 in Chappaqua, N.Y.

Irvin, Rea, 90, cartoonist whose beaver-hatted, monocled Eustace Tilley symbolized the *New Yorker* magazine. May 28 in Frederiksted, Virgin Islands.

Jackson, Mahalia, 60, black gospel queen who joyfully praised the glory of God throughout the world; the granddaughter of a slave, she committed herself to the civil rights movement. January 27 in Evergreen Park, Ill.

Jigme Dorji Wangchuk, king of Bhutan, 45, beloved "dragon king" who attempted to modernize his small Himalayan nation and reduce its isolation from the outside world. July 21 in Nairobi.

Johnson, Howard Dearing, 75, Boston boy who parlayed 28 flavors into a $200 million motel, restaurant, and food-supply corporation. June 20 in New York City.

Jones, Robert Tyre, Jr. ("Bobby"), 69, brilliant golfer whose 1930 grand slam in the U.S. Open, British Open, and the British and U.S. Amateur tournaments is unequaled. December 18, 1971, in Atlanta.

Kawabata, Yasunari, 72, the only Japanese writer ever to win the Nobel Prize (1968); among his best-known books in the West are *Snow Country* and *Thousand Cranes*. Found dead April 16 in Zushi, an apparent suicide.

Kchessinska, Mathilde, 99, *prima ballerina assoluta* with the Russian Imperial Ballet. December 7, 1971, in Paris.

Lazareff, Pierre, 65, French director of the Paris newspaper *France-Soir* and the popular women's magazine *Elle*. April 21 in Neuilly-sur-Seine.

Leakey, Louis S. B., 69, Kenyan-born British archaeologist and anthropologist who discovered the earliest known evidence of human genesis. October 1 in London.

Leoni, Raúl, 67, president of Venezuela from 1964 to 1969; he was the first Venezuelan leader to yield power peacefully to an elected successor from an opposing party. July 5 in New York City.

Levant, Oscar, 65, concert pianist, television personality, and legendary hypochondriac who exposed his neuroses with morbid, sardonic wit. August 14 in Beverly Hills.

Lewis, C(ecil) Day, 68, British poet laureate since 1968. With Auden and Spender, he came to prominence in the radical climate of the 1930's; in later years his classicism predominated, and he successfully translated Vergil. May 22 in London.

Lichine, David (David Lichtenstein), 62, Russian-born ballet dancer, choreographer, and teacher whose most popular work is *Graduation Ball*. June 26 in Los Angeles.

Lin Piao, 63 (?), once regarded as Mao Tse-tung's heir apparent. A confidant of Mao's during the long march of the 1930's, he became minister of national defense in 1959. But Lin became involved in a power struggle and died in a plane crash in Mongolia on September 12, 1971, allegedly while fleeing after an abortive coup. (Death revealed by official Chinese sources July 28, 1972.)

Long, Edward V., 64, former Democratic senator from Missouri (1960–1969). November 6 in Eolia.

Lübke, Heinrich, 77, second president of West Germany (1959–1969). April 6 in Bonn.

Lucas, Dione, 62, English cooking expert whose restaurants, cooking schools, and TV programs espoused Cordon Bleu cuisine. December 18, 1971, in London.

Lyman, Lauren Dwight, 81, Pulitzer Prize-winning aviation journalist. July 11 in Bridgeport, Conn.

Mahendra bir Bikram Shah Deva, king of Nepal, 51, who abolished polygamy and the caste system and introduced land reform. January 31 in Bharatpur.

Maxwell, Marilyn, 49, breezy blonde who starred in Hollywood musicals of the late 1940's. March 20 in Hollywood.

Mayer, Maria Goeppert, 65, German-born theoretical physicist; in 1963, for her research into the shell structure of the atomic nucleus, she became only the second woman ever to win the Nobel Prize in physics. February 20 in San Diego.

McKenney, Ruth, 60, humorous author of the short-story collection *My Sister Eileen*. July 25 in New York City.

Montherlant, Henry Milon de, 76, French novelist and playwright noted for his clear, aphoristic prose and his nihilistic, woman-hating outlook. Shot himself September 21 in Paris.

Moore, Marianne, 84, imagist poet whose carefully crafted verses won every major American literary award; to the public she was known as a loyal Brooklynite and Dodger fan. February 5 in New York City.

Nijinska, Bronislava, 81, Polish-born ballet dancer, sister of the celebrated Nijinsky, and choreographer with the Ballets Russes under Diaghilev in the 1920's. February 21 in Pacific Palisades, Calif.

Nkrumah, Kwame, 62, messianic African statesman who led Ghana to independence in 1957 and became its first president in 1960; he was overthrown six years later, amid charges of megalomania and corruption. April 27 in Conakry, Guinea.

Norell, Norman (Norman Levinson), 72, Seventh Avenue's dean of American designers, whose pure, simple, and traditional fashion lines endured 50 years of changing feminine modes. October 25 in New York City.

O'Connor, Basil, 80, fund-raiser whose March of Dimes collected nearly $1 billion to fight polio. March 9 in Phoenix, Ariz.

Oufkir, Muhammad, 48, Moroccan defense minister. Committed suicide August 17 at Skhirat after allegedly leading an abortive coup.

Pound, Ezra Weston Loomis, 87, American poet, translator, and critic. His theory and practice influenced Eliot, Joyce, and a whole generation of American imagist poets, but his condemnation of *usura* led him to overtly pro-Fascist activities. Extradited for treason after World War II, he was judged insane and held in a U.S. mental hospital for 12 years before returning to Italy. November 1 in self-imposed exile in Venice.

Powell, Adam Clayton, Jr., 63, Baptist minister and Harlem's flashy congressman from 1945 to 1967, when he was barred, he claimed, for flaunting publicly what other men kept secret. He was later reelected and reinstated but stripped of his Education and Labor Committee chairmanship. April 4 in Miami.

Rabin, Michael, 35, violin prodigy who became a world-renowned virtuoso. January 19 in New York City.

Rank, Lord J(oseph) Arthur, 83, wealthy British movie magnate. March 29 in Winchester.

Robinson, Jack Roosevelt ("Jackie"), 53, Hall of Fame infielder who broke major league baseball's color line in 1947 to become a star player for the Brooklyn Dodger's, thus paving the way for black athletes to enter all professional sports. October 24 in Stamford, Conn.

Romains, Jules, 86, French man of letters whose voluminous works encompassed poetry, history, fiction, drama, and philosophy, including *Men of Good Will*, a 6,400-page fictionalized history of Western Europe, 1908–1933. August 14 in Paris.

Ruggles, Wesley, 84, film director and producer whose many films included the 1931 Oscar-winning western *Cimmarron*. January 8 in Los Angeles.

Rushing, Jimmy, 68, Kansas City–born blues man whose pure, high-pitched singing with Count Basie set the swing style for decades. June 8 in New York City.

Rutherford, Dame Margaret, 80, unpredictable grande dame of the British stage and screen, best remembered for her comic portrayals in four Agatha Christie films. May 22 in Chalfont St. Peter.

Saarinen, Aline Bernstein, 58, leading art critic, head of NBC's Paris news bureau, and former hostess of the television show *For Women Only*. July 13 in New York City.

Sambu, Zhamsarangin, 76, president of Mongolia since 1954. May 20 in Ulan Bator.

Sanders, George, 65, sneering sophisticate whose roles in *Rebecca* and *All About Eve* reflected his off-screen personality. April 25 from an overdose of barbiturates in Castelldefels, Spain.

Sarnoff, David, 80, broadcasting giant whose foresight and perseverance built the Radio Corporation of America, with its subsidiary National Broadcasting Company, into one of the most powerful U.S. corporations. December 12, 1971, in New York City.

Shapley, Harlow, 86, renowned U.S. astronomer whose computations located the earth near the edge of the Milky Way. October 20 in Boulder, Colo.

Shawn, Edwin Myers ("Ted"), 80, the father of modern dance. Coming to ballet as therapy for his own paralysis, he developed into America's first great male dancer. With Ruth St. Denis, his wife for 20 years, he cofounded the Denishawn schools; later he started the Jacob's Pillow dance center and summer festival. As a choreographer he devised for his all-male troupe a vigorous, athletic style. January 9 in Orlando, Fla.

Sieff, Israel Moses (Baron Sieff of Brampton), 82, Lithuanian-born British Zionist and philanthropist who headed Marks and Spencer, the department store chain. February 14 in London.

Sikorsky, Igor Ivan, 83, Russian-born aviation pioneer who developed the helicopter. October 26 in Easton, Conn.

Simpson, Kirke Larue, 90, former Associated Press reporter who coined the term "smoke-filled room" in 1920 and won the 1921 Pulitzer Prize for his series on the Unknown Soldier. June 16 in Los Gatos, Calif.

Smith, Betty (Elizabeth Keogh), 75, writer whose first novel, *A Tree Grows in Brooklyn*, won immediate and lasting popularity. January 17 in Shelton, Conn.

Smith, Joseph Fielding, 95, president of the Church of Jesus Christ of Latter-Day Saints. July 2 in Salt Lake City.

Snow, Edgar, 66, American journalist whose *Red Star Over China* (1937) sympathetically portrayed the revolutionaries who would come to power a decade later; he often returned to China in subsequent years. February 15 in Eysins, Switzerland.

Spaak, Paul-Henri, 73, Belgian statesman and a principal architect of European unity after World War II. A lifelong Socialist, he became at 39 his country's youngest president and served in numerous cabinet posts from 1939 onward; the first president of the UN General Assembly, he was also secretary general of NATO (1957–1961). July 31 in Brussels.

Spingarn, Arthur B., 93, civil rights lawyer who headed the NAACP from 1940 to 1966. December 1, 1971, in New York City.

Steiner, Max(imilian) Raoul, 83, film composer whose scores for *The Informer; Now, Voyager;* and *Since You Went Away* each won an Oscar. December 28, 1971, in Hollywood.

Talal, king of Jordan, 63; after his father was assassinated he reigned for 13 months before mental illness forced him to abdicate in 1952. July 8 in Istanbul.

Tamiroff, Akim, 72, Russian-born character actor whose deft way with dialects won acclaim in hundreds of films. September 17 in Palm Springs, Calif.

Tashlin, Frank, 59, Hollywood director who put Jerry Lewis, Bob Hope, and Danny Kaye through their slapstick paces. May 5 in Beverly Hills.

Tazewell, Charles, 72, writer and actor whose children's story "The Littlest Angel" became a perennial Christmas favorite. June 26 in Chesterfield, N.H.

Theiler, Max, 73, South African–born winner of the 1951 Nobel Prize in medicine for developing a yellow fever vaccine. August 11 in New Haven.

Thompson, Llewellyn E., 67, career diplomat who twice was U.S. ambassador to the Soviet Union (1957–1962, 1967–1969). February 6 in Bethesda, Md.

Tiger, Dick, 42, Nigerian boxer who twice held the world middleweight title and once the light-heavyweight title; he lost all his wealth after siding with Biafra. December 14, 1971, in Aba.

Tisserant, Eugene Cardinal, 87, French scholar-priest who became the dean of the Sacred College of Cardinals in 1951. February 21 in Albano, Italy.

Traubel, Helen, 69, the Metropolitan Opera's leading Wagnerian soprano from the 1930's to the 1950's and, subsequently, a showbiz star with Jimmy Durante, Red Skelton, and other comics. July 28 in Santa Monica, Calif.

Traynor, Harold Joseph ("Pie"), 72, fielding and batting star with Pittsburgh Pirates (1920–1937); in 1969 this Hall of Famer was named the best third baseman in history. March 16 in Pittsburgh.

Trendle, George W., 87, former radio executive who rescued Detroit's faltering WXYZ in the 1930's by creating the *Lone Ranger, Sgt. Preston of the Yukon,* and *Green Hornet* adventure series. May 10 in Grosse Pointe, Mich.

Tvardovsky, Aleksandr, 61, Soviet poet and editor whose liberal journal *Novy Mir* was the first to publish Solzhenitsyn. December 17, 1971, in Krasnaya Pakhra.

Vann, John Paul, 47, senior U.S. adviser in Vietnam. June 9 in a helicopter crash in the Central Highlands.

Weiss, George Martin, 78, outstanding baseball executive who built Yankee champions and later directed the Mets. August 13 in Greenwich, Conn.

Wilson, Edmund, 77, essayist, editor, and literary and social critic. He exerted incalculable influence on American letters both directly, by reviewing and encouraging contemporary authors, and indirectly, through pioneering research into early American writers and lesser known foreign literatures. June 12 in Talcottville, N.Y.

Winchell, Walter, 74, brash song-and-dance man whose staccato gossip column and radio newscasts elevated personal piques to national issues. February 20 in Los Angeles.

Wolpe, Stefan, 69, German-born teacher and composer of jazz-inflected serial pieces. April 4 in New York City.

ABBY RAE ZUKERMAN

THINK TANK. Commuting from a support vessel (above, artist's rendering) to this 21-foot-long cylindrical mobile office, U.S. scientists spent three-day shifts off Florida for three months studying marine life, ocean currents, and pollution.

OCEANOGRAPHY. Marine geology. Concern over national stores of minerals and costs associated with environmental problems caused many mining companies to make enormous financial commitments to obtain minerals from the sea. Of particular interest were systems designed to recover manganese nodules, which cover vast areas of ocean floor from depths of 12,000 to 17,000 feet.

Among other companies interested in deep-sea mining, Deepsea Ventures, Inc., a subsidiary of Tenneco, has invested over $20 million obtaining some 13 patents and 27 patent applications for mining deep-sea manganese nodules. Tenneco's system uses an airlift dredge to suck manganese nodules directly from the sea floor dredge-head to the ship's hold. Preliminary chemical hydrometallurgical processes have been tested capable of extracting 98 percent of the minerals from the ore.

A recent survey completed by Lamont Doherty Geological Observatory showed the currently known distribution and concentration of manganese nodules on the ocean floor. The mineral wealth, if it can be economically harvested, is staggering. Governments and industry are actively pursuing programs to recover this natural resource, but the fundamental question of ownership of ocean minerals is a serious obstacle.

Ocean law. The days of "freedom of the sea" are vanishing as interest increases in offshore oil, mineral recovery, and fishery resources. Nations are demanding more and more rights to the sea in return for their investments.

For example, definition of the ore bodies requires extensive, costly, highly visible operations on location. As soon as mining operations begin, the location of the lodes becomes public (international) information. Therefore, each mine site must be protected by governmental lease prior to the outlay of engineering funds.

Accordingly, the U.S. government has been developing a system to give mineral leases to companies for deep-sea mining. However, the United States does not legally own the resources, and both the Soviet Union and Japan have been conducting global mineral explorations and developing and testing deep-sea mining systems. China, admitted to the United Nations Seabed Committee this year, is accusing Japan and the United States of a conspiracy to plunder the wealth of the oceans.

The 91 nations of the United Nations Seabed Committee met in February and July to agree on an agenda for the International Law of the Sea Conference, to be held in 1973. However, little progress was made because of failure to agree on the fundamental question of limiting the boundaries of national waters. Smaller countries, fearful of foreign exploitation of their fisheries and minerals, are claiming a 200-mile limit; the United States and other major powers favored a 12-mile limit, with the condition that free passage be safeguarded through narrow straits such as Gibraltar, the English Channel, and 114 other waterways.

Geophysics. The *Glomar Challenger* continued its worldwide Deep Sea Drilling Project (DSDP), retrieving about 60,000 feet of sediment cores from more than 300,000 feet of holes drilled. Benefits from the expedition include advances in deep-ocean drilling, assessment of mineral deposits in the sea floor, and increased knowledge of sea floor spreading, continental drift, and continental subsidence. In the past year the DSDP documented that the Pacific sea floor shifted 2,000 miles during the past 125 million years and that it moves under the Asian continental block at a rate of 4 inches a year.

In the North Pacific, the National Oceanic and Atmospheric Administration research vessel, the *Oceanographer*, began a three-year study of the earth's oldest oceanic bottom crust—the 250-year-old Pacific Tectonic Plate, which forms a corridor from the Hawaiian Islands to the Marianas Trench. Sea-floor spreading is slowly thrusting the plate under the Philippine sea plate, forming the Marianas Trench (a rift in the ocean floor 36,198 feet deep).

Energy crisis. In February, after three months of court injunctions by environmentalists, the United States canceled the lease sale of Gulf of Mexico oil plots. The resultant lag in further offshore exploration was a serious factor in the energy crisis projected by oil companies. At a time when oil and natural gas utilization is rapidly accelerating, the oil companies are finding it increasingly difficult to maintain

the cyclic process of providing oil (which starts with exploration). U.S. oil company exploration has expanded in Trinidad, Malta, Africa, western Australia, Japan, Thailand, Sumatra, and South America. Such offshore oil activities cause problems over legal control of these resources. Taxation, pollution restrictions and expenses, transportation problems, and increased expense in finding new oil deposits have made the petroleum industry's return on investment below the average for manufacturing in general. As a result, the rate of investment has leveled off, making it doubtful that the industry will be able to meet the demands of the U.S. energy crisis.

Tidal-powered generators and deep-water thermal generators have been proposed to help meet the energy demands of the 1970's. This past year a new concept was introduced—seagoing nuclear power plants. Faced with powerful resistance by environmental groups, electrical companies have turned to placement of nuclear power plants on offshore platforms.

Coral chronometers. One of the more important strides in biological oceanography was the discovery and calibration of annual growth rings in the stony corals that make up coral reefs and atolls. Corals, responding to changes in light from winter to summer, form growth rings in their calcium carbonate skeletons. Researchers from the Hawaii Institute of Geophysics, University of Hawaii, examined corals from Eniwetok. Radioactivity bands in the coral structure caused by strontium-90 were related to a specific series of nuclear tests. By correlating autoradiography and X-radiographs of sections of the coral heads, yearly growth bands were identified similar to those found in trees. Examination of these growth bands can provide valuable information for studies on paleoclimatology, coral reef development, and aspects of pollution.

Monster camera. A monster camera for deep-sea photography was designed at Scripps Institution of Oceanography. The appropriately named camera and electronic flash system has a special trigger baited with hunks of fish or squid. It was lowered into deep water with the idea that elusive sea monsters might grab the bait and take a self-portrait. In 17,000 feet of water a giant amphipod crustacean, 11 inches long, took the bait and was photographed. The crustacean was unknown to science and triggered a new monster effort —a monster trap to catch the unusual animal.

Sea mammals. Naval research on ocean mammals was highlighted by the announcement that naval-trained porpoises were patrolling for enemy frogmen in Vietnam harbors. The docile animals were reportedly equipped with tracking devices and trained to home in on divers in the water. Other mammals were trained to perform useful tasks for the navy. Whales, equipped with special harnesses, were taught to locate and attach lines to sunken torpedos in depths up to 2,000 feet. Sea lions were trained to retrieve smaller objects from depths of 500 feet.

Aquaculture. Ocean farming in the United States took a step forward with the first commercial harvest of 500,000 pounds of pink shrimp from Marifarms, Inc., a shrimp farm in western Florida. The harvested shrimp were said to be of more uniform size and tastier than wild shrimp. They were flash-frozen immediately upon harvesting and sold through regular fishery product outlets in central Florida.

Man Undersea. Small submersibles, habitats, and special scientific diving equipment received a significant financial boost, with the enactment of the National Oceanic and Atmospheric Administration's Man Undersea Science and Technology Office. MUST, with a multimillion dollar a year budget, is the first unified federal effort supporting technical use of the more sophisticated diving systems developed during the past decade. Their first saturation diving experiment was named the Florida Aquanaut Research Experiment. Forty scientists conducted ten projects along the Florida coral reefs, using the University of ,New

Hampshire's Edalhab II underwater habitat and the Woods Hole Oceanographic Institution's ship *Lulu*. Scientists studied the reefs in each area on three- to four-day dives. When finished, the habitat was raised and easily moved from one research site to another.

Ocean buoys. The giant NOAA Data Buoy Program got under way this year with the launching of the first of six prototype, 100-ton data buoys. The buoy was towed to sea and placed 225 miles south of Gulfport, Miss. The buoys will one day circle the globe sending continuous oceanographic and meteorological data via satellite to a special receiving station and computer bank.

RICHARD CHESHER

OHIO. Environment. The general assembly, after laboring for a year, enacted a bill to regulate strip mining, but heavy lobbying by the coal industry took the edge off what could have been landmark controls. In long, acrimonious debates prior to passage, conservationists fought for a tough bill, while mine operators threatened that stringent reclamation requirements would force the closing of mines in coal-rich eastern Ohio. The final version of the bill reduced the time period allowed for backfilling and replanting strip pits, required that cliffs left by digging be leveled to no more than 35 degrees, and stipulated that the land be returned to its best possible use.

After another year-long battle between conservation and industry forces, legislation was enacted setting up a state

AN EARTH-EATING MONSTER, the "Gem of Egypt" rises above the Hanna Coal Company's strip mine in Belmont County, Ohio. After bitter fighting between conservationists and the coal industry, the Ohio state legislature enacted a strip-mining control law.

department of environmental protection to serve as an umbrella for all pollution-control programs. The measure had been a top priority item for Governor John J. Gilligan (D), although he had wanted a more comprehensive bill, giving citizens instant powers to take polluters to court.

Attorney General William J. Brown went to court against a polluter, armed with the state's century-old "bawdy house" law forbidding public nuisances. He won a permanent injunction against a Cleveland firm, which had been discharging 40,000 gallons a day of cyanide and chromic acid into the Cuyahoga River.

Meanwhile, the general assembly extended until July 1, 1974, its ban on gas and oil-well drilling under Lake Erie, but refused to make it permanent. The lake, once declared nearly "dead," appeared to be reviving because of successful antipollution programs.

Education and culture. When its planned $61 million program of state aid to nonpublic schools appeared unconstitutional, the legislature shunned direct assistance and parental grant methods, coming up instead with a proposed credit against the state income tax for those sending children to private and parochial schools. The plan was challenged by the American Civil Liberties Union and later ruled unconstitutional by the U.S. Supreme Court.

John D. Millett, chancellor of the Ohio Board of Regents since its inception, retired to become an educational consultant in Washington.

The Neil Armstrong Aerospace Museum opened this year at Wapakoneta, home of the first man to walk on the moon. Half of its $1 million cost was financed by private subscription, the other half by state funds. The museum contains early airplanes, space vehicles, and some of Armstrong's boyhood mementos, but no permanent display of moon rocks, contrary to expectations.

As the museum was being erected, another Ohio cultural landmark disappeared from the scene, when Crosley Field, 60-year-old former home of the Cincinnati Reds, was razed.

Judiciary. Judge Lloyd O. Brown, a black Democrat from Cleveland, was Gilligan's first interim appointee to the Ohio supreme court. Brown, the only non-Republican on the seven-man bench, was defeated in November.

Economic development. Ohio logged 768 new or expanded firms during the first year of the Gilligan administration, but emphasis on attracting foreign and out-of-state business declined. The Department of Development, which had flourished under the administration of former governor James A. Rhodes (R), was combined with the Department of Urban Affairs.

For election results and campaign highlights, see the special supplement ELECTION '72.

Area and population. Area, 41,222 sq. mi. Pop. (1970), 10,652,-017. Principal cities: Columbus (cap.), 539,677; Cleveland, 750,-903; Cincinnati, 452,524; Toledo, 383,818; Akron, 275,425; Dayton, 243,601.
Government. Gov., John J. Gilligan (D); lt. gov., John W. Brown (R); atty. gen., William J. Brown (D); secy. of state, Ted W. Brown (R); aud., Joseph T. Ferguson (D); treas., Gertrude W. Donahey (D). Legislature: senate, 20 R, 13 D; house, 54 R, 45 D.
Finance (through June 30, 1972). Revenue, $2,019,679,900; expenditure, $1,912,425,152; cash balance, $260,968,183.
Education. Public school districts, 625. Elementary schools, 3,210; enrollment, 1,429,840; teachers, 51,819. Secondary schools, 1,012; enrollment, 738,534; teachers, 48,000. Private and parochial schools, 788; enrollment, 296,510; teachers, 14,113.   LEE LEONARD

OKLAHOMA. Government and politics. The mood of Oklahoma politics was generally placid this year. In a short session, the 33rd legislature voted for establishment of a school of medicine at the University of Oklahoma in Tulsa, in a move to supplement the University Health Sciences Center, located in Oklahoma City. The Health Sciences Center had suffered from grossly inadequate legislative appropriations, necessitating cancellation of some of its health services.

The politics of whiskey took an interesting turn, when state lawmen boarded an AMTRAK train in Oklahoma and arrested the bartender for serving liquor by the drink while operating an open saloon. State law forbids the sale of liquor by the drink, although it may be purchased by the bottle or served by the drink in clubs if members supply their own source. In the legal contest that followed, AMTRAK won a federal district court injunction against Oklahoma, on the grounds that the federal law regulating the operations of AMTRAK precluded state interference. On a related issue, a state organization seeking to legalize liquor by the drink conducted a petition drive for a referendum; however, dry forces challenged the validity of many signatures, thereby winning delays from a sympathetic secretary of state and putting off the final resolution of the question for some time.

Education. School-desegregation controversies swept the principal metropolitan center school districts. Oklahoma City, in particular, was confronted in September with a court-ordered desegregation plan that called for massive busing across the city. But in spite of mass protests against the busing, most school officials expected the plan to prove operative and acceptable in time.

Municipal events. The All-American City award was won this year by Chickasha, a small city southwest of Oklahoma City, for its efforts to reverse the rural-urban population shift plaguing the nation. The city fathers had conducted a successful industrial expansion program, accompanied by energetic efforts in fostering racial harmony and more amicable human relations.

The Association of Central Oklahoma Governments (ACOG) encountered membership disputes that eventually destroyed it. It had been organized by local governments in the Oklahoma City metropolitan area for consolidated planning, coordination, and clearing of federal grant-in-aid proposals. But the Department of Housing and Urban Development (HUD) requires that any such "clearinghouse" for federal grants must represent at least 75 percent of the population of the area. When Oklahoma City withdrew from ACOG, citing a list of grievances, 55 percent of the area population lost representation on ACOG, and HUD was prompted to withdraw its accreditation.

Economic developments. Economic growth was indicated for the first half of the year in a number of sectors. Compared to the first half of last year, retail sales went up 17 percent, while construction soared by more than 85 percent. Demand deposits rose by about 4 percent, while time deposits increased by over 21 percent.

For election results and campaign highlights, see the special supplement ELECTION '72.

Area and population. Area, 69,919 sq. mi. Pop., 2,559,229. Principal cities: Oklahoma City (cap.), 366,481; Tulsa, 331,638; Lawton, 74,470; Norman, 52,117.
Government. Gov., David Hall (D); lt. gov., George Nigh (D); atty. gen., Larry Derryberry (D); aud., Joe Bailey Cobb (D); treas., Leo Winters (D). Legislature: senate, 39 D, 9 R; house, 78 D, 21 R.
Finance (year ending June 1972). Revenue, $1,292,460,155; expenditure, $1,272,781,459.
Education. Public enrollment (est. 1971–1972): elementary, 353,436; secondary, 280,424. Nonpublic enrollment (est. fall 1971): elementary, 9,100; secondary, 3,000. Higher education enrollment (fall 1970): full time, 83,291; part time, 26,251.
                    WALTER F. SCHEFFER

ONTARIO. Politics and government. The year opened with the newly elected Progressive-Conservative government of Premier William G. Davis firmly in power, continuing the 28 years of unbroken Conservative Party rule in Canada's central and most populous province.

One of the most significant acts of the premier was the reorganization of the government. Three secretaries were appointed: justice, Allan Lawrence; social development, Robert Welsh; and resource development, Bert Lawrence. Other government departments have been gathered together

under five superministries: solicitor general, with responsibility for all legal matters; treasury, economics, and intergovernmental affairs; natural resources, which includes the former department of lands and forests, the department of mines, and the department of northern affairs; the former departments of tourism and information and trade development; and the office of the premier.

Continuing its emphasis on concern for the environment, the government of Ontario was a cosigner with the United States of an antipollution pact in April—the Great Lakes Water Quality Agreement. A radio and television campaign against pollution and littering was also introduced.

Economic developments. Throughout the year the public has been harassed by strikes in the public sector: garbagemen, hospital workers, postmen, hydroelectric employees, and air and ground communication technicians have gone on strike in an attempt to win a larger share in the booming economy. At the same time, despite international monetary crises and U.S. restrictive practices, Ontario's industry flourished, especially the construction industry.

As part of the national reaction in Canada to U.S. plant ownership in Ontario, the provincial government took measures to ensure that the majority of boards of directors of all firms in Ontario are Canadian citizens and residents. It also passed legislation making licenses no longer available to insurance agents, brokers, or adjustors if the majority of shares issued by any of their companies are held by nonresidents of Canada. At the same time the Ontario Development Corporation made loans available for up to 50 percent of the cost of buildings and machinery for Canadian-owned companies.

Education. The lack of employment opportunities for university and postgraduate degree holders has made the Department of University Affairs and the university presidents take a second look at plans for expansion in the face of enrollments that remained stationary or declined during the 1971–1972 university year. After university tuition costs were nearly doubled by a recent provincial budget, a number of Ontario students made plans to continue their higher education elsewhere. Students have taken a less militant attitude toward solving their problems, and although a serious confrontation over the use of a new library took place at the University of Toronto, the tension has diminished in the area of education.

Other developments. The development of a second international airport on 18,000 acres of farmland to be expropriated some 20 miles northeast of Toronto, together with an adjoining new "Cedarwood City" of 250,000 people, proposed by the federal-provincial governments, has stirred opposition from environmentalists, transportation planners, and the POP (people or planes) committee.

In August the province was stunned by the revelation of two conflict-of-interest charges in connection with land speculation leveled against the attorney general and the provincial treasurer; the latter, W. Darcy McKeough, resigned his post. In January, Ontario lost its senior citizen, R. Samuel McLaughlin, president of General Motors of Canada and benefactor of universities, hospitals, and public institutions, on the eve of his 100th birthday.

Area and population. Area, 412,582 sq. mi. Pop. (est. 1972), 7,825,000. Principal cities: Toronto (cap.), 1,925,100; Ottawa, 300,000; Hamilton, 297,000.
Government. Democratic parliamentary government. Gov., William Ross Macdonald; prem., William G. Davis.
Finance. Revenue, $4,183,200,000; expenditure, $4,835,700,000.
Education. Total enrollment (1971; ages 5–16), 2,031,360. (Total enrollment is expected to decrease by approx. 5,000 in 1972). Schools, 4,795; teachers, 92,798. Total expenditure for elementary, secondary, and adult education (1970), $1,702,420,000.

WILLIAM A. MCKAY

OREGON. Legislation. An additional cigarette tax, which brought the total tax for each pack to 9 cents, was approved by the voters in a special election January 18 and became effective February 17. The tax, enacted by the 1971 legislature to become effective September 9, 1971, had been successfully referred by its opponents to the general election in November 1972. When it became apparent that this postponement and declining receipts from income and liquor taxes would create a $35 million drop in revenue for 1972, the governor called a special session of the legislature, which met November 16–22, 1971. In addition to setting the date for the special election on the cigarette tax, the legislators ordered a cut of $11.9 million in already minimal state agency budgets and revised the income tax code. Since 1969, state income tax regulations have paralleled federal regulations to simplify filing for the taxpayers, but the revenue loss from recent changes in exemptions and deductions proved unexpectedly large.

Environment. Efforts to reduce air pollution from field burning in the Willamette Valley took two directions. Several prototype mobile burners were given field trials, and the sale of many tons of grass waste to Japanese dairymen seeking a new cattle feed source raised hopes of a new industry for the state.

After a 13-year effort by Oregon congressmen, the Oregon Dunes National Recreation Area was established and dedicated for public use on July 15. The area contains 32,250 acres extending for 40 miles along the coast from Florence to Coos Bay.

Minorities. Settlement of boundary claims, under dispute since 1855, added 61,000 acres to the Warm Springs Indian reservation. Another important event for this group was the opening in July of the new lodge building in their convention-resort center. With improving economic conditions on the reservation, interest has been renewed in Indian cultural heritage, and old crafts such as weaving corn-husk bags and preparing traditional root foods have been revived. Eugene was the scene of the first convention of the National Tribal Chairmen's Association. The meeting brought together leaders from a majority of the Indian tribes to discuss relations with the federal government.

In Woodburn the year-old community service office within the police department successfully served as liaison between local agencies and the large group of Mexican-Americans and Old Believer Russians who have settled in the area recently. Language barriers and cultural differences were considered the underlying causes of the new problems faced by this rural community.

Community activities. The tiny settlement of Ukiah in the Blue Mountains became an incorporated town in May in order to secure the legal right to levy taxes and to receive distributed funds. The citizens of Prineville rejected a 1972–1973 budget which called for a tax-free year. The $37,000 levy which was substituted was allocated for civic improvements beyond those already scheduled to be financed by revenue from the city-owned railroad.

On August 18, Salem dedicated a civic center consisting of a new city hall, firehouse, and library. Although less ornate, the new city hall, fire station, and city shop of Madras were unique in that they were actually built by the city employees. Furthermore, this $52,000 project did not require any special levies or tax increases during the four years of its construction.

For election results and campaign highlights, see the special supplement ELECTION '72.

Area and population. Area, 96,981 sq. mi. Pop. (est. 1971), 2,143,010. Principal cities: Salem (cap.), 72,445; Portland, 383,000; Eugene, 81,385.
Government. Gov., Tom Lawson McCall (R); secy. of state, Clay Myers (R); treas., Robert W. Straub (D); atty. gen., Lee Johnson (R). Legislature: senate, 16 D, 14 R; house, 34 R, 26 D.
Finance (1971). Revenue, $1,175,953,000; expenditures, $1,134,508,000.
Education (1970). Public elementary schools, 1,002; public secondary schools, 325; enrollment, 498,336; teachers, 21,409.

CLARICE KRIEG

PACIFIC ISLANDS. A significant development this year was the continuation and expansion of the South Pacific Forum, first organized at the Wellington (New Zealand) conference in August 1971. This "mini-UN" of the Pacific islands held its second meeting, in Canberra, Australia, in February. The leaders of the five island member countries—Nauru, Fiji, Western Samoa, Tonga, and the Cook Islands—together with representatives from Australia and New Zealand discussed a variety of topics. Foremost among these was trade, a particular wish of the island members being the creation of a free trade area in the South Pacific; to foster trade relations, the Bureau of Economic Cooperation (two-thirds financed by Australia and New Zealand) was set up in Suva, Fiji. The bureau is generally considered to have a formidable task ahead of it.

At the forum's third meeting, held later in 1972, a matter of great concern to the members was the continuation of atmospheric nuclear testing in French Polynesia. The French nuclear tests which were carried out in mid-1972 created a storm of protest throughout the South Pacific. Before the scheduled date of the tests, many efforts were made to stop them, including an impassioned plea by New Zealand at the Stockholm conference on the environment. Nevertheless, the tests went ahead, and at the end of September, New Zealand again protested, this time in an address to the UN General Assembly.

Another matter discussed by the South Pacific Forum was the future of the Pacific Islands Producers Association, which seemed in danger of extinction after the Bureau of Economic Cooperation was created. However, at a PIPA meeting in June, it was decided to extend the association's term for three years, principally because of its involvement in such aspects of regional trade as marketing, shipping, and bulk purchasing of copra.

The 12th South Pacific Conference was held in Apia, Samoa, in late September. Representatives from 18 island countries attended, together with delegates from the United States, Great Britain, France, Australia, and New Zealand. One objective stressed at the conference was long-term planning. After some discussion, a directive was given to the planning committee to prepare a long-term program for consideration at the 1973 conference. In the meantime, the participating countries agreed to increase their contributions by 5 percent; that, together with some voluntary contributions, will bring in an additional $80,000. Approved projects for the future included preparation of new school syllabi, study of the rhinoceros beetle, and research on the ways to solve nutritional problems. One controversial question concerned the first Pacific Festival of Arts, held in May on Suva; although an artistic success, the festival had failed to show a profit and had therefore established no fund for future arts expositions.

American Samoa. Samoan high chiefs called on the U.S. Congress in March to enact legislation enabling the Samoan people to elect their own governors. But Congress deferred action until a congressional subcommittee could visit Samoa for a firsthand look at the situation.

The U.S. Department of Commerce made a grant of $980,000 to develop an 80-acre industrial area at Tafuna, near Pago Pago's international airport. The development will create 300 new jobs. Also during the year the American Samoan government established an environmental quality commission to investigate and control the many environmental problems that have resulted from the imposition of Western culture on the Samoan people.

Cook Islands. In the general elections held on April 11, the Cook Islands Party, led by Albert Henny, again won comfortably. However, on Rarotonga, the most populous island, a 17 percent swing away from the CIP to the Democratic Party made the voting close. Thus, the CIP's overall majority of 65.3 percent in 1968 was reduced to 54.4 percent in 1972, although it still holds 15 out of 22 seats.

Fiji. In a general election held in April, the voters returned to power for another five years the Alliance Party and its leader, Prime Minister Ratu Sir Kamisese Mara.

The basis of the government's planning for the immediate future is the sixth development plan, taking Fiji to 1975. The plan aims to improve education, transportation, and health facilities, especially for rural dwellers. The Fiji government is shortly to take over the dominion's sugar industry, setting up the Fiji Sugar Corporation as a limited liability company in place of the South Pacific Sugar Mills, Ltd., a subsidiary of the Colonial Sugar Refining Company.

During the year, work on Fiji's first national tourism development plan began with the launching of a survey on the future of tourism.

French Polynesia. In midyear the attention of the whole Pacific world was focused on French Polynesia because of the nuclear tests conducted by the French government on Mururoa atoll. Although the explosions were smaller than earlier ones, the protests against them in areas outside French Polynesia were stronger. The bans on shipping imposed by trade unionists in Australia and New Zealand appear not to have affected the islands themselves to any great extent. In fact, French Polynesia itself was probably the calmest place of all during the controversy. The French government plans to continue testing until 1975.

Gilbert and Ellice Islands. A major political change occurred at the beginning of the year when the Gilbert and Ellice Islands Colony became responsible directly to the Foreign and Commonwealth Office in London instead of to the Western Pacific High Commission in the Solomon Islands. The colony will have a governor of its own but will continue to be included in the jurisdiction of the High Court of the Western Pacific. The economy of the colony at present is based largely on Ocean Island phosphate deposits. Since these deposits are expected to be worked out in about eight years, alternative sources of revenue and employment will have to be sought soon.

Nauru. In March elections, all nine members of the Nauru Local Government Council were returned to office. The main function of the council is overseeing Nauru's various commercial enterprises. Parliament underwrites the council's debts for such enterprises but does not have a say in their direction. Island services were improved this year when Air Nauru was granted a full license in August to operate a service twice weekly between Nauru and Melbourne, Australia.

New Caledonia. Although eight political groups were competing, September elections produced a division almost identical to that of the outgoing Territorial Assembly. If anything, the antiautonomists showed a slight gain. Generally, New Caledonians voted for the men who had the best relations with France.

Papua—New Guinea. The year was one of great political advance, based on the February and March general elections for the 100 elective seats in the House of Assembly (seven members are appointed). The enlarged parliament is representative of a wide range of interests and consists predominantly of non-Europeans. As no one party held a majority, a coalition government was formed among Pangu Pati, the People's Progress Party, the New Guinea National Party, the Mataungan Association, and a number of independents. Michael Somare, a young Sepik who, in 1965, was a founder of the progressive Pangu Pati, emerged in his first six months in office as a strong leader.

One of the critical decisions facing the new government was the setting of a date for self-government, and December 1973 was decided on and approved by the House of Assembly. The next decision to be made is on the nature of the constitution. Somare favors a modified parliamentary system; others favor a presidential system. The ultimate decision will rest on the outcome of a submission to be made to the Constitutional Planning Committee.

The government hopes to produce by June 1973 a new economic five-year plan for Papua–New Guinea. A wide spectrum of trading partners is envisaged, but Somare is looking increasingly to Japan, a major buyer of the country's raw products, such as copper ore, timber, copra, and coffee. This increasing interest by Papua–New Guinea in the wider Pacific realm means that Australians will have to change their paternalistic attitude toward the country in order to retain good relations after independence.

Solomon Islands. During the year the British Solomon Islands Protectorate announced export records for both timber and copra. In timber, the production increase of 12.5 percent was in keeping with estimates made in the 1968 white paper on forestry policy. Copra produced by cooperatives, small holdings, and village producers reached an all-time record of 14,332 tons—2,933 tons more than was produced on plantations.

Tonga. Tonga took steps this year to stimulate its tourist industry. The moves included the appointment of an overseas tourist adviser, the formation of a tourist association, the appropriation of government funds for promotional work, the upgrading of the existing airport, the development of beaches, and the erection of tourist accommodations.

U.S. Trust Territory of the Pacific Islands. Negotiations concerning the future status of the U.S. Trust Territory of the Pacific Islands continued this year. A fourth round of talks was held at Palau in April and a fifth round at Washington, D.C., in July. The Palau talks resulted in a significant breakthrough because they guaranteed the four basic requirements of Micronesia: the right to self-determination, the right to decide on its own constitution and laws, the right to control its land, and the right to unilaterally terminate any compact with the United States. The details of the compact, including the length of time of an initial period during which the compact could be dissolved only by mutual consent, were discussed at the Washington meeting. A completed compact, if ratified by the Micronesian Congress and the U.S. Congress, will be put to a Micronesian referendum in 1973.

The negotiations did not cover the future status of the Mariana Islands, which is to be decided through direct dialogue between representatives of the Marianas and the United States. Marianas leaders hope for a close political relationship with the United States.

American Samoa. *Area and population.* Area, 76 sq. mi. Pop. (1970), 27,769.
British Solomon Islands. *Area and population.* Area, 11,500 sq. mi. Pop. (1970), 160,998.
Cook Islands. *Area and population.* Area, 93 sq. mi. Pop. (1971), 21,217.
Fiji. *Area and population.* Area, 7,055 sq. mi. Pop. (est. 1970), 524,457.
French Polynesia. *Area and population.* Area, 1,544 sq. mi. Pop. (est. 1971), 107,000.
Gilbert and Ellice Islands. *Area and population.* Area, 342 sq. mi. Pop. (1968), 57,000.
Nauru. *Area and population.* Area, 8.25 sq. mi. Pop. (1971), 6,927.
New Caledonia. *Area and population.* Area, 7,336 sq. mi. Pop. (est. 1971), 115,000.
Trust Territory of New Guinea. *Area and population.* Area, 92,160 sq. mi. Pop. (est. 1970), 1,800,000.
Territory of Papua. *Area and population.* Area, 86,100 sq. mi. Pop. (est. 1970), 660,000.
Tonga. *Area and population.* Area, 270 sq. mi. Pop. (est. 1970), 88,000.
Trust Territory of the Pacific Islands. *Area and population.* Area, 687 sq. mi. Pop. (1970), 102,250.
Western Samoa. *Area and population.* Area, 1,113 sq. mi. Pop. (1971), 143,547.
KENNETH W. ROBINSON

PAKISTAN. Politics and government. Zulfikar Ali Bhutto —a few days after he had stormed out of a Security Council debate on the Indo-Pakistani crisis—flew to Islamabad on December 20, 1971. Army officers were in a mutinous mood; there were public demonstrations against the regime in several cities; and the discredited and self-indulgent General Agha Muhammad Yahya Khan was burned in effigy by a noisy Peshawar mob. Yahya Khan's army and air force chiefs had forced him to announce his readiness to resign on December 19, and Bhutto's Pakistan People's Party (PPP) seemed to be the only group capable of controlling the situation.

Huge airport crowds chanting "Long live Bhutto, long live Chairman Mao" and "Down with Yahya" greeted Bhutto's return. Four hours later, and only four days after the Pakistani surrender in Bangladesh, he was sworn in as president and chief martial law administrator.

The new regime started off on a liberal note. Bogus by-elections which Yahya Khan had stage-managed in East Pakistan were canceled; a ban on Khan Abdul Wali Khan's National Awami Party (NAP), supported by Pathan tribesmen and holding a majority of provincial assembly seats in Baluchistan and the North-West Frontier Province (N.W.F.P.), was revoked; and the Bengali Awami League leader, Sheikh Mujibur Rahman, was released on January 8 after nine months of imprisonment. Although Bhutto resisted public demands for Yahya Khan's trial, he set up a three-man commission to investigate the Pakistani debacle in the east.

An administrative purge followed. Senior military officers were sacked; several members of the judiciary retired; and Bhutto promised to lead Pakistan back to parliamentary democracy. On the strength of that assurance, his rule was endorsed by 104 votes to 38 when the National Assembly met in mid-April. It was the first time in Pakistan's history that a head of state had been confirmed in office by a representative assembly elected by direct adult franchise.

The honeymoon appeared to be nearing its end, however, with increasing friction between the PPP and the partnership to the NAP with a faction of the Jamaat-i-Islami. Although this coalition in Baluchistan and the N.W.F.P. modified its autonomy demand, it still accused Bhutto of trying to erode its power base in the two provinces bordering on Afghanistan. The threat of civil war in these provinces had still not died down late in the year. In May, Wali Khan narrowly missed being killed in an assassination attempt. And in August his father, the veteran Pathan leader Khan Abdul Ghaffar Khan, warned against another civil war from his exile in Kabul.

In addition, there were strikes and riots by policemen, factory workers, and students in Hyderabad, Lahore, and Peshawar, as well as in Karachi, Rawalpindi, Sialkot, and the hill state of Swat. About 30 people were killed when Sindhis rioted in August for their regional language. Bhutto, himself a Sindhi, initially sent troops but later agreed to recognize Sindhi as the province's official language. The concession provoked an immediate backlash from Urdu-speaking Punjabis, and there were reports in October of a parallel government functioning in Baluchistan. The most serious threat to the government was the resignation on October 6 of Bhutto's deputy, Mian Mahmoud Ali Kasuri, who held the Law and Parliamentary Affairs portfolios. Two other ministers followed Kasuri, and the ruling PPP appeared to be splitting on ideological as well as provincial lines.

Constitution. After a 25-member committee, weighted in favor of the ruling coalition, had unsuccessfully grappled with the problem of drafting a constitution for four months, Bhutto took over the negotiations himself on October 14. Four days of discussions were followed by an all-party agreement on a 200-member national assembly and a senate in which all four provinces will be equally represented: this was the minimum to which Sind, Baluchistan, and the N.W.F.P.—which are apprehensive of Punjabi domination of the assembly—would agree. Bhutto's plea for a presidential form of government was rejected. Instead, the president, elected by both houses, will be a figurehead, and power will be vested in a prime minister who will be re-

OATH OF OFFICE. Pakistan's Zulfikar Ali Bhutto was sworn in as president in April, ending over 13 years of military dictatorship.

AP

sponsible to the national assembly. The draft constitution is expected to be ready by mid-December and to be adopted by April 21, 1973.

If the document is not approved, Pakistan's present constitution, adopted by the current Assembly on August 16, might become permanent. The NAP general secretary, Mahmud al-Haq Usmani, complains that it gives the president the powers of "the [British] governor general of India, the viceroy of India, the American president, and everything else." At the core of the dispute is Pakistan's search for a federal equilibrium—in particular, the refusal of the Punjab to relinquish its decision-making authority. The province accounts for over 57 percent of Pakistan's population, nearly 75 percent of its armed forces, and 55 out of a total of 86 PPP legislators.

Measures such as suspension of fundamental rights, curbs on press freedom, and the reappearance of martial law restrictions as statutory law have further consolidated this hegemony and strengthened federal authority. Punjabi control was further reinforced when Lieutenant General Tikka Khan—whose harshness in crushing a 1962–1963 uprising gained him the sobriquet "Butcher of Baluchistan" and who directed the early stages of the repressive campaign in East Pakistan—replaced the more moderate Lieutenant General Gul Hasan Khan as army chief.

Economic affairs. With a foreign debt estimated at more than $3,000 million, a 5.6 percent decline in industrial production, and the growth rate down from 6.6 to 1.4 percent, Pakistan's economy was in a shambles. Food prices soared when the rains failed, and spiraling inflation accounted for a 17 percent rise in the wholesale price index. The loss of East Bengal removed jute from the export list and deprived Pakistani manufacturers of a captive market which absorbed nearly 40 percent of their output.

Faced with this crisis, Bhutto devalued the rupee by about 57 percent (on May 11), obtained a standby credit of 100 million special drawing rights from the International Monetary Fund, and persuaded the aid-to-Pakistan consortium to reschedule debts amounting to $234 million. But defense spending consumes more than half of substantially reduced central expenditure, Pakistan's national income has been cut drastically, and Bhutto has found it difficult to live up to the radical pledges of his 1970 election manifesto.

Since wholesale nationalization of industries and the expropriation of landlords and capitalists, as set out in the PPP charter, would alienate the Punjab, Bhutto has had to be content with symbolic measures which do not hit too hard. To begin with, senior commerce officials were imprisoned, the passports of 200 prominent industrialists were impounded, and threats were held out against the 22 families who control 80 percent of Pakistan's industrial, banking, shipping, and insurance interests. The aim was to force the repatriation of an estimated $3,000 million, believed to be secreted away in foreign banks by a small group of influential families, but only $25 million trickled back, and the campaign was abandoned by March.

Under an economic reforms order, however, the government has taken control of a number of firms in ten basic industries. This was followed up with modified land reforms which are expected to yield several million acres for redistribution among the landless. At the same time, Bhutto announced large expenditures on agriculture and rural development. But these measures still fall short of expectations raised by the PPP's extreme radical posture during pre-election canvassing. There is unlikely to be enough money to implement promises of free education and higher wages, bonuses, and fringe benefits. Disillusionment exploded in a six-day industrial rampage in Karachi which apparently cost $4.5 million in lost production.

Foreign policy. Pakistan left the Commonwealth of Nations out of pique, but did not seriously pursue a doctrine of regarding it as an unfriendly act for any country to recognize Bangladesh. Nevertheless, Bhutto's main aim is to prevent Bangladesh from acquiring de jure respectability and to oppose changes in the South Asian balance of power arising out of the December war: his explanation for higher defense spending is that, apart from recouping heavy losses of hardware, Pakistan will have to improve its military capacity to maintain its customary political role in the subcontinent. Hence there was a hectic flurry of diplomatic activity as soon as he took over.

But his real courtship is of the United States, the Islamic world, and the People's Republic of China. Bhutto claims U.S. president Richard M. Nixon's personal support for Pakistan. The Indo-Soviet treaty of 1971 has obviously operated in Pakistan's favor. Washington's recognition of Bangladesh does not appear to have affected a friendship which was so demonstrably proved by the U.S. tilt toward Pakistan during the December war. However, Pakistan did withdraw from the Southeast Asia Treaty Organization in November.

Islamic nations have also always stood by Pakistan, and Bhutto's 13-day tour of 14 countries on the eve of his Simla

summit meeting with Prime Minister Indira Gandhi merely underlined an accepted fact. Jordan, Iran, Saudi Arabia, Libya, Abu Dhabi, and Kuwait have wholeheartedly endorsed the Pakistani position in the United Nations and in the councils of the Afro-Asian world.

Chinese support, however, has been both more explicit and more effective. China has provided diplomatic support, eased loan-repayment terms, supplied economic and military aid, and vetoed the Bangladesh application for UN membership. Having emerged as the major Asian power after the 1962 border war with India, China is bound to react strongly to any development which appears to favor India in the leadership stakes. India's close ties with the Soviet Union are an added irritant, but too much should not be made of Peking's ideological affinity with Bhutto's diluted socialism. Chinese diplomatic support for Pakistan, easier repayment terms for a $200 million loan, economic assistance, the UN veto against Bangladesh, and the visit to Islamabad by the Chinese vice–foreign minister, Chiao Kuan-hua, are probably functions of China's suspicion of India.

India. Although Bhutto has talked of accommodation with India, he is not inclined to attach much credence to Mrs. Gandhi's argument that it is in India's interest to ensure the integrity of Pakistan. He may not actually believe that India is out to dismember Pakistan, with the Soviet Union's help, but many Punjabis obviously do; in any case, having preached confrontation for years, Bhutto is to some extent the prisoner of his own past pronouncements.

Kashmir remains the major stumbling block to a normalization of relations. Pakistan wants the prewar situation restored, but the Indian position has hardened since the war and there is no intention of retreating to the 1949 cease-fire line. Pakistan, having launched its main armed thrust in Kashmir, is equally unwilling to surrender two captured border posts. Talks between military commanders and officials, which followed the Simla summit, have clarified both positions, but without much sign of a rapprochement. In fact, much of the goodwill generated in Simla evaporated as the year wore on. The case of more than 91,000 prisoners of war is a far more explosive issue, especially since 70 percent of the ranks are recruited in the Punjab. Bhutto is under great domestic pressure from wives and relatives, but reports that he has started to replace 74,000 regular army men among the POW's suggest that he is not counting on their early return. One theory is that POW's, suspected of indoctrination in captivity, will be demobilized in any case.

Bangladesh. Pakistani National Assembly seats have been allocated to Bengalis, and the names of Sheikh Mujibur Rahman and other Awami Leaguers were included in the list of members. However, Bhutto has continued to blow hot and cold: he claims that "Muslim Bengal will always be part of Pakistan," although this intransigence has not lessened his efforts to get a dialogue going with Rahman. It would appear that Bhutto wants two issues settled to his satisfaction before he recognizes Dacca. He would like guarantees for the future safety of 1.5 million Urdu-speaking Muslims (popularly referred to as Biharis) in Bangladesh, and he must persuade Rahman not to go ahead with the proposed trials of 1,500 prisoners of war as war criminals. Given Pakistan's mood of bitterness and resentment, such trials could mean the end of civilian rule. (*See* PEOPLE IN THE NEWS: Zulfikar Ali Bhutto.)

Area and population. Area, 310,723 sq. mi. Pop. (est. 1971), 57.2 million. Principal cities (est. 1970): Islamabad (cap.), 60,000; Karachi, 2.5 million; Lahore, 2 million.
Government. Republic with unicameral National Assembly with all-party Council of Ministers. Pres., Zulfikar Ali Bhutto; vice-pres., Nurul Amin.
Finance. Monetary unit, Pakistani rupee; R1 = US$0.0925. Budget (est. 1972–1973): development expenditure, Rs4,150 million; deficit, Rs250 million.
Trade (1971). Exports (including reexports and exports to East Bengal), Rs3,488.4 million. Imports (including from East Bengal), Rs4,406.2 million.
SUNANDA K. DATTA-RAY

PANAMA AND THE CANAL ZONE. Panama. *Government and politics.* After four years in power, General Omar Torrijos Herrera consolidated his position as strong man of Panama and wrote a new constitution. On August 6, elections were held for 505 representatives (*corregidores*), two of whom were elected in the Canal Zone, thus increasing Panamanian claims to sovereignty over the area.

The Assembly of Community Representatives met on September 11 and proclaimed General Torrijos "maximum leader of the Panamanian revolution," in addition to reconfirming him as commander and chief of the Panamanian National Guard. Torrijos was given this special title to allow him to keep real power, without being burdened with paper work, which he complained prevented him "from having contact with the people." The Assembly later reelected Demetrio B. Lakas to the largely ceremonial post of president of the republic and Arturo Sucre, member of Torrijos' junta, as vice-president. The new government organization went into effect on October 11, the fourth anniversary of Torrijos' revolution. It was the highlight of several days of public festivities and anti-American speeches.

Foreign affairs. The new constitution, unlike its predecessors, did not accept the U.S. presence in the Canal Zone. Furthermore, the Assembly rejected the annual U.S. payment of $1,930,000 for the use of the canal. It declared that the "Canal Zone . . . has not been purchased, or conquered . . . or its sovereignty been transferred. . . . but it has been occupied arbitrarily." The rejection of the payment was symbolic, because Panama had mortgaged it for several years to come. But these measures gave Torrijos a stronger hand in the negotiations for a new treaty between the United States and Panama.

There were other incidents that helped strain relations with the United States. In March, Congressman John Murphy (D, N.Y.) accused Panama's foreign minister, Juan Antonio Tack, and General Torrijos' brother Moises of involvement in smuggling narcotics into the United States. This move helped to cause the suspension of treaty negotiations and also resulted in the expulsion from Panama of three U.S. narcotics agents.

In June the Panamanian government took over the Electric Bond and Share Company, which supplied Panama City and Colón with telephone, electric, and gas service and was owned by the Boise-Cascade Corporation. The Panamanians maintained the company failed to pay fuel bills, constantly opposed government policy, and had not installed any new equipment. The company replied that it could not modernize, charging that the government set low rates.

There was some uneasiness among business people because of several diplomatic and cultural exchanges with Cuba, which included a Cuban film festival in Panama City and a visit to Havana by a Panamanian cultural delegation, led by the head of the University of Panama, a former Communist.

Economic affairs. Panama made economic progress, and the business community showed confidence in Torrijos. Many projects and buildings were being constructed, including a multimillion dollar airport expansion program and the $40 million Bayono hydroelectric dam. Financed largely with U.S. funds, the $150 million project to close the Darien gap in the Inter-American Highway was reported in progress as well. New programs for 1972 included a hydroelectric plant at La Fortuna, a $6 million project to improve port facilities, and a program to acquire 40 new shrimp boats. A Japanese consortium started to develop copper deposits at Petaquilla, and the first magnetite ore extracted from the sea was exported to Japan in May. There were also closer economic ties with both Costa Rica and Nicaragua.

Other developments. The government planned to build about a dozen new hospitals. Substantial tax increases were levied on cigarettes, liquor, and gasoline. These taxes

434 PARAGUAY

directly affected the middle class, but Torrijos discounted them nevertheless as being pro-American. On the other hand, Torrijos built up support among the working class with a new labor law that set minimum wages, established compulsory collective bargaining, provided a one month's bonus (*aguinaldo*) every year, and protected street vendors and domestic servants.

Canal Zone. In fiscal 1971, transits of the canal were down from 14,829 the year before to 14,829, and the number of Canal Company employees dropped from 12,092 to 11,560. This trend continued in 1972 because of the decline of U.S. involvement in Vietnam. In general, the atmosphere in the Zone and the Republic was one of watchful waiting for the expected showdown between Panama and the United States over the future of the canal.

Republic of Panama. *Area and population.* Area, 29,209 sq. mi. Pop. (est. 1971), 1,500,000. Principal cities: Panama City (cap.), 389,000; Colón, 65,600.
Government. Military government; head, General Omar Torrijos Herrera; for. min., Juan Antonio Tack.
Finance. Monetary unit, balboa; 1 balboa = US$1.00. Budget (1969): balanced at US$130 million.
Trade (1970). Imports, US$240.5 million; exports, US$90.8 million. Principal imports: manufactured goods, machinery, chemicals, fuels, minerals. Principal exports: bananas, petroleum products, fresh shrimps, sugar.
Education (1968). Enrollment: primary, 221,692; secondary, 69,346; higher, 9,390.
Canal Zone. *Area and population.* Area, 553 sq. mi. Pop. (1970), 50,344. Principal towns: Balboa, 2,568; Rainbow City, 2,385; Gamboa, 2,137. Almost 80 percent are U.S. citizens.
Government. Under U.S. control. Gov., Major General David S. Parker.
THEODORE S. CREEDMAN

PARAGUAY. Foreign affairs. The extradition to the United States of a major figure in the international drug traffic put Paraguay in the spotlight in 1972. Auguste Joseph Ricord, a 61-year-old Corsican known as Monsieur Andres in the narcotics trade, was handed over to U.S. authorities and flown under heavy guard to New York City on September 2 to face indictments pending against him in U.S. courts. The circumstances of the lengthy extradition proceedings—which lasted 18 months—soured U.S.–Paraguay relations.

In Washington officials charged that the Paraguayan government had needlessly delayed Ricord's extradition. During the protracted proceedings in the Paraguayan courts, the United States granted Paraguay a lucrative quota in the price-supported U.S. sugar market for the first time in history. There were dark allegations in the U.S. and international press that Paraguay's military dictator, Alfredo Stroessner, was delaying the Ricord extradition to gain other foreign aid benefits from the United States. There were also charges that Stroessner's reluctance was partly motivated by the complicity of high-ranking Paraguayan military officers, whose support he needs to stay in power, in the drug-smuggling operations masterminded by Ricord.

Whether the charges of calculated delay were true or not, Ricord's extradition was arranged only after a visit to Paraguay in late August by Nelson G. Gross, the U.S. State Department's senior adviser and coordinator for international narcotics matters. Gross reportedly told Stroessner that U.S. economic and military aid, worth about $11 million annually, would be terminated unless Ricord were promptly extradited.

In Paraguay and in neighboring Argentina, where Ricord is a naturalized citizen, the case caused ruffled feelings. Officials of both countries complained that Ricord's extradition had been rammed through because of U.S. pressure and without sufficient deference to the slow workings of the Paraguayan judicial system.

Ricord has been involved in criminal activities as far back as World War II, when he was a Nazi collaborator in German-occupied Marseille, France. After the war French courts tried him for murder, armed robbery, and other offenses and sentenced him to death *in absentia* in 1950. By that time, Ricord had taken up residence in Buenos Aires, Argentina, and had become the proprietor of a restaurant, a center for prostitution and other underworld activities. Using the Argentine restaurant and another one he later bought in Asunción as fronts, Ricord directed a global narcotics ring responsible for smuggling an estimated $2 billion worth of heroin and other dangerous drugs into the United States, according to U.S. officials.

Most observers considered it doubtful that Ricord's extradition would affect Stroessner's chances for reelection. Shortly after Ricord was handed over, Stroessner, who has carefully manipulated public opinion over the case to make himself appear strong in the face of U.S. pressures, was confirmed as the candidate for a fifth five-year term by Paraguay's dominant Colorado Party. The elections are scheduled for February 1973.

Economic developments. During 1972, Paraguayan authorities managed to keep meat exports relatively high and to some extent succeeded in pushing diversification of the nation's primarily agricultural output. Production of soybeans for 1972 was estimated at 100,000 tons, more than double the figure for 1971. Earnings from the new U.S. sugar quota were realized for the first time during 1972, and Paraguay also shipped 5,000 tons of refined sugar to Greece.

Although a small and basically resource-poor nation, Paraguay has developed some new exports, chiefly unprocessed and processed lumber products. It found good markets among its neighbors for such other exports as tung and vegetable oils, hides, and tannic acid used in leather tanning.

Paraguay continued to consult with Brazil, its powerful northern neighbor, on the joint development of hydroelectric power on Paraguayan territory. Reportedly, secret negotiations between the two countries are well advanced on the construction of a huge new hydroelectric plant which would be financed largely by Brazilian capital.

There was little progress on persistent domestic problems, among them the continuing heavy migration of people from the countryside to Asunción. At present, well over one-fifth of Paraguay's total population lives in the capital city, and consequently there has been a sharp rise in the demand for consumer goods and jobs.

The government has done little to equalize the distribution of Paraguay's tax burden. Taxes still fall heaviest on productive small businessmen. Smugglers of drugs and other merchandise continue to avoid paying taxes on their lucrative operations. Payoffs and bribes remain commonplace, and corruption among the members of the ruling elite seems to grow the longer Stroessner remains in power.

Area and population. Area, 157,048 sq. mi. Pop. (1970), 2,-395,614. Principal cities: Asunción (cap.), 437,136; Encarnación (est. 1969), 46,000.
Government. Constitutional republic with bicameral legislature. Pres., General Alfredo Stroessner. Dominant party, Colorado.
Finance. Monetary unit, guaraní; G1 = US$0.008. Budget (1969): revenue, US$70.3 million; expenditures, US$82.8 million.
Trade (1968). Imports, US$72.7 million; exports, US$47.5 million. Principal imports: foodstuffs, vehicles and machinery, chemicals, fuels, textiles. Principal exports: meat products, timber, oils, tobacco. Principal trading partners: United States, Argentina, West Germany, United Kingdom.
Education (1968). Enrollment: primary, 400,000; secondary, 45,000; higher, 7,500.
Armed forces. Army, 11,000; navy, 1,700; air force, 800.
NATHAN A. HAVERSTOCK

PENNSYLVANIA. Flood disaster. Torrential rains from tropical storm Agnes in late June caused the worst flooding in Pennsylvania's history. Forty-seven people lost their lives and 250,000 were left homeless in the flood area, which extended from Wilkes-Barre in eastern Pennsylvania to Pittsburgh in the state's southwest corner; property damage was put by the state at over $1 billion, a figure disputed by federal officials. Hardest hit were the towns and cities along the Susquehanna River, including Harrisburg, where

STORM OVER AGNES. At the microphone in a Wilkes-Barre, Pa., press conference, Housing Secretary George Romney clashed with Governor Milton Shapp (right) and hurricane victims who claimed that federal flood relief was inadequate to cover their losses.

the governor's mansion was flooded with 8 feet of water, Wilkes-Barre, where the Susquehanna overflowed 38-foot-high dikes, and Sunbury, where flooding forced the evacuation of 10,000 people.

In the flood's wake came controversy over the adequacy and management of the relief programs to aid flood victims. Months after the waters of the rampaging rivers had receded, thousands were still homeless. Meanwhile, both presidential candidates toured washed-out Wilkes-Barre; the White House catered a picnic for cleanup crews; and Governor Milton J. Shapp, Secretary of Housing and Urban Development George Romney, and a group of flood victims got into a public shouting match in Wilkes-Barre on August 9 over the amount of federal flood aid being provided. Flood relief also became a major legislative issue, with senators and representatives bickering over just how and how much state money should be spent. They finally settled on a figure of $150 million.

Legislation. The legislative session was newsworthy not so much for what it produced as for what it did not. The lawmakers failed to pass bills reducing the legislature's size, establishing a strong no-fault automobile insurance plan, relaxing milk price controls, instituting voting reforms, and beginning the process of amending the state constitution to permit a graduated income tax.

The legislature did reapportion the state's legislative and congressional districts according to population (Pennsylvania's number of U.S. representatives declined from 27 to 25 as a result of the 1970 census); get a state lottery moving, with the proceeds going for tax relief for the elderly; liberalize workmen's compensation benefits; and pass another bill providing financial aid to parochial schools (previous private-school-aid laws have been struck down as unconstitutional first by state courts and then by the U.S. Supreme Court).

The legislators also voted themselves healthy $8,400 a year raises and $2,500 expense accounts, bringing each member's total income (salary and expenses) to $18,100; formerly each legislator made $7,200 a year in salary and had an $8,400 "unaccountable" expense account.

Bicentennial. After much wrangling, Philadelphia lost its position as host to what had been planned as a $600 million commemoration of the United States' 200th birthday in 1976. The National Bicentennial Commission opted for less costly "local celebrations."

Teachers' strikes. The new law setting up collective bargaining and arbitration procedures for disgruntled public workers failed to prevent crippling teachers' strikes throughout the state in September 1972. The walkouts, undertaken primarily to achieve higher pay and a greater role in determining classroom methods, delayed some school openings by as much as a month.

Home rule. A movement snowballed during the year to break the state legislature's hold on communities' decision-making apparatus. Many communities voted to set up home rule charter commissions to determine what type of government each local jurisdiction wanted instead of letting the determination be made by state law.

Culture. Plans for the 1973 Pittsburgh International Exhibition of Painting and Sculpture were canceled by the Carnegie Museum because of construction on a new wing intended to house the Sarah Mellon Scaife collection of impressionist works. The international exhibition had been a major art attraction for more than 70 years.

For election results and campaign highlights, see the special supplement ELECTION '72.

Area and population. Area, 45,333 sq. mi. Pop. (1970), 11,-793,909. Principal cities: Harrisburg (cap.), 65,828; Philadelphia, 1,927,863; Pittsburgh, 512,789; Erie, 125,941; Allentown, 108,926; Scranton, 102,294.

Government. Gov., Milton J. Shapp (D); lt. gov., Ernest P. Kline (D); treas., Grace M. Sloan (D); aud., Robert P. Casey (D); atty. gen., J. Shane Creamer (D); secy. of state, C. DeLores Tucker (D). Legislature: senate, 26 D, 24 R; house, 112 D, 90 R, 1 vacancy.

Finance (fiscal 1973). Budget, $3.67 billion; expected revenue, $3.674 billion. Cash on hand (Sept. 1972), $42 million.

Education (1970–1971). Public elementary schools, 3,442; enrollment, 1,264,247; teachers, 55,270. Public secondary schools, 1,-202; enrollment, 1,099,570; teachers, 53,502. Private and parochial elementary schools, 1,301; enrollment, 387,478; teachers, 13,375. Private and parochial secondary schools, 290; enrollment, 129,673; teachers, 7,643.

RALPH C. BREM

People in the News

AGNEW, SPIRO. *See the special supplement* ELECTION '72.

ALLEN, WOODY (1935–   ). When Allen Stewart Konigsberg was growing up in Flatbush, he used to convulse classmates at Midwood High with his deadpan delivery when he did things like call his alma

WOODY ALLEN

mater "a school for emotionally disturbed teachers" or quip, "I failed to make the chess team because of my height."

Encouraged by their laughter, Konigsberg began sending gags to Walter Winchell and other Broadway columnists, using the name Woody Allen. Unlike most high school comics, Allen sounded as funny to the pros as he did in homeroom. By the time he was 18, he was writing comedy routines for television star Herb Shriner. At 22, he was making $1,500 a week with Sid Caesar.

Today, Allen is considered by many to be the best all-around funnyman in the business, a creative genius whose zany style ranks with the Marx Brothers. He has become, without doubt, the most versatile comedian: light of the late-night talk shows, contributor to *Playboy* and the *New Yorker*, nightclub comic whose patter has been packaged in three LP albums, writer-director-star of such movies as *Bananas* and *Take the Money and Run*, and playwright with two shows to his credit (*Play It Again, Sam* and *Don't Drink the Water*).

This year, Allen turned *Play It Again, Sam* into a box office success movie starring—of course—himself as the hapless failure haunted by the ghost of tough-talking Humphrey Bogart. He also managed to write, direct, and play in a flawed but funny film adaptation of the best seller *Everything You Always Wanted to Know About Sex* (*But Were Afraid to Ask)*.

Woody's favorite role is the loser, a part he embellishes every day. Wispy and dejected-looking, Allen was born in Brooklyn on December 1, 1935, grew to be 5' 6" tall—then stopped forever. Using his life as the launching pad for his bizarre flights of comic fancy, Allen describes himself as a runty little guy growing up in a dead-end neighborhood where, he tells audiences, the kids were so tough they stole hubcaps off moving cars. His family couldn't afford a dog, Allen continues, "So my parents got me an ant. I called it Spot." The laughter only makes Woody sadder. His eyes wide with pained surprise, his forehead permanently corrugated, he goes on to talk in bewilderment about his unhappy first marriage to a girl so childish that "one time I was taking a bath, and for no reason, she came in and sank my boats."

Although Allen leaves his audiences helpless with laughter, he maintains he is deadly serious about his work. "I write comically," he says, "because things look that way to me. But I'm deadly serious. I don't watch funny movies; I watch Ingmar Bergman. He's concerned with the silence of God, and in some small way so am I."

ANDERSON, JACK (1922–   ). "We hit you—pow, then you issue a denial, and—bam, we really let you have it." It was a big year for syndicated columnist Jack Anderson and for his philosophy, as expounded by Anderson associate Brit Hume.

First, Anderson deeply embarrassed the Nixon administration by publicizing the proceedings of a secret December conference on the India-Pakistan war attended by top government officials, including presidential aide Henry Kissinger. Kissinger complained that Anderson had taken his remarks "out of context." Anderson supplied the context by releasing the texts of the official memoranda recording the meetings. For releasing these "secret-sensitive" documents, Anderson was later awarded the Pulitzer Prize.

JACK ANDERSON

436

In February, Anderson was back again with another blockbuster, quoting a memorandum allegedly linking the Justice Department's favorable settlement of antitrust suits against ITT with the company's pledge of $400,000 for the Republican National Convention. Anderson pressed his accusation before the Senate Judiciary Committee, holding up confirmation of Richard Kleindienst as attorney general. Further, he accused ITT of conspiring with the CIA to keep Salvador Allende from assuming the presidency of Chile.

The role of muckraker and scandalmonger seemed an odd one for a nondrinking, nonsmoking Mormon. But Anderson regards himself, with considerable self-righteousness, as a "watchdog on government" and refuses to cultivate high government officials or political leaders as sources. Instead, the column's best information often comes from disgruntled secretaries and fired low-echelon employees.

"People in power get too puffed up with their own importance . . ." notes the round-faced, 50-year-old journalist. "I consider it my function . . . to deflate the windbags. . . . People in power think that their positions entitle them to do as they please. . . ."

Jackson Northman Anderson was born in Long Beach, Calif., on October 19, 1922, but grew up in Utah, where he attended the University of Utah and worked as a reporter for the Salt Lake City *Tribune*. He arrived in Washington in 1947 after spending two years as a Mormon missionary in the South and a stint as an army newsman in China. He went to work as a legman for Drew Pearson, who had started his muckraking column, "The Washington Merry-Go-Round," in 1932.

For several years Anderson was Pearson's low-paid, anonymous investigator. When Anderson finally decided to start out on his own, Pearson begged him to stay and promised he would inherit the column, which he did when Pearson died in 1969. Today, "The Washington Merry-Go-Round" is syndicated in 965 newspapers—300 more than when Pearson ran it—and Anderson's staff has been expanded to four investigative reporters plus two secretaries.

Anderson is considered anti-Nixon in his political outlook, but his most embarrassing moment this year came when he tried to give the Democrats equal time and dealt vice-presidential candidate Thomas Eagleton a low blow in July, hitting him with a "pow" when he didn't have a "bam" to back it up.

On television, Anderson stated that he had proof of half a dozen drunk and reckless driving arrests against Eagleton in his home state of Missouri. Eagleton called the charge "a damnable lie"—and Anderson could not produce any evidence. The reporter finally retracted his statement and apologized personally to Eagleton. "I went ahead with a story that I should not have gone ahead with and that was unfair to you, and you have my apology."

BEARD, DITA (1918–   ). It began in February, when Washington columnist Jack Anderson accused the Nixon administration of dropping antitrust suits against the gigantic International Telephone and Telegraph corporation in exchange for an ITT promise of $400,000 to help underwrite the Republican Convention in San Diego.

As proof of his charge, Anderson released a confidential memorandum allegedly written by a 53-year-old ITT lobbyist named Dita Beard. In the document, Mrs. Beard reported that, at a 1971 Kentucky Derby party, Attorney General John Mitchell had indicated that the cases pending against ITT would be settled in a way favorable to the company. The memorandum went on to state, "I am convinced

DITA BEARD

. . . that our noble commitment has gone a long way toward our negotiations on the mergers eventually coming out as Hal wants them." "Hal" was reported to be Harold S. Geneen, president and chairman of ITT.

Shortly after Anderson released the controversial memorandum, Mrs. Dita Davis Beard dropped from sight. She surfaced days later as a patient in the cardiac unit of Rocky Mountain Osteopathic Hospital in Denver, where doctors pronounced her too ill to testify before the Senate Judiciary Committee.

Weeks later, her doctors finally allowed their patient to be questioned. Seven senators then flew to Denver and gathered around her hospital bed. With an oxygen tube taped to her nose, Mrs. Beard denied writing the memo as published by Anderson. Asked why she had not repudiated it in the beginning, she said that ITT had not believed her denial.

After 2½ hours of testifying, Mrs. Beard clutched her chest and moaned. Apparently it was a heart seizure. The embarrassed senators retreated back to Washington. When doctors announced their

patient could not be questioned again for six months, the investigation dragged on, but without much steam. Richard Kleindienst, the attorney general designate who had asked the Judiciary Committee to reopen hearings on his nomination to check out Anderson's charges, was finally confirmed in June.

Dita Beard was an army brat born in November 1918 at Fort Riley, Kan. Her father, a hard-drinking colonel, treated Dita like a son and taught her to be self-reliant. She made her debut in Washington and then, during World War II, went to North Africa with the Red Cross.

Mrs. Beard's first marriage was to a fighter pilot, her second to Cameron Beard, a flag manufacturer. Both marriages ended in divorce, and she was left with five children. At this point she went to work for ITT as a $30,000-a-year lobbyist.

Admittedly a hard drinker (she tells of packing 12 bottles of liquor with her to Casablanca during the war) and proud of her reputation as a feisty woman, Dita Beard told a reporter before the Senate questioning, "When my health was good, I wasn't afraid of anything. . . . Not even of that bunch of little bums coming out here. But I don't know how I'm going to face it."

BEAUVOIR, SIMONE DE (1908–   ). When France's leading woman intellectual wrote *The Second Sex* in 1949, she thought she knew the answer to the problems of the unemancipated female: switch to socialism. Two decades later, after studying the lot of women in Communist countries, the fine-boned, austere-looking Simone de Beauvoir decided that the cause needed stronger action. In November 1971 she joined with women from around the world in a protest march on Paris and, along with other prominent French women, signed a manifesto declaring she had had an abortion, a criminal act in France.

Communism did not turn out the way Marx had envisioned it as far as women are concerned, the author told a reporter in the new feminist magazine, *Ms.* In Communist countries, as in the capitalist countries, "men have deeply internalized the idea of their own superiority. They are not ready to give up what I call their superiority complex."

If Simone de Beauvoir was angry with the cavalier behavior of men toward women, she was equally furious when she discovered how the world treats its elderly. As she herself approached the traditional retirement age of 65, she turned her attention to what society holds in store for the aged. The result was *The Coming of Age*, whose U.S. edition appeared this year.

"Society looks upon old age as a kind of shameful secret that it is unseemly to mention," she wrote. "As far as old people are concerned, this society is not only guilty but downright criminal." By ignoring the aged, she noted, "we even reach

SIMONE DE BEAUVOIR

the point of turning it [ostracism] against ourselves, for in the old person that we must become, we refuse to recognize ourselves."

Speaking out against society's evils has been a cause for Simone de Beauvoir for four decades. Born in Paris on January 9, 1908, Simone de Beauvoir watched her well-to-do father lose a fortune and sink lower and lower on the social scale. Al-

ZULFIKAR ALI BHUTTO

though at first as devout a Catholic as her mother, Beauvoir later swung over to her father's point of view and became an unregenerate skeptic. "My disbelief never wavered," she wrote.

When she was 20 and a fractious student at France's foremost teacher's college, Beauvoir met 23-year-old Jean-Paul Sartre, the existentialist author who has been her companion ever since. For long years, although both inveighed against the inequities of capitalism, it was Sartre who did the writing. Beauvoir was 40 before she published *The Second Sex*, the best seller which has been translated into 19 languages.

Later she won the coveted Prix Goncourt for her 1954 novel *The Mandarins*. With the prize money she bought a comfortable duplex apartment on a tree-shaded street in Paris. Sartre lives close by. They usually lunch or dine together and spend quiet evenings listening to classical music. Beauvoir also spends long hours answering letters—primarily from women around the world.

In spite of her longtime liaison with Sartre, Beauvoir has become in the past two years an ardent feminist, actively participating in the struggle. In her mind, there is nothing unresolved in this. "Women's liberation," she says, "will surely bring about new kinds of relationships between human beings, and men as well as women will be changed. Women, and men, too, must become human beings first and foremost."

BHUTTO, ZULFIKAR ALI (1928–   ). "I am a man who works 24 hours a day," the new president of Pakistan promised his people in January. The energetic Zulfikar Ali Bhutto had descended on the capital, Islamabad, determined to save what was left of his shattered country.

The bitter civil war between east and west had ended when India joined the Bengali guerrillas and defeated the Pakistani Army in December 1971. What had been East Pakistan proclaimed itself the new nation of Bangladesh.

The Pakistan that remained was in a state of shock. Its president, General Agha Muhammad Yahya Khan, and his military advisers had lost their claim on the government when they lost the war, and hints of a new civil war in West Pakistan were heard. At this point Bhutto, with the help of some of the military, stepped into the presidency.

One of his first acts was to fire most of the top military brass in an attempt to soothe the angry Pakistanis, who felt humiliated by their loss to the traditional enemy—India.

In the past, Bhutto was as anti-Indian as the next Pakistani. But as president he began to talk of a peaceful settlement of differences. (Since India still held more than 91,000 Pakistani prisoners, he had little choice.) He ordered the release of Sheikh Mujibur Rahman, the Bangladesh

hero who had been in a West Pakistani jail since early spring.

The tireless Bhutto also tried to crack down on the "22 families," who controlled a huge portion of Pakistan's wealth, but the rich were too powerful, and Bhutto had to back off in order to preserve the tenuous stability that existed.

Bhutto, who bills himself as "a man of the people," is actually the son of a rich landowner. He was born near Larkana, in the province of Sind. He was graduated from the University of California at Berkeley in 1950 with a degree in political science and then studied law at Oxford.

In 1951, Bhutto married Nusrat Ispahani, a wealthy Iranian. They have four children, including one being educated in the United States.

Bhutto became a United Nations delegate in 1957 and was minister of commerce at the age of 30. As Ayub Khan's foreign minister from 1963 to 1966, he struck up friendly relations with Mainland China.

Pakistan's hard-working, fast-talking president is now credited with rescuing his country from ruin. Ironically, it was Bhutto's Pakistan People's Party which precipitated the disastrous civil war.

LEONID BREZHNEV

Rather than accept Sheikh Mujibur Rahman as prime minister in early 1971, Bhutto refused to participate in the National Assembly. Yahya Khan postponed the National Assembly meeting, and war broke out in East Pakistan.

BREZHNEV, LEONID (1906–   ). When Richard Nixon stepped off the plane at the Moscow airport in May, President Nikolai Podgorny and Premier Aleksei Kosygin of the Soviet Union were on hand to welcome him. But the man the president

really came to see was not there. Leonid Ilyich Brezhnev, secretary general of the Communist Party—and the real leader of the Soviet Union—preferred to wait for a private Kremlin meeting later in the day.

During the week-long summit talks, the president and the party chief sat down and signed a series of documents aimed at bringing the two cold war enemies closer together. Most important, of course, was the agreement to limit nuclear weapons, but there were also promises to pool medical and environmental know-how and a decision to have American and Soviet spaceships meet in orbit in 1975.

Although the Soviet Union currently supplies a large portion of North Vietnam's military assistance, the smiling Brezhnev ignored the recent American decision to mine Haiphong harbor during Nixon's visit, indicating a willingness to bargain with his country's major opponent. "The Brezhnev years have proven that the Soviet Union can get along without a charismatic leader," the New York *Times* observed, "without frenetic changes of direction, without going to the brink of nuclear war, without arbitrary rule and terror."

Brezhnev came to power as Nikita Khrushchev's protégé. Brezhnev followed Khrushchev up the power ladder, faithfully supporting his mentor until 1964, when Khrushchev's erratic behavior grew too outrageous to ignore. Then the protégé joined other Presidium members in ousting Khrushchev. He has never mentioned him in public again, nor did he attend Khrushchev's funeral.

Unnerved by years of one-man rule, the Presidium insisted that a triumvirate of president, premier, and party chief should rule the country. It did not take Brezhnev long to garner most of the power for himself.

As the Soviet and American leaders talked and toasted each other in champagne, Pat Nixon was touring Moscow with Brezhnev's wife, Viktoria Petrovna. The Brezhnevs have two grown children and live in a comfortable five-bedroom apartment. The party chief is known as an avid soccer fan and car fancier who has been seen at the stadium in his Rolls Royce Silver Cloud. In fact, before leaving Moscow, President Nixon presented Brezhnev with a 1972 Cadillac.

The Soviet Union's more relaxed attitude toward the United States follows Brezhnev's plans for a détente with Western Europe. Seven months before Nixon's visit, he happily toured Paris with French president Pompidou, acting, according to one British journalist, just like "your friendly neighborhood superpower."

BUNKERS, THE (1971–   ). Five Emmies. Not bad for the quiet, home-loving Bunkers from Queens. Archie, the blue-collar bigot, got one, and so did his ding-bat wife, Edith. Archie's "weepin' Nellie atheist" daughter, Gloria, shared one, and

THE BUNKERS

the Bunkers' show, *All in the Family*, made it as Best Comedy Series.

Some people didn't think it was so funny, but American television viewers just couldn't get enough of Archie Bunker inveighing ineffectually against the pinkos, the meatheads, the freaks—and, above all, that Polack meathead son-in-law—who threaten his very carefully ordered existence.

Carroll O'Connor, the veteran character actor who plays Archie to choleric perfection, explains his appeal: "Archie Bunker is one of the most indigenous American types. His dilemma is coping with a world that is changing in front of him. He doesn't know what to do, except lose his temper, mouth his poisons, look elsewhere to fix the blame for his own discomfort." In other words, Archie is a little like the rest of us, a real person in the very unreal world of television.

All in the Family is loosely adapted from a popular British program called *Till Death Us Do Part*. When producer Norman Lear tried to sell the idea to ABC, the network paid for two pilots, then backed away from the show's controver-

sial material and free-swinging style. Two years later, CBS picked up the show and ran it as a midseason replacement. The program slept for a few weeks, then took off.

O'Connor, born in New York City on August 2, 1924, came to his current role by a roundabout route that included a B.A. in history from University College, Dublin; three years at the Dublin Gate Theatre; and roles in over 20 films, including *Lonely Are the Brave*, *Cleopatra*, and *Waterhole #3*. In addition to acting, O'Connor has practiced the crafts of playwright, screenwriter, lyricist, singer, and nightclub performer. He wrote the closing theme for *All in the Family*, entitled "Remembering You," and recently included the song in his first album.

Jean Stapleton, who plays Archie's wife, Edith, is also a native of New York City. She appeared in both the Broadway stage productions and the film versions of *Damn Yankees* and *Bells Are Ringing*, and she had featured roles in *Up the Down Staircase* and *Klute*.

Sally Struthers plays daughter Gloria. Born in Portland, Ore., she studied at the

Pasadena Playhouse. In addition to work in television commercials, she played in a supporting role in *Five Easy Pieces*. She also has a role in Sam Peckinpah's new film, *The Getaway*.

Rob Reiner plays meathead Mike Stivic, Gloria's student-husband. The son of actor-writer-director Carl Reiner, Rob was born in New York City and got his break as a writer for the Smothers Brothers. He played in the movie *Summertree* and has appeared on the television shows *That Girl, Gomer Pyle, Beverly Hillbillies, Room 222,* and *Headmaster*.

Observes actor-comedian O'Connor, "I frankly thought the American public was too dour to laugh at itself . . . I was fooled. I'm gratified."

CARLTON, STEVE (1944–   ). It was late in February of this year that left-handed pitcher Steve Carlton got the bad news: he had been traded by the St. Louis Cardinals to the ragamuffin Philadelphia Phillies in exchange for another pitcher, righthanded Rick Wise. In giving up Carlton, the Cardinals knew they were losing a high-quality pitcher, one who in 1969 had established an all-time major league high (since broken) by striking out 19 Mets in one game and who had won 20 games in 1971. However, Cardinal owner Gussie Busch was fed up with his holdouts for higher pay, first in 1970 and again early this year. "I hope he never pitches another inning for us," Busch said in February and then traded him away. Certainly, it seemed unlikely that even someone as capable as Carlton could win another 20 games with the bumbling Phillies.

But Carlton had other ideas, very positive ones. It seems that in 1970 a night watchman in Tucson, Ariz., had sent him a ten-page letter that altered his outlook on life and pitching. Carlton would divulge only that the writer urged him to take a more positive attitude to become a big winner. Steve insisted that the letter enabled him to win those 20 games in 1971. "Defeat?" Carlton said. "I never consider it."

But defeat is a way of life among the Phillies, and on May 30 he lost his fifth straight game and had a 5–6 record. From then on, however, he was almost unbeatable, winning 15 games in succession and finishing the season with a 27–10 record and a league-leading ERA of 1.98. He also led the National League in complete games (30), innings pitched (346⅓), and strike-outs (310). His 27 wins were the most in the majors this year and equaled Sandy Koufax' National League record for the most wins by a lefthander since 1900. What's more, his 27 wins—almost half of the Phillies' 59 victories—were the most victories ever for a pitcher with a last-place team. Naturally, he was the unanimous choice for the Cy Young Award.

With luck, his winning streak might not have ended at 15. As it was, it took 11 innings for the Atlanta Braves to beat him, 2–1, on Mike Lum's broken-bat single

STEVE CARLTON

off a slider. Nevertheless, Carlton's slider, which he picked up while touring Japan with the Cardinals in 1968, was instrumental in his success. Because the pitch had given him a sore arm in 1970, Carlton junked it in 1971, only to take it up again this spring. Thus, aided by a crackling fastball and an "I can win" attitude, Carlton this year was positively the best pitcher around.

WILT CHAMBERLAIN

CHAMBERLAIN, WILT (1936–   ). Time after time, Wilt Chamberlain has said: "Nobody loves Goliath." For no matter how spectacular his feats on the basketball court, he simply could not attain the popularity he longed for. And there has never been any doubt that Chamberlain, all 7' 1½" and 275 pounds of him, was basically correct in his assessment.

Sure, he was able to score prolifically and rebound superbly. He led the National Basketball Association with an all-time high average of 50.4 points a game in 1961–1962, and he scored a record 100 on March 6, 1962. But such feats were both expected of him and sneered at. He was supposedly an individualist, not a team player; and until 1967 he had never played for an NBA title-winning club.

Even when Chamberlain and his Philadelphia 76er teammates ended the domination of the Boston Celtics that year and took the NBA championship, there was only faint praise for Chamberlain. His detractors preferred to indicate that the Celtics had fallen victim to old age, not to Wilt. So, in July 1968, he was traded to the Los Angeles Lakers, a collection of superstars with little team cohesion.

In Los Angeles, however, he began at long last to receive some of the adulation he had been seeking. The first indications came in a roundabout way, after a knee injury shelved him for all except 12 games of the 1969–1970 season. While lying abed, Chamberlain received scads of letters from fans. Los Angeles warmed up to him in other ways. The sweatband that Wilt wears around his forehead during games soon became a fad for Los Angeles youngsters, who would now no more think of playing without a sweatband than they would without sneakers. It was a small thing, but the new respect meant a great deal to Wilt. Not even his new ultra-plush house, valued at between $1 million and $1.5 million and equipped with everything from a 280-gallon sunken marble bathtub to a 1,000-square-foot bedroom, turned off the fans.

Most of all, Chamberlain won new admirers with his all-out play this season. In February he cracked the NBA career rebound record and also became the first to score 30,000 points. More than that, he quashed the redoubtable Kareem Abdul-Jabbar of the Milwaukee Bucks in the NBA semifinals. Playing with more verve, more team-mindedness, and more perseverance than ever, Chamberlain kept up his superlative work against the New York Knicks in the finals. Despite a severe sprain and chip fracture of his right wrist, he played his finest game of the series in the finale, which the Lakers won by a score of 114–100.

For weeks before and after that playoff period, Wilt was flooded with mail. "I think my charisma is that of the frustrated athlete," he said. "I think they can relate to that, and the fact that they have has touched me deeply."

DIMITRIOS I (1914–   ). One by one the archbishops filed past the throne in Istanbul's historic St. George's Church and dropped their votes into a silver urn. When the count was finished, black-bearded Metropolitan Dimitrios, archbishop of Imbros and Tenedos, was the new ecumenical patriarch of the Eastern Orthodox Church, succeeding the late Athenagoras I as spiritual leader of 250 million believers.

When the 58-year-old Dimitrios heard his name called, he rose and walked forward in the eighteenth-century church to accept the traditional kiss on both cheeks from the 14 other metropolitans. He was one of the youngest and least experienced among them.

Athenagoras had died ten days earlier in July, of kidney failure following a hip fracture. The man given the best chance of taking the 86-year-old prelate's place was Metropolitan Meliton, the liberal archbishop of Chalcedon, a suburb across the Bosporus from Istanbul. But the Turkish government was anxious to keep the patriarchy under its thumb. Meliton's name was struck from the list of candidates as being too progressive.

The modest, self-effacing Dimitrios is a close friend of Meliton. Sources in the church believe the rather unworldly patriarch will follow Meliton's more sophisticated lead in matters of church politics.

The Orthodoxy that Dimitrios will preside over is a complex confederation of 15 Greek, Russian, Bulgarian, and Syrian churches ranging from the Patriarchate of Moscow, with 60 million members, to the Church of Sinai, which boasts only 100. Although the ecumenical patriarch's powers within this confederacy are limited, his prestige is great.

The new patriarch has, until now, devoted his time to pastoral duties. He was born Dimitrios Papadopoulos on September 8, 1914, in Istanbul. At 17 he entered the island monastery of Halki near Istanbul, where most of Orthodoxy's outstanding leaders have trained.

Dimitrios was ordained a deacon in 1937 and a priest in 1942. He was consecrated a bishop in 1964 and, in February of this year, appointed archbishop of Imbros and Tenedos, two islands in the Aegean Sea. Dimitrios is unmarried. Although Orthodox priests are allowed to take wives, only celibates are eligible for the rank of bishop.

Guided by Meliton, Dimitrios is expected to work toward Athenagoras' unfulfilled goal—the first synod involving all the Orthodox churches in almost 1,200 years.

EAGLETON, THOMAS (1929–   ). No one wanted to be vice-president more than the handsome junior senator from Missouri. "I'm ecstatically available," the smiling, boyish Tom Eagleton told almost everyone at the Democratic Convention in Miami.

His eagerness was almost unique. None of the other men whom presidential candidate George McGovern had in mind wanted the job. When McGovern finally arrived at Eagleton's name on his list of prospective running mates, he barely got the invitation out before Eagleton interrupted: "Well, George, before you change your mind, I accept."

Although Thomas Francis Eagleton was unknown to most Democrats at the convention, his qualifications made him an appealing number-two man for McGovern. He was a Roman Catholic, a border-state senator, and strongly prolabor. The facts

DIMITRIOS I

that his wife, Barbara, was a coolly beautiful blond and that his two children were charmingly photogenic didn't hurt either.

Born in St. Louis on September 4, 1929, Eagleton was trained for political office from childhood. His father was a hard-driving St. Louis lawyer who wanted his son to be a senator. Tom was given special tutoring in public speaking and international affairs while still at the prestigious St. Louis Country Day School. At Amherst, Eagleton was known as a campus politician. He graduated *cum laude* from both there and Harvard Law School.

At 31, Eagleton became the youngest attorney general in the history of Missouri and, at 35, the youngest lieutenant governor. In 1968 he unseated the Democratic

THOMAS EAGLETON

incumbent in a primary fight and went on to become a U.S. senator.

Eagleton was able to enjoy his vice-presidential nomination for less than two weeks before the roof fell in. It turned out that the candidate had neglected to mention a past history of mental illness to his running mate. In 1960, 1964, and 1966, Eagleton had been hospitalized for exhaustion and fatigue—twice at the Mayo Clinic. On two occasions he underwent electric shock treatment for depression.

When McGovern forces learned that the Knight newspapers planned to publish Eagleton's medical record, the two candidates hastily called a press conference to break the news themselves. McGovern originally said he was "1,000 percent" behind his running mate, but as the controversy grew, he started backing away. Eventually, Eagleton had no choice but to resign his candidacy, and he met with McGovern and agreed to do so. In the history of the major American political parties, he was the first person to resign the vice-presidential nomination after accepting it.

FISCHER, BOBBY (1943–   ). Bobby is "the most individualistic, intransigent, uncommunicative, uncooperative, solitary, self-contained, and independent chess master of all time," observed U.S. grandmaster Larry Evans. "He is also the strongest player in the world. In fact, the strongest player who ever lived." No one agreed with the second part more than Fischer himself, though in winning the

world chess championship at Reykjavík this summer, he proved both parts true.

Before he even got to Iceland, Fischer fussed about money. There wasn't enough to make it worth his while. So an obliging British banker offered to double the pot, making the stakes a record $250,000.

Then Bobby refused to go on with the second game because he said the television cameras bothered him. The cameras were eventually removed. Next it was his chair. It wasn't comfortable. His own special chair was duly flown in from New York. When he showed at all, he showed up late.

Whether this was personal pique or psychological warfare, it may well have thrown Soviet grandmaster Boris Spassky off form. After beating a careless Bobby in the first game and claiming a forfeit in the second, the Russian seemed firmly in command. But in the third game, played at Fischer's insistence in a back room away from the cameras and spectators, Spassky lost to Fischer for the first time in his life.

Games five through ten were a disaster for Spassky. Bobby, an acknowledged master in king's pawn openings, began to vary his gambits. Each midgame maneuver was a brutal challenge that Spassky was unable to fend off. And in the endgame Fischer lived up to his reputation— a precise technician who could exploit small advantages into crushing victories.

Here Boris fought back, but his hopes were short-lived. Fischer's cockiness in game 11 cost him his queen when Spassky, obviously in a prepared variation, offered him a "poisoned pawn" and Bobby bit. The next game was a standoff, but in game 13, Bobby struck back. Spurning another "poisoned pawn," Fischer launched into Alekhine's Defense, a supermodern strategy he had used only five times earlier in his career. When Spassky was caught off guard, the game and match were Fischer's. The two marked time with

BOBBY FISCHER

a series of draws until, characteristically finishing with a win, Fischer was pronounced champion on September 1. His winner's share was $150,000, but for one of the sports world's hottest properties that was only the beginning. Even the $1.75 million suit lodged against him by Chester Fox, the film producer whose cameras had been barred from the hall, barely dimmed his financial prospects.

In triumph Bobby was as unpredictable as ever. At the victory dinner in Reykjavík two days later, after months of haggling over their public matches, Bobby and Boris suddenly found themselves bent over Fischer's pocket chess set, replaying their final game for the benefit of kibitzing grandmasters. Naturally, Bobby had arrived at the ceremonies 45 minutes late,

INDIRA GANDHI

keeping everyone else from eating. As the medals were awarded, Spassky got the larger ovation, but Fischer had the crown, and that was all he wanted or needed.

GANDHI, INDIRA (1917–   ). "I am not a person to be pressured by anybody or anything," the prime minister of India told an American newsman in January. Tiny, imperious Indira Gandhi had made this point the month before when she set India's army against West Pakistan's menacing forces. It took the Indians two weeks to make a shambles of Pakistan's highly touted troops.

In moving against Pakistan, Mrs. Gandhi had ignored the United States. President Richard M. Nixon was furious with the prime minister for not telling him of her plans during a state visit to Washington in November. He instructed his aides to "tilt" in favor of Pakistan in the brief war.

It did not help. By the end of it, India had penetrated deep into Pakistani terri-

tory, both east and west, freed the beleaguered people of the new nation of Bangladesh, and captured more than 91,-000 Pakistanis. The decisive victory left India the dominant power on the Asian subcontinent.

When election time came in March, Indians showed their approval for her bold action by giving Mrs. Gandhi's New Congress Party the biggest majority in independent India's history. In 1971, the prime minister had won parliament but not control of the key state governments. Now her party won large majorities in 14 of the 16 states where elections were held. The two-thirds majority allowed Mrs. Gandhi to pursue her long-stalled plans for aid to farmers and the redistribution of land.

Indira Gandhi is the daughter of the late Jawaharlal Nehru, India's prime minister for 17 years. Her husband, Feroze Gandhi, died in 1960. She became prime minister in 1966.

This July, Mrs. Gandhi met with Pakistan's president Zulfikar Ali Bhutto in the cool Himalayan town of Simla. In a surprising atmosphere of peace, the two leaders spent five days conferring.

Mrs. Gandhi and Bhutto agreed to normalize diplomatic relations on a step-by-step basis, to resume communication links, and to keep talking on other problems. However, Mrs. Gandhi refused to return the Pakistani captives and left the question of who should rule Kashmir unresolved.

"It's just a beginning," Prime Minister Gandhi noted as she emerged from the talks. But, as India approached its 25th anniversary celebration on August 15, it was the most hopeful step toward accommodation with Pakistan since the British left the subcontinent.

ISAAC HAYES

HAYES, ISAAC (1942–   ). He comes on stage dressed in red satin tights and a golden coat of mail under an orange, black, and white cape. A black woman, whose head is shaved as bald as his own, undulates around him in what is billed as "an African dance of adoration," while four bodyguards glower at the audience.

Isaac Hayes doesn't need the flashy entrance. At 30, he is considered one of the top pop stars in the country—a singer with four platinum records (meaning sales of $2 million each) and a composer whose music for the movie *Shaft* won him an Oscar and a Grammy.

If Hayes with his bodyguards and black sunglasses makes a threatening appearance on stage, the image was somewhat diluted on Oscar night when he gently thanked his grandmother for making him what he is today.

Even with his grandmother's help, it's been a long road from Covington, Tenn., where Isaac Hayes was born on August 20, 1942. Raised by his grandparents after his mother died, Isaac knew a life of grinding poverty and back-breaking toil. Searching for something better, the family moved to Memphis, where Hayes drifted into the musical scene before he had graduated from high school.

In 1962, Hayes and lyricist David Porter teamed up to write songs. In 1964, Stax records set them to writing for Sam and Dave—and they produced "You Don't Know Like I Know," "Hold on, I'm Coming," and "Soul Man."

His singing career, Hayes recalls, "began by accident. I was doing great as a producer and songwriter, but one night after a Christmas party at Stax, I was sit-

ting in the studio with a bass player and a drummer when the executive vice-president said, 'Okay, Isaac, now I'm going to record you.' "

The LP, *Presenting Isaac Hayes*, was a modest success and led to his first hit, *Hot Buttered Soul*. By the time Hayes was asked to score *Shaft*, he had sold 6 million records.

In concert Hayes can manage only a few songs each performance because of the "rap." While the organ holds a single note, Isaac extemporizes for as long as ten minutes. Then his rich baritone glides smoothly from blues to soul to pop.

Hayes' latest album is called *Black Moses* and features a poster of him dressed in biblical costume. It is the kind

budge on the pay issue, even after a state of emergency was declared. But when public opinion sided with the miners and a government commission recommended salary increases averaging 20 percent, Heath had to give in.

Five months later Britain was again paralyzed, this time by a wildcat dock strike called to protest the imprisonment of five dockworkers for illegal picketing. This was the first crucial test of a new labor relations bill, the most comprehensive in British history, on which the Heath government had staked a great deal of prestige. The five prisoners became symbols of a union challenge to government power; steel mills were closed down, the newspaper presses silenced, and transpor-

British into paying a much steeper rent for their naval facilities on the island. Most embarrassingly, the compromise agreement with Rhodesia had fallen through when the Pearce Commission, actually fulfilling its mandate, found that Rhodesian blacks would not accept the settlement.

Capping all that, Heath now found himself at his lowest point in the polls since the Conservatives took office over two years ago. The prime minister always insisted that he put principle above power; Labour could hardly wait for the British electorate to put that resolve to the test.

IRVING, CLIFFORD (1930–   ). In January 1971 a minor-league writer named

EDWARD HEATH

CLIFFORD IRVING

HENRY KISSINGER

of overstatement Hayes enjoys—like his fourth car, a Cadillac with custom-built gold bumpers. "I like luxury, man," he explains. "Because that's what I never had."

HEATH, EDWARD (1916–   ). It was Britain's worst year of labor confrontations since the great general strike of 1926. Two disastrous walkouts and a host of lesser shutdowns dealt a damaging blow to Prime Minister Edward Heath's plan to contain wages and stop inflation.

First came the coal miners' strike, which all but crippled the nation during the winter. During the seven-week stoppage, Britons suffered frequent power blackouts, and between 1.5 and 2 million workers were idled. The poorly paid miners, long overdue for a pay hike, demanded increases up to 47 percent, well over the 8 percent national guideline favored by Heath and the 7.9 percent offered by the National Coal Board. At first, the prime minister had refused to

tation all but halted. Only the release of the five dockers on July 26 prevented a general strike of over 9 million workers. The dock strike itself went on for 20 days, with yet another state of national emergency proclaimed.

The failure of Heath's anti-inflationary policy was documented in July. Prices were rising at an annual rate of 12 percent, far above the 5 percent the government was pointing to pridefully earlier in the year. Finally, Heath was forced to impose a wage-price freeze in November, a move he had previously resisted.

Domestic troubles were only part of the prime minister's problem. The margin in the Commons on Common Market entry had dwindled from 112 votes in October to only eight in February. Heath's friend and adviser, William Whitelaw, had proved no more capable of resolving the Northern Ireland conflict than the Stormont government had before him. Dom Mintoff, the Maltese prime minister, had haggled the

Clifford Irving approached a publisher with a tantalizing offer. Would McGraw-Hill be interested in the autobiography of billionaire recluse Howard Hughes? Hughes, a constant source of fascination to the American public, had not been interviewed since 1958, but there was Irving claiming that Hughes was so impressed with Irving's latest book that he had asked Cliff's help in writing his autobiography. Irving produced letters from Hughes to prove his story. McGraw-Hill gave Irving the go-ahead sign.

In retrospect, Irving hardly seems the type Howard Hughes would have chosen to work with. Born in New York City on November 5, 1930, Clifford Irving had married four times and roamed the world experimenting with life-styles before settling down as an expatriate on the Spanish island of Ibiza. His novels were published without a literary ripple, but he never gave up the hope of making it big in the publishing world.

In December 1971, McGraw-Hill announced publication of the book, and *Life* magazine reported it would print a serialization, bought for $250,000. In response, various Hughes henchmen produced a storm of accusations against Irving.

Irving, backed to the hilt by McGraw-Hill and *Life*, insisted he had spent more than 100 hours in secret meetings demanded by Hughes in Mexico, Puerto Rico, and Miami. For proof there were the contracts signed by the billionaire and $650,000 of McGraw-Hill money deposited to H. R. Hughes in a Swiss bank. A firm of highly respected handwriting analysts declared that the depositor's signatures on those canceled checks were authentic.

Hughes at this point became so exercised that he called an unprecedented telephone press conference for reporters who knew him in the old days. Talking from Paradise Island in the Bahamas, he vigorously denied any knowledge of the autobiography.

Throughout the controversy, Irving insisted he had talked with Hughes. But in February 1972, Swiss officials revealed that the Zürich bank account had been opened by a slim woman bearing a Swiss passport in the name of Helga R. Hughes. She signed her name H. R. Hughes, and a few weeks after each deposit she withdrew the money. The Swiss were eyeing Irving's wife Edith, a German-born Swiss citizen. Meanwhile, several U.S. agencies began their own investigations. A heavy blow to Irving's story came from a pretty Danish singer named Nina van Pallandt. Miss van Pallandt told reporters she had been with Irving, day and night, on his five-day trip to Oaxaca, Mexico, so he could not have talked with Hughes.

At the invitation of the U.S. attorney's office in New York, the Irvings returned from Ibiza. Then Irving got a fatal blow. His researcher, Richard Suskind, changed his story. Previously he, too, insisted he had met Hughes, who once offered him an organic prune. Now Suskind testified that he never saw the billionaire. Irving was finally forced to admit his hoax.

In June the bills came due. The Irvings were sentenced in a federal court to 2½ years for Clifford and two months for Edith, as well as a $10,000 fine for each. The week before these sentences were imposed, McGraw-Hill had won a claim of $776,000 against Irving. To make matters worse, the Swiss government was continuing with plans to prosecute Edith. Clifford Irving had at last made his name known, but at a cost, as he told the court, of "my reputation, my honor, the financial debt that may last for years or the rest of my life, and a loss of credibility which is very valuable to me, which I deserve to lose because I lived a year of a lie."

KISSINGER, HENRY (1923–   ). When Richard Nixon was photographed at the historic Peking conference with Mao Tse-tung in February, the smiling man at his elbow was not the secretary of state, as might be expected, but the president's foreign policy expert, Henry Kissinger.

Kissinger had every right to be there. It was he who met secretly with Chinese officials last year and delicately negotiated Nixon's landmark tour—and the Sino-American détente that it symbolized.

But Kissinger the Sino-American go-between played second fiddle to Kissinger the Vietnam peace-broker throughout most of the year. Time and again he met with North Vietnamese negotiators secretly in Paris, until he could claim, as he did late in October, that peace was finally "at hand."

STANLEY KUBRICK

En route to these clandestine peace talks, Kissinger behaved like a secret agent. On one occasion he slipped out of Washington early on a Sunday morning and flew, unannounced, to a German air base near Frankfurt, where he changed planes for the final hop to a French base 9 miles out of Paris. After a ride in a curtained limousine to a "safe" house, he caught a few hours' sleep and then, by another car, went to meet the North Vietnamese negotiators.

Kissinger commands a White House corps of 46 staff members and 105 clerical workers. His demanding meticulousness—and his overweening ego—have caused about a quarter of his team to quit. Those who stay consider Kissinger a genius and tolerate his tantrums. "He makes us do things we never thought we could do," observed one devoted aide.

Nixon regards him almost as highly because Kissinger gives the well-organized president what he wants: a clear-cut list of choices available on a specific prob-

lem and a penetrating analysis of the possible consequences. "The role of the president is not to ratify the compromises of the bureaucracy," points out Kissinger, who is deft at extracting options from all sides and distilling intelligence for his boss.

China was only the beginning of Kissinger's peripatetic year. Before Nixon arrived in Moscow in May, Kissinger went there secretly to work out details of the talks with Leonid Brezhnev. Then he was back again for the actual summit meeting.

Next the president dispatched his aide to patch up strained U.S. relations with Japan, the strongest ally that the United States has in Asia. Within days, Kissinger was back in China, then on to Paris for further peace talks with the North Vietnamese. In August he returned to Moscow for four days of talks with Soviet leaders. On his way back to Washington, the energetic Kissinger stopped off to brief British prime minister Edward Heath and French president Georges Pompidou on the outcome of his Soviet visit.

This brand of personal diplomacy makes Kissinger one of the most powerful men in the administration and a source of fascinating information to the press. Another indication of Kissinger's appeal is the fact that publishers have already bid more than $2 million for his autobiography—a book he hasn't even had time to begin.

KUBRICK, STANLEY (1928–   ). "Although a certain amount of hypocrisy exists about it . . . everyone is fascinated by violence. After all, man is the most remorseless killer who ever stalked the earth." The man talking is movie director Stanley Kubrick, whose current film, *A*

Clockwork Orange, is more than a little violent. It is also the subject of more than a little controversy.

Some observers feel that, in *Clockwork*, Kubrick has reached a new low of radical chic, equating all genital friction with rape, all political activity with fascism, and all mankind with the hero, a fellow whose time seems to be divided equally between bouts of sadism and fits of catalepsy. Others, including Kubrick, have defended the film, asserting that the director has employed a technique which dates back to Chaucer and beyond—that, in fact, he is simply displaying the evils of this world, both actual and potential, to warn the ignorant public against what is and what may be.

Stanley Kubrick has made a career of portraying societies gone haywire—some real, some not. In 1957, he won critical acclaim for *Paths of Glory*, a biting tale of trench warfare during World War I that is still banned in France. He followed this effort with a filmed version of Vladimir Nabokov's bizarre novel *Lolita*, the story of aging Humbert Humbert's lust after a pubescent girl. After *Lolita* came *Dr. Strangelove*, a "what-if" movie in which Kubrick explored the comic possibilities of nuclear annihilation.

Next Kubrick spent four years and $11 million creating *2001: A Space Odyssey*. The critics liked it less than *Strangelove*, but the film attracted large audiences and earned $31 million.

Born in the Bronx on July 26, 1928, Kubrick now lives outside of London with his third wife, Christiane, and their three daughters.

Kubrick's early years in New York City were marked by a supreme indifference to school (he barely graduated from high school) and a preoccupation with still photography. His pictures were published in *Look* when he was 16, and he joined the magazine as an apprentice photographer at 17.

Four years later, Kubrick turned a *Look* article he had done on a young boxer into an amateurish short movie. "The thrill of watching that film," he recalls, "pathetic as it was, was incomparable. . . . I knew after I had made it that I was absolutely hooked."

Kubrick's devotion to cinema has occasionally led him into print. When the Detroit *News* decided that it would no longer carry display advertising for X-rated films, Kubrick waxed indignant in a letter to the paper. Several months later, however, Kubrick made the whole argument moot when he announced plans to withdraw *Clockwork* from circulation and release a recut version. The recut version will carry an R rating rather than an X, expanding the film's distribution potential.

LAND, EDWIN (1909–   ). "I think this camera can have the same impact as the telephone on the way people live," said its inventor modestly. Twenty-four years after Edwin Herbert Land astonished the world with his first Polaroid camera, he was back again with a revolutionary refinement: a vest-pocket model with instant pop-out color pictures that develop outside the camera.

The SX-70, as it is known at Polaroid, is completely automatic as well as compact. The real magic is its self-developing film. Free from the gunky litter that has accompanied the Polaroid process until now, each photograph emerges from the new camera sealed in plastic and dry to the touch. At first the film is a cloudy blue nothing. Then, as the photographer watches, the blue turns into true color in less than four minutes.

Born on May 7, 1909, in Bridgeport, Conn., Edwin Land was pursuing his own creative path even as a boy. When he attended Norwich Academy in Connecticut, he won top grades. His physics teacher cheerfully admits that the brilliant young student was far ahead of him in scientific thinking. As an 18-year-old student at Harvard, Land began experimenting with ways to cut glare by polarizing light. He became so involved in the work that he dropped out of school. Land then continued his experiments in New

JOHN LAVELLE

York City, occasionally "borrowing" a Columbia University physics laboratory by crawling through a window late at night. His lab assistant in those days was his wife, Helen.

In 1937, Land founded the Polaroid Corporation in Boston with the idea of selling Detroit glare-reduced headlights. The scheme failed, but Land's Polaroid sunglasses, based on the same principle, sold very well, particularly during World War II.

Land got the idea for his camera while on vacation in 1943. His impatient young daughter wondered how long she would have to wait to see the photographs just snapped. Intrigued, Land began experimenting. He hit on the idea of a capsule of developing jellies which would break and spread over an exposed negative within the camera. The first Polaroid Land cameras appeared on the market in 1948; to date, some 26 million have been sold.

Land, who is president, chairman, and research director of Polaroid, has given

EDWIN LAND

What Lavelle had done was to augment the escort force upon occasion. Instead of four planes, he would send 16 armed planes to escort a reconnaissance flight. The augmented escort force would proceed to attack radar installations, missile bases, airfields, oil stockpiles, and truck depots.

By his own admission, Lavelle ordered around 20 of these raids between November 8, 1971, and March 8, 1972. Ryan stated that an air force investigation concluded that there had been 28 violations of the rules of engagement involving unauthorized strikes by 147 aircraft.

Lavelle was ordered to retire from service and demoted by one grade, giving him the three-star rank of lieutenant general in retirement. However, the air force establishes pensions on the basis of the rank held prior to retirement, so Lavelle will receive a four-star pension of $27,000 a year.

Lavelle was born in Cleveland on September 9, 1916. He was graduated from John Carroll University there in 1938, and in 1939 he enlisted in the army as an aviation cadet. He assumed command of the Seventh Air Force in July 1971, after tours as commander of the 17th Air Force in West Germany and as director of the Defense Communications Planning Group in the Pentagon.

MARGRETHE II, queen of Denmark (1940–). On a chill January day, Prime Minister Jens Otto Krag stepped to the balcony of Copenhagen's Christiansborg Palace and announced three times: "King Frederik IX is dead. Long live Her Majesty Queen Margrethe II."

After a 24-year reign, Denmark's popular sailor-king was dead at 72 of pneumonia. And with no more ceremony than the traditional words spoken by the prime minister, Frederik's eldest daughter, 31-year-old Margrethe, succeeded him to the throne.

If Margrethe's coronation lacked the pomp the world has come to expect from its dwindling supply of royalty, it was, nevertheless, a royal landmark. She is Denmark's first queen in a millennium of monarchy. Even the national heroine, Margrethe I (1353–1412), never officially became queen because the law at the time did not provide for female succession.

The current queen won her royal prerogative through the democratic process. In 1953, when the Danes realized King Frederik would have no children other than his three daughters, they changed the constitution to allow women to inherit the throne.

Handsome and leggy, Margrethe stands a shade under 6 feet tall. The Danes were mildly worried when their future queen reached the ripe age of 26 without finding a husband. Her youngest sister, Anne-Marie, was long wed to King Constantine of Greece while the unconcerned Margrethe spent her time at far-flung archaeo-

MARGRETHE II

only three press conferences in his entire career. Although Land refuses to talk about his private life, he can wax poetic about the SX-70 camera: "It can make a person pause in his rush through life. It will help him to focus himself on some aspect of life and, in the process, enrich his life at that moment."

LAVELLE, JOHN (1916–). "Everybody knew we were falsifying these reports," the sergeant said later. "Everybody was doing it. I kept on saying, 'Why?' and they said, 'That's the way we do it.'" The murky explanation didn't satisfy Sergeant Lonnie B. Franks, stationed with an intelligence unit at Udorn Air Force Base in Thailand. So Franks wrote Iowa senator Harold Hughes to ask "if this falsification of classified documents is legal and proper." Senator Hughes passed Franks' letter on to Senator Stuart Symington, who in turn passed it on to air force chief of staff General John Ryan. The next day, the air force inspector general, Lieutenant General Louis

Wilson, was on a plane for Vietnam. What he found caused Ryan to relieve General John Daniel Lavelle of his command over the Seventh Air Force, which controls all air force units involved in the Vietnam war.

Lavelle had been pursuing his own interpretation of the rules of engagement. In 1968, President Lyndon Johnson had ordered a halt to the bombing of North Vietnam in an attempt to further peace negotiations. The rules of engagement developed to give that order substance forbade unprovoked attacks upon North Vietnamese territory. There was, however, the possibility of "protective reaction." The United States continued to send unarmed reconnaissance planes over North Vietnamese territory, accompanied by several—usually four—armed escort planes. If the North Vietnamese took certain measures aimed at destroying these planes—such as "locking on" to them with their radar, or firing missiles at them—the escort was authorized to attack the installations responsible.

logical digs. When friends insisted that she look for a suitable mate, Margrethe would reply: ''He has to find me.''

And he did. In 1967, Margrethe married the handsome French count Henri de Laborde de Monpezat. To fit his role as the future consort, Henri changed his name to the more Danish-sounding Henrik and renounced his Catholic faith in favor of his new country's Lutheranism. The royal couple now have two sons, Prince Frederik and Prince Joachim. After her coronation, Margrethe announced that, although she was queen of the country, she was content to be helpmeet at home.

Margrethe Alexandrine Thorhildur Ingrid, born at Amalienborg Castle in Copenhagen on April 16, 1940, is one of the best-trained monarchs in the world. She studied at the universities of Copenhagen and Århus, at the London School of Economics, Cambridge, and the Sorbonne. Her special interests are art and archaeology.

McGOVERN, GEORGE. *See the special supplement* ELECTION '72.

MEIR, GOLDA (1898–   ). Twenty-five unsuspecting travelers massacred at Tel Aviv's Lydda Airport, 11 Israeli Olympic athletes murdered in Munich, an Israeli diplomat in London killed by a letter-bomb—the Palestinian guerrillas were stepping up their attacks on Israel in horrifyingly dramatic ways, and Israel's prime minister, Golda Meir, spent the year in almost perpetual mourning for their victims.

Speaking before the Knesset (parliament), after the Lydda attack, the prime minister condemned Lebanon for ''openly enabling the centers of terrorist organizations to reside in their midst.'' The Popular Front for the Liberation of Palestine, with headquarters in Lebanon, proudly claimed the attack was a fifth anniversary reprisal for the Arab defeat by the Israelis in the six-day war.

About three months later, members of the Black September guerrilla organization scaled the fence at the Olympic Village in Munich and then forced their way into the Israeli quarters, killing two team members and taking nine others hostage. Prime Minister Meir adamantly refused to release 200 Arab prisoners in Israel, the price demanded by Black September in exchange for the athletes, and throughout the day German officials tried to negotiate the release of the nine while the prime minister and her advisers awaited news in the Knesset's underground cabinet room. When the guerrillas and their hostages went to a military airport near Munich, German police sharpshooters attempted to kill the terrorists, but after the exchange of gunfire was over, not only five of the Arabs but also one policeman and all nine hostages were dead.

Although Prime Minister Meir publicly thanked the German government for its desperate efforts, there was considerable criticism within Israel of both the German police action and Israeli intransigence. The incident turned into a personally heartbreaking time for the 74-year-old prime minister. Just as she was about to attend state ceremonies at Lydda Airport for the dead athletes, word came of the death of her 83-year-old sister, who had accompanied Golda Meir when she emigrated from Milwaukee, Wis., to Palestine 51 years before.

Nevertheless, there was the future to consider, and the prime minister had helped secure Israel's future in December 1971 by winning a U.S. promise to sell Israel a fleet of Phantom jets that it had tried unsuccessfully to buy for 15 months. Part of the deal may have been a secret promise by the prime minister to end Israel's opposition to peace negotiations with its Arab enemies in the 1967 war. In February 1972, Israel did express renewed interest in U.S.-initiated negotiation with Egypt on opening the Suez Canal, and in July, after Egyptian president Anwar Sadat ordered Soviet troops out of his country, Prime Minister Meir issued an appeal for direct peace talks. In a speech to the Knesset she reminded the Arabs: ''We have not declared permanent borders, we

LIZA MINNELLI

have not drawn up an ultimate map, we have not demanded prior commitments on matters which must be clarified by means of negotiations."

However, in September, after the Munich and London incidents, Israel let it be known that peace negotiations could not go forward until Palestinian terrorism against Israel was ended.

MINNELLI, LIZA (1946–   ). In nine years she had starred on Broadway, commanded $60,000 a week in Las Vegas for a nightclub act, and played in three films. For all that, Liza Minnelli was still best known as Judy Garland's daughter.

Until this year. When the movie *Cabaret* opened in February, Liza became a superstar on her own. As Sally Bowles, the appealing though amoral American adrift in the decadence of Berlin in the 1930's, she received unanimous raves from all the critics. Suddenly Liza was discovered.

Within a week, her big-eyed, wistful face showed up on the covers of both *Newsweek* and *Time* while fashion editors scrambled to photograph her provocative new wardrobe. She was named the new "Miss Show Biz," and one writer suggested Liza be investigated by the Justice Department as an "entertainment monopoly." For the first time, the daughter could, if not banish the memory of her mother's overwhelming talent, at least put it in perspective as part of her inheritance.

Growing up was a roller coaster ride for Liza. Born in Hollywood on March 12, 1946, Liza May Minnelli was the only child of Garland's marriage to Hollywood director Vincente Minnelli (*Gigi, An American in*

MARTHA AND JOHN MITCHELL

GOLDA MEIR

Paris). She spent the good years in a world of secluded estates with such family friends as Humphrey Bogart and Marilyn Monroe. During the bad times—and there were many after Judy divorced Minnelli and began a self-destructive round of pills, alcohol, and suicide attempts—Liza was forced to become the adult her mother refused to be. Still, Liza insists, it wasn't all grim. She recalls with affection her mother's sense of humor and her bright courage.

By 16, Liza had attended around 20 different schools. It seemed enough, so she quit and spent a year in New York trying for bit parts in the theater. Success came with an off-Broadway revival of *Best Foot Forward*. Next there was the lead in George Abbott's musical *Flora, the Red Menace*. The show was a flop, but Liza won a Tony Award for her Broadway debut. She was 19 years old.

After *Flora*, Liza worked up a sophisticated nightclub routine, then took parts in the movies *Charlie Bubbles, The Sterile Cuckoo,* and *Tell Me That You Love Me, Junie Moon.*

In 1967 Liza married Australian singer Peter Allen, but the relationship fizzled. Her latest love is Desi Arnaz, Jr., the actor son of Lucille Ball. Desi is six years younger than Liza, a fact that doesn't bother her at all. Says Liza, "You grow up early in Hollywood."

Meanwhile, Liza continues a dizzying pace. She loves to work and gives her all at every single performance. "When I'm holding that last note," she explains, "if I never sing again, I know I've held that note properly. I am in the moment of my life."

MITCHELL, MARTHA AND JOHN (1918–   ; 1913–   ). After months of silence, the most outspoken woman of the Nixon administration was back at her old stand: making late-night phone calls to sympathetic reporters. Martha Mitchell, the chatty belle from Arkansas, phoned up UPI Washington correspondent Helen Thomas from a motel in Newport Beach, Calif., and passed on a fascinating piece of news. She had, she said, given her husband an ultimatum to "get out of politics" or she'd leave him.

Delivering herself of that momentous scoop, Martha turned to the news of the day. "I'm sick and tired of the whole operation," she began in answer to a question about the men caught bugging the Democratic national headquarters. The reporter then heard the sounds of a scuffle and Mrs. Mitchell saying, "You just get away," before the line went dead. That was on June 22.

Martha Mitchell checked back with the UPI correspondent in a week. This time she was calling from the secluded West-

chester Country Club in Rye, N.Y., where she had fled after the motel incident.

"If you could see me, you wouldn't believe it," she complained. "I'm black and blue. I'm a political prisoner." Mrs. Mitchell went on to say, "I love my husband very much, . . . but I'm not going to stand for all those dirty things that go on," and told the reporter that five men had entered her room in California, ripped out the phone, and stuck a needle into her backside.

John Mitchell, who is known as a doting husband, flew to New York to comfort his wife. After two days of talking things out, the couple left for their Washington apartment. The same day, Mitchell had lunch with President Nixon and resigned as his campaign manager.

It has not been a vintage year for the dour John Mitchell—at work as well as at home.

On June 17, just five days before Martha Mitchell had the needle stuck in her backside, the Democratic national headquarters in Washington, D.C., had been broken into by a group of men who were closely tied to a committee working for President Nixon's reelection. John Mitchell denied any foreknowledge or complicity on the part of the committee. "We want to emphasize that this man [James W. McCord, Jr.] and the other people involved were not operating either on our behalf or with our consent. I am surprised and dismayed at these reports."

Earlier in the year, Mitchell had been kept busy issuing denials in relation to the ITT scandal. Jack Anderson had alleged that the Justice Department had settled some antitrust suits against ITT in a manner favorable to ITT, after ITT had pledged $400,000 for the Republican Convention in San Diego. Mitchell denied he had had any part in the affair, asserting that he had previously disqualified himself from consideration of the case because his former law firm had once represented an ITT subsidiary.

In September, it was Martha Mitchell who again garnered a headline—she identified the man who had torn her phone off the wall on June 21 as Steve King, who had been assigned to her as a bodyguard at the time. King had recently become head of security for the Committee to Re-Elect the President, after James W. McCord, Jr., had been arrested on June 17 while inside the Democratic national headquarters in Washington.

NICKLAUS, JACK (1940–   ). Jack Nicklaus has won so many golf tournaments and so much money in recent years that maybe he should be memorialized on American currency. Like $2,000 bills with a picture of him encircled by one of his favorite sayings: "There's always room for improvement."

In Nicklaus' case, though, there really isn't that much room left for improvement, especially after this year. Among other

things, the blond Ohio State graduate won the Masters, the U.S. Open, and the $50,000 top prize at the Westchester Classic.

About the only thing he didn't win was the grand slam, his avowed goal. But Nicklaus gave it a good try, by taking the first two events of the four—the Masters and the U.S. Open—and putting up one of the most spirited comebacks ever before losing the British Open. Going into the final round of that tournament, Nicklaus trailed Lee Trevino by 6 strokes. Playing with his typically relentless determination, Jack shot a 4-under-par 32 on the first nine to tie for the lead. One hole —and one birdie—later he was a stroke ahead. Then it was Trevino's turn to unloose some masterful shots, just enough of them to defeat Nicklaus, who finished with a 5-under-par 66, by 1 stroke. "I

JACK NICKLAUS

GEORGES POMPIDOU

was there and let it get away," muttered the disconsolate Nicklaus, for whom anything lower than first place is a letdown.

But his two earlier big victories had helped him attain his long-range goal of 13 major-tournament triumphs, tying him with Bobby Jones: four Masters, three U.S. Opens, two wins in the British Open, two PGA's, and two U.S. Amateurs. And in August at Pinehurst, N.C., Nicklaus added even further luster to his record by taking the U.S. Professional Match Play championship in a showdown struggle with Frank Beard. The win earned him another $40,000 and brought his earnings for the year all the way up to $280,481, thus breaking his own 1971 mark for the most money ever won in a calendar year by a golfer. Furthermore, that victory, his sixth this year and the 43rd since he turned professional in 1962, lifted his total earnings on the tournament trail to an incredible $1,650,000.

NIXON, RICHARD M. *See the special supplement* ELECTION '72.

POMPIDOU, GEORGES (1911–   ). Last year Georges Pompidou was hailed as the statesman who helped Britain win its long-denied entrance into the European Common Market. This year the suave, self-assured French president began acting as autocratic about the European Economic Community as his predecessor, the late Charles de Gaulle, whose pique kept the British out of the organization in the first place.

In March, Pompidou announced a national referendum would be held to give the French a chance to approve or disapprove the treaties allowing Britain, Ireland, Norway, and Denmark to join the EEC—to "express their opinion directly on the new policy of a new Europe." But what the president really wanted was to demonstrate his ballot-box strength both to en-

hance his role in the EEC and bolster his political position at home. After a resounding triumph, he planned to call for early national elections, which must be held by next March. Unfortunately, the referendum backfired—only 46 percent of the electorate bothered to vote yes or no; of those only two-thirds approved entry. Pompidou's prestige suffered a severe blow.

In June the French president began throwing roadblocks in the way of the first summit meeting of leaders of the old and the new EEC countries, scheduled to be held in October in Paris. The member countries, Pompidou complained, were not moving fast enough on behalf of Europe, "to help her find her place, her personality, her influence in the world again."

What the president had in mind was a plan to establish France in its proper place as the political nerve center of the Com-

SHEIKH MUJIBUR RAHMAN

mon Market, a grandiose scheme worthy of *le grand Charles.* London, as Pompidou saw it, would be the financial capital, Brussels would remain the "bread and butter" capital, handling problems like tariffs, while West Germany would still be the industrial center. Not surprisingly, the other Common Market nations opposed his empire-building ideas and called his bluff. Pompidou was forced to back down and agree to hold the October summit conference as planned.

On the home front, Pompidou remained shaken by the government's poor showing in the referendum. In the wake of that and an income tax controversy, he fired Premier Jacques Chaban-Delmas in July and replaced him with Pierre Messmer, a more orthodox Gaullist, in an effort to bolster his ranks, which must face the combined forces of the Communists and

Socialists in the approaching legislative elections.

RAHMAN, SHEIKH MUJIBUR (1920–   ). Half a million cheering Bengalis gathered at the Dacca racecourse in January to welcome the hero of their new nation of Bangladesh. Sheikh Mujibur Rahman appeared surprisingly fit after spending some nine months in a jail cell in West Pakistan.

As Bengalis pelted him with rose petals, the smiling, mustachioed Mujib urged them to forgive the West Pakistanis who he said had killed 3 million of their number during the bitter civil war. "Today I do not want revenge from anybody," Mujib declared. Then he told them firmly, "The unity of the country is ended."

His words crushed West Pakistan's hopes of maintaining a loose confederation between the two distant parts of the

nation. The brutal behavior of the Pakistani Army troops during the nine-month war had made this an impossible dream.

Mujib had been named president of Bangladesh *in absentia.* His first major decision on his return was to set up a parliamentary democracy and switch his title from president to prime minister. Mujib was faced with reorganizing a land so wasted that it was referred to on one occasion as "an international basket case."

First Mujib had to find food and shelter for his ravaged countrymen—including the 10 million destitute refugees now trickling back from India. Promises of food and cash quickly came from India and other nations, and the majority of the world's nations recognized the Bangladesh government. In August, however, the Chinese cast their first veto in the Security Council

to keep Bangladesh out of the United Nations.

Sheikh Mujib was an ardent patriot from boyhood. A landowner's son born March 17, 1920, in East Bengal, then part of British India, he got his first taste of jail as a seventh-grader agitating for the end of British rule.

The new nation of Pakistan was created in 1947 during Mujib's first year at the University of Dacca law school. From the beginning, the more powerful west tried to force its ways on the eastern province. Mujib was thrown into prison again during the language strikes, when the government ordered East Pakistan to switch from Bengali to the West's native Urdu. The sheikh was in jail once more as late as 1968 for demanding better treatment for the Bengalis.

As Bangladesh limped through its first year, the urgent need for food and jobs made the people restless. While Mujib was in Europe for six weeks recovering from a gall bladder operation, there were strikes and demonstrations against the government. But the disorders were quelled, and by November Sheikh Mujib had secured what he called the fulfillment of a lifelong dream—a democratic constitution for his people.

ROSEWALL, KEN (1934–   ). "All I'm doing is postponing the inevitable. This year may be my final fling." So said Ken Rosewall, the Australian tennis player who rejuvenated the hopes of the geriatric set with his on-target shots, his grit and stamina, and his resounding backhands. At an age when most players start reliving past glories rather than envisioning new ones, Rosewall reached his peak.

He should have reached that height in November 1971, when he stunned fellow Australian Rod Laver to win the $100,000 World Championship of Tennis title match. But, as so often has happened to Rosewall, his triumph was played down; too many people thought he was just lucky.

In mid-May of this year, though, Rosewall again made the showdown match of the WCT tournament in Dallas, and again on the other side of the net was none other than Rod Laver. There was little doubt this time that Laver would win the $50,000 top prize, especially since he took the opening set, 6–4.

It was too much to expect that the 37-year-old Rosewall could rally. But Rosewall, taking advantage of numerous double faults by Laver and hammering away with his own relentless backhand, took the next two sets, 6–0 and 6–3. Almost overcome by exhaustion, Rosewall dropped the following set, 6–7, on a tie-breaker. He hung on in the final set at 6–6 to force another tie-breaker that would decide the championship. Laver took a 5–4 lead, had the serve and needed just two points to ensure his victory. Despite his fatigue from almost 3½ hours of extremely intense play, Rosewall solidly drilled back Laver's serves to

regain the lead at 6–5. Then, when Laver rapped Rosewall's serve into the net it was all over.

The short, muscular Rosewall proved himself to be a marvel. His backhand, long called the best since Don Budge, was now rated as the best ever. The staggering span of his high-caliber play was measured by his record: he won his first Australian championship at age 18 in 1953, his fourth this year; he took his first French singles title also in 1953, his second in 1968; he won at Forest Hills in 1956 and again in 1970. His longevity has been amazing, and if 1972 turns out to be his "final fling," it will have been a grand and glorious one.

SADAT, ANWAR (1918–   ). No one was more surprised than the Soviet leaders last July when Egypt's president, Anwar Sadat, suddenly ordered an estimated 15,000–20,000 Soviet military advisers and technicians out of his country. "It is now time to reconsider the policy of extravagant dependence on the Soviet Union," Sadat announced to his people. "That policy, five years after defeat, has not deterred the aggression nor has it restored our rights. The policy of alliance with the devil is not objectionable until it becomes favorable to the devil."

The Soviets should not have been caught off guard by Sadat's action. Three times in the previous 12 months he had flown to Moscow to plead for offensive weapons to match the sophisticated U.S. missiles and aircraft supplied to Israel. Each time the Soviets refused, preferring a Middle East standoff to an out-and-out war.

Meanwhile, Sadat was getting angry complaints from his generals about the overbearing and often derogatory attitude of the Soviet advisers. Egyptian generals were not even allowed to enter some Soviet-run bases without special permission. According to some reports, the generals were so dissatisfied that they threatened the president with a military coup d'etat.

Sadat tried one last appeal to Moscow, and when that failed, he ordered the Soviet troops out and ordered his commanders to take control of all Soviet military equipment and installations in Egypt. It was a move well received by Sadat's people and one that left the Western world wondering who, if not the Soviet Union, would arm Egypt. That answer came in October, when the Soviets agreed to return some of the weaponry and advisers they had earlier been asked to remove.

Before Sadat's dramatic move in July, unrest had grown among Egyptians over their president's vacillating policy toward Israel. He had promised them a "year of decision" in 1971, but he did not act. The inaction was unacceptable to thousands of angry Cairo University students who demonstrated in January with signs declaring: "We must fight." Sadat at-

KEN ROSEWALL

tempted to mollify them by announcing measures to put Egypt's economy on a wartime footing, but his actions continued to lag behind his rhetoric. He apparently realized what other Egyptians refused to believe: that another war with Israel would certainly mean another defeat; Israel's weapons were simply far superior.

Anwar Sadat became president in 1970 because he was a loyal friend and faithful follower of Gamal Abdel Nasser. The two had gone to the Egyptian Military Academy together in 1938 and had later served at the same upper Nile army post. Nasser prized Sadat's friendship, and when he seized power from Faruk in 1952, he gave Sadat a succession of top government jobs, including the vice-presidency. When Nasser died in 1970, Sadat took over, supposedly as an interim leader, and then deftly outmaneuvered the opposition.

SHRIVER, SARGENT. See the special supplement ELECTION '72.

ANWAR SADAT

SONNY AND CHER (1935–   ; 1946–
). Back in the early 1960's, a
hustling songwriter named Salvatore Bono
and Cherilyn Sarkisian, his impassive-
faced, teen-age bride, took a look at the
current crop of rock stars and decided
that all they needed to hit the top was a
catchy tune and a little gimmickry.

So they dressed up in unisex outfits,
wore matching shaggy hairdos, and har-
monized their way through a few slow
rock love songs as the new singing team
of Sonny and Cher.

Only a few months after the Bonos
began as a singing team, they scored big
with a number called "I've Got You,
Babe," followed by four more hits in less
than a year (including "The Beat Goes
On," now the theme song of the *Sonny
& Cher Comedy Hour*).

Today, the couple have dropped their
hippie duds for a groomed and polished
image as television superstars whose
variety show is the Cinderella hit of 1972.

Sonny was born in Detroit on February
16, 1935. His interest in show business
started early, and he left high school in
the 12th grade to pursue his career. He
wrote songs and worked as an artists-
and-repertoire man and producer for a
record company. When he met Cher in
1963, he already had a number of hits
to his credit, including "Koko Joe" and
"Needles and Pins."

Cher was born on May 20, 1946, in
El Centro, Calif., of Armenian, Turkish,
French, and Cherokee Indian descent.
Cher, like Sonny, was bitten by the show
biz bug early. She studied acting with
Jeff Corey and dropped out of high school.

The couple met on a double date the
week Cher turned 17. The meeting was
hardly auspicious. Cher thought Sonny
had a "weird" haircut, and Sonny thought
Cher was "stuck up." First impressions
were overcome, however, and they were
married on October 27, 1964. They have
one daughter, Chastity.

SPITZ, MARK (1950–   ). The paradox
of Mark Spitz is that he has been unsink-
able in the water but has often been in
danger of drowning on dry land—in a
flood of criticism. Spitz has always struggled with his brash personality and has
always been able to alienate people.

As a youngster growing up in California,
Spitz was, he admits, a loner, a brat—and
a very fast swimmer. When he was ten,
his swimming lessons interfered with his
Hebrew lessons. It was never a contest as
to which would be dropped. Rationalizing
his way around the rabbi, Mark's father insisted that "even God likes a winner."

And a winner is what Spitz became. By
the time he entered Indiana University, he
had already set ten world records—but
was perhaps even better known for his
high-voltage ego. That's why, before Spitz
arrived at Indiana, the team's swimming
coach, James ("Doc") Counsilman, pleaded
with his swimmers not to judge Mark on

SONNY AND CHER

MARK SPITZ

his reputation, especially after what happened to Spitz at the 1968 Olympics in Mexico City, where he had boasted he might well win six gold medals. Oh, he won two golds, but both had been in relays; all he had to show for his four individual events was a silver and a bronze. Not a bad haul for any mortal, but then Spitz had been telling the world for so long that he *was* no mere mortal. However, in retrospect, his "failure" in 1968 helped make him both a better swimmer and a better man.

In 1971, Spitz swam as if driven by a propeller blade: he became the first male to win four titles at the national AAU championships, setting three world records in the process; then the next week, while on tour with an American team in East Germany and the Soviet Union, he not only won all seven of his races but also set, individually and with his teammates, four more world records. Largely because of that triumph, Spitz was selected this

fers (endorsements, personal appearances, television, movies) that it was estimated he would reap a $5 million bonanza. All of which seemed to indicate that promoters—as well as God—love winners.

STANFIELD, ROBERT (1914–   ). No one described Robert Stanfield as "dashing," and there were no squeals from the audience as the leader of Canada's Progressive Conservatives plodded around the country to deliver speeches in a lackluster style. Usually clad in a quiet gray suit and white shirt, the candidate himself conceded, "I'm a pretty old-fashioned kind of guy, and not very pretty at that!" Nonetheless, when the votes were counted after the October 30 election, Stanfield's party had come out just about even with the Liberals, in an embarrassing upset of the administration of Prime Minister Pierre Elliott Trudeau. What followed after Canada's closest election was a scramble for support from the 48 de-

elected four times as premier of the province, serving from 1956 to 1967 with so much popularity that Liberal opponents avoided attacking him by name. In 1967 he became the leader of the national Progressive Conservatives, succeeding former prime minister John Diefenbaker.

Trudeau's October 30 defeat was largely blamed on his own aloof campaign style and on disenchantment, especially among English-speaking Canadians, with inflation, unemployment, and the Official Languages Act, which made French coequal with English as the national tongue. Stanfield, an English-speaking Anglican, won strong support everywhere but in Quebec. But he is also credited with organizational ability and with a sincerity of manner that shines in public appearances.

STEINEM, GLORIA (1936–   ). Long, streaked blond hair, tinted eyeglasses, snug jeans—the best known of the feminists is also the best looking. As a result,

ROBERT STANFIELD

GLORIA STEINEM

KAKUEI TANAKA

February to receive the 1972 Sullivan Award as America's outstanding amateur athlete.

But it was at the Olympics in Munich this year that Spitz had a chance to surpass all those accomplishments, for he had earned the right to swim in seven events—both butterfly and freestyle at 100 meters and 200 meters, plus three relays. Spitz, straining valiantly to overcome his bulging self-confidence, refused to make any rash predictions. Instead, he jumped into the pool and swam away with all seven of those golds, topping the 1920 Olympic record of five, and cracked (or helped crack) the world record in each event. When he returned to the United States, he was swamped by so many of-

cisive seats held by minor-party candidates and independents, in which the mild-mannered, craggy-faced man from Nova Scotia remains within inches of realizing his dream of becoming prime minister of Canada.

Stanfield's steady climb toward the summit began back in Truro, N.S., where he was born April 11, 1914, into a political family which, as political cartoonists were wont to remember, made its money manufacturing woolen underwear for the long Canadian winters. An honors graduate of Dalhousie University and Harvard Law School, he began his career as a provincial attorney and Progressive Conservative Party leader. After seven years in the Nova Scotia legislature, he was

young women around the country have taken her distinctive look as their own, making Gloria Steinem as influential a fashion trend-setter as she is a spokesman for women's rights.

A Phi Beta Kappa at Smith College, Steinem is currently an editor of *Ms.*, a new magazine aimed at moving women out of second-class status.

Ms. was previewed in a December 1971 issue of *New York* magazine, and it raised enough money for its first solo flight in July. Steinem describes *Ms.* as a "how to" publication for women—"not how to make jelly but how to seize control of your life."

Born in Toledo on March 25, 1936, Gloria Steinem arrived in New York in

1960 ready to take her place among the serious journalists. Instead she found the market for women writers was in light-weight articles. Her first big success was a 1963 exposé of the life of a Playboy Club bunny, a job Steinem actually held for one month while researching the article. Soon she was turning out quicky pieces for all the women's magazines.

Steinem got her first real chance at political reporting when she went to work for *New York* magazine in 1968. She proved to be a deft, telling reporter with a knack for the jugular.

As part of her journalistic duties, Steinem attended a meeting of the militant Redstockings women's group in 1968. It was revelation time. "I'd always understood what made me angry about the Playboy Club or the double standard or not being able to do political writing or being sent out for coffee. . . . But I didn't realize it was a group problem."

Once she decided men were subjugating women, Steinem joined the movement. She helped organize the Women's Strike for Equality in 1970. The next year she helped to organize the National Women's Political Caucus and the Women's Action Alliance.

When the Democrats met in Miami in July, Steinem was there gleefully counting the new influx of women. At the 1968 Democratic Convention, only 13 percent of the delegates were women. By 1972, thanks to the feminist movement, that number jumped to 40 percent.

Noted Steinem with satisfaction: "We've changed the population here. It almost looks like the country."

TANAKA, KAKUEI (1918–   ). "I am a peasant born," the dynamic, self-made millionaire likes to boast. Ever since he took over as premier of Japan in July, stubby Kakuei Tanaka has attacked his country's considerable foreign and domestic problems with such earthy vigor that the Japanese—accustomed to the slower, more cautious approach of 71-year-old former premier Eisaku Sato—have been left gasping. Indeed, Western reporters in Tokyo find Tanaka's boisterous, back-slapping ways surprisingly reminiscent of the homier American school of politics.

The very fact that Tanaka got elected was an unprecedented event in traditionalist Japan. The son of a provincial farmer, Tanaka has neither education nor aristocratic polish. His predecessors as premier since World War II have all been university-educated, bureaucracy-trained patricians with the powerful family and friends usually necessary for top political jobs in a rigidly stratified society.

Tanaka effectively broke the mold. Born on May 4, 1918, in the village of Nishiyama in Niigata prefecture, on the west coast of Japan's main island of Honshu, Tanaka left home at 15 to work for a Tokyo contractor by day and study the building trade at night. After a brief stint with the army in Manchuria, Tanaka got a medical discharge just before Pearl Harbor and set up his own small construction company just in time to cash in on the wartime building boom.

A rich man before he was 30, Tanaka was elected to the Japanese Diet in 1947. After holding a series of government posts for the ruling Liberal-Democratic Party, he became trade minister under Sato.

Tanaka has taken over the leadership of his country at a time when it faces a period of flux, with new departures in its international relations and a long-overdue recognition of pressing domestic ills.

Late in August, Tanaka traveled to Hawaii for a meeting with President Richard M. Nixon. The primary focus was economic: Nixon asked Tanaka to help cut the large United States balance-of-trade deficit by boosting Japanese imports of U.S. goods, and Tanaka agreed. One of the things that Tanaka got in return was Nixon's blessings on the premier's proposed trip to Peking, which took place in September. While in China, Tanaka met with Party Chairman Mao Tse-tung and Prime Minister Chou En-lai, and the two governments formally agreed to resume diplomatic relations.

Tanaka is one of the first Japanese politicians to make pollution an issue, and his regime will almost certainly bring action on this front, as well as in the areas of housing and mass transportation. The prime minister's best-selling essay, *A Proposal for Remodeling the Japanese Archipelago*, envisions a broad restructuring of Japanese society to achieve "a new era of 'human restoration.'"

TRUDEAU, PIERRE (1921–   ). "Living next door to the U.S. is in some ways like sleeping with an elephant," the Canadian prime minister once observed. "No matter how friendly is the beast, one is affected by every twitch and grunt."

For sophisticated Pierre Trudeau, the problem of coexisting happily with the giant to the south gets knottier all the time. With nationalism burgeoning, there is a growing clamor among Canadians for the United States to pick up its considerable economic and pop-cultural influence and get out. From the prime minister's vantage point, it isn't that simple: high unemployment means that Canada needs foreign investment and the American dollar.

President Richard M. Nixon paid a state visit to Ottawa in April to improve, if not clear, the diplomatic air. He urged a new approach to Canadian-American relations based on recognition of the two countries' "separate identities" and "significant differences."

Nevertheless, at home Trudeau continued to be criticized for his less-than-militant attitude toward the United States. When his government announced in June that it planned to monitor all future investments in Canadian business, the To-

PIERRE TRUDEAU

ronto *Star* labeled the measure as "a feeble, timid gesture." Yet despite the growing criticism, the Liberal leader called for an election in October.

The swinging bachelor is now a settled husband and proud father of a new son, but his style was still in strong contrast to that of his Conservative opponent.

The election results gave Trudeau's Liberals only 109 seats to 107 for the Progressive Conservatives, led by Robert L. Stanfield. Trudeau, observers said, was rebuked for his economic policies and his emphasis on bilingualism, which cost him seats almost everywhere but Quebec. His colorful personality, which had caught the Canadian fancy four years earlier, may have seemed inappropriate in a prime minister. In any case, though his pride was stung by the results, Trudeau decided not to resign immediately. Instead, he will wait until Parliament reconvenes and meanwhile try to court a working majority.

VONNEGUT, KURT (1922–   ). The college students made him what he is today —a millionaire. When author Kurt Vonnegut, Jr., published his first novel, *Player Piano*, in 1952, it sold a meager 3,500 copies. Although critics remained unimpressed with his next four novels, a small but spirited core of devotees was growing on campuses around the country. Seventeen years after his first work, he published *Slaughterhouse-Five*, the latest in his now familiar mix of morality and science fiction. The novel was a runaway best seller. Faced with a demand for his earlier books, publishers then reissued his works in both hardback and paper.

All of which makes the wry, rumpled Vonnegut somewhat uneasy. "I am in the dangerous position now," he says, "where I can sell anything I write. For so long money has motivated me, and now there is nothing to move me off center. I don't know what to do."

After *Slaughterhouse*, Vonnegut turned to playwriting, producing the off-Broadway hit *Happy Birthday, Wanda June* in 1970. A movie of *Slaughterhouse* was released this year, and Vonnegut has formed a company called Sourdough Inc. to oversee other such deals.

One critic analyzed Vonnegut's enormous appeal to the young as being based on "his insistence on the randomness of life." Another found him "articulating the blackest suspicions of a skeptical, cynical generation without running into orgies of hate or ironical partisanship of evil."

Born in Indianapolis on November 11, 1922, Vonnegut served as an infantry combat scout in World War II, was captured during the Battle of the Bulge, and actually lived through the horrific firebombing of Dresden that forms the major subject of *Slaughterhouse*. After the war, he drifted into public relations work, then for years made a living churning out stories for the slicks and sci-fi magazines. He married his wife Jane in 1945, and they live in a farmhouse in West Barnstable, Mass., with their three children and three adopted nephews, the children of Vonnegut's deceased sister.

KURT VONNEGUT

WALDHEIM, KURT (1918–   ). On January 1, 1972, Kurt Waldheim took office as the fourth secretary general in the history of the United Nations. He soon became embroiled in the controversies that go with the job.

There were money problems that even Waldheim's austerity program could scarcely make a dent in. His offer to arbitrate the civil war in Northern Ireland was refused by the British. Like his immediate predecessor, U Thant, Waldheim was denounced by the United States for his statements on Vietnam. Staking all his prestige, he did succeed in getting the General Assembly to debate the hot topic of terrorism, despite Arab and Chinese objections. There was no question about it: despite the controversies, Waldheim was carrying on the activist tradition.

Waldheim was born on December 21, 1918, in St. Andrae-Wörden, a small town near Vienna in Austria. The son of a school inspector of Czech descent (his father had changed the family name from Waclawik when he entered the Austrian civil service), Waldheim grew up as an intensely patriotic lad who volunteered for service in the Austrian Army at the age of 18. After a period of service in which he attained a rank equivalent to corporal, he returned to school, only to have his legal studies at the University of Vienna disrupted by the German occupation of Austria in 1938.

Although they threw his father into jail, the Nazis drafted Waldheim into the German Army as a lieutenant and sent him to the Russian front, where he was severely wounded in the leg. After a lengthy period of convalescence, he was discharged from the army and permitted to resume his studies. He received his LL.D. degree in 1944 and, at the end of the war, joined the Austrian diplomatic service.

Waldheim participated in the negotiations that led to the neutralization of Austria and, in 1955, when Austria joined the United Nations, he became head of the Austrian mission to the UN. From 1968 to 1970 he served Austria as minister of foreign affairs, and in 1971 he ran for the presidency of Austria, losing narrowly with 47.2 percent of the vote.

Waldheim married the former Elisabeth Ritschel on April 19, 1944. The couple has three children.

WALLACE, GEORGE (1919–   ). At the beginning of the year, the feisty governor of Alabama was regarded somewhat patronizingly by Republican and Democratic politicians alike as a spoiler, a role he had played in the 1968 presidential election. But by early May, when George Wallace had won four presidential primaries, finished second in three others, and garnered the largest total popular vote, his opponents were taking him very seriously.

The Wallace of 1972 may have been the same man who stood in the schoolhouse door in 1963 to keep out black students, but, on the surface at least, there was a new Wallace. He had a new and beautiful young wife, Cornelia (whom he married in 1970, two years after his first wife, Lurleen, died of cancer), and a new contemporary wardrobe she had picked out for him. But most important of all, he had a new and different way of talking about the old problems. Wallace described busing in nonracial terms, criticizing it as the "callous, asinine . . . whim of some social schemer in Washington who messed up the schools there and then moved out to Virginia or Maryland." In fact, the major theme of Wallace's primary campaign was that the "working man," who has to "pay through the nose" while the rich are provided with tax loopholes, was being victimized by liberal bureaucrats in the federal government—"pointy-headed intellectuals who can't park their bikes straight."

The Wallace campaign abruptly came to a sickeningly familiar end at a Laurel, Md., shopping center on May 15. During his speech at the shopping center, Wallace stood behind a 600-pound bulletproof podium and was surrounded by Secret Service agents, Maryland county police, and his own Alabama state police bodyguards. But after he finished speaking, Wallace stepped down to greet the crowd. Then, as he worked his way down a line of supporters, a blond young man with opaque sunglasses—Arthur Herman Bremer—pushed his way through the people surrounding Wallace, pulled a .38-caliber pistol from his jacket pocket, and fired point-blank at the governor. Bremer (who, it was later learned, had stalked and intended to shoot President Richard M. Nixon during Nixon's state visit to Canada in April) also managed to wound one of Wallace's bodyguards, a Secret Service agent, and a campaign worker.

Wallace was rushed to Holy Cross Hospital in Silver Spring, Md., where he underwent a five-hour operation, during which a bullet was removed from his intestine. Nine days later, the governor almost died from an abdominal infection and peritonitis. When that infection was under control, surgeons finally went after the bullet that was paralyzing Wallace from the waist down. They found his spinal column bruised but not severed, but whether he would ever walk again was an unanswered question.

KURT WALDHEIM

GEORGE WALLACE

Wallace made a dramatic comeback appearance as he was lifted in his wheelchair up to the speaker's dais at the Democratic National Convention in July to ask for platform planks against busing, for a crackdown on welfare eligibility, and for capital punishment. The delegates applauded and listened politely but voted down the platform requests.

On August 4, the same day Arthur Bremer was found guilty, Wallace unequivocally pulled himself out of the presidential race. When the American Party telephoned the governor from its convention in Louisville, Ky., to ask him to be the party's candidate, Wallace refused. "I regret," he said, "that my physical condition is such that I cannot answer the people's wish to draft me."

WESTWOOD, JEAN (1923–   ). "... I've come to recognize that she represents the new force of women in American political life." With those admiring words from presidential candidate George McGovern on the last day of the Miami convention, Frances Jean Miles Westwood was unanimously chosen to replace Larry O'Brien as chairman of the Democratic National Committee. She is the first woman in either party to hold the prestigious post.

A rough-voiced blond grandmother from Utah, Mrs. Westwood is a seasoned backroom politician (organizer of voter registration drives, state committeewoman, congressional election campaign manager in her home state). "She has boundless energy," notes one friend, "and she has that incredible talent to strip away the peeling and find the core."

WILLIAM WHITELAW

Mrs. Westwood first met George McGovern at the 1968 Democratic convention. She was a Humphrey supporter at the time but was impressed with the antiwar senator from South Dakota. When he asked her to work for him last year, Mrs. Westwood ran the citizens for McGovern campaign in 17 western states. At the July convention, she served as adviser, confidante, and floor leader for the candidate.

Jean Miles was born in the small Utah mining town of Price on November 22, 1923, and she married Richard E. Westwood in 1941. Her husband is currently in the apartment construction business, but for years the couple ran a highly profitable mink ranch.

When Mrs. Westwood thanked the committee for picking her she added, "I'm proud to be your chairman." Someone shouted, "You're the chairwoman." And another contradicted: "No, she isn't, she's the chairperson." "I'm proud to be your chairman," she repeated firmly, observing that the committee faced enough serious national problems without haggling over titles.

WHITELAW, WILLIAM (1918–   ). On March 24, British prime minister Edward Heath suspended the Protestant-dominated government of Northern Ireland and replaced it with a secretary of state directly responsible to London. The man Heath chose for the job was his good friend and adviser, William Whitelaw, a bluff Scottish landowner who had risen steadily through Conservative Party ranks.

"Everyone likes Willie," a friend noted after Whitelaw was picked. "Even the grottiest Irishman should warm to him." "He radiates good will, patience, impartiality," said one of his aides, "but underneath, he's a very cunning man—it's an ideal mix." That combination of attributes had served Whitelaw well in Parliament, where as leader of the House of Commons and a stalwart defender of Conservative interests, he remained on good terms with the Labour Opposition.

Born June 18, 1918, and favored with an upper-class education, William Stephen Ian Whitelaw had shown no remarkable intellectual gifts. In fact, as a politician his outstanding trait was loyalty—loyalty to Heath. "If he told me that tomorrow I should become ambassador to Iceland," Whitelaw once said, "I would go straight to Iceland. I trust his judgment absolutely. I trust him more than I've ever trusted anyone." Assignment to Northern Ireland may represent an even more thankless task.

Whitelaw quickly set to work listening to complaints from all sides. Within two weeks he eased the Catholics' most immediate grievance by releasing 73 persons who had been interned or detained without trial; eight weeks later he reportedly freed another 379. But that still left almost 500 suspected terrorists in prison.

JEAN WESTWOOD

Meanwhile, the Irish Republican Army kept up its barrage of terrorism. And the danger of counterterrorism was on the rise, with the newly formed Ulster Defense Association threatening to act on its own if Whitelaw did not invade IRA sanctuaries in the Catholic "no go" areas.

Yet by late June it looked as if Whitelaw might have achieved the impossible. The Provisional wing of the IRA was offering the first cease-fire in three years. Whitelaw assured the IRA that British troops would "obviously reciprocate." But the truce lasted a mere two weeks, as a housing dispute on July 9 erupted into a pitched battle between Catholic protesters and British soldiers. Whitelaw charged that the IRA had provoked the confrontation to provide an excuse for the resumption of guerrilla activities throughout Ulster.

The net result was a hardening of Whitelaw's position. Reinforcements were requested and sent, and, on July 31, British troops staged an armored invasion of IRA strongholds in Londonderry and Belfast. As Catholic barricades came down, Whitelaw's commander of ground forces announced that "anyone can go anywhere at any time." A new wave of IRA bombings belied his assertion.

After the stick, Whitelaw tried another carrot. The internment camps were to close, he said, and a special tribunal would be empowered to try the suspected terrorists remaining in captivity. But the IRA wasn't biting. As the killings continued and the UDA kept gathering strength, it seemed that no one but his friend Edward Heath was thanking William Whitelaw. NANCY GAY FABER
HERMAN WEISKOPF—*Sports*

PERU. El Niño. The appearance of a warm ocean current off the Pacific coast of Peru last December has been creating economic problems of potentially disastrous dimensions. The Child (El Niño), as the current is called because it appears around Christmas every five or six years, brings warm waters to an area bathed by the icy Humboldt Current. The Humboldt Current is rich in fish, helping to make Peru the largest fishing nation in the world (the fishing industry provides 40 percent of the country's foreign exchange). The Humboldt Current also generates cold air which normally forms a wall off Peru's coast preventing warm Pacific rain clouds from discharging their waters on the coast.

The prolonged stay of the warm current, which usually lasts until April, has practically shut down the fishing industry, and the incursion of Pacific rain clouds is causing serious flooding with increasing loss in crops, roads, and human life. Peruvians were so worried about the unusual length of the phenomenon that they asked experts from the Organization of American States to investigate the causes.

Government and politics. The military government proceeded this year to "democratize" Peruvian society and reinforce its declared policy of international neutrality. The ministry of agriculture announced that almost 5 million acres of farm and grazing land have been expropriated and redistributed between 1967 and the end of 1971. Moreover, a government decree of December 23, 1971, has seen rapid implementation, with 127,000 acres of land expropriated and included in the agrarian reform program.

On February 9, Peru's first Chinese ambassador, Chiao Jo-yu, presented his credentials to President Juan Velasco Alvarado, after a year of exploratory talks on trade and aid between the People's Republic of China and Peru. However, underscoring the position of the government, 12 leftists belonging to the Maoist Revolutionary Vanguard were arrested March 16, according to an Interior Ministry announcement. They were accused of terrorism in the robbing of several banks and the murder of two policemen.

The increased nationalism of the regime was further emphasized with the expulsion of three foreign political activist priests. The Reverend Antoine Bourdom Brun, a 40-year-old French priest, Reverend José Luis Gómez Morales, a 39-year-old Spaniard, and 26-year-old Brazilian Adalberto Garces Lopez were charged with "interference in the internal affairs of Peru." This is the second year that the government has expelled members of religious communities on these grounds.

The sensitivity of the government to any form of criticism, not only from foreigners but from domestic sources as well, came to a head with the government order that Pedro Beltran Espantoso, publisher of Lima's prestigious paper *La Prensa*, sell his stock in the paper. In a pattern typical of other government moves to break up companies, an "industrial community" of *La Prensa* workers bought the 80,000 shares valued at US$163,000. *La Prensa* had been the leading spokesman for the opposition to the regime. The *La Prensa* crisis is typical of a tightening control which the regime has been imposing on all media. On May 17 two broadcasting decrees were issued for radio and television programming. They require a higher "Peruvian" content and the expansion of programs that reflect "humane values" and are "socially useful"; the decrees also prohibit religious, social, or racial discrimination and create a ban on advertising products "outside the reach of the Peruvian masses."

Economy. A subtle improvement in Peru's position toward foreign investment has raised the likelihood of new credit and the extension of foreign debt repayment. Japan has already offered some US$60 million in credit, and 14 New York banks have refinanced US$53.3 million in debts that were to come due in the next two years, extending the repayment schedule to 1973 through 1977.

In a tough approach to foreign investors the government turned over phosphate and potash deposits in northern Peru

CURRENT EVENT. Peruvian fishing yields were disastrously small because of a warm ocean current that infiltrated coastal waters and drove off anchovies used in fish meal, Peru's leading export.

to Minoperu, the state mining corporation. The action came after the government claimed that Bayovar Mining Company, a U.S. firm, and Midepesa Industries of Canada failed to meet government requirements for accelerated development of deposits. Reflecting its desire to accelerate exploitation of resources, Minoperu signed a marketing agreement with two U.S. firms, Cerro Corporation and Southern Peru Copper Corporation, in which the two companies would act as agents for the state corporation. Another agreement was signed with the Romanian firm Geomin to develop the Antamina copper deposits. Peru will hold over 51 percent of the joint venture. Minoperu has also taken over the marketing of zinc, lead, and silver production.

As part of the policy of diversifying its economy, Peru has also been trying to develop its petroleum resources. Petroperu, the state oil corporation, was prepared to sign oil development contracts with the French firm Elf-Erap and the U.S. Sun Oil Corporation. Furthermore, after the successful striking of two high-grade oil wells in Peru's eastern jungle area near the Amazon town of Iquitos, a Japanese company, Marubeni Corporation, offered to finance construction of a pipeline to the Pacific coast. The pipeline, according to estimates reported by the press, would cost over US$400 million. At the same time it was announced that Marcona Mining Company of San Francisco, Calif., planned to invest US$60 million in the construction of an iron ore processing plant in the state of Ica. The urgency with which Peru is pressing, especially in the area of oil production, is

stimulated by the fact that Peru consumes over 100,000 barrels daily in petroleum while the domestic production is only in the vicinity of 66,000 barrels, thus forcing the government to import the balance at great cost in foreign exchange.

Area and population. Area, 496,224 sq. mi. Pop. (est. 1971), 14,000,000. Principal cities (est. 1970): Lima (cap.), 2,200,000; Callao, 330,000; Arequipa, 200,000.
Government. Military rule. Pres., General Juan Velasco Alvarado.
Finance. Monetary unit, sol; 1 sol = US$0.0232. Budget (1970): balanced at US$952 million.
Trade (est. 1971). Imports, US$603 million; exports, US$1.044 billion. Major exports: copper, fishmeal, iron ore. Major imports: manufactured goods, fuel.
Education (1968). Enrollment: primary, 2,334,982; secondary, 470,664; higher education, 111,553.
Armed forces. Army, 35,500; navy, 7,600; air force, 9,000.

STEFFEN SCHMIDT

PHILIPPINES. In late September the Philippines were rocked by its most severe domestic turmoil since the Communist insurgency of the early 1950's. A month of terrorist bombing of public facilities in Manila and Quezon City culminated on September 22 with an assassination attempt on Defense Secretary Juan Ponce Enrile. Six hours later, President Ferdinand E. Marcos responded with the imposition of martial law. All newspapers and radio stations were closed; a few were permitted to reopen following the imposition of strict censorship. Many arrests followed, with several prominent politicians—including the leader of the opposition Liberal Party and two provincial governors—caught up in the government sweep. President Marcos characterized the campaign as an effort to save the country both from Communist insurrection and from criminal and corrupt elements pervading Philippine society.

Government and politics. During the year, a changeover from the U.S. style of government to the British parliamentary system was agreed upon in principle by the Constitutional Convention. But the convention's effectiveness was threatened by the snail's pace of its work and by demoralizing charges of corruption within its ranks. September's martial law crises changed the situation greatly.

The key decision on the choice of a governmental system came in July, with the British parliamentary model winning by a vote of 158 to 120. By then the Con-Con, as it was known in Manila, had been limping along for a year with no end in sight to its appointed task of writing a charter of political and socioeconomic reforms. In May it had been stunned by delegate Eduardo Quintero's allegations of extensive bribery of delegates, even those from the presidential family itself.

On October 20 the Constitutional Convention adopted an article covering the transition from the presidential government to the British-style parliamentary government. The article states that the president will hold the post of prime minister as well, with all the powers of both offices under both constitutions, until he calls on an interim parliament to form a new government. President Marcos then announced that he would submit a draft constitution to the voters in January 1973.

UNDER MARTIAL LAW decreed at 2:00 A.M. on September 23 by Philippine president Ferdinand Marcos, 49 persons, including newsmen and prominent politicians, were arrested. Below, visiting hours for three Filipinos who were caught in the widespread actions.

UPI

In general the government felt confident enough to restore the rights of habeas corpus, suspended during the summer of 1971. But violent demonstrations and guerrilla activity continued unabated. Two groups involved in these actions were identified as the Kabataang Makabayan (Patriotic Youth)—which claimed an active membership of 75,000, and the Maoist New People's Army (NPA). The latter launched several "offensives" against police and government troops and was said to number about 300. The NPA was most active in Isabela Province but also appeared in the provinces of Zambales and Bicol. President Marcos charged that some Philippine rebels had been trained by Indonesian and Chinese Communists, citing evidence supplied by Indonesia's president Suharto. Similar charges were made against some Arab countries allegedly supporting Muslim guerrillas in Mindanao and helping to run secret training camps there. Trouble between Christians and Muslims has been endemic in this area for several decades.

Foreign relations. The popularity of Mrs. Imelda Marcos, first lady of the Philippines, rose during the year. One reason was a lengthy overseas tour she embarked upon which included a meeting with Premier Aleksei N. Kosygin in Moscow. President Marcos dispatched his wife as his official representative and had, at the same time, sent her brother, Governor Benjamin Romualdez, to Peking to assess changes in China's foreign policy after President Richard M. Nixon's visit.

President Marcos made great strides in liberalizing Philippine policy toward the Communist countries. He opened diplomatic relations with Romania and Yugoslavia and granted permission for Communist traders and vessels to enter the country, thus ending a ban that had been in force since 1945.

After the Nixon initiative in China, Marcos attempted to woo Peking but was apparently rebuffed. Later, he seemed to revert to support for keeping up traditional ties with Taiwan. Nevertheless, a new trade era was launched with Peking, the Philippines selling coconut oil and other local products in exchange for 100,000 tons of Chinese rice, ordered via Hong Kong. Peking followed with a donation of 3 million pesos for flood relief after a typhoon struck. Significantly, the grant was one of the largest made by any foreign government.

Meanwhile, Marcos responded to demands of younger-generation critics and launched a campaign to renegotiate the military and commercial treaties with the United States "to give real meaning to our independence." Little progress was made, however, in modifying the terms of the controversial Laurel-Langley agreement on trade and commerce, due to expire in 1974.

Economy. One of the worst disasters in modern Philippine history struck in July when a typhoon washed over the islands with the heaviest rains in more than 60 years. Luzon received 170 inches of rainfall in less than a month. More than 530 people died from the resulting floods and damage was estimated at 2 billion pesos.

This tragedy spoiled what otherwise promised to be a reasonably good year for the economy. The 1971 growth rate of 5.3 percent was expected to be at least equalled. Exports had risen by 15 percent in 1971, with bananas clearly emerging as an important new source of foreign exchange.

Area and population. Area, 115,831 sq. mi. Pop. (1970 census, provisional), 37,008,419. Principal cities: Quezon City (cap.), 585,100; Manila, 1,582,000.
Government. Republic with bicameral Congress. (Undergoing change to a parliamentary system.) Pres., Ferdinand E. Marcos.
Finance. Monetary unit, peso; 1P = US$0.15. Budget (1971–1972), US$640 million.
Trade (1971). Imports, US$1,315,000,000; exports, US$1,103,000,000.
Education (1970). Enrollment: primary, 7,350,000; secondary, 1,921,000; college and university, 700,000.   DICK WILSON

PHOTOGRAPHY. Popularity. Numerous signs indicate that the audience for serious, creative photography is rapidly expanding. The first such portent is the phenomenal increase in the ranks of galleries devoted exclusively to the presentation of photographic imagery. Only five years ago, the number of photographic galleries in the United States could have been counted on one's fingers; and, except for Chicago, there were none at all between the east and west coasts. There are now more than a dozen in New York alone, and it seems likely that within a few years every state will have at least one—more than 20 do already. Original photographic prints still do not sell well, so most photo galleries operate on a shoestring. The mortality rate is exceedingly high, but the number of such births and deaths is at an all-time peak.

Part of the reason for this may be that the collecting of photographs and related material has at last become fashionable. Major auction houses such as Parke-Bernet in New York and Sotheby's in London are now selling photographs and photographica at special auctions, and although the returns have been held down somewhat by the recession, they have nevertheless been surprisingly high. This reflects a gradually increasing public awareness of the significance of photography as an art form. (Also, photography is the only major graphic art form in which a modestly budgeted collector can still build a representative group of central works by key figures in the medium's history without going bankrupt.)

Not unpredictably, the work favored by collectors of photography is generally in the classic vein—images by such early photographers as William Henry Fox Talbot, Julia Margaret Cameron, Mathew Brady, and Timothy O'Sullivan, along with well-established twentieth-century artists like Walker Evans, Edward Weston, and Man Ray. The work of younger photographers, no matter how reasonably priced, is rarely purchased, a fact which has led to another recent phenomenon—the rise of the privately published photographic book.

Private publishing. There is a long tradition of "publishing your own" in photography—indeed, the very first book illustrated with original photographs, Fox Talbot's *The Pencil of Nature* (1844), was issued by its author and sold by subscription. Since then, many photographers have published their own books, but these have been sporadic and unconnected events. Over the past two or three years, however, private publication has been happening more and more frequently, to such an extent that it can now be considered a movement.

Among the leaders in this field are painter Ed Ruscha, who, with 14 small photographic books to his name (the first being *Twentysix Gasoline Stations*, the most recent *Dutch Details*), is surely the most prolific; Lee Friedlander, whose *Self-Portrait* was an instant classic; and Ralph Gibson, who began by publishing his own sequence, *The Somnambulist*, and ended up starting a publishing venture, Lustrum Press, to enable other photographers to do the same.

The motives behind this do-it-yourself tendency are numerous. Pragmatically, it is difficult to get a photographic book published by a large publisher; such books are difficult to manufacture well and usually lose money. However, there is a small but definite market for them, sizable enough to make a small edition—3,000 to 5,000 copies—commercially feasible. Furthermore, the book format is an exciting one for many photographers—a natural one, in fact, for anyone working in sequence form—and a unique way of enlarging one's audience. Since a distributing company—Light Impressions, located in Rochester, N.Y.—has recently been formed specifically for the purpose of marketing photographic books, the idea is bound to spread. Some of the books which can be included in this "movement" are esoteric —such as Geoff Winningham's *Friday Night in the Coliseum*, a document of the wrestling subculture in Houston, Texas,

or Alwyn Scott Turner's *Photographs of the Detroit People* —but many are of general interest and will eventually find a wide audience by this unusual route.

Multimedia. Conceptual art, happenings, and the snapshot aesthetic met again this year, often with better results than expected. Bernadette Mayer, a New York poet, shot an entire 36-exposure roll of color film every day for a month, had them printed by a drugstore processing concession, and mounted "Memory," a show which included all 1,116 images in sequence, accompanied by a taped monologue which used the photos as a jumping-off place. A New York photography critic, teaming up with a well-known photographer, invited 100 New York photographers to photograph each other at a party at a 10th Avenue diner and mounted the results—a group show and essay in comparative style—in a New York gallery under the title "The Market Diner Bash." Several shows—including one in New York and one in Cologne, Germany—were created by giving general instructions for the making of certain kinds of city views and requesting their submission for exhibition purposes.

Exhibitions. The year's exhibits included several major retrospectives, among them Paul Strand's (accompanied by a monumental two-volume monograph) at the Philadelphia Museum. Strand's show prompted a bevy of art critics—who are frequently not well informed about photography—to eulogize his work as the culmination of twentieth-century photography, thus ignoring every development in the medium since 1935. Another retrospective, David Douglas Duncan's, was important as a breakthrough—it was the first photographic exhibit ever held under the auspices of the Whitney Museum of American Art. But the melodramatic presentation of the images—all blown up to larger than life-size—and their illustrativeness made them seem out of place in a museum context.

KODAK AND POLAROID:

Two Titans Think Small

America's two photography giants have developed flashy new mini-entries in the race to snap up a lion's share of the camera market. Right, actress Cybill Shepherd tries out the wallet-sized Kodak model-20 Instamatic, on sale for about $28; the company hopes to sell 4 million small Instamatics a year. Below, the Polaroid SX-70, which closes up to the size of a paperback; less than two seconds after the shutter button is pushed, a solid blue film ejects itself from the SX-70 and automatically develops into a picture, with nothing at all to throw away.

ABOVE, EASTMAN KODAK; LEFT, POLAROID

Books. The relationship between photography and the other arts was the subject of one of the year's more important books, Van Deren Coke's *The Painter and the Photograph.* Coke, who resigned his position as director of the International Museum of Photography at George Eastman House this spring after a surprisingly brief tenure and returned to the University of New Mexico, provided in his book documentation of hundreds of instances in which painters have worked directly from photographs. Although he failed to draw many specific conclusions from his data, Coke demonstrated quite clearly that painting is deeply in photography's debt. And *The Photographs of Thomas Eakins,* by Gordon Hendricks, provided an in-depth look at one painter's use of photography throughout his career.

Among the year's other notable books were Mark Jury's *The Vietnam Photo Book,* unique in its exploration of the manifestations of youth culture—drugs, rock, and bell bottoms—in the military bases in Vietnam; Larry Clark's *Tulsa,* a harrowing and totally committed document of the drug scene in Oklahoma by a sometime participant in it; *Palante: Young Lords Party,* an equally committed and un-"objective" statement by young photojournalist Michael Abramson; Danny Seymour's *A Loud Song,* an ambitious attempt at an autobiography in pictures by a young disciple of Robert Frank, whose own *The Lines of My Hand* reaffirmed his almost single-handed founding of contemporary documentary photography and fully justified his selection by the Rolling Stones as the official photographer for their spectacular American tour and double album, *Exile on Main Street.*

Obituaries. Two deaths this year bereaved the photographic community. The fine young British photojournalist Tony Ray-Jones was stricken by leukemia while on the verge of wider recognition. And Ralph Eugene Meatyard, who had never received the recognition he merited but had just published two books—one a monograph, the other a collaboration with his friend, the poet Wendell Berry—died at the age of 47.

Princeton professorship. A major breakthrough in the academic world's acceptance of photography as a legitimate subject for study was made when Princeton University announced the establishment of the David Hunter McAlpin professorship of the history of photography and modern art. The position will be filled by Peter Bunnell, former curator of the Department of Photography at the Museum of Modern Art. While this development will no doubt accelerate the growth of the academic school of photography, it also indicates that photography is moving faster and faster toward cultural acceptance as a full-fledged art form, with all the rights and privileges pertaining thereto.

A. D. COLEMAN

PHYSICS. Both unemployment and underemployment were widespread among new physics graduates this year, and the prospect was for a continuing tight market. Federal and industrial support of research in physics, although roughly constant in dollars, continued to decline in real terms. Nevertheless, 1972 was an extremely productive and exciting time for physics research. The year saw some pioneering ventures in astrophysics; the initial use, at the National Accelerator Laboratory in Batavia, Ill., of the world's largest accelerator for the study of elementary particles; and the start-up, at the Los Alamos, N.M., scientific laboratory, of still another unique accelerator for probing the nucleus. The year also witnessed new developments in the use of lasers and the publication of a National Academy of Sciences report on the status of physics. The report represented a major effort at introspection by the physics community.

Astrophysics. Nowhere was the pace of activity more rapid than in the study of the physics of the universe, particularly the properties of stars near the end of their lifetimes. The discovery of pulsars by radio astronomers in 1968 led to intensive observation of these objects, which are believed to be rotating neutron stars formed during the explosion of a supernova (a nova is a star that suddenly becomes extremely bright and then fades relatively quickly). Now, investigations by X-ray astronomers have turned up evidence of what may be a still more exotic end point of stellar evolution—the black hole.

Black holes were first predicted some 30 years ago by J. Robert Oppenheimer and others on the basis of Einstein's theory of general relativity; they occur, according to the predictions, when a massive star burns out, loses its ability to withstand gravitational forces, and begins an unending collapse that compresses the star's matter to theoretically infinite densities. Such objects have never been observed directly, and not surprisingly, since they are so compact and of such mass as to trap even light rays. In the terminology of general relativity, the curvature of space in the vicinity of a black hole becomes so great as to reflect all radiation back into the dead star, so that no signals escape. Hence the name. The hope of astrophysicists who want to study black holes for the clues they may shed on the process of gravitational collapse is to identify such an object by means of its interactions with surrounding matter (for example, by studying a binary star system in which one member is a black hole).

The current excitement centers on X-ray data from the first small astronomy satellite (nicknamed Uhuru, the Swahili word for freedom), which was launched in December 1970. The satellite's X-ray experiment, designed by Riccardo Giacconi and his associates at American Science and Engineering, Inc., in Cambridge, Mass., appears to have discovered a new class of objects of a size so small that they may be black holes. Two of these new objects, Centaurus X-3 and Cygnus X-1, appear to be part of binary or other multistar systems.

Cygnus X-1 in particular has X-ray emissions that vary in a complex pattern. Optical observations by C. T. Bolton of the David Dunlap Observatory of the University of Toronto and by Paul Murdin and Louise Webster of the Royal Observatory in Greenwich, England, indicate that a class-B supergiant star in the same region of the sky has an unseen companion that orbits the star every 5.6 days; that companion is assumed to be Cygnus X-1. Gas appears to be streaming from the larger star toward its companion, and the X rays measured by Uhuru might well be given off as the gas is accelerated and compressed by the intense gravitational field of a black hole. This possibility has stimulated additional theoretical calculations of the properties that the radiation should have.

Centaurus X-3 might also be a black hole, but the extreme regularity of the X-ray pulses from it has convinced many astrophysicists that it is some other kind of condensed stellar object, such as a neutron star. Efforts to optically identify the other star or stars that appear to eclipse the Centaurus X-3 emissions regularly are of particular interest because the combination of optical and X-ray data might allow the mass, distance, luminosity, and other features of the condensed object to be determined. As the wealth of data from the Uhuru satellite is evaluated, still other surprises in the X-ray spectrum, until now observable only for short periods with rockets, can be expected.

Neutron stars and black holes are of interest in their own right, but they also provide a means of studying the behavior of matter at densities unattainable on earth. Gravitational collapse, whether of a black hole or of an entire universe, appears to involve some fundamental contradictions between quantum mechanical laws that describe matter under normal conditions and the predictions of general relativity. The resolution of these apparent contradictions will be essential to an understanding of how the universe evolved.

Elementary particles. Physicists who are studying the fundamental structure of matter have been waiting impa-

tiently for several years for the National Accelerator Laboratory (NAL) to begin operation, and in 1972 their waiting finally came to an end. Progress in the study of elementary (subatomic) particles is to a large degree dependent on experiments involving collisions of particles at higher and higher energy levels. Despite some tantalizing findings at the Stanford Linear Accelerator in California and at the Center for European Nuclear Research near Geneva, Switzerland, in recent years, no definitive answers to a host of important questions have emerged. The new and extremely powerful synchrotron at NAL, capable of accelerating protons to energies as high as 500 billion electron volts (Gev), has now become the main focus of research on such questions as the following: Are the proton and the neutron in fact composed of the elusive quarks or partons that have been suggested by theorists as the ultimate building blocks of matter? Do particle collisions at 500 Gev produce phenomena similar to those observed at lower energies or something radically different?

Since the NAL accelerator is six times more powerful than the next largest accelerator (at Serpukhov in the Soviet Union), physicists have high hopes that experiments now being initiated at NAL will settle some uncertainties.

While waiting for new experimental results, the theorists have not been idle, and one result has been considerable progress in the past year in the attempt to form a unified theory of two of the fundamental forces of nature. Four such forces are known—electromagnetic force; gravitational force; the strong nuclear force that controls interactions between protons, neutrons, and mesons; and the weak nuclear force that controls interactions between these particles and electrons, neutrinos, and muons. The electromagnetic force was thought to be well understood, and the nature of the gravitational force as a manifestation of the curvature of space was postulated by Einstein in the theory of general relativity, published in 1916. Less is known about the two nuclear forces, but recently physicists have become aware of some remarkable similarities between the electromagnetic force and the weak nuclear force. At least two theoretical models have been advanced to explain these similarities and to outline a more universal theory. The nature of the strong nuclear force, however, remains an enigma.

Nuclear physics. There was also a major new accelerator for nuclear physicists to use—the 800-million-electron-volt machine at the Los Alamos Meson Physics Facility (LAMPF). The accelerator, which produced its first beam in early June, can make simultaneously available beams of protons, neutrons, muons, and neutrinos in copious numbers, permitting physicists to probe the nucleus far more deeply and precisely than ever before. No results from LAMPF will be forthcoming until next year, when the experimental areas are completed, but the initial experiments have been chosen.

In the meantime, quite a few nuclear physicists have been turning their heavy-ion accelerators, normally devoted to probing the nucleus, to studies of molecular phenomena. When heavy ions collide with other atoms, some unusual X rays are given off that indicate a great deal about the state of the atoms. The technique may prove useful for studying the chemical composition of air pollution particles and for locating impurities in semiconductors. The technique has already led to the apparent discovery of a still more exotic phenomenon involving elements heavier than any yet found in nature or made by man, the so-called superheavies. Scientists have speculated that when two heavy elements collide, their electrons arrange themselves into a short-lived molecular pattern characteristic of the element whose atomic number equals the sum of the two. Thus, it may be possible to study the X-ray spectra of superheavy elements which have not yet been created. Preliminary evidence that just such X rays had been seen was reported, at a conference held in Atlanta, Ga., in April, by P. H. Mokler of the Kernforschung Anlage in Jülich, Germany.

Lasers. One of the most exciting developments of the year was the announcement of new details about the work on laser-induced fusion (the information was declassified by the U.S. Atomic Energy Commission). A scheme that uses many different laser beams to bombard a small pellet of hydrogen isotopes from all directions was revealed. Because the laser beams create an implosion effect that compresses the pellet, as much as 1,000 times less energy is needed to start a fusion reaction. Many physicists now predict that the scientific feasibility of laser-induced fusion will be demonstrated within the next two to four years, either by U.S. or Soviet scientists.

Extremely short pulses of energy are needed to induce fusion reactions, and neodymium glass lasers that can deliver 1,000 joules of energy in less than a nanosecond (one-billionth of a second) are being developed at several U.S. laboratories. The largest so far announced is a 215-joule laser at the Naval Research Laboratory in Washington, D.C. A 600-joule laser has been built at the Lebedev Institute in Moscow. Light from flash lamps "charges" the neodymium glass by storing energy in excited atoms; the energy is released in a pulse that is triggered by the light from another small laser. Several stages of lasers are used, each one amplifying the pulse of light. Because neodymium lasers are extremely inefficient, converting about 0.1 percent of the energy used to drive them into a light pulse, these lasers are not expected to be the basis of operational devices. However, they will permit study of the basic physics of the processes that take place in the pellet as it is heated and begins to react and of the interactions between the laser beams and the pellet.

Although the lasers currently available are still substantially less powerful than those needed for power plants and although many other problems associated with the practical generation of fusion power remain to be solved, the prospects for fusion power are perhaps more encouraging now than ever before. The fusion reaction most likely to be used involves deuterium and tritium. Inexhaustible amounts of deuterium can be found in seawater, but tritium must be produced in fusion reactors from lithium. Even though lithium is not an abundant element, the world's resources are estimated to be large enough to provide a million years' worth of energy at current rates of use. Thus, fusion, if it can be achieved at reasonable cost, would be man's largest source of energy except for sunlight, which itself originates from fusion reactions within the sun.

Lasers have also revitalized the optical sciences and have stimulated a broad range of fundamental and practical work. One application of particular importance is the use of lasers in detection and measurement of air pollutants. Laser-based spectroscopic techniques that began to appear in large numbers in 1972 promise to make remote monitoring a reality. A prototype laser system based on absorption spectroscopy that was developed at the Bell Telephone Laboratories in Murray Hill, N.J., for example, can detect ten gaseous pollutants at concentrations of a few parts per billion. Tunable lasers, whose frequencies can be adjusted for maximum sensitivity to different pollutants, seem likely to be of key importance for monitoring systems, and at least four different types of tunable lasers are undergoing experimental trials—spin flip lasers, tuned by varying a magnetic field; organic dye lasers, tuned by variable diffraction gratings; optical parametric oscillators, in which a crystal is rotated to select the desired tuning; and, perhaps most promising for air pollution work, diode lasers that can be tuned by a variety of means.

Lasers are also provoking revolutions in holography, in communications, and in the measurement of fundamental quantities. For example, two groups of physicists at the National Bureau of Standards in Boulder, Colo., have succeeded in building a methane-stabilized laser whose frequency varies no more than one part in 10^{11}. Highly accurate measurements of its frequency and its wavelength

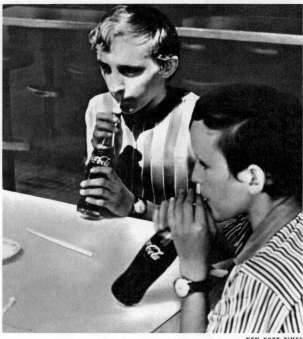

NEW YORK TIMES

NO JOKE—that old symbol of Yankee imperialism is now being peddled in Communist Poland, where admen have undertaken a new kind of cold war campaign. Roadside ad reads: "Cold . . ., wonderful, incomparably refreshing. Demand Coca-Cola wherever you see this sign." At right, Warsaw youths taste the real thing.

have permitted an independent determination of the speed of light (which is the product of frequency and wavelength). The scientists found that $c = 2.9979267 \pm 20 \times 10^8$ meters per second, which agrees with the accepted value. Eventually, the physicists hope, through improvements in their technique, to extend the measurement to within one part in 10^8, a 30-fold increase in precision. Many scientists expect that eventually laser techniques such as these may become the basis for new and more accurate standards of length and frequency.

Status of physics. A final event of no little significance for the future of physics was the publication of a major new report, *Physics in Perspective*, by the National Academy of Sciences. Two years in the making, 1,000 pages in length, the report examines the status of physics and each of its subfields, discussing manpower and funding problems and research opportunities. The work of a committee headed by D. Allan Bromley of Yale University, the report achieves a first by setting some suggested priorities for research in physics. On the basis of purely scientific interest, the report gave top priority to research at the new National Accelerator Laboratory at Batavia; on the basis of both scientific and practical criteria, it gave an overall top rating to research on lasers. The report also identified some 13 additional areas of research—including heavy-ion interactions, controlled fusion, and biophysical acoustics—as areas in which the potential for results of scientific or social importance was great enough, in the judgment of the committee, to warrant increased funding by federal science agencies. The report also recommended a renewed emphasis on broad fundamental training for new physicists in the graduate schools and major efforts to improve the public's understanding of physics and other sciences.

ALLEN L. HAMMOND

POLAND. Poland's relations with the United States and West Germany, countries from which it has long been estranged, underwent substantial improvements during the year. Within two weeks in May, the West German parliament ratified the nonaggression treaty with Poland, and Richard M. Nixon became the first U.S. president in office to visit the country.

These developments in foreign relations overshadowed a domestically busy year in which Poland elected a new parliament, chose Henryk Jabloński to replace Józef Cyrankiewicz in the ceremonial post of president of the Council of State, belatedly adopted a five-year economic plan, eliminated many travel restrictions to and from East Germany and Czechoslovakia, and announced a plan to reorganize the countryside into self-governing districts.

The treaty with West Germany. As Polish commentators noted after West Germany's Parliament narrowly approved the nonaggression treaty, May 17 marked the first time since the end of World War II that Poland felt secure within its borders. At the end of the war Poland was given 40,000 square miles of former German territory east of the Oder

and Neisse rivers and in former East Prussia and Danzig. Ratification of the nonaggression treaty this year meant that West Germany relinquished its claim on these areas, which were formally under temporary Polish and Soviet administration since 1945, pending conclusion of a World War II peace treaty.

The restoration of normal relations with West Germany signified more than territorial security to the Poles. In the first half of this year German exports to Poland rose by 70 percent and Polish exports to West Germany by 40 percent. Last year's trade statistics reflected a similar rise. Both figures were the result of trade agreements made possible by the treaty. An example of new business ties was an 18-month contract for a West German firm to build in Poland two automated meat processing plants at a cost of $52 million. Polish officials hope that many more deals will now be possible, because the nation's industry could benefit greatly from the more advanced German technology.

The Nixon visit. Economics also played an important part in the talks between President Nixon and Edward Gierek, leader of the Polish Communist Party, during Nixon's visit on May 31 and June 1. The two countries agreed to establish a joint commission to expand trade. Poland expressed interest in increasing its purchases of capital goods and licenses to produce capital goods, as well as in obtaining technological assistance in the United States and in negotiating an air transport agreement.

A more dramatic expression of good relations between the Polish and American people, however, was the warm reception given Nixon. Although Polish authorities attempted to play down his visit because they did not want to offend the Soviet Union, crowds estimated at 300,000 turned out to greet him. Although teachers and Communist Party members were reported to have been told to try to keep the crowds small, thousands of Warsaw citizens had waited since dawn to greet Nixon.

Domestic politics and the economy. Parliamentary elections were the first test of the popularity of the new regime, installed after the rioting in December 1970. Although 97.9 percent of the voters backed the approved candidates, there were more cases than usual of unpopular politicians' names being crossed off ballots. Cyrankiewicz's replacement as head

of state marked the end of his political career. As prime minister for many years, he had been blamed for the events leading to the rioting. The 1970 upheaval was also responsible for the 17-month delay in adopting the five-year plan. When parliament finally passed it in June of this year, it contained revisions designed to improve living standards—higher wages, lower prices, and a system of incentives.

The liberalization of travel rules made it possible for Poles to travel to neighboring East Germany and Czechoslovakia without visas for the first time since Communist rule began. In the first six weeks of the new system, 320,000 Poles went to East Germany and 400,000 East Germans visited Poland. But Polish citizens of German background hoping to emigrate to West Germany under the new non-aggression treaty ran into difficulty. Since West Germany and Poland cannot agree on how large this group is, emigration, which had been averaging 3,000 people a month, was slowed to a trickle after about 25,000 persons had left Poland.

A radical plan for administrative reform was announced at the meeting of the Communist Party's Central Committee in late September. Scheduled to go into effect on January 1, 1973, the plan divides the country into 2,300 *gminas,* or districts, headed by appointed *naczelni,* or executives. The *naczelni* will work with the district council, which will collect local taxes and designate expenditures. The plan for decentralization grants a large measure of local autonomy and represents a major step by Gierek in his attempt to modernize the economy.

Church and state. The conflict between the regime and the powerful Roman Catholic Church continued. The church charged that the government was not doing enough in permitting the construction of new churches, alleviating taxation for the church, and fighting pornography. An important step was taken by the Vatican this year in recognizing the bishoprics in the Oder-Neisse territory as Polish rather than German. It was a measure that was welcomed by both the church and the government. Pope Paul VI had waited until West Germany's ratification of the treaty with Poland before naming Polish bishops for the area. There was actually no change in personnel; Polish prelates had headed the bishoprics since the end of World War II but had been called apostolic administrators.

Area and population. Area, 120,360 sq. mi. Pop. (est. 1971), 32,750,000. Principal cities (1970): Warsaw (cap.), 1,308,100; Łodz, 761,700; Kraków, 583,400.
Government. People's republic. Nominally highest government organ, the Sejm (parliament), is elected every four years. Dominant political power is the Polish United Workers' (Communist) Party. Party first secy., Edward Gierek; chmn., Council of State (in effect, president of the republic), Henryk Jabłoński; prime min., Piotr Jaroszewicz.
Finance. Monetary unit, zloty; 1 zloty = US$0.475. Budget (1971): revenue, US$9.5 billion; expenditure, US$9.4 billion. Main sources of revenue: industry, agriculture, shipping. Main items of expenditure: education, welfare.
Trade (1971). Imports, US$2.7 billion; exports, US$2.8 billion. Principal exports: coal, meat and meat products, ships and boats, cotton fabrics. Principal imports: machinery and equipment, fuels, raw materials, agricultural products. Major trading partners: Soviet Union, East Germany, Czechoslovakia, West Germany, Great Britain.
Education. Schooling is compulsory from the 7th to the 17th year. Enrollment (1970): kindergarten, 512,000; elementary school, 5,443,100; high school, 309,700; vocational school, 1,605,000; college and university, 322,100.
Armed forces. Army, 195,000; navy, 22,000; air force, 25,000; security and border forces, 45,000.   DONALD R. SHANOR

POPULATION. Commission on Population Growth. The Commission on Population Growth and the American Future, chaired by John D. Rockefeller III, submitted its final report to the president and Congress in March. The report, *Population and the American Future,* contained the commission's findings and policy recommendations based on two years of deliberations, public hearings, and study of research papers. The public hearings and research papers were published in seven separate volumes.

Research undertaken for the commission covered a broad range of matters relating to population, including demographic, economic, and social aspects of population growth and of population policies; resources and the environment; population distribution; and governmental implications of population change. The commission's findings and recommendations were not limited to a discussion of anticipated changes in population and how the country might accommodate itself to them. The commission also considered the complex ways in which legal, social, and economic structures themselves determine population growth and distribution, and what changes might be made in these structures to achieve, in a manner consistent with democratic ideals, a population level suited to the country's resources and needs.

Study of recent population trends showed major changes in the population between 1900 and 1970, a period of exceptional growth.

U.S. POPULATION CHARACTERISTICS, 1900 AND 1970

	c. 1900	c. 1970
Population	76 million	205 million
Life expectancy	47 years	70 years
Median age	23 years	28 years
Births per 1,000 population	32	18
Deaths per 1,000 population	17	9
Immigrants per 1,000 population	8	2
Annual growth	1.75 million	2.5 million
Growth rate	2.3 %	1.1 %

SOURCE: "POPULATION AND THE AMERICAN FUTURE: THE REPORT OF THE COMMISSION ON POPULATION GROWTH AND THE AMERICAN FUTURE." WASHINGTON, D.C., GOVERNMENT PRINTING OFFICE, 1972.

For the immediate future, the pattern of past growth—especially the "baby boom" after World War II—implies continued growth throughout the remainder of the century even if family size were to drop immediately to an average of two children per family. An average family size of two children would bring the population to 300 million by 2015. An average family size of three children would bring the population to that level 20 years earlier and would add an additional 100 million by 2013.

The commission concluded that gradual stabilization of the country's population was desirable both economically and socially. It also concluded that conscious planning was necessary to achieve stabilization harmoniously and to ensure that policies relating to population growth were consistent with national ideals of promoting equal opportunity and individual dignity.

Recommendations. In order to reduce overall fertility and to equalize opportunities, the commission recommended that discrimination based on sex be eliminated by adoption of the proposed Equal Rights Amendment to the Constitution. In order to enable all Americans to avoid unwanted births and to realize their own family size preferences, the commission recommended that investment in the development of improved means of individual fertility control be increased; subsidized family planning programs be extended; access to abortion be liberalized, with the understanding that abortion not be considered a primary means of fertility control; and all forms of health services related to fertility and infertility be extended and improved. The commission also proposed that present levels of immigration not be increased and that illegal immigration be stopped. With a view to easing the nation's adjustment to changing distributional requirements, the commission suggested that national population distribution guidelines be established and that regional planning activities be increased.

Consistent with its desire for an increase in freedom of choice concerning residential location, the commission recommended that governmental provision of suburban housing for low-income and moderate-income families be promoted. It also proposed that the federal government assist school systems in establishing population education pro-

grams. To provide education for responsible parenthood, the commission suggested that sex education be made available through community organizations and schools. Finally, the commission recommended strengthening the basic statistical and research programs on which all demographic, social, and economic policies depend.

Effect. The commission's report met with a mixed reception from the Nixon administration. In particular, the more controversial recommendations (such as liberalized access to abortion) were singled out for criticism. Other recommendations received relatively little publicity.

Downward U.S. population trend. Figures for the first seven months of 1972 indicate that the United States has reached the lowest fertility rate in its history, 72.7 births per thousand women aged 15 to 44. This figure is 11 percent lower 'than the corresponding figure for 1971 and falls below the lowest full-year U.S. fertility rate ever previously recorded, 75.8, registered in 1936. If this rate were to remain constant, zero population growth would eventually occur within approximately 70 years.

Whether the fertility rate will indeed remain at this low a level is another question. In the short term, demographers had reason for optimism; a survey conducted by the Census Bureau in June showed that married women aged 18 to 24 expected to have an average of 2.3 children each, a figure roughly consistent with replacement level fertility (2.1 children for all women in general). However, when the fertility rate is low, the birthrate is highly sensitive to economic fluctuations. Consequently, the national rate could swing sharply up or down at some time in the future.

World demographic situation. Awareness of the need for every country to have accurate data on the size, composition, and distribution of its population, in order to provide essential economic, social, and medical services, continued to spread throughout the world. The United Nations continued to expand its activities in aiding population data collection and analysis.

Over 60 countries had held national censuses in 1970 or 1971, the first results of which became widely available during the year. Nearly every country has now had at least a basic population count or sample survey within the last ten years, though the scope, detail, and accuracy of the data collected are highly variable. However, two of the world's most populous nations have yet to provide reliable current data even on such basic questions as their total populations.

WORLD POPULATION GROWTH

	Population (in millions) 1971	1972	Births per 1,000 population 1971	1972	Deaths per 1,000 population 1971	1972	Annual percentage of growth 1971	1972	Doubling time[1]
Latin America	291	300	38	38	9	10	2.9	2.8	25
Africa	354	364	47	47	20	23	2.7	2.6	27
Asia	2,104	2,154	38	37	15	14	2.3	2.3	30
Oceania	20	20	25	25	10	10	2.0	2.0	35
North America	229	231	18	17	9	9	1.2	1.1	63
Soviet Union	245	248	17	17	8	8	1.0	0.9	77
Europe[2]	466	469	18	16	10	10	0.8	0.7	99
World	3,706	3,782	34	33	14	13	2.0	2.0	35

SOURCE: REPRINTED WITH THE PERMISSION OF THE POPULATION REFERENCE BUREAU, INC.

[1] *Number of years required for population to double if current growth rate persists.*
[2] *Excluding European portions of the Soviet Union.*

For the People's Republic of China, which contains approximately 20 percent of the world's population, the most recent data are nearly 20 years out of date. Estimates for 1970 range from 753 million people up to 871 million; acceptance of the higher rather than the lower figure would add as much as 3 percent to the estimate of the world's total population.

The other major puzzle is Bangladesh. Estimates for Bangladesh in 1972 range from 70 to 80 million people.

The 1961 census had counted 51 million, with an estimated 5–9 percent undercount. Growth rate estimates at that time ranged from 2 percent a year to over 3 percent; the former would have yielded a population of 65–69 million people in 1970, the latter a population of 75–78 million. Subsequent natural and political disasters claimed the lives of a very large but unknown number of persons. Half a million deaths is a widely accepted figure for the devastating cyclone of November 1970; 1.5 million is an estimate of war-related deaths in 1971.

The latest data currently available reveal the following picture of regional variations in the world's population size and growth rate. The only major difference between the latest estimates available in 1972 and 1971 lies in the size of population; vital rates have remained essentially unchanged, though a very slight downward movement in the growth rate is perceptible. The growth rate remains high in Asia and Oceania and extremely high in Latin America and Africa. If current growth rates persist, the population of Latin America and Africa will double before the end of the century and that of the world as a whole will double before 2010. On a world scale, little has yet been achieved in terms of slowing the pace of growth. Nevertheless, these broad regional figures conceal a number of countries where major advances have been made in the last few years—for example, Taiwan, Hong Kong, Singapore, and Costa Rica.

HILARY PAGE

PORTUGAL. Politics and government. Admiral Américo Thomás, the 78-year-old president and head of state, was reelected in July for a third seven-year term of office. This was regarded as an important indication that the government under Prime Minister Marcello Caetano would continue its program of slow but moderate reform.

Caetano and Thomás, who have worked together effectively since 1968, are respected and popular with the Portuguese people, who are highly conservative by tradition.

The extreme right wing, consisting of big landowners, bankers and industrialists, and top-ranking officers of the armed services, has rallied around Thomás. The center political groupings and general public expect Caetano to introduce much needed social and economic reforms.

On July 22, Portugal signed a treaty with the European Economic Community for a form of association with Common Market members. In a historic about-face, Portugal forged its first links with the new community in Europe and loosened its links with its overseas territories.

Widespread reforms of the 1933 constitution granted varying degrees of self-government and autonomy to Angola and Mozambique, which have ceased to be provinces and have become states within Portuguese sovereignty. The Lisbon government will continue to legislate on matters of common interest, but the overseas provinces will become substantially autonomous regions.

The constitutional changes also provided for widespread judicial reorganization and revision of the penal code. The wings of the security police have been clipped, and the rights of the people in relation to the law and the police are being placed on the statute books.

A new press law introduced in June abolished censorship. However, any published material the government regards as endangering the security of the state or as beyond normal criticism of ministers and government policy could result in fines or imprisonment. Censorship will nevertheless continue for the duration of the present "state of subversion" (a milder form of a state of emergency), declared because of the guerrilla wars in Africa.

Economic developments. The official 1971 balance-of-payment figures show a credit balance of $195 million; the trade deficit was $655 million, and credit in invisible earnings was $825 million, mostly from tourism and remittances by emigrants abroad.

Rising prices and falling production characterized 1972. In Lisbon, from mid-1971 to mid-1972 the cost of living officially rose 11 percent, but some nonofficial figures placed the rise at 16 percent.

Agricultural production is shrinking from lack of manpower, as 1.5 million people have emigrated from Portugal in the past ten years. Summer was disastrous for the olive and tomato crops. Old-fashioned practices have hampered the enlargement and progress of many commercial firms. On the other hand, in some instances industrial growth has been spectacular. The Lisnave ship-repairing and dry dock yards across the Tagus River from Lisbon earned $53 million in 1971 in foreign exchange. This year Lisnave opened the world's largest dry dock for the million-ton tankers of the future.

Work started on the largest shipyard outside Japan in the estuary of the Sado River near Setúbal with an investment of $70 million. It will build tankers up to 700,000 deadweight tons. Building has started on a major new oil refinery at Sines and a petrochemical complex. A new port and industrial city is being built to service them.

To boost industry, the government passed an enabling law opening large areas of Portuguese industry to foreign investment.

The gross national product, growing at a good rate of 7 percent yearly, is still one of the lowest in Europe.

Education. The government has embarked on a program of wide educational reform which will take a decade to complete. According to official figures, 21 percent of the population is illiterate. Some nonofficial figures place illiteracy at 39 percent, including lost literacy. By mid-1972, the school leaving age was raised from ten to 12 years. Lack of school buildings posed an acute problem, as thousands of children were turned away at the October term opening for lack of accommodations.

Area and population. Area, 35,553 sq. mi. Pop. (1970), 8,668,-267. Principal cities (est. 1969): Lisbon (cap.), 830,600; Porto, 325,400.

Government. Corporate republic. Pres., Admiral Américo Thomás; prime min., Marcello Caetano.

Finance. Monetary unit, escudo; 1 escudo = US$0.0380. Budget (1971): revenue, $1,367,760,000; expenditure, $1,367,000,000, including war and general security expenditures of $556,000,000.

Trade (1971). Imports, $1.889 billion; exports, $1.099 million. Principal imports: machinery, electrical and transport equipment, textiles. Principal exports: textiles, wine and agricultural products, machinery. Major trading partners: Great Britain, West Germany, overseas African territories and states, United States.

Education (1971). Enrollment: primary, 1,000,000; secondary, 392,792; universities and colleges, 46,774. Number of schools: 19,-412, including 6 universities, 3 colleges, 59 teachers colleges, 1,950 secondary schools, 17,017 primary schools, 317 infant schools. Number of teachers, 59,897.

Armed forces (est. 1971–1972). Army, 175,000; navy, 20,000; air force, 18,000.   LAURENCE MEREDITH

COLD POWER. As the United States slowly runs out of gas, shipbuilders have come up with a way to import large quantities of natural gas in a contracted, liquefied state. The supercool "Descartes," a French-owned carrier (right) that completed its second transatlantic run early this year, boasts six huge stainless-steel tanks like the one above, designed to hold the liquefied gas at −259° F.

POWER AND ENERGY RESOURCES. The growing debate over the developing U.S. energy crisis was increasingly heard in the courts and the halls of Congress. At least a dozen bills introduced in Congress attempted to modify the National Environmental Policy Act (NEPA). Indeed, energy has become such a politically sensitive issue that the Council on Environmental Quality's annual report to the president, issued August 7, 1972, did not contain a chapter on energy. The council indicated that the energy chapter would not be released until after the November elections were held.

Passed by Congress with bipartisan support in 1969 and signed into law by President Richard M. Nixon on January 1, 1970, the National Environmental Policy Act sets basic federal policy. At the heart of NEPA is section 102, which directs all federal agencies to interpret and administer their authorities in agreement with the new federal code. Subsection 102(2)(C), which has been the basis for a number of environmental lawsuits, requires agencies to prepare a detailed statement of environmental impact for all "major federal actions significantly affecting the quality of the human environment." In preparing these statements, agencies are required to consider alternative actions and to consult with other agencies having expertise in environmental matters. Not surprisingly, this subsection has come under criticism from some development-oriented agencies, and the congressional attack on NEPA centered on attempts to exempt certain projects from NEPA compliance or to allow construction to proceed before final environmental impact statements are filed.

Fossil fuels. *Oil.* One of the most controversial projects to come under the purview of NEPA is the proposed trans-Alaska pipeline. In July 1969 the Trans-Alaska Pipeline System, a consortium later reorganized as the Alyeska Pipeline Service Company, applied for a permit from the U.S. Department of the Interior to construct a 48-inch diameter pipeline to carry oil from Prudhoe Bay on the North Slope to the port of Valdez in southeastern Alaska—a distance of 789 miles—where it would be transferred to tankers for shipment to west coast refineries. In April 1970, after NEPA had been signed into law, Interior agreed to issue permits, but environmental groups promptly obtained an injunction against such issuance on the grounds that Interior had failed to prepare an environmental impact statement in compliance with NEPA. Interior finally released a nine-volume environmental impact study on March 20, 1972. After allowing interested parties only 45 days to analyze the statement and submit responses, Interior Secretary Rogers C. B. Morton announced on May 11 that permits would be issued when the injunction was lifted. Federal District Court Judge George L. Hart, Jr., removed the injunction on August 15, ruling that Interior had complied with the terms of NEPA in preparing the impact statement and reaching its decision. However, the environmental groups which brought the suit —the Wilderness Society, Friends of the Earth, and the Environmental Defense Fund—promptly announced that an appeal would be filed with the U.S. court of appeals in Washington, D.C. Regardless of the decision rendered by the appeals court, the historic case seems certain to reach the U.S. Supreme Court, probably early in 1973.

In its impact study, Interior admitted that the pipeline and subsequent tanker transport of oil would have adverse environmental effects and pose serious environmental risks, including the possibility of large-scale oil spills in Prince William Sound, one of the finest commercial and sports fisheries in the world.

Environmental groups have charged that Interior failed to consider alternatives to the trans-Alaska line, particularly a common-corridor route for an oil and gas line through Canada's Mackenzie River Valley that would carry the oil directly to Edmonton, Seattle, and midwestern markets. Environmental groups and many Canadian officials favor the

Canadian route because they fear oil spills from tanker operations along Canada's west coast if the trans-Alaska route is chosen. Interior agreed that a gas line should eventually be built through Canada. But Interior Secretary Morton argued that U.S. national security requires the immediate construction of the trans-Alaska line (which could be built more quickly than the longer pipeline across Canada), allegedly to relieve the growing dependence of the United States on foreign oil.

This argument appears to be more of an illusion than a realistic possibility, as the following statistics reveal. U.S. consumption of petroleum (including natural gas liquids) in 1971 totaled 5.52 billion barrels, an increase of 2.8 percent over the 5.37 billion barrels consumed in 1970 (1 barrel = 42 gallons). While U.S. crude production declined from 3.52 billion barrels in 1970 to 3.48 billion barrels in 1971, net imports of crude oil and refined products rose from 1.15 billion barrels in 1970 to 1.32 billion barrels in 1971— an increase of 14.8 percent. In 1971, 24 percent of all the petroleum consumed in the United States was imported. Consumption of motor gasoline in 1971 was almost 2.19 billion barrels (91.85 billion gallons), an increase of 3.6 percent over 1970 consumption.

Proved U.S. reserves of crude oil declined from 39 billion barrels at the end of 1970 to 38.06 billion barrels at the end of 1971, a decrease of 2.4 percent. These reserves, which include an estimated 9.6 billion barrels under Alaska's North Slope, constitute about an eight-year supply of crude oil at the 1971 rate of consumption. While more oil will undoubtedly be found in Alaska, the present North Slope reserve constitutes only a two-year supply.

If the trans-Alaska pipeline is built, it is expected to ultimately deliver 2 million barrels a day (or 730 million barrels a year), a quantity equal to 13 percent of all petroleum consumed in the United States in 1971. However, U.S. petroleum consumption increased at an average annual rate of 4.4 percent between 1961 and 1971. If this rate of increase should continue (and some authorities have projected an even higher rate), U.S. petroleum consumption in 1980 will reach 8.2 billion barrels. Thus, even if the trans-Alaska pipeline is operating at full capacity by that time, its full flow would furnish at most 9 percent of the total U.S. petroleum requirement. Thus, given the present rate of increase in consumption, greatly increased imports of foreign oil appear inevitable regardless of whether the trans-Alaska pipeline is built.

National security arguments have provided the rationalization for federal intervention in the crude oil industry in the past. In 1959, imports of foreign oil were rising rapidly, and President Dwight D. Eisenhower, fearful that military intervention or political upheaval in oil-exporting countries could suddenly cut off those imports, imposed mandatory oil import quotas. While import quotas did temporarily reduce U.S. dependence on foreign oil, they also resulted in a more rapid depletion of domestic resources and a less competitive pricing system. As a consequence, American consumers have paid more for oil than they would have in the absence of import quotas.

Rising U.S. oil consumption in the face of declining domestic production during 1971 renewed the controversy over oil import quotas. On May 11, 1972, President Nixon raised by 15 percent the amount of crude oil that can be imported into the United States. This increase allowed the importation of an additional 230,000 barrels of crude oil a day during the remainder of 1972. A further increase in oil import quotas in 1973 seems almost certain, and if U.S. consumption of petroleum continues to increase at a rate of 4.4 percent, the foregoing arguments make it inevitable that the entire oil import control program will have to be scrapped before 1980.

Rising oil imports were also a significant factor in the U.S. Department of the Interior's decision to begin explora-

tory offshore drilling on the outer continental shelf off the east coast in 1972. The drilling, limited by department rules to 300 feet of water, will initially be concentrated in two areas, one about 30 miles off the Delaware–New Jersey coast, the other between Long Island and Cape Cod. Both are among the world's most valuable fishing grounds.

Natural gas. Natural gas is a clean-burning fuel containing almost no sulfur and producing essentially no fly ash during combustion. Partly because increasingly stringent air pollution control regulations have made it a very desirable fuel, natural gas (including natural gas liquids) furnished 36 percent of all the energy consumed in the United States in 1971. Not surprisingly, the potential demand for gas has considerably outstripped the supply. Marketed production of natural gas in 1971 was 22.95 trillion cubic feet, an increase of only 4.7 percent over 1970 production, markedly below the 7.2 percent average annual rate of increase since 1940. Proved reserves declined from 290.7 trillion cubic feet at the end of 1970 to 278.8 trillion cubic feet at the end of 1971, a decrease of 4.1 percent. These reserves represent a 12-year supply at the 1971 rate of consumption.

Coal. Both domestic production and exports of coal declined in 1971. Production of anthracite, lignite, and bituminous coal totaled 564 million tons in 1971, a decline of 8 percent from the 1970 level. Exports declined from 71.7 million tons in 1970 to 57.3 million tons in 1971.

Petroleum. During the past decade world petroleum consumption has increased at an average annual rate of 7.56 percent and in 1971 totaled 17.7 billion barrels. About 17 percent of the 1971 production came from offshore wells, and offshore reserves represent about 20 percent of proved world reserves. Production wells are now being drilled in 600 feet of water, and a test well has been drilled in 1,500 feet of water off California.

The North Sea was the site of a major oil boom in 1972, and by the end of the year proved reserves there totaled about 9 billion barrels. British Petroleum planned to begin construction in 1973 of a 115 mile-long underwater pipeline in 300 to 420 feet of water between Cruden Bay on the northeast coast of Scotland and its offshore oil field. Many Scottish residents fear the operations will pollute Scotland's clean environment.

Electrical energy. U.S. electrical energy production from all sources rose from 1,640 billion kilowatt-hours (kw.-hr.) in 1970 to 1,718 billion kw.-hr. in 1971. Part of this rise is directly attributable to the 1.23 percent increase in popula-

TABLE 1. U.S. ELECTRICAL ENERGY PRODUCTION PER CAPITA, 1940–1971

Year	Production (billion kw.-hr.)	Average annual increase (percent)	Total resident population[1] (millions)	Power production per capita (kw.-hr.)[2]
1940	180	......	132.5	1,360
1945	271	8.56	133.4	2,030
1950	389	7.46	151.9	2,560
1955	629	10.11	165.1	3,810
1960	842	6.00	180.0	4,680
1965	1,158	6.59	193.5	5,980
1970	1,640	7.21	203.7	8,050
1971	1,718	4.73	206.2	8,330

[1] As of July 1.   [2] Totals not exact because of rounding.

tion which occurred between July 1970 and July 1971. However, as the last column in Table 1 illustrates, per capita production rose by 3.5 percent during the year.

Industrial use accounted for about 40 percent of electrical energy consumption in 1971. Residential use consumed 34 percent, commercial use accounted for about 22.5 percent, and miscellaneous uses were responsible for the remaining 3.5 percent. The percentage of the total U.S. electrical energy production consumed for residential use has been increasing, principally because of the growing use of electricity for home heating and airconditioning.

TABLE 2. PERCENTAGE OF U.S. UTILITY ELECTRICAL PRODUCTION, BY TYPE OF FUEL CONSUMED[1]

	1940	1945	1950	1955	1960	1965	1970	1971
Coal	54.6	51.7	47.1	55.1	53.6	54.1	46.1	44.3
Oil	4.4	3.5	10.3	6.8	6.1	6.1	11.9	13.5
Gas	7.7	8.9	13.5	17.4	21.0	21.0	24.3	23.3
Nuclear	....	....	....	....	....	0.4	1.4	2.3
Hydro	33.4	35.9	29.2	20.7	19.3	18.4	16.2	16.5

[1] Totals do not always add to 100 because of rounding.

Production of power from hydroelectric sources increased from 47 billion kw.-hr. in 1940 to 266.3 billion kw.-hr. in 1971. However, the rate of increase has not been as rapid as that of fossil fuel plants; hence, the percentage of electrical power derived from hydro facilities has shown an almost continuous decline (see Table 2). In 1940 only 7.7 percent of utility electricity was generated from combustion of natural gas, while in 1970 gas furnished 24.3 percent. As Table 2 shows, gas furnished a slightly smaller fraction of the electricity generated in 1971; this decline was due chiefly to shortages in supply. Indeed, there was growing sentiment during 1971 and 1972 to impose some "end use" controls on this valuable resource in order to curtail its use for power generation, during which only about 35 percent of the thermal energy available from the gas is converted into electrical energy.

Table 2 also shows that nuclear power, while contributing only 2.3 percent of utility electrical power production in 1971, is by far the fastest growing component. Electrical energy production from nuclear sources increased from 21.8 billion kw.-hr. in 1970 to 37.9 billion kw.-hr. in 1971, an increase of 74 percent in one year. In 1969 there were 11 nuclear power generating plants with a capacity of 2 million kw., about 0.6 percent of the total generating U.S. capacity. By June 30, 1972, there were 26 plants with a generating capacity of 11.8 million kw. operable or licensed for startup, 51 plants with a capacity of 43.99 million kw. under construction, and 66 additional plants with a capacity of 65.88 million kw. which were on order or for which construction permits had been filed with the Atomic Energy Commission. The combined capacity of those operable and under construction represents 14 percent of the total U.S. generating capacity.

Several nuclear power plants now under construction have been delayed as a result of the 1971 Calvert Cliffs decision by the U.S. court of appeals in Washington, D.C. In that decision, the court held that the National Environmental Policy Act required the AEC to consider not only radiological effects but also the full range of environmental impact, including air and water quality and aesthetic and recreational considerations, when reviewing applications for construction permits.

Several plants under construction have required modification to comply with the decision. Unit 1 of the Calvert Cliffs, Md., plant itself has been under construction since July 1969. Originally planned to be operational in June 1972, it is now one year behind schedule. However, other factors appear to have been more significant than environmental control in causing the delay.

Nuclear power plants were the subject of an important U.S. Supreme Court decision rendered in April 1972. By a 7–2 margin the Court held in *Minnesota* v. *Northern States Power Company* that the AEC has exclusive authority to set standards for the release of radioactive emissions from nuclear power plants. The case involved the Monticello plant built by Northern States about 30 miles north of Minneapolis. The company obtained an operating license from the AEC which permitted the release of 41,400 curies a day in radioactive emissions from the stacks. The Minnesota state pollution control agency set a limit of 860 curies per day, just 2 percent of the AEC limit. Minnesota argued that both the state and federal governments had the right to

TABLE 3. PROJECTED U.S. ELECTRICAL ENERGY PRODUCTION AND INSTALLED CAPACITY, 1980–2000

Year	Production (billion kw.-hr.)	Installed capacity (million kw.)	Number of additional 4 million-kw. capacity plants required
1980	3,022	663	69
1990	5,662	1,243	214
2000	10,610	2,328	485

set pollution standards even if the state requirements were more stringent. The Court held, however, that when Congress passed the Atomic Energy Act the federal government preempted state control over matters having to do with nuclear energy.

Between 1955 and 1971, electrical energy production in the United States grew at an average annual rate of 6.48 percent. At this rate of increase, electrical energy production doubles every 11 years. Table 3 gives the projected electrical energy production and installed capacity to the year 2000 if this growth rate is sustained. If, in order to minimize the number of sites required for power generating plants, the additional generating capacity required to supply this energy were provided in the form of 4 million-kw. plants (the largest nuclear plant now under construction is only 1,140,-000 kw.), 485 such plants would be required by the year 2000.

Electrical power production on a scale indicated by the figures in Table 3 would have some serious consequences, but the Federal Power Commission has predicted in its *1970 National Power Survey* that such growth will indeed occur. Projected electrical energy production and generating capacity are essentially identical to those given in Table 3. However, the FPC has predicted major shifts in fuel usage for power generation. Projected distributions of the sources of electrical energy in 1980 and 1990 are shown in Table 4, along with the distribution for 1971. This table shows that nuclear energy, which accounted for 2.3 percent of the electricity produced in 1971, is expected to furnish 49 percent by 1990.

TABLE 4. PROJECTED PERCENTAGE DISTRIBUTION OF ELECTRICAL ENERGY PRODUCTION[1]

	1971	1980	1990
Coal	44.3	36	28
Oil	13.5	13	8
Gas	23.3	13	8
Nuclear	2.3	28	49
Hydro	16.5	10	7

SOURCE: FEDERAL POWER COMMISSION, ''1970 NATIONAL POWER SURVEY''
[1] *Actual 1971 data included for purposes of comparison; percentages do not add to 100 because of rounding.*

Because nuclear power generation on a scale projected for 1990 and thereafter would exhaust domestic reserves of uranium ores within two decades, President Nixon proposed a program in 1971 for development of a breeder reactor by 1980. On January 14, 1972, the AEC announced that the Tennessee Valley Authority and Commonwealth Edison of Chicago had agreed to cooperate in building the nation's first fast breeder reactor demonstration plant. The plant will be located on the TVA system near Oak Ridge, Tenn. Construction was scheduled to begin early in 1973. Because of the serious radioactive waste disposal problems involved, not everyone is enthusiastic about breeder reactor development.

Meanwhile, a classic conservation battle, spawned by growing electrical power consumption, began taking shape. The controversy stems from a proposal, made in October 1971 by the U.S. Department of the Interior and 35 power supply entities in the North Central region, for a 50 million-kw. coal-fired generating complex in the Gillette-Colstrip area of eastern Wyoming and Montana. The capacity of this complex would be more than the present combined utility generating capacity in New York, Pennsylvania, and

Connecticut, and most of the power produced would be transmitted to midwestern load centers at Minneapolis, Des Moines, Kansas City, Mo., and St. Louis. The complex would consume more than 200 million tons of coal a year, all of which would come from strip mines near the power plants. Daily sulfur dioxide emissions would total more than 5,500 tons—a quantity equal to more than five times the daily sulfur dioxide emissions in New York City. Since sufficient cooling water is not available in the area, a massive water importation system was also proposed.

Overall energy consumption. At the heart of all these controversies lies the ever-increasing American consumption of energy. In 1971, U.S. energy consumption totaled 68.99 quadrillion BTU, an increase of 2.3 percent over the preceding year. Since the end of World War II the annual rate of growth has averaged 3.06 percent. Because the earth cannot indefinitely sustain such an exponential growth rate, some major revisions will have to occur in our social and economic policies, which continue to presuppose that exponential growth can somehow be made permanent. These adjustments have been understandably slow in coming, and as 1972 drew to a close the energy crisis appeared as far from resolution as ever.   DONALD F. ANTHROP

PRINCE EDWARD ISLAND. The traditionally placid, uncomplicated life-style of Prince Edward Islanders was shaken somewhat by economic problems this year. A slowdown in the agricultural export market hit the base of the economy and upset the timetable of a 15-year federal-provincial economic development plan, initiated in 1969. Sluggish markets, low prices, high transportation costs, and bad weather all adversely affected the production of strawberries, hay, grains, and (probably) tobacco. To make matters worse, the ruggedly independent islanders, although they had long clamored for the price and market stability of a central selling agency, remained reluctant to forego private deals even if it meant undercutting their own market prices.

School reform. Another painful transformation involved the consolidation of 371 local school boards into six district boards, accompanied by the elimination of many small schools and the advent of busing on a wide scale. The provincial government also relieved local boards of financial control and assumed sole rights to tax property for educational purposes. Real property assessments have been standardized across the island both for urban and rural areas, and a uniform base tax rate has been levied equally on all, with provisions for proportionately higher rates in districts that vote for school facilities over and above the norm.

Fishing and tourism. A high proportion of island farmers are also seagoing fishermen, catching lobsters, scallops, mackerel, cod, and flatfish. The government has been successfully fostering oyster farming in the shallow bays and inlets. Meanwhile, development of sports fishing for bluefin tuna has reached commercial proportions. Tourists and local anglers boated more than 400 tuna from five island ports this season. Tuna are flown fresh to Japanese markets and shipped frozen to Europe.

Tourism showed another 10–12 percent rise; the millionth tourist of the year was ferried from the mainland in late August. Through the development of facilities in various parts of the island, vacation visitors were better dispersed throughout the province, with resultant benefit to local economies.

Area and population. Area, 2,184 sq. mi. Pop. (1971 census), 111,641. Principal cities (1972): Charlottetown (cap.), 18,500; Summerside, 10,042.
Government. Lt. gov., J. George MacKay; prem., Alexander B. Campbell. Legislative assembly: Liberals, 27; Progressive Conservatives, 5.
Finance. Budget (est. 1972–1973): revenue, Can$105,020,711; expenditures, Can$112,016,016.
Education. Enrollment: elementary and secondary schools, 29,251; institutions of higher education, 2,241.   WALLACE WARD

Prizes and Awards

ART

American Academy of Arts and Letters and National Institute of Arts and Letters Awards

Arnold W. Brunner Memorial Prize in Architecture: Richard Meier

Award of Merit Medal for Painting: Clyfford Still

GENE HACKMAN, JANE FONDA, AND WILLIAM FRIEDKIN

WIDE WORLD

Rosenthal Foundation Award: Barkley L. Hendricks

Awards in Art: Richard Aakre; Varujan Boghosian; Lowry Burgess; Mary Frank; Maud F. Gatewood; Herman Rose; Anton Van Dalen

DRAMA, DANCE, AND FILM

Academy of Motion Picture Arts and Sciences ("Oscars")

Best Picture: *The French Connection*

Best Actress: Jane Fonda in *Klute*

Best Actor: Gene Hackman in *The French Connection*

Best Supporting Actress: Cloris Leachman in *The Last Picture Show*

Best Supporting Actor: Ben Johnson in *The Last Picture Show*

Best Director: William Friedkin for *The French Connection*

Best Foreign-Language Film: *The Garden of the Finzi-Continis* (Italy)

Best Documentary Feature: *The Hellstrom Chronicle*

Best Original Song: Theme from *Shaft*, music and lyrics by Isaac Hayes

Best Screenplay Based on Material From Another Medium: Ernest Tidyman for *The French Connection*

Best Original Screenplay: Paddy Chayefsky for *The Hospital*

Special Award: Charles Chaplin

Albert Einstein Commemorative Awards

Performing Arts: Harry Belafonte

Antoinette Perry Awards ("Tonys")

Best Play: *Sticks and Bones*

Best Musical: *Two Gentlemen of Verona*

Best Performances in a Drama: Sada Thompson in *Twigs*; Cliff Gorman in *Lenny*

Best Performances in a Musical: Alexis Smith in *Follies*; Phil Silvers in *A Funny Thing Happened on the Way to the Forum*

Best Supporting Performances in a Drama: Elizabeth Wilson in *Sticks and Bones*; Vincent Gardenia in *The Prisoner of Second Avenue*

Best Supporting Performances in a Musical: Linda Hopkins in *Inner City*; Larry Blyden in *A Funny Thing Happened on the Way to the Forum*

Best Director of a Play: Mike Nichols for *The Prisoner of Second Avenue*

Best Director of a Musical: Hal Prince and Michael Bennett for *Follies*

Cannes International Film Festival (France)

Best Actress: Susannah York in *Images* (England)

Best Actor: Jean Yanne in *We Will Not Grow Old Together* (France)

Best Director: Miklos Jansco for *Red Psalm* (Hungary)

Best Short Subject: Jean Chapot for *Telescopic Rifle* (France)

Special Prize: Raoul Servais for *Operation X-70* (Belgium)

Clarence Derwent Awards (Supporting Performances)

Best Supporting Actress: Pamela Bellwood in *Butterflies Are Free*

Best Supporting Actor: Richard Backus in *Promenade, All!*

Dance Magazine Awards

Judith Jamison of the Alvin Ailey Dance Theater

Anthony Dowell of the Royal Ballet

Drama Desk Awards

Most Promising Playwrights: Jason Miller for *That Championship Season*; Michael Weller for *Moonchildren*; David Wiltse for *Suggs*; J. E. Franklin for *Black Girl*; Richard Wesley for *The Black Terror*; Philip Hayes Dean for *The Sty of the Blind Pig*; J. E. Gaines for *Don't Let It Go to Your Head*

Most Promising Directors: Dan Sullivan for *Suggs*; Gilbert Moses for *Ain't Supposed to Die a Natural Death*

Most Promising Costume Designer: Carrie F. Robinson for *Grease* and *The Beggar's Opera*

Most Promising Scenic Designer: Video Free America for *Kaddish*

Most Promising Composer: Andrew Lloyd Webber for *Jesus Christ Superstar*

Most Promising Lyricist: Micki Grant for *Don't Bother Me, I Can't Cope*

Most Promising Book Writer: Melvin Van Peebles for *Ain't Supposed to Die a Natural Death*

New York Drama Critics Circle Awards

Best Play: *That Championship Season*

Special Citation: *Sticks and Bones*

Best Musical: *Two Gentlemen of Verona*

Best Foreign Play: *The Screens* (France)

New York Film Critics Awards

Best Film: *A Clockwork Orange*

Best Screenplay: Penelope Gilliatt for *Sunday, Bloody Sunday*; Larry McMurtry and Peter Bogdanovich for *The Last Picture Show*

Best Actress: Jane Fonda in *Klute*

Best Actor: Gene Hackman in *The French Connection*

Best Supporting Actress: Ellen Burstyn in *The Last Picture Show*

Best Supporting Actor: Ben Johnson in *The Last Picture Show*

Off-Broadway Awards ("Obies")

Best Theater Piece: *The Mutation Show*

Distinguished Performances: Salome Bey in *Love Me, Love My Children;* Maurice Blanc in *The Celebration: Jooz/Guns/Movies/The Abyss;* Alex Bradford in *Don't Bother Me, I Can't Cope;* Marilyn Chris in *Kaddish;* Ron Faber in *And They Put Handcuffs on Flowers;* Jeanne Hepple in *The Reliquary of Mr. and Mrs. Potterfield;* Danny Sewell in *The Homecoming;* Marilyn Sokol in *The Beggar's Opera;* Kathleen Widdoes in *The Beggar's Opera;* Elizabeth Wilson in *Sticks and Bones;* Ed Zang in *The Reliquary of Mr. and Mrs. Potterfield*

Distinguished Direction: Wilford Leach and John Braswell for *The Only Jealousy of Emer;* Mel Shapiro for *Two Gentlemen of Verona;* Michael Smith for *Country Music;* Tom Sydorick for *20th Century Tar*

Best Music and Lyrics: Micki Grant for *Don't Bother Me, I Can't Cope*

Best Composer: Liz Swados for *Medea*

Best Visual Effects: Video Free America for *Kaddish*

HUMANITARIANISM

Albert Einstein Commemorative Awards
Philanthropy Award: Max Fisher

American Jewish Committee Award
Herbert H. Lehman Human Relations Award: Andrew Goodman

Council of Churches of the City of New York Family of Man Awards
Gold Medallion: Raymond Shaffer
Bronze Medallion for Human Relations: Roy Wilkins
Bronze Medallion for Education: Lord Kenneth Clark for *Civilisation*
Bronze Medallion for Peace: Not given for 1972

National Conference of Christians and Jews Human Relations Award: Chet Atkins

JOSEPH P. LASH

JILL KREMENTZ

JOURNALISM
George Polk Memorial Awards
National Reporting: New York *Times*
Foreign Reporting: Sidney H. Schanberg, New York *Times*
Editorial Reporting: Joseph Lelyveld, New York *Times*
Metropolitan Reporting: Donald Barlett and James B. Steele, Philadelphia *Inquirer*
Public Service: Frances Cerra, *Newsday*
Magazine Reporting: Ross Terrill for "The 800,000,000: Report From China," *The Atlantic*
Television Documentary: Peter Davis, Perry Wolff, Roger Mudd, CBS News
News Photography: Michel Laurent and Horst Faas, AP
Television Reporting: Phil Brady, Peter McIntyre, Lim Youn-Choul, Shunichi Yashuda, NBC News
Criticism: Richard Harwood, Washington *Post*

Overseas Press Club Awards
Best Daily Newspaper or Wire Service Reporting From Abroad: Sidney H. Schanberg, New York *Times*
Newspaper or Wire Service Interpretation of Foreign Affairs: Robert S. Elegant, Los Angeles *Times*
Newspaper or Wire Service Photo Reporting From Abroad: New York *Times*
Magazine Reporting From Abroad: Arnaud de Borchgrave, *Newsweek*
Magazine Interpretation of Foreign Affairs: John L. Cobbs and Gordon L. Williams, *Business Week*
Business News Reporting From Abroad: Leonard S. Silk, New York *Times*
Robert Capa Gold Medal for Still Photography Requiring Courage and Enterprise Abroad: Larry Burrows (posthumously), *Life*
Reporting in Any Medium Requiring Ex-

FRIEDMAN-ABELES
SCENE FROM "STICKS AND BONES"

ceptional Courage and Enterprise Abroad: Nicholas W. Strah, Washington *Star*

Pulitzer Prizes
Commentary: Mike Royko, Chicago *Daily News*
Editorial Cartooning: Jeffrey K. MacNeily, Richmond *News Leader*
Editorial Writing: John Strohmeyer, Bethlehem *Globe Times*
International Reporting: Peter R. Kann, *Wall Street Journal*
National Reporting: Jack Anderson, "Washington Merry-Go-Round"
Feature Photography: Dave Kennerly, UPI
News Photography: Michel Laurent, AP
Photography: Horst Faas, AP
General Local Reporting: Richard I. Cooper and John W. Machacek, Rochester *Times-Union*
Special Local Reporting: Ann De Santis, Stephen A. Kurkjian, and Gerard M. O'Neill, Boston *Globe*
Music Criticism: Frank L. Peters, Jr., St. Louis *Post-Dispatch*
Meritorious Public Service: New York *Times*

LITERATURE
Academy of American Poets Awards
Lamont Prize: Peter Everwine, *Collecting the Animals*
Fellowship: James Wright, *Collected Poems*

American Academy of Arts and Letters and National Institute of Arts and Letters Awards
Gold Medal for the Novel: Eudora Welty
Gold Medal for History: Henry Steele Commager

E. M. Forster Award: Frank Tuohy

Loines Award for Poetry: William Jay Smith

Rosenthal Foundation Award: Thomas McGuane

Morton Dauwen Zabel Award: Donald Barthelme

Awards in Literature: *Poets:* Peter Davison, Pauline Hanson, Michael S. Harper, Ann Stanford. *Novelists:* Harry Crews, Paula Fox, Penelope Gilliatt, Gilbert Rogin. *Playwright:* Israel Horovitz. *Critic:* Walter Kerr

American Library Association Awards

John Newbery Medal: Robert O'Brien for *Mrs. Frisby and the Rats of NIMH*

Randolph J. Caldecott Medal: Nonny Hogrogian for *One Fine Day*

Bancroft Prizes in American History

Carl N. Degler for *Neither Black nor White*

Robert Middlekauff for *The Mathers: Three Generations of Puritan Intellectuals, 1596–1728*

Samuel Eliot Morison for *The European Discovery of America: The Northern Voyages, A.D. 500–1600*

George Polk Memorial Award

Book Award: Erik Barnouw, *A History of Broadcasting in the United States*

National Book Awards

Contemporary Affairs: Stewart Brand, ed., *The Last Whole Earth Catalog*

Arts and Letters: Charles Rosen, *The Classical Style: Haydn, Mozart, Beethoven*

Children's Book: Donald Barthelme, *The Slightly Irregular Fire Engine, or The Hithering Thithering Djinn*

Fiction: Flannery O'Connor (posthumous), *Flannery O'Connor: The Complete Stories*

Biography: Joseph P. Lash, *Eleanor and Franklin*

History: Allan Nevins (posthumous), *Ordeal of the Union,* vols. 7–8

Philosophy and Religion: Martin E. Marty, *Righteous Empire: The Protestant Experience in America*

Science: George L. Small, *The Blue Whale*

Poetry: Frank O'Hara (posthumous), *Collected Poems;* Howard Moss, *Selected Poems*

Translation: Austryn Wainhouse, *Chance and Necessity: An Essay on the Natural Philosophy of Modern Biology* (by Jacques Monod)

Overseas Press Club Award

Book on Foreign Affairs: Anthony Austin, *The President's War*

Poetry Society of America

Melville Cane Award: James Wright, *Collected Poems*

Pulitzer Prizes

Biography: Joseph P. Lash, *Eleanor and Franklin*

Fiction: Wallace Stegner, *Angle of Repose*

Poetry: James Wright, *Collected Poems*

General Nonfiction: Barbara W. Tuch-

man, *Stilwell and the American Experience in China*

Society of American Historians

Francis Parkman Prize: Joseph P. Lash, *Eleanor and Franklin*

Yale University Younger Poets: Michael Casey, *Obscenities*

MEDICINE

Albert Einstein Commemorative Awards

Medical Sciences Award: Dr. George Wald

American Association of Pathologists and Bacteriologists

Gold-headed Cane: Dr. Sidney Farber

MUSIC

American Academy of Arts and Letters and National Institute of Arts and Letters Awards

Charles E. Ives Scholarships: Thomas Janson; Robert Krupnick; Michael Seyfrit

Charles E. Ives Award: Harold Farberman

Marjorie Peabody Waite Award: Vittorio Rieti

Awards in Music: Earle Brown; John Eaton; John Harbison; William O. Smith

National Academy of Recording Arts and Sciences Awards ("Grammys")

Record of the Year: Carole King, "It's Too Late"

Album of the Year: Carole King, *Tapestry*

Song of the Year: Carole King, "You've Got A Friend"

Best Score from an Original Cast Show Album: *Godspell*

Best Original Score for a Motion Picture: *Shaft*

Best Comedy Recording: Lily Tomlin, *This Is a Recording*

Album of the Year, Classical: *Horowitz Plays Rachmaninoff*

Best Rhythm and Blues Song: "Ain't No Sunshine"

Best Country Song: "Help Me Make It Through the Night"

Pulitzer Prize

Music: Jacob Druckman, *Windows*

NATIONAL SERVICE

Albert Einstein Commemorative Awards

Public Affairs: W. Averell Harriman

American Society of Mechanical Engineers

Hoover Medal for Public Service: Luis A. Ferré

RADIO AND TELEVISION

George Foster Peabody Awards

Excellence in Dramatic Programming: NBC

Drama Award: "Brian's Song"

Documentary: "This Child Is Rated X"

Broadcast News: John Rich, NBC News

Radio Public Service: *Second Sunday*

Radio Special Awards: Arthur Godfrey, CBS; "The Heart of the Matter," WCCO, Minneapolis

Television Youth or Children's Program: *To Make a Wish*

Television Special Awards: George Heinemann, NBC; Frank Stanton, CBS

National Academy of Television Arts and Sciences Awards ("Emmys")

Best Program of the Year: "Brian's Song"

Best Actress in a Series: Glenda Jackson, *Elizabeth R*

Best Actress in a Single Performance: Glenda Jackson, segment of *Elizabeth R*

Best New Series: *Elizabeth R*

Best Dramatic Series: *Elizabeth R*

Best Actor in a Comedy: Carroll O'Connor, *All in the Family*

Best Comedy Series: *All in the Family*

Best Variety Series: *The Carol Burnett Show*

Best Variety and Talk Show: *The Dick Cavett Show*

Best Actor in a Single Performance: Keith Mitchell, segment of *The Six Wives of Henry VIII*

Best Actor in a Series: Peter Falk, *Columbo*

Best Variety and Popular Music Show of the Year: "Jack Lemmon in 'S Wonderful, 'S Marvelous, 'S Gershwin"

Best Actress in a Comedy Series: Jean Stapleton, *All in the Family*

Best Performance in Music or Variety: Harvey Korman, *The Carol Burnett Show*

Best Sports Show: *ABC's Wide World of Sports*

Special Award: William H. Lawrence, news coverage

Best Documentary: *The Search for the Nile*

Best General Program: "The Pentagon Papers"

Overseas Press Club Awards

Radio Spot News Reporting From Abroad: CBS News

Radio Interpretation of Foreign Affairs: James Quigley

Radio Documentary on Foreign Affairs: "Return to Peking," NBC News

Television Spot News Reporting From Abroad: Phil Brady, NBC News

Television Interpretation of Foreign Affairs: John Hart, CBS News

Television Documentary on Foreign Affairs: "Terror in Northern Ireland," ABC

SCIENCE

American Chemical Society Awards

Priestley Medal: Frederick D. Rossini

Roger Adams Award in Organic Chemistry: Herbert S. Brown

Award for Creative Invention: S. Donald Stookey

Garvan Medal: Mary Fieser

James T. Grady Award for Interpreting Chemistry for the Public: Victor Cohn

Ipatieff Prize: Paul B. Venuto

ABBY RAE ZUKERMAN

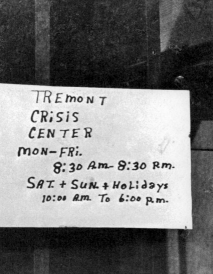

STOREFRONT PSYCHIATRY

Bronx State Hospital for the mentally ill runs neighborhood clinics where people can talk out their problems before hospitalization is needed. At left, three staffers interview a mother who brought in her daughter (back to camera).

BOTH PHOTOS, LEONARD KAMSLER

PROTESTANT AND ORTHODOX CHURCHES. *See* RELIGION: PROTESTANT AND ORTHODOX CHURCHES.

PSYCHIATRY. Community mental health centers. In the 1960's the late president John F. Kennedy funded a national program that was to inaugurate a new era of "moral treatment" for the mentally ill. The purpose of the program was to provide a better alternative to the thousands of underfinanced, overcrowded, impersonal state custodial institutions by establishing local community mental health centers. In addition, the new centers would have psychiatric programs for all social classes and minority groups, the first recognition of the need for an egalitarian and comprehensive psychiatric treatment for all who needed help.

The state hospitals, which had become unbelievably crowded, were regarded as places for "warehousing" people, depersonalizing them as human beings. Under the new humanitarian program, instead of dividing entire state hospitals into divisions for treatment, there were set up in the community local hospitals, day treatment clinics, halfway houses, crisis centers with 24-hour-a-day hot lines, open telephone lines for suicidal persons, walk-in clinics in local hospitals, alcoholic rehabilitation clinics, and drug addiction centers. New local bureaucracies were established to

handle patients, and the state hospitals began releasing patients by the thousands into community facilities. However, many community centers were not completed because of the lack of state and federal funds and the difficulties attendant on the management of a multitude of alcoholic rehabilitative clinics, drug addiction centers, and halfway houses. As a result, county and private hospitals were forced to take in too many patients and soon became unworkable.

Recently, criticisms have begun to appear. One of Ralph Nader's groups charged that the new system is irrelevant and vastly oversold, and that it has spawned a bureaucracy unresponsive to community needs. The National Institute of Mental Health answered most of the criticisms by showing that it was aware of the deficiencies and working to improve them. According to Dr. Morton Wachpress of Hillside Hospital, Glen Oaks, N.Y., by calling on the centers to provide comprehensive treatment for all, the limited staff must function mainly as a consultation and educational service for the entire community, rather than providing actual therapy for the mentally ill. Since the causes of mental illness are largely unknown, prevention through education is very limited at best, and the question has arisen whether any of the facilities are truly achieving their goals. Meanwhile, the state hospital population continues growing.

Basically, says Dr. Theodore Rothman of the University of Southern California, the function of the mental health centers is not political, but scientific; not egalitarian, but therapeutic. Many psychiatrists feel that the mental health centers should be more carefully reevaluated and the confusion cleared. Humanitarianism, while it is now fashionable, is not therapy. Meanwhile, new methodologies need to be developed to determine what has been helpful to the mentally ill, and also what has been harmful to local communities, such as the "dumping" of thousands of unrehabilitated individuals who may be a danger to themselves and the community.

New approaches to drug abuse. The major developments in treating drug abuse this year involved two different methods: (1) controlled substitution for heroin addiction using methadone and (2) blocking the effect of the drug using cyclazocine, chemically similar to nalorphine, which acts as a clinical antagonist to opiates. Increasing sophistication in the use of methadone-controlled addiction has lead to a more careful selection of patients and better control of the substance, and has shown the need for adjunctive group and vocational techniques for optimum effectiveness. The use of methadone maintenance appears to diminish the complicating social and criminal problems associated with addiction. The major remaining problem is that the heroin addict becomes addicted to methadone, which acts as an euphoriant.

On the other hand, a principal feature of cyclazocine is that it extinguishes the conditioned stimulus, i.e., it blocks the drug-induced euphoria. Extinction is best achieved by repeated exposures to a conditioned stimulus without the expected physiological and psychological reward. During the induction phase of treatment, cyclazocine as an effective narcotic-blocking agent is discussed with the addict in individual and in the drug therapy sessions. To prove that this agent blocks heroin's euphoria, the addict is given a small dose of heroin, which then produces no systemic or euphoriant effect.

Encounter groups—their psychiatric limitations. Dr. Morton A. Lieberman of the University of Chicago states that encounter groups have many aliases, e.g., T-groups, sensitivity training groups, human awareness groups, human relations groups, human enrichment groups, Synanon games, marathon groups, sensory awareness, and gestalt groups. An apologist for this popular movement, Dr. Arthur Burton of Sacramento State College, sees "the encounter group" as a community that is set in a framework of honesty and openness and that is enlivening and healing. Encounter groups are "soul" groups, in which the parameters of the human condition are opened for all persons to share. The purpose is to live more freely and to experience more deeply.

A number of critical voices have been heard recently, however. Dr. Robert Merton of Columbia University asserts that in such groups "the borrowed authority of science becomes a powerful prestige symbol for unscientific doctrine." Moreover, encounter groups are not therapeutic but "soul" enriching, and may be dangerous for those susceptible to psychiatric complications. Dr. Burt W. Back of Duke University compares many encounter groups to ancient pilgrimages, as in *The Canterbury Tales*. The present-day pilgrimages are to the encounter centers, where thousands attend on weekends for sessions and marathons. Essentially, they are seeking enrichment of self and loss of alienation.

Dr. Irvin Yalom and Dr. Morton Lieberman have documented a number of mild to severe psychiatric complications arising from encounter experiences. There is no psychiatric examination that will identify persons vulnerable to side effects. The uncontrolled and unpredictable rages of some participants have resulted in broken bones and court suits. In one instance, after a verbal combat a group of females proposed that they would resolve their problems with group sex. Psychologist Dr. Carl Rogers, however, says that he has never seen any psychiatric complications in his encounter groups.

Psychopharmacology and psychochemistry. For the last 15 years, drugs that change the psyche have been used in psychiatry and have helped many patients to free themselves from hospital care and be reintegrated into the community. The most effective drugs in psychopharmacology were reviewed: phenothiazines for psychotic states, such as schizophrenia; the antidepressant drugs tricyclic, imipramine, and amitriptiline, for the relief of depression; diazepam and meprobamate for severe anxiety.

The most exciting new development has been the revival of the use of lithium carbonate, discovered in 1949 by psychiatrist J. F. Cade of Australia. Lithium carbonate has been found to prevent manic-depressive reactions—a first in medical history. After a long study by J. Mendels and then D. W. Goodwin, it was found that both manic and depressive states can be alleviated in a high percentage of cases. This new use of lithium carbonate likewise makes it possible to test the chemical causes of depressions and manic-depressive psychoses.

Some psychiatrists reported findings indicating that schizophrenia may be related to the lack of a certain regulator chemical in the brain which allows the unchecked manufacture and build-up of dimethyl tryptamine (DMT), a powerful psychosis-inducing substance. Synthetic DMT has been used by young people to induce hallucinations.

Alcoholism. Alcohol is now becoming the "in" drug among adolescents, replacing marijuana, according to Morris E. Chafetz, M.D., of the National Institute of Mental Health. He states that in the past ten years the number of girls 18 years and under arrested for intoxication has more than tripled. Arrests of young boys in the same age group have increased 2.5 times. Studies suggest that alcohol abuse is a precursor of "drug switching," more so than marijuana.

The complex social attitudes within which drinking occurs is probably of primary importance in creating a susceptibility to alcoholism. Dr. Chafetz, who is convinced that physicians have turned over the treatment of alcoholics to others, suggests that any program of prevention should take into account the lessons of other cultures. Some cultures, like the Jewish, Italian, and Greek, use alcohol widely but have few problems with it, while the Irish, Scandinavians, French, Germans, and Russians show a greater degree of susceptibility and a larger population of alcoholics. In those cultures where drinking is not a major problem, drinking follows a definite pattern: The beverage is sipped slowly, consumed with food, and is partaken in the company of others in relaxed, comfortable circumstances. Also, drinking is taken for granted in these cultures and given no special significance; that is, no positive sanction is given to prowess in amounts consumed, and drunkenness is socially condemned. Conversely, in cultures with high incidences of alcohol problems, the person involved drinks quickly, often without food, and often in solitary and uncomfortable circumstances. In addition, drinking has a special significance, and there is a prevalence of guilt feelings, conflicts, and ambivalence. Dr. Chafetz concludes that alcoholism may be untreatable.   THEODORE ROTHMAN

PUBLIC HEALTH. Blood transfusions. The complications following blood transfusions received some attention this year. According to a paper published in the *Journal of the American Medical Association,* among 5,000 patients who underwent heart surgery and blood transfusion in 14 university centers, 3 percent developed symptomatic hepatitis, a viral infection of the liver. Ranging from 0 to 9 percent, the risk of hepatitis rose as the proportion of blood coming from banks which paid donors for blood increased.

Writing in *Science,* Dr. Constance Holden urged that the blood banking system develop uniform high standards and inspection procedures and that it change to an all-volunteer

system providing blood with a much lower risk of subsequent hepatitis. These steps would not occur without a significant prod from the federal government, cautioned Dr. Holden. That prod came quickly. The Food and Drug Administration (FDA) moved to require federal registration of intrastate blood collection activities. While the 530 large centers already under federal regulation produce about 85 percent of all donated blood, federal inspection and licensing will now extend to perhaps 3,000 other small centers.

In a related development, Georgetown University Hospital in Washington, D.C., devised an automated system to prevent blood mismatches caused by human clerical errors.

National health insurance. In preelection statements, both the Democratic and Republican parties came out in favor of national health insurance. The Democratic platform set forth the more sweeping plan, one compatible with the proposal of Senator Edward Kennedy (D, Mass.). The Republicans stood with President Richard M. Nixon's proposal for employer-funded health insurance plans with minimum benefit levels and for the encouragement of prepaid group practice organizations.

Delivery of health care. In England the long-awaited white paper on the reorganization of the National Health Service was published this summer. Intended to enable an integrated health service to come into operation in 1974, the white paper proposes abolishing the administrative structure, which is divided into three branches—the hospital service, the local health services, and general practice. As soon as legislation has been passed, area health authorities will be appointed to plan all health needs of the population in their areas. Fourteen regional health authorities will also be formed, with some planning, executive, and supervisory functions. For Scotland, plans for the health service reorganization are further ahead, do not include regional authorities, and involve the establishment of an ombudsman to handle complaints about the health service.

Health manpower problems and the better delivery of health care in the United States continued to provoke interest. Focusing on the problem of foreign medical graduates, Dr. Thomas D. Dublin wrote in the *New England Journal of Medicine* that they comprise one-fifth of active physicians and about one-third of hospital interns and residents. Because their training is sometimes inferior, both before and after coming to the United States, Dublin urged the discontinuance of active recruitment of foreign graduates. Instead, the country must define its manpower requirements and develop its own ways to meet these needs.

Recently returned from a visit to China, Dr. Victor W. Sidel of Montefiore Hospital, New York City, described the expansion of medical services there in recent years. In the rural areas in China, agricultural workers have been trained for activities in environmental sanitation, health education, immunization, first aid, and some aspects of medical care; these "barefoot doctors" are said now to number more than a million. Analogous groups have also been trained in cities, such as "work doctors" in factories and "Red Guard doctors," who are housewives serving as physicians' assistants in neighborhood health clinics.

After repeated delays in organization in Washington, the National Health Service Corps began to provide health care services in 122 urban and rural areas in 39 states and the District of Columbia in mid-1972. The personnel who were assigned are Public Health Service commissioned officers and civil service personnel. While not a permanent solution to the shortage of health manpower, the corps is intended to alleviate some acute problems in geographic distribution of health care services.

Reproduction. The health-related aspects of human reproduction were much discussed in 1972. A marked upsurge of interest occurred in the use of frozen human semen, stored in semen banks and then thawed for administration to the wife of an infertile couple. One writer was impressed by

IN MEMORIAM. Some 400 billboard-size death notices grimly reminded Stockholm residents about the menace of drugs.

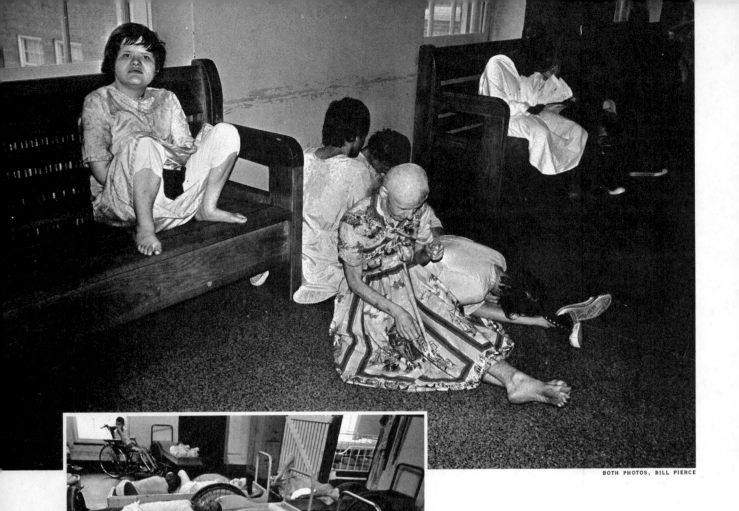

BOTH PHOTOS, BILL PIERCE

Human Wasteland

When Geraldo Rivera, a WABC-TV newsman, brought a camera crew on an unauthorized early-morning visit to Willowbrook State School in Staten Island, N.Y., he found untended children, ill-clothed and dirty, some smeared with their own feces, lying crowded in dingy wards where the only sound was the undertone of a dreary communal wail. The shocking glare of publicity fended off a budget cut and even brought in some additional funds to the state-supported home for mentally retarded children and adults. But most public health officials acknowledged that something more than short-term aid is needed if the 5,300 Willowbrook patients are ever to see any substantial improvement in their lot.

the number of couples seeking such help because the husband had had a vasectomy during a previous marriage.

The Indian government decided to set an upper age limit of 50 years for men undergoing vasectomy. This step followed the discovery that even octogenerians had been pressured into having the operation, apparently so that family-planning workers could collect bonus payments.

The curtain over sexual habits in Scotland was slightly parted by a study in the *British Medical Journal*, written by Dr. C. McCance and Dr. D. Hall. This questionnaire survey of unmarried women undergraduates at Aberdeen University found that about 30 percent had experienced intercourse in the previous six weeks, 86 percent of them with fiancés or steady partners. A survey in France revealed that the French, popularly thought great lovers, actually have rather straitlaced sexual attitudes and habits.

Mental health. Public attitudes toward mental health problems received an airing when Senator Thomas Eagleton (D, Mo.) withdrew as the Democratic nominee for vice-president. Most criticism of Eagleton seemed to be that he had kept quiet about his history, not that he had undergone treatment for depression. After this news broke, the American Psychiatric Association issued a lengthy statement which concluded, "An episode of depression in a person's medical history should be considered in the same manner as a wide range of other successfully treated illnesses."

A study based on the riot situation before it became so serious in Belfast, Northern Ireland, was published by Dr. H. Lyons in the *British Medical Journal*. It confirmed the belief that the frequency of depressive illness falls when it is possible to externalize aggressive behavior. In Belfast the fall was more pronounced in men, was confined to lower-income

478

groups, and was greater in riot areas. In contrast, a more peaceful neighboring county showed a sharp rise in male depressives.

Drug and alcohol abuse. The continuing problem of drug addiction resulted in much discussion this year, but no consensus was reached on how best to control the situation. Writing in *Science*, Henry L. Lennard, Leon J. Epstein, and Mitchell S. Rosenthal claimed that the ubiquitous use of psychoactive drugs forms the rising problem of "internal pollution." It is naïve, they suggested, "to think that the use of another drug can solve the profound and complex task facing us." Supporting this critical view, Dr. F. Heyman wrote in *Society* that methadone maintenance should be a first step in treating a health problem; instead it is being used as a final solution—a legal addiction to replace an illegal one. More cheerful views came from Dr. P. Boyd and colleagues, who treated adolescent heroin addicts in London, England, and from Dr. Vincent P. Dole, involved in the successful detoxification of more than 22,000 heroin addicts in New York City jails.

Placing a different perspective on drugs, however, a 1972 report from the National Institute on Alcohol Abuse and Alcoholism (U.S. Department of Health, Education, and Welfare) pledged a comprehensive federal effort to unify existing treatment, rehabilitation, and preventive programs in this field. It presented figures, based on liquor tax collections, which suggested that alcohol consumption seems to be heaviest in the Pacific states, followed by the New England and Middle Atlantic states, and lowest in the eastern south-central part of the United States. New York City has about 125,000 heroin addicts and more than 600,000 alcoholics. Nevertheless, it spends much more on narcotics control programs than on alcoholism.

Infectious disease. In an effort to reduce the frequency of congenital defects in infants, Illinois passed a new law forbidding issuance of a marriage license except when women have been tested for immunity to rubella (German measles). Some uncertainty remained, however, over the extent to which rubella vaccines could themselves cause congenital defects if they were given accidentally to pregnant women.

State laws requiring smallpox vaccination before entering school, still in effect in more than 20 states in 1972, tended not to be enforced or to be repealed. Meanwhile, the World Health Organization intensified its program of smallpox eradication. Now that pockets of smallpox have been eliminated in Brazil, this disease is believed to be cleared from the Americas.

A perplexing problem in 1972 was the number of reported outbreaks of staphylococcal disease in some hospital nurseries in the United States after the discontinuing of routine bathing of infants with hexachlorophene. Despite the outbreaks, the FDA and the Center for Disease Control (U.S. Public Health Service) continued to advise against using solutions of this drug, which has been shown to cause brain damage in rats and monkeys. France also imposed controls on hexachlorophene preparations when excessive amounts of the agent in talcum powder were believed to have caused the deaths of 39 infants. (*See* CHEMISTRY.)

Kidney disease. The continuing use of long-term dialysis and of renal transplants stimulated further studies of patients with kidney disease in 1972. This year about 6,000 patients in irreversible kidney failure were kept alive by long-term dialysis—the use of machines to eliminate waste matter that would be removed by normal kidneys. About 9 percent of such patients die each year, with suicide an unusually frequent cause of death. Dr. P. McKegney of the University of Vermont College of Medicine urged that patients on dialysis should be allowed to discuss early the possibility that they may not want to live with such artificial help. Such realistic discussions of these feelings could lower the mortality of such patients, he suggested. Two psychiatrists at the University of Colorado Medical School, Dr. D. Fishman and Dr. C. Schneider, wrote of their efforts to predict emotional adjustment of patients and their families during the first year of dialysis. They believed that patients should be selected for this procedure by assessing the expected quality of life as well as the length of survival.

The alternative to dialysis is kidney transplantation. The ninth report of the Renal Transplant Registry, published in the *Journal of the American Medical Association*, showed that 5,952 kidney transplants had been reported to the registry since 1953; possibly many other transplants were carried out but not reported during these years. The trend in recent years has been toward using more cadaver kidneys, with fewer coming from living donors. Between 10 and 20 percent of the recipients die in the year following transplantation, and this outcome has changed little since 1967.

Health testing. Interest continued in 1972 in the possibilities of using many simple tests to detect disease early in people without symptoms. Just as one example, the American Health Foundation opened Health Maintenance Centers, Inc., in New York City to perform a series of tests tailored to the needs of the individual participant. Recent publications from the World Health Organization have cautioned that all new forms of mass health examinations should be fully validated before being introduced as part of the routine health services. Although weight is given to this conservative view, particularly in European countries, automated health testing had many advocates in the United States in 1972.   CHARLES M. WYLIE

PUERTO RICO. Political status. The major issue was whether Puerto Rico should remain a commonwealth associated with the United States, as advocated by the Popular Democratic Party; move toward full statehood, as long proposed by the New Progressive Party; or take the road toward independence, as the Puerto Rican Independence Party (PIP) urged. In August a UN special committee on colonialism approved a resolution, 12–0, with ten abstentions, recognizing the "inalienable right of the people of Puerto Rico to self-determination and independence." The resolution fell short of demands by Cuba, backed by China and the Soviet Union, that the committee classify Puerto Rico as a colony of the United States.

The vote caused a considerable stir in Puerto Rico. Governor Luis A. Ferré termed it "interference" in internal Puerto Rican matters and said he would "refuse to cooperate" with any UN committee looking into the status of the island. The PIP said the UN vote was additional "evidence of world support" for the "deep-seated yearnings of the Puerto Rican people." There was considerable speculation in Puerto Rico that the UN vote might well hasten a new plebiscite on the island's status. In a 1967 plebiscite, Puerto Ricans had voted 60 percent to remain a commonwealth, 39 percent for statehood, and about 1 percent for independence. The results of a public-opinion poll in July 1971 revealed that 63.5 percent supported commonwealth status, 25.4 percent favored statehood, and only 5.2 percent were for independence.

Internal developments. The Ferré government was hard pressed to stem a rising tide of illegal squatting on public land by the homeless. The PIP offered advice and assistance to seven new communities of squatters during the year and viewed the land seizures as a step toward fulfilling the goal of full independence. A law that required special permission before the government could destroy occupied houses stymied the government's efforts to oust the squatters.

A controversial plan to build a 1.2-million-kilowatt nuclear power plant on the south coast of the island was suspended in August by the U.S. Atomic Energy Commission, which ordered the Puerto Rico Water Resources Authority, the government-owned power company, to conduct further geological surveys. The plant was scheduled to have been con-

structed on top of the Esmeralda Fault, which is subject to periodic seismic disturbances.

Economic developments. Continued high unemployment beset the island through the year, and little improvement was made by the Ferré government in bringing down the 12.4 percent unemployment rate registered on January 1, 1972. In fact, there were preliminary reports toward the end of the year which suggested that the unemployment rate may have climbed during 1972. Part of the unemployment problem was due to the increasing migration of Puerto Ricans from the U.S. mainland to Puerto Rico. Throughout the 1960's, the flow of Puerto Ricans to the mainland had helped reduce unemployment, but starting in 1969 a reverse trend became evident. By 1972 more Puerto Ricans were returning than leaving.

The annual per capita income reached $1,564 in 1971, according to statistics released by the Ferré government during the election campaign. By contrast, in 1940, Puerto Ricans earned an average of $120 yearly, and in 1952 the figure was only $279. Opponents of Governor Ferré pointed out that the per capita income figure was deceptive because the urban poor live very close to subsistence and the rural poor have barely made their way out of a barter economy.

Puerto Rico aimed to produce more food and import less from the mainland. Construction was started on new facilities for 16 large privately owned food producers at various locations around the island. These facilities were expected to produce about 25 percent of the island's food needs when in full operation.

For election results and campaign highlights, see the special supplement ELECTION '72.

Area and population. Area, 3,435 sq. mi. Pop. (1970), 2,712,-033. Principal cities: San Juan (cap.), 452,749; Ponce, 128,233.
Government. Commonwealth associated with the United States; population has U.S. citizenship. Gov., Luis A. Ferré.
Finance. Budget (1972–1973): balanced at $976 million.
Trade (1970). Imports, $2.9 billion; exports, $1.8 billion.
Education (1967–1968). Enrollment: primary, 437,206; secondary, 221,687; higher, approx. 45,000.

JAMES NELSON GOODSELL

QUEBEC. Labor unrest. The biggest strike in Canadian history, followed by eight days of tumultuous protest, made labor unrest the outstanding event of the year in Quebec. Adding to the climate of unrest were the high rate of unemployment and the desire of the unions to play a decisive role in determining the social and economic policies of the province.

Three major labor organizations formed a common front against the Liberal government of Premier Robert Bourassa on behalf of 210,000 public service workers in their wage contract negotiations. The three were the Confederation of National Trade Unions, an aggressive outgrowth of Catholic syndicates, headed by Marcel Pepin; the Quebec Federation of Labor, affiliated with many international unions, led by Louis Laberge; and the Quebec Teachers Corporation, under the presidency of Yvon Charbonneau. The public service workers asked for a $100 minimum weekly wage, equal pay for equal work, job security, and annual wage increases during a proposed three-year contract.

After a one-day general walkout on March 28, the strike started on April 11. The government responded with court injunctions ordering maintenance of essential services, mainly in chronic care and psychiatric hospitals. Water workers were also served with an essential service injunction and returned to their jobs. Meanwhile, hospitals operated under emergency conditions; courts and schools were closed, as were the government-controlled liquor stores, license bureaus, income tax and other government offices, and rental and welfare boards.

The government introduced emergency legislation to end the strike. Adopted after 23 hours of nonstop debate in the national assembly, the legislation called for heavy fines for

workers defying the back-to-work order and provided for settlement by government decree if necessary. The legislation also removed the right to strike from public servants (first granted in 1964) until June 1974.

On May 8 union leaders Pepin, Laberge, and Charbonneau were sentenced to a year in jail. They were found guilty of contempt of court for urging Hydro-Quebec and hospital employees to strike in defiance of court injunctions. The next day, the leaders went to jail, and protest walkouts started in ports, schools, and hospitals. Strikes spread to construction sites throughout the province. In the North Shore iron ore city of Sept-Îles, strikers took over a radio station, blocked roads into the town, and closed businesses. Throughout the province, industrial workers walked out, radio stations were occupied, and Montreal transport was disrupted by bombs, nails on bridge approaches, and sit-ins. Strikes closed newspapers in Montreal and Quebec, and French and English journalists walked out on the Canadian Broadcasting Corporation's radio and television stations for one day.

The general strike was formally ended May 17, after thousands of workers decided on their own to return to work. The three jailed leaders were released on May 24 after appeal.

Throughout the summer, negotiations continued between the government and the common front with final settlement due by agreement or through decree, as provided in the new strike-ending legislation.

In all, the strikes were unsuccessful, particularly in the attempt to politicize union members. As a result, the more conservative leaders of the Confederation of National Trade Unions pulled out and started a rival group, the Centrale des Syndicats Démocratiques. The battle for members continued at union meetings and in the courts.

During the general protest strike, 8,000 manual workers were legally able to resume their contract strike against the city of Montreal. Starting May 12, garbage piled up and repairs halted on traffic signals, police cars, street lighting, and street surfaces, and parks, zoos, playgrounds, and swimming pools were closed. After 32 days, the strike ended, but Man and His World, the city's summer fair on the Expo '67 site, was forced to shorten its season by five weeks.

Later, longshoremen staged an eight-week wildcat strike over loading procedures in the St. Lawrence River ports of Montreal, Trois-Rivières, and Quebec City. It was ended by federal back-to-work legislation, as the ports are under federal jurisdiction. Losses were heavy as ships diverted their cargo, although many vessels bypassed the three struck ports and ran cargo into nearby harbors.

Other developments. In June Prime Minister Pierre Elliott Trudeau, Premier Robert Bourassa of Quebec, and Premier Frank Moores of Newfoundland officially opened the giant Churchill Falls power development, 700 miles north of Montreal on the Quebec-Labrador border. The largest single-site power source in the Western world, Churchill Falls cost Can$946 million and was built in five years, although its conception goes back nearly 20 years. Commercial delivery of power to Hydro-Quebec, the government-owned electric utility, started in December 1971, when the first of the eventual 11 turbine-generator units began to operate. Each of the 11 generators will have a capacity of 475,000 kilowatts, for a total of 5,225,000.

Quebec is now looking to the James Bay area, 600 miles northwest of Montreal, where hydroelectric development on La Grande River has the potential development of three times the power of Churchill Falls. Roads and airports are already being built into the area, and this year's contracts are estimated at Can$125 million.

Meanwhile, Premier Bourassa announced the signing of a contract for Hydro-Quebec to supply 800,000 kilowatts of power to Consolidated Edison Company of New York during the summer months, beginning June 1, 1977. Hydro-

Quebec will receive Can$123 million during the first five years of the 20-year agreement.

Area and population. Area, 594,860 sq. mi. Pop. (est. 1970), 6,100,000. Principal cities: Quebec (cap.), 180,000; Montreal, 1,-500,000; Laval, 196,088; Verdun, 80,000; Sherbrooke, 75,690.
Government. Prem., Robert Bourassa.
Finance. Budget (est. April 1, 1970–March 31, 1971): revenue, Can$3,654,548,000; expenditure, Can$3,660,870,000.
Education (1969–1970). Enrollment: kindergarten, 108,200; elementary, 942,800; secondary, 608,800; university, 56,200. Teachers: kindergarten, 2,700; elementary, 34,900; secondary, 22,500; university, 4,300.   JACK MARSTERS

RELIGION. A new wave of Arab terrorism shocked and saddened the Jewish community, with the sudden, violent deaths of Christian pilgrims in Israel, Olympic athletes, and Israeli diplomats. Protestants continued to follow two paths, a growing number engaging in Jesus-centered fundamentalism and a diminishing number pursuing broad social goals. Metropolitan Dimitrios was chosen to succeed Athenagoras I as patriarch of the Orthodox Church. Contrary to his own recommendation that bishops retire upon reaching the age of 75, Pope Paul VI elected to remain in office.

Jewish Affairs

Concern for Jewish survival, security, and continuity was dramatically underscored this year by a series of terrorist acts that shocked the conscience of the world.

Terrorism. On May 30, soon after an Air France jet arrived at Lydda Airport near Tel Aviv, three Japanese gunmen—claimed as agents by the Popular Front for the Liberation of Palestine—retrieved submachine guns and hand grenades from their luggage and began shooting at fellow-passengers and bystanders. Twenty-five civilians died, including 15 Puerto Rican Christian pilgrims, and some 77 more were wounded in this massacre. On September 5, a group of Arab terrorists broke into the quarters of the Israeli team at the Olympics in Munich, immediately killing two men and taking nine hostage. Later that day, all nine athletes, five terrorists, and a West German policeman were killed in a shoot-out at a military air base. Three guerrillas were captured by the police but were later freed in exchange for a hijacked plane. On September 19, one Israeli official was killed and another was wounded by a bomb planted in an envelope received in London. A number of other bombs were discovered in materials addressed to Israeli offices in New York, Paris, Jerusalem, Zaïre, Brussels, and Buenos Aires.

These acts of terrorism, avowedly the work of ultra-extremist Arab groups, were widely condemned by political and religious leaders. They undoubtedly heightened the sense of Jewish solidarity and strengthened the emotional bonds between Israel and the rest of the world. American Jews, of course, shared in this feeling. (One of the murdered Olympic athletes, David Berger, was an American citizen.) American Jews were also concerned by reports of increasing anti-Semitism in Italy, by the growth of anti-Semitic propaganda in Argentina, and by severe discrimination in Syria against native Jews, who are not even permitted to emigrate.

Soviet Jews. Jews saw as another blow against freedom the decision of the Soviet government in August to impose a steeply graduated scale of fees on exit-visa applicants with higher education. While the regulation applies to anyone seeking to emigrate to a non-Communist country, in practice, the Jews were the largest group hit. The fees ranged from more than $4,000 to $50,000, based on a potential emigrant's skills and educational background. Even the lowest sum amounts to more than 2½ years' earnings for a teacher, doctor, or social worker.

Would-be emigrants were stunned and angered. Ten intellectuals led by Benjamin Levich, the highest-ranking Soviet scholar yet to apply for a visa (and be refused),

charged that educated Jews were being penalized for their brains and that scientists were in danger of becoming a new class, "the slaves of the twentieth century." Jews throughout the free world expressed their outrage at the new regulations. Before the imposition of these fees—despite the humiliating restrictions and administrative hurdles involved in emigration—some 20,000 Jews had left the Soviet Union in the first eight months of the year, compared to 15,000 for all of last year. While some contended that the exit fees were intended to stop the brain drain, Jews in the Soviet Union pointed out that some intellectuals denied permission to emigrate were later fired from their jobs.

Anti-Soviet militance. On January 26, a young woman was killed and 13 people were injured when a fire caused by an incendiary device, set apparently to protest Soviet treatment of Jews, broke out in the offices of Sol Hurok Enterprises, an organization that books Soviet performers for U.S. tours. A few minutes before, a similar bomb had exploded at Columbia Artists, another talent organization. Fortunately, there were no injuries at Columbia Artists. Although the Jewish Defense League denied responsibility for the fires, three of its members were indicted on charges of bombing these offices in June.

Electioneering. In the United States, as the wooing of Jewish voters by campaigners for President Richard M. Nixon and Senator George McGovern became more intense, eight major national Jewish groups joined in September in deploring appeals to Jews based on the single issue of United States support of Israel. These organizations, widely representative of American Jewry, asserted that such appeals, "addressed specifically to Jews, stating or suggesting that the votes of all or most Jews for parties or candidates

A RARITY AMONG RABBIS, Sally J. Priesand was ordained at a Cincinnati temple in June by Rabbi Alfred Gottschalk (left). She is the first woman rabbi in the United States and is believed to be only the second female rabbi in the history of Judaism.

UPI

THREE CHEERS FOR JESUS. An estimated 75,000 gospel-preaching young people from 50 states and 60 foreign lands jammed Dallas' Cotton Bowl for "Explo 72," the mid-June rock and religion rally conducted for almost a week by the evangelistic Campus Crusade.

will or should be determined by this consideration alone, are a disservice to the nation and to Jewish voters." The statement emphasized that Jews vote as individual citizens, according to their individual judgments, and that Jews have demonstrated concern for the entire spectrum of issues in American political life.

Among the national issues that emerged as special concerns for Jews was the question of quotas. The very word "quota" has an ugly sound for most Jews, given their efforts to eliminate discrimination in education, housing, and employment; given their support of programs on behalf of disadvantaged minorities; and given the long history of quotas against Jews. In August, Philip E. Hoffman, president of the American Jewish Committee, addressed an open letter to both presidential candidates, asking for their positions on racial, sexual, and ethnic quotas. Both candidates clearly rejected the concept of such quotas. Later Hoffman said, "We will continue to do everything in our power both to resist trends to a quota-oriented society and to expand appropriate efforts to eliminate discrimination wherever it exists."

Similarly, the National Jewish Community Relations Advisory Council, an umbrella group of major Jewish national and local community organizations, condemned the use of "preferential quotas," while strongly supporting programs to equalize opportunities for racial and ethnic minorities.

Interreligious affairs. On the interreligious scene Jews were heartened by the great outpouring of Christian support for Soviet Jewry, dramatized by a two-day National Interreligious Consultation on Soviet Jewry, which brought together leaders of major faith communities in Chicago in March. American Jews were also encouraged by a number of statements and guidelines on Jewish-Christian relations issued by various Christian bodies (Lutheran Council in

the U.S.A., 1971; Roman Catholic Archdiocese of Cincinnati, 1971; United Methodist Church and Southern Baptist Convention, 1972) which urged better understanding between Christians and Jews, condemned anti-Semitism, and repudiated the use of interreligious exchange for purposes of conversion.

At the same time, Jewish religious leaders and many parents were distressed by the increasingly aggressive campaigns of certain Christian missionary groups committed to the conversion of Jews, such as the Jews for Jesus movement. Some concern was also expressed about "Key '73," a forthcoming year of emphasis on evangelism in which a number of mainstream Christian bodies are planning to cooperate. While not specifically directed at the conversion of Jews, such as emphasis raised questions about the future of authentic pluralism in American religious life, to which Jews are heavily committed.

Quality of Jewish life. An intensified concern for Jewish continuity was apparent during the past year as Jews looked to their own community, examining and attempting to enrich the quality of Jewish life. Three major studies on the nature of American Jewish life today and in the future were completed this year. A study of the Union of American Hebrew Congregations, directed by Dr. Leonard J. Fein of Brandeis University, examined the role of the Reform congregation in the life of its members. The results pointed to a profound need for community among temple members and suggested that Reform temples provide richer opportunities for both intellectual and emotional growth in Judaism. The second study, a task force report of the Council of Jewish Federation and Welfare Funds, examined new directions in Jewish communal services. It resulted in the creation of the Institute for Jewish Life to encourage innovative programs in Jewish education and Jewish living experiences.

Finally, a report of the American Jewish Committee task force on the future of the Jewish community indicated a trend toward Jewish inwardness in communal goals and noted a shift in the agenda of Jewish communal services from concern with individual needs to those of Jewish group life, including Jewish education and religious practice.

While differing in emphasis and approach, all three reports point to a growing concern with Jewish identity and group life. Undoubtedly, a central focus of that identity is the feeling of American Jews for Israel, a feeling that is basically nonideological (i.e., Jews support Israel whether or not they consider themselves Zionists) and that views Israel not only as a refuge from persecution but also as a symbol of the Jewish people's renewed capacity for historical self-determination. These emotional bonds play an increasing role in Jewish educational and communal activities.

Woman rabbi. This year marked the ordination of the first woman rabbi in the United States, 25-year-old Sally J. Priesand. Rabbi Sally, as she is known, is believed to be the second woman rabbi in the history of Judaism. She received her degree from the Hebrew Union College–Jewish Institute of Religion in Cincinnati.

MARC TANENBAUM AND JUDITH BANKI

Protestant and Orthodox Churches

Protestants and the Eastern Orthodox Church elected what the press popularly called "new popes" this year. In meetings of the World Council of Churches and the United Methodist Church, platforms were hammered out which reaffirmed liberal positions on social and political issues. Meanwhile, capitalizing on declining attendance and declining support for liberal churches and on the "Jesus movement" phenomenon, more conservative Christians laid plans to evangelize the world in the next decade.

World Council of Churches. Philip Alford Potter, 51, a Methodist from the West Indian island of Dominica, was unanimously elected general secretary of the World Council of Churches (WCC) by its 120-member Central Committee, which met in Utrecht, the Netherlands, in August. Potter succeeded Eugene Carson Blake of the United States. He is the first black to head the WCC, which was founded in 1948 and has 252 member denominations. As general secretary, Potter will be the ecumenical spokesman for some 400 million Christians.

Potter first joined the WCC as a member of its youth division in 1954. During the 1960's, he served for seven years as field secretary for Africa and the West Indies for the British Methodist Missionary Society. At the time of his election as general secretary, he was director of the WCC's Commission on World Mission and Evangelism.

The new general secretary is known for his biblically based social activism in opposition to war and racism. He told *Time* magazine in an interview: "How dare I go well-fed to talk to hungry, unlearned people about the fact that they must be saved, and not roll up my sleeves?" He also stated that, "coming from a slave people in a poor, relatively unknown area of the world, I have a sense of belonging to all men beyond race and class."

Also at the August meeting, the Central Committee called for an end to U.S. involvement in Indochina by the end of 1972. The committee also voted overwhelmingly to sell its financial holdings in corporations operating in or trading with six African nations or areas: South Africa, South West Africa (Namibia), Rhodesia (Zimbabwe), Angola, Mozambique, and Portuguese Guinea. The WCC had about $3.5 million invested with such companies, which, the WCC said, are directly supporting racist policies in the six areas. The vote followed debate on whether the WCC might better protest racism by holding the investments and thereby maintaining access to stockholders' meetings.

The latter protest tactic was used during the year by a number of U.S. denominations which opposed the war in Vietnam. In January the Corporate Information Center of the National Council of Churches reported that the ten largest U.S. denominations held some $203 million in "war industries" stock, and it urged the churches to either "exercise social responsibility" or sell the stock.

The WCC asked its member denominations to also disinvest in companies involved with the six African countries or areas it singled out. It also voted to withdraw funds from banks which have operations in the six areas.

The actions of the Central Committee were criticized in some quarters. Harold Lindsell, editor of the periodical *Christianity Today,* said that the election of Potter "will produce further movement away from the historic mission of the church," which he sees as Gospel evangelism. Others attacked the WCC for becoming involved in African politics, by its stock sale decision and by its financial support ($265,000 since 1970) of black organizations in southern Africa.

The ecumenist leaders of the WCC were disappointed to learn in June that the Vatican was indefinitely postponing any plans to apply for Roman Catholic Church membership in the WCC. The Vatican said it was "unrealistic at present" to set a date for such an application, thereby foreclosing any possibility of Catholic membership before the 1975 WCC assembly in Djakarta. General Secretary Blake said he had been "assured by ecumenists in the Vatican that it is not basically a decision against the World Council of Churches."

Eastern Orthodox Church. His Holiness Athenagoras I, archbishop of Constantinople–New Rome and ecumenical patriarch, died July 6 in an Istanbul hospital at the age of 86. Widely hailed as one of the world's great holy men, Athenagoras, with Pope Paul VI, ended the 900-year battle between Orthodoxy and Roman Catholicism that began with the schism between East and West in 1054. In 1964,

PATRIARCH ATHENAGORAS I, in a reflective mood. The spiritual leader of 250 million Orthodox Christians died in July at 86.

UPI

Athenagoras met with the pope on Jerusalem's sacred Mount of Olives, where the two men exchanged a kiss of peace and prayed together.

Athenagoras was a reconciler. From 1931 to 1948, as archbishop of the Greek Orthodox Church of North and South America, he healed the wounds of a church torn by the politics of the old country. As patriarch for 24 years, he was the spiritual leader of 250 million Eastern Orthodox Christians, although he held jurisdiction over only 3 million of them. His dream was to convene a synod of all Orthodox Christians, the first in nearly 1,200 years, but he had not achieved this goal at the time of his death.

Metropolitan Dimitrios of Imbros and Tenedos was chosen as the new patriarch on July 16 after considerable political interference in the selection process by the Turkish government. Metropolitan Meliton of Chalcedon, a progressive, was reportedly Athenagoras' choice and therefore was considered most likely to head the patriarchate, but the Turkish government struck his name and four others, including that of Archbishop Iakovos of the Greek Orthodox Archdiocese of North and South America, from the Holy Synod's

GETTING TOGETHER in a Unity Week ceremony at New York's St. Patrick's Cathedral: from left to right, the Most Reverend Michael Ramsey, archbishop of Canterbury; Terence Cardinal Cooke, archbishop of New York; and the Greek Orthodox archbishop Iakovos.

PATRICK BURNS/NEW YORK TIMES

list of candidates. Dimitrios I was elected by a vote of 12–3 as the man acceptable to both the Turkish government and the various factions within worldwide Orthodoxy. He was known among churchmen as "the quiet metropolitan." In a press conference after his selection, the 58-year-old patriarch, speaking in Turkish to Greek journalists, said: "I will be a priest. There will be no politics in this church." (*See also* PEOPLE IN THE NEWS: Dimitrios I.)

United Methodist Church. The quadrennial General Conference of the United Methodist Church, meeting in Atlanta, Ga., in the last two weeks of April, approved a new statement of doctrine (the first in 150 years), a new statement of social principles, and a plan for restructuring all of the church's boards and agencies.

The statement of doctrine reaffirms the doctrinal stands of the premerger Methodist and Evangelical United Brethren churches and seeks to make them relevant to today's world. The traditional link between faith and work, for example, is emphasized in the statement that "personal salvation leads always to involvement in Christian mission in the world." The whole statement proved to be rather noncontroversial and was approved 925–17.

Far more controversial was the statement on social principles, a 4,000-word document dealing with sexuality, drugs, civil disobedience, war, and death. One of the most heated debates concerned the statement that homosexuals as well as heterosexuals are "persons of sacred worth." The section was approved only after a phrase was added declaring homosexuality "incompatible with Christian teaching."

Other sections of the statement proclaimed that abortion should be allowed under certain circumstances; that the use of marijuana, like the use of alcohol, is "discouraged"; that people have a right to commit nonviolent acts of civil disobedience provided they accept the costs; that war is incompatible with the teachings and example of Christ and that the church supports individuals who conscientiously oppose all war or any particular war; and that every person has a right to die in dignity "without efforts to prolong terminal illnesses merely because the technology is available to do so."

In a massive realignment of church structure, the United Methodists reduced from 23 to 12 the number of church boards and agencies.

A women's caucus was formed to protest the disparity between women's 54 percent membership in the church and their 13 percent representation in the General Conference. The women won two victories. One was the establishment and funding of a commission on the role and status of women. The other was the removal from the church's *Book of Discipline* of all male-oriented language (such as the use of "he" and "him" as universal pronouns).

Conference delegates were concerned with the escalation of the war in Indochina. The anguish over Vietnam was reflected in prayers and silent vigils, but resolutions on a course of action split the house almost down the middle. By a 5–4 margin the delegates voted to call on President Richard M. Nixon to "cease immediately all bombing," to call on Congress to stop funding "all military activities in Southeast Asia by the end of this year," and to ask U.S. leaders to pledge to pay reparations under UN auspices to victims of the war.

Church growth and decline. The dialectic between authority and freedom has been operative throughout church history. The hierarchical churches—emphasizing dogmatism, personal salvation, exclusiveness, and discipline—have usually managed to remain dominant. Occasionally, as during the 1960's, the forces advocating that the churches be more open, flexible, and socially aware gain greater influence. Church statistics for 1972 showed that the advocates of greater relativism and social activism were declining in popularity.

Although total church membership in the United States continued to rise, membership in major liberal Protestant

denominations either declined or remained static. The United Methodist Church reported 10.7 million members, down from a peak of 11.1 million in 1965. The Episcopal Church claimed 3.3 million members, down from 3.4 million in 1964–1967. The American Lutheran Church, the United Presbyterian Church, the United Church of Christ, and the Christian Church (Disciples of Christ) all experienced similar membership patterns.

In contrast, statistics showed steady membership increases of 2–5 percent since the mid-1960's for more conservative churches: Seventh-Day Adventists, the Church of the Nazarene, Jehovah's Witnesses, the Christian Reform Church, congregations in the Southern Baptist Convention, and various Pentecostal groups, including the Assemblies of God.

The most remarkable increase was reported by the Church of Jesus Christ of Latter Day Saints. The Mormons announced that their membership in the United States had increased by 50 percent to 2.1 million since 1960. "The biggest problem we have is that of tremendous growth," said Harold Bingham Lee after he became the church's 11th president in July. According to the Los Angeles *Times,* the church's "astounding growth" can be attributed to its intensive missionary program: "It constantly keeps approximately 15,000 young men at home and abroad pounding the streets and knocking on doors, seeking converts. These youths labor for two years, always at their own expense, and the list of applicants is longer than the openings."

Similar youthful enthusiasm and dedication were evident among the 75,000 delegates (mostly white, conservatively groomed teen-agers) to Explo 72, held in Dallas, Texas, in mid-June. Jesus rock music and "praise the Lord" cheers filled the Cotton Bowl for six days while Campus Crusade, the organizer of this convention for the less socially radical members of the Jesus movement, taught the delegates how to "evangelize the whole world by 1980."

The evangelical theology of Explo 72 was strictly fundamentalist—and that seemed to be its appeal. The delegates wanted some certainties in life, and they received them in doctrinal form, including statements of the supreme authority of the Bible, the deity of Jesus Christ, the historical fact of the bodily resurrection of Jesus Christ, and the future personal return of Jesus Christ.

Questioning and doubting were "out"; believing and converting were "in." Delegates were told not to participate in antiwar activity but rather to bring peace to the world through Jesus Christ. And they were told how to evangelize the world: each person was to win five other evangelists who were each to win five others and so on until no one was left outside.

The gap between the fervent evangelical movements and the socially and politically involved churches was widely commented on during the year. For example, *Time* magazine attributed part of the "Methodist malaise" to a poll showing that fewer than half of the United Methodist clergy believe that Jesus arose bodily from the grave. That fact was in striking contrast to the unanimity of belief demonstrated at Explo 72.

A much more detailed explanation of the contrast was presented by Dean M. Kelley of the National Council of Churches in his book *Why Conservative Churches Are Growing.* Kelley described the churches that are growing as those that emphasize discipline, missionary zeal, and conformity, that avoid contact with other churches and involvement in social or political issues, and that make clear their belief that they alone have the truth. Kelley characterized the churches that are losing members as those in which political and other concerns had partially supplanted fervent piety and strict Puritanism, in which diversity was tolerated, and in which dialogue with other churches was sought. Efforts to promote interfaith cooperation "may be conducive to brotherhood, peace, justice, freedom, and compassion,"

Kelley wrote, "but they are not conducive to conserving or increasing the social strength of the religious groups involved."

Kelley argued that the purpose of religion is to make people's personal lives meaningful but that, in recent years, the worldly concerns of some churches have tended to dilute and complicate that purpose. "When churches get sidetracked into noble but nevertheless extraneous goals such as changing social structures, then allegiance falters," he concluded.

Others had different theories and conclusions. Some said that the complexity of life today drives some people to seek easy answers (from fundamentalists) and others to seek complicated answers (from psychiatrists), with both trends leading to a decline in liberal-church membership.

The Right Reverend Roger W. Blanchard, executive vice-president of the Episcopal Church, felt that after the violence and social activism of the 1960's, "many people today are looking for a kind of security that fundamentalist churches can provide."

George E. Sweazey, a faculty member at the Princeton Theological Seminary, viewed doctrinal uncertainty as the major problem, maintaining that "if professional theologians can't even say what to believe, what about the average person?"
                                        JAMES H. STENTZEL

Roman Catholic Church

During 1972 much Catholic interest focused on the question of whether Pope Paul VI would follow the recommendation which he had earlier made to the bishops of the world: to retire from office at the age of 75. For some time the pope had shown signs of wearying under the weight of the church's internal worries, notably the birth-control controversy, declining vocations, the drift of young people away from orthodox religion, and a seemingly constant clergy drain. However, September 26, the pope's 75th birthday, came and went, and Paul showed no signs of relinquishing the burdens of the papacy.

During the year Pope Paul continued to come under public criticism from several Catholic quarters for the fashion in which he has presided over the church. Efforts by high-ranking churchmen to stem this criticism were less than totally successful. In February the Very Reverend Pedro Arrupe, superior general of the Jesuits, disclosed the text of a letter in which he urged the 31,700 Jesuits of the world to help foster "love and respect for the person of the Holy Father." His plea was echoed widely, but it failed to halt the issuance of a manifesto in March by 33 of the world's leading liberal Catholic theologians charging Pope Paul and the bishops in general with wielding excessive power in autocratic ways. The theologians also contended that a crisis of leadership and confidence existed in the church because of a failure to initiate meaningful reforms.

Pope Paul did not respond directly, but the Vatican's Gabriel-Marie Cardinal Garrone, prefect of the Congregation for Catholic Education, termed the charges "aggression by criticism" and added that they were "not in the spirit of the faith and in the tradition of the church." In mid-May the Italian Conference of Bishops, clearly speaking on behalf of Pope Paul, sternly warned dissenters that pressure tactics were illicit in the church. The bishops contended that the signers of the liberal manifesto wanted "a church different from the one that Jesus Christ established" and stressed that it was up to "legitimate authority"—the pope and the bishops —to decide what reforms were opportune.

Tisserant papers. In February, Eugène Cardinal Tisserant, 87, longtime head of the Vatican Library and Archives, died; within a few months memoirs of his began cropping up which contained embarrassing and lurid allegations. The most serious was the charge that Pope Pius XI was murdered by means of a poisoned injection contrived by Italian dictator Benito Mussolini. The Vatican emphatically re-

jected the charge "on the basis of direct and irrefutable testimony." Soon after, another Tisserant story made the news. This one alleged that Pope John XXIII conducted a form of election campaign for the papacy and that in the election consistory itself, 18 of the 54 cardinal-electors did not vote for him. The Vatican labeled the story a "great affront" to Pope John's spirit of humility. While issuing its denials, the Vatican braced for what could be a series of allegations based on the Tisserant papers. Before he died, Cardinal Tisserant arranged to have many of his personal papers, including diaries, taken out of Italy to his native France. This was a departure from normal practice, since Vatican cardinals usually consign their papers to the Vatican archives, where they can be scanned and controlled by authorities.

Church art. For some years the Vatican and the Italian government have been concerned over the theft of art treasures from Italian churches. In April it was announced that burglar alarms would be installed in unguarded churches and in many unguarded museums before the end of the year, with the cost to be shared by the Italian government's Treasury Ministry and the Vatican Office for Sacred Art.

The Vatican also moved to tighten its watch in churches where guards have normally been stationed. It took this action after a man wielding a hammer severely damaged Michelangelo's *Pietà* in St. Peter's Basilica. After the incident Vatican officials announced plans to protect its most prominent treasures with unbreakable glass shields. (See ART.)

Other Vatican developments. In January leaders of the Roman Catholic and Anglican Churches announced that, after four centuries of theological controversy, the two churches had reached agreement on "essential" teachings about the Eucharist. A joint statement asserted that Christ is "present" in the Eucharist in a manner that is not dependent upon what participants think. The statement declared: "Communion with Christ in the Eucharist presupposes His true presence, effectually signified by the bread and wine which, in this mystery become His body and blood."

The Vatican ended its running battle with women in miniskirts and men in shorts seeking to enter St. Peter's Basilica and other holy places. For a year the Vatican had stationed nuns at the entrances to these places and refused admission to those it considered scantily or improperly attired. In August the issue was settled when the Vatican instituted a program of lending long black plastic coats to persons it formerly would have turned away.

United States. Bishops and other Catholic officials continued to fight liberalizations of abortion laws and sought repeal of liberalized laws in states where abortion reform had been instituted. In the State of New York, Catholic leaders received a helping hand from President Richard M. Nixon, who wrote a widely publicized letter to Terence Cardinal Cooke in which he expressed support for the cardinal's efforts to secure repeal of the state's abortion law. A repeal bill subsequently passed the New York legislature but was vetoed by Governor Nelson Rockefeller. A few months later results of a Gallup poll revealed that an estimated 56 percent of U.S. Catholics believed that the decision to terminate a pregnancy should be made "solely by a woman and her physician."

With regard to parochial schools, closings continued at the rate of more than one a day, and overall enrollment declined by nearly 300,000 during 1972. The decline was partly accounted for by changing preferences of Catholic parents, many of whom are now content for their children to attend public schools. But a major factor remained the forced closing of many Catholic schools because of escalating expenses. The situation prompted U.S. bishops to quicken their efforts to secure state and federal aid that would be compatible with the federal Constitution, but at year's end no satisfactory legal avenue had been found.

Although school enrollments were decreasing, the Catholic population of the United States increased, by 176,261 persons, to a total of 48,390,990. On the other hand, there were 740 fewer priests in the United States, 416 fewer religious brothers, and 6,731 fewer nuns—evidence that the vocations problem is becoming increasingly serious.

Divorce and remarriage. A new theological contention was brought to the fore in the United States when some of the Catholic Church's traditional positions on divorce and remarriage were challenged. Under Canon Law divorced Catholics incur specific ecclesiastical penalties, including exclusion from reception of the Eucharist and sometimes denial of Christian burial. The charity and theology of the church's old position has long bothered some churchmen, and during 1972 a few dioceses began to experiment with new policy. The dioceses of Boise, Idaho; Birmingham, Ala.; Chicago; Baton Rouge; and Portland, Ore., instituted programs whereby "good conscience" Catholics of stable second marriages—those able to justify within themselves personal situations contrary to the church's traditional discipline—could receive the Eucharist and participate in the sacramental life of the church. The diocesan experimentations were at a point where they included several hundred persons when they were abruptly halted in August on the order of John Cardinal Krol of Philadelphia. Cardinal Krol announced that the question of the rights of divorced and remarried Catholics was under study by the Vatican and that all innovations were to cease pending the study's conclusions.

Catholic peace community. The conspiracy case lodged by the Justice Department against eight Catholic peace activists, including Father Philip Berrigan, S.S.J., came to trial in Harrisburg, Pa., and concluded indecisively for the government. The government charged the activists with conspiracy to kidnap presidential adviser Henry A. Kissinger and to blow up heating tunnels to federal buildings in Washington, D.C., as pressures to bring the war in Vietnam to an end. The trial dragged on for 11 weeks, with the government winning convictions against only two of seven defendants—Father Berrigan and a New York nun, Sister Elizabeth McAlister—and these on the minor charges of smuggling letters to one another through prison walls. In September, Philip Berrigan was sentenced to four two-year terms in jail; Sister McAlister was sentenced to one year in jail and three years' probation. Both sentences are being appealed.

Meanwhile, Father Daniel Berrigan, Philip's brother, was paroled from federal prison in Danbury, Conn., in February; there he had served 18 months of a three-year term for participation in a raid on the Catonsville, Md., draft board in 1968. According to the U.S. Board of Parole, he was released because he was in poor health, but Berrigan himself claimed that he was let go because it was "politically embarrassing for them to keep me there longer."

Catholic women's liberation. The nascent movement to improve women's place in the Catholic Church, specifically by opening up certain ministerial functions to women, suffered a setback in September, when Pope Paul handed down a decree barring women from even the smallest formal role in the church's ministry. On the same day that he announced revision of the traditional stages by which men advance to the priesthood and restated the church's insistence on celibacy for priests and deacons, the pope said that "in accordance with the venerable tradition of the church, installation in the ministries of lector and acolyte is reserved to men." The ruling did not actually prohibit women from performing some altar services, such as the reading of the lessons at Mass, but it did bar them from formal investiture by a bishop to do so.

On other fronts, there were a few modest gains for women, notably in the appointment of women to diocesan administrative posts formerly held by males and in the sexual integration of several hitherto all-male U.S. colleges and

MIXED BLESSING

One of the year's most celebrated cases ended in a mistrial when a federal jury, voting 10–2 for acquittal, failed to reach a unanimous verdict on charges that the Harrisburg seven had conspired to kidnap presidential adviser Henry Kissinger, raid draft boards, and blow up heating tunnels under Washington, D.C. However, two of the seven, Sister Elizabeth McAlister (third from right) and the Reverend Philip Berrigan (inset) were convicted and sentenced on a lesser charge of smuggling letters to and from prison.

universities. Notre Dame University, a male bastion for 130 years, accepted the first women into its undergraduate program—125 as freshmen and 240 as transfers from other colleges into its sophomore, junior, and senior classes.

Iron Curtain Catholicism. The Vatican and the Polish government reached agreement in June on the long-standing question of the church's administration of Poland's western territories. The Vatican acknowledged Poland's control over 40,000 square miles of pre–World War II Germany by naming Polish residential bishops to the area which the Vatican had previously considered nominally German. The territory in question was ceded to Poland under the Potsdam Agreement of 1945, pending final settlement.

In February the Hungarian government accepted the appointment of five new Catholic bishops. Observers saw the move as a sign of further improvement in Vatican-Hungarian relations after the relaxation of tensions in 1971, when Pope Paul prevailed upon Joseph Cardinal Mindszenty to leave his self-imposed asylum at the U.S. Embassy in Budapest and take up residence outside Hungary.

Thirty priests were ordained to the priesthood in Czechoslovakia in June, but church-state relations dipped to a low point in July when talks between the Vatican and the Czech government broke off without results. The Vatican has been unable to appoint a single residential bishop in Czechoslovakia for 23 years and is anxious for a change in Czech policy that would allow such appointments.

In the heavily Catholic Soviet Baltic republic of Lithuania, there were three self-immolations and several demonstrations during the spring demanding freedom of worship and protesting alleged discrimination against Catholics in secular life. In June authorities cracked down, jailing about 200 young people, but religious and nationalist feelings refused to subside.

Spain. Liberalization tendencies in the Spanish Catholic Church were a matter of considerable controversy, high-

lighted by a Vatican document attacking a "reformist" assembly of Spanish Catholic bishops and priests held in 1971. The document originated in the Vatican's Congregation of the Clergy, headed by John Cardinal Wright. It accused the assembly of sacrificing religious values for social values, of favoring Marxist forms of society, of imposing a liberal conformity on the church, and of blurring traditional distinctions between clergy and laity. The document aroused liberal elements of the Spanish church: Madrid's Vincente Cardinal Enrique y Tarancón alleged that the progress of the Spanish church was being undercut by the Congregation of the Clergy in league with a minority of conservative Spanish bishops. Cardinal Tarancón took his case to Rome, where he was backed by both Pope Paul and Jean Cardinal Villot, Vatican secretary of state. Cardinal Wright issued a statement denying that there was any political or ideological intent to the document and downgraded it as a "routine evaluation by this congregation of a meeting of Spanish bishops." The Spanish hierarchy, meanwhile, gave Cardinal Tarancón a "resounding" vote of confidence by reelecting him as their conference's chairman.

Italy. The autonomous administrations of Italy's ten Cassinese Benedictine monasteries, including the famed monasteries of Monte Cassino in central Italy and St. Paul's Outside the Walls in Rome, were dissolved in July, and temporary governing bodies were set up for them under direct Vatican control. Authorities did not specify why the action, unprecedented in Benedictine history, was taken, but there were reports that it resulted from certain modernizing tendencies and the resultant controversy between liberals and conservatives within the ten monasteries. The monastery of St. Paul's Outside the Walls had come under particular criticism after its head, Abbot Giovanni Franzoni, spoke out in favor of conscientious objection, which is illegal in Italy; protested against war in general and the Vietnam war in particular; and objected to Vatican interference in the Italian government's moves to legalize divorce. The temporary governing bodies are to direct the monasteries until new leaderships are chosen next spring. Meanwhile, "apostolic visitations"—or official inspections—are to take place at each of the institutions.

The Netherlands. The Vatican continued its efforts to swing the restive Dutch Catholic Church back from its liberal trends of recent years. Over the demurrer of Bernard Cardinal Alfrink, primate of the Netherlands, Pope Paul in February appointed a conservative, the Most Reverend Johannes Gijsen, as bishop of Roermond. Liberals fought the appointment on the grounds that Gijsen stood apart from the mainstream of Dutch Catholicism.

Switzerland. In June the Council of States of the Swiss Parliament approved a government-sponsored bill to lift a 124-year-old ban on the Society of Jesus (Jesuits) in Switzerland. The council agreed to abolish two articles of the constitution of 1848 which interdicted the Jesuits and banned the founding of new Catholic convents and monasteries. The interdictions were written into the constitution after an insurrection of Catholic cantons in Switzerland's secessionist war of 1847.

France. The French government, the French Catholic Church, and the Vatican found themselves in a potentially explosive situation after information became public in June linking the three to President Pompidou's pardoning of a war criminal, Paul Touvier, 57, whose crimes reportedly included the rounding up of Jews and the torturing and killing of members of the French Resistance during World War II. The initiative for the pardoning was admitted by a French priest working at the Vatican.

Meanwhile, church authorities in France displayed concern over a public opinion poll published in March which showed that although 84 percent of the French population professed to be Catholic, only 21 percent attended Sunday Mass regularly.

Zaïre. Church-state tensions flared in Zaïre, formerly the Belgian Congo, after an editorial in a Catholic weekly attributed to Joseph Cardinal Malula allegedly cast doubts on Zaïre's policy of a "return to African authenticity" and said it was "likely to sow confusion" and "mislead" the people. President Mobutu Sese Seko accused the cardinal of treason and had him banished from the country. A reconciliation was later worked out, but the tension lingered. Still unresolved was the fundamental issue of the respective influences to be exercised by church and government. Especially upsetting to Catholic leaders was the government's drive to implant its National Youth Movement in all schools, including seminaries, and its decision to abolish Christian names and Christian holidays. Catholics make up approximately 40 percent of Zaïre's population.

Peru. Bishop Julio Gonzales Ruiz of Puno, 43, considered one of the most progressive prelates in Peru, was forced by the Vatican to resign his diocese in April. Bishop Gonzales contended that he was ousted because of his "liberal policies" and charged that he was "condemned without trial and without previous notification."

Chile. American Catholic missionaries in Chile followed up their 1971 letter to President Nixon demanding respect for Chilean sovereignty with a 1972 protest over the alleged interference of American corporate interests in Chilean internal affairs. The letter came after reports that International Telephone and Telegraph (ITT), which has vast holdings in Chile, had sought to block the assumption of Salvador Allende Gossens, a Marxist, to the presidency of Chile.   JOHN DEEDY

RETAIL BUSINESS. The passing of pioneers. For the second time within the brief span of two years, death erased the name of a widely known and respected man from the roster of living American retailing pioneers. In 1971, it was James Cash Penney, the founder of the giant retailing firm bearing his name, who passed away; this year, it was Philip LeBoutillier, a former president of Best & Co. Both men were in their 90's when they died, which would appear to belie the idea that the heavy pressures and responsibilities found in retailing tend to shorten the lives of executives in the field.

LeBoutillier gained extensive experience in well-known Rochester, N.Y., Boston, and New York City retailing firms before joining Best & Co. in 1912. When he came to the company, it was a medium-sized New York City women's and children's specialty store enjoying only a local reputation. From this modest position, LeBoutillier promoted Best & Co. into a national institution through the exercise of unusual foresight and drive. Recognizing the sales potential of suburban retailing long before other larger retailers, LeBoutillier pioneered branch store operations by opening store units in suburban areas across the country. In 1919, he instituted one of the first pension plans for the employees of a retailing firm. He was also known as a strong advocate of generous wage and salary policies and for promoting employees from within the organization. Following LeBoutillier's retirement, Best & Co. lost its momentum and finally went out of business about two years before the death of its pioneering architect.

TABLE 1. U.S. RETAIL SALES AND SERVICES SHARES OF PERSONAL CONSUMPTION EXPENDITURES, 1950–1970

Year	Total expenditures (in billions)	Retail sales	Services
1950	$191.0	67%	33%
1955	254.4	64	36
1960	325.2	60	40
1965	432.8	60	40
1970	616.7	57	43

SOURCE: U.S. DEPARTMENT OF COMMERCE

TABLE 2. SHARES OF U.S. NATIONAL INCOME ORIGINATING IN DISTRIBUTION AND SERVICE INDUSTRIES, 1950–1970

Year	National income (in billions)	Retail	Wholesale	Services
1950	$241.1	11.5%	5.5%	9.0%
1955	331.0	10.4	5.9	9.4
1960	414.5	11.0	5.6	10.7
1965	564.3	9.6	5.9	11.4
1970	800.8	15.2		13.0

SOURCE: U.S. DEPARTMENT OF COMMERCE

Store closings. New York City retailers appear to be having more than their share of problems staying in business. In addition to Best & Co., since 1964, five sizable retailing firms located in the area have closed their doors for the last time: John David, Stern's 42nd Street, DePinna, Broadstreet's, and Weber & Heilbroner. The annual sales of the six firms totaled well in excess of $100 million.

Catalog discount showrooms. Catalog selling, discounting, and the warehouse showroom have been combined to create the catalog discount showroom. This innovation in retail marketing features well-known brands of merchandise at discount prices. It is found in both downtown and suburban areas. The typical outlet occupies from 2,000 to 10,000 square feet, of which one-third is allocated to a showroom for displaying merchandise and the remaining two-thirds to warehousing. The method of operation enables a customer to make a selection of merchandise from a catalog at home, travel to a showroom to see and purchase the desired items, and take the purchases home or have them sent. For the operator, the catalog discount showroom should mean greater sales in less space at a lower cost; thus, this innovation is expected to yield a higher return for each dollar of invested capital.

Major retailers are neither fighting nor shunning the catalog discount showroom as they did the discount store 20 years ago. Rather, they are moving aggressively into the field. Among the retail marketing giants that have either opened or are planning to open catalog discount showrooms are Grand Union, Vornado, Mammoth Mart, Giant Food, Dayton-Hudson, Coop Electric Supply of Chicago, E. F. McDonald, Sperry & Hutchinson, Zayre, May Department Stores, Designkraft Jewelry, and Malone & Hyde. Traditional retailers currently contemplating catalog discount showroom operations are Bradlees, Franklin Stores, and W. T. Grant. Trade sources estimate that there are currently in operation about 600 catalog discount showroom firms and that they will do roughly a billion dollars this year. The same sources predict that catalog discount showroom volume will grow to $3 billion by 1975. For comparison with an old established form of retail marketing, the big five in mail order selling—Alden's, Montgomery Ward, J. C. Penney, Sears, Roebuck and Co., and Spiegel—did a total of about $4 billion in 1971.

Television advertising. An ever-increasing number of large and small retailers are discarding the notion that newspapers and other print media are the only effective means of local advertising and are following the lead of Sears by turning to television. The retailers' defection from the print media is transforming local television advertising and is causing both retailers and their suppliers to revamp their marketing and advertising strategies and operations. All types of retailers are asking their suppliers for assistance in planning and using television. Multiunit retailers are demanding that their suppliers provide them with practically tailor-made rather than canned commercials. Department stores are beginning to seek advice from advertising agencies about television advertising. For suppliers, the evolving situation spells the need for more intimate knowledge of local markets; for newspapers and television stations, it means keener competition for local advertising dollars.

Services. Since 1950, consumers have reduced the share of their personal consumption expenditures for goods 15 percent and increased the share for services 30 percent (Table 1). This change in consumer spending patterns has pushed services well ahead of retailing in terms of the sizes of their relative contributions to the national income (Table 2). An article on consumer spending in U.S. News & World Report highlights the growing importance of services to the health of the national economy. The article points out that services have accounted for a major share of all new jobs in the country during the past two decades and that services today employ more persons than manufacturing.

TABLE 3. U.S. RETAIL SALES, JANUARY–JUNE 1972 AND 1971[1]
(in millions)

Group	1972	1971	Percentage change from 1971
Durable goods stores (total)[2]	$ 71,356	$ 62,961	+13
Automotive	41,888	37,376	+12
Furniture and appliances	10,470	9,154	+14
Lumber, building, hardware, farm equipment	12,827	10,949	+17
Nondurable goods (total)[2]	145,406	136,360	+ 7
Apparel	10,704	10,322	+ 4
Drug and proprietary	7,139	6,861	+ 4
Eating and drinking places	16,598	15,324	+ 8
Food	46,378	44,371	+ 5
Gasoline service stations	15,021	14,152	+ 6
General merchandise	36,378	33,028	+10
Department stores	22,171	20,308	+ 9
Mail order houses	2,424	2,028	+20
Variety stores	3,806	3,534	+ 8
Liquor stores	4,581	4,308	+ 6
Total[3]	**$216,762**	**$199,321**	**+ 9**

[1] Seasonally adjusted.　　[2] Followed by selected items.　[3] Total durables plus total nondurables.

SOURCE: U.S. DEPARTMENT OF COMMERCE

Retail sales. For the first six months of 1972, retail sales were 9 percent higher than they were in the same six months a year ago. Measured against the rise in the Cost of Living Index (1967 = 100) from 121.5 in June 1971 to 125.5 in June 1972—about a 3.3 percent increase—the 1972 sales total for the six-month period represents slightly more than a 5 percent gain in physical volume over 1971's first six months. As in 1971, durable goods made a better showing than nondurable goods in the size of their 1972 percentage sales increases. The biggest gainer in terms of relative sales increases, however, was found among nondurables with mail order houses chalking up a whopping 20 percent gain. The next best showing in terms of relative sales increases was made by the lumber, building, hardware, farm equipment classification of retail firms, with a 17 percent increase. The apparel and the drug and proprietary store classifications of stores were at the bottom of the list with 4 percent gains (Table 3).

Since June, retail sales have continued their upward climb. This trend is evidenced by an article in an early September issue of the New York Times which was headlined, "Retail Sales Last Month Rose Strongly to Record."

TABLE 4. U.S. APPAREL SALES, JANUARY–JUNE 1972 AND 1971[1]
(in millions)

Group	1972	1971	Percentage change from 1970
Men's, boy's wear	$ 2,540	$ 2,366	+7
Shoe stores	1,783	1,775	+0
Women's apparel, accessory	4,073	4,023	+1
Other apparel	2,308	2,158	+7
Total	**$10,704**	**$10,322**	**+4**

SOURCE: U.S. DEPARTMENT OF COMMERCE

[1] Seasonally adjusted.

THE BARGAIN BUG sends shoppers browsing through household gadgets and objets d'art, all for sale at a flourishing flea market in Lahaska, Pa.

JANE LATTA

In the article, it was pointed out that 1972 August retail sales were 1.5 percent higher than in the preceding month (July) and 9.5 percent above August 1971.

Apparel sales. For the second consecutive year, apparel firms failed to match the percentage sales gains of the retail trade as a whole during the January–June period. If one discounts inflation, the apparel firms' physical volume during the first six months in 1972 just about matched their 1971 physical volume for the same months. Shoe firms made the poorest showing of the apparel classification of stores—in terms of relative sales gains over the previous year—by just about matching their 1971 January–June dollar sales in the same 1972 months (Table 4). Despite the failure of shoe firms to show a sales gain in 1972 over 1971 during the January–June period, they fared better this year than last, when their sales dropped 13 percent below the previous year.

Discounting. Audits & Surveys, Inc., a marketing research agency, reported that there were 12,400 fewer stores in the country at the end of 1971 than there were at the beginning of the year and that the number of stores had fallen some 60,000 in the last five years. In contrast, *The Merchandiser*, a mass retailing publication, reported that discount department stores had added over 400 units in 1971 and that their total of 4,500 now equaled the number of traditional department stores. The Mass Retailing Institute, in a study entitled "Compensation in Mass Retailing, 1971," estimated that mass retailers' sales totaled $30 billion in 1971 and that they employed from 800,000 to 900,000 people that year. *Modern Retailer*, a second mass retailing publication, reported that mass retailers were projecting another 500–600 new units in 1972.

Automotive sales. Sales of imported and domestic cars in 1971 totaled 10,155,411, topping the 1968 record of 9.66 million, according to the New York *Times*. The 1971 upsurge in car sales carried over into 1972, with a 12 percent increase in automotive sales during January–June 1972 over the same six months in 1971 (Table 3). Figures for the 1972 model year show that manufacturers sold a total of 12,794,000 vehicles, a new record. Of that total, 10,735,000 were passenger cars and 2,059,000 were trucks, including pickups. General Motors captured the largest share of the domestic passenger-car market, selling 49 percent; Ford followed with 30 percent, Chrysler 18 percent, and American Motors 3 percent. Since the 1971 realignment of exchange rates, not only were U.S. auto-makers enjoying record sales, but they appeared successful in their efforts to slow the tide of foreign imports with their new "compacts." "If present trends continue," predicted *U.S. News & World Report*, "sales of foreign models in all of 1972 will amount to 1.5 million—marking the first yearly drop since 1962."

Retail inventories. While retailers increased their inventories of both durable and nondurable goods many millions of dollars from June 1971 to the same month in 1972, they lowered their inventories in relation to sales in both categories of goods (Table 5). The retailers handling durable goods, however, appear to have done a job superior to that done by those dealing in nondurable goods, because

TABLE 5. U.S. RETAIL INVENTORIES[1]

(in millions)

Group	June 1972	June 1971	Percentage change from 1971	Inventory-sales ratio 1972	1971
Durable	$23,306	$22,679	+3	1.98	2.10
Nondurable	28,559	26,855	+6	1.16	1.17
Total	**$51,865**	**$49,534**	**+5**	**1.41**	**1.46**

SOURCE: U.S. DEPARTMENT OF COMMERCE

[1] *Seasonally unadjusted.*

TABLE 6. U.S. PERSONAL CONSUMPTION EXPENDITURES[1]
(in billions)

Group	1972 Second quarter	1972 First quarter	1971 Fourth quarter	1971 Third quarter	1971 Second quarter
Durable	$113.9	$111.0	$106.1	$106.1	$101.9
Nondurable	297.2	288.3	283.4	278.5	277.2
Services	302.4	296.7	290.9	286.1	281.3
Total	**$713.5**	**$696.0**	**$680.4**	**$670.7**	**$660.4**

SOURCE: U.S. DEPARTMENT OF COMMERCE

[1] *Seasonally unadjusted.*

they made by far the greater reduction in their inventory-sales ratios during the year.

Consumer spending. Consumers were on a buying spree that boosted personal consumption expenditures to all-time highs. According to *U.S. News & World Report*, spending for durable goods—automobiles, furniture, household appliances, television sets—paced the upturn in consumer buying; sales of food and clothing were less buoyant, although they, too, were well ahead of the rate for 1971. The same report suggested that the surge in retail sales stimulated the whole economy.

TABLE 7. U.S. CONSUMER CREDIT[1]
(in billions)

	June 1972	June 1971	Percentage change from 1971
Total installment	$114,567	$101,862	+13
Automobile	41,104	36,349	+13
Other consumer goods	32,841	28,976	+13
Repair modernization	4,571	4,186	+ 9
Personal loans	36,051	32,351	+11
Total noninstallment	27,648	25,526	+ 8
Single-payment	10,851	9,862	+10
Charge accounts	8,870	8,214	+ 8
Service	7,927	7,450	+ 6
Total[2]	**$142,215**	**$127,388**	**+12**

SOURCE: U.S. DEPARTMENT OF COMMERCE

[1] *Seasonally unadjusted.* [2] *Total installment plus total noninstallment.*

Consumer credit. Consumers were speeding their rate of borrowing, boosting the annual increase in their total debt from 4 percent in June 1971 to 12 percent in June 1972. Installment credit—the most expensive form of borrowing—claimed the biggest share of the increase in their outstanding debt.

Prospects for 1973. With the upsurge in consumer confidence showing no signs of subsiding, retailers were expected to end 1972 with total sales of between $445 billion and $450 billion—an all-time high. If nothing happens in the next 12 months to destroy consumer confidence, retailers should enjoy another banner year in 1973.

During the coming year, retailers will undoubtedly face their usual quota of problems.

There is the wage-price freeze with its attendant paper work. Despite politicians' promises to the contrary, it hardly seems likely that legislators will repeal the wage-price legislation within the next year.

There is pilferage, with its negative impact on retailers' profits. Although retailers may have succeeded in blunting the upward trend of theft losses, it has been a costly effort in terms of added security procedures, devices, and personnel. Retailers' pilferage losses will probably continue at a prohibitively high level until there is a fundamental change in public morality.

There are the resurgent and innovative types of retail marketing outlets, which traditional retailers need to identify early if they are to initiate essential competitive actions. In these categories of outlets, there are the bantam store and

A&P's WEO (Where Economy Originates) store in addition to the catalog discount showroom and the resurgent mail order and house-to-house selling.

There is consumerism, which will not go away. The consumer's confidence in the economy is at variance with his confidence in the general integrity of retailers and other businessmen. Consumerism is rapidly becoming institutionalized in the form of a consumer complaint industry. In turn, businessmen are seeking persons who can either defuse consumer criticism or blunt the drive for regulatory legislation.

THEODORE D. ELLSWORTH

Advertising

After a two-year leveling-off period, advertising volume in the United States showed a sharp upward trend this year. Robert J. Coen of the media research department at McCann-Erickson estimated for *Advertising Age* that expenditures for the year would total $22.5 billion, an increase of nearly $2 billion over 1971. As the economy continued to rebound from the 1969–1970 slump, many advertisers were stepping up new product introductions and increasing overall promotional effort. Retail and other local advertising appeared to be gaining momentum even faster than national advertising, showing a 12 percent rate of increase compared to 7 percent for national advertising.

Consumer groups maintained their pressures for more stringent governmental control of advertising practices. However, a bill to create a separate consumer protection agency, an expanded version of a measure passed last year by the House, died in the Senate on October 5 when supporters were unable to invoke closure to cut off unlimited debate.

The Federal Trade Commission continued its aggressive stance toward advertising. The "substantiation" program—requiring manufacturers to provide supporting evidence for questionable advertising claims—was extended to additional groups of products, including soaps, cold remedies, and analgesics. After nearly a century of advertising Ivory soap as pure, Proctor & Gamble was asked to provide proof.

Corrective advertising. The procedure enunciated earlier by the FTC in the Profile Bread case, requiring the advertiser to devote 25 percent of his advertising for one year to correcting erroneous impressions, was extended to other advertisers. In the second consent agreement of this kind, the producers of Ocean Spray Cranberry Juice Cocktail agreed in May to corrective advertisements pointing out that their use of the term "food energy" does not include minerals or vitamins but only calories.

Actions instituted earlier by the FTC to require similar corrective action by the Firestone Tire & Rubber Company and the Standard Oil Company of California continued to be strongly contested by both firms, each maintaining that its advertising claims had a sound factual basis. Standard Oil additionally charged the FTC with greatly exaggerating its charges against the company in the original news release on its proposed action and then actually filing a watered-down complaint. A false demonstration complaint filed against E. I. du Pont de Nemours for its "punctured can" Zerox television commercial was ultimately dropped, but not until a great deal of unfavorable publicity had been generated by the FTC action.

Corrective action complaints were also filed against the Sugar Association and three makers of analgesics. The FTC claimed that advertisements suggesting that small amounts of candy or other sugar products eaten shortly before meals could curb the appetite and aid in weight reduction programs were without adequate scientific substantiation. The analgesics manufacturers were told to use corrective advertising pointing out that it had not been established that their respective brands were more effective for relief of minor pain than ordinary aspirin.

Counteradvertising. To many advertising spokesmen the most ominous specter to appear on the regulatory scene was

the concept of counteradvertising. Originating with the anti-smoking messages that were accepted as public service announcements by radio and television stations after the U.S. surgeon general's report on the hazards of cigarette smoking was released, this principle was coming to be applied to any advertising with controversial implications. While some supporters of the idea were trying to apply it to all media, the "fairness doctrine" long recognized by the Federal Communications Commission made television and radio broadcasters particularly vulnerable.

Several groups had already obtained time for counter-messages through court action or threats thereof. Friends of the Earth forced several television stations to carry environmental messages to counteract automobile and gasoline advertising. NBC agreed to carry countermessages for a farm group in opposition to television commercials it had broadcast for the Association of American Railroads. The FTC gave further impetus to this development when it made specific proposals to the FCC for new broadcast regulations to more readily implement counteradvertising efforts. Included were suggestions for providing responses not only to advertisements that raised controversial issues but also to those that did not disclose the negative aspects of their products as well. The proposal unleased a storm of protest from broadcasters and advertisers who contended that practically every advertisement could bring about a claim for a countering response on the part of someone.

Advertising review board. Much attention during the year was focused on the advertising industry's most ambitious self-regulation effort to date—the National Advertising Review Board—set up and administered in conjunction with the Council of Better Business Bureaus. Several consumer groups soon moved to test its effectiveness. Mark Silbergeld, an associate of Ralph Nader, filed complaints with the NARB on the advertising of ten different products, claiming they used "dangling comparisons, rigged demonstrations, and untrue nutritional claims." Erma Angevine of the Consumer Federation of America filed 27 "test cases" with the board.

By the end of the year criticism of NARB operations was being voiced. Action was often very slow, and many months sometimes passed before decisions were rendered. Some complainants suggested that the decisions too often seemed to support the advertiser; interpretation of an advertisement was said to be from the standpoint of the writer of the message rather than from the perception of it by the consumer. There was criticism, including some from members of the board, of the policy of not publicly disclosing board decisions. Late in the year the board was restudying its policy with respect to public release of its decisions.

Media. The financial outlook for advertising media generally was brighter than it had been in several years. Television rebounded strongly from its slump of 1971, which had been brought on by the loss of cigarette revenues and the softness of the economy. Network television was up 9 percent in volume, with national spot and local posting even greater gains. Newspapers continued to show strong growth, with total advertising expenditures in this medium estimated at $6.8 billion for the year, despite the loss of three more metropolitan dailies: the Washington *Daily News*, the Boston *Herald Traveler*, and the Newark *Evening News*. Magazines, one of the financially troubled areas in recent years, posted a 5 percent increase in advertising volume.

Agencies. Despite the generally improving economic picture most advertising agencies voiced only cautious optimism during the year. The annual report of the American Association of Advertising Agencies, released at midyear, disclosed that the agency business had suffered its most unprofitable year in a decade during 1971. Agency profits had averaged only 0.56 percent of billings and 2.87 percent of gross income.

Lennen & Newell, which in 1970 had been among the top 20 agencies in size with $160 million in billings, filed for bankruptcy in February following loss of several key accounts during 1971. The trend toward agency consolidation continued. The biggest merger of the year joined Campbell-Ewald, longtime agency for Chevrolet, with McCann-Erickson and other units of The Interpublic Group of Companies.
See also CONSUMER AFFAIRS.   ROBERT V. ZACHER

RHODE ISLAND. Education. Educational developments were the highlight of the year in Rhode Island, as the state continued through a period of economic depression.

School openings were delayed by teacher strikes in nine districts. More than 50,000 pupils had unexpected extensions of their summer vacations. In addition, two Providence high schools, Mount Pleasant and Central, were closed briefly by violent racial disturbances.

A major step was a decision by Brown University to expand its medical program into a full-fledged medical school—the state's first—together with a decision by the general assembly to partially support the private venture with public funds. Brown was urged to open the school in order to assure the state of a future supply of physicians.

Rhode Island Junior College, a state institution, moved from makeshift quarters into a $17 million "megastructure" in Warwick. The private Vernon Court Junior College in Newport closed, citing bankruptcy.

Unemployment. Unemployment remained extremely high throughout the year, reflecting the sluggish national economy. It appeared that the yearly average unemployment rate for the state would be about 7.5 percent, indicating that about 25,000 persons were without work.

Legislation. The general assembly session was marked by a battle over no-fault automobile insurance. The proposal, strongly supported by Democratic Governor Frank R. Licht but opposed by lawyers, died.

The assembly approved a $345.8 million budget. It decided to allow dog racing, subject to approval by public referendum, but did not move on numerous other gambling proposals, including some for gambling casinos, off-track betting, and state-sponsored sports wagering.

Crime. Raymond L. S. Patriarca, the aging, publicly identified head of organized crime in New England, was found innocent at a retrial of a charge of murder conspiracy, despite the recanting of testimony by a priest who had been his alibi witness. In the trial of another underworld figure, a Providence councilman and another man were indicted for jury tampering.

Major arrests included those of 28 persons for horse-race rigging, 83 in a single raid for gambling conspiracy, and the police chief in the town of Coventry for extortion.

Religion. The Most Reverend Louis E. Gelineau became one of the youngest Roman Catholic bishops in the United States when he took over the diocese of Providence at the age of 43. The Right Reverend Frederick H. Belden assumed the Episcopal bishopric.

Providence. Redevelopment work proceeded apace as finishing touches were put on the new Providence Civic Center, a $17 million combination sports center and convention hall, one major office building was opened, and another was started. Plans were announced for building hundreds of apartment units on the fringe of the downtown area.

Environment. One major project this year was the September cleanup of the Blackstone River banks by an estimated 5,000 to 10,000 volunteers. The men, women, and children who participated worked with an estimated 200 pieces of heavy equipment donated by contractors and created parks where mounds of debris had been dumped.

For election results and campaign highlights, see the special supplement ELECTION '72.

Area and population. Area, 1,214 sq. mi. Pop. (est. 1972), 946,725. Providence (cap.; 1970), 179,213.

Government. Gov., Frank R. Licht (D); lt. gov., J. Joseph Garrahy (D); secy. of state, August P. LaFrance (D); treas., Raymond H. Hawksley (D); atty. gen., Richard J. Israel (R). General assembly: senate, 41 D, 9 R; house, 75 D, 24 R, 1 ind.

Finance (1972–1973). Budget: anticipated revenue and expenditure, $340,111,411.

Education. Enrollment: public (est. 1971–1972), elementary, 106,914; secondary, 83,782. Nonpublic (est. fall 1971), elementary, 35,000; secondary, 10,100. Higher education (fall 1970), full-time, 34,334; part-time, 10,753.   DAVID F. DONNELLY, JR.

RHODESIA. Rhodesia's internal and international affairs were completely dominated during 1972 by developments flowing from the Anglo-Rhodesian accord of November 1971. The agreement, signed by British foreign minister Alec Douglas-Home and Rhodesian prime minister Ian D. Smith, provided a solution for the conflict between the two countries since Rhodesia's unilateral declaration of independence in 1965. Under the agreement the Rhodesian Front (RF), led by Smith, was to remain in power with British recognition—and an end to British economic sanctions against the regime—while gradually extending a greater political voice to the African majority. However, the terms under which Africans would be granted new political opportunities were so complicated that there was no doubt that white domination would persist for several generations. No provision was made to improve the status of the average African in the immediate future.

The Pearce Commission. The one concession that the British government had asked of the white Rhodesians was that the November agreement be subjected to a "test of acceptability" by an independent commission of inquiry. At the time of the commission's appointment at the very end of 1971, it was widely anticipated that it would find the agreement acceptable, an answer obviously desired by both governments concerned.

On January 11, the commission, headed by Lord Pearce, a retired British High Court judge, arrived in Salisbury, sparking the most concerted round of political activity and protest seen in Rhodesia since the early 1960's. An organization called the African National Council (ANC) had been formed in December specifically to fight the agreement. The ANC, headed by Bishop Abel Muzorewa and the Reverend Canaan Banana, disseminated information throughout the country, telling Africans about the settlement and urging them to reject it. The Rhodesian government, on the other hand, had worked to convince the British and the world that the Africans were satisfied under white rule. In its efforts to counter the ANC campaign against the November agreement, the government contended that the proposals were realistic and that Rhodesia's African population would benefit as much as the whites from an end to the sanctions and the infusion of foreign investment and British aid.

At the beginning of the commission's two-month stay, a series of disorders and riots occurred in many of Rhodesia's major urban centers. The Rhodesian police and army were called out to put down the disturbances; more than 30 Africans were killed and thousands were arrested or detained.

Despite the disorders, the Pearce Commission organized meetings throughout the country, from the largest towns to the smallest villages, in its effort to ascertain attitudes toward the settlement. Traveling with Shona and Ndebele translators, the commissioners listened to anyone who wanted to speak, interviewing in the course of its investigation 6,130 whites and 114,600 Africans.

The commission's report. On May 23, two months after its departure from Rhodesia, the Pearce Commission released its report, which found that the November settlement could not be considered "acceptable to the people of Rhodesia as a whole." The report noted overwhelming support for the agreement among whites and in most of the small Asian and Coloured communities, but among the Africans it found widespread "mistrust of the intentions and motives of the Smith Government." It reported that to a great extent the Africans did not so much reject the settlement as they did the entire white government.

COMMISSION OF INQUIRY. Established to sample opinion in Rhodesia on an agreement with Britain to recognize the present government, the Pearce Commission interviewed widely and found the settlement not acceptable to "the people of Rhodesia as a whole."

KEYSTONE © CAMERAPIX

The British government accepted the report's findings, and Douglas-Home announced to the House of Commons that sanctions would be continued. The Rhodesian government, disappointed and angered by the report, claimed that the Africans who had opposed the settlement had been intimidated and that the British government had simply "lost the will to settle." Neither government foresaw the prospect of renewed negotiations in the near future.

Other political developments. After the Pearce Commission left, the ANC was banned from issuing membership cards and was later denied access to funds from outside Rhodesia. The RF continued to augment the powers of the chiefs, who tend to be the most reliable allies of the whites among the African population. It was announced in July that a policy of "provincialization" would be initiated later in the year. This was expected to lead Rhodesia closer to the Bantustan concept of separate government in African enclaves, pioneered in South Africa, as it was anticipated that separate provincial councils for Africans would soon be established in Mashonaland and Matabeleland.

Rhodesia found itself at the center of another major political battle in August, when a crisis arose over its participation in the 1972 summer Olympic games in Munich. Rhodesia had agreed to participate with an integrated team and to accept the British flag and national anthem as its own. However, many African countries, as well as blacks from the U.S. team, threatened to withdraw unless Rhodesia was excluded. After much debate, the International Olympic Committee (by a 36 to 31 vote, with three abstentions) withdrew its invitation to Rhodesia.

Economic developments. Accurate information on the Rhodesian economy continued to be hard to come by. It was, of course, hoped for part of the year that sanctions would soon be lifted, but this did not happen.

In 1971 and 1972, however, the U.S. Senate passed riders to military procurement bills that allowed the United States to import minerals from Rhodesia. Early in 1972 two shiploads of Rhodesian chrome entered Louisiana ports and, when protests were mounted, were offloaded by nonunion labor.

The Rhodesian economy suffered a major blow in June when an enormous fire and explosion at the Wankie Coal Mine ended in the deaths of at least 426 men. The disaster resulted in the complete sealing of a shaft of the mine that produced nearly 50 percent of the output of Wankie coal. There was no indication whether the shaft could be used again. In the face of this loss, Rhodesia will have to intensify its already close economic ties to South Africa—a trend that has been persistent since 1965.

Area and population. Area, 150,333 sq. mi. Pop. (est. 1970), 5,354,000, including 5,100,000 Africans, 228,000 Europeans, and 26,000 Asians and Coloureds. Principal cities: Salisbury (cap.), 435,000; Bulawayo, 281,000.

Government. Self-proclaimed republic. Prime min., Ian D. Smith; pres., Clifford Dupont.

Finance. Monetary unit: Rhodesian dollar; Rh$1 = US$1.57. Budget (1972–1973): revenue, Rh$272 million; expenditure, Rh$288 million.

Trade (1971). Exports, Rh$271 million (compared with Rh$278 million in 1965, the last year before sanctions); imports, Rh$265 million.

Income (1971). 779,000 employed Africans earned Rh$244 million; 108,000 employed Europeans (whites) earned Rh$365 million.

LARRY W. BOWMAN

ROMAN CATHOLIC CHURCH. *See* RELIGION: ROMAN CATHOLIC CHURCH.

ROMANIA. Politics and government. A plenary session of the Communist Party Central Committee, meeting in April, made a large number of changes affecting the party secretariat, the Council of Ministers, and other leading organs of government. The changes, said to continue the process of revamping the secretariat that had been in progress for several years, were in political, ideological, and security matters. However, there were rumors that Communist Party secretary general Nicolae Ceauşescu's position had been endangered by the possibility of an army coup d'état, and there were reports that he had taken over control of the security forces. In a cabinet reshuffle in October, Corneliu Manescu was replaced as foreign minister by George Macovescu.

In May, on the 80th anniversary of his birth, Stefan Foris, who had been secretary general of the Communist Party during World War II, was accorded political rehabilitation. Foris had been removed from his post because of "shortcomings and serious mistakes," arrested in June 1945, and executed in the summer of 1946 without investigation of the charges against him or trial. A meeting of the party Central Committee in 1968, noting the groundlessness of the accusations, had decided on his rehabilitation.

Foreign affairs. In May, as if to belie rumors that his position was menaced by a coup, Ceauşescu made an extensive tour of Africa. In Egypt, his last and most important stop, discussions with Egyptian leaders led to a financial agreement between the two countries. Romania agreed to advance Egypt $100 million as well as a loan to pay for deliveries of Romanian equipment for Egypt's rural electrification projects and a loan to cover delivery of 2,000 tractors and other imports. Ceauşescu's tour reflected Romania's need for new markets for its expanding industry and for new sources of raw materials.

Also in May, Israeli prime minister Golda Meir paid an official visit to Bucharest. It was the first visit by an Israeli prime minister to any East European capital.

On May 16, Ceauşescu and Marshal Tito of Yugoslavia unveiled memorial tablets on the dam of the Iron Gates hydroelectric power project. The dam was constructed over eight years as a joint Romanian-Yugoslavian project and is to be used by both countries. It is 1,447 feet long and has a flow capacity of 547,400 cubic feet per second. The installed power reaches 2,050 megawatts, with an annual power output of 10.4 billion kilowatt-hours. The reservoir has a volume of 70.6 billion cubic feet and a surface area of 66 square miles.

Abrupt cancellation in June of President Ceauşescu's visit to Japan caused ill feeling in Tokyo and speculation that the move had resulted from Chinese pressure.

In July, U.S. secretary of state William Rogers visited Bucharest. During his visit talks were held on expansion of scientific and technological cooperation between the United States and Romania.

Economic developments. Inauguration of the Iron Gates project and other new power generating facilities will bring Romania's electric power output to 44 billion kilowatt-hours this year, compared with 35 billion kilowatt-hours in 1970. A high-voltage line linking the grid of the Soviet Union with that of Bulgaria, which is being built by Romania under an interstate agreement, was scheduled to be finished this year. Romania's first nuclear power station, to be built in cooperation with the Soviet Union, is to be commissioned in 1978.

Important projects with the Soviet Union in the engineering, chemical, metallurgical, food, and light industries were begun this year. Arrangements were also finalized with the Soviet Union for cooperation in the building of dry docks, the purchase of tube, cold, and rolling steel mills from the Soviet Union, and the delivery of a large number of railroad freight cars by Romania to the Soviet Union during the current five-year plan.

A trade protocol this year with the Soviet Union envisaged a 17 percent increase over last year's volume of merchandise trade between the two countries. This growth was to be achieved primarily by a more than 50 percent increase in the exchange of machinery and equipment between the two countries.

Romanian participation, with other Communist bloc countries, in setting up production units in the Soviet Union for the processing of pulp, asbestos, and nickel was being considered.

Area and population. Area, 91,700 sq. mi. Pop. (1972), 20,-600,000. Principal cities (1970): Bucharest (cap.), 1,475,050; Cluj, 202,715; Timişoara, 192,616; Brasov, 182,105; Ploiesti, 162,937.

Government. Socialist republic. Highest organ of government is Grand National Assembly, elected for four years. Pres., State Council, and secy. gen., Communist Party, Nicolae Ceauşescu; prem., Ion Gheorghe Maurer. Communist Party membership (1972), 2,194,627.

Finance. Monetary unit, leu (pl., lei); official rate, 1 leu = US$0.181 (tourist rate, 1 leu = US$0.06). Budget (1970): revenue, 133.3 billion lei; expenditure, 130.9 billion lei.

Trade (1970). Imports, US$1.96 billion; exports, US$1.85 billion.

Agriculture and industry (1970). Agricultural production (in thousands of metric tons): maize, 6,395; wheat, 3,351; barley, 511; potatoes, 2,075. Livestock (in thousands): cattle, 5,035; pigs, 5,972; sheep, 13,836; horses, 686. Industry and mining (in thousands of metric tons): crude oil, 13,377; hard coal, 6,402; lignite, 14,129; iron ore, 881; pig iron, 4,211; steel, 6,517; metallurgical coke, 1,070; aluminum, 89.6; manganese ore, 26.7; cement, 8,127. Electric power, 35 billion kw.-hr. Natural gas, 25 billion cubic meters.

Education (1969). Enrollment: primary schools, 2,886,855; secondary schools, 650,482; institutions of higher learning, 151,705.

RICHARD A. PIERCE

RWANDA. Government and politics.

Rwanda's tranquil political life under President Grégoire Kayibanda was disturbed throughout 1972 by the tragic conflict in neighboring Burundi between the majority Hutu and the politically dominant Tutsi. Rwanda's Hutus, who constitute 90 percent of its population and who have held political power since they overthrew the Tutsi in 1959, watched with some alarm as between 80,000 and 200,000 people, mostly Hutu, died in the turmoil in Burundi (see BURUNDI). Rwanda was faced with an influx of Hutu refugees, but there was little that the Kayibanda government could do to halt the slaughter across the border other than express its concern. The tiny size of its army, few developed resources, and extreme poverty prevented any direct action. Moreover, Rwanda remained entangled by a pact it signed in 1966 with Burundi and Zaïre in which each nation pledged to aid the others in the event that internal rebellions took place in any of the three countries.

A bizarre crisis arose in mid-August, when Uganda's president, General Idi Amin, accused Rwanda of collaboration with Israeli agents seeking retaliation for Uganda's sudden severance of relations with Israel in April. Amin threatened to destroy Kigali, Rwanda's capital, if any Ugandan was harmed as a result of the alleged association with Israel. Despite denials and explanations by President Kayibanda, Amin ordered a full Ugandan military exercise near the Rwanda border to back his warning.

Economic affairs. Several developments on the economic front during 1972 held out at least some promise for Rwanda's future. The third United Nations Conference for Trade and Development (UNCTAD) meeting, in Santiago, Chile, called for special steps to be taken to assist the 25 poorest nations of the world; this list included both Rwanda and Burundi. UNCTAD asked that these poor states be excepted from quota cuts in international commodity agreements and that they be granted more liberalized tariff benefits by richer nations.

The 16th meeting of the Technological Committee for the hydrometeorological survey of the catchments of lakes Victoria, Kyoga, and Albert was held in March, and Rwanda and Burundi were granted an extra US$225,000 to extend their projects. In addition, the European Economic Community, the International Development Association, and the European Development Fund all granted Rwanda credits for different development projects—the most important being a tea factory to be built near Gisakura. These developments, however, will make but a small dent in the extreme poverty of the country.

Area and population. Area, 10,169 sq. mi. Pop. (est. 1971), 3,700,000. Kigali (cap., est. 1969), 16,000.

Government. Republic. Pres., Grégoire Kayibanda.

Finance. Monetary unit, Rwanda franc; 1 Rwanda franc = US$1.0112.

Trade (1971). Exports, US$22 million; imports, US$33 million.

LARRY W. BOWMAN

SASKATCHEWAN. Politics and government.

The New Democratic Party government of Premier Allan E. Blakeney passed 158 bills during the 1972 session of the legislative assembly. The measures included the reduction of the age of majority to 18 years, the establishment of a human rights commission, provision for an ombudsman, and creation of several new departments of government: consumer affairs, continuing education, youth and culture, environment, and Northern Saskatchewan affairs. An independent electoral boundaries commission was also established and a record number of intersessional legislative committees appointed to investigate and recommend policies relating to welfare, agriculture, small businesses, and liquor regulations. Increased benefits were provided under the Workmen's Compensation Act, the Automobile Accident Insurance Act, and the Property Improvement Grants Act.

Late in 1971, David G. Steuart, former provincial treasurer, was elected leader of the provincial Liberal Party and became official leader of the opposition. In three by-elections held since the general election of 1971, the government retained one seat and the Liberal Party two seats, leaving the standing in the legislative assembly unchanged at New Democratic Party, 45 seats, Liberal Party, 15 seats.

Economic developments. This year's crop, while generally good, was subject to reduced returns—owing to early fall frosts and adverse harvesting conditions—and was estimated at well below the total production of 1971. Wheat production, estimated at 308 million bushels, would approximate 80 percent of the 1971 crop, and oats, estimated at 75 million bushels, about 70 percent of 1971 production. Barley, rye, and rapeseed crops were expected to range from 50 percent to 60 percent of the previous year's totals. The population continued to decline, down more than 40,-000 from a peak of 960,000 in 1968. This decline was attributed to the emigration of young people and a declining rate of natural increase. The unemployment rate of 3.7 percent in 1971, well below the Canadian average, remained fairly constant throughout 1972.

Culture and recreation. The Saskatchewan Summer Games held at Moose Jaw in August were a new and major undertaking in the field of amateur sports. The air show at the Canadian Armed Forces Base, Moose Jaw, attracted over 100,000 spectators. National historic sites were dedicated at Fort Esperance, an early North-West Company trading post in the Qu'Appelle Valley, and at Cut Knife, in commemoration of the Cree Indian chief, Poundmaker.

Area and population. Area, 251,700 sq. mi. Pop. (1971), 926,-242 (est. 1972, 916,000). Principal cities (1971): Regina (cap.), 137,759; Saskatoon, 125,079.

Government. Lt. gov., Stephen Worobetz; prem., Allan E. Blakeney.

Finance (est. 1972–1973). Revenue, Can$514,046,680; expenditure, Can$513,195,090. Principal sources of revenue: federal-provincial payments, income taxes, education and health tax, gasoline tax. Principal items of expenditure: education, highways and grid roads, medical and hospital plans.

Education (1970–1971). Enrollment: elementary and secondary schools, 253,929; private schools, 1,381; government correspondence school, 4,580.

Agriculture. Cash farm receipts (1971), Can$911,628,000. Principal crops (in millions of bushels): wheat, 342; barley, 285.

Production (est. 1971). Minerals, Can$381.8 million; construction, Can$229 million; manufacturing, Can$201 million; electric power, Can$72 million; other natural resources, Can$15 million.

ALLAN R. TURNER

SAUDI ARABIA.

King Faisal's prestige and influence both among the Arab countries and in international relations continued to increase this year. The firm but realistic policy

of the Saudi government seemed to ensure, through important negotiations with Aramco (the U.S.-owned Arabian-American Oil Company), that the rapidly increasing flow of oil from Saudi Arabia would continue without interruption. Also this year, the consistent Saudi policy of anti-Communism and friendship with the Western powers played an important role in Egyptian president Anwar Sadat's decision to remove most of the Soviet advisers from Egypt. The policy was also instrumental in the decision by Yemen to resume diplomatic relations with the United States, followed by the resumption of U.S. aid.

Domestic affairs. A record budget for the fiscal year 1972–1973 of 13.2 billion Saudi riyals (SR), or nearly $3 billion, was announced in August. It contained a surplus of SR467.7 million. The Ministry of Finance and National Economy announced that revenues from oil—royalties, income taxes, and pipeline transit fees—would contribute nearly 92 percent of anticipated revenues. Oil revenues were expected to increase by about 23 percent over the 1972 fiscal year, because of both increased prices and production. Budget allocations to educational and cultural affairs were increased by 38 percent and for defense by 3.8 percent. There were decreases in transport and communications and in commerce and industry. Military expenditures accounted for SR3.97 billion, or almost 28 percent of the budget. A major arms purchase, including tanks, was arranged in France in December 1971. In January, ten patrol boats were ordered from Great Britain.

Foreign relations. Relations with France, which have been good, were strengthened by the visits to France of Defense Minister Prince Sultan in December 1971 and of Foreign Minister Sheikh Omar al-Saqqaf in January. Jidda was the site of the third conference of Islamic foreign ministers in February and March, at which 31 countries were represented. The final communiqué of the conference called on UN Security Council members, especially the United States, to force Israel to withdraw from occupied Arab territory. It also reaffirmed the UN General Assembly resolutions opposing the Israeli annexation of Jerusalem. King Faisal's role as a leader among the Muslim nations was emphasized in May when he donated the entire cost for the establishment of an Islamic news agency, which is to be operated by the Islamic secretariat. The news agency issued its first bulletin from Jidda on June 4.

Arab affairs. Saudi Arabia remained the chief supporter of Jordan among Arab nations this year. It was the only state to continue supplying the cash subsidies pledged to Jordan in 1967 and to maintain a small military force in southern Jordan. Continued attempts to mediate between Yasir Arafat of the Palestinian Liberation Organization and Jordan's King Hussein were unsuccessful.

Relations with Egypt, Syria, and Iraq were better than at any time in recent years. The Saudis had long opposed Iraq's membership in the Organization of Arab Petroleum Exporting Countries because they feared Iraq's political radicalism. In March, however, a compromise was arranged, and Iraq, along with Syria and Egypt, was admitted, even though the other two countries are not major oil exporters. Thus, it was hoped, Iraqi radical influence in the organization would be diluted. When Saudi Arabia supported the nationalization by Iraq of the Iraq Petroleum Company in June, King Faisal was hailed as a brother by the ruling Iraqi Ba'ath Party.

Relations with Arab radicals continued to improve this year despite King Faisal's open hostility to the most radical Arab government, that of Southern Yemen, and to the rebels in Oman. Saudi Arabia asserted its power throughout the Arabian peninsula through support of moderate and conservative countries, such as Yemen, Kuwait, Oman, and the United Arab Emirates. The radical Arab nations, in need of Saudi diplomatic and financial support, could offer little resistance.

A major test for Faisal's policy came in negotiations between the Saudis, representing the oil-producing states of the Persian Gulf, and Aramco, representing the oil companies in the area. The major issue was the governments' demand for participation in the oil concessions, initially a 20 percent share but eventually to rise to a controlling 51 percent. In March, Aramco agreed in principle to participation, and in October it was announced that a final agreement had been reached. The settlement was generally regarded as a personal triumph for Saudi Arabia's minister of oil and minerals, Sheikh Ahmed Zaki Yamani, who had developed the concept of participation as an alternative to nationalization. The agreement is expected to set a trend for the industry.

Oil production increased from 190.2 million metric tons in 1970 to 235.2 million metric tons in 1971. Aramco production in the first quarter of this year increased again by 28 percent over the same period in 1971. Mitsubishi, a Japanese company, contracted to build a new oil refinery in Riyadh and to expand the Jidda refinery for the Saudi Petromin company. The cost of $127 million is to be paid in crude oil from the Saudi share of Aramco royalties.

An oil strike in the al-Mazalij area this year was so extensive that it was thought that the new field would equal the Ghawar field, hitherto the largest in the world.

Area and population. Area, 830,000 sq. mi. Pop. (est. 1971), 8,000,000. Principal cities (est. 1965): Riyadh (cap.), 225,000; Jidda, 194,000; Mecca, 185,000; Medina, 72,000.
Government. Absolute monarchy. Effective power in the hands of King Faisal ibn Abdul Aziz, advised by an appointed cabinet.
Finance. Monetary unit, Saudi riyal (SR); SR1 = $0.245. Budget (1972–1973): income, SR13.2 billion; expenditure, SR12.7 billion.
Education (1971–1972). Total enrollment, 560,000.
Armed forces. Army, 35,000; air force, 5,000; navy, 1,000; national guard, 30,000.   RALPH H. MAGNUS

SENEGAL. Politics and government. A cabinet reshuffle was announced June 19. Magatte Lo, formerly chairman of the Economic and Social Council, became minister of state for the armed forces, while Coumba N'Doffene Diouf moved from the Civil Service Ministry to the Ministry of Foreign Affairs. The former foreign affairs minister, Amadou Karim Gaye, assumed Magatte Lo's position on the Economic and Social Council. This was the second consecutive year since the installation of Abdou Diouf as prime minister that Senegal has undergone major cabinet changes.

Foreign affairs. President Léopold-Sédar Senghor was active on several diplomatic fronts. In March he met with President Moktar Ould Daddah of Mauritania and Colonel Moussa Traoré of Mali to establish the Organization for the Development of the Sénégal River (OMVS), a successor subgroup to the defunct Organization of the Sénégal River States (OERS). Headquarters for OMVS will be in Dakar.

After the breakup of OERS in November 1971, President Senghor made visits to Mali and the Ivory Coast in December to explore new avenues of regional cooperation. Senegal joined the Ivory Coast, Dahomey, Mali, Mauritania, Niger, and Upper Volta in signing the founding documents for the West African Economic Community in Bamako on June 3. Less than two weeks later, President Senghor and President Ahmadou Ahidjo signed a friendship agreement in Cameroon. Their aim, Senghor asserted, was to prevent the nations along the Atlantic coast of Africa from dividing into hostile West African and Central African subgroups.

Relations with Portugal remained tense. President Senghor's December visit to Mali ended with a joint condemnation of Portuguese policies on the continent. Then, at the Organization of African Unity ministerial conference in Rabat in June, Foreign Minister Gaye charged that on May 26, Portuguese forces had committed an act of "naked aggression" by killing six Senegalese soldiers near the Guinea (Bissau) border. Retaliatory action, he said, had already been taken. The Portuguese later apologized for another border violation, on October 12.

HEAVY DUTY. The "Doctor Lykes," largest dry cargo carrier in the world, was put into service this year by Lykes Brothers Steamship Company. It features a specially designed stern elevator, capable of lifting 2,000 tons of cargo at a time onto any of the ship's three decks.

In late April the summit conference of the African, Malagasy, and Mauritian Common Organization elected Senghor as OCAMM's president, replacing President Françoise Tombalbaye of Chad, who had resigned in February.

Area and population. Area, 76,124 sq. mi. Pop. (est. 1971), 4.02 million. Dakar (cap.; est. 1969), 581,000.

Government. Republic with unicameral legislature; single-party system. Pres., Léopold-Sédar Senghor; prem., Abdou Diouf.

Finance. Monetary unit, Communauté Financière Africaine franc; 1 CFA franc = US$0.0041. Budget (est. 1972–1973): balanced at 56.5 billion CFA francs.

Trade (1971). Exports, 34.7 billion CFA francs; imports, 60.56 billion CFA francs. Principal exports: groundnuts, groundnut oil, oilcake. Principal imports: petroleum products, rice, wheat, textiles, machinery.

Education (1970–1971). Enrollment: primary, 266,383; secondary, 48,905; technical and professional schools, 9,084. University enrollment (1971–1972), 4,690.

Armed forces (1969). Army, 5,000; police, 4,000; air force, 300.

SHIPS AND SHIPPING. American shipping has been rescued once again. This time it is not a war that seems to offer hope to an otherwise sadly depressed industry but the sale of grain to the Soviet Union, in part, and the decision to relax restrictions on foreign oil imports.

Freighters, oil tankers, and passenger ships are the chief elements of the American maritime scene. Except for a few isolated special ships, the general freighter side of the merchant marine continued to decline this year. The oil tanker business will improve because of increased oil imports, but the long-range view is very dark. The passenger ship industry is almost completely dead, with only brief sparks of life on widely scattered fronts.

LNG carriers. In past years the introduction of a new type of ship marked a milestone in maritime history. To a degree this is again true, and 1972 will be known as the year of the LNG carrier. ("LNG" stands for liquefied natural gas.)

There are only 16 such ships in the world today, all small. Some 100 big ones are needed and all will be huge, meaning a spurt in world shipping. The LNG carrier has come into this prominence because the United States is rapidly using up its supply of natural gas and must import it. In 1958 an American World War II Liberty ship was rebuilt to carry natural gas. Renamed *Methane Pioneer*, it was fitted with five rectangular aluminum tanks to carry gas under great pressure. The highly volatile gas is compressed to one six-hundredth of its normal volume and kept refrigerated at −259° F during the voyage. No other LNG ships were built in the United States between 1958 and 1972, but now whole fleets of them are planned.

Although such specialized ships have not been subsidized in the past, it appears that up to $200 million in government shipbuilding subventions may be authorized for such ships in 1973 by the Maritime Administration of the U.S. Department of Commerce. Some $500 million worth of orders for LNG ships may be placed in U.S. shipyards in 1973, with three times as much being spent for these new ships

497

within five years. This new windfall for American yards is due to what can only be described as a sudden awakening to the need for such ships throughout the world. Foreign yards are already building LNG carriers to capacity, and the U.S. government subsidy will permit American yards to make their prices competitive. Interestingly enough, such basic specifications as hull design, safety rules, and even basic construction principles are far from definite today. The LNG ship is a new frontier in world shipping. And the incentive is a double one. Not only is there a critical shortage of natural gas in the United States, but also the current annual consumption of 22.5 trillion cubic feet is expected to rise to about 40 trillion cubic feet by 1985. By 1980 new ships must be available to import 2 trillion cubic feet of natural gas. Algeria is at present the main source of natural gas imported to the United States.

Oil tankers. Depletion of resources is the key to this year's relaxing of the limits on foreign oil imports. This policy change will benefit the American merchant marine in the short term by reducing the differential between American and foreign tanker rates and possibly permitting a few U.S. oil tankers to find employment on deep-sea foreign oil routes. Today's American coastwise tanker fleet, however, has much to fear from the situation over the long range. The United States is running out of oil, and when it does there will be no more American coastwise oil tanker business. Because of high labor costs, the United States has priced itself out of the world tanker trade; if the coastal tanker trade is lost, the U.S. tanker fleet itself will be out of business. For years the tanker part of the merchant marine has been the only secure, healthy segment of the maritime industry.

The staggering increase in oil tanker size has outmoded all regular American ports with inadequate facilities. Ships drawing 80 to 100 feet cannot come into U.S. harbors, so their oil must be transferred to smaller craft. The future may see half a dozen billion dollar offshore oil-handling complexes far out in the Gulf of Mexico and along the Atlantic and Pacific coasts.

The oil tanker picture will change greatly with a new reliance on oil from abroad. The futuristic offshore port schemes now taking shape on blueprints may well prove the chief source of new business for American-flag tankers, if more and more foreign oil continues to come in on foreign ships. In Texas, Port Arthur, Galveston, and Freeport are planning such a port 65 miles offshore; Houston has one in prospect 40 miles off the coast. An offshore oil-unloading depot is proposed for Louisiana that could handle ships of up to 500,000 deadweight tons.

Container ships. In the more traditional area of development, cargo shipping, one highly untraditional thing happened in 1972. Sea-Land Service, Inc., in September put into operation the first of eight new container ships. Named *Sea-Land Galloway*, the new vessel can make 33 knots, giving it an operating speed greater than even the fastest passenger liners in service. It is 946 feet long, can carry 1,096 containers, and cost $50 million. Its transatlantic run is made in 4½ days; the fastest competitor takes 7½ days. A sister ship is due to operate with the new *Sea-Land Galloway* on the Atlantic, and the six other Sea-Land ships will run in transpacific routes.

By comparison the new container ships of other lines are small indeed, but a word about the new LASH ships is appropriate. ("LASH" means lighter aboard ship.) A huge ship's hull can be used most efficiently to transport self-contained lighters, which can be dropped outside a port and towed in without holding up the "mother ship" for more than a few hours. In addition, they can be loaded at inland river ports a thousand miles from the sea. These ultra-modern ships saw increasing popularity in 1972, with a number of foreign lines launching LASH vessels; previously the LASH had been an American monopoly as far as operation was concerned, a bright spot on an otherwise generally

dark freighter horizon. The first of three quite similar ships was put into service in 1972 by Lykes Brothers Steamship Company, Inc.—the *Doctor Lykes*. Basically like the LASH ship in concept, it uses a large elevator cut into its stern to lift loaded barges in or out of its "honeycomb" hull complex. LASH ships use on-board rolling cranes capable of picking up over 500 tons of cargo in one barge.

U.S.-Soviet grain shipments. Perhaps the biggest single event of the year in the cargo ship sphere was the federal government's decision to sell grain in bulk to the Soviet Union. Although there is a law on the books requiring 50 percent of all aid cargoes (and these shipments are heavily subsidized by the U.S. government) to go in U.S. bottoms, Andrew Gibson, a Department of Commerce official, appeared to be seeking to ensure that one-third of the tonnage would go American. Even one-third would mean a gift of $100 million to U.S. merchant shipping. Labor leaders were pessimistic about how well the sharing might be policed and anticipated that American ships would not get the proportion promised. The problem will doubtless come down to the fact that there are not enough American freighters available to carry one-third of the grain.

Decline of the merchant fleet. The decline of the American cargo fleet has been a growing concern to those who feel that American-flag ships are important to the nation's economy. Not only is the U.S. merchant marine, including the large government-owned fleet of idle tonnage, the smallest of any major power, but it is also the oldest. The average age of American merchant ships as of midyear was 22 years, compared to an average of eight for Denmark and Norway and nine for Sweden, East Germany, and West Germany. As of June 1 there were 1,246 ships in the merchant marine, of which 669 were privately owned. The government-owned ships were largely old World War II standard types. The merchant marine's decline has been relatively steady since the end of World War II, with interruptions created by the Korean and Vietnam wars. The decline has meant increasing unemployment for American seamen.

American shipbuilding has also declined drastically, with only 73 ships of 1,000 or more gross tons on order in American yards as of midyear. These ships had a deadweight of 3,323,102 tons. Japan at the same time was building 611 ships of 62,088,625 tons. Even Spain surpassed the United States in shipbuilding, with nearly three times as much new construction.

Passenger liners. The Norwegians continued to fill the vacuum left by the death of the American liner fleets out of Atlantic and Gulf ports. Not a single U.S. passenger ship sails on either the North or South Atlantic. The flagship of the merchant marine, America's proud superliner *United States,* was turned back by its unhappy owners to the U.S. Navy. Its powerful engine rooms were sealed, and plans were afoot to cut off the tops of its masts and twin stacks to get the vessel under James River, Va., bridges to a freshwater location for permanent reserve lay-up. Two

MAJOR MERCHANT FLEETS OF THE WORLD
(vessels 1,000 gross tons and over; as of January 1, 1972)

Country	Number	Deadweight tons (thousands)
Liberia	1,840	60,992
Japan	2,109	39,142
United Kingdom	1,772	37,065
Norway	1,173	32,374
United States	1,579	21,346
Greece	1,195	18,214
Soviet Union	1,942	14,302
West Germany	993	11,697
Italy	625	9,803
Panama	629	9,140
France	457	9,007

SOURCE: U.S. MARITIME ADMINISTRATION

relatively new U.S. liners, the *Brasil* and the *Argentina*, were sold by Moore-McCormack Lines, Inc., to Holland-America Cruises (a part of the Holland-America Line).

Two of the four regular passenger liners flying the American flag are due to end their service and be retired in 1973 when they are 25 years old and their subsidy ends. They are the *President Cleveland* and *President Wilson*. A sister ship of theirs, the troopship *General M. C. Meigs,* which at one time was going to be rebuilt into a regular peacetime luxury liner, grounded near Seattle and broke in half as 1972 began. Its loss was mourned by shipping enthusiasts who remembered its heroic World War II career. Both the *Cleveland* and the *Wilson* were built from similar P-2 troopship hulls.

The famous *Queen Elizabeth,* largest passenger liner ever built, was destroyed by fire early in the year while nearing restoration in Hong Kong. It was in the process of being returned to service as a floating campus by C. Y. Tung, a Hong Kong shipping executive, when it burned and capsized. The 83,000-ton former British Cunard liner had been retired three years earlier and briefly used as a Florida ship museum. As the year ended, efforts were being made to salvage the former Atlantic sea queen, which had been renamed *Seawise University* by the Chinese owner.

New passenger liners continued to be ordered during 1972, putting the lie to those who declared that liners were a thing of the past. Cruise liners will one day carry just as many passengers on cruises as earlier liners once carried across the oceans. The airplane, by taking thousands of tourists quickly and cheaply across the oceans, has stimulated small cruise ships the world over. Each year two or three dozen fine little liners are put into service on short cruise routes on the Baltic Sea, the Black Sea, the Mediterranean, the Caribbean, and the Sea of Japan, to mention a few major areas. While 5,000-to-10,000-ton overnight ferries are common in most parts of Northern Europe, the waterways of the United States still lack such services, so complete has been the domination of the automobile and the airliner.

End of a nuclear liner. The nuclear passenger ship *Savannah* was laid up early in 1972 at Savannah, Ga.; it will be made into a museum to honor President Dwight D. Eisenhower's atoms-for-peace efforts. In its decade of operation the *Savannah* called at 40 ports around the world to prove that it could visit crowded harbors without exploding or polluting the waters with nuclear material. In one year the vessel went 72,000 miles on 26 pounds of uranium, and it steamed 330,000 miles on its first charge of nuclear fuel. Labor disputes, governmental confusion over the vessel's purpose, and an effort to make the ship pay like any other commercial freighter spelled doom for those high goals. The first vessel with a steam engine to cross any ocean, the original *Savannah* of 1819, was also called a flop and a white elephant. History may yet prove that nuclear power is practical in merchant shipping.   FRANK O. BRAYNARD

SIERRA LEONE. Politics and government. Continuing its cautious policies designed to sustain stability in a faction-ridden nation, President Siaka Stevens' government entered a second stage in its program to assume public control over Sierra Leone's foreign-controlled mining industries. It negotiated a 51 percent holding in the Marampa iron ore mining complex, including a rail line and ore port facilities at Pepel, operated by the formerly British-controlled Sierra Leone Development Company Ltd. (DELCO). Iron ore, representing about one-tenth of Sierra Leone's exports, now joins diamonds, the country's major product, as a predominantly state-owned enterprise.

The partial nationalization of iron helped satisfy the militantly nationalist youth wing of President Stevens' All People's Congress (APC) party. The more conservative military, business, and (largely Creole) civil service interests were offered balancing concessions: Several military and civilian prisoners associated with the coup d'etat of 1967 and the attempted coup of March 1971 were released; Sierra Leone's disagreements with Nigeria were reconciled and a cultural exchange agreement signed with Ethiopia; and an official commission recommended improved compensation for lower civil service employees, who make up the backbone of the APC. A commission was formed in July to recommend a new name for the republic, whose current name is of Portuguese origin.

The state of emergency imposed in 1971 was lifted temporarily in September to permit by-elections in the eastern provinces. The vote produced easy victories for the ruling APC, which nevertheless accused the opposition of fomenting disturbances during the campaign.

Economic developments. Whatever the eventual effects of the diamond and iron nationalizations, Sierra Leone's economy remained in the doldrums. Agricultural production and bauxite mining declined seriously, and prices for all exports except diamonds dropped. The government's budget deficit grew; foreign trade imbalances worsened; state reserves dwindled. The government has been unable to eliminate illegal diamond mining and smuggling, which aggravate the depletion of national resources. Inadequate rice production and overall agricultural depression continue to frustrate the vital campaign for self-sufficiency in foodstuffs.

A new state trading company was given monopoly control over certain imports in order to combat rising domestic prices. The American-owned Sierra Rutile Corporation has begun to operate the formerly defunct but potentially valuable rutile mines.

Sierra Leone declined to join the West African economic community established in midyear by seven French-oriented states. Instead, it pursued discussions of economic integration with Liberia and Guinea.

MILLION DOLLAR DREAM. Sierra Leoneans scour a riverbed in government-controlled mining lands, searching for diamonds. An estimated 60,000 illegal prospectors make a nightly run for the money in a flourishing trade the government seems unable to stop.

ANDREW JAFFEE

Diamond discovery. In February the world's third largest diamond was discovered in Sierra Leone—a 969.8-carat stone the size and shape of a hen's egg and valued at US$11.7 million. It was put on exhibition at Freetown's museum.

Area and population. Area, 27,925 sq. mi. Pop. (est. 1971), 3.1 million. Freetown (cap.), 150,000.
Government. Republic within the Commonwealth of Nations. Pres., Siaka Stevens; prime min., Sorie Ibrahim Koroma.
Finance. Monetary unit, leone; Le1 = US$1.25. Budget (1972–1973): revenue, US$74.1 million; expenditure, US$72.8 million (plus unbudgeted supplements).
Trade (1970). Imports, US$123 million; exports, US$109.3 million. Chief trading partners: United Kingdom, Japan, Netherlands, United States, Italy. Principal exports: rough diamonds, cocoa, coffee.
Education. Primary school enrollment (1969), 139,400 in 976 schools; secondary school enrollment (1970), 26,000 in 66 schools; technical-vocational enrollment (1970), 750; University of Sierra Leone enrollment (1970), 740.   PHILIP M. ALLEN

SINGAPORE. Politics and government.

The government's decision in mid-1972 to allow average salary increases of 10 percent increased speculation that Prime Minister Lee Kuan Yew would soon call for new elections. It was no surprise then when elections were held in September, one year before the mandatory date. In spite of preelection agreements among the opposition to avoid splitting the votes against Lee's People's Action Party (PAP), the five opposition parties and two independent candidates were unable to win even one of the 65 parliamentary seats at stake. The PAP thus repeated its clean-sweep victory of 1968, gaining about 70 percent of the popular vote in the process. There is continuing evidence of a PAP approach to governance which sometimes displays the characteristics of autocracy and puritanism in actions such as suppression of newspapers and banning of foreigners with hair "touching the shirt collar." The latter ruling has forced many long-haired journalists and entertainers (jazz pianist Dave Brubeck among others) to cancel visits to Singapore. In spite of these ostensible departures from democratic practices, the stability and rapid industrial development of the city-state has made for a generally contented electorate.

Economic developments. By dint of intelligent planning and hard work on the part of Singapore's leaders, the challenge posed by the planned pullout of British troops from Singapore—completed late in 1971—has been met. Economic expansion has been rapid enough not only to provide new jobs for 40,000 former base employees but to hire more than 70,000 "guest workers" as well, most of the latter from Malaysia. Unemployment was at an all-time low. The economic growth rate again rose by about 10 percent in 1971. Although the GNP growth rate fell from 17.2 percent in 1970 to 14 percent in 1971, average per capita income—at US$1,075—was up by about 6 percent from the 1970 figure.

Foreign affairs. Prime Minister Lee's first official visit to Malaysia since 1965 took place in April, and in July Singapore abandoned attempts to use the initials MSA (Malaysia-Singapore Airlines) for its new airline, adopting instead SIA (Singapore Airlines). Singapore took a somewhat neutral position on the declaration made by the Malaysian and Indonesian governments of their right to control foreign shipping through the Straits of Malacca. The move was viewed as an indirect threat to Singapore's entrepôt trade position, inasmuch as it might force the major trading nations to press for the construction of a canal or pipeline across Thailand's Kra Isthmus.

Area and population. Area, 224 sq. mi. Pop. (est. 1972), 2,-200,000.
Government. Parliamentary republic, 65-member unicameral parliament. Pres., Dr. Benjamin Sheares; prime min., Lee Kuan Yew.
Finance. Monetary unit, Singapore dollar; S$1 = US$0.339. Budget (1972–1973): US$475 million.
Trade (1971). Imports, US$2.8 billion; exports, US$1.8 billion. Main trade items: petroleum and petroleum products, rubber, timber,

electrical machinery. Chief trading partners: Malaysia, United States, United Kingdom, Japan.
Education (1970). Schools, 564; teachers, 18,978; students, 513,663.
Armed forces (1971). Army, 16,000; navy, 500; air force, 15,000 men and 36 combat planes.   NANCY L. SNIDER

SOCIAL SECURITY.

Two measures captured attention during the year, one dealing primarily with social security, the other with both social security and welfare reform. There was relatively little public debate over actions by Congress to strengthen the social security program. In contrast, the battles over welfare reform were bitterly fought, and relatively few changes in the basic system were made during the 1972 session.

Social security. A 20 percent across-the-board increase in social security benefits, signed into law on July 1, became effective September 1, with the increased payment starting in October. The minimum monthly benefit for one person goes from $70.40 to $84.50 and the maximum from $216 to $258. The average benefit for one person will go from $133 to $161 and for a couple from $223 to $270.

An important new feature of this legislation is that, effective in 1975, the benefit will rise automatically with each 3 percent jump in cost of living. Senator Frank Church (D, Idaho) sponsored this legislation as an amendment to a House bill authorizing an increase in the federal debt ceiling. A problem for beneficiaries who receive supplementary aid from public welfare will be loss of all or part of the supplement unless some federal-state agreement is reached.

On October 14 a Senate-House conference committee approved a bill affecting both welfare and social security. The payroll tax, which had already been raised from 5.2 percent on $9,000 to 5.5 percent on $10,800 to pay for the increase in benefits, was raised again under this bill to 5.85 percent on $10,800 ($12,000 in 1974). The major increased benefits were an extension of medicare payments to 1.5 million persons receiving disability benefits, permission for those over 65 to earn $2,100 a year (instead of $1,680) without loss of social security payments, an increase in widows' benefits from 82.5 to 100 percent of their husbands' payments, and minimum social security payments for those who have worked many years in low-paying jobs. The bill was approved by both houses and signed by President Richard M. Nixon on October 30.

Welfare reform. Differing objectives in the House and the Senate stood in the way of many of the proposals for welfare reform. H.R. 1, embodying the administration's proposals, passed the House in June 1971. It would have assured a family of four an income of $2,400, with aid going to the working poor as well as those unable to work. Federal aid was to be reduced as a family earned more income up to a cutoff point around $4,200. There were strong work requirements in this measure, with reduction of benefits for work refusal by presumably employable family members.

The bill approved by the Senate on October 6, 1972, retained hardly any of the welfare reform provisions that had been discussed earlier. Instead of a guaranteed income for the poor, uniform benefits were voted only for the aged, blind, and disabled with no other source of income. A whole series of welfare reform plans had been killed, and the only survivor was a pilot test of several proposals.

The bill that finally came out of the conference committee on October 14 was only a first step toward a federal take-over of all welfare programs in the United States. The bill provided for uniform federal payments starting in 1974 to approximately 3 million disabled, blind, and aged persons. The payments amount to $130 a month for single persons and $195 for couples. Recipients may also keep up to $20 a month from social security or other pensions and $65 in earned income without losing any welfare benefits.

In addition, states may supplement the federal payments. A guaranteed income for poor families went down to defeat, as did the Senate plan for testing several welfare proposals, a national system for tracing runaway welfare fathers, residency requirements, day care centers, and bonuses for poor people who work. As previously mentioned, this joint social security–welfare bill was signed by the president on October 30.

WIN—Talmadge and workfare. Measures to strengthen employment programs for welfare recipients were intensified on July 1, when an amendment sponsored by Senator Herman E. Talmadge (D, Ga.) went into effect. This extension of the Work Incentive Program (WIN) includes an increased number of recipients of Aid to Families with Dependent Children. Exempt are children under 16 or in school full time, people who are incapacitated, persons needed to care for those who are incapacitated, people who live in remote areas, and mothers or relatives caring for children under the age of six. All others must be available for work training or placed in employment. Training programs are to be directly related to job availability in the area. Services to make employment possible (day care and other baby-sitting services) are federally reimbursable at 90 percent. This program is administered by the departments of Labor and of Health, Education, and Welfare.

Opinions differ sharply over the effectiveness of workfare programs, with proponents for each point of view citing statistics. Early reports in New York State showed that of every 100 persons referred for jobs or training, four were placed. Of those placed, one in three was employed three months or more, and one in three held the job a week or less. Some questions arose about public service employment, with those assigned to work out their welfare support paid at three-fourths of the minimum wage doing work comparable to other employees paid at full scale. There was agreement that continuing widespread unemployment and the historic inadequacies of work training programs were serious handicaps in developing a hoped-for success story. Potential employers were slow to take advantage of the Talmadge amendment, even though they would receive $1,000 for on-the-job training of each welfare recipient and a 20 percent tax credit on the first-year salary paid to a worker who remains on the job for at least two years. Even with these employer incentives, Wisconsin reported that 19,000 persons registered for 300 available jobs.

Court test of New York work rules. In February, a case was brought in a federal court in New York state challenging the constitutionality and conformity with the Social Security Act of the definition under New York law of "employability" as it referred to recipients of Aid to Dependent Children, Aid to Dependent Children of the Unemployed, and Home Relief. Under the New York law, "employable" recipients are required to pick up semimonthly assistance checks in person at employment offices, to take such jobs as are offered, or, if there are no jobs, to work out assistance payments at public jobs provided through the department of social services.

The briefs in the case pointed out the constitutional issues, the arbitrary application of the requirements, and the social welfare policy implications. The cases cover a range of situations. One ADC mother of three was already engaged in a vocational training program. Another plaintiff was training full time as a dental assistant under the WIN program. One plaintiff lived 22 miles from the nearest employment office; others had no public transportation facilities available. One on moral grounds refused employment as a go-go girl in a night club. Another refused domestic work beyond her stipulated seven days a week, eight hours a day job. Late in the year, final disposition of the case had not yet been made.

Redesigning programs. The first step in a major redesign of federally financed social services was taken this year when

some state governments announced that they would henceforward administer welfare payments and social services separately. The objective of this reform measure is to free the social services staff so that they can help each recipient reach his highest potential of self-sufficiency. A plan is to be developed with each client, barriers to reaching the agreed-upon goals are to be identified, and services needed to remove the barriers are to be made available. This system is the basis for measuring the impact of services and identifying which ones helped the client toward his goal and at what financial cost. Among the services to be available and for which the federal government will pay on a 75–25 ratio are employment and education assistance, family planning, health services, homemaker assistance for shut-ins, home management counseling, housing improvement, child care including protective care for abused children, foster care and adoption, day care, and transportation to a hospital or clinic. The projected aggregate ceiling on payments for social services, replacing the system of open-ended matching, will bear directly on how effective this goal-oriented approach will be.

The proposed Allied Services Act, sent to Congress by President Nixon on May 18 but not acted on in this session, supports the president's thrust for decentralization of authority. This bill calls for states and units of local government to establish comprehensive plans for delivering the some 200 different assistance programs now administered by HEW. The bill encourages simpler, more uniform, more flexible service delivery, with greater freedom to develop locally the program most needed. States would be given authority to transfer up to 25 percent of federal funds from one HEW program to another with HEW approval. Planning grants would be made available to the states.

Units of HEW have made available project grants totaling $3 million to test this proposal. In Hartford, Conn., a new citywide system will deliver social services through neighborhood centers. Emphasis is on welfare, social services, mental health, children, and youth. In Louisiana, the governor's office will administer a program meant to consolidate and coordinate the state's social services programs, particularly those under the Social and Rehabilitation Service, the Health Services and Mental Health Administration, and the Office of Education (all agencies of HEW). Programs are under way in Duluth, Minn., and Brockton, Mass., and a plan is being developed for a social indexes base for HEW Region VIII (Montana, Wyoming, Utah, North and South Dakota, and Colorado).

Financing social services. Open-ended appropriations matching payments by the federal government to the states for social services provided under the Social Security Act were lost this year. Early in the year the Senate in its HEW-Labor appropriations bill limited the amount of money available for social services. This provision was eliminated in the bill agreed upon by the conference committee and was one reason given by the president for his July veto.

A second try for a ceiling became a part of the general revenue sharing bill. The conference committee report placed a ceiling of $2.5 billion on social services, to be divided among the states in proportion to population. Broader eligibility standards are provided for services related to care for children whose mothers are employed, in training, or absent from the home; family planning; services related to alcoholism, drug abuse, and mental retardation; and services connected with foster care of children. This measure will mean great changes in most states, with some having sharp cutbacks and others big increases. For example, New York's estimate for fiscal year 1973 was $855 million, but the new legislation provides only $223 million; Kansas projected $8.4 million for fiscal year 1973 and would now receive $27.5 million; Mississippi projected $463.6 million and the new amount would be $27.1 million.

The conference committee bill received final congressional approval on October 13 and was signed by the president on October 20.

Policy directions. The problems Congress faced this year in dealing with social security and welfare reform pointed up the need for a national social report as a guide for decision-making in both the governmental and the voluntary sectors. Senator Walter F. Mondale (D, Minn.) introduced a bill (later passed in the Senate) calling for a council of social advisers in the executive office of the president. One of the council's tasks would be the preparation of an annual social report.

Initial steps toward a social report have been taken. The U.S. Office of Management and Budget is compiling extensive social statistics with a view toward publication in the spring of 1973. A voluntary organization, the National Assembly for Social Policy and Development, completed a study on the feasibility of preparing an annual social report to complement the social statistics prepared by OMB.

Other policy directions appeared in the platform statements of the Democratic and Republican parties. Both parties called for financial support for those unable to provide for themselves. The Democratic platform detailed ways to replace the present welfare system with an income security program to include tax and insurance measures, income from jobs including public service employment when needed, and cash assistance to assure families an income above the poverty level for those employed in training or unable to work.

The Republican platform flatly opposed programs that embrace the principle of guaranteed income. The platform called for support for those persons who through no fault of their own cannot support themselves.

ELMA PHILLIPSON COLE

SOMALIA. Politics and government. On July 3, two former members of the Supreme Revolutionary Council, Muhammad Ainanshe Guled and Salad Gabeyre Kidiye, together with a former army officer, Abdulkadir Abdulleh, were publicly executed by a firing squad at Mogadishu. They had been found guilty of conspiring to overthrow the government and were sentenced by the National Security Court on May 3. The court also sentenced six other defendants to life imprisonment and 20 others to terms varying from one to 30 years, while acquitting 29. Only one other person had previously been executed, the assassin of former president Abdirashid Ali Shermarke.

In January a new campaign was launched to implement the principles of scientific socialism. There were no signs of the representative institutions that President Muhammad Siyad Barre had promised.

Foreign affairs. Somalia continued to play an active part on the African political scene, while strengthening its historic links with the Arab world and its more recent ties with the Communist powers. President Siyad was elected one of the vice-chairmen of the June summit meeting of the ninth assembly of Organization of African Unity at Rabat. His visit in November 1971 to Moscow, where he had talks with President Nikolai Podgorny, was followed by the visit of Soviet defense minister Marshal Grechko to Mogadishu in February. Other state visitors in 1972 were presidents Zulfikar Ali Bhutto of Pakistan and Jean Bedel Bokassa of the Central African Republic.

President Siyad visited Libya, Egypt, Saudi Arabia, and Tanzania. In July, Siyad met with presidents Jafaar al-Nimery of the Sudan and Idi Amin of Uganda in Somalia. President Nimery promised to use his good offices to settle the territorial disputes between Somalia and Kenya, Ethiopia, and the French Territory of Afars and Issas. The same communiqué supported all African liberation movements.

In October, Somalia acted as mediator in the negotiations between Uganda and Tanzania, held at Mogadishu.

Economic affairs. Somalia continued a three-year development plan started in 1971. The government's emphasis was on self-help, but considerable foreign aid was still necessary. A protocol was signed in May on further Somali-Soviet economic and technical cooperation, which included the building of a dam on the Juba River to provide both hydroelectric power and irrigation. The International Development Association and the African Development Bank provided loans for a highway from Berbera to Hargeisa in the north. In January, the Somali shilling was devalued from 7.1 to 6.9 to the U.S. dollar to protect the economy from the repercussions of the world currency crisis.

Education and culture. A commission was set up to decide on an alphabet for the Somali language and then to prepare the first school texts. This decision should end a long and bitter controversy between partisans of different scripts. With one national language instead of the English, Italian, and Arabic currently in use, communication will be simplified and a major barrier to the development of a modern culture will be removed.

Area and population. Area, 246,201 sq. mi. Pop. (est. 1971), 2,900,000. Mogadishu (cap.; 1967), 172,677.
Government. Democratic republic now under military rule. Pres. of Supreme Revolutionary Council, General Muhammad Siyad Barre.
Finance. Monetary unit, Somali shilling; Ss1 = US$0.15. Budget (1971): expenditure, Ss330 million; revenue, Ss316.3 million.
Trade (1971). Imports, US$62 million; exports, US$34 million.
Education (1971). Total enrollment, 55,571.

VIRGINIA LULING

SOUTH AFRICA, REPUBLIC OF. Politics and government. Major changes in South Africa's cabinet were announced on July 31 by Prime Minister Balthazar Johannes Vorster. Most significantly, Connie Mulder replaced Theo Gerdener as interior minister while retaining the portfolios of information, social welfare, and pensions. Gerdener had stressed on June 16 that he was leaving his post to set up a "race relations bureau" and that his resignation had nothing to do with factional disputes within the National Party. But his dissatisfaction with current government racial policies was well known, and his opposition to Vorster's handling of recent student disorders had also been reported.

The disruptions began after a student leader at the all-black University College of the North in Turfloop was expelled for criticizing, in a graduation day speech, the apartheid system and the educational inequalities it had produced. On May 6 it was reported that all of the college's 1,146 students had also been expelled for protesting the original disciplinary action. Both the South African Students Association (all black) and the National Union of Students (all white) called for street demonstrations and a boycott of lectures. A demonstration by 100 students in Cape Town on June 2 was broken up by policemen, and a crowd of about 10,000 persons was dispersed on June 5. Giving full support to the police, Prime Minister Vorster announced a ban on outdoor meetings.

In electoral politics, results were mixed. In March the United Party increased its majority on the Johannesburg city council, with the antiapartheid Progressive Party winning its first seat. The following month the Nationals increased their majority vote in the Oudtshoorn by-election. It was announced in March that at least 30 National Party members had split off to found the new Democratic Party, whose platform stresses improvement in the standard of living for blacks and "better use of African manpower in order to increase productivity." Party leaders did not indicate whether they favored any specific changes in the lists governing which jobs whites and blacks are permitted to hold. In presenting his 1972–1973 budget to the House of Assembly on March 29, Finance Minister N. J. Diederichs indicated that increased use would be made of African labor, especially in export industries, and he urged private employers to cooperate with trade unions in reclassifying

MEETING AMID THE MAIZE. South African president J. J. Fouché (left) strolls alongside his host, Malawi president Hastings Kamuzu Banda. Fouché's visit was the first ever paid by a South African head of state to an independent black nation.

CENTRAL PRESS

job categories. South Africa's economy has been lagging because of a shortage of skilled labor.

Foreign policy. The policy of "dialogue" with black African governments bogged down this year when the new military government of the Malagasy Republic informed an Organization of African Unity meeting in Rabat that it would not adhere to the "outward" policy of its civilian predecessors. However, relations with Malawi continued to improve. President J. J. Fouché paid a state visit to Malawi March 17–24, calling for "peaceful coexistence and cooperation." In December 1971 it had been disclosed that South Africa had agreed to President Hastings Kamuzu Banda's request for arms for possible use against Frelimo infiltrators from Mozambique. South Africa and Malawi concluded an extradition treaty on March 24, 1972.

Bantustans. Two new Bantustans were established in the springtime. On March 23 the legislative council opened for a semiautonomous region to be known as East Caprivi, at Katima Mulilo in South West Africa. Then, on April 11, the Gazankulu Bantustan became operative at Giyani in the Northern Transvaal. Another semiautonomous region, the Transkei, took another step toward self-government on March 30, when five police stations were transferred to black control. Kaiser Matanzima, chief minister of the Transkei territorial government, announced that he would not request autonomy until more white-owned land from surrounding areas had been allotted to the region, but the claims were turned down. Similar and equally unsuccessful demands were made by Chief Justice Mabandla of the Ciskei, which became self-governing on August 1. In November, Bophutatswana also became a self-governing Bantustan.

Economy. After Great Britain announced in June that it would let the pound float on international currency markets, the South African government decided to maintain the tie with sterling. In October the government announced a return to a fixed parity representing a 4.2 percent devaluation from the previous fixed rate but a 4 percent appreciation over then current free market values.

It was announced that the stringent import controls imposed in November 1971 would end sometime in 1973. In their place, the South African government plans to erect tough new tariff barriers to protect the economy from overseas competition. According to Finance Ministry figures, the growth rate, which averaged 6 percent between 1960 and 1970, was only 4 percent in 1971.

Area and population. Area, 472,359 sq. mi. Pop. (1970), 21,-448,169, including 15,057,952 Africans, 3,751,328 whites, 2,018,453 coloureds, and 620,436 Asians. Principal cities (est. 1968): Pretoria (admin. cap.), 492,577; Cape Town (legis. cap.), 625,740; Johannesburg, 1,364,523; Durban, 682,910.

Government. Republic with Parliament and cabinet. Prime min., Balthazar Johannes Vorster.

Finance. Monetary unit, rand; 1 rand = US$1.29. Budget (est. 1972–1973): revenue, R2,803,000,000; expenditure, R2,800,000,000.

Trade (1971). Imports, R2,879,000,000; exports, R1,530,000,000. Principal imports: machinery and transport equipment. Principal exports: food, manufactured goods, minerals.

Education. Africans (1970): schools, 10,125; enrollment, 2,748,-635. Whites: schools (1968), 2,821; enrollment (1966), 822,482. Coloureds (1967): schools, 1,832; enrollment, 453,338. Asians: schools (1968), 358; enrollment (1967), 155,961.

Armed forces. Army (est. 1971): regulars, 5,700; citizen force, 60,000.

South West Africa (Namibia)

Meeting in Addis Ababa on February 4, the UN Security Council once again condemned South Africa for failure to comply with an advisory opinion delivered by the International Court of Justice in June 1971 declaring South Africa's mandate over Namibia illegal. But in a new, Argentine-sponsored initiative, the council also called on Secretary General Kurt Waldheim "to initiate as soon as possible contacts with all parties concerned" to permit the people of Namibia "freely and with strict regard to the principles of equality to exercise their right to self-determination and independence...." Accordingly, Waldheim visited South Africa and South West Africa March 6–10, conferring with Prime Minister Vorster and meeting representatives of nonwhite groups, principally in Ovamboland. On March 8 the secretary general declared that the aim of both the UN and the South African government was "to grant self-determination to Namibia," but he later acknowledged there was a "deep gulf" between their positions

A BLACK DAY
FOR THE
BLACK HILLS

On the night of June 9 a sudden heavy thunderstorm swelled streams in the Black Hills, collapsed the Canyon Lake Dam, and sent floodwaters surging through Rapid City, S.D., in a torrent that claimed an immediate toll of at least 226 persons dead and over 100 persons missing. When the floodwaters subsided, wrecked autos lay strewn in the muddy debris, and about 2,000 families were left with only the wreckage of their houses or mobile homes. Altogether, the flood caused an estimated $120 million in property damage.

which further negotiations would try to bridge. On August 1 a Security Council resolution urged Waldheim to continue his efforts, and in October he named a retired Swiss diplomat, Alfred Escher, as his representative to Namibia.

Ovamboland had earlier been wracked by labor protests demanding a pay increase and, in the words of the South West African Peoples Organization, "abolition of the degrading semi-slavery contracts system." On December 18, 1971, the Johannesburg *Star* reported that an estimated 10,000 Ovambos were on strike, 5,200 of them in Windhoek alone, and that the strike had spread to the Tsumeb Corporation, a leading source of South West African mineral revenue. The strikers returned to work only after the South African government announced on January 10 that new agreements between Pretoria and territorial authorities would replace the contracts system under which, once assigned to a job, the worker was bound to that job for 18 months. In June the *Times* of London reported that eight Ovambo tribesmen had been given suspended jail terms for inciting the strike.

Area and population. Area, 318,262 sq. mi. Pop. (1970), 745,-000, including 340,000 Ovambos, 287,000 other Africans, 90,000 whites, and 28,000 coloureds. Windhoek (cap.; est. 1967), 61,000.
Government. Territory administered by the Republic of South Africa.
Finance. Monetary unit, rand; 1 rand = US$1.29. Budget (1968–1969): revenue, R88,948,000; expenditure, R85,825,000.
Education (1970). Africans: schools, 424; enrollment, 95,302. Whites: schools, 81; enrollment, 22,355. Coloureds: schools, 56; enrollment, 12,270.

SOUTH CAROLINA. Politics and government.
After fighting a losing battle in the federal courts, the general assembly was obliged to revise its 1971 reapportionment plan for the state senate in order to bring about a proper population distribution and do away with residence clauses favoring some counties and senators. Reapportionment tangles kept the legislature in session until late July and caused the June primary to be delayed to August 29 in order to provide adequate time for candidates to file.

In what turned out to be its longest session in history, the general assembly enacted significant legislation providing for automobile safety standards, state aid for local sewer systems, increased benefits for retired state employees, a state-financed health insurance program for state employees, increased workmen's compensation benefits, a department of human relations, substantial salary raises for state employees and public school teachers, and public meetings for all state agencies.

The adoption of recommendations proposed by a panel of business experts brought increased income and savings to the state. While the reorganizational needs of the government continued to be studied, the state ended the year with a $36 million surplus.

Education. In the spring there was some unrest in the public schools, but no major outbreaks occurred and schools quieted down in the fall. Significant gains were made in reaching the goals set by the department of education in its 1970 five-year master plan. This year the state could point to large enrollments in adult education programs and programs for the handicapped, a reduction of the failure rate in first grade, increased enrollment in occupational training, and a decline in the number of high school dropouts. All two-year postsecondary programs, except those controlled by a university, were placed under a special technical educational board, preparing the way for community colleges. Meanwhile, Lander College in Greenwood was made a part of the state system, Winthrop College in Rock Hill became coeducational, and the higher educational commission was strengthened.
Economic developments. The economy improved with the end of the textile slump, a rise in state tax collections, a drop in the unemployment rate, and continued industrial

expansion. Farmers also had a generally good year, although a late frost reduced the peach crop and dry weather in late summer threatened cotton and soybeans. An inland port for Greenville-Spartanburg was created by the Ports Authority, and the state continued a policy of encouraging foreign trade and foreign industrial investments.
Other events. The state stepped up sickle-cell anemia research and opened a marine research laboratory in Charleston County. Action was taken to preserve virgin forests in the Congaree-Wateree and Hell Hole swamp areas. Plans for redeveloping and preserving the downtown section of Columbia were in progress.

State Senator Edgar A. Brown, dean of the South Carolina senate and longtime chairman of its finance committee, retired from politics after 50 years in the legislature.

For election results and campaign highlights, see the special supplement ELECTION '72.

Area and population. Area, 31,055 sq. mi. Pop. (1970), 2,589,-891. Principal cities: Columbia (cap.), 113,542; Charleston, 66,945; Greenville, 61,028.
Government. Gov., John C. West (D); lt. gov., Earle E. Morris, Jr. (D); secy. of state, O. Frank Thornton (D); treas., Grady L. Patterson (D); atty. gen., Daniel R. McLeod (D). General assembly: senate, 44 D, 2 R; house, 113 D, 11 R.
Finance (fiscal year ending June 30, 1971). General fund revenue, $504,540,819; expenditures, $494,388,516.
Education (1971–1972). Public elementary school enrollment, 387,035; public secondary school enrollment, 242,291.

ROBERT H. STOUDEMIRE

SOUTH DAKOTA.
Rapid City and Keystone experienced disaster on June 9 when a dam gave way under pressure during a heavy rainstorm. Water rushed through the canyon below, inflicting a death toll of at least 226 (later estimated at 239) and damage to roads, tourist facilities, and private property appraised in the millions of dollars. Nearly 200 Red Cross workers and 600 volunteers labored to distribute relief supplies and clear away the debris.
Legislation. Democratic governor Richard Kneip proposed a $50 million personal and corporate income tax measure in an attempt to raise more revenue and lessen the tax burden on real property owners. His bill died in the Republican-dominated assembly amid partisan debates, and his hope for distinction in his first term died with it.

Legislators lacked the resources for an adequate appropriations act that could accomplish more than simply continuing programs at existing levels of funding. Other legislation included a law granting persons 18 years of age and older the vote "at any election" in the state. Several acts promised to improve the environment by removing bounties on foxes and wildcats to prevent their extinction; by arranging for a popular referendum on a law permitting open season on mourning doves; and by granting expenditures for water pollution control.
Economic developments. Fiscal 1972 ended with an unobligated cash balance in the state general fund of $9.7 million, an increase of $3 million over the previous year. This resulted chiefly from increased sales-tax receipts, a sign that many people, including farmers and stock-growers, had more money to spend than in 1971. Regular rainfall produced good crops, and favorable market conditions caused livestock prices to improve. Tourism also prospered, as visitor attendance at all popular sites continued to rise (except at Mt. Rushmore, which some tourists avoided because of the flood). However, industrial production did not increase significantly, and the civilian work force was 1 percent smaller than in the previous year.
Education. Budgetary deficiencies brought crisis in public education at all levels, despite improvements in efficiency. Elementary and secondary school administrators noted that their enrollments had increased by more than 19,000 over the past decade, while the number of schools was reduced by more than one-half (1,354 in 1970). University and

college administrators boasted that they had consolidated many programs during the previous two years and had eliminated many others. Yet they all reported a shortage of money and warned of the decline of the quality of education unless they were given more money.

American Indian affairs. Raymond Yellow Thunder, a Dakota Indian, died in February as a result of a beating by non-Indians at Gordon, Neb. Approximately 1,000 young Indians congregated at Gordon to demand justice, and about 330 of them crossed the state line to investigate the alleged abuse of a teen-age boy by the proprietor of a trading post at Wounded Knee. Tempers flared. The protesters abused the proprietor, took Indian artifacts from his museum, and smashed merchandise, inflicting damages estimated at $50,000.

Fortunately, there were peaceful, constructive activities to balance the violence. For example, an adult group worked through the summer to create literature in the Dakota language at Rosebud Reservation. A lecturer from Rosebud taught Dakota language and saw its acceptance as a substitute for modern foreign language requirements at the University of South Dakota. Indian linguists taught Dakota to elementary students on several reservations, and Indian medicine men shared their religious beliefs and ceremonies with non-Indians at several locations.

Area and population. Area, 77,047 sq. mi. Pop. (1970), 665,- 507. Principal cities: Pierre (cap.), 9,699; Sioux Falls, 72,488.
Government. Gov., Richard S. Kneip (D); lt. gov., William Dougherty (D); atty. gen., Gordon Mydland (R); secy. of state, Alma Larson (R). Legislature: senate, 24 R, 11 D; assembly, 46 R, 29 D.
Finance (June 30, 1970). Budget: revenue, $265,804,170; expenditure, $250,830,668.
Education (September 1971). Public elementary and secondary school enrollment, 163,457. Nonpublic elementary and secondary school enrollment, 12,900. Higher education enrollment (1970), 30,- 731.   HERBERT T. HOOVER

SOUTHERN YEMEN (PEOPLE'S DEMOCRATIC REPUBLIC OF YEMEN). Border clashes.

Military clashes occurred this year along Southern Yemen's borders, although the number, identity, and motivation of the combatants were not always clear. Then in October, Southern Yemen and Yemen negotiators reached a tentative agreement to unify the two countries—previously antagonists—within a year.

In February, Aden had claimed that a force of about 2,000 "mercenaries" tried to invade the Beidah region from Yemen but was driven back. Yemen charged that Aden invented border incidents to draw its people's attention away from domestic problems. However, Southern Yemen rebels politically to the right of the Aden government have been in exile in Yemen in recent years. In March, Saudi Arabia accused Southern Yemen of killing 40 rebel leaders lured into the country for an alleged peace conference.

Also in March, scores of deaths resulted from border fighting between Yemen and Southern Yemen until Aden proposed, at the end of the month, a mutual withdrawal of troops from border areas. In May, Oman and Southern Yemen clashed along their common border.

Southern Yemen and Yemen again clashed militarily along their common border in the fall. The Aden government alleged that Yemeni troops had taken over the Red Sea island of Kamaran, which is part of Southern Yemen.

The Aden government repeatedly blamed Saudi Arabian and U.S. "imperialists" for border incursions, charging that invading tribesmen were trained in Saudi Arabia with U.S. equipment. In May the Aden government also accused Great Britain (the former colonial ruler of the Arabian Peninsula) of bombing the island of Socotra, which is part of Southern Yemen, and of landing mercenaries on the mainland. Great Britain denied the accusations.

Assassination attempt. On May 22, Prime Minister Ali Nasser Hassani only narrowly escaped death when an armed assassin burst into his office and began firing. The government branded the attempt the result of a conspiracy between the assassin and elements of imperialism.

Economic developments. Despite loans of $5 million each from Hungary and Czechoslovakia for various economic development projects and an $18 million loan from Libya, the Southern Yemen economy continued to stagnate. The hinterland has always been impoverished, and this year's military clashes upset trade and commerce.

The city of Aden, moreover, is almost at an economic standstill, with the Suez Canal closed, capital fleeing to other Arab states, and commerce subject to shifts in government policy. Since Southern Yemen gained its independence in 1967, Aden's population has declined by 50 percent. Salaries of government employees have been cut by up to 50 percent, the income tax has been doubled, and the cost of living has risen sharply.

Area and population. Area, approx. 111,080 sq. mi. Pop. (est. 1972), 1,810,000. Aden (cap.), 125,000.
Government. Political power is exercised by the three-member Presidential Council: Salim Rubai Ali, pres. of the council; Ali Nasser Hassani, prime min. of Southern Yemen; and Abdel Fatah Ismail, secretary general of the National Liberation Front, Southern Yemen's only legal political party.
Finance. Monetary unit, dinar; 1 dinar = US$2.60.
                                    RICHARD H. PFAFF

SPACE EXPLORATION.

Exploration of space this year was conducted mainly by unmanned satellites and space probes. There was only one manned mission, the lunar exploration by Apollo 16.

At their summit meeting in Moscow this May, President Richard M. Nixon and Soviet leaders confirmed plans for U.S. and Soviet spacemen to fly the world's first joint manned mission in June 1975. These plans call for linking a U.S. Apollo with a Soviet Salyut or Soyuz spacecraft in earth orbit for two days.

United States

Some 25 spacecraft were launched by the United States through October, including one Apollo mission, one Pioneer space probe, five scientific satellites, one operational meteorological satellite, two communications satellites, and some 15 Department of Defense satellites.

Lunar exploration. Apollo 16, commanded by John W. Young, with command module pilot Thomas K. Mattingly II and lunar module pilot Charles M. Duke, Jr., was launched from Cape Kennedy on April 16. The lunar module Orion separated from the command module Casper on schedule. However, because of a malfunction on Casper, the landing of Orion on the lunar surface was delayed for about six hours. The malfunction was corrected, and Orion landed in the moon's Descartes region on April 20. Astronauts Young and Duke spent a total of 20 hours and 15 minutes outside of Orion during their three periods of extravehicular activity. They traveled a distance of more than 16 miles in their lunar rover, collecting rock and soil samples along their route. The astronauts reported that the area was rockier, hillier, and more cratered than previous landing sites.

The astronauts collected 214 pounds of lunar rock and soil. One crystalline rock coated with bluish glass appeared to have the same texture as the anthracite "genesis rock" collected on the Apollo 15 mission; others were pure white, and some were flecked with colored glass. Samples were chipped off of a basalt rock the size of a house.

The portable magnetometer registered unexpectedly high readings. Seismometer readings showed that the topsoil was at least 100 feet thick, much thicker than at previous sites.

While Orion was on the moon, Mattingly, orbiting the moon in Casper, took lunar and astronomic photographs. He located a radioactive hot spot on the eastern edge of the Ocean of Storm and discovered volcanic lava flows

in the mountains near the lunar equator on the far side of the moon.

The lift-off of Orion from the lunar surface was televised in color by a camera on the lunar rover and was seen by millions of viewers throughout the world. Orion redocked with Casper on April 24, and samples, film, equipment, and personnel were transferred to Casper. Orion was jettisoned a day later and went into orbit around the moon.

A hexagonal scientific subsatellite about 30 inches long and 14 inches in diameter, weighing about 90 pounds, was ejected into lunar orbit from Casper on April 24. It carried a magnetometer to measure interplanetary and earth magnetic fields near the moon, a particle sensor to collect data on plasmas and solar flares, and an S-band transponder to detect variations in lunar gravity, caused by mass concentrations of dense material in the moon.

During the return trip to earth, Mattingly made two trips outside the spacecraft to retrieve panoramic and mapping camera film and to deploy, expose, and retrieve a microbial ecological evaluation experiment. Casper splashed down in the Pacific Ocean 1,500 miles south of Hawaii and about 3 miles from the recovery ship U.S.S. *Ticonderoga* on April 27.

In May, seismic instruments at the Apollo 12, 14, 15, and 16 sites recorded the impact of a large meteorite—probably measuring about 10 feet in diameter—near the Apollo 14 site. Vibrations lasted about one hour as a result of the energy release, which was estimated as greater than that of 1,000 tons of TNT. Analysis of the data from this large meteorite impact and from impacts of Apollo S-4B stages indicates that the lunar crust is approximately 37 miles thick, or about twice the thickness of earth's crust, and that the lunar mantle is solid to depths of about 560 miles.

Unmanned research satellites and space probes. In addition to the research carried out by Apollo 16, the United States conducted extensive research from earth satellites and space probes, some of which were launched before this year.

Mars probe. Mariner 9, which reached Mars on November 13, 1971, was still collecting data while orbiting Mars early this year. The television photographs of Mars reveal many surface features, such as the treelike canyon tributaries of valleys that seem explainable only by the presence of running water at some time in the past. There is also evidence of glacial activity near the South Polar Cap that cannot be accounted for by frozen carbon dioxide.

Jupiter probe. Pioneer 10, launched on March 2, is traveling at an average speed of 50,000 miles an hour on a trajectory to pass Jupiter about December 3, 1973. Ten of the 11 scientific experiments are collecting data on interplanetary space and sending it to earth. The 11th experiment will be used only to record heat emissions from Jupiter as it passes by the planet next year. Since July, Pioneer 10 has been in the asteroid belt between Mars and Jupiter. It should pass out of the asteroid belt in February 1973. After passing Jupiter, Pioneer 10 should continue to collect and transmit data to earth out to the orbit of Uranus, more than 2 billion miles away. Then, if the trajectory is not interrupted, Pioneer 10 will escape from the solar system into interstellar space. It carries a pictorial plaque designed to show scientifically educated inhabitants of some other star system, who might intercept it millions of years from now, when Pioneer was launched, from where, and by what kind of beings.

Physics. Scientists continued to analyze data that were obtained by satellites and space probes launched before this year. Several of the OGO, OSO, IMP, Mariner, and OV spacecraft were still operating and providing scientists with new data on the magnetosphere, ionosphere, sun, and interplanetary space.

Explorer 45, launched last November as the first in a series of small satellites, is providing data on particle fluxes, electric fields, and magnetic fields of the magnetosphere.

Explorer 46, a Meteoroid Technology Satellite (MTS), launched on August 13, has three experiments to collect data on the near-earth meteoroid environment and measure its effect on the spacecraft structure.

An orbiting astronomical observatory (OAO-3), called Copernicus, was launched into a nearly circular orbit on August 21. It carries four telescopes and related electronic equipment to observe the celestial sphere from above the earth's atmosphere.

Explorer 47, launched on September 23, carried 13 experiments to measure energetic particles, plasma, and electric and magnetic fields in space.

Applications and technology. The useful application of satellites increased. An earth resources technology satellite, two communications satellites, one meteorological satellite, one amateur radio satellite, and about 15 Department of Defense satellites were launched as of October; several others will be launched before the end of the year.

Earth resources technology satellite. ERTS-1, launched on July 23, is acquiring periodic multispectral images of the earth's surface to support investigations in such areas as agriculture, forestry, and land, water, mineral, and marine resources. More than 300 scientists in the United States and 37 foreign countries are using data from this satellite. Preliminary reports indicate that the imagery resolution usually was sufficient to identify 800 square feet, industrial or commercial centers, major four-lane highways, minor cleared roads, bridges, small canals, railroads, golf courses, orchards, agricultural lands, range lands, forests, and small lakes (350–400 feet wide).

Meteorological satellites. NOAA-2 (National Oceanic and Atmospheric Administration), an improved TIROS operational satellite (ITOS), was launched on October 15 from the western test range in California and was placed in a circular, nearly polar orbit, about 910 miles high. It carries sensors to take daytime and nighttime pictures of the earth's cloud cover, to obtain the atmosphere's vertical temperature and water vapor distribution and sea surface temperatures on a global basis, and to detect the arrival of energetic solar protons in the vicinity of earth.

Communications satellites. NASA launched two more INTELSAT 4 communications satellites for the Communications Satellite Corporation (COMSAT) as of October. Another INTELSAT launching has been scheduled for December.

PIONEER 10, once past Jupiter, will carry this message to the Milky Way. Below, a diagram of Pioneer's trip; center left, earth's position relative to 14 radio-pulsating stars; center right, earthlings measured against the dimensions of the spaceship; top left, a sketch of the two states of the hydrogen atom, meant to serve as a scale for measurements used in the other drawings.

NASA

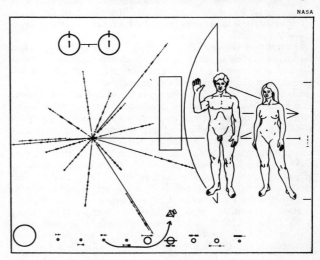

A Little Summit
in Outer Space

In 1975 the world's two spacefaring nations will join forces in the dramatic linkup of a U.S. Apollo craft (left) with a Soviet Soyuz (right). Astronauts will visit back and forth, passing through a cylindrical docking module (center) designed to provide a transition between the pressurized atmospheres of the two ships. Construction of this module (diagrammed on facing page) will give a $250 million boost to the U.S. aerospace industry.

These satellites have a designed capacity of 3,000 to 9,000 telephone circuits and a designed lifetime of seven years.

Amateur radio satellite. An OSCAR satellite carrying an amateur radio relay transmitter was launched with NOAA-2 on October 15. Radio amateurs throughout the world use this satellite for relaying transmissions and for studying radio propagation phenomena.

Soviet Union

Some 70 spacecraft were launched by the Soviet Union as of November. About 57 of the flights were unmanned, earth-orbital missions in the Cosmos series, which has a variety of purposes: reconnaissance, establishment of working and communications systems for military use, technological development, application, and research. A Venus probe, a lunar probe, two Intercosmos scientific satellites, two Prognoz satellites, four communications satellites, and three operational meteorological satellites made up the other 13 spacecraft which were launched as part of the Soviet space program.

Unmanned flights. *Mars probes.* The two Mars probes that were launched last May went into orbit around Mars at the end of November 1971. A capsule released from Mars 3 entered the planet's atmosphere, parachuted down, and soft-landed in the southern hemisphere of Mars last December. The lander was equipped with sensors to measure temperature and atmospheric pressure, a mass spectrometer to determine chemical composition of the atmosphere, an anemometer, and devices to determine the chemical composition and physical and mechanical characteristics of the Martian surface. The lander also contained two television cameras to provide pictures of the landing site. Unfortunately, the successful landing was nullified when television transmissions from the lander ceased 20 seconds after they started.

Soviet scientists reported surface temperatures from $+55°$ F to $-135°$ F and average atmospheric surface pressure at 5.5 to 6 millibars. According to the Soviets, the atmosphere consists largely of carbon dioxide near the surface. They also reported that the surface material is dry sand or dust and that the dark "seas" are generally warmer than the lighter colored "continents."

Venus probes. Venus 8, launched on March 27, made a soft-landing on Venus on July 22 and transmitted one hour of data in the most successful planetary probe achieved by the Soviets. Data included temperature readings, atmospheric pressure, light levels, and wind speed and direction. An attempt to send a second probe to Venus from earth orbit failed; the spacecraft was designated as Cosmos 482.

Lunar probe. Luna 20, launched on February 14, made a soft-landing on the moon in a mountainous area between the Sea of Fertility and the Sea of Crisis on February 21. Samples of rock were obtained by drilling and were returned to earth by rocket for analysis on February 25. Soviet scientists reported that these samples differed greatly from the Luna 16 samples in color, chemical composition, and physical texture.

Luna 19, which went into lunar orbit October 1971, completed its exploration of the lunar surface some 12 months later. It obtained new data on radio reflectivity and on plasmas at or near the lunar surface.

Science and applications. Many of the Cosmos series of satellites carried experiments dealing with particles, fields and radiation in the upper atmosphere, magnetosphere, and interplanetary space. Two Intercosmos research satellites, which are larger and heavier than previous Intercosmos satellites, were launched this year. Intercosmos 6, with experiments supplied by Hungary, Poland, Czechoslovakia, and Romania, was launched on April 7 to investigate high-energy cosmic-ray particles and chemical properties of dust particles in space. Intercosmos 7, with shortwave radiation instruments supplied by the German Democratic Republic and solar X-radiation instruments supplied by Czechoslovakia, was launched on June 30.

Two solar research satellites, Prognoz 1, launched on April 7, and Prognoz 2, launched on June 29, were placed into highly elliptical orbits with periods of about four days.

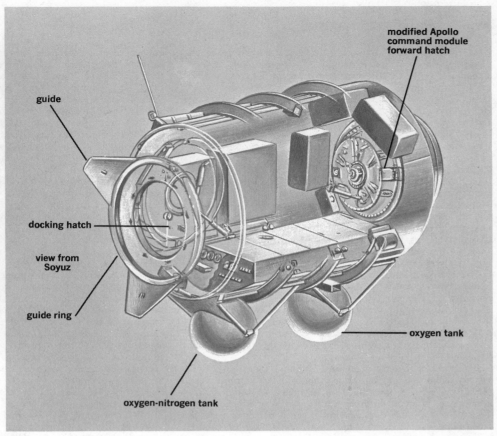

guide

docking hatch

view from Soyuz

guide ring

modified Apollo command module forward hatch

oxygen tank

oxygen-nitrogen tank

AFP FROM PICTORIAL

They are collecting data on solar radio, gamma-ray, X-ray, and plasma emissions, on the earth's magnetic field, and on the interaction of solar plasmas with the earth's magnetic field. Prognoz 2 also carried a French experiment to obtain data on the solar wind.

Meteorology. Meteorological satellites in the Meteor series have been launched at regular three-month intervals since Meteor 6 in the fall of 1970, with the exception of Meteor 10, launched two months late on December 29, 1971. Meteor 12 was launched on June 30 and Meteor 13 on October 27. These Meteor satellites carried experimental systems for obtaining images of clouds and of the earth's surface in the visible and infrared parts of the spectrum and for making quantitative measurements of the components of the earth's radiation on a planetary scale. The data received from these satellites are used by the Soviet weather service and are disseminated to other countries for their use.

Communications. Two communications satellites in the Molniya 1 series and two in the improved Molniya 2 series were launched this year. These satellites are used for radio, television, telephone, and telegraph transmissions both domestically and internationally.

Other Nations and International Organizations

Those countries capable of launching spacecraft continued this year to include experiments designed by other nations on their satellites and to launch other nations' vehicles. NASA launched HEOS A-2 in January and a TD-1A satellite in March for the European Space Research Organization. HEOS carried seven experiments to investigate interplanetary space and the high-latitude magnetosphere. The TD-1A satellite carried seven unique experiments for astronomical, solar, and cosmic research.

A small French satellite, SRET-1, was launched by the Soviets with their Molniya 1 communications satellite on April 4. It carried experiments to study characteristics of solar batteries for space operation and degeneration of solar cells from cosmic-ray exposure in Van Allen belts.

The Japanese launched their second scientific satellite, REXS, on August 19. It carried several experiments to investigate the ionosphere and magnetosphere.

Space research was carried out by many nations through sounding rocket programs, through analysis of tracking and other data obtained mainly from satellites launched by the United States, and through cooperative agreements with NASA. The NASA program involves cooperation with 87 countries. Of these, 28 nations are engaged in space research projects, 22 in tracking and data acquisition, 40 in personnel exchanges, and 84 in ground-based programs relevant to space experiments.

International scientific cooperation was continued through the Committee on Space Research of the International Council of Scientific Unions. Over 800 scientists from 32 nations attended COSPAR's 15th general assembly, held in Madrid in May.   RICHARD Y. DOW

SPAIN. Politics and government. Political reform leaders lost in their struggle against conservatives resisting change under 81-year-old Generalissimo Francisco Franco Bahamonde. Admiral Luis Carrero Blanco, Franco's second-in-command and an extreme conservative, age 69, was named by Franco to succeed him as head of government if the post—now held by Franco—remained unfilled at his death.

Liberals, however, scored in other fields—significantly in the area of the church, whose leaders had hitherto remained unconditional backers of the status quo under Franco. Dramatic change took place at the March conference of Spanish bishops when advocates of reform, led by Vicente Cardinal Enrique y Tarancón, fought off conservatives battling their movement for the divorce of church and state, the correction of economic and social imbalances, and the formation of deeper ties between church and laymen.

Thus, Spain's political and social fabric experienced much tension. Conservatives, perhaps, managed to consolidate political positions, and progressives held more tenuously to theirs.

509

To mark the 36th anniversary of the nationalist rebellion against the Second Spanish Republic, Generalissimo Franco signed a law in July dictating norms for the implementation of the succession. Under the new law, Vice-president Carrero Blanco will assume the premiership at the instant of Franco's death and preside eight days afterward at the formal coronation of Prince Juan Carlos de Borbón as chief of the Spanish state. The law is designed both to set the timetable for Prince Juan Carlos to accede to the throne and to ensure that Carrero Blanco fills the seat of power vacated by Franco. Technically, after Franco's death, a list of three names will be submitted to Prince Juan Carlos from which he, as king, will designate his first premier.

In the interim, Admiral Carrero Blanco will hold the office. Therefore, in light of Franco's public support of his vice-president, it is thought highly unlikely that Carrero Blanco will not figure in the list of three or that Prince Juan Carlos will be in a position to go above him when he already occupies the post.

The church. Partially offsetting the conservative victory, Spain's church was seen moving rapidly to formulate more progressive policies. This stems mainly from the group of new bishops appointed by Pope Paul VI. Under the leadership of Madrid archbishop Vincente Cardinal Enrique y Tarancón, the new bishops defeated by democratic vote a campaign led by conservatives at the conference of Spanish bishops held in Madrid.

Bishop José Guerra Campos, Cardinal Tarancón's adversary, who is a regime churchman and an extreme conservative, lost his key office as secretary of the bishop's conference after a dramatic confrontation with Cardinal Tarancón. Cardinal Tarancón produced a personal message from Pope Paul endorsing his stand. Separation of church and state has been the central issue discussed by the Vatican and Spain in talks concerning reform of the concordat, the document regulating ties between them.

Education. Madrid University and other Spanish universities were in turmoil this year. Academic life was almost completely paralyzed over the implementation of Spain's new education law as students—in pitched open battles against police on university campuses—defied government-appointed university authorities. Students called for improved classroom facilities and increased student representation in the drafting of educational programs. Medical students touched off the rebellion when they went on strike for more classrooms and increased access to hospital facilities related to their medical studies. In July the government hit back, imposing rigid disciplinary controls.

The government-imposed statutes provide for suspension of students who engage in rebellion campaigns and give the new government-appointed rector the right to close down campuses or to transfer the centers of study elsewhere in the event of trouble.

Foreign relations. Spain's foreign ministry, continuing implementation of flexible policies, closed a historical trade agreement with the Soviet Union. It marked the first official de jure recognition between Spain and the Soviet Union after a 36-year estrangement. The implementation of a step-by-step program aimed at restoring diplomatic relations was not expected to take place soon. The official aim was to grant each other's trade missions diplomatic status to foster trade. Soviet oil supplies, which began coming to Spanish refiners in 1964, and Spanish Valencia oranges, which went to the Soviet Union in barter agreements, initiated the trade program that culminated in the trade agreement signed in Paris in September.

Confronted by the enlargement of the European Economic Community, Spain requested renegotiation of the two-year-old preferential trade pact, since Great Britain, an important market for Spanish agricultural products, will be protected by high entry tariffs when it joins the EEC in 1973. Spain's bid was the focus of public controversy

among several European governments. French president Georges Pompidou's statement at a Paris press conference that he favored Spanish entry as soon as possible was met by a formal statement signed by EEC commissioner Altiero Spinelli that the Common Market's political basis does not permit it to consider for membership a country whose internal structure does not reflect the fundamental principles of liberty and democracy that characterize the political systems of all the other member nations.

In the Far East, Spain began a subtle campaign for rapprochement with the People's Republic of China. After opening a consulate in Hong Kong, Spain failed to fill the vacant Spanish embassy post in Taiwan. The People's Republic of China, in recognition of Spain's playdown of ties with Nationalist China, invited Spanish foreign minister Gregorio López Bravo to its UN inaugural reception.

Economy. Spain's gross national product reached over $40 billion, and gold and dollar reserves increased to $4.5 billion. The record economic figures appeared to support those who insist that a strong authoritarian-type government can produce conditions for economic development.

Now recognized as a monetary power, Spain was permitted to observe technical information sessions on the working of the Common Market's currency bloc. In view of the EEC ruling that Spain is not democratic, the gesture was unusual, for the monetary meetings of central bankers from EEC member countries discuss coordination and implementation of monetary policies. Spain's attendance at the EEC monetary council meetings was significant in that it might indicate the possibility of EEC ties with Spain in some new form which does not politically commit the EEC to grant Franco equal status acceptance.

Industrially Spain made two decisions with far-reaching effects, and, significantly, U.S. corporations were partners to the Spanish decisions designed to bolster its bid as a European power. Spain's government-controlled industrial holding agency, Instituto Nacional de Industria (INI), closed a $200 million venture in partnership with Texaco and Chevron to build a refinery at Tarragona, Empresa Nacional de Tarragona. The refinery is 60 percent INI owned, and the balance is shared by Chevron-Texaco with Spain's biggest chemical company, Union Explosivos-Rio Tinto, partly British-owned through the Rio Tinto London-based group of companies. The refinery will supply oil products to the booming Barcelona market and export to European markets through Chevron-Texaco.

The U.S. Steel Corporation, bidding through a partly owned Spanish partner, won the opportunity to build a $1.5 billion steel complex at Sagunto, a Mediterranean location north of Valencia. The steel plant at Sagunto will be among the biggest in the Mediterranean area and will supply steel sheets mainly for Spanish industry. U.S. Steel's partners will be privately owned Spanish economic interests, headed by Altos Hornos de Vizcaya.

Japan made its first investments in Spain when the Mitsui group took a 33 percent interest in a new Spanish petrochemical undertaking and Nissin Steel Company agreed to a 35 percent interest in a stainless steel plant.

Area and population. Area, 194,885 sq. mi. Pop. (est. 1971), 33,600,000. Principal cities: Madrid (cap.), 3,200,000; Barcelona, 2,800,000; Valencia, 614,000; Seville, 610,000.

Government. Monarchy. Ranking government organ is the Cortes (Parliament). Dominant political group is the Falange. Head, Falange and National Movement, Generalissimo Francisco Franco Bahamonde.

Finance. Monetary unit, peseta; 1 peseta = US$0.0160. Budget (est. 1971): balanced at US$4.43 billion.

Trade (1971). Imports, US$4.937 billion; exports, US$2.938 billion.

Education (1967–1968). Primary schools, 118,786; enrollment, 4,179,000; teachers, 60,000. Secondary schools, 3,748; enrollment, 1,089,100; teachers, 59,900. Technical and vocational schools, 834; enrollment, 238,024; teachers, 17,916. Universities (including technical schools), 12; enrollment, 150,000; teachers, 9,604.

Armed forces. Army, navy, and air force, approx. 336,000.

DOMINIC CURCIO

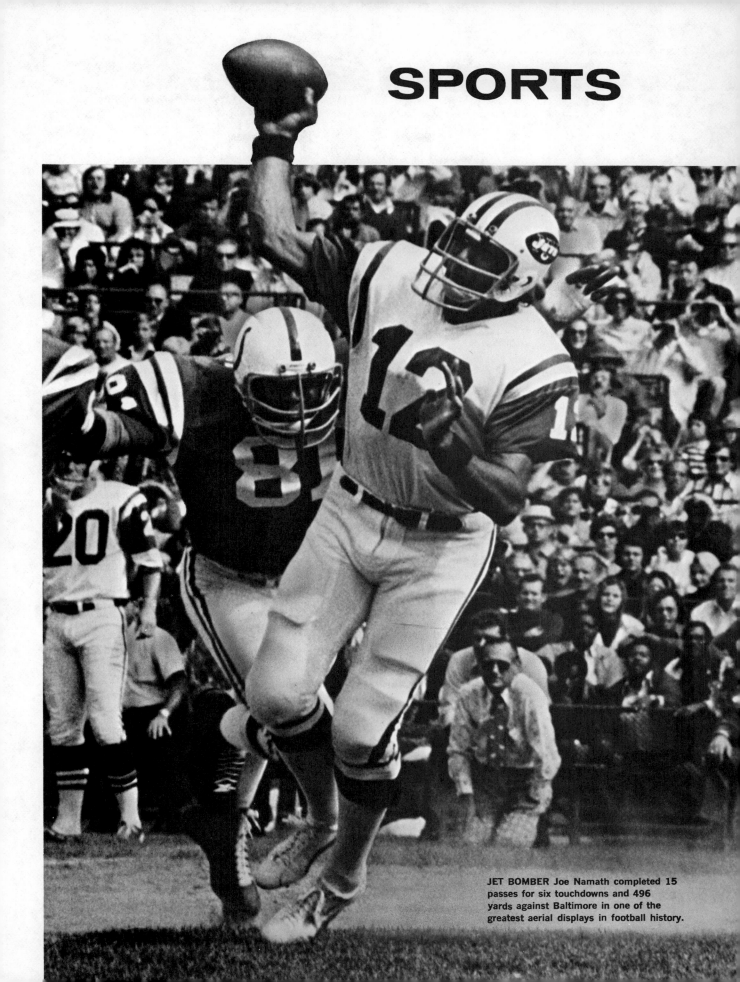

SPORTS

JET BOMBER Joe Namath completed 15 passes for six touchdowns and 496 yards against Baltimore in one of the greatest aerial displays in football history.

HOT WHEELS. Making up for his 1971 disappointment, Mark Donohue set a new speed record to finish first in the Indianapolis 500.

Many questions were raised during this year of frenetic sports activity. Could—or should—the Olympic Games survive the massacre of Israeli athletes or the blatant commercialism, the fierce nationalism, and the outright politics that characterized what was supposed to be a friendly competition among athletes of good will? What would be the final verdicts in all those court cases involving players in every sport who broke contracts in order to jump from one team to another, from one league to another? Would the U.S. Congress ever get around to sanctioning the long-anticipated merger of the American Basketball Association and the National Basketball Association? Would baseball's reserve clause stand up under closer legal scrutiny? How much longer could the National Hockey League hold out against the barrage of heavyweight blows dealt by the upstart World Hockey Association? And, finally, would the U.S. Treasury Department manage to print enough money to enable all those athletes with six-figure and seven-figure salaries to collect their wages?

Well, if sportsmen could not come up with answers to those questions, the world of sports bristled and shook with all the tension and controversy they provoked; and no one can say that nothing was proved. Bobby Fischer proved that there is a limit, but not much, to what a gamester can rightfully demand and get away with. Both the Los Angeles Lakers and the Dallas Cowboys proved that they don't flop in the championship showdown all the time. When Adolph Rupp finally retired as coach at the University of Kentucky, college basketball showed itself able to survive without him, just as it survived the continued dominance of the UCLA Bruins. How baseball would bear up under the repercussions of this spring's player-strike remained to be determined, but it did manage to get along quite nicely with the hairiest show since the House of David, as the Oakland Athletics took the World Series from the Cincinnati Reds in seven games.

It was a year of upsets and near upsets. Soviet ice hockey stars jolted Team Canada all the way down to its skate blades, and the Soviet basketball team finally fouled up America's perfect record in the Olympics. The shock waves from both those Russian performances no doubt will long be felt. Less publicized, yet equally stunning in its own way, was the victory achieved by Jesse Kuhaulua of Hawaii, who became the first foreigner ever to win Japan's sumo championship.

In a very real way, the fiber of sport was tested this year, perhaps as never before. Surely there will be re-evaluations of rules and practices on professional and amateur levels alike, and adjustments will have to be forthcoming. But, if nothing else, these tumultuous 12 months gave strong indications that the realm of sport has enough elasticity and durability to bounce back with the much-needed solutions and keep on rolling along.

HERMAN WEISKOPF

AUTO RACING. Emerson Fittipaldi, a 25-year-old Brazilian who started at the bottom, reached the top in 1972 to become the youngest world driving champion in 22 years. The most successful American drivers were George Follmer of Arcadia, Calif., in sports cars; Joe Leonard of San Jose, Calif., and Mark Donohue of Media, Pa., in Indianapolis-type cars; and Richard Petty of Randleman, N.C., and Bobby Allison of Hueytown, Ala., in stock cars.

Drivers' championship. The world driving championship was decided in 12 Grand Prix races in 12 nations on four continents. The cars, known as Formula Ones, were open-wheel, open-cockpit, single-seat roadsters, with engines limited to three liters. They were similar in appearance, though not always in power, to the cars used in the world manufacturer, the Indianapolis-type, and the Continental 5,000 series.

Emerson Fittipaldi, driving a British Lotus with a Ford engine, won five Grand Prix races—in Spain, Belgium, Britain, Austria, and Italy—in addition to two Formula One nontitle races and several European Formula Two races. Defending champion Jackie Stewart of Scotland, driving a British Tyrrell-Ford, won four Grand Prix—in Argentina, France, Canada, and the United States. The richest of the Grand Prix were the American ($275,000 gross) and Canadian ($200,000).

Fittipaldi, who in 1969 won the British title driving Formula Threes, and in 1970, as No. 1 driver for the Lotus Formula One team, won the U.S. Grand Prix, was plagued by suspension problems and inexperience last year and consequently finished sixth in the world championship series. In 1972, he was first, partly because he thought like a win-

ner. "When I get inside a car," he said, "it is like being out of this world. If I have any other problems, I have to forget them. It is as if I am part of the car."

Manufacturers' title. The world manufacturers' championship was decided in 11 races, but the big five-liter and seven-liter sports cars and prototypes no longer were allowed. Engines were limited to three liters, a change that prompted Porsche, the champion the three previous years, to bypass the series. Ferrari of Italy won ten races and passed up the 11th, the Le Mans 24-hour classic (won by Henri Pescarolo and Graham Hill in a French Matra), because it disliked such a long race. All three manufacturers' races in the United States—at Daytona Beach, Fla.; Sebring, Fla.; and Watkins Glen, N.Y.—were won by a car in which Mario Andretti of Nazareth, Pa., and Jacky Ickx of Belgium alternated as drivers.

Porsche, no longer interested in the manufacturers' series, turned to the Canadian-American Challenge Cup series of nine races for the largest sports cars. Its task was formidable because Team McLaren, which had won 37 of the 43 Can-Am races in the five previous years, had introduced a new car that generated close to 800 horsepower.

Porsche countered with an open-cockpit version of its 910-10, which it had used so successfully in previous manufacturers' series. Its flat, 12-cylinder engine, boosted by two turbochargers originally designed for trucks, produced about 900 horsepower. It helped Porsche win the team title and the individual championship.

Surprisingly, the title went to George Follmer rather than to Mark Donohue, who had seemed ready for an all-conquering year. The 35-year-old mechanical engineer won two races in the Can-Am Porsche, but on July 3, while practicing at Gainesville, Ga., for a Can-Am race, his Porsche came apart at 160 miles per hour and flipped over. Donohue suffered damaged tendons in the left knee and was sidelined for ten weeks.

Follmer, who during the year also won the Trans-American championship for sports sedans and the team title for Javelin in this eight-race series, thus became the No. 1 Can-Am driver for Porsche, winning five races and taking the series title.

USAC and NASCAR. USAC's Championship Trail comprised 11 races for Indianapolis-type cars. Bobby Unser of Albuquerque, N.M., had the fastest car, winning four races and breaking qualifying records at almost every track—his qualifying lap of 199.778 miles per hour was the fastest in the sport's history—but his Eagle-Offenhauser lacked durability. Joe Leonard repeated as series champion in one of the three new Parnelli-Offenhausers, whose turbocharged engines generated almost 900 horsepower. Al Unser and Mario Andretti drove the other two.

When Viceroy cigarettes became a sponsor of the Parnellis, Marlboro cigarettes angrily dropped its $500,000 sponsorship of the USAC races.

Winston cigarettes, however, remained a major sponsor of the NASCAR Grand National series of 32 races, all from 250 to 500 miles. Richard Petty, driving a 1972 Plymouth and then a 1972 Dodge, won the point title for the fourth year in a row, and Bobby Allison, in a 1972 Chevrolet, became the first NASCAR driver in history to win more than $200,000 in consecutive seasons. Among them, Petty, Allison, and David Pearson of Spartanburg, S.C., won three-quarters of the races. Mark Donohue drove American Motors' new Matador, which lacked power and did badly.

The most bizarre and controversial race of the year was the $1,011,846 Indianapolis 500. Gary Bettenhausen of Tinley Park, Ill., Donohue's teammate, was leading with 65 miles remaining when his ignition failed. Then Jerry Grant of Seattle, driving an Eagle-Offenhauser, led until his spark plugs fouled. Thus, Mark Donohue in a Sunoco McLaren-Offenhauser took command with 32 miles left and became the winner. Grant, who finished second, was dropped to

12th place because he received fuel from a teammate's pit reservoir. Thus, instead of winning $95,258, he received $23,853.   FRANK LITSKY

BASEBALL. It was on April Fools' Day that major league players commenced their first all-out strike, but neither the players nor the club owners were fooling. The players had voted 663–10 to strike, and the owners had voted 24–0 to refuse the players' demands for increases in their pension fund. The impasse persisted, and the scheduled opening

THE A'S HAVE IT. Left fielder Joe Rudi climbed the wall to grab a ninth-inning drive from Cincinnati's Denis Menke, saving the second game of the World Series for the Oakland underdogs. The Athletics finally derailed the Big Red Machine in seven.

UPI

![THE BOYS OF SUMMER — ROGER KAHN](book cover)

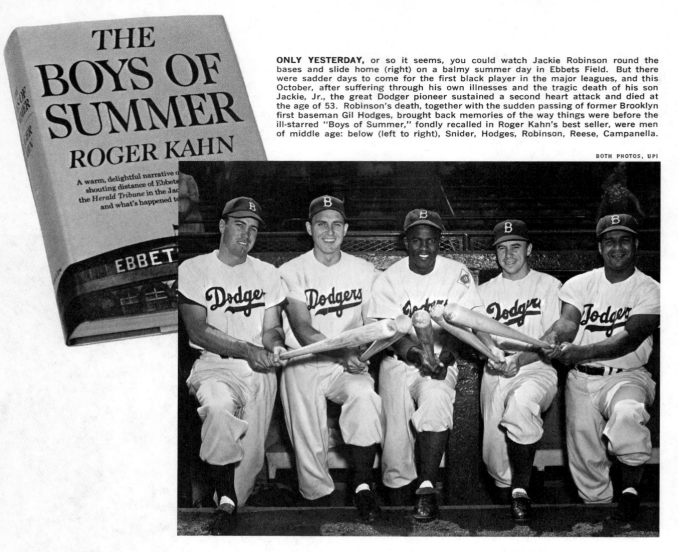

ONLY YESTERDAY, or so it seems, you could watch Jackie Robinson round the bases and slide home (right) on a balmy summer day in Ebbets Field. But there were sadder days to come for the first black player in the major leagues, and this October, after suffering through his own illnesses and the tragic death of his son Jackie, Jr., the great Dodger pioneer sustained a second heart attack and died at the age of 53. Robinson's death, together with the sudden passing of former Brooklyn first baseman Gil Hodges, brought back memories of the way things were before the ill-starred "Boys of Summer," fondly recalled in Roger Kahn's best seller, were men of middle age: below (left to right), Snider, Hodges, Robinson, Reese, Campanella.

BOTH PHOTOS, UPI

day came and went. Finally, on April 13, the owners coughed up more money, but the effects of the strike were to be far-reaching. Eighty-six scheduled games that had not been played would not be made up; these crimped the season's gate receipts and ultimately played a vital role in the scramble for first place in the American League East.

The season itself was strongly influenced by massive trading at the baseball meetings in Arizona four months earlier. That turned out to be the biggest swapping binge of all time—17 trades involving 53 players, many of them well-known frontliners.

National League West. Most significant of all the deals in Arizona was the one in which the Cincinnati Reds obtained speedy second baseman Joe Morgan, outfielder Cesar Geronimo, third baseman Denis Menke, pitcher Jack Billingham, and a minor league outfielder from the Houston Astros in exchange for slugging first baseman Lee May and two others. This change of emphasis from power to speed and team balance paid off; with Morgan stealing 58 bases, the team led the majors with 140. Even though the club's 124 homers ranked just fifth in the league, the Reds won the West by a whopping 10½ games. A few other things helped, too. One was the return of Bobby Tolan, who came back after missing the 1971 season because of a torn Achilles tendon and hit .283, had 82 RBI's, and stole 42 bases. Another was the resurgence of Johnny Bench, the league's Most Valuable Player in 1970, who had slumped horrendously in 1971 but led both leagues this year in homers with 40 and in RBI's with 125. Finally, there was top-notch

relief pitching from Clay Carroll, who set a big-league mark with 37 saves, and Tom Hall, who had been picked up from Minnesota in yet another trade.

May had 29 homers and 98 RBI's for the Astros and, perhaps as important, helped Jimmy Wynn play up to his potential (24 home runs, 90 RBI's, 117 runs scored). But it simply was not the Astros' year, even though they did beat out the Dodgers for second place by one percentage point. Manager Harry Walker was replaced on August 26 by Leo Durocher, who earlier had been canned by the Cubs. Leo made little difference, because the two things the Astros had counted on most had already failed them: their pitching staff had a dismal 3.77 ERA, and the Astrodome roof leaked, forcing the team to honor rain checks for patrons who were dripped on.

One of the biggest of the Arizona deals was the one in which Los Angeles got Frank Robinson from the Orioles. Alas, Robinson hit a mere .251 and, as usual, the Dodgers lacked real sock. They also lacked sure hands, the apex of their inefficiency coming the day they set a club record by making seven errors. Still, there was plenty of good pitching: the club led the league with a 2.78 ERA and 23 shutouts, nine by Don Sutton (19–9, 2.08 ERA) and four by Claude Osteen (20–11, 2.64 ERA). And reliever Jim Brewer's 1.27 ERA was the best in the majors.

There was little to cheer about in Atlanta. Hank Aaron did unload 34 homers and moved to within 41 of Babe Ruth's total, but the Braves' 4.27 ERA was by far the worst in either league. Eddie Mathews replaced Luman

Harris as manager in August, to no avail. Miseries were also heaped upon San Francisco. Juan Marichal hardly earned his $140,000 salary with a 6–16 performance, Willie Mays was traded to the Mets, Willie McCovey's knees buckled, and the club's biggest gamble—trading Gaylord Perry to the Indians for Sam McDowell—was a flop. San Diego was even more hapless. After replacing Preston Gomez as manager, about all Don Zimmer had to cheer about was Nate Colbert's 38 homers and 111 RBI's.

National League East. Pittsburgh's world champions of 1971 lost nine of their first 14 games this season under new manager Bill Virdon. Then the Pirates went to work and made a shambles of the East. Nine Pirates who were used more or less regularly hit from .281 on up. Willie Stargell contributed the power with 33 home runs and 112 RBI's. Steve Blass was 19–8 and Dock Ellis 15–7, but it was the bullpen that really excelled: Rudy Hernandez (1.67 ERA and 14 saves), Dave Giusti (1.92 and 22 saves), and Bob Miller (2.67).

Several Cubs had superb seasons: Ferguson Jenkins (20–12) was a 20-game winner for the sixth straight time; Milt Pappas (17–7) won his 200th game; and the ageless Billy Williams had 37 homers and 122 RBI's and led the league in hitting with a .333 average. But even with Leo out and Whitey Lockman in, the best the Cubs could make was a distant second.

Tragedies befell the Mets, first when manager Gil Hodges died of a heart attack on April 2 and later when a rash of injuries struck the club. Worst of all was Rusty Staub's broken hand, which sidelined him for more than half of the season. Seeing the Mets through it all was Yogi Berra, their new skipper. Another injury, to pitcher Scipio Spinks of St. Louis, helped cripple the Cardinals' pitching staff and ruined their hopes for the season, despite another tremendous year for Bob Gibson (19–11). The Cardinals' .260 batting average was the second best in the majors, but their 70 homers was the second lowest. Matty Alou hit .314 before inexplicably being dealt to the Athletics late in the year.

Clothes are supposed to make the man, and they certainly helped make Ken Singleton of the Expos. On June 20, with his average down to .225 and his eyes puffy, Singleton was sent to an allergist, who found that the wool Expo uniform was to blame. So Singleton switched to a new doubleknit outfit and, presto, his eyes cleared and his average puffed up—all the way to .274. Otherwise, the Expos were cut from the same thin cloth as last year.

Philadelphia had Steve Carlton and not much else. Carlton, picked up in a winter deal that sent Rick Wise to St. Louis, was 27–10, putting him 20 wins ahead of the next pitcher on the staff. (See PEOPLE IN THE NEWS: Steve Carlton.) Things got so bad for the Phillies that Turnaround Night was held: the ushers wore their caps backward, "Goodnight, Sweetheart" was sung at the start of the game, the seventh-inning stretch was taken in the third inning. And still the Phillies lost. Frank Luchessi was bumped as manager, giving way to Paul Owens, who earlier had replaced John Quinn as general manager.

American League East. The race for the top spot came right down to the final games of the season, when the Tigers beat the Red Sox two out of three to take the crown. Norm Cash led the Tigers during the season with 22 homers, and Al Kaline, at age 38, hit .313 as a part-timer and was red hot down the stretch. Steady pitching came from Mickey Lolich (22–14), Joe Coleman (19–14), and relievers Chuck Seelbach and Fred Scherman. Additionally, after being traded to the Tigers from the Phillies, Woodie Fryman was 10–3 and had a 2.05 ERA.

Had the Red Sox picked up Bob Veale from the Pirates a few weeks earlier, they might have overcome the Tigers. Veale got into just six games, won two, saved two, and did not allow a run. Luis Tiant, 1–7 a year ago, was 15–6 this time and took the ERA title at 1.91. Moreover, Tiant kept the surging Sox going with four straight late-season shutouts. The big winner was Marty Pattin (17–13), who came to Boston from Milwaukee. Rookie catcher Carlton Fisk had 22 homers and a .293 average. Meanwhile, Baltimore's three-year American League reign ended because the Birds' .229 batting more than offset their 2.53 ERA, the lowest in the majors. Trading away Frank Robinson seemed to have cost the Orioles his leadership even more than his hitting.

There was no doubt that an early-season trade bringing Sparky Lyle from the Red Sox for Danny Cater kept the weak-hitting Yankees in contention. Lyle won nine games, set a league record with 35 saves, had a 1.92 ERA, and was at his best the day he came in with the bases full and none out and struck out the side on ten pitches. However, another deal may well have cost the Yankees first place. That was the trade that sent Stan Bahnsen to the White Sox for Rich McKinney, who quickly proved he could not play third base.

Cleveland, under new manager Ken Aspromonte, led the East in mid-May, then fell apart. Former Giant Gaylord Perry was 24–16, but Alex Johnson, who was picked up from the Angels, did not pep up the attack with his .239 hitting. Milwaukee's colossal deal with Boston paid mixed dividends: George Scott hit 20 homers and had 88 RBI's and Jim Lonborg was 14–12, but Ken Brett was 7–12, Joe Lahoud hit .234, Don Pavletich did not play, and Billy Conigliaro quit baseball for business in June, taking his .230 average with him.

American League West. Hair, hair, hair—the Athletics were covered with it. Owner Charlie Finley gave $300 to each player who sprouted a mustache for Mustache Day, and many of the A's retained their added growths long after collecting their money. From Fu Manchus to mutton chops to long, flowing locks, the A's had everything except superpitcher Vida Blue, who held out for an enormous raise, did not get it, and spent most of the season out of shape and off form. But Jim ("Catfish") Hunter was 21–7, and Ken Holtzman, acquired from the Cubs for outfielder Rick Monday, was 19–11. Highlighting the offense were Joe Rudi (.305, 19 homers, 75 RBI's), Mike Epstein (26 homers), and Reggie Jackson (25 homers). And Bert Campaneris led the league in stolen bases with 52.

Trades made a contender of the White Sox. Coming from the Dodgers: Dick Allen, who hit .308, powered 37 homers, and had 113 RBI's. Coming from the Yankees: Stan Bahnsen, who, with much bullpen help, won 21 games. Knuckleballer Wilbur Wood was 24–17, and 20-year-old Terry Forster had six wins and 29 saves in relief. The Sox, who were 22½ games out of first place last year, might have won it all had they not lost Bill Melton, the league-leading home run hitter in 1971, because of a bad back.

With three-time batting titlist Tony Oliva plagued with knee trouble and Jim Kaat sidelined with a sore arm, the Twins slumped. Bill Rigney was sacked on July 6 and replaced by Frank Quilici. Kansas City's high hopes were dimmed by clubhouse rumblings that led to the dismissal of manager Bob Lemon at the season's end. The Royals

could hit but not pitch, putting them a cut above California, which could neither hit nor pitch. Their only exception was fastballer Nolan Ryan, obtained from the Mets for shortstop Jim Fregosi. Ryan was 19–16, had a 2.28 ERA, led the league in shutouts with nine, and was tops in the big leagues with 329 strikeouts. New general manager Harry Dalton, fresh from building the Orioles into league champions, hired Del Rice as manager, then fired him at the end of the season and hired Bobby Winkles, a coach with the Angels who had won three NCAA titles with Arizona State.

Ted Williams was not fired. He quit in frustration after four seasons as a manager. His Texas Rangers, formerly the Washington Senators, were last in the majors in batting (.217) and in home runs (56) and last in the league in pitching with a 3.53 ERA.

FINAL AMERICAN LEAGUE STANDINGS
Eastern Division

	Won	Lost	Pct.	GB
Detroit	86	70	.551	—
Boston	85	70	.548	½
Baltimore	80	74	.519	5
New York	79	76	.510	6½
Cleveland	72	84	.462	14
Milwaukee	65	91	.417	21

Western Division

	Won	Lost	Pct.	GB
Oakland	93	62	.600	—
Chicago	87	67	.565	5½
Minnesota	77	77	.500	15½
Kansas City	76	78	.494	16½
California	75	80	.484	18
Texas	54	100	.351	38½

FINAL NATIONAL LEAGUE STANDINGS
Eastern Division

	Won	Lost	Pct.	GB
Pittsburgh	96	59	.619	—
Chicago	85	70	.548	11
New York	83	73	.532	13½
St. Louis	75	81	.481	21½
Montreal	70	86	.449	26½
Philadelphia	59	97	.378	37½

Western Division

	Won	Lost	Pct.	GB
Cincinnati	95	59	.617	—
Houston	84	69	.549	10½
Los Angeles	85	70	.548	10½
Atlanta	70	84	.455	25
San Francisco	69	86	.445	26½
San Diego	58	95	.379	36½

Playoffs. Pittsburgh twice took the upper hand in the National League playoffs by beating the Reds in the first and third games, but Cincinnati would not knuckle under. The Reds took the National League pennant in the decisive fifth contest when Johnny Bench homered in the bottom of the ninth to tie the score at 3–3 and when, two outs and two singles later, they scored again on a wild pitch.

In the American League showdown, Oakland won the first two games, Detroit the next two, coming from behind in the fourth game to score three runs in the last of the 10th. Oakland took the finale, 2–1, but lost Reggie Jackson for the World Series because of a leg injury.

World Series. *First game.* Catcher Gene Tenace, who hit only five homers all year, unloaded two and drove in all three A's runs. Shutout relief work over the final four innings by Rollie Fingers and Vida Blue saved the win.

```
Oakland .................................. 020 010 000—3-4-0
Cincinnati .............................. 010 100 000—2-7-0
  Holtzman (W), Fingers (6) Blue (7) vs. Nolan (L), Borbon (7), Carroll (8)
```

Second game. Leftfielder Joe Rudi homered for the A's and then came up with a game-saving catch in the ninth. After a few more scary moments, Fingers came in to get the final out.

```
Oakland.....................................011 000 000—2-9-2
Cincinnati..................................000 000 001—1-6-0
   Hunter (W), Fingers (9) vs. Grimsley (L), Borbon (6), Hall (8)
```

Third game. The low scoring reached its ultimate minimum, as the Reds hung on for a 1–0 triumph. Even the run was minimal: on Geronimo's single Perez slipped and fell on the soggy turf rounding third. His pratfall unnoticed by the A's fielders, he scrambled home with the game's lone score.

```
Cincinnati..................................000 000 100—1-4-2
Oakland.....................................000 000 000—0-3-2
   Billingham (W), Carroll (9) vs. Odom (L), Blue (8), Fingers (8)
```

Fourth game. Tenace's third homer of the Series kept the A's in front, 1–0, until the eighth, when Bobby Tolan drove in two for the Reds. With one down in the ninth, Gonzalo Marquez got a pinch single, Tenace got a scratch hit, and Don Mincher, obtained from the Rangers in August, got a pinch hit that tied the score. Angel Mangual then got the A's third pinch hit of the inning to drive in the winning run.

```
Cincinnati..................................000 000 020—2-7-1
Oakland.....................................000 010 002—3-10-1
   Gullett, Borbon (8), Carroll (L, 9) vs. Holtzman, Blue (8), Fingers (W, 9)
```

Fifth game. The Reds were six outs from being eliminated, but they rallied when they had to. That man Tenace was at it again, hitting a three-run shot in the second that gave him a record-tying fourth Series homer and put the A's ahead until the eighth. Rose finally put the Reds back in front with a ninth-inning single, but the run barely stood up. Odom, on third base as a pinch runner in the last of the ninth, tried to score on a foul pop but was thrown out on a perfect throw by Morgan for the final out.

```
Cincinnati..................................100 110 011—5-8-0
Oakland.....................................030 100 000—4-7-2
   McGlothlin, Borbon (4), Hall (5), Carroll (7), Grimsley (W, 8), Billingham
   (9) vs. Hunter, Fingers (L, 5), Hamilton (9)
```

Sixth game. The Reds finally unloaded, building a 3–1 lead and then adding a five-run seventh inning. Ross Grimsley won in relief for the second day in a row, Johnny Bench homered, and Joe Morgan and Bobby Tolan ran wild on the basepaths.

```
Oakland.....................................000 010 000—1-7-1
Cincinnati..................................000 111 50x—8-10-0
   Blue (L), Locker (6), Hamilton (6), Horlen (7) vs. Nolan, Grimsley (W, 5),
   Borbon (6), Hall (7)
```

Seventh game. The Reds had stolen 11 bases in 15 attempts in the first six games, so Oakland manager Dick Williams replaced Tenace behind the plate with Dave Duncan, a catcher with a stronger arm, moving his home run star to first. Tenace wound up the day with two hits and two RBI's, but it was Sal Bando whose double over Tolan's head drove across the decisive run. Williams took a chance in the eighth, intentionally walking Bench to load the bases, but his gamble paid off when Fingers got Perez on a sacrifice fly and held off the Reds the rest of the way. Tenace, who had 9 RBI's out of the A's 16-run total, was named by *Sport* magazine as star of the Series.

```
Oakland.....................................100 002 000—3-6-1
Cincinnati..................................000 010 010—2-4-2
   Odom, Hunter (W, 3), Holtzman (8), Fingers (8) vs. Billingham, Borbon
   (L, 6), Carroll (6), Grimsley (7), Hall (9)
```

All-Star Game. It seemed only fitting that Hank Aaron, who hit a two-run homer in the sixth to give the Nationals a 2–1 lead, should be the hero of this, the first All-Star Game played in Atlanta. But it was not to be, for Cookie Rojas gave the lead back to the American League with a two-run pinch homer in the eighth. After the National League tied the score in the ninth, Nate Colbert scored the winning run in the tenth, drawing a walk, taking second on a sacrifice, and romping home on Joe Morgan's single.

```
American League.........................001 000 020 0—3-6-0
National League...........................000 002 001 1—4-8-0
   Palmer, Lolich (4), G. Perry (6), Wood (8), McNally (L, 10) vs. Gibson,
   Blass (3), Sutton (4), Carlton (6), Stoneman (7), McGraw (W, 9)
```

Other highlights. In postseason balloting, Allen and Bench won Most Valuable Player awards, and Gaylord Perry and Carlton took Cy Young honors. Other notable achievements included three no-hitters, by Bill Stoneman of the Expos (his second) and Burt Hooton and Pappas of the Cubs.   HERMAN WEISKOPF

BASKETBALL. Los Angeles was the city of champions this year in both profession and collegiate basketball, as the Lakers won the NBA playoffs against the New York Knickerbockers and UCLA triumphed over Florida State University in the NCAA playoff.

Collegiate Basketball

The University of California at Los Angeles, led by center Bill Walton, a sophomore with a temperament as fiery as his red hair, won its sixth consecutive National Collegiate Athletic Association basketball championship. It was the Bruins' eighth title in the past nine years under coach Johnny Wooden, a record for success unapproached by any other school or coach. UCLA clinched its championship with victories over the University of Louisville (96–77) and Florida State University (81–76) in the finals of the NCAA Tournament at the Los Angeles Sports Arena, but the Bruins' superiority had been established far earlier.

Even before the 1971–1972 schedule began, UCLA was highly rated, although all but one of the important members of the previous year's title-winning team had graduated. The Bruins replaced them with a group of talented sophomores who had been undefeated the season before as members of the UCLA freshman team. Still, the experts had underrated just how good these new young players would be. Led by Bill Walton and guided by the steadying hand of senior guard Henry Bibby, the Bruins advanced to the top spot in the rankings only a few weeks after the season began. They finished the campaign with a perfect, 30–0 record, as they outscored their opponents by an astonishing 30.3 points a game. The winning streak ran UCLA's record to 45 consecutive victories over two seasons.

Bill Walton. Walton, the 6'11" College Player of the Year, was outstanding at all phases of the game. Perhaps no area of his play better typified his precociousness than his defensive rebounding and passing to start the potent UCLA fast-break offense. Walton thoroughly dominated his rivals under the backboards and showed great agility and strength in throwing quick, long, and accurate outlet passes to start the fast break. Many experts already ranked Walton ahead of most professional pivotmen in making this play.

Walton himself remained something of an enigma. Reticent about his basketball achievements, he was nevertheless arrested shortly after the season ended as he stood in the forefront of a group of student antiwar protesters on the UCLA campus. His boyish face and short, tousled red hair gave him the look of the all-American boy, but he was often reported verbally abusing referees and being abrupt to journalists. "I realize I can't keep my whole life private," Walton said during the season. "My basketball life is open to everyone, but what I do off the court . . . is my own business. . . ."

Challengers. UCLA's most likely challenger throughout the season was Marquette University, which had a tall center of its own in Jim Chones, a junior. The two teams were not scheduled to meet in the regular season, but Marquette's

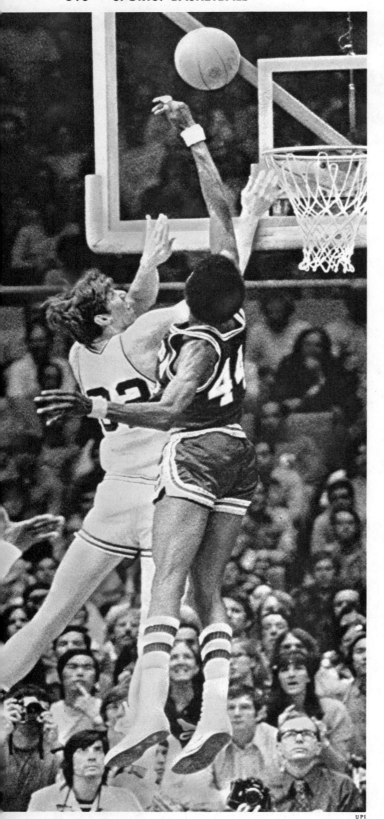

LEADING MAJOR COLLEGE SCORERS

Name	School	Points	Average
Lamar	Southwestern Louisiana	1,054	36.3
Fuqua	Oral Roberts	1,006	35.9
Collins	Illinois State	847	32.6
Robinson	West Virginia	706	29.4
Averitt	Pepperdine	693	28.9
Williamson	New Mexico State	678	27.1
Kohls	Syracuse	748	26.7
Millier	Florida	507	26.7
Taylor	Murray State	538	25.6
Martiniuk	Saint Peter's	611	25.5

undefeated record after 22 games indicated that a showdown would probably come in the NCAA tournament. It never happened. After Marquette's 22nd win, Chones quit the team to sign a $1 million professional contract with the American Basketball Association's New York Nets. Marquette was subsequently eliminated in the preliminaries of the NCAA tourney.

UCLA's other challengers were nearby Long Beach State with its All-American Ed Ratleff, the University of North Carolina and its big man, 6'9" Bob McAdoo, and the University of Pennsylvania, which had two stars in Corky Calhoun and Bob Morse. All of them fell with unexpected ease. Pennsylvania lost to North Carolina in the East Regional finals, Long Beach was defeated by UCLA in the western championships, and then North Carolina fell to unnoticed Florida State in the semifinals of the national championship tournament.

The Seminoles turned out to be the surprise team of the year and gave UCLA a tough game in the finals. Florida State, which had been on NCAA probation the past three years for recruiting violations, scored seven consecutive baskets early in the championship game to take a 21–14 lead. It was the only time all year that UCLA trailed by more than 4 points in a game. But then Walton asserted himself, and the Bruins built a safe 50–39 halftime lead and held off a spirited Florida State rally in the closing minutes of the game.

High scorers and other champions. The season's two highest scorers in major college competition came from schools which only recently began to play big-time schedules. Guard Dwight Lamar of Southwestern Louisiana, an irrepressible shooter at ranges far from the basket, led in scoring with a 36.3 average. He was followed by 5'9" Richie Fuqua, a New York City native who found his way to Tulsa, Okla., to play for the college founded by and named for the radio evangelist Oral Roberts. He scored 35.9 points per game, spurred on, no doubt, by Roberts' inspirational locker room pep talks.

The biggest scorer of them all, however, played in the small college ranks. Kentucky State's 6'8" forward Travis Grant became the first collegiate player ever to score 4,000 points, including 39 against top-ranked Eau Claire (Wis.) State in the finals of the National Association of Intercollegiate Athletics tournament. Kentucky State won that game 71–62.

MAJOR COLLEGE CONFERENCE BASKETBALL CHAMPIONS

Atlantic Coast Conference: North Carolina
Big Eight Conference: Kansas State
Big Sky Conference: Weber State
Big Ten Conference: Minnesota
Ivy League: Pennsylvania
Mid-American Conference: Ohio University
Middle Atlantic Conference: Temple
Midwestern Conference: Northern Illinois
Missouri Valley Conference: Louisville
Ohio Valley Conference: Eastern Kentucky
Pacific Coast Athletic Conference: Long Beach State
Pacific Eight Conference: UCLA
Southeastern Conference: Kentucky
Southern Conference: Davidson
Southwest Conference: SMU
West Coast Athletic Conference: San Francisco
Western Athletic Conference: Brigham Young
Yankee Conference: Rhode Island

UPI

BATTLE OF THE BOARDS. Bill Walton, UCLA's star center, is stopped by Lawrence McCray (44) of Florida State University. Walton led the Bruins to an 81–76 NCAA championship victory.

COLLEGIATE BASKETBALL COACHES' RANKINGS[1]
Compiled by United Press International

1. UCLA (30–0)[1]
2. North Carolina (26–5)
3. Pennsylvania (25–3)
4. Louisville (26–5)
5. South Carolina (24–5)
6. Long Beach State (25–4)
7. Marquette (25–4)
8. Southwestern Louisiana (25–4)
9. Brigham Young (21–5)
10. Florida State (27–6)

[1] *Records include postseason tournament games; poll taken at the conclusion of regular season play.*

Roanoke (Va.) College won the NCAA College Division Championship with an 84–72 victory over the University of Akron, and Vincennes (Ind.) Junior College won its third National Junior College Athletic Association title in seven years by defeating Ferrum (Va.) Junior College, 73–61. The University of Maryland, which like UCLA had many sophomores—including an outstanding young big man in 6'11" Tom McMillen—won New York's National Invitation Tournament, a tourney for good major college teams which failed to qualify for the NCAA championships.

B. PETER CARRY

Professional Basketball

The National Basketball Association's Los Angeles Lakers, who had the best record ever compiled by a professional basketball team, and the American Basketball Association's Indiana Pacers, who survived an unexpectedly poor season, won the championships of their leagues. Meanwhile, Congress continued to hold up legislation that would permit a merger between the two leagues.

The Lakers, who played under a new coach, Bill Sharman, set myriad records, including the most wins (69) and best percentage (.841) in NBA history. At one point in the season, Los Angeles won 33 consecutive games, the longest string of victories by a team in any professional sport. The streak ended in the year's most dramatic game when the Lakers lost, 120–104, to the 1970–1971 champion Milwaukee Bucks in a Sunday afternoon contest which was watched by a standing-room-only crowd at the Milwaukee Arena and viewed by the largest television audience ever to see a professional basketball game.

Before the season began, the Lakers appeared too old and too tired to repeat as champions in the strong Pacific Division. But Sharman's coaching revived his aging superstars, Wilt Chamberlain and Jerry West, and changed the Lakers, who in the past had been a slow-moving, pattern team, into a cohesive, fast-breaking one. The new style helped younger players Gail Goodrich and Jim McMillian blossom to stardom, but it was also daring. No longer did the Lakers wait for 7'1½" Chamberlain, the highest scorer in pro history, to lope downcourt before setting up their offense. Chamberlain instead concentrated on defense and rebounding.

At the end of the ABA's regular season, the Pacers seemed headed nowhere. One of the league's three preseason favorites along with the Utah Stars and Kentucky Colonels, Indiana became bogged down in dissension, ennui, and disorganization. Meanwhile, Utah, the defending ABA champion, won the Western Division title by a surprisingly easy 13 games over the Pacers. In the Eastern Division, Kentucky set a record for victories by an ABA team with 68, and the Colonels' first-year, 7'2" center Artis Gilmore was selected as both Rookie of the Year and the league's Most Valuable Player.

NBA playoffs. The power in the NBA playoffs was concentrated in the Western Conference, where four of the league's five best teams were contestants, including the Lakers, the Bucks, the Chicago Bulls, and the Golden State Warriors. The Bulls and Warriors were so strong, in fact, that both were considered capable of springing upsets over their powerful opponents. Thus, the Lakers, who swept Chicago in four games, and the Bucks, who triumphed by 4–1 over Golden State, were particularly impressive in their first-round victories.

WIDE WORLD

OUTREACHING teammates and opponents alike, superstar Wilt Chamberlain led the Los Angeles Lakers to their first NBA championship, in spite of a bad wrist that hampered his play.

FINAL NBA STANDINGS
Atlantic Division

Team	Won	Lost	Pct.	Games behind
Boston	56	26	.683	—
New York	48	34	.585	8
Philadelphia	30	52	.366	26
Buffalo	22	60	.268	34

Central Division

Team	Won	Lost	Pct.	Games behind
Baltimore	38	44	.463	—
Atlanta	36	46	.439	2
Cincinnati	30	52	.366	8
Cleveland	23	59	.280	15

Midwest Division

Team	Won	Lost	Pct.	Games behind
Milwaukee	63	19	.768	—
Chicago	57	25	.695	6
Phoenix	49	33	.598	14
Detroit	26	56	.317	37

Pacific Division

Team	Won	Lost	Pct.	Games behind
Los Angeles	69	13	.841	—
Golden State	51	31	.622	18
Seattle	47	35	.573	22
Houston	34	48	.415	35
Portland	18	64	.220	51

FINAL ABA STANDINGS
Eastern Division

Team	Won	Lost	Pct.	Games behind
Kentucky	68	16	.810	—
Virginia	45	39	.536	23
New York	44	40	.524	24
Floridians	36	48	.429	32
Carolina	35	49	.417	33
Pittsburgh	25	59	.298	43

Western Division

Team	Won	Lost	Pct.	Games behind
Utah	60	24	.714	—
Indiana	47	37	.560	13
Dallas	42	42	.500	18
Denver	34	50	.405	26
Memphis	26	58	.310	34

LEADING NBA SCORERS

	Points	Average
Kareem Abdul-Jabbar, Milwaukee	2,822	34.8
Nate Archibald, Cincinnati	2,145	28.2
John Havlicek, Boston	2,252	27.5
Spencer Haywood, Seattle	1,914	26.2
Gail Goodrich, Los Angeles	2,127	25.9

LEADING ABA SCORERS

	Points	Average
Charles Scott, Virginia	2,524	34.6
Rick Barry, New York	2,518	31.5
Dan Issel, Kentucky	2,538	30.6
John Brisker, Pittsburgh	1,417	28.9
Ralph Simpson, Denver	2,300	27.4

For practical purposes, the NBA title was settled in the Western finals, which Los Angeles won over Milwaukee, 4–2. The Bucks' Kareem Abdul-Jabbar, the NBA's highest scorer and Most Valuable Player, outdueled Chamberlain, but the Lakers received excellent performances from Goodrich and McMillian. McMillian, who earlier in the year had supplanted retired superstar Elgin Baylor at forward for Los Angeles, scored 42 points in one game, the highest individual total of the series. Still, the 6'5" McMillian felt he was merely an average player on an extraordinary team. "I can't really tell how I fit into this team," he said. "I'm just the little, fat dude wearing No. 5."

After the victory over Milwaukee, the Lakers' final series against the New York Knickerbockers, who had upset the Boston Celtics to win the Eastern Conference championship, was a mere formality. Los Angeles won, 4–1, with Chamberlain dominating, although he played the last game and a half with a chip fracture in his right wrist. The title ended a decade of futility for the Lakers, who had been to the finals seven times in the previous 11 years and had never won.

ABA playoffs. Indiana, which had barely edged out the weak Denver Rockets in the opening playoff round, upset Utah in the Western Division finals, four games to three. The Pacers and Stars continued the closest rivalry in the pros during the series. In 44 games, which were played over three seasons, each team won 22, and the Pacers scored only 7 more points (out of a two-team total of nearly 10,-000) than Utah over that span. In the playoff for the Western championship, Indiana outscored Utah by one basket over seven games and took the title by winning a dramatic seventh game on the Stars' home floor. In the Eastern Division, the New York Nets, another disappointing team during the regular season, pulled off a startling upset of Kentucky in the opening round, with rookie guard John Roche as the Nets' hero. New York beat Virginia for the Eastern Conference championship, but the Nets' magic ended against Indiana in the finals. Led by underrated guard Freddie Lewis, the Pacers took the ABA championship easily, by a score of 4–2. It was the second title captured by Indiana in three years.

Off-court events. The pros were in chaos off the court, and the bright market research projections of two years ago, which foresaw a boom for basketball in the 1970's, had to be shelved largely because the NBA and ABA still could not hammer out a merger. The two leagues had agreed on a merger in May 1971, but to complete the deal they needed an antitrust waiver from Congress. There they were opposed by the well-organized NBA Players' Association, which objected to the waiver because it felt a merger in basketball, like the 1966 pro football merger, would dissipate the salary gains made during the five years of interleague competition for personnel. The players had strong allies in the Senate, particularly Sam Ervin, Jr. (D, N.C.), before whose subcommittee the merger bill was reviewed.

The lack of a merger helped to keep rookies' bonuses and veterans' salaries at record high levels. It also prompted continued jumping of athletes between leagues. Virginia's Charlie Scott and Carolina's Jim McDaniels, two young ABA stars, left to sign more lucrative contracts with Phoenix and Seattle, respectively, in the NBA. The signing of college talent also continued, as both leagues, reacting to pressure from the courts, set up procedures for drafting college players even before their eligibility to play for their schools had expired. The Nets profited most by this system by adding junior All-Americans Jim Chones of Marquette and Brian Taylor of Princeton to their roster. B. PETER CARRY

BOWLING. PBA U.S. Open. Don Johnson of Akron, Ohio, won the $10,000 top prize in the finals of the BPAA U.S. Open, beating George Pappas of Charlotte, N.C., 233–224. Detroit's Bobby Williams, who finished fourth behind

Johnny Petraglia of Brooklyn, N.Y., became the first black bowler to appear on national television since 1962. The tournament was broadcast from Madison Square Garden in New York City on January 8.

Tournament of Champions. Mike Durbin of Chagrin Falls, Ohio, who a year earlier had quit the PBA full-time tour, came roaring out of retirement to win the $25,000 top prize in the $125,000 Firestone Tournament of Champions in Akron, Ohio. In the final match on April 1, Durbin soundly whipped Tim Harahan of Canoga Park, Calif., 258–187.

Other top PBA events. A week after his U.S. Open title, Don Johnson, selected as the 1971 Bowler of the Year, took his second PBA win by defeating Johnny Petraglia, 218–213, in the $50,000 Denver Open. In other top tournaments, part-time tour competitor Bill Beach of Sharon, Pa., won the $60,000 Don Carter Classic to take his first PBA title ever. Gus Lampo of Endicott, N.Y., also notched his first PBA victory in the $77,777 Showboat Invitational in January and then went on to win the Mercury Cougar Open two weeks later, picking up a $10,000 check and a new car. Nelson Burton, Jr., who by mid-September headed the list of the top 20 money winners with earnings of $52,150, won three big championships: the $75,000 Ebonite Open, the $80,000 Miller High Life Open, and the $42,000 Waukegan (Ill.) Open. Larry Laub set a PBA national television scoring record as he won the $50,000 King Louie Open with an aggregate score of 1,021 pins. Texan Butch Gearhart trounced Roy Buckley in the finals of the $80,000 Winston-Salem Classic, 216–169. Earl Anthony, the 34-year-old left hander from Tacoma, took both the Portland (Ore.) Open and the $45,000 Japan Starlanes Open. While on leave from the U.S. Air Force, Sergeant Paul Colwell took two PBA titles in three weeks—the Tucson Open and the Houston Sertoma Open. Johnny Petraglia broke a year-long victory drought on September 11, when he won the $50,000 Bellows-Valvair Open.

ABC championship. Bill Beach defeated Jim Godman of Lorain, Ohio, 889–876 and 919–914, to capture the American Bowling Congress Masters tournament in Long Beach, Calif. In the Classic Division, Teata Semiz won both the all-events and the singles titles.

Women's bowling. The top prize at the Woman's International Bowling Congress tournament was won by Dotty Fothergill of North Attleboro, Mass. She bested Maureen Harris of Madison, Wis., 890–841, in the Queens tournament.

In Denver, little-known Lorrie Koch of Carpentersville, Ill., took the $4,000 top prize in the distaff version of the U.S. Open in late May. The first amateur ever to win this major title, she bested former Bowler of the Year Mary Baker of Central Islip, N.Y.

Patty Costello emerged on top in the Professional Women's Bowling Association by winning the Japan Starlanes Classic in Tucson, Ariz., the PWBA National Championships, and the El Cajon (Calif.) Open. Dotty Fothergill won the Cavalcade of Stars in Wichita, Kan., and Rita Justice captured the Japan Gold Cup in Tokyo.

JOSEPH MARCUS

BOXING. Joe Frazier, fighting just often enough this year to sustain his status as world heavyweight champion, successfully defended his title twice against nonentities. But the man who lost his championship to Frazier, Muhammad Ali, was much busier. Ali, biding his time until his rematch with Frazier, fought five times against some of the division's leading competitors and was primarily responsible for keeping boxing interest alive, at least in the United States. The name of Bob Foster, the world light-heavyweight champion, also kept cropping up in the news media. Foster, a skinny six-footer, defended his 175-pound championship three times, all by the knockout route.

Frazier first took on a former collegian from Southern Methodist University, Terry Daniels, in New Orleans on January 15. A crowd of 7,000 in Rivergate Convention Hall paid about $200,000 to watch Frazier knock Daniels to the floor four times before the referee stopped the slaughter after one minute and 47 seconds of the fourth round. Frazier got about $250,000 for his brief excursion. Daniels won the plaudits of the crowd for his courage and was paid about $25,000 for his foolhardy venture. Daniels said he probably would go back to college and get his degree in government.

Frazier then took on another virtual unknown, Ron Stander, a local bully boy from Council Bluffs, Iowa, on May 25 in Omaha, Neb. Again the champion picked up nearly $250,000 for a short night's work. Frazier battered Stander into a bloody pulp (17 stitches had to be taken to close the facial wounds), and the action mercifully was halted by referee Zack Clayton, acting under a physician's orders, before the bell rang for the fifth round. Stander never went down from Frazier's punches. He proved his courage but also demonstrated why he was a 10–1 betting underdog. And he proved that he did not deserve a title bout. (He was ranked 31st among heavyweights by *Boxing Illustrated*.) Stander's popularity attracted to the Omaha Civic Auditorium a crowd of 9,863 that produced about $240,000 in revenue. For losing his second fight against 23 victories and a draw Stander earned a total of about $45,000.

After his 25th knockout in 29 fights, Frazier announced that he was returning to his plantation home near Beaufort, S.C., his birthplace. He said he would put the title "on vacation" until he is assured $3.5 million to oppose Ali in the title rematch.

Meanwhile, Ali embarked upon his campaign to keep his name before the public with an international tour that found him fighting in four countries in six months.

On April 1, Ali beat Mac Foster in 15 rounds in Tokyo before a near-capacity crowd in the 14,500-seat Hall of Martial Arts. After the bout Ali said, "I gave up trying to knock him out although I had predicted I would finish him in the fifth round. I couldn't knock him down because he was too great. Anyone who could last 15 rounds with me must be great." Foster had won 28 of 29 fights by knockouts—all within eight rounds.

George Chuvalo, the shopworn Canadian, was Ali's next victim, losing in 12 rounds in Vancouver, British Columbia, on May 1. Then it was Jerry Quarry's turn as part of a Quarry Brothers doubleheader in June.

Ali, fighting his way into condition with each succeeding bout, weighed 216½ for the top ranked Jerry Quarry, and the result was proof of Ali's fine physical shape. He rocked Quarry repeatedly with lefts and rights to the face, and the bout was halted 19 seconds into the seventh round of the scheduled 12-round match. A Las Vegas Convention Center crowd of 6,549 paid a state record gate of $349,800 to see the doubleheader that Ali dubbed "The Soul Brothers vs. the Quarry Brothers."

The other half of the Soul Brothers was Bob Foster. The lithe, hard-hitting light-heavyweight champion ended Mike Quarry's championship hopes with a fourth-round knockout. Foster thus defended his title successfully for the tenth time and ended Mike's 36-bout winning streak. Ali collected about $500,000 for his share of the doubleheader, which was seen by millions of fans on closed circuit television. Foster earned $80,000, and Jerry Quarry got $200,000 in losing for the sixth time in 49 fights.

Ali and Foster went their separate ways then, but both kept on winning. Ali traveled to Dublin in July to fight Al (Blue) Lewis, one of the division's tougher men. In Ireland's first major fight in nearly four decades, Ali had to go 11 hard rounds before referee Lew Eskin stopped the fight at one minute 15 seconds of the round.

Floyd Patterson, the only two-time world heavyweight titleholder, was Ali's next opponent. The two met in Madison Square Garden in September, and Ali was awarded a seventh-round knockout after the fight was stopped by a ring physician because of a severe cut over Patterson's left eye. The verdict completed Ali's 38th victory, including 30 knockouts, against one defeat—by Frazier in March 1971. Ali was guaranteed $250,000 against 35 percent of the gate, which came to $512,361 paid by a crowd of 17,378 fans. Patterson was guaranteed $100,000 or 20 percent.

Before meeting Mike Quarry in Las Vegas, Foster had established his sole claim as the champion in Miami Beach on April 7, when he stopped Vicente Rondon of Venezuela at 2:55 of the second round in a scheduled 15-round bout. Rondon had been recognized by the World Boxing Association after that body had lifted the title from Foster for his alleged failure to defend the title within the prescribed six-month period. Foster's victory restored him to the good graces of the WBA. The New York State Athletic Commission, which is generally recognized as the ultimate body, and most other groups had not followed the WBA in its decision to lift Foster's title.

Foster made his third title defense of the year a successful one by knocking out Chris Finnegan of Britain in London on September 26. The end came in the 14th round of the scheduled 15. Foster ended the bout after 55 seconds of the 14th to defend his title for the 11th time since winning it by a fourth-round knockout of the late Dick Tiger of Nigeria in New York in 1968. It was Foster's 54th professional fight and the 33-year-old has won all but five; all his losses were to heavyweights.

Carlos Monzon of Argentina successfully defended his title in the middleweight division three times. He stopped Denny Moyer of Portland, Ore., in Rome in March; Jean-Claude Bouttier of France, at Colombes, a suburb of Paris, in June; and Tom Bogs of Denmark at Copenhagen, August 19. The defeat of Bogs was Monzon's fifth defense of the 160-pound championship he had won from Nino Benvenuti of Italy in 1970 and his 11th knockout in succession.

José Napoles of Mexico, the classy boxing welterweight champion, defended twice, knocking out Ralph Charles of London at Wembley in March and knocking out Adolph Pruitt of St. Louis in the second round at Monterrey, Mexico, in June.

The most exciting new face in the sport was a tough, furious-punching Panamanian, Roberto Duran. On June 26 in the Garden the youngster knocked out Ken Buchanan of Scotland in 13 rounds to win the world lightweight (135-pound) championship. Duran was one of four Panamanians to win world recognition. The others were Enrique Pinder, bantamweight (118-pound) champion; Ernesto Mareel, featherweight (126-pound) champion; and Alfonso Frazer, junior welterweight (140-pound) champion.

DEANE MCGOWEN

CRICKET. For the first time in some years, cricket was left more or less to itself, and the game benefited accordingly. South Africa's tour to Australia, planned for the winter of 1971–1972, was called off by Australia in September 1971 to avoid demonstrations like those that had disrupted the South African Springbok rugby union tour the previous June. Thus, South Africa, still probably the strongest side in the world, has had no chance to prove its superiority since overwhelming Australia in 1969–1970. It seems that unless there is a change in government policy, South Africa's only hope of engaging in international competition depends on whether Australia and New Zealand are prepared to continue playing on South African soil.

Australia. After playing 12 Test Matches without a victory, Australia showed real signs of a revival by holding England, in England, to a two-all draw. Although this meant that England retained the Ashes, the mythical trophy

which means so much to cricket fans in both countries, it was generally agreed by the end of the series that Australia had the better side, at any rate on good pitches. Controversy raged over the pitch for the Fourth Test Match at Leeds, which the Australians felt had been prepared especially to suit England's spinners. (It did.) This was fiercely denied by the local authorities, who claimed that the turf had been stricken with fusarium, a fungous disease which killed the grass.

In the face of some criticism, Australia's selectors had chosen a young side, leaving out three old campaigners—Bill Lawry, Ian Redpath, and Graham McKenzie—who many thought were worth a place. But the Australians now have the makings of a top-notch side for some years to come. Greg Chappell, younger brother of the Australian captain, Ian, is among the two or three best batsmen in the world, and in Dennis Lillee the team has unearthed a genuinely fast bowler. Lillee's 31 wickets in this year's Test Matches were a record for an Australian bowler in England.

England. The English team, led for the past three years by Ray Illingworth, an unbending Yorkshireman, is now disbanding. Despite a defeat by India in 1971, it has had a successful record, but its success was based more on attrition than attack. For the tour to India and Pakistan in 1972–1973, the team selectors turned to new faces, in certain cases because leading players chose not to make the trip. The fact that Illingworth, John Snow, and Geoffrey Boycott were among the missing caused resentment among the Indians and Pakistanis, who felt that their own high standards in recent years warranted the visit of a full English side.

West Indies. The West Indians are also in the throes of rebuilding. Gary Sobers, perhaps the greatest all-around cricketer the sport has known, had an operation on his knee which curtailed his mobility, and there is no certainty of his being reappointed captain of the West Indian team when it receives the Australian side at the beginning of 1973. The team has been searching, so far unsuccessfully, for fast bowlers. In Clive Lloyd the West Indians already possess one of the world's most dangerous batsmen, and Alvin Kallicharran shows equal promise. Both are left-handers, and like Rohan Kanhai, another fine batsman, they come from Guyana, which has now superceded Barbados as the main breeding ground of precocious West Indian talent.

Team rankings. To place the main cricketing countries in an order of merit is not easy; between them all there is little to choose. Even New Zealand was able to hold the West Indies to a draw in a five-match series early in 1972, and no side would go to India or Pakistan confident of victory. New Zealand has a defensive attitude, born of long years of defeat, which now makes the team hard to beat. India's particular strength is in spin bowling, Pakistan's in attractive batting. In 1974 or 1975, if plans for a World Cup of cricket materialize, it should be possible to draw up a valid ranking. The first World Cup tournament is to be held in England, with each of the major cricketing countries then hosting the championship series in turn.

Trends. There is a growing demand for one-day cricket, and with it an increasing spread of sponsorship, much of it by tobacco firms whose advertising scope is limited. English cricket benefited to the tune of nearly £250,000 in 1972 from direct sponsorship, with players able to augment their wages considerably with the prize money they won. Successful cricketers are no longer the paupers of world sport. In South Africa and Australia, one-day competitions attract large crowds, and between England and Australia there will always be a one-day series to follow the main series of five-day matches, as there was this year. In England the most certain sellout of the season is the Gillette Cup final, which attracts 30,000 people to Lord's and could fill

a stadium twice that size. Lancashire won the cup in 1972 for the third successive year.

This growing wealth has attracted to England, just for the summer, a majority of the best overseas players to play for county sides. There are no fewer than 70 of them currently registered, with only Yorkshire holding out against signing anyone not born within the county.

JOHN WOODCOCK

FOOTBALL. Once again the differences between collegiate and professional football were apparent. College competition continued to be dominated by a few powerhouses, while the pros developed a more balanced league with vigorous trading and instituted rules changes to make the game more attractive to fans.

Nothing confirmed the balance of the pros better than the rise of the Miami Dolphins and the collapse of the Baltimore Colts in the fall 1972 season. While the Dolphins, a young team that until two years ago had been a league doormat, inched closer and closer to a division championship, the Colts fell apart, fired their head coach, and went for youth to salvage the year. Even in collegiate ranks a

few giants were toppled, as Nebraska was beaten by UCLA and tied by Iowa State, while Michigan State upset previously unbeaten Ohio State.

Collegiate Football

The 1971 football season starred the running back, rather than the passer, with the Wishbone T the favorite formation. Oklahoma, Michigan, Texas, Colorado, Penn State, Cornell, and Michigan State were the outstanding running teams.

In overall performance, the University of Nebraska varsity outshone all other teams by defeating its 12 opponents during the season and then crushing a proud and supposedly mighty Alabama in the Orange Bowl, 38–6, to be crowned the national champions.

No. 1 Nebraska. There was complete unanimity in ranking the 1971 Nebraska team at the top from the very first weekly poll after the start of the season in September. Week after week throughout the campaign, Nebraska stayed at the top in both the AP and UPI polls, with Notre Dame (the preseason choice for the No. 1 spot by a narrow margin), Texas, Michigan, Oklahoma, and Alabama in close contention.

UPSET BY UCLA. Brad Lyman of the Bruins outruns Cornhusker Joe Blahak to catch a 46-yard pass thrown by quarterback Mark Harmon. The touchdown bomb helped the underdog Uclans topple the mighty Nebraska team from the No. 1 spot in the national rankings.

WIDE WORLD

On November 25, Thanksgiving Day, the unbeaten Cornhuskers and the unbeaten Oklahoma Sooners met in what was labeled the game of the decade. Nebraska had the year's best defensive force, led by Larry Jacobson, Rich Glover, and Willie Harper; and Oklahoma's strong offensive team had compiled awesome running and scoring figures, attacking from the Wishbone T formation with quarterback Jack Mildren, the "triple option wizard," and the devastatingly fast Greg Pruitt. The game, watched by a television audience said to be the largest on record for a college football game (it was beamed by satellite to the Far East and Europe), lived up to its potential in excitement. Nebraska scored early, as Johnny Rodgers ran a breathtaking 72 yards with one of his typically explosive punt returns. But the Cornhuskers found themselves trailing, 14–17, for the first time during the season, when Mildren threw a 24-yard touchdown pass for Oklahoma five seconds before the half ended. After going ahead, the Cornhuskers fell behind again on another Mildren touchdown pass. Then in the closing minutes, Jerry Tagge, who completed 62 percent of his passes for the season, piloted the Cornhuskers 74 yards for the winning touchdown 98 seconds before the end of the game. The final score was 35–31.

Two days later, November 27, Paul ("Bear") Bryant's Alabama powerhouse, which had surprised Southern California at the start of the season and been invincible week after week, faced unbeaten Auburn, led by Heisman Trophy winner Pat Sullivan, the year's most famous quarterback. Alabama crushed Auburn, 31–7, to win the Southeastern Conference championship.

The bowl games. The climax of the season was also ballyhooed to be the greatest college football game ever—No. 1 Nebraska against No. 2 Alabama in the Orange Bowl. Alabama had strength in its use of the Wishbone T and in Johnny Musso, one of the most powerful ball carriers in a year of exceptional running backs. However, the roof caved in early, and Bear Bryant got the most horrendous licking of his career. Two fumbles and an interference penalty set up three Nebraska touchdowns in the first 18 minutes, and Rodgers sped 77 yards on a punt return for a fourth. It was 28–0 at halftime, with Alabama hopelessly beaten.

The 38–6 triumph sealed the national championship for the Cornhuskers, their second straight title. Devaney's satisfaction was all the greater because his Nebraska teams of 1965 and 1966 had lost to Bryant's Alabamans in the Orange and Sugar bowls, respectively. It was Nebraska's 13th victory of the 1971 season, its 23rd consecutive victory, and its 32nd game without a loss over a three-year span.

Other important bowl games did occur, although they were submerged in the excitement of the Orange Bowl match. Michigan had an excellent season, winning all 11 of its games and scoring 409 points, to become the Big Ten champion and to establish a claim to national honors in the Rose Bowl. But, just as it did to a seemingly invincible Ohio State team in 1971, Stanford pulled a win out of the hat when Rod Garcia scored a field goal with 12 seconds left. The final score was 13–12.

Oklahoma proved much too strong for Auburn in the Sugar Bowl at New Orleans, winning 40–22. This victory moved the Sooners into second place ahead of Alabama in the postbowl AP ranking. Colorado, a rank outsider in the preseason appraisals, beat Louisiana State and Ohio State during the season and went on to defeat Houston in the Astro-Bluebonnet Bowl in Houston, 29–17. This bowl win promoted Colorado from seventh place in the early December poll to third place in the postbowl lists, making this the first time since the AP polls were started in 1936 that three teams from the same conference, the Big Eight in this instance, swept the top places in the rankings.

Alabama finished No. 4 and Penn State No. 5. Penn State's 15-game winning streak had been ended by Tennessee, 33–11, in its final regular season game. However, Penn State earned its AP fifth place rating after defeating Texas, the Southwest Conference champion, in the Cotton Bowl, 30–6, and won the Lambert Trophy for the eighth time as the best team in the East.

Postbowl rankings. The Football Writers Association of America, like the AP, picked Nebraska as champion in a poll taken after the bowl games, awarding the Cornhuskers the Grantland Rice Trophy. The FWAA also ranked Oklahoma and Colorado in order behind Nebraska. But it chose Penn State at No. 4 ahead of Alabama. The National Football Foundation and Hall of Fame awarded the MacArthur Bowl to Nebraska, for the first time deferring its vote until after the bowl games because of the Orange Bowl match between the No. 1 and No. 2 teams.

In the final AP ranking, Michigan, which had been fourth in the December poll, placed sixth, behind Penn State. It was followed by Georgia, which lost only to Auburn and which defeated North Carolina, the Atlantic Coast champion, in the Gator Bowl at Jacksonville, Fla., 7–3. Arizona State, the Western Athletic champion, beat Florida State in the first Fiesta Bowl game at Tempe, Ariz., 45–36, and was ranked eighth. Tennessee, a 14–13 victor over Arkansas in the Liberty Bowl at Memphis, was ninth and Stanford tenth. Following the first ten in order were LSU (33–15 winner over Iowa State in the Sun Bowl at El Paso), Auburn, Notre Dame (which lost to Southern California and LSU), Toledo (which won its 35th game in a row by defeating Richmond in the Tangerine Bowl at Orlando, Fla.), Mississippi (45–18 winner over Georgia Tech in the Peach Bowl at Atlanta), Arkansas, Houston, Texas, Washington, and, finally, Southern California.

Awards. Bob Devaney was named "top coach in the universe" in a resolution adopted by the Nebraska legislature and was voted coach of the year by the FWAA, with Bryant second. Devaney became head coach at Nebraska in 1962; in 1963 the Cornhuskers won the conference title for the first time since 1940; in 1965 they won every game on their schedule for the first time since 1915; and in 1966 they won their fourth Big Eight title in a row. The coaches themselves, in a poll taken before the bowl games, picked Bryant for the honor.

The Heisman Trophy was awarded to Pat Sullivan, Auburn's brilliant quarterback. Sullivan's closest rival for the award was the top running back of the season, Ed Marinaro of Cornell. Final statistics showed Marinaro to be the leading rusher of the year, averaging 209 yards a game; the leading scorer, averaging 16.4 points a game; and the No. 1 all-purpose runner, averaging 214.7 yards a game. His three-season career total in rushing, a record-breaking 4,715 yards, was 848 more than the previous total. Marinaro's skill led his team to a share of the Ivy League championship with Dartmouth, the first time the Big Red finished at the top since the league was formally organized in 1956.

Other Heisman Trophy contenders were Greg Pruitt of Oklahoma, Johnny Musso of Alabama, Lydell Mitchell of Penn State, Jack Mildren of Oklahoma, Jerry Tagge of Nebraska, Chuck Ealey of Toledo, Walt Patulski of Notre Dame, Eric Allen of Michigan State, Bill Taylor of Michigan, Bob Moore of Oregon, Terry Beasley of Auburn, and Sonny Sixkiller of Washington. All were backs except Patulski, a defensive end, and Beasley, a wide receiver.

Chosen unanimously by both the AP and UPI for the All America first team offense were Sullivan, Marinaro, and Beasley and guards Royce Smith of Georgia and Reggie McKenzie of Michigan. Other picks for the first team offense were tackles John Vella of Southern California and Jerry Sisemore of Texas A & M, ends Johnny Rodgers of Nebraska and Doug Kingsriter of Minnesota, and center Tom DeLeone of Ohio State. Musso, Mitchell, and Moore were other choices for offense.

The UPI and AP first choices on defense were Patulski and back Clarence Ellis of Notre Dame, back Bobby Majors

WHAT MAKES THOMAS RUN? Sulky, silent Duane Thomas lets his rushing skills speak for themselves. Here, he is set upon by Miami tacklers after another of the short bursts that helped the Cowboys down the Dolphins, 24–3, in the Super Bowl at New Orleans.

of Tennessee, tackles Jacobson of Nebraska and Mel Long of Toledo, middle guards Tony Casanova of LSU and Glover of Nebraska, and linebacker Jeff Siemon of Stanford. Also honored on the defensive team were tackles Sherman White of California and Herb Orvis of Colorado, end Willie Harper of Nebraska, backs Tom Darden of Michigan and Dick Harris of South Carolina, and linebackers Willie Hall of Southern California, Mike Taylor of Michigan, Jackie Walker of Tennessee, and Dave Chaney of San Jose State.

Hall of Fame. Voted into the College Hall of Fame in 1972 by the National Football Foundation and Hall of Fame were Angelo Bertelli of Notre Dame and Bruce Smith of Minnesota (both former Heisman Trophy winners), Bob Fenimore of Oklahoma A & M, Bowden Wyatt of Tennessee, Robert ("Bones") Hamilton of Stanford, Mort Kaer of Southern California, Bill Morton of Dartmouth, Charley O'Rourke of Boston College, Malcolm Aldrich of Yale, and Joe Stydahar of West Virginia. Pioneer players (prior to 1920) voted in were Percy Wendell of Harvard, Ellery C. Huntington, Jr., of Colgate, John O'Hearn of Cornell, Everett Strupper of Georgia Tech, Bart Macomber of Illinois, Ray Eichenlaub of Notre Dame, Henderson Van Surdam of Wesleyan, John Wesley Beckett of Oregon, Douglas Bomeisler of Yale, and Bob Butler of Wisconsin. Ernest R. Godfrey, of Wittenberg and Ohio State, was elected as a pioneer coach. Lawrence ("Buck") Shaw, coach at California, the Air Force Academy, Santa Clara, and other schools, was also honored.

Rule changes. The National Collegiate Athletic Association, meeting in Florida in January 1972, adopted a resolution making freshmen at major colleges eligible for varsity competition in football and basketball starting in 1972. In 1971 small colleges had been given permission to use freshmen on varsity football and basketball teams. Most of the major conferences and Notre Dame, a leading "independent" football power, supported the change.

FINAL COLLEGIATE FOOTBALL STANDINGS

National: Nebraska
Eastern (Lambert Trophy): Penn State
Eastern (Lambert Cup): Delaware
Eastern (Lambert Bowl): Alfred
Ivy League: Dartmouth, Cornell (tie)
Big Ten: Michigan
Yankee Conference: Connecticut, Massachusetts (tie)
Southeastern Conference: Alabama
Atlantic Coast Conference: North Carolina
Southern Conference: Richmond
Mid-American Conference: Toledo
Big Eight: Nebraska
Missouri Valley: Memphis
Pacific Eight: Stanford
Ohio Valley: Western Kentucky
Southwest Conference: Texas
Big Sky: Idaho
Pacific Coast AA: Long Beach State
Western Athletic: Arizona State

The football rules committee of the NCAA adopted 24 rule changes, including one which makes an untouched kickoff going into the end zone a dead ball. Heretofore, a member of the kicking team could fall on a loose ball in the end zone for a touchdown. Another change provides that "when a player is obviously injured" an official timeout not charged to either team may be called; the injured player must be removed for at least one play. A third change makes the wearing of a mouthpiece mandatory starting in 1973.

Obituary. Eddie Kaw, All America halfback on Gil Dobie's undefeated and untied Cornell teams of 1921 and 1922 and the first Cornellian to be voted into the College Hall of Fame, died in December 1971 at Walnut Creek, Calif.   ALLISON DANZIG

Professional Football

Club owners of the National Football League introduced several changes in the game this year, prompted by the continuing improvement in team defenses in recent years. In 1969 the scoring average in the NFL was 42 points a game; in 1971 it was 38. There were 75 fewer touchdowns and 100 fewer touchdown passes in 1971 than in 1969. Thus, in the off-season the club owners attempted to restore the delicate balance between offense and defense and open up the game.

Hash marks. The inbounds markers, known as hash marks, break up the gridiron into 1-yard intervals between the yard stripes. In the past the hash marks were 20 yards in from each sideline, but a new rule moved them to 23½ yards from each sideline, which gave the offense 3½ more yards on each side in which to maneuver, placing a heavier burden on the defense.

The new rule forced changes in defensive concepts. As Mark Duncan, the head of NFL officials, observed, "The defense considered the sideline as an extra man." With a wider area near the sidelines, the defense had new problems.

The tight end—cracking the zone defense. An important change in offensive philosophy concerned the tight end. Previously, his chief concern was blocking, and he seldom was used to catch a long pass. In his new role he was used more often as a deep receiver and thus had to be faster and more agile.

For several years, zone defenses had cut down on the spectacular passing game the spectators seemed to enjoy. In a zone defense the defensive backs and linebackers have zones of responsibility and cover potential pass receivers only in their zones. The alternative is man-to-man coverage. Most teams use both defenses in varying degrees.

The best way to attack a zone is to send potential receivers to the "seams"—the border lines where one defender's responsibility ends and another's begins. Supposedly, long passes are all but impossible to complete against a zone.

In man-to-man situations, double-teaming—putting two defenders on one receiver—also hurts passing attacks. In some cases, both wide receivers (flanker and split end) are double-teamed, leaving single coverage on the other potential receivers, including the tight end. This works when the tight end is a heavier man with little downfield speed.

The new tight ends have the speed. For example, the New York Jets dropped Pete Lammons (6′ 3″, 227 pounds), their tight end for six years, and replaced him with Richard Caster (6′ 5″, 215 pounds), a rookie wide receiver in 1971. Lammons, an excellent blocker, was not fast. Caster once ran the 100-yard dash in 9.5 seconds.

In their second game of the season, the Jets played the Baltimore Colts, whose zone defense was considered the most effective in the game. The Jets won, 44–34, as Joe Namath passed for six touchdowns (one short of the NFL record) and 496 yards (the third highest total in history). Caster caught six passes for 204 yards, including touchdown plays of 80, 79, and 10 yards. Caster's two long touchdowns came on long passes against a zone.

The Colts quarterback was 39-year-old Johnny Unitas, perhaps the finest ever in pro football. He was Namath's boyhood idol (Namath's schoolboy friends called him Joey U.). Ironically, Unitas, who passed for 376 yards against the Jets' defense and was generally having one of his better seasons, was benched in midseason when the floundering Colts fired Coach Don McCafferty, replaced him with John Sandusky, and gave young quarterback Marty Domres the chance to take over.

Attendance. Pro football is more popular than ever. In 1971 regular-season attendance surpassed 10 million for the first time, with a record average attendance of 55,363 per game. The 78 preseason games in 1972 averaged a record 52,951 spectators. (Once, these exhibitions drew 7,000 or 8,000 a game.) The three major networks paid $40 million to televise 1972 games.

One reason for pro football's popularity was balanced competition. Every week, as many as five or six favorites were beaten. After the first nine games of the season, only one team (the Miami Dolphins) was undefeated.

Super Bowl. The Dolphins had been a surprise team in 1971. In the first round of the postseason playoffs, they defeated the Kansas City Chiefs, 27–24, on Garo Yepremian's 37-yard field goal. It came after 22 minutes and 40 seconds of sudden-death overtime in football's longest game ever. The Dolphins went on to win the American Conference championship by defeating the Baltimore Colts, 21–0, while the Dallas Cowboys beat the San Francisco Forty-niners, 14–3, to win the National Conference. In the Super Bowl at New Orleans (January 16, 1972), the Cowboys beat the Dolphins, 24–3, as Roger Staubach, voted the game's most valuable player, passed for two touchdowns and Duane Thomas ran for 95 yards in 19 carries. Dallas set a Super Bowl record of 252 yards gained running.

The scrambling quarterback. Staubach was absent when the Cowboys opened the 1972 season. He liked to run with the ball, which had helped him win the starting quarterback's job in 1971 from Craig Morton, a classic drop-back passer who ran only in desperation. In his first preseason game this year, however, Staubach ran himself into a concussion. In his next exhibition, his six scrambles (unplanned runs) won the game. In his third exhibition, while scrambling, he collided with linebacker Marlin McKeever of the Los Angeles Rams and suffered a separation of the right shoulder (he passed right-handed). When the season began, Morton was the quarterback, and Staubach, his shoulder in a harness, watched from the sidelines.

Trades. Duane Thomas, in two years with Dallas, had become perhaps football's most feared runner. He had also become an enigma and, for management, a problem. In 1971, angry because the Cowboys would not renegotiate his three-year contract, he had refused to report to training camp. He was traded to the New England Patriots, left their camp, returned to Dallas, rejoined the Cowboys after the start of the season, and regained a starting berth. He had refused to talk with teammates or the media. After the season, he had pleaded guilty in Greenville, Texas, to a charge of marijuana possession. In August, the Cowboys traded him to the San Diego Chargers.

In addition to Thomas, the Chargers acquired Tim Rossovich from the Philadelphia Eagles, and Dave Costa from the Denver Broncos. Rossovich was a hippie middle linebacker who ate glass for laughs. Costa was a ten-year defensive tackle and former juvenile delinquent who rebelled when John Ralston, the new Denver coach, outlawed beer at training camp. "Actually," said one observer, "Duane Thomas, Tim Rossovich, and Dave Costa are just like the boy next door, providing the boy next door is Bobby Fischer or Harpo Marx."

Thomas kept reporting to the Chargers and walking out. Finally he stayed, and at midseason he was activated. As for Rossovich, he suffered a torn knee ligament in an exhibition game and was lost for the season. But the Chargers had a fascinating year because their general manager and coach, Harland ("Swede") Svare, had made 21 off-season trades, one more than the record set the year before by George Allen of the Washington Redskins.

There were other major trades, notably for quarterbacks. The Minnesota Vikings, who in 1967 had sent Fran Tarkenton to the New York Giants, got him back, establishing themselves as Super Bowl favorites until slowed by an aging

defense. The Vikings cut loose two quarterbacks, sending Norm Snead to the Giants in the Tarkenton deal and, later, Gary Cuozzo to the St. Louis Cardinals.

Baltimore shipped Earl Morrall to Miami, where he later replaced the injured Bob Griese, then obtained Marty Domres from San Diego to back up Unitas. The Chicago Bears, who for years had had quarterback problems, sent Jack Concannon, one of their two best, to Dallas after Staubach was hurt.

Franchise exchange. The most spectacular trade was created by Carroll Rosenbloom, the 65-year-old owner of the Baltimore Colts. He traded his franchise for that of the Los Angeles Rams. Rosenbloom had become disenchanted with Baltimore. He had feuded with the city over shortcomings at Municipal Stadium, with the Baltimore Orioles baseball team (the stadium's prime tenant), and with the Baltimore public, which did not turn out for preseason games.

On July 13 he swapped franchises with Robert J. Irsay, the principal owner of the Rams. In exchanges of property with no cash involved, there is no capital gains tax, so Rosenbloom got rid of the Colts at no cost. (Had he sold them, he would have had to pay $4.4 million in capital gains taxes.) Irsay, a Chicago businessman, had just purchased the Rams for $19 million, the highest price for a team in any sport.

New coaches. Four teams started the season with new coaches. Two coaches—Lou Saban of the Buffalo Bills and Abe Gibron of the Chicago Bears—had professional backgrounds. The other two—Bill Peterson of the Houston Oilers and John Ralston of the Denver Broncos—came from the college ranks.

Peterson was one of the first college coaches to use a pro offense. After 11 years as head coach at Florida State, he signed a five-year contract in 1971 as head coach at Rice. He broke the contract to join the Oilers for $75,000 a year for 15 years. Peterson succeeded Ed Hughes, fired after one year on the job and many run-ins with the Houston front office.

Denver had previously offered its coaching job to Peterson. When he declined, it turned to Ralston, whose nine years at Stanford were marked by a strong passing game and outstanding quarterbacks, notably Jim Plunkett. In its 12 years as a franchise, Denver had never had a winning season or a successful quarterback.

Saban quit late in the 1971 season after 4½ years as Denver coach. Then he returned on a long-term contract to Buffalo, where he had coached from 1962 to 1965. John Rauch had quit as Buffalo coach before the 1971 season after a policy disagreement with the club owner, and Harvey Johnson, his interim replacement, wanted to return to his job as director of player personnel. Johnson did assume his former position.

Owner George Halas of the Bears, who had picked Jim Dooley four years before as his coaching successor, fired him because the team was a perennial loser. Gibron, a Bears assistant coach since 1965, moved his 300 pounds into the head coach's chair.

After a distinguished career as quarterback of the Green Bay Packers, Bart Starr retired at 38. He was hired by the Packers as an assistant coach.

Associated Press awards. On January 7 sportswriters polled by the Associated Press named George Allen of the Washington Redskins as NFL Coach of the Year. Under Allen the Redskins had their best record in 26 years (9-4-1). Cited as the Most Valuable Player was Alan Page, defensive tackle of the Minnesota Vikings. It was the first time the award had ever been given to a defensive player. Rookie of the Year awards went to running back John Brockington of the Green Bay Packers (offense) and linebacker Isaiah Robertson of the Los Angeles Rams (defense).

FRANK LITSKY

GOLF. While fate shattered his dream of winning the elusive grand slam of golf, Jack Nicklaus was busy this year literally breaking the Professional Golfers Association bank. By late August the hard-driving Golden Bear had already set a new PGA one-season record for winnings, with $280,481, by taking the $40,000 first-place prize in the competition for the $150,000 U.S. Professional Match Play championship.

Nicklaus misses grand slam. The golf world applauded Nicklaus' gallant try for the grand slam, which would have been the first since the great Bobby Jones, who died December 1971, accomplished that feat in 1930.

However, heartbreak came for the 32-year-old Nicklaus in the British Open in July when, with a four-day total of 279, he finished just 1 stroke off Lee Trevino's winning pace. Six shots behind at the start of the final round in Muirfield, Scotland, Nicklaus fought his way back to a 5-under-par 66, but Trevino, with a delicate little chip, shot from the short rough on the 17th hole, saved his par 5, and thus took the second British Open title of his career.

Nicklaus first stirred grand slam hopes in early April by running away from the field in the Masters. That was his fourth victory in the prestigious golf classic since 1962, thus placing him with Arnold Palmer as the only four-time Masters winner.

The next step, in June, was a victory at the U.S. Open at Pebble Beach, Calif. Carding a spectacular four-round total of 290 (71-73-72-74), Nicklaus finished three strokes ahead of Bruce Crampton and won the Open for the third time. This was the 13th major title of his fantastic career—tying him with Bobby Jones—and Nicklaus nailed down the win with two crucial birdies, on the 15th and 17th holes; the latter, a tremendous No. 1 iron shot that landed 2 inches from the cup, was almost a hole in one. Victory was certain after that, and his 3-putt bogey on the 18th had no effect on the outcome. After the disappointment in Scotland, Nicklaus finished 13th in the PGA tournament, taken by South Africa's Gary Player.

Year of the playoffs. If the PGA year seemed longer to some pros than normal, it was—because of a record 13 playoffs. And it all started in the first major tournament of the year, the $125,000 Glen Campbell-Los Angeles Open. George Archer won it on the fifth day of play, shooting a 5-under-par 66 to beat out Tommy Aaron and Dave Hill. Among the other playoff winners were Tony Jacklin, who parred the first extra hole to take the Greater Jacksonville Open; George Archer, who beat Tommy Aaron on the second hole of sudden death in the Greater Greensboro Open; and Bobby Mitchell, whose 20-foot birdie putt on the first extra hole gave him a 1-stroke victory over Jack Nicklaus in the Tournament of Champions. Also, Chi Chi Rodriguez won his first tournament in four years by besting Billy Casper with a birdie on a 19th-hole playoff in the Byron Nelson Golf Classic, Australia's David Graham bumped in a 10-foot birdie putt on the second extra hole to snatch the Cleveland Open from fellow countryman Bruce Devlin, and Lou Graham broke out of a four-way tie with Hale Irwin, Larry Ziegler, and David Graham to win the Liggett and Myers Open.

Women's pro golf. Janie Blalock caused shock waves on the 1972 Ladies Professional Golf Association tour this June when she filed a $5 million suit against the LPGA after being suspended for a year on charges of violating golf ethics. Earlier, she had been disqualified in the Bluegrass tournament in Louisville, Ky., for an improperly marked scorecard. However, a federal judge in late June ordered the LPGA to allow her to play pending settlement of the suit.

Kathy Whitworth was once again the top money winner on the LPGA circuit. She won four tournaments, including the Alamo Ladies Open, the Raleigh Golf Classic, the Knoxville Ladies Open, and the Southgate Ladies Open.

Her win in the Knoxville, with a 54-hole total of 210, boosted her earnings to $41,737 by August.

Miss Blalock won three tournaments, including the LPGA's richest event, the Dinah Shore–Colgate Winners Circle championship. She finished three shots ahead of Carol Mann and Judy Rankin, 213 to 216, to take home the first-place check of $20,000. Her other titles came in the Suzuki International Golf tournament and the Dallas Civitan Open. In other women's play Betsy Cullen won the $85,-000 Sears Women's World Golf Classic; Betty Burfeindt, who earlier won her first professional championship in the Birmingham Centennial Classic, captured the $50,000 Sealy-LPGA Classic, and Susie Berning grabbed her second tour win in eight years by finishing one shot ahead of Kathy Ahern, Pam Barnett, and Judy Rankin in the $38,500 U.S. Women's Open. Kathy Ahern triumphed by 6 strokes over Janie Blalock in the Eve-LPGA championship to take the $7,500 top prize.

Amateur golf. Perseverance finally paid off for Vinny Giles, who won the U.S. Amateur championship after three straight years of finishing second. This time he ended at 285, 3 strokes better than the second-place finishers, Ben Crenshaw and Mark Hayes.

In other men's competition, Danny Edwards of Oklahoma State University won the North and South Amateur championship, Ben Crenshaw took the Trans-Mississippi, Bill Rogers won the Southern Amateur, and Tommy Evans triumphed in the Dogwood Classic in Atlanta.

Jane Bastanchury Booth won the North and South Women's Amateur crown; Beth Barry won the Southern Women's Amateur, Ann Laughlin of the University of Miami won the National Women's Collegiate, Alice Dye the Eastern Amateur, and Mary Ann Budke the U.S. Women's Amateur.

International competition. The United States retained the coveted Curtis Cup in Western Gailes, Scotland, in June, scoring a 10–8 victory over Great Britain. An even share of the final day's matches, three foursomes and six singles, allowed the American team to hold onto the winning margin it had gained the previous day. Members of the winning U.S. team were Jane Booth of Palm Beach Gardens, Fla., Barbara McIntire of Colorado Springs, Beth Barry of Mobile, Ala., Hollis Stacy of Savannah, Laura Baugh of Long Beach, Calif., Martha Kirouac of Rancho Bernardo, Calif., and Lancy Smith of Snyder, N.Y. Also in international play, Mickey Walker of England won the British Women's Amateur championship.   HAL HAYES

GYMNASTICS. The Japanese men, as expected, retained their reputation as the world's best gymnasts. At the Olympic competition they easily took the team championship and swept 15 individual titles in seven events. The Russians and East Germans, who placed second and third respectively, together garnered the remaining six medals.

Perhaps overshadowing the men, the women gymnasts, particularly the Russians, put on an unforgettable Olympic display. And outstanding among the gold-medal Soviet team, which has so long dominated this competition, was tiny 17-year-old Olga Korbut. Winner of three medals, she performed stunts on the uneven bars that had never before been accomplished. Her compatriot, Ludmila Turishcheva, retained the gold medal as the all-around gymnast. Here, the best American showing was made by Cathy Rigby, who placed tenth.

NO SLAM. Showing great form and concentration, Jack Nicklaus hits the green to maintain his lead at Pebble Beach. Big Jack went on to win the U.S. Open, his 13th major golf title, but hopes for a grand slam faded when Lee Trevino took the British Open in July.

WIDE WORLD

RINGED VICTORY. Japanese gymnast Akinori Nakayama won a gold medal for top form in the rings competition in Munich. Nakayama also dazzled judges in an international meet at Penn State, where he was given a perfect score for his performance on the high bar.

UPI

Earlier, one of the most dazzling performances in gymnastics history was put on by Olympic medal-winner Akinori Nakayama of Japan during a two-day U.S.-Japanese meet at Penn State University Park in late January. His lowest score for the entire evening was 9.35, and his average for the six events was a spectacular 9.75. Nakayama was literally perfect in his final routine, all the judges awarding him 10's for his performance on the high bar. It was the first time ever during an international match in the United States that any contestant had ever been judged to be flawless. As expected, the Japanese men defeated the U.S. squad, 286.20 to 277.90. But the American women, led by Cathy Rigby, upset their Japanese counterparts, 188.95 to 187.20.

Southern Illinois came up with two individual titlists—Gary Morava in vaulting and Tom Lindner on the horizontal bar—and took its fourth NCAA championship. The Salukis, runner-ups a year ago, put on a strong performance to defeat Iowa State, the defending champions, 315.925 to 312.325. Southern Illinois dedicated its triumph to gymnast John Arnold, who was killed in a car accident two years ago while the team was traveling to a dual match. Iowa State's Russ Hoffman won on the side horse, the first contestant ever to take the event three times. Although he did not win any individual events, Steve Hug, who is currently a sophomore at Stanford University, won the all-around title.

NCAA CHAMPIONSHIPS IN GYMNASTICS
Iowa State, April 8–10

Team: Southern Illinois
All-around: Steve Hug, Stanford
Horizontal bar: Tom Lindner, Southern Illinois
Free exercise: Odess Lovin, Oklahoma
Side horse: Russ Hoffman, Iowa State
Rings: Dave Seal, Indiana State
Vaulting: Gary Morava, Southern Illinois
Parallel bars: Dennis Mazur, Iowa State

She had to come from behind to do it, but when it was all over Linda Metheny had won her third successive AAU all-around title and her fifth in all. Cathy Rigby took an early lead but was then slowed down by an injured thigh and overtaken by her opponent. In the men's competition the winner was Makoto Sakamoto, a 5′ 1″ dynamo, who thwarted Yoshi Takei's attempt to win the all-around title for a third straight time. HERMAN WEISKOPF

HARNESS RACING. Albatross. Albatross, a spectacular four-year-old pacer, broke world records twice during the summer and was expected to retain the Harness Horse of the Year honor. On July 1 at Sportsman's Park in Chicago the champion, who is trained and driven by Stanley Dancer, paced a mile over a ⅝-mile course in 1:54⅗—the fastest time ever posted in a race by a harness horse. On September 19, Albatross set another world mark; his 1:55⅗ time in a race at the Delaware (Ohio) County Fairground was

the fastest ever recorded by a harness horse on a half-mile track.

By October the Kentucky-bred son of Meadow Skipper had earned $340,000 for the year and had pushed his earnings total over the $1 million mark by August. Earlier, in April, the Hanover Shoe Farms purchased the horse for $2.5 million. His major victories included the $50,000 Provincial Cup, the $80,425 American-National, the $91,000 Realization Pace, the $58,295 Matron, and the $59,400 Canadian Pacing Derby. Albatross was not always a winner, however. He lost five times, twice to Nansemond and three times, early in the year, to the Isle of Wight.

Speedy Crown. Speedy Crown, the 1971 Trotter of the Year, enhanced his reputation and his owner's bank account with splendid victories that included foreign competition. The son of Speedy Scott swept three big races this summer at Roosevelt Raceway in New York. After taking the $92,505 Realization, the prize trotter, with Howard Beissinger at the reins, captured the $125,000 International Trot on July 15, the first American horse to do so in eight years. However, since the great French horse, Une de Mai, had been scratched from the race because of tightened muscles, it was felt that Speedy Crown's victory in the 1¼-mile race was not over the best. The next week, in the special $150,000 Challenge Match race, Speedy Crown beat Une de Mai by a length. Fresh Yankee, who had finished three-quarters of a length behind the winner in the International, was third in the 1¼-mile match race.

Super Bowl takes Triple Crown. Super Bowl lived up to the first part of his name when he won the Kentucky Futurity on October 6 and became the sixth winner of trotting's Triple Crown. First, the son of Star Pride, with Stanley Dancer driving, took the famed $119,090 Hambletonian in straight heats at Du Quoin, Ill., on August 30. He then triumphed in the $93,097 Yonkers Futurity a month later. After the first race it was announced that he had been syndicated to the Hanover Shoe Farms for the remarkable sum of $1 million.

Strike Out. Strike Out, a three-year-old Canadian pacer, captured the $104,916 Little Brown Jug at the Delaware (Ohio) County Fairground. The son of the great Bret Hanover bettered his sire's world record for pacing on a half-mile track with a time of 1:56⅗ on September 21, under the guidance of Keith Waples. This May, Strike Out was beaten by his half-brother Hilarious Way in the $107,097 Cane Pace at Yonkers.

For the first time in a major harness race in the United States a dead heat was recorded. The oddity occurred in the $92,110 Adios Stakes at The Meadows, near Pittsburgh, on August 12. Strike Out, with Waples at the reins, and Jay Time, guided by Gene Riegle, crossed the line together and after long study of the photos, the judges declared a dead heat. The time was 1:59⅖.   DEANE McGOWEN

HORSE RACING. The saga of Riva Ridge. The major disappointment for followers of thoroughbred racing was the failure of Riva Ridge to capture the Triple Crown. There was plenty of rain on May 20 at Pimlico, and the heavily favored colt, who had won the Kentucky Derby two weeks previously, bogged down on the sloppy track to finish fourth, out of the money, in the $187,800 Preakness Stakes.

The impressive record with which the Meadow Stables three-year-old entered the season made him top ranked in his class. With his performance at the $49,700 Blue Grass Stakes on April 27, his owners felt sure that the Triple Crown was forthcoming, starting with a victory in the 1¼-mile Kentucky Derby on May 6. Ridden by Ron Turcotte, Riva Ridge did indeed get off in front in that $182,000 event, gradually widening his margin and finishing 3¼ lengths ahead of No Le Hace, whose drive down the stretch had overtaken Hold Your Peace for second place.

After Riva Ridge had shown enough speed to lead the Derby all the way, many thought that he would have no trouble in the shorter Preakness; a crowd of 48,721, a Maryland record, made him a 1–5 favorite. But at the start of the 1 3/16-mile race, Bee Bee Bee, a little-known Maryland-bred colt owned by William Farish, went to the front and stayed there. At the three-quarters mark, Riva Ridge had moved into second place but faded off in the slop to finish fourth, behind No Le Hace, who rallied from last place in the field of seven, and Key to the Mint.

Lucien Laurin, Riva Ridge's bitterly disappointed trainer, found fault with Turcotte's riding, but he had no complaints with the running of the $155,900 Belmont Stakes on June 10; his colt charged to the front in a field of nine, finishing seven lengths ahead of Ruritania. Key to the Mint wound up fourth, five lengths behind Cloudy Dawn, and No Le Hace was sixth.

Extending his domination to the west coast, Riva Ridge beat out two of the west's leading three-year-olds, Bicker and Quack, in the $109,900 Hollywood Derby on July 1. Riva Ridge picked up $59,900 in that tough victory, giving him $358,887 for the season and $862,150 for his career. However, in his next big east coast race, the $100,000 Monmouth Invitational Handicap on August 5, Riva Ridge finished fourth, as Freetex, an 11–1 shot, won. Suspicious of his logy performance, the colt's owners had blood and urine tests taken after the race. Sure enough, a blood test showed traces of a tranquilizer which, according to technicians, could have been injected from eight to 48 hours before the race. Monmouth, the FBI, and the Thoroughbred Racing Protective Bureau all launched separate investigations of the affair.

Key to the Mint. Key to the Mint, who had not been eligible for the Kentucky Derby, campaigned actively after the Belmont. He won the Brooklyn Handicap on July 8, beating ten older horses in the field of 12, and took the Whitney and the Travers stakes at Saratoga Springs the following month. In the Travers, Key to the Mint earned $66,600 for his owner, Paul Mellon, raising the horse's 1972 earnings to $255,037.

Late in the season, Riva Ridge and Key to the Mint clashed in the $115,500 Woodward Stakes at Belmont Park on September 30, with the Rokeby Stable colt winning the 1½-mile test over a sloppy track in 2:28.4. Riva Ridge finished a weary fourth in the heavy going, the same track conditions that cost him the Preakness. Key to the Mint picked up $69,300 for his seventh victory in 11 starts this season, his fourth stakes victory in succession and his sixth of the year.

Other winners. In a meeting of two Kentucky Derby winners in the Stymie Handicap on September 20 at Belmont, Riva Ridge was beaten by four-year-old Canonero II, the victor at Louisville in 1971. Canonero set a track record and tied the American mark for 1⅛ mile in 1:46⅕, beating Riva Ridge by five lengths. The three-year-old, however, carried 123 pounds to 110 for the older horse.

In an unusual match race, two horse owners decided to see who had the better mare. Fletcher Jones, the owner of Typecast, and Leonard Lavin, who owns Convenience, each put up $100,000, with Hollywood Park adding $50,000, for a winner-take-all $250,000 purse in the 1⅛-mile race on June 17. Convenience, a four-year-old filly ridden by Jerry Lambert, beat Typecast, a six-year-old mare with Bill Shoemaker up, in a photo finish. Convenience had beaten Typecast by a half-length two weeks before in the $105,900 Vanity Handicap.

Quack, ridden by Donald Pierce, captured the $175,000 Hollywood Invitational Gold Cup on July 15 by 5½ lengths. Beating 12 older horses in a field of 13, he equaled the U.S. record on a 1¼-mile dirt course in 1:58.2. The Kentucky-bred colt, owned by Millard Waldheim of Bwamazon Farms, had previously won the $100,000 California

VIVA RIVA! Ahead all the way, top-ranked Riva Ridge fired past the finish line in a spectacular performance at Churchill Downs. But hopes for a Triple Crown bogged down on a rainy Pimlico track when the three-year-old finished a disappointing fourth in the Preakness.

Derby in April. The Gold Cup victory raised his earnings for the year to $273,450.

An American horse, Droll Role, won on soggy surf in the International at Laurel, Md., in November.

European races. This year American horses continued to dominate England's horse racing classics. Boucher, owned by Ogden Phipps of New York, captured the $131,482 St. Leger at Doncaster. When the American-bred horse, ridden by English champion Lester Piggot, beat Steel Pulse on September 9, he got even for a previous loss suffered by his trainer, Vincent O'Brien. In the Irish Sweepstakes Derby, Steel Pulse defeated the O'Brien-trained Roberto. Owned by John W. Galbreath, Roberto was named for Roberto Clemente of the Pittsburgh Pirates, also owned by Galbreath. The horse had won the Epsom Derby by a nose over Rheingold on June 7, becoming the fourth American-bred in five years to win the historic event at Epsom Downs, England. He also ended the 15-race winning streak of Brigadier Gerard in the Benson and Hedges Gold Cup in New York. However, on September 10, Roberto lost by a length to Japanese-owned Hard to Beat, the French Derby winner, in the $45,000 Prix Neil at Longchamps.

Shoemaker ties stakes record. In racing in California, Bill Shoemaker was in the midst of most of the action, as usual. On February 21 the world's most successful jockey tied Eddie Arcaro's record for stakes victories by winning both divisions of the San Luis Obispo Handicap at Santa Anita for his 554th stakes triumph of 1972. By late July he had 571 stakes victories and had pushed his career total for winners past 6,390. But even he had a bad streak—a string of 18 straight stakes without a win until Buzkashi triumphed in the $83,300 American Handicap in July.

DEANE MCGOWEN

ICE HOCKEY. Birth of the WHA. The 1971–1972 hockey season came to be known as the year of the endless winter because it didn't seem to end in mid-May when the games ended. Remarkably, interest in hockey increased during the summer, principally because of the new World Hockey Association.

Organized rather unobtrusively in 1971, the WHA did not receive much attention until January 1972, when it became obvious that the new league would challenge the established National Hockey League for customers, with teams in 12 cities—New York, Winnipeg, Chicago, Edmonton, Los Angeles, Quebec City, Philadelphia, St. Paul, Ottawa, Boston, Houston, and Cleveland—all of them raiding the NHL for first-rate players.

UPI

GONE BUT NOT FORGOTTEN. Chicago Black Hawk superstar Bobby Hull (9) knocked in the 600th goal of his National Hockey League career in a game in March against Boston. Three months later he defected to the World Hockey Association in a player war with the NHL.

Gary L. Davidson, the Southern California attorney who had organized the American Basketball Association in 1967, was named president of the WHA, and by February 1972 the NHL began losing players to the new league. Bernie Parent, a gifted young goaltender, disclosed that he had agreed to play in the WHA for the 1972–1973 season at more than three times the salary he had received in the NHL. One by one, other NHL players defected to the rival organization. On June 27, Bobby Hull, who had played 15 seasons with the NHL Chicago Black Hawks, signed a 10-year, $2,750,000 contract as player-coach of the WHA Winnipeg Jets. Professional hockey's most popular player—he was the first hockey player to appear on the cover of *Time*—Hull gave the WHA the credibility it needed and inspired other National League players to defect. On July 27, goalie Gerry Cheevers and defenseman Ted Green of the Bruins also switched over.

The unexpected emigration from the NHL caused great concern in the old league. Its quality already diluted by expansion, the NHL admitted two new teams, the Atlanta Flames and the New York Islanders, for the 1972–1973 season; the league also plans to increase its membership to 18 in 1974–1975, with the addition of Kansas City and Washington, D.C.

To stem the loss of players to the WHA, NHL lawyers sought to find a legal means to save NHL rosters from total depletion; they based their case on a clause in the standard NHL player's contract that allows a team the option of signing a player for the following season before he can play elsewhere. The NHL successfully obtained temporary injunctions against the defectors, but these were lifted by a federal court judge in November, and the former NHL stars began playing for their new WHA teams.

The demand for new players forced NHL teams to sign inexperienced junior players developed in Canada and, of course, to pay higher and higher salaries. Bill Harris was signed to a three-year contract by the New York Islanders for $300,000, although he had never played professional hockey. Some clubs signed U.S. Olympic skaters.

The NHL season. While the WHA-NHL war carried hockey interest to a new high throughout North America, it overshadowed an exciting 1971–1972 season dominated by the Boston Bruins, who finished 10 points ahead of the New York Rangers during the regular East Division race, while the Chicago Black Hawks finished comfortably atop the West Division.

Phil Esposito, the Bruins' center, led the league in scoring with 66 goals and 67 assists for 133 points, marking the second straight season he had finished first in scoring. Boston defenseman Bobby Orr was second in scoring; he won the Norris Trophy as the league's best defenseman for the fifth consecutive year and the Hart Trophy as Most Valuable Player for the third consecutive year, and he was named to the first-team All Stars. In addition, Orr won the Conn Smythe Trophy as Most Valuable Player during the Stanley Cup playoffs.

In their path to the world championship, the Bruins played in their typically aggressive style, stressing heavy body checks, hard shooting, and speed that confounded their opponents. Boston defeated Toronto, four games to one, in the opening Stanley Cup round and routed the St. Louis Blues in four straight games of the second round. Meanwhile, the New York Rangers advanced to the finals by first eliminating the defending champion Montreal Canadiens in six games and then the Chicago Black Hawks in four consecutive games.

The confrontation of New York and Boston in the finals offered fans the definitive contrast in styles; the Rangers relied more on finesse, while the Bruins played aggressively. The Bruins opened the series with two straight victories at Boston Garden and went on to win the Stanley Cup, 4–2.

International competition. As expected, the Soviet Union won a gold medal at the Winter Olympics in February at Sapporo; the United States finished a surprising second. (*See the special article: THE XX OLYMPICS.*)

Czechoslovakia won the world amateur hockey title in Prague in April by defeating the Soviet Union. It was the first time since 1962 that the Soviet team had not won the championship.

In September a series of eight games was initiated between a select team of Canadians from the NHL coached by Harry Sinden and a team composed of the leading players from the Soviet Union. Team Canada did not include such star players as Bobby Hull, who had jumped to the WHA, and Bobby Orr, who was recovering from knee surgery. After an unexpected 7–3 loss in the opening game in Montreal, Canada won 4–1 in Toronto, played to a 4–4 tie in Winnipeg, and lost 5–3 in Vancouver. When the series resumed in Moscow, Canada lost 5–4, won 3–2, squeezed out a 4–3 victory, and in a dramatic finale won the eighth game 6–5 in the last 34 seconds of play, with Paul Henderson of the Toronto Maple Leafs scoring the winning goal. Team Canada thus won the series, 4–3–1. The games presented a contrast in hockey styles. The Soviet style was characterized by excellent conditioning and extensive training that allowed the team to maintain a very fast pace, precise passing, and an unemotional attitude. Vladislav Tretiak, the goalie, was particularly outstanding. The Canadian team, which was not so well conditioned as the Soviets, had a less patterned offense that relied on the slap shot and a more aggressive defense. Some observers felt that the next time there is a series with the Soviet Union, one of the regular NHL teams should play, rather than a specially formed All Star unit.

EAST DIVISION

	Won	Lost	Tied	Goals for	Goals against	Points
Boston	54	13	11	330	204	119
New York	48	17	13	317	192	109
Montreal	46	16	16	307	205	108
Toronto	33	31	14	209	208	80
Detroit	33	35	10	261	262	76
Buffalo	16	43	19	203	289	51
Vancouver	20	50	8	203	297	48

WEST DIVISION

	Won	Lost	Tied	Goals for	Goals against	Points
Chicago	46	17	15	256	166	107
Minneapolis	37	29	12	212	191	86
St. Louis	28	39	11	208	247	67
Pittsburgh	26	38	14	220	258	66
Philadelphia	26	38	14	200	236	66
California	21	39	18	216	288	60
Los Angeles	20	49	9	206	305	49

LEADING SCORERS

	Goals	Assists	Points
Phil Esposito, Boston	66	67	133
Bobby Orr, Boston	37	80	117
Jean Ratelle, New York	46	63	109
Vic Hadfield, New York	50	56	106
Rod Gilbert, New York	43	54	97

STAN FISCHLER

ICE SKATING. Ard Schenk of the Netherlands may not have been the whole story of skating during 1972, but he was enough of it to overshadow nearly everybody else.

Speed skating. Ard Schenk's dominance of men's speed skating was almost total—he won three out of four races at both the Olympics and at the European Championships in Davos, Switzerland, and he swept all four contests (he shared first place with Roar Gronvold in the 500 meters) in the World Championships in Oslo.

His two strongest events were the 1,500 and 5,000 meters, in which he won the Olympic, World, and European titles. Schenk's times were relatively unspectacular, mostly because of poor ice conditions, but he made up for that in March at the Inzell Golden Skates Competition in West Germany. There he covered the 1,500 in 1:58.8, just 0.1 second slower than the world record he set in 1971, and the 5,000 in 7:09.8, bettering his own previous world mark of 7:11.

In the 10,000, Schenk won both the Olympic and World titles. Earlier, at the European Championships, Schenk's teammate Kees Verkerk scored the biggest upset of the season by winning the 10,000, as Schenk faded to fourth. Despite that defeat, Schenk easily won the overall title at both the European and World championships. And at the Golden Skates meet he broke his own world overall record with a 167.420 score.

The only event that Schenk did not dominate was the 500, in which Erhard Keller won his second straight Olympic title with a slow 39.44. Keller had bettered his own world record from 38.42 to 38.3 at Inzell in early January, only to have Leo Linkovesi of Finland reduced that to 38 at Davos less than a week later. But Linkovesi was a soundly beaten sixth at Sapporo, and at the Golden Skates meet he could only take third in 38.5, as both Keller and Hasse Börjes of Sweden equaled his 38 record. Most of the top sprinters, including Keller, passed up the World and European meets, enabling Schenk to take the European title in 39.38 and share the World crown with Roar Gronvold of Norway in 40.18.

The Golden Skates meet also produced two world records in events not usually on the men's schedule. In the 1,000 meters Keller blazed a 1:18.5 to snap Schenk's record of 1:18.88, and Schenk cut more than four seconds off his own 3,000-meter mark with a 4:08.3 clocking.

On the women's side there was no one to match the dominance of Schenk, and competition was much better balanced. The greatest drama was provided by Anne Henning, of Northbrook, Ill., who won the Olympic 500-meter title despite interference from Canada's Sylvia Burka, the other skater in her heat. Her time of 43.73, an Olympic record, was good enough to win but well short of the world record of 42.5 she had set a month earlier in Davos. Because of the interference she was allowed to skate a second time and set another Olympic record of 43.33. Indirectly, however, the mishap and the strain of her double effort may have cost her the gold medal in the 1,000 the next day. She had been favored in the event, having set a world record of 1:27.3 a month earlier. But this day she could manage only a 1:31.62 for third place, as Monika Pflug of West Germany won in 1:31.4.

In the 1,500 another Northbrook skater, Dianne Holum, was the winner, upsetting Stien Baas-Kaiser of the Netherlands. But Baas-Kaiser turned the tables in the 3,000. She defeated opponent Holum by a margin of more than six seconds.

Ironically, the best all-round woman speed skater of the year didn't win any Olympic gold. That was Atje Keulen-Deelstra of the Netherlands, who won the overall titles at both the women's World and European championships. She took the 1,000 and 1,500 events at the World meet, held in Heerenveen, the Netherlands, in early March, with Stien Baas-Kaiser taking the 3,000 and Dianne Holum winning the 500. In the European meet the only double winner was Ludmila Titova of the Soviet Union, who took the 500 and 1,000.

Figure skating. The 1972 figure skating season was nearly a carbon copy of the year before, except that the well-established champions added Olympic gold medals to their World titles. In the men's singles Ondrej Nepela of Czechoslovakia easily won the Olympic title in a relatively unexciting competition. He then repeated the performance to win his second straight title in the World Championships at Calgary, Alberta, in March. As expected, Beatrix Schuba of Austria won both the Olympic and World women's titles, with Karen Magnussen of Canada second and Janet Lynn of the United States third on both occasions. Like Nepela, she wrapped up both titles on the compulsories, easing in with uninspired free-skating performances. Trixi Schuba easily repeated as European champion, while Janet Lynn narrowly won the U.S. title.

In the pairs competition the Soviet duo of Irina Rodnina and Alexei Ulanov continued to reign supreme, winning the Olympic gold medals and taking their fourth straight World title. The Russians also repeated as European champions, and the United States title was taken by Jo Jo Starbuck and Ken Shelley of Downey, Calif.

In ice dancing competition the World title was won by Ludmila Pakhomova and Alexander Gorshkov of the Soviet Union. The United States champions were Judy Schwomeyer and James Sladky, and the European title was taken by Angelika and Erik Buck of West Germany.

ROGER ALLAWAY

JUDO. Tom Rigg, after winning a silver medal in the 139-pound division at the World University championships in July, attributed his success to luck—a good draw and a day when he couldn't do anything wrong. Luck and a good draw may well have helped Rigg, but in the end it was his Morote Seoi-nage (shoulder throw) which probably helped him the most during his bouts at the Crystal Palace in London. He was the only American to win a medal in London, where, as expected, the Japanese took the golds in all six classes.

Rigg, a freshman engineering student at the University of South Florida, also put his Morote Seoi-nage to good use at the NCAA championships earlier in the year by finishing in first place at 139 pounds. Despite Rigg's victory and those of teammate Tom Masterson, who won at 154 pounds and was also the grand champion, South Florida did not come away with the team title. That was taken by San Jose State, which came up with three champions.

AP

SKATING DUTCHMAN Ard Schenk was the star of the Winter Olympics. Easily overpowering his fellow skaters in the 1,500-meter and 5,000-meter competitions, he sped through the 10,000-meter competition and went home from Sapporo with a total of three gold medals.

There were some 500 contestants on hand at Temple University in Philadelphia in late April, and they were all primed and ready to win AAU titles, as well as berths on the Olympic team. It had been announced that the winners of the six categories would automatically be selected to represent the United States at the Olympic Games in Munich but alas, the tournament became gripped by confusion. So much so that another tryout was held in Washington, D.C. It was at those final trials that two of the winners at Temple—Brian Yakata of New York City in the 139-pound class and Doug Graham of San Jose State in the 205-pound-and-under division—were bumped off the Olympic squad by Ken Okada of Los Angeles and James Wooley of Houston, respectively.

NCAA JUDO CHAMPIONSHIPS
Missouri Western College, April 8

139 pounds: Tom Rigg, South Florida
154 pounds: Tom Masterson, South Florida
165 pounds: Louis Gonzalez, San Jose State
176 pounds: Tom Cullen, Kent State
205 pounds: John Reed, San Jose State
Unlimited: Dave Long, San Jose State
Grand champion: Masterson

In Olympic competition the Japanese dominated the lighter weights, with three gold medals—Takao Kawaguchi, Toyokazu Nomura, and Shinobu Sekine. However, the gold medals in the heavier events were taken by Wim Ruska of the Netherlands in the heavyweight and open divisions and light-heavyweight Shota Chochoshvili of the Soviet Union.

AAU JUDO CHAMPIONSHIPS
Temple University, April 29–30

139 pounds: Brian Yakata, New York
154 pounds: Pat Burris, Anaheim, Calif.
176 pounds: Irwin Cohen, Chicago
205 pounds: Doug Graham, San Jose State
Heavyweight: Doug Nelson, Sacramento
Open: Johnny Watts, U.S. Air Force

HERMAN WEISKOPF

LACROSSE. The University of Virginia, a team which almost did not qualify for the national championship tournament, won its first official NCAA title in 1972. The Cavaliers, who had shared the unofficial championship (decided by a poll of a panel of coaches) in 1970, before the NCAA established its playoff for lacrosse, endured almost two years of disappointment before overcoming Johns Hopkins University, 13–12, at College Park, Md.

In 1971 heavily favored Virginia surprisingly lost the inaugural NCAA tournament in the first round to the U.S. Naval Academy. That defeat taught them a lesson for the 1972 playoff which many of the traditional lacrosse powers have yet to learn: the tournament is everything. Since previous records no longer determine the champion, even a team that goes through its whole schedule undefeated can lose the title; one loss in the playoffs and you're out.

Armed with this new wisdom, however, Virginia took the regular season of 1972 too casually. The Cavaliers lost four games and won 11 and trailed at half time of their season finale against Washington and Lee University. Had they lost that game, they would not even have been invited to the tournament. However, the Virginia defense, considered the team's weakness because of its inexperience, held Washington and Lee scorers in check for most of the final 30 minutes, while the offense staged a rally to win, 10–9.

NCAA tournament. In the opening two rounds of NCAA play, Virginia needed no late-game rallies, as it easily defeated the U.S. Military Academy, 10–3, and then a surprising new power, Cortland (N.Y.) State College, 14–7. Meanwhile, Johns Hopkins, which had won 11 of its 12 games during the regular season, was adding to its impressive record with victories of 11–5 over Washington and Lee and 9–6 over the University of Maryland, to whom the

Blue Jays owed their sole regular-season defeat. Earning a berth in the finals marked a return to form for Hopkins, which as the nation's most powerful lacrosse school had suffered through its worst season ever in 1971. A group of new, young players led by sophomore attackman Jack Thomas, who finished the year with 34 goals and 41 assists, turned a predicted rebuilding year for the Blue Jays into a near championship season.

At the start of the title game on June 3, Hopkins looked like a sure winner, scoring easily on its first two shots. But before the record crowd at College Park could settle back in their seats, the Cavaliers parried with three goals on their first three shots. The lead seesawed for the remainder of the game. Twice Hopkins held the lead by two goals, and twice Virginia led by a three-point margin. Then, with just over four minutes to play and the score tied at 12–12, Virginia midfielder Pete Eldredge fired in his team's winning goal—a high 20-foot shot into the upper right corner of the net. It was Eldredge's fourth score of the day.

Players honored. To his four-goal performance in the NCAA title game, midfielder Pete Eldredge added three more goals and one assist in the annual postseason North-South College All Star Game and earned a sweep of all major individual honors for the year. He was named Most Valuable Player in the nation, in the North-South game, in the NCAA tournament, in the early-season Hero's Tournament in Baltimore, and on his team; he also received the Enners Award as the nation's outstanding lacrosse player. Selected to the All America team for the second consecutive year, he became the first player ever to twice win the Richard Seth Award, given annually to Navy's outstanding individual opponent.

Other first-team All Americans were: goalie, Les Matthews (Hopkins); defense, Ed Haugevik (Rutgers), Larry Story (Yale), and Tom O'Leary (Army); midfield, Richard Kowalchuk (Hopkins) and Doug Schreiber (Maryland); attack, Jay Connor and Jack Thomas (both from Virginia), and John Kaestner (Maryland).

Other championships. The Carling Lacrosse Club defeated the Long Island (N.Y.) Athletic Club, 9–8, in its home town of Baltimore to take the national U.S. Club Lacrosse Association championship. This was Long Island's first loss in the championships since the club was established in 1968. In Geneva, N.Y., Hobart College outscored Washington College of Chestertown, Md., 15–12, in the first U.S. Intercollegiate Lacrosse Association championship tournament for small colleges, held at Hobart in May. The South defeated the North, 18–14, in the June North-South College All-Star Game, also played at Hobart.

The winners of other major leagues and divisions were: Washington and Lee (South Atlantic Division); Franklin and Marshall College (Central Atlantic Division); Adelphi University (New York Metropolitan Division); Cortland State (Central New York Division); Ithaca College, Albany State College, and Clarkson College of Technology, tied (Northern New York Division); Cornell University (Ivy League); Boston State College and Springfield College (Colonial Division); University of Massachusetts (Northeastern Division); Denison University and Kenyon College, tied (Midwest Division); U.S. Air Force Academy (Rocky Mountain Division); and San Francisco Lacrosse Club (Northern California Division). B. PETER CARRY

POWER BOATING. The 1972 powerboat year was dominated by Bobby Rautbord's triumph in offshore racing and Bill Muncey's unlimited hydroplane success. Both Rautbord and Muncey grabbed early leads and held them to the end to win their respective championships in the two exciting and rugged sports.

Muncey, a 43-year-old Seattle native now living in California, had the kind of year in his unlimited hydroplane, *Atlas Van Lines,* that dreams are made of. He won all but

HYDRO POWER. Bill Muncey and his "Atlas Van Lines" hydroplane won the Gold Cup title in June and set speed records all year.

one regatta, took 22 out of 25 heats, finished every race he started, and set enough records to rewrite the American Power Boat Association yearbook.

Rautbord, whose home is in Miami Beach, Fla., captured the Union of International Motorboating (UIM) title, which is equivalent to the world championship of ocean powerboat racing, by building a lead with early victories in South America, Spain, and Norway, and then hanging on as a succession of challengers wore out their hulls and burned out their engines in futile attempts to catch him.

Muncey's 7,000 pound hydro seemed to set records wherever it raced. Although world records are unofficial in the unlimited hydro world, Muncey set such "historic" marks as the fastest recorded time for a 15-mile heat over a 2½-mile course (110.655 miles an hour) and the fastest time for a single lap in competition (115.979).

Ironically, the year's most exciting race was the only one that Muncey did not win: the President's Cup in the nation's capital. Since Muncey had captured the Gold Cup, the most prized possession in the unlimited hydro sport, as well as the UIM world championship race two weeks before that, he was a prohibitive favorite to win in Washington, D.C.

However, it was *Pride of Pay 'N Pak* from Seattle that won the cup in a dramatic fashion. Its owner had changed drivers at the last moment, and it was Bill Sterett, Jr., a son of the former national champion, Bill Sterett Sr., who dueled the fast *Atlas* over the entire Potomac River course. Finally, Muncey gave way, but, as it turned out, for the only time all year.

Rautbord raced a 36-foot Cigarette named *Fino* not so much for speed marks but rather to finish first without getting maimed or killed. Battling waves all over the globe, Rautbord guided his boat to five victories and two second places to win the Sam Griffith Memorial Trophy as the best ocean racer in the world.

Rautbord had several pretenders to the throne: first, Vincenzo Balestrieri of Italy, who had won the world title twice; then, 50-year-old Sandy Satullo of Cleveland, who won the first four races he had ever entered; and finally,

Carlo Bonomi, also of Italy, a banker racing the world circuit seriously for the first time.

Bonomi came the closest, winning four races, mostly in the last half of the schedule. To overtake Rautbord's record, he had to win the last two contests, however, and when he could only gain a second in the next-to-last Miami-Nassau race, Rautbord had the title clinched.

Bob Magoon of Miami Beach, who did not campaign outside American waters, edged Satullo for the national championship, and another Floridian, Steve Shere, captured the national outboard championship for offshore drivers.

WORLD OFFSHORE POWERBOAT RACES
Argentina (February 5): Bobby Rautbord, Miami Beach
Uruguay (February 12): Rautbord
Sam Griffith (Miami, May 5): Sandy Satullo, Cleveland
Trofeo Baleares (Spain, May 21): Rautbord
Bahamas 500 (June 9): Satullo
Makarska-Rosetto (Yugoslavia, July 7): Vincenzo Balestrieri, Italy
Tvedestrand (Norway, July 8): Rautbord
Naples (Italy, July 16): Carlo Bonomi, Italy
Hennessy Grand Prix (Pt. Pleasant, N.J., July 19): Satullo
Viareggio (Italy, July 23): Balestrieri
Ile des Embiez (France, August 6): Bonomi
Öregrund (Sweden, August 13): Rautbord
Poole (England, August 19): Bonomi
Hennessy Long Beach Cup (California, August 19): Dante Tagnoli, Oakland
Cowes (England, September 2): Bonomi
Grand Prix du Leman (Switzerland, September 24): Ronald Hoare, England
Miami-Nassau (October 13): Robert Magoon, Miami Beach
Hennessy Key West (November 11): Magoon

UNLIMITED HYDROPLANE RACES
Champion Spark Plug (Miami, May 21): Bill Muncey, Atlas Van Lines
Kentucky Governor's Cup (Owensboro, June 11): Muncey
Gold Cup (Detroit, June 25): Muncey
UIM World Championship (Madison, Ind., July 2): Muncey
President's Cup (Washington, D.C., July 9): Bill Sterett, Jr., Pride of Pay 'N Pak
Atomic Cup (Pasco, Wash., July 23): Muncey
Seafair (Seattle, August 6): Muncey

PARTON KEESE

ROWING. The Olympics. In early September the black-shirted New Zealand crew rowed to glory in the Olympic final for eight-oared shells at Obershleissheim, West Germany. Superbly conditioned by six months of rowing on the icy waters of the River Avon, the poised and powerful Kiwis nosed out in front at the start and never dropped their beat below 39 strokes a minute throughout the 2,000-

meter course. Well ahead with 500 meters to go, they had more than enough stamina to hold off a surging U.S. eight, who won the silver medal by 0.06 second over the East Germans.

The East Germans dominated Olympic competition, however, winning three gold medals. The Soviet Union won two golds, with West Germany and New Zealand each taking one.

That silver medal was the only one taken by American oarsmen in the games, but their success and the success of the four-with-coxswain in reaching the final vindicated the decision of the U.S. Olympic Rowing Committee to pick All Star lineups for these teams from a list of 400 candidates. From that list 50 men were picked to attend a training camp at Hanover, N.H. The group was then pared to 16 before the eight and four-with-coxswain were chosen.

The only other American to make the Olympic finals was single sculler, Jim Dietz of the New York Athletic Club, who finished fifth behind competitors from the Soviet Union, Argentina, East Germany, and West Germany. Earlier, in July, Dietz had easily won the 2,000-meter elite singles title at the 99th annual national championships at Philadelphia and had captured the championship singles and open singles events at the Royal Canadian Henley Regatta at St. Catherines, Ontario.

Other events. Crews from Harvard University and Kent School in Connecticut both won trophies at England's Henley Royal Regatta in July. The Harvard freshman lightweights, unbeaten during the season, took the Thames Challenge Cup, and Kent, likewise undefeated, won the Princess Elizabeth Challenge Cup.

In early June the University of Pennsylvania won the varsity eights title at the Intercollegiate Rowing Association Championships at Syracuse, N.Y., for the fourth time in six years. Earlier the Quakers had lost the Adams Cup race against Harvard when their shell capsized and had finished a disappointing fifth in the Eastern Sprints final, won by Northeastern at Worcester, Mass. But this time they led from the start of the title race and finished more than a length ahead of Brown. Wisconsin, which earned third place, won the Ten Eyck Trophy for the best overall showing in the three-day regatta.

Other standout oarsmen besides Dietz at the national championships were Larry Klecatsky of the New York Athletic Club, who won the elite 150-lb. singles and the elite 145-lb. quarter-mile singles titles, and John Van Blom of the Long Beach (Calif.) Rowing Association, who upset Dietz in the elite quarter-mile singles and teamed with Tom McKibbon to win the elite doubles. McKibbon and Van Blom also earned U.S. Olympic berths in that event. The Undine Boat Club of Philadelphia nosed out the Potomac Boat Club of Washington, D.C., for team honors.

DAVID M. PHILIPS

SKIING. World Cup Alpine champions Gustavo Thoeni of Italy and Annemarie Proell of Austria were the two outstanding performers of the 1972 skiing season. But this was an Olympic year, and despite their season-long efforts, Thoeni and Miss Proell had to yield public attention to the three top skiing celebrities at Sapporo, Marie-Thérèse Nadig of Switzerland, Yukio Kasaya of Japan, and the nonparticipant Karl Schranz of Austria.

Alpine skiing. The biggest story of the year took place off the slopes, with the feud between Karl Schranz and International Olympic Committee president Avery Brundage which ended in Schranz' disqualification from the Winter Olympic Games. For more than a year Brundage had threatened a wholesale barring of the top Alpine skiers,

HIGH STYLE. Japan's Yukio Kasaya glided to victory in the 70-meter ski jump at Sapporo; compatriots placed second and third.

charging that they had allowed their names and photographs to be used by ski equipment manufacturers for advertising purposes. But when the Japanese Olympic Organizing Committee pleaded that this would ruin the games, Brundage settled for singling out Schranz, the downhill favorite whose income as an "amateur" skier has been estimated as high as $50,000 a year. Schranz, who had earlier vowed to take court action, took his suspension calmly, maintaining that many other skiers were equally guilty of commercialism; he also talked the Austrian team out of its plans to boycott the games in protest. Then, returning home to a hero's welcome, Schranz announced that he was retiring from competition.

Back at Sapporo, Schranz' Austrian teammates were being shut out of the gold medals by the surprising Swiss team, which took three of the six Alpine races.

In the men's competition, the first two races went according to form, with Bernhard Russi of Switzerland winning the downhill and Thoeni taking the giant slalom. But the third, the slalom, saw one of the greatest upsets in skiing history, as the heavily favored Thoeni was beaten by Francesco Fernandez Ochoa of Spain, a relative unknown who thus became the first Spanish athlete ever to win a medal in the Winter Olympics.

In the women's competition the form charts went completely to pieces. Annemarie Proell, considered a cinch to win the downhill and giant slalom and a possible winner in the slalom, lost both the downhill and the giant slalom to Marie-Thérèse Nadig, a pudgy Swiss teen-ager, by margins of 0.32 second and 0.64 second, respectively. The Austrian girl's hopes for a gold medal ended when she fell in the slalom, as Barbara Ann Cochran of the United States won by only 0.02 second over France's Danielle Debernard.

On the season-long World Cup circuit Miss Proell suffered no such frustrations. Officially, she clinched her second straight title on March 1, when she won a giant slalom at Heavenly Valley, Calif., in 1:48.96. But in fact, the outcome had been a foregone conclusion ever since February 2, when Miss Proell's only serious rival, Françoise Macchi of France, was injured during practice at Sapporo.

Miss Macchi had taken the lead in cup points in early January, winning four straight races to open a 150–113 gap over Miss Proell. But the Austrian star had regained the lead by a 203–187 margin before Miss Macchi's injury. In the final standings, Miss Proell ended with 269 points to 187 for Miss Macchi, 128 for Britt Lafforgue of France, 120 for Monika Kaserer of Austria, and 111 for Miss Nadig, who, despite her two Olympic victories, did not win a single World Cup race all season.

The men's World Cup competition, in contrast to the women's, offered a frantic five-way battle which was not decided until the final run of the giant slalom—the season's last race—at Pra Loup, France, on March 19.

The leader during most of the season was Henri Duvillard of France. But during the final series of five races, the best performances the Frenchman could muster were a pair of fourth places. Thoeni, who had trailed Duvillard by 117–107 going into that final week, finished second in the next-to-last race and took the lead for the first time over Duvillard, 134–131. In the final race, Thoeni had to beat Duvillard to win the cup for the second straight year, and he did, finishing second again to gain a 154–142 advantage in the final standings. Third was Edmund Bruggmann of Switzerland, with 140; fourth, with 125, was Jean-Noel Augert of France; and fifth, with 114, was Russi, who had been only 3 points off the lead with four races left. Russi also set a world record: his average speed of 66.4 miles an hour during a downhill race at Val Gardena, Italy, on March 15 was the fastest ever recorded under racing conditions.

The University of Colorado won the NCAA skiing championships, sending the University of Denver to only its fifth defeat in the last 19 years.

Nordic skiing. Yukio Kasaya of Japan was easily the star of the show on the Nordic side of the sport. He provided one of the supreme thrills of the Olympics in the 70-meter jumping event, soaring to distances of 275 feet and 264 feet to give the host country its first gold medal ever in the Winter Olympics. Kasaya's victory was no great shock, but what was a surprise was that his teammates, Akitsugu Konno and Seiji Aochi, took the silver and bronze medals. The Japanese did not fare so well in the 90-meter jump; Kasaya could manage only a seventh-place finish, as Wojciech Fortuna of Poland won the gold medal with a best leap of 364 feet.

In cross-country skiing at Sapporo, the Russians were the best, although they did not attain the dominance enjoyed by the great Norwegian team at the last Olympics. On the men's side, Soviet star Viacheslav Vedenine took the 30-kilometer event, Sven-Ake Lundback of Sweden the 15-kilometer, and Norway's Paal Tyldum the 50-kilometer. The Russians also won the men's 40-kilometer relay, with Vedenine beating out the Norwegian anchor man by ten seconds after having trailed by a minute at the start of the leg. Among the women, the Soviet Union's Galina Kulakova won both the 5-kilometer and 10-kilometer races and anchored the Soviet 15-kilometer relay team to an easy victory.

The Nordic combined champion was Ulrich Wehling of East Germany. Wehling finished only fourth in the jumping portion of the event and third in the cross-country but won the overall title on balance.

Magnar Solberg of Norway won his second straight individual biathlon title, but the Russians took the biathlon relay.   ROGER ALLAWAY

SOCCER. The opening rounds of the qualifying trials for the 1974 World Cup, the powerful display of the West German national team, several high transfer fees involving top players, and the continuing escapades of the controversial George Best highlighted the 1972 soccer season.

British football. Stoke City, Leeds United, and Derby County all provided their followers with some thrilling moments during the season. On March 4, Stoke City recorded the first major British title in its 100-year history when it defeated Chelsea, 2–1, in the finals of the English League Cup before a crowd of over 100,000 at London's Wembley Stadium. George Eastham scored the winning goal for the Stokers after Peter Osgood had tallied for Chelsea to tie the count earlier in the second half.

The century-old English Football Association Cup was captured on May 6 by Leeds United, which won a hard-earned 1–0 victory over the defending champion, Arsenal. With nine minutes gone in the second half Allan Clarke sent a header past Arsenal goalie Geoff Barnett for the lone score of the match, played before a crowd of over 100,000 at Wembley.

The battle for the Football League's First Division crown was close all season, but when it was all over in May, Derby County had emerged with the title by compiling 58 points—just one more than Leeds, Manchester City, and Liverpool, which tied for second place.

Francis Lee of Manchester City was the top scorer in the First Division with 33 goals, six less than the number recorded by this year's Golden Boot Award winner, Gerd Müller of West Germany. English National Team goalie Gordon Banks was named English Footballer of the Year.

And as for Manchester United forward George Best, his season was marked by referee-baiting, suspension, and then finally the announcement of his retirement—that is, until he changed his mind and decided to stay on for at least one more year.

In other championships, a three-goal spurt ten minutes into the second half gave the Stafford Rangers a 3–0 victory over Barnet and the title in the FA Challenge Trophy.

The FA Amateur Cup was won by Hendon over Enfield, 2–0. Aston Villa defeated Liverpool, 1–0, and then 4–2 in overtime to win its first FA Youth Cup. In Watney Cup play the Bristol Rovers topped Sheffield United, 7–6, in penalty shots after the two teams had played to a scoreless tie in regulation time.

Transfer fees. In an effort to bolster their competitive edge, several English clubs paid high transfer fees to acquire the players they wanted. Manchester United bought winger Ian Moore for $520,000 from Nottingham Forest and paid Scotland's Aberdeen $300,000 for halfback Martin Buchan. Manchester City gave the Queens Park Rangers $520,000 for forward Rodney Marsh, while Coventry City gave Hull City $220,000 for Chris Chilton. Allan Ball was transferred to Arsenal from Everton for $520,000.

Scottish football. Partick Thistle spoiled Glasgow Celtic's bid for another Scottish Football Association triple by upsetting Celtic, 4–1, in the finals of the Scottish League Cup held early in the season. But Celtic regained its prestige and ran off with the First Division title, compiling a record of 28 wins, four ties, and only two defeats for 60 points, ten more than second-place finisher Aberdeen, which had the league's highest scorer in Joe Harper. To cap off the season, Celtic walked all over the Hibernians, 6–1, in the finals of the Scottish FA Cup, played before an estimated crowd of 135,000 at Hampden Park. Dixie Deans got three goals, Lou Macari two, and Billy McNeill one.

British Home Tournament. England and Scotland shared the British International Home Tournament championship, each winning two and losing one. For a while it seemed Scotland would win the competition so long dominated by England. Northern Ireland won a stunning 1–0 victory over England, which then came back to beat Wales and Scotland. Northern Ireland placed third even without the services of George Best, and Wales was last.

European championships. The West German national team showed why they must be favored to win the 1974 World Cup in Munich when they captured the biennial European Nations' Cup in Brussels this June. In the smashing 3–0 victory over the Soviet Union, Gerd Muller scored two goals and Herbert Wimmer the other.

The European Cup Winners' Cup championship ended in a riot, as the Glasgow Rangers topped Moscow Dynamo of the Soviet Union, 3–2. Several thousand fans flown in from Scotland invaded the pitch at Barcelona just before the final whistle blew. Dynamo, in an appeal, claimed that the fans had injured one of their players. As a result, the Rangers were banned from international competition for two years, later reduced to one year. The Rangers were paced by two goals from Jimmy Johnstone and one from Colin Stein, building a 3–0 lead before the Soviet Union got tallies from Eshtrekov and Makhovikov.

Tottenham Hotspur topped the Wolverhampton Wanderers, 3–2, in a two-game total-goal series for the European Fairs Cup. Martin Chivers' two goals were the highlight for Tottenham. Roma of Italy blanked Blackpool, the defending champion from England, 3–0, to win the annual Anglo-Italian Cup championship. In the European Cup championship Johan Cruyff, voted Footballer of the Year in Europe, scored both goals as Ajax of Amsterdam defeated Inter-Milan (Italy), 2–0, to win its second consecutive championship.

Other championships. Often tabbed the Mini World Cup despite the fact that many nations did not take part, the Independence Cup was played in Brazil with the host nation topping Portugal, 1–0, to win the title on a goal by Jairzinho in the final minute. Yugoslavia topped Argentina, 4–2, for third place.

At the Olympics, Poland took the gold medal in soccer by defeating Hungary, the defending champion, 2–1. East Germany and the Soviet Union tied 2–2 to share the bronze medal. The U.S. team, after a scoreless deadlock against Morocco, was blanked 3–0 by Malaysia and 7–0 by West Germany.

North American Soccer League. The New York Cosmos defeated the St. Louis Stars, 2–1, in the championship game of the NASL's sixth season. The Cosmos took the lead on a goal at the 4:23 mark by Randy Horton, but the Stars tied the game seven minutes into the second half on a tally by player-coach Casey Frankiewicz. Finally, the Cosmos won the match on a penalty shot by Josef Jelinek with 4:18 remaining. With just 53 seconds left to play, an apparent tying goal by the Stars' Willy Roy was disallowed.

In the regular season, St. Louis, with seven American-born players on its starting team, won the Southern Division title with 69 points, on a record of seven wins, three ties, and four defeats. The Cosmos won the Northern title with a record of seven wins, four ties, and three defeats, for 77 points.

Randy Horton won the league scoring title with nine goals and four assists for 22 points. He was also named the NASL's Most Valuable Player. Top goalie was Kenny Cooper of Dallas, with an 0.86 goals against average. St. Louis goalie Mike Winter, with an 0.92 average, was Rookie of the Year, while Casey Frankiewicz was named top coach.

U.S. championships. Walt Smotolocha scored the only goal as the Elizabeth Soccer Club of New Jersey topped the San Pedro Yugoslav-Americans, 1–0, and won their second U.S. Dewar's Challenge Cup in the past three years. Kevin Missey's first-half goal gave the Busch Bavarians of St. Louis a 1–0 win over the Portuguese Soccer Club of New Bedford, Mass., for the National Amateur Cup championship. The National Junior Cup was won for the second straight year by the St. Louis Seco Jets, who defeated Baltimore's Casa Bianco, 2–1.

American Soccer League. Charles Roberts' goal with 35 minutes remaining gave the winner of the Midwestern Conference, the Cincinnati Comets, a 2–1 win over the defending champion New York Greeks and the American Soccer League title. The Greeks, who won the Northern Conference crown, had already defeated the Southern titleholders, the Philadelphia Spartans, 2–0.

U.S. national team. The U.S. World Cup team was eliminated in its first qualifying test for the 1974 World Cup competition, to be held in Munich. The Americans lost to and tied the Canadians and then were defeated twice by Mexico, which advanced into the second round.

JOSEPH MARCUS

SWIMMING. In an Olympic year competitive swimming usually flourishes, but in 1972 worldwide and American swimming blossomed as never before.

All 16 world records for men were broken, 11 by Americans. Twelve of the 15 world records for women were shattered—six by Americans and four by 15-year-old Shane Gould of Australia.

In the swimming portion of the Olympic Games in Munich from August 27 to September 4, 11 world records were broken and two equaled in the 15 men's events and 11 of 14 were broken in women's competition. At the U.S. Olympic trials in Chicago (August 2–6), American men broke seven world records and equaled one, and the women bettered four.

Mark Spitz. The Swimmer of the Year—and the Olympics' most celebrated athlete—was 22-year-old Mark Spitz of Carmichael, Calif., a June graduate of Indiana University and cocaptain of the school's champion swimming team. Spitz alone bettered world records 12 times in seven events, and at the Olympics he captured an unparalleled seven gold medals, swimming his races in world record times. At the National AAU short-course swimming championships in Dallas (April 6–9), Spitz won three individual events—the 100-yard freestyle and the 100-yard and 200-yard butterfly—and narrowly lost the 200-yard freestyle to

Steve Genter. He also won the Kiphuth Award as the meet's high scorer. Earlier, at the NCAA championships at West Point, N.Y. (March 23–25), he won two individual titles—the 100-yard and 200-yard butterfly—and became the third swimmer in history to win a single event four times.

At the Olympics, Spitz' world records came in the 100-meter (51.22 seconds) and 200-meter (1:52.78) freestyle, the 100-meter (54.27) and 200-meter (2:00.70) butterfly, the 400-meter (3:26.42) and 800-meter (7:35.78) freestyle relay, and the 400-meter medley relay (3:48.16). (See PEOPLE IN THE NEWS: Mark Spitz.)

Other record breakers. Roland Matthes, a tall 22-year-old East German, won the 100-meter and 200-meter backstroke events at the Olympics, the latter in a world record time of 2:02.82. He also broke his own world record in the 100-meter backstroke twice within two days at an international meet in April, his time: 56.3.

The other individual record-breakers among Americans were all Californians—15-year-old Rick DeMont of San Rafael (15:52.91) and then 25-year-old Mike Burton of Carmichael (15:52.58) in the 1,500-meter freestyle, Kurt Krumpholz of Santa Clara in the 400-meter freestyle (4:00.11), Gary Hall of Garden Grove in the 400-meter individual medley (4:30.81), and John Hencken of Cupertino in the 200-meter breaststroke (2:21.55). World records also went to Brad Cooper of Australia in the 800-meter freestyle (8:23.8), Gunnar Larsson of Sweden in the 200-meter individual medley (2:07.17), and Nobutaka Taguchi of Japan in the 100-meter breaststroke (1:04.94).

Hall, Spitz' college roommate, had a frustrating year. He won both the 200-yard and 400-yard individual medleys at the AAU and NCAA championships, the Santa Clara (Calif.) International Invitational meet (June 23–25), and at the U.S. Olympic trials. By the Olympics he had expected to have more speed, but instead of winning two gold medals, he finished fourth and fifth in the Olympic finals.

Women's records. When the year began, Shane Gould held four world freestyle records for women, and when she swam the 100 meters in 58.5 on January 8, she held all five. Later, during the summer games she bettered world and Olympic records for the 200-meter (2:03.56) and 400-meter (4:19.04) freestyle and the 200-meter individual medley (2:23.07). She retained her 1971 record for the 1,500-meter freestyle but lost the 800-meter freestyle record to Jo Harshbarger of Bellevue, Wash. (8:53.83), and then Keena Rothhammer of Santa Clara, Calif. (8:53.68). In addition to her three gold medals, she took a silver in the 800-meter freestyle and a bronze in the 100-meter freestyle. Then she said, "I'm tired and looking forward to school. I wish to be an ordinary teen-ager." Despite her wishes, there is no way she could be considered ordinary.

Neither could 15-year-old Melissa Belote of Springfield, Va., who won both the 100-meter and 200-meter backstroke races in the U.S. Olympic trials and in the Olympics and set world records for 200 meters of 2:20.64 and 2:19.19. She also set an Olympic record in the 100 meters of 1:05.78. After the games she returned to her sophomore year in high school.

In the AAU championships, Miss Belote, not yet a star, finished only fifth in the 200-yard and seventh in the 100-yard races. Susie Atwood of Long Beach, Calif., won both AAU backstroke finals for the fourth year in a row, but settled for one silver and one bronze medal in the Olympics.

World records also fell to 15-year-old Cathy Carr of Albuquerque, N.M. (1:13.58) in the 100-meter breaststroke; Karen Moe of Santa Clara, Calif. (2:15.57) in the 200-meter butterfly; Mayumi Aoki of Japan (1:03.34) in the 100-meter butterfly; Gail Neall of Australia (5:02.97) in the 400-meter individual medley, and U.S. teams led by 16-year-old Sandy Neilson of El Monte, Calif., in the 400-meter freestyle relay (3:55.19) and 400-meter medley relay (4:20.75).

Diving. Micki King of Hermosa Beach, Calif., a 28-year-old air force captain, won the Olympic women's diving title off the 3-meter springboard, and her AAU indoor victory at 3 meters was her tenth national title. Ulrika Knape of Sweden took the gold medal in the platform diving contest. In the men's competition Dick Rydze of Pittsburgh, a 22-year-old medical student who took first place in the AAU indoor platform championship, placed second in the Olympics behind Klaus DiBasi of Italy. In springboard diving Vladimir Vasin of the Soviet Union won the gold medal and ended the 60-year domination of the event by the United States. Craig Lincoln of Minnesota made the best U.S. showing, finishing in third place after Italy's Franco Cagnotto.

FRANK LITSKY

TENNIS. Dispute settled. The ten-month dispute between the International Lawn Tennis Federation and the World Championship of Tennis organization ended in late April. The settlement of the dispute, which had led to the disbarment of such top WCT-contracted players as Ken Rosewall, Rod Laver, and Arthur Ashe from the major federation-sanctioned championships since January, came in time for the 1972 U.S. Open title at Forest Hills in September but too late for Wimbledon in July.

The agreement, announced in London on April 26 by ILTF president Allan Heyman and ratified on July 12, not only resolved the items of conflict—which included WCT demands for a high percentage of the gate receipts and the right to choose the balls to be used—but restructured the entire tennis establishment. Particularly significant was the provision to phase out WCT contracts with the professionals, thus obliterating the distinction between contract and independent pros. The latter maintain allegiance to their national associations (who belong to the ILTF) and thereby had been eligible for the Davis Cup team while earning big prize money. Under the settlement, the player would also come under the "umbrella" of his national association as his WCT contract expired. However, the professionals, fearing excessive control by their national association, organized the Tennis Players Association to protect their interests.

In exchange for the concessions made by the WCT the agreement further stipulated that the federation and its 96 member national associations would sanction all WCT-sponsored events, at standard sanction fees, and that all pros would be allowed to compete in both WCT and ILTF tournaments—for the same prize money and without traveling expenses or contract guarantees from the WCT.

Moreover, the truce provided for a coordinated schedule to eliminate conflicts between events of comparable importance. Lamar Hunt, head of the WCT, was given control of the schedule dates for the first 4½ months of the year. In addition, the WCT agreed to set up two separate schedules to allow maximum participation. Under this plan 64 men (33 contract players and 31 selected non-WCT players) would be divided into two groups of equal strength, each playing 11 events. The top four in each group would then qualify for the eight-man $100,000 finals in Dallas, May 9–13, the winner of the finals receiving a top prize of $50,000.

Women's tennis shines. The women's division at Wimbledon and elsewhere furnished exceptional appeal this year.

Wimbledon. The long-awaited semifinal between the two most popular young players of tennis—Chris Evert, the 17-year-old sensation of the 1971 season, and 20-year-old Evonne Goolagong, last year's Wimbledon champion—seesawed endlessly, the pace becoming more and more furious. Finally, Miss Goolagong defeated her opponent, 4–6, 6–3, 6–4. But in the final she too was defeated, as Billie Jean King took her fourth Wimbledon title, 6–3, 6–3. Mrs. King had already put out Rosemary Casals and Virginia Wade to reach the final.

GOOD AS GOULD. Australian swimming ace Shane Gould set a new world record of 4:19.04 in winning the Olympic 400-meter freestyle.

WIDE WORLD

U.S. Open. Mrs. King, who set a record for a woman athlete by earning $117,000 in prize money last year, passed the $100,000 mark again in 1972, when she retained the United States Open championship over Kerry Melville of Australia, 6–3, 7–5. Miss Melville, unseeded, had unexpectedly beaten Miss Evert in the semifinals, 6–4, 6–2, using the drop shot and volley to marked advantage and holding her own in driving exchanges. However, the most stunning defeat was that of Miss Goolagong to an 18th-ranked American, Pam Teeguarden of Los Angeles, 7–5, 6–1, in the third round.

Other champs and championships. The comeback of Margaret Smith Court, after a 13-month retirement, marked the 1972 season. In the first match of her comeback, on July 28 in Cleveland, she lost to Miss Evert, 6–3, 6–3, in the first Bonne Bell Cup competition between teams from Australia and the United States. Although Miss Evert also beat Miss Goolagong, 6–3, 4–6, 6–0, Australia won the series, 5–2.

Miss Evert also led the United States team to a 5–2 victory over Great Britain in the Wightman Cup at Wimbledon in mid-June. Making her debut at Wimbledon, she won both of her singles matches against Joyce Williams and Virginia Wade and the doubles with Patti Hogan.

Miss Evert won her first major tournament by besting Miss Goolagong in the $60,000 U.S. Clay Court final, 7–6, 6–1, after defeating Mrs. Court, 6–3, 7–6. Then she lost her semifinal match in the $18,000 Virginia Slims Classic in Newport, R.I., 6–3, 6–0, to Mrs. Court, who picked up her first major victory as she beat Mrs. King in the final, 6–4, 6–1. However, Mrs. King topped Mrs. Court in the richest women's event, the $40,000 Four Roses tournament.

Nancy Richey Gunter defeated Miss Evert in the Virginia Slims Masters tournament at St. Petersburg, Fla., and in the Caribe Hilton tennis final in Puerto Rico. She also topped Mrs. King in the Maureen Connolly Brinker tournament at Dallas, 7–6, 6–1, and again in the final of the $25,000 Virginia Slims Denver final, 1–6, 6–4, 6–3. But at Forest Hills she was put out in the first round by Kazuko Sawamatsu of Japan.

In distaff tennis politics women professionals announced plans in October to organize independently from the USLTA as the Women's International Tennis Federation.

The group planned to compete for bigger prize money without paying sanction fees to either the USLTA or the ILTF.

However, complications developed in November when the new organization entered into a "mutual recognition" agreement with the predominantly black American Tennis Association, under which from three to six players will be selected to qualify for the 18 Virginia Slims–WITF tournaments. While bringing more black pros into the "big money," the agreement is seen as a challenge to the USLTA, which, should it disbar WITF members for not paying sanctions, must take the same action against the ATA.

Men's competition. As stunning as were the setbacks to Miss Goolagong, Miss Evert, and Mrs. Gunter in the U.S. Open championships, they were overshadowed by the fearful toll taken of the top players in the men's division.

U.S. Open. Four unseeded players reached the quarterfinals while Ken Rosewall, 1972 Player of the Year; third-seeded Rod Laver; and fifth-ranked John Newcombe all were eliminated. Stan Smith, the defending champion and the 1972 Wimbledon winner, lost in the quarterfinals to sixth-seeded Arthur Ashe, 7–6, 6–4, 7–5, after narrowly surviving his match with Spain's Andres Gimeno. A rejuvenated Ashe, who then toppled Cliff Richey in the semifinals, and Ilie Nastase, who won his match with Tom Gorman, 4–6, 7–6, 6–2, 6–1, won the right to face each other in the finals.

There, Ashe seemed to have it all wrapped up, ahead two sets to one. Even in the fourth set, Ashe, with his scorching service and backhand delighting the record gallery, enjoyed a tremendous advantage. With the score at 3–1 and 3–0 in his favor, he had only to hold service twice to win the match. But he could not maintain his form, and at that point, Nastase, who had seemed indifferent about winning, staged a spectacular comeback to take the set, 6–4, and the next, 6–3. The final score was 3–6, 6–3, 6–7, 6–4, 6–3. Nastase's rather undecorous behavior during the match appeared to have irked Ashe and won the active disfavor of the gallery when he protested a call by directing a ball toward service lineman Jack Stahr. Nastase, rewarded with a cash prize of $25,000, a car, and a Grand Prix bonus of $1,250, became the first Iron Curtain champion of the U.S. Open.

UPI

POPPERFOTO

WOMEN'S LOB. Three young stars on the upswing: Evonne Goolagong (left), 1971 Wimbledon champ; Chris Evert (center), a teen-ager who led the U.S. team to a Wightman Cup victory; and Billie Jean King (right), the leader of the women's rights movement in tennis who took first place at Wimbledon and Forest Hills this year, pushing her 1972 earnings over the $100,000 mark in the process.

Davis Cup. For the fifth consecutive year Stan Smith of Pasadena, Calif., clinched an American victory in the Davis Cup competition. On the soft clay courts of Bucharest, with a promising 2–1 lead in the three-out-of-five match series, Smith battled with Romania's burly Ion Tiriac, who, many felt, benefited from numerous questionable line calls and the rabid but understandable partisanship of the crowd. Against this and his opponent's barrage of irritating remarks and distracting behavior, Smith dropped two of the first four sets but kept his cool long enough to take the fifth set and the victory. The final tally for the match: 4–6, 6–2, 6–4, 2–6, 6–0.

Other men's events. At Wimbledon, with many top players absent, Stan Smith took the prestigious championship over Ilie Nastase, after defeating Jan Kodes of Czechoslovakia. After his smashing victory in the U.S. Open, Nastase beat out Tom Gorman, 6–4, 3–6, 6–3, to capture the Rainier International Classic in Seattle. The same week Arthur Ashe was able to beat Roy Emerson in the championship match of the $50,000 Rothmans' WCT International in Montreal. In May, Ken Rosewall topped fellow Australian Rod Laver, 4–6, 6–0, 6–3, 6–7, 7–6, in a thrilling 3½-hour battle to win the $50,000 first prize in the $100,000 WCT tournament in Dallas. Earlier in April, Rosewall had trounced Cliff Richey, 2–6, 6–2, 6–2, in the finals of the WCT North Carolina National Bank Tennis Classic in Charlotte. Also in April, Rod Laver won a surprisingly easy victory in the $50,000 River Oaks Tennis tournament.

ALLISON DANZIG

TRACK AND FIELD. This year saw both a rise in the world record for the pole vault and a decline in the track career of Jim Ryun. Those were two highlights of an Olympic year in which American track and field supremacy was severely challenged.

Pole vaulters reach new heights. When the year started only one man—Christos Papanicolaou of Greece—had vaulted over 18 feet, and he had done it only once, in 1970. By the end of 1972, Bob Seagren of Los Angeles and Kjell Isaksson of Sweden had raised the world record four times, and a total of six men had cleared 18 feet.

In Austin, Texas, on April 8, Isaksson vaulted 18′ 1″ despite a tender thigh muscle that continued to bother him all year. A week later, at Los Angeles, he did 18′ 2¼″. Five weeks later, in a workout at El Paso, Texas, he cleared 18′ 9″ on his third attempt (practice vaults are not accepted as records). Two days later, on May 23, in a special AAU meet at El Paso, both Seagren and Isaksson did raise the official record to 18′ 4¼″.

Six weeks later Seagren went even higher. On July 2 in the U.S. Olympic trials at Eugene, Ore., he cleared 18′ 5¾″, thereby regaining sole possession of the world record. Jan Johnson of the University of Alabama and Steve Smith of Long Beach (Calif.) State both vaulted 18′ ½″ for second and third and also made the Olympic team. Dave Roberts of Rice University, who had cleared 18′ ¾″ in the national AAU championships, managed only 17′ 8½″ in the Olympic trials, good enough to make any Olympic team except the one he was attempting to make.

The 25-year-old Seagren, the 1968 Olympic gold medalist, was a fiery competitor in the 1972 games—his oft-injured knees held up, but his favorite vaulting pole never made it. The poles that Seagren and Isaksson had used all year, Catapoles, were made of a new fiberglass weave and were lighter and slightly thinner than their predecessors. In July the International Amateur Athletic Federation, the governing body of track and field, ruled that poles—specifically, the new Catapole—could not be used in the Olympics unless they had been in general circulation at least a year. Seagren called the move "100 percent politics," blaming it on Wolfgang Nordwig of East Germany, who contended he had not had access to the new pole. However, George Moore, the manufacturer, stated that he had sent Catapoles to every top vaulter in the world, including six sent to pole-vaulter Nordwig.

In August, the ban was reversed and then reinstated 48 hours before the Olympic vaulting event. Thus, Seagren had to use a strange pole, which carried him over 17′ 8½″, good only for second place. Nordwig won at 18′ ½″.

After the competition, Seagren not only refused to shake hands with the winner but as he walked past an IAAF official instrumental in the ban, he dropped his old-style pole in the man's lap.

Jim Ryun. Jim Ryun's track career has produced many records but not this year. His 1966 and 1967 world marks for 880 yards (1:44.9), 1,500 meters (3:33.1), and 1 mile (3:51.1), still stood after the 1972 season. However, though his talent was untarnished, his desire and concentration wavered and he ran erratically throughout 1972.

On March 4, in Los Angeles, Ryun ran a mile in 4:19.2, finishing 150 yards behind the winner, Tom Von Ruden. "I didn't conquer Jim Ryun," said Von Ruden. "Something else did. He seems to be running without motivation."

On April 22, on his home track in Lawrence, Kans., Ryun won a mile in 3:57.1 and seemed ready to complete his comeback. His 4:09 mile a week later at Des Moines was blamed on dysentery, but his ninth-place 4:14.2 finish at the Dr. Martin Luther King, Jr., International Freedom games in mid-May was something else. His coach, Bob Timmons, said the absence of many top milers created a negative competitive response from him.

Then, in the Olympic trials at Eugene, Ore., Ryun barely missed qualifying for the 800-meter team but won the 1,500-meter final in 3:41.5. With an Olympic berth assured, Ryun won the mile in Toronto in 3:52.8, the third fastest in history (he had run the two faster miles himself).

But again Ryun's hopes were frustrated—in Munich he did not even qualify for the Olympic 1,500, an event he was favored to win. His big chance lasted less than three minutes, when he fell in his heat after colliding with another runner. By the time Ryun got up, he was 50 meters behind, and he could not close the gap.

Track winners. Aside from the pole vault, the year's most fascinating competition came in the distance runs. The major prizes went to Lasse Viren of Finland, Emiel Puttemans of Belgium, and Steve Prefontaine of Coos Bay, Ore.

Viren, a slender, 23-year-old policeman, broke three world records within a month. On August 14, he set a record of 8:14 for 2 miles. Then, in the Olympics, he won the 5,000-meter and 10,000-meter finals, the 10,000 in the world-record time of 27:38.4. Valery Borzov, the Soviet sprinter, was the only other double track winner at Munich, with victories in the 100-meter and 200-meter dashes. On Sep-

OLYMPIC POLE-ITICS. East Germany's Wolfgang Nordwig used a standard pole to vault to victory in the Munich games. Competitors complained that he would never have won had they been allowed to use new fiberglass Catapoles, on which they had confidently practiced.

tember 14, at Helsinki, Viren lowered Ron Clarke's six-year-old 5,000-meter record to 13:16.4.

Viren's 5,000-meter record lasted only six days. Puttemans broke it September 20 in his native country, when he set two world records in one race—12:47.6 for 3 miles and 13:13 for 5,000 meters. Six days before, Puttemans broke Kipchoge Keino's seven-year-old 3,000-meter record with a time of 7:37.6 at Aarhus, Denmark.

Prefontaine was a 21-year-old junior at the University of Oregon, a short, cocky folk hero whose popularity inspired the "Go Pre" T-shirts many people wore at his home track in Eugene, Ore. There at the Olympic trials, Prefontaine set an American 5,000-meter record of 13:22.8 which equaled the third-best world time ever. After it was all over

he took a victory lap wearing a "Stop Pre" T-shirt designed by rivals. He ran fourth in the Olympic 5,000.

U.S. Olympic trials and joys. In the Olympic track competition at Munich the United States and the Soviet Union each won six gold medals in the 24 men's events. This represents a decline for the Americans, who had won 12 golds in the 1968 Mexico City games.

Offsetting Ryun's disappointment in the 1,500-meter event, there was one surprise victory for the United States when Dave Wottle, the tall golf-capped Ohioan, shot from behind and then squeaked past Russia's Yevgeny Arzhanov, the world's top-ranked half-miler, to win the closest 800-meter race in Olympic history. Both men were clocked at times of 1:45.9.

544

In addition to facing impressive competition, the U.S. track team suffered from its share of internal problems. There was the case of Rey Robinson and Eddie Hart, who both set world marks of 9.9 in the 100-meter dash at the U.S. Olympic trials and who, through the carelessness of their coach, missed their quarterfinal heat in that event. Thus, the title of the world's fastest human went, in a 10.14 time, to Valery Borzov. Robert Taylor, who just made his heat, came in second.

Among the Americans who did well at the Olympics and throughout the year were Rod Milburn in the high hurdles, Frank Shorter in the marathon, Larry Young in the 50-kilometer walk, and Randy Williams in the long jump.

Women. The leading women in track were Renate Stecher of East Germany and Ludmila Bragina of the Soviet Union. Stecher won both Olympic sprints, and during the year she tied the world records of 11 seconds for 100 meters and 22.4 for 200 meters. Miss Bragina accomplished one of the most amazing feats in track history by breaking the world record for 1,500 meters three times in two days (4:06.9 to 4:06.5, 4:05.1, and 4:01.4, the last in the Olympic final) and also setting a record for 3,000 meters (8:53.0). Among gold medal–winning nations, East Germany topped the list with six and West Germany took four.

Nina Kuscsik of Huntington Station, N.Y., a 33-year-old mother of three, made history in the Boston Marathon, a race of 26 miles 385 yards, when women were allowed for the first time to run in the same race with men. She led the female finishers in 3:08:58 and was the first woman to finish in the AAU national marathon (3:21:03). Her goal, she said, was "to present an image that makes running look human for women."   FRANK LITSKY

WEIGHT LIFTING. There was never any question about what team would win the AAU championship, and just as expected, the York (Pa.) Barbell Club won the title for the 41st consecutive time. The big question at the meet was whether super-heavyweight Ken Patera of the York squad would become the first American ever to clean-and-jerk 500 pounds. Three times in the past he had cleaned that much weight but each time had failed to raise it overhead.

Patera, a former NCAA indoor shot-put champion while at Brigham Young University, had injured his knee and back while training for the AAU showdown in Detroit, but he was otherwise well prepared. Physically, his weight was at a whopping, albeit highly desirable, 335 pounds, and since this would be his final U.S. weight lifting competition because of plans to become a professional wrestler after the Olympics, he was also mentally ready to make the big lift. And make it he did, hoisting a total of 501½ pounds. Patera also set national and American records by lifting a total of 1,339¼ pounds in the three types of lifts.

AAU SENIOR WEIGHT LIFTING CHAMPIONSHIPS
Detroit, June 10–12

Flyweight: John Yamauchi, Hawaii, 595¼ pounds
Bantamweight: Salvador Dominguez, York, Pa., 672½
Featherweight: Philip Sanderson, Los Angeles, 744
Lightweight: Dan Cantore, San Francisco, 931½
Middleweight: Fred Lowe, York, Pa., 992
Light-heavyweight: Michael Karchut, River Forest, Ill., 1,041¾
Middle-heavyweight: Rick Holbrook, York, Pa., 1,129¾
Heavyweight: Frank Capsouras, York, Pa., 1,157½
Super-heavyweight: Ken Patera, York, Pa., 1,339¼

Aside from Patera, there were three other men who successfully defended their titles: bantamweight Salvador Dominguez, light-heavyweight Mike Karchut, and middle-heavyweight Rick Holbrook. Lightweight Dan Cantore of San Francisco also put on an exceptional performance at the AAU championships by establishing three national and American marks: 303¼ pounds in the press, 358¼ pounds in the clean and jerk, and a total poundage of 931½.

The Olympic weightlifting crown was won by super-heavyweight Vasily Alexeyev of the Soviet Union, who

hoisted a three-lift total of over 1,410 pounds to set a new Olympic record. In this event, dominated almost exclusively by East European nations, Bulgaria topped the list with six medals, including three golds.

HERMAN WEISKOPF

WRESTLING. The big story: Chris Taylor. In a sense, the Cyclones of Iowa State had been suffering from a surfeit of success in recent years. Attendance had declined at home matches, and many of those fans left as soon as their team was assured of another victory. But this year the attendance soared and once reached 10,100 for a match against arch rival Oklahoma State, the largest crowd ever to witness an amateur wrestling match in this country. What's

AN UPLIFTING VICTORY. Soviet super-heavyweight Vasily Alexeyev upheld his reputation as strongest man in the world by hoisting a three-lift total of over 1,410 pounds for an Olympic gold medal.

KEYSTONE

more, the fans did not leave early this season, for leaving early would have meant missing that enormous heavyweight, the spectacular Chris Taylor.

Taylor, a 6'5" junior from Dowagiac, Mich., is so big that the only place on campus he can weigh himself is at the meat laboratory, where he sends the scale soaring up to well over 400 pounds. Amazingly agile despite his bulk, Taylor proved himself on the wrestling mat this season, where he had one draw and 32 wins—24 of them by pins—in dual meets.

The Olympics. At the Munich Olympics this year Taylor captured a bronze medal; however, many felt that officiating errors in his first-round bout with world champion Alexander Medved may have cost him the gold. On the whole, the Americans made an unexpectedly strong showing in the wrestling competition. To Taylor's bronze, add three gold-medal performances by lightweight Dan Gable, welterweight Wayne Wells, and light-heavyweight Ben Peterson and two silver medals won by bantamweight Rick Sanders and Ben's brother, John Peterson, a middleweight.

U.S. championships. Possibly because of Taylor's renown, attendance records were set at this year's NCAA tournament at the University of Maryland, where 42,500 attended the six sessions. For the finals, 12,000 spectators showed up, setting another all-time high for an amateur match in the United States. And Taylor did not disappoint his followers, as he scored a 6–1 victory over the defending heavyweight king, Greg Wojciechowski of Toledo. With Taylor's help, Iowa State won the team title for the third time in four years. Carl Adams (158 pounds) and Ben

TOP HEAVY. Chris Taylor, the 400-pound-plus wrestling champ from Iowa State, gave West Germany's Wilfried Dietrich a weighty problem in the Olympic Greco-Roman grapple. Dietrich won, but Chris Taylor remained a very big man on the Iowa campus.

UPI

Peterson (190) were the other Cyclones winners, who outscored Michigan State 103–72½.

Greg Johnson of the Spartans became a three-time champion in the 118-pound division. Two of his teammates, brothers Pat and Tom Milkovich, also won, with Pat becoming the first freshman to take an NCAA gold medal since 1947. Little Clarion (Pa). State College sent only two wrestlers to the tournament, but both of them—134-pounder Garry Barton and 150-pounder Wade Schalles—were winners. And Schalles, who pinned four of his five opponents, was named Outstanding Wrestler.

NCAA WRESTLING CHAMPIONSHIPS
University of Maryland, March 10–12
118 pounds: Greg Johnson, Michigan State
126 pounds: Pat Milkovich, Michigan State
134 pounds: Gary Barton, Clarion State
142 pounds: Tom Milkovich, Michigan State
150 pounds: Wade Schalles, Clarion State
158 pounds: Carl Adams, Iowa State
167 pounds: Andy Matter, Penn State
177 pounds: Bill Murdock, Washington
190 pounds: Ben Peterson, Iowa State
Heavyweight: Chris Taylor, Iowa State

For the third straight time the New York Athletic Club won the freestyle title and the Minnesota Wrestling Club the Greco-Roman competition at the National AAU Wrestling Championship in April. Dave Hazewinkel of Minnesota won his fourth Greco-Roman championship in a row at 125½ pounds, and three men were winners in both styles: Jay Robinson at 180½ pounds, heavyweight Wojciechowski, and Wayne Baughman at 198 pounds. For Baughman these were his 13th and 14th NAAU titles.

HERMAN WEISKOPF

YACHTING. Newport-to-Bermuda. Shouldering its way to the finish line in 20-foot to 30-foot waves and through frequent, violent squalls that reduced visibility to zero, the 48-foot British sloop *Noryema* became the first non-American yacht in 66 years to win the Newport-to-Bermuda race, the last of a series of four races. Skippered by 64-year-old Ted Hicks, who filled in for owner Ron Amey, the Sparkman & Stephens-designed yacht beat 177 rivals, three of which were dismasted in what many veteran Bermuda race hands described as the worst racing conditions within memory. A tropical depression materialized unexpectedly southwest of Bermuda and moved northward, battering the fleet for 30 hours with winds of near-hurricane force and making the landfall for yachts trying to finish at that point an extremely dangerous proposition. A number of yachts hove-to for as long as 12 hours rather than risk damage on the coral reef which protects the eastern end of the Bermuda islands.

Of the record 178 entries, 27 were foreign. Many of them had been attracted to the Newport race by the increasingly popular Onion Patch Trophy competition among three-boat national teams held earlier, and five of the 27 foreign yachts finished among the top three in their respective classes. In the 18-boat race for the Onion Patch Trophy, the U.S. team, consisting of Jesse Phillips' 56-foot sloop *Charisma*, David Steere's 56-foot sloop *Yankee Girl*, and Wallace Stenhouse's 49-foot sloop *Aura*, easily won over a field from five other nations, with 281 points to 206 for second-place Great Britain.

Transatlantic competition. For the second time since the event was inaugurated in 1960 a French yacht won the singlehanded transatlantic race, sponsored by the London *Observer*. The 67-foot ketch-rigged trimaran *Pen Duick IV*, skippered by Alain Colas, sailed from Plymouth, England, to Newport, R.I., in 20 days, 12 hours, and 15 minutes, breaking the previous record by a margin of more than five days.

The 128-foot three-masted schooner *Vendredi Treize*, the largest single-handed vessel ever built, had been ex-

SAILSMANSHIP. The "U.S. 600," skippered by Buddy Melges, slips ahead of the pack (right) in Olympic Soling-class competition.

pected to finish first but arrived more than 17 hours behind the winner. This was much to the dismay of the schooner's owner, French movie producer Claude Lelouch, who was in Newport preparing for the triumph that never came.

Of the 55 yachts that actually started the race, though not all at the same time, 12 retired and 40 reached Newport before the race officially ended.

Light winds, which had hampered the single-handers after their first week at sea also slowed the fleet making the transatlantic Race of Discovery from Bermuda to Spain. The winds were so light that the 73-foot ketch, *Jubilee III,* the eventual winner in Class A, made only 38 miles in one 24-hour period. Richard S. Nye's 48-foot sloop *Carina,* which had won the Newport-to-Bermuda race in 1970, earned Class B and fleet honors in the race. *Noryema* was the winner in Class C, and Morton Gibbons-Neff's *Prim* took Class D.

Olympics. Buddy Melges was the only American skipper to win a gold medal in the Olympic games at Kiel, Germany, when he took first place in the Soling class. Glen Foster of New York City won a bronze medal in the Tempest class, and Donald Cohan of Philadelphia took the bronze medal in the Dragon class. Other Olympic gold medal winners were Rodney Pattison of Great Britain in the Flying Dutchman class, Serge Maury of France in the Finn class, David Forbes of Australia in the Star class, Valentin

Mankin of the Soviet Union in the Tempest class, and John B. Cuneo of Australia in the Dragon class.

Other winners. One of the year's most outstanding achievements was turned in by 23-year-old Argyle Campbell of Newport Beach, Calif., who won the Congressional Cup for the second time in a week-long match-racing series at Long Beach, Calif., in March. The field of ten included 1970 America's Cup helmsman Bill Ficker and crews from Hawaii, Canada, Australia, and New Zealand. In 1971 Campbell had helped the University of Southern California win the championship in the North American Intercollegiate dinghy competition.

Edwin Sherman, Jr., of St. Petersburg, Fla., won a hammer-and-tongs match race from his nearest rival on the final day in capturing the senior men's North American championship and the Mallory Cup at Marina Del Rey, Calif.

Sally Lindsay, representing The Dinghy Club of Swampscott, Mass., won the women's senior North American championship at Rocky River, Ohio. To make the finals she had to defeat last year's Adams Cup winner, Romeyn "Rusty" Everdell, in a district elimination.

Clark Thompson of Houston, Texas, won the North American junior championship at Jackson, Miss., for the Sears Cup, and Craig Thomas of Seattle won the North American singlehanded championship for the O'Day Trophy.

DAVID M. PHILIPS

WEST GERMANY (WOLFGANG ZIMMERER, DRIVER)

CH. CHINOE'S ADAMANT JAMES

CHAMPIONS IN

Event	Winner	Event	Winner
ARCHERY		**CYCLING**	
World men	John Williams, Cranesville, Pa.	World pro sprint	R. van Lancker, Belgium
World women	Maureen Bechdolt, Loveland, Ohio	World women's sprint	Galina Ermolava, U.S.S.R.
U.S. men	Kevin Erlandson, Sacramento, Calif.	U.S. sprint	Gary Campbell, Paramount, Calif.
U.S. women	Ruth Rowe, Pittsburgh, Pa.	World pro road	Marino Basso, Italy
		U.S. road	John Howard, Springfield, Mo.
BADMINTON		Tour de France	Eddy Merckx, Belgium
U.S. men	Sture Johnsson, Sweden		
U.S. women	Eva Twedberg, Sweden	**DOG SHOWS**	
All-England men	Rudy Hartono, Indonesia	Westminster, New York City	Ch. Chinoe's Adamant James, English
All-England women	Noriko Nakayama, Japan		springer spaniel
		International, Chicago	Ch. Joanne-Chen's Maya Dancer, Maltese
BARREL JUMPING			
World	Roger Wood, Portland, Ore.	**FENCING**	
		U.S. foil	Bert Freeman, Philadelphia
BIATHLON		U.S. épée	James Melcher, New York City
United States	Pete Karns, Jackson, Wyo.	U.S. saber	Alex Orban, Yonkers, N.Y.
		U.S. women's foil	Ruth White, Baltimore
BILLIARDS			
World three-cushion	Raymond Ceulemans, Belgium	**FIELD HOCKEY**	
World pocket	Irving Crane, Rochester, N.Y.	World Cup women	Netherlands
U.S. pocket	Steve Mizerak, Carteret, N.J.	U.S. men	Westchester, N.Y.
U.S. women's pocket	Jean Balukas, Brooklyn, N.Y.		
		GAELIC FOOTBALL	
BOBSLEDDING		All-Ireland	Offaly
European four-man	Switzerland (Hanruedi Müller, driver)		
European two-man	West Germany (Wolfgang Zimmerer,	**HANDBALL**	
	driver)	USHA three-wall	Lou Russo, New York City
		USHA four-wall	Fred Lewis, Miami Beach, Fla.
CANOEING		YMCA four-wall	Paul Haber, Chicago
U.S. 1,000-meter canoe	Roland Muhlen, Newport Beach, Calif.	AAU one-wall	Steve Sandler, New York City
U.S. men's 1,000-meter kayak	Pete Weigand, Newport Beach, Calif.		
U.S. women's 500-m. kayak	Marcia Smoke, Niles, Mich.	**HORSESHOE PITCHING**	
U.S. men's kayak slalom	Eric Evans, Hanover, N.H.	U.S. men	Elmer Hohl, Wellesley, Ontario
U.S. women's kayak slalom	Caroline Ashton, Kensington, Md.	U.S. women	Mrs. Ruth Hangen, Buffalo, N.Y.
CASTING		**ICEBOATING**	
U.S. all-around	Steve Rajeff, San Francisco	North American	Jan Gougeon, Bay City, Mich.
U.S. all-distance	Zack Willson, Delaware, Ohio		
		LUGE (TOBOGGANING)	
COURT TENNIS		U.S. men	Terry O'Brien, Plattsburgh, N.Y.
World	Jim Bostwick, Brookville, N.Y.	U.S. women	Kathleen Homstad, Missoula, Mont.
U.S. open	Bostwick		
		MODERN PENTATHLON	
CROSS-COUNTRY		World military	Captain Charles Richards, Tacoma
International men	Gaston Roelants, Belgium	United States	Richards
International women	Joyce Smith, Britain		
		MOTORCYCLE RACING	
CURLING		U.S. grand national	Mark Brelsford, San Bruno, Calif.
World	Canada (Orest Meleschuk, skip)		
U.S. men	Grafton, N.D. (Robert LaBonte, skip)	**PADDLEBALL**	
U.S. women	Wilmette, Ill. (Mrs. Gerry Duguid, skip)	United States	Dan McLaughlin, Ann Arbor, Mich.
		PARACHUTE JUMPING	
		World men's overall	Clayton Schoelpple, Hartwood, Va.
		World women's overall	Barbara Karkoschka, East Germany
		U.S. men's overall	Roy Johnson, Warren, Ohio
		U.S. women's overall	Susan Rademakers, Oakland, Calif.

RUTH WHITE

PAUL HABER (LEFT)

OTHER SPORTS

Event	Winner	Event	Winner
POLO		**SOFTBALL**	
U.S. open	Milwaukee	World men's fast pitch	Canada
U.S. 20-goal	Red Doors Farm, Barrington, Ill.	U.S. men's fast pitch	Raybestos Cardinals, Stratford, Conn.
U.S. collegiate	Connecticut	U.S. women's fast pitch	Raybestos Brakettes, Stratford, Conn.
		U.S. men's slow pitch	Jiffy Club, Louisville
QUARTER HORSE RACING		U.S. women's slow pitch	Riverside Ford, Cincinnati
All-American Futurity	Possumjet		
		SQUASH RACQUETS	
RACQUETBALL		North American men	Sharif Khan, Toronto
U.S. men	Charles Brumfield, San Diego, Calif.	U.S. men	Vic Neiderhoffer, Berkeley, Calif.
U.S. women	Jan Pasternak, Houston, Texas	U.S. women	Mrs. Nina Moyer, Pennington, N.J.
RACQUETS		**SQUASH TENNIS**	
World	William Surtees, Chicago	U.S. open	Dr. Pedro Bacallao, New York City
United States	Surtees	U.S. amateur	Bacallao
ROLLER HOCKEY		**SUMO WRESTLING**	
World	Spain	Emperor's Cup	Jesse Kahaulua (Takamiyama), Honolulu
ROLLER SKATING		**SURFING**	
World men	Michael Obrecht, West Germany	U.S. men	Dale Dobson, San Diego, Calif.
World women	Petra Hausler, West Germany	U.S. women	Mary Setterholm, Corona Del Mar, Calif.
U.S. men	Michael Jacques, Norwood, Mass.		
U.S. women	April Allen, Houston	**SYNCHRONIZED SWIMMING**	
		U.S. indoor	Gail Johnson, Santa Clara, Calif.
ROQUE		U.S. outdoor	Miss Johnson
U.S. first division	Jack Green, Long Beach, Calif.		
U.S. second division	Jack Roegner, Decatur, Ill.	**TABLE TENNIS**	
		U.S. men	Dal Joon Lee, Parma, Ohio
RUGBY		U.S. women	Wendy Hicks, Santa Barbara, Calif.
Rugby Union	Wales		
U.S. collegiate	Palmer College, Davenport, Iowa	**TEAM HANDBALL**	
		World women	East Germany
SHOOTING		U.S. men	Adelphi University
Rifle			
U.S. small-bore, position	David Boyd, Quantico, Va.	**TRAMPOLINE**	
U.S. small-bore, prone	Presley Kendall, Atlanta	U.S. men	Dieter Schulz, West Germany
Pistol		U.S. women	Alexandra Nicholson, Rockford, Ill.
U.S. all-around	Bonnie D. Harmon, Columbus, Ga.		
Skeet		**VOLLEYBALL**	
U.S. all-around	Tony Rosetti, Biloxi, Miss.	USVA men	Chart House, San Diego, Calif.
Grand American Trapshoot		USVA women	South Texas, Houston, Texas
Men	George Mushrush, Fairfield, Ohio	AAU men	Sand and Sea, Santa Monica, Calif.
Women	Charlotte Wells, Middletown, Ohio	AAU women	Region 13 Seniors, Los Angeles
SHUFFLEBOARD		**WATER POLO**	
U.S. winter	Romie Schneider, Boynton Beach, Fla.	U.S. men's outdoor	Concord (Calif.) Dolphins
U.S. summer	Lary Faris, Cincinnati	U.S. women's outdoor	Coral Gables, Fla.
SKIBOBBING		**WATER SKIING**	
World men	T. Graeber, Italy	U.S. men's overall	Mike Suyderhoud, Petaluma, Calif.
World women	M. Geissler, West Germany	U.S. women's overall	Liz Allan Shetter, Winter Park, Fla.
SNOWMOBILE RACING		**WHEELCHAIR GAMES**	
Winnipeg to St. Paul	Yvon Duhamel, Valcourt, Quebec	United States	Illinois Gizz Kids
SOARING			
World	G. Ax, Sweden		
United States	H. Ray Gimmey, Sacramento, Calif.		

SRI LANKA. Politics and government. Ceylon was declared the republic of Sri Lanka on May 22, when the Constituent Assembly adopted a new constitution. This date will replace February 4 as Independence Day. (Lanka is the Sanskrit name of Ceylon.) No change of personnel was involved: Prime Minister Sirimavo Bandaranaike remained in office, and Governor-general William Gopallawa was renamed president. The House of Representatives became the National Assembly, and its members will serve six-year terms; the Senate had been abolished last September. The new Appeals Court, which replaces the Privy Council, had been set up last November. Sri Lanka will remain in the British Commonwealth.

The new constitution was adopted by a 120 to 16 vote. The United National Party, under former prime minister Dudley Senanayake, voted against it in protest against the nomination of the head of state by the prime minister, the subordination of the judiciary to the National Assembly, the investing of almost all powers in the political executive, and the taking away from the courts of the power to determine the constitutionality of legislation.

Opposition unity between parliamentary leader J. R. Jayewardene and party leader Dudley Senanayake became strained as a result of Jayewardene's unsuccessful efforts to join Mrs. Bandaranaike's left-wing coalition government. These differences were patched up, however, when the new constitution came into effect without any additions to the government.

The (Moscow-oriented) Communist Party, which is part of the government coalition, split over the subject of the Criminal Justice Commission bill, which set up a special court to try those involved in the insurgency last April. In this court, which would also try currency offenders, normal rules and procedures can be disregarded and no decision can be appealed. Four Communist legislators refused to vote in favor of this bill, and the junior minister who voted for it was suspended by the party. The other Communist member of the government, Minister of Housing Pieter Keuneman, was fortuitously out of the island when the vote took place. There was also internal dissension over the bill in the small Peking-oriented Communist Party, which does not support the government.

The trial of 41 leaders accused of treason in the 1971 insurgency finally started in June. The special commission which had been established to try the offenders was staffed by members of the regular judiciary, although the commission is considered by many to remain a potential danger to normal democratic principles of justice. There had been dissatisfaction, both at home and abroad, over the length of time so many persons had been interned without being brought to trial, and a former British legislator, Lord Avebury, who tried to inspect the prison camps was unable to do so. However, Douglas Hyde, renegade Communist and former editor of the British *Daily Worker*, was later able to make a private inspection, and he praised the government for its treatment of the internees. After much criticism of the continued emergency regulations, censorship of the press was lifted in May. Sensational escapes from a number of internment camps were reported on the eve of the trials.

Economic development. Finance Minister N. M. Perera, Trotskyist member of the government coalition, introduced in his budget a ceiling on expendable income of 2,000 rupees per month (about US$312) and a limitation of land holdings to 50 acres per person; this should bring the government an estimated 500,000 extra acres. Pressure from left-wing elements in the coalition to reduce this figure to 25 acres per family was resisted. Perera's attempt to reduce food subsidies was less successful than his other proposals for change.

The Ceylon rupee, which was linked to the U.S. dollar last November, was again linked to the pound sterling this July. Ceylonese subjects resident abroad were ordered to remit 10 percent of their earnings to Ceylon. The budget deficit was reckoned at 400 million rupees.

To encourage domestic food production, the government banned importation of chilies and potatoes. In addition, importation of rice will be completely stopped at the end of 1973.

Foreign affairs. In early July, Prime Minister Bandaranaike paid a state visit to Peking, where she was warmly received. China again granted Ceylon interest-free loans—307 million rupees and an additional 150 million rupees in convertible currency. It also gave Ceylon five gunboats for use on patrol (primarily to stop illegal immigration from India). Arrangements were made to begin a regular service of cargo liners between Ceylon, China, and Japan in October. Meanwhile, Ceylon's own merchant fleet was increased from one vessel to three.

Education and culture. Tentative efforts were made to establish controls on two sections of society that have often acted as pressure groups in Ceylon—students and Buddhist monks. The four universities and the Government Technical College were combined into a single university with five campuses. A program of rationalization of faculties among these campuses was proposed, although it was strongly resisted by both staff and students. A register of Buddhist monks was compiled for the first time—hitherto all estimates of their total numbers have been guesses. The register shows that there are approximately 18,000 Buddhist monks in Ceylon today.

Area and population. Area, 25,332 sq. mi. Pop. (1971), 12,-747,755. Principal cities: Colombo (cap.), 563,705; Dehiwela, 154,-313; Jaffna, 106,856; Moratuwa, 95,395.
Government. Republic within the British Commonwealth. Pres., William Gopallawa; prime min., Mrs. Sirimavo R. D. Bandaranaike.
Finance. Monetary unit, rupee; 1 rupee = US$0.1575. Budget (1970–1971): revenue, 2,878 million rupees; expenditure, 3,809 million rupees.
Trade (1971). Imports, US$334 million; exports, US$327 million. Principal exports: tea, rubber, coconut products. Principal trading partners: United Kingdom, China.
Armed forces (1970). Military, 10,691; police, 12,843.

CHRISTOPHER B. REYNOLDS

STAMPS AND STAMP COLLECTING. U.S. developments. The focus of the philatelic world was on the U.S. Postal Service, with its innovations in hobby promotion and stamp design. Foremost among the former was the publication of a colorful book, *Stamps and Stories*, combining a priced catalog of all U.S. issues, a technical guide, and a history of the nation as shown on stamps. The book was produced by the Scott Publishing Company, Omaha, and is sold in cloth and paper bindings. Special philatelic gift shops were opened in large metropolitan offices, and the Philatelic Automatic Distribution Service was established to merchandise souvenir album pages for new issues.

A departure in design was the four-element two-cent Cape Hatteras National Seashore commemorative in the national parks centennial series. Each stamp is an entity, but blocks of four combine to complete a larger design. Other parks honored for the first time were Wolf Trap Farm Park for the Performing Arts in Virginia, City of Refuge National Historical Park in Hawaii, and Mount McKinley National Park in Alaska. The eight-cent stamp of the series repeated in multicolor the Old Faithful design on the 1934 Yellowstone stamp.

Se tenant arrangements for four different designs in a sheet were utilized for the wildlife conservation and American bicentennial issues. The latter was also furnished in first day cover form with a Bureau of the Mint medal attached. Other special issues commemorated poet Sidney Lanier, fictional hero Tom Sawyer, the Peace Corps, mail order business, and the Olympic Games. Osteopathic medicine, pharmacy, family planning, and the Parent-Teacher Association furnished socially oriented themes. A new face

in the regular series was New York mayor Fiorello La Guardia on a 14-cent denomination, and another new face —Santa Claus—appeared on one of the Christmas stamps. To celebrate the 125th anniversary of U.S. stamps and to salute stamp collectors, an eight-cent stamp based on the Benjamin Franklin issue of 1847 was released to the public on November 17.

Highlighting new postal stationery were five large pictorial postal cards issued for the Tourism Year of the Americas. Printed in black and orange on beige stock, each has an imprinted stamp design with tourist-oriented theme; on the picture side are four reproductions of tourist sites.

Stamps in space. A negative aspect of American philately was the revelation that astronauts David R. Scott, Alfred M. Worden, and James B. Irwin of the Apollo 15 moon mission of 1971 had carried at least 632 unauthorized covers. One hundred of these reached a German dealer, who sold 99 of them for about $1,500 each. This violation of NASA rules resulted in the reprimanding and re-assignment of Scott and Worden, and Irwin resigned to go into religious work.

World developments. The traditional omnibus issues dominated international philately, with the majority devoted to the Olympic Games, the 25th wedding anniversary of Britain's Queen Elizabeth, the UNESCO campaign to save Venice, and the World Health Organization's drive against heart disease. Climaxing the fellowship aspect of the hobby was Belgica, the two-week exhibition held in Brussels during the summer.   BARBARA R. MUELLER

SUDAN. Government and politics. On March 27, after almost 17 years of unremitting civil war, a peace treaty was concluded between Sudan's central government and the Anyanya rebels in the south. Under the terms of the treaty, the three southern provinces of Bahr al Ghazal, Equatoria, and Upper Nile were combined to form a single, self-governing region operating within the Sudanese political framework. A 12-member high executive council was formed on April 4 to govern the new region. An elected regional assembly will have power to legislate on local matters.

A 12,000-man Sudanese army will remain stationed in the region, but its personnel will be divided equally between northerners and southerners. The city of Juba was chosen as the new capital of the southern region.

On June 15 the ruling Revolutionary Command Council was dissolved, with the political power of Sudan transferred to a 15-member political bureau of the Sudanese Socialist Union, the country's only legal political party.

Foreign relations. Sharp improvement in Sudan's relations with its African neighbors to the south followed the ending of the Sudanese civil war. Sudan's border with Uganda was reopened for the first time in five years and a defense agreement was concluded with that country; both Chad and Uganda promised Khartoum that no support would be given to anti-Sudanese rebels in the future.

Sudan also moved closer to the West. Diplomatic relations were established with the Vatican and, in July, resumed with the United States (they had been broken off in 1967). In April, Foreign Minister Mansour Khaled visited Washington, where he obtained promises of aid to help Sudanese rehabilitation. During the same period, President Jafaar al-Nimery toured the oil-rich Arab states of the Persian Gulf in search of economic assistance. One result was a $4 million grant from Qatar to aid development programs in the southern region.

Economic developments. The cost of Sudan's civil war was staggering, absorbing more than half the military budget, tying up three-fourths of the army, and prohibiting expenditures on economic development. Almost 500,000 southerners were killed in the fighting, another half million were rendered homeless, and almost 1 million died through war-induced famine and disease. Already among the most underdeveloped countries in the world, Sudan now faces the task of reconstructing an impoverished region left devastated by war, its countryside depopulated and towns swollen with homeless, jobless refugees. A proposed irrigation canal across the Nile bend in the area of Malakal is expected to provide some economic relief. However, the immediate future for the southern region continues to seem bleak at best.

SOUVENIRS. The Apollo 15 astronauts were reprimanded by NASA in July for smuggling at least 623 stamped, canceled envelopes aboard their moon ship for commercial gain; 100 of them reportedly reached a stamp dealer, who sold them for about $1,500 each.

NEW YORK TIMES

THIS ENVELOPE WAS CARRIED TO THE MOON ABOARD THE APOLLO 15 #100 OF 300 TO THE LUNAR SURFACE IN L. M. "FALCON"

FIRST MAN ON THE MOON

A DECADE OF ACHIEVEMENT   UNITED STATES IN SPACE

Area and population. Area, 967,500 sq. mi. Pop., 15,100,000. Principal cities: Khartoum (cap.), 220,000; Juba, 120,000.

Government. Effective political power vested in the political bureau of the Socialist Union Party. Pres. and prime min., Jafaar Muhammad al-Nimery; for. min., Mansour Khaled.

Finance. Monetary unit, Sudanese pound. S£1 = US$2.94. Budget (1972): revenue, S£191,200,000; expenditure, S£255,-500,000.

RICHARD H. PFAFF

SWAZILAND. Politics and government. This year's general elections, the first since independence, provided a great deal of interest and some important surprises. The ruling Imbokodvo National Movement, led by Prince Makhosini Dlamini and backed by the *ngwenyama* (paramount chief), Sobhuza II, won 21 out of 24 seats. However, the Ngwane National Liberatory Congress (NNLC), led by Dr. Ambrose Zwane, ran better than expected, even though the party had split into two factions prior to the balloting. The vote totals were Imbokodvo, 164,493; NNLC-Zwane, 38,554; NNLC-Samketi, 6,393; the United Front of Obed Mpangele, 797; and the Progressive Party of Albert Nxumalo, 582. Dr. Zwane and two other members of the NNLC were elected to the House of Assembly.

The new government included Prince Makhosini as prime minister, Zonke Khumalo as deputy prime minister, Polycarp Dlamini as minister of justice, Robert Stephens as minister of finance, Simon Nxumalo as minister of industry, mines, and tourism, and Stephen Matsebula as minister of foreign affairs. Although the forces of the monarchy are still very much in control of the political system, the inclusion of the opposition in national political life should stimulate greater interest in politics and stave off the possibility of Swaziland becoming a one-party state.

Economic developments. The economy continued to show steady growth. A new international hotel was begun, as was a new fertilizer factory, an oil-processing plant, and a knitwear garment facility. Other projects under consideration by year's end included a plastics factory, an iron ore smelting unit, a cotton spinning facility, and an electrical wire production firm. Most importantly for the immediate economic outlook, through the considerable efforts of Dr. S. T. M. Sukati, ambassador to the United States and high commissioner to Canada, Swaziland's sugar quota was increased from 7,000 to 30,000 tons. This will help to prevent severe dislocation in the Swazi sugar industry when Great Britain joins the Common Market. In addition, the United States authorized a $1.2 million loan for agricultural development to improve livestock production and to carry out other programs designed to benefit the average Swazi farmer. A major target of the plan will be to develop the underutilized grassland, heretofore used only for grazing.

Area and population. Area, 6,705 sq. mi. Pop. (est. 1971) 420,000, including 9,000 persons of European descent. Mbabane (cap.), 15,000.

Government. Constitutional monarchy within the Commonwealth of Nations. King, Sobhuza II; prime min., Prince Makhosini Dlamini; ambassador to the United States, Dr. S. T. M. Sukati.

Finance and trade. Monetary unit, South African rand; R1 = US$1.29. Chief exports: iron ore, asbestos, sugar, timber products, and citrus fruits.

Armed forces. None.

Education (1969). Primary schools, 361; enrollment, 63,000. Secondary schools, 40; enrollment, 6,300.

CHRISTIAN P. POTHOLM

SWEDEN. Politics and government. After a relatively tame budget debate, the Riksdag and the government faced a deepening economic crisis as a rate of unemployment comparable to that of the 1930's forced the adoption of drastic measures. The Riksdag lowered income taxes for lower- and middle-income groups, extended the value-added tax to 20 percent, and, with some dissent, increased excise duties on tobacco, spirits, and other luxury items.

The Riksdag also revised procedures to attain a more effective management of its time on the basis of a year's

experience with a unicameral system. It also passed laws for the preservation of recreational areas and for environmental purposes, approved antipollution and antidumping legislation, and reduced the number of police and judicial districts.

A constitutional reform bill was also introduced that would make the king a symbolic head of state and authorize the speaker of parliament to appoint the premier-designate to form a government. Future premiers would appoint the cabinet without the royal consent and would have the decisive vote at deadlocked cabinet meetings. The bill, which would also lower the voting age from 20 to 18, has to be approved by two sessions of parliament, with an election in between; the next scheduled elections are in September 1973.

Foreign affairs. The Swedes have formally declined membership in the European Economic Community (Common Market). However, a free-trade agreement with the Common Market, signed July 22, will probably ease the transition when Denmark, Britain, and Ireland join the EEC on January 1, 1973. The agreement allowed entry of more than half of Sweden's exports under nominal tariffs and provided Sweden with some protection for its own markets. Also in July a reasonably satisfactory agreement dealing with forest products was signed with Britain and Norway.

The World Conference on the Human Environment, sponsored by the United Nations, convened in Stockholm in June. The conference welcomed proposals for worldwide pollution controls but also furnished a rostrum for Prime Minister Olof Palme's bitter attack on American policies in Southeast Asia. The Riksdag also adopted strong protests against the bombing of North Vietnam. Sweden joined with other countries in pressing for UN action and for a denunciation of the bombing by Secretary General Kurt Waldheim.

Economy. The rate of unemployment in January ranked as the highest since the depression years, and it continued during the remainder of the year. The government encouraged private investment with tax advantages, assumed loans to enterprises with economic problems, and attempted to strengthen companies involved with foreign export. Parliament's approval was sought for a fund of more than a half billion kronor, partially to support firms with potential export markets. Price controls had ended in January, and when prices continued to rise there were public demonstrations against food prices. Despite predictions of economic improvement, unemployment, business failures, wage and price increases, larger foreign trade deficits, and inflation continued unchecked.

One of the largest grain harvests of recent decades, with a 1.5 million ton surplus to market abroad, benefited neither the farmer nor the consumer, since the farmer stood to receive no advantages from lower international grain prices and the housewife saw the same or higher food prices.

Church-state relations. A government commission reported favorably on the disestablishment of the state church by 1983, with obvious support in the Riksdag for the move. The church would no longer be responsible for the census and other duties for the state; the government, however, would guarantee salaries and pensions and the maintenance of churches for both congregational and historic reasons. The report recommended a gradual transition in several stages.

Area and population. Area, 173,666 sq. mi. Pop. (est. 1971), 8,091,782. Principal cities (1971): Stockholm (cap.), 740,486 (greater Stockholm, 1,344,748); Göteborg, 451,806 (greater Göteborg, 677,548); Malmö, 265,505; Västerås, 116,648; Uppsala, 127,448.

Government. Constitutional hereditary monarchy with unicameral parliament (Riksdag). King, Gustaf VI Adolf; prime min., Olof Palme; for. min., Krister Wickman; fin. min., Gunnar Sträng; def. min., Sven Andersson.

Finance. Monetary unit, krona; 1 krona = US$0.211. Budget (1972–1973, in billions of kronor): revenue, 47.8; expenditure, 42.2.

Major sources of revenue: income and property taxes, value-added tax, excise tax, auto tax. Principal items of expenditure: social welfare, education, defense, communications. Gross national product, 181.45 billion kronor.

Trade (1971, in billions of kronor). Exports, 38.3; imports, 36.2. Principal imports: textiles, foodstuffs, machinery, chemicals, fuel, transport, electrical machinery. Principal exports: wood products, pulp and paper, machinery, transport, iron and steel. Principal trading partners: West Germany, United Kingdom, Denmark, Norway.

Agriculture and industry. Agricultural production (1970–1971, in metric tons): milk, 1,220,445; cheese, 62,911; butter, 39,087. Industrial production (1971, in millions of metric tons): textiles, 86.8; iron and steel, 11.8; pulp, 6.77; paper, 4.23.

Education (1970–1971). Enrollment: elementary, 863,151; secondary, 103,672; folk high schools, 13,722; universities (5), 124,440.

Armed forces. Army, 12,000 officers and noncommissioned officers, 40,000 trainees, and 45,000 reserves; navy, 16,000; air force, 9,000, including civilian employees.   RAYMOND E. LINDGREN

SWITZERLAND. Politics and government.
Women's suffrage was extended this year to local and cantonal affairs as women voted in a number of Swiss cantons and half-cantons in a referendum on March 5 and in the annual assemblies of all electors (Landsgemeinden) on April 30.

In a letter to the Defense Ministry in early February, 32 Catholic and Protestant clergymen announced their refusal to serve in the army or engage in other forms of military service, as required of all Swiss men. Stating that the Swiss army "makes less and less sense in the international context and serves little other than economic and financial interests," the signers received the support of 43 other clergymen. According to the Defense Ministry, the clergymen will be individually liable to prosecution for refusal to answer a call-up for basic training or refresher courses. (In place of a standing army, Switzerland has a militia formed of all able-bodied men, aged 20 to 50, who can be called to arms at any time.)

In an attempt at dramatizing their demand for the establishment of part of the German-speaking Bern canton as an autonomous French-speaking Jura canton, a group of 30 Jura separatists, members of the militant group Les Béliers (The Rams), occupied the Swiss embassy in Paris on July 13. In Bern, an illegal protest was staged by several hundred separatists on June 17 over the Bern voters' rejection of a proposal linking Jura school systems with those of French-speaking cantons. On July 16, a bomb explosion that wrecked a munitions depot in a Jura village was attributed to the separatist Jura Liberation Front.

Within three years a referendum on a constitutional amendment liberalizing abortion will be held now that a petition has been signed by about 60,000 people.

Foreign affairs. On July 22 trade pacts were signed in Brussels by members of the enlarged European Economic Community and those members of the European Free Trade Association, including Switzerland, not seeking membership in the EEC. The agreements provided for a 20 percent annual reduction of tariffs on most industrial goods traded over a period of five years, beginning April 1, 1973. By July 1, 1977, the tariff is to be eliminated.

The International Committee of the Red Cross announced on June 5 that an international conference to revise the 1949 Geneva conventions on warfare will be sponsored by Switzerland in 1974. During May, experts from 77 countries met in Geneva to work on additions to the conventions that would cover victims of wars and civil strife.

On July 12, East Germany and Switzerland signed an agreement in Bern, to take effect August 10, for an exchange of trade missions to carry out certain consular functions between the two countries.

Switzerland and Italy signed an agreement on April 20 to protect Lake Maggiore and Lake Lugano from water pollution.

Monetary developments. Two referenda were approved on June 4 to extend two 1971 enactments permitting the government to exercise emergency powers in case of serious disturbances in international monetary relations and to maintain a certain control over the building sector to lessen the risks of inflation.

In reaction to the floating of the British pound, the government announced on June 27 that nonresidents would not be permitted to buy property in Switzerland and banks would not be allowed to invest, or arrange the investment of, foreign funds in Swiss securities.

Other developments. Novelist Clifford Irving and his wife Edith were indicted for fraud by the Swiss government on January 31. First claiming that he had written a biography of billionaire Howard R. Hughes with Hughes' cooperation, Irving later admitted the work was a hoax. The Swiss action resulted from Edith Irving's cashing $650,000 in checks intended for Hughes in one Swiss bank and depositing the sum in another Swiss bank under the name of Helga R. Hughes. Mrs. Irving, a Swiss national, is awaiting trial in Switzerland, after having served a prison sentence in the United States.

In an exception to the law guaranteeing the inviolability of Swiss bank accounts, the Swiss Justice Ministry froze over $500,000 in numbered bank accounts belonging to three alleged international drug dealers. Acting on information supplied by French and U.S. authorities, the Swiss government took its first action against narcotics smugglers attempting to take advantage of the secrecy of Swiss bank accounts.

Area and population. Area, 15,940 sq. mi. Pop. (1970 census), 6,269,783. Principal cities (est. 1970): Bern (cap.), 166,200; Zürich, 427,600; Basel, 213,400; Geneva, 171,900; Lausanne, 138,700; Luzern, 73,100.

Government. Federal republic. Chief executive authority is the seven-man Bundesrat (Federal Council). The electorate (all Swiss citizens over 20) elects representatives to the bicameral Federal Parliament every four years (last election, 1971). Pres., Nello Celio; vice-pres., Roger Bonvin. (Bonvin will be 1973 pres.)

Finance. Monetary unit, Swiss franc; SF1 = US$0.2635. Budget (est. 1970): revenue, 7,571,047,000 Swiss francs; expenditure, 7,594,210,000 Swiss francs.

Education. Universities (1968–1969), 7, and 3 federal institutes; enrollment, 38,462.

Armed forces. Universal compulsory military service.

FELICE BERGEN

SYRIA.
Developments in the Middle East during 1972—highlighted by Egypt's expulsion of its Soviet military advisers—had the net effect of intensifying Soviet-Syrian relations. As a result of these developments, the future of the Federation of Arab Republics (FAR)—comprising Syria, Egypt, and Libya—looked bleak. As Egypt and Libya moved away from Soviet ties, they simultaneously sought closer cooperation with each other. The Soviets, meanwhile, took an active role in Syria's domestic politics through the Syrian Communist Party, traditionally the strongest Communist party in the Arab world.

Politics and government. In March, Syria created a National Progressive Front, consisting of four left-wing parties plus the Ba'ath Party. The four minor parties had two delegates each on the Front's central committee; the Ba'ath had nine. Among the leftist groups, only the Syrian Communist Party was thought to have any significant popular support. Participation of the Syrian Communists in the Front was ensured through the efforts of the Soviet deputy premier, Kyril Mazurov, during his visit to Damascus in February. The move met resistance from elements within the party who wished to remain independent of the Front. Meanwhile, many Ba'athists, including Defense Minister Mustafa Tlas and Vice-President Mahmoud Ayoubi, had pressed for complete abolition of the Communist Party, with its members to be absorbed in an Arab Socialist Union. The Soviets, needless to say, refused to agree to this arrangement.

In April, a serious split developed within the ranks of the Syrian Communist Party. The party's central com-

mittee was evenly divided over the question of retaining veteran party chairman Khalid Bakdash. Embarrassingly bitter accusations were exchanged by both sides, each accusing the other of "deviationism" and anti-Soviet attitudes. In July, the opposing leaders were called to Moscow and a compromise was reached. The Soviets were aware that President Hafez al-Assad needed the full support of a united Syrian Communist Party in order to ward off the leaders of his own Ba'ath Party who opposed cooperation with Syrian Communists and the Soviets.

In March, elections were held for local council seats, part of President Assad's double-edged program to decentralize and institutionalize the revolutionary regime. In a burst of political fervor, 6,897 Front-aligned candidates turned out to run for 644 available seats.

Arab relations. The FAR began administrative operations in December 1971, with Ahmed Khatib, a Syrian, acting as federal prime minister. Federation headquarters had been established in the Cairo suburb of Heliopolis. Difficulties quickly arose on two fronts at the FAR's June Presidential Council meeting at Mersa Matruh, Egypt. Libya's Colonel Muammar al-Qaddafi voiced open hostility to the Soviets, setting the stage for Egypt's sudden reversal, on July 18, of its pro-Soviet policy. At the time, Syria was deeply committed to bringing off new military and economic deals with the Soviets and was, furthermore, midway through the construction of the Soviet-aided Euphrates Dam. Syrian leaders thus found good reason to be cautious.

Foreign relations. Two prominent Soviet officials, Deputy Premier Kyril Mazurov and Defense Minister Marshal Andrei Grechko, visited Syria in February and May, respectively. Mazurov signed an agreement providing Soviet economic and technical backing for Syria's third five-year plan (1971–1975). Military matters were also discussed in both meetings. Although Syria had reiterated its opposition to a formal treaty with Moscow, the Soviets promised an increased supply of modern weapons, including the latest type of SAM missiles. As a result, the total Soviet arms commitment to Syria reached about $700 million. In July, President Assad visited Moscow. The two states "agreed on measures that will increase the military capability of the Syrian Arab Republic." A former chief of staff of the Syrian army, Assad had criticized both the quality and quantity of Soviet military aid. Arriving home from Moscow, he announced that he was now satisfied. On August 12, Assad stated that Syria would not follow Egypt and would keep its Soviet advisers (estimated at 2,500).

Meanwhile, Syria continued to enjoy good relations with the People's Republic of China. In May, Foreign Minister Abdul Halim Khaddam signed an economic and technical cooperation agreement in Peking and received an interest-free loan of $23.8 million.

In its confrontation with Israel, Syria suffered a severe tactical blow with the capture on June 21 of five high-ranking Syrian officers by an Israeli raiding force in southern Lebanon. These officers no doubt knew the details of the recent Syrian-Soviet military aid agreements. In September, Israel mounted a series of heavy bombing raids against Syrian targets. The attacks, following on the Palestinian guerrilla massacre of Israeli Olympic athletes in Munich, were ostensibly aimed at guerrilla operations within Syria and constituted the heaviest such raids since the 1967 war.

Economic developments. Syria cooperated in Iraq's nationalization of the Iraq Petroleum Company (IPC) by taking over the Syrian section of the IPC pipeline. Syria had received $71 million in transit fees from the pipeline in 1971. To help replace the lost revenues, the Organization of Arab Petroleum Exporting Countries (OAPEC)—which Syria had joined in March—offered the Syrians an interest-free loan of $16.3 million.

The government experienced some success in its efforts to encourage the repatriation of Syrian capital which had

fled the country in recent years. During 1971, it announced the return of $15.4 million. Syria also sought to encourage its human resources to return to the homeland. On February 14, one year's amnesty was offered "with no questions asked" to all former civil servants, technicians, and students who had quit the country.

Area and population. Area, 71,498 sq. mi. Pop. (est. 1972), 6,440,000. Principal cities (1969): Damascus (cap.), 813,008; Aleppo, 589,482; Homs, 236,478; Hama, 217,602.
Government. Nominally a constitutional republic. Pres., Hafez al-Assad.
Finance. Monetary unit, Syrian pound; S£1 = US$0.240. Budget (1971–1972): ordinary, US$381.1 million; development, US$384 million. Defense expenditures: 60 percent of (ordinary) budget.
Trade (1969). Imports, US$370 million; exports, US$207 million. Oil production (1971), US$86.4 million.
Education (1968–1969). Primary and secondary students, 1,100,-896; teachers, 34,994.
RALPH H. MAGNUS

TANZANIA. Government and politics. Throughout 1972 the government of Tanzania, headed by President Julius K. Nyerere and the Tanganyika African National Union (TANU), gave priority to internal developments. The most important step taken during the year was the implementation of a policy of decentralization that diffused responsibility for Tanzania's economic development throughout the country.

On January 27 the TANU executive committee announced that new steps would be taken that were "rooted in the Arusha Declaration and the policy of socialism and self-reliance." The Arusha Declaration, a policy document and guide promulgated in 1967, was based on the assumption that Tanzania, as a poor country, could not expect much aid from wealthy countries and would therefore have to rely upon its own hard work to grow and prosper. The new decentralization policy was firmly linked to this goal of self-reliance and was, indeed, the most extensive effort yet made to implement the declaration's objectives.

The major thrust of the campaign was to remove decision-making from the capital of Dar es Salaam and place it in the hands of regional and district groups. The essential idea was to decentralize power—to base Tanzanian development on the principle that "more and more people must be trusted with responsibility."

To give effect to this, several steps were taken. The old system of local government was abolished and replaced by new district development councils. These councils were given direct responsibility for local commercial and industrial projects, roads, water, health services, and primary education. Each region was made responsible for its own activities, with a minimum of interference from the central government. Civil servants are now to be regionally assigned and to be responsible to regional directors of development, rather than to the central bureaucracy in the capital. Local administrators were warned that they would be treated as "saboteurs" if their projects became entangled in new bureaucratic procedures.

The intent of the new measures was clear. Nyerere and TANU had decided that Tanzanians must understand the full meaning of self-reliance and that the only way this could be done was to force regional and district groups to assume full responsibility for their own development. It was naturally hoped that Tanzanians would thrive on the challenge, but it was also accepted that those who worked harder would have better opportunities.

In order to show that TANU was determined to make decentralization work, a major cabinet reshuffle took place in which five ministers were named as new regional commissioners. They will continue to have ministerial status, but their new responsibility will clearly be to the growth and development of their regions. In other cabinet changes, D. Bryceson, the white minister for agriculture and cooperation, was dropped, as were A. M. Babu (economic affairs and development planning) and P. Bomani (commerce and

industry). Other new ministers included John Majecela (foreign affairs), Cleopa Msuya (finance), and Saidi Maswanya (home affairs).

The most difficult and trying political event of the year occurred in April when Sheikh Abeid Karume, first vice-president of Tanzania and chairman of the Zanzibar Revolutionary Council, was assassinated at the headquarters of the Afro-Shirazi Party on Zanzibar island. Karume had been the head of the government on Zanzibar since January 1964, when he led the African ouster of the Arab government and had overseen Zanzibar's union with Tanganyika to form the United Republic of Tanzania. Karume had, however, resisted complete union in many ways, and Zanzibar under his leadership had often acted virtually as a separate entity. Karume was succeeded by Aboud Jumbe, Zanzibar's minister of state, as head of the Zanzibar Revolutionary Council and first vice-president of Tanzania.

Foreign affairs. Troubles with and within neighboring states continued to plague Tanzania during 1972. Relations with Uganda deteriorated further during the year for reasons generally related to Ugandan unhappiness over Tanzania's support for Uganda's former president Apollo Milton Obote, who fled to Tanzania after he was overthrown by General Idi Amin. Nyerere's refusal to recognize Amin and Amin's condemnations of Tanzania for harboring fugitives from Uganda—despite Tanzanian denials—impaired the smooth running of the East African Community, of which both countries, with Kenya, are members. The situation was further worsened by Amin's expulsion of Asians from Uganda; similar anti-Asian sentiment exists in Tanzania, although the government has not taken such radical measures. Intermittent border skirmishes between the two countries

led to an outbreak of more substantial hostilities in September, when Tanzanian forces crossed into Uganda. A settlement was quickly reached, but relations remained cool.

Tanzania's support of Frelimo liberation army forces, which has been challenging Portuguese rule in neighboring Mozambique, posed other problems during the year. In April the government announced that its forces had shot down a Portuguese plane over Tanzanian territory. A few days later, in a possibly related incident, significant damage was caused by sabotage at the Tanzanian high commissioner's office in London.

The country was also affected by the violence between Hutus and Tutsis in Burundi, as thousands of Hutus streamed into Tanzania to escape the bloodshed. A Tanzanian member of parliament was reported killed when he crossed the border in an attempt to investigate the situation.

In other developments, presidents Nicolae Ceauşescu of Romania and Jafaar Muhammad al-Nimery of the Sudan paid state visits to Tanzania. The country also continued its active support of liberation movements in southern Africa. Major Hashim Nbita, a former TANU executive secretary, became the new executive secretary of the Organization of African Unity's Liberation Committee.

Economic developments. More than most poor nations, Tanzania has squarely faced the reality of its poverty and has attempted to define a national policy—the commitment to socialism and self-reliance contained in the Arusha Declaration—to deal with its problems. Nevertheless, Tanzania has been a willing partner in development schemes that do not threaten its integrity and independence.

Tanzania's efforts to help neighboring Zambia break its ties with the white-dominated states of southern Africa in-

MOURNERS included top Tanzanian officials at the funeral of Sheikh Abeid Karume, the Zanzibari leader who was assassinated in April.

KEYSTONE © CAMERAPIX

volved various important projects. The two countries are being linked by the new Tan-Zam Railroad, currently under construction with Chinese assistance. In addition, a 50 percent expansion of the Tazama oil pipeline, which connects Dar es Salaam with the Zambian copper belt, is being undertaken in 1972–1973. The projects have been funded by a $3.2 million grant from the African Development Bank.

The government announced during the year that it intended to buy out between 20 and 25 British farmers who own about 500,000 acres in the West Kilimanjaro region. The announcement reflected TANU's view that it is not in the interest of a developing socialist state for so few people to own so much land.

New moves to broaden Tanzanian tea production were made during the year. Britain announced that it would drop its opposition to a £4.3 million World Bank loan to Tanzania for a small tea scheme. Later in the year the International Development Association announced a $10.8 million credit for a small-holder tea development project. The government hopes to involve 13,000 people in this project.

Like most poor countries, Tanzania has suffered from a dwindling reserve of foreign exchange in recent years as a result of inflation in the industrialized countries and the limited rise in the value of its own exports. In the new budget, consumer taxes were increased and new efforts were made to control imports. Despite its difficulties, however, Tanzania recorded a real growth rate of 4.5 percent in 1971, and it was expected that this rate could at least be sustained.

Area and population. Area, 362,820 sq. mi. Pop. (est. 1971), 13,630,000. Dar es Salaam (cap.; est. 1970), 345,000.
Government. Independent republic within the Commonwealth of Nations. Pres., Julius K. Nyerere; 1st vice-pres., Aboud Jumbe; 2nd vice-pres., R. Kawawa.
Finance. Monetary unit, Tanzania shilling; TSh1 = US$0.1415. Budget (est. 1971–1972): expenditure, TSh2.74 billion.
Trade (1971). Exports, TSh2.7 billion; imports, TSh1.95 billion. Major trading partners: United States, United Kingdom, People's Republic of China, West Germany.   LARRY W. BOWMAN

TELEVISION AND RADIO BROADCASTING. Ventilated video.

There was a big change in television this year, as programming became permissive. Turning its back on a straitlaced past, the industry shucked its corset of taboos and beamed a new liberality into the nation's living rooms. While talk shows, it seemed, could now discuss anything from lesbianism to venereal disease, dramas also discovered a new freedom. Even Marcus Welby, M.D., was allowed to encounter an unwed girl seeking an abortion, along with the modern mama who had, unavailingly, supplied her with The Pill. And on an ABC Movie of the Week, Hal Holbrook played a homosexual who had to explain to his young son his particular feeling for another man.

Network censors were not always so quick with their scissors in snipping out segments and phrases from theatrical films brought to television. In showing Love Story, with Ali MacGraw and Ryan O'Neal, ABC cut out the four-letter words, but abandoned its scruples when it came to certain other words of three letters or five. CBS televised The Damned, originally an X-rated movie, and, although network censors did extensive editing, they retained enough offensive material to yield many letters of protest. However, the networks did draw the line in some cases. One network watched a private screening of Carnal Knowledge, only to decide that, once the necessary cuts were made, there would hardly be any movie left to show.

The upsurge of ethnic comedy, spurred by the past success of CBS's All in the Family, helped television to throw off many of its inhibitions. As ethnic comedies multiplied, they also gained the leeway to try for even racier laughs through gag lines and situations dealing with sex. A case in point was Maude, a situation comedy that made its debut in the fall over CBS, starring Beatrice Arthur in the title role.

The character Maude had first appeared on All in the Family as the left-leaning cousin of Archie Bunker's wife, Edith. Executive producer Norman Lear, decided to tap her for a spinoff series, in some ways bolder than the original. For example, the staff and production crew taped the first two-part episode in which Maude becomes pregnant and considers an abortion, while her husband (played by Bill Macy) mulls over the possibility of a vasectomy. Although CBS asked for a rewrite on the script and waited until late in the year to give final approval, it was interesting that the network was willing even to consider giving topics like abortion and vasectomy a place in situation comedy.

As All in the Family began its third season, it was now well established that Archie Bunker's passion was not limited to right-wing politics. One episode was built around his pointed interest in the physical attractions of the wife of a former air force buddy. In other episodes, Archie occasionally alluded to Edith's menopause, a subject that was treated in full in one of the year's more unusual shows.

With some trepidation about public acceptance, NBC introduced Sanford and Son, a comedy about the stormy relations between a black father (Redd Foxx) and son (Demond Wilson) in the junk business. Based primarily on generation-gap humor, the series also produced its share of ethnic gags and managed to score a high audience rating.

Bridget Loves Bernie, a new comedy on CBS, built its situations around a hotbed of Jewish-Catholic in-law jokes. Harking back to Abie's Irish Rose of the 1920's, it had a girl (Meredith Baxter) from a well-to-do Catholic family marry a boy (David Birney) of much less affluent Jewish stock. Meanwhile, NBC introduced an adventure series with an ethnic touch, starring George Peppard as Banacek, an insurance investigator of Polish descent. Time magazine commented that, in between his sleuthing, Banacek was "a walking lightning rod for Polish jokes."

Late-night shows. Both CBS and ABC, after suffering many years of rating losses with their late-evening talk shows, finally decided to make changes. The prime problem for the two networks was Johnny Carson's Tonight show on NBC, which kept stealing away a sizable chunk of the late-night audience.

CBS had come close to canceling the Merv Griffin Show on several occasions but was always deterred by the lack of a suitable replacement. Forgoing the idea of doing original programming, CBS early this year replaced Griffin with feature films. The movies were a big success—much bigger than CBS had anticipated—although they snatched most of their audience not from NBC's Tonight show but from the Dick Cavett Show on ABC.

In the spring ABC announced that if Cavett's rating did not improve considerably by late summer, the show would be replaced in September. It seemed then that this was ABC's way of putting Cavett on notice—that the network already had decided to drop him in September. But ABC did not foresee the thousands of letters that poured in from people who usually do not write a network, urging that Cavett not be dropped. Accordingly, network officials made a compromise and announced that, beginning in January 1973, Cavett would be on one week out of four, while Jack Paar, returning to late-night television, would fill up another week of each four-week period. The other two weeks would be occupied by comedy-variety and drama shows.

Public television. In early summer, the U.S. Congress took up a bill authorizing $155 million over two years for the Corporation for Public Broadcasting (CPB). The bill sailed through the House of Representatives and breezed through the Senate. Never before had CPB been on the threshold of such good fortune; but the bill was vetoed by President Richard M. Nixon, and the bonanza never materialized.

Nixon, who had proposed a one-year grant of $45 million, contended that public television should be held accountable for its actions at the end of each year. But his veto also

Pinko

DINGBAT

Hippie

MEATHEAD

stifle

ARCHIE'S OFFSHOOTS. When loud-mouth Archie Bunker weaned American audiences from their diet of familial blandness, comic writer Norman Lear produced two more abrasives: below, Sanford and Son squabbling in the family junkyard; right, Edith Bunker's liberated cousin Maude, in a breast-beating session with Walter, Maude's latest husband, and Carol, her divorced daughter.

NBC

CBS

CBS

brought to the forefront what was already known to be a difference of philosophy between the White House and CPB. The Nixon administration favored decentralization of public television, with most of the federal funds to be allocated to individual stations; in administration eyes, CPB already exerted too much influence as distributor of programming to the more than 200 public television stations across the country.

The employment of newsman Sander Vanocur by the CPB-funded National Public Affairs Center for Television also helped heat up the controversy about public-television

funding. Vanocur's $85,000-a-year salary brought charges from some quarters that public television was not being administered properly.

After Nixon vetoed the $155 million two-year authorization for CPB, John W. Macy, Jr., president of the corporation, resigned his $65,000-a-year post. Henry Loomis, who was elected as the new CPB president by its board of directors, has indicated he believes local stations should have "a considerable voice in national programming."

Special events. When President Nixon visited the People's Republic of China, American television cameras got their

first look behind the bamboo curtain. Some fascinating pictures were sent back live via satellite, although the Chinese exerted strict control over what was shown. Later in the year, American television followed Nixon to Moscow. During the president's visit there, he went on Soviet television to address the Soviet people, in a speech beamed by satellite to U.S. audiences.

The Democratic and Republican national conventions were televised from gavel to gavel by NBC and CBS. ABC, which limited its coverage to shorter wrap-ups, succeeded in luring many viewers from politics to entertainment.

The Public Broadcasting Service, a noncommercial system serving public television stations, did not cover the Democratic convention, but it did televise the Republican convention. In a move which distressed many local managers, the National Public Affairs Center for Television, which produced the programs, decided simply to put its cameras on official proceedings and avoid any analysis or political commentary. While correspondents Sander Vanocur and Robert MacNeil refused to participate in this type of coverage, saying it restricted their roles as journalists, Bill Moyers, who conducts a weekly public-affairs program on public-television stations, accepted the assignment. As it turned out, Moyers did engage in commentary here and there.

A highlight of the year's special events coverage was the televising of the Winter Olympics in Japan by NBC and the XX Olympic Games in Munich by ABC. The popularity of the summer spectacle gave ABC tremendous ratings for two weeks of prime time. When Arab terrorists moved into Olympic Village in Munich and held nine Israeli athletes as hostages, ABC also had a spectacular news story in its lap, and Jim McKay, an ABC sportscaster, switched from effusive sports reporting to a restrained commentary on the tragedy that shocked the world.

Another event that built great interest as it unfolded was coverage by public television of the world championship chess match between Bobby Fischer of the United States and Boris Spassky of the Soviet Union. No television cameras were permitted on the site of the match in Reykjavík, Iceland, but move-by-move reports were telephoned to a television studio in Albany, N.Y., where chess grandmaster Shelby Lyman re-created each move on a chess board and managed to fill in the intervals with a ready flow of strategic commentary. Lyman became quite a celebrity during the long-drawn-out chess match. The programs were carried in New York by WNET/13.

Children's television programming. Under pressure both from the public and from the federal government, ABC and NBC proposed a cutback of one-third in commercials on Saturday morning children's programs, while CBS proposed that the reduction be applied to all programs for children. Later, the National Association of Broadcasters, a trade organization, adopted a new code similar to what ABC and NBC had proposed. In another development, three major drug companies—Miles Laboratories, Bristol-Myers, and Hoffmann-LaRoche—announced they had dropped all vitamin pill advertising in children's shows. Their action came in the wake of various reform campaigns pushed by Action for Children's Television.

Meanwhile, U.S. surgeon general Jesse L. Steinfeld released a controversial study of the impact of televised violence on children. The study, undertaken by a 12-man committee of experts in various fields, pointed to an increase in violence in children's cartoons, but also found indications that the causal relation between viewing violence and doing violence operates only on children already predisposed to aggressive behavior. Critics found the report ambivalent and criticized the fact that the television industry had been given veto power over the selection of members to serve on the committee drafting the study.

Senator John Pastore (D, R.I.), chairman of the Senate Commerce Subcommittee on Communications, who had re-

quested the study in the first place, called hearings in March to clarify its findings and obtain recommendations for action. All parties testifying seemed to agree that the report justified the conclusion that televised violence plays some role in stirring up children's aggressions; and Nicholas Johnson, maverick commissioner of the Federal Communications Commission, went so far as to charge television with having "molested the minds of our nation's children to serve the cause of corporate profit." Network officials stressed the limited nature of the findings, but ABC president Elton H. Rule promised plans to de-emphasize violence in future cartoon series, and CBS president John Schneider promised to give consideration to the number, scheduling, and treatment of action-adventure shows on CBS. Senator Pastore closed the hearings with the admonition that strong action be taken about the problem, offering the suggestion that the government, as a first step, devise an index to measure the amount of violence on American television.

Government and broadcasting. The Justice Department filed an antitrust suit against ABC, CBS, and NBC charging the networks with an illegal degree of control over program production, through extensive financial interests in programs produced by others. The suit also sought to block the networks from producing their own programs, although the networks said they actually produce very few of their own.

Broadcasters were alarmed by the Federal Trade Commission's endorsement of countercommercials and its proposal to the FCC that counteradvertising be made enforceable. Under the proposal, television and radio would have to make time available to persons or groups who wanted to make counterclaims in response to certain commercials. Industry officials contended that countercommercials would destroy broadcast advertising and spread chaos to other media as well.   VAL ADAMS

TENNESSEE. Legislation. During the regular legislative session a united Democratic majority, overriding a veto by Republican governor Winfield Dunn, passed a congressional redistricting plan intended to give them five or six of the state's eight seats in the U.S. House of Representatives. The Democrats also enacted over the governor's veto a reapportionment of the state house of representatives which increased their majority by ten seats. Suits filed by Republicans against the reapportionment laws were dismissed by the U.S. district court in Nashville. The governor successfully vetoed bills legalizing certain types of gambling devices and exempting veterans organizations from paying the gross receipts tax on liquor by the drink.

The session produced several other significant pieces of legislation. Legislators adopted a $1.6 billion budget, rewrote the state's election laws, required that conflicts of interest be disclosed by state officials, and instituted statewide systems of emergency medical services and alcoholic rehabilitation. Also, new state departments of transportation and of economic development were created; strip-mining legislation was strengthened; and a tax was levied on all coal mined in the state.

On August 3, voters approved an amendment to the state constitution providing for classification of property for taxation at different rates. Railroads and other utilities, whose rates were increased, filed suits against the law.

Hijacking. State residents were alarmed in November when three men who had hijacked a Southern Airways jet threatened to crash it into the Atomic Energy Commission's Oak Ridge plant. After the hijackers were given the ransom they demanded, they headed for Cuba, and the plant, which had been on safety alert, resumed normal operations. The hijackers were later jailed by Cuban authorities.

Economy and ecology. Tax collections in May increased 47 percent above the same month in 1971, and employment climbed to a record high. The prospects for continued economic improvement were increased by an Atomic Energy

TEXAS 559

Commission decision to locate the nation's first breeder reactor power plant in Roane County near Oak Ridge. The $500 million project of the TVA and Commonwealth Edison of Chicago was scheduled for completion in 1980.

Work on the TVA Tellico Dam across the Little Tennessee River was halted in January by a temporary federal court injunction favoring environmentalists; the court action was later unsuccessfully appealed. Afterward, former TVA chairman Arthur E. Morgan advocated that the $69 million Tellico project be shelved and the area be used for the benefit of the Cherokee Indians. This year the TVA did close the generating unit at Nolichucky Dam near Greeneville, creating a waterfowl sanctuary at the site.

While environmentalists continued the appeals process, work began on the $386 million Tennessee-Tombigbee Waterway, a controversial project designed to link the Tennessee River system with the Gulf of Mexico. Some feared the system would damage the ecosystem of the Tombigbee River, but in August a federal judge lifted a temporary injunction against construction, stating that a legally proper environmental impact statement had been filed.

Education and culture. Court-ordered racial integration involving a considerable amount of student busing proceeded, despite delays and some popular opposition, in the four major cities of the state, Memphis, Nashville, Knoxville, and Chattanooga. But a federal court order to integrate the black Tennessee State University in Nashville remained largely unfulfilled, as proposals to unite it with the Nashville center of the University of Tennessee or with other white Nashville colleges failed to gain approval.

On July 1 all the institutions of higher education in the state, except for the state university, came under the control of a newly created 11-member board of regents, and the jurisdiction of the state board of education was limited to elementary and secondary public education.

Area and population. Area, 42,246 sq. mi. Pop. (1970), 3,924,164. Principal cities: Nashville (cap., figure includes the metropolitan government of Nashville and Davidson County), 447,877; Memphis, 623,530; Knoxville, 174,587; Chattanooga, 119,082.
Government. Gov., Winfield Dunn (R); lt. gov., John Wilder (D); treas., Thomas H. Wiseman (D); cont., William R. Snodgrass (D). General assembly: senate, 20 D, 12 R, 1 A; house, 55 D, 44 R.
Finance (1970). Revenue, $1.03 billion; expenditure, $993.4 million.
Education (1971–1972). Public elementary schools, 1,299; secondary schools, 490. Enrollment, elementary and secondary schools, 667,316; teachers, 40,608. Private and parochial schools, 175; enrollment, 41,748; teachers, 2,863. STANLEY J. FOLMSBEE

TEXAS. Crime. The scandal surrounding the collapse of the Sharpstown State Bank in Houston continued to dominate the legislative scene. House speaker Gus F. Mutscher, his executive assistant S. Rush McGinty, and state representative Tommy Shannon of Fort Worth were given five-year suspended prison sentences after conviction of conspiracy to accept a bribe. The bribe was in the form of loans from financier Frank Sharp's bank which were then used to purchase quick-profit stock in a firm controlled by Sharp, who was seeking passage of legislation. Mutscher resigned his post as speaker.

Former state representative Walter L. Knapp, Jr., of Amarillo was convicted of using state-issued postage stamps to buy a truck and was sentenced to four years in prison.

Legislation. The legislature held three special sessions. The first was called for March 28 by Governor Preston Smith after the U.S. Supreme Court ruled that the law requiring candidates in Texas primaries to pay high filing fees was unconstitutional because it discriminated against poor candidates. The legislature passed a bill to provide state financing for the party primaries. It also approved a billboard removal and junkyard screening act so that Texas would not be penalized $24 million in federal funds under the Highway Beautification Act. The second session, which opened June 14, was necessary because in 1971 the governor

had vetoed the 1972 portion of the state budget. The legislative session passed a $4.1 billion appropriation bill, the largest ever. The house chose Rayford Price of Palestine as speaker. The senate rejected Governor Smith's appointment of Larry Teaver as a member and chairman of the state board of insurance. Smith grumbled about this for a while and then summoned the legislature into special session on September 18 with instructions to rewrite the state's insurance laws.

The state is also faced with a drastic change in financing public education. A federal court ruled in San Antonio that the present system is unconstitutional because the use of local property taxes to raise each school district's share of the cost results in discrimination against poor districts. Several state commissions are looking into alternatives; the ruling is being appealed.

Economy. The employment picture remained bright. As fall began, Austin had only 2.8 percent unemployment and Houston, Dallas, Lubbock, Wichita Falls, and Abilene had less than 4 percent. In Houston, with the Apollo moon-exploration program nearing an end, about 1,200 employees at the Manned Spacecraft Center were notified that they would be losing their jobs. The Skylab project, however, is expected to keep space activity thriving. The demand for beef caused some rise in farm income, which totaled $3.3 billion in 1971. Oil production was set at 100 percent of capacity for months because of the energy demand.

Municipal developments. Houston planners presented the city with a mass transit proposal calling for expenditure of $1.4 billion to construct 81 miles of rapid transit, including

RISING TEXAS STAR. Frances "Sissy" Farenthold, a state legislator who almost captured the gubernatorial nomination in Texas this year, meets the press in Miami. The reformer ran second in the balloting for the Democratic vice-presidential nomination.

NEW YORK TIMES

BLUE BELL

COTTON CRAZE

Cotton had a ball in knits and corduroys this year; even the little black book was available in blue denim (right). Synthetics also did well. Above, the girl sports softly casual jeans of polyester and velour with a cotton-knit Western shirt; her boyfriend wears sculptured corduroy slacks and a plaid shirt made from a cotton-polyester weave.

a subway. In San Antonio, a court ruling stymied a plan to build a highway through famed Breckenridge Park. New Braunfels recovered slowly from a May 13 flash flood on the Guadalupe and Comal rivers that killed 17, including the mayor's wife.

Culture. Three major museums opened. In Fort Worth, the Kay Kimbell Art Museum, with a wide-ranging collection of old and modern masters, occupies a $6.5 million, highly original structure designed by Louis I. Kahn of Philadelphia. The Art Museum of South Texas occupies a new building on the bay in Corpus Christi. The Amarillo Art Center opened on the Amarillo College campus.

For election results and campaign highlights, see the special supplement ELECTION '72.

Area and population. Area, 267,339 sq. mi. Pop. (1970), 11,196,730. Principal cities (1970): Austin (cap.), 251,808; Houston,

1,232,802; Dallas, 844,401; San Antonio, 654,153; Fort Worth, 393,476; El Paso, 322,261.

Government. Gov., Preston Smith (D); lt. gov., Ben Barnes (D); atty. gen., Crawford C. Martin (D); secy. of state, Robert Douglas Bullock (D); treas., Jesse James (D); cont., Robert S. Calvert (D). Legislature: senate, 29 D, 2 R; house, 139 D, 11 R.

Education (1971–1972). Elementary schools, 3,257; junior high schools, 818; high schools, 1,165. Total enrollment, 2,818,400; total teachers, 141,500.   LESLIE H. BENNETT

TEXTILE INDUSTRY. The textile industry experienced a return of both confidence and optimism after several years of depressed sales, lower employment, and generally chaotic conditions. Like other industries, textiles had suffered one of its worst declines during the 1970–1971 recession, but the general economic upturn in late 1971 and early 1972 was reflected in improved sales and rising prices. The U.S. Federal Trade Commission reported that first-quarter sales were $5.9 billion, compared with $5.3 billion in 1971. The American Textile Manufacturers Institute reported that total mill employment in May reached 994,000, the highest monthly total since January 1970. The consumption of cotton, wool, and synthetic fibers was also up.

In contrast to last year's wide fluctuation in styles, shoppers could be a little more confident that their purchases would not be obsolete the next month, and this confidence, together with slightly more spending money in the U.S. economy, put life back into the marketing picture.

Imports. The voluntary textile quotas negotiated by the Nixon administration with Japan, Hong Kong, South Korea, and Taiwan in 1971 helped slow the rate of imports and provided U.S. textile men with incentives and opportunities. (Before the quotas, imports had risen an average of 20 percent annually, and U.S. manufacturers had lost well over $1 billion in business. Competition in knit fabrics and knit apparel was especially severe.) Some manufacturers felt the impact of the quota system was not strong enough, noting that there would be an estimated 15–18 percent increase of imports in 1972 over 1971. The American Textile Manufacturers Institute noted a slight increase in total cotton, wool, and man-made fiber imports from May to June. However, the new quotas and, according to some observers, the devaluation of the dollar were expected to moderate the flow of imports and free U.S. manufacturers from the fear of overwhelming and unstoppable imports.

Cotton. One major reason for the overall prosperity of the textile industry was that cotton was once again a profitable business. Cotton had been pushed increasingly out of the picture by man-made textiles, high prices, and oversupply. However, the "jeans revolution" around the world sparked the need for cotton in denims, corduroys, and velveteens and brought cotton to the attention of the world's designers and manufacturers. Designers found new, more sophisticated uses for the once lowly denims and corduroys not only in men's apparel but also in women's suits and casual wear. Cotton prices that had reached a low of 22.6 cents a pound in 1971 reached over 35 cents a pound in 1972. Few industry experts would predict how long the cotton boom would last. One key could be the export market; the world supply of cotton was estimated at 55 million bales, while world consumption was 54.4 million in 1971 and expanding. However, world consumption of man-made fibers also expanded and could weaken cotton's hold on the market in the year ahead.

Knits. With the development of the double-knit machine and the popularity of easy, form-fitting apparel, knits maintained a peak of popularity that is only beginning to even out with a drop in yarn and fabric prices and a general leveling off of demand. But apparel makers believed knit fabrics would dominate the textile industry for the next decade and went so far as to predict that knits would represent 75 percent of all apparel by 1980. The popularity of knits and the overall improvement in the textile financial

position were reflected in the improvement of net earnings by the larger apparel companies. Preliminary figures on the net profits of 26 apparel companies surveyed by the First National City Bank of New York in May showed profits were up an average of 25 percent over the first quarter of 1971.

Wool. The wool market shared some of the spin-off from the general upturn in textile fortunes, but not by much. Wool had lost out in popularity during the past ten years to man-made fibers. In 1961 the output of wool goods came to 287 million yards while in 1971 it was 140 million yards, a decline of over 50 percent, and further declines were predicted. However, because of increased exports of wool by domestic producers, U.S. manufacturers experienced a shortage during 1972, boosting the price of wool fabrics. Production for 1972 was estimated at 79.3 million pounds, down 7 percent from 85.2 million pounds in 1971. The world production of wool remained fairly stable. The estimate for the 1971–1972 season was 3.45 billion pounds.

Man-made fibers. Man-made fibers continued in a strong position with some indications of a leveling off in demand and consumption. The textile Economics Bureau, Inc., reported that in 1971 global production of all fibers reached a record 50 billion pounds. The total capacity of the 1,100 textile plants turning out man-made fibers was expected to be 25.7 billion pounds and to reach 27.7 billion pounds by the end of 1973. The actual output for 1972, however, reached 20.58, which was about double what it had been eight years before. The United States, the largest producer of man-made fibers, produced 5.68 billion pounds in 1972, Japan 3.6 billion pounds, West Germany 1.7 billion pounds, and the Soviet Union 1.58 billion pounds. Polyester fibers, used in both knit fabrics and in permanent press fabrics, accounted for much of the man-made fiber business, followed by the acrylics, nylon, and acetates. U.S. producers braced themselves for stiffer competition from their European counterparts.

Other developments. While the textile industry in general reflected good times, some individual companies had problems. Celanese Corporation, one of the largest producers of synthetic fibers, plastics, and chemicals, had to lay off about 1,300 workers, mostly in white-collar jobs. It also reported a second-quarter drop in earnings and announced a reorganization of its top executive personnel. An incomplete product line, with heavy reliance on polyesters and acetates, poor planning, unsuccessful foreign ventures, and sagging prices were some of the reasons given for its poor performance.

Burlington Industries, the largest textile firm in the United States, reached $1.7 billion in sales in 1971 but then suffered a series of poor fiscal earnings. Some observers thought Burlington waited too long to get into knitted fabrics and put too much emphasis on worsted fabrics. However, Burlington improved toward the end of the year, when it posted both a third-quarter gain of 18 percent in net earnings and a 10 percent gain in sales over the same quarter last year. Botany Industries, Inc., a major men's apparel manufacturer, filed for reorganization under Chapter XI of the Bankruptcy Act. The company had announced a $23.5 million loss for the year ending July 31, 1971, and it reported a $2 million deficit for the first half of 1972.

Home sewing has been growing into a tremendous industry within the past few years, and by 1972 one estimate was that one-third of all women's garments were made in the home. The market for retail piece goods, sewing notions, and patterns was estimated at between $2.5 billion and $3 billion. This market has grown in recent years at an annual compound rate of about 15 percent. This growth was attributed to the greater individuality of women in American society and their interest in creative expression, greatly improved sewing machines, a richer variety of patterns, and a much better selection in fabrics. As a result, there are an

estimated 10,000 stores offering fabrics and related items and accounting for 40 percent of the home sewing market. Department stores, discount stores, and other stores make up the other 60 percent. One of the largest chains of fabric retailers is House of Fabrics, Inc., based in Sun Valley, Calif., which hoped to add from 50 to 60 new stores to its chain of 279 stores around the country. Its total sales in 1971 were $55.9 million, up from the $44.3 million of the year before. Net earnings were $2.9 million.

DUNCAN G. STECK

THAILAND. Politics and government. In the wake of the 1971 coup which set aside Thailand's parliamentary constitution, the ruling National Executive Council has placed major stress on maintaining public order and has not hesitated to apply the death sentence to convicted murderers. March brought the arrest of three former parliament members who had filed a criminal suit against the government. The group alleged that Field Marshal Thanom Kittikachorn and other military leaders were guilty of rebellion against the state for having overturned the constitutional system. In July the three were convicted of trying to overthrow the National Executive Council and were sentenced to prison terms of up to ten years. In May the Council announced its decision to delay the promulgation of an interim constitution. Although Thanom had earlier indicated his intention to resign as commander of the armed forces, in July the government extended his term of office for another year.

Insurgency. Thailand's Communist insurgency appeared to be on the rise. In February, Lieutenant General Saiyud Kerdphol, director of the Communist Suppression Operations Command, stated that the insurgents were stronger than ever. This remark was borne out by the extensive number of successful ambushes against government forces and by evidence of the use of modern weapons such as AK-47 rifles, rockets, mortars, and plastic mines. In January a major military operation, reportedly involving more than 10,000 Thai regulars backed by artillery and aircraft support, was launched near the Laotian border at the junction of the three northern provinces of Phitsanulok, Phetchabun, and Loei. The operation centered on the Phu Hin Longkhla plateau, the site of an insurgent base complex. The operation, which lasted into April, had an inconclusive result. Snipers inflicted heavy casualties on the Thai side, enabling the estimated 2,500 insurgents to escape without difficulty. A sign of the government's desperation came with a decision in July to evacuate civilians from seven northern areas—including a 50-mile strip along the Mekong River border with Laos—to permit the adoption of a scorched earth policy against the guerrillas. Another counterinsurgency move was the accelerated construction of strategic highways through Communist-infiltrated areas, especially in the north. Twice during the year, guerrilla attacks were mounted on U.S. air bases: in January at Utapao and in June at Ubon.

Foreign affairs. U.S. vice-president Spiro T. Agnew visited Bangkok in May in an attempt to allay Thai anxiety over President Richard M. Nixon's visit to Peking in February. Agnew provided assurances that the United States would stand by its SEATO commitment to defend Thailand against foreign aggression. The U.S. military response to the North Vietnamese offensive at the end of March led to an increased use of Thai airfields for the bombing of North Vietnam and a corresponding increase in Thai-based U.S. military forces. In May the Americans reactivated the Takhli air base, 100 miles north of Bangkok, and, in June, the Nam Phong base, 260 miles northeast of the capital. At the beginning of 1972, U.S. military personnel numbered 32,000; by June the total had risen to 50,000. Indeed, U.S. troop concentrations in South Vietnam were reduced in part as a consequence of the transfer of military personnel to Thailand. Thus, by mid-1972, there were more U.S.

forces in Thailand than in South Vietnam. It was also reported that 525 U.S. military advisers were training Thai troops in counterinsurgency techniques.

In August, General Praphas Charusathien, deputy chairman of the National Executive Council, announced a reversal of government policy when he asserted that the government could not support the neutralization of Southeast Asia at a time when Thailand was still facing Communist aggression. This position was underscored in September by Sunthorn Hongladarom, the incoming Thai secretary general of SEATO, who avowed that the countries of the region were facing a dangerous threat of Communist subversion and insurgency. In August, nonetheless, Thailand moved to improve its relations with the People's Republic of China by sending a Ping-Pong team to take part in the Asian championships in Peking. It was reported that Prasit Kanchanawat, a government official who had traveled to Peking ostensibly as an adviser to the Thai team, had taken part in talks with Chinese premier Chou En-lai.

Economic developments. The Thai economy continued to have its problems, despite increasing U.S. military investments in the country. A severe drought during the 1971–1972 growing season raised the grave specter of a rice shortage for domestic consumption. The influential Bangkok Bank, meanwhile, observed caustically that the benefits of development were being reaped by only a small nonagricultural minority.

During the year reports abounded of a renewed interest in the construction of a canal across the Thai Isthmus of Kra. The Kra canal was represented as an alternative route to the politically congested Straits of Malacca, jointly claimed by Indonesia and Malaysia as territorial waters. However, no firm decision on the canal was reached by the Thai government, and it was widely felt that the necessary dredging and maintenance would prove prohibitively expensive without earnest foreign assistance.

Area and population. Area, 198,500 sq. mi. Pop. (est. 1971), 37.4 million. Bangkok (cap.), 2,040,000.

Government. Monarchy, governed by military oligarchy headed by Field Marshal Thanom Kittikachorn. King, Bhumibol Adulyadej.

Finance. Monetary unit, baht; 1 baht = US$0.0483. Main sources of revenue: taxes, duties, and government enterprises.

Trade (1971). Exports, US$810 million; imports, US$1.3 billion. Principal exports: rice, rubber, maize, wolfram, sugar, tin, teak. Principal imports: motor vehicles, iron and steel, industrial machinery, petroleum products. Major trading partners: Japan, West Germany, United Kingdom, United States, Singapore, Hong Kong.

Agriculture and industry. Rice production, 14,000,000 metric tons; cement, 2,000,000 metric tons.

Education. Literacy rate: 70 percent. Seven universities; military, naval, air force, and police academies.

Armed forces (1971). Army, 130,000; navy, 21,500 (including 6,500 marines); air force, 23,500; volunteer defense corps, 10,000; border police, 8,000.   MICHAEL LEIFER

THEATER. Resident theater. A new toughness seemed to be developing among American resident theaters, as each realistically faced the problems of function and survival. There were more changes than usual in the artistic leadership of these theaters, which perhaps reflected the concern of boards of directors about supplying their communities with a wide spectrum of popular theater.

Realistically, too, both government and corporations increased their support of theater. The National Endowment for the Arts continued to receive the blessing of President Richard M. Nixon, and Congress allocated $38.2 million for fiscal 1973, a modest increase from the $29.75 million it allocated for fiscal 1972. And President Nixon reiterated his intention to continue to strengthen support of the arts in order "to improve the quality of life for all our people." The Democratic presidential candidate, Senator George McGovern (S.D.) quickly pledged that he, too, would strengthen government support not only of the artistic institutions but also of the artists, who in his opinion are shockingly underpaid for their work. McGovern also criticized an alleged

instance of censorship by National Park Service officials of *An Unpleasant Evening With H. L. Mencken,* presented at Ford's Theater, which is administered by the National Park Service.

It also appeared that the nonprofit Kennedy Center for the Performing Arts not only would draw good audiences for star revivals but also might become a major contributor to the American theater scene. The Kennedy Center chairman, Roger L. Stevens, managed to obtain a revolving fund from private donors to make possible new productions that could go on tour after their Washington engagement. Two of these, *The Country Girl* with Jason Robards, Jr., Maureen Stapleton, and George Grizzard and the very moving *Lost in the Stars* with Brock Peters, went on to enrich the Broadway season.

Around the country, resident theaters enjoyed a sound year. In Washington, D.C., Arena Stage received the Margo Jones Award for its encouragement of new playwrights over the years, and, appropriately, several of its productions were new works: Michael Weller's *Moonchildren,* a comedy about the younger generation rejecting the real world with put-ons; Jay Broad's *A Conflict of Interest,* an intriguing drama dealing with an event that bore some resemblance to the resignation of Abe Fortas from the Supreme Court; and Günter Grass' *Uptight,* a philosophical comedy about political activism and the generation gap. In addition, Arena Stage invited two productions from other theaters to play in Washington. One was Donald Driver's *Status Quo Vadis,* a comedy about class distinction which had first been done at Chicago's Ivanhoe Theater. The other was *Tricks,* a musical version of Molière's *Scapin,* which originated at the Actor's Theater of Louisville. Similarly, the Washington Theater Club presented *Lady Audley's Secret,* a musical spoof of Victorian England, which came to them from Chicago's Goodman Theater. Indeed, there seemed to be emerging a pattern of exchange of successful productions between resident theaters, in which these companies would use the best of what was developing around the country as well as the latest from Broadway and London.

In Los Angeles, where the handsome new Shubert Theater opened with a financially unsuccessful presentation of the Broadway production of *Follies,* the smaller Mark Taper Forum broke all previous box-office records with its west coast production of *Don't Bother Me, I Can't Cope.* And the Company Theater scored with Elaine Edelman's rock "musical tragidity" about motherhood and Middle America, called *Mother of Pearl.*

San Francisco's American Conservatory Theater revived *Private Lives,* and the Noel Coward comedy proved so popular that the ACT is planning to keep it in its 1973 repertoire. In Seattle, Paul Zindel's *And Miss Reardon Drinks a Little,* which had had a disappointing run on Broadway, was so well performed by the Seattle Repertory Theater that it played to capacity audiences for its entire run. And in the same city the enterprising A Contemporary Theater presented the professional pilot production of N. Richard Nash's *Echoes,* a study of two lovers who try to preserve in the real world the happiness they found together while in an asylum. *Echoes* was the American Playwrights Theater selection for the 1972–1973 season and will be played at scores of college and resident theaters.

The American College Theater Festival brought ten productions to the Kennedy Center. The most important of these was the University of Minnesota's staging of Dr. Ronald J. Glasser's book about treating soldiers wounded in Vietnam, *365 Days.*

In Minneapolis the Tyrone Guthrie Theater had a popular success with its revival of John Steinbeck's *Of Mice and Men,* and most boldly it attempted a complex production of Anthony Burgess' adaptation of *Oedipus,* written in a newly evolved language which the author called Indo-European. The Milwaukee Repertory Theater astonished

JOSEPH PAPP'S
CHAMPIONSHIP SEASON

It was a remarkable year for Joseph Papp, as his pioneer ventures in public theater began to draw recognition from critics and money from foundations. "That Championship Season" (below), produced at his downtown theater (right), won the Drama Critics Circle Award as best play of the season, and his musical version of "Two Gentlemen of Verona" (below), transferred to Broadway from Central Park, won another Drama Critics Circle Award and became a smash hit.

FRIEDMAN-ABELES

KEN REGAN/CAMERA 5

FRIEDMAN-ABELES

563

everyone by breaking box-office records with Nagle Jackson's staging of several English medieval religious dramas, *The English Mystery Plays,* and also did well with a Georges Feydeau farce, *Cat Among the Pigeons.* In Buffalo, Joseph H. Dunn's American Contemporary Theater broke new ground with its demanding, experimental version of Samuel Beckett's novel *The Unnameable.*

The Theater Company of Boston returned to life with David Wheeler's staging of *The Basic Training of Pavlo Hummel,* with Al Pacino exciting as a misfit soldier destroyed by the pressures that push him to a false bravado. In New Haven, the Long Wharf Theater presented the first American showing of David Storey's *The Contractor,* and brought in Stacy Keach in an inventive *Hamlet.* And the Yale Repertory Theater scored both with Christopher Walken in Camus' *Caligula* and the Brecht-Weill musical *Happy End.*

The summer Shakespeare festivals appeared to thrive. The Shakespearean Festival of Canada at Stratford, Ontario, impressed some with *King Lear* and Musset's *Lorenzaccio* with actress Pat Galloway in the male title role. At Stratford, Conn., the American Shakespeare Festival found good audiences for *Julius Caesar, Antony and Cleopatra,* and Shaw's *Major Barbara.* The New Jersey Shakespeare Festival made an auspicious start in its new home in Madison, N.J., with a women's lib versus male chauvinist pig version of *The Taming of the Shrew.* And the Great Lakes Shakespeare Festival imported director Charles Marowitz from England to stage his scrambled version of *Hamlet.*

Subsidized theater in New York City. This year's Vernon Rice Award went to the Chelsea Theater Center of Brooklyn, whose revival of *The Beggar's Opera* and whose highly original staging of Allen Ginsberg's *Kaddish* were so well received that they were moved to regular runs in off-Broadway playhouses. Most important of all was the CTC's production of *The Screens,* Jean Genet's enormous play about the Algerian revolution. With costumes by Willa Kim that caught both the poetry and the humor of the play, and an outstanding performance by Julie Bovasso as the mother, the Chelsea production realized this formidable work well enough for it to be voted the New York Drama Critics Circle Award as the best foreign play of the season. In addition to all this, it came up with a new musical, *Lady Day,* a passionate tribute to the late singer Billie Holiday.

Joseph Papp continued to astonish everyone with his productivity. An improved version of the musicalized *Two Gentlemen of Verona* that the New York Shakespeare Festival had presented in Central Park the previous summer became a Broadway hit and won the "Tony" award as the season's best musical. And from this summer's festival, a turn-of-the-century updating of *Much Ado About Nothing,* with background music by Peter Link, proved so popular that it, too, was moved to Broadway. In addition, the NYSF mounted an impressive production of *Hamlet* with Stacy Keach, James Earl Jones, and Colleen Dewhurst. Downtown, NYSF's Public Theater, which in fall 1971 moved David Rabe's *Sticks and Bones* to Broadway where it won the "Tony" award as the season's best dramatic play, came up with a remarkable performance of a new play by Jason Miller called *That Championship Season.* The drama stunningly caught the flavor of bigotry, sleazy politics, and distorted values in a small Pennsylvania city.

The La Mama Experimental Theater Club received praise for its repertoire of three musical dramas, and Andrei Serban's experimental version of *Medea,* a magnificent exercise in theatrical dedication and art, was sent to Europe for an extended tour. The Judson Poets' Theater and its merry pastor-composer, Al Carmines, exploded with four inspired musical odysseys. *Wanted* dealt with the subject of law and order. *Joan* featured a rebellious East Village girl whose "voices" led her to bomb a bank. *A Look at the Fifties* was a satirical study of American mores of 20 years ago. And

The Life of a Man emerged as an overreaching but memorable effort to follow a man from womb to grave through a wide variety of social and educational experiences.

The black theater continued to contribute richly. Richard Wesley's *Black Terror* began the previous year at Harlem's New Lafayette Theater and then was restaged again in order that La Mama's Ellen Stewart could take it to the Venice Biennale as the American entry, together with a program of four one-act plays by Ed Bullins. Philip Hayes Dean's *The Sty of the Blind Pig,* a haunting study of slow-dying atavisms that plague black people, was the highlight of the Negro Ensemble Company season. And out of many other interesting black writers whose work was presented at La Mama, the Public, the New Lafayette, the NEC, and the Henry Street Playhouse, the most promising seemed to be actor-playwright J. E. Gaines, whose *Don't Let It Go to Your Head* was a stimulating drama about an ex-convict.

The Repertory Theater of Lincoln Center appeared to be solving its financial problems with an assist from a smash hit revival of *Man of La Mancha* which relieved the RTLC of a heavy summer maintenance expense. At the Beaumont it mounted a splendid revival of Arthur Miller's *The Crucible,* a good if not successful try at realizing Edward Bond's original but difficult *Narrow Road to the Deep North,* Ellis Rabb's melancholy staging of *Twelfth Night,* and the New York premiere of Maxim Gorki's *Enemies.* At the Forum, the RTLC drew praise for attempting Peter Handke's bizarre *The Ride Across Lake Constance;* was attacked by playwright Ed Bullins for alleged distortions of his play, *The Duplex;* won awards for its production of David Wiltse's *Suggs,* a fine new play about the impact of New York City life on a complaisant young man; and mounted a Samuel Beckett Festival comprising *Happy Days, Act Without Words I, Krapp's Last Tape,* and the world premiere of *Not I.* However, when money could not be raised for any other productions at the Forum, the artistic director submitted his resignation. At its new Joseph E. Levine Theater in the Broadway area, Circle-in-the-Square opened with a revival of O'Neill's *Mourning Becomes Electra.*

Unsubsidized theater. The transfer of *Two Gentlemen of Verona, Sticks and Bones, That Championship Season,* and *Much Ado About Nothing* was only part of subsidized theater's gift to Broadway. Robert Bolt's *Vivat! Vivat Regina!* starring Eileen Atkins as Elizabeth I and Claire Bloom as Mary, Queen of Scots, was originally produced in England as part of the Chichester Festival. Michael Weller's *Moonchildren* was picked up from the Arena Stage in Washington, D.C. A revival of Georges Feydeau's farce, *There's One in Every Marriage* was the work of the Shakespearean Festival of Canada. Clifford Odets' *The Country Girl* was mounted originally for the Kennedy Center, as was the stirring new production of the Maxwell Anderson–Kurt Weill musical, *Lost in the Stars.* And *Don't Bother Me, I Can't Cope,* Micki Grant's musical that balanced the black people's pain from injustice with their warm capacity for love and friendliness, was originally the product of Vinnette Carroll's Urban Arts Corps.

Of those shows produced from scratch by Broadway producers, the most successful was Neil Simon's *The Sunshine Boys,* a black comedy about two retired vaudeville comics, played by Sam Levene and Jack Albertson. Arthur Miller's latest effort, *The Creation of the World and Other Business,* in which the playwright humorously retells the myths of God and Lucifer, Adam and Eve, and Cain and Abel, had a mixed reception. Paul Zindel's *The Secret Affairs of Mildred Wild* starred Maureen Stapleton as a Kewpie doll wife of a candy store proprietor. By coincidence there were two plays about the widow of Abraham Lincoln. The first, starring Eva Marie Saint, dealt with her early life with her husband. The second, starring Julie Harris, concerned itself with the period when the older Mrs. Lincoln was committed to a

mental institution. Bob Randall's slight comedy about a brief encounter, *6 Rms Riv Vu,* featured a beautifully honest portrayal by Jane Alexander. And off Broadway a double bill, *The Real Inspector Hound* and *After Magritte,* both by Tom Stoppard, delighted audiences for months.

Of the other new musicals, *Sugar,* based on the film *Some Like It Hot,* managed to run despite an unenthusiastic critical reception. *Grease,* a lively show about high school life in the late 1950's as seen in retrospect, developed gradually from modest Chicago and off-Broadway beginnings to become a Broadway success. And *Pippin* by Roger O. Hirson and Stephen Schwartz managed to make a medieval young man's quest for fulfillment theatrically effective. The new Gerome Ragni and Galt MacDermot musical, *Dude,* adventurously remodeled the inside of the Broadway Theater into a one-ring circus, but its antics were confusing and erratic. MacDermot also did the music for *Via Galactica,* whose plot involved space travel and which was the inaugural attraction at the Uris Theater.

Foreign stars contributed, too. Melina Mercouri tackled *Lysistrata* with the help of some songs by Peter Link, and Alan Bates brought his highly acclaimed portrayal of a neurotic professor in Simon Gray's *Butley* to Broadway. Most exciting of all was the visit of Nuria Espert's Company from Madrid. The company performed Victor Garcia's staging of Lorca's *Yerma* on a huge trampoline, which was pulled into a variety of interesting and resilient shapes.

HENRY HEWES

TOGO. Politics and government. The major political event of the year was the long-postponed referendum and legitimation of President Étienne Eyadema's five-year-old military government. The referendum, held on January 9, asked: "Do you want General Eyadema to continue the functions of president of the republic entrusted to him by the army and the people?" The answer was yes, 867,941; no, 878. Earlier, General Eyadema had offered several times to return the government to civilian rule, but each offer had purportedly been rejected by civilian leaders fearful of further political instability. The vote clearly reaffirmed Eyadema's popularity with the electorate. Bolstered by this support, Eyadema gave absolute pardon to all those sentenced in the wake of the abortive coup of August 8, 1970.

Foreign affairs. Togo, long the most bilingual and bicultural of the West African states, continued to seek to serve as a potential bridge between English-speaking and French-speaking nations. Togo reaffirmed its basic ties with the French-speaking states by hosting the African, Malagasy, and Mauritian Common Organization (OCAMM) meetings in April. However, economic and ethnic realities have brought it closer than any other of the former French territories to integration with English-speaking Ghana and Nigeria. In early May, Nigeria and Togo tentatively joined together to form the nucleus of a West African common market.

Togo's close ties with Ghana were formalized during 1972 with the first regular meetings of the Ghana-Togo Joint Commission for Cooperation. The discussions focused mainly on methods to ease the movement of goods and people between the neighboring countries.

Economic developments. The Togolese economy continued its brisk activity of the previous year. Cocoa and coffee production were forecasted to equal or exceed the record crops of 1971, and phosphate and palm oil output remained high. In 1972, Togo began working toward the primary objective of its public sector development, which is to expand cocoa and coffee output by more than one-third before turning to crop diversification and industrial development. Unlike other major producers of the two crops, however, Togo will depend heavily on a publicly owned corporation and plantation-style organization rather

than on smallholders to achieve its production goal quickly. France's Aid and Cooperation Fund will finance most of the development.

Privately financed industrial development during the year included a major expansion of Togo's textile industry and the construction of a refinery to handle crude oil imported from Nigeria.

Area and population. Area, 21,850 sq. mi. Pop. (est. 1971), 1.9 million. Lomé (cap.; est. 1970), 135,000.
Government. Military republic. Pres., General Étienne Eyadema.
Finance. Monetary unit, Communauté Financière Africaine (CFA) franc; 1 CFA franc = US$0.0041. Budget (est. 1972–1973): 12.3 billion CFA francs.
Trade (1971). Exports, 13.6 billion CFA francs; imports, 19.5 billion CFA francs. Principal exports: phosphates, cocoa, coffee, cotton. Principal trading partners: France, the Netherlands, West Germany.
Education (1971–1972). School enrollment: primary, 257,877; secondary, 24,521; technical, 2,506.   GEORGE LAMSON

TRANSPORTATION. The first U.S. international transport exhibition was held at a 360-acre site at Dulles International Airport, Washington, D.C., opening on May 27. Helped by excellent weather and considerable publicity, Transpo '72 attracted 1.5 million people who were treated to a fine display of modern and World War II aircraft and many novel surface transport systems, which, although not so spectacular, were nevertheless of significance for the future. U.S. secretary of transportation John A. Volpe made this statement: "Transpo '72 was not just an aerospace show but was a new kind of industrial marketplace where creativity and innovation were on display covering the total transportation industry."

The wide range of new and experimental "people movers" was an indication of the coming revolution in new ground transportation systems.

Many U.S. companies had laid out complete tracked systems, and many visitors were able to experience their speed and quietness. Among the exhibits, the Transportation Technology, Inc., Otis PRT system demonstrated air cushion suspension and electromagnetic linear induction motors for propulsion, and the Westinghouse Air Brake Company showed a monorail as used at Houston Airport. Then, there was Bendix Corporation's "dashaveyor," which is summoned to the station by the waiting passenger at the press of a button and operates under computer control to select the quickest and safest route to its destination. However, the general introduction of such new rail systems will be expensive, and whether the average American can be weaned away from his automobile remained problematical.

Unexpectedly, short takeoff and landing (STOL) aircraft and quiet air transports did not play a large part in the demonstration. Apparently, new intercity links, whether they be aircraft, high-speed rail, or air cushion vehicles on tracks, were still quite some way off in 1972.

Rail. The Bay Area Rapid Transit (BART)—the first such system in the United States in 50 years—was introduced in San Francisco in September. This railway joins the three bay area counties of San Francisco, Contra Costa, and Alameda by a 75-mile network of tracks with 33 stations. Although electric commuter railways are commonplace in Europe, this ultramodern testament to automation, built to compete with the heavily relied upon automobile, has aroused great interest not only among the people of San Francisco but also among government bureaucrats, automobile manufacturers, city planning officials, and specialists in transport design and operations. It took 15 years of planning and eight years of construction before BART could begin operations; it had to overcome such difficulties as decisions on the location of the railway and its stations. The success of BART may not depend so much on its speed, smoothness, safety, and use of electronic automatic systems as on its costs compared to other systems. Mass transit system costs depend critically on labor rates, which normally amount to 70 per-

cent of total operating costs. If BART succeeds economically, it will give encouragement to the nearly 30 cities that are building or expanding commuter railways.

Aerospace technology influenced the design of the BART vehicles, which are built of a light alloy and employ sophisticated electronic computers for vehicle speed control, signaling, and passenger handling. Furthermore, a development in track maintenance was announced in September, when a laser gyroscope system was put into use to measure minute changes in vehicle attitude. Through analysis of these changes small variations in track profile and alignment can be detected and subsequently corrected.

In Europe the first experimental version of British Rail's fastest train, the 150-mile-per-hour advanced passenger train (APT), began a series of test runs in July. This radical development incorporates new wheel and spring suspension and a mechanism that tilts coaches on turns so as to allow use, with very little alteration, over existing railway tracks that are not designed for this high speed. The experimental test program was planned to last from three to four years, during which two prototypes, one electric and the other gas turbine powered, would enter passenger evaluation service.

In Germany, Messerschmitt-Bölkow-Blohm continued prototype testing of a new principle of suspension for high-speed trains—magnetic levitation. This was proposed for the German Hochleistungsschnellbahn railway as a means of rationalizing freight and passenger services by the latter part of the 1970's. Other tests have been made with superconducting magnets for the same purpose.

In April, Battelle Research Center in Geneva, Switzerland, released a novel design of a tube train—propelled by compressed air. Electrically driven blowers mounted in concrete supports provide air pressure alterations so that pressure is increased behind the train and reduced in front of it. By this means, noise and pollution effects are avoided, and power requirements are reduced to a small fraction of normal values.

Ships. Early in the year pictures first began to appear of the extensively equipped flagship of the Soviets' ten-vessel space tracking fleet, *Yuri Gagarin*. The 750-foot-long vessel, weighing 53,500 metric tons, is powered by gas turbines and carries two dish antennae 80 feet in diameter and up to 100 other smaller antennae for use on several wave bands. Furthermore, the ship is equipped with special stabilizers and can move sideways for accurate positioning.

Communication between ships and their shore stations would be revolutionized by the proposal of the International Maritime Satellite Consortium (IMSCO) for the use of three communication satellites to provide an instantaneous telephone service for 1,500 ships. At present, the average cargo ship transmits only 25 words per day, and the time for a ship to transmit a message and receive a reply is often as long as 12 hours.

The United States Maritime Administration started experiments in the fall on a satellite system for maritime traffic. The system would transmit precise navigational information and hence could lead to improvement of ship control and avoidance of sea collisions.

A quiet transformation was in progress in the North Sea region, where more large fields of oil and gas were discovered during the year and vast operations of oil drilling and piping were under way. In one case, the American Marathon Shipping Company took over some of the Clyde shipyards to build offshore drilling rigs. However, there were likely disadvantages from this exploitation. Common turbulent and stormy conditions were likely to fracture pipelines and together with drill rig accidents might lead to serious oil pollution of the shorelines and seabed in the area. Whether the North Sea becomes a marine desert will depend on future decisions on the use of special techniques and the introduction of pollution control vessels.

Air transport. After the cancellation of the U.S. supersonic transport (SST) in 1971, the U.S. government paid back the vast sums owed to the manufacturers and the airlines. However, a technology transfusion program was organized by the National Aeronautics and Space Administration (NASA) so that the promising lines of research already developed in aerodynamics, structures, propulsion, and systems could continue until such time as an SST might become economically viable.

The Concorde, the SST designed and constructed jointly by Britain and France, continued to progress in spite of some environmental opposition and a mounting development bill approaching $2.6 billion. Two prototypes and one preproduction Concorde were assembled in England in January. In June and July the British prototype flew to the Far East on a sales tour, eventually reaching south Australia and Japan. Seventy hours of flying was achieved in 30 days. After the British Overseas Airways Corporation (BOAC) and Air France had placed orders in July for five and four Concordes respectively, the People's Republic of China ordered two from France and one from Great Britain.

Air hijacking. Air hijacking continued to threaten passenger safety and convenience and airline revenues during 1972. Airline personnel took the initiative in protesting such "piracy." In June pilots and maintenance men carried out a one-day work stoppage to dramatize their demands for more stringent antihijacking controls. Also, Captain Charles Dent of United Airlines chartered a Pan American World Airways Boeing 747 and invited United Nations staff to join 30 pilots and stewardesses who had experienced hijackings in an airborne conference on the problem.

In February a Lufthansa Boeing 747 en route from New Delhi to Frankfurt was successfully hijacked with 187 passengers and crew and diverted to Aden in Southern Yemen. There was widespread international criticism of the West German cabinet decision to pay the $5 million ransom to the guerrillas who had taken over the plane. In the United States, during the first half of the year, there was a rash of hijackings; some of these criminal exploits led to loss of life. The Federal Aviation Administration investigated antihijacking procedures used by airlines in an attempt to tighten regulations. During 1972, 1,500 sky marshals rode in passenger cabins to foil hijacking attempts. However, the aim of the national long-term policy was to prevent hijacking on the ground with improved checking procedures, including vehicle searches, spot investigation of personal identification, magnetometer checks, and behavior profile.

Airline woes. The International Air Transport Association (IATA) estimated that the scheduled airlines suffered a net loss of $400 million in 1971, during which the passenger and cargo traffic registered its lowest growth for over a decade. In addition, the difficulties of the scheduled airlines continued to worsen because of further inroads by the chartered and nonscheduled tour operators into the transatlantic flight business. The fierce fare battle at the heart of this problem was discussed at the IATA international meeting held in London in September. Laker Airways, a British charter airline, proposed a sky train service which could offer a single fare of $79 for a London-New York flight in winter ($91 in summer) by dispensing with booking agencies and free meal and refreshment services. Subsequently, Trans-International Airlines, the Oakland (Calif.)-based supplemental carrier, asked the Civil Aeronautics Board to approve a one-way New York to London sky bus service at a fare of $75.

New aircraft. The Lockheed L-1011 Tristar, powered by the RB-211, entered service with Eastern Airlines and Trans-World Airlines in April, thus successfully resolving a financially uncertain situation occasioned by the restructuring of Rolls Royce, Ltd. In August, British European Airways ordered 12 Tristars with a further six options; this

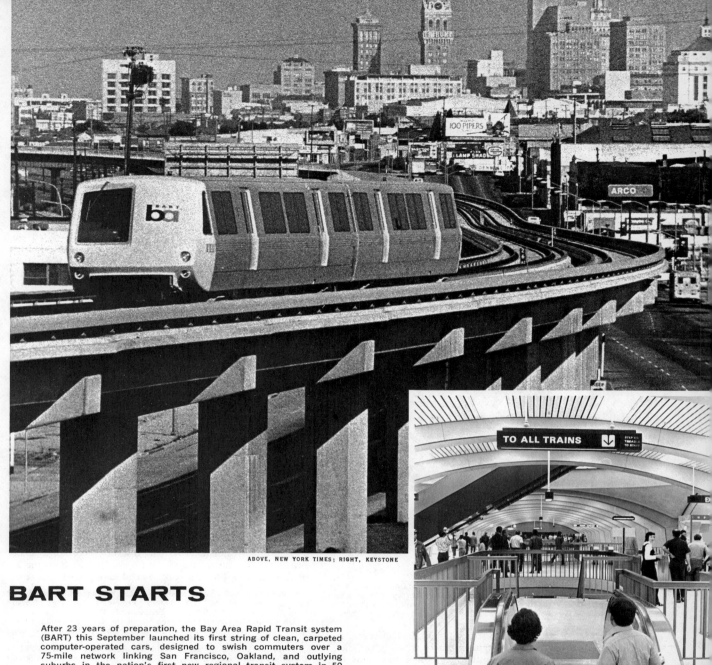

BART STARTS

After 23 years of preparation, the Bay Area Rapid Transit system (BART) this September launched its first string of clean, carpeted computer-operated cars, designed to swish commuters over a 75-mile network linking San Francisco, Oakland, and outlying suburbs in the nation's first new regional transit system in 50 years. Above, a test run near downtown Oakland; right, the Central Berkeley Station. Planners hope the $1.4 billion system can operate deficit-free and set a modern pace for mass transit.

coincided with the announcement that the British government was to back development of a larger model, the RB-211 engine, thereby ensuring larger versions of the Tristar. The new engine proved to be remarkably quiet, and sound measurements taken by the Federal Aviation Agency showed it to be well below the regulation values.

Road transport. Road safety is still a very live issue with governments, individual authorities, and automobile manufacturers and has promoted new international cooperation in road research.

Road safety. The Organization of Economic Cooperation and Development (OECD), which has 23 regular member nations, announced a third cooperative international program which would stress studies on the effects of law enforcement on driver behavior and the reduction of traffic accidents, the scientific assessment of the influence of roads

and traffic on urban environment, and techniques to improve urban life by curbing the use of motor vehicles.

Rapid progress was made in road tests of experimental safety vehicles (ESV), particularly in countries outside the United States, which responded to the tough U.S. specifications. The German Volkswagen ESV developed passive seat restraints which are automatically adjusted when the engine is started, and at the moment of collision a special sensing device regulates the gas pistons to take up the slack in body belts and the belts around the occupants' knees. The German Mercedes-Benz was equipped with a long hood with a large crash zone ahead of the engine and front and rear bumpers of energy-absorbing design. In contrast, the Japanese Toyota had a fiber-reinforced plastic body, an air bag that inflates on impact to restrict passenger movement, and an engine designed to fall below the body in a crash.

OLD   NEW

NEW DIRECTIONS

On roadside signs across the United States, words are giving way to a new system of pictures and symbols similar to that already used in Europe. Experts say the symbols are more quickly grasped than words. To ease the transition, subtitles will be added.

Pollution. The new auto truck legislation effective in California during 1972 set engineers there on a big program to measure vehicle noise, identify its source, and come up with a series of simple solutions. First, attention was paid to giant trucks to reduce their exhaust noise as well as significant fan and transmission noise, which is more difficult to cure than other noise without incurring substantial additional cost. Progress was made in reducing the irritating noise of the tracked snow vehicles, one of the newest intruders of the wild lands.

In an attempt to beat the 1975 California limits for exhaust emission, Mercedes-Benz demonstrated a city bus run on natural gas. The bus, which contains the gas in refrigerated insulated tanks under the body, has demonstrated significantly lower emission levels for carbon monoxide (8 percent) and nitric oxides (76 percent) than required. A disadvantage, however, is that fuel consumption is 15 percent greater than that of a diesel engine which has the same output.

Resource demands. At an international conference in London in September, the long-term effects of the demands of transport on world energy supplies were debated. In the OECD countries, which account for 83 percent of Western petroleum consumption, transport consumes 43 percent of

the total, of which 31 percent is used by road vehicles. Although road traffic congestion has not yet been brought under control, thought is already being given to the question of priorities allocated to overall transport resources.

PAUL M. DANFORTH

TRINIDAD AND TOBAGO. Government and politics. A controversial eight-month national state of emergency banning political gatherings was lifted in mid-June. The emergency declaration, imposed in October 1971, was the second in two years. The government had justified its action on the grounds of deteriorating labor relations that had caused a halt in the construction of a US$80 million petroleum desulfurization plant. In a further act of conciliation, the government also granted amnesty to 19 soldiers serving sentences for mutiny and released 29 other military and political detainees. All had been arrested for their alleged connection with an army mutiny that had taken place in April 1970, an event that touched off the first state of emergency.

Trinidad and Tobago's relations with Jamaica became strained temporarily at the end of 1971 when delegates attending a Caribbean Ecumenical Consultation staged a boycott to protest both the continuing state of emergency and a sedition bill introduced by the government of Prime Minister Eric Williams. The resolution to stage the boycott was introduced by a Jamaican, prompting Williams to lodge a formal protest with the Jamaican prime minister, charging an "unnecessary and unwarranted intrusion of Jamaican citizens into the affairs of Trinidad and Tobago."

Health crisis. A polio epidemic struck the island nation during January–February, taking more than a dozen lives and infecting nearly 180 others. The annual pre-Lenten carnival—for which Trinidad is famous—had to be postponed until May, resulting in a loss of about US$1 million in tourist revenues. Primary school classes, scheduled to resume after the Christmas holidays, did not begin until mid-February. A massive immunization program was undertaken to inoculate all children between the ages of three months and six years.

Miscellaneous. Trinidadian novelist V. S. Naipaul, a long-time resident of Great Britain, received a major British literary prize—the Booker Prize for Fiction—for his book *In a Free State*, a collection of short stories.

Area and population. Area: Trinidad, 1,864 sq. mi.; Tobago, 116 sq. mi. Pop. (est. 1971), 1,100,000. Principal cities: Port of Spain (cap.; est. 1968), 100,000; San Fernando, 50,000.

Government. Independent member of the Commonwealth of Nations. Bicameral legislature. Prime min., Eric Williams; gov. gen., Sir Ellis Clarke.

Finance. Monetary unit, Trinidad and Tobago dollar; TT$1 = US$0.52. Revenue (1970), US$183 million; expenditure, US$204 million.

Trade (1970). Exports, US$505 million; imports, US$571 million.

Education (1967–1968). Enrollment: primary and intermediate, 233,164; secondary (government and assisted), 27,094; university (1971), 1,660.

C. G. LINDO

TUNISIA. Politics and government. President Habib Bourguiba, unlike the proverbial old soldier, has refused to fade away, even after more than two years of illness. Rather than laying down institutional roots for his Destour Socialist Party, the "supreme warrior" has reasserted his personal style of presidential monarchy. All this to the consternation of the young "liberals" in the party, who had hoped to build a regime with enough durability to survive its revered founder.

The liberals had demonstrated their strength at the DSP congress, held in October 1971, by winning the greatest number of votes for their delegates to the party's central committee and by passing a motion that the political bureau be elected by the central committee rather than appointed by the president. Having thus lost effective control of the congress, Bourguiba beat a tactical retreat and managed to

have the final vote postponed. He then proceeded to select 20 of the more amenable members of the 58-man central committee as candidates for the 14-member political bureau. Ahmed Mestiri, the most prominent liberal on the central committee, was left off Bourguiba's list.

His health apparently restored, Bourguiba flexed his political muscles anew in January 1972 and had the party excommunicate Mestiri for continuing to express dissent publicly and for refusing to make apologies to the president. In March the political bureau announced its support for the creation of the office of vice-president to ensure orderly presidential succession, should the need arise. But in late June, Bourguiba ended the debate by declaring that in the event of succession the prime minister would automatically serve out the president's five-year term.

At the local level, however, some of the reforms espoused by party liberals began to take effect. In early 1972, 108 intermediate party units—called circumscriptions—were created as links between local party branches and the "committees of coordination" heading the party in each of Tunisia's 13 governorates. The officers of the circumscription are democratically elected by the branches and are permitted to communicate directly with the central political bureau. Moreover, the committees of coordination, elected by the circumscriptions, are not to be presided over by the governors of their respective provinces. Hence, local party functionaries gained a greater measure of autonomy, at least on paper.

Municipal elections were held throughout Tunisia on May 14, amid widespread public apathy. Regularly every three years the party presents single slates of candidates for each municipality; since 1957, independent candidates have not been allowed to compete. Party nomination procedures remain complex and Byzantine: this year, in an apparent attempt to broaden the party's base, some nonparty people suddenly found themselves listed, while respected party veterans found that they had been screened out by higher authorities.

Foreign affairs. Bourguiba proved to the world by his showy summitry that he was back in the saddle, ably assisted by his brilliant foreign minister, Muhammad Masmoudi. Bourguiba received Algerian president Houari Boumedienne in April and returned the visit in May, marking the first top-level contacts between the two neighboring states since Algeria gained independence in 1962. While Bourguiba, moderate and realistic as always, continued to disagree with Boumedienne's calls for resumption of the war with Israel, the two leaders agreed to consolidate bilateral relations in technical and commercial fields, to coordinate their negotiations with the Common Market, to resume faltering efforts toward an economically united Maghreb (including Morocco), and to work toward a pan-Mediterranean security conference. Also in May, Bourguiba met in Tunis with Egyptian president Anwar Sadat.

Bourguiba's summitry reached its peak in June. First he attended the Organization for African Unity meeting in Rabat, Morocco; then he joined Morocco's King Hassan and Boumedienne for a quick Maghreb summit meeting; and two weeks later he paid an official visit to France, conferring with President Georges Pompidou and cementing the relationship so carefully built up by Masmoudi after Bourguiba's 1964 nationalization of lands owned at the time by French settlers.

Economic developments. Prime Minister Hedi Nouira continued to liberalize Tunisia's economy, weighed down by excessive state control up until 1969. On February 14 a new investment code was passed. Modeled on Singapore's, the law was designed to attract private foreign investment on advantageous terms, even if it meant risking some economic independence.

Worker unrest gave the regime some minor headaches. In 1971 the veteran trade union leader Habib Achour had publicly protested that promised wage increases were not being given. There were strikes in February, and by the spring of 1972 the DSP had decided to infiltrate the trade union movement, provoking dissension in order to eventually remove some current labor leadership.

Education and culture. The most intense challenge to Bourguiba came from the students. The Tunisian generation gap, widened by the cynical control exercised by the DSP over the General Union of Tunisian Students, burst in early February into a virtual insurrection of high school and university students against Bourguiba's regime. The university faculties of law and letters were closed and did not reopen until April.

Area and population. Area, 63,379 sq. mi. Pop. (est. mid-1971), 5.3 million. Principal cities (1966): Tunis (cap.), 642,384; Sfax, 249,990; Bizerte, 95,000.
Government. Republic. Pres., Habib Bourguiba; prime min., Hedi Nouira.
Finance. Monetary unit, Tunisian dinar; DT1 = US$2.12. Budget (est. 1972): balanced at DT175 million.
Trade (1970). Imports, US$305 million; exports, US$181 million. Principal trading partners: France, Italy, United States, West Germany.
Agriculture and industry. Agricultural production (1969, in thousands of metric tons): cereals, 450; fruits, 73. Minerals (in thousands of metric tons): crude oil (1970), 4,600; phosphate rock (1970), 4,250; iron ore (1969), 945. Industry (1969, in thousands of metric tons): superphosphates, 333; cement, 582.
Education (1969–1970). Enrollment: primary, 912,646; secondary and technical, 163,353; university, 9,413.
Armed forces. Total, 20,000.   CLEMENT HENRY MOORE

TURKEY. Politics and government. Military and political leaders worked without much apparent success during the year to resolve Turkey's deep-seated political and constitutional crisis. Nihat Erim's "above-party" government, formed in March 1971 after top military chiefs forced the resignation of Prime Minister Süleyman Demirel and his Justice Party government, grappled with major reform issues but was unsuccessful in mobilizing broad parliamentary support for its program. The continuation of martial law in 11 of Turkey's 67 provinces helped Erim's government curtail terrorism and violence from right- and left-wing extremists. In February, 227 left-wing activists connected with the Dev Genc (Revolutionary Youth) organization and the Turkish People's Liberation Army (TPLA) were put on trial before the military tribunal in Ankara. In early March the general staff announced the dismissal and arrest of 57 junior officers on charges of participating in left-wing activities and distributing arms to terrorists. Despite the rigors of military law, however, terrorist incidents erupted again in March. On March 27, members of the TPLA kidnapped one Canadian and two British radar technicians, civil employees assigned to NATO forces in Turkey, and held them for ransom in return for the release of three terrorists sentenced to death in Ankara. Prime Minister Erim refused to make the exchange, and on March 30 the three hostages along with ten terrorists were killed when police attacked the house in the village of Kizildere where they were hidden.

The tragedy at Kizildere deepened the frustration of military leaders over the lack of progress toward an overall settlement of Turkey's political difficulties. Indirect efforts to force reform by coercing civilian leaders to act in concert had produced meager results, yet senior officers were reluctant to seize power directly. A military coup, they feared, would ruin Turkey's international image, destroy the professionalism of the armed forces, and, perhaps, unleash destructive political ambitions among Marxist and Nasserite officers in the middle and junior grades of the officers' corps.

President Cevdet Sunay, himself a former general and chief of staff, acted as mediator between the military staff and the civilian government. In a stern letter to the leaders of Turkey's four major political parties, made public on April 3, President Sunay declared that the democratic

THE MARBLE RECESSES OF THE SERAGLIO where sybaritic sultans of the Ottoman Empire used to consort in splendor with concubines and slaves have now been restored and opened to tourists at a dollar a head. Located inside Istanbul's 500-year-old Topkapi Palace (above), the harem afforded reigning sultans every possible felicity, including a private view of the women's pool. Meanwhile princes of the realm were allotted chambers (right) in which to pass their days doing nothing but reading the Koran or writing poetry.

regime and national integrity were in danger. He requested a temporary suspension of parliamentary rules in order to enable the Erim government to rule by executive decree. The inability of Parliament and the political parties to agree on this proposal, however, resulted in Erim's decision to resign as prime minister on April 17. President Sunay designated Ferit Melen, defense minister in the Erim cabinet, as acting prime minister and charged Senator Suat Hayri Ürgüplü with the task of organizing a new "above-party" government.

Ürgüplü's effort to establish a broadly multipartisan cabinet was complicated by a serious power struggle within the Republican People's Party (RPP), Turkey's second-largest political organization. Deepening animosity between RPP moderates, headed by 87-year-old party chairman İsmet İnönü, and the Socialist wing of the party, headed by former labor minister Bülent Ecevit, came to a head at a special party convention on May 6 and 7. Although Kemal Satir and other İnönü supporters had taken the initiative to call the extraordinary meeting, the Ecevit group dominated the proceedings. Party delegates voted 709 to 507 in support of Ecevit's "left-of-center" program and forced İnönü to resign the party chairmanship. Ecevit was elected to succeed İnönü as party chairman and set about the task of expelling prominent RPP moderates from the party.

Political tensions were heightened by additional terrorist incidents. Four guerrillas hijacked a Turkish airliner to Sofia, Bulgaria, on May 3 in an unsuccessful effort to secure the release of leftists jailed in Ankara, and on the next day gunmen wounded General Kemalettin Eken, chief of the gendarmerie and Turkey's fifth-ranking military officer, in an unsuccessful attempt to either kidnap or assassinate him. In response to these incidents the government hanged three condemned members of the TPLA in Ankara on May 6. Four university students hijacked a Turkish plane to Sofia, Bulgaria, in October and, in vain, demanded the release of 13 leftist prisoners. The hijackers freed their hostages and were granted political asylum in Bulgaria.

On May 15, after Ürgüplü's failure to form a working political coalition, President Sunay asked acting Prime Minister Melen to form a government. Melen's new cabinet, approved on May 22, was broadly representative of the political spectrum. It included as ministers eight members of the Justice Party, five from the Republican People's Party, and two from Turhan Feyzioglu's Reliance Party, in addition to nine nonpartisan technocrats and one presidential appointee. Premier Melen vowed to achieve a return to normal conditions in time for the parliamentary elections due in October 1973 and moved to deal with the difficult problems left unsolved by the Erim government. By the end of the year, however, Prime Minister Melen's government appeared to be sinking deeper into the political quagmire. Both the RPP on the left and the Justice Party on the right were attacking proposed constitutional amendments to curb terrorism, and in November the RPP decided to withdraw from Melen's coalition government. İnönü thereupon withdrew from the party and announced his decision to leave the assembly and seek a Senate seat.

In August, with Parliament producing much talk but little action, changes in the military high command raised serious questions about Turkey's political future. After a tense period of backstage maneuvering, General Memduh Tagmaç, who resigned as chief of staff on August 29, was replaced by General Faruk Gürler, who was among the signers of the March 1971 ultimatum against the Demirel government. The shift in military leadership gave a radical and

and interests of the Turkish and Greek Cypriot communities." The Turks interpreted the statement as signifying Soviet recognition of Turkey's contention that Cyprus is inhabited by two distinct communities and not, as President Makarios would argue, by one Greek nation with a resident Turkish minority.

While keeping the Soviet Union politely at arm's length, the Turkish government, with a nervous eye on growing Soviet diplomatic and military influence in Syria and Iraq, drew closer to the United States. Prime Minister Erim visited Washington in March primarily in search of military assistance and new weapons with which to modernize Turkey's armed forces. Although Turkey received an average of $115 million a year in U.S. military aid between 1965 and 1970, the level of support in 1971 fell to $60 million. President Nixon pledged to ask Congress for $115 million worth of defense support again for Turkey in fiscal 1973.

The top priority item on Erim's shopping list was a request for F-4 Phantom jets to balance the 36 Phantoms sold to Greece in March. Turkey regarded the Greek Phantom jets as threatening because, with their extended range and fire power, they undermined Turkish air superiority over Cyprus. In August the United States announced plans to provide an equal number of Phantoms to Turkey with deliveries to begin in 1973. For its part, the Turkish government, with left-wing dissidents more firmly under control, announced plans to reopen Turkish ports to units of the U.S. Sixth Fleet. In addition, despite widespread domestic opposition, Ankara reaffirmed its promise to ban cultivation of the opium poppy after this year's harvest.

The Cyprus problem remained a dominant foreign policy concern in Turkey during the year although Ankara played a subdued role in the situation. News in January that President Makarios had imported $2.5 million worth of armaments from Czechoslovakia raised strenuous Turkish protests until the weapons were surrendered to United Nations' custody. The Turkish government supported the resumption of intercommunal talks in July and provided an expert legal adviser to participate in them.

Liu Chun, Communist China's first ambassador to Turkey, presented his credentials in Ankara in May; Turkey recognized the People's Republic of China last year.

Economics. The Turkish economy showed signs of stabilization this year, after a combination of inflation and industrial stagnation last year. Industrial investment underwent a brisk upsurge during the year in response to more settled political conditions. The Bandirma sulfuric acid plant, one of the first industrial projects in Turkey to be built with Soviet technical assistance, began trial runs in May before going to full production, with a planned capacity of 120,000 tons of acid a year.

The project to bridge the Bosporus between Ortakoy and Beylerbey, begun in 1970 as a means of breaking the transit bottleneck in Istanbul, made satisfactory progress during the year. The two 540-foot towers were completed and construction of the main cables was begun. The bridge is scheduled to open for traffic in 1973 and will be the fourth-longest suspension span in the world.

The Turkish Petroleum Corporation brought two new oil wells into production in southern Turkey and announced an allocation of $6 million to continue oil-prospecting operations during the year. Oil-poor Turkey at present produces 1 million tons of crude oil a year, roughly one-quarter of its annual requirements.

Eastern Orthodox patriarch. Athenagoras I, the ecumenical patriarch of Istanbul and spiritual leader of 250 million Eastern Orthodox Christians, died in Istanbul on July 6 at 86 years of age. The patriarchate's Holy Synod of 15 archbishops elected Dimitrios, archbishop of Imbros and Tenedos, as Athenagoras' successor after the leading candidate, Archbishop Meliton of Chalcedon, had been identified as unacceptable by the Turkish government.

activist cast to the general staff. General Tagmaç was a political conservative who exerted a restraining influence on top military leaders. General Gürler, whose views are seconded on the staff by air force chief General Muhsin Batur, is known to be impatient with endless political debate and the resultant delays in legislative action. With the RPP split down the middle and Demirel's Justice Party seemingly assured of an easy win in next year's election, General Gürler and his staff may be inclined to jettison democratic procedures in favor of more direct control.

Foreign affairs. Turkey's political instability injected a note of hesitancy in the government's foreign policy operations. The ebullient self-confidence of the 1960's, when Turkey assumed the role of Mediterranean mediator between Christendom and Islam and between the Communist bloc and the West, has been largely dissipated. Relations with Moscow were troubled by evidence that the Soviet Union is lending support to the TPLA and other left-wing guerrilla organizations through intermediaries in East Germany, North Korea, and the Palestinian resistance movement. Soviet president Nikolai Podgorny arrived in Ankara on April 11 for one week, returning President Sunay's state visit to Moscow in 1969. The timing of the visit, which followed terrorist outrages and coincided with Premier Erim's resignation, was unfortunate, and the Turkish response was polite rather than warm. President Podgorny's suggestion that the two countries renew the 1925 treaty of friendship and cooperation, which Stalin abrogated unilaterally in 1945, received no Turkish encouragement. From Ankara's point of view, President Podgorny's visit produced one positive result. In the final communiqué President Podgorny referred to the Cyprus problem and stated that a solution on the island should protect "the legitimate rights

Area and population. Area, 301,382 sq. mi. Pop. (est. mid-1971), 36.5 million. Principal cities (est. 1965): Ankara (cap.), 905,700; Istanbul, 1,743,000; Izmir, 411,600.

Government. Republic with bicameral Grand National Assembly. Pres., Cevdet Sunay; acting prime min., Feret Melen.

Finance. Monetary unit, Turkish lira or pound; TL1 = US$.0725. Budget (est. 1969–1970): revenue, TL24.5 billion; expenditure, TL25.7 billion.

Trade (1970). Imports, US$886 million; exports, US$589 million. Principal imports: machinery, transportation equipment, petroleum products. Principal exports: tobacco, cotton, fruits. Major trading partners: United States, West Germany, Great Britain, Belgium-Luxembourg.

Agriculture and industry (1968, in thousands of metric tons). Agricultural production: wheat, 9,602; barley, 3,560; corn, 1,000. Industrial production: coal and lignite, 8,447; cement, 4,893; crude petroleum, 3,103.

Education (1968). Primary and first level: students, 4,794,237; teachers, 113,211. Secondary level: students, 1,063,546; teachers, 41,588. Third level: students, 143,279; teachers, 7,627. Special: students, 12,749; teachers, 570.

Armed forces (1970). Army, 390,000; navy, 37,500; air force, 50,000.

VICTOR R. SWENSON

UGANDA. Returning from a three-nation diplomatic tour in February, Ugandan president Idi Amin said that he had tried to "put the country on the map" and promote its social and economic development. After a year marked by a small war, an expulsion order for some 50,000 Asians, and a crescendo of frenetic presidential pronouncements, no one could deny that Amin had achieved the former objective, if not the latter.

Asian ouster. Stating that they had "frustrated the attempts by Ugandan Africans to participate in the economic and business life of the country," Amin decreed as of August 9 that British Asians and citizens of India, Pakistan, and Bangladesh must get out within 90 days or "face the consequences." Later he accused them of plotting against his regime and warned that Asians remaining after the deadline would be placed in camps or unused government hospitals. Estimates vary as to how many fled the country before November 8 to face an uncertain future in Britain or elsewhere.

Invasion. In mid-September more than 1,000 troops, most of whom were believed to be guerrillas loyal to former Ugandan president Apollo Milton Obote, infiltrated Uganda from Tanzania and captured three towns before they were beaten back. President Amin retaliated with bombing raids against Tanzania and claimed that Tanzanian troops were involved and that President Julius K. Nyerere was collaborating with the British government in a plot to take over Uganda before the deadline arrived for expulsion of the Asians. Both countries denied the accusations. By early October, Amin had apparently wiped out all opposition and reached an agreement with Nyerere easing the tension between the two countries.

Other developments. Early in the year a reporter for the London *Observer* cited evidence of a massive campaign of terror, in which Amin's troops rounded up and killed thousands of Lango and Acholi tribesmen who had been in the army at the time of Amin's coup in January 1971. A government statement denied that any such atrocities had taken place.

During the September uprising, a U.S. Peace Corps trainee was fired upon and killed as he rode through an area where fighting was going on. An investigative commission reported in July that two bodies found near a barracks and burned on orders of a Ugandan army officer were apparently those of American journalists reported missing in Uganda the previous summer.

Relations with Israel plummeted early in the year. In March, Amin closed the Israeli embassy and severed diplomatic relations; later he turned the Israeli ambassador's house over to Palestinian groups and sent a message to UN secretary general Kurt Waldheim in which he said that he was able to understand why Adolf Hitler had killed 6 million Jews.

Area and population. Area, 91,134 sq. mi. Pop. (1969 census), 9,548,847. Kampala (cap.; est. 1969), 332,000.

Government. Republic with unicameral legislature within the Commonwealth of Nations. Pres., Idi Amin.

Finance. Monetary unit, Uganda shilling; Sh1 = US$0.1415. Budget (est. 1972–1973): revenue, Sh1,390 million; expenditure, Sh1,430 million.

Trade (1971). Exports, Sh1,672 million; imports, Sh1,362 million.

WILLIAM A. McGEVERAN, JR.

JOHN READER

ASIAN-OWNED shops in Kampala, Uganda, were closed for business as merchants and their families, evicted from the country by presidential order, waited in hotel rooms for air passage to London or Bombay.

UNION OF SOVIET SOCIALIST REPUBLICS.

UNION OF SOVIET SOCIALIST REPUBLICS. The most important meeting between Soviet and American leaders since World War II and the forced departure of the Soviet military from Egypt overshadowed the more immediate concerns of the Soviet consumer faced with the effects of a poor harvest caused by unfavorable weather.

The summit. U.S. president Richard M. Nixon brought home with him numerous agreements that he and the Soviet leadership had negotiated during his week-long stay in the Soviet Union at the end of May. It marked the first time that an American president in office had visited the Soviet Union in peacetime. For a while it even appeared doubtful that the meeting between the leaders of the world's two nuclear superpowers would take place at all. A scant two weeks before his scheduled departure President Nixon ordered the mining of Haiphong and other North Vietnamese ports to prevent the flow of arms and other military equipment to Hanoi—equipment that was principally supplied by Soviet ships. The Soviet leadership did not cancel or postpone the summit as some in the West had predicted. By temporarily averting their gaze from Vietnam, they underscored their hope (shared by Nixon) that the meeting would result in a new, more stable and constructive era of Soviet-American relations, a consideration which to them held higher priority than the war in Indochina. Undoubtedly, Soviet leaders were much annoyed that the North Vietnamese launched a major offensive against the South just before Nixon's arrival but not before or during his visit to the People's Republic of China in March.

SALT. Among the agreements reached, the most sought after was the limiting of defensive and offensive strategic weapons. The details had been worked out during the long and painstaking SALT (strategic arms limitation talks) negotiations, which lasted 2½ years with 130 separate meetings alternating between Helsinki and Vienna. Finally, in Moscow, both sides were able to compromise on this life and death issue. They agreed to limit each country to 200 defensive missiles (ABM's), 100 at each of two sites. One of these could be around each nation's capital, the other around an offensive missile site, such as the American ABM facility in North Dakota. Offensively both sides agreed to freeze the number of land and submarine missiles at their present levels. On the basis of the accord the Soviets will have an edge on land-based ICBM's, 1,618 to 1,054, but the United States will maintain superiority because the number of multiple warheads carried by each missile is unaffected by the freeze. The United States has missiles that carry up to ten independently targeted nuclear warheads (MIRV's); at the present time, Soviet multiple warheads cannot be individually directed. The United States maintains the overwhelming edge of 5,700 to 2,500 warheads.

The agreement will not necessarily slow down the costly arms race but will cause it to become qualitative. Both sides, in all probability, will direct their efforts toward replacing old missiles with new, sophisticated models. To prevent this, new SALT negotiations started in Geneva on November 21. The arms accord was passed by the U.S. Senate and the Supreme Soviet in September and a treaty was signed in October.

Other agreements. The leaders of both countries also agreed on setting up a series of joint committees to exchange information and to work for solutions in problem areas of mutual concern: a joint committee on the environment to study problems of water, air, and soil pollution and measures to control man's impact on the environment; a joint committee on medicine to coordinate research on heart disease, cancer, and other problems of public health; a joint commission on science and technology to recommend exchanges and combined research in these fields. These committees began their work soon after the summit.

In space, a joint docking of manned spacecraft in flight is planned for 1975. When the two space ships are linked, American astronauts and Soviet cosmonauts will begin cooperative activities, including exchange of crewmen. There will also be cooperation in space medicine and space meteorology.

The summit did not wipe out the many problems that still exist between the Soviet Union and the United States, nor were any of the agreements shatterproof. It did emphasize to all that the leadership of the two mightiest nations—despite continuing differences over Vietnam, the Middle East, and the Indian subcontinent were striving for agreement, based on mutual self-interest, on a wide range of issues which could lay the groundwork for future accord in still other areas.

Soviet-American trade. High on the Soviet priority list was the effort to significantly increase trade with the United States, to provide the long-ignored Soviet consumer with wider choices and higher quality goods, and to import American technology in the many areas in which the Soviet Union is still behind. American business interests are also hopefully eyeing the potential of the Soviet market. The issue of American credits, favorable tariff treatment, and a settlement of the old Soviet Lend-Lease debt left over from World War II was too complicated to unravel in May; agreement was not reached until October, as part of a comprehensive trade pact.

An immediate fruit of the summit was the July 8 announcement that the Soviet Union had signed a three-year agreement for the purchase of at least $750 million worth of American grain, the largest grain deal ever made between the two countries. By early September the Soviets had already purchased more than $1 billion in foodstuffs for this year alone. Since the United States will not have to buy anything in return from the Soviet Union, the deal will balance off a significant part of the American balance-of-payment deficit during each of the next three years. The grain deal, by itself, exceeded last year's import-export total between the two countries. It was the most dramatic of several accords reached between Soviet agencies and American firms.

Meanwhile, a comprehensive trade agreement, the first since the early years of the cold war, was being intensively negotiated. High-ranking officials of the new joint Soviet-American commercial commission crossed and recrossed the Atlantic, Commerce Secretary Peter G. Peterson flew to Moscow in July, as did presidential assistant Henry A. Kissinger in September.

On October 18 a significant trade agreement was signed that included payment by the Soviets of $722 million in World War II debts, most of it on the condition that the United States extend most-favored-nation treatment (that is, the lowest regular tariff rates) to the Soviets. The U.S. government Export-Import Bank was authorized to extend credits and guarantees for the sale of goods to the Soviet Union. The last Lend-Lease repayment is due in the year 2001. Most-favored-nation status was in doubt, however, because of an amendment introduced in the Senate that would forbid trade concessions to any country imposing high exit visa fees. In August, Moscow had imposed such fees on those seeking to emigrate, mainly Jews. Hardly by coincidence, 19 Jewish families were given permission to go to Israel without the usual fees ($195,000 worth) on the same day that the trade agreement was signed.

Middle East. *Soviet exodus from Egypt.* Anwar Sadat, the president of the Arab Republic of Egypt, on July 18 told an unprepared world that he had ordered Soviet military advisers and experts to leave his country and place Soviet bases and equipment under the exclusive control of Egyptian forces immediately. To the astonishment of many, Moscow complied with Egypt's demand. About 20,000 Soviet pilots, missile crews, and advisers quickly departed with their families, taking their advanced SAM missiles with them.

Sadat's decision, which probably took even the Soviets by surprise, had been building for more than a year, during which time he had made three trips to Moscow. On each occasion he had vainly sought to secure certain offensive weapons: MIG-23 fighter-bombers and surface-to-surface missiles to counter American-made Phantom jets flown by Israeli pilots. With an offensive arsenal, Sadat had hoped to be able either to recapture the territories lost in the 1967 war or to threaten Israel with a preemptive strike, thereby forcing it to return the occupied lands by negotiations.

Soviet leaders maintained a different perspective. They were convinced that the Egyptians were still incapable of handling sophisticated weapons and would be defeated again in another round of fighting with Israel. Second, if another Arab-Israeli war broke out, with Soviet troops in Egypt, the Soviet Union faced military confrontation with the United States, which it was determined to avoid at all costs. Under such circumstances the Kremlin's unsatisfactory alternatives would be to confront the United States by actively aiding Egypt against Israel or to stand by passively while their ally was defeated once more. With a new Moscow-Washington relationship evolving, touched off by President Nixon's summit meeting with General Secretary Leonid I. Brezhnev, Soviet leaders had too much at stake to allow this new stage in U.S.-Soviet relations to be jeopardized by Egypt's recklessness. Sadat read these signals clearly and hence took his abrupt action.

Sadat's long-standing anti-Communism, which led him to pursue policies opposed by Moscow, was another reason for Soviet nonsupport. When the Soviet Union and Egypt signed a 15-year treaty of friendship and cooperation in May 1971, the Egyptian president was eliminating the left wing of his regime by arresting Ali Sabry and his pro-Soviet faction. In July of the same year, and against Moscow's wishes, Egypt actively helped the Sudanese government to crush a Communist-led coup d'etat in Khartoum.

Despite the sudden and abrupt expulsion of Soviet military advisers, Egypt remains linked to the Soviet Union by huge financial obligations and the promise of unfinished aid projects and trade patterns which are virtually impossible to reverse over the short run. The total Soviet investment in Egypt is estimated at about $6 billion, of which $2 billion has gone for nonmilitary projects. Of these the most important investments were the Aswan High Dam, a steel complex, a land reclamation project of 200,000 acres, textile factories, and oil prospecting. Egypt had been paying for these—as well as for MIG jets, missiles, and Soviet military advisers—by selling the Soviets cheap consumer goods. Even the military ties between the two countries were not broken completely, for in October the Soviets agreed to return some SAM-6 missiles to Egypt.

Syria, Iraq, and el-Fatah. Moscow had begun to diversify its political investment in the Arab world well before the blow came from Cairo, by building up its position elsewhere in the Middle East. Hedging its bet in Egypt, the Soviet Union signed a 15-year friendship treaty with Iraq, which Premier Aleksei Kosygin personally delivered and signed in Baghdad in April. Relations with Syria—which can offer alternative ports if Alexandria should no longer be available to the Soviet Mediterranean fleet, as well as air bases for Soviet squadrons—were decidedly improved when Marshal Andrei A. Grechko, the Soviet defense minister, signed a large new arms deal for Syria in Damascus in May. These indicators and the news that the Soviet Union had made its first direct arms delivery to el-Fatah Arab commandos showed that the Soviet Union was solicitous of improving its influence even with the fedayeen (and Syria which shelters them) to counterbalance its loss of leverage in Egypt.

Accord on West Berlin. The foreign ministers of the United States, the Soviet Union, France, and Great Britain signed a comprehensive agreement on Berlin in June which will put an end to a quarter century of periodic crisis and uncertainty over the divided city. For the West Berliners the accord will ease their isolation considerably. They will now be able to drive or take trains 100 miles across East Germany to and from West Germany without being subjected to harassment or time-consuming controls. The Soviet Union agreed, for the first time, to share responsibility with the three Western powers in guaranteeing access routes to West Berlin. For up to 30 days a year West Berliners will also be permitted to visit East Berlin and East Germany, from which they had been barred since 1966 and 1952 respectively. Divided family members living in both Germanies will thus be able to see each other once more on a regular basis.

The four-power agreement was regarded as a sign of Soviet willingness to make significant concessions to the West to gain further support for a European security conference, for which Soviet leaders have been lobbying in recent years. After hard negotiations, the basis of the accord was agreed upon in August 1971, but the official signing was held up by the Soviet Union pending the ratification by the West German Parliament of a goodwill treaty signed by Chancellor Willy Brandt and the Soviet leaders in 1970. In that treaty West Germany gave up its claim to substantial amounts of territory lost to Poland and the Soviet Union after World War II. After a long and stormy debate the goodwill treaty was ratified in May, making the Berlin accord possible.

Sino-Soviet relations. The chilly atmosphere prevailing between Moscow and Peking blocked them from providing quick aid to their North Vietnamese ally after that country's ports had been closed down by American mines. Before the mining, 85 percent of North Vietnam's supplies came by sea, mostly from the Soviet Union. Yet, the Soviet Union and China have been unable to reach an agreement that would permit increased Soviet aid by land shipment across China. In August at the United Nations the two largest Communist powers clashed over the admission of Bangladesh to the world body. The Soviet Union, India's ally, strongly backed Bangladesh's entry, which was vehemently opposed by the People's Republic of China, a Pakistan supporter. Nor have the two nations, who share a 2,000-mile frontier, been able to make progress in the often-interrupted border talks over disputed territory that were begun three years ago.

Politics. The only significant change in the aging Soviet leadership was the demotion in May of Pyotr Y. Shelest, the first secretary of the Ukrainian Communist Party. The 64-year-old Shelest, a full member of the Politburo, was named deputy premier of the Soviet Union—a lesser position since none of the other eight deputy premiers holds Politburo status. Vladimir V. Shcherbitsky, 54 years old, a close supporter of party leader Brezhnev, was appointed in Shelest's place as first secretary of the Ukraine, one of the top five political positions in the country. The Ukraine is the second largest republic, with 42 million inhabitants. Since Shelest's demotion came on the eve of President Nixon's visit, when the Soviet leadership would want to present a united front, speculations were raised that Shelest, a hawk during the Czechoslovak crisis of 1968, favored breaking the American blockade of North Vietnamese ports or at least canceling Nixon's visit in protest. Another view suggested that Shelest was removed principally for not being sufficiently vigilant in dealing with increased Ukrainian nationalist sentiments among intellectuals and young people.

Economic affairs. For the first six months of 1972 the Soviet economy, despite production setbacks caused by a severe winter, achieved a 6.8 percent rise in the total value of industrial production over the first half of 1971. The midyear output rate, therefore, almost equaled the 6.9 percent growth rate planned for 1972. However, labor productivity, one of the most important indicators of economic

WIDE WORLD

KREMLIN CONFERENCE. U.S. president Richard Nixon and Soviet Communist Party secretary Leonid Brezhnev, aided by an interpreter (back to camera), talked privately for two hours shortly after the president arrived in Moscow for his nine-day summit visit in May.

progress, continued to lag behind, increasing only by 5.4 percent, thereby falling substantially short of the 6.1 percent rate set for 1972.

The attempt to raise labor productivity has been seriously hampered by the heavy consumption of vodka by Soviet workers, which rose markedly when the five-day workweek was introduced in 1967. Analyses of drinking patterns indicated that absenteeism in industry after holidays and paydays resulted in idleness of costly equipment, a high rate of below-standard products, and the disorganization of assembly line operations. For these reasons the Soviet government, in its most recent drive against alcoholism, on June 16 ordered a sharp reduction in the sale of vodka, prohibiting its purchase in stores on weekends and holidays and requiring strict enforcement of the limitation on retail hours to 11:00 A. M. through 7:00 P.M. on weekdays. Whether these measures will prove effective or will give rise to illegal purchases and distilleries remains to be seen.

Agriculture. A harsh winter and a rainless summer resulted in a relatively poor harvest of an estimated 167 million metric tons of wheat in 1972. Although this figure was the average yield for the previous five-year plan (1966–1970), it fell far below the expected goal of 190 million tons and well below the 1971 gross of 181 million tons. To bridge the gap between expectation and actual yield the Soviet Union was forced to purchase millions of tons of grain and foodstuffs from the West, most of which came from the United States. The more than $1 billion that the Soviets will pay for the American grain this year alone will be the largest commercial transaction between the two countries since the Lend-Lease agreement of World War II.

Although Soviet citizens were not told of the foreign grain purchases in the controlled press, Soviet shoppers—noticing the spotty offerings of vegetables usually available in early September—began to form lines in front of vegetable stores, particularly for potatoes, despite official appeals against hoarding and promises that potatoes, a staple of Russian diet, would be in sufficient supply during the coming winter. Part of the 25 million tons of grains and foodstuffs purchased will be delivered to Soviet bloc countries of Eastern Europe, including Poland (which receives about 1.5 million tons yearly), Czechoslovakia, and East Germany.

The total cost for Western grain will be over $1.3 billion in hard currency. This sum exceeds the annual value of all Soviet imports of Western equipment and technology from 1966 to 1970 and may force the Soviet Union to resume substantial sales of gold after several years of modest offerings in order to build up its hard currency holdings.

Dissidents. Soviet dissidents who openly and daringly defy the authorities fall mainly into two categories. The first, the intellectuals, few in number but including figures of international renown, oppose the regime on moral and legal grounds. The second, members of various nationality and religious groups with a potentially huge following, demand greater political, cultural, and religious freedoms for their people. Both groups were subjected to harsh crackdowns by the regime.

Intellectuals. The "Democratic Movement"—composed primarily of intellectuals but with many of its key activists in prison, Siberian exile, or forced internment in mental hospitals—suffered another loss in June when the previously jailed Pyotr I. Yakir (whose father, a general, was shot by Stalin on trumped-up charges of treason) was imprisoned and charged with anti-Soviet activities. Yakir was only one of many intellectuals who were arrested, received warnings to stop their activities, or saw their homes searched by the security police.

The authorities so far have failed to suppress the *Chronicles of Current Events,* the most successful Soviet underground publication, despite a secret Central Committee decree of December 1971 ordering its elimination. The *Chronicle* has continued to appear, as it has for four years, at regular bimonthly intervals, recording objectively the cases of individuals who have been persecuted by the regime for various heresies. A voice which the regime has so far not dared to still is that of the Soviet Union's great novelist Aleksandr I. Solzhenitsyn. In the lecture published in Stockholm in August that he would have delivered had he been permitted to accept in Moscow the Nobel Prize he won in 1970, Solzhenitsyn denounced those governments who by use of censorship prohibit the free development of a nation's literature, "Because that is not just a violation against 'freedom of print,' it is the closing down of the heart of the nation, a slashing to pieces of its memory."

Jewish emigration. This was the best year yet for Jewish emigration. In the first eight months of 1972 about 20,000 Jews had already been permitted to leave, compared with the 15,000 that were released during the whole of 1971. Jewish intellectuals, who previously had had greater trouble in receiving permission to emigrate than blue-collar workers and pensioners, were faced with a new government regulation in August that imposed a steeply graduated scale of fees on applicants with higher education. The fees ranged from more than $4,000 to $50,000. Jews are the most highly educated ethnic group in the Soviet Union; the fact that the new exit fees were timed to coincide with the height of Soviet Jewish emigration to Israel was an attempt to discourage a Jewish exodus.

Even before the fees were instituted, emigration applicants faced great difficulties. They had no assurances that their papers would be processed once they were filed. Most of those who applied were immediately discharged from their jobs and then faced threats of prosecution for lack of employment, and those of the appropriate age faced sudden military conscription.

The new exit fees brought protests from the international community and threatened to affect the ratification of a Soviet-American trade agreement reached on October 18. (On that day, 19 Jewish families were exempted from the usual fees.)

Other nationalities. In May, Roman Kalanta, 20, a member of the Young Communist League and a Catholic, set fire to himself in Kaunas, Lithuania's second largest city, in protest against religious restrictions. On the day of Kalanta's burial thousands of Lithuanians took to the streets shouting "Freedom for Lithuania." The demonstrations lasted for two days and had to be suppressed by the army. At least 200 were arrested and faced trial. Lithuania is the only Catholic republic in the Soviet Union, and its population of 3 million harbors deep-rooted religious and nationalist feelings in opposition to Soviet rule. Two months before Kalanta's self-immolation, 17,000 Lithuanians signed an open letter that was sent to the United Nations deploring the deportation of Catholic bishops, the arrest of priests, and the closing of churches.

Nearly 30 years after the German occupation of the Soviet Crimea, four Crimean Tatars were sentenced and executed in July for collaborating with the German military during World War II. The trial, which was given wide publicity in the press, appeared designed to support the regime's refusal to allow Crimean Tatars to return to their homeland. In 1944, 200,000 Crimean Tatars were deported to Soviet Asia for their alleged collaboration with the Germans. Since 1967, the Tatars have been officially exonerated but refused permission to resettle in the Crimea, despite repeated requests and petitions signed by thousands of Tatars in Central Asian exile.

Sports. Soviet men and women athletes had a field day at the Summer Olympic Games in Munich. They won 99 medals, of which 50 were gold, outdistancing their closest rivals, the Americans, who won 94 medals, only 33 of which were gold. Outstanding achievements were recorded: In basketball, for the first time in the history of the Olympic Games, an American team failed to win the gold medal, losing a highly controversial final game to its Soviet opponent, 51–50. In track and field Valery Borzov established himself as the fastest human by winning the 100- and 200-meter dashes, and Nikolai Avilov emerged as the best all-around athlete by winning the decathlon. In weight lifting, Vasily Alexeyev laid claim to the title of the world's strongest man by lifting more than anyone else in the superheavyweight category. And, in gymnastics, Olga Korbut, 17, put on dazzling performances to win two gold medals. Other Soviet victories were registered in water polo, canoeing, springboard diving, sharpshooting, wrestling, boxing, and women's volleyball.

The U.S.S.R. national hockey team played the cream of the Canadian professional hockey players in September in a series of eight games, four in Canada and four in the Soviet Union, and almost scored a startling upset. The series ended with four victories for Canada and three for the Soviet Union with one tie. The Canadians came from behind and won the series by taking the last three games by a single goal each, scoring the deciding goal in the final match with only 34 seconds left in the contest. The Soviet skaters outscored their highly touted rivals 32 goals to 31 in the series and proved that they were hockey equals of Canada in every respect.

World chess championship. Boris Spassky of the Soviet Union lost his world chess title to Bobby Fischer of the United States in Reykjavík, Iceland, on September 1. The score was 12½ to 8½. Fischer won seven games outright against Spassky's three. This marks the first time that someone other than a Soviet citizen has held the world title since 1946. The matches were full of controversy. Bobby Fischer forced a delay in the opening game by refusing to show up until the prize money for the tournament was raised. He then forfeited the second match by not appearing because he objected to having the games filmed. When Fischer took a commanding lead, Soviet officials charged that Fischer was using electronic devices and a chemical substance to weaken Spassky's power of concentration. After careful investigation by Icelandic officials, these charges were proved to be groundless.

Area and population. Area, 8,599,300 sq. mi. Pop. est. 1971), 245,070,000. Principal cities (1970): Moscow (cap.), 7,061,000; Leningrad, 3,950,000; Kiev, 1,632,000; Tashkent, 1,385,000; Baku, 1,261,000; Kharkov, 1,223,000.
Government. Socialist republic. Pres., Presidium of the Supreme

SPEAKING OUT. Aleksandr Solzhenitsyn, with his wife and son, is interviewed in his apartment by a Western newsman. Days later the Soviet government blocked plans for a private ceremony in which the author was to receive his 1970 Nobel Prize for literature.

HEDRIK SMITH/NEW YORK TIMES

Soviet, Nikolai V. Podgorny; chmn., Council of Ministers, Aleksei N. Kosygin; gen. secy., Communist Party, Leonid I. Brezhnev.

Finance. Monetary unit, ruble; 1 ruble = US$1.25. Total budget (1972): revenue, 173.8 billion rubles; expenditure, 173.6 billion rubles.

Trade (1971). Imports, US$12.5 billion; exports, US$13.8 billion.

Education (1969). Primary and secondary schools, 197,000; enrollment, 49.4 million. Technical colleges, 4,196; enrollment, 4.3 million. Higher educational establishments, 800; enrollment, 4.5 million.

Armed forces (1970). Army, 2 million; air force, 500,000; navy, 500,000; border guards and security troops, 350,000.

HENRY W. MORTON

UNITED ARAB REPUBLIC. *See* EGYPT.

UNITED KINGDOM OF GREAT BRITAIN AND NORTHERN IRELAND.
During 1972 the British government completed the legislative preliminaries for assuming full membership in the European Economic Community (Common Market) on January 1, 1973. At the same time, the government had reason to be disappointed with the economy's lack of response to the new prospect thus opened up. Nor did the absence of enthusiasm among the British public for a continental future give way to a more eager mood as the time for joining the market approached. It had been the hope and intention of the government to bring to Europe a renewed national confidence and a buoyant economy. Yet, with only three months still to go, industrial investment was sagging, unemployment remained at a high level, and the pace of inflation was causing general alarm.

This combination of unfavorable trends caused the Conservative government to reverse its method of economic management in the autumn. It had come to power in the summer of 1970 preaching the virtues of competition, incentives, and reduced state intervention in industrial affairs, including wage bargaining. But the combination of sagging industrial investment, high unemployment, a weak pound, and rampant inflation caused it to go into reverse. By early November the government temporarily abandoned a fixed exchange rate, re-created machinery for dispensing public subsidies to ailing industries and firms, and introduced a statutory wage-price freeze for from 90 to 150 days.

Meanwhile, the government's responsibilities in Northern Ireland became no easier in spite of the apparently simplifying stroke of suspending the provincial parliament and government and appointing a member of the United Kingdom cabinet to assume full control.

Approach to Europe. The political debate about Britain's membership in the European community continued throughout the year. At the popular level, no great heat was engendered. The opinion polls, for what they are worth in a matter of this kind, did not show any marked change in favor of the government's policy, as its advocates had expected to happen when Common Market membership became a *fait accompli*. Misgivings about membership have been tempered by a feeling that there is probably no satisfactory alternative—even the Europeanists lean heavily on that argument—and this does not make for political excitement. In the House of Commons, however, passionate arguments left wounds that will take a long time to heal.

The necessity of passing legislation to pave the way for accession to European community treaties (which Britain signed in Brussels early in the year) provided opponents of British membership with the opportunity that they felt they had hitherto been denied: the opportunity to subject the implications of the government's policy to systematic criticism. In October 1971 the Commons had voted in principle in favor of entry, the terms of which were then known only in outline form. The majority was 112, as more Labourites cross-voted in favor than Conservative members cross-voted against, and that majority had been enshrined by the Europeanists as representing the "true" opinion of the Commons. But on second reading (on February 17, 1972) of the essential constitutional bill, the majority was a bare eight, 309–301. Prime Minister Edward Heath was on record as having said before taking office that no government could take Britain into the Common Market without the wholehearted consent of Parliament and the people. That slender majority on second reading plus such indications as there were of the state of public opinion were paraded as evidence that Heath had broken a pledge.

The 1972 constitutional bill exposed the full extent of the abatement of parliamentary sovereignty entailed by British membership in the European community, and that was the issue on which the bill's opponents seized. Led by Michael Foot from the Labour benches and Enoch Powell from the Conservative benches, the critics fought the bill clause by clause. On some votes, the majority fell as low as three or four, but no vote was lost by the government. The bill received the royal assent before Heath took off in October for a summit conference of members and prospective members of the European community. The way was then clear for Britain to become a member of the Common Market on January 1, 1973, as scheduled.

All this left the Labour Party in serious disarray. The position on which party leader Harold Wilson sought to maintain a semblance of party unity was one which called for rejection of the terms of entry negotiated by the Conservatives, "renegotiation" of the terms by a future Labour government, and submission of the results of the renegotiation to the British people in a referendum. This policy, which stopped short of straight opposition to Common Market entry, was approved at the Labour Party conference in October together with a resolution in apparent conflict with it. Thus, a formal schism in the party was avoided between the minority with European convictions and the majority, which has become increasingly unfriendly to Europeanism. The position of the minority became difficult in spite of Wilson's skillful bridge-building. Roy Jenkins, who began the year as deputy leader of the party, retired to the back benches when the leadership espoused the idea of a national referendum on the Common Market issue. He was joined by other former ministers in the Labour government, including George Thomson, whom Heath later appointed to be one of the two Common Market commissioners supplied by Britain. The other is Sir Christopher Soames, a former Conservative minister and more recently ambassador to France. He is given much of the credit for melting the icy relationship that existed between Paris and London after Charles de Gaulle's two vetoes of British entry into the European community. Both British commissioners are substantial political figures, and their appointment is believed, in Britain at least, to set a new standard at the commission in Brussels.

Inflation and unemployment. The British economy exhibited an unusual combination of features during the first nine months of 1972. National output was rising again after the recession of 1970–1971 and by autumn had achieved an annual growth rate of nearly 5 percent. Unemployment, which passed the 1 million mark in the winter, remained obstinately high. The rate of increase in average weekly earnings was in double figures. The retail price index was rising at a rate of more than 6 percent a year. Industrial investment was at a low ebb. The balance-of-payments current account surplus declined to £77 million in the second quarter of 1972, having stood at £295 million a year before. The money supply was allowed to expand at an unprecedented rate, and in the second quarter the annual rate of increase was almost 35 percent. Of the many manifestations of inflation the most conspicuous was the rise in house prices—up 18 percent on the average in the first six months of the year.

Early in the year, the government gave first priority to the reactivation of economic expansion. The budget in the spring was expansionary in tone; credit restraints were relaxed; and public spending was increased.

In June the downward trend of the payments surplus and the upward trend of inflation precipitated a sudden and massive run on sterling. The authorities, instead of defending the pound's parity (it had been valued in the 1971 Smithsonian Agreement at a middle rate of approximately $2.60), suspended dealings and announced that the pound would be allowed to float temporarily. In May, Britain, as a prospective member of the European community, had entered into an agreement to hold European currencies in a fixed relationship to each other, with only a narrow margin of fluctuation permitted. The flotation temporarily annulled that agreement as far as Britain was concerned. The pound fell initially to $2.41 and then to $2.34 by late October.

The high level of unemployment provided one motive for the government's embracing of expansionary policies. But public anxiety about unemployment was superseded by public anxiety about price inflation. The inflation was widely believed to be caused by excessively high wage settlements, which raised industrial costs and then prices.

The Conservative government had come to office with a temperamental dislike of wage and price controls, official norms, or anything that could be described as a comprehensive prices and incomes policy. Price rises were to be checked by the stimulation of greater competition, and government interference in collective bargaining over wages was to be confined to that large number of employees for whose wages the government is directly or indirectly responsible—civil servants, local government staffs, and those working in publicly owned industries. If it had worked, that policy would have discriminated against people in public employment in comparison with the majority whose wages were not subject to official restraint. But it did not work. In 1972, first the coal miners and then the railwaymen secured wage settlements at a figure well beyond what the government had in mind. (The strike by the miners, who won 20 percent wage increases, left many Britishers without heat or electricity.) Throughout the year, the general size of wage settlements was far in excess of anything that could be justified by reference to improvements in productivity, and the government came under growing pressure to adopt a more effective incomes policy.

At the end of September, Heath responded. He had earlier restarted tripartite talks—between the government, the Confederation of British Industry (CBI), and the Trades Union Congress (TUC)—about measures to combat inflation. After the second formal meeting, the prime minister published specific proposals. First, the government reaffirmed and extended its commitment to achieve an annual growth rate of 5 percent over the next two years, a rate of growth well ahead of anything seen in Britain since World War II. Second, for 12 months there would be a nationwide limit on wage increases of £2 a week for a normal working week. This limit would apply to everyone from managing directors to office cleaners. In that way the real wages and relative position of lower-paid workers would be improved. Third, over the same 12-month period, price increases would be kept within 4 percent for manufactured products and within 5 percent for retail goods. It was Heath's purpose to achieve these measures of restraint by voluntary means.

The initial response of the TUC was to put up counterproposals and keep the dialogue going. However, the failure of these talks to bear fruit was a major factor in the pound's decline. On November 5, Heath created the new Ministry for Trade and Consumer Affairs; the new minister, Sir Geoffrey Howe, was expected to spearhead the government's efforts to hold down prices. But more urgent measures were needed, and the very next day Heath imposed a freeze on wages, prices, rents, and dividends. Increases will not themselves be illegal, but it will be illegal to persist in an increase after receipt of a cancellation order. The government did not disclose its long-term intentions.

Bitter labor conflicts earlier in the year made the trade unions reluctant to become working partners with the Conservative government. One source of conflict was the operation of the Industrial Relations Act, a reform of trade union law. The TUC resolved that unions should not register under the act (they are not required to register, but if they do not, they forfeit important legal immunities), and it predicted that the invocation of the law would merely worsen industrial relations. That prediction proved correct in the short run. The act, which went into effect in February, had hardly been in force for four months when three leaders of London's dockers were jailed under its provisions. The act had been drafted so as to avoid, if possible, that kind of inflammatory action, but it proved in this case not to be possible, as the union leaders refused to defend themselves in the Industrial Relations Court, which they claimed had no jurisdiction over them. A national dock strike was immediately called. However, there was found to exist a person previously unknown to the public called the official solicitor, who was able to apply to the court for the release of the imprisoned men, which ended the strike.

Another part of the Industrial Relations Act was tested beginning in April, when the railwaymen began work slowdowns (or industrial action) in support of their wage claim. The minister for employment invoked the new power to impose a "conciliation pause," during which a return to normal working practices is required. When the interval passed without a settlement being brought any nearer, the minister invoked the power to order a balloting of the unions' members on the question of the proposed industrial action. The balloting resulted in an overwhelming vote in favor of industrial action, in other words, in support of the union leadership. A final settlement in June gave the railwaymen 13.5 percent wage increases.

THE DUKE OF WINDSOR, who gave up his throne to marry the woman he loved, died in France at the age of 77. At left, he poses with his mother, Queen Mary; above, he gives his first radio speech as Edward VIII, a title he held for less than a year. At right, the duke and duchess of Windsor arrive in England together after 30 years of marriage, for the first time since he abdicated his kingly office.

The new Industrial Relations Act contributed nothing to the resolution of the railwaymen's dispute, and unions and the Labour Party argued strenuously that the act should be repealed or at least radically amended. The government was reluctant to alter the act, but its reluctance became less marked as it saw that the concession might be a necessary part of the price for the unions' cooperation in policies to combat inflation.

Another source of friction between the government and the unions was the allegedly "divisive" character of the government's fiscal and social policies. Particular exception was taken to the government's reform of public housing finance. Subsidies for such housing had grown up over time into a system which failed to ensure either that the total sum was distributed in a way that was proportionate to the housing needs of the administering councils or that all individual tenants in need of assistance (and only such tenants) received aid. The government's measures to remedy those defects entailed a sharp rise in the general level of public housing rents coupled with a more generous system of rebates available to those tenants who could prove need.

The combination of economic and political pressures caused the government to diverge from its spoken intentions in another way also—in a newfound readiness to come to the aid of "lame ducks" of industry. That phrase was minted in a celebrated speech by John Davies, then minister for trade and industry, in the early confident days of the present government. The speech gave notice that failing enterprises with poor prospects of profitability should expect no more special financial assistance from public funds. They

would have to live or perish in a tougher milieu than that provided by the previous Labour government. This doctrine did not last through 1972. Upper Clyde Shipbuilders in Glasgow, Scotland, was the place of its interment. A great deal of public money had been put into those shipyards over the years, but the assistance did not prevent them from sliding into liquidation and being on the verge of shutting down, in whole or in part. The shipyard workers organized a "work-in," in which they more or less took over the running of the yards, and the government came under intense pressure not to permit the addition of these workers to the already heavy unemployment on Clydeside. And so, the yards were yet again reorganized, and another £35 million of public money was made available.

Northern Ireland. On March 24, Prime Minister Heath announced in the House of Commons the suspension of the Northern Ireland Parliament and government for a period of at least a year. The United Kingdom government was to assume direct control of the administration of the province. The decision was taken against the background of political deadlock and a deteriorating security situation.

The year had opened with reasonably optimistic assessments by the British Army commanders in Ulster about the chances of reducing Irish Republican Army (IRA) violence to what was imprecisely called an "acceptable level." However, the actual incidence of bombing and shooting obstinately refused to conform to that prediction. Meanwhile, elected representatives of the Roman Catholic community were boycotting almost all the institutions of the state to protest the policy of internment without trial of suspected

terrorists. That policy, introduced in August 1971, was considered by Catholics to be enforced with bias, there being no Protestants of Unionist persuasion among the internees.

Things were made dramatically worse by the disorders in Londonderry on January 30, which came to be called "bloody Sunday." When an illegal Catholic march in protest against internment was blocked by British troops, Catholic youths began stoning the army barricades. A detachment of the Parachute Regiment was ordered to make a snatch raid to grab some of the youths, and the troops' incursion took them into the Bogside, a Catholic enclave which had more or less withdrawn itself from the authority of the United Kingdom.

In the shooting that broke out (started by the soldiers, said the Bogsiders; started by the IRA, said the soldiers), 13 civilians were killed. There were no military casualties. The loss of life sent a wave of anger through the Catholic community, temporarily ruptured good relations between

the governments of Great Britain and the Irish Republic, provoked the sacking of the British embassy in Dublin, and made any hope of political reconciliation in Northern Ireland seem infinitely remote.

Brian Faulkner's provincial government had no responsibility for the conduct of the soldiers, and the police on the spot, for whom Faulkner did have responsibility, had advised against the raid into the Bogside. Nevertheless, Faulkner came under increasing pressure from the Heath government in London to repair the situation by making further political concessions to the Catholics. The concession that Heath most wanted Faulkner to make was the transfer to Westminster of all authority over internal security and policing. This Faulkner was not prepared to do, and his refusal was the immediate cause of his dismissal.

The man whom Heath selected to administer the province was William Whitelaw, a former chief whip of the Conservative Party and, at the time of his selection, leader of the House of Commons. He set about his task with a

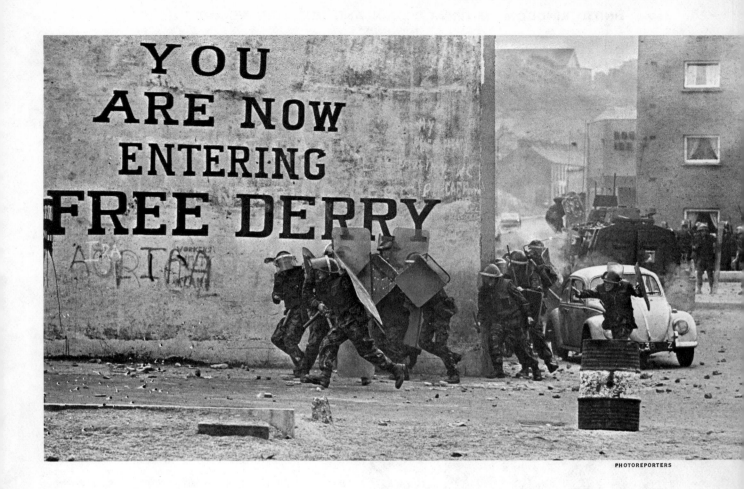

YOU
ARE NOW
ENTERING
FREE DERRY

THE STRUGGLE FOR ULSTER

Bloody riots by day and secret executions by night continued to heat up tensions between Catholics and Protestants in war-torn Northern Ireland. At left, combat practice for Protestant women of the secret Ulster Defense Association. Above, snatch squads in operation at "Free Derry," the Catholic Bogside enclave in Londonderry. At right, the ruins of a wedding reception; guests were warned to flee a Belfast hotel by terrorists who then blasted it with a 50-pound charge.

581

determination to get himself personally trusted by all sections of the community.

On the Catholic side, his advent was well received. The Stormont government had been suspended (never, the Catholics believed, to be restored). Whitelaw seemed to understand them, and he at once set about releasing some of the internees. The Provisional wing of the IRA kept up hostilities, but the Officials, the more ideological of the two factions, declared a truce. Whitelaw's appointment, of course, gave no similar satisfaction to the Protestant side. There was a sudden flow of support for the Vanguard, an ultraloyalist movement formed by William Craig, a former minister for home affairs. Mammoth rallies of protest and strikes by Protestant workers took place on March 27–28. But such manifestations of discontent were manageable, and the dreaded "Protestant backlash" did not occur.

In the early summer Whitelaw began to make contact through intermediaries with the leadership of the Provisional IRA. In great secrecy some of their number were flown to London for talks with Whitelaw, and early in July a truce was declared. The full circumstances of the agreement were obscure, but it was evidently not the wholly unconditional cease-fire that it was represented as being in London. The four days that were set between the announcement of these arrangements and their implementation were used by some Provisional units for an intensification of the bombing and shooting. The truce itself lasted little more than a week and then collapsed with reciprocal accusations of bad faith. Whitelaw's readiness to treat with the Provisional IRA—

NO LIGHT FOR SORE EYES. A nurse at London's Royal Eye Hospital worked by candlelight during blackouts caused by a coal strike.

© TIMES OF LONDON

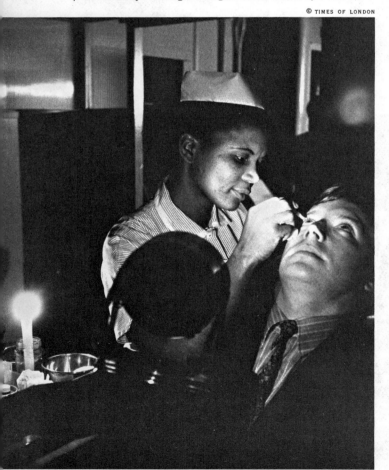

something which he had given the impression he would not do—unsettled the Protestant community and aroused in some sections of it a sense of betrayal.

Part of the trouble was the political disorientation of the Protestant community, a disorientation which was accelerated by the suspension of Stormont. The Unionist Party (of which Faulkner was the leader) was subject to erosion at both ends. Some defected to the Alliance Party, a recently formed organization which stands for nonsectarian and conciliatory policies within the framework of the United Kingdom. Others defected to the Vanguard movement or to the Loyalist Association of Workers, a tough-minded body of people with its roots in the shipyards of Belfast. The Reverend Ian Paisley, the Protestant extremist of whom so much once was heard, had dropped into the background. His response to the suspension of Stormont was to demand total integration of Northern Ireland into the United Kingdom, on the model of Scotland.

Meanwhile, there had grown rapidly in size, organization, and menace a Protestant paramilitary force called the Ulster Defense Association. Its purpose was to give muscle to the Protestant-Unionist cause or, alternatively, to prepare against the possibility of "betrayal" by providing for the armed defense of the Protestant community. It became increasingly active during the summer months, reinforcing its demand for the removal of barricades around the Catholic "no go" areas by erecting its own in Protestant areas.

Whitelaw's next major initiative was a response to this rising demand for action against IRA sanctuaries. The army moved in strength into the Bogside and Creggan in Londonderry and into comparable areas in Belfast. The bloodshed that had been so confidently predicted in the event of a military invasion of these areas did not occur. The IRA, in accordance with the classic doctrine of guerrilla warfare, melted away, regrouped, and fought on.

At the same time Whitelaw was trying hard to restart a political dialogue in Ulster. He called a conference of all parties represented in the suspended Stormont Parliament. The three parties representing the nationalist-republican tradition, of which the Social Democrat and Labour Party (SDLP) is the largest, declined to attend before the last internee was released. Paisley's party also declined, although for another reason. That left the Unionists, the Alliance Party, and the tiny Northern Ireland Labour Party as participants. The conference was held in the last week in September at Darlington in the north of England.

The participants were invited to submit position papers in advance. The Unionists called for the restoration of Stormont in strengthened form with straight majority government but conceded to the minority a number of parliamentary committee chairmanships, a much modified Special Powers Act (which had been the legal justification for internment without trial), and a bill of rights. Alliance and Labour wanted a provincial assembly having less power than before, with Westminster responsible for security and police. The SDLP, although absent from the conference, published its proposals: that the United Kingdom government should declare that a united Ireland is in the best interests of all concerned and that, in the interval that would elapse before unification could be achieved by agreement, Northern Ireland should be under the joint sovereignty of the United Kingdom and Irish Republic, whose representatives would severally approve legislation passed by the provincial assembly; policing would also be the joint responsibility of those two governments. Needless to say, such diverse proposals were not capable of reconciliation at the Darlington conference.

On October 30 the British government released for consideration a paper drafted by Whitelaw proposing an "assembly of authority" (legislature) for Northern Ireland in which Protestants and Catholics would have proportional representation; the assembly was not to have control of the

police—which would remain with London. The paper also promised that Ulster "will remain part of the United Kingdom as long as that is the wish of the majority of the people."

The day after the paper was released, the government introduced legislation in Parliament to authorize a plebiscite in Northern Ireland. Prime Minister Heath visited Ulster that same month.

Between August 1969 and September 1972 the total number of people killed in Northern Ireland in connection with the civil strife were 386 civilians, 144 soldiers, and 23 policemen; since the middle of 1970, 6,000 people were injured in a way that required hospital treatment.

Immigration. Feelings of hostility or uneasiness were aroused in some sections of British society by the announcement in August from President Idi Amin of Uganda that he intended to expel within three months all those Asians living in Uganda who, having not taken out Uganda citizenship, were in possession of British passports. There was vagueness about the number of people: at least 50,000 was the initial estimate of the probable number of immigrants to the United Kingdom, but official spokesmen later reduced the figure to 30,000–40,000, partly because of offers from some other countries to provide sanctuary. There are, the British government calculated, about 300,000 people in former British colonies who, having no local citizenship, are similarly entitled to refuge in Britain if expelled from their countries of residence. In 1968 the Labour government got legislative authority to control by quota the entry of these passport holders, but it was admitted during the passage of the legislation that any immigrants who had nowhere else to go would, in the end, have to be admitted.

As soon as it was apparent that General Amin meant what he said, the British government acknowledged its obligation and began to make preparations for the reception of the refugees. It was supported in this effort by the leaders of the Labour and Liberal parties. As in the past, Enoch Powell, articulating the fears and prejudices of a sizable proportion of the population, opposed the admission of the immigrants. He disputed the government's claim that Britain was obligated to admit all the refugees. Such is the confusion in which the law of citizenship stands in the United Kingdom that there is genuine obscurity about the government's legal obligation. But many people feel that Britain, as the former colonial ruler of these citizens, has incurred a clear moral obligation.

Rhodesia. Toward the end of 1971, Sir Alec Douglas-Home, the foreign secretary, had reported agreement with Prime Minister Ian D. Smith of Rhodesia over terms for a constitutional settlement of the Rhodesian dispute. The terms fell, or were claimed to fall, within four of the "five principles" first enunciated by Sir Alec when previously in office and accepted by all parties in Britain as the test of acceptability. The four included unimpeded progress toward majority rule and guarantees against retrogressive amendment of the constitution. The fifth principle was acceptability of any settlement to the people of Rhodesia as a whole. In order to ascertain whether that criterion was satisfied, the British government sent out a commission to consult directly with all sections of Rhodesian opinion. Lord Pearce, a former appeals judge, was chairman of the commission. Throughout January and February, as the Pearce commission moved around Rhodesia, it became increasingly clear that the verdict of the black Rhodesians on the proposed settlement was a resounding "no." And so the Pearce commission found. On receipt of that report, the foreign secretary declared that the proposals would be shelved, the status quo maintained, and the economic sanctions kept in being.

Other events. The North Sea oil fields continued to provide evidence of abundant reserves, much of them under

that part of the seabed to which Britain lays claim. More than 500 exploration drillings have been made at a cost of more than £250 million. It is estimated that by the mid-1980's production should be between 1 million and 3 million barrels a day, a useful source of supply to have under national control as world supplies become depleted and more difficult to count on with certainty. But the North Sea reserves will be expensive to exploit, requiring an investment of perhaps £1,500 million.

The Anglo-French supersonic aircraft Concorde had received 12 firm orders by October 1972. The purchasers included the two countries making the aircraft and Mainland China and Iran. The British prototype went on a demonstration flight to the Far East. Twenty-two production models had been authorized to be manufactured.

Lord Longford, Irish peer, former Labour cabinet minister, prison reformer, and prominent Roman Catholic layman, having failed to persuade the government to establish an official inquiry into the pornography trade and its effects, set up his own commission. Its findings expressed a judgment very different from that of the United States presidential commission on the same subject, and it recommended sweeping legal changes of a restrictive kind. The only proposal likely to be adopted is one increasing penalties for publicly displaying pornographic materials.

The treasures of Tutankhamen were put on display in the British Museum by arrangement with the Egyptian authorities. The display lasted from April until December.

The duke of Windsor, formerly King Edward VIII, died at his home in France on May 28. He was buried at Frogmore in Windsor Great Park. Prince William of Gloucester, ninth in succession to the throne, was killed when a light aircraft he was flying crashed on August 28.

The deaths occurred also of Sir Francis Chichester, who in 1966–1967 sailed single-handed around the world, and of Cecil Day Lewis, Britain's poet laureate. Lewis was succeeded in that honorable sinecure by Sir John Betjeman, writer of sometimes mocking, sometimes poignant verses and an eccentric conserver of England's architectural past.

See also PEOPLE IN THE NEWS: Edward Heath and William Whitelaw.

Area and population. Area, 94,214 sq. mi. Pop. (1971), 55,521,534: England, 45,870,062; Scotland, 5,227,706; Wales, 2,723,596; Northern Ireland, 1,525,187; Jersey, 72,532; Guernsey and assoc. islands, 52,708; Isle of Man, 49,743. Principal cities: London (cap.), 7,379,014; Birmingham, 1,013,366; Glasgow, 897,848; Edinburgh, 448,895; Cardiff, 278,221.
Government. Monarchy; queen, Elizabeth II. Conservative Party in government. Prime min., Edward Heath; for. secy., Sir Alec Douglas-Home; chancellor of the exchequer, Anthony Barber; home secy., Robert Carr; def. min., Lord Carrington.
Finance. Monetary unit, pound sterling; £1 = US$2.34. Revenue (1971–1972; in millions), £18,873. Expenditures: social security, £4,426; education, £3,092; defense, £2,725; health, £2,553; housing, £1,272.
Trade (1971; in millions). Exports, £9,170; imports, £9,840.
Gross national product (1971; in millions), £47,746.
Armed forces. Army, 186,000; air force, 112,000; navy, 84,000.
T. J. O. HICKEY

UNITED NATIONS. The welcome process of superpower détente was not matched by any apparent interest on the part of the big powers in greater use of multilateral diplomacy or machinery, except to deal with environment and terrorism. On the security front the Security Council's inability to act as war flared between India and Pakistan simply highlighted the continuing erosion of the commitment to UN principles and procedures. The new secretary general, Kurt Waldheim, warned that balance-of-power diplomacy which ignores the interests of the majority of medium and small powers cannot provide a durable system of world order in the twentieth century.

New officers. On January 1, Kurt Waldheim, a former foreign minister of Austria who was serving as his country's permanent representative to the UN, began a five-year term

as the UN's fourth secretary general (*see* PEOPLE IN THE NEWS). He succeeded U Thant of Burma, who was appointed in November 1961 and reappointed in December 1966.

The late Ralph J. Bunche, undersecretary general for special political affairs, was succeeded by Frank Bradford Morse, then a Republican member of Congress from Massachusetts. Other senior appointments included Tang Ming-chao of China as undersecretary general and Helvi Sipila of Finland as assistant secretary general, the first woman to receive a high-level appointment.

Membership. The United Arab Emirates became the 132nd UN member on December 8, 1971.

China as a great power. Predictions that China would adopt the role of spokesman for the Third World, which holds a commanding UN majority, have been largely borne out. As expected, the People's Republic of China has been vehement in its anti-Soviet stance. By comparison, its anti-U.S. rhetoric has been fairly mild. However, China has not proven immune to the dilemmas that faced other great powers in the UN. For example, as the Soviet Union, long the champion of majority concerns, increasingly opted for pragmatic maneuvering on issues of peace, security, and disarmament, its would-be leadership role became blurred. British and French indifference to the UN, stemming from their Suez humiliation in 1956, has become monumental. The United States, too, has become steadily less committed to multilateral approaches, to the point of being actively delinquent (along with France and the Soviet Union) on some of its financial obligations. For example, the United States is importing Rhodesian chrome in defiance of Security Council sanctions, while withholding assessed dues from the International Labor Organization. Further, although an agreed scale of financial assessments was approved in 1971 which set the United States contribution at 31.52 percent (considerably less than under a strictly applied ability-to-pay formula), the United States is already negotiating a reduction to 25 percent. This figure may soon be imposed by a Congress still smarting at the UN expulsion of Taiwan, which took place when the People's Republic of China, with U.S. support, was voted in.

The balance sheet on China is mixed. As expected, it has been vocal on behalf of the poor (as in the UN Conference on Trade and Development), and the powerless (as on African issues). But during the 1971 war between India and Pakistan, Peking sided strongly with the repressive Pakistani regime against Soviet-supported India; then, this August 25, it cast its first veto, against the admission of Bangladesh (formerly East Pakistan) to the UN. At the United Nations Conference on the Human Environment, held in Stockholm, Peking sought to air such issues as U.S. practices in Vietnam, racism, and colonialism. But this was balanced by its insistence (along with France) on continuing to conduct nuclear tests in the atmosphere. As the Soviets learned earlier, these two roles—champion of the oppressed and balance-of-power practitioner—contain some built-in contradictions. As it turned out, it was U.S. leadership that was able to prevail in the 1972 General Assembly over combined Chinese and Soviet pressure to debate the continuing UN role in Korea, as the item was deferred for another year.

Peace and security. *India, Pakistan, and Bangladesh.* Pakistan's brutal suppression of East Pakistan's demands for greater autonomy, which had sparked the flight of some 10 million refugees to India between March and October 1971, finally resulted in Indian support for an independent East Pakistan—Bangladesh. As contending forces mobilized along the borders during November, the secretary general's offer of good offices foundered on the irreconcilable Pakistani insistence on unconditional troop withdrawals and Indian insistence on prior cessation of acts of violence and a political settlement. On December 3, Indian units attacked the main part of Pakistan along a 500-mile front, including

the long-sensitive areas of Kashmir and Jammu, over which two wars had already been fought (1947–1949 and 1965). On December 4, Pakistan declared a state of war with India, and India then formally recognized an independent state of Bangladesh.

The Security Council proved powerless to act. China and the United States gave strong diplomatic support to Pakistani demands for an unconditional cease-fire, an approach vetoed five separate times by the Soviets. At the same time, however, support was lacking for Soviet demands for a political settlement. The war ended with the surrender of Pakistani forces in Bangladesh on December 16. On December 21 the Security Council adopted a resolution calling for a cessation of all hostilities and for troop withdrawals in Kashmir, to be supervised by the UN military observer group which was still on the scene from previous conflicts. The secretary general was authorized to help with the appalling humanitarian problems generated by the war.

Terrorism. In the wake of the September murder of 11 Israeli athletes by Arab terrorists at the Olympics in Munich, Secretary General Waldheim took the unusual step of personally proposing that the assembly consider an item on measures to prevent terrorism and the spreading rash of deliberate violence on innocent parties for political purposes. The Munich tragedy was the latest in a series for which Palestinian extremists claimed credit. However, the secretary general's concern grew out of a more general trend toward what he termed "senseless violence," a trend that this year required the assembly to operate under the tightest security in its history. China and the Arab states opposed the Waldheim initiative, and the Soviet Union abstained. While the item was accepted on the agenda, many Africans were opposed to it, because of their conviction that terrorist tactics may be necessary to correct what they consider a greater evil, white racism in southern Africa. The United States strongly supported the item and on September 25 proposed a draft convention aimed at curbing terrorism.

The U.S. resolution also called on states to ratify the Tokyo, Hague, and Montreal conventions requiring return of hijacked airplanes and their occupants and the extradition or prosecution of hijackers. Attempts to reach conclusions on collective sanctions (such as suspension of service) against those who assist hijackers failed in the Security Council in June, but the subject was taken up again at a Washington conference of members of the International Civil Aviation Organization in September. Should negotiations for a treaty succeed, it would be the first agreement since the 1945 UN Charter that obliges nations to act collectively against a violating country.

Middle East. Of all the year's events in the chronically turbulent Middle East the only ones to come before the UN Security Council involved Israeli reprisals against Lebanon, where the majority of Palestinian groups are headquartered. On February 28 the council unanimously condemned Israeli raids into Lebanon after alleged border incursions. The UN observer unit on the border was subsequently boosted from seven to 21. On May 8, terrorists threatened to blow up a Sabena jet with 101 passengers aboard at Lydda Airport but were foiled; on May 30, 25 passengers were killed and some 77 were wounded when three Japanese gunmen, agents of the Popular Front for the Liberation of Palestine, fired into a crowd of more than 250 people, also at Lydda; from June 21–23 Israel launched major raids with tanks and aircraft against guerrilla encampments inside Lebanon, citing border terrorism as the provocation. On June 26, with the United States and Panama abstaining, the council condemned Israel.

Further Israeli reprisals against Lebanon after the Munich killings prompted another council condemnation of Israel on September 10; this time the United States vetoed the resolution (the second veto in U.S. history) because of failure to condemn equally the provocation. With the Gunnar

THE UNITED NATIONS—1973

General Assembly

PRESIDENT   Stanislaw Trepczynski, Poland

MEMBERS

Vice-Presidents

China
Colombia
Cyprus
Ethiopia
France
Haiti
Iceland
Libya
Mauritania
New Zealand
Paraguay
Philippines
Rwanda
Syria
Union of Soviet
    Socialist Republics
United Kingdom
United States

Afghanistan	Cyprus	Ireland	Netherlands	Spain
Albania	Czechoslovakia	Israel	New Zealand	Sri Lanka
Algeria	Dahomey	Italy	Nicaragua	Sudan
Argentina	Denmark	Ivory Coast	Niger	Swaziland
Australia	Dominican Republic	Jamaica	Nigeria	Sweden
Austria	Ecuador	Japan	Norway	Syria
Bahrain	Egypt	Jordan	Oman	Tanzania
Barbados	El Salvador	Kenya	Pakistan	Thailand
Belgium	Equatorial Guinea	Khmer Republic	Panama	Togo
Bhutan	Ethiopia	Kuwait	Paraguay	Trinidad and Tobago
Bolivia	Fiji	Laos	Peru	Tunisia
Botswana	Finland	Lebanon	Philippines	Turkey
Brazil	France	Lesotho	Poland	Uganda
Bulgaria	Gabon	Liberia	Portugal	Ukraine
Burma	Gambia	Libya	Qatar	Union of Soviet
Burundi	Ghana	Luxembourg	Romania	Socialist Republics
Byelorussia	Greece	Malagasy Republic	Rwanda	United Arab Emirates
Cameroon	Guatemala	Malawi	Saudi Arabia	United Kingdom
Canada	Guinea	Malaysia	Senegal	United States
Central African	Guyana	Maldives	Sierra Leone	Upper Volta
Republic	Haiti	Mali	Singapore	Uruguay
Chad	Honduras	Malta	Somalia	Venezuela
Chile	Hungary	Mauritania	South Africa	Yemen
China	Iceland	Mauritius	Southern Yemen	Yugoslavia
Colombia	India	Mexico	(People's	Zaïre
Congo, Republic of the	Indonesia	Mongolia	Democratic	Zambia
Costa Rica	Iran	Morocco	Republic of	
Cuba	Iraq	Nepal	Yemen)	

International Court of Justice[1]

President[2]
Muhammad Zafrulla Khan, Pakistan (1973)

Isaac Forster, Senegal
    (1982)
André Gros, France
    (1982)
José Maria Ruda,
    Argentina (1982)
Nagrenda Singh, India
    (1982)
Sir Humphrey Waldock,
    United Kingdom
    (1982)
Louis Ignacio-Pinto,
    Dahomey (1979)
Platon D. Morozov,
    U.S.S.R. (1979)

Federico de Castro,
    Spain (1979)
Hardy Cross Dillard,
    United States (1979)
Eduardo Jiménez de
    Aréchaga, Uruguay
    (1979)
Sture Petren, Sweden
    (1976)
César Bengzon,
    Philippines (1976)
Fouad Ammoun,
    Lebanon (1976)
Manfred Lachs, Poland
    (1976)
Charles D. Onyeama, Nigeria (1976)

[1]All terms are for nine years and expire February
5 of the year indicated. [2]A new president is to be
chosen after February 5, 1973.

Security Council[1]

Australia (1974)
Austria (1974)
China
    (permanent)
France
    (permanent)
Guinea (1973)
India (1973)
Indonesia (1974)

Kenya (1974)
Panama (1973)
Peru (1973)
Sudan (1973)
U.S.S.R.
    (permanent)
United States
    (permanent)
Yugoslavia (1973)

[1]All terms of nonpermanent members of this and
other councils expire on December 31 of the year indicated.

Economic and Social Council

President[1]
Karoly Szarka, Hungary

Algeria (1975)
Bolivia (1974)
Brazil (1975)
Burundi (1974)
Chile (1974)
China (1974)
Finland (1974)
France (1975)
Haiti (1973)
Hungary (1973)
Japan (1974)
Lebanon (1973)
Malagasy Republic (1973)
Malaysia (1973)

Mali (1975)
Mongolia (1975)
Netherlands (1975)
New Zealand (1973)
Niger (1973)
Poland (1974)
Spain (1975)
Trinidad and Tobago
    (1975)
Uganda (1975)
U.S.S.R. (1974)
United Kingdom (1974)
United States (1973)
Zaïre (1973)

[1]New president to be elected in 1973.

Secretariat

Secretary General

Kurt Waldheim, Austria

Trusteeship Council

President
W. Tapley Bennett, Jr., United States

Australia[1]	France[2]	United Kingdom[1]
China[2]	U.S.S.R.[2]	United States[1]

[1]Administering power. [2]Permanent member of
Security Council not administering power.

CLEANING UP THE WORLD

The United Nations Conference on the Human Environment triumphed over predictions of disruption and stalemate and made some progress in international environmental cooperation at its meeting this June in Stockholm's People's Center (above). Pressured perhaps by youthful lobbyists like the girl at right (draped in nonreturnable beer cans from around town), the 1,200 delegates from 114 countries ratified a common declaration of environmental principles, created a permanent UN secretariat for environmental affairs, and approved several measures for monitoring air and water pollution.

Jarring mediation mission stalled all year, the four-power talks marking time, and the U.S. initiative toward reopening the Suez Canal aborted, Israeli foreign minister Abba Eban asserted that no negotiations of any kind would be held until terrorist activity ceased.

Cyprus. Intercommunal tension on Cyprus, which had been increasing since Greek-Turkish Cypriot talks deadlocked the previous September, intensified again early in the year. The Greek government demanded that Cypriot president Makarios modify his government. Makarios in turn revealed the acquisition of substantial arms placed under the exclusive control of the Greek Cypriot guard, arms which the Turkish Cypriots regarded as a direct threat. With the active cooperation of both Greek and Turkish governments, the force commander of UNFICYP, the UN peacekeeping force, was able to arrange for storage of the arms under a system of double locks, with one set of keys for the Cypriot government and one for UNFICYP. Subsequently the intercommunal talks were reactivated. On June 15, for the 21st time, the Security Council approved a six-month extension of the UN force.

The environment. *Conference at Stockholm.* Despite potentially crippling political obstacles, the United Nations Conference on the Human Environment, held in Stockholm, June 5–16, succeeded brilliantly in achieving the first global consensus on ways to preserve and enhance the planet. Three major goals were achieved: agreement on the Declaration on the Human Environment, stating 26 principles; adoption of an action plan comprising 200 specific short-range tasks that can begin soon; and a recommendation for new UN machinery, including an environment fund, which will provide a focus for international activities in the environmental field.

The conference was attended by 114 countries, representing 90 percent of the world's population. In addition to the sessions of the 1,200 accredited delegates, the conference featured parallel meetings of nongovernmental organizations, a Swedish government-sponsored environmental forum, and a "hog farm" (or tent city) housing 600 members of the counterculture, with its own program. Glaringly absent from Stockholm were representatives of the Soviet Union and other Eastern European nations (except Romania and Yugoslavia), in protest against the General Assembly's earlier decision to limit attendance to members of the UN and its specialized agencies, thus excluding East Germany.

The dominant question at the conference was how to reconcile the developed countries' wish to halt the environmental havoc that has accompanied industrialization with the developing countries' need for technology to overcome their poverty and deprivation. The conference succeeded beyond expectation in fostering greater understanding on both sides, including a realization that their goals need not, as feared, be mutually exclusive. (*See* ENVIRONMENT.)

Outer space. On March 29 the UN-drafted Convention on International Liability for Damage Caused by Space Objects was opened for signature. The Committee on Peaceful Uses then turned to a draft treaty concerning the moon and the regulation of objects launched into space.

Law of the sea. A comprehensive conference on the law of the sea is to be held in 1973. The UN's Preparatory Committee, newly increased from 86 to 91 (including China), is focusing on proposals for an international regime for the seabed and ocean floor, while considering methods and criteria for sharing the benefits of exploited ocean resources. The tasks of reconciling the interests of individual states with those of the international community and of then redefining the international laws that should apply may prove too complex to be resolved in the short time remaining.

Southern Africa. For the first time in 20 years the Security Council met away from headquarters, in Addis Ababa,

Ethiopia, from January 28 to February 4. The purpose was to highlight the frustrating set of colonial and racial problems that persist in the white-dominated areas of southern Africa.

Rhodesia. The continuing effort to unseat the Ian Smith regime through UN efforts focused on two areas: First, a Security Council majority vote on February 4 asked the British government not to implement the Home-Smith proposals that set out the conditions for British recognition of the regime. The council resolution was vetoed by the United Kingdom, which subsequently abandoned its proposals after the Pearce Commission had reported overwhelming black opposition within Rhodesia. Second, the General Assembly, Security Council, and the committees on colonialism and apartheid attempted to persuade the United States to seek a reversal of the congressional action that permits importation of Rhodesian chrome in violation of Security Council sanctions (the U.S. Senate reaffirmed that policy in June).

Namibia. Backed by International Court of Justice affirmation of UN responsibility for Namibia and by the Security Council directive on February 4 to initiate contacts with all parties, Secretary General Waldheim was invited to South Africa and Namibia, March 6–10. This was the first direct contact the UN has had with the area. In September he named Alfred M. Escher of Switzerland as his "representative regarding Namibia." While South Africa will not permit Escher to have an office in the territory, it has agreed to permit visits.

Portuguese territories. For the first time an official UN mission visited a "liberated" area. In April a three-member group appointed by the Committee on Colonialism visited parts of Guinea (Bissau) at the invitation of the nationalist liberation movement, PAIGC. Traveling on foot for seven days, the mission reported unceasing harassment by Portuguese jet aircraft and helicopters and impressive PAIGC achievement in the political, administrative, judicial, social, health, and educational fields.

Development. *UNCTAD.* Three thousand representatives of 141 countries, including China, attended the third session of the UN Conference on Trade and Development held in Santiago, Chile, from April 13 to May 21. Reported progress toward the goals of the second development decade, which will require considerable modification of the developed countries' traditional trading practices, was generally regarded as disappointing.

UNDP. The UN Development Program has a new administrator, Rudolph A. Peterson, as well as a newly enlarged 48-member governing council and a new system of country programming. Seeking ways to assist the 25 least developed countries, which have a limited capability to absorb external aid, the council has selected six for intensive study—Afghanistan, Haiti, Lesotho, Rwanda, Upper Volta, and Yemen.

Human problems. The secretary general dispatched humanitarian missions to Bangladesh, Sudan (after a prolonged civil war ended), and Burundi (where mass killing was reported).

Disaster relief. On December 14, 1971, the General Assembly authorized the secretary general to appoint a disaster relief coordinator. His nominee, Faruk N. Berkol of Turkey, will serve for five years. The secretary general was also empowered to draw on up to $200,000 per member country for any one disaster.

Drug abuse. From March 6 to 24, 96 states and five observers were represented at a UN conference in Geneva which adopted a protocol to the 1961 Single Convention on Narcotic Drugs strengthening the role of the International Narcotics Control Board. Pledges to the UN Fund for Drug Abuse, established by the General Assembly in 1970, totaled $2.8 million for the first year.

LINCOLN P. BLOOMFIELD AND IRIRANGI C. BLOOMFIELD

PRESIDENT NIXON briefs congressional leaders on his trip to China after giving them gifts from Peking.

UNITED STATES

This section is divided into the following articles:

FOREIGN RELATIONS   SUPREME COURT
NATIONAL DEFENSE   BUDGET
CONGRESS

Foreign Relations

Behind the movement, heralded in 1972, toward a new era in international affairs was Washington's increasing willingness to accept the consequences of the Soviet victory in World War II and Mao Tse-tung's triumph in China. Official American rhetoric no longer regarded the existence of two Communist-led giants as a serious threat to Western security. President Richard M. Nixon's trips to Peking in February and to Moscow in May symbolized new relationships between three states with the power to reshape world politics. Clearly, the erosion of cold war assumptions afforded new opportunities for international maneuvering.

President Nixon's decision to focus national attention on foreign affairs in 1972 resulted in the most extensive exercise of personal diplomacy conducted by any national leader in modern times. His summit talks started in December 1971 with Prime Minister Pierre Elliott Trudeau of Canada and continued into the summer of 1972 with Premier Kakuei Tanaka of Japan. Through a series of conversations with European and Asian leaders, conducted both at home and abroad, the president sought to reaffirm ties with allies and to establish new relations with the Communist powers.

Europe. *The Moscow summit.* What crowned the months of summitry was President Nixon's trip to Moscow in late May. Indeed, the Moscow summit dominated the year of

U.S.-Soviet relations, for it reflected the conviction among both Soviet and American spokesmen that, despite differences over Indo-Pakistani relations and Vietnam, agreements could be reached that would permit both nations to live together with greater confidence and decency.

Nixon's welcome in Moscow was cordial but subdued. From his arrival, the American and Soviet negotiators proceeded to discuss every major world problem. Unable to come to agreement on Vietnam or the Middle East, they pledged to strive for a better relationship by binding the two countries together so tightly with joint committees and projects that only with difficulty could remote conflicts of interest disrupt their mutual determination to avoid direct confrontations.

Eventually they endorsed a series of agreements that had been carefully prepared in advance. These covered health research, pollution control, a future linkup of astronauts in space, and the avoidance of naval incidents at sea. To achieve a more stable balance of terror at existing nuclear levels, the negotiators at Moscow signed two nuclear arms pacts, one limiting the installation of antiballistic missiles to two locations in each country, the other freezing offensive weapons at current levels for five years, ensuring numerical superiority for Soviet missiles. In large measure, this nuclear formula had been reached at the strategic arms limitation talks in previous months. The Moscow agreements imposed no restraints on the qualitative improvement

of existing weapons; thus, Secretary of Defense Melvin Laird made it clear that expenditures for missile development would not be curtailed.

Back in Washington, the president assured Congress that the nuclear arms pacts would prevent the arms race from spreading but would not endanger U.S. security; the nation would remain the most powerful on earth. This assurance did not convince Senator Henry Jackson (D, Wash.), who offered a resolution requiring any future U.S. negotiator to demand the numerical equality of American and Soviet nuclear power. In early August the Senate approved the ABM agreement by a vote of 88–2, after only one day of debate. But the president's endorsement of the Jackson resolution, coupled with the subsequent retreat of administration officials from certain of Jackson's interpretations of his own amendment, clouded Senate debate on the five-year interim agreement. Not until September, after five weeks of bitter argument, did the Senate approve the second nuclear arms pact as amended.

At Moscow the questions of trade, credits, equal tariff treatment, and the settlement of the old World War II lend-lease debt proved too complicated to be resolved by high-level conversations and remained unsettled until October, when a comprehensive trade agreement covering these and other matters was concluded. Meanwhile, progress continued on other fronts. In July the two countries signed an agreement calling for the United States to sell at least $750 million in grain to the Soviet Union between 1972 and 1975; in fact, sales for 1972 alone exceeded $1 billion.

Berlin agreement. In May, after much political wrangling, the West German Bundestag ratified nonaggression treaties with the Soviet Union and Poland. This reluctant endorsement of Chancellor Willy Brandt's *Ostpolitik* opened the way for the June 3 signing of the Soviet-American-British-French agreement on Berlin. The brief ceremony, held in Berlin, capped a 26-month effort to remove that city from its formerly central position in the cold war. The agreement did not alter the legal status of West Berlin; it sought rather to help West Berlin's more than 2.1 million people escape much of the friction created by the city's division. The precise terms, announced by East and West German officials in December 1971, would enable people to travel back and forth under simplified procedures eliminating much of the previous delay and harassment.

European security. Bonn's action on the nonaggression treaties encouraged negotiations on two related questions—European security and troop reductions across Central Europe. Late in May, the NATO foreign ministers, at their spring meeting, anticipated the signing of the Berlin agreement by announcing that preparatory talks would begin with Soviet-bloc nations on a European security conference, to begin at Helsinki in the fall. These talks were expected to lead to an all-European conference, including Canada and the United States, sometime in 1973.

Agreement on troop withdrawals remained elusive. Europe's NATO partners, especially West Germany, still opposed the reduction of U.S. force levels on the continent, fearing that any limitation of the American military presence in Europe would result in the eventual subordination of European politics to Soviet interests. To many European officials, only an East-West agreement on mutual force reductions would render any U.S. troop withdrawal acceptable. Washington insisted only that talks on troop reductions be limited to those countries whose forces actually confronted one another in Central Europe.

The Far East. *Vietnam.* Having failed in three years to terminate the American involvement in the Vietnam war, President Nixon entered the new year emphasizing his past and continuing efforts at peace. On January 25 he revealed that his adviser Henry Kissinger had, since August 4, 1969, conducted 12 secret negotiating sessions with top North Vietnamese envoys in Paris. At the same time he unveiled

an eight-point peace offer—not entirely new—which included a cease-fire; the withdrawal of American forces within six months after a peace agreement, in exchange for the release of American prisoners of war; a pledge that the Vietnamese would be permitted to determine their own political future, with the United States abiding by the outcome; and the promise that South Vietnamese president Nguyen Van Thieu would step down one month before an election. Hanoi rejected the proposal outright, while Thieu denied that he had agreed to resign and made clear that Saigon would accept no territorial concessions, no neutrality, and no coalition government. Meanwhile the president announced his plan to reduce United States forces in Vietnam to a residual force of between 25,000 and 35,000 men by November. Simultaneously he reminded Hanoi that the United States still maintained effective power in Asia by sustaining the heaviest air war against North Vietnam since 1968.

During March the Paris peace talks collapsed, compelling the president again to entrust the success of his policies to Vietnamization. But Vietnamization, which still required a high level of U.S. logistical support, could not prevent the massive North Vietnamese offensive which opened late in March. Nixon struck back with massive bombing runs of B-52's and other aircraft over Hanoi, Haiphong, and other key targets. The bombing, said the administration, would protect American troops, sustain the withdrawal program, and protect South Vietnam from the invasion. Even as the destruction mounted, U.S. officials expressed doubt about its effectiveness. Battlefield reports were not encouraging.

Humiliated and frustrated by the North Vietnamese success, the president reached for another "contingency plan" to end the fighting. Early in May he informed the nation that he had ordered the mining of Haiphong harbor and other ports to stop the flow of weapons and supplies to the North Vietnamese Army. Simultaneously he unleashed air and naval bombardments to cut the rail lines from China. Ultimately the bombing and the mining did buy time on the battlefield; the destruction stalled the North Vietnamese, helping Saigon's forces recapture some lost ground.

Meanwhile, the president searched for a negotiated settlement. Late in April he announced that the United States would resume negotiations in Paris, but the revived talks remained hopelessly deadlocked. During the summer months, Kissinger's well-publicized trips to Paris, Moscow, Peking, and Saigon sparked rumors of an impending settlement. Washington and Hanoi seemed to agree on the need for political change in Saigon, but they disagreed on the means to achieve it; Thieu's role in Saigon's future remained the key to a settlement in 1972, just as it had been four years earlier. However, on October 26 Hanoi disclosed that there had been a breakthrough in the Paris negotiations between Kissinger and Le Duc Tho on October 8, and both sides appeared to have reached a general agreement on a nine-point plan for ending the war and establishing a new political order in South Vietnam. The agreement, which the United States was to have signed by October 31, according to Hanoi, provided for a cease-fire in South Vietnam and the withdrawal of American troops within 60 days, during which time all captured military personnel and foreign civilians would be repatriated, with North Vietnam accounting for all American prisoners and men reported as missing in action throughout Indochina. Although the agreement was not signed by the October 31 deadline, U.S. officials remained confident that peace was near. But as Election Day passed, both the rhetoric and the fighting continued to escalate. Hanoi renewed its insistence on Thieu's ouster, and the Saigon government denounced what it considered certain crucially vague passages about its future. Even as Henry Kissinger prepared for yet more talks with Le Duc Tho, U.S. bombers struck throughout Indochina. It seemed increasingly likely that even the signing of an agreement would bring no quick end to the war.

UPI

WIDE WORLD

WIDE WORLD

Travels With Henry

For presidential aide Henry Kissinger, the year was a dizzying round of diplomatic journeys. Above, in Moscow with Soviet ambassador Dobrynin; above right, in Peking with Communist Party officials; right, in Japan with Prime Minister Tanaka.

The Peking summit. Behind the president's carefully planned trip to Peking in February 1972 was not only the Sino-Soviet rivalry but also China's emergence as a major factor in the burgeoning Asian balance of power. Critics who feared that the Peking trip would astonish and antagonize the country's Asian allies still agreed generally that U.S. interests demanded better communications with Peking. A reconciliation with China, moreover, would remove from Vietnam the specter of Chinese expansionism that long served as the rationale for American containment policy in Southeast Asia.

Nixon's welcome in Peking was modest but correct. Despite the subsequent cordiality the U.S.-Chinese reconciliation was far from complete. For the president the visit was a historic event, "a week that changed the world." Peking gave up its official hostility but gained an occasion for warning the Soviets, isolating Japan, and threatening Taiwan. In fact, the Peking summit proved to be less an ex-

ercise in diplomacy than a television spectacular for the benefit of American viewers.

The final communiqué dwelt on disagreements, especially that over Taiwan. The president acknowledged that Taiwan's future was a question to be resolved by the Chinese people. The United States would reduce its forces on Taiwan as tension in the area diminished, but it would not cut its ties with the Nationalists. On the Vietnam issue the two nations again agreed to differ. Elsewhere the communiqué was more positive. The two countries agreed to respect "the sovereignty and territorial integrity of all states." Neither would seek hegemony in the Asia-Pacific region, and both would oppose the efforts of any other country to do so. They agreed on the importance of broadened contacts, increased trade, and further diplomatic consultation. For the moment, Peking refused to accept a permanent diplomatic representation, but the two nations maintained constant diplomatic association through their ambassadors.

To reassure Washington's Asian allies that this new relationship with China had not cast them adrift, the president sent Assistant Secretary of State Marshall Green to visit their capitals. Green's reception in Taipei was cool, for the Nationalist Chinese felt especially threatened by Nixon's tacit recognition of Peking's legitimacy. The destruction of the 20-year illusion that the Chiang Kai-shek regime was indeed the government of all China exposed Taipei to increased opposition at home and increased isolation abroad. In Manila, Green insisted that U.S. policy toward the SEATO allies had not changed. In Bangkok he assured Thai officials, "We will faithfully honor all of our treaty commitments. Our close bonds with our friends are vital to the success of our foreign policy." Still, the new lines of conflict suggested by the changing American perception of China and the growing Sino-Soviet confrontation across Asia undermined the validity of alliances which had assumed a Kremlin-based Communist monolith threatening Asia's independence. Now, many agreed, U.S. interests favored a true neutrality for Asian states that Washington once viewed as strategic partners.

Japan. Nowhere was the impact of the Peking summit more pronounced than in Japan. Having followed the U.S. lead in Asia, Tokyo was especially vulnerable to any change in American-Chinese relations. With its industrial and commercial vitality, Japan had emerged as a major influence in Asian affairs; yet as long as Japan eschewed military power it could guarantee its security only by sustaining a mutuality of interest with the United States, which itself demanded a high level of cooperation with the United States on military and diplomatic questions. Far Eastern experts warned Washington that cordial U.S.-Japanese relations, the key to Pacific stability, could no longer be taken for granted.

Issues other than defense troubled U.S.-Japanese relations in 1972. Japan's huge dollar accumulation had long created pressures in Washington to curb Japanese imports. President Nixon's measures of August 1971, to overcome deficits in the United States balance of payments, shocked and angered the Japanese. Nevertheless, with U.S. trade as their lifeline, the Japanese had no desire to imperil their markets by encouraging commercial reprisals. Thus, early in 1972, Tokyo adopted measures to promote imports, curtail exports, and encourage the movement of Japanese capital abroad. Thereafter, the United States pressed the Japanese to take positive action to pare their country's trade surplus with the United States.

Quite understandably, the Japanese were ruffled when President Nixon planned the Peking summit without consulting them. In January, Premier Eisaku Sato urged Nixon at the Western White House in San Clemente to avoid any agreements which might affect Japan adversely. To ease Japanese apprehensions, Secretary Green briefed the Tokyo government in March on Nixon's Peking trip, which Japan had followed with cynicism and alarm. In June, after an embarrassing postponement, Kissinger traveled to Tokyo to reassure the Japanese that Washington would continue to regard Japan as its permanent ally in the Pacific. What eased the tension somewhat was Okinawa's formal reversion to Japanese control in May (the United States retained the right to nonnuclear facilities on the island).

Kakuei Tanaka's accession to the Japanese premiership in July opened a new era in Japan's external relations, for Tanaka shared few of the convictions of his predecessor. He favored close ties with the United States but was equally determined to normalize Japanese relations with China. He promised American trade officials in late July that he would work toward cutting the trade imbalance. At his summit conference with Nixon at Honolulu in late summer, Tanaka agreed to a $1.1 billion reduction in the trade imbalance (considerably less than the Nixon administration desired), but it was clear that the old "special relationship" between Tokyo and Washington was gone. Japan had left its postwar client status to become a friendly rival for power and influence in the Pacific.

The Middle East. For the United States the perennial Arab-Israeli conflict remained an issue less of immediate than of long-range concern. The U.S. compromise plan, which Secretary of State William P. Rogers had placed before the UN in October 1971, carried the burden of Washington's peace efforts. But Israeli premier Golda Meir regarded the Rogers formula, which supported Egypt's demand for an interim agreement to reopen the Suez Canal, as an abandonment of Israel's negotiating position. Israel, she complained, would never agree to a political settlement which jeopardized its security and would withdraw no troops from the eastern bank of the Suez unless the United States agreed to support the Israelis in case of an Egyptian violation of any territorial arrangement. Israel, moreover, demanded a long-term commitment of U.S. military assistance in exchange for a withdrawal from Arab lands. Egyptian president Anwar Sadat, convinced that peace was impossible, called on the Egyptian Army to prepare for trouble. The Middle East entered 1972 hovering between peace and war.

Suddenly, during July, events in Egypt offered some promise of a turnabout. Having failed to come to terms with the Kremlin over additional Soviet arms for Egypt, Sadat announced the termination of the Soviet military mission in Egypt and ordered the expulsion of Soviet advisers. Even the return of some advisers in October left the Soviet presence at its lowest level since 1955.

Nevertheless, continued Arab terrorism, especially along Israel's borders with Lebanon, Syria, and Jordan, convinced the Israelis that the Arab states were unwilling, perhaps unable, to make peace and that Israeli interests lay in military reprisals rather than diplomatic maneuvering. Siding with Israel in the UN, the United States vetoed a Security Council resolution which condemned Israel for its reprisals against Syria and Lebanon but refused to condemn the terrorist acts of the Arabs, only the second veto in U.S. history. On September 28, President Sadat again rejected an interim peace settlement and refused direct negotiations with Israel. Peace remained as elusive as ever.

Latin America. As the major powers moved toward the creation of a new world order, they increasingly consigned the Third World to the periphery of international affairs. U.S.-Latin American relations reflected the growing tension between rich and poor nations, for Latin Americans continued to condemn Washington for its lack of concern about their economic plight.

In November 1971, 21 Latin American countries, led by Brazil, submitted the proposition to the industrialized countries at the UN that political security could not exist without economic stability. They condemned especially the United States, Japan, the Soviet Union, and the members of the European Economic Community. Even Mexico sought to curb its economic ties with the United States because of the special restrictions imposed on Mexican trade. During April, President Nixon informed Latin American leaders at the White House that the United States recognized the diversity of views in Latin America and would attempt to deal realistically with governments as they existed. During June, former treasury secretary John Connally toured Latin America, visiting Venezuela, Colombia, Brazil, Argentina, Bolivia, and Peru. In each country he discussed trade but warned his listeners that the United States would probably limit its foreign aid and investments, especially to countries which had expropriated American firms.

President Nixon, addressing the annual meeting of the World Bank and International Monetary Fund in September, declared that self-interest, not benevolence, would determine this country's future international economic policy. The

administration made its attitudes even clearer when it unsuccessfully attempted to deny a third term to Pierre-Paul Schweitzer as managing director of IMF because he had urged then-secretary Connally to devalue the dollar against gold at a time when the United States had refused to do so. The U.S. government also put former defense secretary Robert S. McNamara on probation for reappointment to the presidency of the World Bank because McNamara had permitted loans to Bolivia, Peru, and Chile, all of which had nationalized American private investments. When its loans were suspended late in September, Chile denounced the World Bank as a tool of the United States. Observers believed that Washington's relations with Latin America had deteriorated to the lowest level in memory.

See also the special article WORLD POWER.

NORMAN A. GRAEBNER

National Defense

If 1972 had not been a presidential election year, the achievement of the first strategic nuclear arms limitation agreement in history would stand alone as the most dramatic story of the year in the area of national defense policy. However, the presidential candidate of the Democratic Party, Senator George McGovern (S.D.), sparked great political controversy by proposing a large cut in the defense budget.

The McGovern-Nixon debate. McGovern argued that a cut of $30 billion, or almost 40 percent of the present defense budget, would not jeopardize national security and would allow a reallocation of national resources to meet the demands of the wars against poverty, pollution, unemployment, and urban decay. President Richard M. Nixon, on the other hand, contended that a defense budget re-

EXPLOSIVE ISSUE. At a congressional hearing in June, former four-star general John D. Lavelle (right) attempted to justify the raids he had authorized over North Vietnam. Claiming the strikes violated the rules of engagement, U.S. Air Force chief of staff John D. Ryan (left) had relieved Lavelle of command and had ordered his retirement at three-star rank but with full pension.

UPI

duction of any amount would make the United States a "second-rate power," would seriously undermine U.S. interests in the world, and would increase unemployment at home because such a large segment of the American economy is dependent on military expenditures.

The presidential campaign of George McGovern served to focus the criticism of American defense spending that had been increasing in Congress and within large segments of the general public since the outbreak of the Vietnam war. The defense budget for 1972–1973 was $85 billion, with the Vietnam war responsible for much of the recent rapid increase. Public and congressional pressures had resulted in some small reduction in the Nixon administration's budget requests, as well as in terminations of several controversial weapons systems and restrictions on the purchase of other systems experiencing serious cost overruns. Affected items included the controversial F-111 fighter-bomber, the very expensive C-5A giant transport plane, and the new F-14 fighter plane. However, it was not until McGovern became a presidential candidate that anyone of political prominence proposed a major, across-the-board reduction in total defense spending.

The McGovern position on defense expenditures not only was in sharp contrast to that of the Nixon administration but also was a significant departure from past Democratic Party policies. In 1968 the Democratic party platform had endorsed President Lyndon B. Johnson's handling of the Vietnam war, had rejected proposals for unilateral withdrawal from Vietnam, and had urged a "substantially larger" U.S. commitment to NATO. The platform contained no specific language on defense programs and not even broad directives on how much should be spent for national defense. In contrast, the McGovern platform called for an immediate end to American involvement in Vietnam, a total U.S. withdrawal from all of Southeast Asia, a partial withdrawal of U.S. military forces from Europe, and a $30 billion cut in the defense budget.

McGovern's proposed military budget envisioned a phased reduction of defense spending over a three-year period ending with fiscal year 1975. In that year (beginning July 1, 1974) the defense budget would be $55 billion as compared to $85 billion. The military programs that would be most affected included virtually all of the Nixon administration's proposed new strategic nuclear weapons systems, as well as the total amount of military manpower.

Bombers. Among the weapons to be eliminated was the B-1 bomber, the proposed replacement for the B-52 strategic bomber, which is now almost 20 years old. The B-1 is bigger and faster, and it carries a wider assortment of bombs and missiles than the B-52. Rather than argue as many others have that the manned bomber is an obsolete weapon in the missile age, McGovern simply proposed that the monies now allocated for research and development of the B-1 be spent instead on upgrading the old B-52. A large ultimate savings would result because the B-1 will be at least five times as expensive as the B-52 to buy.

MIRV's. A major target of McGovern's criticism of President Nixon's military policies was the program to deploy MIRV's, or multiple independently targetable reentry vehicles, on most, if not all, intercontinental ballistic missiles. MIRV's were originally developed to overcome antiballistic missile (ABM) defenses by forcing the defender to deal with many warheads rather than a single missile over each target. However, with ABM's now virtually eliminated by the SALT agreements, MIRV has been retained as a means of vastly increasing the number of targets that can be struck without increasing the number of missile launchers; and the launcher is far more expensive than the warheads are.

Because MIRV is not, comparatively, an expensive weapons program, McGovern's criticism appeared to be directed more at arms control considerations than at potential budg-

etary savings from its elimination. He argued that MIRV raised for the first time the possibility of an effective nuclear first-strike strategy which might make nuclear war more likely. Because the United States would have many more warheads (5,200 in total) than the Soviet Union would have missiles to attack (approximately 2,400), a U.S. first strike might hope to knock out most if not all of the Soviet missiles before they could be fired. At any rate, MIRV's possessed by both sides would greatly increase the fear that the other side might try a first strike, and pressures to undertake preemptive nuclear war would increase the chances of an irrationally determined nuclear war.

Sea-based missiles. McGovern went beyond opposition to multiple warheads by questioning the continued reliance on land-based missiles when technological improvements like MIRV made them very vulnerable to nuclear attack. Furthermore, the land-based missiles merely duplicated the strategic nuclear capabilities of the Polaris/Poseidon missile-firing submarine fleet. Therefore, McGovern proposed that programs to improve the land-based missiles be stopped and that greater reliance be placed on the Polaris deterrent.

McGovern's preference for reliance on the submarine-launched strategic nuclear missile system did not lead him to endorse the Nixon administration's proposal for developing the new Trident submarine as a replacement for the aging Polaris. The Trident, or ULMS (undersea long-range missile system), is much larger than the Polaris and carries more missiles with a longer range. It is also more expensive than any other weapons system presently proposed.

Manpower reductions. In addition to these strategic nuclear programs, McGovern proposed cutting military manpower from 2.3 million men (as of June 1972) to 1.7 million men. To accomplish this reduction, McGovern proposed a complete U.S. withdrawal of personnel from Southeast Asia and South Korea, and a decrease in U.S. forces in Europe to 130,000 men as compared to the present level of approximately 300,000.

Bargaining chips. McGovern's recommendations, ironically, added up to a return to the policies of Republican president Dwight D. Eisenhower. McGovern has proposed a virtual return to a doctrine of massive retaliation, as articulated by Eisenhower, in which a minimum nuclear force is retained to deter nuclear war and conventional forces are kept to an absolute minimum, based on the argument that the United States cannot and should not become involved in conventional wars abroad. The proposed defense budget of President Nixon, on the other hand, is justified by the same arguments used by Democratic presidents John F. Kennedy and Lyndon B. Johnson, under whom the present defense establishment was in large part created.

President Nixon has argued that unilateral American military cuts would leave the United States at the mercy of the expanding military forces of the Soviet Union. The Soviets now enjoy an advantage over the United States in many categories of nuclear and conventional weaponry. The Nixon administration argued that American restraint in defense expenditures would not encourage reciprocal Soviet restraint but would result in an even larger Soviet strategic advantage and in Soviet efforts to exploit that advantage. Furthermore, the administration argued that the only means of securing additional arms control agreements with the Soviet Union is to go ahead with all of the presently proposed military weapons programs. The "threats" these new weapons pose to the Soviet Union are believed to be "bargaining chips" in future arms control negotiations: the United States will have something to bargain away and the Soviets will have an incentive to bargain.

Consequently, even though the first SALT agreements have been reached, the administration has proposed an increase of $6 billion in the defense budget for fiscal 1974. This is by far the largest increase requested by President Nixon during his term in office. In addition, the fiscal year 1973 defense budget request has already been increased by a $2.2 billion supplemental request to cover the increased costs incurred in meeting the North Vietnamese offensive of spring and summer 1972. Many observers had hoped that a successful outcome of the SALT talks would mean a reduction in defense expenditures, but, in fact, Secretary of Defense Melvin R. Laird testified to Congress that the Department of Defense would not support congressional ratification of the SALT agreements if all of the new weapons programs proposed by the administration were not approved at the same time. We have, therefore, the strange occurrence of an arms control agreement resulting in an increase in the arms race and in the defense budget.

Arms reductions under Nixon. One of the least understood aspects of the defense budget requests of the Nixon administration is that, although the budget totals have consistently increased from 1969 onward, the net effect has been an actual reduction in military capabilities. The only additions to the strategic nuclear forces have been the initial stages of the MIRV program for both the land-based and sea-based missile systems. The conventional forces have been reduced in terms of both manpower and equipment. Inflation has significantly increased the costs of previously authorized weapons systems, and the all-volunteer army has required drastic increases in military pay, with personnel costs now accounting for over 55 percent of the total defense budget. These additional costs have completely offset the hoped-for "Vietnam dividend," the budget savings expected from a reduction in the American effort in Vietnam. Of the $6.3 billion increase in this year's defense budget, Secretary of Defense Laird has testified that some two-thirds is to cover pay increases for the all-volunteer army. The remainder is for "technological improvements" in the strategic nuclear forces.

Administration victories. Attempts were made in Congress during 1972 to place a lower ceiling on defense expenditures and to eliminate those weapons systems opposed by George McGovern. In each case the administration's requests for increased expenditures and for new weapons were upheld by Congress.

SALT agreements. The SALT (strategic arms limitation talks) agreements of 1972 constituted the first successful effort to limit the number of nuclear weapons deployed by the Soviet Union and the United States.

There seems little doubt that after three years of deadlocked negotiations the Nixon administration was under considerable pressure in the spring of 1972 to accept certain questionable and controversial terms to achieve an agreement at the SALT talks. It was during the president's trip to Moscow in May 1972 that the final terms of the SALT agreements were determined and the result publicly announced. With the failure of the recent trip to China to produce significant diplomatic breakthroughs, there was strong incentive to produce tangible results from the Moscow trip. This pressure was underlined by the fact that the United States had mined the harbors of North Vietnam only weeks before, in defiance of possible retaliation from the Soviet Union. Thus, eleventh-hour concessions on the SALT negotiations plus a generous U.S. trade offer to the Soviet Union may have been aimed at convincing the Soviets that their greater interests lay in not retaliating against the mining of the North Vietnamese harbors. A second source of pressure was the presidential election and the need for a good campaign issue to offset the criticisms of military policy coming from the Democratic presidential candidates.

The resulting SALT agreements were neither a complete nor a permanent agreement to limit nuclear weapons. There were two separate agreements. One covered only ABM's and restricted each side to 200 launchers in two ABM

sites, with one to go around each nation's capital city. The second was an "interim" agreement on offensive weapons that lasts only five years or until a permanent agreement can be reached. Lengthy lists of "interpretations" accompany this interim agreement. That is, a number of issues could not be resolved, so both the Soviet Union and the United States attached their own interpretations of what the agreement meant, thereby providing excuses for abrogating the treaty if the other side does not live up to the interpretations.

The interim agreement did not reduce the number of land-based and sea-based missiles possessed by either side. It simply "froze" the totals in existence or "under construction" on July 1, 1972. Because the Soviet Union had been conducting a major buildup of strategic forces and the United States was not at the time of the agreement, the United States conceded to the Soviets a significant advantage in the total numbers of strategic missiles. The Soviet Union is limited to a total of 2,358 missiles, and the U.S. ceiling is 1,710 missiles. In mid-1972 the United States had 1,054 land-based missiles and 656 missiles on nuclear submarines, with an allowable maximum under the treaty of 710 on submarines. (But any increase over 656 must be offset by equivalent reductions in older land-based or sea-based missiles.) The Soviet missile fleet is limited to 1,618 on land and 740 at sea, except that up to 210 of the land-based missiles may be dismantled and replaced by submarine-launched missiles. Critics of the interim agreement oppose the numerical superiority granted to the Soviets and, especially, the fact that their larger missiles give them an even larger relative advantage in destructive power.

Against criticisms of the agreements, the administration has argued that without the agreements the Soviet strategic nuclear advantages would have been even greater. The administration contends that by 1977 (the termination date of the agreement) the Soviets would have had 3,200 total strategic missiles instead of the 2,358 to which they are now restricted. Because the United States has not planned for a buildup in total numbers of missiles, it has not lost any ground by accepting the agreements.

Beyond these limits on the total number of missiles, there are no restrictions on qualitative changes in those missiles and no limits on numbers of bombers, on air-defense systems, on antisubmarine systems, on air-breathing missiles (which fly nonballistic trajectories), or on tactical nuclear weapons. As a consequence, the administration has proposed that the United States push ahead at a maximum rate to take advantage of these loopholes in the agreements to offset the advantages granted the Soviet Union in numbers of intercontinental ballistic missiles. The final result of the SALT agreements may be the end of one kind of arms race and the beginning of a new one—a race with an even greater tendency toward instability.

Vietnam. George McGovern got his early impetus as a presidential candidate by being one of the earliest and most outspoken Senate critics of the Vietnam war. However, President Nixon was able in large part to defuse the Vietnam issue by late summer of 1972 by eliminating the American ground combat involvement in Vietnam and by announcing an end to the draft by mid-1973. Several events did occur in 1972 which kept the Vietnam issue alive. A major North Vietnamese offensive in the spring and summer succeeded in capturing and holding, in some instances for many months, several key cities in South Vietnam. The U.S. response was to renew the bombing of North Vietnam, including the Hanoi area, and to undertake the mining of the harbors in North Vietnam, announced in a speech by President Nixon on May 8. In addition, the United States increased its forces just outside of South Vietnam—in Thailand and at sea—to a total of between 40,000 and 50,000 men.

The decision to resume bombing of North Vietnam and to mine the harbors was surprising for a number of reasons.

The bombing of North Vietnam from 1965 through 1968 had not proved to be very effective and the political criticism it created within the United States seemed to argue against resuming such an effort. Mining had always been rejected in the past because of the risk of war with the Soviet Union or China, both of whom used North Vietnamese ports to supply that country with its necessary war-supporting matériel. Furthermore, it had been argued that mining would not be effective because of alternative land routes through China into North Vietnam and the possibility of unloading Soviet and other boats onto smaller craft at sea and then sneaking them into North Vietnamese waters. In fact, all of these arguments were raised in National Security Study Memorandum No. 1, which was ordered by presidential assistant Henry Kissinger in 1969. That study was leaked to the press by critics of administration policy in Vietnam after the resumption of bombing in early 1972 because its conclusions were that bombing and mining would not have a significant effect on the war in South Vietnam. In the months since the bombing and mining were begun, the fears of a confrontation with the Soviet Union or China have been allayed, but there has been no apparent effect on the North Vietnamese military effort in South Vietnam.

The Lavelle affair. Another event which raised renewed questioning of U.S. policy in Vietnam was the revelation in the summer of 1972 that the United States had been bombing North Vietnam without provocation for some months before the North Vietnamese offensive. Since the 1968 bombing halt, the administration's stated policy was to bomb only antiaircraft sites in North Vietnam and then only in "protective reaction strikes." This meant attacking these sites only if U.S. planes were fired upon or if the antiaircraft radars were "locked onto" American planes in a manner suggesting attack. In a scandal reminiscent of the unprovoked My Lai massacre, General John D. Lavelle, commander of the Seventh Air Force in Vietnam, was demoted to lieutenant general and retired from the service when it became known that he had ordered attacks on North Vietnamese targets without provocation and apparently without authority from Washington.

As explained in congressional investigations of the events, Lavelle and his subordinates had made up false intelligence reports of antiaircraft attacks on U.S. planes and had used them to justify bombing targets other than antiaircraft sites in North Vietnam. On more than 20 occasions, attacks which were later described as "protective reaction" bombing missions were in fact unprovoked bombings of North Vietnamese targets. Lavelle claimed that General Creighton W. Abrams, commander of U.S. forces in South Vietnam, and Admiral Thomas H. Moorer, chairman of the Joint Chiefs of Staff, knew of his actions. In any event, Lavelle received full retirement pay; no other officer or enlisted man was disciplined. Ironically, Lavelle was relieved of his command just a few days before the all-out bombing of North Vietnam was resumed.   JAMES L. FOSTER

Congress

The second session of the 92nd Congress brought to a climax four years of confrontation between a Republican president and a Democratic majority in the Capitol. When the senators and representatives returned to their deliberations in early January, they had already established one of the lowest records in history of cooperation between the executive and legislative branches of the government. And in an election year no one expected that record to improve.

Thus, it came as no surprise that 1972 was a year of much rhetoric and a low level of legislative production. This was particularly true in the Senate, where no fewer than five members campaigned actively for the Democratic presidential nomination and were eager to establish records of opposition to President Richard M. Nixon.

Much of the confrontation between the Nixon administration and Congress focused on two principal issues: In foreign affairs, antiwar forces in Congress attacked the president's policies in Vietnam and sought to limit both his war-making powers and the degree to which he could enter into foreign agreements without the consent of Congress. On the domestic front, old issues of spending dominated much of the conflict, with the president accusing the lawmakers of fiscal irresponsibility. During the summer he vetoed an appropriations bill for the departments of Labor and Health, Education, and Welfare because it provided more money than he had asked for. As the fall election campaign progressed, the president repeatedly linked his promise of no tax increase in a second Nixon administration with passage by Congress of a ceiling on federal spending. On October 10 the House voted to set a ceiling of $250 billion for the fiscal year July 1, 1972–June 30, 1973, and to give the president authority to trim or eliminate federal programs to keep total spending under that amount. The measure did not pass in the Senate, but presidential aides said that Nixon was nevertheless likely to withhold enough appropriated funds to stay below the $250 billion ceiling.

On October 27, after Congress had adjourned, Nixon vetoed nine bills which he claimed were too expensive. The measures included a new appropriations bill for the Labor Department and HEW and bills authorizing funds for flood control and rehabilitation of the handicapped.

Despite the partisanship displayed and the paucity of legislative achievement, there were actions of historic moment. After 49 years of trial and failure, Congress passed a constitutional amendment to place women on an equal footing with men in all aspects of the law. It also passed an election-year act requiring public disclosure of the sources of financial contributions to candidates for federal office and limiting the amounts those candidates could spend for television campaigning. Further, Congress enacted revolutionary legislation for sharing federal tax collections with the hard-pressed state and local governments.

Responses to the president. The revenue-sharing action represented a significant break with precedent. For as long as anyone in office could remember, Congress had been voting money to be distributed among the states, but the grants were always for specific purposes and included specific directions and regulations as to how the money could be spent. But in his 1971 State of the Union address, President Nixon called for distribution of some federal revenue among the states, to be used as they and their constituent local governments might see fit.

Nixon asked for two forms of revenue sharing. One would give federal money, with no strings attached as to use, to state and local governments to meet their individual needs. The other would partially replace existing grants to the state and local governments for a wide variety of specific purposes, such as housing, rural development, and manpower training; under the president's plan, money would be given to the governments to be spent within one of those broad categories, but the governments would have wide leeway as to planning for and allocation of funds among specific projects.

Congress, reluctant to untie the purse strings, soon came under concerted pressure from state officials, who had long found it difficult to collect enough taxes to meet the states' fiscal obligations, and from big-city mayors, who were faced with even more serious financial problems. Finally, right before adjournment this year, both houses completed action on legislation to distribute $5.3 billion in fiscal 1973

BEDSIDE AFFAIR. ITT lobbyist Dita Beard, flanked by her doctors (left) and her attorney (right), waits to testify from her Denver hospital bed before Senate Judiciary subcommittee members. The hearing was terminated when she complained of pains in her chest.

UPI

in restriction-free grants to states and localities; President Nixon signed the bill. (Congress will continue to vote specific-purpose funds along traditional lines.)

Congress partially yielded to the president's wishes on another domestic question of significance, but this action —on the question of school busing—was clearly a reaction to public rather than presidential pressures. Final action came on June 8, when the House upheld a compromise version (already approved by the Senate) of an amendment to a higher education bill. As it was enacted, the amendment required the postponement, until all appeals had been ruled on or until January 1, 1974, of all federal district court orders requiring the transfer or transportation of students to achieve racial balance in public schools. It also limited the use of federal funds for such a purpose and prohibited any busing that would entail a health risk or that would transfer a student from one school to another of inferior capabilities (*see* CIVIL LIBERTIES AND CIVIL RIGHTS).

Even as he signed the bill, however, Nixon complained that Congress did not go far enough. In a March 17 message to Congress, the president had asked for legislation restricting the power of federal courts to issue new busing orders. On August 18 the House did pass a measure prohibiting the courts from ordering busing across school district boundaries, but in the Senate a bipartisan group of liberals filibustered the measure to death in the October preadjournment rush.

Higher education. The higher education bill to which the first antibusing measure had been attached was itself a significant piece of legislation. It set up an emergency fund to help colleges and universities in financial distress; it gave to institutions of higher education, for the first time in U.S. history, federal money with no strings attached as to use; and it outlined a potentially important new scholarship program (*see* EDUCATION).

Equal rights. Final congressional action on another historic measure came with ease this year when the Senate passed and sent to the states for ratification a constitutional amendment guaranteeing the same rights to men and women. The House had passed the same amendment in 1971. In the Senate the vote was 84–8, giving the amendment 22 votes more than the two-thirds majority necessary for passage.

In its final form the amendment read simply: "Equality of rights under the law shall not be denied or abridged by the United States or by any state on account of sex."

The constitutional amendment was the first of two significant equal rights questions settled by Congress during the year. In the second, after seven years of effort, Congress passed a measure giving the Equal Employment Opportunity Commission the power to seek court action in cases involving discrimination in job practices.

Public interest legislation. Congress, acting to clean up the nation's lakes and streams, approved and sent to the president in the fall a bill intended to end the discharge of pollutants into U.S. waterways by 1985. More specifically, the bill authorized $24 million over nine years, primarily to help state and local governments construct sewage treatment facilities; required industrial plants discharging waste into waterways to use the "best practicable" pollution control equipment by 1977 and the "best available" by 1983; and in order to enforce that requirement, mandated that only those industrial firms obtaining state or federal permits could discharge waste into the waterways. Nixon vetoed the bill, claiming it was too costly, but both houses of Congress overrode the veto by wide margins.

Congressional efforts to establish a special federal agency to represent consumers in court actions and federal administrative proceedings were thwarted by a Senate filibuster in October. But both houses did vote to establish an independent commission to set mandatory product safety standards. Nixon signed the product safety bill.

Social welfare. The three-year congressional effort to reform the nation's welfare system also ended in failure in October when the Senate voted to test on a small scale three different reform plans over the next five years. None of the three alternatives—the Nixon proposal for a $2,400 guaranteed annual income benefiting the "working poor" as well as the unemployed and unemployable, a more liberal plan for a $2,600 guaranteed income and automatic increases tied to the cost of living, and a conservative plan linking welfare benefits with a strict work or job-training requirement—could attract enough votes to win passage. The House had previously passed the president's welfare plan, and the House-Senate conference committee could not reach a compromise and deleted all reform proposals from the final welfare bill, which did the following: liberalize social security and medicare benefits, set up a federal corporation to provide custodial day care for children of working mothers, and federalize welfare payments to the aged, the blind, and the disabled.

On June 30, Congress completed action on a measure increasing social security payments by 20 percent.

Kleindienst nomination. Some of the tone of confrontation between Congress and the president came outside the legislative sphere. It developed from a nomination that was expected to face—and in fact originally encountered—little opposition in the Senate. This was the president's naming of Richard G. Kleindienst to succeed Attorney General John N. Mitchell, who resigned to manage Nixon's campaign.

The Senate Judiciary Committee had already cleared Kleindienst for what was expected to be a routine vote when syndicated columnist Jack Anderson accused him on March 1 of "telling an outright lie" by denying participation in a controversial out-of-court settlement of antitrust suits against the International Telephone and Telegraph Corporation. The Justice Department had initiated legal action to force ITT to divest itself of three subsidiaries, but in the settlement, ITT was allowed to keep the largest and most valuable firm, the Hartford Fire Insurance Company.

Anderson said that, contrary to Kleindienst's denials, the nominee had held secret meetings on the case with Felix G. Rohatyn, an ITT director. In further testimony on March 2, Kleindienst admitted having four meetings with Rohatyn and arranging for Rohatyn to explain to other Justice Department officials ITT's side of the antitrust case, but Kleindienst denied knowledge of any possible link between the out-of-court settlement and a pledge of up to $400,000 from another ITT subsidiary to help support the Republican National Convention.

Such a link was alleged by Jack Anderson on February 29 when he published a purported memorandum by ITT lobbyist Dita Beard stating that ITT's "400,000 commitment . . . has gone a long way toward our negotiations on the mergers eventually coming out as [ITT] wants them. Certainly the president has told [Attorney General] Mitchell to see that things are worked out fairly. . . . Mitchell is definitely helping us."

The alleged memo, whose content was disputed by ITT and Justice Department officials (including Mitchell), had closed with the words, "Please destroy this, huh?" Instead, it nearly destroyed Kleindienst. But he survived some of the year's most dramatic congressional scenes, including sickbed testimony from Mrs. Beard, and nearly four months after he was nominated, Kleindienst was finally confirmed as attorney general. (*See also* PEOPLE IN THE NEWS: Jack Anderson and Dita Beard.)

Foreign policy. Most of the heat—if little of the action—in the conflicts between the president and Congress concerned foreign policy. One source of controversy throughout the Nixon administration has been the Senate's repeated attempts to attach to legislation amendments aimed at forcing a total withdrawal of United States troops from South Vietnam. Repeatedly in the past, these efforts failed for

THE SENATE: NINETY-SECOND CONGRESS, SECOND SESSION[1]
Spiro T. Agnew, president

State	Senator	Began office	Term expires	State	Senator	Began office	Term expires
ALABAMA	John Sparkman, D	1946	1973	MONTANA	Mike Mansfield, D	1953	1977
	James Allen, D	1969	1975		Lee Metcalf, D	1961	1973
ALASKA	Ted Stevens, R	1968	1973	NEBRASKA	Roman Hruska, R	1954	1977
	Mike Gravel, D	1969	1975		Carl Curtis, R	1955	1973
ARIZONA	Paul Fannin, R	1965	1977	NEVADA	Alan Bible, D	1954	1975
	Barry Goldwater, R[2]	1969	1975		Howard Cannon, D	1959	1977
ARKANSAS	John McClellan, D	1943	1973	NEW HAMPSHIRE	Norris Cotton, R	1954	1975
	J. W. Fulbright, D	1945	1975		Thomas McIntyre, D	1962	1973
CALIFORNIA	Alan Cranston, D	1969	1975	NEW JERSEY	Clifford Case, R	1955	1973
	John Tunney, D	1971	1977		Harrison Williams, Jr., D	1959	1977
COLORADO	Gordon Allott, R	1955	1973	NEW MEXICO	Clinton Anderson, D	1949	1973
	Peter Dominick, R	1963	1975		Joseph Montoya, D	1964	1977
CONNECTICUT	Abraham Ribicoff, D	1963	1975	NEW YORK	Jacob Javits, R	1957	1975
	Lowell Weicker, Jr., R	1971	1977		James Buckley, Cons.-R	1971	1977
DELAWARE	J. Caleb Boggs, R	1961	1973	NORTH CAROLINA	Sam Ervin, Jr., D	1954	1975
	William Roth, R	1971	1977		B. Everett Jordan, D	1958	1973
FLORIDA	Edward Gurney, R	1969	1975	NORTH DAKOTA	Milton Young, R	1945	1975
	Lawton Chiles, D	1971	1977		Quentin Burdick, D	1960	1977
GEORGIA	David H. Gambrell, D[3]	1971	1973	OHIO	William Saxbe, R	1969	1975
	Herman Talmadge, D	1957	1975		Robert Taft, Jr., R	1971	1977
HAWAII	Hiram Fong, R	1959	1977	OKLAHOMA	Fred Harris, D	1964	1973
	Daniel Inouye, D	1963	1975		Henry Bellmon, R	1969	1975
IDAHO	Frank Church, D	1957	1975	OREGON	Mark Hatfield, R	1967	1973
	Len Jordan, R	1962	1973		Robert Packwood, R	1969	1975
ILLINOIS	Charles Percy, R	1967	1973	PENNSYLVANIA	Hugh Scott, R	1959	1977
	Adlai Stevenson III, D	1971	1977		Richard Schweiker, R	1969	1975
INDIANA	Vance Hartke, D	1959	1977	RHODE ISLAND	John Pastore, D	1950	1977
	Birch Bayh, D	1963	1975		Claiborne Pell, D	1961	1973
IOWA	Jack Miller, R	1961	1973	SOUTH CAROLINA	Strom Thurmond, R[8]	1956	1973
	Harold Hughes, D	1969	1975		Ernest Hollings, D	1966	1975
KANSAS	James Pearson, R	1962	1973	SOUTH DAKOTA	Karl Mundt, R	1948	1973
	Robert Dole, R	1969	1975		George McGovern, D	1963	1975
KENTUCKY	John Cooper, R[4]	1956	1973	TENNESSEE	Howard Baker, Jr., R	1967	1973
	Marlow Cook, R	1968	1975		William Brock III, R	1971	1977
LOUISIANA	Elaine S. Edwards, D[5]	1972	1972	TEXAS	John Tower, R	1961	1973
	Russell Long, D	1948	1975		Lloyd Bentsen, Jr., D	1971	1977
MAINE	Margaret Chase Smith, R	1949	1973	UTAH	Wallace Bennett, R	1951	1975
	Edmund Muskie, D	1959	1977		Frank Moss, D	1959	1977
MARYLAND	Charles Mathias, Jr., R	1969	1975	VERMONT	George Aiken, R	1941	1975
	J. Glenn Beall, Jr., R	1971	1977		Robert T. Stafford, R[9]	1971	1977
MASSACHUSETTS	Edward Kennedy, D	1962	1977	VIRGINIA	Harry Byrd, Jr., ind.	1965	1977
	Edward Brooke, R	1967	1973		William Spong, Jr., D	1966	1973
MICHIGAN	Philip Hart, D	1959	1977	WASHINGTON	Warren Magnuson, D	1944	1975
	Robert Griffin, R	1966	1973		Henry Jackson, D	1953	1977
MINNESOTA	Walter Mondale, D	1964	1973	WEST VIRGINIA	Jennings Randolph, D	1958	1973
	Hubert Humphrey, D[6]	1971	1977		Robert Byrd, D	1959	1977
MISSISSIPPI	James Eastland, D[7]	1943	1973	WISCONSIN	William Proxmire, D	1957	1977
	John Stennis, D	1947	1977		Gaylord Nelson, D	1963	1975
MISSOURI	Stuart Symington, D	1953	1977	WYOMING	Gale McGee, D	1959	1977
	Thomas Eagleton, D	1968	1975		Clifford Hansen, R	1967	1973

[1] As of Oct. 12, 1972. [2] Also served in the Senate from Jan. 3, 1953, to Jan. 3, 1965. [3] Appointed to fill vacancy caused by death of Richard Russell, D, Jan. 21, 1971. [4] Also served in the Senate from Nov. 6, 1946, to Jan. 3, 1949, and from Nov. 5, 1952, to Jan. 3, 1955. [5] Appointed to fill vacancy caused by death of Allen Ellender, D, July 27, 1972. [6] Also served in the Senate from Dec. 1948 to Jan. 1964. [7] Also served in the Senate from June 30, 1941, to Sept. 28, 1941. [8] Also served in the Senate from Dec. 24, 1954, to Apr. 4, 1956. [9] Appointed to fill vacancy caused by death of Winston Prouty, R, Sept. 10, 1971.

State	D*	Name	State	D*	Name	State	D*	Name
ALA.	1.	Jack Edwards, R	FLA.—cont.			LA.—cont.	7.	John B. Breaux, D[10]
	2.	William Dickinson, R		11.	Claude Pepper, D		8.	Speedy Long, D
	3.	Elizabeth Andrews, D[2]		12.	Dante Fascell, D	ME.	1.	Peter Kyros, D
	4.	Bill Nichols, D	GA.	1.	G. Elliott Hagan, D		2.	William Hathaway, D
	5.	Walter Flowers, D		2.	Dawson Mathis, D	MD.	1.	William Mills, R[11]
	6.	John Buchanan, R		3.	Jack Brinkley, D		2.	Clarence Long, D
	7.	Tom Bevill, D		4.	Benjamin Blackburn, R		3.	Edward Garmatz, D
	8.	Robert Jones, D		5.	Fletcher Thompson, R		4.	Paul Sarbanes, D
ALAS.		(at large)		6.	John Flynt, Jr., D		5.	Lawrence Hogan, R
		Nick Begich, D		7.	John Davis, D		6.	Goodloe Byron, D
ARIZ.	1.	John Rhodes, R		8.	W. S. Stuckey, D		7.	Parren Mitchell, D
	2.	Morris Udall, D		9.	Phil Landrum, D		8.	Gilbert Gude, R
	3.	Sam Steiger, R		10.	Robert Stephens, Jr., D	MASS.	1.	Silvio Conte, R
ARK.	1.	Bill Alexander, D	HAW.		(at large)		2.	Edward Boland, D
	2.	Wilbur Mills, D			Spark Matsunaga, D		3.	Robert Drinan, D
	3.	John Paul Hammerschmidt, R			Patsy Mink, D		4.	Harold Donohue, D
	4.	David Pryor, D	IDA.	1.	James McClure, R		5.	——[12]
CALIF.	1.	Don Clausen, R		2.	Orval Hansen, R		6.	Michael Harrington, D
	2.	Harold Johnson, D	ILL.	1.	Ralph Metcalfe, D[6]		7.	Torbert Macdonald, D
	3.	John Moss, D		2.	Abner Mikva, D		8.	Thomas O'Neill, Jr., D
	4.	Robert Leggett, D		3.	Morgan Murphy, D		9.	Louise Hicks, D
	5.	Phillip Burton, D		4.	Edward Derwinski, R		10.	Margaret Heckler, R
	6.	William Mailliard, R		5.	John Kluczynski, D		11.	James Burke, D
	7.	Ronald Dellums, D		6.	George Collins, D[7]		12.	Hastings Keith, R
	8.	George Miller, D		7.	Frank Annunzio, D	MICH.	1.	John Conyers, Jr., D
	9.	Don Edwards, D		8.	Dan Rostenkowski, D		2.	Marvin Esch, R
	10.	Charles Gubser, R		9.	Sidney Yates, D		3.	Garry Brown, R
	11.	Paul McCloskey, Jr., R		10.	Harold Collier, R		4.	Edward Hutchinson, R
	12.	Burt Talcott, R		11.	Roman Pucinski, D		5.	Gerald Ford, R
	13.	Charles Teague, R		12.	Robert McClory, R		6.	Charles Chamberlain, R
	14.	Jerome Waldie, D		13.	Philip Crane, R		7.	Donald Riegle, Jr., R
	15.	John McFall, D		14.	John Erlenborn, R		8.	James Harvey, R
	16.	B. F. Sisk, D		15.	Clifford D. Carlson, R[8]		9.	Guy Vander Jagt, R
	17.	Glenn Anderson, D		16.	John Anderson, R		10.	Elford Cederberg, R
	18.	Robert Mathias, R		17.	Leslie Arends, R		11.	Philip Ruppe, R
	19.	Chet Holifield, D		18.	Robert Michel, R		12.	James O'Hara, D
	20.	H. Allen Smith, R		19.	Tom Railsback, R		13.	Charles Diggs, Jr., D
	21.	Augustus Hawkins, D		20.	Paul Findley, R		14.	Lucien Nedzi, D
	22.	James Corman, D		21.	Kenneth Gray, D		15.	William Ford, D
	23.	Del Clawson, R		22.	William Springer, R		16.	John Dingell, D
	24.	John Rousselot, R[3]		23.	George Shipley, D		17.	Martha Griffiths, D
	25.	Charles Wiggins, R		24.	Melvin Price, D		18.	William Broomfield, R
	26.	Thomas Rees, D	IND.	1.	Ray Madden, D		19.	Jack McDonald, R
	27.	Barry Goldwater, Jr., R		2.	Earl Landgrebe, R	MINN.	1.	Albert Quie, R
	28.	Alphonzo Bell, R		3.	John Brademas, D		2.	Ancher Nelsen, R
	29.	George Danielson, D		4.	J. Edward Roush, D		3.	Bill Frenzel, R
	30.	Edward Roybal, D		5.	Elwood Hillis, R		4.	Joseph Karth, D
	31.	Charles Wilson, D		6.	William Bray, R		5.	Donald Fraser, D
	32.	Craig Hosmer, R		7.	John Myers, R		6.	John Zwach, R
	33.	Jerry Pettis, R		8.	Roger Zion, R		7.	Bob Bergland, D
	34.	Richard Hanna, D		9.	Lee Hamilton, D		8.	John Blatnik, D
	35.	John Schmitz, R[4]		10.	David Dennis, R	MISS.	1.	Thomas Abernethy, D
	36.	Bob Wilson, R		11.	Andrew Jacobs, Jr., D		2.	Jamie Whitten, D
	37.	Lionel Van Deerlin, D	IOWA	1.	Fred Schwengel, R		3.	Charles Griffin, D
	38.	Victor Veysey, R		2.	John Culver, D		4.	G. V. Montgomery, D
COLO.	1.	James McKevitt, R		3.	H. R. Gross, R		5.	William Colmer, D
	2.	Donald Brotzman, R		4.	John Kyl, R	MO.	1.	William Clay, D
	3.	Frank Evans, D		5.	Neal Smith, D		2.	James Symington, D
	4.	Wayne Aspinall, D		6.	Wiley Mayne, R		3.	Leonor Sullivan, D
CONN.	1.	William Cotter, D		7.	William Scherle, R		4.	William Randall, D
	2.	Robert Steele, R[5]	KANS.	1.	Keith Sebelius, R		5.	Richard Bolling, D
	3.	Robert Giaimo, D		2.	William Roy, D		6.	W. R. Hull, Jr., D
	4.	Stewart McKinney, R		3.	Larry Winn, Jr., R		7.	Durward Hall, R
	5.	John Monagan, D		4.	Garner Shriver, R		8.	Richard Ichord, D
	6.	Ella Grasso, D		5.	Joe Skubitz, R		9.	William Hungate, D
DEL.		(at large)	KY.	1.	Frank Stubblefield, D		10.	Bill Burlison, D
		Pierre duPont, R		2.	William Natcher, D	MONT.	1.	Richard Shoup, R
FLA.	1.	Robert Sikes, D		3.	Romano Mazzoli, D		2.	John Melcher, D
	2.	Don Fuqua, D		4.	M. G. Snyder, R	NEBR.	1.	Charles Thone, R
	3.	Charles Bennett, D		5.	Tim Carter, R		2.	John McCollister, R
	4.	Bill Chappell, Jr., D		6.	William P. Curlin, Jr., D[9]		3.	Dave Martin, R
	5.	Louis Frey, Jr., R		7.	Carl Perkins, D	NEV.		(at large)
	6.	Sam Gibbons, D	LA.	1.	F. Edward Hébert, D			Walter Baring, D
	7.	James Haley, D		2.	Hale Boggs, D	N. H.	1.	Louis Wyman, R
	8.	C. W. Young, R		3.	Patrick Caffery, D		2.	James Cleveland, R
	9.	Paul Rogers, D		4.	Joe Waggonner, Jr., D			
	10.	J. Herbert Burke, R		5.	Otto Passman, D			
				6.	John Rarick, D			

State	D*	Name	State	D*	Name	State	D*	Name
N. J.	1.	John Hunt, R	OHIO	1.	William Keating, R	TENN.	1.	James Quillen, R
	2.	Charles Sandman, Jr., R		2.	Donald Clancy, R		2.	John Duncan, R
	3.	James Howard, D		3.	Charles Whalen, Jr., R		3.	LaMar Baker, R
	4.	Frank Thompson, Jr., D		4.	William McCulloch, R		4.	Joe Evins, D
	5.	Peter Frelinghuysen, R		5.	Delbert Latta, R		5.	Richard Fulton, D
	6.	Edwin Forsythe, R[13]		6.	William Harsha, R		6.	William Anderson, D
	7.	William Widnall, R		7.	Clarence Brown, R		7.	Ray Blanton, D
	8.	Robert Roe, D		8.	Jackson Betts, R		8.	Ed Jones, D
	9.	Henry Helstoski, D		9.	Thomas Ashley, D		9.	Dan Kuykendall, R
	10.	Peter Rodino, Jr., D		10.	Clarence Miller, R	TEXAS	1.	Wright Patman, D
	11.	Joseph Minish, D		11.	J. William Stanton, R		2.	John Dowdy, D
	12.	Florence Dwyer, R		12.	Samuel Devine, R		3.	James Collins, R
	13.	Cornelius Gallagher, D		13.	Charles Mosher, R		4.	Ray Roberts, D
	14.	Dominick Daniels, D		14.	John Seiberling, D		5.	Earle Cabell, D
	15.	Edward Patten, D		15.	Chalmers Wylie, R		6.	Olin Teague, D
N. MEX.	1.	Manuel Lujan, Jr., R		16.	Frank Bow, R		7.	Bill Archer, R
	2.	Harold Runnels, D		17.	John Ashbrook, R		8.	Bob Eckhardt, D
				18.	Wayne Hays, D		9.	Jack Brooks, D
N. Y.	1.	Otis Pike, D		19.	Charles Carney, D[15]		10.	J. J. Pickle, D
	2.	James Grover, Jr., R		20.	James Stanton, D		11.	W. R. Poage, D
	3.	Lester Wolff, D		21.	Louis Stokes, D		12.	Jim Wright, D
	4.	John Wydler, R		22.	Charles Vanik, D		13.	Graham Purcell, D
	5.	Norman Lent, R		23.	William Minshall, R		14.	John Young, D
	6.	Seymour Halpern, R		24.	Walter Powell, R		15.	Eligio de la Garza, D
	7.	Joseph Addabbo, D	OKLA.	1.	Page Belcher, R		16.	Richard White, D
	8.	Benjamin Rosenthal, D		2.	Ed Edmondson, D		17.	Omar Burleson, D
	9.	James Delaney, D		3.	Carl Albert, D		18.	Robert Price, R
	10.	Emanuel Celler, D		4.	Tom Steed, D		19.	George Mahon, D
	11.	Frank Brasco, D		5.	John Jarman, D		20.	Henry Gonzalez, D
	12.	Shirley Chisholm, D		6.	John Happy Camp, R		21.	O. C. Fisher, D
	13.	Bertram Podell, D	ORE.	1.	Wendell Wyatt, R		22.	Bob Casey, D
	14.	John Rooney, D		2.	Al Ullman, D		23.	Abraham Kazen, Jr., D
	15.	Hugh Carey, D		3.	Edith Green, D	UTAH	1.	K. Gunn McKay, D
	16.	John Murphy, D		4.	John Dellenback, R		2.	Sherman Lloyd, R
	17.	Edward Koch, D	PA.	1.	William Barrett, D			(at large)
	18.	Charles Rangel, D		2.	Robert Nix, D	VT.		Richard W. Mallory, R[20]
	19.	Bella Abzug, D		3.	James Byrne, D	VA.	1.	Thomas Downing, D
	20.	——[14]		4.	Joshua Eilberg, D		2.	G. William Whitehurst, R
	21.	Herman Badillo, D		5.	William Green, D		3.	David Satterfield III, D
	22.	James Scheuer, D		6.	Gus Yatron, D		4.	Watkins Abbitt, D
	23.	Jonathan Bingham, D		7.	Lawrence Williams, R		5.	W. C. Daniel, D
	24.	Mario Biaggi, D		8.	Edward Biester, Jr., R		6.	——[21]
	25.	Peter Peyser, R		9.	John Ware, R[16]		7.	J. Kenneth Robinson, R
	26.	Ogden Reid, R		10.	Joseph McDade, R		8.	William Scott, R
	27.	John Dow, D		11.	Daniel Flood, D		9.	William Wampler, R
	28.	Hamilton Fish, Jr., R		12.	J. Irving Whalley, R		10.	Joel Broyhill, R
	29.	Samuel Stratton, D		13.	R. Lawrence Coughlin, R	WASH.	1.	Thomas Pelly, R
	30.	Carleton King, R		14.	William Moorhead, D		2.	Lloyd Meeds, D
	31.	Robert McEwen, R		15.	Fred Rooney, D		3.	Julia Butler Hansen, D
	32.	Alexander Pirnie, R		16.	Edwin Eshleman, R		4.	Mike McCormack, D
	33.	Howard Robison, R		17.	Herman Schneebeli, R		5.	Thomas Foley, D
	34.	John Terry, R		18.	H. John Heinz III, R[17]		6.	Floyd Hicks, D
	35.	James Hanley, D		19.	George Goodling, R		7.	Brock Adams, D
	36.	Frank Horton, R		20.	Joseph Gaydos, D	W. VA.	1.	Robert Mollohan, D
	37.	Barber Conable, Jr., R		21.	John Dent, D		2.	Harley Staggers, D
	38.	James Hastings, R		22.	John Saylor, R		3.	John Slack, D
	39.	Jack Kemp, R		23.	Albert Johnson, R		4.	Ken Hechler, D
	40.	Henry Smith III, R		24.	Joseph Vigorito, D		5.	James Kee, D
	41.	Thaddeus Dulski, D		25.	Frank Clark, D	WIS.	1.	Les Aspin, D
				26.	Thomas Morgan, D		2.	Robert Kastenmeier, D
				27.	William S. Conover, R[18]		3.	Vernon Thomson, R
N. C.	1.	Walter Jones, D	R. I.	1.	Fernand St. Germain, D		4.	Clement Zablocki, D
	2.	L. H. Fountain, D		2.	Robert Tiernan, D		5.	Henry Reuss, D
	3.	David Henderson, D	S. C.	1.	Mendel Davis, D[19]		6.	William Steiger, R
	4.	Nick Galifianakis, D		2.	Floyd Spence, R		7.	David Obey, D
	5.	Wilmer Mizell, R		3.	William Jennings Bryan Dorn, D		8.	John Byrnes, D
	6.	Richardson Preyer, D		4.	James Mann, D		9.	Glenn Davis, R
	7.	Alton Lennon, D		5.	Tom Gettys, D		10.	Alvin O'Konski, R
	8.	Earl Ruth, R		6.	John McMillan, D	WYO.		(at large)
	9.	Charles Jonas, R						Teno Roncalio, D
	10.	James Broyhill, R				WASH., D.C.		(delegate)
	11.	Roy Taylor, D						Walter Fauntroy, D
N. DAK.	1.	Mark Andrews, R	S. DAK.	1.	Frank Denholm, D	P. R.		(resident commissioner)
	2.	Arthur Link, D		2.	James Abourezk, D			Jorge Córdova, D

* D stands for Congressional District. [1] As of Oct. 12, 1972. [2] Elected to fill vacancy caused by death of George Andrews, D, Dec. 25, 1971. [3] Elected June 30, 1970, to fill vacancy caused by death of Glenard P. Lipscomb, R, Feb. 1, 1970. [4] Elected June 30, 1970, to fill vacancy caused by death of James B. Utt, R, Mar. 1, 1970. [5] Elected Nov. 3, 1970, to fill vacancy caused by death of William L. St. Onge, D, May 1, 1970. [6] Elected to fill vacancy caused by death of William L. Dawson, D, Nov. 9, 1970. [7] Elected Nov. 3, 1970, to fill vacancy caused by death of Daniel J. Ronan, D, Aug. 13, 1969. [8] Elected to fill vacancy caused by resignation of Charlotte Reid, R, Oct. 1, 1971. [9] Elected to fill vacancy caused by death of John Watts, D, Sept. 24, 1971. [10] Elected to fill vacancy caused by resignation of Edwin W. Edwards, D. [11] Elected May 27, 1971, to fill vacancy caused by resignation of Rogers Morton, R. [12] Vacancy caused by resignation of F. Bradford Morse, R, May 1, 1972. [13] Elected Nov. 3, 1970, to fill vacancy caused by resignation of William T. Cahill, R, Jan. 19, 1970. [14] Vacancy caused by death of William Ryan, Sept. 17, 1972. [15] Elected Nov. 3, 1970, to fill vacancy caused by death of Michael J. Kirwan, D, July 27, 1970. [16] Elected Nov. 3, 1970, to fill vacancy caused by death of G. Robert Watkins, R, Aug. 7, 1971. [17] Elected Nov. 2, 1971, to fill vacancy caused by death of Robert Corbett, R, Apr. 25, 1971. [18] Elected to fill vacancy caused by death of James Fulton, R, Oct. 6, 1971. [19] Elected to fill vacancy caused by death of L. Mendel Rivers, D, Dec. 28, 1970. [20] Elected to fill vacancy caused by resignation of Robert Stafford, R, Sept. 16, 1971. [21] Vacancy caused by resignation of Richard Poff, R.

WIDE WORLD

WILLIAM H. REHNQUIST (1924–   )

At 47, William H. Rehnquist became one of the youngest men ever to take a seat on the Supreme Court. In December 1971 he replaced Justice John M. Harlan, who had resigned in September because of ill health.

Born in Milwaukee, Wis., Rehnquist received both his undergraduate and law degrees from Stanford University. After graduating at the top of his law school class in 1952, he served for one year as law clerk to Supreme Court Justice Robert H. Jackson, during which time he urged Jackson to oppose the Court's landmark school desegregation decision, *Brown* v. *Board of Education*, because "it was not part of the judicial function to thwart public opinion except in extreme cases."

From 1953 until 1969, when he became assistant attorney general in the Nixon administration, Rehnquist practiced law in Phoenix, Ariz. In 1964 he was a speechwriter for Barry Goldwater during the Arizona senator's campaign for the presidency.

lack of support from the House. But this year, the Senate itself narrowly voted down a withdrawal amendment that it had passed earlier in the year. The amendment, which would have cut off funds to support U.S. troops involved in the war, dependent on the concurrent release of U.S. prisoners, was defeated 45–42 on September 26. Senator Edward W. Brooke (R, Mass.), the amendment's sponsor, attributed its failure to the absence of four Senate doves on the day of the vote. However, some senators conceded privately that enthusiasm for end-the-war amendments had waned.

The end-the-war effort was only one of the conflicts between Nixon and Congress on foreign policy. In another, the Senate, long seething over what it regarded as usurpation of power, started action to limit the president's authority to make war without the consent of Congress. In the end it passed a bill that would permit the president only 30 days of military action without specific authorization from Congress. The House followed suit with a somewhat milder measure, but late in the session, the two bills could not be reconciled by a conference committee.

In a closely related action, the Senate passed and the House accepted a bill requiring the president to submit the texts of all international agreements to Congress. Like the war powers bill, this was a reflection of growing discontent in Congress over the dominance of the executive branch in the making of foreign policy.

In a year of confrontation, there was one note of harmony. The Senate overwhelmingly endorsed the treaty concluded in Moscow by the president and Soviet leaders to limit the installation of antiballistic missile systems. But even this action was accompanied by an expression of discontent over another U.S.-Soviet agreement. In approving a five-year pact limiting offensive nuclear arms, the Senate added to its resolution a demand that any future renewal of the agreement give the United States a better deal. The House again accepted the Senate version.

People in the news. House leadership was thrown into turmoil when a plane carrying Majority Leader Hale Boggs (D, La.) and Representative Nick Begich (D, Alaska) was lost over Alaska in mid-October. Both were reelected. Two controversial former representatives died this year: Adam Clayton Powell (D, N.Y.), the most powerful black person in Congress until barred from the House in 1967 (he was later reinstated but stripped of his Education and Labor Committee chairmanship), and Martin Dies, the first chairman of the House Committee on Un-American Activities. Former senator Daniel B. Brewster (D, Md.) was convicted in November of accepting an unlawful gratuity from a lobbyist for Spiegel, Inc.   WILLIAM ROBBINS

Supreme Court

The justices. The Supreme Court began 1972 with a full nine justices after the nominations of Lewis F. Powell, Jr., and William H. Rehnquist were approved by the Senate in late 1971. The new justices replaced John M. Harlan and Hugo Black, both of whom resigned in September 1971 because of ill health and died soon after.

Justice Rehnquist came under intense criticism during the year for his refusal to disqualify himself from cases before the Supreme Court in which he had helped prepare or had publicly defended the government's position while he was a member of the Justice Department. Rehnquist maintained that every judge comes to the Court with strong opinions, even if they have not been well publicized.

Capital punishment. The most important constitutional case of 1972 in the area of criminal law was *Furman* v. *Georgia* (92 S. Ct. 2726), handed down on June 29, which held unconstitutional the death penalty as it was being administered in the United States. The decision was by a 5–4 vote, and each judge wrote a separate opinion.

Several themes dominated the opinions of the majority, who all concluded that the death penalty violated the Eighth Amendment's prohibition of "cruel and unusual punishment" but could not agree on why. Justice William O. Douglas was impressed with the fact that the judges and jurors who imposed the death penalty were given uncontrolled discretion to determine who should die and who should be imprisoned. "No standards," he wrote, "govern the selection of the penalty," which he alleged was being applied prejudicially against the poor and minorities.

Justices William J. Brennan and Thurgood Marshall read the Eighth Amendment as prohibiting any punishment that does not "comport with human dignity" (quote from Brennan's opinion), and they concluded that execution was such a punishment. Both justices had to confront the facts that the death penalty existed when the Eighth Amendment was adopted and had generally been retained by state legislatures since that time. Both answered that the meaning of the amendment was not frozen by the eighteenth century's understanding of what was cruel or unusual but properly derived substance from today's ethics and culture.

Justices Potter Stewart and Byron R. White were concerned that the death penalty was "wantonly and freakishly" imposed (quote from Stewart's opinion) on only a small fraction of the convicted felons who could have been executed. Justice White, in particular, was impressed with the point that, because the death penalty was so infrequently imposed, there was little reason to believe that it served any rational purpose, such as deterring crime.

LEWIS F. POWELL, JR. (1907–   )

On December 6, 1971, Lewis F. Powell, President Nixon's third Supreme Court nominee from the South, was overwhelmingly confirmed by the Senate and became the first southerner in two decades to take a seat on the Court. A life-long Virginia resident, Powell earned a bachelor's and a law degree at Washington and Lee University and a master's degree at Harvard Law School. From 1937 until the time he was confirmed, Powell was associated with a Richmond-based law firm, one of Virginia's oldest, and from 1952 to 1961 he served on the Richmond school board, where he helped implement that city's first moves toward school integration.

A nationally respected lawyer, Powell headed the American Bar Association (1964–1965), the American College of Trial Lawyers (1969–1970), and the American Bar Foundation from 1969 until his appointment to the Supreme Court. Powell was also a member of the federal Commission on Law Enforcement and Administration of Justice.

WIDE WORLD

The dissenters—Chief Justice Warren E. Burger and Associate Justices Harry A. Blackmun, Powell, and Rehnquist—emphasized that the death penalty had been used throughout U.S. history and that the justices had no effective way of measuring whether the national moral climate had changed to the extent that what had long been considered acceptable punishment now no longer comports with human dignity. Justice Powell recalled that the death penalty for airline hijackers had recently been voted by Congress.

Because only a minority of the justices found the death penalty cruel and unusual per se, the Furman case left unanswered the question of whether a nonarbitrary way of administering the penalty—for example, a law mandating the death sentence for all convictions of a certain type—would be constitutional.

Other criminal law issues. Until a few years ago, a person on parole or probation was thought to occupy such a status as a matter of grace and, therefore, thought to have no right to challenge the reasons for revocation. This year, in *Morrissey* v. *Brewer* (92 S. Ct. 2593), the Supreme Court held that the due process clause of the Fourteenth Amendment required the following minimum hearing procedures when parole or probation has been revoked: written notice of the claimed violations of parole or probation; disclosure to the accused of evidence against him; an opportunity for the accused to be heard in person, to present witnesses and documentary evidence, and to confront and cross-examine adverse witnesses (unless the hearing officer specifically finds good cause for not allowing confrontation); a decision by a "neutral and detached" hearing body, such as a parole board, the members of which need not be judicial officers or lawyers; and a written statement by the fact finders as to the evidence relied on and the reasons for the decision. The Supreme Court's opinion, written by Chief Justice Burger, did not reach the question of whether the assistance of counsel at the revocation hearings is constitutionally required. In a dissenting opinion, Justice Douglas argued that the accused did have the right to counsel and that his hearing must precede his imprisonment for allegedly violating probation or parole. The Court's ruling left the question of the accused's freedom pending the outcome of his hearing to the preliminary hearing officer.

The right to counsel for persons accused of crime was greatly expanded in *Argersinger* v. *Hamlin* (92 S. Ct. 2006). Ever since the Supreme Court's landmark 1963 decision in *Gideon* v. *Wainwright* (372 U.S. 335), it has been the law that alleged felons are entitled to counsel at their trials. *Argersinger* extends the right to counsel to embrace any case in which the accused could be imprisoned if convicted.

An investigation by a grand jury or other government agency is frequently blocked because needed witnesses invoke the Fifth Amendment privilege against self-incrimination. Many states and the federal government have enacted statutes empowering prosecutors to offer immunity from prosecution in return for witnesses' testimony. In general, it had been thought that the government must promise exemption from all prosecution with respect to the events about which a witness testifies. But this year, in *Kastigar* v. *United States* (92 S. Ct. 1653), the Supreme Court held that the Constitution merely requires that the evidence received and derived from the testimony given cannot be used in a later trial of the witness. The defendant in *Kastigar* argued that it would be extraordinarily difficult for a defendant who had been a grand jury witness to show that evidence introduced at his trial did, in fact, come from independent sources and not from his own testimony. The Court answered by placing the burden of proof on the government to establish clearly the source of the evidence.

In *Barker* v. *Wingo* (92 S. Ct. 2182), the Court dealt with the meaning of the Sixth Amendment right to a speedy trial. Justice Powell's opinion of the Court rejected the point that, after a certain period of time, the speedy trial guarantee requires that a case be dismissed. The opinion also rejected the opposite position that the speedy trial right does not come into operation until a defendant has demanded to be tried. The constitutional right can be determined, the Court said, only on an ad hoc basis in which various factors are weighed and balanced: the length of the trial delay, the reasons for the delay, the defendant's manner of asserting his right, and the degree of prejudice to the defendant resulting from the delay.

In American courts a jury is generally required to reach its decision by a unanimous vote. If a verdict cannot be unanimously agreed to, the jury is dismissed as a "hung jury," and the case is retried. This year, however, in *Johnson* v. *Louisiana* (92 S. Ct. 1620) and *Apodaca* v. *Oregon* (92 S. Ct. 1628), the Supreme Court upheld state laws providing for convictions by less than unanimous action (by a 9–3 vote in Louisiana and by a 10–2 vote in Oregon). The statutes were challenged primarily on the grounds that the unanimity requirement was essential to support the constitutional principle that an accused is entitled to the standard of proof beyond a reasonable doubt. A majority of the Court decided, however, that the fact that some jurors were not convinced by the evidence did not mean that others had not employed the strict standard of proof required in criminal cases. Another argument against non-unanimous verdicts was that jury members with the minority viewpoint would not be heard because the majority possessed sufficient votes for a conviction or a verdict of not

guilty. A majority of the justices found no reason to assume that adequate discussion would not take place. The dissenters in both cases—Justices Douglas, Stewart, Brennan, and Marshall—urged that the unanimity rule be kept as a kind of prophylactic rule to encourage full discussion. Justice Powell's opinion of the Court in *Apodaca* announced that a 10–2 verdict was constitutionally permissible only in cases coming from the states and that the Sixth Amendment would still require a unanimous verdict in federal cases.

In the 1968 case *Terry* v. *Ohio* (392 U.S. 1), the Court held that, under certain circumstances, a police officer may constitutionally stop a suspicious person and make an on-the-street "threshold investigation" to determine the person's name and whether his purposes are noncriminal. As an incident to such a stop, the Court held, the police had a right to "frisk" the suspect to search for weapons. The Court's decision this year in *Adams* v. *Williams* (92 S. Ct. 1921) expanded this power considerably by permitting a "stop and frisk" based on information supplied by an unidentified informer. Threshold investigations will thus be much easier to justify.

In *Kirby* v. *Illinois* (92 S. Ct. 1877), the Court backtracked on one of the criminal law cases decided by the Warren Court. *United States* v. *Wade* (388 U.S. 218), decided in 1967, had held that an accused person must be offered counsel at a police lineup. *Kirby* limited *Wade* to cases in which formal proceedings of some sort had been begun against the suspect. Therefore, under *Kirby*, the right

NO MORE WAITING. The future became clearer for this inmate of San Quentin's "death row" and for 600 other U.S. prisoners awaiting capital punishment when the Supreme Court, in a historic 5–4 decision, called the penalty unconstitutional as presently applied.

WIDE WORLD

to counsel does not extend to a lineup conducted as part of a general police investigation.

Government surveillance. In *United States* v. *United States District Court* (92 S. Ct. 2125), the federal government claimed the right to undertake—without court authorization—wiretapping and other electronic surveillance of alleged domestic subversives. The Supreme Court ruled, however, that a court order was required to protect U.S. citizens' Fourth Amendment right to be free from unreasonable searches and seizures.

In another case, the Court ruled that federal courts would not hear cases involving the constitutionality of U.S. Army surveillance of civilians unless a plaintiff could show that he had suffered some specific harm as a result of the surveillance. Justice Rehnquist cast the deciding vote in the 5–4 ruling.

Consumer protection. Traditionally, the seller of goods under a conditional sales (installment) contract has had swift relief in the event payments are not continued. In a typical case a seller can, by legal process, repossess the items sold without a hearing taking place before official action occurs. This time-honored practice was limited in *Fuentes* v. *Shevin* (92 S. Ct. 1983), which held that parties who have a property interest have a constitutional due process right to notice and some sort of hearing before the loss of that interest. A buyer under a conditional sales contract was said to have the interest of "continued use and possession of the goods."

Justices White, Burger, and Blackmun dissented, claiming that the hearing would offer little protection to the buyer and pointing out that modern statutory reform efforts, such as the Uniform Commercial Code, had still retained the seller's right to summary repossession.

Teachers' rights. *Board of Regents* v. *Roth* (92 S. Ct. 2701) raised the issue of the rights of a nontenured teacher in a state college system. David Roth had been engaged for one year and was told in February that he would not be reappointed; no reasons were given. Roth alleged that the failure to rehire him was not grounded in dissatisfaction with his teaching or scholarship but in his expressions of criticism of the college administration.

Justice Stewart, writing for the Court, held that Roth would be entitled to a hearing only if he had lost liberty or property. His subjective expectation of being rehired was not, in Justice Stewart's view, property. He had lost no reputation or opportunity for other state employment.

Justice Douglas dissented on the grounds that, given the assertion of First Amendment rights by Roth, a hearing should take place, even though one need not be held for other sorts of challenges to college administration decisions. Justice Marshall's dissent contained a statement going far beyond present law: "Every citizen who applies for a government job is entitled to it unless the government can establish some reason for denying the employment."

In a companion case, *Perry* v. *Sindermann* (92 S. Ct. 2694), the Court recognized that a teacher could have tenure rights even if he did not have a contract formally giving him tenure, depending on the university's practices in respect to rehiring. The Court returned the case to the trial court for a determination on whether Robert Sindermann, who also claimed he was dismissed for exercising his First Amendment right of free speech, did in fact have tenure.

Freedom of speech and press. *Healy* v. *James* (92 S. Ct. 2338) upheld a First Amendment right of students to form campus organizations at public colleges and universities. A state institution had prohibited formation of a chapter of Students for a Democratic Society. The prediction that the group would be disruptive, the alleged adherence of the group to a philosophy of violence, and the group's national affiliation with other SDS chapters were not sufficient reasons, the Court said, to deny the students their right of political association. College administrators could seek to

curb the group only after some overt destructive act had taken place.

In *Kleindienst* v. *Mandel* (92 S. Ct. 2576), the right of free speech yielded to the special power of the federal government to control the visits of foreigners. The Immigration and Nationality Act provides that aliens who "advocate" or "publish" the doctrines of "world Communism" are ineligible for a visa to visit the United States. Ernest E. Mandel, a Belgian Communist editor, applied for a visa, which he could obtain only if the attorney general of the United States waived the statutory inhibition. Secretary of State William P. Rogers recommended the waiver, so that Mandel could speak at the numerous U.S. universities (including Columbia, Stanford, and Harvard) which had invited him, but then Attorney General John N. Mitchell refused to waive the act. Justice Blackmun, writing for the Court, declared that, if on the face of things there is a bona fide reason to refuse a waiver, "the courts will neither look behind the exercise of discretion nor test it by balancing its justification against the First Amendment interests."

The definition of freedom of the press was addressed in *Branzburg* v. *Hayes* (92 S. Ct. 2646), an opinion covering three similar cases in which newsmen refused to appear and testify before state or federal grand juries concerning the sources of news stories. The newsmen argued that, to gather news, a reporter must often agree not to identify the source of his information. Thus, to require testimony revealing sources will chill the First Amendment right of freedom of the press because fewer persons will communicate with reporters.

Five justices—White (who wrote the opinion of the Court), Burger, Rehnquist, Powell, and Blackmun—voted to compel the reporters to appear and testify. Justice White wrote that any abridgment of freedom of the press must be balanced against the great public need for broad, soundly executed grand jury investigations, and he found only "incidental" and "uncertain" abridgment to balance.

Justices Stewart, Brennan, Marshall, and Douglas dissented. Stewart, expressing a broad definition of freedom of the press, wrote: "The right to gather news implies, in turn, a right to a confidential relationship between a reporter and his source." Douglas predicted that "fear of accountability will cause editors and critics to write with more restrained pens."

The Court declined to review a contempt sentence imposed on a newsman, William T. Farr, for refusing to state which lawyers in the Manson case had violated a trial publicity ban and leaked information to him. Because California has a law specifically protecting newsmen, the trial judge did not issue the contempt citation until Farr left the Los Angeles *Herald-Examiner* for a job in a district attorney's office, long after the trial was over.

In *Lloyd Corporation, Ltd.* v. *Tanner,* the Court ruled that leafleters could be prohibited from distributing literature in a shopping center, because the center is private property. The leafleters had claimed a First Amendment right to hand out their material.

Pentagon papers. In *Russo* v. *Byrne,* the court denied an appeal by lawyers in the Pentagon papers case to stay the trial pending a hearing on their charges that legal conversations had been recorded by a government wiretap. Justice Douglas had stopped the trial in July, with a jury already empaneled.

Rights of parenthood. The Court turned down without comment an appeal by Olga Scarpetta, the natural mother of "Baby Lenore," and permitted the child to remain with Nick and Jean De Martino, her adoptive parents.

Environmental law. By a 4–3 vote, the Supreme Court dismissed a suit by the Sierra Club to prevent construction by the Walt Disney organization of a $35 million recreation area on public land in California. The Court ruled that the conservation group had no standing to sue because it could not show that any of its members would be specifically harmed by the Disney project.

In another case, the Court refused to review a Federal Power Commission ruling allowing the Consolidated Edison Company to build a power plant at Storm King Mountain along the Hudson River.   MONRAD G. PAULSEN

Budget

President Richard M. Nixon's budget message for the fiscal year 1973 demonstrated, among other things, that government deficits were not the property of any one political party; government spending would increase whether the economic weather was fair or foul; the federal budget was beyond anyone's control; and fiscal policy was a textbook rather than a real-world concept.

Contemplated expenditures. The January message estimated total expenditures for fiscal 1973 (July 1, 1972, through June 30, 1973) at $246.3 billion, or about 6 percent more than the actual 1972 expenditures.

Spending for defense, space research, foreign aid, veterans, interest, and general government would remain approximately the same as in fiscal 1972. Outlays for farm subsidies and natural resources would be down. But spending for health and welfare, education, and income security would be much higher. The 15 percent increase in welfare payments would be less than the 29 percent and 24 percent increases in 1971 and 1972, but the total budget for the Department of Health, Education, and Welfare would be much higher than that for the Department of Defense.

The president proposed a 5 percent increase in social security benefits, which would have brought income security outlays to almost $70 billion, but Congress once again surpassed the proposal and raised benefits by 20 percent, making income security the largest single budget category.

Estimated revenues. The budget estimated federal income for fiscal 1973 at $220.8 billion, based on assumptions of a $1.145 trillion gross national product, a 5 percent unemployment rate, a 16 percent increase in corporate profits, and increases in the rate of Social Security taxes from 5.2 percent to 5.4 percent and in the wage base on which the tax is paid from $9,000 to $10,200. These assumptions were more realistic than those of 1972, but the raise in the social security wage base still depended on congressional action.

The budget message revised the contemplated deficit for 1972 to $38.8 billion and estimated the 1973 deficit at $25.5 billion, or less than $1 billion on a full employment basis.

The accuracy of budget estimates. Most outside observers took sharp issue with the budget estimates for 1972, and the record sustained their opinion. In July, the final figures for fiscal 1972 showed that receipts had exceeded the budget estimates by over $10 billion and that spending had been $5 billion less than contemplated. The deficit was $23 billion, or $3.6 billion on a full employment basis. The

THE ACCURACY OF OFFICIAL U.S. BUDGET ESTIMATES[1]
(in billions of dollars)

Fiscal years[2]	Estimates[3]	Realized	Difference
1961	+5.9	−2.3	−8.2
1962	+1.3	−5.8	−7.1
1963	+1.8	−4.0	−5.8
1964	−10.3	−4.8	+5.5
1965	−2.9	−2.7	+0.2
1966	−3.9	−3.3	+0.6
1967	+0.5	−1.5	−2.0
1968	−10.3	−25.1	−14.8
1969	−8.0	+3.2	+11.2
1970	+3.4	−2.8	−6.2
1971	+1.3	−23.0	−24.3
1972	−11.6	−23.0	−11.4

SOURCE: SALOMON BROTHERS

[1] (+) represents surplus, (−) represents deficit
[2] Represents cash budget data from 1961 to 1967 and unified budget after 1967
[3] As estimated in presidents' annual budget messages

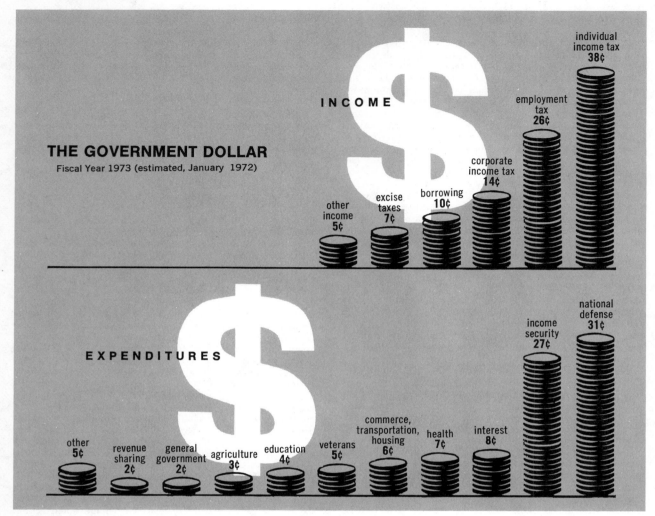

THE GOVERNMENT DOLLAR
Fiscal Year 1973 (estimated, January 1972)

INCOME

other income 5¢
excise taxes 7¢
borrowing 10¢
corporate income tax 14¢
employment tax 26¢
individual income tax 38¢

EXPENDITURES

other 5¢
revenue sharing 2¢
general government 2¢
agriculture 3¢
education 4¢
veterans 5¢
commerce, transportation, housing 6¢
health 7¢
interest 8¢
income security 27¢
national defense 31¢

administration then estimated the deficit for 1973 at $27 billion, but again private economists were skeptical. Believing that the administration would not be able to hold total spending to $250 billion and that Congress would both substantially exceed that amount and hold back increases in the social security base, they estimated the deficit at $35 billion.   HERMAN E. KROOSS

Area and population. Area, 3,615,123 sq. mi. Pop. (est. Aug. 1, 1972), 208,976,000. Principal cities (1970 census): Washington, D.C. (cap.), 765,510; New York, 7,771,730; Chicago, 3,325,263; Los Angeles, 2,782,400; Philadelphia, 1,927,863; Detroit, 1,492,914.

Government. Executive branch. Pres., Richard M. Nixon; vice pres., Spiro T. Agnew. Cabinet: secy. of state, William P. Rogers; secy. of the treasury, George P. Shultz; secy. of defense, Melvin R. Laird; atty. gen., Richard G. Kleindienst; secy. of int., Rogers Morton; secy. of agric., Earl L. Butz; secy. of comm., Peter G. Peterson; secy. of labor, James D. Hodgson; secy. of health, education, and welfare, Elliot L. Richardson; secy. of housing and urban development, George W. Romney; secy. of transportation, John A. Volpe. Judicial branch (U.S. Supreme Court). Chief justice, Warren E. Burger. Associate justices: Harry A. Blackmun, William J. Brennan, Jr., William O. Douglas, Thurgood Marshall, Potter Stewart, Byron R. White, Lewis F. Powell, Jr., and William Rehnquist.

Finance. *See* UNITED STATES: Budget.

Agriculture and industry. Chief agricultural products (est. 1972): corn, 4,947,996,000 bu.; wheat, 1,540,792,000 bu.; cotton, 13,343,000 bales; tobacco, 1,720,270,000 lbs. Livestock (1971): cattle, 40,624,- 656,000 lbs.; swine, 22,927,995,000 lbs. Fuel and power (1970): coal, 599,000,000 tons; crude petroleum, 3,516,000,000 bbl.; natural gas, 22,200,000,000,000 cu. ft.; electricity, 1,644,000,000 kw.-hr.

Trade (1970). Imports, $40 billion; exports, $43.2 billion. Chief exports: machinery, grains and preparation, chemicals, automobiles and parts. Chief imports: petroleum and petroleum products, machinery,

automobiles and parts, metals. Major trading partners: Canada, Japan, West Germany, Mexico, the Netherlands, United Kingdom.

Education (1972). Public day schools, 90,821; elementary, 64,- 539; secondary, 23,972; combined, 2,310. Enrollment (public and private): elementary, 35.9 million; secondary, 14.1 million; institutions of higher learning, 9 million.

Armed forces (est. 1971). Army, 1,107,000; air force, 757,000; navy, 623,000; marines, 212,000.

UPPER VOLTA. Politics and foreign affairs. Upper Volta's new civilian government, still headed by General Sangoulé Lamizana, completed its first full year in an atmosphere of apparent calm.

The year saw major advances in West African cooperation, and Upper Volta played its role. In June, Upper Volta reaffirmed its basic ties with the other former French colonies of West Africa (except Guinea) by joining the new West African Economic Community. The WAEC set up an "organized zone of exchange" for agricultural goods; in addition, it sought to reestablish some degree of mutual cooperation in industrial and trade matters. Most importantly, it planned to establish a preferential tariff system for the region's industrial goods, produced largely in Senegal and the Ivory Coast. Of the poorer interior countries, Upper Volta will probably be the least affected, since it already depends heavily on imported Ivory Coast goods, and the Ivory Coast, in turn, on Voltaic meat and foodstuffs.

Upper Volta also continued to work concretely toward closer cooperation with an English-speaking neighbor, Ghana. An obvious first step was a formal border demarcation.

Upper Volta, Mali, and Niger convened a ministerial-level meeting of the Liptako-Gourma Integrated Development Authority in Ouagadougou in February. The group is seeking multilateral development of the rich copper, manganese, limestone, and phosphate deposits that straddle the region's international frontiers. The major barrier to economic exploitation of these minerals has been the lack of rail transport for heavy products.

Economic developments. While there is a great deal of long-run development potential implicit in these mutual projects, Upper Volta's current economy continued to lag. Cotton and peanut production did not rebound despite improved weather, and the official statistics showed a growing trade deficit and a decline in exports of 6 percent. Moreover, Upper Volta's "invisible" exports of meat and foodstuffs to the Ivory Coast and its income from the earnings of Voltans working abroad dropped with the depression in the Ivorian economy. As if to underline this, President Lamizana stated in November 1971 that the 1972–1973 budget would reflect the austerity that must remain "a rule of conduct as long as domestic resources are less than domestic needs."

Area and population. Area, 105,869 sq. mi. Pop. (est. 1971), 5.5 million. Ouagadougou (cap.; est. 1971), 125,000.

Government. Republic with unicameral parliament. Pres., Sangoulé Lamizana; prime min., Kango Ouédraogo.

Finance. Monetary unit, Communauté Financière Africaine franc; 1 CFA franc = US$0.0041. Budget (est. 1972–1973), 10.82 billion CFA francs.

Trade (1971). Imports: 14.05 billion CFA francs; exports: 4.41 billion CFA francs. Principal exports: livestock, cotton, almonds.

Education (1971–1972). Enrollment: 106,060 in 624 elementary schools; 8,810 in 46 secondary schools; and 1,271 in 12 technical schools.   GEORGE LAMSON

URUGUAY. Politics and government.

Seldom has a Uruguayan chief executive entered office with a more disheartening set of problems than those confronting Juan María Bordaberry, who assumed the presidency on March 1. Most crucial of the tasks facing the wealthy rancher and handpicked heir of former president Jorge Pacheco Areco was how to put an end to urban terrorism—a campaign of kidnapping, killing, and lawlessness led by the Tupamaros, Uruguay's superbly organized guerrilla movement.

During much of the year preceding the presidential election, the Tupamaros had foresworn violence in the hope that a leftist coalition candidate could gain a legitimate victory at the polls. The so-called "Tupamaro truce" persisted for 2½ months after the elections, or up until mid-February 1972. The balloting had been close, and the Tupamaros decided to wait until Bordaberry's slim victory was certified.

Once Bordaberry was officially proclaimed the winner, the Tupamaros swung back to the offensive, commandeering a radio station to proclaim that the truce was over. In April, Tupamaro guerrillas assassinated four people, including two former high-ranking government officials. At Bordaberry's command, the Uruguayan police and armed forces responded, shooting 16 persons, many of whom were just standing in front of a Communist Party headquarters.

Amid the carnage, Bordaberry issued a declaration acknowledging that "a state of internal war" existed. The president also set about making peace with his political opposition to ensure majority support for stiff new law-and-order provisions and for the adoption of urgent measures to revive the Uruguayan economy.

On September 1; government forces wounded and captured Raúl Sendic, widely credited with being the founder of the Tupamaro movement. Sendic's arrest, plus the capture of others reported to be important guerrilla leaders, gave hope that the war on terrorists might be paying off.

Economy. With violence still erupting on the streets, Bordaberry attempted to grapple with the nation's staggering economic problems. The troubles included record budgetary deficits inherited from the previous administration, raging inflation—the price of transportation in Montevideo,

for example, had increased by more than 300 percent annually since 1968—and perhaps worst of all, the sharp decline in beef production, Uruguay's chief export earner.

On June 16, as the Uruguayan economy neared a state of collapse, Bordaberry announced the achievement of a national accord between his administration and enough elements of the defeated Blanco Party opposition to permit legislative action on several drastic economic measures. To bolster the nation's dwindling beef exports, the Bordaberry regime announced an unprecedented four-month ban on all domestic beef sales. The meat ban came as a particular shock to residents of a nation with the world's highest rate of per capita beef consumption. The prohibition, scheduled to last from July 15 to November 15, was expected to free 100,000 tons of beef for export, thereby earning $86 million for 1972 (compared with $56 million earned from 88,000 tons of exports in 1971). The administration also attempted to reopen slaughterhouses and packing plants closed down by skyrocketing production costs. Further, the government acted to halt the massive drives of Uruguayan cattle across the border to Brazilian slaughterhouses. Reliable estimates indicated that at least 250,000 head of Uruguayan cattle were driven across the border in 1971.

Area and population. Area, 72,172 sq. mi. Pop. (est. 1971), 2,900,000. Principal cities (est. 1968): Montevideo (cap.), 1,348,-000; Las Piedras, 90,000

Government. Constitutional republic with bicameral legislature. Pres., Juan María Bordaberry.

Finance. Monetary unit, peso; 1 peso = US$0.00125. Budget (est. 1969): revenue, US$278.8 million; expenditure, US$299.7 million.

Trade (1968). Exports, $179 million; imports, $165 million. Exports (1970), $233 million. Principal exports: wool, meat and meat products. Principal imports: raw materials, fuel and lubricants. Leading trade partners: United States, Brazil, United Kingdom, West Germany.

Education (1968). Enrollment: primary, 318,624; secondary, 189,204; higher, more than 43,000. NATHAN A. HAVERSTOCK

UTAH.

To more than 60 percent of Utah's residents, the death on July 2 of Mormon Church president Joseph Fielding Smith meant a change in their religious leadership for the second time since 1970. Smith died at the age of 95, after succeeding the late David McKay almost three years earlier as the tenth president of the Church of Jesus Christ of Latter Day Saints. The church, with 3 million members worldwide, has been headquartered in Salt Lake City, Utah, since the first Mormon migrations left Illinois over 125 years ago. Smith was a grandson of Hyrum Smith, whose brother, Joseph Smith, organized the church in 1830. The new president is Harold B. Lee, a former teacher and successful businessman.

Crime. Utah was thrust into national headlines when, on April 7, a man commandeered a United Air Lines 727 jetliner and extorted $500,000 from the airline in San Francisco, then parachuted from the plane over Provo. On April 9, a 29-year-old student at Brigham Young University, Richard McCoy, was arrested and charged with the crime. A law enforcement major at BYU and a Vietnam war veteran, McCoy was found guilty and sentenced July 10 to 45 years in a federal penitentiary.

Government. Unexpectedly strong economic trends more than met state government projections for the fiscal year 1972. The state concluded the year with a $17 million general fund surplus. This surplus permitted Governor Calvin L. Rampton to reduce the statewide property tax from 7.2 mills to 4.6 mills. The 2.6 mill decrease, or $2.60 on $1,000 assessed valuation, was applied to the property owners' 1973 tax bill. The surplus resulted from higher than anticipated sales tax and income tax collections.

Legislation. During the legislature's 1972 budget session, the state of Utah for the first time assumed full financial responsibility for state and local school employee retirement contributions. The move is expected to add $10.6 million to state costs next year, and more thereafter.

Medicine. Dr. Willem J. Kolff, professor of surgery and head of the Division of Artificial Organs of the University of Utah College of Medicine, won the $35,000 Harvey Prize. The international recognition was for "pioneering work in the development of artificial organs." Dr. Kolff's twin coil artificial kidney, introduced in 1956, was the first such disposable device available to surgeons and made kidney dialysis possible throughout the world.

Utah Biomedical Test Laboratory, located at the University of Utah's Research Park, was named during 1972 one of the three most outstanding research laboratories built during 1971. The award was made by *Industrial Research* magazine. The facility tests and evaluates artificial hearts and other heart-lung devices.

Sports. The Utah Stars of the American Basketball Association won the league's Western Division by 13 games and advanced to the semifinals of the ABA championships, only to be defeated, four games to three, by the Indiana Pacers. The Pacers proceeded to defeat the New York Nets for the title, succeeding the Stars as ABA champions of the 1970–1971 season.

At the 1972 Olympic Games in Munich, Jay Silvester, an Orem, Utah, resident and BYU faculty member, won the silver medal in the discus, an event in which he is coholder of the world's record.

For election results and campaign highlights, see the special supplement ELECTION '72.

Area and population. Area, 84,916 sq. mi. Pop. (1970 census), 1,059,273. Principal cities (1970 census): Salt Lake City (cap.), 175,885; Ogden, 69,478; Provo, 53,131.
Government. Gov., Calvin L. Rampton (D); secy. of state, Clyde L. Miller (D); atty. gen., Vernon B. Romney (R); aud., Sherman J. Preece (R); treas., Golden L. Allen (R). Legislature: senate, 16 R, 12 D; house, 38 D, 31 R.
Finance (1971–1972). Budget: revenue, $531,561,145.59; expenditure, $526,052,065.45. Principal sources of revenue: sales tax, income tax, property tax, motor fuel tax, and cigarette tax. Main expenditures: education, health and welfare, and highways.
Education (1971–1972). Elementary school enrollment, 183,000. Secondary school enrollment, 144,000. Teachers, 12,000. Private and parochial schools, 25; enrollment, 4,000.

HARRY E. FULLER, JR.

VENEZUELA. The political pot began to boil as Venezuela prepared for the December 1973 presidential elections. During 1972, President Rafael Caldera, who had won his post by taking less than 30 percent of the popular vote, was hard pressed to get the Congress to enact new legislation. Opposition to Caldera mounted as the nation's all-important petroleum production declined while unemployment rose sharply.

Politics and government. In early 1972, Venezuela's two major political parties selected candidates for the following year's elections. The opposition Democratic Action Party selected Carlos Andrés Pérez, a longtime politician and former party chief. The ruling Christian Democrats, whose incumbent president is barred from immediately succeeding himself, chose Lorenzo Fernández, Caldera's former interior minister.

During the year, Venezuela witnessed the emergence of a third party coalition called La Nueva Fuerza (The New Force), comprising diverse leftist factions. The group was in some ways comparable to the Popular Unity coalition through which Chile's Socialist president Salvador Allende achieved power in 1970. The big question, however, as the Venezuelan political campaign kicked off in September, was what role—if any—would be taken by former dictator Marcos Pérez Jiménez, who ruled the country from 1952 to 1958. In the months leading up to the election, it was still unclear whether the Venezuelan government would permit Jiménez' name to appear on the ballot. Although he won a Senate race in absentia during the 1968 elections, Jiménez was prohibited by a technicality from taking his seat in the chamber.

Declining petroleum production. Over the past two years, Venezuela has slipped in its ranking (to fall behind both Saudi Arabia and Iran) among the world's petroleum-producing nations. Several factors have contributed to the decline, including increases in world oil reserves, a drop in demand for Venezuelan oil because of unseasonably warm winters in temperate zones, and Venezuela's decision to take over foreign-owned petroleum concessions—a move that has made foreign investors leery of making further investments in the nation's still substantial petroleum reserves. During the first six months of 1972, Venezuelan oil production—previously accounting for 20 percent of the nation's GNP and providing roughly two-thirds of all government revenues—declined to 3.2 million barrels a day, down nearly 14 percent from a 3.7 million average in 1971. Royal Dutch Shell, an important producer of Venezuelan oil in an industry that had been 98 percent foreign controlled in the past, actually operated in the red during the first quarter of 1972—marking the first time that firm had shown a loss in more than half a century of operations in Venezuela.

As oil revenues have declined, foreign companies have been reluctant to make new investments that would help step up production. Their confidence has been dampened by provisions of Venezuela's Hydrocarbons Reversion Act, passed in December 1971. Under the new law, all foreign-owned petroleum concessions are to revert to state ownership, without compensation, beginning in 1983.

Economic nationalism. Venezuelan officials justified the law in the name of a new policy called democratic nationalism. Backed by widespread popular support for any moves that would end the country's reliance on foreign entrepreneurs, the government has moved toward state control of all key operations in the petroleum, natural gas, and mining sectors. During 1972 the Venezuelan Petroleum Corporation, a governmental body created to take over the petroleum business as foreign concessions are phased out, announced that a Venezuelan tanker fleet will be organized to carry an increasing proportion of Venezuelan oil into world markets.

As the Venezuelan economy enters a transitional period, moving away from an excessive reliance on petroleum, the Venezuelan government is seeking to create new sources of productive wealth both on the farm and in industry. As part of this drive, huge sums have been devoted to the development of potentially fertile lands in the southeast near Ciudad Bolívar. With the help of international development financing agencies, the government has embarked on construction of a giant hydroelectric power complex on the Caroní River. With a projected final capacity of 6 billion kilowatts, the Caroní project has already begun to supply electricity to new industries that are drawing on the Guayana region's substantial resources in iron, bauxite, and other commercial minerals. In developing these resources, the government has stressed the application of the latest advances in science and technology. It has also sought to diversify the sources of its earnings—in tourism, government officials reported a threefold increase in the number of tourists during the 1966–1971 period.

Dispute with Colombia. Venezuela continued to be sorely vexed by its many-faceted dispute with Colombia. During the year, little progress was made in resolving a major sore point: the allocation of oil reserves believed to lie beneath the continental shelf of the Gulf of Venezuela, territory jointly claimed by the two countries. Adding to the dispute was the question of the large-scale illegal movement of Colombians into Venezuelan territory. Conservative estimates indicate that at least 500,000 Colombians now live in Venezuela, having crossed the border in search of the higher wages prevalent in the oil-rich Venezuelan economy. Aroused by exaggerated press accounts, Venezuelans have claimed that the Colombian immigrants are stealing jobs, contributing to depressed wages, and adding to the nation's high crime rate. For their part, Colombians—also partly in-

spired by sensational press reports—have expressed outrage at the treatment being accorded their compatriots living in Venezuela. To make matters worse, both nations—and particularly Venezuela—have been outfitting their armies with expensive new equipment. In 1972, arms outlays by Venezuela included $60 million for French tanks suited to the kind of mountainous operations that might be required along the Colombia-Venezuela border. In recent years, Venezuela is reported to have purchased in excess of $300 million in armaments, including late-model French supersonic fighters. Guyana, another neighbor with whom Venezuela has a territorial dispute, has joined Colombia in voicing alarm over these developments. The arms buildup has also proved worrisome to many Venezuelans, who view the arms purchases as a costly means for shoring up the stability of Venezuelan regimes of whatever party.

Andean Common Market. By late 1972, diplomatic sources in Caracas reported that Venezuela was close to joining the Andean Common Market, an economic alliance comprising Bolivia, Colombia, Ecuador, and Peru. As a preliminary to joining the market, Venezuela—already designated as host nation for the new Andean Development Corporation—terminated its reciprocal trade treaty with the United States.

Area and population. Area, 352,144 sq. mi. Pop. (est. 1970), 10,800,000. Caracas (cap.; including metropolitan area), 2,130,000.
Government. Federal republic with bicameral legislature. Pres., Rafael Caldera.
Finance. Monetary unit, bolívar; 1 bolívar = US$0.228. Budget (1969): balanced at 9.28 billion bolívars.
Trade (1968). Exports, US$2.9 billion; imports, US$1.46 billion. Oil and gas output (1970) averaged a record 3,708,000 barrels a day.
NATHAN A. HAVERSTOCK

VERMONT. Legislation. The Vermont general assembly passed some significant legislation in 1972 in the areas of criminal law, consumer protection, and the environment. One of the acts passed was a revision of the criminal code, providing that offenders be sentenced to the custody of the corrections commissioner and making misdemeanors of offenses calling for penalties of less than five years' imprisonment. Another act strengthened consumer protection, and a separate act mandated the posting of the prices of the 100 most commonly prescribed drugs to permit comparison shopping. The most restrictive legislation in the United States affecting the operation of snowmobiles was enacted, calling for prior written permission by landowners before the snowmobiler can drive over their land. Divorce is now permitted after six months' separation, instead of the earlier two-year requirement. A 4-mill tax was imposed on all containers until July 1, 1973, when nonreturnable malt and soft-drink beverage containers will be banned. A new campaign spending law permits a gubernatorial candidate to spend up to $40,000 in both primary and general election campaigns; other state candidates are permitted to spend $20,000.

Landmark litigation. An unprecedented lawsuit was filed in the U.S. district court at Burlington on June 20. The plaintiff was Florida conglomerateur Glenn W. Turner, and he was suing the state of Vermont, the Council of Better Business Bureaus, and the attorneys general of 26 states on charges of conspiracy to deprive him of his civil and constitutional rights to do business in interstate commerce and conspiracy to put him and his companies out of business. The Turner suit seeks punitive and compensatory damages totaling $567 million.

Economic developments. Although Moody's dropped Vermont's AAA credit rating to AA late in September, a $4 million bond offering a week later attracted a record 37 bids and a 4.7 percent interest rate. Bank deposits (time and demand) as of June 30 reached $1.712 billion, up $200 million over the same period in 1971. Employment in

August was 191,450, up 1.6 percent over the same month a year ago. Unemployment was at the 5.8 percent mark, compared to last year's 5.9 percent.

The 540-megawatt Vermont Yankee nuclear power plant at Vernon in southeastern Vermont went "on line" under a temporary full-power license from the Atomic Energy Commission in October. The virtual doubling of the plant's cost was attributed to two years of delay resulting from environmental opposition, and energy costs were estimated at nearly 14 mills per kilowatt-hour.

Area and population. Area, 9,609 sq. mi. Pop. (1970 census), 444,732. Principal cities: Montpelier (cap.), 8,609; Burlington, 38,-633; Rutland, 19,293; Bennington, 14,586; Brattleboro, 12,239; Barre, 10,209.
Government. Gov., Deane C. Davis (R); lt. gov., John S. Burgess (R); secy. of state, Richard C. Thomas (R); atty. gen., James M. Jeffords (R); treas., Frank H. Davis (R); aud. of accts., Alexander V. Acebo (R). Legislature: senate, 22 R, 8 D; house, 96 R, 54 D.
Finance (fiscal year ending June 30, 1972). Revenue, $301,-621,590; expenditure (including bond sales), $356,859,759. Main sources of revenue: personal income taxes, sales tax, and liquor and tobacco taxes.
Education (1971–1972). Primary schools, 401; enrollment, 71,-133; teachers, 3,153. Secondary schools, 68; enrollment, 45,642; teachers, 3,160.
ROBERT W. SMITH

VETERINARY MEDICINE. Newcastle disease. Early this year, the incidence of Newcastle disease, a viral infection affecting poultry and ornamental birds, reached disaster proportions in eight counties of southern California. The U.S. Department of Agriculture soon decided on a policy of total eradication by slaughter of affected and exposed birds, with indemnity to producers for birds destroyed. From March to August some 4 million laying hens in 105 commercial flocks were killed. Then, in September, the virus was detected on the world's largest egg farm, which has some 2.8 million hens, bringing the total number of chickens, turkeys, ducks, and pet birds affected to more than 8 million. This outbreak was traced to imported birds sold by a pet shop in southern California.

As in previous outbreaks of exotic disease among various animal species in the United States, considerable controversy developed over the merits of total eradication. Most birds destroyed in this outbreak were not known to be affected, and since many had been vaccinated against the disease, only about 15 to 20 percent were expected to die. Mortality in unvaccinated birds is usually 100 percent. At $2 indemnity per bird, the total cost of the operation was expected to exceed $20 million, compared with losses to the poultry industry of perhaps $500 million if the disease had been allowed to run its course.

Disease control programs. The national hog-cholera eradication program reached the point where 46 states had not reported a case of the disease for a year; only New Jersey, Texas, North Carolina, and South Carolina had not been declared cholera-free by late July. An outbreak on two farms in New Jersey involved some 6,000 hogs, for which $482,000 was paid in indemnity. Previously, the disease had cost American hog producers some $50 million annually—about 20 percent of profits. (The cost of vaccination, outlawed since 1970, was the major expense of keeping the disease under reasonable control.) Sporadic outbreaks in several states made it unlikely that the goal of total eradication—set a decade ago for December 1972—would be reached. Even so, more than 99 percent of U.S. swine were in cholera-free states by September.

In February the U.S. Department of Agriculture announced a stepped-up program to eliminate brucellosis from livestock by the end of 1975, five years earlier than originally scheduled. The disease causes abortion in cattle and decreases the productivity of other domestic animals. In man, both the bovine and porcine strains cause undulant fever, an occupational hazard of slaughterhouse workers and

others having contact with infected animals. By midyear 24 states had been declared brucellosis free, but 20 percent of all U.S. cattle were in the three states that had made the least progress—Texas, Nebraska, and Mississippi.

Venezuelan equine encephalomyelitis, which spread to the United States from Mexico in June 1971, affected approximately 3,400 horses (about 1,500 fatally) in Texas. More than 4,000 veterinarians vaccinated some 2.8 million horses in 19 states between June and November—about 95 percent of the horses in these states. In addition, 13.5 million acres of the Gulf coast were sprayed by air to suppress virus-carrying mosquitos. These measures, together with continued vaccination, apparently prevented another outbreak of the disease this year.

Rabies. The problem of bat rabies remained acute in Latin America, where more than 1 million cattle and horses were killed by vampire bats last year. Earlier methods of reducing the bat population by using dynamite and flamethrowers killed beneficial species as well. However, U.S. researchers have recently developed a chemical means of control. An anticoagulant compound smeared on captured bats kills them within 24 hours after they are released, but before they die they transfer the compound to others of their species by physical contact, so that each treated bat kills another 20 to 30. On some Mexican ranches this method has reduced by 97 percent the number of horses and cattle bitten.

Diethylstilbestrol feeding. In August the Food and Drug Administration (FDA) banned the use of the synthetic sex hormone diethylstilbestrol in cattle feeds, the ban to take effect as existing supplies were depleted but not later than January 1, 1973. Large amounts of the hormone, which had been used for about 15 years to promote the growth of beef cattle and to improve meat quality, had produced cancer in laboratory animals. Tissue residues were found in cattle if prescribed withdrawal times were not observed before slaughter. Although these residues have not been demonstrated to cause cancer in persons eating the meat, FDA officials were unwilling to assume there was no risk. Until the ban was announced, about 75 percent of cattle fed for slaughter received the hormone, and it was estimated that its discontinuance might increase the cost of beef by as much as 10 cents a pound. Use of the hormone in the form of pellets implanted under the skin was still permitted.

Computer medicine. Veterinary scientists at Ohio State University, working with dogs, developed a computerized system for diagnosing heart disease. The method, which is applicable to man, involves feeding medical records, together with X-ray and electrocardiographic data, into a computer programmed to sort out diagnostic categories of heart disease.

The first dog in history to receive a cardiac pacemaker recently returned for a five-year checkup at the age of 14. Veterinarians at the University of Pennsylvania had inserted the pacemaker when the dog failed to respond to medical treatment for heart disease.   J. F. SMITHCORS

VIETNAM. While the public peace talks in Paris remained stalemated, a clear breakthrough was scored in secret negotiations between President Richard M. Nixon's adviser for national security, Henry Kissinger, and a member of the North Vietnamese Politburo, Le Duc Tho. This breakthrough, announced by both U.S. and North Vietnamese officials in late October, followed a year of intensified action on the battlefield. Communist forces in March launched their most ambitious offensive since Tet in 1968, and U.S. bombing over all of Indochina reached levels unprecedented in the history of the war.

Peace Talks

Throughout the summer Henry Kissinger and Le Duc Tho met with increasing frequency, spurring speculation by Sep-

tember that an agreement to end the war was imminent. The discussions between Kissinger and Tho were conducted in deep secrecy, leaving the world at large to wonder what progress, if any, was being made. From comments of those closely involved, however, it became apparent that the chief stumbling block was how political power was to be organized in postwar South Vietnam. The United States appeared to want new elections carried out under the aegis of the existing South Vietnamese constitution. The other side seemed to be arguing that this would give South Vietnam's president, Nguyen Van Thieu, too much control over the outcome, even though he had supposedly agreed to step down 30 days before the balloting. They demanded that Thieu be replaced by a three-part (Communist, neutralist, anti-Communist) coalition, which would convene a national assembly that would have the tasks of drawing up a new constitution and holding elections. Washington officials had been criticizing this plan as merely a device to ensure Communist domination of any future Saigon government by ensuring that the so-called neutralist members of the coalition would be sympathetic to the Communist side.

A significant question in the negotiations was the fate of President Thieu, who for five years had been the keystone of U.S. policy in South Vietnam. In late October the North Vietnamese, seemingly reversing a long-held position, hinted that they would accept Thieu as head of the anti-Communist group in a coalition Saigon regime. At the same time Kissinger flew to Saigon for five days of highly secret talks with Thieu, who had run for president in 1971 on a "four no's" policy: no political role for the Communists in South Vietnam, no coalition, no territorial concessions, and no neutralism.

On October 24, one day after Kissinger returned to Washington from Saigon, the New York Times reported that Thieu was preparing a decree, to be released in the event of a bilateral cease-fire agreement between Washington and Hanoi, making it a capital crime in South Vietnam to be a Communist or be associated with Communists. Hanoi subsequently reiterated its insistence that Thieu's resignation accompany any peace agreement.

Just how close the U.S. and North Vietnamese positions were became clear on October 26, when Hanoi disclosed that Kissinger and Tho had agreed on a cease-fire in South Vietnam, withdrawal of U.S. troops within 60 days, and repatriation of foreign civilians and military personnel. About the war in Indochina and the postwar government of South Vietnam the agreement was much less precise—indeed, vague enough for Kissinger to claim, later the same day, that although peace was "at hand," several details remained to be worked out. One crucial provision—South Vietnamese elections in which Communists could participate, supervised by an international commission—aroused Saigon's fiercest rhetoric.

Hanoi claimed that the United States had agreed to sign the agreement by October 31, an assertion disputed by Kissinger. In any case, as the deadline passed, both sides escalated the fighting in an effort to secure as much territory as possible before a cease-fire. Throughout the diplomatic maneuverings of November, it became clear that Saigon, Hanoi, and Washington had placed very different interpretations on what such agreement would mean for the future of South Vietnam.

The War

Communist offensive. Since October 1971 allied officials had been predicting a large North Vietnamese offensive, probably centered on Kontum in the Central Highlands. There was abundant evidence of a buildup of men and supplies in that area. When the attack came, however, it surprised Saigon by its scope and intensity. The first blows came March 30 across the demilitarized zone separating

NAPALM meant for Communist troops was accidentally dropped on South Vietnamese children at Trangbang in June (above). Phan Thi Kim Phuc, at the center of this much publicized photo, was later located and given medical treatment in a Saigon hospital.

the two Vietnams. An estimated 12,500 to 15,000 North Vietnamese troops easily pushed through the inexperienced 3rd Division, which had been strung along the northern front. In less than a week the North Vietnamese had captured the upper half of Quangtri Province. Within a few days two other fronts were opened, one in Binhlong Province, about 80 miles north of Saigon, and one in Kontum Province. The Communist offensive crested in early May with the routing of South Vietnamese forces in the remainder of Quangtri Province and the capture of its capital, Quangtri City. This was the first time in the war that the Saigon government had lost a provincial capital. Elsewhere, the cities of Anloc (in Binhlong Province) and Kontum were subjected to extremely long and violent sieges, but they held.

Credit for the initial successes of the North Vietnamese was given, to a large degree, to their adoption of two new weapons—tanks and heavy artillery. Typically, an assault would open up with a massive barrage from 130-mm. guns, which would be followed by attacks by Soviet-built T-54 tanks and then by infantry. The South Vietnamese, at first, had neither the experience nor the weapons to cope with the tanks and fell back in disarray. However, with the passage of time the South Vietnamese acquired the ability to deal with the tanks. Nor for that matter were the North Vietnamese very proficient in their use. Instead of massing them on the attack, the North Vietnamese would most often send them into action piecemeal, allowing them to be picked off with relative ease. Moreover, the tanks and the large artillery pieces required a sophisticated logistics system that the North Vietnamese found they were unable to sustain under the allied bombing campaign.

Eventually, the South Vietnamese went on the offensive themselves. The encirclements at Anloc and Kontum were broken, and on September 15, Saigon announced that its troops had retaken Quangtri City. (By that time the "city" was completely in ruins as a result of the artillery fire by both sides and the massive U.S. bombing.)

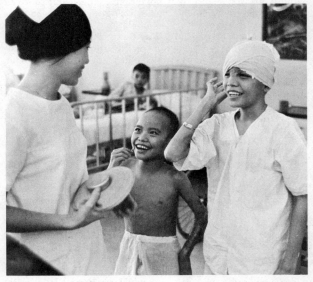

In the fall, the Communists seemed to be concentrating their efforts on trying to envelop and isolate South Vietnam's major cities, notably Saigon and Danang. There was also renewed pressure in the Central Highlands, where several government outposts fell. Although the fortunes of both sides were continually rising and falling in these smaller actions, a slight edge seemed to belong to the Communist forces.

In the Mekong Delta the fighting was never as dramatic as the actions in other parts of the country, but the Com-

EXODUS. As the North Vietnamese hold over Anloc loosened in mid-June and the road to the south was opened to civilians, refugees poured out by the thousands, dodging snipers along the way.

munists also increased their operations. The delta, south of Saigon, is South Vietnam's richest rice-growing area and has more than 40 percent of its population. For several years the region had been regarded as the most pacified in all of South Vietnam. But beginning in the spring, several thousand Communist troops were infiltrated from Cambodia. The result was a general deterioration of security. It is believed that the Communists were more than willing to avoid any large-scale confrontation with the government in the delta while they rebuilt their political infrastructure in expectation of a final negotiated agreement and eventual elections.

The 1972 Communist offensive was costly for both sides. The official figures given in Saigon for the number of men killed during the first six months of the drive were more than 15,000 South Vietnamese troops and about 83,000 North Vietnamese and Vietcong troops. Although these statistics were not regarded as accurate by independent observers, they were seen as a rough measure of the level of combat.

Judged on the purely military criteria of ground seized and casualties inflicted, the Communist offensive was not too successful. However, the Communists almost certainly had other goals which they may feel are even more significant over the long run and which they may have come closer to achieving. These goals probably included the following:

• Disruption of the Saigon government's efforts to extend its control and influence over the countryside (the so-called pacification program). Close to 1 million more refugees, by conservative estimates, were added as a result of the offensive to the government's already severely taxed relief rolls.

• Demonstration to the American and South Vietnamese people, both wearied by years of conflict, that the Com-

munists retained the ability to mount a powerful military threat. By this demonstration the Communists apparently sought to influence the attitudes of Washington and Saigon toward the peace negotiations.

• Decimation of the elite of the South Vietnamese combat force, the so-called strategic reserve of marines, paratroopers, and rangers. These troops are an important element in the vital military support for President Thieu.

• Disruption of the South Vietnamese economy, already weakened by the loss of millions of dollars in spending by U.S. servicemen.

North Vietnamese officials professed to see the offensive as an unqualified success that would destroy President Nixon's policy of Vietnamization and hasten the ouster of President Thieu. (In October, U.S. advisers began a retraining program for the entire South Vietnamese Army, a move which some observers interpreted as a tacit admission that Vietnamization was at least a partial failure.)

Little effort was made, in contrast to previous years, to conceal the fact that North Vietnamese forces were fighting in the South, a policy shift which may have been intended to dilute the position of the National Liberation Front.

U.S. response. President Nixon's response to the Communist offensive was to order an immediate removal of the four-year-old restrictions on U.S. bombing of North Vietnam. Once again, as in 1967 and 1968, American planes roamed widely over the North, striking at transportation systems and manufacturing facilities. Nixon went on national television to explain his decision to the American people. "All that we have risked and all that we have gained over the years now hangs in the balance," he maintained, and he declared that "we will not be defeated, and we will never surrender our friends to Communist aggression." The speech brought strong criticism from congressional foes of the president's war policy. Senator J. W. Fulbright (D, Ark.), chairman of the Senate Foreign Relations Committee, said his reaction to the speech was "one of acute depression and sadness for our country, that after all these years of destruction of life and property, there is no end to this epic tragedy in sight."

On May 8, after the fall of Quangtri Province, Nixon went a step further and ordered the mining of the sea approaches to North Vietnam in an attempt to prevent further shipments of military supplies. But the mining of North Vietnamese waters did not completely seal off North Vietnam. Movement of matériel by rail from China was increased, and the North Vietnamese were also able to bring in supplies by small lighters from Chinese freighters anchored just outside the areas where the mines were strewn. Supplies from the Chinese ships were also put into buoyant plastic containers, which were then dumped into the sea to be floated ashore by the tide. The Soviet Union reportedly resorted to an airlift to ferry in some of the larger items needed by the North Vietnamese. U.S. military authorities in Saigon estimated in early fall that North Vietnam was getting at least 25 percent of the quantity of supplies it had been receiving prior to resumption of full-scale bombing.

As it had frequently done in the past, North Vietnam charged that U.S. planes were attacking civilian targets, such as schools and hospitals. In early spring it also revived the accusation that the United States was attempting to destroy the intricate system of dikes that held back North Vietnam's powerful rivers from its farming and population centers. Similar charges were made by Westerners who were permitted to travel in the North at the time. Pentagon spokesmen denied that the dikes were being targeted as a matter of policy. They acknowledged the possibility that some could have been hit either by accident or, if antiaircraft weapons were emplaced on them, when U.S. planes attacked those emplacements. The period of greatest flood

danger was the rainy season from July to September. Those months passed without flooding.

On October 11 an American bomb, which U.S. officials later were to say misfired, wrecked the building of the French diplomatic mission in Hanoi and fatally injured the mission chief, Pierre Susini.

Many observers felt that U.S. air strikes against North Vietnam and in support of South Vietnamese ground troops were decisive in blunting the Communists' spring offensive. In the first eight months of 1972, American planes dropped 800,000 tons of bombs throughout Indochina. This figure surpassed the total for all of 1971 and was well on its way to becoming a record for any one year in the war. Official cumulative figures showed that from February 1965 to the end of August 1972 American planes had dropped more than 7.5 million tons of explosives—about 3½ times the tonnage expended in World War II by all the allies in all theaters of that war.

U.S. ground combat ended. The combat role for U.S. ground troops in Vietnam was formally ended on August 12 in a low-key ceremony at Danang. There the colors of the 3rd Battalion of the 21st Infantry were furled. President Lyndon B. Johnson had first committed U.S. troops to combat in South Vietnam in 1965.

The end of the U.S. combat role did not mean an end to all risks for the remaining American servicemen in Vietnam. Thousands were still assigned to such potentially dangerous jobs as providing base security at Longbinh or advising South Vietnamese ground combat units. However, the biggest contingent of Americans remaining—about 12,000 men—was assigned to largely technical tasks connected with air operations against Communist forces inside South Vietnam.

The reduction of U.S. personnel inside South Vietnam (the total was to be down to 27,000 by December 1) continued throughout the year, but a buildup of units of the Seventh Fleet offshore and of air squadrons based in Thailand brought an overall increase in the number of U.S. military personnel in the Indochina area. Some 39,000 men were assigned to the U.S. armada in the South China Sea, and between 40,000 and 50,000 U.S. servicemen were stationed in Thailand.

Nature of Communist rule. There were indications that Communist rule in the areas occupied during 1972 was considerably less harsh than it had been in similar circumstances during the Tet offensive of 1968. In the earlier period, the Communists had carried out thousands of political executions, especially in the area around the old imperial capital of Hué. Those executions and similar campaigns in other eras of Communist ascendancy had created in South Vietnam and in the U.S. government a fear of what President Nixon called a "bloodbath" should the Communists ever gain power in Saigon. This fear had been questioned by some as historically unjustified, and many observers felt that the Communists themselves had come to regard their actions in 1968 as a mistake which hardened opposition to them even among those who were against the regime of President Thieu. Therefore, the experience of Communist rule during 1972 in Binhdinh Province, located along the central coast, was studied carefully.

The northern area of the province, around the district town of Bongson, was under the undisputed control of the Communists for a three-month period from late April to late July. The area is estimated to contain about 200,000 people, most of them farmers. The Communists took over administration of the hamlets and villages with meticulous thoroughness, imposing a tightly regimented rule involving restricted travel, forced labor, high taxes, and compulsory political indoctrination. There were executions, according to civilians who lived through the period, of local

BOMBING THE NORTH. This photo, released by Communist sources, allegedly shows the aftermath of American bombing of Haiphong harbor in April; the ship at left was said to be a Soviet vessel. President Nixon further extended the bombing of North Vietnam on May 8.

officials identified with the government in Saigon (estimates of the number killed ranged from 250 to 500). But there was apparently nothing like the wholesale slaughter that had characterized the 1968 offensive. There were also reports that several thousand persons had been taken to indoctrination centers in the Communist stronghold in the Anlao Valley to the northeast of the province. These reports, however, were not confirmed.

Abrams departs. In June, General Creighton W. Abrams ended five years of service in Vietnam, four of them as U.S. commander there. He returned to Washington to become army chief of staff. During his years in Vietnam, General Abrams had presided over the reversal of U.S. military policy. He was assigned the decidedly difficult task of directing the safe withdrawal of some 500,000 men from an area still wracked by fighting.

Prior to the 1972 Communist offensive General Abrams was known to believe that the South Vietnamese armed forces had developed to the point where they could hold their own in any battle with the Communists. He was said to have dropped that opinion after the disasters of the spring, when only U.S. air power was able to blunt the offensive. The general was also reportedly embarrassed by the failure of his own intelligence staff, despite the array of electronic gadgetry available to it, to predict the scope and power of the spring offensive.

Unauthorized bombing. The last months of General Abrams' tour were marked by a major scandal. It became known that his deputy for air operations, General John D. Lavelle, had ordered unauthorized bombing raids on North Vietnam during late 1971 and early 1972, in violation of the guidelines laid down by civilian leaders in Washington. General Lavelle had also required his subordinates to falsify their after-action reports to conceal what he had done.

When this became known, Lavelle was fired from his job and demoted from four-star to three-star general. But he was then allowed to retire at a full general's pension, which was supplemented by 70 percent disability benefits, giving Lavelle an annual income of $27,000, of which $24,100 is tax free. An air force lieutenant brought court-martial charges against Lavelle, but on October 24, Secretary of the Air Force Robert Seamans, Jr., said that Lavelle would not be court-martialed and that no further action against him was planned. No action was taken against any of the pilots who made the unauthorized raids.

Vann dies. An American who in a decade of service in South Vietnam, in both military and civilian capacities, had achieved a powerful role in shaping U.S. policies there was killed June 9 when his helicopter went down at night during a flight between Pleiku and Kontum. The official, John Paul Vann, 47, was regarded at the time of his death as the third most important member of the American mission in South Vietnam—despite his seemingly subordinate position as chief civilian adviser to the Second Military Region.

Operation Sherwood Forest. It was disclosed in July that in 1966 and 1967 U.S. forces in Vietnam attempted to destroy by fire large patches of South Vietnam's tropical forests. The object of these operations, code-named Sherwood Forest and Pink Rose, was to deny cover to Vietcong and North Vietnamese troops. A Pentagon spokesman denied allegations that any attempt had been made to create fire storms such as had been touched off during World War II in the German cities of Dresden and Hamburg; those storms caused the deaths of hundreds of thousands of civilians.

The experiment in South Vietnam failed because even in the dry season the trees stayed too damp to burn. But whatever the outcome, it was another addition to the list of controversial efforts by the U.S. military to manipulate the environment in South Vietnam and the rest of Indochina for tactical purposes. Other efforts included chemical defoliation, artificial rainmaking, and the plowing of forests.

South Vietnam

Erosion of democracy. President Thieu tried to increase his personal power considerably and thereby further weakened South Vietnam's democratic institutions. He justified his moves by pointing to the magnitude of the Communists' military threat and the prospect of a negotiated settlement, which he alleged would pit an efficient Communist political organization against the myriad political factions in the South. On August 11 he gave a speech in Quinhon which seemed to sum up his attitude. "In the South here," he said, "our political parties are small and disunited, we are too complacent, and most important, our democracy is disorderly, it presents many gaps."

To close those so-called gaps, Thieu took several steps: He declared a state of martial law, giving the national police force authority to arrest thousands of suspected Communists or Communist sympathizers. He pushed a bill through the National Assembly which permitted him to rule by decree in the national security and economic fields. He abolished election of officials in hamlets and villages, the nation's most basic levels of government, allegedly because these units had been found to be infiltrated by Communists. He put most common crimes under the jurisdiction of military courts and stiffened the penalties for them. He compelled newspapers to post $47,000 bonds, thereby forcing the closing of 14 of South Vietnam's 41 daily newspapers. He dismissed a number of top commanders who performed badly during the Communist offensive, thereby greatly increasing his personal control of the military establishment.

Thieu's opposition, largely rooted in the old Vietnamese nationalistic parties and in one of the Buddhist groups, was helpless to challenge Thieu's growing power.

Inflation and unemployment. The economy of South Vietnam experienced a troubled year. South Vietnam had already been suffering from unemployment because of the great reduction in the number of U.S. military bases. The Communist offensive, besides vastly increasing the number of refugees dependent on government aid, raised havoc with the distribution system. Rice, once South Vietnam's leading export, rose in price more than 50 percent in some areas. Officials anticipated having to import between 100,000 and 200,000 tons of rice before the year was out, despite a domestic crop which was said to be one of the best ever. There was also a sharp decline in the output of crude rubber, South Vietnam's second best money earner. The decline occurred primarily because many of the rubber plantations are in the area around Locninh and Anloc, the scene of heavy fighting in the late spring.

Total government spending during 1972 was estimated at $840 million. With government tax revenue and U.S. aid able to supply only about three-quarters of that sum, Saigon borrowed from the National Bank to make up the deficit; in other words, it simply printed more money, a step which greatly increased the rate of inflation. A deficit similar in size to 1972's was envisioned in the Thieu government's $1 billion budget proposed for 1973. The largest allocation—more than 64 percent—was to be for the war and national security. In contrast, education would get 6 percent and social welfare 4.9 percent of the budget in 1973.

Area and population. Area, 67,108 sq. mi. Pop. (est. 1971), 18.3 million. Saigon (cap.; est. 1966), 2 million.
Government. Constitutional republic with bicameral National Assembly. Pres., Nguyen Van Thieu.
Finance. Monetary unit, piaster; 1 piaster = US$0.0025.

North Vietnam

War effort. The government of North Vietnam admitted an unusually high number of Western correspondents, especially Americans, during the year. They all reported finding hard-working people resolutely going about their tasks in the face of the most intensive bombing campaign in the history of warfare.

The correspondents also reported that they had been impressed by the seemingly endless movement of supplies to the war front. They said this movement was carried out by a variety of means, some of them simple, some of them ingenious. Truck traffic moved largely at night to lessen the risk of air attack, the trucks being pulled off to the side of the road under the cover of trees during the day. Great stocks of supplies were said to be stored along every roadway, to be moved south in a shuttle system. Frequently, a pontoon bridge would be used during darkness at key crossings and then floated away before dawn to give U.S. reconnaissance planes a picture of a bridge that remained bombed out.

The correspondents reported that there seemed to be an adequate supply of basic consumer goods. However, North Vietnamese officials publicly complained about the prevalence of black market activities and warned that black market operators would be severely punished. North Vietnam was also suffering from a great manpower shortage despite a mobilization decree shortly after the spring offensive began.

Political developments. Two men were appointed this year to fill long-standing vacancies on the 11-member Politburo of the Lao Dong (Workers) Party. Named were Tran Quoc Hoan, the minister of public security, and General Van Tien Dun, chief of staff of the armed forces. There were conflicting interpretations of the import of these choices. One group of observers believed the promotions represented no more than a recognition of the growing role of technicians in the governing of North Vietnam. There was another line of thought which saw the appointments as one manifestation of a policy debate over Hanoi's fundamental strategy. In this view, the appointment of General Dun represented a dilution of the position of Defense Minister Vo Nguyen Giap as North Vietnam's leading authority on military affairs. Giap had gained world fame as the conqueror of the French at Dienbienphu in 1954. He is also generally regarded as the advocate of the so-called decisive battles of 1968 and 1972.

Oblique criticism of this strategy as reckless and costly appeared during the year in the theoretical journal *Tuyen Hoan.* The articles' main thesis was that support for the war in the South must not come at the risk of the socialist development of the North. The primary responsibility for defeating the U.S. forces and the Thieu regime, the articles asserted, lies with the insurgent forces in the South. *Tuyen Hoan* seemed to be preparing its readers for the possibility of North Vietnam's cutting back on the extent of its involvement in the war in order to devote its resources and energy to building up the socialist system at home. The North Vietnamese official most identified with this "dovish" approach was Truong Chinh, a Politburo member and long one of the party's leading theoreticians.

Pilots released. The North Vietnamese released three U.S. pilots to a group of American antiwar activists in September. The three were navy lieutenants Norris A. Charles and Mark L. Gartley and air force major Edward K. Elias. Elias and Charles had been prisoners of war only a few months, but Gartley had been held since August 1968. The three men accepted as a condition of their freedom that they return to the United States on commercial airline flights, not on a U.S. military plane. At various stopovers en route to New York, the antiwar group—the Committee of Liaison—held press conferences in which President Nixon's Vietnam policy was attacked.

Upon their arrival in New York the three pilots were met —before they left the plane—by U.S. military officials who told them they were to be sent immediately to military hospitals. Gartley's mother, in tears, protested that "we just want him to ourselves for a few days," and Gartley, obviously irritated, told the officials, "You may have pushed this a little too far." In an airport press conference, David Dellinger, who cochairs the liaison committee, claimed that

the pilots had been promised by U.S. officials in Europe that they could speak with the press in New York; he also claimed that the U.S. military's actions jeopardized further prisoner releases.

Area and population. Area, 61,294 sq. mi. Pop. (est. 1971), 21.6 million. Hanoi (cap.; est. 1966), 644,000.
Government. People's republic. Pres., Ton Duc Thang; prem., Pham Van Dong; Communist Party first secy., Le Duan.
Finance. Monetary unit, dong; 1 dong = US$0.3175.

JOHN SHARKEY

VIRGINIA. Legislation. Governor A. Linwood Holton convened the general assembly on January 12 for its first regular biennial 60-day session under Virginia's newly adopted state constitution. In alternate years the assembly will meet in regular 30-day sessions, primarily to deal with interim fiscal matters. A record $5.036 billion budget was adopted for 1972–1974. The major tax increase was a two-cents-per-gallon additional motor fuel tax, estimated to raise an extra $103 million for the state's 1,400-mile network of arterial highways.

The general assembly gave financial assistance to local governments by assuming in a $140.6 million budget item the full burden of payments for major categories of welfare, previously borne partially by city and county governments. Local governments were also granted authority to levy service charges against tax-exempt properties, other than churches and parsonages, for fire, police, and trash collection services.

Full voting rights were granted to 18-year-olds, and the legal age of majority for purposes of assuming financial obligations and performing other legal actions was also lowered from 21 to 18. Sexual sterilization laws for males and females were liberalized. A reorganization of state administration, permissive in nature, was authorized, to permit installation of a six-member cabinet of secretaries in the governor's office.

In September the Virginia supreme court of appeals ruled unconstitutional a tuition grant plan under which the general assembly had hoped to give aid to students attending the state's private colleges.

Floods. The most extensive flooding ever recorded in Virginia's major river basins followed the passage over the Appalachian highlands June 19 and 20 of tropical storm Agnes. Floodwaters crested at 36.5 feet on June 22 at the city locks on the James River in Richmond, the highest in 200 years. Richmond's water and sewage treatment plants were inundated, and U.S. Army and National Guard troops assisted in hauling fresh water to Richmond and maintaining damage control. State government operations not of an emergency nature were suspended for three days because flood waters knocked out the electrical substation that powers Capitol Hill. Fredericksburg on the Rappahannock River, sections of Alexandria, Arlington, and Fairfax County, and dozens of smaller communities along streams throughout northern and central Virginia were hard hit. Interstate highway 95 was blocked at two points. State damages were estimated at more than $200 million, including $16.2 million in Richmond, and the loss of 17 lives was attributed to the floods.

On the night of September 2, a combination of the highest tides of the fall season and a surprise northeastern storm caused extensive flood damage in the Hampton Roads area cities of Norfolk, Newport News, Hampton, and Virginia Beach. An oceangoing tugboat and barge, seeking shelter from the storm in Chesapeake Bay, were blown into the Chesapeake Bay Bridge-Tunnel, and the only direct transportation link between mainland Virginia and its two eastern shore counties was severed. The U.S. Navy provided emergency ferry service while repairs were made.

In early October heavy rains again caused extensive flooding in central Virginia. This time the James River crested

at 28 feet, 19 feet above flood level. Damages were in excess of $19 million, and at least six lives were lost.

History and culture. Archaeologists from the College of William and Mary in Williamsburg, using clues found in English colonial records, discovered the site of Flowerdew Hundred Plantation, an early 17th-century settlement. The first excavation yielded clues that pointed to a probable construction date of 1620. The town's site is Windmill Point, on the western side of the James River in Prince George County, upstream from Jamestown.

For election results and campaign highlights, see the special supplement ELECTION '72.

Area and population. Area, 40,817 sq. mi. Pop. (1970), 4,648,-494. Principal cities: Richmond (cap.), 249,621; Norfolk, 307,951; Arlington, 174,284; Virginia Beach, 172,106; Newport News, 138,177; Hampton, 120,779; Alexandria, 110,938.
Government. Gov., A. Linwood Holton (R); lt. gov., Henry E. Howell, Jr. (ind.); atty. gen., Andrew P. Miller (D); treas., Walter W. Craigie, Jr. (R); cont., David B. Ayers, Jr. (R); speaker of the house, John Warren Cooke (D). Legislature: senate, 33 D, 7 R; house, 74 D, 23 R, 3 ind.
Finance (1972–1974 biennium). Balanced budget of $5,036,-133,570. Principal sources of revenue: sales tax, income tax, motor fuel taxes. Principal expenditures: public education, health and welfare services, highways.
Education (spring 1971). Elementary and special schools, kindergarten through grade 7: enrollment, 708,619; teachers, 29,549. Secondary schools: enrollment, 404,509; teachers, 21,753.

WILLIAM R. SAUDER

WASHINGTON. Politics and government. On January 10, Governor Daniel J. Evans (R) convened a second special session of the 42nd legislature. Lawmakers agreed to devote the first two weeks to drawing the new district boundaries which a federal court had ordered completed by February 25. But Republican and Democratic leaders failed to reach agreement, and the legislature adjourned on February 22, leaving the problem to the federal court. The court appointed Richard Morrill, a University of Washington geography professor, to draw up a reapportionment plan, which was made effective in April. Senate Democrats and the Washington State Labor Council appealed unsuccessfully for a stay of the plan, pending review by the federal courts. On October 10 the U.S. Supreme Court unanimously and without comment let stand the U.S. district court's reapportionment of legislative and congressional districts.

Governor Evans presented the legislature with a program for economic recovery, designed to provide immediate jobs for the 10 percent of the work force still unemployed as of January, and then 20,000 new jobs each year for ten years. He requested an increase in the gasoline tax and a $500 million package of bond issues to help finance the program with the aid of local and federal matching funds. The legislature approved the overall plan, but cut the bond package by $95 million and threw out the gasoline tax, stipulating instead that the plan be funded largely with general fund surplus revenue when it should reach a stated sum. Legislators then tacked on a $50 million bond issue to finance community college construction. A supplemental appropriation of $87.5 million, about $6.5 million more than the governor had requested, was passed, with no accompanying increase in taxes. The new appropriations included $19.5 million to maintain state support for schools and $9.7 million to cover a 3 percent cost-of-living increase for public employees.

In other legislation, referendum bills were passed to regulate lobbyists and campaign expenditures, and a revision of the public employees retirement plan increased benefits by 15 to 20 percent and gave women the same retirement benefits as men. Women also benefited from a measure giving equal rights to both husband and wife in most areas of property management and from a constitutional amendment prohibiting discrimination by sex.

Economic developments. Many sectors of the economy were enjoying a normal growth rate by June. The Boeing Company added 2,000 workers, raising its work force to over 39,000, with an increase of several thousand more likely by the year's end. Employment and production also rose in the machinery, fabricated metals, aluminum, wood products, truck, railcar, and shipbuilding industries. Both residential and nonresidential construction gained, retail sales increased in the large cities, and foreign trade totaled more than $2.5 billion through July, an increase of 16.5 percent over the same period in 1971. But although personal income showed an 8.3 percent increase over 1971, the statewide unemployment rate was a disquieting 8.7 percent.

Municipal developments. Construction began on Expo '74, the international exposition on the environment scheduled to open in Spokane on May 1, 1974, to coincide with the city's centennial celebration. The $60 million project was to transform a blighted downtown area along the Spokane River into a 100-acre park and cultural center.

For election results and campaign highlights, see the special supplement ELECTION '72.

Area and population. Area, 68,192 sq. mi. Pop. (1970), 3,409,-169. Principal cities: Olympia (cap.), 23,111; Seattle, 530,831; Spokane, 170,516; Tacoma, 154,581.
Government. Gov., Daniel J. Evans (R); lt. gov., John A. Cherberg (D); atty. gen., Slade Gorton (R); secy. of state, A. Ludlow Kramer (R). Legislature: senate, 29 D, 20 R; house, 51 R, 48 D.
Finances (1971). Revenue, $2,185,468,000; expenditure, $2,475,-307,000.
Education (October 1971). Elementary schools: enrollment, 427,-401; teachers, 15,998. Secondary schools: enrollment, 377,648; teachers, 15,991.

HAZEL EMERY MILLS

WASHINGTON, D.C. Education. A strike of schoolteachers closed the city school system for two weeks in September. The strike was settled when school officials agreed to higher pay, the providing of additional supplies, and the hiring of additional personnel whose posts had been dropped from the city budget. The strike was conducted by the Washington Teachers Union, part of the AFL-CIO, which represents about 3,600 of the city's 7,000 teachers. Congress subsequently granted the teachers a 12 percent pay increase, raising some taxes to provide the needed money.

Financial problems continued to plague the school system during the year. A congressional committee found that the schools had illegally overspent their budget. Slashes in the current budget led to the teachers' strike. The school administration warned that $10 million would have to be cut from the budget for the 1973–1974 fiscal year unless more income were provided.

As the fall term opened, the city opened its first "tower" school, the eight-story Woodson High School. School Superintendent Hugh J. Scott, who often has clashed with the city's elected school board, hinted that he may leave his post in 1973.

Prisons. Several days after eight prisoners, some of them accused or convicted murderers, broke out of the century-old Washington, D.C., jail, about 50 convicts gained control of a cellblock there. They lured Kenneth J. Hardy, the city's director of corrections, into the prison on the pretext of negotiating demands, then kept him and 11 guards hostage for 22 hours. After making threats on Hardy's life, they ended the uprising and freed him when a judge agreed to hear their grievances.

The city's other penal institution, a reformatory at nearby Lorton, Va., was the scene of several escapes and a five-day work stoppage by inmates in prison workshops. Hardy granted the prisoners' demands for better food and living conditions.

Transportation. Congress voted full financing of the region's 98-mile Metro rapid transit system, assuring its completion by 1979. Construction was under way on 15 miles of line, mainly subway in the downtown area.

Congress also authorized the Metro transit agency to acquire the region's four privately owned bus companies,

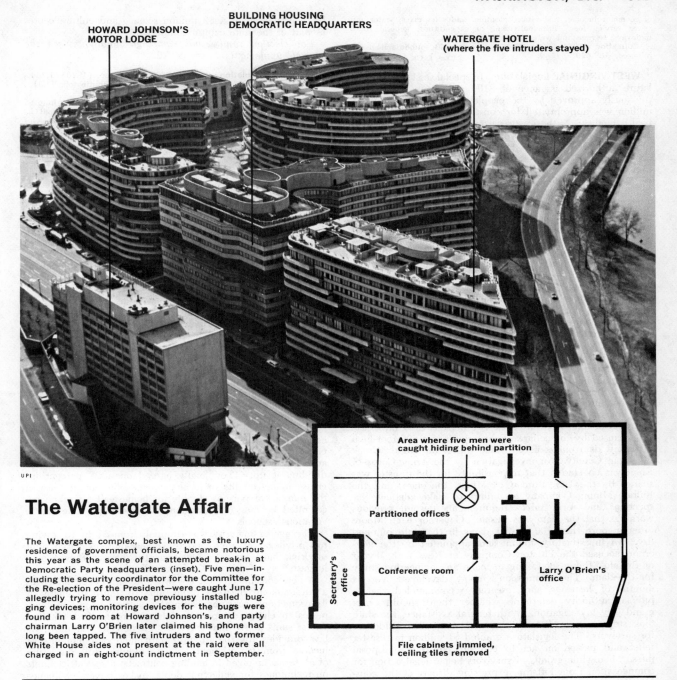

HOWARD JOHNSON'S
MOTOR LODGE

BUILDING HOUSING
DEMOCRATIC HEADQUARTERS

WATERGATE HOTEL
(where the five intruders stayed)

UPI

Area where five men were
caught hiding behind partition

Partitioned offices

Secretary's
office

Conference room

Larry O'Brien's
office

File cabinets jimmied,
ceiling tiles removed

The Watergate Affair

The Watergate complex, best known as the luxury residence of government officials, became notorious this year as the scene of an attempted break-in at Democratic Party headquarters (inset). Five men—including the security coordinator for the Committee for the Re-election of the President—were caught June 17 allegedly trying to remove previously installed bugging devices; monitoring devices for the bugs were found in a room at Howard Johnson's, and party chairman Larry O'Brien later claimed his phone had long been tapped. The five intruders and two former White House aides not present at the raid were all charged in an eight-count indictment in September.

which have experienced sharp declines in riding as rising costs forced fare increases.

Government. Representative John L. McMillan (D, S.C.), longtime chairman of the House D.C. Committee and a conservative influence in city affairs, was defeated for renomination to Congress. President Nixon appointed John Nevius to replace Gilbert Hahn, Jr., as chairman of the appointive City Council, which had six Republicans (the legal maximum) and three Democrats as members.

Congress authorized the construction of a convention hall as a memorial to former president Dwight D. Eisenhower and approved the redevelopment of Pennsylvania Avenue between the Capitol and the White House. The city's glass-

walled Martin Luther King Memorial Library, built downtown at a cost of $18 million, was opened to the public.

Other developments. The Washington *Evening Star* bought out the Washington *Daily News*, an afternoon tabloid newspaper. Under the name *Evening Star-News*, the merged newspaper reported substantial circulation gains.

Hurricane Agnes struck in June, causing significant damage, mainly in the Virginia suburbs, and the loss of at least ten lives in the area.

Area and population. Area, 69 sq. mi. Pop. (1970), 756,510.
Government. Mayor comm., Walter E. Washington; deputy mayor comm., Graham W. Watt; city council chmn., John Nevius.
Finance (fiscal 1973). Budget, $833,800,000. Principal sources

of revenue: income, real estate, gasoline, and sales taxes; water and sewer service fees. Principal items of expenditure: general fund, highways, sewage and water facilities.

Education (1971–1972). Public schools, 163; public school enrollment, 139,629.   JACK E. EISEN

WEST VIRGINIA. Legislation. In special session, the legislature authorized issuance of $100 million in road bonds previously approved by the people. In regular session, $6 million was appropriated for construction of a new mental health facility. Authority was extended for construction of 14 community mental health centers and eight mental retardation centers in a long-range program. An unusual new act provides for oil and gas exploration at very deep levels under the earth. Land and mineral interests are to be pooled for the drilling of wells that go below 6,000 feet, some as deep as 22,000 feet.

The legislature failed once again to reapportion itself as required by recent federal court decisions. This year the house and senate functioned in violation of federal court guidelines for equal representation. Major bills rejected by the legislature, but certain to come up again, provided for strip mine abolition, no-fault automobile insurance, consumer protection, unionization of public employees, dog racing, and bonuses for Vietnam veterans.

Economic developments. A sharp decline in coal production, mainstay of the state's economy, marred a generally favorable picture. Through the first seven months of the year, production was off 12.7 percent, compared to the same period the previous year. Sporadic wildcat strikes and tightening of safety and environmental requirements hindered the industry's efforts. Average weekly earnings in the industry climbed 10 percent. Electric power production was up 26.8 percent, the largest increase among the state's economic indicators. Unemployment was generally higher than last year and stood at 6.8 percent in mid-August.

Industrial disaster. At least 107 persons died in a flash flood caused by the collapse February 26 of a 200-foot-high makeshift dam made of coal mine wastes on Buffalo Creek in Logan County. An investigation by the Army Corps of Engineers concluded that responsibility for the disaster was shared by the U.S. Bureau of Mines, the state, and the Buffalo Mining Company for failure to make adequate inspections and meet safety requirements despite previous warnings that the dam was unsafe. Governor Arch Moore ordered more than 100 similar dams in the state pumped dry. An investigatory commission, appointed by the governor, accused the Pittston Company of New York, owner of Buffalo Mining, of failing to make an engineering study for the dam. The commission's report, developed over six months of hearings and research, recommended that a judicial authority determine whether there should be a grand jury investigation. With federal assistance, the state took steps to provide mobile homes and other residences for survivors. The legislature granted $1 million in disaster relief and passed an act to control coal refuse disposal piles. Meanwhile groups of survivors began legal action for compensation from Pittston, expressing dismay at the company's tardiness in meeting their claims and anger that it continued to operate while they went unpaid for the losses caused by the disaster.

Education and culture. A full-scale public kindergarten program was launched with the help of $3.5 million in new financing by the state. About 30,000 five-year-old children are eligible under the program. Approximately 40,000 employees of county boards of education and higher education institutions were brought under a new major medical and life insurance program. The state pays 70 percent of the entire cost, and employees contribute 30 percent.

Charleston philanthropist William J. Maier, Jr., announced that a family foundation will give about $2 million for a health education center, to be established in Charleston as an affiliate of West Virginia University. Plans proceeded

for construction of a $9 million science and culture center as part of the state capitol complex.

For election results and campaign highlights, see the special supplement ELECTION '72.

Area and population. Area, 24,282 sq. mi. Pop. (1970), 1,744,-237. Principal cities: Charleston (cap.), 71,505; Huntington, 74,315; Wheeling, 48,188.

Government. Gov., Arch A. Moore, Jr. (R); secy. of state, John D. Rockefeller IV (D); treas., John H. Kelly (D); aud., Denzil L. Gainer (D); atty. gen., Chauncey Browning, Jr.; agric. comm., Gus R. Douglass (D). Legislature: senate, 23 D, 11 R; house, 68 D, 32 R.

Finance (fiscal 1972). Budget: $884,845,986, including $372,-032,207 in general revenue, $469,373,948 in state road funds. Expenditures, $795,803,910.

Education (1971). Public elementary schools, 967; pupils, 236,-559; teachers, 10,151. Public secondary schools, 341; pupils, 181,-829; teachers, 8,529. Private and parochial schools, 58; pupils, 11,-018; teachers, 629.   JOHN G. MORGAN

WISCONSIN. Politics and government. The state legislature, having practically knocked itself out last year in an unprecedentedly long budget battle, was content to meet for a two-month session, from mid-January to mid-March, to review budget activities and pass a small number of significant bills, then wind things up with a special three-day session in April.

Legislators had heard numerous protests from the folks back home after corporation and personal income taxes were raised in 1971 to pay for the record $2 billion state budget covering the two-year period ending June 30, 1973, so they were pleasantly surprised to find, when they reconvened in January, that the state was getting $34 million more revenue than it had expected. This disclosure, however, also generated more protests. Several groups of farmers and rural taxpayers voted to withhold their property taxes, and more than 1,000 protesters showed up at the state house demanding tax relief.

The result of such actions was a budget review that allocated nearly $38 million to property tax relief, with Democratic governor Patrick J. Lucey and the Republican senate and Democratic assembly jockeying over the details of dividing it up. They finally agreed on a 27 percent increase in tax credits to local property bills, an increase in the number of persons eligible for homestead tax relief, accelerated business depreciation, and increased state aid to vocational schools.

The age of majority was dropped from 21 to 18, giving full privileges of adulthood to 18-year-olds—even the right to drink hard liquor, which was the barrier fought over longest.

A new consumer credit law was put into effect, hailed as a landmark in consumer protection. In return for many of its protections, consumer supporters agreed to permit businesses to charge 18 percent interest on the first $500 of debts; sums above that pay only 12 percent interest. The law provides for the exemption of increased amounts of income from garnishment actions, requires full disclosure of all terms involved in lending contracts, places strict limits on techniques for collecting debts, makes buyers of finance contracts responsible for defects in merchandise covered by the contracts, and requires that lien holders on automobiles get court orders before seizing the cars.

The legislature also reapportioned congressional districts, cutting the number from ten to nine because the state lost one representative as a result of the 1970 census, and reapportioned state senate and assembly districts for the 1972 election.

The hardest fought battle was over aid to the parents of private school pupils. Supporters of such aid in the form of income tax credits got a tie vote at one point but could not win passage.

Reports by the governor's task forces raised a number of controversial issues. One recommendation, for example, was that prostitution be legalized. Another asked for the elim-

ination of prisons, replacing them with rehabilitation centers near the home communities of offenders.

Economic developments. National figures showed that Wisconsin is among the highest states in total taxation, which some critics deplore as a detriment to economic growth. However, manufacturing—the mainstay of the state's economy—continued a slow but steady rise from the start of the year. Employment was up, and retail sales totals were at a record level, as were total personal incomes and average weekly earnings of manufacturing workers. In addition, Governor Lucey pointed out that new industry and business formations were replacing those that had ended production in the state. He also said that Wisconsin offered its residents a desirable quality of life, a low crime rate, a high education level, and a high level of services to go with the high tax rates.

Tourism fell off somewhat after two consecutive record years. This was blamed on a rather wet summer, which also cut down on some agricultural production. The state continued to lead all others, however, in production of milk, cheese, vegetables for canning, and malt liquors and in several manufacturing categories, such as various types of paper, huge power cranes, and small gasoline engines.

For election results and campaign highlights, see the special supplement ELECTION '72.

Area and population. Area, 56,154 sq. mi. Pop. (1970), 4,417,-933. Principal cities: Madison (cap.), 173,258; Milwaukee, 717,099; Racine, 95,162; Green Bay, 87,809; Kenosha, 78,805.
Government. Gov., Patrick J. Lucey (D); lt. gov., Martin J. Schreiber (D); atty. gen., Robert W. Warren (R); secy. of state, Robert C. Zimmerman (R); treas., Charles P. Smith (D). Legislature: senate, 20 R, 12 D, 1 vacant; assembly, 66 D, 34 R.
Finance (fiscal year ending June 30, 1973). Approximately $2 billion budget for two-year period; revenues from taxes, federal aid, licenses, and fees. Approximately 63 percent allocated to education at all levels, 27 percent to welfare and social services, 10 percent to general expenses.
Education (1971–1972). Public elementary schools, 1,739; teachers, 26,806; pupils, 580,296. Private elementary schools, 732; teachers, 6,489; pupils, 157,453. Public high schools, 633; teachers, 23,727; pupils, 419,625. Private high schools, 80; teachers, 1,760; pupils, 30,942. Public institutions of higher learning, 45; students (est. fall 1972), 150,000. Private institutions of higher learning, 35; students (est. fall 1972), 27,000.   HYMAN CHESTER

WORLD ECONOMIC REVIEW. The year 1972 saw the major economic powers of the world enter upon a new period of economic growth. This step forward, however, occurred against a background more troubled than at any time since the end of World War II.

The absence of major progress in negotiating a formal replacement for the Bretton Woods monetary system threw a partial eclipse over the postwar pattern of international economic cooperation.

Moreover, many industrialized nations found that their accustomed patterns of economic growth were threatened by the resurgence of an inflation with which they did not fully know how to cope. A combination of factors—a shift in the mix of economies to sectors in which there is less productivity growth, changing attitudes to work, competition for funds from both public and private sectors—seemed to have produced a situation in which the traditional use of fiscal and monetary policy was not enough to maintain stable prices. Yet, neither those countries that had tried direct incomes policies (controls over wages and prices) for an extended period (Great Britain in the 1960's), nor those that had not (West Germany) were certain that they had found the answer.

The Smithsonian Agreement. The international monetary system, which had been through a series of crises in recent years, began 1972 with the promise of some respite. On December 18, 1971, the major nations of the world signed the Smithsonian Agreement, so named because it was worked out in a conference held at the Smithsonian Institution in Washington, D.C. President Richard M.

Nixon called it "the most significant monetary agreement in the history of the world." Although some observers thought this an overly generous characterization, the agreement did bring to a close a four-month period of currency floats that had begun on August 15, 1971, when Nixon unilaterally ended the Bretton Woods system by cutting the tie of the U.S. dollar to gold for international purposes.

The Smithsonian Agreement was notable chiefly for the realignment of currencies it achieved. To effect this agreement, the United States backed down from its historic opposition to devaluation. The value of the dollar was changed from one thirty-fifth of an ounce of gold to one thirty-eighth of an ounce; this action amounted to an 8.57 percent devaluation.

Because the United States did not agree to exchange its gold for dollars held by foreign central banks, the devaluation had little meaning other than as a face-saving gesture for foreign nations that had to take the step (unpopular with major exporting interests) of revaluing (valuing upward) their currencies. In terms of changing the value of their currencies in relation to gold, these nations did not need to revalue as much as they would have had to without a U.S. devaluation. In the figure of actual trading importance—the change of parity in relation to the U.S. dollar—the United States obtained about a 12 percent devaluation on a weighted basis. Japan, which had not revalued since 1948, went from 360 yen to the dollar to 308, a change of about 17 percent. West Germany, which had had a 5 percent revaluation in 1961 and a much larger one in 1969, revalued again, this time by about 12 percent, going from 3.66 marks to 3.22 marks to the dollar.

Speculation starts anew. The United States could not officially change the price of gold until Congress acted. The administration announced that before submitting the gold bill to Congress it would get some trade adjustments from the Common Market, Japan, and Canada. This process dragged on for over two months. After getting some token changes from the Common Market countries and from Japan, but nothing from Canada, the administration finally presented the gold bill, and it duly passed. In the meantime, as it had become clear to foreign traders that the dollar would not immediately become convertible again, speculation resumed. The position of the dollar was also not helped by the record trade deficit of the United States in the first quarter of 1972. It became clear that the benefits of devaluation would take several quarters to be felt.

Role of gold still a question. After several months of intermittent speculation, amid charges by some foreign countries that the United States was delaying negotiation of the rest of the monetary agreement envisioned at the time of the Smithsonian talks, it became clear that the dollar was still the kingpin of international trading, and that it would be some time before all the nations could agree on a formal system to replace Bretton Woods. Would gold continue to play a role? It it did, at what price? Speculation in the first half of 1972 raised the free market gold price to almost $70 an ounce, or close to double its new official value. Some experts felt that the free market price would eventually lead to a new, much higher official price. To others, the free market situation only underscored the futility of continuing to try to use gold as the basis for the system (especially because gold was playing an increasing role as an industrial commodity).

But, if gold was to be phased out, were the major nations ready to accept some paper unit, such as the International Monetary Fund's special drawing rights, in its place? And what about the 60 billion in dollars held by foreign central banks? Some countries thought these dollars should be funded for a five-year period by a special issue of U.S. bonds. Other countries were more concerned that future additions to their U.S. dollar holdings be protected from exchange losses, in case of a second dollar devaluation.

Step toward European monetary integration. At the same time, the Common Market nations were playing out another monetary game. The Smithsonian Agreement had permitted nations to widen the bands within which their currencies could trade. Previously set at 2.25 percent, these were widened to 4.5 percent (2.25 percent either way from parity). This alteration meant that central banks would not be called upon to defend their nations' currencies as frequently and that speculators would bear more risk themselves. But in Europe, where the original six had a general commitment to achieve monetary union by 1980, the nations of the European Economic Community set about to narrow the bands within which their own currencies could move to 2.25 percent.

At a meeting in Rome in September, the members of the EEC moved further to implement this "snake in the tunnel" plan, as it was called. Their finance ministers agreed on a plan to set up an incipient central bank, the European Monetary Cooperation Fund.

On October 19 the Common Market leaders reached agreement on a plan that went farther than had been expected. The monetary fund (a $1.4 billion line of credit) was to be set up on April 1, 1973. A timetable for the further development of the fund was also agreed to.

Importance and difficulty of reaching new accord. The technicalities of monetary reform escape much of the public. But the issue is vital for at least two reasons. First, foreign trade and investment will eventually suffer if the major participants in the international economy do not have confidence in the system. Second, although reform involves monetary details, some of which are necessarily complex in themselves, the success of reform at this point depends on the political will of the major nations involved, and the outcome will thus be an augury of the degree to which these countries may be willing to submerge purely national interests for the sake of international cooperation.

Although the International Monetary Fund set up a group of 20 nations to negotiate reform, there was still no clear agenda. The less developed countries wanted reform tied to more aid. The United States wanted reform to be tied to trade talks, because it feels that much of its trade deficit is the result of restrictive practices abroad. Undersecretary of the Treasury Paul A. Volcker commented that, although a complete agreement within two years might be desirable, such a schedule seemed too short for considering all the diverse viewpoints. But it seemed almost certain that another crisis over the dollar at this point would lead to restrictive measures (such as the French two-tier system) that would begin to curtail the flow of trade and investment.

U.S. economy returns to good growth track. Economically, the United States enjoyed the best overall year since 1967, using the combined major criteria of economic growth, stable prices, and level of employment. The gross national product seemed likely to fulfill the Nixon administration's prediction of 6 percent real growth for the year. The controls program had reined in inflation and, although the jobless rate was still high, the numbers of those employed were reaching new highs each month. (See EMPLOYMENT.)

What happened in the United States was of interest not only to Americans. The U.S. economy still produces between 40 and 50 percent of the goods and services produced in the non-Communist world each year, and trends in the United States have a direct bearing on other nations.

Controls. Although the inflation rate was coming down by 1971, the U.S. economy was only slowly responding to monetary stimulus, and there were abundant fears that the recovery would either abort itself or lead to a new round of inflation. This was the background against which President Nixon announced a 90-day wage-price freeze on August 15, 1971, followed in November by a phase two set of controls over wages and prices.

A year's experience with controls offered inconclusive proof of their viability as a permanent tool. To some extent they interfere with a free market economy, but in other respects they may actually improve the operation of segments of the economy that are not free enough in practice.

"Poor devils! Tell them we have a special on cake!"

In any case, the immediate results looked impressive. Inflation had run at a 5.9 percent rate in 1970. In 1971, partly because of the wage-price freeze, it declined to 4.3 percent. And with 1972 two-thirds over, it had further declined to a 3.2 percent annual rate. From August 1971 to August 1972, the consumer price index climbed only 2.9 percent.

Argument over fairness of controls. Labor claimed that the pattern for wage hikes had been adhered to much more rigidly than the rules for pricing. Labor in general had been held to a 5.5 percent annual increase, although there were some exceptions in the months immediately following the freeze. Business, for its part, claimed that the gross profit margins it was supposed to follow (no higher than the average of the best two of the last three years) would cut into the normal profit growth expected during the upswing of the business cycle. In March, four of the five labor members of the 15-member Pay Board resigned.

Renewed inflation a threat for 1973? As 1972 drew to a close, the main concern of economists was whether the continuing business upturn and a federal budget badly in deficit would so compete for funds in 1973 as to bring about another bout of tight money and high interest rates, thus braking the economy before full employment was achieved. Given even the possibility of these conditions recurring, it seemed unlikely that the administration would wish to abandon the controls program, authority for which runs out on April 30, 1973. Indeed, in July and August wholesale prices moved disturbingly higher (at about a 7 percent annual rate), causing additional concern about inflation. Some of the changes in the wholesale index, though, were caused by soaring food prices (a real problem, but not one directly related to the rest of the inflation battle) and by the fact that some firms marked up their prices as much as allowed under the controls but were not making all their sales at the posted price.

Federal budget growth. One way to keep a discipline over the economy was to control the growth of the federal budget. The federal deficit of $23 billion in the fiscal year 1972, ending June 30, 1972, was expected to increase to $30–35 billion in fiscal 1973. President Nixon asked Congress to enact a $250 billion spending ceiling for fiscal 1973, but Congress had already approved expenditures exceeding that figure. Because many programs, such as social security, are not set by Congress each year, the actual size of the discretionary budget is only a fraction of the total—about $80 billion. To cut back the total in any substantial way would mean to deal severely with the programs in the $80 billion figure, including the many new and popular ones in the areas of health, education, manpower training, and pollution. It appeared that some kind of tax increase would be necessary in 1973 to head off renewed inflation, and that this increase might well come as part of a tax reform package that would cut back some of the tax shelters most used by people with high incomes.

Jobless rate slow to come down. Unemployment remained in the 5.5 percent area, down only about half a percentage point from its recession high. Many economists said that because of the influx of teen-agers and women into the labor force it would remain difficult to get the jobless rate below 5 percent. Actual civilian employment grew in the year from July 1971 to July 1972 from 79 million to 81.7 million.

Restoration of productivity growth. Productivity also grew in 1972, reflecting in part the particular phase of the business cycle when it normally improves. Pessimists had been saying that the shift to a service-oriented economy meant the end of the historic curve of productivity increases averaging about 3 percent. Although a long-run trend is not reestablished by a year or two, the direction of the curve in the past two years has tended to run against the arguments of the pessimists. With an improvement of 3.4 percent in 1971, the figure increased even faster this year,

at a 4.4 percent rate during most of 1972. If this trend continues, it will reestablish the productivity curve along the favorable trendline of the early 1960's. Moreover, U.S. productivity was rising while that of many of its foreign competitors was leveling off. This trend, if prolonged, will mean easier markets for price-competitive U.S. exports.

By late 1972, all major segments of U.S. industry were involved in the business upturn. Housing had led the way (and was still strong), followed by consumer durables, such as automobiles. Finally in 1972 the long-awaited rise in business inventories began to take place, as well as additional business spending on capital equipment. Then there were signs that a slower growth in consumer durables was being replaced by a boom in food, clothing, and other nondurables, finally bringing together all segments of the economy as beneficiaries of the upturn.

Other major countries. The economies of Western Europe and Japan as a group had a slackening in their growth during 1970 and 1971, a reaction in large part to the 1969–1970 U.S. recession. During 1972 they began to emerge from this slack period. In general they were about a year behind the current business cycle in the United States. Already, however, inflation was high, and several nations faced the same dilemma that confronted the United States before wage-price controls were imposed.

European countries and Japan faced two new problems as they attempted to reflate their economies. First, the devaluation of the dollar took away a trading advantage many of their industries had enjoyed. Thus, it forced some degree of rethinking about the source of the next phase of economic growth in several countries, most notably in Japan. Second, the advanced industrial nations that offered an array of social services (that is, the welfare state) were reaching the point where the taxes to pay for increased public spending were colliding with the expectations of the private sector. The competition for funds tended not only to heighten inflationary tendencies but also to increase social tensions. This situation was noticeable in Sweden.

West Germany. The business slowdown of 1971 in West Germany ended early in 1972. The slowdown had been due in part to the uncertainties caused by the floating of the West German mark. Although German exports faced harder competition after the revaluation in December 1971, major uncertainty was at least removed, improving the business atmosphere. The German automobile industry, in particular, faced new competition from both American and Japanese small cars. However, total production in Germany was expected to climb by 2.5 percent, with the increase accelerating as the year progressed.

During the 1971 slowdown, joblessness reached only about 1 percent, and the number of foreign workers even increased. Thus, the acceleration of the German economy began at a time when there was very little slack in it. With inflation already running about 5 percent, the Germans faced the now familiar problem of speeding up their economy without doing the same thing to the inflation rate.

France. In France, real growth was expected to be more than 5 percent for the year. The French economy is in many respects the obverse of the West German (a factor that must be taken into account in conjecturing on the further development of the Common Market). Although both countries provide a wide range of social services through the public sector, in Germany the private sector is one of the freest in the world. On the other hand, much of the private sector in France is indirectly guided by way of the government's control over much of the banking system. Although social and political turmoil in France a few years ago received considerable attention, the country's economic growth (with the exception of 1968) has been sustained. In 1972, the government introduced various credit measures to encourage additional investment, and it also increased its investment in the nationalized part of French industry.

Italy. Italy did not do so well as its neighbors to the north. Although it appeared that its 1972 growth of about 2.5 percent would surpass 1971, a combination of labor problems, inflation, and an uncertain political outlook held back business investment. Many businessmen complained that social conditions in Italy kept them from making an adequate profit, and increasing numbers of firms turned to the state-owned Instituto di Ricostruzione Industriale to be taken over.

Great Britain. Progress was also uncertain in Britain during the year. The economy was slowed in the early months by the coal miners' strike. In late spring, with the inflation rate the highest of any major European power, the trade deficit growing again (Britain normally has a trade balance in the red), and speculation over the immediate effect on Britain of its entry into the Common Market in 1973, there was another run on sterling. Rather than risk damaging the domestic economy by defending the new values set in December 1971, the British government floated the pound sterling in June. It quickly declined from $2.60 to less than $2.45. When inflation continued rampant into November, Prime Minister Edward Heath imposed a wage-price freeze to last between 90 and 150 days.

Japan. The Oriental *Wunderkind* emerged from what it called its longest postwar recession. The Japanese identify as recession a pause in their rate of growth, which had continued at unusually high levels all during the 1960's. It appeared that the Japanese economy would grow between 7 and 8 percent for their fiscal year, which ends March 31, 1973, compared to only 5 percent in the previous year.

Japan's export industries had long benefited from a yen exchange rate that was too low; it had not been adjusted since 1948, when Japan was rebuilding. When the yen was revalued at the end of 1971, it was widely assumed that this action would lead to some reorientation of Japanese industry, with perhaps more attention paid to building up the domestic infrastructure. However, it appeared that the Japanese trade surplus would still be in excess of $8 billion, almost as much as in the previous year. Late in August, Premier Kakuei Tanaka and President Nixon met in Hawaii to discuss, among other things, the balance of trade between their two countries. Premier Tanaka agreed to a significant boost in Japanese imports of American products, to take place within the near future.

Soviet Union. With the world's second largest economy, the Soviet Union now has a gross national product approaching half that of the United States. But it was in evident difficulty as it went through the second year of unsatisfactory agricultural yields; and in industry productivity declined. The problem was serious enough for the Communist Party to start new workers' "competitions."

Negotiations for a major trade agreement with the United States brought the Soviet Union a big step closer to large-scale exchange with the economies of the non-Communist world. The Soviet Union also agreed to buy large quantities of U.S. wheat over a three-year period. It appeared that the Soviets had purchased one-fourth of the entire 1972 U.S. wheat crop.

China. President Nixon's trip to China in February also began to open wider the door to trade with that country, although not on the scale immediately in prospect with the Soviet Union. In September, the Boeing Company sold ten 707 airliners to the People's Republic; the $150 million order was the largest commercial sale thus far to China.

Developing nations. No summary statement applies equally to that extremely diverse group lumped together as the Third World countries. Most of them continued to find it difficult to raise per capita incomes in 1972. What economic growth there was was partially or even largely diluted by generally high birthrates.

The oil-exporting nations turned in the best performance. The value of their petroleum exports was up substantially (about one-quarter) as the result of new contracts negotiated with the major oil companies. However, the wealth of the major oil-producing nations, most of which have small populations, had little spillover effect on the rest of the developing world.

Other developing nations—the ones that have reached the point of exporting some manufactures—had a better year in 1972 than 1971, as the major industrial nations entered a new period of growth. But developing nations still dependent for their exports on agricultural products, minerals, and metals did not, as a whole, share in the more general prosperity. The prices of many of their exports remained severely depressed, still reflecting the recent period of slow-down in business growth in almost all the industrial nations.

Even among the developing nations showing good growth, such as Brazil and Mexico, there were warnings from economic experts that the fruits of growth were not percolating through to all citizens and that, in fact, the gap between rich and poor was increasing.   RICHARD NENNEMAN

WORLD LITERATURE. The major story in world literature was the awarding of the 1972 Nobel Prize to Heinrich Böll, the 54-year-old West German novelist, playwright, and short story writer. The Swedish Academy cited Böll for his "sensitive skill" and "broad perspective," contributing to "a renewal of German literature." Böll's works, which mainly treat the impact and horror of war and the German postwar mentality, are published in both East and West Germany. The academy cited Böll's most recent novel, *Gruppenbild mit Dame* (to be published in the United States as *Group Portrait With Lady*), as his "most grandly conceived work." In the United States, Böll is best known for *The Clown* and *Billiards at Half Past Nine.*

Italy. Leonardo Sciascia, one of Italy's finest prose stylists and unquestionably the most distinguished interpreter of the strange mores of his native Sicily, published an important new work, *Il contesto* (The Context), this year. Sciascia's earlier novels were in the realistic tradition; his latest work, although as stylistically lucid and laconic, is more complex and is influenced by the French, rather than the Italian, new novel. It probes Sicilian life, not by depicting its obviously ugly and violent side, but by concentrating on the middle class and even the superliterate. As a whole, the novel (*à la* Robbe-Grillet) is conceived of as a kind of conundrum; at times the wisdom of its insights and even the force of its frequent ironies seem to be undetermined by an arch-literariness—and Sciascia hardly escapes this criticism by describing *Il contesto* as a parody. Nonetheless, it is as exciting as a good thriller and much deeper and more revealing.

Mario Tobino, a distinguished psychiatrist as well as novelist, added immeasurably to his already high reputation with *Per le antiche scale* (Down the Ancient Steps). This subtle and sympathetic exploration of madness and its origins, closely influenced by his own experiences as a doctor, recalls his novel of nearly 20 years ago, *Le libere donne di Magliano* (The Madwomen of Magliano), rather than the more recent *Il clandestino* (The Underground), for which he won the 1962 Strega Prize. The implications of *Per le antiche scale* are inescapable: an acquisitive and aggressive society drives a wedge between the aspirations and the sense of reality of sensitive people, and their intellects give way in despair. Dr. Tobino implies, in fact, that some kinds of madness represent a state in which the emotions are healthy while the reasoning powers are in a process of disintegration. This is a tragic and deeply felt novel, which tells the layman much more about its subject than any textbook of psychiatry.

Dino Buzzati (Traverso), Italy's leading practitioner of the genre of fantasy, died at the age of 66. He will be remembered mainly for his delightful children's book *La famosa invasione degli orsi in Sicilia* (The Bears' Famous

MCGRAW-HILL

THE 1972 NOBEL PRIZE for literature went to Heinrich Böll, a popular West German novelist, short story writer, and playwright.

Invasion of Sicily) of 1946 and for *Il deserto dei Tartari* (The Tartar Steppe) of 1940. But his posthumous collection of short stories and sketches, *Le notti difficili* (The Difficult Nights), contains much excellent work in his familiar role as gentle and whimsical but ironic questioner of conventional notions of reality.

Giorgio Bassani, frequently regarded both in Italy and elsewhere as the best writer of fiction of his generation, continued to scrutinize and uncover the patterns inherent in the predicament of Italian Jewry (specifically in Ferrara) between the wars with *L'odore del fieno* (The Scent of Hay), which collects short stories (some are very brief indeed) and an unfortunately ponderous and solemn final essay on his own work. Nothing here is as substantial as the brilliant novel *Gli occhiali d'oro* (The Gold-rimmed Spectacles), but the writing remains acute, evocative, and psychologically penetrating.

Franco Cordero is less well known than the preceding writers, but his two new books—one, a novel called *Opus,* and the other, an "anthropological analysis of Pauline Christianity," *L'Epistola ai Romani*—seem certain to establish him as a first-class writer. The novel, a lucid and bitter account of a Roman Catholic priest's loss of faith and subsequent decline into death, needs to be read in the light of Cordero's highly unorthodox but profoundly interesting nonfiction work. The latter sets out to demonstrate that the primary aim of the Pauline theology is to neutralize willy-nilly the powers of thought.

Maria-Luisa Astaldi, author of an influential biography of Tommaseo, has written what is perhaps the most important European biography of the year, *Manzoni,* on Italy's great novelist. The biography is as fully documented as one could wish, but its form resembles that of a novel. The result is an invaluable study of an enigmatic personality.

France. Nathalie Sarraute, justly regarded as one of the initiators of the French *nouveau roman,* published one more of her subtle exposures of the meagerness and meanness of what passes for civilized social intercourse. *Vous les en-*

tendez? is as meticulous a tracing of "tropisms"—the involuntary impulsive patterns that precede all speech—as any of her previous novels. The ostensible subject here is a piece of ancient sculpture, the property of an art lover whose entire snobbish world comes under Sarraute's minute and savagely satirical scrutiny.

Marguerite Duras has gained a wider fame than Sarraute but is disliked more by literary critics. The prose poetry of *L'amour* is repetitious and will not enhance her reputation. The subject is an insoluble erotic situation involving three people, but the treatment is unnecessarily obscure. The author's sincerity is not in question, but this work well indicates the element of pretentiousness in Duras's writing.

A more interesting and enterprising novel was Jean d'Ormesson's *La gloire de l'Empire.* This mock history of the world up to the foundation of the Holy Roman Empire is unquestionably a remarkable book; the author is an expert parodist of various styles, including the omniscient one affected by epic historians. D'Ormesson raises serious questions about the meaning of history, and his work has been conceived at a very high level of intelligence.

André Pieyre de Mandiargues is best known as a novelist, but he is also a short-story writer, poet, and essayist. *Mascarets* collected eight of those tales the French call *récits,* in each of which the author demonstrates his skill in constructing an unfamiliar, "unreal," but nonetheless entirely valid world. His *Bona: l'amour et la peinture* is a fascinating, unusual, and moving book about his wife, the painter Bona Tibertelli. *Troisième Belvédère* consists of interesting essays.

The veteran American novelist Julien Green, who has (except during World War II) made his home in France and written in its language, published the ninth installment of his famous journals, *Ce qui reste du jour,* which covers entries for the years 1966–1972. There are interesting comments on his readings in French and English literature and some accounts of his own novels published in this period. This year has also marked the issue of the first volume of Julien Green's *Oeuvres complètes.* The first four volumes of the *Oeuvres complètes* of the French eroticist and novelist Georges Bataille (who died in 1962) also appeared; apart from many otherwise inaccessible book reviews and essays by this interesting and original synthesizer, these volumes incorporate his famous *L'Histoire de l'oeil,* one of the most important of the handful of pornographic novels of this century that have literary significance.

Jean-Paul Sartre published further installments of his *Situations,* records of his responses to events between 1968 and the present. As always, they are lucid and provocative; perhaps their most interesting aspect is their indication of the author's seemingly final departure (prompted by the invasion of Czechoslovakia) from Soviet-style Communism.

Four leading French poets published new volumes. Yves Bonnefoy, born in 1923 and generally regarded as the most important poet of his generation, published (in Geneva) *L'Arrière-pays,* an autobiographical report on the poet's search for the lost paradise—the beauty beyond beauty—that has marked all his work as poet, traveler, and art critic. It is a chaste, in some ways neoclassical, work. Bonnefoy's near contemporary—and in many ways kindred spirit—Philippe Jaccottet, collects his prose poems in *La Semaison,* some of which have appeared before; they are clotted, severe, and classical in the manner of Bonnefoy. Jacques Dupin collected his poems in *L'Embrasure,* another severe, aesthetic, and metaphysical grouping which gives more comfort to the reader than the author finds in his bleak appraisal of life. But it is a fine poetry of unresolved tension between despair and hope. André du Bouchet's poems in *Qui n'est pas tourné vers nous* express their author's distrust of the surface of the world in the more abstract form of technique: white spaces play as much part as words in these elaborately constructed graphic poems.

Spain. Max Aub was born in France in 1903 but is a naturalized Spaniard and writes in Spanish. He was for many years one of Franco's bitterest enemies, and his work was strictly proscribed; now, however, he is back in Spain, and the publication of four of his earlier novels in that country must be regarded as something of an event, since he is a gifted and versatile writer. In particular, his meticulously "documented biography" of *Jusep Torres Campalans,* an in fact imaginary Catalan postimpressionist painter, deserves the new lease on life that it has been given. His best book, it belongs more to the world of 1972 than to that of its original publication (1958).

Sweden. Per Olov Enquist has established himself as a major novelist with his substantial and psychologically acute study of the world of athletics, *Sekonden* (Second), which is probably one of this year's most distinguished books. The protagonist, Christian, has acted as a second to his father, a fairly successful boxer. Abandoning boxing, the father becomes an outstanding hammer thrower, but just as the world championship comes within his reach, he is caught cheating. Long afterward, his father dead, Christian seeks to learn what led him to cheat and contemplates the meaning of an athlete's existence. There seems to be nothing that Enquist does not know about athletics, and the book is a profound examination of its implications in human life.

Germany. It has taken nearly a quarter of a century for Arno Schmidt to become established as "Germany's Joyce," the most important German experimental writer of the postwar era. Now, however, since the publication of his magnum opus *Zettels Traum* in 1970, a decipherment industry on a Joycean scale is going on in Germany. His new work, *Die Schule der Atheisten,* is like *Zettels Traum* inasmuch as it is a facsimile reproduction of the author's own 10-inch by 12-inch typescript page. It is a fantastic work, not by any means always immediately coherent, but it is rich in the same kind of possibilities as was Joyce's *Finnegans Wake* and points to Schmidt's possessing something of the same kind of erudite, poetic, punning, and yet essentially humanitarian vision as that of Joyce.

A younger writer, G. F. Jonke, who had previously made something of a reputation with *Geometrischer Heimatroman* (1970), published *Die Vermehrung der Leuchttürme.* This book, essentially a mixture of allegory, fantasy, and the *Märchen* of E. T. A. Hoffmann (now an all-pervasive influence in West German literature), was not wholly a success; the author hovers too indecisively between the three genres. But it is an impressive book, and the theme—of suddenly multiplying lighthouses—is often handled with great imaginative power (as distinct from calculated allegorical cunning).

Stefan Andres, author of the famous *Wir sind Utopia,* died in 1970, but this year saw the publication of his last novel, *Die Versuchung des Synesios.* This story of the conversion of Synesios, bishop of Libya, has not the impact of his masterpiece or even of his later, more comic novels with an Italian setting, but it is a solid work, showing much understanding of its subject.

Soviet Union. Things have become worse, rather than better, for Soviet writers: there has been no relaxation of pressure on those who do not conform to the party line. One poet, Joseph Brodsky, previously sentenced as a "parasite," has left the Soviet Union and is now poet-in-residence at the University of Michigan. But some good writers not in disfavor have, by dint of special circumstances, published within the Soviet Union. Karlo Kaladze, Georgia's best poet, has been translated by Pasternak (said to have owed his life to Stalin's approval of his Georgian versions), Yevtushenko, Zaboletsky, and others. His *Stikhotvoreniya i poemy,* a retrospective selection of his works in Russian translation, is a pleasing volume of robust and sunny poems. Chingiz Aitmatov is from the Central Asian republic of Kirghizia and writes in its language, Kirghiz. His *Povesti gor i stepei* (Tales of Mountains and Steppes) has been issued in a Russian translation; the stories have lyrical power and grandeur and amply demonstrate that not all Lenin Prize winners are subservient and creatively lifeless.

Aleksandr I. Solzhenitsyn's first volume of his new long novel *August 1914,* published in Russian and in English translation, cannot be issued in the Soviet Union. Dealing with the life of an officer of the tsarist Russian army that suffered devastating defeat at the hands of the Germans at the beginning of World War I, it is a novel of epic sweep—at which the Russians are masters—and it seems (although we must await its completion) to be of profound historical mastery. Solzhenitsyn's suppressed acceptance speech for the 1970 Nobel Prize, which he was not allowed to go to Stockholm to receive, has now been made public in the West. As courageous as one would expect from this courageous man, it spares neither Russian tyranny nor Western complacency but strikes a notable blow for the autonomy of art.   MARTIN SEYMOUR-SMITH

WYOMING. Wyoming commemorated the centennial of the creation of Yellowstone National Park this year. A centennial dinner at Cody drew a crowd of 1,700 persons, including Nellie Tayloe Ross, who in 1925 became the first woman to be elected governor of a state.

Court decisions. As a preliminary to the elections, the Wyoming supreme court in July held that Wyoming's 82-year-old voting residency law, a provision of the state constitution since 1890, was in effect unconstitutional because of a U.S. Supreme Court decision handed down earlier in the year, and that any otherwise eligible voter could exercise the franchise on the basis of a residence in the state and a county for a period of 30 days, plus residence in the precinct where he would vote for ten days.

Another important court decision, rendered only a week earlier, dealt with a suit filed in U.S. district court in Cheyenne challenging the constitutionality of the act of the 1971 legislature reapportioning the Wyoming house and senate on the basis of the 1970 census. A three-judge federal court heard the case in April and found the act constitutional, noting that "...the 1971 act only made changes which reflect population fluctuations."

The Wyoming supreme court upheld a ruling by Judge John F. Raper of Laramie County district court rejecting a legal challenge to the 1970 election of State Representative Dean T. Prosser, Jr., to the Wyoming house of representatives from Laramie County. The suit had noted that the house in which Prosser resided at the time of his election was located 700 yards beyond the state border with Colorado, which runs through the 12,000-acre ranch owned by Prosser and members of his family. Judge Raper had held that Prosser's birth in Laramie County and his indicated continuing residence there, including his voting in the county and state and taking part in community activities for more than 30 years, all strongly indicated that the county and state were his intended residence.

Industry. Despite challenges raised by environmentalists, construction continued on a $300 million coal-fired, steam-generated electric plant near Rock Springs. The plant, which will produce a total of 1.5 million kilowatts, is a joint venture of the Pacific Power and Light and Idaho Power companies. The U.S. Department of the Interior, through its Bureau of Land Management, granted rights-of-way for transmission lines from the Bridger project across southwestern Wyoming and into Idaho.

The Wyoming water development program, a subdivision of the state engineer's office, which is the state's preeminent water authority, issued an in-depth study of industrial development in northeastern Wyoming which showed that the coal-rich area would exceed its present water resources between the years 2000 and 2020 if current industrialization

trends continued. It recommended consideration of importation of water by pipeline from the Yellowstone or Bighorn rivers or from as far away as the Green River in southwestern Wyoming. The report quoted a study by Cameron Engineers, carried out for the state department of economic planning and development, to the effect that coal production, which totaled 850,000 tons in 1967, would increase in the area to more than 230 million tons in the year 2020 and that this trend would be accompanied by an increase of 31 times in present employment by the year 2000 and 57 times the current employment in the year 2020. Subsequently, both governors Stanley Hathaway of Wyoming and Forrest Anderson of Montana asked the federal government to designate a single federal agency to carry out a resource study of the two states.

Earlier in the year, the Reynolds Metals Company announced that it hoped to organize a consortium of companies for the construction of a gaseous diffusion plant at Lake DeSmet between Buffalo and Sheridan in northeastern Wyoming. The plant, which Richard S. Reynolds, Jr., chairman of the board of the Reynolds Metals Company, estimated would cost $2.2 billion, would utilize coal and water to operate the plant, which would enrich uranium for nuclear-powered electric generating plants. Reynolds estimated the project could be completed by the end of the present decade. If built, it would be the single largest industrial project in the history of Wyoming.

Late in the year, the Burlington Northern Railroad announced plans for construction of a 126-mile branch line from Gillette to Douglas to ship low-sulfur coal from northeastern mines to major power plants in the south and east. If approved by the Interstate Commerce Commission, the $32.5 million project will be the longest new railroad line to be built in the United States since 1931.

For election results and campaign highlights, see the special supplement ELECTION '72.

Area and population. Area, 97,914 sq. mi. Pop. (1970 census), 332,416. Principal cities: Cheyenne (cap.), 40,914; Casper, 39,361; Laramie, 23,143.

Government. Gov., Stanley K. Hathaway (R); secy. of state, Thyra Thomson (R); aud., Everett T. Copenhaver (R); treas., James Griffith (R). Legislature: senate, 11 D, 19 R; house, 20 D, 40 R, 1 ind.

Finance (fiscal 1971). Budget: revenue, $225,491,905; expenditure, $200,704,128.

Education (1970–1971). Elementary schools, 294; junior high schools, 49; senior high schools, 73. Total public school enrollment, 86,885. Institutions of higher learning, 7; total full-time enrollment, 11,702.　　　　　　　　　　　　　　JAMES M. FLINCHUM

YEMEN. Military confrontations.

On October 28 the governments of Yemen and Southern Yemen (officially the People's Democratic Republic of Yemen) agreed to unite. They also agreed to withdraw troops from their common frontiers and to open their borders. The agreement ended several months of extremely intense fighting between the two countries. Numerous border clashes in February and March threatened to escalate into a full-scale war until Southern Yemen proposed, at the end of March, a mutual withdrawal of troops from border areas. Heavy fighting, including aerial and artillery bombardment and resulting in at least 200 casualties, recurred in late September. On October 9, one day after an Arab League mediation committee arrived in Sana (the Yemeni capital), Southern Yemen accused its neighbor of attacking and occupying the Red Sea island of Kamaran, part of Southern Yemen.

Yemen claimed during the year that it took military action only in response to incursions into its territory by Southern Yemen troops trying to suppress antigovernment rebels operating from Yemen. The Sana government also alleged that Southern Yemen, in order to distract public attention from domestic economic problems, fabricated reports that its territory was being invaded. For its part, Southern Yemen maintained that it was being attacked by

THE LOWER FALLS of a Yellowstone River canyon illustrate how Yellowstone National Park has managed to attract tourists during a total of 100 years since its opening in 1872 by President Grant.

"mercenaries" and by Yemeni and Saudi Arabian troops attempting to implement a United States–Yemeni–Saudi plot to overthrow Southern Yemen's Marxist government.

Foreign relations. The trend in Yemen's foreign relations since the civil war ended in 1969—a gradual drift to the right—continued in 1972. The year was marked by increasingly close ties with conservative Saudi Arabia, by the resumption of diplomatic relations with the United States, and by a decline in the influence of the Soviet Union.

By 1972 approximately 100 Soviet military advisers remained in Yemen, most of them engaged in air force training. In addition, as a result of President Abdul Rahman Iryani's December 1971 visit to Moscow, further Soviet aid—a loan of $84 million and $15 million worth of MIG-17 aircraft and other military equipment—was delivered.

Meanwhile, Saudi Arabia was attempting to persuade Yemen to oust the Soviet advisers, who were already allegedly in disfavor with the Yemeni chief of staff, Major General Hussein Massouri. A Saudi military mission arrived in Yemen in May and promised that Saudi Arabia could and would replace Soviet personnel and aid.

On May 21, symbolizing the strengthening of Saudi-Yemeni ties since the two countries agreed in 1970 to establish diplomatic relations, Sheikh Musaed al-Sideiri presented his credentials as the first Saudi ambassador to republican Yemen. In June, Yemeni premier Mohsen al-Ayni visited Saudi Arabia, reportedly to seek a budget subsidy.

U.S. secretary of state William P. Rogers made an unscheduled stop in Sana on July 2 to meet with Premier al-Ayni. After the meeting al-Ayni announced that diplomatic relations with the United States, which had been broken in 1967, would be resumed. On July 14 the United States announced the resumption of economic aid to Yemen.

The recent trend in Yemen's foreign policy was discussed by Premier al-Ayni when he stopped in Moscow on his return from a visit to Peking in July. Despite reports published in a Cairo newspaper in August (after President Anwar Sadat had ordered Soviet military advisers out of Egypt) that Yemen would follow Egypt's lead, Premier al-Ayni stated on August 12 that the Soviets would remain. Nevertheless, there was no doubt that the Soviet position in Yemen had deteriorated since the civil war of the 1960's.

The economy. Yemen eagerly sought economic aid from all possible sources. Its economy has not yet recovered from the civil war and drought of recent years. During 1972, aid was received from the United Arab Emirates, Qatar, Iraq, Iran, West Germany, Mainland China, Saudi Arabia, Great Britain, the Soviet Union, and the United States. In addition, the World Bank lent Yemen $7.7 million for road construction.

The plight of the Yemeni economy was underscored by the foreign trade figures for 1971: imports were valued at $34.3 million, but exports totaled only $6 million. The budget deficit for 1971–1972 was estimated at more than $16 million. Yemen's total foreign debt was estimated at more than $190 million.

Crackdown on high officials. On May 22, Premier al-Ayni prohibited all government ministers and public officials from chewing kat and ordered all kat bushes on state-owned land destroyed. Kat is a mildly narcotic plant which grows wild and is cultivated in the southern Arabian Peninsula. Kat chewing is probably more common in Yemen than tobacco smoking is in the United States, but Yemeni officials tend to think that it lowers efficiency. Kat had already been banned in the armed forces. It has been estimated that 20 percent of the cultivable land in Yemen is planted in kat bushes; much of this land could no doubt be used for one of Yemen's few export crops, such as coffee.

Area and population. Area, 75,300 sq. mi. Pop. (est. 1971), 5,900,000. Principal cities: Sana (cap.), 120,000; Ta'izz, 80,000; Hodeida, 90,000.
Government. Constitutional republic. Legislative body: Consultative Council of 159 members (20 appointed, 139 indirectly elected). Executive body: Presidential Council of 3 members. Pres., Abdul Rahman Iryani; prem. and for. min., Mohsen al-Ayni.
Finance. Monetary unit, riyal; 1 riyal = US$0.205.
Armed forces. Official U.S. estimate (1968), 8,000. There are extensive tribal forces that can be mobilized.
Education (1969–1970 school year). Schools, 768 (744 primary, 20 intermediate, 4 secondary); teachers, 1,703; students, 69,460 (64,404 boys, 5,056 girls). RALPH H. MAGNUS

YUGOSLAVIA. Politics and government. Croat separatism continued to threaten the solidity of the Yugoslav federation. The movement was spearheaded by members of the Ustaše, a neofascist organization whose World War II forebears ruled Croatia under Hitler and have agitated for Croatian secession ever since. Particularly active among Yugoslav workers living in Sweden, Ustaše agents have managed to extort funds for terrorist acts by threatening fellow Yugoslavs and their families. In February, Ustaše terrorists placed a bomb on a Yugoslav Airlines flight from Stockholm to Belgrade. The plane crashed in Czechoslovakia, killing 27 of the 28 persons aboard. A few hours later, another bomb went off on an express train near Zagreb, injuring six passengers.

The incidents were timed to coincide with a meeting of Yugoslav political leaders in Belgrade, convened to debate the separatist problem. Many speakers at the meeting called for a return to a tougher brand of Communism, with Soviet-style "democratic centralism" replacing Marshal Tito's more liberal "self-management socialism." Beleaguered by the sharp criticism, the government moved against the terrorists with stepped-up secret police activity, especially in Croatia, and with wholesale ousters and arrests. Nevertheless, in June, a band of about 50 Croat émigrés illegally crossed the border from Austria and established a base in the central highlands near the Bosnian town of Bugojno. In a pitched battle, government forces killed 12 of the invaders and wounded another dozen, while others escaped into the mountains. Officials were especially shocked over the age of the invaders—most were in their early twenties and had left Yugoslavia only in the last few years. Officials had previously maintained that the Ustaše comprised only die-hard fascists of an older generation.

In its trials of newly arrested subversives, the government moved cautiously, avoiding any action that would create an aura of martyrdom. In June, four former municipal officials charged with committing counterrevolutionary attacks on the state through hostile propaganda received relatively light sentences of 6 to 15 months. Trials of dissident Croat students and intellectuals dragged on inconclusively through the rest of the year.

In June, a party commission questioned the low proportion (28.8 percent) of workers in the Yugoslav League of Communists, advocating a campaign for the recruitment of workers in the party on the grounds that "there must be both a relative and absolute workers majority."

The aging Tito undertook a campaign to rebuild a strong party as his successor. This effort resulted in October in the resignation of the two main leaders of the Communist Party in Serbia, who were charged with "liberalism" and following an independent line. New leaders were named.

Tito is 80. On May 21, the nation celebrated Marshal Tito's 80th birthday, a tribute to the unflagging energy of Europe's most venerable Communist leader and a reminder, perhaps, of how much the nation's unity still depended on the force of his personality.

Foreign affairs. In April, Yugoslavia appealed to the governments of several nations—and in particular Sweden—requesting the adoption of strong measures to control expatriate anti-Yugoslav terrorist organizations. The requests were met with expressions of sympathy, but little else.

On May 17, Marshal Tito and Romanian party chief Nicolae Ceaușescu met on the Danube to inaugurate the Iron Gates power and navigation system. The giant project, under construction for eight years, will eventually have an annual power output of 10.4 billion kilowatt-hours, with production to be shared jointly by the two countries. Tito and the liberal-minded Ceaușescu emphasized the growth of cooperation in all fields between Yugoslavia and Romania since the leaders last met in November 1971.

Area and population. Area, 98,766 sq. mi. Pop. (est. 1971), 20,504,516. Principal cities (est. 1971): Belgrade (cap.), 1,209,360; Zagreb, 503,000; Skopje, 228,000; Sarajevo, 227,000; Ljubljana, 182,-000.
Government. Socialist federal republic; a federation of the republics of Serbia, Croatia, Slovenia, Bosnia-Hercegovina, Macedonia, and Montenegro. Highest organ of state authority is the five chamber Federal Assembly. Pres. of republic and secy. gen. of Communist League of Yugoslavia, Marshal Tito; pres. of Federal Assembly, Mijalko Todorovic; prem., Dzemal Bijedic.
Finance. Monetary unit, dinar; 1 dinar = US$0.0625. Federal budget (1970): revenue, 26.07 billion new dinars; expenditure, 23.33 billion new dinars.
Trade (1970). Imports, US$2.87 billion; exports, US$1.68 billion.
Agriculture and industry. Agricultural production (1970, in thousands of metric tons): corn (maize), 6,928; wheat, 3,792; potatoes, 2,964; tobacco, 48. Livestock (1970, in thousands): sheep, 8,974; pigs, 5,544; cattle, 5,029; horses, 1,076. Mineral and industrial production (1970, in thousands of metric tons): lignite, 27,779; cement, 4,399; crude oil, 2,854; steel, 2,228; bauxite, 2,098; antimony, 1,999; pig iron, 1,377; iron ore, 1,301; hard coal, 643; magnesite, 512; mercury, 533; lead ore, 126.7; copper ore, 90.8; aluminum, 47.7. Electric power, 26,024 million kw.-hr.
Education (1969). Enrollment: primary schools, 2,857,291; secondary schools, 705,746; institutions of higher learning, 239,701. RICHARD A. PIERCE

YUKON TERRITORY. Government and politics. Petitions and public protests highlighted the political life of the Yukon Territory this year. When the territorial council introduced a health insurance plan, citizens petitioned Commissioner James Smith for a plebiscite on the question. But

the demand was rejected, the council passed the plan, and protests multiplied because of growing resentment over predominant federal control of territorial affairs. While a mob surged menacingly around the council chamber, members debated and defeated a motion calling for dissolution of the council and new general elections. A majority of Yukon voters then signed a petition requesting Governor General Roland Michener to dissolve the council; but he refused to do so.

The Yukon has been making slow and erratic progress toward autonomy since the time of the Klondike Gold Rush. The establishment in 1970 of a governing executive committee, composed of two elected councillors as well as three federally appointed officials, apparently did not help much in reducing chronic protests against federal control. Somewhat ironically, the governor general, on a visit to the territorial capital in March, gave the council its first mace, the traditional symbol of parliamentary authority.

Economic developments. Economic growth slowed down, as international and Canadian market conditions continued to bring cutbacks in mineral exploration. Also, Donald S. Macdonald, federal minister of energy and resources, announced an embargo on oil search permits in the Yukon, as well as in the Northwest Territories. However, tourism was expected to increase in value to at least $14 million by the end of the year. Zinc and lead remained the territory's most important mineral products; in 1971 zinc production went up 169 percent and lead increased by 166 percent, but gold production decreased in volume by 30 percent.

The 1972–1973 budget amounted to more than $39 million, compared to $29.6 million in 1971–1972. The increase was caused by collective salary agreements signed in 1971 and by new programs such as the take-over of the Alaska Highway System. Maintenance of the system was expected to cost the territory $5 million.

Sports. The biennial Arctic Winter Games opened at Whitehorse, the territory's capital, on March 6. The Yukon barely won by amassing 38 points compared to Alaska's 37½, but Alaska won the greatest number of medals.

Area and population. Area, 202,076 sq. mi. Pop. (1971 census), 18,390. Whitehorse (cap.), 11,217.
Government. Comm., James Smith.
Finance (est. 1972–1973). Expenditure, Can$39,361,606.
Education (1971). Total enrollment, 4,521.   J. A. BOVEY

ZAÏRE. The Republic of Zaïre, known until October 27, 1971, as the Democratic Republic of the Congo, saw during 1972 the continuation of economic and political trends that had emerged the year before: a persistent slump of export earnings (caused largely by the low level of world copper prices) and a further drift toward one-man rule cloaked in the rhetoric of a skin-deep cultural revolution.

"Zaïrian authenticity." Initially treated as a whim by foreign observers, the change of the country's name from the Congo to Zaïre (a name based, ironically, on an inaccurate sixteenth-century Portuguese rendition of the Kikongo word for river) turned out to be only the first step in a well-orchestrated campaign in search of "Zaïrian authenticity." In November 1971, shortly after the inauguration of the campaign, the government, still led by General Mobutu, introduced a new national flag, bearing a handheld red torch within a yellow circle on a field of lime green. The names of the country's major cities, including the capital, Kinshasa (formerly Léopoldville), had been Africanized on the sixth anniversary of the country's independence in 1966, shortly after Mobutu's take-over. A further and this time thoroughgoing wave of name changes was announced in January 1972. Most prominent, the mineral-rich former secessionist province of Katanga was renamed Shaba (Swahili for copper); this, together with the dropping of the name Congo, was viewed as representing a desire to erase some of the turbulent memories linked

with the old terms. Other significant changes affected two cities: Luluabourg, which became Kananga, and Port-Francqui, renamed Ilebo. Lake Léopold II—surely the most gratingly colonial name still in use in the country—was finally renamed Lake Mai-Ndombe; Stanley Pool, a broad section of the Congo River (itself officially changed to the Zaïre River) named for the British explorer Henry M. Stanley, became Malebo Pool.

The authenticity campaign reached even further, however. Statues and monuments associated with the colonial regime were removed throughout the country. All remaining European names were ordered removed from maps and street signs, and European family names borne by Zaïrian citizens of mixed descent were banned in favor of African names.

Conflict with the church. It was not the elimination of European family names, however, but that of Christian names that brought out the strongest reaction against the new policy. Initially, the government's official position had been that Christian names would be tolerated, although their abandonment was strongly encouraged by the president's decision to change his own name from Joseph Désiré Mobutu to Mobutu Sese Seko. At this point, the appearance in a Catholic weekly of an article—allegedly inspired by the country's senior Catholic churchman, Cardinal Malula—in which the policy of authenticity was criticized precipitated a vigorous attack on the part of President Mobutu against the Catholic clergy in general and against Malula in particular. As Malula prudently left Kinshasa for a trip to the Vatican, his residence was taken over by the youth wing of the Mouvement Populaire de la Révolution (MPR), Zaïre's only political party. Mobutu vowed that the cardinal would never again occupy his archepiscopal seat. From Rome, Pope Paul VI issued a conciliatory ruling that the use of African names for Christian baptism was perfectly acceptable, but an appeal on behalf of Malula by the conference of Zaïrian bishops led to a stiffening of the government's position on church-state relations. Several Belgian missionaries were expelled from the country. Public personalities were enjoined against taking part in any religious ceremonies in an official capacity, and Catholic seminaries were ordered to allow the setting up of party youth committees among students or else be closed down. When this latter measure was accepted by the bishops, the party claimed that nothing now stood in the way of a reconciliation, and by mid-May Cardinal Malula was quietly allowed back in Kinshasa.

Government and politics. As the MPR opened its congress in Kinshasa a week later on May 21, the fifth anniversary of the inauguration of the one-party system, Mobutu's victory over all forms of organized opposition was so manifest that he could afford to decline the life presidency that the party offered him. The Catholic Church, a virtual state within a state for nearly a century, had come to terms with the regime. Student opposition was muted and almost every surviving civilian political figure was in exile, jail, or forced retirement. To the already long list of those members of the independence generation who have been purged or executed was added in July the name of Losembe Batwangele (better known as Mario Cardoso), foreign minister until February and a former member of the College of Commissioners, who fled to Portugal and was stripped of his nationality. At least a dozen personalities of lesser fame also suffered penalties ranging from death to dismissal during the course of the year—a relatively modest total under this distinctly repressive regime.

The army, understandably regarded as a key factor for the stability of the Mobutu regime, remained ostensibly loyal (notwithstanding a minor plot in December 1971 involving ex-Colonel Honoré Kudiakubanza), and Mobutu saw to it in July that overseas-trained officers were not blocked from further promotions by the aging generals who had been

promoted from the ranks of noncommissioned officers after independence: in July, no fewer than ten generals, including Mobutu's own uncle, General Bobozo, were honorably but firmly retired to make room for younger blood.

The tightening of power in the hands of Mobutu and a handful of associates was put in sharp focus at the end of August when the government and the executive committee of the single party were merged into a single National Executive Council. With that decision, the rubber-stamp legislature receded yet a little further into the background.

Economic developments. While the political situation was reasonably stable, the economic picture was marred by the continued weakness of world copper prices, which had resulted in a 13 percent drop of export earnings and in an $82 million balance-of-payments deficit for 1971. The country's currency reserves declined from $224 million to $166 million during the same period. Copper production from Gécamines (the former Union Minière), the government-owned copper corporation, continues to increase regularly, however, at an annual rate of about 6 percent. Total output was expected to approach 430,000 tons during 1972. The Zaïrian-Japanese mining consortium, Sodimico, will go into production in 1973 and should help boost the country's total copper output to 800,000 tons within a decade. The world's largest hydroelectric complex is being developed in Inga. An aluminum smelter and a steel plant (initially fed with scrap, later with domestic ores) are already going into operation. Both Ford and General Motors are building major motor vehicle plants near Kinshasa.

While the country's long-term economic future is not in doubt, short-term prospects remain somewhat uncertain. The growth rate of Zaïre's gross domestic product (GDP) subsided to 4.6 percent in 1971. The 1971 budgetary deficit of $120 million was apparently reduced by half in 1972, and the government devoted 24 percent of the budget to expenditures on capital investment for development.

Foreign affairs. Internationally, Zaïre has long aspired to play a role commensurate with its size and wealth. However, its pivotal position between East and West Africa and between ex-French and ex-British territories has often placed it in a peripheral diplomatic position on the continent. Zaïre came to realize that, in spite of its being the largest member of the Francophone African, Malagasy, and Mauritian Common Organization (OCAMM), it could never really be part of what is essentially a family of former French territories. In announcing its intention to withdraw from OCAMM in April, Zaïre indicated that it could not let itself be tied to any one linguistic or regional group and that its national interest was, in effect, to play the field. In fact, for the first time since attaining independence, Zaïre in 1972 had no conflict with any of its neighbors. At the same time, the decision by the West African members of OCAMM (along with Mali) to organize the West African Economic Community (WAEC) left OCAMM's central African members in an awkward left-out position that Zaïre may be tempted to exploit in an effort to revive the idea of an Equatorial African union. Chad and the Central African Republic have in the past been receptive to this concept. Mobutu's visits to Gabon, Togo, and Guinea may or may not have been part of a grand design, but it is interesting to note that some French circles interpreted these moves as part of a U.S.-inspired plan to weaken French positions in sub-Saharan Africa. African influence has clearly been very strong in Kinshasa, while Belgian influence has been slowly but visibly declining. Mobutu's decision in August to reduce Belgium's share of Zaïre's total imports to a maximum of 15 percent was only another event in a long series of minor frictions between the two countries.

Area and population. Area, 905,567 sq. mi. Pop. (est. 1972), 18,250,000. Kinshasa (cap.; est. 1970), 1,500,000; Lubumbashi (1966), 233,145; Kisangani (1966), 149,887; Kananga (formerly Luluabourg; 1966), 140,897; Likasi (1966), 102,200.

Government. Republic. Single party, Mouvement Populaire de la Révolution (MPR). Pres., General Mobutu Sese Seko.

Finance. Monetary unit, zaïre; 1 zaïre = US$2.05. Budget (1972): $660 million (including $160 million development expenditure).

Trade (1971). Exports, $693.2 million; imports, $622.2 million. Production: copper, 405,832 tons; manganese (1970), 346,950 tons; cobalt, 14,518 tons; zinc, 120,000 tons; palm oil, 210,000 tons; coffee, 1.2 million bags; diamonds (est.), 12 million carats.

Education (1969–1970). School enrollment: primary schools, 3,-039,279; secondary schools, 246,413; higher education (1971–1972), 12,852.

EDOUARD BUSTIN

ZAMBIA. Politics and government.

The political climate in Zambia clouded up in February when President Kenneth D. Kaunda jailed opposition leader Simon Kapwepwe, along with more than 100 of his followers in the United Progressive Party (UPP), and announced that Zambia was to become a one-party state. Although Kaunda's own United National Independence Party (UNIP) enjoyed a clear majority in the National Assembly, Kapwepwe had defeated a UNIP candidate to win a seat in the December 1971 by-elections. Harry Nkumbula, whose African Congress Party (ANC) had picked up three seats, branded the move to one-party government as "far worse" than the proposed Anglo-Rhodesian settlement of which Kaunda had been so critical in the past.

The president defended the change as reflecting the will of the people and blamed the UPP in particular for numerous acts of violence, including an abortive attempt to blow up UNIP headquarters in the capital city of Lusaka. He appointed Vice-President M. Mainza Chona as head of a commission charged with drawing up a new constitution, which, he said, would retain a democratic government.

All in all, it was a tense year in Zambia. A few weeks before his imprisonment, Kapwepwe had to flee to a nearby hospital after he was set upon and beaten by an angry crowd on a street in Lusaka. In June someone sent a bomb inside a parcel addressed to President Kaunda; it reportedly exploded in his office, seriously injuring a secretary. In March police arrested 97 members of the fanatical Lumpa religious sect on charges of trying to revive the movement banned seven years before, when Alice Lenshina led a revolt in which hundreds of people were killed.

Foreign relations. Addressing the Conference of Nonaligned Nations in Guyana, President Kaunda called for more constructive action in building peace; addressing a meeting of the African-American Conference in Lusaka, he called upon the United States to improve its relations with African nations by taking positive action against racism and colonialism in southern Africa.

After a five-day visit to Zambia, Romanian Communist Party leader Nicolae Ceauşescu promised technical, educational, and cultural cooperation between the two countries.

In August the government announced that Zambian villages bordering the Portuguese colonies of Angola and Mozambique would be evacuated to guard against future incursions by Portuguese troops; the Portuguese newspaper *Diario de Noticias* denied that any incursions had taken place.

Economy. In spite of increases in agricultural production, the Zambian economy continued to deteriorate because of a decline in the output and market price of copper, the country's main export. Government officials were optimistic that the situation would improve; but, meanwhile, it was found necessary to ban 18 categories of goods from being imported and to levy increased duties on others.

Area and population. Area, 290,586 sq. mi. Pop. (est. 1971), 4,400,000. Lusaka (cap.; 1971), 238,200.

Government. One-party republic within the Commonwealth of Nations. Pres., Kenneth David Kaunda.

Finance. Monetary unit, kwacha; K1 = US$1.41. Budget (1972): expenditure, K429.5 million.

Trade (1969). Exports, K766.5 million; imports, K311.8 million.

WILLIAM A. McGEVERAN, JR.

UPI

LING-LING, one of the panda pair donated by the Chinese after President Nixon's visit, settles down to a piece of honey-bread toast in her airconditioned suite at Washington's National Zoo.

ZOOLOGY. With increasing concern about the widespread use of DDT and similar insecticides, attention has been focused on broader understanding of their mode of action and on the development of less persistent or more specific insecticides. Recent advances in insect physiology suggest techniques useful for this approach.

Insect tissue culture. Insect cells differentiate during development but, unlike vertebrate cells, cannot become generalized when allowed to divide unchecked. It is also very difficult to provide conditions for growth and survival outside the insect body, because insect blood contains a great variety of sugars, salts, and amino acids and, unlike vertebrate plasma, cannot be collected in large quantities.

The recent development of both suitable culture solutions and suitable insect material for culture—notably by Imogene Schneider of Yale University and Herbert Oberlander of Brandeis University—has enabled the course of biosynthesis and the mode of hormone action to be examined in greater detail than before.

Schneider's first experiments with adult buds of the fruit fly showed that the buds would develop in the presence of the moulting hormone ecdysone. Since then, James Fristrom and his co-workers at the University of California at Berkeley and David S. King of the Zoecon Corporation have tested the relative efficacy of various analogues of insect hormones. Using leg buds of the wax moth, they obtained development with concentrations of beta-ecdysone similar to those estimated to be present in the living insect, and they showed that the response depended on the dose of hormone. Analogue hormones inokosterone and rubrosterone derived from plants were 100 and 10,000 times less effective, respectively.

Development of adult structures does not occur in the presence of juvenile hormones. Using beta-ecdysone to promote development, Fristrom and King tested the relative efficacy of Farnesol, a synthetic hormone, and of a natural hormone derived from the *Cecropia* silk moth. They found that these hormones inhibited development, but with decreasing effect. Whereas the moulting hormone promotes synthesis of ribonucleic acid (RNA), juvenile hormones inhibit this process. The moulting hormone produces its full effect in six hours, but this effect can be inhibited for another four hours by juvenile hormones, so the two types of hormones probably act at different points in the cell cycle.

The idea that there is a threshold for the action of the hormones is borne out by the experiments with cockroach leg tissue of Edwin P. Marks of the U.S. Agricultural Research Service. He showed that single large doses of beta-ecdysone or repeated small doses caused cuticle growth similar to that occurring at moulting, but that single small doses had no effect. Where treatment was prolonged, single doses at weekly intervals produced a set of five cuticles during the experiment, but a smaller continuous dose produced a single thick cuticle during the same 40-day culture period. This evidence suggests that, once activated, the cells' synthetic activity continues in the presence of the appropriate hormone, but that a threshold dose of hormone produces a cycle of synthesis.

Insecticide action. In vitro studies of the physiology of insects are useful in understanding how insecticides work. Recently, Simon Maddrell and S. E. Reynolds of Cambridge University have examined the effect of various types of insecticides on hormone release in the blood-sucking bug *Rhodnius.* They find that the alkaloid nicotine, the organophosphate TEPP, and the carbamate Zectran all cause similar simultaneous release of two separate hormones that are not normally released together. DDT causes these hormones to be released at different times, which would imply that there is no simple universal process involved in the functioning of insecticides. However, it does appear that insecticides work by disrupting the central nervous system, which would cause both paralysis and general release of the hormones regulated by that part of the nervous system which is responsible for metabolic control. Death of the insect may then occur from normal metabolic failure.

Maddrell and Reynolds suggest that hormonal insecticides should be developed; these would have the advantage of being both specific to insects and biodegradable. It is clear, too, that biological assays of such insecticides are now available.

The songs of whales. A remarkable series of recordings has been made from naval hydrophone installations in the Atlantic and Pacific oceans by Frank Watlington of Palisades Sofar Station, Bermuda, and Roger Payne of Rockefeller University. Although there is only circumstantial evidence, it is likely that these records, which appear as songs lasting from seven to over 30 minutes, are produced by humpback whales and are used in communication.

Most striking is the individuality of the songs. Analyses made by Payne and Scott McVay of Princeton University have shown that if one individual repeats its song, the repetition is practically note perfect and follows the order of the phrases with great precision. Songs usually start with a theme of rapid pulses that may alternate with sustained notes. The next theme includes short, shrill upward glissandos, and the song concludes with a series of lower notes that may fall in pitch. While the thematic content does not vary, phrases in a theme may be developed or omitted in later repetitions of the song by the same whale. The songs are of great beauty and cover a band of frequencies easily audible to man. It is still not clear how the songs are produced, nor is there any information about the function of the song or the sex of the singer. Whales are highly intelligent, and it is not surprising that their songs are of such beauty and complexity.

See also the special article Social Insects.

Henry C. Bennet-Clark

Chronology

DECEMBER 1971

2 The dollar fell to new lows on international money markets. Earl Butz was confirmed as U.S. agriculture secretary.

3 War erupted between India and Pakistan.

4 General Motors announced the recall of 6.7 million vehicles to correct defects.

6 Pakistan broke diplomatic relations with India after New Delhi recognized Bangladesh; the United States branded India the "main aggressor" in the conflict. The U.S. Senate confirmed Lewis Powell, Jr., as Supreme Court justice.

7 The Soviet Union announced that an instrument capsule from its Mars 3 spacecraft had landed on Mars five days earlier.

8 Chilean president Allende announced a government take-over of food distribution.

9 President Nixon vetoed a comprehensive child development bill.

10 William Rehnquist was confirmed by the Senate as Supreme Court justice.

12 Belfast terrorists shot and killed a Protestant senator, John Barnhill, as violence in Northern Ireland continued.

14 After meeting with President Pompidou of France, President Nixon agreed in principle to devalue the dollar.

16 Indian troops captured Dacca and accepted an East Pakistani surrender.

17 Fighting in West Pakistan ended with a truce arranged on India's terms.

18 In negotiations with nine other leading non-Communist nations, the United States agreed to devalue the dollar and remove the import surcharge, in exchange for upward revaluations by West Germany and Japan.

20 Zulfikar Ali Bhutto was sworn in as president of Pakistan after Yahya Khan resigned.

21 The Security Council elected Kurt Waldheim of Austria to succeed U Thant as secretary general of the United Nations.

24 The Italian Electoral College chose Giovanni Leone as president after 23 ballots in 16 days.

29–30 President Nixon and West German Chancellor Brandt conferred in Florida.

30 Ending five days of bombing over North Vietnam, the heaviest since 1968, the U.S. command threatened further attacks if the Communist military buildup continued.

JANUARY 1972

2 President Bhutto ordered the nationalization of major Pakistani industries.

3 William Tolbert was inaugurated as president of Liberia.

4 Senator Edmund Muskie (Me.), already considered the front runner, formally entered the Democratic presidential race.

5 President Nixon ordered development of the $5.5 billion space shuttle.

7 After conferring for two days, President Nixon and Premier Sato agreed on the return of Okinawa to Japan.

8 Sheikh Mujibur Rahman was released by Pakistan, as former president Yahya Khan was placed under house arrest.

10 Senator Hubert Humphrey (D, Minn.) announced his presidential candidacy.

12 Sheikh Mujib became prime minister of Bangladesh, appointing his first cabinet.

13 A military coup was reported in Ghana. President Nixon announced new cuts that would halve U.S. troop strength in Vietnam by May. Governor George Wallace of Alabama entered the presidential race.

14 King Frederik IX of Denmark died at 72, to be succeeded by Margrethe II.

16 Anti-Marxist candidates won Chilean by-elections. Dallas took the Super Bowl.

18 British and Common Market officials completed negotiations on terms for entry.

22 Denmark, Norway, and Ireland signed the Treaty of Brussels providing for Common Market entry; voters in all three countries must ratify the terms.

24 The Soviet Union recognized Bangladesh. President Nixon proposed a record $246.3 billion budget.

25 President Nixon charged that, in secret talks with Henry Kissinger, North Vietnam had rejected an eight-point peace plan.

27 Commerce Secretary Stans resigned to become chief Nixon campaign fund-raiser; Peter Peterson was named to replace him.

30 On "Bloody Sunday," British troops killed 13 Catholics in Londonderry. Advised that Britain, Australia, and New Zealand would recognize Bangladesh, Pakistan withdrew from the Commonwealth.

31 Hanoi claimed that Washington had not seriously considered its nine-point peace plan, submitted in secret. King Mahendra of Nepal died at 51; Birenda Bir Bikram Shah Deva succeeded him.

FEBRUARY

2 The British embassy in Dublin was fire-bombed. John Ross Marshall was named prime minister of New Zealand, replacing Keith Holyoake.

3 The Winter Olympics opened in Sapporo. Communist negotiators in Paris offered a revised peace plan.

4 At a Security Council meeting in Addis Ababa, Britain vetoed a resolution condemning an Anglo-Rhodesian accord.

6 Israel canceled a jet purchase from France after reportedly negotiating the purchase of U.S. Phantoms and Skyhawks.

8 Britain declared a state of emergency, as a coal strike entered its 30th day.

10 President Nixon reaffirmed support for the Thieu government and warned that Hanoi must respond to the latest U.S. peace proposal before any new offer would be made.

11 More than two months after the election, Juan Bordaberry was finally named president of Uruguay. A U.S.-Soviet joint medical research agreement was disclosed. Archbishop Makarios reportedly received a Greek ultimatum for increased influence over Cyprus.

14 The Nixon administration ordered further relaxation of U.S.-Chinese trade policy.

15 A military coup ousted Ecuador's president, José María Velasco Ibarra. In a televised speech, French premier Jacques Chaban-Delmas denied tax fraud charges.

18 The Nixon administration declared congressional restrictions on aid to Pakistan no longer valid.

21 President Nixon arrived in Peking.

22 The vacationing ruler of Qatar was deposed by his cousin.

24 The Communist delegations to the Paris peace talks walked out to protest recent U.S. bombing of North Vietnam.

26 In Italy, Premier Giulio Andreotti and his nine-day-old cabinet resigned after a Senate vote of no confidence. The Sudanese government and leaders of the southern rebel movement reached an agreement ending a 17-year civil war.

28 After a week of talks in Peking, President Nixon and Premier Chou En-lai issued a joint communiqué in which the United States promised gradual troop withdrawals from Taiwan; both nations vowed greater cultural and trade relations. The UN Security Council condemned Israeli reprisal raids against Lebanon.

MARCH

1 Acceding to Greek demands, Archbishop Makarios reportedly agreed to surrender secretly imported arms to a UN commission. Israel and Syria bombed each other's front lines.

2 Acting attorney general Richard Kleindienst, appointed to replace John Mitchell, denied arranging a settlement of three ITT antitrust suits in exchange for pledges to help finance the Republican convention in San Diego.

5 The Soviet Union gave assurances of aid to the visiting Sheikh Mujib.

6 UN Secretary General Waldheim arrived in South Africa for talks on Namibia.

7 Senator Edmund Muskie won the New Hampshire presidential primary.

8 A new executive order revised classifications of government documents after repeated security leaks.

10 Lon Nol assumed absolute power in Cambodia.

12 In India, the ruling New Congress Party won 70 percent of state assembly seats.

13 Clifford and Edith Irving pleaded guilty to criminal charges arising from the fraudulent "autobiography" of Howard Hughes. President Nixon ordered stricter antiterrorist measures on U.S. airlines. Britain formally agreed to full diplomatic relations with China.

14 Governor George Wallace easily won the Florida primary.

15 King Hussein of Jordan revealed a plan to convert his kingdom into a federated state that includes the Israeli-held West Bank.

16 President Nixon called for new laws to forbid court-ordered school busing.

19 India and Bangladesh concluded a 25-year friendship treaty.

20 The U.S. Interior Department called the trans-Alaska pipeline essential despite environmental risks.

22 The Senate gave final approval to the Equal Rights Amendment prohibiting discrimination based on sex.

23 After four labor leaders left the Pay Board, President Nixon reconstituted it as a seven-man public group.

24 Britain suspended provincial government in Northern Ireland and imposed direct rule from London.

28 Arabs on the Israeli-held West Bank voted in the first general election since 1963. The Polish Parliament elected Henryk Jablónski as president.

30 In the heaviest Communist assault in four years, South Vietnamese bases along the DMZ were attacked.

APRIL

1 U.S. military sources revealed that thousands of Communist troops had swept across the DMZ into the South.

4 Senator McGovern won the Wisconsin Democratic primary. The United States formally recognized Bangladesh.

5 The jury in the Harrisburg seven case deadlocked over conspiracy charges after convicting the Reverend Philip Berrigan and Sister Elizabeth McAlister on lesser charges. The U.S. Department of Justice filed antitrust suits against the major American television networks.

6 American bombers struck troop concentrations and missile sites north of the DMZ, as North Vietnamese forces continued their assault on Quangtri. Egypt severed diplomatic relations with Jordan.

7 Four gunmen assassinated Sheikh Abeid Karume, ruler of Zanzibar since 1964.

10 Officials of 70 nations, including U.S. and Soviet dignitaries, signed a treaty outlawing biological weapons. An earthquake in southern Iran claimed at least 5,000 lives.

11 Representative Cornelius Gallagher (D, N.J.) was indicted for tax evasion, perjury, and conspiracy.

13 President Nixon arrived in Canada to confer with Prime Minister Trudeau. The first general strike in baseball history ended after 13 days.

16 American planes bombed Hanoi and Haiphong for the first time since 1968.

17 Nihat Erim resigned as premier of Turkey; Ferit Melen replaced him.

19 North Vietnamese MIG's attacked U.S. warships in the Gulf of Tonkin.

21 Martial law ended in Pakistan.

23 French voters approved a treaty which provided for admitting Britain, Ireland, Denmark, and Norway to the Common Market.

25 In presidential primaries, Senator Humphrey won Pennsylvania and Senator McGovern won Massachusetts; Senator Muskie trailed in both.

26 President Nixon announced the withdrawal of 20,000 more U.S. ground troops from Vietnam by July 1.

27 Senator Muskie withdrew from active campaigning for the Democratic presidential nomination. Returning after their 11-day trip with over 200 pounds of moon rocks, three Apollo 16 astronauts made a safe Pacific splashdown. Public Vietnam peace talks resumed in Paris. West German chancellor Willy Brandt barely survived a parliamentary no-confidence vote.

30 Le Duc Tho of North Vietnam arrived in Paris to resume secret peace talks with U.S. representatives.

MAY

1 South Vietnamese forces abandoned Quangtri City. Millions of U.S. firms were exempted from wage-price controls.

2 Senator Humphrey won the Indiana and Ohio primaries. FBI director J. Edgar Hoover died at 77. Canada announced plans to tighten controls on foreign takeovers of domestic businesses.

4 Public peace talks in Paris were again suspended.

5 The Republican Party switched its convention site from San Diego to Miami.

6 European and Japanese steel-makers agreed to restrict exports to the United States.

8 President Nixon ordered the mining of Haiphong and other North Vietnamese ports and the severance of supply routes with China.

9 Unofficial totals showed that Christian Democrats had won nearly 40 percent of the vote in Italian general elections. Israeli paratroops foiled a hijacking attempt in Tel Aviv.

10 By an overwhelming margin, Irish voters approved Common Market entry.

12 The two Germanys initialed a transportation treaty.

15 Governor George Wallace of Alabama was shot while campaigning in Laurel, Md.; the police arrested Arthur Bremer. After more than 27 years of U.S. rule, Okinawa formally reverted to Japan.

16 Governor Wallace swept the Michigan and Maryland primaries. President Nixon announced that Treasury Secretary John B. Connally had resigned; George Shultz was named to replace him.

17 The West German Bundestag approved friendship treaties with Poland and the Soviet Union.

21 At the Vatican, Michelangelo's Pietà was damaged by a fanatic.

22 The U.S. Supreme Court upheld, 5–4, the constitutionality of nonunanimous verdicts in state criminal cases.

23 The Pearce Commission found an Anglo-Rhodesian compromise unacceptable to Rhodesians "as a whole."

29–30 Cease-fire in Northern Ireland was proclaimed by the Official wing of the IRA but rejected by the Provisional wing.

30 President Nixon left the Soviet Union after a nine-day visit during which he and Soviet leaders signed two strategic arms limitation pacts, agreements for cooperation in space and on the high seas, and a joint declaration of principles for future U.S.-Soviet relations. Three Palestinian-trained Japanese gunmen attacked civilians at Lydda International Airport near Tel Aviv, killing 25 and injuring 77.

JUNE

1 Iraq nationalized an oil combine producing 10 percent of Middle Eastern output.

3 In Berlin, a four-power agreement was signed clarifying that city's status.

4 Angela Davis was acquitted on capital charges by an all-white California jury.

5 Police broke up antigovernment demonstrations in two South African cities.

6 Senator McGovern won the California and New Jersey presidential primaries.

8 After long debate, the Senate confirmed Richard Kleindienst as attorney general.

12 Retired lieutenant general John Lavelle admitted that, as U.S. air commander for Southeast Asia, he had ordered bombing of unauthorized North Vietnamese targets. The U.S. Supreme Court, in separate rulings, required legal representation for any offense punishable by jail and permitted racial bias in private clubs publicly licensed to serve liquor.

14 The United States banned the use of DDT almost totally, as of December 31.

16 The UN Conference on the Human Environment ended in Stockholm; during the 12-day meeting, representatives of 114 nations had endorsed a declaration of principles, a new environmental agency, and an "action plan" against pollution.

17 Eisaku Sato announced his retirement as Japanese premier. Five men were arrested at Democratic Party headquarters in Washington's Watergate area.

19 World airline pilots held a one-day strike for stiffer antihijacking measures.

20 Senator McGovern won the New York primary.

21–23 Israeli forces attacked several areas along the Lebanese border.

23 The British pound was allowed to float. Five eastern states were declared disaster areas, as Hurricane Agnes caused the worst floods in U.S. history. Signing the school aid bill, President Nixon called its antibusing provisions not strict enough.

26 A new Italian centrist government was sworn in under Premier Giulio Andreotti. To curb rising meat prices, President Nixon ended U.S. meat import quotas. A cease-fire by IRA Provisionals took effect.

27 Palestinian guerrillas agreed to curb Lebanese border activities.

28 Announcing new troop cuts, President Nixon promised that no draftees would be assigned to Vietnam.

29 A sharply divided Supreme Court barred discretionary death penalty statutes; another decision held that journalists could not withhold confidential information from grand juries. U.S. controls were tightened on nonwholesale food prices.

JULY

1 President Nixon signed a bill increasing social security benefits by 20 percent.

3 At Simla, Indian and Pakistani leaders agreed on mutual troop withdrawals and step-by-step normalization of relations.

4 A joint communiqué revealed that North and South Korean representatives agreed on principles for reunifying the nation.

5 Selection by a Liberal-Democratic caucus as party president ensured Kakuei Tanaka's election by Parliament as Japanese premier. After Premier Jacques Chaban-Delmas was forced to resign, French president Pompidou chose Pierre Messmer for the post.

6 Athenagoras I, ecumenical patriarch of the Eastern Orthodox Church, died at 86.

8 President Nixon announced major grain sales to the Soviet Union.

9 IRA Provisionals rescinded their cease-fire, as new violence erupted in Ulster.

11 After many delays, the chess match between Bobby Fischer and Boris Spassky opened in Reykjavík.

12–13 Meeting in Miami, Democrats nominated Senator McGovern for president on the first ballot; McGovern then named Senator Thomas Eagleton of Missouri as his vice-presidential choice.

13 Public peace talks resumed in Paris.

16 Metropolitan Dimitrios was chosen to head the Eastern Orthodox Church.

18 President Sadat ordered Soviet advisers out of Egypt.

19 The United States intervened on currency markets to protect the dollar.

22 President Nixon announced his decision to retain Spiro Agnew as his vice-presidential running mate.

25 Senator Eagleton admitted that he had twice received shock treatments to cure nervous depression.

26 Labor unrest mounted throughout Britain, but a general strike was averted.

27 Another 4,000 British troops were committed to Northern Ireland, totaling 5,500 in July and 21,000 overall.

28 Official Chinese sources acknowledged the death last September 13 of former defense minister Lin Piao, allegedly while fleeing after an abortive coup. A U.S. government report admitted damage to North Vietnam's dikes but called the bombing "unintentional." The death toll in Burundi's civil war was put at 80,000–120,000 since the end of April.

31 At McGovern's request, vice-presidential nominee Eagleton announced his resignation. British troops invaded Catholic "no go" areas in Ulster.

AUGUST

2 Egyptian and Libyan leaders agreed on steps toward unity for the two nations. U.S. authorities banned, as of January 1, 1973, a steer-fattening hormone linked to cancer.

3 The Senate approved, 88–2, the U.S.-Soviet pact limiting defensive missiles.

4 Ugandan president Idi Amin ordered the expulsion by November 7 of over 50,000 Asians holding British passports.

5 Stringent new controls were imposed on South Vietnamese newspapers.

8 The Democratic National Committee approved Sargent Shriver as McGovern's new vice-presidential running mate.

12 One day after the last U.S. ground combat unit in Vietnam was deactivated, B-52's carried out what were called the heaviest raids ever against the North.

15 Reports indicated that well-educated Soviet Jews were being charged heavy exit fees to emigrate to Israel.

16 King Hassan II of Morocco barely escaped death when his plane was strafed by his own air force.

17 U.S. biologists at Brookhaven announced the first nonsexual growth of hybrid plants from artificially fused cells.

18 Moroccan defense minister Muhammad Oufkir, after committing suicide, was blamed for leading the coup against Hassan. The U.S. government beat back attempts by auto-makers to raise prices on 1973 models.

19–20 South Korean floods took over 368 lives and left over 326,000 homeless.

21 Chilean president Salvador Allende declared a state of emergency in Santiago Province to quell rising protests.

22 Threatened with a black boycott, Olympic officials barred Rhodesia from the games.

22–23 Republicans renominated the Nixon-Agnew ticket; antiwar demonstrations failed to disrupt the Miami convention.

25 In the Security Council, China vetoed a Bangladesh bid for UN entry.

26 The General Accounting Office charged the Finance Committee to Re-Elect the President with violating U.S. election laws.

29 Britain froze a $24.5 million loan to Uganda, as controversy mounted over whether to accept the expelled Asians.

30 Full Red Cross talks opened in Pyongyang between the two Koreas. After 20 years in office, Premier W. A. C. Bennett of British Columbia was forced to resign. Further U.S. troop cuts in Vietnam were announced. Larry O'Brien, McGovern's campaign chairman, threatened to quit in the face of widespread disorganization.

SEPTEMBER

1 Bobby Fischer won the world chess championship. President Nixon and Premier Tanaka agreed on steps to reduce the U.S. trade deficit with Japan. Raúl Sendic, founder of the Tupamaros, was captured in Montevideo. Rioting Protestants attacked British soldiers in Belfast.

4 Mark Spitz won his seventh Olympic gold medal, an all-time record.

5 A day-long drama that began when Arab guerrillas raided Israeli Olympic quarters, killing two athletes, ended with the death of nine more Israelis, five terrorists, and one German policeman after a shoot-out at a military air base. A 17-nation conference rejected a strong U.S.-Canadian draft proposal to curb air piracy.

6 The South Vietnamese government abolished elections in the nation's hamlets.

10 U.S. jets bombed the main railroad and highway bridge in Hanoi.

14 The U.S. Senate approved, with reservations, a U.S.-Soviet agreement to limit offensive missiles. Secretary of Agriculture Butz denied any knowledge of tipoffs from U.S. officials that had allowed grain exporters to reap profits from a special subsidy.

15 Henry Kissinger met with North Vietnamese negotiators in their 17th secret peace meetings. Some opposition publications were permanently closed by the South Vietnamese government. Two former White House aides and five others were indicted on charges of having conspired to break into Democratic National Committee headquarters.

16 Israeli armed forces clashed with Lebanese and Palestinian units.

17 Three U.S. prisoners of war were freed in Hanoi.

21 The United States and the Soviet Union agreed to launch 30 joint environmental protection projects. Britain replaced internment in Northern Ireland with special court proceedings.

23 Martial law was declared in the Philippines. It was reported that guerrilla army invaders from Tanzania had been repulsed by Uganda six days earlier. The UN General Assembly agreed to debate political terrorism.

25 Norwegian voters rejected membership in the Common Market.

26 After mass arrests of Communists, Philippine president Marcos revealed a sweeping land reform program.

30 Premier Tanaka left China after negotiating an agreement for the full restoration of Sino-Japanese relations in return for an end to Chinese demands for war indemnities. Japan also recognized the Peking regime as the sole legitimate government of China.

OCTOBER

2 Guerrillas attacked a U.S. air base at Udon in northeastern Thailand.

3 Only hours after a national referendum had endorsed his policy of Common Market entry, Danish premier Jens Otto Krag resigned for personal reasons.

5 Negotiators reached preliminary agreement on terms for the take-over of Western oil holdings by five Arab countries.

6 East Germany declared amnesty for prisoners estimated in the thousands. France and Poland signed a friendship treaty.

10 The Supreme Court declared direct tuition grants for parochial schooling unconstitutional. In a televised speech, Senator McGovern announced his plan to end the Vietnam war.

11 U.S. warplanes accidentally bombed the French diplomatic mission in Hanoi.

12 Henry Kissinger returned from an unprecedented four days of secret Paris talks. A national state of emergency was declared in Chile.

15 Israeli bombers attacked guerrilla bases in Syria and Lebanon. U.S. B-52's hit targets throughout Indochina.

17 In South Korea, martial law was invoked and all political activities halted, pending constitutional changes.

18 New U.S.-Soviet trade agreements were signed, including the settlement of Soviet lend-lease debts; apparently under U.S. pressure, the Soviets began waiving exit fees for some emigrating Jewish families. The 92nd Congress adjourned after overriding a water pollution bill veto and refusing to enact new presidential powers to limit spending.

20 President Nixon signed a $30.2 billion revenue-sharing bill.

22 The Oakland A's beat the Cincinnati Reds in the World Series.

26 Hanoi radio reported that the United States had promised to sign, by October 31, a peace agreement providing for a Vietnam cease-fire, U.S. troop withdrawals, the release of American prisoners held by the North, and internationally supervised elections to decide South Vietnam's future; later that day, Henry Kissinger declared peace was "at hand" but claimed the October 31 deadline was based on a "misunderstanding." A military coup was reported in Dahomey.

28 South Vietnam's foreign minister called the peace plan "surrender."

29 Hijacking a West German jet, guerrillas won the release of three Arabs imprisoned since the Olympic shootings.

30 Prime Minister Trudeau lost his parliamentary majority in Canadian elections. President Nixon signed a new social security bill.

NOVEMBER

1 At Egypt's request, the Soviets reportedly agreed to restore SAM-6 missiles.

2 Prime Minister Trudeau declared he would not resign his office.

4 North Vietnamese negotiators agreed to further secret peace talks in Paris.

5 After a Chilean government ultimatum, labor leaders sent strikers back to work.

6 A wage-price freeze was imposed in Great Britain. The two Germanys concluded a treaty establishing formal diplomatic relations.

7 President Nixon was reelected with 60.9 percent of the vote; Democrats kept majorities in the House and Senate.

8 Pakistan withdrew from SEATO.

13 Representatives of 91 nations approved a convention restricting marine waste disposal. Japanese premier Tanaka dissolved the House, calling elections for December 10.

14 For the first time, the Dow-Jones stock average closed above 1,000.

15 It was announced that Canada, Indonesia, Hungary, and Poland had agreed to oversee a Vietnam cease-fire.

17 Former president Juan Perón returned to Argentina after 17 years in exile.

19 Chancellor Brandt's coalition government won an increased majority in West German national elections.

20 As both sides continued their military buildup in Vietnam, Henry Kissinger and Le Duc Tho resumed secret talks in Paris.

21 South Korean voters ratified constitutional changes permitting President Park Chung-hee to hold power indefinitely. Border clashes broke out between Syria and Israel. An appeals court voided all convictions in the "Chicago seven" case.

22 Unable to resolve Belgium's ethnic divisions, Premier Gaston Eyskens resigned.

23 The Bolivian government imposed a state of siege to suppress labor unrest.

24 A 39-day search failed to find House Majority Leader Hale Boggs, lost in Alaska.

25 Apparently hitting a snag, Tho and Kissinger adjourned their talks. New Zealanders elected a Labor government headed by Norman E. Kirk. Jordan claimed to have thwarted an attempt, financed by Libyans, to overthrow King Hussein. Negotiations on antihijacking measures opened between Cuban and U.S. representatives.

27 Irish prime minister Jack Lynch sought new powers to curb IRA terrorism. Prime Minister Trudeau announced 18 cabinet changes.

28-29 President Nixon named three cabinet appointments: Elliot Richardson to Defense; Caspar Weinberger to Health, Education, and Welfare; and Peter Brennan to Labor.

Index

Entry in **BOLDFACE CAPITALS** refers to an article title. Page number in *italics* indicates that the reference is to an illustration or table.

PHOTO CREDITS